YÉIL KUNDAYAAYÍ

ADVENTURES OF RAVEN

Tlingit Raven Stories

Classics of Tlingit Oral Literature, Volume 5

TITLES IN THE SERIES

CLASSICS OF TLINGIT ORAL LITERATURE

VOLUME 1

Haa Shuká, Our Ancestors: Tlingit Oral Narratives

Edited by Nora Marks Dauenhauer & Richard Dauenhauer

VOLUME 2

Haa Tuwunáagu Yís, for Healing Our Spirit: Tlingit Oratory

Edited by Nora Marks Dauenhauer & Richard Dauenhauer

VOLUME 3

Haa K̲usteeyí, Our Culture: Tlingit Life Stories

Edited by Nora Marks Dauenhauer & Richard Dauenhauer

VOLUME 4

Anóoshi Lingít Aaní Ká, Russians in Tlingit America: The Battles of Sitka, 1802 and 1804

Edited by Nora Marks Dauenhauer, Richard Dauenhauer & Lydia T. Black

VOLUME 5

Yéil Kundayaayí, Adventures of Raven: Tlingit Raven Stories

Edited by Nora Marks Dauenhauer, Richard Dauenhauer, Will Geiger & Jeff Leer

YÉIL KUNDAYAAYÍ

ADVENTURES OF RAVEN

Tlingit Raven Stories

Edited by

Nora Marks Dauenhauer, Richard Dauenhauer,
Will Geiger *&* Jeff Leer

UNIVERSITY OF WASHINGTON PRESS
Seattle

SEALASKA HERITAGE INSTITUTE
Juneau

SEALASKA HERITAGE INSTITUTE
105 Heritage Way, Suite 201
Juneau, Alaska 99801
www.sealaskaheritage.org

UNIVERSITY OF WASHINGTON PRESS
uwapress.uw.edu

Sealaska Heritage Institute is a tribal organization founded in 1980 to perpetuate and enhance Tlingit, Haida, and Tsimshian cultures of Southeast Alaska. SHI also conducts social scientific and public policy research that promotes Alaska Native arts, cultures, history, and education statewide. The institute is governed by a Board of Trustees and guided by a Council of Traditional Scholars, a Native Artist Committee, and a Southeast Regional Language Committee.

Design by Nobu Koch.

COVER IMAGE: Totem pole carved circa 1984 by Nathan Jackson and Steve Brown, currently located in the Sealaska Corporation building in Juneau, Alaska. Raven is depicted with the ear tufts, beak, wings, and tail of a raven, while clutching the Box of Daylight with human hands. Smiling, he is poised to remove the lid and break daylight over the former world of darkness. Jackson's Tlingit name, Yéil Yádi, means 'Raven Child', alluding to Raven stealing the daylight in the form of a human child. Photo by Nobu Koch. Courtesy of Sealaska Corporation, SCC.1984.002.001.

Library of Congress Control Number: 2025948049
ISBN 9780295754802 (paperback)

∞ This paper meets the requirements of ANSI/NISO Z39.48-1992 (Permanence of Paper).

K̲eixwnéi kaadé,
Xwaayeenák̲ kaadé.
Ch'a tleix̲ hasdu káa daak k̲aa sag̲ahaa.

To the memory of Nora Marks Dauenhauer
and Richard Dauenhauer.
May their memory be eternal.

… the perfect narrative
emerges through the layering
of numerous retellings.

–Walter Benjamin, "The Storyteller"

TLINGIT RAVEN STORIES TOLD BY

K̲uchéin, Frank Italio (1870–1956)
Chalyee Éesh, Andrew Wanamaker (1886–1969)
Shaadaax', Robert Zuboff (1893–1974)
Kaasgéiy, Susie James (1890–1980)
Naakil.aan, Frank Dick Sr. (1899–1992)
Daanawáak̲, Austin Hammond (1910–1993)
Yakwx̲aan Tláa, Katherine Mills (1915–1993)

WITH TRANSLATIONS BY TLINGIT ELDERS

Kaax̲k̲aatuklag̲é, Kenneth Grant
Kaxwaan Éesh, George Davis
Shak'sháani, Marge Dutson
Kingeestí, David Katzeek
Keiyeeshí, Bessie Cooley
K̲aanák̲, Ruth Demmert
Anáalahaash, Sam Johnston
K̲aakal.aat, Florence Sheakley

WITH TRANSCRIPTION, TRANSLATION, AND RESEARCH CONTRIBUTIONS BY

G̲unaak'w, Fred White
K̲aagwáask', Ishmael Hope
X̲'aagisháawu, Keri Eggleston
X̲'unei, Lance Twitchell
Dzéiwsh, James Crippen
Koolyéik, Roby Littlefield
Kathy Kolkhorst Ruddy

AND WITH REVIEW BY

Amy Fletcher
Mari Kramer

CONTENTS

LIST OF FIGURES

Foreword

By Rosita Ḵaaháni Worl

The recent appearance, or shall we say the reappearance, of White Raven has led to great excitement among Alaska Natives throughout the state. As I write, daily postings of him are seen on social media. Long captivated by Raven stories, Natives know that at one time Raven was white, and they now hope—with the appearance of White Raven—that others will be convinced that the stories of Raven are true.

Folklorists and anthropologists, who have portrayed Raven as a culture hero, a trickster, or transformer, have written books analyzing Raven stories. Daanawáaḵ, Austin Hammond, former leader of the Lukaax̱.ádi Raven clan, who is one of the storytellers in this collection of Raven stories, describes the significance of Raven in a single sentence, "Raven shows us how to live." Daanawáaḵ in simple terms further explains, "Sometimes Raven is powerful and wise, and at other times Raven seems foolish." He also spells out a powerful lesson that we, who live in a period of climate and environmental change brought on by human action, should heed, "For Raven taught us, if we live with the land, not against it, the land will take care of us. The land, the river, they hear us!"

The Southeast Alaska Natives had to convince the Christians who first arrived in Alaska that they did not conceive of Raven as a god. However, as late as 2023, the Ketchikan School District was challenged in court that a poster that was displayed in a school violated the constitutional rule of separation of church and state. The tribal poster included a value cited as "Reverence for the Creator". Experts testified that the Elders, who had developed the list of tribal values and whose first languages were Tlingit, Haida, and Tsimshian and not English, were referring to Raven rather than to a Christian god. The Central Council of the Tlingit and Haida Indian Tribes of Alaska, which supported the convening of Elders to compile the tribal values, currently includes the list on its website. It also includes a reference to the Tlingit Raven story entitled, "Raven and the Creation Story". The Ketchikan School District ultimately won the case, but it demonstrated the continued misunderstanding of Southeast Alaska Natives' perception of Raven.

The Raven stories included in this publication will describe how Raven through his antics created the world. Raven stories continue to be popular among the Tlingit, Haida, and Tsimshian. The original stories are complex, humorous, and sometimes filled with raucous sexual adventures. Raven stories are not about what is viewed as proper behavior, but what is not acceptable behavior.

Raven stories in their entirety are not always appropriate for younger readers. However, taking our lead from Daanawáak̲, who emphasized the need to ensure that our grandchildren learn the lessons of Raven, Sealaska Heritage Institute began publishing the Baby Raven Reads series that includes Raven stories adapted for children.

The Raven stories project had its beginnings some fifty years ago with revered scholars Nora and Dick Dauenhauer, who collected oral narratives from storytellers and orators. As we say in Tlingit, "Nora and Dick Walked Into the Forest", along with the storytellers who shared their stories, before they could see the publication of their monumental collection. The collection became so large that the Raven stories are divided between two volumes, of which this is the first.

Within the last decade, we've had other scholars and interested parties, such as X̲'unei Lance Twitchell and Keri Eggleston, work on various aspects of the Raven project. However, bringing it to the finishing line have been two dedicated linguists, Jeff Leer and Will Geiger, along with anthropologist Thomas Thornton. Both Leer and Geiger have offered detailed analysis of the Tlingit transcriptions of the stories and explanations of the narratives when the English translations are bound to raise questions in the minds of readers. While their linguistic analysis may only be read or understood by other linguists, their work offers lasting contributions to ongoing and future scholars studying the Tlingit language, which is nearing its end of birth speakers.

Thomas Thornton graciously agreed to write the introduction after it became clear that we could not use the Dauenhauers' magnum opus 250-page introduction, which was not only lengthy but dated in its academic review. However, the Dauenhauer introduction is a brilliant analysis of Raven stories and should be made available. Thus, SHI will publish it in a forthcoming publication in its Box of Knowledge series.

We applaud Thornton, who in his introduction has accomplished a great feat in synthesizing the meaning of Raven stories and gives coherence to the cycle of stories. He also successfully brings Raven stories and lessons into the present period in addressing the climatic and environmental challenges facing society and embraces Daanawáak̲'s lesson, "If we live with the land, not against it, the land will take care of us!"

Current and future generations including Indigenous peoples, scholars, and the public will have the benefit of Raven stories and lessons that had their beginnings thousands of years ago. We owe the storytellers, Nora and Dick Dauenhauer, and the cadre of contributors including Jeff Leer, Will Geiger, and Thomas Thornton, and the SHI media team a debt of gratitude for this first volume of Raven stories.

Guest Introduction

Raven, Resilience, and Adaptation:
The Art of Disruptive Innovation and Practical Wisdom

By Thomas F. Thornton

> *[Raven] did a lot of funny things around there, shaping the land.*
> –Anonymous Yakutat Tlingit to Frederica de Laguna[1]

Among the Tlingit and other peoples of the northern Northwest Coast of North America, Raven is an incomparable *being*—a culture hero, a trickster, a transformer, disruptor, and (re)organizer *par excellence*—who plays a foundational role in shaping the world. At the same time, Raven is an irrepressible *agent*—of knowledge, motivation, materiality, relationality, causality, and transformation in the cosmos. Even more, he possesses an irrepressible opportunistic outlook, incomparable energy, relentless resilience, and astonishing adaptive capacity. Through these unique traits, as one of the Raven storytellers in this volume, Daanawáak̲, Austin Hammond, once pointed out: Raven shows us how to live.

> Raven knew what was good for us and taught the Tlingit how to live. Raven exists in our legends and in our lives. Sometimes Raven is powerful and wise, and at other times Raven seems foolish. But always the stories of Raven hold special meaning for us. It was Raven who hung by his beak suspended from the clouds at the time of the Great Flood. It was Raven who taught our people to catch salmon. These are the stories my grandfathers passed on to me. These are the things I'm trying to teach my grandchildren. It is these stories which help guide our people as we live with the land … For Raven taught us, if we live with the land, not against it, the land will take care of us. The land, the river, they hear us![2]

The notion of Raven, through his culture-hero, trickster, and transformer roles, becoming an agent of practical knowledge and practical wisdom—a guide for how to live through both positive and negative examples—is an important but perhaps not-so-obvious lesson of this set of Raven narratives and of the Raven cycle of stories more generally. For Raven is no sage, but rather a restless rogue. Yet, through his doings Raven provides humanity with a surprisingly comprehensive set of experiential lenses for contemplating our complex, capricious, and contingent world, both socially and ecologically. His crazy, larger-than-life adventures show humans that being in the world involves continuous adaptation and (re)negotiation of boundaries (physical, social, moral) among a host of beings and forces that also inhabit (and may seek to control parts of) the planet, and with whom one may need to strategically collaborate or compete. Raven's wisdom on how to live with and not against nature, as Daanawáak̲ wisely points out, is borne of these deep, wide, and troublesome involvements.[3]

This lesson has continuing relevance and special salience in this era of accelerating changes in nature: dangerous climate change, increasing environmental pollution, intensifying competition for natural resources, and the like. Our environment is changing, the science says, and there is likely to be no new 'normal' but rather more extreme events and uncertainty. What is more, humans are now identified as the main cause of these disruptive changes to earth systems, so much so that the term Anthropocene, 'the age of humans', has been coined to replace the previous, more stable Holocene, as human impacts have become a major driver of earth systems. Thus comes the imperative that we must mitigate and adapt to climate change now, or else the results will be catastrophic for humanity, and especially for peoples in marginalized and overburdened areas, who tend to face a disproportionate share of climate impacts, as in the Arctic.

Somewhere between mitigation (reducing harmful actions on the environment) and adaptation (adjusting to environmental impacts that cannot be mitigated) lies what has come to be termed the 'resilience gap'. It is in this gap where Raven conspires and cavorts, and where the exigencies of life and livelihood play out. The adventures of Raven address the fundamentals of resilience in a changing environment. And in doing so they not only turn the idea of the human-centered Anthropocene on its head, but also give us a more compelling framework of practical wisdom—an 'ecology of mind'[4] and more-than-human model—for confronting the enormous and complex communication and collective action challenges we face in responding to environmental dynamics and change.

Currently, in the mainstream, we lack such a narrative frame and conceptual model, as most of the approaches we have to address this gap are not very Ravenesque. Raven narratives are not only climate encounters but geologic, planetary, world, and cosmos-making encounters. In this sense, as argued elsewhere,[5] they are very relevant to this disruptive period we have come to term the Anthropocene. Raven narratives avoid the guilt of the moral jeremiad (against human greed and expansion), subvert the hubris of the 'march of progress' and eco-modernist 'technofix optimism', and instead accept the fact that disruptive forces, like humanity, like Raven and other powerful forces in the world, have always created and transformed earth systems in ways that reconfigure the planet and its constituent beings in novel, unanticipated, everchanging dynamic ways. As an agent of metamorphosis, Raven may be the best embodiment and protagonist we have of planetary metamorphisms, cycles, fluxes, and reactions. So, when we think about pluralizing science, we should think not only of the disruptive anarchy and panarchy of Raven but also his 'resilience' and 'adaptation' with respect to both initiating and responding to change. Raven stories are not just timeless cosmic plots, but pathways for contemplating and negotiating social and ecological change.

With Raven order can come from chaos, transformation from calamity, and largesse from selfishness, or vice versa. Anthropologist Robert Pelton, writing of similar trickster figures in West Africa, offers this archetypal characterization: "Loutish, lustful, puffed up with boasts and lies, ravenous for foolery and food, yet managing always to draw order from ordure, the trickster appears in the myths and folktales of nearly every traditional society."[6] As this portrayal makes clear, it is difficult to typecast a trickster like Raven as a mere rogue, an unprincipled disruptor, a maker of messes, as he is also the source of vital innovations and (re)configurations upon which life depends. Most of all, Raven is never singular, never static, but rather everchanging, always dynamic. Disruptive innovator, clever outlaw, con artist, provocateur, Raven transcends boundaries, catalyzes reactions, and reshapes social and environmental relations amidst the ferment and the firmament. 'Where would we be without him?', elders sometimes muse. Still stagnating in the proverbial 'primordial soup', a student of Northwest Coast Raven cosmologies might conclude, with no sun, moon, stars, land base, fresh water, fire, tides, critical foods, or much else that we depend on. Ultimately, without Raven we risk not being fully human and not being fully *in* and *of* the world. Raven's adventures show us how we continuously define ourselves and our world through how we relate to it, both consciously and unconsciously.

Stories of Raven, often termed the Raven cycle, comprise a master narrative of creation and evolution that is unsurpassed in world literature. Raven stories have been transmitted orally since time immemorial and recorded as written texts for some 250 years in Alaska, since the time of Russian colonization. Raven's 'mischief' caught the ire of early Protestant missionaries, especially, some of whom equated Raven with the devil in particular (as did some of their converts), and idolatry and savagery more generally. Missionaries saw Raven's version of creation and the Flood story as analogous, if not ultimately antithetical, to Genesis, and a potential leverage point for conversion to Christianity. Early anthropologists, such as Franz Boas,[7] John Swanton,[8] and especially Paul Radin,[9] in contrast, recognized Raven tales for their value as a cultural framework not only for understanding the origins and development of the cosmos, but also as a 'mirror for man' in terms of the human psyche—a complex and tense admixture of self-interestedness and social obligation, autonomy and dependency, transparency and deception, which must be continually rebalanced and renegotiated in one's trajectory through life.

Radin, placing Raven in the universal trickster hero-and-fool genre of folklore, declared that in trickster we find "the original plot" that no human "generation can do without".[10] For Radin, the problem of the trickster was basically a psychological one, and "only if we view it as primarily such, as an attempt by man to solve his problems inward and outward, does the figure of trickster become intelligible and meaningful."[11] Similarly, psychoanalysts like Carl Jung and Sigmund Freud saw the trickster as a manifestation of the unconscious, embedded in the human psyche. Jung posited the trickster as an archetype of the unconscious, "a collective shadow figure" dancing in the "waterfall" between humans' more "primitive" subconscious (animalistic, below/base) and individualistic, "higher" consciousness (god-like, above), never letting us forget the tension, contradictions, and hilarity in trying to negotiate between the two levels.[12] A Freudian perspective, on the other hand, views the trickster as embodying the fundamental tension between the id (repressed base desires), ego (conscious self), and super-ego (social mores and values).[13] Many of these authors have drawn on the Raven cycle of narratives as exemplary of these more universal cultural roles and psychological themes in human mythology and folklore.

Perhaps the most important thing about Raven, beyond his multiplicity of roles, however, is that, as a cosmic *agent*, he is never static in life or in lore. Again, Radin sums up the pattern neatly for trickster figures in general:

> The symbol which Trickster embodies is not a static one. It contains within itself the promise of differentiation, the promise of god and man. For this reason every generation occupies itself with interpreting Trickster anew. No generation *understands him fully but no generation can do without him*. Each had to include him in all its theologies, in all its cosmogonies, despite the fact that it realized that he did not fit properly into any of them, for he represents not only the undifferentiated and distant past, but likewise the undifferentiated present within every individual. This constitutes his universal and persistent attraction. And so he became and remained everything to every man—god, animal, human being, hero, buffoon, he who was before good and evil, denier, affirmer, destroyer and creator. If we laugh at him, he grins at us. What happens to him happens to us.[14]

As the antithesis of stasis, of inertia, of the status quo, of those (besides himself) who would hoard their treasures rather than distribute them, Raven is never satisfied with existing circumstances. He is always looking for and leading us to more, consistent with the role of ravens in many human cultures as guides and in augury.[15]

'Raven is walking along the beach,' narrations of Raven's adventures often begin, inviting listeners to follow his jaunty moves. Motion is the norm and disruption the tool, it seems, in every Raven story. And out of the ordure (the havoc, the mess!) that Raven wreaks in his wanderings comes a new order, but by then the trickster is off to his next adventure, grinning (cawing!).

While generalizations about the nature of culture heroes and trickster-transformers like Raven can be useful in understanding similar characters across cultures, they have limitations as well. One problem with the universalist perspectives is that they can flatten the uniqueness of individual Raven narratives as well as regional differences in manifestations of the culture hero and trickster. Del Hymes elaborates on this diversity in his overview essay on myth in the Northwest Coast Volume (7) of the *Handbook of the North American Indians*:

> In the north Raven is the gluttonous, lecherous trickster-transformer, center of very extensive cycles of stories among the Tlingit, Haida, and Tsimshian. From the Bella Bella southward as far as the Quileute and the Southern Coast Salish, Raven is a gluttonous trickster but not a transformer, and Mink is Raven's rival in lechery. Among the Southwestern Coast Salish and Chinookans the trickster-buffoon is Bluejay. [...] Coyote is a trickster-transformer on the Lower Columbia (Chinookans), in the inland valleys of western Oregon (Kalapuyans, Takelma), and on a part of the Oregon coast (Alseans). Among the Tillamook the trickster is Ice [... and so on].[16]

Beyond regional differences within the Northwest Coast culture area, there are also individual differences in the style, oeuvre, and gestalt of specific narrators, who may revel in certain particulars, connections, or details relating to their communities, histories, and environs, as much as the broad motifs of Raven's wanderings and deeds. Raven stories are never recounted purely by rote; rather, there is always a critical individual context to their disseminations and elaborations—a social and geographic life to the stories. For Radin it was clear that "we cannot properly and fully understand the nature of these problems or the manner in which they have been formulated in the various trickster myths unless we study these myths in their specific cultural environments and in their historic settings."[17] This precept led Radin to study myth and narrative not just horizontally or comparatively, but also vertically through deep, individual life histories and autobiographies he collected from gifted Indigenous philosophers and storytellers, especially the Winnebago brothers Sam and Jasper Blowsnake with whom he formed a unique partnership. Similarly, many scholars among the Tlingit have taken this lead and adopted the life history approach in working intensively with individual leaders and storytellers as culture bearers.[18]

Despite the pioneering work of Boas, Swanton, de Laguna, and others, it has taken a new generation of scholars, working collaboratively with storytellers, to flesh out their important social, cultural, and environmental contexts. This new scholarship has enabled a freer and fuller appreciation of Raven stories, not merely as folklore or cultural artifacts, but as genuine oratory, art, 'edutainment', and inspiration. Nora and Richard Dauenhauer and their collaborators on this volume of Raven narratives exemplify this new model, which is caringly attentive to the particulars of individual stories. Strongly grounded in linguistics, comparative studies, and the social and intellectual genealogies of individual stories and storytellers, the Dauenhauers and their co-editors manage to bring Tlingit Raven stories alive in new ways, enriching their context and adding dimensions and nuances that are often lost in translation, abstraction, or universalist interpretations. We are enormously indebted to them for this monumental effort, which has yielded this opus in both Tlingit and English from coastal Tlingit communities in Alaska. Some 50 years in the making, this book is destined to become the definitive work on Raven narratives, setting a standard for appreciative inquiry of this deep and abiding, highly entertaining, and ever-rich and relevant oral literature. If Raven stories show us how to live, as Daanawáak̲ states, then this volume shows us how to understand and appreciate all that Raven and Raven storytellers have to teach us.

Putting Raven Stories Together: Challenges and Organizational Themes

As so much is attributed to Raven by so many people and peoples across the scales of time and space, there are necessarily challenges in putting a book like this together. I want to point to a few of these organizational issues and themes.

Perhaps the major challenge, with the quantity and variety of Raven stories, is what to include or not to include. While most well-known, and a few less well-known, Raven stories are included in this volume, it cannot be said to be comprehensive, for Raven is never fully captured. There are seemingly countless variations on every Raven story, according to individual storytellers' renderings in particular contexts. Furthermore, while some variations are included here, even variations by the same storyteller (e.g., Shaadaax', Robert Zuboff) for different audiences, there are necessarily many other versions that are omitted. Additionally, there are doings attributed to Raven that do not necessarily have rich narratives to accompany them, or at least not stories that are still known. For example, many features of the landscape are attributed to Raven's work, especially anomalous or outstanding geographic sites (a theme taken up further below), but not all are backed by detailed stories. Another challenge is how much to contextualize Tlingit Raven narratives in the larger canon of Raven stories and those of similar characters in world folklore. Originally, this book manuscript contained a nearly 250-page introduction by the Dauenhauers that sought to place the unique Tlingit corpus of Raven stories within the larger literature and tradition of tricksters and culture heroes around the world.

Brilliant in its synthesis but unfortunately too lengthy to include here, a separate publication is planned for this essay.

Another challenge is how to organize a book of Raven narratives. Time and space are fundamental considerations. With respect to time, Raven stories do not follow a simple chronology. This is one reason why the stories are considered a 'cycle'. As a transformer, Raven is always disrupting and rearranging (more than actually creating) and there is no grand plan or simple progressive sequence to a higher or utopian end. Narrators may create their own sequences or connections between stories in the cycle, as we find among master storytellers K̲aadashaan and Deikeenaak'w in Swanton's *Tlingit Myths and Texts* and those represented in this book. With the Raven and a range of other oral history narratives in mind, Frederica de Laguna proposed classifying Tlingit temporality into four categories (mythic, legendary, historical, modern) in order to place them in time sequence that could articulate with Western historiography.[19] Obviously, most Raven stories were classified deep in her 'mythic' (*tlaagú*) category. But not all Raven stories can be bound by this category, and his discovery of whiskey, for example, appears to have a much shallower historical context. Moreover, Tlingit narrators are not particularly concerned with chronology so much as plot. The Dauenhauers suggested two types of Raven stories in time: *tlaagú*, 'what-is-old' (ancient or mythical) and *shkalneek*, 'what is told' (or 'a telling'). *Tlaagú* is sometimes glossed as ancient, mythic, or eternal, but it is complex and not simply a term or subgenre applied to narratives. As de Laguna observed, "[*Tlaagú* stories are understood to be] true, but refer to a time so remote that one does not expect events to have the realistic qualities of the present, nor can one expect to understand clearly how or why things happened."[20] Anthropologist Richard Nelson, in *Make Prayers to the Raven*, calls this temporality "distant time",[21] primordial time, which, importantly, continues to affect the present. The world-shaping occurrences from *tlaagú*, including such things as major geological shifts or formations, are encoded in Raven's doings. Here we see Raven also as culture hero, unsurpassed in his capacity to both stimulate and respond to environmental change at a grand earth systems level. He alternately instigates or struggles with profound disruptions in the natural order, like fiery volcanic eruptions and titanic floods, which are foundational elements of the geography of the North Pacific Rim, among the most dynamic and dramatically active landscapes in the world. This *longue durée* of geologic time is the stage for Raven as a world-maker and as an adaptive and resilient being and force within a tumultuous cosmic and geological matrix.[22]

The Raven cycle of culture hero and world-maker stories typically include the following narratives: 1) Raven survives the great Flood, brought on by his jealous uncle; 2) Raven proceeds to bring land back to the world by harvesting (with the help of sea otter) some sand from the depth of the flooded lands, which he scatters to create the Aleutian Islands and other parts of Alaska; 3) Raven steals the sun, the moon, and the stars from his grandfather (*Naas Shaak* 'Head-of-the-Nass-River' or *Naasshagiyéil* 'Raven-of-the-Head-of-Nass-River') thus giving light to the day and night sky; 4) Raven forces the Little-Elder-Who-Enlarged-the-Tide (a.k.a. Old Woman of the Tide) to move the tides daily for access and productivity; 5) Raven steals fresh water from his brother-in-law, Petrel, to make the rivers and lakes; 6) Raven cons Pygmy Owl into helping him obtain fire from a source flaring up over the open ocean (apparently a volcano); 7) Raven captures salmon and other food sources by pulling the floating Salmon Box to shore with his borrowed magic Octopus Tentacle Cane; and 8) Raven transforms humans into leaf-like kin, lively and short-lived, from the stone-like, slow, and long-lived beings they once were. Stories may or may not proceed in this order and may be further linked to each other in various ways. As well, there are other non-Raven origin stories that complement, or perhaps even precede, the Raven cycle, such as the origin and separation of the Sun and Moon, portrayed as brother and sister, of Thunder (from *Xeitl* 'Thunderbird') and Earthquakes (from *Haayeeshaanák'u* 'Old-Woman-Underneath'), also sometimes represented as siblings, and of the *Lḵ'ayáak'w*, associated with the origin of Rainbows,[23] or more commonly the Milky Way. Unlike Raven, these figures may not rise to the level of a culture hero who transforms existing beings into their present forms, defines social roles and cultural norms, and teaches people various survival skills; and some of the brother-sister stories may be marked by incest events.[24] Yet, like Raven stories, they are associated with disruption and the shaping of the cosmos.

Another subset of Raven stories concerns more mundane and less world-making events, although they may involve transformation. Raven's impacts in these stories are consequential but less cosmic. These include Raven and Bear, Raven and the Blueberries, Raven and Whiskey, and the like. There are many more in this category than can be included in one volume, and some, like Raven and Fog Woman, could certainly be considered as part of the grand Raven cycle,[25] reflecting the fuzziness and fluidity that arises whenever we try to neatly classify or categorize this boundless trickster-transformer.

This leads us to another challenge for this book: conceptualizing and placing Raven in space. Just as he works at a multiplicity of temporal scales, Raven also works at a wide range of spatial scales, from the cosmic to the subtidal to the landscape level. In addition to liberating the skies from darkness in the Container of Daylight story, we find Raven at specific localities like the Nass River (a setting for the Container of Daylight story), Dry Bay (where Raven broke open the Container of Daylight), Akwe River (site of Raven's tracks from dragging in the Salmon Box and other stories), and the Hazy Islands (site of Petrel's freshwater spring). Yet other sites associated with Raven's doings do not necessarily have epic stories associated with them. The creek at Saginaw Bay on Kuiu Island, recently rechristened with its

Raven name, *Skanáx̱*, is a good example. The meaning of the Tlingit name *Skanáx̱* is said to be related to the name of a village on the eastern shore of Saginaw Bay where Raven was greeted by a cacophony of clams squirting water on its fertile beaches. When he alighted there, Raven at first tried to name the place after the Nass River (which he thought it resembled, visually) but, being overwhelmed by the noisy clams, so named it *Skanáx̱* instead, after the clamorous shellfish.[26] The story is not elaborate but gives us a sense of another important role of Raven: namer.[27] Similarly, another site in Saginaw Bay is associated with Raven: *Yéil Kawóot* 'Raven Beads'.[28] This site houses a unique form of round, center-holed fossils, known as chrinoids, which are well preserved in the limestone bench forming the inside shoreline of Saginaw Bay. Raven is said to have fashioned these beads into a necklace for his wife. Other such sites associated with Raven can be found in proximity to nearly every major traditional Tlingit, Haida, and Tsimshian community.

The spatial and temporal dimensions of Raven's activities combine in landscapes that are especially dynamic and discontinuous with their surroundings. A good example of this is the Alsek River–Dry Bay drainage, referenced in the stories of Frank Italio, Frank Dick, Katherine Mills, and Robert Zuboff in this volume and in other Raven narratives.[29] This dramatically rugged region contains the highest mountains, broadest glacial forelands, and most ever-shifting rivers in *Lingít Aaní* 'Tlingit Country' and, correspondingly, features the highest density of Raven placenames. Here, even names that do not reference Raven directly can be the result of his interventions. As an example, Bear Island, the major island feature in Dry Bay, is called *Yáay* 'Humpback Whale' or *Yáay X'áat'i* 'Humpback-Whale Island', for it is here that the whale Raven entered through its blowhole, to feast on its blubbery innards, finally was beached.[30] Raven "wished the Whale to strand on a fine sandy beach" and thus the Alsek delta is said to be sandy as a result.[31] As the narratives detail, it was here that people living in the east side of Dry Bay heard Raven calling and dragged the whale ashore and flensed it, eventually opening a hole big enough for Raven to escape the whale's belly exclaiming "Caw!", his signature cry of trickster triumph, having cheated the people out of much of the whale meat and fat.

Raven's food quest is also evident in his geographic tracks in Dry Bay, at Akwe River, which are produced after he drags in the famous *Kudatankahídi*, or 'Salmon Box', a repository of jumping fish and other seafoods, to shore. The Salmon Box was heavy and Raven's effort to pull it ashore, aided by the magic Octopus Tentacle Cane, left indelible landmarks on the land including at *Yéil Áx̱ Daak̲ Uwanugu Yé* 'Where Raven Scooted Back [Kicking Up the Sand]' and *Yéil Áa Yoo Akaawajiyi Yé* 'Where Raven's Feet Worked into the Mud Dragging [the Salmon Box]'.[32] Many in Yakutat have seen these Raven tracks, and some were taken there and shown them as an illustration of Raven's work on the land. As de Laguna records: "Canoe Prow House of the Tłukʷax̣ʌdi [Lukaax̱.ádi] refers to the enclosed prow of this canoe [the

Salmon Box], and the Tł’ᴜknax̣ᴀdi [L’uknax̱.ádi] use a dance paddle shaped like the [Octopus Tentacle Cane]. The point, ’Atuqka, was ‘a place just like the prow of a canoe.’”[33] The entire peninsula between the rivers defining this place was referred to as *Yaakw Shaká*, literally ‘Canoe Prow’, and linked to Raven’s original Salmon Box.

Another key result of this story, like that of “Raven Goes Down Along the Bull Kelp” and “Raven and the King Salmon”, is that Raven, as culture hero, brings food to the people. Food sources that have been previously inaccessible are made available to the people, who previously were poor and struggling. This aspect of the Raven cycle is very important and exemplifies Raven as a hero to the people, as emphasized by Katherine Mills, who ends her telling of “Raven and the Salmon Box” in this way:

Áwé	Well,
yáa—yá Yéil aadé haa éet wudishiyi yé áyá.	This—this is how Raven helped us.
Ách áyá k̲’anashgidéi k̲u.oo kagéi kaawaháa	This is how poor people came to have access to salmon,
yá shkalneek.[34]	this very story.

The same is true of Raven’s sharing of the sun, the moon, the stars, tides, and fresh water with the people. However, rather than being caught and brought to shore, these essential life elements are released from those seeking to hoard them from circulation.

Alsek River–Dry Bay is also a site where Raven is said to have opened the Box of Daylight he stole from his grandfather at Nass River.[35] In doing so, he not only released the sun, the moon, and the stars into the cosmos, but also frightened everything else, including the rocks and the mountains, which vacated the coastal land from Dry Bay all the way to Ocean Cape, near Yakutat, leaving the vast, sandy forelands that define this coast today, as Fred White notes. It was also in this area that Raven obtained the first plants and other earthly material from the sea otters after the great Flood.[36]

Another critical aspect of Southeast Alaska geography that comes to us courtesy of Raven’s disruptions is that of the great Flood. In this story, often marking the beginning of the Raven cycle, Raven enables his own birth into a human family and provokes his maternal uncle (known as Yook̲is’kook̲éik, ‘Tide-Commander’), who has killed all his previous newborn nephews for fear he might be displaced. However, Raven, whom Frank Italio calls «lyax̱dats’éini súk»[37] ‘a troublemaker-to-be’, outsmarts Yook̲is’kook̲éik, avoiding every deadly trap his uncle sets. Repeatedly stymied in his attempts to rid himself of Raven, his uncle finally invokes a great Flood to wipe Raven from the face of the earth. The Flood manifests not as torrential rainfall, as in the Biblical flood. Instead, it comes as a great tidal inundation, indicative of the floods at the end of the Pleistocene and the retreat of the Last Glacial

Maximum. After saving his mother, Raven escapes the rising tides by flying upward and clinging to the atmospheric clouds. Raven survives, dropping onto a kelp patch on the flooded Earth, and, with the help of a sea otter, proceeds to remake the land for human habitation, exemplifying the principles of formation and transformation for which he is famous.

The Flood story emphasizes another important organizational theme in the Raven cycle, along with space and time: material transformations. Material transformations are at the heart of Raven's dynamism, catalysis, disruption, and reconfiguring. In this sense, Raven may represent carbon—the building block of life—personified, and the carbon cycle—the rearranging or carbon atoms between Earth, its organisms, and the atmosphere—perpetuated through his ceaseless activity and shifting materiality. In numerous Native American traditions Raven begins his existence in pure white form, "only to be permanently blackened by his own misadventures with fire and its sooty, hydrocarbon emissions. Viewed as an interspecies transformer and an agent of metamorphosis, Raven may be the best embodiment and protagonist we have of carbon's metamorphisms, cycles, fluxes and reactions."[38] This is well emphasized by Swanton's interlocutor, Ḵaadashaan, who relates that Raven endured the Flood by turning to rock.[39] After the Flood, Ḵaadashaan states that Raven also tried to make humans out of rock, as he had been born, but when he did so humans proved too slow, so he chose to fashion them out of leaf instead. Unlike stones, which are slow and long-lived, leaves are fleeting, and according to Swanton's interlocutor, Deikeenaak'w: "That is why there is death in the world. If men had come from the rock there would be no death."[40] Robert Zuboff puts it similarly in this volume:

Át wulis'eeséyáx̱ áwé yatee	When he converted this leaf
yáa kayaanée	into his brother,
du kéek'x̱ awulyeix̱í.	it moved like it was blowing in the wind.
Tleidooshú jinaak táakw,	Sixty years,
dax̱adooshú jinkaat táakw,	seventy years
yéi áyá haa kanax̱ yoo at yateek.	is how long it takes for old age to overtake us.
Yáa kayaank'ée áyá	It's out of this little leaf
haa éex̱ awliyéx̱ yáa Yéil.	that Raven made us.
Yéi áyá dutláakw	This is how they tell the story
yáa Yéil.[41]	of Raven.

On the other hand, because he originated from stone, Susie James remarks in her story of the Flood, «tle noow yáx̱ gíwé wootee wé Yéil ḵu.aa, / yá lingit'aaní awliyex̱i Yeil»[42] 'Raven was like a fortress, I suppose, / this Raven who arranged the world'. And when the people came to escape the great Flood elsewhere, they imitated Raven in enclosing themselves in great stone nests high in the mountains—not quite the high clouds that Raven clung to, but the highest landmarks that surrounded their settlements. Here, as Robert Zuboff details, people built their stone forts, or *xóowx'* (also translated as 'monuments' or 'cairns'), «yá a t'éi ḵoowaneix̱i»[43] 'behind which the people found shelter' using ropes to tie themselves, their dogs (kept to ward off the bears, also swimming for refuge), and their canoes to prevent them from being washed away. The petrified ropes are still preserved in places like *S'ex'aayihéen Shaa* (a high mountain near the narrator's village of Angoon).[44] Most Tlingit villages have stories of their refuge mountains, and stories of migrations in the wake of the great Flood that took them to the interior, or elsewhere, until they could return to their (often transformed) coastal homelands.[45]

These themes of Raven as a force of almost infinite variation, temporality, spatiality, and materiality all converge on what is perhaps the most important theme in Raven's teachings on how to live: how to survive *and* thrive creatively. Raven's anarchic creativity and ways of being show us how to navigate, negotiate, and adapt successfully in a world where there is always disruptive and indeterminate change, stress, want, webs of interdependence, and unintended consequences that haunt and constrain us, be it on a vast geological timescale or a local social or geographic one. Raven stories provide a compelling heuristic to comprehend this existential fate of ours to which we must respond individually, socially, and ecologically. Such adaptation takes two things that Raven teaches by both positive and negative example: practical knowledge and practical wisdom.

The Practical Knowledge and Wisdom of Raven in the Anthropocene

Practical knowledge and wisdom are concepts often overlooked in academic studies of trickster-transformers, including Raven. Yet, this is precisely what narrators often emphasize when they suggest that "Raven shows us how to live." Raven's intersubjective manipulations of earth systems and his fellow species reveal the integrity, balance, exigencies, and contingencies of life on Earth, which every inhabitant must know something about in order to survive, if not thrive. Indeed, elsewhere[46] we have proposed that Raven, through his schemes and machinations, exhibits what James Scott has termed *mētis*: "the indispensable role of practical knowledge, informal processes, and improvisation in the face of unpredictability."[47] Raven is a master of this mode of practical knowledge discovery even though his novel approaches and improvisations do not necessarily produce (only) their intended outcomes.

Raven's other crucial modality is as a transcender of conventional boundaries. He marries other species, becomes their offspring, and otherwise pushes beyond the conventional limits of intersubjectivity and interanimation, such that seemingly nothing is beyond his realm of manipulations. In this respect the Raven of the 'Ravencene' anticipates humanity (anthropos) of the Anthropocene,[48] both as an agent (or 'driver') of change through his hubris, appetites, and aspirations to control things for his own purposes, and as a resilient respondent to change (through coping, mitigation, adaptation, etc.) when earth systems and their constituent elements prove too powerful, dynamic, or complex to be harnessed in such a way. It is yet to be seen whether humanity will prove as resilient as Raven, but Raven is there for us as an object of contemplation, a 'mirror for [hu]man[ity]' in Radin's terms. I would go further to suggest that Raven also is an agent for inter-species communication. As such, Raven can be conceived as both a boundary species, who transforms and transcends his own species identity, and a boundary object. Just as tricksters are liminal beings,[49] operating betwixt, between, and beyond conventional species and organism boundaries, boundary objects are those "both plastic [flexible] enough to adapt to local needs and … yet robust enough to maintain a common identity across sites."[50] As such, boundary objects help to bridge gaps between different parties' social and conceptual worlds. Practically, Raven does this by linking nearly every dimension of the cosmos—from water to fire to light—to the social and conceptual worlds of humans and other species. In this way, Raven is more than a 'mirror for man'—he embodies, as a boundary object, the radical interdependence of Earth's systems and constituent beings in a way that makes our own interconnectedness to the living animate cosmos and its inhabitants more comprehensible and negotiable. This is why Raven stories are good to remember and good to think about in a wide variety of contexts where social, moral, and ecological boundaries have been, are being, or need to be disrupted, transcended, restored, or reconfigured.

The strategic negotiation and transcending of conventional boundaries is key to acquiring what Barry Schwartz and Kenneth Sharpe term *practical wisdom*, "a kind of moral jazz". Practical wisdom "sometimes depends on rules and principles—like notes on the page and the basic melodies in jazz. But rules by themselves can't do the job. Moral improvisation is the interpretive tune we play around these notes and melodies in order to do the right thing."[51] As these authors further stress, echoing Aristotle, wisdom is the "master virtue",[52] the key to human happiness and well-being, which depend on moral experience and empathy with others, not abstract rules. Without the practical wisdom that comes from moral know-how, our virtues can quickly turn to disastrous liabilities: recklessness rather than courage, blind loyalty rather than commitment, egotism rather than empathy. Raven stories reveal the boundaries between these virtues and liabilities across a vast moral and biophysical spectrum. Furthermore, because Raven's appetites and improvisations occur at the individual, interspecific, and cosmic scale, and lead through both positive and negative example, we see what it means to 'do the right thing', individually, socially, and collectively as moral beings in an ecosystem of sentient beings. Perhaps it is no coincidence, then, that elders like Daanawáak̲ are led to reflect on Raven's world-making adventures as a source of wisdom. And to the extent that Raven's wisdom resides in peoples' deep understandings of his activities on the land, we can also say, echoing Keith Basso's book on Western Apache storytelling and sense of place, that Raven's 'wisdom sits in places'.[53]

In this way, Raven proves to be a moral compass and ecological consciousness. He embodies the way of knowing that the anthropologist and philosopher of science Gregory Bateson outlines in his book *Steps to an Ecology of Mind*. 'Ecology of mind' is a holistic, integrated perspective, which does not limit itself to the simple measures and dissection of worldly phenomena, by counting and weighing, but rather trains itself to apprehend and respond to the broad systemic patterns and open-ended processes that define our being in a world that is constantly creating, conditioning, and transforming us. That is, a world that is *alive*, *interdependent*, and *relational*.

Raven stories encode these 'steps to an ecology of mind' by engaging the fundamental planetary patterns and processes in relation to human and other-than-human ways of thinking and being in the world. Mind and materiality are never static or separable, or limited to a single body. As a result, Raven is never just a simple bird, or a simple god, but a composite stone, fortress, catalyst, conniver, improviser, boundary-spanner, jester, and so much more. Even in transformation, Raven is always more than an individual organism: through his doings and interactions, he literally constitutes the earth system as we know it and becomes a primal force in its evolutionary processes and transformations. He survives and endures not simply because he is an extraordinary being adapting to his environment, but because Raven is *being and environment in co-production*. Raven's improvisational "moral jazz" is the manifestation, realization, and becoming of an ecology of mind and being in an interdependent world of lively, sentient beings. Ultimately it is the understanding and negotiation of this complex relational world, and all of its craziness, change, and contingency, that leads to practical knowledge and practical wisdom.

Enduring Raven: Heritage and Destiny

Raven endures because he still has much to offer. As the incredible embodiment of powerful, contingent, collaborative, and conflicting appetites and forces that make physical and social existence possible and a continuous drama, this trickster-transformer-worldmaker offers innumerable lessons to ponder as we peruse his peregrinations with the master narrators we encounter in this collection. Perhaps no other creature can boast as much of how he made and transformed the world—and boast Raven does!

Pessimists may see a great reckoning ahead in this new epoch we call the Anthropocene, a payback for the havoc humans have wreaked on the planet in the industrial age. Optimists, on the other hand, see opportunities for humans to embrace their dominance and engineer a better world. Yet one can argue that these opposing visions are themselves products of human conceit—Raven-like boasts, if you will. As Raven narratives remind us, both these extreme visions are flawed and anthropocentric. Great floods, darkness, famine, and other disasters have all been visited on Earth before, with profound winners and losers, but the people survived, rock-like on the mountaintops. And when the topography and ecology changed after the Flood, Raven made humans more leaf-like, and showed them how to adapt, flexibly and resiliently as such. Moreover, Raven gave the people the benefit of hard-learned practical wisdom to navigate the complex, dynamic, ever-transforming, non-linear world that they inhabited—practical wisdom and an ecology of mind being indispensable virtues that human and other-than-human beings needed to survive in the world they were co-producing.

As Raven also shows us, hubris and the aspiration to engineer the cosmos to our selfish ends have always been with us. Yet, for humanity, as for Raven, things rarely work out as planned, and when we insult or push planetary boundaries too far, there are unanticipated consequences: other living beings, including the rocks, the waters, and the glaciers, may push back, putting humans in jeopardy. Thus, an ecology-of-mind awareness and attentiveness toward earth systems and other-than-human beings and how we affect and relate to them is requisite if we are to survive the so-called Anthropocene. This is but one of many lessons of Raven and why each of these *shkalneek*, these wise 'tellings' of his doings, should and will endure. Before there was the Anthropocene there was the *Ravencene* and it was bigger, more dramatic, and more all-encompassing and vitally connected than its anthropocentric counterpart.

What is more, Raven never died. According to Frank Italio in this volume, Raven still lives in a rock house west of Yakutat, where he retired after completing his cycle of major deeds on Earth.[54] Thus, the many manifestations of Raven's work endure. In one form or another, they will always be with us to instruct and to ponder—that is, if we remember the stories. The gifted orators represented in this book did remember, and through them the editors have reinvigorated and co-produced the Raven cycle of stories in a most entertaining and edifying way, thereby surfacing the deepest truths of being and becoming in the cultural-ecological matrix of the land and its inhabitants. Because these orators have carried and communicated these wise tellings, the practical knowledge and wisdom of Raven remains alive and relevant, resilient and adaptive, inspirational and hilariously amusing for generations to come. Accordingly, Raven will continue to accompany the people and guide them, with his moral jazz and razzmatazz, as Lingít *shagóon* (heritage and destiny), for the next generations of worldmaking.

Preface

1 COMMENTS FROM NORA MARKS DAUENHAUER & RICHARD DAUENHAUER

Why More Raven?

Raven is beyond doubt the most familiar figure in Tlingit folklore. His existence and exploits have been documented and discussed by outside observers for almost 240 years (since 1788),* but Raven stories have never before been published in Tlingit! All previous versions have been in Russian, German, and English. Essentially, this volume presents the first Raven stories ever published in the original Tlingit. (Actually, we should hasten to modify this sweeping statement; the sole exception to this is the 1973 booklet of a Raven story by Robert Zuboff published in Tlingit only, without English translation, under the imprint of Tlingit Readers, Inc., and subsumed in this volume.) Even John Swanton, who in 1909 published the first Tlingit-language texts, and who collected and published some of the most comprehensive Raven cycles (in English), missed Raven in Tlingit. The older fieldwork and publication by Swanton and others have been a source for generations of subsequent retellings in English and other languages, each more removed in time and place from the original. The present volume is a bit of a paradox: it is nothing new, yet everything new. It presents the first Tlingit Raven stories ever published in the original language text, as transcribed directly from tape recordings of oral performance, and accompanied by facing English translations and detailed annotations.

---

* As far as we know, the first published reference to Tlingit Raven dates from June 1788, when the Russian navigators Gerasim Izmailov and Dimitri Bocharov visited Yakutat and described their contact with the Tlingits.

The Place of This Book in the Series

The present volume, fifth in the series *Classics of Tlingit Oral Literature*, continues the documentation of Tlingit oral literature, featuring in this case Raven stories, which form a major genre distinct in style, content, and function from the genres introduced in previous books in the series.

Volume 1, *Haa Shuká, Our Ancestors: Tlingit Oral Narratives*, is an introduction to Tlingit social structure and oral literature. It presents the concept of *at.óow* 'clan crests, possessions' and shows how at.óow are acquired through events in the lives of ancestors, and are remembered in myth, legend, and song.

Volume 2, *Haa Tuwunáagu Yís, For Healing Our Spirit: Tlingit Oratory*, is an introduction to Tlingit traditional spirituality and world view. It expands the concept of at.óow and shows how the clan crests are used, and how the social structure works. Through documentation of ceremonial oratory, this book illustrates the connection between verbal and visual art, between ritual and myth, and examines the potlatch as a unifying event in Tlingit folklife.

Volume 3, *Haa K̲usteeyí, Our Culture: Tlingit Life Stories*, is an introduction to Tlingit social and political history—the context in which the other genres of oral literature and folklife evolved and function today. It also provides more detail about the lives of the tradition bearers featured in the other volumes, showing not only the background they bring to their stories and speeches, but the importance of oral literature, visual art, at.óow, and other aspects of Tlingit folklore in their lives.

Volume 4, *Anóoshi Lingít Aaní Ká, Russians in Tlingit America: The Battles of Sitka, 1802 and 1804*, relates this history with accounts from both the Tlingit and Russian point of view.

Each volume in the series introduces a different genre of Tlingit oral literature and explains its position and function in Tlingit culture. Raven stories occupy a unique position and function in Tlingit oral literature. Ancestral narratives (featured in *Haa Shuká*) tend to be 'heavy' and deal with the serious side of legend and history. Oratory (featured in *Haa Tuwunáagu Yís*) might be called the gem in the crown jewels, especially at its ritual best. As a strategy for the removal of grief, speeches can be humorous (as they often are at Forty-Day Parties) or serious. But if the crest or ancestral narrative is the quintessential genre of tragedy, then Raven stories comprise the genre of comedy. Raven hops here and there, from serious origin myth to absurd comic relief. In many ways, Raven is elusive and harder to get at. The stories often illustrate human weaknesses demonstrated through negative examples, but also expressed as comedy, typically in a bewildering combination of the sacred and the scatological. Ultimately, this is not unlike tragedy in its focus and depiction of the 'tragic flaw' that destroys otherwise noble people, whether Shakespearian or Tlingit.

History of the Book

The present volume was to be our first book. But in the course of field-testing our working drafts in the mid 1980s we found Raven to be far less accessible to college students and the general reader than clan-crest stories and oratory. Despite their complexity and seriousness, the crest stories and speeches for the removal of grief were far easier for people to understand and appreciate. We think this is because the first questions of access the serious genres raise are 'within acceptable parameters'. They are technical and informational. But with Raven stories the problem was—and is—humor. Not that humor should be a problem, or that there is anything wrong with humor. But the unfortunate social reality is that humor is notorious for not translating well across cultural boundaries. We found ourselves to be the only ones laughing, and having to explain why we think the stories are funny. It's no fun explaining a joke to people who don't get it. Humor, social satire, and parody depend for their comic effect on prior knowledge of what is correct or expected. Only then can we laugh at the distortions, or at what goes wrong.

Ten years later, we frequently observe audiences at dramatizations of Raven stories feeling uneasy, wanting to laugh, but unsure if it's okay, asking if it's okay to laugh (yes), or if it shows disrespect for sacred traditions (no). Is it politically correct to laugh at Raven? (We can answer that question only with more of Raven.) Some viewers have been shocked and outraged, storming out of the theater in disgust, to pen angry letters to our office.

So, poor Raven got shunted down the literary line until we couldn't stand it anymore. We're laughing even harder at the stories now, and we hope that readers will laugh along. (We're tired of laughing in our private sleeve.) But the wait has been worth it. We've learned a lot more about Raven and other tricksters along the way. We've learned that tricksters can be serious business, and that beyond the slapstick on the surface, there can be more profound levels of understatement. We hope that the previously published volumes in this series will provide a literary and social context for the comedy in this one.

Nora Marks Dauenhauer & Richard Dauenhauer
Juneau, 1998*

* Note from Geiger and Leer: This is the date of the most recently modified draft preface that we could locate from among the Dauenhauers' estate.

2 COMMENTS FROM WILL GEIGER & JEFF LEER

Project Origin and Development

The original vision of this book was that of Nora and Richard Dauenhauer, so it is unfortunate that neither lived to see it completed. On June 12, 2014, they gave a joint lecture on the present volume, which was then still in developing form. Reflecting on the life of the project and what could be considered its inception, Nora pointed to a specific moment: "I came across a man in Angoon. His name was Bob Zuboff, Robert Zuboff, and he was very generous with me. I asked him if I could tape and he agreed."* The visit Nora paid to Zuboff's home, tape recorder in tow, took place in 1972. By that timeline, the present volume is now over fifty years in the making. At long last, following Zuboff's death two years after telling his stories to Nora, the publication of four intervening volumes on different topics, Richard's untimely death only two months after the June lecture, Nora's passing three years later, and the fate of the project changing hands multiple times, the words Zuboff generously shared to set this project in motion endure here half a century later in written form. Alongside Zuboff, six other storytellers are featured in this volume: Frank Italio of Yakutat, Andrew Wanamaker of Sitka, Susie James of Sitka (originally from Hoonah), Frank Dick of Yakutat, Austin Hammond of Haines, and Katherine Mills of Hoonah. Their words form the heart of this volume and are among the finest recorded examples of the classical art of Tlingit storytelling.

Contributions Over Time

As the original principal editors, Nora and Richard prepared many of the draft transcriptions and translations and developed a well-defined scope and structure for the book. In the intervening period since Richard's death on August 19, 2014, and Nora's on September 25, 2017, the content and organization of the book has been significantly revised, redacted, and modified, but much of the original framework remains in place. Numerous additional individuals, fluent Tlingit elders, and editorial teams have contributed to this volume. The stories were recorded by Frederica de Laguna, Jeff Leer, Henry Davis, Nora Dauenhauer, Mary Pelayo, Fred White, Gordon Sandy, Tim Wilson, and Edna Belarde Lamebull. Contributions to the written material were made by Fred White, Keri Eggleston, Lance Twitchell, Ishmael Hope, James Crippen, Helen Sarabia, Michael Travis, Linda Belarde, and Kathy Kolkhorst Ruddy while the Dauenhauers were still alive. After Richard and Nora passed, the project stagnated somewhat but members of this team continued the effort along with

* Interested readers are encouraged to view the recording of this lecture, which was the Dauenhauers' final joint statement on the project before their passing. The recording is held in SHI's archive (MC002, series 17, item 47) and is available on SHI's YouTube channel.

Sergei Kan. Fluent speakers Bessie Cooley, George Davis, and Marge Dutson advised members of this team in parsing lines of the Tlingit texts and discerning their meaning. In 2018 Twitchell reviewed a large portion of the material with Davis and Dutson. Will Geiger, working on the staff of Sealaska Heritage Institute (SHI), simultaneously began reviewing the texts independently and corresponded with Twitchell on revisions.

In 2020 Jeff Leer was coaxed out of retirement in order to see the project through to completion and joined the SHI staff to form the final editorial team with Geiger. We (Geiger and Leer) worked together on the material sporadically throughout 2020–2024. The Tlingit texts were reviewed while weighing the transcription against digitally cleaned-up versions of the original audio. The English translations were reviewed once the transcriptions had been more or less completed. The notes to the stories were substantially expanded and revised throughout the process. We consulted fluent speakers Ruth Demmert, Sam Johnston, Bessie Cooley, Kenneth Grant, Florence Sheakley, and David Katzeek on issues of translation and grammatical form. Roby Littlefield provided some crucial information about the spellings of names and clan affiliations, relying on lists of names and other information she had privately gathered at numerous ceremonies in Sitka. Our last joint effort was the remaining work to complete the front matter, editors' introduction, appendixes, notes, and final adjustments to the transcriptions and translations.

Upon considering the sheer volume of the texts, notes, and introductory material that would be necessary to publish what had become known as 'the Raven Book' in one volume, it became clear that the only way to come out with a high-quality publication within a reasonable time frame would be to separate the book into two volumes. Thus, this publication is roughly only half of the Dauenhauers' original vision. Even after reducing the scope of the project, we routinely passed one deadline after another and completion of the book took years longer than anticipated. In this volume we have prioritized the inclusion of narratives told as 'extended tales' or 'cycles', i.e., those in which multiple episodes from Raven's many adventures are told as an integrated sequence.

We must acknowledge the individuals who helped complete the final phases of proofing and designing the book. Amy Fletcher provided comprehensive editorial feedback on multiple iterations of the manuscript, correcting many granular errors and greatly improving the book's overall tone and organization. The manuscript also benefited from careful reading by Therese Pokorney and Mari Kramer, who jointly undertook the laborious task of cross-checking every reference and citation. Kramer also copyedited the final drafts of the manuscript with great attention to detail. The layout and design of the book was envisioned and executed by Nobu Koch with assistance from Fletcher and Kramer.

The Editorial 'We'

Although we find the use of the editorial 'we' somewhat off-putting, it has inexorably found its way into most of the material written in the voice of the editors (the preface, editors' introduction, notes, and appendixes). Section 1 of this preface is taken directly from the Dauenhauers' draft manuscript, so in that case 'we' preserves the voices of Nora and Richard. In section 2 of this preface, the editors' introduction, and the appendixes, 'we' refers to Geiger and Leer. Leer wrote the linguistic exposition (appendix 1); Geiger wrote §§1 and 2 of the editors' introduction; §3 of the editors' introduction was written jointly. Everything was jointly reviewed and edited until mutual agreement was reached. In the notes to the stories, the editorial 'we' often refers to Geiger and Leer, but in many other places it was already used in notes written by earlier (often unspecified) editors or teams of editors that were left unaltered by the final team; since the final team agreed with the earlier editors, the editorial 'we' is valid in these cases as well. In general, most of the notes focusing on technical aspects of grammar were written by Leer and most of the notes focusing on literary and rhetorical aspects of the stories were written by Geiger. Rarely, there were differences of opinion among editors as to what the speaker actually said or how to translate it. In such cases, rather than decide which interpretation is 'better' by editorial fiat, we discuss the differences in interpretation in the notes, specifying who provided which opinion and how they supported it.

Copyright and Royalties

Clan ownership and systems of oral copyright are essential features of Tlingit culture and these are central topics in the first two volumes in this series. Many stories from Tlingit oral tradition, especially those dealing with the experiences of clan ancestors and the acquisition of clan crests, are the real and sacred property of Tlingit clans. Even though the Raven stories form a distinct genre that is in general not subject to the same forms of oral copyright as the crest and ancestral narratives, questions of copyright and royalties for a book on Tlingit oral literature are relevant to the Tlingit community and should be explicitly addressed. Copyright of the material in this book is held by SHI. Any royalties that accrue from the sales of the book after meeting expenses for its production and publication go to SHI and are applied to future education-related projects. The editors were salaried or contracted by SHI to write and edit the book but receive no income from its sale.

Description and Goals of the Book

At the heart of this book are fifty Raven stories by seven Tlingit storytellers that were recorded between 1952 and 1989. The stories are presented with the transcribed text of the original Tlingit on the left-hand page and a facing English translation on the right-hand page. Detailed notes provided in the back of the book focus heavily on issues of grammar and translation, and to a lesser, but significant, extent on matters of oral-literary form and cultural context. Leading into the texts is an editors' introduction that discusses features of the context, composition, and characters of the stories as well as editorial decisions that bear on the manner in which the stories are presented to the reader on the page.

The development of the book's introduction in the history of this project deserves mention. Among the documents left behind when the Dauenhauers passed away was a manuscript primarily authored by Richard and originally intended to serve as the introduction to the present volume.* The draft introduction, penned primarily in 1998, includes, among other topics, an extensive scholarly engagement with ideas about the meaning and social function of Raven and other trickster figures across cultures, the position of the Raven genre in the general system of Tlingit oral literature, and a review of the nearly 200-year-long written record about Raven. The manuscript was in a state such that its inclusion in full here would have required editorialization beyond recognition of the original scope, form, and style that Richard had set forth. With the most heavily redacted draft comprising roughly 250 pages, its inclusion would have dramatically increased the width of the book and the timeline for copyediting and typesetting. We thus opted to exclude it from the volume but to make it available as a separate publication in order to preserve Richard's significant contribution to the scholarship on Raven and Tlingit oral literature. The manuscript will be made available as an independent text titled *Hilarious Raven, Being of Wantonness and Wit* through SHI's Box of Knowledge series.

This volume thus lacks the extensive discussion of the character Raven that the Dauenhauers originally envisioned. In the editors' introduction we address some of the same topics, such as the position of the Raven genre within Tlingit oral tradition and the kind of being Raven appears to be in the stories, but in less comprehensive detail. In the second section of the introduction, the cast of characters, we discuss the character Raven with the focus being the statements made about him by the storytellers of this volume and other tradition-bearers and scholars. Following after Raven is a similar treatment of a significant number of the characters that readers will encounter within the stories of this volume with comparative analysis of the storytellers' treatment of each.

In line with the prior volumes in this series, the major scholarly goal of the book is to present a substantial collection of primary data—the stories themselves—as accurately and meaningfully as possible. As an additional goal, we have gone to considerable lengths in the notes to explicate grammatical features of the Tlingit

* MS052, box 48, contains multiple iterations of the draft introduction, mostly from the period 1996–1998; the most recent is a 2015 version edited by Michael Travis after Richard's passing.

texts in hopes that the book may serve as another tool in the arsenal of students and teachers of the Tlingit language. In our comments on the storytellers' words—which go at times into granular detail—we often make use of a technical linguistic vocabulary. Appendix 1, a linguistic exposition, provides a description of many of the grammatical concepts and vocabulary items used throughout the book; in the notes to the texts, we often cross-reference relevant sections of this appendix rather than repeatedly describing the meaning of the technical terms in each case. Similarly, for discussion of the stories' characters and certain aspects of oral-literary form, the notes often direct readers to relevant sections of the editors' introduction. In preparing these texts, we have learned and continue to learn a great deal about the Tlingit language from these storytellers. We encountered several phenomena of Tlingit grammar that were either underdescribed or unmentioned in the linguistic literature, so students and scholars will find something new not only in terms of oral literature but also in the field of Tlingit grammar. We have strived to be as accurate as possible in the presentation and interpretation of the stories and accept any errors, oversights, or misinterpretations as our own.

Will Geiger & Jeff Leer
Juneau, May 2025

YÉIL KUNDAYAAYÍ

ADVENTURES OF RAVEN

Editors' Introduction

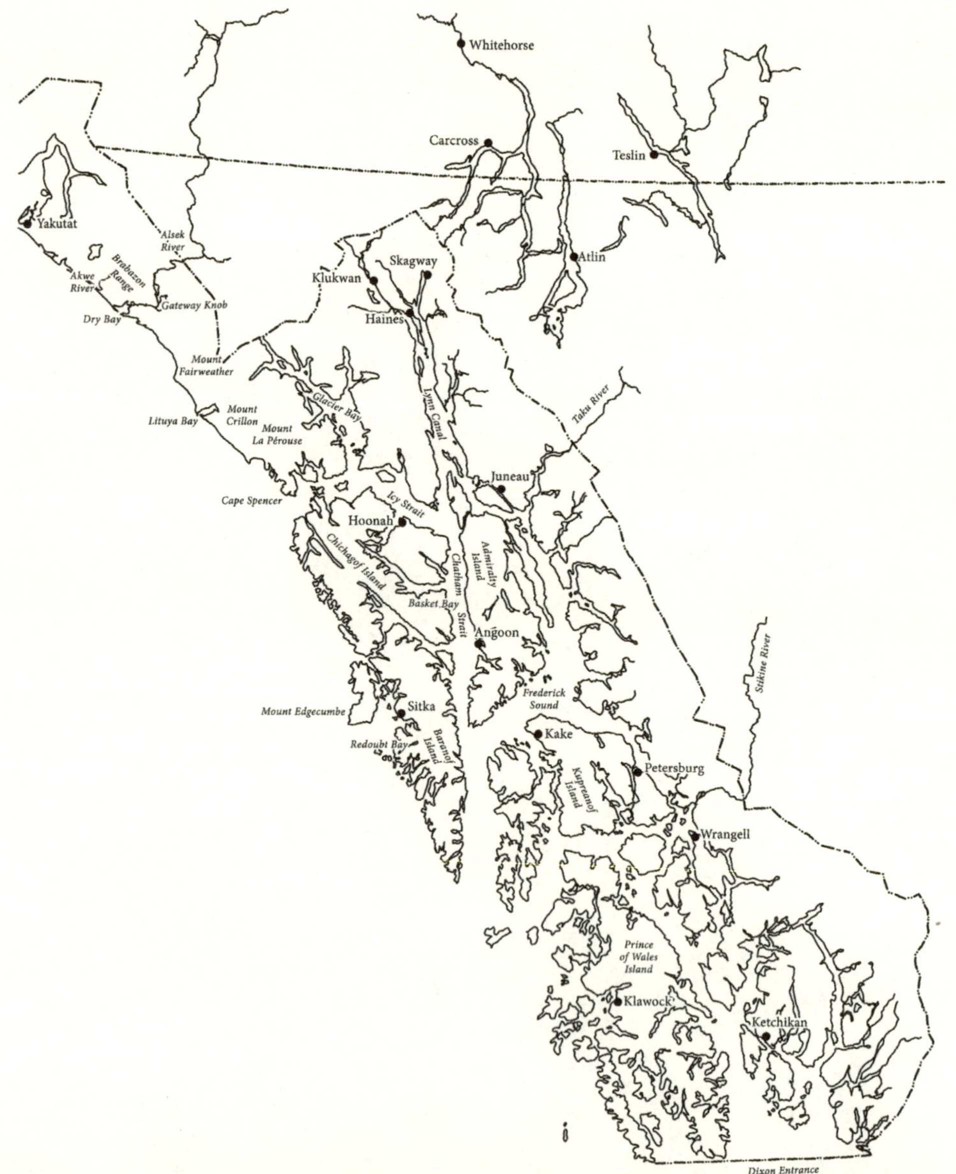

FIGURE 1. Map of Tlingit Country.

THE SUBJECT of this volume is the bewildering figure known in Tlingit as Yéil and in English as Raven. Raven's adventures cover a vast range of experiences from the permanent reconfiguration of the cosmos to the short-lived satisfaction of scandalous appetites. The narratives depicting these antics unfold in fluctuating combinations of weighty myth and uproarious comedy. The fifty stories included in this volume were recorded from oral performances in the Tlingit language throughout the period 1952–1989. These are the words of seven of the period's great storytellers: Frank Italio, Andrew Wanamaker, Robert Zuboff, Susie James, Frank Dick, Austin Hammond, and Katherine Mills. Individually, each story and storyteller offers a unique perspective on Raven and the art of storytelling. Together, they give a taste of the general spirit of Tlingit Raven stories as a classical oral literary genre as it existed in the minds and words of elder storytellers of the mid-to-late twentieth century.

The focus of this introduction is the context, composition, and formatting of the Raven stories of this volume. Section 1 introduces the reader to the dramatic setting within the stories, the context within which they were told, and some characteristics of the form and style of the oral narratives. Section 2 introduces the characters that appear throughout this collection of stories, discussing them in light of the specific ways they are deployed and referred to by the storytellers. Section 3 describes features of the formatting of the stories as they appear on the page, covering editorial decisions involved in preparing the written and translated forms of the stories and what certain features of the texts are meant to communicate to the reader. Readers seeking a comprehensive background on Tlingit society and oral literature are referred to the prior volumes in this series, which go into detail describing Tlingit social structure, cultural practices, spirituality, visual art, geography, history, and politics, and analyzing how these relate to genres and specific texts of Tlingit oral tradition.[1]

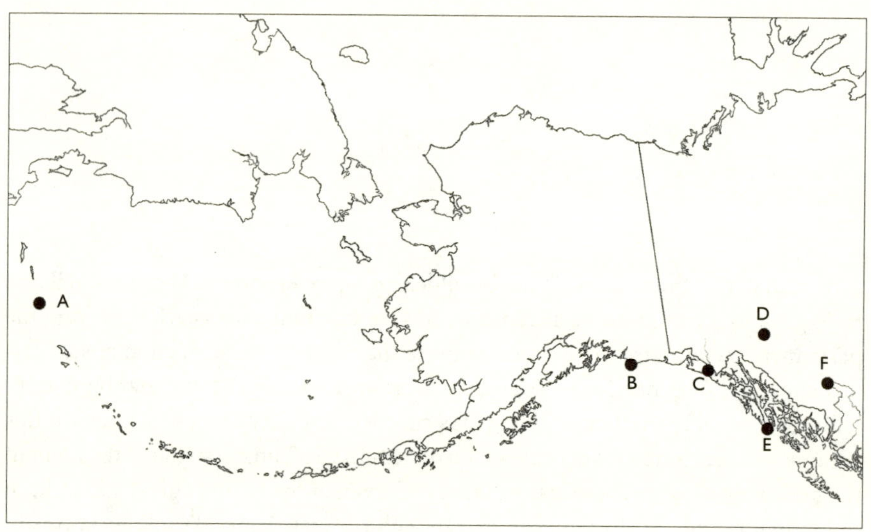

FIGURE 2. The range of Raven's antics in this volume.

A. Tip of the Aleutian Chain (§1.1.1.1). Where Raven fell to after dangling from the sky by his nose.

B. Near Kayak Island (§1.1.1.2). Where Raven harpooned a whale from his skin kayak.

C. Dry Bay (§1.1.1.3). Where Raven floated ashore in a dead whale, pulled ashore the Salmon Box, and broke daylight on the world, among many other things.

D. Near Teslin (§1.1.1.4). Where Raven walked around barefoot.

E. Hazy Islet (§1.1.1.5). Where Raven stole fresh water from his brother-in-law Petrel to disperse throughout the world.

F. Head of the Nass River (§1.1.1.6). Where Raven obtained the Container of Daylight and other heavenly luminaries.

1 NOTES ON CONTEXT & COMPOSITION

1.1 *Space*

We will first consider the setting of the stories and the storytelling in space. The principal dramatic setting of the Tlingit Raven stories is the homeland of the Tlingit people. This extends along the coast of Southeast Alaska northeast towards the Copper River and southeast to Dixon Entrance, also reaching northwest into the interior along the Chilkat River and into northwestern British Columbia and southwestern Yukon (see figure 1). This region is home to the world's largest temperate rainforest, with much of the lower elevations covered by stands of evergreens and dense underbrush. Hundreds of streams and rivers supporting wild runs of salmon flow through the forests to the ocean. The typically rocky and steep coast encompasses the 300-mile Alexander Archipelago, which contains over 1,000 islands of varying sizes separated from the mainland by winding ocean channels. Mountains along the coast rise directly out of the water, typically to elevations of 2,000–4,000 feet. Glaciers periodically spill into the ocean and reach into heavily iced interior mountain ranges that are punctuated occasionally by peaks over 10,000 feet.

The Raven stories are intimately connected to this landscape and natural environment. In addition to serving as the stage upon which Raven acts, many of the stories explain how features of this environment came to be arranged as they are. Raven's adventures are often localized by storytellers in specific places, such as the bank of the Akwe River, where Raven is said to have removed the lid from the Container of Daylight. Some of the specified locations lie outside of Tlingit Country, such as the head of the Nass River, from where Raven obtained the container. In many other cases, the events are not overtly connected to any particular place and it is up to the audience to make imaginative sense of the setting.

1.1.1 *The Spatial Setting Within the Stories*

We will take a cursory survey of the places Raven visits in the stories of this volume in order to orient readers in space. A few of these locations will serve as opportunities for discussing features of oral literary composition, looking at how and to what effect the storytellers depict Raven in these places. We will begin at the western extreme and generally move east and southeast.

1.1.1.1 *The Tip of the Aleutian Chain*

The furthest west that we find Raven in this volume is well outside of Tlingit Country on a floating bed of kelp in the Pacific Ocean near the end the Aleutian Islands. This would seem to place Raven somewhere between Attu Island and the Russian Commander Islands. Raven falls from the sky onto a floating bed of kelp and gets a sea otter to bring him gravel from the ocean floor, which Raven uses to create the Aleutian Islands one by one. Raven moves to each newly created island until he reaches the mainland, from there setting off on another adventure.

1.1.1.2 *Near Kayak Island*

If one follows the bending course of the Aleutian Islands, as Raven did, the nearest location where he appears in this volume is roughly 2,000 miles to the east, near the now-abandoned town of Katalla. In Italio's narrative of 1954, islands in this vicinity are related to an instance in which Raven was hunting a whale from a skin kayak. This whale, with Raven's harpoon sticking out from it, became modern-day Kayak Island, referred to by Italio with the placename «Yáaÿ»[2] 'Whale', while Raven's skin kayak became Wingham Island, which Italio calls «Káayaakw»[3] (itself a Tlingit borrowing of the Sugpiaq name for the nearby Kayak Island, *Kayaaq* 'Whetstone'). The northern-most Tlingit community today is Yakutat, about 175 miles east of Kayak Island. At the time of European contact, Tlingit groups were expanding westward of Yakutat toward the Copper River. The whale and Raven's skin kayak lie roughly in the vicinity of the western-most reach of historical Tlingit expansion.

1.1.1.3 *Dry Bay*

Raven was particularly active in the area known in Tlingit as *G̱unaax̱oo*, which refers to the vicinity of Dry Bay roughly sixty miles east of Yakutat. The Tlingit people of the Dry Bay region are referred to as *G̱unaax̱oo Ḵwáan* 'People of Dry Bay'. Two storytellers of this volume, Italio and Dick, lived for many years in Dry Bay and the surrounding areas. We will touch on a few notable places where Raven appears in this area, particularly near the mouths of the Akwe and Alsek rivers, and what the storytellers have to say about the setting.

1.1.1.3.1 *The Akwe River*

Roughly thirty-five miles southeast of Yakutat and just west of Dry Bay is *Aakwéi*, the Akwe River. In the stories of Italio and Dick, it was on the bank of the Akwe that Raven broke daylight over the world. Upon Raven's arrival at the Akwe with the Container of Daylight, Dick depicts him sitting to take a break:[*]

Tlax̱ wáa-áa-áa yóo
    koogútgoo sáyáa
	After walking here and there for a
	    lo-o-ng time,

át uwagút Aakwéi.	he came to the Akwe River.
Aakwéi á—	Indeed, the Akwe—
du ta.eetí,	this is where you find the imprint of where he lay,
át tux̱'ada.àayi yé.[4]	the place where he had been sitting on his butthole.

[*] Story extracts are given with original Tlingit quotation left, English translation right.

In addition to altering the geography with his anus, when Raven eventually opened the Container of Daylight it was apparently such a frightening event that even the rocks and trees fled from the area.[5] Italio and Dick tell us that Raven first sets out from the Akwe River to obtain the Container of Daylight from the head of the Nass River, then returns again to the Akwe. Today these locations lie roughly 400 miles apart.

1.1.1.3.2 *The Alsek River*

Multiple events involving Raven transpired at the mouth of *Aalséix̱*, the Alsek, a major river that originates in the Yukon, flows through British Columbia, and empties into the Gulf of Alaska at Dry Bay. We will look at scenes from two stories that are often set at the mouth of the Alsek, "Raven and the Whale" and "Raven and the Salmon Box", to see how the storytellers relate to the setting.

1.1.1.3.2.1 *A Fine Sand Beach*

Raven at one time decided to fly through the blowhole of a humpback whale. Once inside, Raven hosted for himself a high-seas barbecue consisting of the whale's meal of herring and, once that was depleted, the whale's internal organs. Its vital organs having been cooked and eaten from within, the whale perishes. With Raven trapped inside, the whale's carcass—coaxed by Raven's wishmaking—eventually floats ashore at a fine sand beach.

Italio and Dick, both of whom lived in Dry Bay where they set this scene, approach the setting in a similar way. In their stories, the whale lands at the Alsek and becomes an enduring part of the landscape. While we were unable to discern the placename from the recording (indicated below by '{...}'), the feature of Italio's passage we are trying to highlight is that he connects the whale of the narrative to a specific place near the Alsek:

Atx̱ áwé deisguch oolx̱éis',	So next he gradually started wishing,
«Yak'éiyi l'éiwdéi-éi-éi-éi!»	"To a fine sand bea-ea-ea-each!"
yóo áwé oolx̱éis'.	that's what he was wishing for.
«Yak'éiyi l'éiwdéi-éi-éi!»	"To a fine sand bea-ea-each!"
Wáananée sáwé l'éiw kaléit wulihásh.	Eventually it drifted to a beautiful sand beach.
[...]Ayóo Aalséix̱ {...} áwé yóo duwasáakw.	[...]It is called {... at} the Alsek River.
Yéilch yíkde wdak̲eeni yáaÿ áwé.[6]	That is the whale that Raven flew into.

Dick similarly states that the whale became a geographic feature at the river mouth:

Haa, áyáa awdlix̱éis',
«Yak'éiyi l'éiwdéi-éi-éi!
Aalséix̱ wát!»
Ách áwé Aalséix̱ wátnáx̱
  ÿan wulihásh.
Áwoo á yáa yeedát,
wéi yáay.
[...]Yá x'áat' tlein[...]
Á áwé wéi yáay yéeyi.[7]

Well now, he made a wish,
"To a fine sand bea-ea-each!
The mouth of the Alsek!"
So he drifted ashore along the
  mouth of the Alsek.
It is there now,
that whale.
[...]A big island[...]
that is what used to be the whale.

For Italio and Dick, the geography of Dry Bay is in part the setting and in part the result of events depicted in the narrative. What is now an island at the mouth of the Alsek was at a previous time a whale whose innards Raven feasted on at sea. The distinction between the whale of the story and the island of the river mouth has a parallel in the formal characteristics of the storytelling—that between the narration of the story's plot and the interpretation of the story's significance. In their narration, Italio and Dick establish the setting of the story in the landscape of Dry Bay; in their interpretation, they present the story as an explanation of one of the region's geographical features. They include their own editorial commentary as part of the performance and offer the audience a roadmap for relating the story to the observable world.

In the same story as told by Mills of Hoonah, however, the setting of this scene is handled a bit differently. From her we hear:

Áwé tle a yíkde éex',
«Yak'éiyi l'éi-éi-éiwt kwshé
  x̱at g̱alahaash.
Yak'éiyi l'éiwt g̱alahaash yá yáay,»
  yóo áwé a yíkdwe éex'.
Ch'áakw éex'i áwé
tóo aawanúk yan wulihásh
  yú yáay.
Yá teet du een át x̱'awdiyeeḵ.
Awsikóo yan áyú wlihásh.[8]

Then he was hollering inside it,
"Oh, let me float to a fine sand
  bea-ea-each.
Let this whale float to a fine sand
  beach," he was hollering inside it.
After hollering for a long time
he felt the whale float ashore.
The undertow was pulling it about in
  the breakers with Raven inside.
He knew he had floated to
  the beach.

Mills never uses a placename or connects the story to any specific time or place. Other than the formulaic opening and closing lines of her story, «Tléix' yateeyi aa áwé» 'There's this one [story]' and «Yéi áyá yan shuwjix̱ín yáat'aa» 'That's how this one ends',[9] she adheres strictly to the process of the plot and overlays it with no interpretation or commentary. She places the task of interpreting the story's setting and significance entirely in the audience's hands. The experience of the audience here seems to approximate that of Raven, who is sealed within the cold dead whale: our only impressions are waves and a shoreline, and we are otherwise left in the dark. Listeners and readers with prior knowledge or opinions on the story may be inclined to imagine a specific setting they are familiar with, such as the mouth of the Alsek. For others, the image may remain as minimal as Mills' depiction and simply amount to 'a beach'.

Italio and Dick shift between narrating the plot and interpreting the significance of the narrative. In doing so, they give the story an explanatory force and locate one of Raven's experiences in a specific place. Such interpretation and commentary are regular features of Tlingit Raven stories, and whenever present they are considered integral features of the story's overall composition. These are not, however, obligatory, as shown in the case of Mills, who remains uninterruptedly within the plot of the story. With her, the setting is unelaborated and never related to a specific place. Neither of these amounts to a more 'correct' or 'better' way of telling the story; they are two examples of how the setting may be handled stylistically in the course of a storyteller's performance and each offers a different experience to the audience. These also do not characterize any of these three storytellers' styles as a whole. From one scene to the next, and one storytelling situation to the next, a given storyteller may alter the style or level of detail with which they depict a location as they see fit.

Having touched on what is different in their approaches to the setting, we should also note that the three passages above share a great deal in common, the central feature being Raven's verbalized wish. Italio, Dick, and Mills impersonate Raven wishing to float to a 'fine sand beach'. They all use the Tlingit phrase *yak'éiyi l'éiw*, literally meaning 'sand (or sand beach) which is good, fine, nice'. They also all share a common pattern of intonation, emphatically sustaining the vowel of *l'éi-éi-éi-éiw* or the postposition attached to it, *l'éiwdéi-éi-éi*. This sort of formulaic consistency, found especially in the speech attributed to the stories' characters, is a common thread throughout the whole of the Raven genre.

1.1.1.3.2.2 *The Landing of the Salmon Box*

Raven had another experience at the mouth of the Alsek, in which he pulled ashore a massive floating house-like structure known as the *Kudatankahídi* or 'Salmon Box'. The versions of this story contained in this volume demonstrate the degree to which storytellers may closely align in their approach to the tale, while for others the major ideas may be notably different.

Zuboff and Mills employ the same two themes in their tellings of this story. First, by pulling the Salmon Box ashore, Raven established the river- and stream-based salmon runs. When the Salmon Box was in its original position before Raven pulled it ashore, it was out in the middle of the Pacific Ocean and the contents (most importantly salmon, but other marine life as well) were inaccessible to the people of the era, who are described specifically as impoverished. As a result of Raven's actions, Zuboff (speaking in 1972) states:

Yáa k̲'anashgidéi k̲áa kagéix'
aa kahéix̲ yá héen yíkdáx̲
yáa atyana.á tlein.
Aadé haa kagéi kaawahayi yé.[10]

Poor people
now have access to a portion of
this great salmon run.
This is how we gained access to it.

And Mills (speaking in 1989):

Áwé
yáa—yá Yéil aadé haa éet
  wudishiyi yé áyá.
Ách áyá k̲'anashgidéi k̲u.oo
  kagéi kaawaháa
yá shkalneek.[11]

Well,
this—this is how Raven
  helped us.
This is how poor people came to
  have access to salmon,
this very story.

Raven's establishment of the salmon runs allowed poor people to access one of the most important food sources in the region and this has been a principal resource of the Tlingit people to the present day. There is a shared sense of humility in both passages, with the two storytellers identifying with the poor people of the story.

The second theme used by Zuboff and Mills has to do with the physical remnants of this event at the mouth of the Alsek. During Raven's struggle to pull the Salmon Box ashore, his feet sunk into the ground under the great forces involved and his footprints became solidified in the land near the river mouth. Zuboff and Mills accentuate the idea that his large footprints lie in an area that gets pummeled by ocean swells (the mouth of the Alsek being exposed to the Gulf of Alaska), but remain in place and cannot be filled in. Zuboff states:

yáa teet tlénx',
ch'a aan tléil kei—
tléil kei shaahíkch,
yáa du x̲'us.eetí áa yéi yatee.
Ch'oo yáa yeedádidé áa yéi yatee
Yéil x̲'us.eetí.[12]

these huge waves—
no matter how big the waves are,
the indentations never get filled in;
Raven's footprints remain there.
To this very day Raven's footprints
are still there.

And Mills:

Du x̲'us.eetí tlénx' tle áa yéi yatee.
Ch'u yeedát de tlél aax̲ unahéich.
K̲ushtuyáx̲ wáa koogeyi héen a
  káa yóo jisatángi sá, yóo teet
  tlénx', ch'a aan hél aadé kéi
  shaagaaheegi yé du x̲'us.eetí.[13]

His huge footprints are still right there.
They haven't been erased even to this day.
No matter how much water rolls
  over them, even with those huge
  breakers, there's no way his
  footprints can get filled in.

These passages are congruent in the ideas they express and the linguistic material which gives them form. Both evoke a sense of immensity through the waves and footprints and strike a common emotional tone in the way the storytellers affirm the permanence of something that should conceivably have been eroded. In thinking about the literary form of the Raven stories, it is notable here that in the same story, scene, and setting we find two storytellers from different communities, recorded roughly seventeen years apart, utilizing a common group of ideas, feelings, sounds, and syntactic structures. As seen in Raven's wish for a fine sand beach, the storytellers are drawing from a shared body of oral material and arranging it according to a conventionalized compositional style.

In Dick's telling of the story, however, the ideas he puts forward are notably different. The contents of the Salmon Box, the salmon runs, and Raven's footprints are never mentioned. Dick's story is important—and unique in this volume—in that it depicts Raven not only altering the landscape, but prefiguring aspects of the background of Tlingit clans that would inhabit the areas where Raven was active. Dick states that Raven pulled the Salmon Box ashore at a place called «G̱aaw Aanée», a name which we are unable to translate beyond 'G̱aaw Country' or 'Land of G̱aaw'.[14] From there, Raven dragged the Salmon Box (described by Dick as a *hít* 'house') across the land, leaving an imprinted trail:

Áx' áyáa yéi téeyeen yáa Yakwdèiyée,	It is here that this Canoe Trail used to be,
áyá yá hít a kaanáx̱ yan awsiyig̱i Yakwdèiyée[.][15]	the Canoe Trail over which he pulled the house[.]

The placename used by Dick, *Yakwdeiyée* 'Canoe Trail', is found in the Tlingit placename atlas *Haa Léelk'w Hás Aaní Saax'ú* at the mouth of the Alsek as «Yéil Yakwdeiyí» 'Raven's Canoe Trail'.[16] Dick continues, stating that the final resting place of the Salmon Box was the site of a historical Tlingit village. He tells us:

Gus'éix̱ á,	It was at [the village named] *Gus'éix̱*;
a káx' áyáa wdudliyéx̱ tle	there they built
yáa Diginaa Hít.[17]	Far-Out House.

Dick refers here to the house and clan from which he descends, Diginaa Hít, the 'Far-Out House', of the L'uknax̱.ádi clan of the Raven moiety. He then describes a section of the remnants of the Salmon Box as «yóo a shaká yáx̱ kaaxadi yé»[18] 'place which is shaped like a canoe prow', and says it was here that Shakahít 'Canoe-Prow House' stood, referring to a house of the closely related Lukaax̱.ádi clan, also of the Raven moiety. Affirming how crucial Raven's actions with the Salmon Box were in establishing the background of his people, Dick states:

Ách áyáa ch'u tle ch'oo aadáx̱ áyáa Lingítx̱ haa wsitee.[19]	So it was from this very event that we became Tlingit.

Raven alters the landscape and in so doing paves the way for the area's Tlingit residents, which includes the narrator and his ancestors.

Between Zuboff, Mills, and Dick, the themes that emerge in their stories share common features in that Raven alters the landscape and affects the lives of the local people. They are all geographic and cultural-historical. In the details, Zuboff and Mills differ significantly from Dick. In the first case, Raven leaves behind footprints and establishes the salmon runs; in the second, Raven leaves behind a large house-like structure and shapes the history and identity of two Tlingit house groups. In the first, the Salmon Box is relevant due to its contents; in the second, the empty container takes the foreground. In the first, destitute people gain access to a replenishing food source; in the second, two specific Tlingit house groups form a cultural identity. In the first, the people in question are poor people in general; in the second, it is the ancestors of two specific Tlingit lineage groups. These two approaches to the story are complementary when taken together, each addressing aspects that go unstated in the other.

1.1.1.4 *Near Teslin*

The furthest northwest that a storyteller places Raven in this volume is near the village of Teslin, Yukon, one of the major population centers of Inland Tlingit people (alongside Atlin and Carcross of British Columbia). Zuboff states that when his people were living in the interior in the village of Teslin, Raven walked around a nearby lake and left behind his footprints:

Yáa—yáa daḵká,
áa yéi haa natée
yáa daḵká,
á áyá áx̱ yaawagút
yáa áa tlein x̱'ayaax̱.
A x̱'ayaax̱ áyá áx̱ yaawagút
yáa—yáa Táslanx' yéi haa teeyí.
[…]S'é káx̱ ayaawagudéyáx̱ áwé
yatee du x̱'us.eetée.

Yáa du x̱'ustl'eeḵ eetí áa yéi yatee
ḵa yáa du x̱'eitákw
eetí áa yéi yatee
kaltéelḵ.[20]

In the—the interior,
when we were living
in the interior,
this is when he walked around
the shore of this big lake.
It was this shore that he walked around
when we lived in—in Teslin.
[…]His footprints leave the
impression that someone was
walking around on the clay.
The prints of his toes are there,
and his heel
prints are there,
barefoot.

This occurs early on in Zuboff's performance, which consists of six consecutive Raven stories. The image of Raven walking barefoot in the interior is not involved in the plot-development of any of the ensuing stories. It rather frames and sets the tone for the overall narration. It is an instance of what Richard Dauenhauer referred to as a "narrative frame", that being "a matrix in which the story proper is set."[21] The narrative frame is an important compositional element found generally throughout Tlingit oral narrative and readers will encounter a number of examples in this volume. Dauenhauer continues, "The relationship of the frame or matrix to the story itself may vary from interesting but coincidental to absolutely indispensable. But in all cases it is of great personal interest to the tradition bearer, and in most cases the significance rises to a community level as well."[22] Those familiar with Zuboff's storytelling will recognize that 'when we were living in the interior' is of great personal interest to him, this being perhaps his most treasured and regularly employed theme.[23] His framing here rises to a community level in that he establishes a historical link between his own people (the K̲ak'weidí and Deisheetaan clans of Angoon, where the performance was recorded) and the people of Teslin, thus subtly evoking the history of his and related clans' migration from the interior to the coast. The framing also functions to attune the audience to the narrator's attitude toward the material he is about to deliver: Raven is presented as the historical contemporary of the common ancestors of the people of Teslin and Angoon.

The first two sentences in this passage also offer an example of the poetic aspect of Tlingit oral narrative. The two sentences form a 'chiasmus', with the order of elements in the first sentence reversed in the one that follows and several terms altered rather than exactly repeated: 'when we were living / in the interior, / this is when he walked around / the shore of this big lake' is repeated in reverse order as 'It was this shore that he walked around / when we lived in Teslin'. At an informational level, the repetition emphasizes the importance Zuboff places on the idea that his people used to live in the interior cotemporaneous with Raven. At a poetic level, it creates a sense of balance through the symmetry of the two successive statements. The way he repeats and alters the terms within this structure creates additional layers of symmetry and parallelism: *Yáa—yáa dak̲ká*, literally 'This—this interior', in the opening of the first sentence is followed first by the shortened *yáa dak̲ká* 'this interior' and then replaced at the end of the second sentence with *yáa—yáa Tásl̲an* 'this—this Teslin'. The repetitions of *yáa* and the combination *yáa—yáa* create a beautiful rhythm and acoustic symmetry within and across lines that we were unable to recreate in the translation. These are typical features of Zuboff's compositional style.

1.1.1.5 *Petrel's Fresh Water*

In some cases, none of the storytellers of this volume locate a certain episode in space, but connections between the story and physical location are made by other tradition bearers. Like the different settings for the location of the beaching whale, these raise the question of whether or not the audience should localize the events of a certain story through comparative means. Here we take the example of "Raven and Fresh Water", wherein Raven steals the world's only source of fresh water from his brother-in-law *G̱anook* 'Petrel', who had been keeping it for himself in his home in a bentwood box. This volume includes versions of this story told by Dick and Hammond, neither of whom relate Petrel's home to an observable location or describe the area in any detail. However, we find other tradition bearers connecting this event to a small rocky island known in Tlingit as *Deikinoow* 'Far-Out-to-Sea Fort' and in English as Big Hazy Islet. Deikinoow is one of five small islands known in English as the Hazy Islands, which lie roughly twenty miles south of *Shee* (Baranof Island) and the same distance southwest of *Kuyú* (Kuiu Island). The islands have no western cover and are fully exposed to severe ocean weather in the Gulf of Alaska. In 1904, Ḵaadashaan, John Kadashan, told the anthropologist John Swanton, "Petrel (Ḳanū´k [G̱anook]) [...] was the keeper of the fresh water, and would let none else touch it. The spring he owned was on a rocky island outside of Kuiu, called Dekī´nū [Deikinoow] (Fort-far-out), where the well may still be seen."[24] In 1997, Gux̱tlèn, Clara Peratrovich, stated, «Wéi Dèikinòow ka, héen áa yéi yatèe we Dèikinòow. Ya a shakée, G̱anòok Héenak'u yôo twasáakw we héen. Laḵt yax̱ yatèe we héen àanax̱ kèi déich ye.»[25] This translates as 'On Far-Out-to-Sea Fort, there is a creek there on Far-Out-to-Sea Fort. At the top of [Far-Out-to-Sea Fort], the creek is called Petrel's Little Creek. The place through which the water flows up is like a bentwood box.'

It is possible that Dick and Hammond expected their audience to be familiar enough with the story to know this detail in advance, and assumed it was unnecessary to elaborate on the location. If we could have asked them, they may have agreed that Deikinoow was the location of Petrel's house. Taking this premise, we could superimpose the location specified by Kadashan and Peratrovich onto the unelaborated setting of Dick's and Hammond's stories. These external sources of information could be as a chemical bath to an exposed but undeveloped photograph: when combined, a latent image becomes vivid and we see Raven approaching Petrel's house on an austere, storm-battered island surrounded by open ocean. On the other hand, it could be presumptuous and incorrect to assume that Dick and Hammond understood the story in the same way as Kadashan and Peratrovich. If we were able to ask them, they might have localized it somewhere else or declined to do so at all. Unable to know, and wanting to avoid imposing anything extraneous, we could take a more conservative approach and interpret each text strictly on its own terms. Restricting ourselves to the boundaries of each text, we could view the narrators' lack of elaboration as a feature of the drama. This could be taken as a formal complement to the subject matter, such that the audience's experience approximates that of the mission-driven Raven: as if experiencing a kind of tunnel vision, the only distinguishable features of the setting are those that are salient in the task of obtaining the water (Petrel, the house, the box, and, as readers will see, dog poop). There are no rules dictating when it is or is not appropriate to interpret one text in light of another. Our preferred approach is to do both: compare wherever possible, without pigeonholing one storyteller's material by way of another, while also appreciating each story on its own terms as a whole unto itself.

1.1.1.6 *The Head of the Nass River*

The final location we will mention is the place from which Raven obtains the Container of Daylight. This is uniformly said to be *Naas Sháak* or *Náas Sháak*, meaning 'Head of the Nass River', being based on the placename *Naas*, or its high-toned variant *Náas*, referring to the Nass River. Pronunciations of this placename by speakers of this volume are linguistically interesting in that we hear them often pronouncing it with high-tone forms.[26] The name has been otherwise uniformly documented only with low tone.[27] The lower reaches of the river lie at the southern-most end of Tlingit Country and the furthest south that we find Raven in this volume is in his journey to its headwaters. While the place from which Raven obtained the Container of Daylight is well-established in name, we are not certain of the exact location in space—if it is even meant to be exact. It would presumably be somewhere within the Spatsizi Plateau, also known as the Sacred Headwaters, in the interior of British Columbia. This expansive mountainous plateau contains a lush matrix of lakes, ponds, and creeks which form the source of three massive salmon-bearing rivers: the Nass, the Skeena, and the Stikine.

1.1.1.7 *Elsewhere*

The locations we have touched on are distributed across and beyond the major extent of Tlingit Country and give a sense of how intimately bound together the Raven stories are with the landscape. It should be kept in mind, though, that it is just as common to find Raven in an unstated and unelaborated location as it is in one with a placename or contemporary landmark. Raven is often simply 'walking around' pondering what to do next. These situations leave the setting rather open to interpretation, but it is not for that reason simply an empty form or blank slate. Raven is not, for example, in an arid desert or the high arctic. The default backdrop is typically a generic slice of Tlingit Country on the Pacific Northwest Coast.

1.1.2 *The Spatial Setting of the Storytelling*

Having surveyed the spatial setting within the stories, we will now briefly consider that of the storytelling. It is at times necessary to take account of the setting of the storytelling performance in order to make sense of the setting in the story. In James' version of "Raven and the Whale", she places the whale landing near «Ltu.áa tliyaanax̱.á»[28] 'the far side of Lituya Bay'. Italio, referring to a place where Raven was eating sea urchins, similarly says, «Ltu.áa tliyaanax̱.áwu»[29] 'it is on the far side of Lituya Bay'. Both storytellers say the same thing, but they are referring to exactly opposite directions. James, speaking in Sitka, means the northwest side of Lituya Bay; Italio, speaking in Yakutat, means the southeast side. We have done our best to clarify ambiguity that arises from relative directional references like these in the notes to the stories.

In addition to the broader geography of Tlingit Country, the more immediate physical setting of the performance may become relevant. Hammond was recorded telling "Raven Gets His Nose Yanked Off" in Portland, Oregon, during a conference on Alaska Native art at the Portland Art Museum. As the story progresses, Raven is in the act of stealing bait from fishermen's halibut hooks when he is suddenly hooked through the nose. As Raven is getting pulled up towards the boat, Hammond states, «Altín wé yaakw tayee, k'e hé dikée»,[30] which approximately means 'He (Raven) was watching the bottom of the boat, say, for instance, there above'. The implication is clarified on the recording by Anna Katzeek, who provided a live line-by-line English translation of Hammond's story, "He could see under the bottom of the boat, just like you see the ceiling."[31] If we were present at the performance, or had a video recording, we would likely see Hammond gesture toward the ceiling with his hands or eyes. The narrator makes use of the infrastructure in the performance setting, inviting the audience to look up ominously at the ceiling and imagine themselves in Raven's predicament, looking up at the bottom of a canoe's hull.

Most of these stories were recorded in rather intimate and unostentatious settings, often in the comfort of a home with no more than a few people present.[32] Italio was recorded in 1952 in a house in Yakutat in the company of his friend Minnie Johnson, the anthropologist Frederica de Laguna, and possibly the latter's collaborator Catharine McClellan; two years later de Laguna recorded Italio in the company of his friend Helen Bremner and perhaps one or two others.[33] Wanamaker was recorded in his home in Juneau by Jeff Leer, at the time a recent high-school graduate with an interest in the Tlingit language. Zuboff was recorded in his home in Angoon by Nora Dauenhauer. James was recorded in her home telling the stories to her daughter. Dick was recorded in his home by his grandson. Mills was recorded in Anchorage; we do not have a record of the details, but there are only three or four distinguishable additional voices.

Hammond's Raven stories had a rather different format. The bulk of his stories included here were recorded in a radio studio in Haines, Alaska, in 1985, to be broadcast the next year. This is an interesting performance situation in that the audience it was addressed to was not physically present and there was a significant delay between the storyteller's performance and its reception by an audience. This is an innovative technological strategy within the broad picture of Tlingit oral tradition, but it was not unprecedented. For instance, de Laguna reported the use of phonograph recordings at funerary ceremonies in Yakutat as early as the 1950s, with recordings of songs made at an earlier date by a deceased relative being played for attendees of the individual's memorial ceremony. As another example, before his death in 1967, Jim Marks was recorded telling the history of a mourning song belonging to his clan, the Chookaneidí of the Eagle moiety, with the intent that the recording be played on the occasion of his own memorial ceremony. The speeches from his 1968 memorial, including his own posthumous contribution, form the central example of Tlingit oratory in ceremonial context in the Dauenhauers' *Haa Tuwunáagu Yís*. Jim Marks was the stepfather of brothers Austin Hammond and Horace Marks. Horace made the recording of Jim and was in the studio with Austin for the recording of his extended Raven tale. Note also that Jim Marks was Nora Dauenhauer's father's eldest brother.

While Hammond's performance setting in a studio, with a recording technician and his brother Horace, was rather private, the fact that the recording was intended to be broadcast over the radio meant that Hammond would have a large and very public audience. This may have been an influence in Hammond's stylization of the story in the fashion of public oratory: the performance is mostly serious in tone; lines of speech are regularly punctuated with the affirmations *aaa* 'yes' or its shorter form *aa*; he constructs extended metaphors; he at times approaches a monotone chanting-like delivery; and a significant amount of the performance is dedicated to interpretation and exegesis. In contrast, none of these oratorical features are found in the final story from Hammond, "Raven Gets His Nose Yanked Off", mentioned above, which was recorded in a different time and place. The tone in that case is much more comical and light-hearted. Roughly a dozen or more people, including Mills, were present, and laughing heartily, at the performance. Hammond may have experienced this as a more relaxed context compared to speaking to a radio audience. On the other hand, the unavoidably comical nature of this particular story may have been the deciding factor.

1.2 *Time*

We will now touch on the temporal setting of the events depicted in the stories and the historical context in which the stories were told.

1.2.1 *The Temporal Setting Within the Stories*

Many events of the stories are set in a mythic past when the world and humankind were being modified and rearranged into their present experiential form. The stories do not depict an event of creation from a state of nothingness. Raven comes onto the scene with much of the world already in place. He is born to a woman who has already lived a life of hardship; he walks on the land and canoes on the ocean; he meets other individuals who have habits, homes, and relatives. Some of the beings Raven interacts with, such as Petrel and Unfazable-Little-Elder, give the impression of having already lived full lives with a great depth of experience and accumulated wisdom.

In Hammond's "Raven and Petrel" we receive an impression of Raven's and Petrel's own perceptions of prior states of the world while it was in an earlier process of formation. In a verbal exchange in which each attempts to demonstrate that they are older than, and therefore superior to, the other, the two characters allude to epochs of an ancient past. Hammond begins with Raven inquiring of Petrel:

«Ax̱ káani,	"My brother-in-law,
[goot'a]g̱áan sáyá ḵiydzitee?»	about when were you born?"
Aaa, aag̱áa áwé yéi yaawaḵaa hú ḵu.aa,	Yes, then his brother-in-law said,
«Ch'u kaat'tín x̱á ḵux̱wdzitee.»	"I was born a contemporary of primitive digging sticks."
[…]Aag̱áa hú ḵwá yéi yaawaḵaa wé Ÿéil, «Há.	[…]Then Raven said, "Hah.
Atk'átsk'oo síyá wa.á yeisú!	Well now, you're just a boy yet!
X̱át ḵu.aa ch'ul Haayeetl'óoḵk'u daak sh ulhaashjí áyá ḵux̱wdzitee—	I, however, was born before the Little-Liver-Beneath-Us floated itself out—
aaa, ldakát át ch'ul daa sá	yes, before anything
gági uxeexjée.»[34]	emerged."

Petrel appears to suggest that he was born in the same era as that in which an (or the) elementary form of technology came about. Raven, on the other hand, claims that he was born at an earlier time before anything at all had emerged into being, including an entity called *Haayeetl'óoḵk'u*, literally meaning 'Little-Liver-Beneath-Us'. This liver appears in the written record as far back as the writing of Saint Veniaminov, who rendered it in Cyrillic in 1840 as "Агитл̀юк8", which represents *Haaÿeetl'oog̱ú* or *Haaÿeetl'óog̱u* 'Liver-Beneath-Us'.[35] Following Raven's inquiry of when Petrel was born, Veniaminov includes Petrel (rather than Raven, as in Hammond's telling) relating his existence to this liver, "'Since the time,' responded Kanuk [G̱anook] 'when from below […] the liver emerged.'"[36] It occurs also in the English Raven story told to Swanton by a man named Deikinaak'w in 1904, "And Petrel answered, 'I have been living ever since the great liver came up from under the earth. I have been living that long.'"[37] The Tlingit phrase meaning 'before the Little-Liver-Beneath-Us floated itself out' appears in one of Leer's manuscripts from 1976 with the free translation, "from almost the beginning of time".[38] We do not have any profound insights about the significance, symbolic or otherwise, of this liver other than that it is associated with a formative period of the world or broader cosmos.[39] This liver and surrounding dialogue between Raven and Petrel make an important contribution to the dramatic setting of Raven's adventures: the world in which Raven acts is not freshly formed, but is already endowed with a mythic antiquity of its own.

This gives an impression of Raven's own retrospective view of the past from his perspective in the midst of the drama. From our perspective as readers and listeners in the twenty-first century, the time-setting within which we generally find Raven acting is an ancient era when many of the world's features and phenomena were established but not yet in a state such as we experience them today. Things such as salmon runs, fresh water, and daylight did exist, but they were in highly concentrated states, often constrained in containers in single locations. Many of Raven's adventures consist of him craftily obtaining these entities and dispersing them into their present, more diffused, forms.

The sense of temporal distance between Raven's adventures and a historical period involving ancestors of the Tlingit people may depend upon the perspective of the individual storyteller or the themes of the particular story. Events such as the birth of Raven, the opening of the Container of Daylight, the dispersal of fresh water, the establishment of the salmon runs, and the shaping of the world's geographic features would seem to necessarily belong to an early category of Raven's adventures in which he was affecting the organization of major features of the world. On the other hand, stories such as those depicting his whale-organ barbecue, his scheme to eat a deer through the anus, and his pilfering of bait from fishermen's halibut hooks would not seem to necessarily belong to a remote past and could be construed as a more latter-day category of Raven stories. These general groups suggest a distinction between earlier, more serious, myth and later, more comic, trickster tales. However, in the stories of this volume, the time-boundaries between Raven's experiences relative to one another and to the contemporary era seem too fluid for this scheme to hold up. De Laguna concluded in attempting to differentiate mythic, legendary, and historical events recounted in Tlingit oral narrative, "it is neither possible to arrange mythical events in any temporal sequence, nor can one tell when historical time began. [...] In some sense, 'myth' time is a timeless eternity."[40] The attitudes of the storytellers also make the boundary between serious mythic deed and comedic trickster antic hard to maintain. Italio, for instance, seems to find Raven consistently hilarious whether he is trying to rearrange the world or satisfy a hunger pang.

Other stories and events bring Raven much closer to the present day. In a story told by Charlie White of Yakutat in 1952, Raven gets drunk on Russian whiskey and turns the Russians' schooner to stone.[41] Raven's experimentation with alcohol in that story could be placed in history no earlier than the late eighteenth century, when the first Russian ships came near Yakutat. Raven's existence is brought into more immediate history in this volume. Near the end of his 1954 story, Italio states:

Áwéi yeedát héinax̱.aadé kdunéek.	Even now people say he lives over that way.
Áhu hú,	He's there,
tle yáa tl'átgi shú.	right at the end of the land.
Yéil	Raven
áx' yéi yatee.	lives there.
Té	He uses a stone
hítx̱ awliyéx̱.[42]	as his house.

Italio here offers a fitting image with which to conclude the discussion of the setting of Raven's adventures in time, not only because it fits into a timeline within the stories and brings Raven's existence up to the present era, but because it has symbolic and aesthetic value in relation to another image from the earlier end of Raven's life, that of the conditions of his birth. Before—and in order to bring about—Raven's birth, a grief-stricken woman who would go on to become his mother was instructed to find a small unblemished stone from the lowest exposed area near the water's edge at low tide. She was to pick this rock up, heat it in a fire, and swallow it. It was this stone that became a baby in her womb and was born to become Raven. The image of the stone at the water's edge containing Raven-to-be is the balancing antecedent to that of the stone at the edge of the land containing Raven after his many experiences. There is continuity and symmetry in this juxtaposition. He is pictured at the tail end of his adventures in a situation structurally analogous to that in which he initially took shape. In both, he inhabits stone, the source and symbol of his permanence and immortality.[43] He is found in both cases at the juncture of land and water; his emergence from and return to a liminal region at the threshold of opposites is reflected in his deeds and identity—he is ambiguity personified. There is also a sense of sequential development and resolution when moving from one image to the next. In the little low-tide stone, he is pure potentiality; if he can be said to exist, it is as an unrealized desire or potency. In the stone house, he is the fulfillment and long-standing actuality of what was only latent in the former; he is Raven after the fact of his innumerable deeds and experiences. Implied and embraced between these dual images of Raven dwelling within stone is the entire temporal sweep of his emergence and ensuing adventures.

1.2.2 *The Historical Setting of the Storytelling*

While many of these Raven stories and the elements they are composed from are undoubtedly of ancient origin, no cultural or artistic tradition is static throughout history. The recordings of this volume span the period of 1952–1989. At the time of the performances five of the seven storytellers were in their eighties and the other two were in their seventies.[44] These texts thus represent a sample of the Tlingit Raven story genre as it existed in the elder generations of the mid-to-late twentieth century. They are a small sample of a larger body of audio-recorded Tlingit Raven stories, itself a tiny fragment of the oral tradition of the era and as a whole. As far as we are aware, the recordings taken by de Laguna in 1952, including those of Italio in this volume, are the earliest audio recordings of Tlingit Raven stories.

There are a few important sources of Raven stories from the century prior to those featured in this volume. First to mention is Swanton's *Tlingit Myths and Texts*, published in 1909 and featuring material collected in 1904. Swanton provides two significant extended Raven tales (sequences of interconnected stories), which were told to him in English but are not verbatim texts. The prose of the stories was modified to an unknown extent by Swanton and he does not give any indication of the nature of his adjustments, so it is hard to know the degree to which these reflect the storytellers' original compositions. Some of the more scurrilous details involving genitals, anuses, and fecal matter are rendered in Latin. The sources of these two Raven tales were Deikinaak'w (c. 1828–1928) of Sitka and K̲aadashaan, John Kadashan, (1834–1914) of Wrangell. These men would have respectively been seventy-six and seventy during their work with Swanton in 1904.[45] Another notable source is Veniaminov's *Notes on the Islands of the Unalashka District*, originally published in 1840, which contains a fairly comprehensive recapitulation of a number of Raven's adventures. These are synthesized summaries based on information Veniaminov gathered from a variety of sources and not texts by individual storytellers. Despite issues in Swanton's and Veniaminov's handling and presentation of the stories, they provide valuable material for comparison of thematic features of the stories and occasional vocabulary items, especially names, that were rendered in Tlingit. We generally find consistency with the stories of this volume, many examples of which are discussed below in the cast of characters and the notes to the stories.

The historical specificity of the storytelling in this volume is apparent at times in the texts through references to tape recorders, state-administered permitting systems, iron plumbing, spaceships, modern surgical procedures, and the legal battle for land claims—phenomena which, several generations prior, simply did not exist either in Southeast Alaska or in the world. Grammatical features of the texts are also a testament to their historical moment. In contrast with the present state of the Tlingit language in living communities—which have overwhelmingly shifted to English monolingualism—the words of the elders in this volume now represent a classical era of Tlingit speech and oral literature. In this vein, readers will find references to 'classical Tlingit' throughout the notes in descriptions of grammatical features of the stories.[46]

The Tlingit language has undergone an enormous transition over roughly the past century and a half in terms of the number of people who speak the language, and over roughly the past half-century in terms of the patterns of speech used by those who have continued to speak it. Individuals who learned Tlingit as children and who continue speaking it to this day number no more than perhaps a few dozen, and those with extensive control of grammar and vocabulary, and especially of the form and style associated with the oral literary genres, are incredibly scarce. The primary source of these changes in the composition of the speaking population and of the speech itself is an assimilationist agenda imposed on Tlingit society by Presbyterian missionaries and the US government beginning in the late nineteenth century, a major tenet of which was the elimination of the Tlingit language and the substitution of English in its place. This process took shape in the decades following the 1867 Treaty of Cession, by which the Russian empire sold their claim to Alaska to the United States.[47] The Tlingit language has since been increasingly supplanted by English as the primary language used by Tlingit people in the home, public affairs, commerce, and ceremonial settings. For detailed accounts of this historical process and its consequences for the Tlingit language and culture, we refer the reader to the Dauenhauers' extensive work on the subject.[48]

Over time, as English gradually took a firmer hold in the Tlingit community, the elders who still fully controlled the classical language became increasingly isolated, and many of those who continued to speak the language began to discard or lose contact with some of the more arcane features of the grammar and had fewer opportunities to hear and practice the specialized elements of speech and stylization associated with the oral literary traditions. Many grammatical resources which are used in great abundance by the storytellers in this volume have largely fallen out of use in contemporary Tlingit; for example, one will rarely hear examples of the consecutive, conditional, and contingent verb modes from Tlingit speakers today, these having been almost entirely supplanted by subordinative verb forms.

Regarding the genre of Tlingit oratory, the Dauenhauers wrote in 1990, "Even fluent speakers of Tlingit comment frequently that they don't know 'old time Tlingit.' 'Old time Tlingit' does not refer to archaic grammar or vocabulary (although they may be part of it) but more to matters of form and rhetorical style—specifically the ability to use metaphor and simile with reference to visual art and the spirituality it represents."[49] We use the term 'classical Tlingit' along similar lines as the Dauenhauers' 'old time Tlingit',[50] though we admittedly give more weight to elements of grammar and vocabulary, which we consider to be among its defining features, whether these are used in ordinary conversational speech or with special rhetorical stylization or literary forms. In terms of literary form and style, the Raven stories do certainly have classical features beyond matters of grammar. An important example in this context is the 'formula', an idea we will discuss in more detail below. Practiced storytellers obtain these formulas through ample exposure to the literary resources of the oral tradition. They develop a repertoire of highly conventionalized phrases and lines and are able to employ and creatively recombine them in the composition of their narratives.

Commenting on the speeches published in *Haa Tuwunáagu Yís*, the Dauenhauers noted that the speeches "may be considered a 'vintage crop' of oratory by the last generation of traditionally raised elders. [...] Their speeches are presented here as examples of the past and as models for the present and future."[51] The seven storytellers featured in this volume of Raven stories are of generally the same era as the orators the Dauenhauers reference and we likewise consider their stories to be a 'vintage crop' of Raven stories from a classical era of Tlingit speech and oral literature. They, too, are beautiful examples of the past and important models for present and future storytellers, scholars, and community members.

1.3 *Culture*

We will now touch on the cultural context of the Raven stories.

1.3.1 *Raven and Tlingit Social Organization*

Tlingit society is broadly organized into two moieties: Raven (also known as Crow) and Eagle (also known as Wolf).[52] Each moiety consists of numerous clans, with clan (and therefore moiety) membership determined by matrilineal descent. Many patterns and concepts of traditional Tlingit culture relating to the identity and interaction of moieties and clans remain vital in the present day; others have significantly changed.[53] According to the traditional pattern, the moieties exist for the purpose of exogamy, that is, to facilitate a pattern of marrying outside of one's own group; Ravens would marry Eagles and vice versa. Each moiety is considered the 'opposite' of the other; they may mutually refer to each another as *guneitkanaayí*, usually translated as 'opposite clan' or 'opposite moiety' (the Tlingit word *naa* may mean either 'clan' or 'moiety').

One of Raven's functions as a symbol within Tlingit culture is to differentiate the moiety groups. Much of the crest iconography of the clans of the Raven moiety represents or alludes to the character Raven, and such images are used exclusively by clans of the Raven moiety. Similarly, the clans of the Eagle moiety have unique crests that no Raven clans use. These basic facets of Tlingit culture (matrilineal descent, exogamy, and crest symbolism) provide important context for reading the stories. Raven's interactions with Brown Bears, Killerwhales, and his brother-in-law Petrel (all of which serve as crests of Eagle-moiety clans) have symbolic overtones of the relationship between opposite intermarrying clans. Raven's treatment of his opposites (often cheating, murdering, and eating them) tends to be the extreme antithesis of proper social conduct.

We should briefly dispel some potential misconceptions about Raven as a crest figure with which people identify. George Thornton Emmons' ethnographic monograph from fieldwork in the late 1800s states, "There is no idea [in Tlingit culture] of actual descent from the crest animal".[54] De Laguna similarly notes that "members of the Raven moiety trace their totemic affiliation (not genetic descent) to Raven. My informants [...] deny that one ever prayed to Raven."[55] He is neither a deity to which one prays nor a patriarch who established a bloodline. As a figure of crest imagery and social differentiation, he is an original, principal, and unifying symbol in the identity of the clans of the Raven moiety. However, not all images or artifacts depicting a raven necessarily allude to the character Raven; neither does all clan-related nomenclature (e.g., names of clans, houses, people, artifacts) that includes the word *yéil* 'raven'. Sometimes a raven is simply a raven.

1.3.2 *Raven Stories and At.óow*

Clans possess tangible and intangible items known in Tlingit as *at.óow*. This word is typically translated as 'possessions' or 'property'. At.óow are the property of a clan, not of an individual. They may be physical objects such as areas of land, Chilkat robes, ceremonial hats, bentwood boxes, and masks. They may also be less tangible entities such as personal names, iconographic images, songs, spirits, and stories. These items of real and symbolic property are transmitted and inherited across generations through a clan's matrilineal line. In the case of stories having the status of at.óow, especially those that relate to the experiences of a clan and its ancestors, the story and the right to tell the story are considered the real and sacred property of a clan. This can be understood as an Indigenous system of oral copyright that places boundaries on the right to use and reproduce specific materials.

The concept of at.óow holds a crucial position within Tlingit culture and has featured prominently in prior volumes in this series. The relationship that exists between at.óow and oral narratives dealing with the experiences of clan ancestors is a central theme of volume one. The material and metaphorical uses of at.óow in ceremonial oratory are at the heart of volume two. In addition to patterns of marriage mentioned above, many ceremonial processes depend upon the complementary and reciprocal interaction between clans of opposite moieties. The spirits, songs, and symbols held by different clans may be used in ceremonial contexts to enact a kind of balance and unification between the distinct and opposite groups. Focusing on the category of shamanic spirits, the Dauenhauers write:

> [I]t is significant in traditional Tlingit pre-Christian religion (shamanism of a circumpolar type) that the entire ethnic population did not have equal access to all the spirits of the group, but that each clan had its own, revealed to its

> shamans, and passed down as part of the clan inheritance. [...] Thus any traditional ceremonial event depends on the reciprocal exchange between clans of opposite moieties; both halves are needed to complete the whole.[56]

A complex cultural system exists in which a form of balance and wholeness takes shape through the interaction of distinct social elements, each of which possesses their own unique symbols and spirits embodied in at.óow.[57] Traditional laws govern the use and inheritance of at.óow, preventing them from being frivolously used or evoked by just anyone. The Dauenhauers, however, add that "familiarity with the songs and stories of all clans is basic to traditional Tlingit education."[58] The spirits, songs, stories, and other at.óow of all clans should be known by everyone, but they may not be evoked, sung, told, or used without the proper permission or recognition of the owning clan.

A notable feature of the Raven stories that sets them in contrast to other genres of Tlingit oral tradition is that they exist, as it were, in the public rather than private domain and do not follow the usual pattern of clan ownership. Everyone should know them, and anyone can tell them. Richard Dauenhauer found this aspect of the Raven genre striking in his 1975 doctoral dissertation:

> The Raven stories occupy a strange position in Tlingit oral tradition. Whereas most oral materials are owned and passed along reciprocal lines from tradition bearer to audience, the Raven cycle is the only extensive shared body of oral literature in Tlingit. Any person can tell a Raven story. [...] The Raven stories [...] need more attention *as part of the total system*, especially in view of their unique median position in a structure otherwise typified by polarity and oral copyright.[59]

The same view was maintained decades later in the Dauenhauers' draft materials for this volume: "Where does Raven fit in Tlingit oral literature[?] Not surprisingly, he is a boundary figure and Raven stories seem a boundary genre. They are not clan owned, as are the legends of at.óow and the songs."[60] While a deep association exists between the character Raven and clans of the Raven moiety, the stories that recount Raven's deeds and experiences are not governed by the same copyright laws that generally apply to songs and ancestral narratives. Indeed, this volume contains almost no discussion or mention of clans at all. Across the fifty stories included here, a clan is mentioned by name in only two cases. The first case is humorous and light-hearted, with James impersonating Raven claiming to be the fraternal niece of James' own clan, the Chookansháa (the title of the women of the Chookaneidí clan);[61] in this situation Raven has just transformed himself into a woman and is trying to convince a canoe of Killerwhales that 'she' is a desirable bride of noble pedigree. As the supposed fraternal niece of this clan, Raven is claiming that her father's sisters are the Chookansháa and, therefore, in a roundabout way, that her father is Chookaneidí. Since clan identity is inherited through the mother's side, a child would traditionally be the opposite moiety of their father. Thus, even in his guise, Raven the character remains identified with the Raven moiety. The killerwhale is a crest exclusive to Eagle-moiety clans, so the marriage is formally appropriate (though the disguised Raven's motives and actions within this union are profoundly nefarious). The second mention of a clan name occurs as part of a standard personal introduction given by Mills just before her first tale, "Raven and the Salmon Box", in which she states her name, clan, village, and house.[62] In this case there is a possibility that by identifying herself as a woman of the T'ak̲deintaan clan before telling this story, Mills is indirectly stating that she and her clan have a certain right or claim to the narrative. On the other hand, she may simply be identifying herself as a formality for the recording.

The most consequential example for the relationship between the Raven stories and clan ownership in this volume occurs in Dick's telling of "Raven and the Salmon Box". He mentions the names of two houses, Diginaa Hít 'Far-Out House' of the L'uknax̲.ádi clan and Shakahít 'Canoe-Prow House' of the Lukaax̲.ádi clan, both of which are clans of the Raven moiety. The physical houses, the houses' names, and iconography and artifacts associated with the houses—all of which have connections to the story of "Raven and the Salmon Box"—are clan property of the Lukaax̲.ádi and L'uknax̲.ádi. Yet the story in the abstract remains part of the distinct genre of Raven stories and is not restricted to being told by members of any particular clan. In addition to Dick, who was himself L'uknax̲.ádi, this volume contains versions of the story by Zuboff of the K̲ak'weidí, James of the Chookaneidí, and Mills of the T'ak̲deintaan. In contrast to Dick, these latter three do not relate the story to the development of the houses, which is unlikely coincidental. To do so would involve moving across genre boundaries from that of the Raven stories to that of clan history. For Dick, on the other hand, being L'uknax̲.ádi and a well-regarded oral historian of Far-Out House, moving between such genres in this context poses no sort of oral copyright issue.

This relationship between the clan houses and the story of "Raven and the Salmon Box" shows that the Raven stories, while forming a genre distinct from the ancestral narratives, are nonetheless enmeshed within the system of clan ownership and oral copyright. In addition to the houses mentioned by Dick there are many items of at.óow that depict Raven during one of his adventures and are the property of a specific clan. Examples include a ceremonial hat belonging to the L'uknax̲.ádi clan that Louis Shotridge referred to as the "Barbequing Raven Helmet",[63] alluding to the story of "Raven and the King Salmon" (told in this volume by Dick and Mills), which is still used in ceremonies today; another is a hat held at the Seattle Art Museum belonging to the G̲aanax̲.ádi clan depicting Raven with the head of a raven and arms of a human clutching the Container of Daylight and alluding to the story of "Raven and the Daylight" (told herein by Italio, Wanamaker, James, Dick, and Hammond).[64]

The general pattern would appear to be that specific embodiments of themes and events in Raven's adventures—executed in forms such as material artifacts, iconographic images, songs, and names—can and do become at.óow, while the themes, events, and stories in the abstract and to which they allude do not. In an analogous way, the transcriptions and translations of the stories in this volume (their embodiment in letters) are held under copyright by Sealaska Heritage Institute, but these stories in the abstract—which have been and will be told in many other times and ways—are not.

Considering the role of property in the subject matter of the stories themselves, it is tempting to relate this position of the Raven genre on the boundaries of clan ownership to Raven's own behavior. His way of relating to the property of others usually consists of craftily stealing it in order to destroy its status as a private possession, often accomplished either by dispersing it for general use (as with fresh water and the heavenly lights) or consuming it for his own immediate satisfaction (as he does with his brother's cache of oil, a beached whale being processed by villagers, and the bait on fishermen's halibut hooks). The supreme example is Raven stealing the daylight itself, the most prized and closely guarded treasure of a wealthy man at the head of the Nass River, and thereupon releasing it into thin air. In cases like these, Raven's behavior undermines, or at least pokes fun at, the sanctity of property and other facets of Tlingit culture.

1.3.3 *Raven Stories as Framework of Culture*

The Tlingit historian and anthropologist Stoowuḵáa, Louis Shotridge, (1883–1937) makes some comments relevant to the discussion of culture. For generational reference, he was thirteen years younger than Italio and born within the decade prior to Wanamaker, James, and Zuboff. His words are valuable as an example of how a Tlingit intellectual who was a contemporary of the storytellers in this volume, steeped in his own traditions as well as a trained scholar of anthropology, would frame the significance of the Raven stories. In a short preface to his series of Raven stories written in English, "The Journey of the Raven", he writes:

> Sometimes something comical, only accidently, would appear in a legen[d], and our young listeners had received this in a waggish spirit, which encourage[d] those old fellows of facetious nature to add more, often in an exaggerated manner, to those parts that had raised mirth. But it was the method of a droll which played a havoc with the true quality of many an important legend, such is very true in the general run of the "Journey of the Raven", that noble old myth which well deserved its position as being a foundation to all that pertains to the creation of things in the Tlingit world.[65]

The element of comedy is presented as a kind of accident of history, a deviation resulting from whimsical elders pandering to juvenile amusement. The stories appear as internally split between a refined aristocratic aspect (the myth conceived in its "true quality" is "noble" and "old") and that of unsophisticated frivolity. The description of the frivolous and comedic aspect, involving the introduction of "havoc" by the combination of "a waggish spirit" and "facetious nature", would seem to rightly describe Raven's typical behavior in the stories. We would expect Raven to play the role of a vulgar rascal rather than an earnest dignitary. Shotridge suggests that the playful exterior of the tales of Raven's journeys may be deceiving, and that they contain deeper and more serious matters pertaining to the foundational philosophies of the culture. He felt, rightly, that the academic and popular impression of the Tlingit people at his time was in many ways factually incorrect and morally unjust. He writes:

> The writer is aware that, in pursuance of the injust[ice] that has been done to the interpretation of the true conception of the Tlingit people, a contribution showing some refinement, to represent a character which has been more familiar as that of a savage, would appear too civilized. Hence, it is with a risk, of a supposition of misrepresentation, that the interpretation of the myth in the following pages is offered.[66]

Shotridge was responding to a situation in which an opposition between Native savagery and White civilization was taken as axiomatic. He felt it necessary to correct the record, but in doing so risked a misrepresentation different in form but related in kind. The concern is that of inadvertently allowing one's adversary to control the terms of the debate. By assuming as his target a misconception that rests on the opposition between savage and civilized, he would risk simply recasting the Tlingit people into the more preferable of inherently unjust terms. His minimization of Raven's scurrilous side may largely be a rhetorical strategy to intervene against racist assumptions about Indigenous people among his contemporaries. Framing of the serious-scurrilous distinction aside, the crucial idea that Shotridge puts forward is that, to him, a just and truthful conception of the Tlingit people necessarily requires plumbing the depths of the Raven myths.

Following Shotridge, a consideration we hold for ourselves—being neither ethnically Tlingit nor anthropologists—is that there is little better way to learn about Tlingit culture than by studying the oral literature. While there is certainly utility in explicating features of Tlingit culture in order to contextualize and better understand Raven, we for the most part assume the converse premise that the oral literature is a key framework for contextualizing and better understanding the broader cultural system. As Shotridge states above, the stories are the outward form of "a foundation to all that pertains to the creation of things in the Tlingit world." And while these stories are Tlingit in form and origin, their significance is not restricted to better understanding a particular culture. Shotridge perceives them as a philosophical discourse, the underlying subjects of which are embodied in the outward form of mythic narrative.[67] Though typically comic in tone and at times intensely culture-specific, the Raven stories are of universal significance in their concern with themes confronted by all people and cultures, such as paradox, desire, and deception.

1.4 *Tradition*

We will now consider the relationship between the Raven stories and oral tradition, aspects of which may be sought directly in the storytellers' choice and arrangement of words. A striking feature of these stories is the regular appearance of certain combinations of words and phrases. Many of these are so recurrent in the Raven stories, with a great enough distribution and stability from one storyteller to the next, that they may be regarded as a unifying feature of the genre. We consider these recurrent words and phrases to be 'oral formulas', a concept borrowed from oral-formulaic theory, also known simply as oral theory, which was originally developed by Milman Parry and Albert Lord in the study of Homeric epic and South Slavic narrative song and has since been applied to numerous other oral and written traditions.[68] Applying and adapting these concepts to Tlingit oral literature has significantly deepened our own appreciation of the Raven stories. It is also theoretically consistent with the Dauenhauers' approach to the presentation and analysis of Tlingit oral literature. In volume two in this series, on Tlingit oratory, they write,

> We have been influenced, at a more general level, [...] by the work of Albert Lord and Milman P[a]rry on Homeric and South Slavic oral literature. Though our efforts are more modest in comparison, [...] we aspire to similar goals[.... A]lthough we are not dealing in Tlingit with heroic poetry and metrical composition in the European oral tradition and strictest definition, many important concepts apply to Native American oral literature.[69]

We will review some of the basic ideas of this approach to oral literature and discuss several formulas from within the volume.

1.4.1 *Composition by Formula and Theme*

The concept of the 'oral formula', or simply 'formula', gained footing through Milman Parry's analysis of repeated and relatively fixed phrases in Homeric epic poems in the 1920s and 1930s. Parry was able to demonstrate that Homer's written poems were composed using a diction and style that were not the product of individual literary genius, but which had necessarily developed over generations through oral tradition. The ideas of the formula and 'oral-formulaic composition' were further developed by Parry and his student Albert Lord through the study of the living oral tradition of South Slavic narrative song, culminating in Lord's publication *The Singer of Tales* in 1960. One of their major contributions was a shift in perspective from that of the audience to that of the performer. While the repetition of certain conventionalized patterns of speech may satisfy the aesthetic tastes of a traditional audience, these recurrent spoken elements serve a pragmatic role for the oral performer. Lord writes of Parry's initial insight, "the repeated phrases were useful not, as some have supposed, merely to the audience if at all, but also and even more to the singer in the rapid composition of his tale."[70] The oral poet, singer, or storyteller who does not read from a text or follow some other fixed external guide must compose their tale while in the act of telling it. There is an urgency to their practice, "[their] problem is to construct one line after another very rapidly. The need for the 'next' line is upon him even before he utters the final syllable of a line."[71] Oral narrative is not composed *for* performance, but *in* performance. The formulas serve as ready-made groups of words and lines which can be called to mind quickly, even reflexively, while the performer composes each subsequent line of their tale. They thus not only establish the traditional aesthetic features of the stories but belong to the traditional technique of the storytelling.

Like oral epic poetry and heroic song, Tlingit oral narratives are not recited from memorization. Neither are they invented from scratch in each instance. Each telling of a story is neither completely the same nor entirely novel. The practiced poet, singer, or storyteller fashions their material by drawing as needed from a mental collection of compositional units that have been acquired through exposure to their mentors and other practitioners of the art form. The two basic units of oral composition identified by Parry and Lord are 'formula' and 'theme'. Formulas have the form of sound and are found at the level of the line. Themes have the form of ideas and are found at the level of narrative structure. Lord writes, "I have called the groups of ideas regularly used in telling a tale in the formulaic style of traditional song the 'themes' of the poetry. [...] The theme, even though it be verbal, is not any fixed set of words, but a grouping of ideas."[72] Themes are the patterns of ideas and scenarios that give the narrative its structure. Formulas are the acoustic forms into which these ideas have been cast.

One of the fundamental themes at work in the Raven stories, and in many other genres and traditions the world over, is that described as 'lack and lack liquidated'.[73] The theme consists of two ideas that belong together as an ordered pair: an initial lack and the subsequent overcoming of this lack. The range of details and situations with which this theme can be employed are endless. Raven's mother-to-be lacks a child that can survive the wrath of her murderous brother; the lack is liquidated through the birth of Raven, who is born from a stone and invincible. Raven loses his own eyeballs and so fills the voids with blueberries. Poor people lack access to salmon; Raven hauls the Salmon Box ashore. The world lacks daylight, fresh water, tidal cycles, and fire; Raven obtains these and disperses them. Another essential thematic lack driving this genre is Raven's experience of hunger; he (temporarily) liquidates this lack by finding something to eat, including a whale, a Brown Bear couple, a Killerwhale husband, a king salmon, a Deer, and many other things. The folklorist Alan Dundes' observations on the centrality of the lack–lack liquidated theme in the Indigenous narrative traditions across North American ring true for the Tlingit Raven stories:

> [T]here is in one sense a surplus in that for one individual at least, there is a concentration of an item in one place. On the other hand, because of the concentration, there is an insufficiency of the same item in other areas. Folktales can consist simply of relating how something in excess may be lost or something lost or stolen may be found. Both of these situations fall under the rubric of moving from disequilibrium to equilibrium.[74]

Not all Tlingit stories using the lack–lack liquidated theme are Raven stories, and not all stories of Raven are centered around his hunger as the instigating lack. But for the Raven stories that use his hunger as a basic motivation in the plot, part of what makes him such a dynamic and well-suited figure for this theme is that he is a bottomless pit that can never be satiated. It is impossible to satisfy his hunger, so a Raven story resulting in a feast is never a permanent or complete resolution. The movement in the direction of the equilibrium of satiation springs immediately back to the disequilibrium of hunger. Raven by necessity ventures off in search of something else and the cycle is perpetuated.

Another crucial theme in the Raven stories is 'trickery and complicity'.[75] In the first element of this pair, Raven uses deceit to trick someone; in the second, the victim submits to the deception and thereby unwittingly helps Raven accomplish his goal. This theme regularly intervenes between the two elements of the lack–lack liquidated pair. For instance, Raven is hungry (lack), so he concocts a plan to convince Deer to walk across a rotten log, claiming that it is sturdy (trickery); when the Deer eventually submits and walks across the log (complicity), he falls to his death and Raven eats him (lack liquidated). This sequence—lack, trickery, complicity, lack liquidated—is a classic thematic structure of a Raven story.[76]

As different as Tlingit oral narrative is from Homeric epic poetry and Slavic heroic song in form and subject matter, they are comparable at least in terms of compositional technique. Lord describes "the technique of composition of oral-traditional epic" as "composition by formula and theme."[77] Upon reading or listening to even a handful of Raven stories, it becomes apparent that the storytellers share a common scheme of ideas (themes) that go together with conventionalized and often relatively fixed ways of putting them into words (formulas). It also becomes apparent that from one storyteller to the next, and even from one telling to the next of the same story by the same storyteller, the level of detail in some particular situation may vary; major events may occur in different sequences and similar scenarios may occur with a range of different actors. This aligns with Lord's observation that the singer of oral-traditional narrative song "thinks of his song in terms of a flexible plan of themes, some of which are essential and some of which are not."[78] There is no fixed scheme or script for the storyteller to consult. They may envision in advance a general plan of what to cover and in what order and level of detail, but in the course of telling their story they may decide to elaborate on one idea in great detail, pass over another with few words, or let the associations that arise in the act of telling lead the way. The Raven stories are composed by formula and theme according to a flexible plan.

This provides a useful way of considering Italio's tales in this volume, which were recorded two years apart and are notably different in structure. In his 1952 tale, the arrangement of themes is for the most part linear and orderly, with the extended tale consisting of five discrete stories told in a connected sequence. In his 1954 tale, on the other hand, flexibility seems to have become more dominant than planning, with spontaneous associations of words and ideas directing the composition; there are at least four distinguishable stories involved, but their themes and images are so intermeshed, non-linear, and fragmentary in the telling that they do not form a cycle so much as a collage. Both tales employ many of the same formulas and themes, but they differ dramatically in order and detail. Lord writes, "All singers use traditional material in a traditional way, but no two singers use exactly the same material in exactly the same way. The tradition is not all of one mold."[79] This idea holds for the tradition and genre as a whole and even for the individual storyteller.

A formula expresses an idea in a certain combination of words. A question arises as to why a certain idea becomes fixed in a particular group of words rather than another. In the Homeric case, many formulas may be demonstrated to exist in order satisfy the metrical conditions of the verse. A line in the scheme of Homeric verse (dactylic hexameter) contains six metrical feet each consisting of a fixed pattern of short and long syllables. The role of meter was central in Parry's original definition, "The formula in the Homeric poems may be defined as a group of words which is regularly employed under the same metrical conditions to express a given essential idea."[80] The formulas aid the epic poet in setting their tale to the rhythmic scheme required by the verse-form. The poet may draw on their mental collection of formulas in order to accomplish the versification of their story's ideas while composing their tale rapidly in performance.[81]

In Tlingit oral narrative, however, lines are not formed according to a metrical scheme; there is no requirement for lines to contain any number or quality of syllables.[82] It is often possible, however, to distinguish the delivery of Tlingit oral narrative from ordinary speech by a more prominent and stylized use of pause and intonation. This produces a rhythm, the most basic aspect of which is an alternation of sound and silence. Dennis Tedlock's concept of the 'line' in Zuni and K'iche' oral traditions is applicable here as well, "between two silences is an unbroken sequence of sounds I call the line."[83] Also consistent with Tedlock's account, "the speaker may go on without interruption indefinitely, the ultimate limitation being an exhaustion of the capacity of the memory or the lungs."[84] The length and internal structure of a Tlingit line is highly variable. A line may be as short as a single syllable, or, especially in the case of James, may contain several independent clauses and upwards of thirty syllables. At the present stage of our research, if we were to specify a verse-form for Tlingit oral narrative it would be something like 'unrhymed free verse delimited by breath'.[85] While it is possible that further research could disclose prosodic tendencies that we do not yet understand, the more likely conclusion is that acoustic rhythm does not play a primary role in the formation of lines of Tlingit oral narrative.

Compare these nearly identical passages from Zuboff's separate tellings of "Raven and the Salmon Box", told less than two months apart in the year 1972, in which Raven approaches a man named X̱'enax̱g̱aatwaayáa and speaks to him:

RZ I, 50–54:	«Ḵúnáx̱ áyá yak'éi yáa—yáa ax̱ sáḵsi. Tlax̱ tléil áyá aan at woox̱sat'úkx̱aa. Tlax̱ ḵúnáx̱, ḵúnáx̱ yak'éi.[»]	"This—this bow of mine is very fine. I simply never miss with it. It is very, very fine.["]
RZ II, iii, 58–64:	«Tlax̱ ḵúnáx̱ áyá yak'éi yáa ax̱ chooneidí. Tlax̱ tléil— tléil tlákw gaaw áyá aan at woox̱sat'úkx̱aa. Tlax̱ ḵúnáx̱ yak'éi yá ax̱ chooneidí.[»]	"This arrow of mine is so very fine. I simply never ever at any time miss with it. This arrow of mine is so very fine.["]

There are no metrical schemes involved here to explain the makeup of either passage or how one may have evolved into the other. Where the first case has Raven referring to «ax̱ sáḵsi» 'my bow' (also by extension meaning 'my bow and arrow'), the second has «ax̱ chooneidí» 'my arrow'. The first case has «tláx̱ tléil áyá» 'simply never', which in the second is more embellished as «tláx̱ tléil— / tléil tlákw gaaw áyá» 'simply never / ever at any time'. If one is counting syllables, the two passages lack internal order and are notable for their differences. However, the central idea of Raven speaking boastfully and hyperbolically about his seemingly magical hunting implement remains consistent; what Raven deceptively refers to here is really a live magpie, a fact that he conceals from X̲'enax̲gaatwaayáa. In sound, syntax, and style, both passages, each consisting of three sentences, are largely identical. Both share Zuboff's regularly used device of repetition with slight variation, especially the first and third sentences of each passage, and the only vocabulary-level differences are *tlákw gaaw* 'at all times', *sák̲s* 'bow', and *chooneit* 'arrow'. At the level of syntax, idea, and the rhythm of their spoken delivery, the two formulaic passages are significantly congruous.

Even though meter was basic to Parry's definition of the formula, the concept remains applicable to the Tlingit narratives. "[O]ne may state the principle as follows", Parry writes, "the formulas in any poetry are due, so far as their ideas go, to the theme, their rhythm is fixed by the verse-form, and their art is that of the poets who made them and of the poets who kept them."[86] He defines the formula "in the Homeric poems" strictly in relation to metrical conditions, but the more general principle holds that the formulas "in any poetry" are fixed by the verse-form of their tradition. The existence of formulas in Tlingit oral literature is not precluded by the absence of meter. The acoustic rhythm of Tlingit formulas is determined by their grammatical form and the speaker's use of pause and intonation. Parry's original concept of the formula remains valid, but a more suitable definition is needed. Michael Foster's discussion of formulaic composition in Iroquois oratory, which the Dauenhauers highlighted in *Haa Tuwunáagu Yís*, proves useful. Foster noted the existence of clearly formulaic but non-metrical patterns of speech, leading him to modify Parry's definition to better suit the Iroquois situation. He defines the formula as "a recurrent phrase expressing a conventionalized idea and capable of multiple combination[s] with other such phrases in the discourse."[87] This is an appropriate definition of the formula for the Tlingit oral literary traditions.

1.4.2 *Formulas Found in the Raven Stories*

Formulas of various types exist generally throughout Tlingit oral narrative. Whether the topic is an individual's life story, the experience of a clan's ancestors, or Raven, formulas telling of the movement of time, for example, are used ubiquitously. Some prevalent examples are *wáananée sáwé* 'eventually' *wáaykunayáat' sáwé* 'after a while', *k̲eina.áa* 'the next day' (lit. 'when it dawned'), and *yaa k̲eiga.áa* 'as dawn was approaching'. A less widely attested formula for the passage of time and scene resolution is used in this volume by Dick. Five times in his extended Raven tale, he uses a rather obscure word *ldinax̲k'iyéide*, in these cases meaning roughly 'sooner or later', in combination with verbs in the consecutive mode. The formula could be roughly described as *ldinax̲k'iyéide* + CONSECUTIVE·VERB 'sooner or later, once VERB [took place]'. It is a fixed pattern but allows for significant flexibility in that different verbs may be employed within the syntactic framework to fit the situation at hand. Compare:

FD iii, 48:	Ldinax̱k'iyéide yan asnée wéi hít	Sooner or later, once he finished the houses
FD v, 57:	Ldinax̱k'iyéide ash eedéi sh ilháa áwé tsáa	Sooner or later, once [Petrel] finally yielded to him
FD vi, 68:	Ldinax̱k'iyéide yan awusnée á	Sooner or later, once he finished with this
FD vii, 1:	Ldinax̱k'iyéide {yan at dax̱} sanée—[88]	Sooner or later, once he was finished with everything—
FD xii, 31:	Ldinax̱k'iyéide a jeet at shulaxéex áwé	Sooner or later, once he had used up all of [his wife's] provisions

We can add to this comparison Dick's use of the formula roughly six months later in the story of "The Woman Who Married the Bear", found there as «Ldinax̱k'iyéidei yan at dux'áan» and translated by the Dauenhauers as "After they had dried plenty of fish".[89] Dick uses the formula in oral narrative composition generally; it is not restricted to the Raven or ancestral genres. His use of the formula serves a common function in each of the six cases, indicating the finality of some process after the passage of an undefined period of time. The repetition of this formula across five episodes of his extended Raven tale establishes a sense of parallelism and continuity (dramatic and acoustic) throughout the overall performance.

While Dick is the only storyteller in this volume who uses this combination often enough to discern its formulaic character, comparison with its use by his brother-in-law Italio suggests that it has seen wider circulation:

Italio:	Ldinax̱k'iyéide yan kalakóox áwé tsáa ajeewanáḵ.[90]	Sooner or later, once the tide had finally drained away completely, [Raven] released [Little-Elder-Who-Enlarged-the-Tide].
Dick:	Ldinax̱k'iyéide ash eedéi sh ilháa áwé tsáa ajeewanáḵ.[91]	Sooner or later, once [Petrel] finally yielded to [Raven], [Petrel's smokehole spirit] released [Raven].

Here the same basic formula and the main verb that follows to complete the line and sentence are in both cases identical. More examples would be needed to prove this is more than coincidental, but these together make it tempting to consider *ldinax̱k'iyéide* + CONSECUTIVE·VERB + *áwéi tsáa ajeewanáḵ* 'sooner or later, once VERB finally [took place] did SUBJECT release OBJECT' to constitute a further elaboration of the formula. Whereas the formula *ldinax̱k'iyéide* + CONSECUTIVE·VERB allows for a fixed structure to be adapted to various narrative environments by placing different verbs within the framework, the two uses of *áwé tsáa ajeewanáḵ* '[once that finally happened] did he release him' show a fixed verb form being adapted to different narrative environments by associating different characters with the arguments of the verb. In both cases *ajeewanáḵ* means 'SUBJECT released OBJECT'; with Italio, *ajeewanáḵ* refers to Raven releasing Little-Elder-Who-Enlarged-the-Tide (used in the story "Raven Goes Down Along the Bull Kelp"), while with Dick, *ajeewanáḵ* refers to Petrel's smokehole spirit releasing Raven (used in the story "Raven and Fresh Water"). For Italio, Raven is the subject and agent of the verb; for Dick, he is the object being acted upon. The actors and surrounding details are variable, but the formulaic words and thematic structure remain steady. The basic idea of the formula could be described 'scene transition following apprehension and release'; in their respective narrative contexts, the formula comes right as Raven has irreversibly enacted the liquidation of the story's major thematic lack—the tidal cycle in the case of Italio; fresh water in the case of Dick.

Another example of formulaic affinity appears near the end of "Raven and the Whale" when Raven prepares to gorge himself in solitude after convincing the local villagers to abandon the provisions they laboriously prepared from the beached whale along with what remained of the unprocessed carcass:

Dick:	A shóo yéi wootèe hóoch ḵu.aa[92]	He, on the other hand, sat down to eat it (the whale meat and rendered oil)
Mills:	Yú yáay tlein a shóox' yéi wootee[93]	He settled down to eat that huge whale
Italio:	Ts'as daneitx' áwés a shóo ÿan x̱'eiwatée[94]	He lay there with his mouth open ready to devour the oil from those many grease boxes

The most recurrent rendering is *a shóo(x') yéi wootee* 'he was poised before it'. With Italio, the verb in the formula takes a different form, but the use of *a shóo* 'poised before it' along with the verb root *tee~* 'be' in this context makes for a clear family resemblance.

The formula *a shóo yéi wootee* 'he was poised to eat it' also has a broader utilization outside of the story of "Raven and the Whale". Wanamaker uses it in the opening lines of "Raven and the Daylight" to refer back to the conclusion of his preceding story, "Raven and His Uncle". Following a cataclysmic flood caused by Raven's uncle, a massive ebbing event left the tidelands and all manner of marine life exposed for the surviving people to collect. In order to get this food for himself, Raven inveigles a group of these survivors into abandoning the mass of food they've gathered. Between the people abandoning their food and Raven venturing off into the dark world in search of the daylight, Wanamaker states:

á áwé a shóo yéi wootee[95]	he was all set to eat it (the abandoned food)

In addition to the formulaic words, there is a thematic affinity perceptible in, on the one hand, "Raven and the Whale" by Italio, Dick, and Mills, and, on the other, this transition between "Raven and His Uncle" and "Raven and the Daylight" by Wanamaker. The formula announces the transition out of the 'trickery–complicity' theme (Raven deceives the villagers; the villagers fall for the deception) and into 'lack liquidated' (Raven is poised for a feast). Though the stories and the details have changed, the same thematic structure is punctuated by the same formula.

This formula appears again in yet another story, "Raven and the Brown Bear Couple" by Mills. After Raven manages by crooked means to kill his Brown Bear auntie and her husband, he settles himself down to feast on their bodies along with their catch of halibut. Mills uses it twice within five lines:

K'e a shóo yéi wootee wé— wé Xóots dleeyí ḵa wé— wé du aat dleeyí ḵaa ldakát wé cháatl. Tle ch'a tléináx̱ hóoch áwé a shóo yéi wootee.[96]	He stayed there, you see, to feast on the— the Bear's flesh and his— his auntie's flesh and all that halibut. He was the only one there feasting on it.

The previous examples involved Raven tricking a group of people into abandoning their food. Here he rather tricks his interlocutors into becoming his food. Here again, the formula describes the passage out of 'trickery–complicity' (Raven enacts successive tricks against the two bears; each bear falls for the lethal deception) and into 'lack liquidated' (Raven is poised for another feast). The thematic structure and the formula together form a unit of traditional compositional style. They belong to the corpus of ideas and words obtained from the past and kept in circulation by these storytellers.

In addition to the formulas speaking of the passage of time and finality of scenes, many of which are utilized across genres and storylines, there exists a stock of formulas for which specific moments in specific Raven stories serve as the exclusive context for their use.[97] These are hallmarks of the traditional diction of the Raven genre. We will take as an example the phrase uttered by Raven while stranded on the fine sand beach and sealed within the cold, dead humpback whale. Stuck inside the whale, Raven calls out an obscure exhortation so that the local villagers who find the whale will cut him free. These peculiar words are typically heard reiterated by the villagers. The formula occurs in eleven instances across each of the four versions of the story in this volume. They are all clearly fashioned from a common stock, though not all are identical. Those from brothers-in-law Italio and Dick are, however, verbatim repetitions. Italio uses the formula three times in his story, twice attributed to Raven, once to the villagers recounting what they heard:

«Aadóo sá k̲aa kaanáx̲ ang̲axaashée-ée-ée-ée yáaÿ yíkdáx̲ kéi x̲duk̲een?»[98]	"Who could cut a hole over a fello-o-o-ow so a fellow could fly up out of a whale?"

Minnie Johnson interjects into Italio's performance to offer her own slightly more embellished form and used it also in a version she told to de Laguna in English:

«Aadóo sgé k̲aa yéx̲ aanÿédi súk k̲aa kaanáx̲ ang̲axaash yáaÿ yíkdáx̲ kéi x̲duk̲een?»[99]	"Who, being nobility material like a certain fellow, could cut a hole over a fellow so a fellow could fly out from inside a whale?"

James uses her formulation five times, thrice from Raven, twice by the villagers:

«Aa sgí k̲aa kan̲ax̲ ang̲axaashák'óo- óo-óo yáaÿ yíkdáx̲— yáaÿ yíkdáx̲ kei x̲duk̲ee-ee-een?»[100]	"Who could cut a li-i-ittle hole over a fellow so a fellow could fly-y-y up out of a whale?"

Dick's formula, used twice, is identical with that used by Italio. It is said once by Raven, once by the villagers:

«Aadóo sá k̲aa kaanáx̲ ang̲axaashée-ée-ée yáay yíkdáx̲ kéi x̲duk̲een?»[101]	"Who could cut a hole over a fello-o-ow so a fellow could fly up out of a whale?"

Mills uses a shorter variation twice for Raven's wish:

«Aadóo sgí k̲aa kaanáx̲ kéi ag̲axaash?»[102]	"Who could cut a fellow out of here?"

She then uses a slightly different version of the formula in the villagers' recollection; the difference in meaning is incredibly marginal:

«Aadoo sgí k̲aa kaanáx̲ kéi k̲ugaxaash?»[103]	"Who could cut an opening over a fellow?"

The words and ideas remain relatively stable in all cases, though nearly all of these storytellers have put a slight twist on the exact phrasing.

The formulaic elements in Raven's speech often consist of rather convoluted constructions that are somewhat out of the ordinary. Here Raven refers to himself in the fourth person using *k̲aa* and *du-*, both generally meaning 'someone' or 'a person', which we have translated as 'a fellow'. The obscurity and long-windedness of Raven's speech adds to its comedic value alongside its deviant craftiness. His words first coax the villagers into cutting him free and then serve him again later for another purpose. Once free, he flies off and primps himself up to then appear before the village disguised as a lone traveler. He inquires about the whale, asking if any odd sounds might have been heard from within it:

Italio:	«Tlél shéyágúshé a yíkde ḵukawdu.áax̱ákw wé yáaÿ?»[104]	"Mightn't any mysterious sounds have been heard coming from inside the whale?"
James:	«Héigíl ch'a ḵukawdu.áax̱ákw a yíkde?»[105]	"Mightn't any mysterious sounds have been heard coming from inside it?"
Dick:	«Héhe! Tléil shéyákwshé a yíkde ḵukawdu.áax̱ákw?[...»][106]	"Hey-hey! Mightn't any mysterious sounds have been heard coming from inside it?["]

When the villagers affirm that they did in fact hear something in the whale and reiterate Raven's own words back to him, Raven uses this as leverage suggesting that it is a bad sign he has seen before and will surely cause the death of the whole village unless they leave everything in place and move away. Raven uses speech here to manipulate the villagers in two successive 'trickery–complicity' sequences; the same words first cause the villagers to unwittingly assist him in getting free and then to believe the idea that the whale must be abandoned. He then has a feast announced by the formula discussed above, *a shóo(x') yéi wootee* 'he was poised before it'.[107] His conniving words are the mediating term in a satisfying reversal: Raven in the stomach of the whale leads to the whale in the stomach of Raven.

Readers will encounter numerous other such formulas belonging to specific instances throughout the Raven stories. Several are discussed in the cast of characters and the notes to the stories, but we have not commented on, or likely even noticed, all in this volume. The purpose here is not to exhaustively catalogue or analyze the formulas, but to make the reader aware of this important feature of the stories and the storytelling and to suggest lines of inquiry for students and scholars of Tlingit language and oral literature.

1.4.3 *Final Considerations*

It is abundantly clear from oral tradition and the ethnographic record that the Tlingit people have long considered the use of words to be a matter of great importance and sensitivity. Based on discussions with Kadashan in 1904, Swanton observed, "in olden times people were afraid of employing trifling words because they thought that everything was full of eyes looking at them and ears listening to what they said."[108] Kaséix̱, Selina Everson, a woman of the Deisheetaan clan, related such a principle to Will Geiger in 2015, «Ch'a ldakát át a tuḵwáani ḵudzitee, ách áwé sh x̱'adusht'íx'x̱», meaning 'Everything has an indwelling spirit, which is why people control their speech.'[109] In ancestral narratives, careless or offensive speech often has disastrous consequences. In ceremonial oratory, eloquent speech has a transformational capacity in confronting death and grief. With the Raven stories, speech is routinely employed towards devious ends and is meant to be shocking, comical, confusing, and contradictory. The words are at times ridiculous, but they are not for this reason trifling or uncontrolled. The time-tested and highly structured formulas in the Raven stories are a clear sign that these words have been deliberately crafted for their purpose.

Though they are necessarily kept and transmitted by specific individuals, oral-traditional formulas are not the invention of any one storyteller. They are packages of sounds and ideas that have been formed and handed down by generations of departed storytellers. By the fact that they are so conventionalized and habitually employed, the formulas suggest a kind of consensus within the tradition regarding the manner of putting certain ideas into words. They offer a sense of what has been valued over time as the right way to say something worth thinking about. Attention to the ways they are put to use by specific storytellers allows for the appreciation of an oral style which is simultaneously individual and traditional without contradiction.

In "Tradition and the Individual Talent", the poet and literary critic T.S. Eliot writes, "No poet, no artist of any art, has his complete meaning alone. His significance, his appreciation is the appreciation of his relation to the dead poets and artists."[110] Although Eliot had the written literary traditions of Europe in mind, the ideas hold true for Tlingit oral literature. When we appreciate the craft of the seven storytellers of this volume, we appreciate their mentors and theirs in turn, and theirs, who together shaped the whole of the tradition. Eliot states further, "not only the best, but the most individual parts of [an artist's] work may be those in which the dead poets, his ancestors, assert their immortality most vigorously."[111] This well describes some of the richness of the formulaic diction of the Raven stories. Beyond their usefulness for composition in performance, they are a means of enacting a kind of parallelism not at the level of the poetic composition of a story, but at the level of the symbolic composition of the tradition. Rather than the repetition of sounds and ideas across successive lines or passages of a story, the formulas create a repetition of sounds and patterns of thought occurring across successive generations of living and dying storytellers. This can be connected to broader themes of traditional Tlingit spirituality, which is expressed in ceremonial ritual and oratory as 'imitating one's ancestors.'[112]

Italio provides a rich example. In both 1952 and 1954, he punctuates his performances by singing a sequence of two songs (songs, which take oral-formulaic composition to the extreme, are often key features of the stories). The world enveloped in darkness, Raven has managed to obtain the Container of Daylight from his grandfather at the head of the Nass and now sits holding the container on the shores of the Akwe to where he has fled. The songs enter at the high point of dramatic tension and mark the transition between two fundamental contrasting states: the ancient world as it existed in darkness and the current world we experience today illuminated in the cycle of day and night. Preparing to open the container and irreversibly transform the cosmos, Raven breaks into song. Here we see that Raven, too, was a practicing oral literary artist. The first song is sung while he is on the verge of opening the container, the second while directly in the act of doing so. Before singing the first song, Italio states:

1952:	tle áx' áwé kéi	then right there he started singing
	shikaawashée	a song
	ch'a hú chush daat x̱á.	about himself, you see.
	Yéil	Raven,
	du x̱'asheeyí áyá yáadu á,	this right here, this is his song;
	yá kéi kḵwashee	it is Raven's song, which I will
	Yéil x̱'asheeyí á. […]	now sing. […]
	Ch'a hú áyú sh toodé	He himself was composing this song
	shukalx̱úx̱s'.[113]	in his mind.
1954:	Ch'a hú du x̱'asheeyí áyáa yáa Yéil,	This is Raven's very own song; he was
	de shukalx̱úx̱s'.	already composing the song.
	Ch'a hú sh toodé shukalx̱úx̱s'.[114]	He himself was composing the song
		in his mind.

Raven obtained the Container of Daylight from his grandfather at the head of the Nass; Italio obtained the songs from his grandparents in Dry Bay:

1952:	Ax̱ léelk'uch áwé […]	It was my grandparent […];
	du x̱'éitx̱ áwé x̱wsikóo	it was from their lips that I came
	hé G̱unaax̱oo.	to know it in Dry Bay.
	Hasdu x̱'éitx̱ áyá x̱wsikóo yá	It was from the lips of my
	Yéil x̱'asheeyí.[115]	grandparents that I came to
		know this song of Raven's.
1954:	X̱wasikóo, ax̱ léelk'u has	I know it; it was from the lips of
	x̱'éitx̱ x̱wasikóo.[116]	my grandparents that I came to
		know it.

Even the way Italio makes his attribution ('I came to know it from their lips') has a formulaic ring to it. If we assume a standard twenty-five-year generational gap, we can imagine Italio's grandparents at his age (eighty-two and eighty-four at the times of performance) teaching the song to a young Italio (roughly age thirty) in Dry Bay around the year 1900. We imagine further that his grandparents heard the songs from their own grandparents, and them again in turn from earlier sources, and so on.

At the level of the story, Raven is singing on the dark shores of the Akwe; at the level of the tradition, the songs have passed through generations to be heard by Italio from his grandparents in Dry Bay around the turn of the twentieth century; at the level of the individual artist, Italio is consciously singing the songs in a house in Yakutat in the 1950s.[117] The songs are simultaneously the utterance of the mythic Raven, the deceased ancestors, and the living Italio, each of whom become, for a moment, a parallel reflection of the others. This is in a sense a compact image of the tradition itself: the action of the tale, the deceased keepers of the tradition, and the individual artist together form a dynamic living whole. We find Italio's delivery of the songs to be among the most potent and creative images of the volume; and yet, it is certainly one of the most traditional, for Italio is simply imitating his grandparents.

Serious and even spiritual connotations may be drawn from the idea of verbal art traversing generations by way of the ear and mouth. More light-heartedly, the formulaic speech in these stories gives a taste not only of powerful and beautifully formed words but a sense of humor and a cause for laughter that has been handed down and shared by generations. One wonders how many times over how many years the phrases attributed to Raven and his surrounding cast have been uttered and how much laughter they have provoked. The storytellers in this volume struggle at times to speak their lines through fits of laughter. From questions about the spirit of words that endure across generations to the elegance of their spoken form, the potency of their symbolism, and the hilarity of the antics they depict, the diction and style with which these storytellers have crafted their tales offer a feast for our contemplation and enjoyment.

2 CAST OF CHARACTERS

In this section we explore the major characters that appear throughout the stories of this volume. Focusing on the characters, by looking at the specific ways individual storytellers deploy and refer to them, is a useful way of developing and deepening an appreciation of the general mythological and literary situation surrounding Raven. The names of the characters are often suggestive of their attributes or narrative function. The speech acts of many of these actors tend to contain the most palpably formulaic elements of the Raven genre. In comparing the names, roles, and speech of the characters while adhering closely to the words of several storytellers, we hope to demonstrate some of the unity and diversity within the oral tradition. We find much in the way of uniformity and shared common ground, yet we also find a great deal of variation and divergence. In many cases, some or all storytellers employ the same name for the same character with the same role. In many other cases, significant differences exist between one storyteller and the next, or between groups of storytellers, regarding the form of characters' names, who exactly certain names refer to, what kind of beings the characters are, and the function or significance attributed to characters in the action of the stories.

This is not an exhaustive list of characters that appear within this volume, let alone in the broader canon of Raven's adventures. For those characters that are discussed, there is much more that could be said about them beyond what is written here and there are still numerous recorded, written, and living sources of information that can enrich and broaden our understanding. The characters are numbered for ease of cross referencing in the notes to the stories.

2.1 *Yéil, Raven*

Without doubt, the most widely known and infamous character of the entire Tlingit oral tradition is the being known in Tlingit as Yéil and in English as Raven. While *yéil* (phonetically [jé:ɬ]) is the common noun that refers to 'ravens', Raven himself is not exactly—at least, not exclusively—a bird.[118] Though his identity is thoroughly ambiguous, he regularly appears in the narratives as a person-like being who, at some point after his birth, received the name Yéil. While it would be dubious to claim that Raven is simply a person, it is at least clear that this is the form he takes in his initial appearance as a living being in the stories of this volume. Compare, for instance, these formulations referring to Raven after his birth as he is coming of age: Italio states, «Shde ḵáax̱ sateeyí áwé…»[119] 'Now that he was a man…'; Wanamaker, «Ḵáax̱ nastée áwé du káakch kaawaḵaa»[120] 'When he became a man, his uncle sent him on a mission'; and Zuboff, «ḵáak'wx̱ yaa nastéen»[121] 'he was becoming a little man'. All of these refer to Raven 'becoming' a man in the sense of growing up from infancy, not in the sense of transforming or transfiguring himself into a male human. There are numerous other instances within this volume in which the storytellers use the word *ḵáa*, which means 'man' or 'person', in reference to Raven.[122]

Yet, while the prevailing image of Raven in these stories is that of a *ḵáa* 'man', he is no ordinary person and is indeed often found cawing like a raven and flying and hopping around in a bird-like manner. One could contend that Raven's ambiguous depiction as a human with raven-like characteristics reflects an underlying animist cosmology in which animals and other non-human entities are understood to experience themselves as human persons and share the same spiritual substance as ordinary human beings. However, the exact nature of the affinity that exists between the mythic Raven and observable ravens is not entirely clear; one cannot say absolutely whether Raven acts like ravens or if ravens act like Raven. In the stories in this volume, he appears variously in the bodily forms of a stone, a man, a crane- or snipe-like bird with a long beak, a raven, an evergreen needle, a human baby, and a woman. Because he so readily changes from one form to another, he is in a sense all of these things, and, therefore, not entirely or exclusively any one of them. To further complicate the matter, in a 2014 lecture on this volume Nora Dauenhauer remarked, "To me, Raven is several people," after which she simply raised her hands and shrugged.[123] She appears to view Raven as a name through which multiple individuals—notably, "people"—have converged into a single symbolic identity.

Raven's birth seems to always involve his soon-to-be mother receiving assistance from a being who instructs her to find a small impervious stone from the region of the low tide, to heat it in a fire, and then to swallow it. It is this stone, often referred to specifically as a *shanyaateiyí* 'stone of the low-tide region',[124] that becomes a child in the woman's womb and is born to become Raven. One could thus consider Raven's initial appearance in the narratives to be in the form of this seemingly inert small stone lying at the edge of the minus tide, rather than the boy born to the woman who swallows it. Italio in fact says just this, «Shanyaateiyí áwé Yéilx̱ sitee»[125] 'A low-tide stone, that is Raven'. Being originally made of stone makes Raven indestructible and immune to his uncle's attempts to kill him. As Wanamaker puts it, «Tléil ách g̱waajaag̱i át ḵoostí shanyaateiyíx̱ sateeyích Yéil»[126] 'There is nothing that can kill him because he is a stone from the edge of the minus tide'. Italio similarly formulates this notion:

Yú shanyaateiyíx̱ sateeyích áyú tlél
    aadé ux̱dishaani yé, tlél tsú aadé
nag̱waanaawu yé.[127]
	Because he is a low-tide stone
	    he cannot grow old, nor
	can he die.

Storytellers do not share the same perspective on when and how Raven received this name. We can compare a handful of examples on the theme of Raven's naming to gain a glimpse of the variation that exists from one storyteller to the next. Zuboff says in one instance that Raven's mother gave him this name when he was born:

Á áyá ḵug̱astée áyá Yéil tle yóo aawasáa tsu.[128]	So when he was born she (his mother) even named him Raven.

In a different performance, Zuboff himself offers an alternative account of the naming, not on the terms of the internal process of the narrative, but in terms of his own personal and historical perspective,[129] attributing the naming to Tlingit people generally and suggesting that Lucifer and Yéil could be considered different names applied to the same being by different peoples:

Á áyá yáa— yáa Dikée Aanḵáawu kooḵénayi— dleit ḵáach yéi yasáakw *Lucifer*— hú kwshéiyá yáa Lingítch ḵu.aa yéi uwasáa Yéil.[130]	So this— this angel of God— white folks call him Lucifer— I suppose this is who the Tlingit named Raven.

Italio, on the other hand, presents an entirely different picture, directly stating an opposite opinion of Zuboff's first account above, «tlél ch'a du tláach áwé yéi wusá Yéil yóo»[131] 'it was not his mother who named him Raven'. For Italio, this being was not originally named Raven and the first time he was ever called by this name it was in the form of a curse from an elderly man known as Little-Elder-Who-Enlarged-the-Tide (discussed in §2.9), who, out of annoyance, addressed him as «Yéil Tl'éetl'i»,[132] literally meaning 'Shitty Raven'. When interpreting this moment in Italio's narrative, Minnie Johnson (a friend of Italio who served as an interpreter for de Laguna) stated, "That's how that old man named that Yeł [Yéil]. That's the first time he heard his own name."[133] Elsewhere, Italio elaborates, «Yéi du ÿáa wduwasáa Yéil [...] l at yéx̱ yóo unasgít yís»[134] 'He was given the name Raven [...] for his inappropriate behavior'.

There are more accounts in published sources outside this volume. John Kadashan told Swanton in 1904 that Raven received this name when he was born in the form of a human baby at the headwaters of the Nass and the figure known as *Lyóo.at.uwajeegi Shaanák'w* 'Unfazable-Little-Elder' (discussed in §2.8) looked into his eyes and remarked, "His eyes look like the eyes of Raven"; Kadashan continues "That is how he came to get the name Raven."[135] We find yet another explanation in Louis Shotridge's short written piece "Raven in Eyre",[136] where he states— in agreement with Kadashan— that it was "Ancient Wisdom" (Shotridge's English moniker for Unfazable-Little-Elder) who named him Raven. Shotridge's account differs from Kadashan's in that Raven had sought out and approached Unfazable-Little-Elder in some unspecified time and place prior to Raven's adventure to the headwaters of the Nass River. Shotridge gives "Procreator" in parentheses immediately after the name "Raven", apparently as an epithet meant to explain the implication of the use of the name Raven in this context, and states that the elderly woman named him thus "because she knew that the new being came to exist as a proxy for Justice."[137]

While Shotridge's use of "Procreator" is not a literal translation of the name Yéil, it should be noted that while the noun *yéil* does ordinarily mean 'raven(s)', the root of this word has a broader range of possible meanings and connotations that bear strongly on the behavior of this character. This is the root of verbs meaning 'lie', 'cheat', 'deceive', 'fool', 'trick', and the like in forms such as *liyéili* 's/he is cunning, tricky'; *k̲'aliyéil* 's/he is a (habitual) liar'; and *awliyél* 's/he tricked, fooled, deceived him/her'. Raven is usually found tricking and cheating others so that he can eat the fruits of these people's labor or even so that he can eat these people themselves. At other times, though, Raven is found deceiving and fooling people so that he can release a hoarded or isolated resource: fresh water, the tides, the salmon runs, and the daylight were either hoarded by private individuals or accessible only to a wealthy few until Raven strew them throughout the world.[138] George Johnson (a Yakutat man who spoke Tlingit, Eyak, and English) summarizes these aspects of Raven succinctly, "He does things for people [and] does lots of crooked work too."[139]

2.2 *K̲inyukookook̲éik; Raven's Mother*

James is the only storyteller who mentions a name of Raven's mother in this volume and this is the only spoken source that we are aware of. She pronounces the name twice as «K̲inyukookook̲éik»[140] in her performance of "Raven and His Uncle". The only analysis we can come up with for this name is that it is a deformation of a hypothetical original version of the name, of which we can conceive of two possible forms: *K̲inyookook̲éik*, which would be a compacted nominal form of the phrase (*a*/*du*) *k̲ín yoo akuwak̲éik* 's/he commands him/her/it less than, short of (it/him/her)'; or *K̲inyook̲ukook̲éik*, which would be a compacted nominal form of the phrase (*a*/*du*) *k̲ín yoo k̲ukuwak̲éik* 's/he commands people less than, short of (it/him/her)'.[141] Scruples aside, it is tempting, based on the grammatical form of the woman's name, to consider it as a sort of companion name to that of her brother *Yook̲is'kook̲éik* 'Tide-Commander' (both being elaborations of the verbal noun *yookook̲éik* 'commanding'), but this is a tenuous speculation, especially because we have no indication from any source that the woman ever 'commanded' anything at all, let alone in a like or lesser manner than her brother. The one other reference to the woman's name in this volume further shrouds it in uncertainty; Dick states in the first recorded line of his multi-episodic performance, «Hél k̲u.as x̲wasakú du saayée yáa shaawát» 'I don't, however, know the name of this woman'.[142]

The only other sources we are aware of that attest a name for this woman come from Russian missionaries. In 1840, Saint Veniaminov wrote that he had been informed that Raven's mother received assistance from a killerwhale and recorded her name in Cyrillic script.[143] The name occurs three times in his text, each with a slightly different spelling: first as "Китх8ги́нси", second as "китх8гинси", finally as "Китх8ги́нса".[144] Veniaminov glosses the name as "Daughter of the Killer Whale".[145] We believe that Veniaminov's spellings approximate the name *Kéet K̲uháan Sée*, literally meaning 'Daughter of Killerwhale People', in which *k̲uháan* is the archaic uncontracted form of *k̲wáan* 'tribe, people, collectivity'.[146] Sergei Kan transliterates Anatolii Kamenskii's 1906 rendering of the name similarly as "Kitkukhinsi"; like Veniaminov, Kamenskii glosses the name as "daughter of a killerwhale".[147] Notably, he describes the woman as "choosing heron or *tliak* [*láx̲*] as her husband."[148] In a similar vein, in reference to the woman, Italio at one point describes the leader of the Killerwhale People, Hole-in-the-Dorsal-Fin, as «du wadák'u»,[149] literally 'her young man', but more idiomatically meaning 'her boyfriend', implying that the woman and Hole-in-the-Dorsal-Fin had an intimate (though in this case apparently extramarital) relationship.

2.3 *Yoo̲kis'koo̲kéik, Tide-Commander; Raven's Maternal Uncle*

Yoo̲kis'koo̲kéik is the name of Raven's maniacal maternal uncle. Prior to Raven's birth, whenever this man's sister would birth a child he sees to it that it is murdered. He typically accomplishes this in one of two ways: In the performances by Italio and Dick, he sends his slaves to kill the child; in the performances by James, Zuboff, and Wanamaker, he sends for his sister's child to 'assist' him in working on one of his lethal traps, such as an unfinished dugout canoe, which clenches over the child and crushes it. Upon learning of Raven's existence, Tide-Commander again seeks to have his nephew put to death.

Italio, James, and Zuboff use the most common form of the name, Yoo̲kis'koo̲kéik.[150] From Dick we can hear it pronounced as «Yóo̲kis'koo̲kéik»,[151] which is identical other than that it contains the high-toned variant of the preverb *yóo=* (this is simply dialectal variation). Wanamaker pronounces it twice, once surprisingly as «Yoo̲kis'koo̲kéigi»[152] and once later in the narrative with the usual form «Yoo̲kis'koo̲kéik»;[153] the form *Yoo̲kis'koo̲kéigi* has the trappings of an actor noun, but Wanamaker's use of the more common pronunciation later in the narrative suggests that it was a simply an isolated idiosyncrasy. The name Yoo̲kis'koo̲kéik is a truncated nominal form of the phrase *k̲ées' yoo akuwak̲éik* 'he commands the floodtide back and forth' with the noun *k̲ées'* 'floodtide' incorporated into the verb as prefixed *k̲is'-*. Strictly speaking, the nominal form *yoo̲kis'koo̲kéik* literally means 'commanding the floodtide' (i.e., the act of commanding the floodtide), but we have translated the name throughout the English texts as 'Tide-Commander'.

Italio and Dick emphasize that Tide-Commander is himself the moon. Dick states:

Dís,	The moon,
Yóo̲kis'koo̲kéik á.	that is Tide-Commander.
Yéi duwasáakw.	That is his name.
Át akaawa.aak̲w yáa dís.	The moon has command over the tide.
Yá k̲ées'	At his word
du x̲'ayáx̲	the floodtide
daak̲ déich.[154]	rises.

Italio similarly says:

yú dís áyú,	the moon
du káakx̲ sitee, yá lingit'aanikáx' k̲wá yéi yatee yú dís,	is his (Raven's) uncle; but the moon was here on the earth.
tléil yú dikéex̲ wulxáat'.[155]	It wasn't suspended above in the sky.

One can readily understand why Yoo̲kis'koo̲kéik 'Tide-Commander' is a fitting name for the moon, since it is the primary controller of the movements of the tide on Earth. Italio elaborates further that people were so fearful of the power that this man wielded though his control over the floodtide that they became his slaves, «Ldakát yá lingit'aanituḵwáani áyá gooxx'úx̱ awliyéx̱ yú dís»[156] 'The moon had made all of the world's inhabitants into slaves'. Italio is the only one in this volume to state explicitly that Tide-Commander, after flooding the earth, ascended into the sky in order to escape the flood;[157] we can infer this to be his final act as a person on Earth, after which he became the moon as it is now. There is no explicit connection made between Raven's uncle and the moon in the performances by James, Wanamaker, and Zuboff; in their texts, the uncle silently fades away from the narrative foreground after flooding the world.

2.4 *Gushtuwool, Hole-in-the-Dorsal-Fin; Raven's Father*

Gushtuwool 'Hole-in-the-Dorsal-Fin' is the name of a killerwhale who comes to the aid of Raven's mother-to-be (the sister of Tide-Commander) and instructs her as to how she can successfully bear a child that will not die at her brother's hand or command. His crucial instruction is for the woman to go and find a stone from the region of the low tide, to heat it in a fire, and to swallow it. The name Gushtuwool is a compound of *goosh* 'dorsal fin', *tu-* 'inside', and *wool* 'hole', together meaning 'Hole-in-[the-]Dorsal-Fin'. As the name suggests, Italio states, «A goosh tóonáx̱ ḵuwawóol»[158] 'There is a hole in his dorsal fin'. The name and bodily configuration of Hole-in-the-Dorsal-Fin immediately call to mind the depiction of killerwhales in Tlingit crest imagery and visual design (found also in that of the Haida and Tsimshian) in which they are ubiquitously depicted with a hole in the dorsal fin.

Italio describes Hole-in-the-Dorsal-Fin as the «Kéet Aanḵáawu»[159] 'Killerwhale Headman' or 'Killerwhale Chief' (i.e., the principal leader of the *Kéet Ḵwáani* 'Killerwhale People'), and states that he is Raven's father,[160] owing to the fact that he effectuated the successful birth and survival of Raven. Italio also refers to him at one point as «du wadák'u»[161] 'her boyfriend' (i.e., the lover of Raven's mother-to-be). Minnie Johnson expressed the same understanding in a version of the story she told in English in 1954, "The killerwhale heard a girl weeping and crying because she lost all her children. [...] He came ashore and turned into a human being. He gave her instructions on how to take care of her children next time she get that way. That's how Raven was born. He's Killerwhale's son."[162] Italio is the only storyteller in this volume to refer to this character by this name. For James, Zuboff, and Wanamaker, it is *Láx̱'* 'Heron' who comes to the woman's aid. Dick, on the other hand, does not use a personal name or relate this figure to any animal, portraying the entity in a sort of haziness as «ch'a ksiyéiyi át» 'a strange being'.[163]

2.5 *Láx̱', Heron; Raven's Father*

The figure referred to as *Láx̱'* 'Great Blue Heron' by James, Zuboff, and Wanamaker plays essentially the same role as that of Hole-in-the-Dorsal-Fin; it is typically one or the other of these characters who comes to the aid of the ailing woman, and the two never occur together in the same story. *Láx̱'* is a common noun meaning 'great blue heron', but we treat the use of Láx̱' in the narratives as a proper noun referring to a specific individual and translate it simply as 'Heron'. Like Hole-in-the-Dorsal-Fin, Heron assists the sister of Tide-Commander and instructs her as to how she can conceive a child that her brother cannot kill. Kamenskii described Raven's mother-to-be as "choosing heron or *tliak* [*láx̱'*] as her husband."[164] For the same reason that Italio regards Hole-in-the-Dorsal-Fin as Raven's father, James states that Heron is the father of Raven because, as she tells the story, it was Heron who oversaw the successful conception and survival of Raven:

Láx̱' ÿéetx̱ wusitee.	He became Heron's son.
Du éeshx̱ wusitee.	He became his father.
Yéil éeshx̱ wusitee Láx̱',	Heron became Raven's father
yú té yú shaawát x̱'éide akawuṉáayi yátx̱ wusteeyích áwé.[165]	because the stone that he had appointed for the woman to swallow became a child.

2.6 *Éenyeekóon, Flicker-Pits; Raven's Uncle's Wife*

Raven's uncle Tide-Commander had a wife that he jealously guarded. He made a habit of putting his wife in a box, tying the box shut, hoisting the box into the rafters of his house, and leaving her in this condition whenever he went away. The despotic lengths to which Tide-Commander went to isolate his wife relate directly to his murderous relationship with his sister's children. When his sister would birth a male child, Dick impersonates Tide-Commander's directive to his slaves:

«Yijáḵ!	"Kill it!
Yijáḵ,	Kill it,
ax̱ shát éex̱ oongaanóok.»[166]	or it might bother my wife."

Once grown enough to understand the situation, Raven learns from his mother what she endured at the hand of her brother, Tide-Commander; this provokes Raven to seek out his uncle's wife in an act of revenge for the murder of his would-be siblings and the torment endured by his mother.[167] The name of Tide-Commander's wife is *Éenyeekóon*, which is based on the nouns *(du) éenÿee* '(his/her) armpit' and *kóon* 'northern flicker'. The northern flicker is a small migratory bird with vibrant, colorful, and speckled plumage; these feathers are often used to adorn the frontlet headdresses known as in Tlingit as *shakee.át* 'thing atop the head', used by many tribes across the Northwest Coast. Strictly speaking Éenyeekóon translates as 'Armpit Flicker(s)' or 'Under-Arm Flicker(s)', but these had too strong a connotation of 'one who flicks armpits', so we have translated the name, still fairly literally, as

'Flicker-Pits'. Italio is the only storyteller in this volume to mention this character by name; we variously heard him pronounce it as «Éeneekóon» and «Éenyeekóon».[168] Dick does not refer to her by name, but mentions «a éenyee kóoni»[169] 'the flickers of her armpits'. James, Wanamaker, and Zuboff also tell the story of "Raven and His Uncle", but for all three of them this character figures in no way into the plot of the story.

It is not clear to us from the texts how Italio and Dick picture the configuration of the woman and the birds and what exactly Raven does to them. Based on the verbs they both use,[170] it appears that Raven apprehends her and 'plucks' (i.e., violently snatches) the whole birds from under her arms, rather than plucking the feathers from the birds' skin. Minnie Johnson, on the other hand, in her own storytelling as well as in her interpretations of Italio's, seems to view Raven's uncle's wife as having flicker feathers in place of armpit hair, rather than having live flickers under her arms; she states, "He [i.e., Raven] got the woman out and he pulled out all the hair from under her arms. And then he threw it up the smokestack {i.e., smokehole. The hair was flicker feathers (kun ṫawu [*kóon t'aawú*])}."[171] Louis Shotridge presents a different clarifying image, "Jealousy [Shotridge's title for Tide-Commander] had a wife, a being who represented Vanity, from whom came forth conceit. She was guarded by four (eight in some versions) tiny and very delicate Flickers, two birds being concealed in each arm-pit, and this possession constituted her great pride."[172] She is described also by Veniaminov:

> The wife had eight small live birds, reddish in color, which are found in California. The Koloshi [i.e., Tlingits] call these birds kun (kóon). She (the wife) had four birds at each side, in constant attendance. Whenever the wife, no matter how modestly, dealt with a man other than her husband, the birds flew away from her side. Her husband was so jealous that whenever he had to be absent, he locked her up in a chest.[173]

Kamenskii similarly comments, "The only time they flew away from her, was when the woman favored somebody in her husband's absence."[174] The depictions of Veniaminov and Kamenskii suggest a sexual connotation in Raven's apprehension of Flicker-Pits. While never made overt by Italio or Dick, it is not difficult to imagine the existence of a covert sexual element in their tales, in which the woman's sexual desirability would be condensed in the symbolic form of the flickers. The woman serves in the narratives as the object of rapacious male jealousy (that of Tide-Commander) while her flickers become the instruments through which rivalry and revenge is staged between adversarial men (Raven seeks out the woman and releases the flickers as a provocation against Tide-Commander). Raven's apprehension and release of the birds can thus be interpreted as a transmuted sexual conquest, whereby the motive is not Raven's sexual appetite for the woman, but his desire to antagonize the woman's possessive husband.

2.7 *Gus'x̲lugook̲, Pokes-Nose-Into-Clouds; Raven's Bird-Skin Suit*

Italio and Dick use the name «Gus'x̲lugook̲»[175] 'Pokes-Nose-Into-Clouds' in their performances of "Raven and His Uncle" to refer to a bird Raven kills with an arrow in order to harvest and make use of its skin. They are the only two storytellers in this volume to involve such a creature; in the versions of "Raven and His Uncle" by James and Wanamaker, as well as "Raven and the Flood" by Zuboff, Raven flies to the sky without the explicit involvement of a bird's skin. In a 1963 performance of "Raven and His Uncle" Jimmie Johnson refers to the *Gus'x̲lugook̲*, but in his version Raven has his mother enter its skin in order to keep her safe during the flood.[176] As Italio and Dick tell the story, Raven dons the skin of this bird in order to take on its bodily form, which enables him to pierce the bird's long beak into the permeable substance of the sky and thereby escape the flood set loose by Tide-Commander after Raven makes unwanted contact with his wife. Their descriptions of the bird's physical form are limited to brief statements about its beak; Italio states, «yóo lukoowáat'»[177] 'its beak is quite long'; and Dick, «a lú yéi koowáat' yóo kdunéek wéit'át»[178] 'they say that creature has a very long beak'. The name *Gus'x̲lugook̲* is a truncated nominal form of the verb phrase *góos'x̲ lugook̲* 'it pokes its nose into clouds'; we have translated it in the texts as the proper noun 'Pokes-Nose-Into-Clouds'. We have no evidence suggesting that the name *gus'x̲lugook̲* is used to refer to any kind of bird other than this mythic creature Raven makes use of.

There are a number of references to the bird in published texts, though none using the name *gus'x̲lugook̲*. Minnie Johnson refers to the bird in English as a "snipe"[179] in her English interpretation of Italio's performance. She states in a version of the story she told in English, "He's got the skin of some kind of sharp-nosed bird."[180] Kadashan describes it as "a large bird which was very pretty and had a bill that looked like copper",[181] and says of Raven, "he got into the skin of the white bird with copper-colored bill."[182] Veniaminov refers to "a large bird resembling a magpie" and states that it "had a long tail and a very long narrow and glistening beak, as strong as iron."[183] Veniaminov rendered the Tlingit name of the bird in Cyrillic as "к8цгат8ли",[184] which would be romanized as *kutsgatúli*. The standardized Tlingit form is *gus'ÿadóoli*, literally meaning 'crane of the cloud face', which is a common noun for a 'snipe' or 'sandpiper'.

In terms of Raven's development from a stone at the edge of the minus tide to the cunning raven-like rearranger of the world, a notable feature of the versions by Italio and Dick in this volume is that the first time Raven achieves the ability to fly in the form of a bird, it takes place neither by transforming himself into a raven nor by making use of the skin of a raven. The image is that of a young adult man donning the skin of a bird resembling a snipe or a crane and taking on its physical form.

2.8 *Lyóo.atkoowajeegi Shaanák’w ~ Lyóo.at.uwajeegi Shaanák’w, Unfazable-Little-Elder; Raven’s Grandmother*

The name and actions of an elderly woman who appears at various points throughout Raven’s adventures present her as a figure of unique intuitive power and wisdom. She seems to know the answer to whatever obscure question is put before her and can immediately perceive the disguised identities of things (including Raven himself) that go unrecognized by others. She knows who is keeping the tide high and preventing it from receding when Raven comes asking. When the young woman at the head of the Nass is laboring in pain and her baby will not come, this figure is summoned and intuits that the baby (who is really Raven) does not want to be born on expensive pelts and so suggests using moss instead, which proves to be the appropriate material. She alone recognizes Raven by his eyes when he is finally born in the form of a human baby and nearly spoils his whole plan to obtain the Container of Daylight by announcing his identity to the family he was born to. When she recognizes Raven in this situation, the five storytellers who tell “Raven and the Daylight” in this volume impersonate her in formulaic fashion. While holding the newborn Raven, the storytellers have her say:

Italio (1952):	«Éh! Ax̱ dachx̱ánk’, de ch’a Yéil waaḵx̱ x̱áa sitee,» yéi ash yawsiḵaa. «De ch’a Yéil waaḵ x̱áashé.»[185]	“Eh! My dear grandchild, those are Raven’s very eyes,” she said to him. “Now those must be Raven’s very eyes.”
Wanamaker (1966):	«De ch’a Yéil waaḵ x̱áashgé.»[186]	“Now those must be Raven’s very eyes.”
Dick (1983):	«Hehéi-éi! Héi-ei, ax̱ dachx̱ánk’.» […]«Dei ch’u Yéil waaḵ x̱áashé, ax̱ dachx̱ánk’.»[187]	“Hey-he-ey, he-ey, my dear grandchild.” […]“Now those must be Raven’s very eyes, my dear grandchild.”
James (1972):	«Tlaagóo-óo-óo! Ax̱ dachx̱ánk’! Ch’a Yéil waax̱ x̱áashé, ax̱ dachx̱ánk’.» […]«Ch’a Yéil waaḵ x̱áashé, ax̱ dachx̱ánk’.»[188]	“Incredible! My dear grandchild! Now those must be Raven’s very eyes, my dear grandchild.” […]“Now those must be Raven’s very eyes, my dear grandchild.”
Hammond (1985):	«Ée! Cha Yéil waaḵ x̱áashé!»[189]	“Ew! Now those must be Raven’s very eyes.”

With Italio, James, and Dick having her address Raven as *ax̱ dachx̱ánk’* ‘my dear grandchild’, we thus consider this character to be Raven’s grandmother.[190]

The translation of this character's name involved significant discussion and repeated revision. Hammond simply refers to her as «shawat.shaan»[191] 'an old, elderly woman'. Wanamaker similarly refers to her as «shawat.shaanák'w»[192] 'a little elderly woman'. James refers to her with the Tlingit name «Lyóo.at.uwajeegi Shaanák'w».[193] In a performance not included in this volume, Charlie Joseph can be heard referring to this character with a form identical to James'.[194] Italio and Dick call her «Lyóo.atkoowajeegi Shaanák'w»;[195] this form serves as the primary basis for our interpretation of the character's name. The form used by Italio and Dick is based on the attributive form of the verb phrase *tlél yóo at koojeek*; the affirmative counterpart of that verb phrase is *yóo at kuwajeek*, which is typically translated 's/he is curious, wondering, interested', so it would seem natural for its negation, *tlél yóo at koojeek*, to mean 's/he is not curious', 'she does not wonder', or 'she does not find anything of interest'. However, the implication does not at all seem to be that the woman is imaginatively dull or lacks curiosity, but rather that she never succumbs to mystification or perplexity when confronted by phenomena that would leave others confounded or oblivious. Her mental processes transcend the states of curiosity, wondering, pondering, and the like, enabling her to directly apprehend the truth or conclusion of whatever matter she is confronted with. She proceeds straight to the truth with no intervening guesswork. Dick takes a brief discursus in his performance of "Raven and the Daylight" to consider this figure out loud:

Héil x̱wasakú daak̲wéit sá yéi s asáagu.	I don't know what sort of thing (i.e., being, creature) it is that they call by that name.
Tléil yóo at koojeek.	She doesn't get perplexed.
Tle yax̱ at kaneek.[196]	She just tells things the way they are.

We have tried to reflect the general significance of these considerations while remaining faithful to the grammatical form in translating her name as 'Unfazable-Little-Elder'.

We find this character appearing in a variety of older texts as well. Veniaminov refers to her as "a very ancient crone".[197] Kamenskii mentions her as an "old woman".[198] Swanton rendered the name from Kadashan as «Łiu´wᴀt-uwadjī´gî-can»[199] (i.e., *Lyoo.at.uwajeegi Shaan*) and «Łiu´wᴀt-uwadjī´gî-canᴀ´kᵘ»[200] (i.e., *Lyoo.at.uwajeegi Shaanák'w*) and translated these as "He-who-knows-everything-that-happens";[201] interestingly, the character is referred to there with the English masculine pronouns "him" and "he".[202] Swanton rendered it once from Deikeenaak'w with marginal differences as «Łūwat-uwadjī´gî-cānᴀ´k!ᵘ» (i.e., *Lyoo.at.uwajeegi Shaanák'w*), that time surprisingly translated as "Woman-always-wondering";[203] that she is presented as a woman is unsurprising—this is congruent with nearly all other sources—but the gloss 'always wondering' is the exact opposite of what we take her name to mean. Shotridge has more substantial comments on the character, "There existed also a being who was the Ancient Wisdom, (Łyù-àt-ʋ̀wàdjìgì Cà˙n [*Lyoo.at.uwajeegi Shaan*]) Ancient One who has no more to learn, in whose capacity lay discerning and judging[,] sounding what was true and what was false."[204] Elsewhere Shotridge refers to her as "the goddess of Destiny".[205] John Harrington recorded a series of Raven stories that were told in English by George Johnson in Yakutat in 1940,[206] in which Johnson states, "Raven find out all these things from old lady prophet what knows all things in world"; Harrington scribbled in the margin of that page in barely-legible handwriting, "old lady = tlu aht koowagi-gee sha nuku",[207] which we can safely interpret as *Lyóo.atkoowajeegi Shaanák'w*. Further on Johnson states, "this prophet [… her] name means there's nothing she don't know".[208] De Laguna rendered John Ellis' reference to her as «łyú'ᴀt kuwadjiki cawᴀt» (i.e., *Lyóo.atkoowajeegi Shaawát* 'Unfazable Woman'); Ellis elaborated in English, describing her as "a 'woman that has nothing to worry about' because she knows everything. There's nothing she can't think about."[209] Considering all this together, it seems that one could even go so far as to consider this character an 'oracle'.

In terms of the form of the character's name, we find agreement between Italio, Dick, Johnson, and Ellis (all of Yakutat) on the one hand, who use the attributive verb form *Lyóo.atkoowajeegi*, and agreement between James, Shotridge, Kadashan, Deikeenaak'w, and Joseph on the other, who use *Lyóo.at.uwajeegi* (lacking the prefix combination *k+u-*).[210] Maggie Dick of Yakutat (Italio's sister and Frank Dick's wife) used both forms.[211] The latter form would apparently be based on the hypothetical verb phrase **tlél yóo at ujeek* (which we suppose to have the same meaning as *tlél yóo at koojeek* 'she isn't curious, mystified, ponderous, doesn't wonder'), but we have never encountered such a form and it was unrecognized by our consultants.[212]

2.9 *Yax̱ K̲ées' Shakawdzinugu Shaanák'w ~ K̲ées' Yax̱ Ashakawdzinugu Shaanák'w ~ K̲ées' Yax̱ Shakawdzinugu Shaanák'w, Little-Elder-Who-Enlarged-the-Tide*

After Tide-Commander floods the world, the tide recedes a certain distance but stops with the water still at an elevated level. The tide is so high that the seafood of the intertidal region is essentially inaccessible. In the three performances in this volume of "Raven Goes Down Along the Bull Kelp" (FI I, ii; SJ V; and FD vii) an elderly person known as Little-Elder-Who-Enlarged-the-Tide is the one responsible for maintaining the tide at this level. James and Dick refer to this figure as a «shawat.shaanák'w»[213] 'little old woman', while for Italio it is a «k̲áa shaanák̲w»[214] 'little old man'. In Italio's 1952 performance, it is Unfazable-Little-Elder who informs Raven that this elderly person is the cause of the tidal stagnation; she says to him:

[«]Ḵáa shaanák'w a x̱ánt aldél [...].	["]A little old man watches over [the tide ...].
Tlél aadé ÿan kux̱likooxu ÿé.	There's no way the tide can dry up completely.
Chaa ch'a hú du jeenáx̱ áwé tsá yánde kux̱lakóox[.]»[215]	Only by his doing will the tide go out[.]"

The three storytellers' pronunciations of the name are extremely similar, though none are identical. Italio uses the form «Yax̱ Ḵées' Shakawdzinugu Shaanák'w»[216] (with unmodified *ḵées'* 'floodtide' between *yax̱=* and the verb word, thus seemingly in the position of an incorporated object); from James we hear «Ḵées' Yax̱ Ashakawdzinugu Shaanák'w»[217] (with *ḵées'* outside the verb phrase and coreferential with the verbal object prefix *a-* 'it'); and from Dick, «Ḵées' Yax̱ Shakawdzinugu Shaanák'w»[218] (with *ḵées'* outside the verb phrase, but with no verbal object prefix *a-*). The word *ḵées'* means 'floodtide' (as found prefixed in the name *Yooḵis'kooḵéik* 'Tide-Commander') and the final term *shaanák'w* means 'little elder, old person'. The verb itself presents some difficulties. It is an elaboration of the intransitive verb theme *O-sha-ka-d-nook~ (na)* 'for O to swell up, become enlarged', as in sentences such as *xákwl'i shakawdinook* 'soapberries swelled up, became enlarged (i.e., when whipped)' and *k'óox yaa shakandanúk* 'rice is swelling (i.e., when cooking)';[219] these examples correspond well with the image of the ocean waters 'swelling' and remaining in an enlarged state. The technical scruples aside, we translate the character's name in all instances in the texts as 'Little-Elder-Who-Enlarged-the-Tide'.[220]

Before going to visit the little elder, Raven obtains *nées'* 'sea urchin(s)' in order to use them as a torture device against the little elder as part of the plan to get the tide to subside and expose the seafood. In Italio's text, Raven tries numerous times unsuccessfully to swim down to the base of the bull kelp where the urchins live (he is apparently too buoyant) before eventually making it and snatching up some urchins. In James' text, Raven tries but never succeeds and so eventually recruits 'Little Mink' (discussed in §2.11),[221] who goes down and brings urchins up to Raven. In Dick's text, Raven seems to get ahold of them on his own; Dick states «du jeet kaawasóos, gwál déex̱»[222] 'he got ahold of maybe two of them' (literally, 'they fell into his hands, maybe two'). The visual depiction of this moment in the narrative is a crest image known formally as *Geesh Daax̱ Woogoodi Yéil* 'Raven-Who-Went-Down-Along-the-Bull-Kelp' and depicts Raven descending along the stipes of kelp.[223]

When Raven finally appears before Little-Elder-Who-Enlarged-the-Tide, he comes up beside the little elder, who is trying to sleep by a fire, and begins hogging the fire's heat while incessantly repeating that eating the inner meat of sea urchins has made him feel cold. The verbal interactions that ensue between Raven and Little-Elder-Who-Enlarged-the-Tide are noteworthy for their formulaic consistency. In the phrase attributed to Raven we find:

Italio (1952):	«Nées' gehéen tlax̱ x̱at sawli.át',»[224]	"Sea-urchin juice has really made me chilly,"
Italio (1954):	«Nées' gehéeni x̱at sawli.át'.»[225]	"Sea-urchin juice has made me chilly."
James (1972):	«Nées' gehéenák'w áwé x̱at sawli.áat',[»][226]	"Sea-urchin juice has made me chilly,["]
Dick (1983):	[«]Nées' gehéenak'u áyá x̱at sawli.át'.[»][227]	["]Sea-urchin juice has made me chilly.["]

The little elder can only stand Raven's blathering for so long. Once thoroughly annoyed, and disbelieving that Raven could have obtained seafood such as urchins with the tide elevated as it is, the little elder barks another formulaic expression back at Raven:

Italio (1952):	«Cha goot'ayéigaa sá wulaaÿi léin áwé a kát eeyanís', cha Yéil Tl'éetl'i?»[228]	"Sir, when exactly would there have been a tideflat exposed by low tide for you to have eaten sea urchins, you Shitty-Ass Raven?"
Italio (1954):	«Chaa gutgiyéigaa sá wulaayi léin áyóo a kát eeyanís', cha Yéil Tl'éetl'i?»[229]	"Sir, when exactly would there have been a tideflat exposed by low tide for you to have eaten sea urchins, you Shitty-Ass Raven?"
James:	[«]Gwátk sá woolaaÿi léin áwé a kát eeyaṉís'? [...]Gwátgiÿéigaa sá ÿan uwalaÿi léin áwé a kát eeyanís'?»[230]	["]When was there a tideflat exposed by low tide for you to have eaten sea urchins? [...]When exactly was there a tideflat sufficiently exposed by low tide for you to have eaten sea urchins?"
Dick:	[«]Daagu x̱'áanáx̱ sá woolaayi léin áwé keenéek?»[231]	["]What stretch of time are you talking about during which a tideflat would have been exposed by low tide?"

While these do not have the same thoroughgoing uniformity as the statement attributed to Raven, they still exhibit great consistency in form and idea.

At roughly this point Raven draws out the urchin shell and begins stabbing the spines into the little elder's rear end, causing the little elder to scream in pain. Here another formula emerges:

Italio (1952):	[«]Déi, Yéi-éi-éi-éil! G̱aagwaalaa déi Yéil!»[232]	["]Enough, Ra-a-a-aven! The tide could go out any minute, Raven!"
Italio (1954):	«Déi, Yéil, gwaag̱aalaa!»[233]	"Enough, Raven, the tide could go out any minute!"
James:	[«]Lí déi-éi Yéi-éi-éil, gwaag̱aalaa dei, Yéil![»][234]	["]Stop it now, Raven, or the tide could go out any minute, Raven!["]
Dick:	«Déi gaag̱waalaa, Yéi-éi-éil![»][235]	"Enough! The tide could go out any minute, Ra-a-aven!["]

The little elder seems to be warning Raven that the tide is liable to go down if he doesn't quit stabbing him or her with urchin spines. This is, of course, exactly what Raven wants, so he doesn't relent until the tide recedes to a satisfactory level. The dialogue between Raven and Little-Elder-Who-Enlarged-the-Tide in this interaction demonstrate the fact that there is a proclivity for the speech acts of the characters in the narratives to contain the most highly formulaic expressions.

Shotridge writes briefly of this encounter, stating that Raven

> came upon the ancient one who was seated upon the magic trap-door, – the only passage through which the tide may ebb and flood. The ancient one was the mother of 'He-who-commands-the-sea'. When Raven appeared the goddess of tide was very indifferent of his presence, and immediately turned her back upon the visitor.[236]

While none of the storytellers in this volume refer to such a "magic trap-door", one could imagine Raven's act of stabbing the little elder's rear end as a way of getting him or her out of the seated position over the passage-way. The little elder's butt may have been too sore to sit on again after being jabbed with urchin spines. It is not clear who Shotridge refers to by "He-who-commands-the-sea"; it is certainly reminiscent of the name of Raven's uncle Yook̲is'kook̲éik, which literally means 'commanding the floodtide', but Shotridge never refers to Raven's uncle by that name, using rather the moniker "Jealousy".[237]

As a final note on this character, Italio is unique among the storytellers of this volume to state that it was Little-Elder-Who-Enlarged-the-Tide who bestowed the name Yéil upon the being known by this name. Minnie Johnson, in her interpretation of Italio's performance, stated that when the little elder addressed him as *cha Yéil Tl'éetl'i!* 'you Shitty Raven!' this was "the first time he heard his own name."[238]

2.10 *X̱ashak'ákwk'; K'áxw(k'), (Little) Pygmy Owl; Raven's Younger Brother*

The names *X̱ashak'ákwk'* and *K'ákw* (as well as the diminutive *K'ákwk'*) are used to refer to a character that appears alongside Raven in a number of adventures. For some storytellers, X̱ashak'ákwk' is the name of a kind of bird known as a *k'ákw*. For others, X̱ashak'ákwk' is a person and never associated with a bird. For yet others, the name X̱ashak'ákwk' is not used and the character is referred to only as K'ákw or K'ákwk'.

The species of bird that the noun *k'ákw* refers to is not entirely clear. We find a number of references to some kind of hawk or owl in recordings, texts, and lexical materials, but we have been unable to definitively link the name *k'ákw* to a specific species.[239] Based on all the data available to us, we have surmised that a likely candidate is the northern pygmy owl, followed by the northern saw-whet owl, and have settled on translating the proper noun K'ákw(k') in the texts as '(Little) Pygmy Owl', though the reader should note that this translation is tenuous and provisional.[240] Simply using 'Owl', 'Small Owl', or 'Little Owl' seemed overly generic, especially because these glosses would be better suited for the much more common Tlingit noun *dzísk'w*, which refers to owls in general without specification of species or size.

The name X̱ashak'ákwk' is a diminutive form of X̱ashak'ákw, which would appear to be a verbal noun formed from the unattested verb *x̱ashik'ákw* 'it has *k'ákw* fur' (i.e., 'it has pygmy-owl fur').[241] Italio, Dick, and Hammond use the name X̱ashak'ákwk' at least once in their performances. Zuboff refers only to «K'ákw»[242] 'Pygmy Owl' (which we treat in most cases as a proper noun). James uses the diminutive form «K'áxwk'»[243] 'Little Pygmy Owl' and the non-diminutive ergatively marked form «K'áxwch»[244] (which is *K'áxw* plus the ergative suffix *-ch*).

Just as there is variation in the form of the name, the roles and activities attributed to X̱ashak'ákwk' and K'ákw vary from one storyteller to the next, though there is considerable overlap. Italio gives an account of the origin of X̱ashak'ákwk' in which Raven—walking along the beach just after his visit to Little-Elder-Who-Enlarged-the-Tide—rouses up a piece of driftwood with the exhortation,

«Sheenú!	"Get up!
Ax̱ kéek' sákw, sheenú!	My little-brother-to-be, get up!
X̱ashak'ákwk'u sákw!»[245]	X̱ashak'ákwk'-to-be!"

Raven has to try a number of times before one of the logs stands and walks properly, and Italio says that the only one to do so was made of «sáḵs»[246] 'yew'; this piece of yew driftwood thus became Raven's younger brother, X̱ashak'ákwk'. Italio never clearly associates X̱ashak'ákwk' with a *k'ákw* or any other creature. Italio refers to him as «du kéek'»[247] 'his (Raven's) younger brother', and impersonates Raven addressing him with the vocative form «kík'»[248] 'younger brother'. The kinship term *(du) kéek'* '(his/her) younger sibling' refers to a younger sibling of the same gender; when speaking of a woman *du kéek'* means 'her younger sister' and when speaking of a man *du kéek'* means 'his younger brother'. Because we typically construe Raven as a man, we translate Italio's and Dick's reference to X̱ashak'ákwk' as Raven's 'younger brother'; he is the one implied in the title of FI I, iii, and FD viii, «Yéil Du Kéek' K̲ut Awulyeilí» "Raven Deceives His Younger Brother". Once the piece of yew wood is up and walking (and with the tide having just receded to expose the seafood after Raven's visit to Little-Elder-Who-Enlarged-the-Tide) Raven sets X̱ashak'ákwk' to work harvesting whales and other fat-rich seafood; unlike Raven, his brother works diligently enough to amass a large store of wooden boxes full of grease. Hungry Raven (lack) concocts a plan to stage a fake attack on their house by an illusory war party (trickery), sending X̱ashak'ákwk' charging outside to defend them (complicity); Raven then proceeds to chug all the oil in his brother's absence (lack, temporarily, liquidated).

Dick identifies X̱ashak'ákwk' with the bird *k'ákw* and describes him as «du xwáayi» 'his (Raven's) sidekick'.[249] In instances in which Dick impersonates Raven addressing X̱ashak'ákwk', however, Raven uses the vocative form «kík'»[250] 'younger brother'. Dick employs the same theme as Italio, in which Raven solicits X̱ashak'ákwk' to amass a large store of food, only to guzzle it all down while X̱ashak'ákwk' rushes outside to fend off a phony invasion. This theme and some form of the name appear in the Raven story told by Kadashan as well, "A man there, named CAq!ᵘk!ᵘ, collected all kinds of big sea animals, as whales and seals, at the time of this great ebb and made a great quantity of grease out of them, while Raven collected only small fishes like cod and red cod and obtained but a few stomachs full of oil. He would eat this up as fast as he made it, but his companion worked hard so as to have a large quantity on hand."[251] The form as written in Swanton, «CAq!ᵘk!ᵘ», likely contains typographical errors; taken at face value it would seem to represent something like Shák̲'wk', but is probably Shak'ákw or Shak'ákwk'. The same theme occurs in the text from Deikeenaak'w as well, "After that the sea went down so far that it was dry everywhere. Then Raven went about picking up the smallest fish, as bull heads and tom cod, which he strung on a stick, while a friend who was with him at this time, named CAk!A´kᵘ, took large creatures like whales. With the grease boiled out, CAk!A´kᵘ filled an entire house, while Raven filled only a small bladder."[252] In this case, Swanton's «CAk!A´kᵘ» clearly represents *Shak'ákw*, which is a stripped-down version of X̱ashak'ákwk', lacking the prefix *x̱a-* 'fur' and the diminutive suffix *-k'*.

Dick also invokes X̱ashak'ákwk' in the episode in which Raven obtains fire. Raven solicits X̱ashak'ákwk' to fly out over the open ocean and bring back some of the fire which can be seen there flaring up. X̱ashak'ákwk' is said to have originally possessed a very long bill, but through the process of bringing back the fire, it burnt back all the way to his face. As Dick tells "Raven Goes Down Along the

Bull Kelp", when Raven is busy stabbing urchin spines into the rear end of Little-Elder-Who-Enlarged-the-Tide, it is X̱ashak'ákwk' whom Raven sends to report on the status of the tide until it is satisfyingly low; this contrasts with James' telling, in which Raven sends Gidzanóok' (discussed in §2.12) to check on the level of the tide, and with Italio's, in which Raven never sends anyone on this errand.

While Zuboff never invokes the name of X̱ashak'ákwk', he employs a theme found also in Italio's account of how X̱ashak'ákwk' came about—that of Raven rousing up a piece of plant matter to become his younger brother. In Zuboff's telling, Raven first rouses up a stone to be his younger brother, but this creature proves too slow for Raven's liking, so Raven pushes him down into the earth and tries again using a leaf. Zuboff never attributes any name to the newly fashioned brother, and rather than being associated with the *k'ákw*, this being he formed from a leaf becomes the progenitor of modern humans:

Yáa kayaank'ée áyá	It's out of this little leaf
haa éex̱ awliyéx̱ yáa Yéil.[253]	that Raven made us.

The last line is more literally 'It is this little leaf / [that] Raven made into us'. While stone is an impervious and long-lasting substance, leaves wither and decay. Humans now experience death in what Zuboff considers to be relatively short order due to the fact that Raven's brother's body was formed from this perishable substance.

In Zuboff's performance of "Raven and Fire", it is K'ákw whom Raven solicits to fly out to sea and bring back some of the fire that could be seen flaring up over the ocean. Hammond likewise refers to K'ákw as the one to fulfill Raven's request for assistance getting ahold of the fire. Hammond notably refers to him once as a «yées ḵáa»[254] 'young man'. Near the end of his performance of "Raven and Fire", Hammond clarifies the identity of the character he had been referring to throughout the story as K'ákw, saying:

Ách áwé K'ákw—[...]	So Pygmy Owl—
X̱ashak'ákwk' yóo wduwasáa[...].	He was named X̱ashak'ákwk'[...].
Hú áyá X̱ashak'ákwx̱ sitee.[255]	He is X̱ashak'ákw.'

A common theme in this story is Raven issuing words of encouragement to X̱ashak'ákwk' while he endures the pain of carrying the fire back in his bill, with Raven telling him that his actions would be of benefit to everyone in the world. Hammond uses this as a metaphor for the pain of undertaking difficult tasks in life, which, while personally painful, can be of universal benefit to others.

2.11 *Lukshiyáank', Little Mink; Raven's Sidekick and Decoy-Baby*

James is the only storyteller in this volume to involve Little Mink. She varies between two different nouns that both refer to the mink. In some cases she uses the more common form «Lukshiyáank'»[256] 'Little Mink' (the diminutive form of *lukshiyáan* 'mink'), which we generally treat as a proper noun, and in one instance uses «wé Lukshiyáan ÿádi»[257] 'the baby Mink'. She sometimes switches to the form «Leineitk'óoxk'u»,[258] which also means 'Little Mink'; this is a diminutive form of the word for mink found attested in Carcross, «lìnèt k'ûxu»[259] (i.e., *leeneit k'óoxu*), where *leeneit* is the Interior Tlingit variant of Coastal Tlingit *leineit*, which appears to be a contraction of *lein-.át* 'tideflat-thing'. As the narrative progresses, James switches to a more common term for mink, *lukshiyáan*.

In James' telling of "Raven Goes Down Along the Bull Kelp", Raven sends Little Mink to swim down to the base of the bull kelp and fetch him sea urchins, which Raven then goes on to use as a weapon against Little-Elder-Who-Enlarged-the-Tide. In James' "Raven Gets Herself Married to a Killerwhale" the mink serves as Raven's fulcrum in compounding layers of deception that develop between him and the Killerwhales. Raven transforms himself into a woman and pretends that, in James' words, the «aawasháadi Leineitk'óoxk'u»[260] 'Little Mink that he (Raven) had seized' is her infant baby (with the use of the verb *aawasháat* 'he caught, grabbed, seized, snatched it', the mink has clearly been brought along against its will). Raven gnaws on the mink's ears to make it scream in pain, creating the illusion of a fussy baby. Raven obtains globs of fat from the supply the Killerwhales are transporting in their boat, claiming she will use it to pacify her 'baby'. Of course, Raven impulsively gobbles the fat up for herself while no one is looking. These antics with the baby allow Raven to strike up a conversation and ingratiate herself to the skipper of the Killerwhales' boat and ultimately become his bride. Raven claims that her baby's name is «G̱ayes'katleik̲wtík'i»,[261] which would seem to mean 'Iron-Berry Rope'. The Killerwhale skipper, now Raven's husband, as a result of marrying her, effectively becomes Raven's baby's father and takes on the name «G̱ayes'katleik̲wtík'i Éesh»[262] 'Father of Iron-Berry Rope'.

As one might expect, a marriage to Raven does not last or end well. Before long, Raven secretly murders her husband, stabbing him in the chest with a sharpened stick and claiming to the man's relatives that he has suffered a fatal heart attack. Raven proclaims that her husband's final wish was to be buried atop a certain point of land; in fact, Raven simply wants the body placed out of the villagers' sight so that she, in the guise of a mourning widow, can set to devouring her husband's flesh. Pretending to mourn her husband in solitude, while really gnawing away at his corpse, Raven sings a lamentation invoking the name G̱ayes'katleik̲wtík'i Éesh. Even by Raven's standards, the breadth of illusion and mendacity in this scene is astounding: a fallacious lamentation at a fraudulently specified burial site for a deceived husband and falsely self-presumed adoptive father, the death of whom by first-degree murder was accepted by the family as the result of natural causes, and whose acquired title was based on a concocted name of a phony baby carried by a sham woman who only married the man in order to murder and make a meal of him.[263]

2.12 *Gidzanóok'* ~ *Gidzanóox'*; *Raven's Sororal Nephew*

A character going by the name *Gidzanóok'* or *Gidzanóox'* appears alongside Raven in the texts of James, Zuboff, and Mills. The form of the name used by Zuboff and Mills is *Gidzanóox'* (with final /x'w/), while James uses *Gidzanóok'* (with final /k'w/). The name is unanalyzable. The initial syllables *gidza-* make it seem possible that it was borrowed from the Tsimshian language, Sm'algya̱x. If so, we would expect Gidzanóok' to be the more original form of the name and that the element *nóox'* in the variant Gidzanóox' was introduced by Tlingit reanalysis, since *nóok'* is meaningless in Tlingit, whereas *nóox'* means 'shell', and the Sm'algya̱x sound system contains the glottalized velar stop [k'] but does not contain the glottalized velar fricative [x']. Kadashan mentioned this name as well as another that also begins with *gidza-* in the Raven story he told in English to Swanton, "He [Raven] had two slaves after that, named Gîdzag̱ē't and Gîdzanū'q!u. This is why the natives here had slaves. It was on account of his example."[264] The first, «Gîdzag̱ē't», would seem to represent *Gidzag̱eit*, an unanalyzable name of which we have not located any other examples. Due to Swanton's lack of precision with velar and uvular consonants, we cannot be certain whether his «Gîdzanū'q!u» represents *Gidzanóok'* or *Gidzanóox'*.[265]

While Kadashan described him as Raven's slave, this is never indicated by the storytellers in this volume, though he does seem to do Raven's bidding. He makes a brief appearance in James' performance of "Raven Goes Down Along the Bull Kelp". While busy stabbing the rear end of Little-Elder-Who-Enlarged-the-Tide with urchin spines, Raven calls out, «Ch'a goox' sáwé, ‹Gidzanóok'!›»,[266] apparently an elliptic way of saying something like "At some point [Raven called out], "Gidzanóok'!"' Once he has the attention of Gidzanóok', Raven has him run to see how far the tide has receded and report back until Raven is satisfied and releases the little elder. In Dick's telling of this story, it is X̱ashak'ákwk' (§2.10) who fills this role.

Zuboff and Mills involve this character in their performances of "Raven and the Salmon Box". Two versions of this story by Zuboff are included in this volume. In one instance he states:

Du kéilk' áyá k̲udzitee, Gidzanóox'.[267]	He had a sororal nephew, Gidzanóox'.

In the other telling of the same story he adds:

Áwé du kéilk' áwé du eenx̲ sitee, Yéil. Wé Gidzanóox' yóo duwasáagu ts'axweil áwé.[268]	Now his sororal nephew was with him, with Raven. He's the crow that they call Gidzanóox'.

Mills' reference to Gidzanóox' is closely parallel to Zuboff's; she states:

Du een yéi jine aa,	The one who was working with him,
du kéilk' k̲u.aawé—Gidzanóox'	his sororal nephew, in fact—
yóo áwé duwasáakw	Gidzanóox' was the name
wé yéil.[269]	of that raven.

Zuboff and Mills both describe him as Raven's *kéilk'*, the translation of which is ambiguous without knowing whether Gidzanóox' is male or female. This inalienable kinship term refers to one's sister's children, so if the child is male *du kéilk'* means 'his/her sororal nephew', but if the child is female *du kéilk'* means 'his/her sororal niece'. We have defaulted to the assumption that this is Raven's nephew. Where Zuboff and Mills differ is in the bird with which they associate Gidzanóox': for Zuboff, he is a *ts'axweil* 'crow', while for Mills he is a *yéil* 'raven'. In Zuboff's and Mills' stories, it is Gidzanóox' who reminds Raven to invoke the name of X̲'anax̲gaatwaayáa in song in order to activate the power of the latter's Octopus Tentacle Cane and thus successfully pull the Salmon Box ashore.

2.13 *The Heavenly Luminaries: K̲ei.á Daakeit, the Container of Daylight; Dís Daakeit, the Container of the Moon; K̲utx̲.aÿanahá Daakeit, the Container of the Stars*

Before Raven broke the daylight over the world, it was kept in a container by a wealthy man at the head of the Nass River who is referred to variously as *Naasshagiyéil* 'Raven-of-the-Head-of-the-Nass' and *Naas Sháak* 'Head-of-the-Nass' (discussed in §2.14). This man kept other heavenly luminaries alongside it as well, such as the stars and the moon, though the exact number of containers and what each contained within varies between storytellers. While these containers are not characters, per se, their significance in the narratives is so pronounced that they deserve mention.

The most common form of the name used to refer to the container that held the daylight is «K̲ei.á Daakeit»,[270] which we translate as a proper noun, 'Container of Daylight'; this is the pronunciation used by Italio, James, Dick, and Hammond. Wanamaker is the only outlier, using the form «K̲ee.á Daakeit»[271] 'Container of Daylight' (*k̲ee.á* and *k̲ei.á* are simply dialect variants) alongside «K̲ee.á Daakak̲óok»[272] 'Box of Daylight' and the possessed form «K̲ee.á Daakak̲óogu»,[273] which we also translate as 'Box of Daylight'. We invariably translate the inalienable noun *daakeit* as 'container' in the texts, reserving the word 'box' for the noun *k̲óok* or the elaborated form *N daakak̲óok(-u)*. The word *daakeit* 'container' is a compound formed from the elements *daa-* 'around' *ka-* 'surface' and *-.át* 'thing' and does not necessarily denote a wooden box.

Like the daylight, the stars figure into all versions of the story in this volume. Italio and Hammond use the parallel title 'Container of Stars', Italio using the form

«Ḵutx̱.aÿanahá Daakeit»[274] (with the archaic sound /ÿ/) and Hammond using essentially the same form «Ḵutx̱.ayanahá Daakeit».[275] James, Wanamaker, and Dick refer to the stars, but don't use the proper noun for the container. James uses «ḵutx̱.aÿanahá» alongside the overt plural «Ḵutx̱.aÿanaháax'w»;[276] Dick uses «ḵutx̱.ayanahá»;[277] and Wanamaker uses «ḵutx̱.ayanaháa»,[278] all of which mean 'stars'.

The storytellers of this volume do not all regard the situation with the moon in the same way. Hammond is the only one in this volume to use the title «Dís Daakeit»[279] 'Container of the Moon'. James and Wanamaker refer to the *dís* 'moon', but never in combination with a term meaning 'box' or 'container'. Italio is unique among the storytellers in this volume in that he explicitly excludes the moon from among the man's possessions, «Yú dís ḵwá ch'a tlákw ḵudzitee»[280] 'The moon, though, has always existed'. Dick similarly only ever mentions the daylight and the stars, so it would seem that for him as well the moon is not present in the man's house. This could potentially be explained by the fact that Italio and Dick, brothers-in-law both from Dry Bay, are also the only two storytellers in this volume who make a point of stating that Raven's uncle, Tide-Commander, is himself the moon.

For Italio and Dick, there are two celestial bodies in containers: the stars and the daylight. For Wanamaker and James, there are three: Wanamaker refers to the stars, the moon, and the Container of Daylight;[281] alongside the stars and the moon, James' references to the final item vary between «Ḵei.á Daakeit»[282] 'Container of Daylight' and «g̱agaan»[283] 'the sun'. Hammond is unique in this volume in that he perceives the sun and the daylight as distinct entities each housed in a separate container; for him, there are four: the stars, the moon, the sun, and the daylight—obtained and released by Raven in that order. He refers to

yáa g̱agaan a daakeidí yík[284]	the sun in its container

and

ḵei.á a daakeidí yík[285]	the daylight in its container

as separate items in a list along with the Container of the Stars and the Container of the Moon.

The images that develop in the narratives concerning the physical form of the containers are also worth considering. While the containers are popularly referred to as 'boxes' in English, and are referred to in the same way in Tlingit by Wanamaker and Hammond with the noun «ḵóok»[286] 'box(es)', and once as «a daakaḵóogu»[287] 'its box' (i.e., that of the sun) by James, we find a number of instances in which the containers appear to be spherical rather than cubic. Speaking of the Container of Stars, Italio remarks, «K'út' yéx̱ kaaxát»;[288] this phrase literally means 'it is shaped like an egg' or 'it resembles an egg', but idiomatically translates as 'it is round'. James states quite the same, but uses the corresponding plural verb to describe the three entities, «k'wát' yáx̲ áwé kadax̲dixwás' a daaká»[289] 'the outer surfaces [of the containers] were spherical'. Dick agrees and gets more specific, likening the containers to the size of balloons, «gwál wéi *balloon* yáx̲ gíyú kakoodagei»[290] 'maybe they (the containers) were spheres the size of balloons, I suppose'.

All who tell this story in this volume (Italio, Wanamaker, James, Dick, and Hammond) describe Raven 'rolling' the objects around while playing with them, which also suggests a ball- or sphere-like form.[291] In this context the question arises as to whether Raven is rolling the containers or the luminaries themselves after temporarily removing them from their containers. James, for instance, states that Raven would pull the lid back on the moon's container and the inside of the house would be flooded with daylight, «Ÿanáatx̲ yaa ax̲út'jin, ách áwé neil tle áa k̲ee.éix̲»[292] 'He kept prying the lid off, so daylight kept breaking inside of the house', so here we can imagine him rolling a brilliantly glowing moon around inside the house. For Italio, though, it is clearly the containers themselves that little Raven was rolling around; he states that it was like the atmosphere became ablaze «wé a daakeidí gáant aklajóox»[293] 'when he rolled the [stars'] container outside'. Aside from Italio's explicit clarification that Raven was rolling the containers, most instances in the other texts simply leave us uncertain when it comes to picturing Raven's manner of play with the luminaries—whether they are in or out of their containers.

Depictions of the containers in older texts similarly suggest spherical configurations. Shotridge writes, "Along the walls of the great room, in the house of the god of light [i.e., Naasshagiyéil], were hung cases of various shapes and sizes."[294] He refers in one instance to "the box"[295] which held the stars. When it comes to the moon, he writes, "He [i.e., Raven] cried so much that it was thought he would cease to exist, this the grandfather also feared, when he at last ordered: 'Go, untie the case which is round, maybe by it my grandchild will have joy.' After the spherical object was placed before him the child ceased to cry, and with mirth began to roll about the great ball."[296] Here again we see the theme of Raven rolling around playfully with a spherical container. In describing Raven's act of releasing the moon, Shotridge writes, "at the moment an opportunity occurred, he untied the drawstrings; stretched wide the opening of the case. – Like that happened to the stars the great ball of light drifted through the smoke-hole, also into the heavens, and there was the moon."[297] This container appears to be spherical with a drawstring closure, so this is certainly a bag-like configuration. In reference to that which held the daylight, Shotridge does not elaborate on the size or shape, but refers to it as a "magic case".[298] In the Raven story Deikeenaak'w told to Swanton in English, we find a similar situation with spherical objects bound in textile-like material rather than boxes, "Round bundles of varying shapes and sizes hung about on the walls of the house. When the child became a little larger it crawled around the back of the people weeping continually, and as it cried it pointed to the bundles. This lasted many days. Then its grandfather said, 'Give my grandchild what he is crying for. Give him that one hanging on the end. That is the bag of stars.'"[299] Shortly after, however, Deikeenaak'w refers to not a bag or bundle but a box, "Now just one thing more remained, the box that held the daylight, and he cried for that."[300] His grandfather again relents, "Untie the last thing and give it to him."

The statements Shotridge and Deikeenaak'w attribute to the grandfather relate to a noteworthy feature of the texts that involves the containers—the command issued by the owner of the containers (Raven's now-grandfather, i.e., Naasshagiyéil or Naas Sháak) for one of them to be given to Raven. Here, as in many other similar cases, we find notable consistency between storytellers in the use of a formulaic expression that occurs in the narrative through the speech of a character. We hear the grandfather command:

Italio:	[«]Du jeet kaÿlakél' déi ax̱ dachx̱ánk'! Du jeet kaÿlakél'!»[301]	["]Untie it for my dear grandchild now! Untie it for him!"
Wanamaker:	«Du jeet kaylakél' déi! Du jeet yití!»[302]	"Untie it for him now! Give it to him!"
Dick:	«Du jeet kiylakél' ax̱ dachx̱ánk'! Du jeet kiylakél'!»[303]	"Untie it for my dear grandchild now! Untie it for him!"

The situation gets more interesting with James. When it first comes to the stars, we find consistency with the others:

«Du jeet kaÿlakél' déi!»[304]	"Untie it for him now!"

When it comes next to the moon, however, she changes the verb slightly (the fricative element *l-* of the verb's classifier is absent), saying:

«Du jeet kaÿkél' déi ax̱ dachx̱ánk'! Du jeet kaÿkél'! Du jeet kaÿkél'!»[305]	"Untie it for my dear grandchild now! Untie it for him! Untie it for him!"

Finally, when it comes to the sun, we again hear:

«Du jeet kaÿlakél' déi! Du jeet kaÿlakél' déi ax̱ dachx̱ánk'! Du jeet kaÿlakél'!»[306]	"Untie it for my dear grandchild now! Untie it for him! Untie it for him!"

The containers would have been tied upon the wall or in the rafters of the house, so untying them in this situation is the means of bringing them down from their place of storage; this would have been a typical storage location in a traditional Tlingit house, and relevantly here happens to be out of a baby's reach. The fact that the imperative verb includes the second-person plural subject prefix indicates that it is addressed to multiple people; perhaps the order is given to slaves or attendants of the household, but who specifically is addressed by this command is not explicated in the narratives.

In every instance of the formulaic expression other than James' isolated use of *kay̆kél'* in relation to the moon, the verb is based on the theme *O-ka-S-kéil'*~ 'for S to untie O' and includes the non-thematic fricative element *l-* of the classifier, which here we can only explain as having a configurational (also called 'classificatory') function, denoting that the syntactic object of the verb, that being the entity which is to be untied, is classified as a 'composite' (also called 'complex' in Tlingit linguistic literature) object. It would be regular for a bag or bundle to be classified in such a way, but it would be irregular for a wooden box to be classified in this way. For instance, when speaking of a wooden box, one would use the positional verb *át tán* 'it is lying there' (with no classifier elements), but if speaking of a bag or a long flexible object such as a bundle, one would use *át satéen* 'it is lying there' (with the fricative element *s-* denoting the composite configuration of the bag, due to its being composed of numerous interwoven strands and overlapping folds), and if the configurational *s-* were removed from the latter phrase, *át téen* 'it is lying there' would typically denote a compact object such as a rock. In the case of the containers, if the command were for a box to be untied and given to him, the appropriate form would be *du jeet kaykél'* 'you folks untie it and give it to him' (lacking *l-*).[307] This is the very form used by James in relation to the moon; yet, she uses the fricative element when it comes to the stars and the sun. It is possible that she perceived the moon's container as having a different composition than that of the sun and stars; it is also possible that this was a momentary slip-up which she would have altered to *kay̆lakél'* had she been asked—we cannot know.

Overall, the ubiquity of the *l-* element of the classifier suggests that the formulaic expression *du jeet kay̆lakél'*, which certainly predates all of these storytellers who attest it in this volume, may have developed on the basis of an image in which the containers consisted of bags or bundled textile-like material rather than wooden boxes. Alternatively, the image could be that of a box within a bag or swathed within cloth or folded hide. This would align well with the state of affairs as found in Shotridge's depiction of the moon's container and Deikeenaak'w's image of round bundles, as well as Italio's, James', and Dick's reference to the spherical configuration of the containers and the common theme of Raven rolling them about inside the house. While there is no way of verifying the hypothesis that an image such as a bagged up sphere or a box swathed in cloth so as to form a spherical bundle was necessarily involved in the genesis of the formulaic expression *du jeet kaỳlakél'*, it is at the very least an interesting alternative to hold in mind while reading and listening to the texts and imagining what things must have looked like in the house while the containers hung about the walls with Raven crying and pointing at them; what Raven would have seen as someone untied these objects and placed them in his hands; and how he might have looked as a toddler playing with them, rolling them around, and releasing their contents.

However, even if the configuration of the object of the verb in the formulaic expression could be verified, a single image cannot be generically imposed across the texts. In Hammond's telling, for instance, the containers are depicted unambiguously as boxes. He is the only storyteller among this group who does not make use of the formulaic expression discussed above. From him we hear the grandfather issue commands such as, «Du jeet yisa.ín ax̱ dachx̱ánk' yá ḵóok»[308] 'Hand my dear grandchild the box', in which the verb is based on the theme *O-S-s-.een~* 'for S to handle O (a container bearing contents)' and the object is specified as a *ḵóok* 'box'. In James' text we find:

G̱agaan áx̱ daaḵ aawatée, dís, ḵutx̱.aỳanahá.[309]	He (Head-of-the-Nass) had hung up the sun, the moon, and the stars.

in which the verb theme cannot denote a box or a bag, so in this instance it would seem that James is focused on the celestial bodies themselves, regarded individually as compact objects with no specification about the form of the containers; it may even be that in her mind at this moment the luminaries were not in containers at all.

Further, in the texts in which we find explicit references to spherical containers, the storytellers' choice of words at other times depicts these very same entities in a rigid box-like configuration. Immediately after describing the Container of Stars as round, Italio says, «héide shuwjix̱een»[310] 'it (the container's lid) opened'; the verb phrase used here denotes the movement of the wooden lid of a rigid container from a closed to an open position, not the opening of a bag closed by a drawstring. Speaking of when Raven released hints of daylight from the Container of Daylight before entirely breaking it open, Italio says, «yóo wánde a yanáa als'óox̱'»[311] 'he kept nudging the lid open in the direction of the distant shore', in which *a yanáa* 'its cover, lid' also necessarily denotes the lid of a box-like container. Dick, who also describes the containers as having a round balloon-like configuration, likewise uses *a yanáa* when Raven opens the Container of Daylight, «ḵúnáx̱ x'éig̱aa a yanáax̱ ayaawax̱út'»[312] 'he (Raven) pulled its cover all the way off'.

There are thus not only differences between storytellers in the depiction of the containers but multiple images comingled together in the figure of the same container within individual texts, with each respective image assuming a more salient focus at different moments in the narrative. This bundling together of incongruous images in the same entity can be interpreted from a number of angles. It may be that the containers initially consisted of wooden boxes swathed in cloth so as to form a sphere that could be rolled around, with the act of unveiling the underlying box-form simply going unstated by the storyteller. It may be that in the mind of a single storyteller the form of a container may fluctuate with circumstance because its form in the narrative is malleable and subordinate to its relationship with other terms and processes of the narrative—at one moment it is a sphere so that baby Raven may playfully roll it around; at another it is a box so that Raven can reveal a sliver of light by cracking open its lid and then yank it off completely. As discussed in §1.4, it may rather be that, by virtue of their oral-traditional form, the stories themselves are in a sense composite objects, with each storyteller composing their material by drawing from a repertoire of formulaic elements that has come down to them from a variety of sources, not all of which must necessarily share a common origin or a uniform picture of the narrative.[313]

2.14 *Naasshagiyéil, Raven-of-the-Head-of-the-Nass; Naas Sháak, Head-of-the-Nass; Raven's Grandfather*

The man who possessed the Container of Daylight resided at the head of the Nass River. It is to this man's daughter that Raven causes himself to be born in his plot to obtain the Container of Daylight and break its contents over the world. Italio and Wanamaker are the only two storytellers in this volume to refer to this man by the name *Naasshagiyéil* 'Raven-of-the-Head-of-the-Nass'.[314] Because Raven is born to this man's daughter, Italio states:

Náasshagiyéil du léelk'ux̱ áwé wsitee.[315]	Raven-of-the-Head-of-the-Nass became his (Raven's) grandfather.

It is notable, and somewhat perplexing, that the man who is to become Raven's grandfather has the word *yéil* 'raven' as the head noun of his name. We do not have any great explanations for this fact but consider it to be a kind of riddle lying deep within the inner recesses of the myth. If only we could ask Unfazable-Little-Elder.

In Wanamaker's performance of "Raven and the Daylight", the Night-Dwellers (discussed in §2.16) invoke this name in a jeering response to Raven after he claims that he will break daylight over them if they don't give him something to eat, «Naasshagiyéil yádi gwáawéigé wa.é!»[316] 'Oh, so you must be the child of Raven-of-the-Head-of-the-Nass!', and again later in the same performance, «Ách áwé wé aantḵeení yéi yaawaḵaa, ‹Goodáx̱ Naasshagiyéil sá?›»[317] 'So the townspeople said, "Where does this Raven-of-the-Head-of-the-Nass hail from?"' Italio, James, and Dick all use essentially the same formulation as Wanamaker, but they use variations on the form *Naasshagiyát* 'Child-of-the-Head-of-the-Nass' (with *ÿát* 'child' rather than *yéil* 'raven' as the head noun). It is these references to 'Raven-of-the-Head-of-the-Nass' or a 'Child-of-the-Head-of-the-Nass' that lead Raven to voyage to the headwaters of the Nass River and find a way to be born there as a child in order to obtain the Container of Daylight.

James uses a different name for this man. She states clearly, «Naas Sháak yóo áwé duwasáakw wé k̲áa»[318] 'That man's name is Head-of-the-Nass'. She also describes him as the «Naas Sháak Aank̲áawu»[319] 'Headman (or Chief) of the Headwaters of the Nass', as does Wanamaker.[320] Dick does not mention the man's name at all. Hammond mentions the name Naasshagiyéil, attributing it not to the man who becomes Raven's grandfather, but to Raven himself. For Hammond, Naasshagiyéil is a name appropriated and used by Raven after having stolen the Container of Daylight from the head of the Nass:

Ách áwé Yéilch átx̲ layéix̲
Naasshagiyéil.
Aaa, áx̲ kawdudlisáy
  Naasshagiyéil.[321]

That is why Raven uses [the name]
Raven-of-the-Head-of-the-Nass.
Yes, from this he became known as
  Raven-of-the-Head-of-the-Nass.

Similarly, after having stolen and broken the daylight, Wanamaker states, «Yá lingit'aaní g̲eix' k̲ee.á awliyéx̲ yá Yéil, Naasshagiyéil» 'Raven—[that is,] Raven-of-the-Head-of-the-Nass—made daylight appear throughout this world',[322] in which Naasshagiyéil is clearly used as a designation for Raven after his successful voyage to the head of the Nass. One possible, admittedly speculative, way of reconciling the different designations of this name—some storytellers applying it to the man at the head of the Nass from whom Raven stole the Container of Daylight, others applying it to Raven himself after his return from the Nass with the Container of Daylight—would be to understand Naasshagiyéil as the name of the being who possesses or is most strongly associated with the daylight, in which case Raven, through the act of stealing the Container of Daylight, simultaneously steals the associated title.

The name appears in a number of texts as well. Shotridge writes, "In course of time Master Maul [i.e., Raven before he was known as such] learned that there could be light in the world. He learned also of the existence of the 'Affluent-supreme Raven,['] (/Kà/ Nà·s-càkì Yé·ł) a being who was highest of all beings and in whose power was concealed all luminaries of heaven and earth, the covetousness of which Master Maul had heard expressed by the less fortunate beings."[323] Shotridge's «Nà·s-càkì Yé·ł» is clearly Naasshagiyéil, but we cannot account for what he writes as «/Kà/» (i.e., *ka*) just before the main portion of the name. George Johnson colorfully translates the name along similar lines as Shotridge, stating in English, "His grandfather was Rich King Nass."[324] Kadashan makes reference to him in the Raven story he told in English to Swanton, "[T]here lived in a house at the head of Nass river a being called Raven-at-the-head-of-Nass (Nās-cA´kî-yēł)."[325] Kadashan also uses the name in an example of a speech for the occasion of a mortuary totem pole raising; it is a magnificent example of how the Raven stories can be employed in Tlingit oratory. The speech involves an extended metaphor based on themes and images from the "Raven and the Daylight" story. Kadashan equates his ailing, mournful spirit to the world of darkness. His relatives, the addressees of his speech, are metaphorically likened to Raven's grandfather, Naasshagiyéil. Kadashan expresses his request that they raise the pole through the image of Raven begging his grandfather to give him the Container of Daylight. The prospect of his relatives raising the pole is equated with Naasshagiyéil giving up the daylight to Raven, which is thereby suggested to be the seminal act that allowed light to break over the world of darkness. It is noteworthy that in the picture Kadashan paints Naasshagiyéil is in no way simply a dupe or passive victim of robbery, but a principal agent in the process that brought the daylight out of its container. Through the material act of raising the pole, Kadashan's relatives would thus act in the likeness of Naasshagiyéil and set in motion the metaphorical breaking of daylight, thereby transforming and healing Kadashan's own darkened, saddened spirit.[326]

2.15 *Wé Yées Shaatk', the Young Woman; Daughter of Raven-of-the-Head-of-the-Nass and Raven's (Surrogate) Mother*

The young woman who births Raven at the head of the Nass is never referred to by name by any of the storytellers in this volume. We have been unable to find a name for her attested in any recorded or written source. She is the daughter of Naashshagiyéil—the man who possesses the Container of Daylight at the head of the Nass River—and it is into her that Raven sneaks in the form of an evergreen needle—or some other speck of matter—in order to turn into a fetus in her womb and be born as her child. She is often referred to simply as *du sée* 'his daughter', in which cases the listener is expected to understand that this means 'the daughter [of Naasshagiyéil]'. She is also referred to by Italio as an «aanÿédi»[327] 'noble person, aristocrat', indicating that she is considered to be a member of the nobility or an aristocratic family, and as «wé shaawát»[328] 'that woman'. James refers to her as «wé shaatk'»[329] 'that young, adolescent woman' and «yées kaÿát»,[330] which apparently means 'young woman (of childbearing age)' or the like; she also refers to her as «du tláa»[331] 'his (Raven's) mother' after the woman births Raven. In Wanamaker's text we find «du sée»[332] 'his daughter', «yées yát»[333] 'young (virgin) girl', and «wé shaatk'»[334] 'that young, adolescent woman'. Dick similarly refers to her as «du sée»[335] 'his daughter' and «wé shaatk'»[336] 'that young, adolescent woman'. Hammond refers to her as «du sée»[337] 'his daughter', «[ha]sdu sée»[338] 'their daughter' (in Hammond's text the man at the head of the Nass lived with a wife), «yá yées shaawát»[339] 'this young woman', «wé yées shaatk'»[340] 'that young, adolescent woman', and «wéi shaawát»[341] 'that woman'; we translate his use of *yées shaatk'* as 'young virgin', in part because Hammond explicitly compares her to the biblical figure of the Virgin Mary, but also because this seems to be the closest approximate term in Tlingit to the English 'virgin'.

2.16 *Yax̱taattuḵwáani, The Night-Dwellers; G̱ákw Sax̱a Ḵu.oo, the People-Who-Eat-Gnarly-Driftwood*

When Raven is journeying about trying to figure out how to obtain the Container of Daylight, he emerges on the far side of a river across from a group of people who are fishing in the water.[342] These people are the *Yax̱taattuḵwáani*, which we have translated as 'Night-Dwellers'. While Italio is the only storyteller in this volume to refer to them by this name, we take it to be an emblematic title for these beings.[343] In a performance of "Raven and the Daylight" by Charlie Joseph, he can be heard referring to them in two instances as «Yax̱taattuḵuháani»,[344] which is identical to Italio's form with the exception that Joseph uses the more archaic uncontracted form *ḵuháani* 'people of' in place of *ḵwáani*. All the elements of this name other than the initial *yax̱-* are transparently analyzable as *taat* 'night', *tu-* 'inside', and *ḵwáani* 'people of'. We cannot definitively analyze the initial element *yax̱-*. One possibility is that it could be the combining form of the relational noun *ÿaax̱* 'bank, side, edge (of body of water, trail, table, etc.)', as found in, e.g., *áa (x̱'a)ÿaax̱* 'lakeshore', *héen x̱'aÿaax̱* 'shoreline', *dei ÿaax̱* 'side of path, trail, road', and *nadáakw ÿaax̱* 'table-side'. This could conceivably be the same element as found in *Yax̱ Ḵées' Shakawdzinugu Shaanák'w* 'Little-Elder-Who-Enlarged-the-Tide' (§2.9) and Minnie Johnson's form of the name for the Salmon Box, *Yax̱kadatankahídi* (§2.18). If that were the case, it could conceivably refer to the 'edge' or 'cusp' of the night. The name Yax̱taattuḵwáani or some similar form is surely the source of Shotridge's English references to these figures as, "the beings-of-the-dark" and "the beings-of-darkness".[345]

Italio says of these people, «Shaaḵ ÿátx'i áyú dusdeek»[346] 'They were dipnetting bits of driftwood'. Dick similarly refers to them as «wéi Shaḵyátx'i Isdik Ḵu.oo»[347] 'People-Who-Dipnet-Bits-of-Driftwood'. James refers to them by what we take to be a proper title, «G̱ákw Sax̱a Ḵu.oo»[348] 'People-Who-Eat-Gnarly-Driftwood' and clarifies that they were eating «shaaḵ ÿátx'i»[349] 'bits of driftwood' (*shaaḵ ÿátx'i* in each of these cases is literally 'driftwood children'). Hammond, on the other hand, refers to them as «yá saak isdeegí» 'these eulachon dipnetters'.[350] Wanamaker refers to them with less specificity as to what they were harvesting as «yá hintaak.ádi yéi adaane aantḵeení»[351] 'these villagers who were gathering seafood'.

When Raven emerges across the river from these people, he calls out to them, telling them to come pick him up or to give him something to eat. Although he initially has no way of doing so, Raven claims that he could break daylight on them with the words *Yee káa ḵei.á nḵwaak'oots!* '[Watch out or] I might break daylight on you folks!' This is an essential element in the traditional diction of the Tlingit Raven genre; of the formulas that are exclusive to the Raven stories, this is the most consistent and widely-shared one in the volume, occurring in eleven combined instances from each of the five storytellers who tell "Raven and the Daylight" (Italio, James, Wanamaker, Dick, and Hammond).[352] The Night-Dwellers' reply to Raven is also notably formulaic:

Italio:	«Hadóo! Chaa goodáx̱ Naasshagiyét sáyú ḵei.á du jee yéi ng̱atee?»[353]	"Good grief! From where does the Child-of-the-Head-of-the-Nass hail that he should possess daylight?"
Dick:	«Héhéhé! Goodáx̱ Naasshagiyát Ḵei.á Daakeit du jee yéi ng̱atee?»[354]	"Heh-heh-heh! From where does the Child-of-the-Head-of-the-Nass hail that he should possess the Container of Daylight?"
James:	«Dláa! Naasshagiyátk'w Ḵei.á Daakeit ang̱a.oo!»[355]	"Give me a break! This Precious-Little-Child-of-the-Head-of-the-Nass is evidently supposed to own the Container of Daylight!"
Wanamaker:	«Naasshagiyéil yádi gwáawéigé wa.é!»[356]	"Oh, so you must be the child of Raven-of-the-Head-of-the-Nass!"

Calling Raven *Naasshagiyát* 'Child-of-the-Head-of-the-Nass' seems to have a rhetorical force similar to addressing someone who is acting self-important or overly demanding as 'Your Highness' in English. This name *Naasshagiyát* is a crucial element in the plot. Through what was apparently leveled at Raven as an insult, the Night-Dwellers provide Raven with two crucial pieces of information he was lacking and which ultimately lead to him breaking daylight over them as he threatened. The name encodes the location where he must seek the daylight (*Naasshagi-*, the headwaters of the Nass River) and the form he must assume in order to obtain it (*yát* 'a child' born thereof). Raven thus wanders to the head of the Nass and is born to a young woman in the form of a human baby.

No storyteller in this volume explains how knowledge of the daylight came to these beings who inhabited a world deprived of it. One such explanation is found in a 1954 recording of X̱ux'awdu.oo, Maggie Dick, the sister of Italio and the wife of Frank Dick. Before singing a song attributed to Raven, she says:

Yax̱taattuḵwáani keekáx' áwé daak uwagút.	He emerged across the river from the Night-Dwellers.
[...]«Yee káx' ḵei.á nḵwaak'oots!»	[...]"Watch out or I might break daylight on you folks!"
yóo áwé ḵudaayaḵá yóo Yéil.	Raven said to those people.
Tlél wuduskú daaḵwéi sá yéi ḵudaayaḵaayí yú Isdik Ḵu.oo.	Those Dipnetting-People didn't know what he was saying to them.
Ách áwé wéi Lyóo.at.uwajeegi Shaanák'w du ÿís wuduwax̱oox̱.	So they called upon Unfazable-Little Elder to make sense of him.
[...]Tle yóo shaanák'w yéi yaawaḵaa, «Hadáw!	[...]The little elder said, "Good grief!
Gootx̱ Naasshakeeyéil ḵei.ách du jee yéi ngatee, yóo Yéil Tl'éetl'i!»	From where does the Raven-of-the- Head-of-the-Nass hail that he should possess daylight, that Shitty Raven!"
[...]Ch'u tle aadáx̱—ch'u tle aadáx̱ wudihaan, tlél tsu yéi yawuḵaa.	[...]So then—so then he stood up and said no more.
Tlei woogoot Náas Sháakde yóo Yéil.[357]	Raven just set out for the Head of the Nass.

As she tells it, the Night-Dwellers do not initially understand what Raven means by *ḵei.á* 'daylight' and so call upon Unfazable-Little-Elder to enlighten them. In a single stroke, Unfazable-Little-Elder provides the Night-Dwellers with knowledge of what their world lacks and Raven with knowledge of how to liquidate it.

Once Raven, after a long intervening process, obtains the Container of Daylight and flees with it from the head of the Nass, he returns to the same river, emerging again across from the Night-Dwellers. He again calls out to them, insisting with the same words that they pick him up or provide him something to eat, and issuing the same warning that he could break daylight on them. He cracks the lid of the Container of Daylight open slightly, letting out a sliver of light, to demonstrate that he is in fact in possession of the daylight.[358] Even when the Night-Dwellers, fearful of the daylight, hasten toward Raven before he makes good on his warning, Raven yanks the lid completely off the container and daylight bursts forth over the world in all its glory. The Night-Dwellers scatter in terror to escape the light. In the frenzied scramble, they proliferate into groups, seeking refuge in various regions of the earth—now the domain of animals.

This scene occasions a rare and formulaic verb form that we find used by each of the storytellers that tells "Raven and the Daylight" in this volume with the exception of James, the recording of whose performance was cut short by the end of the tape before she reached this scene. The form in question, *atkaawa.át* 'they rushed (en masse)', occurs in this volume exclusively at this moment when the Night-Dwellers flee from the light.[359] Italio in 1952 states:

<table>
<tr><td>Héende yóo atkaawa.át
yú lingít
wé k̲ei.á jinák̲.[360]</td><td>Those people
rushed into the water
to escape the daylight.</td></tr>
</table>

We hear from Italio in 1954:

<table>
<tr><td>Wéi
dáak̲t woo.aadi át k̲u.aa áwé
dak̲dachóon áwé atkaawa.át
yú shaa ÿaadé.[361]</td><td>Those
animals that roam inland, however,
rushed straight inland and up
onto the mountainsides.</td></tr>
</table>

In Wanamaker's text we find:

<table>
<tr><td>Héende aa atkaawa.át wé
aantk̲eení,
a x̲oo.aa k̲u.aa atgutóode
atkaawa.át.[362]</td><td>Some of the townspeople rushed
into the water,
and others rushed into
the forest.</td></tr>
</table>

From Dick we hear:

<table>
<tr><td>Yá dzix̲áawu át yáx̲ yateeyi aa
k̲wás dák̲de atkaawa.át.[363]</td><td>But the ones that were like fur-
bearing mammals rushed inland.</td></tr>
</table>

And Hammond relates:

<table>
<tr><td>Aaa, aag̲áa yóot k̲aa luwagúk̲.
Héende aa atkaawa.át
k̲a dák̲de aa atkaawa.át.
Aaa, tsaax̲ aa wsitee.
Taanx̲ aa wsitee,
cheech,
k̲a yá yáay, woosh g̲uwanáade át,
yá héen táade atkaawa.adi aa.[364]</td><td>Yes, then the people ran away.
Some rushed into the water
and some rushed up into the forest.
Yes, some of them became seals.
Some of them became sea lions,
porpoise,
and whales, various creatures,
the ones that rushed into the water.</td></tr>
</table>

The theme in all these cases involves the Night-Dwellers, who were apparently human beings wearing blankets made of various animal skins, proliferating into the various animal species that now roam about the land and sea. Those wearing seal-skin blankets rush into the water, becoming seals; those wearing marmot-skin blankets rush to the mountainsides, becoming marmots.

Thus, when Raven broke the daylight he not only brought illumination to a world of darkness, but as a consequence caused what was initially a gathered human collective to become diffuse and multitudinous animal species. This is a potent image of transformation—a speed-of-light passage from mythic unity to empirical dispersal. The depictions of this event in oral literary form by the storytellers in this volume erect a vital aesthetic and conceptual background against which to consider the well-known Tlingit—and broadly Indigenous—cosmological principle in which animals, being enveloped by a skin, are understood to be at a deeper level people cloaked beneath blankets. Those interested in the structuralist interpretation of myth may notice that this scene involves not the development of human culture out of an original animal condition or state of nature, but exactly the opposite: here we see human culture as the original condition from which animal nature emerges and distances itself.

2.17 *X̱'anax̱gaatwaayáa and His Náaḵw Tl'eeg̱í Wootsaag̱áa, Octopus Tentacle Cane*

During his endeavor to pull the *Kudatankahídi* 'Salmon Box' (discussed in §2.18) ashore at Dry Bay near the mouth of the Alsek River, Raven appeals to a man named X̱'anax̱gaatwaayáa. The man possesses a powerful implement known as the *Náaḵw Tl'eeg̱í Wootsaag̱áa* 'Octopus Tentacle Cane', which is uniquely suited to this task. The cane is tipped with, or entirely formed from, an octopus tentacle, enabling it to wrap around objects and cling onto them with its suckers. Dick is unique in this volume for describing features of the cane and Raven's apparent modification of it:

ts'ítskw x̱'eitákw aa tás,	the tendon of a songbird's heel
á áyáa wóoshde awlitsóow	was what he used to connect
yáa náaḵw tl'eigée,	the octopus tentacles;
déex̱ a x̱'aan yatee,	it has two tips
aadé kdlixwás'.[365]	that hang from it.

De Laguna recorded a similar statement from Emma Ellis in 1952, "He used bird muscles to pull it ashore they say."[366] The cane possesses other special properties as well, such as being able to extend out over great distances (the Salmon Box being located far out on the open ocean), but in order to activate its latent powers the one wielding the cane must sing a certain song, the lyrics of which invoke the name of X̱'anax̱gaatwaayáa. It is by using this cane and singing the song that Raven is able to grab hold of the Salmon Box and pull it ashore. A real carved wooden staff of the same name, *Náaḵw Tl'eeg̱í Wootsag̱áa*, decorated in the likeness of an octopus tentacle is among the at.óow of the L'uknax̱.ádi clan to this day.

The form of the man's name as given by most speakers is *X̱'anax̱gaatwaayáa*. This is the form used, for instance, by Mills. Zuboff pronounces the name with a slight difference, as *X̱'enax̱gaatwaayáa* (with *x̱'e-* rather than *x̱'a-*). James, on the other hand, pronounces the name as *X̱'anax̱.waatgwaayáa*, in which the consonants /g/ and /w/ are metathesized and the /g/ is rounded to /gw/. Dick mentions neither the man's name nor that of his cane in his telling of the story. The form of the name is so opaque that we are unable to analyze it or give a translation. Although the first portion *x̱'anax̱-* has the appearance of the compounded form of (*a*) *x̱'éináx̱* 'through the mouth, entrance of (it)', it is also possible that *x̱'anax̱-* could come from (*a*) *x̱'anyaax̱* 'blocking the entrance, path of (it)'. Therefore the entire name remains open to interpretation.

2.18 *Kudatankahídi, the Salmon Box*

The *Kudatankahídi* was an entity, typically referred to as a floating *hít* 'house', that was positioned out on the ocean and contained all manner of salmon and other fish. Being confined to this house out on the ocean, the salmon were inaccessible as a food source for commoners and poor folks (Zuboff tells us that rich people were the only ones that could obtain them).[367] The Kudatankahídi is most commonly referred to by Tlingit people in English as the 'Salmon Box', which is how we translate it in the texts, though this is not the literal meaning. The Tlingit name does not contain any elements meaning 'salmon' or 'box'. The final three syllables form a possessed compound noun, (*N*) *kahídi* meaning 'house upon (N)'. The initial syllables, *kudatan-*, are more difficult to account for; they are quite reminiscent of the verb *kadutáan* 'fish jump' or 'fish are jumping', but there is no way to derive the form *kudatan-* from that verb by ordinary grammatical processes, or for the verb (however modified) to become the possessor of *kahídi*. Because we are unable to definitively analyze the name, we default to the customary English name 'Salmon Box' for the translation.

The most common form of the name is *Kudatankahídi*, but, as it turns out, none of the storytellers in this volume say the name in exactly that way. From James, we hear «Atÿana.á Daakahídi»,[368] meaning 'House of Fish Runs', as well as «Atkudatankahídi»[369] (with initial at-), which we translate as 'Salmon Box'. From Zuboff, we hear «Kutatankahídi»[370] pronounced clearly in all instances with *Kutatan-*, phonetically [k^{wh}ut^{h}at^{h}an], rather than the more common *Kudatan-*, phonetically [k^{wh}utat^{h}an]. And from Mills, we hear «Kudataankahídi»[371] with long *taan-* rather than short *-tan-*. Dick never mentions the name, but refers to «yóo-óo-óo deikéenáx̱ át lahashji hít»[372] 'a house floating around wa-a-y out on the ocean'. Minnie Johnson seems to have provided yet another variation in a story told on May 1, 1954. De Laguna rendered her words as «Yax̣kadatan ka hidi 'an'awsiyaq»,[373] which would apparently represent *Yax̱kadatankahídi ÿan awsiyék̲* 'He (Raven) pulled the Yax̱kadatankahídi (Salmon Box) ashore'.

Raven used the *Náak̲w Tl'eeg̲í Wootsaag̲áa* 'Octopus Tentacle Cane' that he obtained from X̱'anax̱g̲aatwaayáa to pull the Salmon Box ashore in Dry Bay near the mouth of the Alsek River. By doing so he established the salmon runs, which have since provided an ample supply of food to the people living along salmon streams and the coast. While bringing the contents of the Salmon Box ashore established the salmon runs, the Salmon Box itself became part of the landscape in Dry Bay. The resting place of the Salmon Box, at the former village called *Gus'éix̱*, became the site of two Tlingit clan houses of the Dry Bay area, the Lukaax̱.ádi house *Shakahít* 'Prow House' (this name commemorating a canoe prow-like feature of the Salmon Box) and the L'uknax̱.ádi clan house *Diginaa Hít* 'Far-Out House'.

2.19 *G̱anook, Petrel; Raven's Brother-in-Law*

The character *G̱anook* 'Petrel' appears in this volume in narratives by Hammond and Dick. Like Raven, Petrel's name uses a common noun for a type of bird. Also like Raven, the mythic figure Petrel is more akin to a person than a bird in these tales. The noun *g̱anook* is typically glossed simply as 'petrel', but the specific referent is likely either the fork-tailed storm petrel (*Hydrobates furcatus*) or the Leach's storm petrel (*H. leucorhous*), though the term could likely encompass both.[374] These are small pelagic birds that spend most of their life on the open ocean, only coming ashore for short periods to breed. The mythic Petrel's history and deeds, as well as his status within the system of Tlingit clans and crest imagery, are rather mysterious and underelaborated when compared to Raven. Shotridge, remarking on the *G̱anook S'áaxw* 'Petrel Hat', states that the piece "represents the most ancient being in Tlingit mythology".[375] While Raven is the forebear of the Raven moiety of Tlingit society, Petrel is sometimes suggested to be in a similar sense the original progenitor of the Wolf, or Eagle, moiety, though this is not a clear-cut or universal understanding of his significance in the clan and crest system.[376]

Dick and Hammond both refer to him as «du káani»[377] 'his (Raven's) brother-in-law', which clearly demarcates a cross-moiety relationship between Raven and Petrel. In Hammond's performance of "Raven and Petrel", the two men come upon one another while canoeing on the open ocean and Raven addresses him as «ax̱ káani» 'my brother-in-law'. Raven then tries to engage Petrel in a match of one-upmanship by proclaiming that he is far older than Petrel and mockingly claiming that Petrel's stated birth-epoch was recent history. Hammond describes this use of words as «Woosh kaanáx̱ yoox̱'adatánk»,[378] a verbal noun phrase we translate as 'dominating one another verbally'. Petrel easily subdues Raven with the use of his *K̲ugwáas' S'áaxw* 'Fog Hat', which, when placed on his head, causes a thick fog to engulf their surroundings. Frightened and unable to navigate, Raven, huddled in his boat, cries out for his brother-in-law's help and concedes that Petrel is in fact the more ancient one.

In the theme of Raven being turned black by being covered with soot in a smokehole during an attempted escape, there is variability in what Raven is escaping with, whom he is escaping from, and who is responsible for covering him with soot. Petrel is frequently regarded as the one responsible for causing Raven, who was originally white, to become black in this manner; this is the situation in the stories of Hammond and Dick. As they relate, Petrel was at some ancient time the keeper of all the fresh water in the world, which he hoarded in a box in his house. Raven manages to steal and disperse this water throughout the world, dramatically altering the geography of Tlingit Country with the establishment of all the major rivers and making fresh water available to all the coastal villages in the form of creeks and tributaries. Hammond explicitly mentions the «T'aaḵú» 'Taku River', «Lḵoot» 'Chilkoot River', «Jilḵáat» 'Chilkat River', and adds «tle yú nánde, Yakutat» 'and [those of] Yakutat to the north'.[379] Dick names the «Iḵhéeni» 'Copper River', «Aalséix̱» 'Alsek River', and the «T'aaḵú» 'Taku River', with the addition, «wáa sá yakoogéi yáa héen tlénx'»[380] 'however many of those big rivers there are', and even states, of the final portion of water Raven released from his mouth, «Áyá éil' tleinx̱ wusitee»[381] 'It became the ocean'. As Raven is in the process of escaping through the smokehole, holding in his beak the water that would become all these rivers, Petrel commands the spirit residing in the smokehole of his house to seize hold of Raven. While his spirit holds Raven in place for a time, Petrel makes a fire below Raven, blackening him with soot. This explains why Raven and the ravens we observe today are as black as coal.

2.20 *Xóots Wooshdasháay, the Brown Bear Couple; Raven's Paternal Aunt and Her Husband*

One of Raven's adventures involves him paying a visit to *Xóots wooshdasháay* 'a [married] Brown Bear couple'. This volume includes performances of this story by Wanamaker, Dick, and Mills. Raven showcases his trickery and crooked desires in his interactions with the Bear couple, turning seemingly friendly favors (taking the Male Bear out halibut fishing after the Bear's spell of bad luck and preparing the day's catch as dinner for the Female Bear) into gruesome murders: Raven solicits the Male Bear to unwittingly and lethally castrate himself; as for the Female Bear, he feeds her hot rocks hidden within halibut stomachs, boiling her from the inside out. After thus murdering his auntie and his auntie's husband, Raven enjoys feasting on their flesh and the remaining halibut.

The three storytellers uniformly refer to the Female Bear as *du aat* 'his (Raven's) paternal aunt' (which we translate in the texts as 'his auntie'), and the Male Bear as *du aatx̱úx̱* 'his (Raven's) auntie's husband'. When Raven returns to the Female Bear's home after stashing the body of her husband, we find another formulaic expression in the question she asks Raven; note, again, the occurrence of this formulaic element in the quotation of a character:

Wanamaker:	«Ha goo sákwshé gwé i aatx̱úx̱ ḵu.aa?»[382]	"Now, I wonder, where is your auntie's husband?"
Dick:	[«]Haa goosú i aatx̱úx̱ ḵu.aa?»[383]	["]So where is your auntie's husband, anyhow?"
Mills:	«Ha goosóo wé i aatx̱úx̱ ḵu.aa?»[384]	"So where is is your auntie's husband, anyhow?"

This illustrates the traditional Tlingit practice of showing respect to the person addressed by referring to the addressee's relationship with the person in question rather than the speaker's relationship with the person. In English we would expect the Female Bear to say, 'Where is *my* husband, though?', whereas in Tlingit she asks Raven, 'Where is *your auntie's* husband, though?"

The kinship term (*du*) *aat* '(his/her) paternal aunt' refers to a person's father's sister. Because Tlingit society is divided into two moieties and involves matrilineal descent with exogamous cross-moiety marriage, one's father, as well as one's father's sisters, would have traditionally belonged to a clan of the opposite moiety. Further, the term (*du*) *aat* '(his/her) paternal aunt' includes not only the father's biological sisters, but all women of the father's clan. The interactions between Raven and his paternal aunt are thus charged with a strong socially transgressive overtone in that he does not relate to her in the socially expected respectful manner. He rather lies to her, murders her in a brutal fashion through trickery, and eats her.

2.21 *Yoo<u>k</u>, Cormorant; Raven's Sidekick*

Yoo<u>k</u> 'Cormorant' is a sort of sidekick figure alongside Raven during the episode with the Brown Bear couple, told by Wanamaker, Dick, and Mills. The three storytellers refer to him as *Yoo<u>k</u>* 'Cormorant'; Dick and Mills additionally use the diminutive form *Yoo<u>k</u>k'* 'Little Cormorant'. Wanamaker states, «Yóot'át áwé Yéil du xwáayi<u>x</u> sitee, du koo<u>k</u>énayi<u>x</u> sitee» 'That creature (Cormorant) was Raven's sidekick, his messenger'. Dick describes him as «du xwáak'u» 'his (Raven's) sidekick, buddy, lackey' and Mills states:

Yoo<u>k</u> yóo áwé duwasáakw	Cormorant is the name
yá Yéil een	of the one who was travelling about
át kawdiyaayi aa yá gaaw.[385]	with Raven at the time.

In the three tellings, Cormorant goes out halibut fishing with Raven and the Male Bear and is witness to Raven's murder of the Bear. In order to prevent Cormorant from reporting this to the Bear's wife, Raven solicits Cormorant to stick out his tongue with the formulaic phrase, «I lóot' daa<u>k</u> tsaa<u>k</u>!»[386] 'Stick your tongue out!' Raven then rips out Cormorant's tongue, after which he can only make unintelligible noises, which explains the way the call of these birds now sounds. Raven eventually banishes Cormorant to live on the ocean reefs, which is now a common place to find cormorants dwelling.

2.22 *Ch'a.aan; Raven's Made-Up Word for a Dead Humpback Whale*

The name *ch'a.aan* occurs in this volume in the story of "Raven and the Whale" as told by Italio. It (or a trace of it) occurs in the same story by Dick, but in much subtler fashion. The *ch'a.aan* is not so much a character or even an entity at all, but rather a peculiar word that Raven uses to refer to what is really a humpback whale that has died and floated ashore. This is the whale that Raven flew into and eventually killed by having a barbecue for himself consisting of its visceral fat and internal organs while inside of it. When villagers find the whale's beached carcass they begin processing the meat and blubber to become a great supply of food. After a series of intervening events, Raven presents himself to the villagers as a rugged and wise lone traveler, telling them that he has seen such a creature before and it is not a whale but something called a *ch'a.aan*. This is a ruse to fool the villagers into thinking it is a dangerous creature that is unfit for consumption and that it will bring harm to the entire village if they don't leave all the meat in place and move away. The name *ch'a.aan* is either a meaningless nonce word (a made-up word created for one-time use) or a pun on the phrase *ch'a aan*, which means 'nonetheless' or 'despite that'. We have simply left it untranslated as a nonce word in the English text, but if we were to take the word as a pun, this portion of Italio's "Raven and the Whale"—which features Raven addressing the villagers—could be interpreted as:

«Haaw.	"Well.
Tléil yáay̆ ásgíwé.	It seems that it is not a whale.
Tléil yáay̆ áwé.	That is not a whale.
Ch'a.aan áwé,	That's a nonetheless,
ch'a.aan.»	a nonetheless."
«Ch'a.aan» yóo áyú aawasáa hóoch k̲u.aa.[387]	A "nonetheless" is the name he came up with for it.

The term seems to have made its way into Dick's performance of "Raven and the Whale" as well, also in Raven's address to the villagers. He says, «Áwé ch'a aan wuduwax̲áa» 'Despite that (i.e., strange sounds having been heard from inside the whale), the people ate it (the whale)'.[388] In this case, Raven never uses the word *ch'a.aan* outright to refer to the whale, so this seems to be a subtle pun which could also mean 'the people ate the *ch'a.aan*'; if we stretch the pun to its limit, the sentence means both 'nonetheless, the people ate it' and 'the people ate the nonetheless'.

It is entirely possible that Dick had no intention of punning on Raven's nonce word *ch'a.aan* with his use of *ch'a aan* 'nonetheless' in this instance, but the appearance of this combination of syllables at this moment in the narrative seemed too formulaic to write off as coincidence, especially since we find the term in older texts as well, such as the Raven story Deikeenaak'w told in English to Swanton:

> When [Raven] thought the people were through making oil, he dressed himself up well and repaired to the town. There he said to the people, "Was anything heard inside that tc!ān [*ch.a.aan*] (his word for whale)?" and one answered, "Yes, a queer noise was heard inside of the whale." "I wonder what it was," said Raven.

> After their food was all prepared Raven said to the people, "Long ago, when a sound was heard inside of a tc!ān [*ch'a.aan*], all the people moved out of their town so as not to be killed. All who remained were destroyed. So you better move from this town.[389]

Once the villagers move off, convinced that the so-called *ch'a.aan* is no good to eat or even reside by and leaving the whale's carcass along with all the processed meat and blubber in place, Raven has a feast for himself.[390]

2.23 *Other Characters*

Many other important characters and entities appear throughout this volume. Of note are the *yáay* 'humpback whale' that Raven flies into and kills by having a barbecue consisting of its internal organs (in FI I, iv; SJ ix; FD vi; and KM V); the *yáxwch'* 'sea otter' that assists Raven by bringing gravel up from the ocean floor so that Raven can create the Aleutian Islands (in SJ ii, and RZ II, vi); the *t'á* 'king salmon', which Raven provokes with the use of the *s'oowk'* 'little greenstone' (in FD ix and KM II); the various little birds that Raven solicits to help with cooking the king salmon (in FD ix and KM II); *G̱uwakaan* 'Deer', whom Raven befriends in order to kill and eat, beginning with the anus, which Raven decides would be the most apt point of entry (in KM IV); Raven's own dislodged nose, which fishermen yank off while Raven is snacking on the fat used as bait on their halibut hooks (in SJ x and AH II); the *Haayeetl'ôok̲k'u* 'Little-Liver-Beneath-Us' referenced in the verbal battle between Raven and Petrel over which is the more ancient being (in AH I, i); and still many others.

3 NOTES ON FORMAT & THE EDITORIAL PROCESS

3.1 *Issues Encountered in Transcription and Translation*

The reader will note that there are a number of places, especially in the earliest recordings, where we were unable to resolve what the speaker was saying. This is often due to the relatively poor audio quality of the older recordings, particularly those that were captured on reel-to-reel recorders. Despite the fact that these older recordings have been 'cleaned up' by digital enhancement, there often remain examples of distortion and noises whose sources are unclear: did the sounds in question come from the speaker's mouth or were they somehow introduced by the recording process? In a number of cases it is clear that the speaker's words have been obscured by someone talking or laughing in the background, or by someone moving the microphone or tapping on the table or drumming. In such cases we have commented on the probable source of the distortion or disruption in the notes. In cases where we were unable to hear what a speaker pronounced and were unable to reasonably infer what they would have said, we simply left these instances untranscribed with '{...}' in place of the indiscernible words.

3.2 *Treatment of False Starts*

Because it bears heavily on the relationship between the recording of the original performance and what is found on the page, we owe it to the reader to explain our treatment of false starts—where the speaker starts to say something and stops, then resumes either with the same phrase or with a different one. In cases where it is clear from the recordings themselves what the false start is and how the speaker resolves it, we have simply omitted the false starts from the narratives, reasoning that reflecting all of the many false starts in the text would be a hindrance rather than a help to the reader; they would add a great deal of clutter to the texts without providing much of value to offset the messiness. However, numerous instances of false starts that may be confusing to the reader and those listening to the original audio are mentioned in the notes. Furthermore, as noted above, special issues and problems that have hampered us in our ability to interpret the speaker's Tlingit speech are dealt with in notes throughout the texts.

3.3 *Notes and Commentary*

We have used notes to explain rarely encountered features of Tlingit grammar to readers who are interested in grammatical analysis. Such explanation is often provided for verb forms and verbal constructions that we believe could be difficult to parse due to their complexity and/or their rarified nature. The primary intended audience for these notes is the serious student of Tlingit grammar and oral literature. There are also numerous instances in which literary, conceptual, and cultural matters are commented upon, which may be of interest to the general reader.

3.4 *Division and Organization of the Narratives*

The texts in this volume are divided and notated based on four categories: storyteller, tale, episode, and line.

3.4.1 *Storyteller*

The individual storyteller is the first basis upon which the material in the book is organized. Each of the seven storytellers' material is presented as a unit. These units are arranged chronologically based on the date of recording, with Italio's 1952 stories being the oldest and Mills' February 1989 stories being the most recent.[391]

3.4.2 *Tale*

What we label as a 'tale' is the broadest compositional unit.[392] It refers to the whole of a given performance, whether it is short and simple or long and elaborately structured. A 'tale' in this useage typically corresponds to an entire recorded storytelling session and may thus refer to a single isolated story or a multi-episodic 'cycle' of Raven's adventures. We may distinguish 'discrete tales' consisting of a single story from 'extended tales' consisting of multiple successive and interconnected stories.[393] Hammond' "Raven Gets His Nose Yanked Off" is a discrete tale consisting of one story. James' "Raven Who Flouts Convention" is an extended tale containing eleven successive episodes. In some cases, such as those of Italio's "Raven Who Breaks All the Rules" and Wanamaker's "Raven's Clever Mind", the extended tale is the result of recording sessions from multiple days. When it is clear, as in these cases, that the storyteller resumed the narration in such a way as to intentionally produce continuity with the previously recorded material, we take this to represent an extension of the same tale. For the purpose of labeling the texts, the Tlingit term corresponding to 'tale' is *tlaagú*, which could be translated as 'myth', 'legend', 'tale', 'fable', or 'story'. If a fitting title for a tale is not immediately obvious, we supply a title based on a line from the tale itself that relates thematically to the overall content of the performance. For example, Wanamaker uses the phrase «Du satoowú áwé»[394] 'That's how clever he is' twice in reference to Raven's cleverness and ingenuity, and additionally states «Ch'a du x̱'asatoowú áwé yéi yatee Yéil ḵu.aa»[395] 'That's how clever Raven was with words'. We thus derive the title «Yéil Satoowú» "Raven's Clever Mind" for the whole of the extended tale.

3.4.3 *Episode*

What we designate as an 'episode' is a subdivision of an extended tale. If a performance consists of several successive stories, and if these can be divided into relatively discrete narrative units, these segments are labeled episodes. For the purpose of labeling the texts, the Tlingit term corresponding to episode is *shkalneek*, which could be translated as 'story', 'narrative', or 'narration'. In most cases, a well-known Tlingit title exists for each episode in Raven's adventures. The titles applied to the episodes are usually based on the major entity with which Raven is preoccupied (e.g., «Yéil ḵa Du Káak» "Raven and His Uncle" and «Yéil ḵa Ḵei.á» "Raven and the Daylight") or a salient image or act from the plot (e.g., «Yéil Du Loowú Kéi Wudusyeeg̱í» "Raven Gets His Nose Yanked Off" and «Yéil Geesh Daax̱ Wugoodí» "Raven Goes Down Along the Bull Kelp").

3.4.4 *Line*

The final subdivision of the texts is the line. The overall guiding principle for the organization of lines in the Tlingit text is consistent with the previous volumes in this series and other scholarly treatments of Native American oral literature. A line is defined here as an uninterrupted sequence of sounds falling between two silences.[396] When the speaker has initiated their tale, we turn the line upon a significant pause. As you might imagine, this sometimes raises the question of what constitutes a 'significant' pause. If the pause is obviously momentary, only a fraction of a second long, we do not consider it to be significant, whereas a pause of roughly half a second or more would usually be considered significant. There are many cases where we have been forced to rely on our personal judgment as to whether to treat a given sequence as one line or two lines. When a speaker pauses for an exceptionally long time (five seconds or more) we insert a blank line to reflect the break in the discourse. This also raises the question of which pauses should be considered motivated compositional units of the narratives (perhaps used to increase the tension of a particularly dramatic moment, to reflect the fact that a character has paused to think, or to establish a series of lyrical repetitions or contrasts) and which should be considered unmotivated pauses that were not intended to be meaningful elements of the composition (perhaps resulting from the speaker simply becoming momentarily tongue-tied or having to clear their throat or regain their breath). We have opted against arbitrating between motivated and unmotivated pauses and simply turn the line whenever a pause occurs. The lines are thus divided on a phonic, and not a grammatical or strictly rhetorical, basis; this is meant to serve as a means, however imperfect, of reflecting on the written page the oral cadence of the original performances. Line numbers are assigned to all spoken lines of text. Numbers are not assigned to blank lines denoting pauses of exceptional duration nor to performance notes indicating laughter, drumming, clapping, interruptions, etc.

3.4.5 *Story (More Generally)*

We should note that 'tale' and 'episode' as described above are categories we have applied to the storytellers' material for the purpose of organizing the book and distinguishing between elements of the performances. These are imperfect terms that do not necessarily reflect an internal Tlingit understanding of narrative form and type. While externally derived and imperfect, we felt that it was important to delineate the cases in which the storytellers' performances consist of multiple interconnected stories and that this was a suitable method.

Outside of the use of 'tale' and 'episode' for organizational purposes, we more generally refer the storytellers' material as 'stories' in a less formal and restricted sense. 'Story' and 'storyteller' have been established as standard terminology in the prior volumes in this series and 'story' is the most common word used by Tlingit storytellers themselves when talking about their material in English. Zuboff and Mills, for example, were excellent storytellers in both Tlingit and English and both regularly used the word 'story'. The corresponding and most common Tlingit term the storytellers apply to their material in this book is *shkalneek*, meaning 'story' or 'narrative'. *Shkalneek* and 'story' have a broad range of applicability to narratives of all types and are used by the storytellers and the Tlingit community.

3.5 *Punctuation*

In a departure from earlier volumes in this series, punctuation is used solely for grammatical purposes and does not signal—especially in the case of commas and periods occurring before the end of a line—that the speaker made a momentary pause or changed the inflection of their voice.[397] Rather, such punctuation is provided to clarify the syntactic structure of phrases within a single line, or when syntactically related clauses and phrases span multiple lines. Less frequently, the speaker may include two or more independent clauses within a single line, which we separate with a period or sometimes with a comma depending on the relationship between the two statements. Semicolons are not used in the Tlingit transcription, but they are used in the English translation.

3.6 *Shorthand Notation of the Texts*

We use a system of shorthand notation in this volume which is based on traditional methods used for dramatic works and long narrative poetry. This system allows for precise citation of the storytellers' words and for ease of cross-referencing within the volume. All pages of the storytellers' texts as well as those of the notes to the texts display the corresponding storyteller, tale, and/or episode number, and line numbers in the upper margin.

Storytellers are referenced by first and last initial (FI, AW, RZ, SJ, FD, AH, KM) and numbers are assigned to all tales, episodes, and lines of narrated texts. Tales are numbered with small-capital roman numerals (I, II, III, IV, ...); episodes are numbered with lowercase roman numerals (i, ii, iii, ...); and line numbers are given in Arabic numerals (1, 2, ...). Storytellers' initials are given first; tale number, episode number, or both, follow next in that order; line numbers are given last.

Following are examples of this notation. 'RZ I' refers to the whole of Robert Zuboff's first tale, which is his "Raven and the Salmon Box (telling 1)". 'SJ iii' refers to the third episode, "Raven and Fire", of Susie James' one tale; because her material consists of a single extended tale, it would be redundant and uninformative to indicate 'tale I' in each instance, so we leave the tale number aside—the same holds for the texts of Wanamaker and Dick. 'KM VI, 4, 9, and 17,' refers to lines 4, 9, and 17 of Katherine Mills' sixth tale, "Why Raven is Always Hungry". 'FI I, iv, 5–8,' refers to lines 5–8 of the fourth episode of Frank Italio's first tale, "Raven and the Whale". There are two subsequent treatments of Hammond's telling of "Raven Gets His Nose Yanked Off", which makes for the most cumbersome notation. Given first as 'AH IIa' is a verbatim transcription containing Hammond's spoken Tlingit as well as a live line-by-line English translation by Anna Katzeek that occurred as part of the same performance. Given next as 'AH IIb' is a text of the excerpted Tlingit lines of Hammond's tale and a facing English translation by the editors. Thus, 'AH IIa, 83,' refers to line 83 (a line spoken in English by Katzeek) of the first rendition; 'AH IIa/b, 82/48,' refers to line 82 in the first rendition as well as line 48 in the second (both referring to the same Tlingit line by Hammond).

3.7 *Some Notes on the English Translations*

Although it is often possible to translate from one language into another closely related language almost word for word, we almost always run into situations where a literal word-for-word translation is not possible. The less closely the two languages are related, the less likely that a literal word-for-word translation would produce intelligible results. In the present case, in which Tlingit and English are grammatically worlds apart, literal word-for-word translations from Tlingit that would make sense to the English reader are rarely achievable. Overly literal translations would also fail to capture the elegant and lyrical qualities of the Tlingit narratives. It is almost always the case that some details or nuances of the Tlingit narrative are not directly translatable into clear English prose. While we have strived for a middle ground between, on the one hand, literal fidelity to the grammar of the original texts, and, on the other, literary fidelity to their aesthetic flavor, our English translations should not be taken as literal translations nor even as complete translations of the Tlingit. Here we reaffirm the Dauenhauers' perspective in the introduction to the first volume in this series, "In the final analysis, of course, a person who wants to savor the Tlingit original will have to read the texts in Tlingit. We hope that for many readers, the English translation will provide easier entry into the rich oral style of the originals. For most readers, who will not attempt to read the Tlingit texts, we hope that our efforts do justice to the artistry of the composers."[398]

In addition to the issues of word-for-word translation, in many cases it is not advisable, sometimes even impossible, to create a line-by-line translation that is clear to the English-speaking reader. In such cases we again follow the Dauenhauers' precedent, which involves translating two or more Tlingit lines as a unit and distributing the English translation among the lines in such a way that the word order is intelligible and aesthetically pleasing in English without the words on one line necessarily corresponding to the Tlingit words on the same line. To see how this works in practice, let us take a few examples:

Lines 169–70 of Italio's "Raven and His Uncle" (FI I, i, 169–70):

Tle a tóode woogoot	His mother	169
wé du tláa.	then entered it.	170

A more literal translation of the Tlingit (separating the lines with a slash) would be '(just) then into it went / that his mother'. It would have been possible to translate line-by-line as follows: 'Then she went into it, / that mother of his', but we have opted for the less convoluted and more natural translation given above, where on line 170 of the English we find the translation of line 169 of the Tlingit, and vice versa.

Lines 37–38 of Mills' "Raven and the Brown Bear Couple" (KM III, 37–38):

Deisgwach shaawahík hasdu een	Their boat	37
wé yaakw.	eventually filled up on them.	38

A maximally literal translation of the Tlingit would be 'eventually it filled up with them / that boat', but this would also be maximally confusing for the English reader. The context here is that the boat that these people (Raven, the Male Bear, and Cormorant) are sitting in is being inundated with halibut. Even though it is clear in the Tlingit text that the boat is not being filled with people, but rather with halibut, and that the people just happen to be sitting in the boat when this occurs, this fact is totally obscured if we use a literal English translation.

Lines 41–44 of Italio's "Raven the Troublemaker" (FI II, 41–44):

Du shátt x̱'eitáang̱aa	His slaves just kept going killing them off	41
x̱áa ḵoodé tle ajáḵx̱	at his command—	42
[du] x̱'ayáx̱—	at her brother's command,	43
du éek' x̱'ayáx̱.	so that none of her children could communicate with his wife, you see.	44

A maximally literal translation of the Tlingit in this case would be:

Lest s/he/it speak to his wife,
you see,
toward the (undefined) area s/he/it/they just kill(s) him/her/it
according to [his] words—
according to her brothers' words.

In the relatively free translation provided initially, lines 41, 42, 43, 44 of the Tlingit text correspond respectively with 44, 41, 42, 43 in the English translation. The process of translating sentences such as this, which are composed of multiple clauses and span multiple lines, involves translating the group of Tlingit lines into English as a unit, then distributing this translation among the lines available for the English translation. Additionally, the Tlingit text does not contain words meaning 'his slaves' or 'her children'; the Tlingit uses only third-person pronouns without specifying the referent and we have supplied these English references for clarity. Further, in line 43 of the Tlingit, the word *du* 'his' (i.e., the man named *Yooḵis'kooḵéik* 'Tide Commander, the brother of Raven's soon-to-be mother) of *du x̱'ayáx̱* 'according to his command' is not audible on the recording; we expect that it really was pronounced by Italio, but below the threshold of reproducibility on the tape. Because we logically expect it to be there, but are unable to hear it, we set it in brackets to indicate that it was inserted by the editors without being audible to them.

3.8 *Songs*

A number of these stories include songs as components of the performance. When a storyteller breaks into song, the lyrics are indented and set in italics. Each line of lyrics is capitalized, and for the most part punctuation is omitted. We have translated Tlingit lyrics into English only when their meaning is readily apparent.

Six songs are found in this volume, some of which are performed more than once. In his "Raven and the Daylight", Italio sings a pair of songs that were composed and sung by Raven when he broke the daylight; Italio performs the same pair of songs again in his 1954 tale.[399] In "Raven and the Salmon Box", Zuboff performs a song that Raven used to activate the power of the Octopus Tentacle Cane, enabling him to use the cane to pull the Salmon Box ashore; Zuboff sings this song in both of his two performances of the story in this volume.[400] James sings three songs. The first, in "Raven Hosts a Potlach", is a song to which Raven's nephews, the Plovers, come dancing into the house during a potlatch hosted by Raven.[401] The second, in "Raven Gets Herself Married to a Killerwhale", is a feigned mourning song sung by Raven, who has taken the guise of a woman and pretends to sing a lament over her dead Killerwhale husband after slyly murdering him.[402] The third, in "Raven and the Whale", is attributed to a little elder among a crowd of villagers who are butchering a beached whale; when the villagers make a cut that allows Raven to burst forth from the whale and fly off, the elder begins singing to him.[403]

3.9 *Tlingit Interjections*

Another practice that we have adopted in our English translations has to do with interjections that occur rather frequently in the Tlingit texts but for which it is difficult or impossible to find a corresponding English interjection. Some interjections have been assigned more-or-less equivalent translations in English, such as *haaw*, *haa*, or *ha* 'well, …'; *aaa* or *aaá* 'yes'; *ha.é!* 'wow!'; *déi!* 'now!'; *hadóu!* 'good grief!'; *hadláa!*, *dláa!*, or *dláh!* 'goodness!'; and *jíh!* 'gee!' Other interjections have simply been rendered with an approximate English phonological equivalent, such as *aa* 'ah', *ei!* 'ey!', *ei-ei-ei* 'ey-y-y', *éh!* or *é'!* 'eh!', *íh!* 'ih!', *hé'!* 'heh!', *hí'!* 'hih!', *aahá!* or *haahá!* 'aha!', *ehehehei!* 'eh-heh-heh-hey!', *hm-m!* 'hm-m!', *mmm!* 'hmm!', *éhhhh!* 'ahhhh!', *aahóhó!* 'ah-ho-ho!', *hóhó!* 'hoho!', and *hohohohou!* 'hohohoho!' Note in particular that the frequently occurring interjection *aa* is a shortened form of *aaa* or *aaá* 'yes'; although we have rendered it into English as 'ah', not only does it serve (like English 'ah') to indicate that the speaker is contemplating what to say next, but it also indicates that the speaker is affirming what they had previously said. The reader should therefore keep in mind that Tlingit *aa* has elements of both 'ah' (i.e., 'I'm thinking') and 'yes' (i.e., 'I'm affirming what I just said') included in it, even though we uniformly render it as 'ah'.

3.10 *Spelling Conventions and Special Linguistic Features of the Tlingit*

3.10.1 *Variable Vowel Length*

As an editorial practice, we have taken pains to reproduce the speech in the texts as exactly as possible within the limits of our ability to do so—with the exception of false starts, which we have discussed above. We have been careful not to standardize vowel length in suffixes such as the possessive and subordinative suffix *-ÿi*[404] (which can be heard pronounced variously with a short or long vowel), the decessive suffix *-ÿin* (also heard variously with a long or short vowel), the allative postposition *-de* 'toward' (also occurring as long *-dei*); enclitics such as *áyá* and *áwé* (also occurring as *áyáa* and *áwéi*); and particles such as *de* 'already', *tle* 'then', *ch'u* 'still' and *tsu* 'again' (also *dei*, *tlei*, *ch'oo*, and *tsoo*).

3.10.2 *The Archaic Sound /ÿ/*

We have used a few special markings to draw the reader's attention to special features of the dialect or idiolect of the narrator. In some of the older texts, particularly in the speech of Italio, we find many instances of the sound /ÿ/, an unrounded high back sonorant [ɰ]. In modern Tlingit, this sound has merged with ordinary /y/. (Historically, /ÿ/ appears to be a denasalized variant of [ŋ], i.e., the English sound /ng/ as in 'sing'.) In classical Tlingit, the consonant /ÿ/ was regularly rounded to /w/ next to a rounded vowel (/u/ or /oo/). We find this particularly in Italio's texts, where, for example, underlying *yóo ÿán* 'yon mainland' is pronounced *yóo wán*. Another feature of this phoneme /ÿ/—but not of ordinary /y/—is that it tends to be suppressed after an obstruent consonant. So, for example, a sequence like *dleit yáx̱ ÿatee* 'it is white' (literally, 'it is like snow') tends to be pronounced *dleit yáx̱atee* (with no break between *yáx̱* and [*ÿ*]*atee*; it doesn't sound like ˣ*yáx̱ atee*, because if these were pronounced as separate words, we would expect to hear a glottal stop before the *a-* of ˣ*atee*). For this reason, when we expect to hear /ÿ/ (or /y/ that we know was originally /ÿ/) at the beginning of a word but don't hear it on the recording, we write the character ⟨ÿ⟩ to alert the reader to the fact that the underlying form of the word begins with /ÿ/ even though we can't hear any consonant there.

3.10.3 *Treatment of Denasalized /n/*

In James' texts, the reader will note that there are quite a few instances of the 'underlined *n*', i.e., ⟨n̠⟩. This indicates that the speaker pronounced what would normally be an /n/ either without nasalization or with incomplete nasalization, resulting in a sound like English /l/ or a sound intermediate between English /n/ and English /l/.[405] In contrast, the Tlingit orthography uses a different spelling convention for instances, especially in Interior Tlingit, where a voiced lateral sonorant [l] (identical to English /l/) is found in a few words and names borrowed from Athabaskan or from English, which are written as /l̠/, e.g., in Teslin *l̠áadiyou* [lá:tiyo:] 'radio' and the *Kwaashk'ik̲wáan* personal name *Lil̠áa'* [ɬilá:ˀʔ] (or *Lal̠áa'* [ɬalá:ˀʔ]), which is Eyak by origin. However, this consonant does not occur in any of the texts of this volume.

3.10.4 *Emphatic Tone Modification*

A second type of special marking has to do with emphatic pronunciation of long low-toned syllables. Normally, what we call long low-toned syllables are pronounced with either completely low pitch or with a pitch contour that starts fairly low and drops even lower, but not dramatically lower. However, when a speaker puts special emphasis on a low-tone syllable, the pitch level will start from a relatively high level and fall dramatically. This effect is very similar to the long 'fading vowels' of Tongass Tlingit (which correspond to long low-toned vowels elsewhere in Tlingit), where the pitch begins at a relatively high level and drops rapidly towards the end of the vowel due to the fact that the speaker rapidly reduces the amount of air flowing through the voicebox.[406] We call attention to such emphasized low tones where they occur in these texts by putting a grave accent over the first letter of the long vowel. An example from James is «tsu awsiteeni át áwé wé hít tlèin»[407] 'the next thing [Raven] saw was a *huge* house', in which the emphasis on the long low syllable of *tlein* 'big, large' is manifested by the pitch level falling rapidly from high to low, whereas the ordinary pronunciation of this word uses a relatively low consistent pitch level. Wherever possible, we have used italics in the English translation in order to approximate this kind of emphatic speech.

3.10.5 *Dialectal Tone Variability With Certain Preverbs*

Four of the Tlingit directional proclitics, informally known as 'preverbs', exhibit dialectal tone variation. Most preverbs are consistently pronounced with low tone by all speakers. However, four common preverbs, *kei=* 'up', *ÿei=* 'down, getting off (a boat or vehicle)', *yoo=* 'repeatedly, back-and-forth', and *ÿeik̲=* 'down to the beach', are pronounced with high tone, i.e., as *kéi=*, *yéi=*, *yóo=*, and *yéik̲=*, by the majority of present-day Northern Coastal Tlingit speakers, who represent the communities of Hoonah, Sitka, Haines, Klukwan, and Yakutat. The only speakers in this volume who use the low-toned versions of these preverbs are Zuboff (Angoon), Wanamaker (Sitka), and Hammond (Haines)—though we find sporadic high-toned preverbs in Hammond's speech. The low-toned forms are used also by Ruth Demmert of Kake (a key consultant on the texts and translations of this volume) and by all Interior Tlingit speakers encountered by Leer. Nellie Willard of Klukwan, as recorded in the late 1960s by Leer, used these low-toned versions as well; the fact that Hammond used the high-toned versions periodically seems to indicate that the high-toned versions of these preverbs were in the process of being adopted by Chilkat-area (Haines and Klukwan) speakers only recently.

3.10.6 *Downdrift*

Those among the users of this book that are comparing the text with the audio recordings should be aware of a phenomenon that linguists call 'downdrift'. This refers to the natural tendency to lower the pitch levels of both high and low tones throughout the course of the utterance. Low tones become gradually lower, but it is the lowering of high-tone syllables that we notice the most. Therefore, at the end of a sentence it may be difficult to distinguish a high tone from a low tone in the recordings of some speakers. Gillian Story has this to say about downdrift, "Extralinguistically, the sentence may be defined as a complete utterance. It is potentially bounded by indefinite pause though frequently it comprises more than one pause group. In narrative, it is characterized by ritardando and a gradual downdrift in pitch."[408]

3.10.7 *Rhetorical Questions*

The reader will note the liberal use of rhetorical questions in these texts. Many of these we were able to translate into English as questions, but some of them defy a precise English translation. Some of the trickier examples of these begin with *goosú* 'where (is it that …)'; examples from the texts are:

Italio:	Goosú tlax̱ yéi yaawat'ay̆i át l x̱'éi oodanoogún?[409]	How is it that she hadn't felt such a hot object in her mouth?
	Goosú kdagaax̱í?[410]	What happened to all the crying? (lit. Where is/was it that he's wailing?)
Hammond:	Goosú wé ḵuwdagwáas'i?[411]	Where did the fog go? (lit. Where is/was it that it was foggy?)

Another type of hard-to-translate rhetorical question is formed with *daat yáx̱ sá*, literally 'like what', e.g.:

Dick:	Daat yáx̱ sá wdlit'íx'[412]	He had become extremely stiff
James:	Daat yáx̱ sáyóo kaligéi a yee yú du hídi.[413]	The inside of his house was so very beautiful.

Other rhetorical questions may be translated either as questions or as indefinite expressions in English. There are numerous instances of these in the texts. Compare the following two examples:

James:	Yaakw—gootx̱ sáwé yaakw du jeet wujix̱ín?[414]	A boat—where did this boat come from that he got his hands on?
Dick:	Áwé, haaw, goodáx̱ sáwé du jeet uwaxíx wé s'áax̱' yook'óo?[415]	Then, well, he got ahold of a little cod stomach from somewhere or other.

This last sentence could equally well have been translated, 'Then, well, where did this little cod stomach come from / that he got his hands on?' Conversely, the first example could have been translated, 'A boat—he got his hands on a boat from somewhere or other.'

Finally, some rhetorical questions are most naturally translated as questions in English. A couple examples will suffice to illustrate this point:

Italio:	daaḵwéit yaanawádi yáx̱ sáwé yatee?[416]	what sort of thing grows so fast as this anyway?
Dick:	Goox' sáyú awsiteen Yéil?[417]	Where had she seen Raven?
Mills:	Áwé ch'a wáa-áa sáyú tsú du x̱'éit aa gasnee wé yaaw?[418]	Just ho-ow could Raven get a taste of the herring?

3.10.8 *Change of /ch/ to /t/ Before Sibilants and Shibilants*

A regular feature of Tlingit phonology is the change of syllable-final /ch/ to /t/ before a syllable beginning with a sibilant (/dz/, /ts/, /ts'/, /s/, /s'/) or a shibilant (/j/,

/ch/, /ch'/, /sh/). This may occur across word boundaries, as heard in regularly used combinations like *aadóoch sá* 'who', often pronounced *aadóot sá*, as well as *daatch sá* 'what', often pronouced as *daat sá*. Other examples from Interior Tlingit are found with compounds consisting of *shich-* 'female' and an animal name, e.g., *shitdzísk'w* 'cow moose' (underlyingly *shich-dzísk'w*) and *shit.s'aax̱* 'female marmot' (underlyingly *shich-s'aax̱*). Some examples from the texts are Italio's pronunciations of «Gáant kanalÿichji át áyá, kóon»[419] 'It's something that flies outside, the flicker', in which *kanalÿichji át* is pronounced *kanalÿitji át*, and «Ch'ul áx' áwé udaxeechjí áwé ḵuwdzitee»[420] 'Before she even made an effort, he was born', in which *udaxeechjí* is pronounced as *udaxeetjí*. This is an aspect of orthographic convention which has not been entirely settled. We have generally transcribed instances of this phenomenon in the texts with the underlying /ch/ rather than the pronounced /t/ while providing a comment on the pronunciation in a note.

3.11 *Conventions of Tlingit Word Division*

Over time, the policies on separation of words or parts of words have evolved and some details remain unresolved. For example, *at x̱á* was once the standard spelling for the declarative phrase 's/he/it is eating', the imperative phrase *at x̱á!* 'eat!', and the noun 'food', but now the noun form meaning 'food' is written as one word, *atx̱á*. This helps remind the reader that the noun functions as a single unit in speech; for example, the possessed form, as in *ax̱ atx̱aayí* 'my food', is formed in the same way as nouns that are not composed of units that would be written as separate words as part of the verb phrase, such as *du nanaayí* 'his/her/its death', with the possessed form of *naná* 'death'. Furthermore, there is a circumfix *ka-l-*NOUN*-ḵ* 'NOUN-less, without NOUN' that can freely be added to nouns, so, for example, one can say *kal.atx̱áaḵ* 'without food'. The same considerations apply to nouns that have conventionally been written as two or more words, such as *yéijiné* 'work, job' (previously written *yéi jiné*), *yoox̱'atánk* 'speech, language, word, sentence, phrase' (previously written *yoo x̱'atánk*) and *shyáa.awudané* 'self-respect' (previously written *sh yáa awudané*), since we can say *ax̱ yéijineiyí* 'my work, my job' and *kalyéijinéiḵ* 'without work, jobless', *ax̱ yoox̱'atángi* 'my language, my words' and *kalyoox̱'atángiḵ* 'without a word, speechlessly', as well as *ax̱ shyáa.awudaneiyí* 'my self-respect' and *kalshyáa.awudanéiḵ* 'without self-respect'. It is only when composite nouns have lexicalized status that they can appear within the circumfix *ka-l-*NOUN*-ḵ*; consequently, the fact that such composite nouns—which in our experience are all verbal nouns—can occur inside this circumflex indicates that they are in fact indivisible lexical units, i.e., words.[421] Note also that some noun phrases that translate in English as ordinary nouns are not possessable; therefore, these are not written as single words. For example, *áa yéi jidune yé* 'office', literally, 'the place where people work' is not possessable; the Tlingit way of saying 'my office' is *áa yéi jix̱ane yé*, literally, 'the place where I work'; here the English possessor 'my' corresponds to the Tlingit verbal subject prefix *x̱a-* 'I'. Similarly, *ḵóo at.latóowu* 'teacher, the one whose duty it is to teach people (*ḵóo*)' is not strictly possessable. The classical Tlingit way of saying 'my teacher' is *x̱áa at.latóowu* or *ax̱ ée at.latóowu* 'the one whose job it is to teach me (*x̱áa* ~ *ax̱ ée*)'; here the English possessor 'my' is expressed in Tlingit as either the object of the postposition *-x'*, here *x̱áa* 'to me' (the truncated form of *x̱áax'*),[422] or as the nominal object *ax̱* 'me' of the semantically empty postpositional base plus locative postposition *ée* (the truncated form of *éex'*).

We have adopted the practice of writing the possessive pronoun *hasdu* 'their, them' as a single unit; the same applies to the contracted form *sdu* (when following a word ending in a vowel, the human pluralizer *has* typically contracts to *s*, with the initial syllable /ha/ simply disappearing). The convention has been to write this combination as two words, i.e., *has du* and *s du*. Crippen advanced the practice of using the single-word spellings *hasdu* and *sdu* in his dissertation "The Syntax in Tlingit Verbs" with a cogent justification, "*du* 'his/her' alone is the singular third-person human possessive; only with *has* does *du* denote plural human possession. This *has* does not combine with any other possessive pronouns so the *has* + *du* structure is unique."[423] In addition to this, we also feel it would be more intuitively apprehensible for the learner to see *hasdu* and especially *sdu* occurring as units rather than two words.

We have also decided to join to the verb certain components which have traditionally been written as separate 'words'. One example is the element *ash-* found in the verbs of playing that have the prefix string *ash-ka+u-d-l-ROOT*',[424] such as *ashkoolyát* 's/he/it is playing', *ashkoolch'éit'aa* 's/he is playing marbles', etc., which were previously written *ash koolyát, ash koolch'éit'aa*, etc. This practice helps alert the reader to the fact that this *ash-* is quite different in character than the salient third-person object pronoun *ash=*, which is always written as a separate word. Similarly, the rare thematic proclitic *ÿaa=* that refers to mental states and events is often shortened when it follows the relational noun *daa* 'about' and immediately precedes the areal prefix *ḵu-*, in which case *ÿa-* is written as part of the following verb word, as in *ax̱ daa ÿaḵushusigéi* (also *ax̱ daa ÿaa ḵushusigéi*) 'I understand (it)'. The 'mental' proclitic *ÿaa=* is not to be confused with the 'directional' proclitic *ÿaa=* that occurs in the progressive epiaspect and generally translates as '(moving) along'.

A special problem is presented by sentences like *héende aa atkaawa.át* 'some of them rushed into the water' (see §2.16 for a discussion of the formulaic use of this verb in narrative context). At first glance, this verb appears to have two proclitic pronominals, *aa=* 'some' and *at=* 'thing(s), something', but these proclitics are as a rule mutually exclusive. These cannot cooccur for the same reason that one cannot say **aa haa wsiteen* 'some saw me' or **at x̱at woot'ei* 'something found me'. In Leer's "Verb Books" we find «aax̱ has kawdi.át» and «aax̱ has at kaawa.át» given as semantic equivalents, both translated there as "[they] left there one by one"; in these cases, *at-* and the *d-* element of the classifier appear to have an identical function. The verb may be inflected for various subjects, e.g., *aax̱ has atkaawa.át* 'they (several people) rushed away from there' (with third-person plural human subject), *aadé atkawduwa.át* 'the people rushed toward there' (with fourth-person human subject), *héende aa atkaawa.át* 'some rushed to the water' (with partitive subject), or *dák̲de atkaawa.át* 'they (animals) rushed inland' (with third-person object).[425] It, however, cannot be inflected for different objects; one cannot substitute an object in place of *at-*. Another interesting feature of this verb is that it remains Ø-conjugation (displayed by the short high-toned stem in the affirmative perfective mode) even when preceded by the directional postpositions *-de* 'toward' and -(*dá*)*x̱* 'from', which would ordinarily trigger *na*-conjugation. The facts together lead us to construe *at-* in this verb as something other than an ordinary pronominal and we therefore treat it as a frozen element of the verb theme in this special case and write it as part of the verb word.

Other common expressions consisting of a fixed combination of elements are also written as one word, such as *ax̱oo.aa* 'some of them', *ax̱ een.aax'w* 'my family' (literally, 'the ones with me'), and conventionalized phrases with *wáa ... sá* 'how' such as *wáananée sá* (or *wáannée sá* or *wáanée sá*) 'eventually, at some point', *wáanganeens* or *wáageens* 'sometimes', *wáaykuwáat' sá* 'how long?' etc. Note especially that we write *a yáx̱* 'like it' as two words when it literally means 'like it', but as one-word *ayáx̱* when it means 'accordingly, properly, correctly, the right way'.

Ḵuchéin X̱’éidáx̱ Tlaagú
Stories by Frank Italio

FIGURE 3. This may be the only photograph that exists of Frank Italio. This is a detail of a larger image taken on glass plate in Dry Bay, c. 1918. He stands inside *Xeitl Hít* 'Thunderbird House', a Shangukeidí clan house erected in Dry Bay in 1909. Behind him is the *Xeitl X̱'éen* 'Thunderbird Screen', which now resides at the Alaska State Museum in Juneau. Photo by Fhoki Kayamori. Courtesy of Bryn Mawr College Special Collections, BMC-1975-06, box 13, folder 2. See de Laguna, *Under Mount Saint Elias*, plate 215, 1144–55, for the full image and further details and identification.

BACKGROUND NOTES. The first tales of this volume were told by K̲uchéin, Frank Italio, of Yakutat, Alaska.* He was a member of the Shangukeidí clan and a child of the L'uknax̲.ádi. He was born on July 7, 1870, and passed away on April 20, 1956. These performances were recorded in Yakutat by Frederica de Laguna on three separate occasions in 1952 and 1954. Italio was eighty-two and eighty-four years of age at the times of these recordings and passed away two years after the 1954 performance. The recording quality is extraordinarily good given the era.

On August 29, 1952, Italio began an extended tale consisting of "Raven and His Uncle" (FI I, i), "Raven Goes Down Along the Bull Kelp" (FI I, ii), and the first half of "Raven Deceives His Younger Brother" (FI I, iii, 1–133); de Laguna's reel-to-reel tape ran out after about twenty-four minutes of narration, abruptly cutting off the performance. Italio resumed the tale on September 13, completing "Raven Deceives His Younger Brother" (FI I, iii, 134–64) and following this with "Raven and the Whale" (FI I, iv) and, lastly, "Raven and the Daylight" (FI I, v). Although fifteen days passed between the two recording sessions, Italio created a seamless transition by resuming exactly where the tape had cut the story short. Together these clearly form a cohesive and intentional sequential narration, so we consider all of the 1952 material to constitute a single extended tale consisting of five episodes. The title we have applied to the 1952 tale taken as a whole is «L At Yéx̲ Yóo Udzigitgi Yéil», in English "Raven Who Breaks All the Rules", which is based on a line from the text, «Yéi du ÿáa wduwasáa Yéil [...] l at yéx̲ yóo unasgít yís»† 'He had been given the name Raven [...] for his inappropriate behavior'. The theme of Raven breaking rules, disrupting

* Minnie Johnson states on a recording that Italio had a second name in addition to K̲uchéin. It sounded to us like *K̲'adaahéets'i*, but the recording was not clear enough to be certain. MC047, "02-05 Explanation of Song for Thunderbird Screen".

† FI I, iii, 23–24. See the note to that line for further discussion.

established states of affairs, and generally acting mischievously is present throughout the five episodes of this tale.

On May 7, 1954, during de Laguna's second major research trip to Yakutat, Italio again told her an extended tale of Raven's adventures. We have used the title «Lyax̱dats'éinix̱ Siteeyi Yéil», in English "Raven the Troublemaker", based also on a line from the narration in which Italio refers to Raven as «lyax̱dats'éini súk»* 'a troublemaker in the making' or 'a troublemaker-to-be'. This tale contains a variety of themes from Raven's escapades all mingled together and does not lend itself to being divided into discrete episodes.

Present with Italio and de Laguna at the 1952 recordings was Minnie Johnson, a L'uknax̱.ádi woman whose Tlingit name was Ts'oowdalé. De Laguna and Johnson are occasionally heard on the recordings and their lines of speech are identified in the text. Johnson was a close friend of Italio and a regular consultant and interpreter for de Laguna. Working from the tape recordings on three separate occasions (September 2, 13, and 14, 1952), Johnson provided an English interpretation of Italio's 1952 performance to de Laguna, which is published in volume 2 of *Under Mount Saint Elias.*† Johnson's interpretations provided key insights for the transcription and translation of Italio's performances and we cite her words amply throughout the notes to Italio's texts; many instances that would have left us scratching our heads were illuminated in crucial ways by her interpretations. During the recording of Italio's 1954 performance, Helen Bremner, who was G̱alyáx̱ Kaagwaantaan with the Tlingit name S'uk̲lakéi, was present to serve as the interpreter for de Laguna and her lines of speech are identified in the text of "Raven the Troublemaker". John Ellis, a K̲ookhittaan man whose Tlingit name was K̲áataan, provided an English interpretation for de Laguna from the tape; the text of Ellis' interpretation appears in *Under Mount Saint Elias* as well.‡ Ellis' interpretations were also of great value in the process of transcribing and translating the 1954 performance.§

REMARKS ON NARRATIVE STRUCTURE. De Laguna notes that her interpreter John Ellis described Italio's 1954 narration as "mixed up" because "the episodes were not told in very connected fashion."¶ Elsewhere de Laguna commented, "On May 7, 1954, Frank Italio again told the whole story of Raven in Tlingit, though evidently a shorter and confused version."** The reader or listener is likely to understand the moti-

* FI II, 173. See the note to that line for further discussion.

† De Laguna, *Under Mount Saint Elias*, 848–51.

‡ Ibid, 855–57.

§ De Laguna notes, "John Ellis, was both patient and skilled in questions pertaining to Tlingit linguistics." Ibid, vi. When de Laguna returned to Yakutat in February 1954, she rented a house belonging to Ellis. Ibid, 9.

¶ Ibid, 855–56.

** Ibid, 1152.

vation for these characterizations when reading the 1954 text (FI II) after having read the 1952 material (FI I). The composition of the two tales is palpably different. However, because we have relied so heavily in matters of interpretation on de Laguna's publication in which Italio's material is described in this way, we feel it important to caution against the idea that Italio was confused in his 1954 performance or that the tale represents some sort of aesthetic or conceptual decline on his part.

The early work of Richard Dauenhauer is instructive in this regard. In his 1975 doctoral dissertation, "Text and Context of Tlingit Oral Tradition", Dauenhauer applied structuralist and formalist techniques of literary analysis to Tlingit oral texts. He appealed to a common distinction in these fields between 'syntagmatic' and 'paradigmatic' approaches to the study of literary texts, which is useful in thinking about the compositional differences in Italio's performances. A syntagmatic approach focuses primarily on the linear sequence of events in a narrative, much like the syntactic order of terms in a sentence. A paradigmatic approach, on the other hand, attempts to uncover an underlying system of associated terms and concepts that form a coherent whole irrespective of the linear order in which they appear in a narrative. Rather than preferring one approach over the other, to Dauenhauer the effectiveness of each approach is in large part dependent on the material in question, "T.S. Eliot, Gottfried Benn, Paavo Haavikko and others are impossible to read unless the images are arranged in paradigmatic form, much the same as finding common denominators in fractions. [...] This contrasts with the reading of a poet such as Robert Frost, for whom the images may be taken in the linear sequence in which they are presented, i.e., in syntactical order."* We can follow Dauenhauer's thinking when it comes to Italio's texts, though rather than dealing with different authors, we are dealing with a single storyteller composing related material in different ways at different times. Italio's 1954 text is more akin to Dauenhauer's depiction of Eliot, Benn, and Haavikko and his 1952 material is closer to the depiction of Frost.

The narrative elements in Italio's 1952 tale have a clearly discernible linear movement, with the order of events in the plot corresponding closely to the order in which the action is narrated. For the most part, one thing leads to the next. The composition has a syntagmatic organization and lends itself to a reading in which the imagery is taken in the order Italio presents it: Raven is born; he bests his jealous uncle; his uncle floods the world; Raven seeks a way to make the flood subside; he obtains sea urchins as a tool to accomplish this goal; he goes to Little-Elder-Who-Enlarged-the-Tide with the urchins in his pocket; etc. Italio's presentation of the material in this tale is relatively straightforward and readers without prior exposure to the oral tradition surrounding Raven will not have much difficulty following along. In the 1954 tale, however, the sequential order in which Italio presents the images

* Dauenhauer, "Text and Context of Tlingit Oral Tradition", 42–43, note 14.

and events, and the images and events he chooses to present, have little to do with the chronology of underlying plot elements. This tale is difficult to make sense of unless the reader or listener has some prior understanding of Raven's deeds and is able to separate the array of images from the order in which they are narrated and reassemble them in their mind. One thing often does not lead to the next in a causal or developmental way; Italio leaps abruptly between discontinuous images and partially elaborated scenes. Italio begins with events surrounding Raven's birth, jumps to Raven calling across the Akwe River to the Night-Dwellers, from there moves to Raven's interaction with Little-Elder-Who-Enlarged-the-Tide, then to Raven's interaction with his uncle's wife, returns again to the Akwe, is soon back again with Little-Elder-Who-Enlarged-the-Tide, then moves far to the west with Raven hunting a whale from a skin kayak, then to Raven's activities at the head of the Nass River, and finally returns once more to the Akwe with Italio singing the two songs Raven composed on the river's shore. The composition of this tale is more paradigmatic than syntagmatic; the tale's material is controlled less by a plot that progresses from scene to scene than by a body of associated images and ideas. The "common denominator", in Dauenhauer's terms, is of course the figure of Raven. We can agree with Ellis that Italio in 1954 presented the material in a 'mixed-up' fashion, but we take this in a purely descriptive sense: it is as if Italio selected a handful of themes and images pertaining to Raven from among his total mental collection, shuffled them together, and spread them out before us to form a collage.

PHONOLOGICAL NOTES. Italio tends to pronounce two common postpositions, *P-dáx̱* 'from P' and *P yáx̱* 'like P', as *P-déx̱* and *P yéx̱*, respectively. In some old Tlingit songs we also find that *yáx̱* 'like' is pronounced *yéix̱* when it is lengthened to fit the melody of the song, so we can conclude that *P yéx̱* is actually an older form than *P yáx̱* 'like P'; note that Frank Dick also uses *P yéx̱* alongside *P yáx̱*. Furthermore, Italio and Dick (both of Yakutat) tend to pronounce words like *N sákw* 'N-to-be, future N' and *deisgwach* 'gradually' as *N súk* and *deisguch*. We have done our best to write these elements as Italio pronounced them in each instance instead of applying a standardization.

Also of note is the fact that we often find cases in these recordings of Italio where we do not hear the possessive pronoun *a* 'its; his/her/their (recessive)' where we would expect it to occur before relational nouns. In such cases, it could be that he simply did not use any such pronoun; it may be that in his day and age, third-person pronominals with obvious third-person reference might have been omissible. We find hints of this with other speakers, such as Susie James, who says, «L k̲'adaat k̲aa tooshtí»,* nobody paid any attention to what he said', in place of the plainer version,

* SJ xi, 15.

«tléi-éil du ḵ'adaat ḵaa tooshtí»,* which she in fact uses later on in the same story; the possessive pronoun *du* is missing in the first variant. And we find lexicalized constructions where nobody uses a third-person possessive pronoun before certain relational noun plus postposition combinations, e.g., «x̱'ét ashukaawax̱ích»,† 'he slammed the lid shut', where there can be no possessive pronoun before *x̱'é-t* (literally, 'mouth-to'). This leads us to believe that, at least in some of these cases, the third-person possessive pronoun was simply omitted by Italio as superfluous. On the other hand, we have to reckon with a different possibility, namely that in some cases he did provide the possessive pronoun *a*, but that he did so with very low volume, such that it was below the threshold of reproducibility on the recording. This might also account for some instances where we could not hear the stem of the verb, or where we heard only the initial consonant of the verb stem.

* SJ xi, 234.

† FI I, iii, 127.

I. L At Yéx̱ Yóo Udzigitgi Yéil

Shkalneek i. Yéil ḵa Du Káak

Yéil, {…}x̱ siteeyi át
ḵa yú dís—
  TS’OOWDALÉ: *Dei ÿaa kanilaník áwé.*
yú dís áyú,
du káakx̱ sitee, yá lingit’aanikáx’ ḵwá yéi yatee yú dís,
tléil yú dikéex̱ wulxáat’.
Haaw,
x̱at x̱’akakg̱eenéek ágé? Ách áyá {…},
ách áwé tléil—.
  TS’OOWDALÉ: *Yá a tóode yoo x̱’eeyatangi át áwé, tlákw ÿaa kaklaneek.*
Aaá.
Áwé
yáa tl’atgikáa yéi teeyí,
yú dís ḵu.aa,
ldakát lingit’aantuḵwáanich áyú du jee akawdlix̱éitl’.
Yá ḵées’
du jeenáx̱ kawuhaaÿích,
Yooḵis’kooḵéik yóo áyú duwasáakw yú dís.
Lingítch yéi yasáakw
Yooḵis’kooḵéik.
Á áwé,
áwé yáa—
yáa tl’atgikáa yéi teeyée áwé,
du dlaak’ jeex’ tlél yát awuswáat.

I. Raven Who Breaks All the Rules

Episode i. Raven and His Uncle

Raven, a being that is {…},
and the moon—
  MINNIE JOHNSON: *You're already telling the story.*
the moon
was his uncle; but the moon was here on the earth.
It wasn't suspended up above in the sky.
Well,
are you going to interpret what I say? This is why {…},
that's why I'm not—.
  JOHNSON: *It's this recorder you are speaking into; continue telling the story.*
Okay.
So,
when he was here on the earth,
the moon, that is,
all of the inhabitants of the world were afraid of what he could do.
Because the tide
was under his authority,
the moon was called Tide-Commander.
The Tlingit people call him
Tide-Commander.
So,
when—
when he was on the earth,
he did not allow any children to be raised in his sister's care.

Du dlaak' k̲udzitee.
Tle yéi k̲unastéeni áwé
du goox̲x'ú yéi ayanask̲éich—.
Ldakát yá lingit'aantuk̲wáani áyá goox̲x'úx̲ awliyéx̲ yú dís.
Yú du jee akoolx̲éitl'—yá k̲ées'i akoolx̲éitl' k̲u.aa áyú yóo kaawagei,
ch'u tle ch'a aadóo sá yéi ayawsik̲aa tle du jeex̲ goot,
tle ch'a hú.
Á áwé,
áx' áwé
yéi yaawak̲aa—.
Yú du dlaak',
wáanée sáwé
hóoch'x̲ wusitee du wátx'i. Ch'u tle áwé
goox̲x' áwé yéi ayanask̲éich,
«Aadé naÿ.á!
Daa sáyú k̲uwdzitee?»
«K̲áa áyú.»
«Agajaak̲!
Agajaak̲!» tle yóo aÿanask̲éich du dlaak'.
Aadé k̲ukunak̲éich.
Du x̲'ayáx̲ áwé tle oojaak̲ch. Tsu yú du dlaak'
    du jee akwdlix̲éitl' yú k̲ées'.
Ách
tle oojaak̲ch wé shaawát du wádi,
k̲áax̲ wusteeyí
tsoo shaawátx̲ sateeyí
yéi kawduneegí.
Yú du shát eedé ÿax̲ ÿagax̲dusk̲áa.
Ách áwé ch'u tle tsu oojaak̲ch tle yú shaawát tsú
du x̲'ayéx̲.
Tlél k̲waayú ín áyú du x̲'awoolnáx̲ unashú
áa yóo k̲aa jikungak̲éigín áwé.
Tléik'.
De ch'a hóoch' áwé, aadé kdunik yé áyá, du x̲'ayéx̲ áyú.
Du x̲'éix' áyú akawdlix̲éitl' yú—
yú du dlaak' k̲u.aa.
Aadéx̲ áwé,
wáananée sáwé,
hóoch', de ÿát du jeet shoowaxíx.

He had a sister.
As one was being born,
he would tell his slaves—.
The moon had made all of the world's inhabitants into slaves.
The fear of his power—the fear of the floodtide had become so pervasive that
whomever he told to do so would submit to his power,
his alone.
So,
at that point
he said—.
As for his sister,
eventually
all her children had been eradicated.
He would just tell the slaves,
"Go there!
What is it that has been born?"
"It's a male."
"Let my slaves kill it!
Let them kill it!" he would say to his sister.
He would send people there.
They would kill it at his word. Even his sister was afraid
of his power and the floodtide.
That's why
they would always kill the child of that woman,
when it was determined
whether it was male,
or even if it was female.
Someone could smuggle a message to his wife.
That's why they would still kill it, even if it were a female,
at his command.
But there was no obsidian sticking up through her doorway
whenever he would order people there to do it.
No.
That's all there was to it. This is the way it is told; it was as he commanded.
His sister lived in—
in fear of his pronouncements.
So then,
eventually,
that was that; she ran out of children.

«Ei-ei áyáa-áa-áa!»
X'aa luká áwé áa g̱ax̱ nuch
wé shaawát,
x'aa luká.
Wáanée sáyá Kéet du eeg̱iyáa yaawagóo.
Tle anax̱ ÿánde akaawanáa wé aanḵáawuch.
Gushtuwool
yóo duwasáakw
Kéet Aanḵáawu.
Du eeg̱aÿáanáx̱ ÿan uwaḵúx̱,
tle ash x̱áni yéi uwagút.
«Wáa sáyá x̱'ayeeḵá yáat?»
«Aaa, ax̱ ÿátx'u sáani ax̱ jeet shoowaxíx, cha Aanḵáawu.
Hóoch'.
Hasdu ítde áyá yéi x̱'ayax̱aḵá.
Yú ax̱ éek' x̱'ayéx̱ áyú.»
Awsikóo hóoch ḵu.aa
yú ḵées' du jeenáx̱ kawuhaayí.
Tléil wáa sá—tléil wáa sá aÿawusḵaaÿí áwé ch'u tle,
aan—
aan wudzigeet.
Du kinaak.ádi tle kaax̱ kéi awditée,
yú du doogú áyá. Ch'u shóogu lingítx̱ sitee
yú Gushtuwool ḵu.aa.
Tle wé shaawáttin áwé
at géide s wudzigeet tle.
Haaw,
atx̱ áwé ÿan aÿawsiḵáa,
«Yá ts'ootaatx' yan wulaayí ch'u tle yú ḵées'—
ḵées' áx̱ laa ÿé,
aadé áwé kg̱eegóot.
Áx̱ ÿaa ḵikg̱eetées'.
Té aax̱ ÿit'eiÿí yéi kugeiyí,
daakdadúgu ch'u tlei ch'a k'idéin
atx̱ kéi kg̱eetée.
Tle gankáa daak gag̱eetée.
Gankáx' áwéi ÿakg̱isat'áa.
Ḵúnáx̱ tl'éx̱ yáx̱ ÿawut'aaÿí áwé tsá
kéi kg̱ilaxwéin tle kikg̱eenóot'.

"He-ey aya-a-ah!"
On the tip of a point of land the woman
would weep,
on the tip of a point.
At some point a flotilla of Killerwhales appeared offshore from her.
The Killerwhale Headman commanded the flotilla ashore.
Hole-in-the-Dorsal-Fin
is the name of
the Killerwhale Headman.
He landed at the shore below her,
got out of his canoe, and walked up to her.
"What are you carrying on about here?"
"Yes, O Headman, all my children have died off on me.
They're all gone.
I am crying for their loss.
They were killed at my brother's command."
Hole-in-the-Dorsal-Fin himself knew
that the floodtide was under her brother's control.
Without—without saying anything to her,
with her—
he performed the act with her.
He took off his coat,
which was his skin. You see, Hole-in-the-Dorsal-Fin
was the same as a human being.
He and the woman just
performed the unnatural act.
Well,
after that he explained the plan to her,
"In the morning when the tide has gone all the way down,
you will go to
the place the tide recedes to.
You should proceed to search about there.
When you find a stone there that's this big,
a solid one without blemishes, you should very carefully
pick it up from there.
Then you are to put it in the fire.
You are to heat it up in the fire.
Only once it's really nice and warm,
you are to scoop it up and swallow it.

Tléil x̲'éi kg̲idanook,»
yóo áwé ash daaÿak̲á.
Ayéx̲ áwé yéi jeewanei wé shaawát.
Haaw,
k̲eina.áa,
k̲eix̲'é áwé sh wudzix̲ék̲.
Éi! Yan kawlikúx wé k̲ées'.
Áx̲ ÿaa nagúdi yá éik̲ awsiteen wé té, yéi kugoogek'i té.
Tle k'wát' yáx̲ kaaxát, daakdidúk tle.
Tle dáak̲x' daak̲ uwagút, tle gankáa daak aawatée.
Gankáa daak atée áwé
tl'éx̲ yáx̲ ÿaawat'áa, aadé ash shukoojeis' yéyéx̲
a yeenáx̲ ayaawatsák̲ tsu daa sá.
Du lakát akaawag̲íx'i
tlél x̲'éi awdanook, áwé tle aawanóot'.
Goosú tlax̲ yéi yaawat'aÿi át l x̲'éi oodanoogún?
Hóoch'.
Tle tlél daa sá du yíkde tóo oonook tsú.
Du yík ÿawut'aaÿí áyú aadé tóo akg̲wanóok yóo a daa tuwatee.
Tléik'.
Ei-ei-ei-ei wáannée sáwé
deisguch
dís—
du dísi yaa shunaxíx.
Dís yaa nas.át.
Áyá tsá hóoch'i aaÿí ÿawdzik̲een.
«Líl i éek' wak̲shiyeex' k̲u.aa,
yéi k̲usteech yéix' i yétx'i x'wán,»
ÿan yóo ash yasik̲éik,
wé—wé du wadák'u.
Aadéx̲ áwé,
hóoch',
ch'a yant'éix' áwé ÿatwoo.oo.
Tle tlél tsu du toowú tín tsú utí,
ch'a wéit'át tuwáx' kwshéiwé du éet wudasheeyí.
Ei-ei, deisguch yaa nawát,
deisgwach yaa nawát.
Ch'a yant'éix' áwé áx' yaa anaswát.
Du x̲ánt u.aatch wé du éek' goox̲x'ú, tléik',

You won't feel the heat in your mouth,"
he said to her.
The woman did just that.
Well,
the next day
she roused herself at daybreak.
Ey! The tide had completely dried up.
As she was walking down the beach she saw the stone, a tiny stone.
It was just round and solid with no imperfections.
Then she walked further up from the beach and put it on the fire.
When she put it on the fire,
it became nice and hot; just as he instructed her
she poked something or other down under it.
When she tossed it into her mouth,
she didn't feel the heat; she just swallowed it.
How was it that she hadn't felt such a hot object in her mouth?
That's all there was to it.
She didn't feel anything inside her body either.
She thought she was going to feel her insides getting warm.
Nope.
Ey-y-y-y, eventually,
gradually,
her menstrual cycles—
she stopped having her menstrual cycles.
The months were passing.
Finally, the last new moon came.
"Don't give birth where your brother can see;
be sure not to have this child where your children were born,"
 he kept warning her,
that young man of hers.
Then,
that was that;
she gave birth in seclusion.
She no longer had reservations
as to whether that creature intended to help her.
Ey-y, the child was gradually growing up,
gradually growing up.
She was raising him in seclusion.
Her brother's slaves would come to her, but no;

a waak̲ nák̲ oolsínch.
Wáanée sáwé deisgwach at t'úkt wé neil.
Áwé tsáa káx̲ akanasteech chooneit yéx̲.
Áa at t'úkt wé neil.
Yax̲.atg̲wakú keitl yaanawádi yéx̲ áwé ÿatee.
Éh!
Shde k̲áax̲ sateeyí áwé,
yéi áwé ch'a hú chooneit chush jiyís awdliyéx̲ tle.
Ÿan alyéix̲déx̲ áwé
woogoot. Aan nagútch.
Wáananée sáwé
x'éig̲aa
at uwat'úk.
Jiwdihoo wé gáaxw,
áwé aawat'úk.
De ash een ÿan akaawaník yú du káak aadé yéi jine yé
du tláach k̲u.aa.
(DU JÍN AAWAT'ÁCH)
Éh!
Atx̲ tóot awsitáa, adax̲ daak̲ awsitáa.
Tle du tláa x̲ánt awustaaÿée áwé
alx'éesh.
Yá a dix̲'kaanáx̲ áwé aawak̲'ék'w
du tláa—
du tláach.
Ch'u tle yóo áwé daatx̲ aawatee, tle a kíjitín,
ldakát tle a x̲'oosí,
tle yéi áwé.
Chaa ch'a aag̲áa áwé tsáa wé k'eeljáa yéi aÿakdatée áwé
yéi aÿawsik̲aa du tláa,
«K'e tóox̲ nagú, atléi, k'e tóox̲ nagú.»
Tle a tóode woogoot
wé du tláa.
Ík̲de yéik̲ nashíx—
he.é—tle daak jiwdihóo.
Du kaadé yóo
teet yóo wuneeyí áwé tle a taÿeedé kát shaadax̲eechch.
Du kaanáx̲ kéi u—
diginaa áwéi-éi át wulitéet.

she would hide the child from their eyes.
Eventually he was shooting a bow and arrow around the house.
At last he would don a string of little sticks to use as arrows.
He would shoot arrows at things inside the house.
As the proverb goes, he was growing up as fast as a dog.
Eh!
Now that he was a man,
he made his own arrows for himself.
When he was done making them,
he left. He always brought them along.
At some point
he actually
shot something.
A duck was swimming on the water,
so he shot it.
His mother had already informed him of
what his uncle was up to.
  (SLAPS HANDS)
Eh!
He picked up the duck, took it for himself, and then brought it up.
When he brought it to his mother,
she skinned it.
She slit it open along the back,
his mother—
his mother did.
Then she took the skin off the body like this, wings and all,
  and even the feet,
just like that.
Only when the storm wind was picking up
did he say to his mother,
"You should get inside this duck skin, mother, you should get inside it."
His mother
then entered it.
She began running down to the beach—
gosh—and swam out to sea on the surface of the water.
When the waves
come over her, she would just dive beneath them.
{When the waves washed} over her
she bobbed along on the waves out toward the o-open water.

Ei-ei-ei,
wáananée sáwé de
yan jiwdihóo.
Ax̱'eiwawóos', «Wáa sás i ée ÿatee?»
«Tle atk'é áhé,» yóo,
«Tle ch'u shóogu yáax' {ḵux̱wasteeyéyéx̱} x̱á x̱áa ÿatee,»
yóo áwé adaaÿaḵá
du ÿéet.
Atx̱ áwé du aayée sákw
aawat'úk.
Á ḵu.aa
yá a lú—
Gus'x̱lugooḵ
yóo áyú duwasáagu át áyú—
yóo lukoowáat'.
Áwé a shanáa daak aawatée.
Tle a tóox̱ wugoodí áwé tle kindachóon kéi wdiḵín.
Tle yú xáats't áwé wdiḵín.
Éh!
Tle yú du lú
wáa sá koowáat' tle a yéx̱ a tóode yawdig̱eech.
Ch'a át áwé sh wudlitool.
Tlél tsu ch'a gég̱aa yóo anasneech, tléik'.
Wáannée sáwé
áa g̱unéi akawlitéx̱'.
Tle daak sh wudix̱ích yínde,
tle yáa tl'átgi káa ÿaa wdzigeet.
Tle k'idéin awsinee, k'idéin atéen.
De a kát woosh kát ÿawdidaa yú du káak ḵu.aa.
Wáannée sáwé deisguch
dulnáax'w íḵdé.
G̱una.aandé kg̱waḵóox̱.
G̱una.aant wuḵoox̱ akwshitán.
Éh!
Ch'u tle yaa ÿakandaÿíg̱i yant'éide,
tle yáax' áwé tle aadé woogoot.
Tsu yeekawliyáat'éyáx̱ áwé.
Hé'!
Wé goox̱x'—

Ey-y-y,
eventually
she swam ashore.
He asked, "How is it for you?"
"This is a neat thing," she said,
"To me, you see, it's just like it was when I lived my life here before,"
she told
her son.
After that, he shot one
to serve as his own.
But the beak
of the one he shot for himself—
it was the creature that is called
Pokes-Nose-Into-Clouds—
it had a long beak.
He took the skin off over its head.
When he had donned the skin, he just flew straight up.
Raven just flew up to the firmament.
Eh!
He stuck the entire length
of his beak into it.
He just spun himself around.
He wasn't just doing this for fun, no.
Eventually
he began to twist it free.
He then hurled himself downwards
and fell down onto the ground.
He cleaned up the skin and carefully stored it away.
He would stop by at intervals to keep an eye on his uncle.
At some point,
bundles were gradually being taken down to the beach.
His uncle was going to travel to some other town.
He was in the habit of going around to different towns.
Eh!
As he was disappearing from sight behind a landmass,
Raven started walking toward his uncle's house.
It seems to have taken a really long time.
Heh!
Those slaves—

aax̱ at wujix̱einéyáx̱ áwé ÿatee wé neil.
Haaw.
Tle yéi aÿawsiḵaa, ax̱'eiwawóos',
«Goosú yú shaawát?
Yú ax̱ káak shát goosú hú?»
Yú s'eyatóot áwé du een wuduwach'íx̱', «Yóodu hú.»
Át awdlig̱ín, át gwáa akawliyaa. Ḵóok yíkt—
ḵóok yíkt as.áa yú du shát.
Tle dzeit át ashawsitán,
áa kéi uwagút.
Ch'u súg̱aa áwé a shuyeedé g̱ax̱.istí wéit,
yú goox̱x',
wé ḵées' kakg̱wadaaÿí.
Anax̱ aÿawsi.ín tle,
tle gánde.
Gáanx' áwé tsáa ÿanáax̱ aÿawlik'úts.
Daax̱ aÿawlik'úts
ách kawdudzi.ax̱u át.
A yíknáx̱ kéi aawax̱út' wé du káak shát.
A jín yéi awsinei—
Éeneekóon áyú aawasháa—
tle atx̱ áwé ax'óol'.
Gáant kanalÿichji át áyá, kóon.
«Gáant,» yóo áwé x̱'aÿaḵá.
Kalÿíchx',
tle kalÿíchx', tle kalÿíchx' du jeedáx̱,
tle héinax̱.á aa tsú.
Ch'a wéix' áwé du x̱einínáx̱ kawdliyeech.
«Ax̱ adée!»
tle yóo waawaḵaa,
Yooḵis'kooḵéik ḵu.aa, «Ax̱ adée!
Daa sákwshé
(AT.SHOOḴ)
a tóonáx̱ ayadlaḵx'u
át áyú gé?
Ḵúx̱de déi!»
Tle ḵúx̱de akaawanáa.
Aahá.
Hóoch'.

the inside of the house was in shambles.
Well.
Then he said to them, he asked them,
"Where is that woman?
My uncle's wife, where is she?"
They pointed him to the inside of the gable of the roof, "There she is."
He looked at it; lo and behold, his uncle had left her dangling there. In a box—
he had his wife sit in a box.
So Raven propped up a ladder
and climbed up to her.
There, at the foot of the ladder, those slaves were wailing
in anticipation,
fearing that the tide might return.
Raven just carried the box through there
and outside.
Once he was outside he snapped the lines over the cover of the box.
He snapped them off all around it,
the lines with which it had been bound.
He pulled his uncle's wife up out of the box.
He grabbed her by the arm—
his uncle had married Flicker-Pits—
and he was just plucking the flickers out.
It's a creature that flies outside, the flicker.
"*Gáant*," is what it says.
They were flying,
just flying, just flying out of his hands,
and the ones from the other armpit too.
Right there those flickers caught up with his uncle.
"My precious stuff!"
Tide-Commander said,
"My precious stuff!
What could it be,
(LAUGHTER)
that creature that's getting bunches of flickers from in there;
is that what's going on?
Go back now!"
He just ordered the boat to go back.
Aha.
That was that.

Ḵux̲ wudiḵúx̲.
Tlei tléil adax̲ gwáayá a tú du shát.
Tle yéi áwé
at wooxoon
tle yáa dikéede.
Wé dís ḵu.aa, wé Yooḵis'kooḵéik, hú áwé,
ách áwé dikée kéi uwaxíx, ch'a hú du ḵées'i jináḵ.
Aaa.
Shaawatl'ít' áyá lingit'aaní.
Ḵées' akawsidaa.
Hóoch'.

Shkalneek ii. Yéil Geesh Daax̲ Wugoodí

Ei-ei-ei!
Tle xáats't wudiḵín.
Du tláa tsú ch'u yéi áwé át jiwdihoo.
Tlél du tóon at utí.
Ÿax̲ has aÿawlijáḵ yóo oowajée.
Ei-ei-ei!
Aadéx̲ áwéi-éi-éi
deisguch yáa yéi naléin.
Ehehehei!
Ch'oo shóogu át kaawadayi yé.
Ch'u shóogu át kaawadaÿi ÿé.
Wáananée sáwé áa yéi akawlitéx̲'
tle daak sh wudix̲ích yínde.
Íh!
Ḵúnáx̲ yú
nées' áa yéi yateeyi yé,
ag̲áa áwé tle át wudiḵín. {A kináak ḵwá ḵukaawaḵín.}
G̲eesh
yínde kdixwás'.
Geesh áyá.
Yá aadé kdixwas'i yéix' áwé yéi yatee wé át,
wé nées'.
Ách áwéi
geesh daax̲ áwé yéi woogútch aadé
du jeet aa g̲axeexít.

He returned in his boat.
But then, lo and behold, his wife was no longer inside the box.
Just like that,
he got ready to go
up above.
Now that moon, Tide-Commander himself,
 that's why he rose up into the sky, escaping his own floodtide.
Yes.
The world was covered in water.
He had caused the floodtide to flow.
That was that.

Episode ii. Raven Goes Down Along the Bull Kelp

Ey-y-y!
Raven had flown to the firmament.
And his mother continued swimming around on the water.
She wasn't concerned about anything.
Tide-Commander thought he had killed them off.
Ey-y-y!
After that,
the tide gradually started going out here.
Eh-heh-heh-hey!
The tide level remained the same.
The tide level remained the same.
At some point, Raven twisted his beak out like that
 and flung himself down below.
Eh!
Then he flew
right to where
the sea urchins were. {He flew over them.}
Stipes of bull kelp
were dangling downward.
It was bull kelp.
Those things, sea urchins,
were at the place where the kelp was anchored.
That's why
Raven kept going down along the bull kelp towards the sea urchins
so that he could get ahold of some.

Tle a k̲índáx̲ áwé kei ulhaashch.
Déi!
Wáananée sáwé aÿaawadlaak̲
tle wóosht ayaawakwách.
Aan kei wlihásh.
Dáak̲x’ áwé daak̲ uwagút.
Áx’ áwé anées’.
«L-l-p!»
Anallúk’ch.
Ch’a yáat áwés x̲’akandukeich.
«L-l-p!»
tle yéi.
L a daat tooshtí.
Tle tsu g̲una.aa.
Chaa ch’a wáananée sáwé de át jiwdigút
wé aadé x̲’akdukaa ÿé.
«Aa sáyá! Aa sáyá de k̲aa x̲’akwdakaa! Aa sá!»
Hm-m!
A ÿaanáx̲ aksagóo, wé g̲íl’ ÿaanáx̲,
wé nís’aa.
Tle ÿakawduwahanéyáx̲ ÿatee.
Ltu.áa tliyaanax̲.áwu
wé áx’ aawanis’i yé.
Tle hóoch’.
Aÿakaawahán wé g̲íl’.
{Naalx̲’} yóo duwasáakw wé g̲íl’,
Yéilch ÿakaawahani g̲íl’.
Tlél yéi dusáakw Yéil, yóo.
Áwéi
Yax̲ K̲ées’ Shakawdzinugu Shaanák’wch áwé tsá yéi uwasáa.
Ash yáa aawasáa Yéil, yóo.
Á áwéi-éi-éi woogoot.
Yáax’ áwé Lyóo.atkoowajeegi Shaanák’w x̲ánt uwagút.
«Daa sákwshíyáagé
ách tléil—
tlél k’idéin yéi uléich gé yáa k̲ées’,» yóo,
«Daa sákwshíyáagé yéi sitee?»
«Héh!
A x̲ánt x̲á aldél tsu.

He kept floating up just shy of the sea urchins.
Now!
Eventually he reached them
and scooped them up together in his hands.
He floated up with them.
He walked inland up from the beach.
That's where he was eating the sea urchins.
"Slurp!"
He kept sucking the meat out.
Right nearby, somebody kept imitating his slurping,
"Slurp!"
just like that.
He didn't pay it any attention.
Then he heard another one.
So at last he went to where the person was imitating his slurping sounds
to attack him.
"Who is it! Who is this imitating a person's sounds now! Who!"
Hm!
He was jabbing a knife for prying open sea urchins
into the face of that cliff.
It's as if the cliff were cut into strips.
The place where he ate sea urchins
is on the far side of Lituya Bay.
That's all there was to it.
He had cut the face of that cliff into strips.
That cliff is called {*Naalx̱'*},
the cliff whose face Raven cut into strips.
He wasn't called Raven back then.
It was
Little-Elder-Who-Enlarged-the-Tide who first named him that.
He bestowed the name Raven on him.
So the-e-en Raven set out walking.
Here he came up beside Unfazable-Little-Elder.
"I wonder why
it should be the case
that the tide doesn't go out so well?" Raven said,
"I wonder why this should be the case?"
"Heh!
He watches over it.

Ḵáa shaanák'w a x̱ánt aldél, yóot'aa aÿa.óo.
Tlél aadé ÿan kux̱likooxu ÿé.
Chaa ch'a hú du jeenáx̱ áwé tsá yánde kux̱lakóox,»
yóo áwés.
{keitl ḵunáax̱i}x̱ awliyéx̱.
Tle aadé woogoot a x̱ánde.
Awsiteen.
Ei! Gwáawé gánt uwatáa
du díx̱'—.
«Éhhhh,»
tle yóo waawaḵaa.
De a dzúkde yanax̱ ayaawataan.
«Nées' g̱ehéen tlax̱ x̱at sawli.át',»
yú.á.
Yéi áwé.
Wáannée sáwé
de ash x̱'akaadáx̱ áa yéi nasgéet áwé
tsá yéi ash ÿawsiḵaa,
«Cha goot'ayéig̱aa sá wulaaÿi
léin áwé a kát eeyanís',
cha Yéil Tl'éetl'i?»
Tle Yéil ash yáa aawasáa.
Hóoch'.
«Tsu g̱unayéide igax̱dusáakw ltín.»
Aahá,
tle át jiwdigút.
Kindatóog̱un aawax̱eech.
Wé nées' daaklik'áts' x̱á kwshíyú yéi nateech.
Tuḵdaanáx̱ áwé aksagóo.
«Tóo nú!
Nées' nóox'u tóo nú!»
«Déi, Yéil!» kéi kawdigáx̱,
«Déi, Yéi-éi-éi-éil!
Déi, Yéi-éi-éi-éil!
G̱aag̱waalaa déi Yéil!»
Aaá!
Ts'as tsu a tóot awsinée wé
«G̱aag̱waalaa Yéil,» yóo ÿawuḵaaÿí.

A little old man watches over it; he owns that thing.
There's no way the tide can dry up completely.
Only by his doing will the tide go out,"
she said.
{...}.
Then he went there to him.
He saw him.
Eh! Look at that! He slept next to the fire,
with his back to it.
"Ahhhh,"
Raven said.
Raven stuck a piece of firewood behind the old man's back.
"Sea-urchin juice has really made me chilly,"
Raven said.
That's how it went.
Eventually,
once the old man was through waving off Raven's blathering,
he said to Raven,
"Sir, when exactly would there have been a tideflat
exposed by low tide for you to have eaten sea urchins,
you Shitty-Ass Raven?"
He just bestowed the name Raven on him.
That was that.
"They're going to start calling you by a different name now, just watch."
Aha,
then Raven came and attacked him.
He flipped him upside down.
Those sea urchins have sharp spines; they're like that, I guess.
Raven jabbed them all over his butt, saying,
"Feel the burn!
Feel the burn of the sea-urchin shell!"
"Enough, Raven!" he cried out,
"Enough, Ra-a-a-aven!
Enough, Ra-a-a-aven!
The tide could go out any minute, Raven!"
Yes!
He just poked those sea-urchin spines into him again as he was saying,
"The tide could go out, Raven."

Ldinax̲k'iyéide yan kalakóox
áwé tsáa ajeewanák̲.
Tle aawax̲ích tle.
Hóoch'.

Shkalneek iii. Yéil Du Kéek' K̲ut Awulyeilí

Aag̲áa áwé woogoot.
Shaak̲x' ashasanúkx̲.
«Sheenú!
Ax̲ kéek' sákw, sheenú!
X̲ashak'ákwk'u sákw!»
yú.á,
Yéil.
(AT.SHOOK̲)
TS'OOWDALÉ: {...} *he does remember all that.*
KUX̲AANGUWUT'AAN: *So that's the end of that story.*
«K'e neesheex!»
Ts'as nalk̲áchch.
Tle yanax̲ yéi oogook̲ch.
Tsaa ts'a yóot'át áwé tsá sák̲s yóo dusáagun,
yóot ixkéex' ka.éix̲.
T'aawyáat' aaní áa ka.éix̲in áwé wéit'át.
Sák̲s x̲'aan yéx̲ nateech.
Áwé ax̲áax̲ tsú s alyeix̲ín.
Á áwé tsá
k'idéin woogoot.
Hóoch', tle du kéek'x̲ wusitee.
«Ts'as yáaÿ x'wán x̲'akla.ísh, kík'!
Ts'as yáaÿ!» yú.á.
Hú k̲u.aa wé s'áax̲' áwé ax̲'akla.eesh Yéil.
(AT.SHOOK̲)
Yéi du ÿáa wduwasáa Yéil—
e-eh—l at yéx̲ yóo unasgít yís.
Éh!
Awliyéx̲.
É'! Has astéix̲, hú tsú.
Wé s'áax̲' áwé adáakw.
Ách áwé tlél utáa s'áax̲',

Sooner or later, once the tide had finally drained away completely,
  Raven released him.
Then Raven just gave him a good thrashing.
That was that.

Episode iii. Raven Deceives His Younger Brother

Then Raven set out walking.
He was rousing up pieces of driftwood.
"Get up!
My little-brother-to-be, get up!
X̱ashak'ákwk'-to-be!"
he said—
Raven said.
  (LAUGHTER)
  JOHNSON: {…} *he does remember all that.*
  FREDERICA DE LAGUNA: *So that's the end of that story.*
"Why don't you run!"
All they could do was limp along.
Raven kept poking them down into the ground.
And so finally he tried that thing called yew;
  it grows way down in the south.
That stuff used to grow in American Indian country.
Yew wood is red.
They used to make paddles out of it as well.
This was the first one
that walked properly.
That was that; it just became his younger brother.
"Be sure to string up just whales, little brother!
Just whales!" he said.
Raven, however, was stringing up cod by the gills.
  (LAUGHTER)
He had been given the name Raven—
e-eh—for his inappropriate behavior.
Eh!
He made it.
Eh! They kept boiling the catch, even Raven.
He was rendering oil from the cod.
That's why cod aren't fat,

Yéilch wudaagóoch.
Yóot'át tsú, náaḵw—
náaḵw tsú aawadákw.
De ch'a a taaÿí áyóo a daaleilíx̱ sitee á ḵu.aa.
Hé'!
Hóoch' áwé.
Wáannée sáwé deisgwach
has ḵuwa.óo.
É'!
Du daneitx'í X̱ashak'ákwk'
ÿaa tandag̱át.
Éh! Du x̱'ax̱ánt at shoowaxíx Yéil.
Ash x̱'éix̱ at gug̱ateex̱ yóo áyú oowajée du kéek'.
Atk'é yáx̱ ágé x̱'éix̱ at gug̱atée?
Éh!
Wéi s'áax̱' yoowú áwé
a ÿaanáx̱—
s'aaḵ kawál'ti a ÿaanáx̱ yéi akootsaaḵch.
Ch'u tle a kaadé koolx'áas,
    ch'a a yee x̱'eit'áx̱ch.
A yee nateich.
Wáa sá hóoch'x̱ wusitee.
Deisguch hóo-óoch',
shoowaxeex.
Éh!
Shunaxéex áwé
tlél aadé adaang̱waanéiyi yé du kéek'.
«Wáa óosh daax̱ané?»
Wáannée sáwé a káx̱ tuwditaan,
«Héik'!
X̱áa adawóotl ÿaḵasaháa!»
Yéi áwé tle woogoot x̱aaÿasahéix̱.
Ch'a ldakát át yóo kdliyichgi át ḵa át loowagoog̱u át
tle yéi áwé aÿawsiháa,
    a x̱oo yóo kaawagút.
«Aadé kḵwagóot.
Yéi
yú neildé jóon kax̱laneegí,
‹G̱unéide ax̱waajoon, kík',

because Raven rendered the fat from them.
And that other creature, the octopus—
he rendered the fat from the octopus, too.
Where the fat was, now it's just flabby loose skin all over.
Heh!
That was that.
At some point they were gradually
settling into the area.
Eh!
As for X̱ashak'ákwk', his grease boxes
were stacking up.
Eh! Raven had run out of things to eat.
He thought his younger brother would be feeding things to him.
Was he going to feed him something good?
Eh!
Through the side of
a cod stomach—
he kept poking a bone fragment through the side of it.
The rendered oil was just cascading down onto the ground;
    he kept opening his mouth beneath it.
He would sleep beneath it.
Somehow it vanished.
Gradually, it ran out;
that was that.
Eh!
When it ran out
Raven could not figure out a way to deal with his younger brother.
"What could I do about this?"
Eventually Raven thought something up for it,
"Say!
How about I gather up a war party!"
So he set out to gather a war party.
He gathered together
all manner of creatures that fly and creatures that run around,
    parading back and forth among them.
"I'm going to walk over there.
Then,
as I narrate my dream in the house,
'I had a strange dream, little brother,

g̲unéide.
X̲áa haa káa wdinaak̲ yóo ax̲ajóon.›
Tle yóo ÿaa ÿanx̲ak̲éinitín a káa kéi gax̲yidanáak̲ yóo hít k'iyee.»
Yéi áwé ÿan aÿawsik̲áa.
Aadé woogoot tle aadé yaa nagut ÿé, tle tá.
Deisguch akéet.
Wáannée sáwé, «Mmm, mmm, mmm, mm, mm.»
Wáa sá át nax̲dux̲íjín
Yéil,
«Mmm, mmm, mm, mm, mm.»
Haahá!
Kawdixíl'.
Ch'a yéi x̲áawé,
«Hadóu! Wáa sá tsú x̲'aÿeek̲á?»
yéi ash ÿawsik̲aa du kéek'.
Ash t'éini woojeil, kéi wdzigít.
Kindachóon wujik̲aak̲.
«Éh!
G̲unéide awx̲aajoon kík'.
G̲unéide awx̲aajoon.
{...}, i gu.aa yáx̲ x'wán!
X̲áa áyú haa káa wdinaak̲ yóo ax̲ajóon,
x̲áa.
Áyá ch'u tle yéi iyax̲wsik̲aa,
‹X̲ashak'áa-áa-áakwk'!
Yux̲ neeshee-ee-eex!›
Ch'a yá neilnax̲.á áyú ch'a yóo x̲at dzigítk x̲át k̲u.aa.»
(AT.SHOOK̲)
«Tle yá neilnax̲.á áyá ax̲ lakaadé kanax̲lal'úx',»
yóo kwshéiwé.
(AT.SHOOK̲)
Éh!
Hóoch' áwé.
Yéi áwé ch'u tle,
ch'oo kéex' áwé yéi yaa sh kanalnígi, «G̲unéide awx̲aajoon.
X̲áa haa káa wdinaak̲,»
tle yóo ÿaa sh kanalnígitín áwé,
hóoch'.
K̲aa yayík wuduwa.áx̲ a daadé wéit.

a strange one.
I was dreaming that a war party stood against us.’
Just as I am saying this, you are all to make a stand behind the house.”
Those were the instructions he gave them.
So he went to where he was going and slept.
After a while he was snoring.
Eventually he went, “Mmm, mmm, mmm, mm, mm.”
When he had been tossing and turning for some time,
Raven would go,
“Mmm, mmm, mm, mm, mm.”
Aha!
His brother was worried.
And just like that,
“For gosh sakes! What on earth are you mumbling about?”
    his brother said to him.
He stroked Raven’s back; he woke up.
He sat straight up.
“Eh!
I had a strange dream, little brother.
I had a strange dream.
{...}; be of good courage!
I was dreaming that a war party stood against us,
a war party.
So I just told you,
‘X̲ashak’áa-áa-áakwk’!
Run outsi-i-ide!’
But as for me, I was in the house in the grip of a shamanic frenzy.”
    (LAUGHTER)
“I was inside pouring oil into my mouth and gulping it down,”
    he must have thought.
    (LAUGHTER)
Eh!
That was that.
And so, just as
he was telling the story out loud, “I had a strange dream.
A war party had stood against us,”
as he was telling the dream like this,
that was that.
They could hear the sound of people around the house there.

Ch'u aadé sh x̲'adajunéyáx̲ áwé,
«X̲ashak'áa-áa-áak'w, yux̲ neeshee-ee-eex!»
Tle yux̲ wujixeex.
Yux̲ jiwdigoot X̲ashak'ákwk'.
Éh!
Hú k̲u.aa áwé ch'a wé neil áwé,
tsu ch'u yux̲ ÿaa nashíxitín áwé,
ÿanáax̲ ayawlik'úts wé daneit—
du daneidí.
Tle a táax̲ ÿawdig̲eech.
Akawlil'úx'.
(AT.SHOOK̲)
Haa, tlax̲ wáa sákwshígí du éet yaan.uwaháa gí?
Éh!
Atx̲ áwé tsu tléix'.aa
tsu tléix'.aa,
de hóoch'i aaÿí.
Éenaa áwé wooch ítx̲ akoox̲áat'ch.
«Ah-ho-ho-ho-ho! K̲aa s'aag̲í {… een} x̲aat'óok.»
«K̲oowaják̲,» yóo kwshéiyú.
Éh!
Wáananée sáwé
hóoch'.
Neil wujixíx.
«De wáa sáwé déi k̲eeshinóok!»
A kaadé sixát.
Tle a kaadé x̲'ét ashukaawax̲ích du húnx̲w,
wé lák̲di yíkde.
Hóoch'.
Tle du waak̲ tsú {…}.
A yíx' áwé kindachóon woonook.
Íh! Sh daat akawdlil'úx' tle wé eex̲.
{…} (CH'ÉEN YAN WUDIYÍK̲)
Áwé {…}
ash wooyaa yú
du kéek'.
Ash wooyaa yú shaa ÿaadé.
Yéi duwasáakw Ch'eek'áa.

It was just like the way he had pretended to dream,
"X̲'ashak'áa-áa-áak'w, run outsi-i-ide!"
Then he ran outside.
X̲ashak'ákwk' charged outside to fight.
Eh!
Raven, however, just stayed in the house;
as soon as X̲ashak'ákwk' started running out,
Raven broke the lines over the covers of the grease boxes—
his younger brother's grease boxes.
He just dunked his face into the box of oil.
He drank it all up.
(LAUGHTER)
Well, he must have been really hungry, right?
Eh!
After that, another one,
and another one,
and then the very last one.
{He kept snapping tongs to make a loud noise.}
"Ah-ho-ho-ho-ho! Wow, I shot a person's bone {with a …}."
"He killed someone," X̲ashak'ákwk' probably thought.
Eh!
Eventually,
that was that.
X̲ashak'ákwk' ran into the house.
"What the heck are you doing!"
Raven was sticking out of the box.
So he flipped his older brother headlong into the bentwood box
and slammed the lid shut.
That was that.
His eyes {…} as well.
He sat straight up inside it.
Ih! He just guzzled up all the oil around himself.
{…} (END OF TAPE)
Then {…}
his younger brother
packed him on his back.
He packed him on his back to the face of a mountain.
It is called *Ch'eek'áa*.

A ÿaatx̱ daak wududzigíx',
 «Yéil a ÿaatx̱ daak wudusg̱éex'i yé»,
wé láḵt du een.
Ch'a yeisú tléix' ÿan wusxeexí áwé
ÿanáatx̱ yóot wujix̱ín,
daax̱ ÿawlik'úts.
Tle a yíknáx̱ yóot wudiḵín.
Ách áwé tlél du túg̱aa ushteex̱ ách kadus.ax̱w át.
«Daa sá ách x̱at keesa.aax̱w kík'?»
tle yóo wanaḵéich.
«Haa, tíx' x̱áayá!»
«Hei-ei-ei.
Ahóu! Kát ách wooch katoos.aax̱u át, ch'u tlaagóodáx̱—»
 (**AT.SHOOḴ**)
Aahóhó!
«—yéi x̱á taashukáx̱ kalxwás'ch gé?
Lax̱'éis'i kax̱aadí {…} á áwé.»
Áwé oosg̱áax̱.
Chaa ch'a ách kadus.áax̱w áwé tsá du túg̱aa wootee.
«Taashukáx̱ kalxwás'[ch] x̱áayá. Á áwé
haa tlaakáak hás ách woosh kas.aax̱u át.»
 (**AT.SHOOḴ**)
Hóhó!
Aadé at ḵukg̱wanuk yé áyá ch'u tle tsu súg̱aa aawatee.
Haaw,
aadéx̱ áyá
daak ash sag̱éex',
tléix' ÿan wusxeexí áwé a yíknáx̱ yóot wudiḵín.
Tle wdiḵeen tle.

Shkalneek iv. Yéil ḵa Yáaÿ

Ch'a yéi x'aak'w—
x'aak'w ÿat'éix' áwé sh daawdlig̱oo wé eex̱,
eex̱ x̱oot aaÿí ÿéeÿich.
Aadéx̱ áwéi-éi-éi
du kéek' ḵwa tle ḵut aawax̱eech,
tle tlél awuskú.
Teet x̱'atóode woogoot.

The bentwood box together with Raven
was thrown off the side of that mountain, which is
"the place from the side of which Raven had been thrown down".
As soon as it bounced once,
the lid flew off
and the strings around it snapped.
He just flew off out of the box.
Now then, he was never satisfied with those lashings.
"What are you tying me with, little brother?"
Raven kept saying.
"Well, it's rope, of course!"
"He-e-ey.
Oh! What we formerly used to tie each other up since ancient times—"
(LAUGHTER)
Ah-ho-ho!
"—you see, they hang down along the berm of the beach, don't they?
The beach rye roots {...}, that's what it is."
He was requesting it.
He wasn't satisfied until it had been bound with it.
"They hang down on along the beach, you see. That's what
our mother's uncles used to bind each other with."
(LAUGHTER)
Hoho!
Raven had anticipated how the situation was going to unfold.
Well,
so then,
when he threw Raven off the cliff
and the box bounced once, he flew out of it.
Then he just flew off.

Episode iv. Raven and the Whale

Just some little point—
behind a little point of land he wiped the oil from his body,
because he had been sitting in oil.
And the-e-en
he ditched his younger brother,
who didn't realize what Raven was up to.
Raven walked out into the curl of the waves.

Awsiteen wé yáaÿ
du t'ikát woox'aak.
Tle tsu héinax.aadé.
Wáanée sáwé a kináa wdikín.
Hí'!
Tle ayáx x'akunalgeich anax diséigu yé,
sh tóoch dlichéesh a yíkde wdakeení.
Wáananée sáwé a yíkde wdikeen.
Hóoch'.
A niÿaax' áwé wjikaak.
«Éh! Neil gwáayá!»
Tle neil[x] áwé du waakx' wusitee wé yáaÿ yík.
Hé'!
Taaÿ kwá ch'a yéi du ÿadaax dixwás',
a yiktaaÿí.
Áwé ch'u tle
a yíx' shóot awdi.ák.
(AT.SHOOK)
Neil gwáawéigé?
A yíx' shóot awda.aagí áwé aawaják.
Áwéi-éi-éi deisguch
du een át wootáan.
Tle ldakát yéide kahéix du daa
tsu du shakée yax gáas', goot'á sá
wuyíkt wusgeedí.
Yéi áwé
aawaják.
Ajáak,
du toowúch ku.aa anax kei kgwagóot
tsu yú anax neil wudakeeni yé.
Ajáak áwé át uwagút.
Tle yéi de tle kawdidóok.
Tle hóoch'.
Yóo wunaawóoch áwé yéi wsinei.
Hóoch' áwé.
Atx áwé deisguch oolxéis',
«Yak'éiyi l'éiwdéi-éi-éi-éi!»
yóo áwé oolxéis'.
«Yak'éiyi l'éiwdéi-éi-éi!»

He saw the whale
swimming around offshore from him.
Then it turned the other way.
Eventually Raven appeared flying over it.
Hih!
The blowhole kept opening big enough
so that he thought he would be able to fly into the whale.
At some point he flew into it.
That was that.
He landed on the near side of it.
"Eh! So this is a home!"
The inside of the whale became a home in his eyes.
Heh!
Fat was just hanging down all over around his face,
its visceral fat.
So he just
built a fire inside it.
(LAUGHTER)
So that was a home, huh?
When he built a fire inside it, he killed it.
So-o-o, gradually
it started jumping out of the water with him inside.
Then the fat got all over his body
and it kept falling over his head, everywhere,
as he tumbled about through space.
That's how
he killed it.
When he killed it,
he thought he could climb back out through the same place
through which he had flown inside.
Once he killed it, he walked up to the hole.
It was completely sealed shut.
Then, that was that.
That whale's dying caused this to happen.
That was that.
So next he gradually started wishing,
"To a fine sand bea-ea-ea-each!"
this is what he was wishing for.
"To a fine sand bea-ea-each!"

Wáananée sáwé l'éiw kaléit wulihásh.
Aaa.
Át laháash áwé
hóoch'.
Ḵul.áx̱s' du daadé.
Lingít
du daadé kg̱wagóot.
Wáannée sáyá aawa.áx̱ yóox̱'ala.átk
du daadé.
Haahá!
Wuduwat'ei
wé yáaÿ.
Áyóo Aalséix̱ {...} áwé yóo duwasáakw.
Yéilch yíkde wdaḵeeni yáaÿ áwé.
Duléich wé l'éiw—.
L'éiwx̱ sateeyí
tléil té á.
Aadé oolx̱éis'i yé.
Tle ch'a wáananée sáwé
deisguch
yóox̱'ala.átk wóochx̱ ÿaa nas.áx̱.
Wáannée sáwé a yíkde wuduwa.áx̱,
«Aadóo sá ḵaa kaanáx̱ ang̱axaashée-ée-ée-ée
yáaÿ yíkdáx̱ kéi x̱duḵeen?»
«Géh!
Daa sá wduwa.áx̱?»
tle yóo ḵuwaawaḵaa.
Yóox̱'atánk x̱áawé wduwa.áx̱.
Yóox̱'atánk áwé.
Tle yeekawliyáat'éyáx̱ áwé tlei tsu,
«Aadóo sá ḵaa kaanáx̱ ang̱axaashée-ée-ée-ée...
TS'OOWDALÉ: *«Ḵaa yéx̱ aanÿédi súk ḵaa kaanáx̱—»*
...yáaÿ yíkdáx̱ kéi x̱duḵeen?»
Wáa sá?
TS'OOWDALÉ: *«Aadóo sgé ḵaa yéx̱ aanÿédi súk*
ḵaa kaanáx̱ ang̱axaa[sh]?»
«Aan—Aanÿédi?» Tlél ḵwaawé yéi x̱wa.aax̱.
«Aanÿédi?»
Aag̱áa gé aanÿádi ḵudzitee yéi i toowúch?

Eventually it drifted to a beautiful sand beach.
Yes.
When it drifted there,
that was that.
He was listening intently to his surroundings.
A human
was going to come by him.
Eventually he could hear conversation
around him.
Aha!
People had found
the whale.
It is called {… at} the Alsek River.
That is the whale that Raven flew into.
People were yelling.
Being sandy,
there are no rocks there.
That's how he had wished it.
Eventually,
gradually,
the sounds of their conversations were mingling together.
At some point a sound came from inside the whale,
"Who could cut a hole over a fello-o-o-ow
so a fellow could fly up out of a whale?"
"Geh!
What was that noise?"
somebody said.
In fact what they heard was speech.
It was speech.
It went on for a long time, so once again he said,
"Who could cut a hole over a fello-o-o-ow…
JOHNSON: *"Nobility material like a certain fellow—"*
…so a fellow could fly up out of a whale?"
What?
JOHNSON: *"Who, being nobility material like a certain fellow, could cut a hole over a fellow?"*
"Nob—nobility?" That's not the way I heard it, though.
"Nobility?"
So you think that the nobility existed at that time?

(AT.SHOOK̲)
Aaa. Ch'a yéi áwé x̲'aÿak̲á. Yéi áwé.
Cha ch'a ayáx̲ áwé a x̲oo.aach yéi ÿaa kaklaníkch.
Haaw.
Yéi áwé.
Wáanée sáwé wduwaxaash.
Wé a yíkde áyú
ÿakawdudlixásh.
Tle ÿaa ÿakandulxáshi yóo woosh dakán yóo ndusnée áwé—
hí'!
Ch'u kunask'eich ágíyá a taaÿí
yá aadé kunaskakch yé.
Aaá,
aatlénx'.
Kée—ch'a yéi k̲aa ÿax̲oot áwé wdik̲ín.
«X̲'óo! X̲'óo! X̲'óo!»
Aaá.
Wuduwa.áx̲.
Tle kindachóon áwé kei ndak̲ín.
«X̲'óo! X̲'óo! X̲'óo! X̲'óo! X̲'óo! X̲'óo! X̲'óo!» yóo wduwa.áx̲ch.
Ch'u de yóodáx̲ tsú áyú tle yóo kínde k̲ut sawdzi.aax̲.
Tle yú xáats' tóode áwé tle k̲ut wooxeex, tle hóoch'.
Áx' áwé yeenaa yú lingít
k̲ut akaksayáa áwé tsá yóo wdik̲een.
TS'OOWDALÉ: *Hé'!*
Aanáx̲ aan yáa kg̲wagut yé,
yú tliyaax' áwé tl'atgikáa yéi wootee.
Daak̲ kandujél.
De aa dus.ée.
Aa dus.ée lák̲díx' x̲oodé, taaÿ.
Wáananée sáwé
aan yáa uwagút.
Tle a shóonáx̲ áwé át uwagút
wé aan.
«Tlél shéyágúshé a yíkde
k̲ukawdu.áax̲ákw wé yáaÿ?»
«Tléik'.»
«Tléik'.»
«Tléik'.»

(LAUGHTER)
Yes. That's just what he said. That's right.
And that's just exactly how some people continue telling it.
Well.
That's right.
Eventually they cut it.
The people cut
into the whale.
As the people began cutting it open like that and pulling the sides apart—
hih!
Apparently the opening was still too small
because of how thick the fat was at that place.
Yes,
huge pieces.
Up—he flew out right among the people's faces.
"*X̱'óo! X̱'óo! X̱'óo!*"
Yes.
That's what the people heard.
Then he just started flying straight up.
"*X̱'óo! X̱'óo! X̱'óo! X̱'óo! X̱'óo! X̱'óo! X̱'óo!*" that's how it sounded.
From a distance he flew high up and out of earshot.
Then he disappeared into the sky and that was that.
So at that point, once the people had started hauling it away
down below, he finally flew off that way.
JOHNSON: *Heh!*
The whale meat was on the ground further over from
the side along which Raven was going to approach the town.
The people were carrying it up from the beach and putting it away.
They were already cooking some of it.
They were cooking some of the fat to be stored in bentwood boxes.
Eventually
he appeared before the village.
He just walked right up to it, along the end of
the village.
"Mightn't any mysterious sounds have been heard
coming from inside the whale?"
"No."
"No."
"No."

Tle tsu tliÿa.aa ÿé,
«Tlél shéyágúshé a yíkde k̲ukawdu.áax̲ákw wé yáaÿ?»
Wáannée sáwé k̲únáx̲ aan yá du kaanáx̲ awuxaashi aax'w,
áa neil uwagút.
«Éh!
Tlél shéyágúshé a yíkde k̲ukawdu.áax̲ákw
wé yáaÿ?» yóo.
«Aaa.
A yíkde k̲uwduwa.áx̲, a yíkde.
A yíkde k̲uwduwa.áx̲.»
«Wáa sá ák.wéigé?»
«‹Aadóo sá k̲aa kaanáx̲ angaxaashée-ée-ée-ée
yáaÿ yíkdáx̲ kéi x̲duk̲een?›
yóo x̲áawé.»
«Gwáa! Gwáa!»
Du x̲'éit uwashée.
«Haaw.
Tléil yáaÿ ásgíwé.
Tléil yáaÿ áwé.
Ch'a.aan áwé,
ch'a.aan.»
«Ch'a.aan» yóo áyú aawasáa hóoch k̲u.aa.
«Tle t'áatx̲ kei naalagás'ch.
T'áatx̲ kei naalagás'ch.
K̲utx̲naax'ák̲wx̲ sitee ltín wéit'át
a t'áak du.oowú,» yú.á.
K̲ashde sh x̲'alk'átl'x̲ áwé.
(**AT.SHOOK̲**)
«K̲utx̲naax'ák̲wx̲ sitee,
tlél a t'áak du.úx̲x'.»
Haaw.
Yéi áwé,
du x̲'ayéx̲ áwé tle t'áatx̲ naawligáas'.
Tliyéix' aan wudiláx̲.
Wé yéi át a t'áak wuduwa.úx̲x',
ayéx̲ áwé tle naawligáas'.
(**AT.SHOOK̲**)
Hóoch'!
De yóodáx̲ áwé k̲ux̲ wudik̲ín.

Then he asked again on the far side,
"Mightn't any mysterious sounds have been heard coming from inside the whale?" Eventually, accompanied by the very ones who had cut him free,
he went inside the house.
"Eh!
Mightn't any mysterious sounds have been heard coming from inside the whale?" he said.
"Yes.
Somebody heard someone inside it, inside it.
Somebody heard someone inside it."
"What did it sound like, huh?"
"'Who could cut a hole over a fello-o-o-ow
so a fellow could fly up out of a whale?'
indeed, that's how it sounded."
"My goodness! My goodness!"
Raven touched his mouth.
"Well.
It seems that it is not a whale.
That is not a whale.
That's a *ch'a.aan,*
a *ch'a.aan.*"
A "*ch'a.aan*" is the name Raven came up with for it.
Raven said, "In this situation the clan just picks up and moves away from behind the *ch'a.aan.*
The clan just picks up and moves away from behind it.
That's the death of a clan, you see, when people live behind it," he said.
I thought he was the type to keep his mouth shut.
(LAUGHTER)
"It's the death of the clan;
people don't keep ownership of the lands behind it."
Well.
Just so,
as he instructed, the whole clan migrated from behind the whale.
The town withered up as it was.
They had been living in a number of places up behind that creature,
but, as he had instructed, the whole clan migrated away.
(LAUGHTER)
That was that!
Then he flew back from way over there.

Ts'as daneitx' áwés a
shóo ÿan x̱'eiwatée.
Aadáx̱ áwé wé át
a ksadóok awsik'ít'.
Aadéx̱ áwé ḵut woogoot tle tsu.
Hóoch'.

Shkalneek v. Yéil ḵa Ḵei.á

Haaw.
Áyáa
Ÿax̱taattuḵwáani keekáa daak uwagút.
Adusdeek.
Shaaḵ ÿátx'i áyú dusdeek.
«Ax̱ shóodéi-éi-éi!»
ana.éex'ch diÿáanax̱.aadé.
«Ax̱ shóodéi-éi!»
L x̱'adaat ḵaa tooshtí de {…}
héide áwé tsu éex' duwa.áx̱ch.
Wáananée sáwé yéi ÿaawaḵaa,
«Ax̱ shóodéi-éi!
Yee káa ḵei.á nḵwaak'oots!»
Haahá!
Yan kawdudli.áx̱.
Áwé yá ÿan wudag̱aawadi aa ách áwé
du x̱'éix̱ akawliyáakw, wéix' du éet x̱'awduwatán tle,
«Hadóo!
Chaa goodáx̱ Naasshagiyét sáyú
ḵei.á du jee yéi ng̱atee?»
Tle ch'u tle áa shukawdujaaÿéyáx̱ áwé woonei ḵei.á áa yéi yateeyi yé.
Ách áwé tle woogoot Náas Sháakde.
Yéil á.
Haaw,
Nasshagiyéil yóo duwasáakw
wé a x̱ánde yaa nagut aa,
wé Ḵei.á Daakeit du jee yéi yateeyi aa,
ldakát át,
Ḵutx̱.aÿanahá Daakeit.
Yú dís ḵwá ch'a tlákw ḵudzitee.

He lay there with his mouth open ready to devour the oil
  from those many grease boxes.
So then he devoured that stuff
hook, line, and sinker.
After that, he just walked off and disappeared again.
That was that.

Episode v. Raven and the Daylight

Well.
Now,
he emerged across the river from the Night-Dwellers.
They were dipnetting.
They were dipnetting bits of driftwood.
"Come get me-e-e!"
he kept hollering to them across the river.
"Come get me-e!"
The people didn't pay any attention to what he was saying,
  but they could now hear the hollering over there.
Eventually he said,
"Come get me-e!
Watch out or I might break daylight on you folks!"
Aha!
They figured out where the sound was coming from.
So the elderly ones
discounted what he was saying and spoke up to him on the spot,
"Good grief!
From where does the Child-of-the-Head-of-the-Nass hail
  that he should possess daylight?"
It was as if they had given him directions to where the daylight resided.
So then he set out walking towards the headwaters of the Nass River.
This was Raven.
Well,
Raven-of-the-Head-of-the-Nass was the name of the man
  whom Raven was going to visit,
the one who possessed the Container of Daylight,
everything,
the Container of Stars.
The moon, though, was always in existence.

Haaw.
Tle át wugoodée áwé,
wé du sée—
x̱'wáal' tóox̱ s'é sh ḵuwdli.oo—
láḵdi x'eesháa
daaḵ nadus.ín du x̱'eis.
Tle yá x̱'awooldáx̱ áwé a kaadé sh wudig̱éex'.
X̱'wáal'
tóox̱ sh ḵuwdli.oo.
Tle neildé yaa nadus.íni xáanaa,
xi.aat yáx̱ ḵuteeÿí,
tle téilt akawligán
káa kéi wududzitée.
«X̱'wáal' gwáayá a kát wulihaash!»
Kaax̱ héit wuduwag̱íx' tle.
(AT.SHOOḴ)
Haa,
hóoch' áwé.
Atx̱ áwé tsu ḵeina.áa,
atx̱ ḵeina.áa tsu xáanaa eeti.aa—
xáanaa áwé
g̱ítg̱aa tóox̱ sh ḵuwdli.oo.
Awsikóo
yáa ḵ'watlgeig̱anx̱áas'ináx̱ adaná
yú aanÿédi.
Anax̱ áwé oodanáaÿch.
Anax̱ adana yé ḵudzitee.
Tle yá ḵ'watlg̱eig̱anx̱áas'i tayeex̱ áwé kei sh wuditsáḵ,
gítg̱aa tóox̱ sh ḵuwdli.oo.
Tle koodlidéin ÿaa aa nanút'i
áwé tsá a yíkde, hóoch'.
Tlél áx̱ jiyawuxaash.
{X'éigaa} áwé alḵáx̱ch, tléik'.
Wáanée sáwé deisguch ilḵú wé aanÿédi.
Ilḵú.
«Kéi kg̱eelḵóo ltín.»
Tle yan ilḵóo du yídáx̱ kéi kawdak'éet'i
áwé át akandulgánch.
Daa sá awunóot'i tléil wuduskú.

Well.
When he arrived
for the man's daughter—
he first fit himself inside a down feather—
a bentwood pail
was being taken back to her room for her to drink from.
So he hurled himself down into the pail from the doorway.
He had fitted himself inside of
a down feather.
As the pail was being brought into the house that evening,
with the world being dark like dusk,
they lit a pitchwood torch
and raised it over the pail.
"Hey, there's a down feather floating around on the surface!"
They just took him out and tossed him aside.
(LAUGHTER)
Well,
that was that.
Then the next day—
the next day after that evening—
in the evening
Raven had fitted himself inside an evergreen needle.
He knew
that the noble child
drank from the place where the bentwood pail was lashed together.
She always drank from there.
There was a place from which she drank.
Then, concealed inside an evergreen needle, he just shoved himself up
under the place where the box was lashed together.
As she was finally taking a great big gulp of it,
he slid into her and that was that.
She couldn't have anticipated what was coming.
She {really} tried to cough it up, but no.
Eventually the noble child started vomiting.
She was vomiting.
"You'll just throw up, see."
When she was through vomiting, when it had all come out of her,
a torchlight was shone around.
No one knew what she had swallowed.

Wáannée sáwé de kát seiwax’áḵw, hóoch’.
Tlél du yíkde tóo oonookch tlex̱ niyís.
Tle atk’átsk’ux̱ áwé du jee wsitee.
Deisguch du dísi ḵudzitee.
Dís
yaa anastúw, ÿaa anatúw, ÿaa anatúw aadé,
hóoch’ {ḵu.aa l}tín dís nóogu tlél du jee.
Wáananée sáwé
yan ÿakaawagéi.
Gánde sh kát ḵuwdzihaa tle,
ei-ei-ei-ei,
gánde.
Tlákw—.
Áyá wdudliyéx̱ du daakahídi, cháash hít.
Tle a yee kéi kawduwaháa kóoḵ,
a táa yéi ḵukg̱wastée.
Yóot’át áwé k’óox doogú áwé a táade kdusyáa du éesh x̱’ayéx̱.
Éh! A táade kdusyáa tle.
Yéi kéi shadulhéek áwé tsáa
tláakw kaaxát wé shaawát.
A káa daak unookch.
Tle a káa daak wunoogóo áwé
tle du éetx̱ ḵunas.héich.
Tlél tsu wáa sá utée nuch, atx̱ áwé tsu a kaax̱ woonúkch.
K’iyeekaax̱ wunoogú
    áwé du éet toodataanch,
tléik’!
Wáananée sáwé de
yéi ÿaawaḵaa
wé du éesh ḵu.aa,
«K’e Lyóo.atkoowajeegi Shaanák’wg̱aa ang̱agoodí.»
Ách áwé tle du eeg̱áa aawagoot.
Haat uwagút
wé Lyóo.atkoowajeegi Shaanák’w.
Tle x̱áawé yéi ÿaawaḵaa wé—
wé shawat.shaanák’w,
«Ax̱ dachx̱ánk’!
K’e s’íx’g̱aa,
k’e s’íx’g̱aa wéit’át shákdéwé yéi sitee.

At some point she forgot about it, and that was that.
She didn't feel anything inside of her for this whole time.
He became a boy in her womb.
Eventually her time of the month came.
She was counting and counting and counting
the months,
but it had stopped, see; she didn't have her menstrual cycle.
Eventually
her baby came to full term.
The baby decided it was time to make its exit,
eh-eh-eh-eh,
to the outside world.
Always—.
They built a house for her to stay in, a bough hut.
A pit was dug out inside it;
he was to be born in the pit.
They were lining the bottom of it with marten skins at her father's request.
Eh! They were just lining the pit with them.
When it was finally filled all the way up,
the woman came into labor.
She kept moving herself so as to sit over the pit.
When she sat over it,
her pains would go away.
She would be okay again; then she would scoot back away from the pit again.
When she would scoot away from the back wall,
  the baby would communicate its desire to come out to her,
but no!
Eventually
he said—
her father, that is—
"Let someone go fetch Unfazable-Little-Elder."
So someone went after her.
Unfazable-Little-Elder
came by.
The little old woman
just said,
"My dear grandchild!
How about moss,
maybe moss would be the right thing.

Shk'e wé k'óox doogú.
Á áwé ách áwé tlél yéi ḵoosteech.»
Áwé shk'e aadé ndag̱at
yé k'óox doogú káa {...}.
(AT.SHOOḴ)
Yéi áwé.
Tle—
tle
a táatx̱ kéi kawduwajél.
S'íx'g̱aa atx̱ kawdudli[jeil], kéi shawdudli[.át]—éh!—
k'idéin,
a x̱'adaaÿax̱t'áayi tsú.
Wáannée sáwé, aaá,
tuwditaan.
A káa daak uwanúk
wé shaawát.
Ch'ul áx' áwé udaxeechjí áwé ḵuwdzitee.
Kei kawdigáx̱ a táade—wé kóoḵ táade.
Aaá!
Mmm.
Kaatx̱ aawanook, a táatx̱ kéi wdudzinúk.
Éh!
Tle wé loon, yéi x̱áa kunageich loon,
a kát áwé kdus.aax̱wch atk'átsk'u, s'íx'g̱aach shaadulhíkch.
Yéi áwé
du jinikát kawdudzi.áx̱w.
Ch'a yéi jidu.aax̱w.
Ḵaa jix̱oox̱ ÿaa nasgít.
Wáanée sáyá wé Lyóo.atkoowajeegi Shaanák'w jeet wududzinúk.
Tle atx̱ awsinook.
«Éh!
Ax̱ dachx̱ánk',
de ch'a Yéil waaḵx̱ x̱áa sitee,» yéi ash yawsiḵaa.
(AT.SHOOḴ)
«De ch'a Yéil waaḵ x̱áashé.»
Waḵltáax̱ at kasgix'x̱éyéx̱ áyá ḵuwanóok wé atk'átsk'u.
Aa! Daagáa de ch'a ayak'w.uwagwál wé shawat.shaanák'w.
Éh,
hóoch'.

Well, it's those marten skins, isn't it?
That's it. That's the reason it hasn't been born yet."
Now just imagine how high the marten skins would be piling up
{if everyone were to be born on them}.
(LAUGHTER)
That's how it went.
So,
they just
removed all the skins from the pit.
Moss was gathered and piled up—eh!—
nicely,
and boards were placed around the sides of the mouth of the pit.
Eventually, yes,
the baby communicated its desire to come out.
The woman
moved herself so as to sit over the pit.
Before she even made an effort, he was born.
He started crying at the bottom—at the bottom of the pit.
Yes!
Hmm.
She picked him up; he was taken out of the pit.
Eh!
Then the bark—the bark is this big, you see—
infants are tied onto them and they're filled with moss.
That's how
they tied down his arms.
They tied his arms down just so.
He was being passed from person to person.
At some point he was placed in the arms of Unfazable-Little-Elder.
She just picked him up.
"Eh!
My dear grandchild,
these are Raven's very eyes," she said to him.
(LAUGHTER)
"Now those must be Raven's very eyes."
It was like the boy was throwing darts at her through his pupils.
Ah! He'd have liked to hit that little old lady in her little old face.
Eh,
that was that.

Dláh!
Yéi áwé ch'a tléix' ÿan uwatée wéit,
k̲wáak̲x̲ daak̲ ÿawdusk̲aaÿí.
Atx̲ áwéi-éi-éi deisguch,
deisguch, yéi—
daak̲wéit yaanawádi yáx̲ sáwé yatee?
Tléix' dís áwé ch'u tle át wudig̲wáat'
wé atk'átsk'u.
Hohohohou!
Ÿaa nawát á
du jee.
Deisguch áwé neil ÿeet wudig̲wáat'.
Haa wáa yóo tukwdasháat sáwé
kanax̲dag̲aax̲ít tuwatee.
Ha-ha-ha-haaw.
Dei shé kei kdig̲áax̲ á.
Tle k̲aa jeex' ÿatx̲ wudusnoogú tle
yóo k̲aa jee shukdax̲'ax̲'w nuch yóo.
Wáananée sáwé,
«Haaá!
Yóot'át áwé.»
Du léelk'uch áwé wsiteen.
«Ach'éx̲'t x̲áayú,
yú—
yú áx̲ ÿakawdzidux'u át áwé.
Du jeet kaÿlakél' déi ax̲ dachx̲ánk'!
Du jeet kaÿlakél'!»
K̲utx̲.aÿanahá Daakeit áwé du jeet kawdudlikél'.
K'út' yéx̲ kaaxát, éh!
Ch'a daadé sh yawdzigoo, hóoch'.
Goosú kdag̲aax̲í?
Wáananée sáwé héide—de héit gíyá x̲á neil yeet
akawuljooxú ák.wé?—
héide shuwjix̲een.
Tle gáant akawlijúx.
«Ax̲ adée!
Yéi anax̲saneet áwé ltín.»
Héik'!
A daadé áwé ch'u tle dé du yoowú du x̲'éi ÿan uwatée Yéil,

Goodness!
So at that point his identity had been divulged
due to the fact that a person had put him in a
precarious position with their words.
So the-e-en, gradually, gradually—
what sort of thing grows so fast as this anyway?
The boy
was crawling around after one month.
Hohohoho!
He was sure growing
in her care.
He was gradually crawling all about inside the house.
Well, once he made up his mind,
he decided to cry for it.
We-e-e-ell.
Gosh, he really started wailing.
Whenever someone would pick him up to hold him,
he would squirm out of their reach in convulsive fits.
Eventually,
"Oh, yes!
It's that thing."
His grandfather had seen it.
"He keeps pointing at it, you see,
at that—
at that thing tied up over there.
Untie it for my dear grandchild now!
Untie it for him!"
It was the Container of Stars that was untied for him.
It was round, eh!
He was just simply captivated by it, and that was that.
What happened to all the crying?
Eventually—I suppose he must have already rolled it here and there
inside the house, right?—
the lid to the container flew open.
He just rolled it outside.
"My precious stuff!
You see, he orchestrated the situation just so he could do that."
Hey!
Raven could almost taste his excitement over

wé gáant akawlijuxu, hé’!
K̲uwlix̲’aanéyáx̲ áwé k̲uwatee,
k̲utx̲.aÿanahá,
wé a daakeidí gáant aklajóox.
Deisguch—
deisguch a kayaax̲ yaawak̲eich wé k̲ei.á.
K̲ei.á awdzig̲áax̲.
K̲ei.á áyú oosg̲áax̲ tle.
Wáananée sáwé déi du jeet kawdudlikél’.
Éh!
Yanáa ax̲las’úx̲ún áwé ch’u tle déi ash ujaak̲ch sh.iltí.
Éh!
«Goodé sáwé wuduwadzòo,
wéit’aa k̲wá?» hú gí yéi x̲’[ayak̲á].
(AT.SHOOK̲)
Jíh!
Hóoch’.
Éh!
Wáanée sáwé
ch’as gaankaadé du waak̲, ch’as gaankaadé
wé atk’átsk’u, ch’as gaankaadé.
Ch’ool du éex̲ k̲aa jiyawuxaashí
áwé jig̲eit awdish[át].
Gáant wudik̲ín.
«G̲óo-óo!»
Hóoch’ á.
Yéil aan gáant wudik̲ín wé K̲ei.á Daakeit.
Hóoch’!
Ch’u tle wé Ÿax̲taattuk̲wáani
keekaadé áwé tle aan woogoot.
Aadé aan nagóot áwé
keekáa daak uwagút.
Tle—
tle áx’ áwé kéi shikaawashée
ch’a hú chush daat x̲á.
Yéil
du x̲’asheeyí áyá yáadu á, yá kéi kk̲washee Yéil x̲’asheeyí á.
Ax̲ léelk’uch áwé {Seiwusx̲’een}
du x̲’éitx̲ áwé x̲wsikóo hé G̲unaax̲oo.

the container that he had rolled outside, my!
It was like the whole atmosphere was aflame
with stars
when he rolled the container outside.
Little by little—
little by little he kept {hinting about} the daylight.
He cried for the daylight.
It was the daylight that he was crying for then.
Eventually it was untied and given to him.
Eh!
Whenever he would nudge the lid off a bit he would be filled with joy.
Eh!
"Where did that one
get launched off to?" did Raven-at-the-Head-of-the-Nass say that?
(LAUGHTER)
Gee!
That was that.
Eh!
Eventually,
his eyes were fixed on the smokehole, right on the smokehole;
the boy's eyes were just fixed on the smokehole.
Before anyone could anticipate him doing so, Raven picked it up and tucked it into the crook of his arm.
He flew outside.
"Ca-aw!"
That was that.
Raven flew outside with the Container of Daylight.
That was that!
Then he took it to the opposite side of the river from
the Night-Dwellers.
When he went there with it,
he emerged across the river from them.
Then—
then right there he started singing a song
about himself, you see.
Raven,
this right here, this is his song; it is Raven's song, which I will now sing.
It was my grandparent {Seiwusx̱'een}; it was from their lips that I came to know it in Dry Bay.

Hasdu x̲'éitx̲ áyá x̲wsikóo
yá Yéil x̲'asheeyí.

(SHUX'WÁA AAYÍ KÉI SHIKAAWASHÉE)

K̲ee.á haa aa haa aa haa
K̲ee.á haa aa haa aa haa haa
K̲ee.á haa yee hee aa haa yaa
K̲ee.á haa yee hee ayei
K̲ee.á haa aa haa
K̲ee.á haa aa haa
I jiyís ágíwé héit'aa
Náas Sháax' duwa.uwu k̲ee.á haa aa haa?
Aadéi hei kéi neegút Yéil-ei—

Ch'a hú áyú sh toodé shukalx̲úx̲s'.

Hei aa haa haa
K̲ee—

De du jeehú á yú k̲ei.á.

.á haa—

Taakát tada.áa, tayeet adatéen.

aa haa haa yaa
K̲ee.á haa yaa ayei
K̲ee.á haa aa yaa
K̲ee.á haa aa haa
I jig̲eiwú gí héi
Náas Sháax' duwa.uwu k̲ee.á haa aa haa?
Sh jeedéi hei keedanéek Yéil-ei

Shux'aa yéi ÿawuk̲aaÿí,
«Yee káa k̲ei.á nk̲waak'oots!»
á áyá shukawdlix̲úx̲ ch'a hú,
chush tóot.

Aa haa haa
K̲ee.á haa yee hee aa haa

Haaw.
Du x̲'éit k̲uwdzi.áx̲ yóo Ÿax̲taattuk̲wáanich.
Tliyéix' yéi woonei.

It was from the lips of my grandparents
that I came to know this song of Raven's.

(HE BEGINS SINGING THE FIRST SONG)

Daylight
Daylight
Daylight
Daylight
Daylight
Daylight
Is it for you, the one just there,
The daylight kept at the Head of the Nass?
You are going up thither, Raven

Raven himself was composing this song in his mind.

Hei aa haa haa
Day—

Now he has possession of the daylight.

light—

He's sitting on the riverbank with the container underneath himself.

light
Daylight
Daylight
Daylight
Is it in the crook of your arm, this
Daylight kept at the Head of the Nass?
You say that it is your own, Raven

What he said at first,
"Watch out or I might break daylight on you folks!"
—these were the very lyrics he himself composed
in his own mind.

Aa haa aa haa
Daylight

Well.
The Night-Dwellers were listening to what he was singing.
They became still.

K̲ee.á aa yei yaa ayei
K̲ee.á haa haa

Hóoch' á.
Tléix'.aa,
k̲únáx̲ a kát k̲ei.á aawak'óodzi aa áyá yáat'aa,
yáa kéi kakk̲washée.

(DAX̲.AA KÉI SHIKAAWASHÉE)

Yee hee hee
A káa haa k̲ee.á haa aaha
Yéil-ei hei hei yaa
Yee hee hee
A káa haa k̲ee.á haa haa yaa
Unax̲duwak'óots shéi

Áwé
ch'u tle áwé déi aawasáa
k̲ei.á akg̲wak'óodzí.

Yee hee hee
A káa haa k̲ee.á haa haa haa
Unax̲duwak'óots shéi aa haa yaa
Yee hee hee
A káa haa k̲ee.á haa

Aadé a kaax̲ ÿawjik̲ák̲.
Héende yóo atkaawa.át
yá lingít,
wé k̲ei.á jinák̲.
Yá
tsaa x'óow yéi dag̲aa.uwu aa yú héende lugúk̲x'.
Ch'a yáa
atgutú aa át—
dáak̲t woo.aadi át yéi dag̲aa.uwu aa
áwé k̲wá dak̲dachóon
ÿaa ndakél'.
S'aax̲ x'óow s'aatx'í tle yú shaa ÿaadé.
Áwé s'aax̲x̲ wusitee
wé a x'óowu s'aatx'í yéi áwé.
Ch'a daa sá duwax'uwu át tle áx̲ yóo k̲usiteek

Daylight
Daylight

That's the end.
The other song,
this is the very one to which he broke daylight;
this is the one I will sing now.

(HE BEGINS SINGING THE SECOND SONG)

Yee hee hee
On them daylight
Raven
Yee hee hee
On them daylight
Could presumably be broken

So now
he is announcing
that he is going to break daylight.

Yee hee hee
On them daylight
Could presumably be broken
Yee hee hee
On them daylight

He scooted off the container toward them.
These human beings
rushed into the water
to escape the daylight.
The
ones wearing seal blankets ran helter-skelter into the water.
And the
creatures which are of the forest—
those who were wearing the blankets of the creatures that roam the inland,
however, were fleeing
inland.
The owners of the marmot blanket just went to the mountainsides.
The owners of marmot blankets
became marmots.
Whatever they were blanketed with is what the people became

k̲eina.áa,
k̲ei.á.
Haaw.
Aaa.
A ká wé k̲ee.á.

Yee hee hee
Sh kooldéix̲'een k̲áa aa haa
Yéil-ei hei yaa haa
Yee hee hee
A káa haa k̲ee.á haa haa yaa
Unax̲duwak'oots shéi hei hei yaa
Yee hee hee
A káa haa k̲ee.á haa haa yaa
Unax̲duwak'oots kwshéi aa haa aa haa haa
Yee hee hee
A káa haa k̲ee.á haa haa haa
Yéil-ei hei hei yaa yee
Wóosht k̲eeya.ayi saa haa

De wóoshde yaa yéi ndaneen wé k̲ei.á.

Unax̲duwak'oots kwshéi

Hóoch' áwé.

(KUX̲AANGUWUT'AAN TU.ÓOXS'I YEITK' AWLI.ÓOX)

TS'OOWDALÉ: *Haaw.*
Á áwé k̲ei.á aawak'oots héit.
Aakwéi yóo duwasáagu yé áwé áx'
Ÿax̲taattuk̲wáani keekáa daak uwagút.
TS'OOWDALÉ: *Haaw.*
Áx' áwé k̲ei.á yéi awsinei
Yéil.
Ách áwé tlél té á.
Tle yá haandé aa wdikéil' de k̲a yú tliÿaa niyaadé.
Tsu tle attugáni yéx̲ yatee á k̲u.aa,
tlél tsu yéi kakoogeÿi aa té át uteen.
Yéi áwé.
Haaw, hóoch' áwé.
Déi áwé.

after the daylight
broke.
Well.
Yes.
The daylight was upon them.

Yee hee hee
A man had shamed himself
Raven
Yee hee hee
On them daylight
Could presumably be broken
Yee hee hee
On them daylight
Could presumably be broken
Yee hee hee
On them daylight
Raven
The name of the daylight that had surely been gathered together

The daylight was already gathering together.

It could presumably be broken

That's the end.

(DE LAGUNA BLOWS PITCHPIPE)

JOHNSON: *Well.*
It was just over there that he broke the daylight.
It was at the place called the Akwe River that he
walked out across the river from the Night-Dwellers.
JOHNSON: *Oh.*
That's where Raven
established daylight.
That's why there are no rocks there.
Some of them fled this way and some off in the other direction.
And the place where the sand is like gunpowder,
however, there aren't even any rocks of considerable size there.
That's right.
Well, that's the end.
Enough now.

II. Lyax̱dats'éinix̱ Siteeyi Yéil

KUX̱AANGUWUT'AAN: *Do you want to sing another one?*
Hóoch' áwé.
Ch'a yéi déix̱ áwé aa x̱aa.áx̱ch,
ch'a yéi déix̱ áwé x̱wsikóo.
Shaÿadihéin.
X̱áat Ḵwáan{i ...}, ḵaa Sheen X̱'ayeeyéigi,
Yakwshakahéadi, yéi áwé.
KUX̱AANGUWUT'AAN: *Does he know any of his other—of his other songs, of G̱oochdáa?*
Yú—
yú Yéil,
has awsikóo gé yá tl'átgi káx' ḵuwusteeyí?
S'UḴLAKÉI: *Aaá. Aadóo sá?*
A káx̱ has x̱'anawóos' Yéil x̱á.
S'UḴLAKÉI: *De x̱áa s awsikóo.*
Wáa sá?
S'UḴLAKÉI: *Has awsikóo Yéil.*
Aa, yá tl'átgi káa ḵuwusteeyí?
S'UḴLAKÉI: *Aaa.*
Ḵa yú du éesh,
du éesh áktsú has awsikóo?
S'UḴLAKÉI: *Huh-uh.*
KUX̱AANGUWUT'AAN: *Say, that—Is he going to tell a Raven story? or a Raven song?*

II. Raven the Troublemaker

DE LAGUNA: *Do you want to sing another one?*
That's all.
There are just two songs that I hear;
there are just two that I know.
There are lots of them.
The "Salmon People" {…} and the "Spirit Awaiting the Bailer",
the "Canoe Prow Cover", songs like that.
DE LAGUNA: *Does he know any of his other—of his other songs, of G̱oochdáa?*
Do—
do they know that Raven
was born on this land?
HELEN BREMNER: *Yes. Who?*
Ask them about Raven, then.
BREMNER: *They already know, you see.*
Huh?
BREMNER: *They know about Raven.*
Ah, that he was born on this land?
BREMNER: *Yes.*
And his father,
do they know about his father as well?
BREMNER: *No.*
DE LAGUNA: *Say, that—Is he going to tell a Raven story? or a Raven song?*

Kéet K̲wáani áwé.
Kéet áwé du éeshx̲ sitee Yéil.
A goosh tóonáx̲ k̲uwawóol.
Á áwé
yéi duwasáakw Gushtuwool. Chʼa yéi sh wudisáakw.
Á áwé—
áwé yá tlʼatgikáxʼ
k̲uwdzitee
hú, Yéil.
Shanyaateiyí áwé Yéilx̲ sitee.
Yáadáx̲ yú ík̲de áa ÿan uwalayi yé,
aadáx̲
yú shaawátch kéi uwatée du x̲ʼayáx̲—
yú Gushtuwool x̲ʼayéx̲.
Du éekʼ jiyeexʼ tle
tlél chʼoo ÿát ooswátx̲ du jeexʼ.
Yú dís áwé du éekʼx̲ sitee
wé shaawát.
Áwé tlél ÿát awuswáat.
Du shátt x̲ʼeitáang̲aa
x̲áa k̲oodé tle aják̲x̲
[du] x̲ʼayáx̲—
du éekʼ x̲ʼayáx̲.
Yú k̲éesʼ du jeenáx̲ kawuhaaÿích k̲waawé tlax̲ yéi áa akwdlix̲éitlʼ.
Yéi áwé.
Tle shaawátx̲ siteeyi aa tsú tle aják̲x̲
du shátdei woondusk̲aag̲áa.
Tle ash x̲ʼayáx̲ aják̲x̲.
Áwé wé shanyaateiyí áwé tsá
yantʼéi awsiwát chʼa yú Kéet K̲wáani x̲ʼayéx̲.
Á áwé uwawát.
Áwé chʼu yeedát k̲udzitee, héinax̲.aadé kdunéek. Héinax̲.áhu hú,
Yéil.
Yú shanyaateiyíx̲ sateeyích áyú tlél aadé ux̲dishaani yé, tlél tsú aadé
nag̲waanaawu yé.
Ldakát yáa lingitʼaanigei yóo kaawagút.
K̲ateeyi
yáaÿ yíkde wdak̲eení tlél—
tlél wunaa.

He was a member of the Killerwhale Tribe.
A Killerwhale is Raven's father.
There is a hole in his dorsal fin.
So,
his name is Hole-in-the-Dorsal-Fin. That is just what he named himself.
So,
it was on this land
that Raven himself
was born.
A low-tide stone, that is Raven.
From here towards the beach where the tide is at its lowest ebb,
from that place
that woman picked it up just like he said—
like Hole-in-the-Dorsal-Fin said.
Under the control of her brother
she still had never had a child grow up in her care.
The moon was the brother
of that woman.
He never let her raise a child.
His slaves just kept going and killing them off
at [his] command—
at her brother's command,
so that none of her children could communicate with his wife, you see.
She was terrified of the floodtide because he had control over it.
That's how it was.
The slaves even killed those that were girls
so that no one could smuggle a message to his wife.
They would just kill the child at his word.
At last it was the low-tide stone that
she raised in hiding as the Killerwhale Person had instructed her.
That's the one that grew up.
He is alive even now; it is said that he's over this way. He's over this way,
Raven.
Because he is a low-tide stone he cannot grow old, nor
can he die.
He has paraded throughout the entire world.
Even
when he flew into a whale, he didn't—
he didn't die.

Du een ÿan wulitít.
Yáaÿ yíkde wdak̲eení,
áyá aadé tuligéiyi yé yáat.
Á áwé k̲ei.á yéi awsinee hú áyá yáa Yéilch.
Héiʼ!
G̲unaax̲oo shgé,
Aakwéi yóo duwasáagu yé,
áxʼ áwé k̲ei.á aawakʼoots.
Yax̲taattuk̲wáani keekáa daak uwagút áxʼ.
Tléil awuskú k̲ei.á
gooxʼ sá yéi teeyí.
Áwé chʼa yóox̲ʼatángích áwé ax̲ʼawuliwóosʼ,
«Ax̲ shóodéi!» yéi x̲ʼayak̲á,
«Ax̲ shóodéi!
Yee káa k̲ei.á nk̲waakʼoots!»
Dax̲.aa yéi ÿanak̲áa áwé tsá,
«Yee káa k̲ei.á nk̲waakʼoots!»
«Goodáx̲ Naasshagiyét sáyú k̲ei.á du jee yéi nag̲atee?»
    yóo ÿawdudzik̲aa.
Tle aawa.áx̲.
Ách áwé tle Náas Sháakde woogoot
Yéil k̲u.aa.
Tlél—tlél chʼa du tláach áwé yéi wusá Yéil yóo.
Wé
k̲éesʼ káx̲ duldél
k̲áa shaanákʼw.
Áwé
a x̲áni neil wujik̲ák̲
hú k̲u.aa.
Áwé,
«Néesʼ g̲ehéeni x̲at sawli.átʼ.»
Tle
a dzúkde yanax̲ aÿag̲atánch wé gán.
A dzúkdáx̲ tóode akawsiháa,
    gánt uwatáa.
Á áwé
yéi ash yawsik̲aa,
«Chaa gutgiyéigaa sá wulaayi léin áyóo
a kát eeyanísʼ, cha Yéil Tlʼéetlʼi?»

It was washed ashore with him.
When he flew into the whale,
the interior of the whale was as spacious as this house.
Then Raven himself caused daylight to break forth.
Hey!
It was at Dry Bay, I guess,
the place called the Akwe River,
where he broke daylight.
It was there that he emerged across the river from the Night-Dwellers.
He didn't know
where the daylight was.
So he asked them with just these words,
"Come get me!" he said,
"Come get me!
Watch out or I might break daylight on you folks!"
Only when he said for the second time,
"Watch out or I might break daylight on you folks!"
did they say to him, "From where does the Child-of-the-Head-of-the-Nass
hail that he should possess daylight?"
His ears perked up.
So Raven just set out walking towards
the Headwaters of the Nass.
It wasn't—it wasn't his mother who named him Raven.
The
tide was guarded
by a little old man.
So,
Raven hopped
into his house.
Then he said,
"Sea-urchin juice has made me chilly."
Raven just
kept sticking a piece of firewood in the ground behind the old man's back.
Raven appropriated the fire for himself from behind the elder's back
and slept by the fire.
So then
the old man said to him,
"Sir, when exactly would there have been a tideflat exposed by low tide
for you to have eaten sea urchins, you Shitty-Ass Raven?"

yóo ash yawsik̲aa.
Ách áyá tle kindatóog̲oon aawax̲eech.
Tuk̲daanáx̲ akawsigóo wé nées' daakak'áts'i.
Kadag̲áax̲ ash jeedé. Deisguch yéi naléin, deisguch
yánde ÿaa kanalkúx.
«Déi, Yéil, g̲waag̲aalaa!» yéi ash daaÿak̲á.
«Yéil», yéi áwé. Ách áwé Yéil
yóo wduwasáa.
—Ná!
Yáat'aach kei lagwaal.—
Haaw.
Yéi áwé.
Áwé
yan kalakóox áwé
ldakát át x̲oot uwaláa:
yáaÿ,
tsàa,
daak̲wéit sáyá héen tak.ádi.
Ch'a yá shaa x̲'áakx' áwé yéi téeyeen yóo k̲ées' kanadá
wé dís k̲ées' akawusdaaÿí.
Á áwé, aag̲áa áwé,
a éenyee kóoni wuyíkt aawax'úl'
wé du káak shát.
Du dlaak' jeex' ÿét l awuswáadeech
áwé yéi awsinee.
Tle kawdliyíchx'.
Éenyeekóon áyú aawasháa.
Áwé tle kawdliyíchx'.
Aaa.
Yéi áwé.
Áa k̲ux̲ dagóot áwé wéit,
wéi atx̲ woogoodi yé,
aag̲áa áwé wé—
du jeehú á wé k̲ei.á—
Yax̲taattuk̲wáani keekáa daak uwagút
ch'a g̲una.aa shaÿadáax̲.
A keekáa daak góot áwéi yéi aÿawsik̲aa,
«Ax̲ shóodéi!
Yee káa k̲ei.á nk̲waak'oots!»

he said to him.
So he then flipped the old man upside down.
Raven jabbed those urchin spines around his butt.
The old man was squealing in Raven's grip. Gradually the tide
started going out; it was gradually drying up.
"Enough, Raven, the tide could go out any minute!" he said to him.
"Raven," that's what he called him. That's how he came to
have the name Raven.
—Here!
Start drumming with this one.—
Well.
That's how it went.
So,
when the tideflats dried up completely
the tide went out revealing all sorts of creatures:
whales,
seals,
all kinds of sea creatures.
The floodtide used to remain up between the mountains
when the moon caused it to flood.
So, at that time
he plucked the flickers from his uncle's wife's armpits
and threw them into the air.
Raven did this to his uncle's wife because his uncle
had prevented his sister from raising any children.
Then the flock of flickers flew off.
He had married Flicker-Pits.
The flock just flew off.
Yes.
That's how it went.
When he returned to that place,
to the place where he had set out from—
that time
he had possession of the daylight—
he emerged again across the river from the Night-Dwellers,
this time more boldly.
When he emerged he said to them from across the river,
"Come get me!
Watch out or I might break daylight on you folks!"

«Tléik'!
Wáa sá?»
Akoolx̱éitl' x̱á woosh kát ÿawdixún,
tsaa x'óow s'aatx'í—
tsaa x'óow s'aatx'í, daa sá, ldakát át.
Yáa naag̱as'éi x'óowx̱ dulyéix̱, ḵaa
s'aax̱ x'óow.
Áwéi
ḵei.á yéx̱
yóo wánde a yanáa als'óox̱—
hé'—
tle ḵeiwa.aa.
Hhhh!
Tle yéi áwé,
tle tsaa x'óow s'aatx'í héent loowagúḵ tle.
Tle tsaax̱ wusitee.
Wéi
dáaḵt woo.aadi át ḵu.aa áwé daḵdachóon
áwé atkaawa.át yú shaa ÿaadé.
Tlél tsu té át uteen yú G̱unaax̱oo áx'
ḵei.á aawak'oodzi yé, ch'u tle yáadáx̱
ch'u tle yáa té S'etáḵdáx̱ shgé.
S'etáḵ, tlél áa yéi s utéeyin S'etáḵ,
tle atx̱ áwé tle yóo tliyaadé tle yóot,
tle yóo
Laaḵ'ásgi X'aaÿí, Diyáay tliyaanax̱.á, naaléi tsú.
Tle át áwé shukatán wé téix', át wudikel'i yé áwé.
Woosh dakán áwé wdikéil'.
Haaw, ḵei.á áa yéi awusneeyée—
a kát ḵei.á aawak'oodzi aa shí
x̱wasikóo—
ha ch'a tlax̱ ḵútx̱ ḵu.aa áwé
yawdi.aa
tle ḵei.á wuk'oodzí.
Ḵa-a-a-a-a
yú
ḵei.á anak'óotsdáx̱, hóoch'.
Tle déi k'idéin xeewa.átx̱.

"No!
What's going on?"
The owners of seal blankets—
the owners of seal blankets, of whatever, of every creature,
peered at each other in terror.
They made blankets out of foxes and
blankets out of marmots.
And so,
like the coming of dawn,
as he was nudging the lid open a bit towards the distant shore—
heh—
the dawn just broke.
Ahhhh!
Just like that,
the owners of the seal blankets just ran into the water.
They became seals.
Those
animals that roam inland, however, rushed straight inland and up onto the mountainsides.
There's not even a single rock there in Dry Bay where he broke the daylight; all the rocks are gone from right here, and the rocks are gone from the Situk River, I suppose.
The Situk, they never used to live there at the Situk,
and from there over to the far side, way over there,
over to
Cape Fairweather on the far side of Bear Island; it's a long ways, too.
That is the extent of the range of the rocks, which is the place the rocks fled to. They fled in different directions.
Well, when Raven made the daylight come about—
I know
the song to which he broke daylight—
well, the breaking of daylight
had been put off
for too long.
A-a-a-a-nd
after
he broke the daylight, that was that.
Dusk would now keep recurring in proper fashion.

Yéil
yéi duwasáakw—ch’u tle yéi wduwasáa Yéil yú—
yú ḵáa shaanák’wch aadé uwasayi yé yáx̱.
Shux’aa ḵwá tlél yéi dusáagoon.
Áwé
nées’ daakak’áts’i
tuḵdaanáx̱ akawusgóowuch áwé yéi aawasáa
lyax̱dats’éini súk.
Ldakát yéide yóo kawdzigít yá lingit’aanig̱ei. Áwé wéit,
yóot’aa gé yisikóo, Káayaakw?
Áwé du [di]yeegooleidée áwé du yaagú, Yéil yaagóo áwé.
Áwé a ká duwa.óo shgé.
Yú a shaká áyú
ch’u tle yóo anax̱ kawdi.áa.
Áwé diyeegooleit áwé.
Yá «Atx̱án» yóo duwasáagu át ḵwá wé
    Yáaÿ t’aḵkaadé duwatéen.
Á ḵwás
du áadaÿi.
Áadaa áwé
Atx̱án.
Adax̱ ḵwáwé kéi aawaxásh
taaÿ ÿatx̱,
áwé ch’a koogéiyi áwé
ch’a wé éil’ káx’
téix̱ aa wsitee.
Ḵa yú wánt aa kaawaháa shgé,
Ḵaataanaa wát.
A shóonáx̱ aa wduwaxásh.
Á áwé,
hú áwé Yéil áwé yéi ḵuwanóok.
Du hídi ḵwaawé yáanax̱.át la.áa.
Áwé
du katseesí tsú anax̱ naashóo.
Tsu tlax̱ yéi a daax̱ aa ÿawlis’ís.
Éh!
Áwéi yeedát héinax̱.aadé kdunéek.
Áhu hú,
tle yáa tl’átgi shú.

Raven
is his name—he was named Raven,
just as that little old man had named him.
That wasn't originally his name though.
It was because
he had been jabbing those sea-urchin spines
around the old man's butt that he gave the name Raven to
this troublemaker in the making.
He performed his antics everywhere throughout the world. That place,
that one way over there, do you know it, Wingham Island?
His boat was a skin kayak; that was Raven's boat.
People own property there, I suppose.
The prow of the boat
just sticks up like this.
It's a skin kayak.
And this natural feature they call "Near the Creature" can be
seen to the side of Kayak Island.
Now, that
is his harpoon.
It's a harpoon,
the natural feature called "Near the Creature".
From there, however, he cut hunks off
from the side of the fat
and threw them every which way;
out on the ocean
some of the hunks of fat turned to stone.
And some ended up on the mainland, I suppose,
at the mouth of Katalla.
Some were cut from the end of it.
Now then,
it was Raven himself who was doing this.
His house, though, is located over on this side.
And
his buoy is sticking up there, too.
Some of the pieces of fat were blown right around it.
Eh!
Even now people say he lives over that way.
He's there,
right at the end of the land.

Yéil
áxʼ yéi yatee.
Té
hítx̱ awliyéx̱.
Yéi áwé.
(AT.SHOOḴ)
KUX̱AANGUWUTʼAAN: *Is he gonna sing the songs that go with the story he's been telling? Ask him if he would do that.*
SʼUḴLAKÉI: *I tuwáxʼ gé sigóo eesheeyí wéi A Kát Ḵei.á Aawakʼoodzi Shí.*
Wáa sá?
SʼUḴLAKÉI: *A Kát Ḵei.á Aawakʼoodzi Shí áwé kéi kg̱eeshée.*
Wáa sá—
A Kát Ḵei.á Aawakʼoodzi Shí yóo gé?
SʼUḴLAKÉI: *Yéi ák.wé iyasáa?*
Aaá, A Kát x̱á Ḵei.á Aawakʼoodzi Shí.
SʼUḴLAKÉI: *Chʼa wáa sgís kei kg̱eeshée. Hél du.aax̱ch.*
Aaa, x̱wasikóo.
X̱wasikóo, ax̱ léelkʼu has x̱ʼéitx̱ x̱wasikóo.
Ax̱ kagwaalí áyá ax̱ tuwáa sigóo.
Wé gaaw ḵu.aawé, tléikʼ—
tsʼa yéi, tsʼa yéi.
Kʼe wéitʼát áwé.
(AT.SHOOḴ)
Haaw.
Shuxʼaa
kéi akaawashiyi aa—
dei du jeehú á yóo ḵei.á.
De Náas Sháakdáx̱ yaa woogoot.
Atkʼátsʼkux̱ wusitee, Náas Sháakxʼ ḵu.aa
ḵuwdzitee.
Aanÿádi éet sh jiwdliháa.
Á áwé
ḵugastéedáx̱ áwé,
aag̱áa áwé
ldakát át awdzigáax̱ yú neil yee du léelkʼw.
Náasshagiyéil
du léelkʼux̱ áwé wsitee.
Daa sá—Ḵutx̱.aÿanahá Daakeit
shuxʼáanáx̱ du jeet kawduwakélʼ.

Raven
lives there.
He uses a stone
as his house.
That's how it is.
(LAUGHTER)
DE LAGUNA: *Is he gonna sing the songs that go with the story he's been telling? Ask him if he would do that.*
BREMNER: *Do you want to sing the Song to which Raven Broke Daylight?*
What?
BREMNER: *You're going to sing the Song to which Raven Broke Daylight. How about—*
The Song to Which Raven Broke Daylight, is that the one?
BREMNER: *Isn't that what you called it?*
Yes, the Song, indeed, to which Raven Broke Daylight.
BREMNER: *You can just sing it however you want. They haven't heard it yet.*
Yes, I know it.
I know it; it was from the lips of my grandparents that I came to know it.
I want my drumstick.
That drum there though, no—
just so, just so.
How about that thing over there?
(LAUGHTER)
Well.
The first
song he began singing—
he already had possession of the daylight.
He had already walked down from the Headwaters of the Nass.
He had become a boy; it was at the Headwaters of the Nass, though, that he was born.
He had spirited himself into the body of the noble girl.
So,
after he was born,
that was when
he begged his grandfather for everything in the house.
Raven-of-the-Head-of-the-Nass
became his grandfather.
Now, what was it?—It was the Container of Stars that was first untied for him.

Íh! Tle gáant akawuljooxú ch'u tle ldakát yá lingit'aaníx'
yéi woonee yú k̲utx̲.aÿanahá.
Áwé a ítdei tlél óosh sh daják̲x̲ ug̲aax̲.
Áwé ch'a aadé ash six̲ani yéich áwé du dachx̲án,
wé Naasshagiyéil k̲u.aa, tle tsoo
wé k̲ei.á a jeedéi akaawanáa.
«Déi!
G̲aa déi yatee,» yóo tuwatee.
Atx̲ haat góot áwé wé Yax̲taattuk̲wáani
keekáa daak uwagút.
Ch'a hú du x̲'asheeyí áyáa yáa Yéil, de shukalx̲úx̲s'.
Ch'a hú sh toodé shukalx̲úx̲s'.

(SHUX'ÁA AAYÍ KEI SHIKAAWASHÉE)

K̲ee.á haa aa haa aa haa haa
K̲ee.á haa aa haa aa haa haa
K̲ee.á haa yee hee yee hee
Aa haa haaha
K̲ee.á haa yee hee ayei
K̲ee.á haa aa haa
K̲ee.á haa aa haaha
I jiyís ágíwé héit'aa
Náas Sháax' duwa.uwu k̲ee.á haa haa haa
Aadé hei kéi neegút Yéil-éi hei heihe
Aa haa haa haa
K̲ee.á haa yee hee hee
Aa haa haa haa
K̲ee.á haa yei yaa ayei
K̲ee.á haa aa haa
K̲ee.á haa aa haa

(CH'ÉEN TLIYÉI YÉI WOONEE)

—aa haa
Náas Sháax' duwa.uwu k̲ee.á haa aa haa
Sh jeedé hei keedanéek Yéil-ei hei heihe
Aa haa haa haa
K̲ee.á haa yei heihe
Aa haa aa haa
K̲ee.á haa yei yaa ayei
K̲ee.á

Ih! When he rolled it outside, the stars
just ended up all over the world.
So after that, he nearly cried himself to death.
Because of the way Raven-of-the-Head-of-the-Nass loved his grandchild,
he gave the order
to relinquish to him the daylight as well.
"Enough!
I give up; it's okay," his grandfather thought.
Then when he came here, he emerged across the river
from the Night-Dwellers.
This is Raven's very own song; he was already composing the song.
He himself was composing the song in his mind.

(**HE BEGINS SINGING THE FIRST SONG**)

Daylight
Daylight
Daylight
Aa haa haaha
Daylight
Daylight
Daylight
Is it for you, the one just there,
The daylight kept at the Head of the Nass?
You are going up thither, Raven
Aa haa haa haa
Daylight
Aa haa haa haa
Daylight
Daylight
Daylight

(**LAPSE IN RECORDING**)

—aa haa
The daylight kept at the Head of the Nass
You say that it is your own, Raven
Aa haa haa haa
Daylight
Aa haa haa haa
Daylight
Daylight

Hóochʼ.
Hóochʼ áwé.

(KUX̱AANGUWUTʼAAN TU.ÓOXSʼI YEITKʼ AWLI.ÓOX)

{…} A kát áwé áa.

(DAX̱.AA KEI SHIKAAWASHÉE)

Yee hee hee
A káa haa ḵei.á haa aa haa
Yéil-ei hei hei heihe
Yee hee hee
A káa haa ḵee—

(CHʼÉEN YAN WUDIYÍḴ)

That's the end.
That's the end.

(DE LAGUNA BLOWS PITCHPIPE)

{...} He was sitting on it.

(HE BEGINS SINGING THE SECOND SONG)

Yee hee hee
Daylight
Raven
Yee hee hee
Daylight—

(END OF TAPE)

Chalyee Éesh X̱'éidáx̱ Tlaagú
Stories by Andrew Wanamaker

FIGURE 4. Andrew Wanamaker wearing a ceremonial wool applique tunic. Partially visible is the image of an eagle seated on its nest, a crest of Ch'áak' Kúdi Hít 'Eagle Nest House', a clan house of the Kaagwaantaan. Sitka, c. 1960. Photo by Martin Strand. Courtesy of Sealaska Heritage Institute, PO004, box 12, item 240.

ANDREW WANAMAKER, whose Tlingit names were Chalyee Éesh and Wooshkeenáa, was born in Sitka, Alaska, on January 11, 1886, and passed away in Sitka on May 13, 1969. He was Kaagwaantaan of Ch'áak' Kúdi Hít 'Eagle Nest House'. In 1899, Wanamaker's older brother signed him up to attend Sitka Industrial and Training School, an assimilationist Presbyterian mission school for Alaska Natives that later became Sheldon Jackson School, and he resided there for five years. There he met his wife, Jean Wanamaker, and later lived near the school in the 'Cottages', a community comprised primarily of former students and their families. This community included prominent Native boat builders, musicians, and political organizers. He recalls:

> The people around the Cottage, they were building boats. Peter Simpson, George Howard, John Willard, three of them were building sealing boats. They were doing a lot of sealing out on Biorka Island and everybody was busy. So I organized a little band. I found a little crooked horn some place. I used to blow on that. And they got me a good horn later on, double bell baritone. We used to go out to Biorka Island with our band. And we used to come in for Decoration Day. We used to lead the parade. The Marines used to stand behind us.*

Along with other Sitka Training School students and Cottage residents, Wanamaker played an important role in the founding of the Alaska Native Brotherhood (ANB). As he remembers some of the early organizing efforts:

> In 1911, Mrs. Brady† was teaching down in the public school and she found out we were trying to organize. So she invited us to come to Juneau for the teachers' conference. Five of us: Peter Simpson, Ralph Young, Frank Price, Willie Wells,

* MC059, item 4. This recording contains Wanamaker discussing, in Tlingit and English, some memories of his childhood and early days of the ANB; spoken commentary follows by A.P. Johnson.

† The wife of former Alaska governor and co-founder of Sitka Training School, John Brady.

FIGURE 5. The Cottages Band. Sitka, c. 1905. Left to right, top row: William Wells, Ray James, Andrew Wanamaker, Sergius Williams (?), Cyrus Peck, UNK. Bottom row: Louis Simpson, Albert James (?), Tom Walton, George Howard, John Willard, UNK, Don Cameron, John Cameron. Image courtesy of Alaska State Library, Historical Collections. Sheldon Jackson College Collection, SJC-wurster 1-37.

> Andrew Wanamaker. [...] We went—five of us went and we adjourned to meet there again, to meet in Juneau again. So next year we went there and that's the time we organized, 1912.*

The Dauenhauers commented that the founding of the ANB "was a social, political, and educational landmark in the history of the aboriginal inhabitants of North America because the ANB was to become the first organization of its kind on the continent."† Wanamaker held various offices within the ANB throughout his adult life.

He served also as a Presbyterian lay minister in Klukwan, Petersburg, and Klawock. In the 1930s and '40s he piloted ships belonging to the National Mission of the Presbyterian Church throughout Southeast Alaska for church activities. These ships included the *Princeton* and its well-known successor the *Princeton Hall,* built in Sitka in 1941. He and Jean became the adoptive parents of Elizabeth Peratrovich, known for her role in ushering in the first anti-discrimination law in the US, which passed through the Alaska Territorial Legislature in 1945.

* MC059, item 4.

† Dauenhauer and Dauenhauer, *Haa Ḵusteeyí,* 84.

One of the early goals of the ANB was securing US citizenship for Alaska Natives, which was not automatically granted to Natives born within the US until the passage of the Indian Citizenship Act of 1924. This is an important aspect of the historical and political context in which the storytellers of this volume lived. In 1915, a territorial act allowed Native individuals to receive citizenship on a case-by-case application basis. The formal conditions included an examination by teachers of a government school and signatures of five white US citizens attesting that the applicant was "found to have abandoned all tribal customs and relationships, [to] have adopted the ways and habits of a civilized life and to be properly qualified to intelligently exercise the obligations of an elector in the Territory of Alaska"; the applicant was also required to swear "an oath duly acknowledged to the effect that such applicant forever renounces all tribal customs and relationships".* These documents would then go to a judge of the district court to be considered for approval.

Andrew Wanamaker's US citizenship was granted by a judge on April 29, 1919.† While Wanamaker ostensibly swore at age thirty-three to permanently renounce all tribal customs and relationships, he stayed true to many aspects of traditional Tlingit culture. He, for example, assumed the traditional leadership role of Ch'áak' Kúdi Hít of the Sitka Kaagwaantaan clan. And, as his narratives demonstrate, he not only continued to speak Tlingit until the end of his life but maintained masterful control of classical Tlingit oral-literary style.

One of Wanamaker's contemporaries, a man named Don Cameron, is worthy of mention as a way of establishing connections between specific individuals in the written record of Tlingit oral literature. Like Wanamaker, Cameron attended Sitka School, resided in the Cottages, played in the Cottages Band, was an ANB member, and belonged to the Kaagwaantaan clan. The two of them appear to have submitted their applications for citizenship together as part of a coordinated effort, their certificates having been completed before the same notary public on February 1, 1919, and showing seven of eight identical signatories.‡ The two men can be seen pictured in multiple group photographs from circa 1905, around the time when Cameron served as an interpreter and consultant for anthropologist John Swanton. Two stories in English and three in Tlingit told by Cameron in Sitka in 1904 were published in Swanton's 1909 *Tlingit Myths and Texts*, which remains one of the cornerstone publications of Tlingit oral literature. Swanton's text and the present volume, published over a century apart, share a common foundation in these peers who together attended school, lived, and sought recognition of their rights in Sitka in the early twentieth century.

---

* "Act to define the political status of certain Native Indians within the Territory of Alaska," Alaska State Library, Historical Collections.

† Alaska State Archives, AS29459.

‡ Ibid. Signatories on both certificates include former Alaska Governor John Brady and renowned photographer E.W. Merrill.

FIGURE 6. Andrew Wanamaker singing and dancing in the Eagle Nest House. Sitka, c. 1960. Courtesy of the Sitka Public Library, Romain Hardcastle Collection, 01-070.

Late in his life, Wanamaker moved to Juneau, Alaska. The Raven stories presented here were recorded by Jeff Leer at Wanamaker's Juneau home, probably in the summer of 1966, Wanamaker being roughly eighty years old at the time. The title we have applied to Wanamaker's extended tale taken as a whole is «Yéil Satoowú», translated as "Raven's Clever Mind", based on three lines found within the tale. Twice Wanamaker uses the phrase «Du satoowú áwé»* 'That's how clever he (Raven) is' in reference to Raven's witty manner of exploiting situations that present themselves to him; elsewhere he states, «Ch'a du x̱'asatoowú áwé yéi yatee Yéil ḵu.aa»† 'That's how clever Raven was with words', using the same phrase but with the addition of the prefix *x̱'a-* 'mouth, speech', referring to Raven's special ability to exert his influence with the use of choice words.‡

* AW i, 59, 66. Literally, 'That's his cleverness, wittiness'.

† AW iii, 44. More literally, 'Raven, though, that's just how his verbal cleverness is'.

‡ The phrase *du satoowú* 'his cleverness, clever mind, ingenuity, wit, astuteness' uses a possessed (and apparently inalienable) verbal noun corresponding to the stative verb *sitóo* 's/he is clever, ingenious', which is formed from the root *N tú* 'the inside of N' which also occurs with the possessive suffix as *N toowú* 'N's inner being, mind, soul, (metaphorically) heart'. Combining this with the denominal string *O-s/l-NOUN·ROOT* 'for O to have NOUN·ROOT' yields *O-s-tóo* 'for O to be clever, ingenious' (more literally, 'for O to have interiority, a mind [of their own]'; more freely, 'for O to be provided with a mind').

FIGURE 7. Andrew Wanamaker (left) and Alex Andrews (right) seated in the Eagle Nest House, the house's crest displayed behind them. Sitka, c. 1960. Courtesy of the Sitka Public Library, Romain Hardcastle Collection, 01-062.

Wanamaker tells his stories in a straightforward manner, without much in the way of flashbacks, elaboration, or commentary. He was surely aware that the young man recording these stories was a novice learner of the language, and perhaps because of this, he tried to keep the telling short and sweet. Nevertheless, the phrasing and imagery are eloquently delivered, and we find a number of places where the archaic language and formulaic phrases that are integral parts of these stories have left us groping for explanations.

Yéil Satoowú

Shkalneek i. Yéil k̲a Du Káak

Yook̲is'kook̲éigi áwé du kéilk'i hás aják̲x̲in ch'u tle k̲uwusteeyí.
Hasdu tláa áwé át nasg̲áx̲jin.
Wáananée sáwé yaa nasg̲áx̲i áwé wuduwa.éex',
«Daa sáwé daadé eeg̲áax̲?»
Tle k̲ux̲ wudihán, tle awdlig̲een.
Awsiteen Láx̲'.
Yéi ash yawsik̲aa, «Ax̲ yátx'i áyá tlél uwátx̲.»
Ách áwé Láx̲' yéi ash yawsik̲aa,
«Shanyaadé nagú.
Té k'wát' aadáx̲ kei kakg̲eetée neildé, yakakg̲isat'áa, kakg̲eenóot'.»
Ách áwé a x̲'ayáx̲ yéi jeewanei.
Wé shanyaateiyí ayakawsit'áa, akaawanóot'.
Á áwé du kát yátx̲ wusitee.
Ách áwé k̲uwdzitee Yéil.
Tléil ách g̲waajaagi át k̲oostí shanyaateiyíx̲ sateeyích Yéil.
K̲áax̲ nastée áwé du káakch kaawak̲aa,
ch'a tlákw yá du húnx̲w aadé ajak̲x̲éyáx̲,
«Yú dáax̲ yíkde nagú, nadaax̲!»
Aadé woogoot du káak x̲'ayáx̲.
A yíx̲ woogoot wé dáax̲.
Tle a yíx̲ wugoodí áwé du káa kawdix̲'áx̲'w.
Ách áwé du t'eey áwé woosh dakán yéi awsinee,
tle kaawawál' wé dáax̲.

Raven's Clever Mind

Episode i. Raven and His Uncle

Tide-Commander used to kill his nephews as soon as they were born.
Their mother would walk about weeping.
One time as she was walking along weeping someone called to her,
"What are you crying about?"
She stopped in her tracks and looked.
She saw Heron.
She told him, "My children never grow to adulthood."
So Heron told her,
"Go to the edge of the lowest tide.
You are to pick up a round stone from there, heat it up, and swallow it."
So she set about doing what Heron had told her to do.
She warmed up the stone from the edge of the lowest tide and swallowed it.
Then it became a child in her womb.
So Raven was born.
Nothing could kill Raven because he was a stone from the edge of the lowest tide.
When he became a man, his uncle sent him on a mission,
which is how his uncle used to kill his older brothers, saying,
"Get inside that unfinished canoe and hew it out!"
He went to it as his uncle had instructed him.
He got down inside the unfinished canoe.
As soon as he got down inside it, it closed over him.
So he pushed his elbows apart,
and the unfinished canoe cracked open.

Ách áwé tsu akaawaḵaa,
«Yú aas nalg̱eech!»
Ách áwé aadé woogoot.
Ch'u tle shux'áa ádi awulx̱óot'i du káa kaawasóos
wé yalik'ats'i néix̱'.
Tlél ash wujaaḵ.
Shanyaateiyí áwé Yéil, ách áwé tlél ash wujaaḵ.
Du káak tsu ash kaawaḵaa,
«Nagú, yú náaḵw jáḵ!»
Aadé woogoot.
Náaḵw tlein áwé, ḵustin náaḵw awsiteen.
Át góot áwé át x̱'eiwatán,
«Náaḵwk'wátsk'ux̱ inastí!»
Aak'wáchk'ux̱ wusitee, aawajáḵ.
Du káak jeedé awsitaa.
Du káak x'áant uwanúk awusteení.
Ash g̱ajaagít áwé du káakch kaawaḵaa,
tlél ash wujaaḵ.
Hóoch ḵu.aa áwé aawajáḵ wé náaḵw.
Du kéilk' tlél ash g̱waajaag̱i át.
Ách áwé du káak Yooḵis'kooḵéik yéi yaawaḵaa,
«Ḵées' kang̱adaa!»
Yéilch sakóo, du tláa yéi ayawsiḵaa,
«Yá s'ús' tóode áwé kg̱eeshéex,»
Yéil yéi yaawaḵaa,
«X̱át ḵu.aa gus'tóode kḵwadaḵéen, yei kḵwalasháat.»
Ách áwé du tláa s'ús'x̱ wusitee.
Gus'tú awlisháat Yéil.
Yá ḵées' kawudaayí, cha ch'a ḵux̱ daláa,
Yéil tsu yá diyée yawdiḵeen.
Awsiteen ldakát át a yeex̱ woolaa.
Yéilch g̱astéen ldakát hintaak.ádi,
ag̱áa áwé tsáa yéi daaduné ḵaa atx̱aayí sákw áwé yá
lingit'aanée wooneix̱i aa.
Yéil ḵu.aa eex̱ at yoowú tóox' yéi aya.óo.
Akakawlitsáḵ a tóonáx̱.
Kadutl'óoḵ, a tayeet sh istáan, du lakaadé kdutl'óoḵ Yéil ḵu.aa.
Du satoowú áwé.
Ch'a ldakát ḵaa atx̱aayí áwé yéi ndusnée yéi yaawaḵaa Yéil,

So again his uncle sent him out,
"Fell that tree!"
So he went to it.
Just when he first started chopping it, sharp shards of marble
fell down onto him.
It didn't kill him.
Raven was a stone from the edge of the lowest tide, so it didn't kill him.
His uncle sent him off again,
"Go kill that octopus!"
He went there.
He saw a large octopus, a giant octopus.
When he came to it, he spoke to it,
"Become a baby octopus."
It became a tiny baby octopus, and he killed it.
He brought the carcass to his uncle.
His uncle was furious when he saw it.
His uncle had sent him there so that the octopus would kill him,
but it didn't kill him.
To the contrary, Raven killed the octopus.
Nothing could kill his nephew.
So his uncle Tide-Commander said,
"Let the floodtide flow!"
When Raven found out about this, he told his mother,
"You must quickly get inside this harlequin duck,"
Raven said,
"As for me, I'll fly into the cloud bank and latch onto it."
So his mother became a harlequin duck.
Raven latched onto the cloud bank.
When the floodtide flowed, after it had finally receded,
Raven circled back, flying down below.
He saw that the tide had receded underneath everything.
When Raven had seen all the seafood,
only then did the people who were spared gather
their food supply.
But Raven had some oil stored in an animal stomach.
He poked a hole in it.
It was dripping; Raven lay down beneath it and it dripped into his mouth.
That's how clever he is.
When they had gathered all their food, Raven said,

«Tlél ushik'éiyi át áwé!
Yax̱ yee yagux̱lajáaḵ!
Líl yeex̱áaḵ!»
Ách áwé wé aantḵeení a náḵ wuligáas'.
Ch'a hóoch ḵu.aa aawax̱áa ldakát wé aantḵeeních yéi wsineeyi atx̱á.
Du satoowú áwé.

Shkalneek ii. Yéil ḵa Ḵee.á

Yá aantḵeení a náḵ na.áat yá atx̱á tlein akaneegích,
«Ḵutx̱ ḵaa shugux̱laxéex,»
á áwé a shóo yéi wootee.
Yax̱ ayasax̱áa yá atx̱á tlein, yá lingit'aaní
tóode woogoot.
Ḵukawjigít yá lingit'aaní.
Áwé awsikóo yá Naas Sháak aanḵáawu áa yéi yatee.
Du ádix̱ sitee ḵutx̱.ayanahá ḵa dís ḵa Ḵee.á Daakeit.
Áwé a niyaadé woogoot.
A niyaadé yaa nagúdi, aantḵeení aseiwa.áx̱ hintaak.ádi
yéi s adaaneiyí.
Ách áwé ax̱'eiwawóos' yá hintaak.ádi yéi adaane aantḵeení,
«Ax̱ x̱'éit aa ywú!»
Tlél du x̱'éit ḵuwus.aax̱.
Yéil yéi yaawaḵaa, «Yee káa ḵee.á nḵwaak'oots!»
Kawduwashooḵ áwé,
«Naasshagiyéil yádi gwáawéigé wa.é!»
Ách áwé g̱unayéi uwagút a niyaadé.
Át uwagút wé aanḵáawu áa yéi yateeyi yé.
Du sée ḵudzitee, yées yátx̱ sitee.
Du goox̱ú du daa yoo jikwli.átk wé yées yát.
Áwé awsiteen Yéilch wé shaatk'i goox̱ú ash daa yoo jikool.átgi,
héen ash x̱'éit awus.eení.
K'idéin a kát ḵutées' wé héen agux̱danaayí.
Ách áwé Yéil akaawa.aaḵw s'eex tóox̱ ḵuwul.oowú.
Tlél ayawudlaaḵ.
Wé shaatk'ích wusteení, yú héen kaadáx̱
yóot oog̱éex'ch.
Ách áwé g̱ítgaa tóox̱ sh ḵuwdli.oo.
A gukshitú áa yéi sh wudi.oo.

"That stuff is no good!
It will kill you all!
Don't eat it!"
So the people moved away from their food supply.
He himself ate all the food that the townspeople had put up.
That's how clever he is.

Episode ii. Raven and the Daylight

When the people left the large store of food because Raven had told them, "It will kill off the people,"
he was all set to eat it.
When he had eaten up this great store of food, he walked out into the world.
The world was dark.
Now he knew that a headman lived at the Head of the Nass.
He owned the stars and the moon and the Container of Daylight.
So Raven went in that direction.
As he was walking in that direction, he heard the voices of townspeople gathering seafood.
So he made a request of those townspeople who were gathering seafood,
"Send some over for me to eat!"
They didn't listen to him.
Raven said, "Watch out or I might break daylight on you folks!"
They made fun of him,
"Oh, so you must be the child of Raven-of-the-Head-of-the-Nass!"
So he started off in the direction of the head of the Nass River.
He came to where the headman lived.
He had a daughter, a young woman.
The young woman was attended by her slave.
Then Raven saw the young woman's slave attending her and giving her water to drink.
The slave carefully examined the water when she was going to drink it.
So Raven tried fitting himself inside a piece of dirt.
He didn't make it.
When the young woman saw it, she would pick it off the water and throw it away.
So he fit himself inside an evergreen needle.
He positioned himself in the corner.

Awdlix̱éis' wé yées yát anax̱ ax̱danaa.
Ách áwé a niyaanáx̱ awdináa wé héen.
Du ulx̱éis'i áa uwaháa.
Wé shaatk'ích ch'u tle awunóot'i áwé tsáa awsikóo.
Á áwé yátx̱ du káa wsitee.
Du káa yan wuwáadi du yádi, yei ḵukg̱wasteeyí du yádi,
aag̱áa áwé ts'as x̱'alitseeni aa at doogú du tayeedé kdusyáa,
wé yát a káa ḵug̱aag̱asteeyít.
Tlél a káa ḵuwustee.
Ách áwé shawat.shaanák'w wuduwax̱oox̱.
Yéi yaawaḵaa, «S'íx'g̱aa ḵu.aa haat yéi saní!»
Du x̱'ayáx̱ áwé haat yéi wdudzinée.
Cha ch'a wé s'íx'g̱aa káx' áwé tsáa ḵuwdzitee.
Wé atk'átsk'u ḵug̱astée a káx',
aag̱áa áwé wé shawat.shaanák'w yéi yaawaḵaa,
«De ch'a Yéil waaḵ x̱áashgé.»
Ách áwé wé atk'átsk'u g̱unayéi uwawát.
Át nadag̱wáat' awsiteen yú neilx' yéi yateeyi ḵutx̱.ayanaháa.
Ayáx̱ áwé aawag̱áx̱t, tlél x̱'awdanaaḵ.
Ách áwé du léelk'w yéi yaawaḵaa,
«Du jeet kaylakél' déi! Du jeet yití!»
Du jeet wuduwatée, aag̱áa áwé tsáa sh wudlik'átl'.
Aan ḵus.ook'.
Ch'áakw aan ḵus.ook'ú, aag̱áa áwé gáanx' gus'tóot aawag̱íx'.
Ách áwé dikéex' yéi yatee ḵutx̱.ayanaháa.
«Ax̱ adée!» yéi yaawaḵaa du léelk'w.
Á áwé tsu awsiteen wé dís du hídi yeedé.
Áwé tsu aawag̱áx̱t, tlél x̱'awdanaaḵ.
Ách áwé du léelk'w yéi yaawaḵaa,
«Du jeet kaylakél' déi!»
Du jeet kadukéil' áwé tsáa x̱'awdináḵ.
Á áwé tsáa gáanx' aan ashkawdliyát.
Át akanalgwátlch, aan shóode yoo akligwátlk.
Áwé neilx̱ aklagwáatl du léelk'uch unaḵéetg̱aa áwé.

He prayed that the young woman would drink from that side.
So she drank the water from that side.
His prayer came true.
The young woman didn't realize what had happened until she had swallowed it.
Then Raven became a child inside her womb.
When her baby had come to full term, when her baby was about to be born,
they spread out precious pelts beneath her
so that the child would be born on them.
It wasn't willing to be born on them.
So they called in a little old woman.
She said, "Bring moss instead!"
It was brought as she had instructed.
So it was finally upon the moss that he was born.
When the boy was born on it,
the little old woman said,
"Now those must be Raven's very eyes."
So the boy began to grow up.
As he was crawling around he saw the stars inside the house.
So he made a big fuss over it, and wouldn't stop crying.
So his grandfather said,
"Untie it for him now! Give it to him!"
They gave it to him, and then he finally quieted down.
He was playing with it.
After playing with it for a long time, he went outside and threw it up into the clouds.
This is why there are stars above.
"Oh, my precious stuff!" his grandfather said.
Then again he saw the moon in his grandfather's house.
And again he made a big fuss over it; he wouldn't stop crying.
So his grandfather said,
"Untie it for him now!"
After they untied it and gave it to him, he finally stopped crying.
Then at last he played with it outside.
He would roll it around; he kept rolling it to the end of the town and back.
Then he would roll it into the house so his grandfather wouldn't be suspicious of him.

X'oon yagiyee shunaxéex sáwé tsu ch'u yéi
áwé akawligwáatl.
Wé aan shóot aklagwáatl áwé dikéet akawligwátl.
Ách áwé du léelk'w a daadé toowú woonéekw.
Atx̱ áwé tsu aawag̱áx̱t wé Ḵee.á Daakeit.
Du léelk'w tuwáx' tlél wushgóo du jeet kawdukéil'i.
Tlél sh wulk'áatl' a daadé wé Ḵee.á Daakaḵóok.
Wé g̱aax̱ tle yaa ash najáḵ.
Ách áwé du léelk'w áwé yéi yaawaḵaa, «Du jeet kaylakél' déi!»
Ách áwé du jeet kawduwakél'.
Gáanx' áwé aan ashkawdliyát.
A yanáatx̱ áwé yaa ayíshch.
Yéi áwé aan ashkoolyát.
Ch'a wé dís aadé aan ashkoolyat yé, a yáx̱ áwé aan káx'
aan ashkoolyát Ḵee.á Daakeit.
Ch'áakw áwé aan ashkawdliyát.
Tlél déi du léelk'w ash wuḵeet ḵa wé aantḵeení.
Aag̱áa áwé át ḵoowaháa, aan wudiḵeen Ḵee.á Daakaḵóogu.
Ḵúnáx̱ áx̱ siteeyi Yéilx̱ wusitee.
Aag̱áa áwé yá lingit'aaní kaadé yóot uwagút.
Át uwagút wé áx' hintaak.ádi l du x̱'éit
wuduwawuwu yé, kag̱ít tú áwé.
Tsu yéi yaawaḵaa, «Ax̱ x̱'éit aa ywú!»
Tlél du x̱'adaat ḵaa tooshtí.
Ách áwé yéi yaawaḵaa, «Yee káa ḵee.á nḵwaak'oots!»
Ách áwé wé aantḵeení yéi yaawaḵaa,
«Goodáx̱ Naasshagiyéil sá?»
Ách áwé a yanáatx̱ ayaawax̱út' ch'a yéi gugéik'.
Aag̱áa áwé wé aantḵeení ák' aawahín wé Ḵee.á Daakaḵóok du jee yéi teeyí.
Aag̱áa áwé déi ldakát yanáatx̱ ayaawax̱út'.
Héende aa atkaawa.át wé aantḵeení,
a x̱oo.aa ḵu.aa atgutóode atkaawa.át.
Ách áwé hintaak.ádi a dleeyí ḵudzitee,
wé Yéilch a káa ḵee.á wuk'oodzídáx̱ áwé a dleeyí
ḵudzitee daḵka.ádi yáx̱.

After a number of days had passed, he again started rolling it in the same manner.
After rolling it to the end of the town he rolled it up into the sky.
So his grandfather grieved over it.
After that, once again he put up a big fuss about the Container of Daylight.
His grandfather didn't want them to untie it for him.
Raven wouldn't shut up about the Box of Daylight.
The crying was just killing him.
So his grandfather said, "Untie it for him now!"
So they untied the box and gave it to him.
He played with it outside.
He kept pulling the lid off a little bit.
This is how he was playing with it.
Just as he had been playing with the moon, so now he was playing in the town with the Container of Daylight.
He spent a lot of time playing with it.
His grandfather and the townspeople were no longer suspicious of him.
Finally the time came; he flew off with the Box of Daylight.
He became Raven in his true form.
Then he went forth into the world.
He came to the place where the people wouldn't send him over any seafood; it was in darkness.
Again he said, "Send some over for me to eat!"
Nobody paid any attention to his words.
So he said, "Watch out or I might break daylight on you folks!"
So the townspeople said, "Where does this Raven-of-the-Head-of-the-Nass hail from?"
So Raven yanked the lid off just a little bit.
Then the townspeople believed that he had the Box of Daylight.
Then finally he yanked the lid off altogether.
Some of the townspeople rushed into the water,
and others rushed into the forest.
Because of this, sea creatures have flesh;
since Raven broke daylight on them, they have flesh like land-dwelling creatures.

Shkalneek iii. Yéil k̲a Xóots Wooshdasháay

Yá lingit'aaní geix' k̲ee.á awliyéx̲
  yá Yéil—Naasshagiyéil.
Aag̲áa áwé g̲unéi uwagút yá lingit'aaní tóode.
Aag̲áa áwé shux'áa awsiteeni át áwé
wé s'eek̲ hít k'iyeenáx̲ naashóo,
áwé tle át uwagút.
Déix̲ Xóots ásíwéigé, K̲áa Xóots du sháttin.
Áwé aadé woogoot.
Tle áa neil wugoodí yéi yaawak̲aa Yéil,
«Ax̲ aatx̲úx̲ wa.é síwéigé!»
Tlél aag̲áa yoo toodatángin wáa sáyá yakg̲wak̲aayí,
ch'u tle áwé tlákw a yís yan uwanée, tle yóox̲ at teeyín.
Yéi áwé yanak̲áa áwé tle du x̲'éix̲ at wuduwatee wé wooshdasháaych.
Atx̲'éeshi du x̲'eis wududliwás.
Áwé atx̲'éeshi dulwáas,
aag̲áa áwé wé K̲áa Xóots du jín gánt awsitán.
Wé du jín gánt awustaaní áwé a tóonáx̲ eex̲ kawduwatl'úk̲,
wé Yéilch aan gax̲aayít wé eex̲.
Du x̲'aseiyée yawdudzi.ín wé eex̲, áwé du atx̲'éeshi aan aawax̲áa,
wé K̲áa Xóots jínnáx̲ kawduwatl'ug̲u eex̲.
Áwé a yáax' áwé hú tsú chush yáax' x̲'éix̲ at wuditee.
Yéi áwé atx̲'éeshi x̲'éix̲ anatée,
hú tsú du jín gánt awsitán Yéil.
Tlél tsu daa sá a tóonáx̲ kawdutl'ook̲,
ts'as tlaax̲ yáx̲ áwé woonee.
Áwé xáanaa áwé du aatx̲úx̲ch yéi yawsik̲aa,
«Cháatl, cháatl kasyeek̲ daak gax̲took̲óox̲ seig̲áneen.»
Hú tsú áwu, wé Yook̲.
Yóot'át áwé Yéil du xwáayix̲ sitee, du kook̲énayix̲ sitee.
Áwé tle k̲eena.áa daak has uwak̲úx̲.
Áwé ch'a x̲áat x̲'úx̲u áwé du wantóo awlisín Yéil k̲u.aa.
A kát has k̲óox̲ wé éet, héeni aawataan du tíx'i.
Yéil tle héeni anatáan áwé, g̲unéi aawax̲út' du katseesí.
Áwé wé Xóots aayí tsú tle héeni awutaaní áwé, tlél tsu wáa sá yoo uneek.
Tlél tsu cháatl kei ooyík̲ch du náxu.
Áwé Yéil ax̲'eiwawóos',
«Daa sákwshéwéigé aan idanák̲ws' gé, ax̲ káalk'w?»

Episode iii. Raven and the Brown Bear Couple

Raven—Raven-of-the-Head-of-the-Nass—made daylight
appear throughout this world.
Then he began to walk into the world.
Then the first thing he saw was
smoke rising from the rear of a house,
so he went to it.
It turned out that there were two Bears, a Male Bear and his wife.
So he went there.
Just as he went inside, Raven said,
"So it must be *you* who are my auntie's husband!"
He never had to search his mind for what he was going to say,
he was always prepared for it, he would just come up with something to say.
When he said that, the couple fed him.
They roasted some dryfish for him.
So when they roasted the dryfish,
the Male Bear put his paw in the fire.
When he put his hand in the fire, oil dripped out of it
so Raven could eat the dryfish with oil.
They placed the bowl of oil before him and he ate his dryfish with
the oil that dripped out of the Male Bear's paw.
So in turn Raven reciprocated by feeding the Bear as well.
So when Raven fed him dryfish,
Raven likewise put his hand in the fire.
There was nothing at all dripping out of his hand;
it just withered up.
Then that evening his auntie's husband said to him,
"Halibut—we're going to go out halibut fishing tomorrow."
He was there too, Cormorant.
That animal was Raven's sidekick, his messenger.
Then the next day they went out.
But Raven had some salmon flesh hidden in his inside pocket.
When they arrived atop the halibut hotspot, he put his line in the water.
When Raven put his line in the water, a halibut began tugging on his buoy.
But when the Bear put his in the water, nothing ever happened.
Not even one halibut would take a nip at his halibut hook.
Then he asked Raven,
"What could it be that you're baiting your hook with, nephew?"

«Ha yá ax̱ leiwadaaleilx'isáani áwé.»
Ách áwé wé Xóotsch ḵu.aa aax̱ wulixaash wé du láaw.
Áwé wé yaakw, áx' áwé tle g̱unayéi jiwdigút.
Áwé du xwáayi ḵu.aa yéi ayawsiḵaa,
«Wé katsees yát idaḵín!»
Ayáx̱ áwé katsees yát wudiḵín.
Áwé tle du jig̱eit ash uwajáḵ wé Xóots.
Ch'a du x̱'asatoowú áwé yéi yatee Yéil ḵu.aa.
Áwé tle sh wudijáḵ wé Xóots ḵu.aa.
Áwé yánde g̱unayéi s ayaawax̱áa.
Yánde yaa s gaḵóox̱ áwé, wé du xwáayi yéi ayawsiḵaa,
«K'e i l'óot', k'e i l'óot'!»—
áwé s'é wé du sháax̱ yaa nashíx—
«K'e i l'óot' daak tsaaḵ!»
Du l'óot' daak awsix̱út', á áwé aax̱ aawak'oots.
Áwé, «Úsh k'e x̱'anidataan!»
«Ráaraaraaraa.»
Tlél aadé x̱'einax̱ditaani yé.
De ch'a hóoch' áwé, «Ráaraaraaraa.»
Yéi áwé altin ḵáa yoo x̱'ayatánk.
Áwé yan has uwaḵúx̱.
Wé du aat ash x̱'eiwawóos',
«Ha goo sákwshé gwé i aatx̱úx̱ ḵu.aa?»
«Aatlein du jeet at yawlil'íx'. Héináx̱
    áwé shakals'óow.»
Áwé tle akawlixaash wé cháatl.
Yat'aayi té áwé a yoowú tóot akaawachák.
Yéi áwé ayawsiḵaa a daat,
«Tlél dutáax'. Tléik', ax̱ jig̱eit áyá tlél dutáax',
    tle dunút'x'w áwé.»
Wé du kooḵénayich ḵu.aa áwé akang̱aneegít sayahéi.
«Ráaraaraaraa!» de ch'a hóoch' áwé aadé yéi yanaḵéich yé.
«‹Héende aa kanataan,› akanéek.
‹Héende aa kanataan,› yéi yanaḵéich.»
Áwé tlél ash wuḵeet,
x'éig̱aax̱ oowajée wé du aat ash x̱'awuwóos'i.
Áwé anút'x'w wé cháatl yoowú.
Yax̱ yakawdlichák wé yat'aayi té.
Áwé tle ash uwajáḵ wé Shéech Xóots.

"Well, it's the little folds of foreskin around my penis."
So the Bear cut off his penis.
Then he started to flail about in the boat.
Then he said to his sidekick,
"Fly to the side of the buoy!"
Accordingly, Cormorant flew to the side of the buoy.
So Raven's artifice killed the Bear.
That's how clever Raven was with words.
Now the Bear had killed himself.
So they started to take the dead Bear to shore.
As they were going toward shore, he said to his sidekick,
"Let's see your tongue; let's see your tongue!"—
at that moment he was running neck and neck with Cormorant—
"Go ahead and stick your tongue out!"
He yanked Cormorant's tongue out and snapped it off.
Then he said, "Just you try to talk now!"
"Rarararah."
Cormorant couldn't speak.
All he could say was, "Rarararah."
That's how the man who witnessed the fatal event spoke.
Then they came ashore.
His auntie asked him,
"Now, I wonder, where is your auntie's husband?"
"A bunch of his gear got broken. He's just over there
chopping limbs off trees."
Then he butchered the halibut.
He packed hot stones into the stomach.
He told her, in reference to the halibut stomachs,
"It isn't to be chewed. No, one does not chew my special recipe;
one simply swallows it in mouthfuls."
But his messenger wanted to tell her what was really going on.
"Rarararah!" is all he kept saying.
"'Put some hooks in the water,' he's saying.
He keeps saying, 'Put some hooks in the water.'"
So she wasn't suspicious of him;
his auntie thought he was telling the truth when she asked him.
So she was swallowing the halibut stomachs by the mouthful.
The hot stones were packed inside them.
So that's what killed the Female Bear.

Yéil áwé ch'a du jig̲eit hú tsú ash uwaják̲,
yat'aayi té a tóot akaawajeli cháatl yoowú
awunút'x'u áwé.
Ash jáak̲ áwé tsáa, yóot ayawsinák̲ wé du xwáayi k̲u.aa.
Tle ch'a tléindruáx̲ áwé aawax̲áa wé déix̲ Xóots Yéil k̲u.aa.

She, too, was killed by Raven's artifice
when she swallowed the halibut stomachs into which
he had put the hot stones.
After this had killed her, Raven finally chased his sidekick away.
Raven ate the two Bears all by himself.

Shaadaax' X̲'éidáx̲ Tlaagú
Stories by Robert Zuboff

FIGURE 8. Robert Zuboff in Angoon, June 1971, wearing the *S'igeidi S'áaxw* 'Beaver Hat' and a ceremonial robe, both at.óow of his clan, the K̲ak'weidí. Photo by Jon Lyman. Courtesy of Sealaska Heritage Institute, PO004, box 7, item 81.

ROBERT ZUBOFF, whose Tlingit name was Shaadaax', was a member and leader of the Angoon K̲ak'weidí clan and a child of the Dak̲l'aweidí. He was born on October 14, 1893, making him seventy-eight years old when these performances were recorded, and he passed away on April 19, 1974. Zuboff was a highly respected orator and storyteller among his contemporaries and he is remembered as such today by the living Tlingit community and students of Tlingit grammar and oral literature. His speech is deliberate, dignified, and carefully articulated. See *Haa K̲usteeyí* for a short biography of Zuboff.*

The first of Zuboff's stories presented here was the first Raven story ever published in the Tlingit language, originally appearing in 1973 as a small Tlingit-only paperback titled *K̲udatan Kahídee, Shaadaax' X̲'éidáx̲ Shkalneek: The Salmon Box, told by Robert Zuboff.*† Zuboff was recorded telling this discrete tale by Kanáash, Henry Davis, in Angoon in June of 1972. The cover design of the original paperback is reprinted below (figure 9).

Zuboff's second tale, consisting of six episodes, was recorded by Nora Dauenhauer in Angoon on July 21, 1972. The full recording actually features Zuboff telling nine sequential stories, but we have only included the six that feature Raven.‡ The third

---

* Dauenhauer and Dauenhauer, *Haa K̲usteeyí*, 612–16.

† The booklet has been digitized and made available by the Alaska Native Language Archives as item number TL973Z1973a.

‡ Zuboff tells these stories in this order: «Dukt'ootl'» "Black-Skin"; «Gantutl'úk'x̲u» "The Wood Worm"; «Yéil k̲a X̲'aan» "Raven and Fire"; «Yéil Lingít Awulyeix̲í» "Raven Makes Humans"; «Yéil k̲a Kutatankahídi» "Raven and the Salmon Box"; «Yéil k̲a Du Káak» "Raven and His Uncle"; «Yéil k̲a Aangalak̲ú» "Raven and the Flood"; «Yéil Ana.óot Aaní Awulyeix̲í» "Raven Makes the Aleutian Islands"; and «Ana.óot Shkalneegí» "Aleut Story". The final story is an account of the origin of sea otters. The original tape recording of Zuboff's performance is no longer extant, but there are a number of transfer copies. MC005, tapes 125; 126, side a; 126, side b; 127, side b; and 128, side a, all contain portions of the full performance, but begin or end (or both) in the midst of Zuboff's

episode of this extended tale provides a second instance of Zuboff telling "Raven and the Salmon Box"; the two versions are not identical and provide an opportunity to compare how a single storyteller may make differing compositional decisions when telling the same story on separate occasions. The title we have applied to this extended tale taken as a whole is «Lingit'aanitóox̱ Yakawdiyayi Yéil» "Raven Who Ventured Through the World", which is based on the concluding lines:

Á áyá yáa—	This is the place
aadáx̱ áwé—aadáx̱ áwé yáa lingit'aanitóox̱	from which—from which Raven proceeded
yakawdiyáa	to venture
yáa Yéil.*	throughout the world.

The phrase *lingit'aanitóox̱ yakawidyáa* 'he ventured, voyaged, travelled throughout the world' is based on the verb theme *O-ka-d-ÿaa*` 'for O to travel, go, voyage, move (by uncertain means)' and contains the derivational string *P-x̱ ÿa-u-* 'moving sideways, in an arc, circuitously along P', the postposition P in this instance being *lingit'aanitú* '(the space) within the world'. Taken all together this yields the hazy image of Raven journeying throughout the world—by means uncertain—along a curving, meandering path.

One of the many interesting features of Zuboff's speech is that he occasionally uses a variant of the perfective prefix that occurs only in the Teslin dialect of Tlingit; the Teslin form is *m-*, while all other dialects use *w-*. The dialect spoken by Zuboff normally does not contain the phoneme /m/ at all. In Teslin, when the perfective prefix *ÿu-* follows a vowel and precedes a CV- prefix, it contracts to *m-* where the rest of Tlingit speakers would have *w-* instead. Zuboff was keenly aware of the close relationship between the Deisheetaan of Teslin and the closely-knit K̲ak'weidí and Deisheetaan of Angoon, holding his Teslin relatives in high regard and perhaps considering their dialect as more original in some respects than the Angoon dialect. While the sound /m/ as a rule is not found outside of the Teslin dialect, it appears that Zuboff uses this sound in a deliberately archaizing manner, recruiting the patterns of speech associated with the origin of his people's migration to the coast for stylistic purposes. His occasional use of the Teslin *m-* perfective may be his way of paying tribute to the place from which his people migrated to the coast many generations prior. Note that Zuboff refers to «yáa Tásl̲anx' yéi haa teeyí»† 'when we lived in Teslin' as contemporaneous with Raven's own adventures in the interior. For example, Zuboff clearly pronounces the

narration. Tape 343, side a, is the most complete, containing an unbroken recording of the whole performance other than the final portion of the last story, which is continued on tape 343, side b.

* RZ II, vi, 55–58.

† RZ II, i, 24.

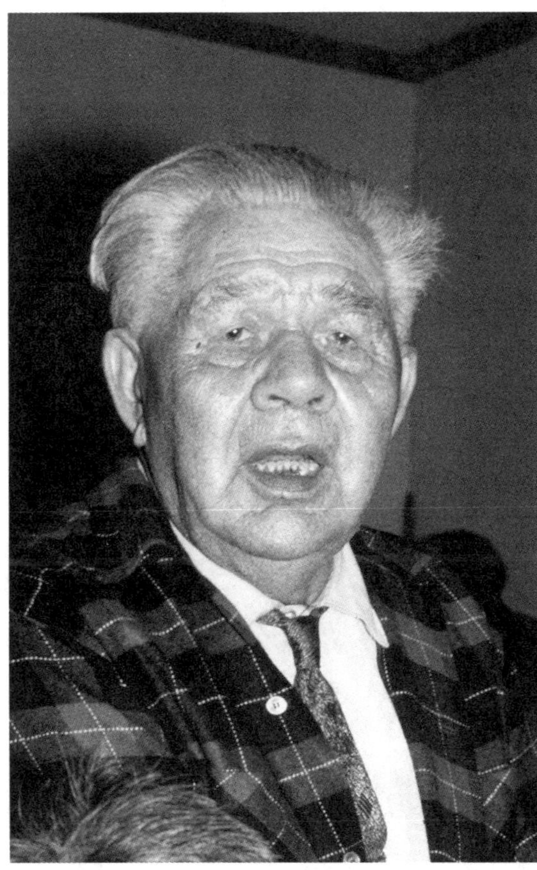

FIGURE 9. (ABOVE) The original cover of the 1973 paperback edition of Zuboff's "Raven and the Salmon Box", published by Tlingit Readers Inc. (retranscribed and translated as RZ I in this volume), featuring a four-color design on white stock by X'aashuch'eet, Robert Davis.

FIGURE 10. (LEFT) Robert Zuboff in Angoon, c. 1974. Photo by Cyril George. Courtesy of Sealaska Heritage Institute, PO077, box 37, item 1324.

Teslin *m*- perfective in the phrase «a t'éinax̱.áx̱ áyá yamdik̲ín»* 'he (a magpie) flew around behind it (a mountain goat)'; the corresponding form in all other dialects would be *a t'éinax̱.áx̱ áyá yawdik̲ín*. Other examples from Zuboff's texts include «héendáx̱ áyá aa kamdi.áa»† 'some of them (mountains) rise up out of the water' (corresponding to *…aa kawdi.áa*) and «du lú áyá áa yoo akamlitíx̱' yá xáats'»‡ 'he (Raven) unscrewed his beak from the sky' (corresponding to *…yoo akawlitíx̱'*).

* RZ II, iii, 82.

† RZ II, v, 75.

‡ RZ II, v, 95.

I. Yéil k̲a Kutatankahídi (shux’áa aayí)

T’éex’in
yá lingit’aaní.
The first beginning of the world,
everything was very, very hard.
T’éex’in.
K̲únáx̲ t’éex’in.
Yáa—yá atyana.á áyú—
yá x̲áat
yoo yaa.éik
yáa k̲utaanx’ yáa yeedát.
Wéi gaaw k̲u.aa tléil—
tléil áwé yáni yéi utí.
Yú deikée góos’ yáx̲ áwé
áa ya.éix̲ wé x̲áat.
Tléil áwé aadé
yáa k̲’anashgidéi k̲áa x̲’éit
aa koox̲dihaayi yé
wé x̲áat—
yáa yaaw
k̲a yáa saak
k̲a yáa wooch g̲uwanáade x̲áat:
cháas’,
téel’,
t’á,

I. Raven and the Salmon Box (telling 1)

This world
used to be a hard place to live in.
In the first beginning of the world,
everything was very, very hard.
It was hard.
It was very hard.
The fish runs—
the salmon
regularly migrate
in the summer these days.
But at that time it wasn't—
it wasn't on the mainland.
The salmon would migrate
way out along the cloud banks on the horizon.
There was no way
a poor person
could procure any
of those fish to eat—
the herring
and the eulachon
and the different kinds of salmon:
humpies,
dog salmon,
king salmon,

deikée ádi áwé.
Ch'a áa isx̱ítt'.
Ch'a áa isx̱ítt'.
They spawned right there
at the Pafísifik Óoshan.
Á áyá ch'as aanḵáawux̱ siteeyi ḵáa
áyá áa daak kudayeich—
aanḵáawu,
jee yéi at yateeyi ḵáa.
Yáa ḵ'anashgidéi ḵáa ḵu.aa áyá
yáa aanḵáawu áyá ax̱'eiltínch.
Áyá a daa yoo tuwatánk
yáa Yéilch.
Át woogoo-oo-oo-oot.
Át kawdiyaa-aa-aa-aa.
Tléináx̱ yateeyi ḵáa jeex' áwé
yéi yatee
wé Naaḵw Tl'eeg̱í Wootsaag̱áa.
Yéi duwasáakw yáa ḵáa
X̱'enax̱g̱aatwaayáa.
Hú ḵu.aa áyá
sáḵs áyá aya.óo,
Yéil ḵu.aa.
Sáḵs áyá aya.óo.
Áyá X̱'enax̱g̱aatwaayáa x̱ánt uwagút.
«Ḵúnáx̱ áyá yak'éi
yáa—yá ax̱ sáḵsi.
Tlax̱ tléil áyá
aan at woox̱sat'úkx̱aa.
Tlax̱ ḵúnáx̱, ḵúnáx̱ yak'éi.
Iyatéen ágé yóo—
yóo jánwu?
Yóo shaa yát woogoodi jánwu gé
iyatéen?»
«Aaá,»
yóo x̱'ayaḵá
X̱'enax̱g̱aatwaayáa,
«Aaá.»
«Ha cha ch'a yáatx̱ áwé

things from out at sea.
They would spawn right there.
They would spawn right there.
They spawned right there
at the Pacific Ocean.
Only a man who is well-to-do
would travel out there—
a rich man,
a person who has property.
But the poor man
could only stare while the rich man ate.
This is what Raven
was contemplating.
He went a-a-a-all over.
He ventured a-a-a-all around.
There was a certain man
who had
the Octopus Tentacle Cane.
This man's name was
X̲'enax̲gaatwaayáa.
Raven, on the other hand,
owned a bow,
Raven did.
He owned a bow.
So he went to X̲'enax̲gaatwaayáa.
"This—this bow of mine
is very fine.
I simply never
miss with it.
It is very, very fine.
Do you see that—
that mountain goat over yonder?
Do you see
that mountain goat walking on the mountainside?
"Yes,"
said
X̲'enax̲gaatwaayáa,
"Yes."
"Well, I'll take a shot at it

aadé kk̲wat'óok.
K'e latín.»
Yáa du chooneidí k̲u.aa
ts'eeg̲eenée áyá.
Yá Yéil, ts'eeg̲eenée áyá
yáa—yáa du chooneidí.
His arrow was a magpie,
Dleit K̲áa x̲'éinác̲.
Áwé yaa ndak̲íni áwé,
tle yaa ndak̲íni,
áwé yáa—yá jánwu t'éix̲—
a t'éinax̲.áx̲ áwé yawdik̲ín.
Áwé daak
áwé awlidlékw.
Tlei daak wudzigít wéi jánwu diyínde.
«Iyatéen gé aadé yak'eiyi yé
ax̲ chooneidí?
X̲waat'úk.
Tlél gé aadé wéi i Náak̲w Tl'eeg̲í Wootsaag̲áa daséix'án,
yáa ax̲ chooneidí x̲áa?
Can I trade with you?»
«Aaá.
Yóo—yóo—yóo atyana.á
áwé kwshé
yóo yax̲'áagi yéi yatee?
Atyana.á
ák.wé?
A yís ák.wé?»
«Aaá.
A yís.»
«Haa tlél aadé yangiyadlaag̲i yé,»
yóo ash daayak̲á X̲'enax̲g̲aatwaayáa,
«Tlél aadé yangiyadlaag̲i yé
cha ch'a x̲át ax̲ saayí átx̲ ilayeix̲í,
x̲át ax̲ saayí átx̲ ilayeix̲í
aag̲áa tsáa yakg̲eedláak̲.»
Yéi x̲'ayak̲á Yéil,
«Yak'éi,
átx̲ guk̲alayéix̲ i saayí.»

from right here.
Just watch."
But his arrow
was a magpie.
This Raven, his arrow
was a magpie.
His arrow was a magpie,
to say it in English.
So, as it was flying,
as it was flying,
it flew around
behind the mountain goat.
And then
the magpie startled it, causing it to fall off the cliff.
The mountain goat fell down below.
"Do you see how fine
my arrow is?
I hit it.
Why not trade my bow and arrows
for your Octopus Tentacle Cane, you know?
Can I trade with you?"
"Yes.
It's the salmon run
way out on the ocean,
isn't it?
The salmon run,
is that it?
Is that what it's for?"
"Yes,
that's what it's for."
"Well, there's no way you can get it,"
X̱'enax̱gaatwaayáa said to him,
"You can't get it
unless you use my name,
only if you use my name
will you get it."
Raven said,
"Okay,
I'll use your name."

Aan áwé woogoot wé Náaḵw Tl'eeg̱í Wootsaag̱áa ayanadláaḵ.
Yaakwdáat haanaanax̱.á,
Aalséix̱ wát áwé át uwagút
Yéil.
Wé Aalséix̱ wátdáx̱
áwé du Náaḵw Tl'eeg̱í Wootsaag̱áa
anax̱ ax̱'eiwataan
Kutatankahídi.
Kutatankahídináx̱ ax̱'eiwataan.
Áwé yánde asaheiyí áwé
yadali átx̱ wusitee du jeex'.
Yaa ash jigatánch.
Yaa ash jigatánch.
Áwé du kéilk' áwé du eenx̱ sitee,
Yéil.
Wé Gidzanóox' yóo duwasáagu ts'axweil áwé.
Áwé yaa ash jigatáan
áwé du káak,
wé du kéilk'ich áwé
yéi adaayaḵá
«Góok! Góok! Góok! Góok!
Shukanalx̱oox̱ déi!»
yóo áwé,
«Shukanalx̱oox̱ déi!»

(AT.SHÍ)

Ou hee yei
Ou hee yei
Ou hee yei
Aa haa yaa haa
Yei hei
Ou hee yei
Aa yaa haa
X̱'ei-naax̱-g̱aat-waa-yaa
Ou yaa
Ou hee yei

Tlákw áx̱ shukalx̱oox̱ú
X̱'enax̱g̱aatwaayáa,
naaléi áa yaa asyiḵji yé yánde.

When he obtained the Octopus Tentacle Cane, he took off with it.
On this side of Yakutat
Raven came to
the mouth of the Alsek River.
From the mouth of the Alsek River
he hooked his
Octopus Tentacle Cane
onto the Salmon Box.
He hooked it onto the Salmon Box.
But when he wanted it to come ashore
it became a heavy thing for him to wrangle.
It kept overpowering him and pulling him around.
It kept pulling him around.
Now his nephew was with him,
with Raven.
He's the crow that they call Gidzanóox'.
As it was pulling
his uncle along,
his nephew
said to him,
"Come on! Come on! Come on! Come on!
Invoke the name now!"
he says,
"Invoke the name now!"

(**SINGING**)

Ou hee yei
Ou hee yei
Ou hee yei
Aa haa yaa haa
Yei hei
Ou hee yei
Aa yaa haa
X̱'ei-naax̱-g̱aat-waa-yaa
Ou yaa
Ou hee yei

Every time he invoked the name
X̱'enax̱g̱aatwaayáa,
he would drag it in a long way toward shore.

Tlákw áx̲ shukalx̲oox̲ú
naaléi áa yaa asyik̲ji yé.
Wáananée sáwé
yán ayaawadlaak̲.
Aalséix̲náx̲ áwé yan awsiyík̲.
Ch'u yá yakyee l'éiw kalag̲é áwé
áa yéi yatee,
Aalséix̲ wát.
KANÁASH: *Aa, yóot, Yaakwdáat x̲án áwé kwshé?*
Uh-huh, Yaakwdáat x̲án áwé,
haanaanax̲.á, Yaakwdáat haanaanax̲.á.
Yáa áx̲ woolaayi yé k̲u.aa áwé
du x̲'us.eetí áa yéi teex̲
Yéil.
Yáa gus'yaadáx̲ jinli.aadi yé,
yáa *óoshan swells,*
yáa teet tlénx',
ch'a aan tléil kei—
tléil kei shaahíkch,
yáa du x̲'us.eetí áa yéi yatee.
Ch'oo yáa yeedádidé áa yéi yatee
Yéil x̲'us.eetí.
Aanáx̲ áyá yan awsiyík̲
yán,
yá Kutatankahídi.
Yan asyéek̲ áyá
ch'a ldakát aantk̲eení áyá oox̲oox̲
a yaagú teen.
«Haadé yee yanagú,»
yóo x̲'ayak̲á,
«Haadé yee yanagú.»
Yáa yaakw ashawulheegí,
«Yáa goo sá i tuwáa sigóo
aadé áyá yakg̲eex̲áa,
goo sá.
You tig it wherever you wand it,
wherever you wand it.»
Á áyá yáa yeedát yáa—
it is a salt-water fish now.

Every time he invoked the name
he would drag it in a long way.
Eventually
it reached the shore.
He dragged it ashore by the Alsek River.
Even today fine white sand
is there at
the mouth of the Alsek.
HENRY DAVIS: *Isn't it way over there near Yakutat?*
Uh-huh, it's near Yakutat,
on this side, on this side of Yakutat.
And Raven's
footprints remain there,
where the beach is exposed by the tide.
Where the waves roll in from the cloud banks,
these ocean swells,
these huge waves—
no matter how big the waves are,
the indentations never get filled in;
Raven's footprints remain there.
To this very day Raven's footprints
are still there.
That's where he pulled it ashore
to the mainland,
this Salmon Box.
When he had pulled it ashore
he was inviting all the townspeople
to bring their canoes.
"Come in your canoes,"
he says,
"Come in your canoes."
When they had filled the canoes, he said,
"You can take it
wherever you want to,
wherever.
You take it wherever you want it,
wherever you want it."
And now today
it is a salt-water fish now.

It goes up to fresh water and spawn in there.
Yáa ḵ'anashgidéi ḵáa kagéix'
aa kahéix̱ yá héen yíkdáx̱
yáa atyana.á tlein.
Aadé haa kagéi kaawahayi yé.

It goes up to fresh water and spawns in there.
Poor people
now have river access to a portion of
this great salmon run.
This is how we gained access to it.

II. Lingit’aanitóox̱ Yakawdiyayi Yéil

Shkalneek i. Yéil ḵa X̱’aan

Sheyadihéin yáa—
yáa shkalneekx’i sáani.
Tléil áyá daa sá a eetée yéi wutee
yáa lingit’aanikáx̱’,
ch’a ldakát át ḵwá a káa yéi wootee.
Yáa x̱’aan—
tléil áyá x̱’aan a tóo yéi utéeyin yáa aas
ḵa yáa wás’x̱’.
Tléil daa sá áx̱ akoogaan.
Yóo deikée yax̱’áak áyú, wáa sákwshíyú kaawahayi
    yóo—yóo—yóo yax̱’áak?
Á ḵu.aa áyáa anax̱ kei akagánch
yáa x̱’aan.
Á áyá yáa—
yáa Dikée Aanḵáawu kooḵénayi—
dleit ḵáach yéi yasáakw *Lucifer*—
hú kwshéiyá
yáa Lingítch ḵu.aa yéi uwasáa Yéil.
Yáa—yáa daḵká,
áa yéi haa natée
yáa daḵká,
á áyá áx̱ yaawagút
yáa áa tlein x̱’ayaax̱.
A x̱’ayaax̱ áyá áx̱ yaawagút,
yáa—yáa Táslanx’ yéi haa teeyí.

II. Raven Who Ventured Through the World

Episode i. Raven and Fire

There are a lot of these—
these little stories.
After the flood, nothing was where it had been
in the world,
but everything was still on the earth.
This fire—
at that time there was no fire in the trees
or in the various bushes.
Nothing could burn.
How in the world did fire end up way out there
    on the open ocean?
But fire kept flaring up
out there.
So this—
this angel of God—
white folks call him Lucifer—
I suppose this is who
the Tlingit named Raven.
In the—the interior,
when we were living
in the interior,
this is when he walked around
the shore of this big lake.
It was this shore that he walked around
when we lived in—in Teslin.

A t'áak áyá yáa áa tleinx̲ sitee.
Áyá teyak̲áash áyá kamdziyík̲.
S'é káx̲ ayaawagudéyáx̲ áwé yatee
du x̲'us.eetée.
Yáa du x̲'ustl'eek̲ eetí áa yéi yatee k̲a yáa du x̲'eitákw
eetí áa yéi yatee,
kaltéelk̲.
Á áyá yáa yeedát
k̲udziteeyi aa áyá
gaaw kei has akg̲watan g̲anúgún áwé
g̲uneitkanaayí áyá aadé has akunak̲éich
yóo Yéil x̲'us.eetí kei x̲dultl'eedít.
It is a human being tracks,
k̲áa x̲'us.eetí áyú.
Á áyóo yóo Yéilx̲
katusanéek.
Yei sh kalhéich yáa k̲áa.
He's invisible man.
Ldakát yéide át kawdiyaa.
Kéetx' áyá tsú
sh wulsháayin.
Shaawátx̲ wusitee.
Shaawátx̲ wusitee.
Aadé át k̲uwdi.oowu yé.
Áyá yáa yeedát
yóo deikéenáx̲ kei kaganji x̲'aan,
á áyá yáa yánde asayahéi,
yáa yánde.
Áyá K'ákw áyá du lú áyá yayát' shóogunáx̲,
yáa K'ákw.
G̲altóot áyá adatéen
yáa náak̲w loowú,
yáa K'ákw x̲ánt góot.
«Tlél gé aadéi
ax̲ jiyís yan aa yagisiyeegi yé
yóo x̲'aan?»
«Tléik'!
Tlél aadé!

Inland from there is a big lake.
There are imprints on the slate rocks.
His footprints leave the impression that someone
    was walking around on the clay.
The prints of his toes are there, and his heel
prints are there,
barefoot.
So those who are alive
today,
whenever they are about to take up the drum,
they send the opposite moiety there
to clear the debris out of those Raven footprints.
They're a human being's tracks;
they're a man's footprints.
This is who we identify
as Raven.
This man makes himself disappear.
He's the invisible man.
He's had all kinds of experiences.
He even got a Killerwhale
to marry him.
He became a woman.
He became a woman.
This is how he changed forms.
And now,
the fire that kept flaring up way out at sea,
this is what he wanted to bring to the mainland,
to the mainland.
The Pygmy Owl originally had a long nose,
the Pygmy Owl.
Raven had an octopus nose
in his pocket
when he came to Pygmy Owl.
"Couldn't you
take some of that fire in your beak
and bring it ashore for me?"
"No!
No way!

Ax̱ loowú ḵwá aadáx̱ gug̱agáan.
Ax̱ loowú aax̱ gug̱agáan.»
«Yak'éiyi aa áa yéi kḵwa.oo wé i loowú.
Eetiyeyáanáx̱ kei kg̱wak'éi áa yéi kḵwa.oo aa i loowú.»
Á áwé yan áwé ayakaawaḵáa yáa K'ákw
Yéil.
Ách áwé yéi yaawaḵaa, «Yak'éi,
yak'éi, kakḵwa.aaḵw
aadé daak x̱wadaḵeení.»
Aax̱ áwé át daḵéen áwé
ayawsiyeeḵ wéi x̱'aan
yánde.
Du loowú daaḵ nagán.
Du loowú daaḵ nagán.
Yéil jeenáx̱ yan ayasayéeḵ áwé
yá aasx'i x̱oodé áwé
aa uwalít,
ḵa yá wás'x'i x̱oodé tsú aa uwalít,
ḵa yá téix' x̱oodé tsú aa uwalít
wé x̱'aan,
wé x̱'aan.
Ách áyáa
yáa aas
shóox̱ tuda.aak.
X̱'aan a tóo yéi wootee.
Áx̱ akagaan
ḵa yáa wás'.
Yáa té tsóo
x̱'aan a tóowu.
Wóosht wudag̱áadi
yíḵdlaa áa yéi yoo yaneek.
K'e aadé yateeyi yé
yáa shkalneek.
Dleit ḵáach
tléil tlax̱ yéi a daa yoo x̱'eitánk.
Yá Adam and Eve aklanik nuch dleit ḵáach.

My beak will burn off.
My beak will burn off."
"I'll replace that beak of yours with a nice one.
The beak I'll put on you will be better than ever."
So Raven
talked Pygmy Owl into it.
So he said, "Okay,
okay, I'll try
to fly out there."
After that, when he flew out there
he took that fire in his beak and brought it
ashore.
His beak was burning away.
His beak was burning away.
When he brought the fire in for Raven to wield,
Raven scattered
some among the trees,
and he scattered some among the bushes too,
and he scattered some among the stones too,
that fire,
that fire.
This is why
we make fires
with tree wood.
Fire came to be inside it.
Tree wood catches fire,
as well as bushes.
Rocks, too,
have fire in them.
When they are struck together
they make sparks.
Notice the way
this story is.
White folks
don't even talk that way about it.
White folks always tell the story of Adam and Eve.

Shkalneek ii. Yéil Lingít Awulyeix̲í

Á áyáa
yáa—
yá át kundayáa
yáa Yéil
shóogunáx̲,
té áyá ashawsigút.
«Sheedagú!
Ax̲ kéek'x̲ inastí!»
Aag̲áa áyáa
yiwooyáat'
aag̲áa yei k̲utoosteech yé
yáa lingit'aanikáx',
dax̲atwooshú
hándít táakw,
nas'gatwooshú
hándít táakw,
gooshúk̲
hándít táakw,
yéi
k̲uditsáakw wé gaaw.
Á áyá ch'a tleidahéen áyáa—
gwál g̲agaan gíyá yawsit'áax̲'án—
áyá yéi ayawsik̲aa du kéek', «Héeng̲aa neesheex kík'.
Héeng̲aa neesheex.
X̲at shaawakúx.»
Á áwé lich'éeyák̲w áwé.
Wé té yéeyi áwé
du kéek'x̲ awliyéx̲.
Áyá x'áan du tóo yéi woonee.
Yanax̲ yei aawagúk̲.
«G̲íg̲aa déi! G̲ígaa, ch'a téix̲ inastí.»
Ch'a yáa a tuwánt tin kayaank'ée áyá ashawsigút,
«Sheedagú!
Ax̲ kéek'x̲ inastí.
Héeng̲aa neesheex.»
Át wulis'eeséyáx̲ áwé yatee
yáa kayaanée

Episode ii. Raven Makes Humans

So now—
now,
when Raven
was venturing around
in the beginning,
he roused up a stone.
"Get up!
Be my younger brother!"
At that time
our lifespans
were long
in this world;
seven
hundred years,
eight
hundred years,
nine
hundred years,
that's how long
people lived at that time.
So one time—
perhaps it was hot in the direct sunlight—
he told his younger brother, "Go run and get some water, little brother.
Run and get some water.
I'm thirsty."
Now his younger brother was slow.
He had turned what used to be stone
into his younger brother.
So anger welled up within Raven.
He pushed him down onto the ground.
"Useless! You're useless; just be a stone."
He roused up this little leaf lying beside the stone.
"Get up!
Be my younger brother!
Run and get some water."
When he converted this leaf
into his brother,

du kéek'x̱ awulyeix̱í.
Tleidooshú jinkaat táakw,
dax̱adooshú jinkaat táakw,
yéi áyá haa kanax̱ yoo at yateek.
Yáa kayaank'ée áyá
haa éex̱ awliyéx̱ yáa Yéil.
Yéi áyá dutláakw
yáa Yéil.

Shkalneek iii. Yéil ḵa Kutatankahídi (dax̱.aa)

Yagéi
aadé yoo kwdiyeigi yé
yáa atyana.á.
Yá ḵutaanx' áyá yoo at yaa.éik.
Yáa x̱áat—
wooch g̱uwanáade x̱áat áyá yoo yaa.éik.
Shayadiheni yéix'
atkookeidíx̱ x̱waliyéx̱
yáat'aa shkalneek,
yáa yoo at ya.éigi.
Shóogunáx̱
yú deikée yax̱'áak—
in the middle part of the Pafísifik Óoshan—
áyá áa yoo at yaa.éik.
Ch'u tle ch'a á áyá áa at dax̱ítt'
yáa deikée.
Á áyáa
aanḵáawux̱ siteeyi ḵáa áyá
hú áyá áa daak ḵúx̱ch.
Du x̱'éix̱ aa kdahaa
yáa x̱áat.
Yáa
eesháanx̱ dax̱siteeyi aa ḵu.aa áyá
tléil aadéi sdu x̱'éit aa koox̱dihaayi yé.
Tlax̱ ḵúnáx̱ yat'éex'
yáa ḵustí.
Á áyá a daa yoo tuwatánk
yáa Yéilch.

it moved like it was blowing in the wind.
Sixty years,
seventy years
is how long it takes for old age to overtake us.
It's out of this little leaf
that Raven made us.
This is how they tell the story
of Raven.

Episode iii. Raven and the Salmon Box (telling 2)

The fish migration
is a big
event.
In the summer the fish run.
The fish—
all kinds of fish migrate.
On many occasions
I have used this story
of the fish run
as a parable.
In the beginning,
out in the deep sea—
in the middle part of the Pacific Ocean—
is where they would run.
That is the very place where fish would spawn,
out in the ocean.
So,
a person who was rich
could go out there by boat.
He would procure some of these fish
to eat.
As for the
people who were poor, though,
they couldn't get any to eat.
Life
was very hard for them.
This is what Raven
was thinking about.

A daa yoo tuwatánk.
Yá dleit ḵáach aadé yasáagu yé, Déivín yóo has ayasáakw.
He done a lot of good for us.
Ch'a Déivínx̱ sateeyí teen,
he done a lot of good for us.
Yáa atyana.á—
yáa yax̱'áak áyá áa at ya.éix̱.
Á áyá áa yéi yatee
yá Kutatankahídi.
Ch'a á áyá áa isx̱ítt' yáa x̱áat.
Á áyá yánde áyá asayahéi
yáa Yéil.
Aag̱áa
yáa yán ayanadláḵni
yáa ḵ'anashgidéi ḵáa
kagéix' tsú aa kakg̱wahéix̱.
Áyú tléinteam x̱ yateeyi ḵáa jeex' áyú yéi yatee
yáa Náaḵw Tl'eeg̱ée
Wootsaag̱áa.
Yéi duwaasáakw yáa ḵáa
X̱'enax̱gaatwaayáa.
Yáa Yéil ḵu.aa áyá
sáḵs áyá du jeewú á,
sáḵs.
Aan áyá
át kawdiy[aa].
Áyá yáa Yéil
X̱'enax̱gaatwaayáa x̱ánt góot áyá,
aan sh kadashéix̱'.
«Tlax̱ ḵúnáx̱ áyá yak'éi
yáa ax̱ chooneidée.
Tlax̱ tléil—
tléil tlákw gaaw áyá
aan at woox̱sat'úkx̱aa.
Tlax̱ ḵúnáx̱ yak'éi
yá ax̱ chooneidí.
Iyatéen ágé yóo—
yóo shaa shakéet woogoodi jánwu?
Iyatéen ágé?»

He was pondering it.
The way white people refer to him, they call him the Devil.
He done a lot of good for us.
Even being that he's the Devil,
he done a lot of good for us.
The fish run—
the fish would run in the middle of the ocean.
This is where
the Salmon Box was.
The fish would spawn at this very place.
This is what Raven wanted
to come ashore.
Then,
once he brings it to shore
the poor people
will always have access to some too.
Now a certain man had
the Octopus Tentacle
Cane.
The name of this man was
X̱'enax̱g̱aatwaayáa.
But Raven
had a bow,
a bow.
He travelled around
with it.
When Raven
went to X̱'enax̱g̱aatwaayáa,
he was bragging about it.
"This arrow of mine
is so very fine.
I simply never
ever at any time
miss with it.
This arrow of mine
is so very fine.
Can you see that—
that mountain goat over yonder that's walking around on the mountain top?
Can you see it?"

«Aaa.»
«K'e latín!
Ch'a yáadáx̱ áwé kḵwat'óok aadé. K'e latín!»
Ch'a yáa—
ch'a yáa diyéedáx̱ áwé
aawat'úk.
Yáa du chooneidée—
ts'eeg̱eenée áyá
du chooneidíx̱ sitee,
ts'eeg̱eení.
Hú áyá yóot wudiḵín.
Aadé yaa ndaḵín.
Át daḵéen áyá ch'u tle yáa—
yáa shaa ḵa yáa jánwu
a t'éinax̱.áx̱ áyá yamdiḵín áyá, daak áyá awlidlékw.
Daak wudzigít diyínde yáa jánwu.
Yéi yaawaḵaa Yéil,
«Iyatéen gé?
X̱waat'úk yóo jánwu.
Diyínde daak wudzigít. Iyatéen gé?»
«Aaá.»
«Tléil gé aadé yáa ax̱ chooneidée
i Náaḵw Tl'eegée Wootsaag̱áa
daséix' wooḵasitaani yé?»
X̱'enax̱gaatwaayáa yéi yaawaḵaa,
«Yóo deikéex' yéi yateeyi yóo—
yú Kutatankahídi,
yú áa at ya.éix̱ yé,
áyá gúshé yánde seeyahéi?»
«Aaá.»
«Tlél aadéi yangiyadlaagi yé.
Chaa ch'a x̱át ax̱ éex̱ shikeelx̱oox̱ú,
x̱át ax̱ éex̱ shikeelx̱oox̱ú,
ch'a tlákw yaa shikanilax̱úx̱u,
ax̱ éex̱ shikeelx̱oox̱ú,
aag̱áa tsáa yakg̱eedláaḵ
Kutatankahídi yan yisayeeg̱í.»
Yéil yéi x̱'ayaḵá
«*Okay. Okay.*

"Yes."
"Just watch!
I'll take a shot at it from right here. Just watch."
From just—
from just down below,
he shot it.
This arrow of his—
a magpie
was his arrow,
a magpie.
He was the one that flew off.
He flew toward the mountain.
When he got to
the mountain and the mountain goat
he flew around behind it and startled it, causing it to fall down.
The mountain goat fell down below.
Raven said,
"Do you see?
I shot that mountain goat.
It fell down below. Do you see it?"
"Yes."
"Why not trade
this arrow of mine
for your Octopus Tentacle Cane?"
X̱'enax̱gaatwaayáa said,
"That Salmon Box
way out there on the open ocean
where the fish run is,
I suppose you want to bring it ashore?"
"Yes."
"There's no way you can get it.
Only when you invoke my name in song,
when you invoke my name in song,
when you go along singing my name constantly,
only when you invoke my name in song
will you manage
to bring the Salmon Box ashore."
Raven said,
"Okay. Okay.

I éex̱ shukakḵwalx̱oox̱.
All right. All right.»
Á áyáa
ayaawadlaaḵ yáa Náaḵw Tl'eeg̱í Wootsaag̱áa yáa Yéil.
Aalséix̱ wát áyá át uwagút,
yáa Aalséix̱ wát.
Yáa—yáa teet tlénx',
yáa—yáa gus'yaadáx̱ jinli.aadi
teet tlénx',
ḵa deikée áyá
yá Aalséix̱,
the big ocean swells are rolling in all the time.
Á áyá yan wulaayí áyá áa yeiḵ uwagút,
yá Aalséix̱ wát.
Yáa Náaḵw Tl'eeg̱ée—
yáa Náaḵw Tl'eeg̱ée áyá
anax̱ ax̱'eiwataan
yáa Kutatankahídi.
Yáa atyana.á tlèin áyá
yánde asayahéi,
éil' ka.ádee áyá
yáa—yáa wooch g̱uwanáade x̱áat,
éil' ka.ádi.
Á áyá ch'u tle yáa Náaḵw Tl'eeg̱ée Wootsaag̱áa
anax̱ ax̱'ewutaaní teen áwé
g̱unayéi ash jeewatán.
G̱unayéi ash jeewatán, yaa ash jinatán.
Áyáa kei shukaawashée,

(AT.SHÍ)

Ou yaa haa ha
Ou hee yei he
Ou hee yei he
Ou hee yei he
Ou hou yaa haa
Yei hei hei he
Ou hee yei he
Ou hou yaa ha
Yei hei

I'll invoke your name.
All right. All right."
So
Raven obtained the Octopus Tentacle Cane.
He came to the mouth of the Alsek,
the mouth of the Alsek River.
These—these huge breakers,
these huge breakers that
are constantly rolling in from the cloud banks
and out on the ocean,
offshore from the Alsek,
the big ocean swells are rolling in all the time.
When the tide went all the way out, he went down to the beach
at the mouth of the Alsek.
The Octopus Tentacle—
it was the Octopus Tentacle
that he hooked onto
the Salmon Box.
He wanted to bring the huge fish run
ashore:
sea creatures,
different kinds of marine
fish.
Now just as soon as he hooked the Octopus Tentacle Cane
onto the Salmon Box,
it began to pull him along.
It began to pull him along; it was pulling him along.
He started to sing the song,

(SINGING)

Ou yaa haa ha
Ou hee yei he
Ou hee yei he
Ou hee yei he
Ou hou yaa haa
Yei hei hei he
Ou hee yei he
Ou hou yaa ha
Yei hei

Du kéilk' áyá ḵudzitee,
Gidzanóox'.
Yéi ash daayaḵá, «Góok! Góok! Góok! Góok! Góok!
Shukanalx̱oox̱ déi!»
yóo áwé ash daaÿaḵá.

Hei yaa haa ha
X̱'ei-naax̱-g̱aa-twaa-yaa ha
Oo yaa haa ha
Ou hee yei he
Ou hee yei he
Ou hee yei he
Aa haa yaa haa
Yei hei hei he
Aa hee yei he
Aa haa yaa haa ha
X̱'ei-naax̱-g̱aat-waa-yaa ha
Oo-oo-oo-oo

Gwál jinkaat kaay yéi gíyá yaa oosyíḵch
áx̱ shukalx̱oox̱óo X̱'enax̱g̱aatwaayáa.
Á áyáa
ch'u yáa yeedádidéi áwé
áa yéi yatee du x̱'us.eetí Yéil yáa Aalséix̱ wát.
Tle áx̱ wulaayée yá l'éiw kalag̱é
áa yéi teex̱ du x̱'us.eetée.
Áyá yan asyéeḵ áyá
yáa—
yá du x̱oonx'ée áyá aawax̱oox̱, «Haadé yee
    yanagóo-óo-óo! Haadé yee yanagú!
Ch'a goo sá i tuwáa sigóo x'wán aadé.
Ch'a goo sá i tuwáa sigóo aadé.»
Yaduskúx̱x' áyá.
Á áyá ch'a ldakát—
ch'a ldakát yéi kaawaháa
yáa atyana.á.
Yáa héen yíx'—
héen yíx' kei isx̱ítch.
Du tuwáadáx̱
yáa eesháan kagéix'—

Raven had a nephew,
Gidzanóox'.
He said to Raven, "Come on! Come on! Come on! Come on! Come on!
Invoke the name now!"
he said to him.

Hei yaa haa ha
X̲'ei-naax̲-g̲aa-twaa-yaa ha
Oo yaa haa ha
Ou hee yei he
Ou hee yei he
Ou hee yei he
Aa haa yaa haa
Yei hei hei he
Aa hee yei he
Aa haa yaa haa ha
X̲'ei-naax̲-g̲aat-waa-yaa ha
Oo-oo-oo-oo

Maybe he would pull it in ten miles at a time
when he would invoke the name X̲'enax̲g̲aatwaayáa in the song.
So,
to this very day
Raven's footprints are there at the mouth of the Alsek River.
When the tide is out on the fine white sand,
his footprints remain there.
So after he pulled it in,
he called
his relatives over, "Bring your boats on o-o-over!
Bring your boats on over!
Take it wherever you want it.
Take it wherever you want it."
They transported loads of fish by boat.
And so,
fish runs
take place all over the place.
In the river—
they go up to spawn in the river.
Because of him
the poor have access to—

haa kagéix' kaawaháa
yáa yeedát.
Áyá dleit ḵáach
á tsú haa jeedáx̱ wootee.
Daa sákwshéwé yéi has ayasáakw *permit.*
X̱ach a tuwáadáx̱ áwé tsáa
haa x̱'éix̱ aa kdahaa yeedát—
yóo *permit* tuwáadáx̱.
Ch'a a g̱óot ḵu.aa ch'u tle.
Héix' áyú haa ádee áyú.
Tléil áyá ayáx̱x̱ usiteeyi ḵáa
dénageit.
Yéi ax̱ tutéeyin dénageitx̱ x̱at g̱adulyeix̱ée
aag̱áa yáa *Alaska* dulgeiyág̱u yé.
X'oon táakw sáyá
dak'éet'
yáa
ax̱ tóoch wulchéeshin
a daa yoo x̱'ax̱atángi yáa *Alaska*,
yáa aangalaḵú shukát
yáa yéi haa wuteeyí,
yáa haa jineiyí,
yáa xóowx'
ḵa yáa tíx',
yáa uháan,
yáa Aangóon t'áak,
yáa shaa.
Á áyá
xóow áwu á, ḵa yáa tíx' tsú áwu á.
Ách áyú ax̱ tóoch lachéeshin
a daa yoox̱'atánk.
Shóogunáx̱
yan née
yáa lingit'aaní,
a daa yoo x̱'ax̱atangi nuch.

we have access to these fish
nowadays.
Now the white folks
have taken that away from us as well.
There's some sort of thing they call a "permit".
It turns out that we only have access to fish
by the authority of a permit now—
by the authority of a permit.
But we're better off without it.
And here it is our own fish.
Our delegate
was an unworthy person.
I used to feel they should have made me a delegate
when they were doing Alaska land claims.
After so many years
had elapsed
I felt
that I could
talk about
the fact that we lived here in Alaska
before the flood,
and about our works:
the cairns
and the rope,
about ourselves,
and the mountain
inland behind Angoon.
So,
the cairns are there and the rope is there, too.
That's why I felt suited
to talk about it.
I always talk about
the time when
the world
was first created.

Shkalneek iv. Yéil k̲a Du Káak

Á áyá yáa—
yáa k̲áa
yéi áyá sh disáakw Yook̲is'kook̲éik.
L ushik'éiyi k̲áa áyá
yáa Yook̲is'kook̲éik
yóo sh disáagu.
Du dlaak'
yádi áyá ch'u tle aják̲x̲.
Tléil áyá du tuwáa ushgú tsu du t'ak̲káa yéi aa teeyí
yáa k̲ées' át akaawa.aagu k̲áa.
Ch'a tlákw áyá yankát wudáayin
ch'áakw k̲u.aa.
Yáa Yook̲is'kook̲éik
tle ch'a hú du tuwáadáx̲ áyá tsá g̲unayéi léix̲in.
Á áyá tsu—
tsu yáa du dlaak' yádi awujaag̲ée áyá
yáa shaawát
éek̲x̲ áyá yaa nagút,
éek̲x̲
yaa nasg̲áx̲.
Á áyá Láx̲' áyá du x̲ánt uwagút, «Wáa sá x̲'ayeek̲á, cha shaawát?»
«Ha ax̲ éek'ch x̲á
uwaják̲ ax̲ yádi.
Ách áyá
tuwunéekw áyá yéi x̲at x̲'alayéix̲.»
Aan yan sh kawdliník
yá Láx̲'tin.
Ách áwé yáa Láx̲'ch yéi yawsik̲aa,
«Dáa ch'a át aneelg̲een,
cha shaawát,
át aneelg̲een.
K̲únáx̲ daakdidugu aa té
kagat'ei,
k̲únáx̲ daakdidugu aa, tlél uwak̲as'i aa.
K̲únáx̲ daakdidugu aa kayit'eiyí,
yéi kakoogenk'i aa, kananóot'.»
A x̲'ayáx̲ áwé

Episode iv. Raven and His Uncle

Now this—
this man
calls himself Tide-Commander.
He's an evil man,
the one who calls himself
Tide-Commander.
He just kept on killing
his sister's children.
This man who controls the tide
didn't want anybody else there beside him.
It was perpetually high tide
long ago.
The tide could not begin to go down
unless Tide-Commander wished it to do so.
So after
he had killed another of his sister's sons,
this woman
was walking along a beach,
crying her way along
the beach.
Then Heron that came to her, "Why are you crying, good woman?"
"Well, my brother, you see,
has killed my child.
So
grief is making me weep like this."
She told her whole story
to this Heron.
So Heron said to her,
"Pray, look around,
good woman,
look around.
Find
a stone that's solid with no blemishes,
one that's solid, one with no cracks.
When you find one that's really solid,
a small one, swallow it."
She searched around

át k̲oowashee.
Wáananée sáwé awsiteen daakdidugu aa té.
Akaawanóot'
yú Láx̲' x̲'ayáx̲.
Tléil yeewuyáat'i áyá
g̲unayéi dís wusi.át
yáa shaawát.
Yátx̲ yaa nastéen du káx'
yáa té.
Té áyá.
Á áyá k̲ug̲astée áyá
Yéil tle yóo aawasáa tsu.
Yáa du éek'ch tléil wuskú
yát awu.oowú.
Yaa nawát.
Yaa nawát.
Wáananée sáyá
k̲áak'wx̲ yaa nastéen.
Gwál jinkaat táakw
k̲a dax̲adooshú,
jinkaat táakw
k̲a nas'gadooshóox̲ sateeyí gíyá
akawunáa,
«I káak x̲ánde nagú.
I káak x̲ánde nagú.
Gwál wudashee
ash tuwáa usgú, i káak.»
Áwés yéi yaawak̲aa, «Yak'éi, aadé kk̲wagóot
ax̲ káak x̲ánde.»
Át ishéex áwé
ax̲'eiwawóos' du káak,
«Tlél gé i jiyís yéi nk̲wasineeyi át?»
«Aaá,
ax̲adáax̲ áwé, héi dig̲inaa, héi dig̲inaat tán
ax̲ dáax̲i.
A yikl'oowú áwé,
a yikl'oowú aan
ax̲ eedé kg̲idashée.»
K̲u.een át áyú,

as he had told her to.
Eventually she saw a perfectly solid stone.
She swallowed it
as Heron had told her to.
Before long
the months of this woman's pregnancy
began to pass.
This stone was becoming a child
in her womb.
It was a stone.
So, when he was born,
she even named him Raven.
Her brother didn't know
that she had borne a child.
He was growing.
He was growing.
Eventually
he was becoming a little man.
Perhaps
when he was seventeen years old,
or even
eighteen years old,
she sent him off,
"Go to your uncle.
Go to your uncle.
Perhaps your uncle might
want some help."
So he said, "Fine, I'll go
to my uncle."
When he ran there
he asked his uncle,
"Don't you have anything for me to do?"
"Yes,
I'm hewing out a canoe up toward the forest; it's lying up there,
the canoe I'm hewing out.
The wood needs to be adzed out,
you can help me with
adzing out the wood."
It's a murderous thing,

yóo yaakw,
yóo—
yóo Yooḵis'kooḵéik
du yaagú.
Du g̱aatáyee áwé.
Lingít áwé
tle wóoshdáx̱ yoo ayatáx'k
wéi yaakw.
It's one of his traps.
Aadé l ushik'éiyi yé áwé wé ḵáa.
Tle a yíx̱ wusheexí teen áwé, a yík ax̱óot'i teen áwé
yaa ash kanatáx', yaa ash kanatáx',
yaa ash kanatáx'.
Áwé tlax̱
ḵúnáx̱ yaa ash kanatáx'i teen áwé
yáa du t'éey teen áwé, yá du t'éey teen áwé, daak ayaawat'íy.
Wóochdáx̱ wudig̱áat wéi yaakw.
Áwé du káak x̱ánde woogoot tle.
Du káak x̱ánt góot áwé,
«Wáa sá tle haat iyagút?»
yóo ash yawsiḵaa.
«Ha yaa x̱at kanatáx' x̱áawé wéi yaakw,
ách áwé wóochdáx̱ daak yax̱waat'íy.»
Éh! X'áande áwé yaa nanúk
wé Yooḵis'kooḵéik.
«Iyatéen ágé yóonáx̱ naashuwu aas?»
«Aaá.»
«Áa kei lag̱eech.
Ax̱ tuwáa sigóo wéi—
wé aas.»
Ín áyú
a yée ka.éix̱
wé aas.
Ín a yée ka.éix̱
wé aas.
Ít'ch áyú,
ít'ch, yéi kwdiyáat' wé ít'ch.
Ḵaa tóode
kadugáas'.

that canoe,
that—
that canoe belonging to
Tide-Commander.
It's his trap.
The canoe
bites
a person in half.
It's one of his traps.
That's how evil that man was.
As soon as Raven jumped inside of it, as soon as he set to adzing it out,
it started clenching over him; it was clenching over him;
it was clenching over him.
As it was very
tightly closing over him,
using his elbows, using his elbows, he elbowed it open.
The canoe split in two.
Then he went to his uncle.
When he came to his uncle
his uncle asked him,
"Why did you come back?"
"Well, that canoe was closing in on me,
so I elbowed it apart."
Eh! Tide-Commander's
ire was growing.
"Do you see that tree standing way over there?"
"Yes."
"Cut it down.
I want
that tree."
Obsidian
was growing within
that tree.
Obsidian was growing within
that tree.
It's glass,
glass—the glass shards were quite long.
They would plummet and embed themselves
inside a person.

Yú aas yíkdáx̱ kadugáas' tle
    ḵaa tóode.
Ḵu.een át áyú.
Áwé a k'éet góot áwé, a k'éet ayalax̱óot' áwé
    du shanax̱wáayi,
du kaadé kadugás'x'.
Ch'a yáa du dukkaadáx̱ ḵu.aa áwé
kashx̱'éel'.
Yáa du dukkaadáx̱ kashx̱'éel'.
As'óow,
as'óow,
as'óow,
as'óow.
Áwé kei awlig̱ích.
Kei alg̱éech áwé du káak x̱ánde woogoot.
«Ha wáa sá haat iyagút?»
«Ha de kei x̱wlig̱ích x̱áa yú aas.»
Ag̱ajaag̱ít áyú asayahéi yáa du kéilk'
Yooḵis'kooḵéik.
Ag̱ajaag̱ít áyú.
Ḵúnáx̱ áyú x'áant uwanúk.
Áwé yéi ayawsiḵaa,
«Iyatéen gé yú tliyaa,
yú ḵudziteeyi—
ḵudziteeyi át,
ḵudziteeyi náaḵw?
Ax̱ tuwáa sigóo kélk', ax̱ tuwáa sigóo
yú ḵudziteeyi
náaḵw.»
Yú ḵudziteeyi át yoo ḵusinút'kw.
Ash nax̱sanóot'it áwé.
Ḵudziteeyi át
yoo ḵusinút'kw.
Aadé g̱unayéi wugoodée áwé
du táanayi—
du táanayi yéi adaané, ch'a aadé yaa nagut yéide áwé.
Ashalach'úḵs'.
Ashalach'úḵs'
yáa du táanayi.

They would plummet out of that tree and embed themselves
right inside a person.
It's a murderous thing.
When he came to the base of the tree, when he set his axe
to the base of the tree,
heaps of glass shards would shower down on him.
But they just kept sliding right off
the surface of his skin.
They kept sliding off the surface of his skin.
He chopped
and chopped
and chopped
and chopped.
He felled the tree.
When he had felled it, he went to his uncle.
"Well, why did you come back here?"
"Well, I have already felled that tree, you see."
Tide-Commander
wanted it to kill his nephew.
He wanted it to kill him.
He became so angry.
He said to Raven,
"Do you see over there on the far side,
that giant—
giant thing,
the giant octopus?
I want it, nephew, I want
that giant
octopus."
That giant thing swallows people.
He wanted it to swallow him.
The giant thing
swallows people.
As Raven started to walk there,
his octopus hook—
he was working on his octopus hook while he was walking there.
He was lowering and raising it.
He was lowering and raising
his octopus hook.

Ax̱'akas'eet áyá.
Áyá a x̱'awoolt góot áyá yéi ayawsiḵaa—
yáa du yoox̱'atángi áwé ch'a yú du káak aayí yáx̱ áwé litseen—
«Sh kag̱eelhá!»
yóo áwé ayawsiḵaa yá ḵudziteeyi náaḵw,
«Sh kag̱eelhá.»
Yaa nallenéyáx̱ áwé yatee,
yéi yaa gunasgéink'.
Tlax̱ yéi gunasgéink',
aak'wátsk'u náaḵwx̱ nastée áwé tsáa,
aawak'íx̱'.
Du x̱iksháat aawax̱ích
du káak x̱ánde.
Du káak x̱ánt góot áwé
tle yáa tl'atgikát aawax̱ích
yáa du káak hídi.
«Sh neelwáat!» yóo ayawsiḵaa,
«Sh neelwáat!»
Áwé yáa neilx' áwé yaa sh nalwát, yaa sh nalwát. Ch'u tle yáa neil yeex̱ áwé yaa kanalx̱'íx',
du koolgeiyí
wé náaḵw.
Kadagax̱éyáx̱ x̱'ayaḵá wé du káak, «A g̱óot!
A g̱óot, gánde!
A g̱óot!
A g̱óot!»
Akawulx̱óox̱udáx̱ áyú—
kei x̱'ayadlúxch á ḵúnáx̱—
áwé tsu át x̱'eiwatán,
«Sh kag̱eelhá tsu,
sh kag̱eelhá.»
De yéi yaa gunasgéink'.
Du yoox̱'atángi ch'u tle ch'a yáa du káak aayí yáx̱ áwé litseen.
Ag̱ajaag̱éet áyú asayahéi yáa du kéilk'.
Tlax̱ yéi gunasgéink' áwé,
yáa náaḵwk'wátsk'ux̱ nastée áwé,
aadáx̱ awsitaa,
héent aawax̱ích.

He was hafting the hook to the shaft.
When he came to the entrance he said to it—
his words are just as powerful as his uncle's—
"Make yourself shrink!"
he said to the giant octopus,
"Make yourself shrink."
It was as if it were melting away;
it was becoming smaller.
When it became very small,
when it finally became a tiny octopus,
he hooked it.
He threw it over his shoulder
and went to his uncle.
When he came to his uncle,
he threw it on the floor
of his uncle's house.
"Make yourself grow!" he said to it,
"Make yourself grow!"
It started growing inside the house; it was growing larger
    and larger. It was getting so large that it started pressing
    against the sides and roof of the house;
that's how large
the octopus was.
His uncle said, as if wailing, "Get rid of it!
Get rid of it, take it outside!
Get rid of it!
Get rid of it!"
After asking him over and over—
Tide-Commander was really getting worked up about it—
Raven spoke to it again,
"Make yourself shrink again,
shrink yourself down."
Now it was getting smaller.
His words are just as powerful as his uncle's.
The uncle wanted the octopus to kill his nephew.
When it became very small,
when it became a tiny octopus,
Raven picked it up
and threw it into the water.

Shkalneek v. Yéil k̲a Aangalak̲ú

Héent awux̲eejéech áwé—
yáa du káak k̲u.aa
yáa du kéilk' ag̲ajaag̲ít áwé asayahéi—
ách áwé yáa k̲ées' aawax̲oox̲,
«K̲ées', g̲unayéi ikadá déi!»
Daak̲ kanadéin.
Tlél awuskú Yéil
yóo du káakch wux̲oox̲ú.
K̲EIXWNÉI: *Daat x̲'áax' sáyú ashik'áan yú du keilk'ihás?*
Tléil áyú du tuwáa ushgú du t'ak̲káx'
át at kawdu.aag̲óo.
Tléil du tuwáa ushgú du t'ak̲kaanáx̲
át at kawdu.aag̲óo.
Ách áwé wéi du kéilk'
ag̲ajaag̲ít asayahéi.
Tlél awuskú Yéil
du káak
k̲ées' awux̲oox̲ú. Daak̲ kanadéin, daak̲ kanadéin.
Tle ch'as de ash x̲ánde yaa kagadáa, tle yéi ash x̲ánt
kadáa áwé awsiteen,
wé du kéilk'ích wusiteen.
Át x̲'eiwatán wé k̲ées',
«Tleiyéix' yan ikadá.
Tliyéi yan ikadá.
Tléil yan x̲at unéiych.»
Ch'u tle tliyéit kadéin.
Yóo du yoox̲'atángi ch'u tle ch'a yú du káak aayí yáx̲ litseen.
Tle ch'a tleiyateeyiyéit kadéin tle.
Du chooneidée ashawlitleik̲w.
Gáant wujixíx Yéilk'.
Yéi duwasáagu át
hintaakx'wás'g̲i.
Gáaxw áyá.
Hintaakx'wás'g̲i áyá aawat'úk.
Á áyá yáa—
yá a doogóo—
yá a doogú tóox̲ áwé awsinook

Episode v. Raven and the Flood

Because he threw it in the water—
his uncle, though,
had wanted it to kill his nephew—
this is why Raven's uncle called the tide,
"Tide, start coming in now!"
The tide was coming in.
Raven didn't know
that his uncle had called up the tide.
NORA DAUENHAUER: *Why did he hate his nephews?*
He didn't want anyone besides himself
making decisions.
He didn't want anyone second-guessing him
in making decisions.
That's why he wanted the tide
to kill his maternal nephew.
Raven didn't know that
his maternal uncle
had called the tide. It was coming in, it was coming in.
Only when it was coming in toward him, when it had come right up to him, did he see it;
his nephew saw it.
Raven addressed the tide,
"Stand still and stop flowing.
Stand still.
I'm not ready yet."
The tide stood still.
His words are as powerful as his uncle's.
The tide just stood still.
He grabbed his bow and arrows.
Little Raven ran out.
There is a thing called
a bufflehead.
It's a duck.
It was a bufflehead that he shot.
So its—
its skin—
Raven set his mother

du tláa,
yáa Yéil
du tláa.
«Ch'a yáa el'kát igux̱laháash,
atléi, ch'a yáa el'kát.
Tléil wáa sá ikg̱watee.
X̱át ḵu.a kei kḵwadaḵéen
ch'u tle yóo xáats',
xáats'dei kḵwadaḵéen x̱át ḵu.aa.
Áa yéi x̱at gug̱atée.»
Wé du tláa yan asnée,
aag̱áa áwé
yéi yaawaḵaa,
«*Okay*, g̱unayéi ikadá
cha ḵées',
g̱unayéi ikadá.»
Daaḵ kanadéin.
Daaḵ kanadéin.
Aag̱áa áyá uháan tsóo
shaa kát wutuwa.át.
Shaa kát wutuwa.át
yáa ḵées' náḵ.
Á áyáa
yá ḵaa ji.eetx'ée
yáa shaax'w yax̱oo ch'oo yáa yeedádidéi
áa yéi yatee, yáa xóowx',
yáa xóowx'
yá a t'éi ḵoowaneix̱i,
yáa a t'éix', ḵa yáa tíx',
ch'áagu ḵáawu tíx'i,
á tsú.
Yáa
S'ex'aayihéen Shaa—
yáa Tsaagwáa a x̱'aká áyá—
yéi duwasáakw.
A shakéewu aa yáa xóow
ḵa yáa tíx'.
Áyá yáa haa keitlx'ée áyá haa káx̱ at wootee.
Ch'a héendáx̱ áyá aa kamdi.áa

inside this bufflehead skin,
Raven's
mother.
"You'll just float around on the ocean,
mom, just right on the ocean.
You will be fine.
As for me, I'll fly up
to the firmament
I'll fly up to the firmament though.
I'll stay there."
When he had gotten his mother ready,
he then
said,
"Okay, start coming up,
O tide,
start coming up."
It was coming up.
It was coming up.
Then we, too,
went up onto the mountains.
We went up onto the mountains
to get away from the flood.
So,
there are artifacts
here and there in these mountains even until today.
They are still there, these cairns,
these cairns
behind which the people found shelter,
behind these, and rope,
the rope of ancient people,
that too.
This
Hood Bay Mountain—
it's at the entrance of Hood Bay—
this is what it's called.
Atop it are some cairns
and rope.
Now, it was our dogs that kept us safe.
Some of these mountains

yáa shaax'w.
Á áyá yáa haa keitlx'ée áyá
yá xóots
nakwaanée
ch'a góot.aa daadáx̱,
ch'a g̱óot.aa daadé,
nakwaanée, yáa xóots,
yáa haa keitlx'ée áyá
haa káx̱ aawasháa.
Yáa xóots
aawasháa.
Yáa aangalaḵú,
wáa yikunayáat', tlax̱ wáa yikunayáat' sáwé,
ḵúx̱de yóo wdinee
yáa aan wulḵoowú.
Íḵde g̱unayéi uwaláa.
Áyáa awsikóo áyá yáa Yéil
íḵde g̱unayéi wulaayí.
Á áyáa
du lú áyá áa yoo akamlitíx̱' yá xáats'.
Aadáx̱ áyá yei nasgít
yáa diyínde. Naaléi yá aax̱ yei nasgit yé.
Ch'a wé diyée áwé áx̱ wulixáat'i dís áwé.
Áyá yáa—
yáa yaa ndaḵin át
nás'k ux̱éeych
a daadé,
yá dís daadé.
Hú ḵu.aa áyá naaléi áyá aadáx̱ yei nasgit yé.
Alx̱éis' áyá du tóo yéi yatee.
«Yeedát
ch'as geesh kadootl
káa x̱at wudzigeet,»
yóo áyá alx̱éis'.
«Yeedát s'é geesh—
sú kadootl káa x̱at wudzigeet,»
yéi áyá alx̱éis' Yéil.
X'oon sákwshé uwax̱ée aag̱áa yei nasgit yé.
Gwál yeewuyáat'

rise right up out of the water.
And our dogs protected us from
these swimmer
bears,
going from surrounding one bear
to surrounding another
of these swimmers, these bears;
it was our dogs
who were barking to protect us.
They barked
at the bears.
This flood,
after a long time, after a very long time,
the flood receded
from the land.
The tide began to ebb from the land down toward the beach.
Now Raven knew
that the tide had started ebbing down toward the beach.
This was when
he unscrewed his beak from the sky.
He was falling downward from there.
The place that he started falling from was a long way off.
The moon was suspended down below the place from which he fell.
Now,
a space ship
takes three days
to get there,
to get to lunar orbit.
But as for him, the place that he started falling from was a long way off.
He had a wish in mind.
"Now
if only I could fall
onto a bed of bull kelp,"
he was wishing.
"Now if only I could fall onto bull kelp—
onto a bed of giant kelp,"
Raven was wishing.
He fell for who knows how many days and nights.
A lot of time probably passed

aag̲áa yei nasgit yé.
He's falling down from the sky.
Naaléi
aax̲ yei nasgit yé.
Wáananée sáwé
yá geesh—
yáa sú kadootl káa wdzigeet.
Tléil áwé yán duteen,
yóo deikée yax̲'áak.
Éil' tlèin ká áyá
áa wdzigeet.
Tléil yán duteen.
Tlél tsú goo sá duteen.
Naasa.áa yáx̲ áyá ash een kayaxát.

Shkalneek vi. Yéil Ana.óot Aaní Awulyeix̲í

De ch'a hóoch' áyá ax̲satinji át áyá yáa yáxwch'.
Yáxwch' áyá ax̲satínch.
De ch'áakw shéyá k̲udziteeyi át áyá yáa—
yáa yáxwch'.
De ch'a hóoch' áyá yei astinji át.
Á áyá ch'u tle—
tle a yát x̲'awdliyóo.
«Ax̲ yak̲áawu,» yóo,
«Ax̲ yak̲áawu,
ch'u tle ágéyóo
yáa éil',
yáa diyée a takáx' gí yax̲ eex'aak?»
yóo áyá ax̲'eiwóos'.
«Aaá,
a takáx' x̲áa yax̲ x̲ax'aak.»
«Yá héen táade yix'aagí,
dáa
l'éiw ax̲ jee kei kakwaach.
L'éiw ax̲ jee kei kakwaach,» yóo áyá adaayak̲á yáa yáxwch'.
A yáx̲ áwé diyínde nax'áak áwé
l'éiw áwé
ash jee kei akaawakwách,

during his fall.
He's falling down from the sky.
The place he fell from
was far away.
At some point
he fell on bull kelp—
on this bed of giant kelp.
There was no land to be seen
out there on the ocean.
He fell
onto the *great* ocean.
Land was not to be seen.
Nothing was to be seen anywhere.
The kelp bed was like a sewing kit with Raven cocooned inside.

Episode vi. Raven Makes the Aleutian Islands

The only things he kept seeing were these sea otters.
These were sea otters that he kept seeing.
They were apparently giant beings long ago, these—
these sea otters.
They were the only things he could see.
So he just
addressed one of them with a kinship term.
"My partner," he said,
"My partner,
do you ever
swim down to the bottom
of the ocean?"
he asked it.
"Yes,
sure, I swim to the bottom."
"When you swim to the bottom,
do
bring me a handful of gravel.
Bring me a handful of gravel," he said to this sea otter.
Accordingly, when he swam down
he brought up a handful
of gravel for him,

k̲únáx̱ wé át wulihaashi yé
Yéil
wé sú kadootl ká.
Wé sú kadootl kaadáx̱ áwé
g̲unayéi akaawag̲ích wé téix' sáani, yá téix' sáanix̱ siteeyi aa.
Yá téix' sáanix̱ siteeyi aa áwé
tle x'áat'x̱ yaa nastéen.
Yá kei akag̲íx'ji
tle x'áat'x̱ yaa nastéen,
tle x'áat'x̱ yaa nastéen,
tle x'áat'x̱ yaa nastéen.
Ch'u tle yóo yánde—ch'u tle yóo yánde yan akaawag̲ích.
A kaanáx̱ áwé
yáa—yáa yánde yan akaawag̲iji
yáa téix' sáani,
a kaanáx̱ áwé
yan uwagút,
yánde.
Á áwé yáa yakyee
dleit k̲áach yéi yasáakw
Aleutian Islands,
Aleutian Islands,
yóo naakée.
Yá gus'yaadéi—
gus'yaadéi daak wudlik̲ée yá x'áat'x',
    aadáx̱ yánde ksixát.
K'e aadéi yateeyi yé yáa shkalneek,
yáa aangalak̲ú.
Tléil yáa lingit'aani teen áwéi wdulyeix̱,
á wé x'áat'áx'w sáani.
Yá aangalak̲ú ít áwé
Yéilch áwé áa yéi woo.oo,
Yéilch.
Á áyá yáa—
aadáx̱ áwé—aadáx̱ áwé yáa lingit'aanitóox̱
yakawdiyáa
yáa Yéil.

right where Raven
was floating
on a bed of giant kelp.
From the bed of giant kelp
he started to toss the little pebbles, the ones that were little pebbles.
These ones that were little pebbles
were turning into islands.
As he tossed them up,
they were just turning into islands,
just turning into islands,
just turning into islands.
He tossed them toward the mainland, toward the mainland.
Across these—
these little pebbles
that he had tossed toward the mainland,
across these
he crossed over
to the mainland.
It is these that today
white people call
the Aleutian Islands,
the Aleutian Islands,
far off to the west.
Toward the cloud banks—
these islands sit facing out toward the cloud banks,
    extending from there to the mainland.
See how this story is,
the story of the flood.
Those islets
were not created with the world.
After the flood,
Raven put them there,
Raven did.
This is the place
from which—from which Raven proceeded
to venture
throughout the world.

Kaasgéiy X̲’éidáx̲ Tlaagú

Stories by Susie James

FIGURE 11. Susie James c. 1960. Courtesy of Sealaska Heritage Institute, PO 004, box 7, item 38.

OUR NEXT STORYTELLER is the redoubtable Kaasgéiy, Susie James, a Chookanshàa (woman of the Chookaneidí clan) and a child of the T'ak̲deintaan. She was born on August 10, 1890, and passed away on November 3, 1980. A short biography of James can be found in *Haa K̲usteeyí.*[*] She grew up in Hoonah, Alaska, and moved to Sitka as a young woman, where she lived for the rest of her life. James was a nearly monolingual Tlingit speaker and a dynamic storyteller who spoke animatedly and at an incredibly fast pace. The speed of her delivery coupled with the gradual deterioration of the original recording and the cassette copy has made it difficult to resolve her every utterance to our satisfaction. She was recorded in September of 1972 by her daughter K̲aatéix̲', Mary Pelayo, so she would have been eighty-two at the time of this performance. Pelayo is heard on the recording a few times asking clarifying questions and responding to her mother.

The title selected for the extended tale taken as a whole, «L At Ÿáx̲ K̲oowanoogu Yéil» "Raven Who Flouts Convention", is based on James' statement «Tléil at ÿáx̲ k̲oonook»[†] 'He (Raven) behaves unconventionally', which she delivers through a bout of laughter upon Raven losing both of his eyeballs and placing blueberries in the empty sockets to fill the voids.

Of special note in these stories are the names by which James refers to three characters. She is the only storyteller known to us who provides a recorded pronunciation of the name of Raven's mother, the form she uses being K̲inyukookook̲éik. In her tale's fourth episode, "Raven and the Salmon Box", the character usually known as X̲'anax̲gaatwaayáa (or X̲'enax̲gaatwaayáa, per Robert Zuboff) is referred to as X̲'anax̲.waatgwaayáa. She also uses the form Gidzanóok' (rather than Gidzanóox' as used by Zuboff and Katherine Mills) to refer to one of Raven's lackeys. These

---

* Dauenhauer and Dauenhauer, *Haa K̲usteeyí*, 284–87.

† SJ vi, 47. See the note to that line for discussion.

FIGURE 12. Robert Zuboff and Susie James in the Sheldon Jackson College print shop, Sitka, August 1973, watching the first paperback editions of their stories come off the press (the texts of which were later updated and published in *Haa Shuká*), eight months before Zuboff passed away. Photo by Richard Dauenhauer. Courtesy of Sealaska Heritage Institute, PO 004, box 6, item 91.

characters and their names are discussed in §§2.2, 2.17, and 2.12 of the editors' introduction.

The recording upon which the written form of this tale is based consists of three audio files. The first two, which comprise the vast majority of of the tale, correspond to the two sides of the cassette tape upon which Pelayo recorded her mother.* The tale is divided into eleven episodes, the last of which, "Raven and the Daylight", was cut short by the tape in the midst of the action. We thus cannot know whether James would have concluded the tale at the resolution of this eleventh episode, or if she would have continued on with further episodes. To create a more satisfying ending to the final episode and the entire tale, we have cheated a bit and spliced in a three-and-a-half-minute segment from a different and unrelated recording session in which James again tells "Raven and the Daylight". The recording from which this final portion of the text is derived was made by Nora Dauenhauer in Sitka four months prior on May 14, 1972.†

---

* MC005, tapes 346, side 1, and 346, side 2. Tape 346, side 1, corresponds to SJ i–vii, 70; tape 346, side 2, corresponds to SJ vii, 71–xi, 239.

† MC005, tape 17, side a. The final lines of the last episode, SJ xi, 240–322, are drawn from 22:38–25:56 on this recording.

Like Mills of Hoonah, Frank Italio and Frank Dick of Yakutat, and Austin Hammond of Haines, James uses the high-toned version of the preverbs *kei=*, *ÿei=*, *yoo=*, and *ÿeiḵ=*, so that they appear as *kéi=*, *yéi=*, *yóo=*, and *yéiḵ=* in her speech. In a number of instances, however, she can be heard using the low-toned forms *yei=* and *kei=* and we have made an effort to transcribe the tone as she pronounces it in each instance rather than standardizing them all as high.*

There are a few instances where we clearly hear the obsolete consonant /ÿ/ in her speech, which we write as such. There are cases where we do not hear any consonant where we would historically expect /ÿ/ after another consonant; in these cases as well we supply the missing consonant, writing it as ⟨ÿ⟩ so as to alert the reader to the fact that where they might expect the consonant /y/, no consonant was heard. Readers will also notice the use of an underlined ⟨n⟩ in these texts. James often partially or completely denasalizes the pronunciation of the phoneme /n/ (the alveolar nasal [n]), which results in a sound closely resembling the /l/ of English 'long' (the lateral approximant [l]); such instances are transcribed as ⟨n̲⟩. And, as in the recordings of Italio, we find a number of instances where the possessive pronoun *a* 'it, its, there' might be expected to occur but is either not audible or definitely not pronounced.

* We are unable to explain what conditions her sporadic tone-lowering with *yei=* and *kei=*. The only notable pattern we find is the use of low-toned *kei=* following *anax̱* 'through/via it/there', though that pattern does not hold in all instances.

L At Ÿáx̱ Ḵoowanoogu Yéil

Shkalneek i. Yéil ḵa Du Káak

Ch'a yaa nasg̱áx̱ áyóo shaawát.
Ḵinyukookooḵéik yóo duwasáakw yú Yéil—
yú Yéil tláa ḵu.aa.
Áwé ch'a yaa nasg̱áx̱ áwéi-éi.
Du yátx'i áwé tle a.een wé du káakch,
tle a.een.
Tle yú dáax̱ yíkde akawuḵaayí áwé tle
    du káa kdax̱'áx̱'wx̱,
tle ash jáḵx̱.
Wé du dlaak' ÿátx'i áwé yéi adaané
Yooḵis'kooḵéik ḵu.aa.
Ách áwé wáanée sáwé déi guṉayéi—
guṉayéi wdzigáx̱ wé shaawát.
Á áwé tle aatlèin g̱áax̱.
Áwé yú taashukát han Láx̱' áwé yéi ash yawsiḵaa,
«Wáa sáwé tsú x̱'ayeeḵá, shaawát?»
Áwé tle a dayéen áwé áa yax̱ uwahán, «Aa sá x̱áat x̱'eiwatán?»
Ch'as yú Láx̱' áyú, tle ash dayéen hú tsú áa yax̱ uwagút.
«Wa.é ák.wé x̱áat x̱'eeyatán?»
«Aaá.»
«Ha yú ax̱ éek' áwé, Yooḵis'kooḵéik yóo duwasáakw.
Áwé tle ax̱ yádee áwé, tle yei ax̱oox̱ch, ‹Haagú!
Ax̱ éet idashí!
Ax̱ éet idashí!›

Raven Who Flouts Convention

Episode i. Raven and His Uncle

A woman was just walking along weeping.
K̲inyukookook̲éik was the name of Raven's—
of Raven's mother.
She was just walking along wee-eeping.
Raven's uncle would slaughter her children;
he just slaughtered them.
When he would send one of her children into that unfinished canoe, it would clench over him;
it would kill the child.
This is what Tide-Commander
would do to his sister's children.
That was why she eventually set about—
that woman set about weeping.
She was crying *so* much.
So, the Heron standing on the river flat said to her,
"What ever are you crying about, woman?"
She turned to face him, "Who spoke to me?"
Only Heron was there, and he likewise turned to face her.
"Was it you who spoke to me?"
"Yes."
"Well, it's my brother; his name is Tide-Commander.
He summons my children, 'Come here!
Help me!
Help me!'

Tle yú dáax̱ yíkde akawunáayi áwé tle—
tle ash jáḵx̱ wé dáax̱.
Á áyá du eedé yóo x̱'ayax̱aḵá.
A jiyeet áyá yaa nx̱asg̱áx̱.»
«Ahóu.
Óu.
Ch'a yaa ḵigeelt'éet, ch'a wéix̱ yaa ḵigeelt'éet.
Ch'a yaa ḵugatées'.
Tlax̱ yéi kagoogek'i aa té ysateení, daakdidugwéyáx̱ yateeyi aa té,
yisateení áwé tle
aax̱ kéi kg̱eetée, tle gakg̱idatée.
Tle i lakaadé yiteeyí áwé kakg̱eenóot'
wé té,»
yóo ash yawsiḵaa yú—yú Láx̱'.
Áwé a x̱'ayáx̱ áwé tle yaa ḵunalt'éet.
Wáanée sáwé awsiteen daakdidugu téik', yéi kagoogéink'.
Áwé tle aax̱ akaawatee,
tle akaawanóot' tle.
Tle akananóot' ásíwégé tle—
tle yátx̱ du jee wsitee wé té,
yátx̱.
Ách áwé,
ách áwé Láx̱' du wéetx̱ wusitee Yéil ḵu.aa.
Láx̱' ÿéetx̱ wusitee.
Du éeshx̱ wusitee.
Yéil éeshx̱ wusitee Láx̱',
yú té yú shaawát x̱'éide akawuṉáayi
yátx̱ wusteeyích áwé.
Aatx̱ ḵug̱astée áwé du yádi
tle noow yáx̱ g̱íwé wootee wé Yéil ḵu.aa,
yá lingit'aaní awliyex̱i Yéil.
Aag̱áa áwé tle yéi ash yawsiḵaa,
«Haat g̱agoot s'é wé i yéet, hé ax̱ dáax̱i yíkdáx̱ kínde ag̱als'óowu yú—
yú l'oowú.»
Áwé tle át uwagút. «Aadé i káakt idashí.
Aadé nagú.»
Át uwagút.
«Goosú i shanax̱wáayi, goosóo?»
Tle ash jeet awsitán.

When he sends my child into that unfinished canoe,
that canoe just kills him.
This is my lament for them.
It's under this burden that I'm pacing forth my mourning."
"Oh my.
Oh.
Just go on beachcombing; head right over there and go on beachcombing.
Just keep searching.
When you see a very small stone, a stone that is completely solid,
when you catch sight of it
you'll pick it up; you'll pick it up as your own.
Then when you put it in your mouth, you'll swallow
that stone,"
that—that Heron said to her.
So she went along beachcombing as he instructed.
Eventually she saw a small, solid little pebble.
So she just picked it up
and swallowed it.
I suppose that once she swallowed it
the stone became a child for her to bear,
a child.
This is how,
this is how Raven became Heron's son.
He became Heron's son.
He became his father.
Heron became Raven's father
because the stone that he had appointed for the woman
    to swallow became a child.
After that, when her child was born,
Raven was like a fortress, I suppose,
this Raven who arranged the world.
Then Tide-Commander said to her,
"Have that son of yours come over now; let him chop the—the wood
out from within my unfinished canoe."
So he went there. "Go there and help your uncle.
Go there."
Raven came to him.
"Where is your axe, where is it?"
He handed it to Raven.

Tle ayáx̱ áwé yaa ḵunas'úw tle.
Yan tadanóok áwé a yíx' tle
a taka.ádi ḵínde as'óowu áwé tle ash káa yaa kandax̱'áx̱'w tle.
Tle ash káa yaa kandatúlitín áwé tle yóo aawat'íy tle.
Awut'éeyi, awut'éeyi áwé tle wóoshdáx̱ wudig̱áat wé dáax̱.
Tle a yíkdáx̱ kéi uwagút tle,
tle át awsitán du shanax̱wáayi. «Náa!
I x̱út'ayi.
Wé dáax̱ ḵwá tle kaawawál'.»
«Háa! Wáa sáwé tsú ysinei?»
«Ha, ch'a x̱áa kaawawál'.»
«Ha yóode nagú yú aas!
Yóox̱ daaḵ uwa.áa aas déix̱.
Nalg̱eech aadáx̱!
Nalg̱eech!»
Tle át uwagút.
Tle shunax̱wáa awsitaan aadé.
Agukg̱wax̱óot'i áwé tle yá a yík ásíwé ín áwu á wé aas.
Hé'! Tle wé ash daadé áwé
yakdag̱éech yú ax̱óot'i wé aas.
Tle du daadáx̱ áwé kask'óot wé ín.
Ch'a yák'w {...} tle kéi awlig̱ích.
Tle wé tléix'.aa tsú agoowax̱út',
tle kéi awlig̱ích á tsú.
Tle wool'éex'.
Át góot áwé, «Náa! Yáadu i shunax̱wáayi.
X̱walig̱ísht' yú aas.»
«É!» X'áan áwé du tóo yéi woonei
Yooḵis'kooḵéik ḵu.aa.
«Yóo—yú x'aa tóowu á náaḵw, aadé nagú aag̱áa.
Aadáx̱ daak lak'éex̱',» tle yóo ash yawsiḵaa.
Tle náaḵw shak'íx̱'aag̱áa atgutóot uwagút tle.
Tle awlis'úw wé yóo ksatan aa—k'íx̱'aa yáx̱ kasatan aa wé aas, sheey.
Asÿádi, asÿádi awlis'úw.
Aag̱áa áwé tle aadé aan woogoot tle.
Tle a x̱'awoolt wugoodí áwé tle yéi ayawsiḵaa wé n̲áaḵw,
«Sh kag̱eelhá, n̲áaḵw.

As he was told, he started chopping inside the canoe.
When he sat down inside it
and chopped just shy of the very bottom, it began clenching over him.
As it was rolling up over him, he simply elbowed it open.
When he elbowed it, when he elbowed it, that canoe just split apart.
So he just got up and stepped out of it
and took the axe to his uncle. "Here!
Here's your adze.
But the canoe cracked."
"What! What ever did you do to it?"
"Well, it just cracked, you see."
"Well, go over there to those trees!
There are trees standing up over there, two of them.
Fell them from there!
Fell them!"
So he went there.
He took an axe to it.
When he was about to chop the base of it, it turned out that
there was obsidian in the tree.
Heh! Shards of obsidian
were shooting at his body when he chopped the tree.
But the obsidian just bounced off his body.
He felled it in short order.
Then he chopped the base of the other one
and felled it as well.
It broke.
When he went to his uncle, he said, "Here! Here's your axe.
I felled the trees."
"Eh!" Tide-Commander
was seething with anger.
"There's an octopus inside that—that point; go there and get it.
Gaff it out from there," he said to Raven.
So Raven went into the woods to fetch an octopus head-gaff.
He chopped one that was curved—one that was curved like a gaff,
a tree limb.
A sapling, he chopped down a sapling.
Then he just took it over there.
When he came to the entrance, he said to the octopus,
"Shrink yourself down, octopus.

Sh kag̲eelhá.
Sh kag̲eelhá.»
Tle yéi áwé gawsigéink' wé náak̲w, tle ashaawak'íx̲'.
Tle aax̲ daak awulkéet'i tle yá du x̲iksháax̲ áwé ayawsig̲éex', tle yú du káak hídidé.
Tle héide ashuwutaan̲í áwé tle anax̲ neil aawax̲ích,
«Sh neelwáat!
Sh neelwáat, cha n̲áak̲w!»
Tle wé du káak, «Náa! Yáadu wé náak̲w.»
Tle aadé neil awux̲eejí teen áwé yaa shanahík wé du hídi du een wé—.
«H-h-h-h! Haagú! Haagú! Gáande nastí!
Gáande nastí wé náak̲w!
Gáan!»
«Ha, ch'al cháa eex̲oox̲ kát!»
«Gáande nastí! Tlél ax̲ tuwáa ushgú.»
Hé'! Tle wéi yaa shanahík wé náak̲w
wé du hídi.
Áwé tle aax̲ awsitaan du k'íx̲'ayi.
«Sh kag̲eelhá, náak̲w!» tle yóo ayawsik̲aa.
Tle yéi sh kanalhéin.
Tle ashaawak'íx̲' tsu.
Tle yóo-óo-óot,
a daat góot áwé wé át kéi awlik'ix̲'i yé aadé kéi ashawlix̲út' tle.
Aag̲áa áwé tlél aadé yéi oonax̲sineiyi yé.
A yís x'áant uwanúk wé du—du kéilk'.
Áwé tle yéi ayawsik̲aa wé k̲[ées'],
«Néi! Cha k̲ées'!
G̲unayéi ikadá!
G̲unayéi ikadá, cha k̲ees'!
G̲unayéi ikadá!»
Aag̲áa áwé tle tláakw áwé g̲unayéi kaawadáa wé k̲ées'.
Áwé tlax̲ tlél tsu aadé nax̲wdzigeedi yé.
Du tláa k̲u.aa wé naaleyiyéidáx̲ áwé a x̲ánt uwagút wé
wé—.
A nák̲ woogoot wé du tláa.
Áwé tle du sák̲si áwé ashawlitleik̲w.
«Néi!

Shrink yourself down.
Shrink yourself down."
Then the octopus became small, and he just gaffed it by the head.
When he pried it loose, he threw it over his shoulder and went straight to his uncle's house.
When he opened the door, he threw it inside,
"Grow yourself big!
O octopus, grow yourself big!"
Then he said to his uncle, "Here! Here's the octopus."
As soon as he threw it inside the octopus started filling up his house with his uncle still inside.
"He-e-e-ey! Come here! Come here! Take it outside!
Take the octopus outside!
Outside!"
"Well, as if that were a polite way to ask for it!"
"Take it outside! I don't want it."
Heh! The octopus was filling up
his house.
So then Raven picked up his gaff hook.
"Shrink yourself down, octopus!" he said to it.
It shrank itself down.
He gaffed it by the head again.
Then, wa-a-ay in the distance,
when he came around to the place where he had gaffed it, he just dragged it up there by the head.
At that point there was nothing his uncle could do to him.
He was furious with his—his nephew.
Then Tide-Commander said to the tide,
"Hey! O tide!
Start coming up!
Start coming up, O tide!
Start coming up!"
Then the tide started coming up fast.
There was really nothing else that Tide-Commander could do.
That—
that child of hers came to her from afar.
He had gone away from his mother.
He snatched his bow and arrows.
"Hey!

K̲ées’!
Ch’a tliyéix’ s’é yan ikadá!
Ch’a tliyéix’ s’é yan ikadá!» yóo ayawsik̲aa.
«Ch’a ax̱ daat át yéi kk̲wasanéi.»
Ch’a a yáx̱ áwé tliyéi yéi wootee wé k̲ées’.
Tle tláakw áwé yú du tláa x̱án.
Aawat’úk wé
gáaxw t’ooch’.
Át jinaskwánch. Yeedát tlél yéi át k̲oostí, gáaxw t’ooch’.
Wáa sáyá at woonei?
Áwé tle aawat’úk.
Tle awut’óogu een áwé a shanaa.át daak akaawas’él’ tle wé gáaxw.
Tle du tláa x̱ánde,
K̲inyukookook̲éik.
«Atlée,
shakg̲watl’éet’ yá lingít’aaní.
Haagú,»
yóo ayawsik̲aa du tláa, «Haagú.
De ch’a wé ax̱ káak yoo.atkoo.ák̲wgu x̱áawé.
K̲ées’ aawax̱oox̱.
Ách áwé shakg̲watl’éet’ yá lingít’aaní.
Yá gáaxw tóox̱ daak̲ gú!
Yá gáaxw doogú tóox̱ daak̲ gú!»
A yáx̱ áwé tle a tóox̱ áwé daak̲ uwagút wé—wé gáaxw doogú.
«Ch’a yá lingít’aaní kát igux̱latéet. Tléil wáa sá ikg̲wanei,» yóo ayawsik̲aa.
«Ch’a yá lingít’aaní kát igux̱latéet. Tléil wáa sá ikg̲wanei.»
Aag̲áa áwé tle tsu áa k̲ux̱ wudigút, yan asnéi k’idéin.
«Háa,
góok déi! Cha k̲ées’,
g̲unayéi ikadá déi!
Ch’a yá ax̱ káak aadé at koo.ag̲wéyáx̱ g̲unéi ikadá!»
Aag̲áa áwé tle g̲unayéi kaawadáa wé k̲ées’.
Tle yá lingít’aaní áwé yaa shanatl’ít’.
L aadé n̲ax̱wdzigeedi yé hú k̲u.aa, wéi—wé Yéil,
«Wáa sá óosh gé k̲ux̱aanóok?»
Wáannée sáwé,
«Xáats’t k̲adak̲eení,» yóo tuwditaan.
«Xáats’t k̲adakeen.»
Tle wdak̲eení áwé kindachóon—ei-ei-ei-ei—

Tide!
Hold still for a moment!
Hold still for a moment!" he said to it.
"I have a job to do."
Just like that, the tide became still.
Then he went quickly back to his mother.
He shot a
black duck.
They swim around on the surface of the water. Such creatures do not exist now, black ducks. What happened?
So he just shot it.
As soon as he shot it, he peeled the skin off over the head of the duck.
Then he returned to his mother,
K̲inyukookook̲éik.
"Mother,
the world will be flooded.
Come here,"
he said to his mother, "Come here.
That is my uncle's scheme, you see.
He has summoned the tide.
That is why the world will flood.
Get inside this duck!
Get inside this duck skin!"
As he instructed she got inside the—the duck skin.
"You'll just float over the world. Nothing will happen to you," he said to her.
"You'll just float over the world. Nothing will happen to you."
Then, once he had fixed her up nicely, he went back.
"Well,
go ahead! O tide,
start flowing now!
Start flowing as my uncle commands!"
That was when the tide started to flow.
The world began filling with water.
There was nothing Raven could do though,
"What might I do?"
Eventually he thought,
"Let me fly to the firmament!
Let me fly to the firmament!"
Then as he was flying straight up—ei-ei-ei-ei—

tle yú xáats't áwé wdiḵín.
Tle yá du lú áwé tle a tóode
yéi woonei, wé xáats' tóode.
Ch'a wuyíkt áwé wlig̱eiḵ hú ḵu.aa.
Shaawatl'ít' yá lingit'aaní tle.
Ch'a yoo akayikkasinúkk, «Wáa sákwshé, wáa sákwshé
de at yatee.
Gwál yéi unaléin gíyáa {...} de.»
Ch'áa-áa-áa-áakw át wulg̱eig̱í—x'oon sákwshéyá
áa uwax̱ée—
yáax' áwé, «Haahá.»
Du tóog̱aa áwé yaa woolaa de.

Shkalneek ii. Yéil Ana.óot Aaní Awulyeix̱í

Aag̱áa áwé tle—
tle yéi alx̱éis',
«Sú kadootl káx' kwshé x̱at g̱aag̱asgeet.
Sú kadootl káx' kwshé x̱at g̱aag̱asgeedée.»
Yóo áwé
tután hú ḵu.aa, Yéil.
«Sú kadootl káa x̱at g̱aag̱asgeet.»
Tle ch'u yéi áwé tle yéi tutáni áwé tle aadáx̱ tóot—
aadáx̱ tóot wudiyéḵ du lú, tle guṉéi
wdzigít héende.
Ḵaatéix̱': *Daa sáwé yéi duwasáakw sú?*
Haa!
Haa, ha x̱áawé wéidu á sú. Geesh—
geesh—geeshtín kawust'éex'i
tle yaakw yáx̱ nateech.
Kasat'éex' nooch héen x̱ukáx',
sú.
Ḵaatéix̱': *Mm.*
A shaayí áa yéi nateech, a shax̱aawú áa yéi nateech.
Héen táanáx̱ kínde koos.áaych.
Tle a káx' áwé wdzigeet tle.
Éh! Kudaseig̱ákw áwé tlax̱ niyís.
Ch'áakw a kát satáan.
De du daadé áwé aya.ax̱ji át áwé,

he flew right to the firmament.
Then his beak pierced into it,
into the firmament.
So he was just dangling in thin air.
The world had become flooded.
He was monitoring the sound of it. "I wonder, I wonder
how things are now.
Maybe the tide is going down now."
After dangling about there for a lo-o-o-o-ong time—who knows
how many days he stayed there—
at this point he said, "Aha!"
He thought the tide had flowed out enough.

Episode ii. Raven Makes the Aleutian Islands

So then—
then he was just wishing,
"Let me fall on a bed of giant kelp.
Let me fall on a bed of giant kelp."
That's what
Raven was hoping for.
"Let me fall on a bed of giant kelp."
Then, just as he hoped, his—
his beak retracted from the firmament and he started
to fall towards the water.
MARY PELAYO: *What is it that's called* sú*?*
Well!
Well, there is giant kelp there, you see. Bull kelp—
bull kelp—when it gets caked together with bull kelp
it is like a boat.
It hardens on the surface of the water,
this giant kelp.
PELAYO: *Mm.*
It has a head; it has hair.
It grows up from the bottom of the sea.
That's what he landed on.
Eh! He was gathering breath for the rest of his journey.
He lay there limp for a long time.
There was something he could hear around himself,

«H-h-h-h!»
kéi dusáaÿch.
Éh! Áwé tle aag̱áa áwé ḵutées̓.
Daa sá, daa sá diséikw?
Wáanée sáwé tle ch’a áa altin yéinááx̱ áwé kei sh wudix̱ích wé yáxwch̓.
Yáxwch’ ásíwéigé.
«Sée.aach,»
yóo kwshé duwasáakw yáxwch’?
ḴAATÉIX̱’: *Sea otter.*
Sée.aat.
«Éi!» tle aawa.éex̓,
«Ax̱ páatṉiyée,
haagú!
Haagú! K’aagú!
K’aagú!
H-h!
Tlél gé aadé x̱áat g̱idisheeyi yé?
L’éiw káx’ gé yax̱ eeltsees yú diyéex’?»
«Aaá,» tle yóo ash ÿawsiḵaa,
«L’éiw káx’ áyá ÿax̱ x̱altsees.»
«Ah!
Ax̱—ax̱ x̱oonée! Wáa sás i ÿát x̱’ex̱wdliyóo?
L’éiw ax̱ jeet kakwách!
L’éiw káa neeltsees, yú l’éiw aax̱ kagakwaach.
Ax̱ jeet kakwách l’éiw
wé diyéedáx̱!»
Aag̱áa áwé tle kát shawdix̱ích wé yáxwch’ík’ ḵu.aa tle.
Ch’áakw dateeyí áwé tsu
aawa.áx̱ a daséigu.
Gwáa, tle yá ach x̱án
anax̱ kei sh wudix̱ích.
Anax̱ kei jiwdihóo.
Tle ash jeet áwé akaawakwách wé l’éiw.
Hahá!
Ash jintáa yan akakwáach áwé tle wáa sá du toowú yatee.
Anóoshan Áanan
tliyaanax̱.á áwé yú.á,
tax’aaÿí tle yóo-óo deikéet aksixát wé tax’aayí.
Áa wdzigeedi yé áwé.

"H-h-h-h!"
someone kept exhaling.
Eh! So, he was looking for it.
What was it? What was breathing?
Eventually a sea otter popped up right along where he was watching.
It turned out to be a sea otter.
"Sea otter,"
isn't that what *yáxwch'* are called?
PELAYO: *Sea otter.*
Sea otter.
"Hey!" Raven called out to him then,
"My partner,
come here!
Come here! Why don't you come here!
Why don't you come here!
H-h!
Isn't there any way you can help me?
Do you swim down to the sand below?"
"Yes," the sea otter said to him,
"I swim down to the sand."
"Ah!
My—my friend! How shall I address you?
Bring me a handful of sand!
Swim over the sand; grab a handful of sand.
Bring me a handful of sand
from down there!"
Then the little sea otter dove down.
After a long time
he heard its breathing again.
Wow, he popped up
right next to him.
That's where he swam up.
Then he gave Raven a handful of the sand.
Aha!
When he put it in Raven's palm, Raven felt so good.
It is on the far end
of the Aleutian Islands, they say,
that he stretched a rocky peninsula wa-a-ay out into the ocean.
That's where he fell.

Á áwé daak̲ áwé akanalít wé l'éiw—
wé té.
Tle kéi akawug̲éex'i áwé, «X'áat'x̲ nax̲satee!»
Éh! Tle x'áat'x̲ áwé nasteech.
Tle a kaadé áwé kdak̲ínch,
tle a káx' áwé g̲anúkch,
kudaseig̲ákw nuch.
Ch'áakw kudaseig̲ákw, áwé tsu kéi
    aa koog̲éex'ch.
«X'áat'x̲ nax̲satee!»
Tle tsu x'áat'x̲ yoo siteek tle tsu.
Wé té áwé daak̲ akanalít.
Tle tsu kdak̲ínch a kaadé.
Haa!
Dawóotl yéidaané áwé yaa ndak̲ín.
Yáax' áwé tle a káa gashk̲ák̲ch.
Ch'áakw kudaseig̲águ áwés tsu ch'oo yéi,
ch'u yéi adaaneiyí áwé tle wéi—
tle wéi ÿánnáx̲ ÿan akaawalít
wé té.
Á áwé tax'aayí kwlaÿát'x̲ sitee wé tax'aayí,
Anóoshan Áanan tliyaanax̲.á.

Shkalneek iii. Yéil k̲a X̲'aan

K̲únáx̲
kulix̲éitl'shán a x̲oo ayagaax̲datéen wé tax'aayí.
Át dak̲éen áwé, ÿan dak̲éen áwé tle,
kudaseig̲ákw ch'a áx'.
Ch'áakwx̲ nastée áwé tsá g̲unayéi uwagút.
Wáa sá kaawahayi át áyú deikéede duwatéen.
Anax̲ kei kagánch wé x̲'aan.
Áwé tle héit'át x̲ánt áwé ugootch,
«Néi!
Yú deikéede kwshé daak idak̲een, yú x̲'aan
    ax̲ jeenáx̲ ÿan ÿasaÿék̲.
X̲'aan áyú yú deikéenáx̲ kei kagánch.»
«Hadáa! Tlél aadé.
Tlél—tlél ax̲ tuwáa ushgú,» tle yóo wandusk̲éich.

That's where he was tossing the gravel—or rather, the rocks—
toward the mainland.
When he threw up a handful he would say, "Let it become an island!"
Eh! They just became islands.
Then he would fly to one,
sit right down on it,
and catch his breath.
He was catching his breath for quite a while; then he
would toss another one.
"Let it become an island!"
They just kept becoming islands as well.
He was tossing rocks toward the mainland.
Then he would fly off to the next one.
Wow!
He was making a lot of commotion as he flew along.
Now and then he would land on one of the islands.
While he was catching his breath again for a long time in the same way,
as he kept doing this,
he cast the stones
down along the shore.
So the rocks became a long rocky peninsula, the rocky peninsula
on the far end of the Aleutian Islands.

Episode iii. Raven and Fire

It's very
frightening whenever it's stormy among the islands of that peninsula.
When he flew there, when he landed,
he stopped right there to catch his breath.
Only after a long time did he begin walking.
Some sort of thing could be seen way out to sea.
Fire was flaring up along the horizon.
He would go around to the nearby creatures saying,
"Hey!
You should fly way out there and take that fire in your beak and
bring it ashore so I have control over it.
There's fire flaring up way out at sea."
"Oh no! No way.
I don't—I don't want to," they would tell him.

Wáannée sáwé K'áxwk'u x̱ánt uwagút.
Hh!
«Hadáa! Aadé daak idaḵeen!
Ax̱ x̱oonée!
Ax̱ x̱ooní, x̱áat idashí! Yú x̱'aandé daak idaḵeen!
Ax̱ jeenáx̱ ÿan ÿasaÿéḵ.»
Áwé aadé daak wudiḵín wé K'áxwk'.
Ách áwé du lú yéi goowáatl'.
Wé a shú óosh kei uwagán du lú.
A jeenáx̱ ÿan aÿawsiÿéḵ wé x̱'aan.
Ách áwé du jee yéi wootee wé x̱'aan hú ḵwaa, Yéil.
Wáa sákwshé aawa.oo a daakeidí. Gwál a daakeidí awu.oo.
Ách áwé x̱'aan du jee yéi wootee.
Yú K'áxwch du jeenáx̱ ÿan ÿawsiÿéḵ
wé x̱'aan.

Shkalneek iv. Yéil ḵa Atkudatankahídi

Aadáx̱—
aadáx̱ tsu g̱unayéi góot áwé
tsu awsiteeni át áwé wé hít tlèin.
Héi'!
Héen x̱ukát áwé wlihaash á ḵu.aa.
Yéi-éi-éi a kát wudziḵín kéidladi, tle a kaadé sixát wé kéidladi.
«Daa sákwshíyóo gé?»
Tlax̱ áwé l yóo akoojeek, «Daa sákwshíyúgé?
Yú kéidladi a kát wudziḵín gé?
Ha ch'a hít yáx̱ x̱á ax̱ tuwáa ÿateeyi át áyú.»
Deikée-ée-éede duwatéen.
Áwé tle atgutóot uwagút.
«Aadóo sgé ḵaa x̱ooníx̱ nax̱sateeyí,
aadóo sgé?»
Yaa ḵunalwás' áwé, «Aadóo sgé ḵóot g̱adashee?
Aadóo sgé ḵóot g̱adashee?»
Wáanée sáwé wé hít x̱'awoolt uwagút.
Hít awsiteen
wé shaa x̱'áak.
Áwé tle a x̱ánt áwé uwagút.
«Haa, wáa sá ḵeeyanéekw?» tle yóo ash yawsiḵaa.

At some point he went up to Little Pygmy Owl.
Hh!
"Oh my! You should fly out there!
My relative!
My relative, help me! Fly out to the fire!
Take it in your beak and bring it ashore so that I have control over it."
That Little Pygmy Owl flew out there.
That's why his beak is so short.
The end of his beak had practically burned up.
He brought the fire ashore in his beak so that Raven had control over it.
That's how he got the fire, Raven that is.
Somehow he bought a container for it. Maybe he bought a container for it.
That's how he got ahold of fire.
That Pygmy Owl brought fire ashore in his beak so Raven
had control over it.

Episode iv. Raven and the Salmon Box

From there—
when he started off again from there,
the next thing he saw was a *huge* house.
Hey!
It was floating out there on the sea.
The gulls were swarming onto it, the gulls were just streaming toward it.
"Whatever can that be?"
Although he knew exactly what it was, he said, "Whatever can that be?
Are those gulls swarming onto it?
Well, it seems to be something like a house to me, indeed."
It could be seen wa-a-ay out there.
So he went into the woods.
"Who should be a fellow's relative,
who should it be?"
He was going around asking people, "Who should help a fellow out?
Who should help a fellow out?"
At some point he came to the door of a house.
He saw a house
in between the mountains.
He went up to a person.
"Well, what are you up to?" he asked Raven.

«Wáa sáwé k̲eeyanéekw?»
«Ha yú deikéede duwatini át áwé ax̲ tuwáa sigóo ÿax̲wadlaag̲ée,
yú deikéede duwatini át.
Kéi-éi-éidladi áyú a kát wudzik̲ín k̲únáx̲.
Ch'a hít yáx̲ áyá ax̲ tuwáa ÿateeyi át áyóo.
Tlax̲ yú kéidladi a káa yéi yakoogéi.
Áwé ax̲ tuwáa sigóo yax̲wadlaag̲ée.
A ÿís áwé wdashee x̲ax̲oox̲,
ax̲ éet g̲adusheeyí.»
Áwé tle yéi ash yawsik̲aa,
«Wáa sá iduwasáakw?
Wáa sá iduwasáakw?»
«Haa Yéil yóo x̲á x̲at duwasáakw.
Yéil yóo x̲at duwasáakw.
Ha wa.é k̲u.aa wáa sás iduwasáakw?» tle yóo ash yawsik̲aa.
«Ha X̲'anax̲.waatg̲waayáa x̲áayá x̲át,
X̲'anax̲.waatg̲waayáa áyá x̲át.
Haagú neildé!»
Tle héide áwé ashoowataan du hídi.
Éh!
Daat yáx̲ sáyóo kalig̲éi a yee yú du hídi.
Yá a kat'óotx̲ áwé daak̲ ÿaawatán wé Náak̲w Tl'eig̲í Wootsaag̲áa.
Tle yáat'át áwé tle
áx̲ daak̲ ayaawatán.
«Yáat'át i éet k̲ahées'i kwshé, yáat'át?
Ch'u tle yóo hít ÿayidlaag̲í tle aan ax̲ x̲ánx' k̲úx̲de kgidagóot kwshé?»
yóo ash x̲'awóos', k̲aax̲'awóos' ash jeet aawatée.
«Aaá.
Ha tle yú hít ÿax̲wadlaag̲í x̲á tle i jeedé kk̲watáan tsu.
Tlél aadé i jeetx̲ nak̲waataani yé ch'a tleix̲.»
«Ahóu, x'éig̲aa kwshé?»
«Aaá, x'éig̲aa x̲áawé.
X̲aadé x̲áawé kg̲idashée.
Ách áwé ÿanx̲adlák̲ni áwé tsu i jeedé kk̲watáan.»
«Ha yak'éi.»
Aag̲áa áwé tle ash ée akawdli.aax̲ wé shí,
kéi akakg̲washee shí
yú hít g̲unayéi saxíxni yánde.
Á k̲u.aawé k̲ut x̲waag̲éex' wé shí.

"What are you up to?"
"Well, that thing that can be seen way out there, I'd like to get it,
that thing that can be seen way out on the ocean.
Gulls are rea-ea-eally swarming onto it.
It looks just like a house to me.
There are so many seagulls on it.
That's what I'd like to get my hands on.
That's what I'm asking for help for,
so someone might help me."
Then he said to Raven,
"What is your name?
What is your name?"
"Well, my name is Raven, you see.
Raven is my name.
Well, what about you, what's your name?" he said to him.
"Well, I'm X̲'anax̲.waatg̲waayáa, you see.
I'm X̲'anax̲.waatg̲waayáa.
Come on in!"
Then he opened the door to his house.
Eh!
The inside of his house was so very beautiful.
Halfway up the wall hung the Octopus Tentacle Cane.
He had this thing
hanging on the wall.
"How about I lend you this thing?
As soon as you get the house, you'll return to me with it, right?"
he asked him; he posed a question to Raven.
"Yes.
As soon as I've gotten that house I'll bring the cane back to you again.
I couldn't keep it from you forever."
"Aho, that's the truth?"
"Yes, that's the truth for sure.
You're going to help me, you see.
That's why if I manage to get it, I'll give this back to you again."
"Well, good."
That's when he taught Raven the song,
the song Raven was going to sing
when the house started moving toward shore.
But I've lost the song.

Tle ax̱ toowú néekw nuch a daadé.
Yáax' áwé
át uwagút.
Tle a káa ÿan ax̱'eiwatán
wé hít káx'.
Ch'a yá haanaa ch'a a yahaayí kát
áwé ax'aatán.
Aan áwé daaḵ k'ul'gasteech,
há!
Ch'u yéi adaaneiyí áwé deisgwach—deisgwach
haanaa kaawaháa, deisgwach haanaa,
yú hít.
Wáa sáyú haadé g̱unayéi wsixíx.
Wáananée sáwé ḵúnáx̱—
ḵúnáx̱ ash een dákde g̱unayéi wlihásh.
Aag̱áa áwé
X̱'anax̱.waatg̱waayáa aawa.éex'.
Ashí wé shí ḵu.aa,
«X̱'aṉax̱.waatg̱waayáa-áa-áa-áa, x̱áat idashée-ée-ée-ée!»
Aag̱áa áwé tsá
tsu wánde g̱unayéi awsiÿéḵ.
Ch'u yéi adaaÿaḵaayí áwé deisgwach ÿán—
ÿán ÿaa aÿanadláḵ.
Deisgwach ÿán ÿaa aÿanadláḵ, ch'u yéi adaaÿaḵaaÿí.
Wáananée sáwé ḵúnáx̱ yan awsiÿéḵ.
A yíkde woogoot.
A yíkde nagóot áwé
awlisín s'é, wé Náaḵw Tl'eigí Wootsaag̱áa ḵwá awlisín.
Aag̱áa áwé tsá
a yíkde woogoot.
«Héi'!
Atÿana.á Daakahídi ásíwéigé?»
Ldakát át áyú a yee, yú eetx'í yáx̱ dagaatee áyú,
héide ashug̱éech.
Daa sá:
s'áax̱',
yaaw,
cháatl,
ldakát yú héen táak

I always feel bad about this.
So at this point
he went there.
He just placed the tip of the cane
on top of the house.
Toward himself, this way, Raven placed the point of the cane over its silhouette.
He was pulling the bottom-heavy house along toward land with the cane, ha!
As he was doing this, it gradually—gradually shifted this way, gradually shifted this way,
that house.
Somehow it was beginning to move this way.
At some point, it really—
it really began to float back out with him.
That's when
he called on X̱'anax̱.waatg̱waayáa.
He was singing that song,
"X̱'aṉax̱.waatg̱waayáa-áa-áa-áa, he-e-elp me-e-e-e!"
It was only then
that he started pulling it to shore again.
As he was saying that to him, it was gradually
reaching the shore.
It was gradually reaching the shore, just as he was saying that to him.
Eventually he pulled it all the way to shore.
He went inside it.
As he went inside,
he first hid that Octopus Tentacle Cane; he hid it.
Only then
did he go inside.
"Hey!
Oh, so that's the House of Fish Runs, isn't it?"
There was every conceivable creature inside it; there were room-like partitions here and there; he threw the doors open.
Whatever:
gray cod,
herring,
halibut;
that house

át kawdziheeni át áyú shaawahík,
yú hít.
ḴAATÉIX̱’: *Daat kaadáx̱ sáwé sh disáakw hú ḵu.aa, X̱’anax̱.waatg̱waayáa?*
Haa tlél x̱á wduskú,
shaakaḵáaw̱oo áyú.
Shaakaadáx̱ lingít áyú hú ḵu.aa, atgutú—
atgutuḵáawux̱ áyú sitee.
X̱’anax̱.waatg̱waayáa, daat kaax̱ sákwshíyú sh wudisáa.
Yú shikax̱úx̱s’i tóox’ ḵwá duwasáakw.
Tle atk’é shí áyú, áwé yaa ḵux̱wlig̱át áwé á ḵu.aa.
Áwé yéi x̱aan sh kalneek wéi—
wé i shatx̱ix̱úx̱.
Yóox’ wududzikóo Aangóonx’ yú.á.
Kéi akaawashée.
Áwé x̱áa ax̱latóowut daaÿax̱aḵá, áwé tlél tsu ÿan ḵuwuteen.
Áwé wáannée sáwé
yéi ash yawsiḵaa,
«Héi’!
Yaaw!»
Du xwáax’u ḵwá wáa sá yakoogéi: ts’ítskw, ldakát át, shoox̱’.
Ldakát át áwé woosh kanax̱ akaawataan du xwáax’oo.
Hás áwé has at gakg̱was.ée. «At gaÿis.í!
At gaÿis.í!
At.éewu yéi naÿsané!»
Ayáx̱ áwé tle tláakw áwé at.éewu yéi daaduné,
tle tláakw,
tséekx’ gandaa.
Ldakát—ldakát yéide
aléet yá aanx’i tóode.
Aag̱áa áwé tsáa
at g̱ax̱aat tuwatee.
A náḵ awlikéil’, a ÿís sh wudliyél wé
    ts’ítsgux’ sáani.
S’íx’g̱aa sháax̱ awdzitee, áwé a x̱oot jiwdigút.
    Áwé tle a náḵ has wudikéil’ wé sdu at.éewu.
    Aag̱áa áwé tsá tláakw awsinei.
Hóoch’! Ldakát yú tséek wáa sá yakwligéi
    ÿax̱ aÿawsix̱áa.
Ÿax̱ aÿasax̱áa áwé tsá tsu,

was full of all things
that swim underwater.
PELAYO: *What did he name himself after, this X̱'anax̱.waatg̱waayáa?*
Well, nobody really knows;
he was a mountain man.
He was a man from the mountains, of the forest—
he was a man of the forest.
I wonder what X̱'anax̱.waatg̱waayáa named himself after.
He's named in the lyrics to the song.
The song is a really good one, but I've forgotten it.
Your older sister's husband
told me the story.
It's still known there in Angoon, they say.
He sang it.
I asked him to teach it to me, but he didn't come back again.
Eventually
one of his crew said to Raven,
"Hey!
Herring!"
He had a big crew, though: songbirds, all kinds of birds, robins.
He herded up his whole crew.
They were going to cook themselves a meal. "Cook yourselves a meal!
Cook yourselves a meal!
Make some cooked food!"
Accordingly they quickly made some cooked food,
quickly,
with barbecue sticks around the fire.
He was flinging them into all the villages
every which way.
And only then
did he decide to eat.
He chased them away; he pretended to be something else
so as to scare away the songbirds.
He put moss on his head and went charging in among them.
They all ran away scared, abandoning their cooked food.
Only then did he get busy with it.
All gone! All of the barbecue sticks, however many there were,
he ate up all the meat on them.
Having eaten them all up

tsu áa ajikawsiháa, «At gaÿis.í!
At gaÿis.í! Kḵwatáa. At gaÿis.í!»
Tle tsu s at gawdzi.ée wé ts’ítsgux’ sáani
ldakát woosh g̱unayáade át.
Aadáx̱—
aadáx̱ tsu a jináḵ ak’éet’dáx̱ áwé tsá tsu g̱unayéi
uwagút haanaa niÿaadé.
Áyú yéi kdunéek yú l’éiw,
tle sakwnéin áyú oowaÿáa yú l’éiw,
yóonax̱.á.
Móon haanaanax̱.á gíyú l’éiw tlein áwu á.
A yahaayí áyá x̱wsiteen wé l’éiw.
Yú áx̱ daaḵ anasÿeḵ yé yóo—
yóo ḵuwanéekw du x̱’oos.
Du x̱’oos wáa sá kdlixwás’ tle a yáx̱ kadixwás’
yú l’éiw ká.
Yú teet áa litseeni yé tlél aax̱ uhéix̱
yú du x̱’us.eetée
yú l’éiw ká.
Yú Atkudatankahídi áx̱ daaḵ awsiÿeg̱i yé,
ch’u shóogu aadé kínde akaawatsex̱i yé káa g̱aag̱aléin
tlél tsu aax̱ yóo uhéik, du x̱’oos wáa sá kdixwás’ Yéil tle á áwé.
Áx̱ daaḵ awsiyeg̱i yé yú yaakw—
yú hít áx̱ daaḵ awsiyeg̱i yé tsóo, a ta.eetí tsú ch’u tle
woosh dakáṉ yú l’éiw,
yú sakwnéin yáx̱ yateeyi l’éiw ḵu.aa.
Ch’a aan áyú yú teet jinastaanch, tlél aax̱ oos.héix̱
yú du x̱’us.eetí.

Shkalneek v. Yéil Geesh Daax̱ Wugoodí

Aadáx̱ haadé g̱unayéi góot áwé
awsiteen wé—
Ḵées’ Yax̱ Ashakawdzinugu Shaanák’w áwé awsiteen, a yáa uwagút.
Áwé tle—
tle yéi tuwdisháat, «K’e ḵux̱ ḵadagoot ḵúx̱de.»
Ḵux̱ wudigút tsu.
Áwé Leineitk’óoxk’u áwé tle du x̱ánt wujixíx.
Yá—

he set them to work on it again, "Cook yourselves a meal!
Cook yourselves a meal! I'm going to sleep. Cook yourselves a meal!"
Then those songbirds cooked themselves a meal again,
all different kinds of things.
After that—
only after eating all the food from their supply did he again
    start going in this direction.
They say the sand there—
the sand over on the far side
is just like flour.
I suppose there's a big sand beach on this side of the moon.
    I saw a picture of the sand.
The place where he pulled it in,
he did that with his feet.
The way his feet were shaped, that's how the surface of the
    sand is shaped as well.
Where the breakers are really strong his footprints
never wash away
from the surface of the sand.
At the place where he pulled the Salmon Box ashore,
when the tide goes out over the very place where he kicked up sand,
it never washes away; however Raven's feet are shaped, that's what's there.
Where he dragged ashore the canoe—
where he dragged ashore the house, it left an imprint as well
where the sand is pushed apart,
that fine powder sand.
Nevertheless, even the constant breaking of waves never
    washes his footprints away.

Episode v. Raven Goes Down Along the Bull Kelp

When Raven started walking this way,
he saw—
he saw Little-Elder-Who-Enlarged-the-Tide; he approached her.
So then
he got an idea, "I ought to stroll on back."
He went back again.
Little Mink ran over to him.
This—

yá tax'aayí kát áwé áa hú ḵu.aa.
«Néi! K'aagú! K'aagú!
K'aagú chx̱ánk'! K'aagú! Haagú!»
Yú diyée
akoo.aaḵw s'é hóoch, wé geesh daax̱ yéi gútch
wé néesde.
Áwé kakax̱duḵéin k'oodás' káx' yéi
Geesh Daax̱ Woogoodi Yéil yóo duwasáakw.
Ei, wé néesg̱aa wé héen takaadé ÿax̱ ÿagút.
Tlél yóo awoodláḵkw.
Wé Lukshiyáank' áwé a káx̱ akawliník, «Haat tí yú nées'!
Haat tí! Aadé nagú!»
Áwé aadé wjixeex ash jiyís. Ash jeet aawatée.
Aag̱áa áwé tle g̱altóode awditee.
Gwál x̱'waash gíyú,
ayáx̱gwá nées'.
Tle át uwagút
wéit, wé shaanák'w x̱án. Gánt uwatáa.
Du díx̱'t áwé kawsit'áx̱' wé x̱'aan.
A keeká áwé neil wujiḵáḵ,
«Éh!
X̱at seiwa.át'.
Nées' g̱ehéenák'w áwé x̱at sawli.áat',
nées' g̱ehéenák'w.»
L ash ḵ'adaat tooshtí.
X'oon.aa yéi yanaḵáa sáwé déi yéi ayawsiḵaa, «Hadáa!
Gwátk sá woolaaÿi léin áwé a
kát eeyaṉís'?
Júk!
{…} ṉagú gánde!
Nagú gánde!
Nagú gánde! Wáa sás ikaawaháa!
Wáa sá ikaawaháa, wáa sá!
Gwátgiÿéig̱aa sá ÿan uwalaÿi léin áwé a
kát eeyanís'?»
«Éh! Hadáa!
Ax̱waanís' x̱áa.
Áyá x̱at sawli.át'.»

Raven was sitting on this peninsula.
"Hey! Come here! Come here!
Come here, grandchild! Come here! Come here!"
First Raven kept trying to go
way down there along the bull kelp
toward the sea urchins.
So thus, on {a ceremonial jacket}
it's called Raven Who Went Down Along the Bull Kelp.
Eh, he was trying to go to the sea floor to get sea urchins.
He never made it.
It was Little Mink whom he talked into doing it, "Bring me that sea urchin!
Bring it here! Go there!"
He ran down there for him. He gave it to him.
Then Raven put it in his pocket.
It could have been a big red sea urchin, I suppose,
or rather a green sea urchin.
He went to
the little elder's place. She slept by the fire.
The fire was radiating heat toward her back.
He hopped inside across from her,
"Eh!
I'm cold.
Sea-urchin juice has made me chilly,
sea-urchin juice."
She didn't pay any attention to what he was saying.
After he had said this so many times, she said to him, "Enough!
When was there a tideflat exposed by low tide for you
  to have eaten sea urchins?
Scram!
Get out of here!
Get out!
Get out! What's wrong with you!
What's wrong with you, anyway!
When exactly was there a tideflat sufficiently exposed by
  low tide for you to have eaten sea urchins?"
"Eh! For goodness' sake!
I did indeed eat sea urchins.
That's what chilled me."

Tle yá—
yá a gáni áwé tle a díx̱'náx̱ ayag̱atánch tle.
Áwé a daat áwé unookch hú ḵu.aa.
Hm, wáananée sáwé dé ash káa jiwdigút tle.
Tle {…} áwé wé du gáni áwé tle x'ús' yáx̱ ash sháa aawataan.
Aag̱áa áx' áwé déi tle a kaanáx̱ ÿan jiwdigút.
Áyú áa yax̱ aawax̱ích yindatáan.
A dex̱'k'idaat áwé aawag̱éex' wé nées'.
«Lí déi-éi, Yéi-éi-éil!
Lí déi-éi, Yéi-éi-éil,
g̱waag̱aalaa déi, Yéil!
G̱waag̱aalaa déi, Yéil!
Lí déi, Yéil!»
«Yéex̱!»
Ch'a goox' sáwé, «Gidzanóok'!»
«Héi!»
«A keekánde neesheex, wé—
wé léin, wáa sá ÿaa woolaa?»
«Ḵaa shoowú yéx̱ ÿaa woolaa!» Neil wujixíx—
neil usheexch.
Du xwáax'u x̱oowdudlisáay.
Aag̱áa áwé yeisú dé,
«Ts'ig̱inéi!
A keekánde neesheex.
Wáa sá ÿaa woolaa?»
«De ÿánde ÿaa naléin, de ÿaa kanalkúx.»
Á áwé tsu.
Áwé tle ldakát yá lingit'aaní áyá kawlikúx yú.á.
Aag̱áa áwé tsá hú ḵu.aa át ashukaawag̱íx' wé—
wé shawat.shaaṉák'w.
Aag̱áa áwéi
akaawa.aaḵw wugoodí íḵde—héi-éi'.
Ldakát át tlein a x̱oot uwaláa.
«Yee gu.aa yáx̱ x'wán!»
wé du xwáax'u,
«Yee gu.aa yáx̱ x'wán!
Ch'as yatáaÿi át dáḵde yéi naysané,
ch'as yatáaÿi át.»
Hú ḵu.aa áwé tle

So, he—
he would shove a piece of her firewood down along her back.
Then he would sit down by the fire.
Hm, at some point she jumped up on him.
So {. . .} she took that piece of wood of hers to his head like a club.
And at this point he attacked and overpowered her.
He flipped her over onto her belly.
He bounced the sea urchin over her butt.
"Stop it now, Raven!
Stop it now, Raven,
or the tide could go out any minute, Raven!
Watch out or the tide could go out any minute, Raven!
Stop it now, Raven!"
"Eek!"
At some point Raven called out, "Gidzanóok'!"
"Hey!"
"Run to check on the—
the tideflat. How far the tide has gone down?"
"It has gone down as far as half a man!" He ran inside—
he would run inside.
Raven's gang was called together.
Then at last Raven said,
"Magpie!
Run down to check on it.
How far has the tide gone down?"
"It is almost all the way down now; the beach is drying up now."
So he jabbed her again.
Then beaches went dry the whole world over, they say.
Only then did he toss aside that—
that little old woman.
That was when
he tried to go down to the beach—he-ey.
The tide went out among all of this great variety of creatures.
"Keep fighting the good fight!"
he said to his crew,
"Be of good courage!
Bring up only fat things,
only fat things."
As for Raven,

s’áax̱’ áwé ax̱’akla.eesh,
s’áax̱’.
Tle yéi-éi-éi-éi x̱’akuwáat’ ax̱’akawul.eeshí áwé
gunayéi oosyeek̲ch.
Léin—
léin ÿát’ áx̱ gug̲alaa yé
tle áx’ áwé a x̱’atóox̱ axáash.
Yáax’ áwé tsu g̲unayéi oosxáat’ch.
Daak̲ kagadéini, aadé daak̲
kakg̲wadaa yé,
léin ÿát’
aadé kakg̲wagei yé,
yéi áwé a x̱’atóode axáash.
Tle hóoch’i aayí—
nas’gi.aa, tle yú aas shuwee
a x̱’atóode axáash.
Tle yéi áwé
a daa yéi jiné
wé k̲ées’ aadé kakg̲wadaa yé.
Daak̲ at kadujéil tlein áwé, «Haa!
G̲unéix’ áwé ikakg̲wadáa, de yan x̱wasinéi.
Nas’gidooshú yeekáx’ áwé
daak̲ kakg̲wadéich,
léin wúx̱—
léin wúx̱ k̲a léin ÿát’.»
Yáax’ áwé
neil uwagút, hóoch’.
Satáan.
Wé s’áax̱’ yoox’ú sáani áwé awsinéx̱t’.
A tú áwé wé eex̱ áa yéi aya.óo. A tayee áwé át ishk̲úx̱
Yéil k̲u.aa, du x̱’éide kdutl’óok̲.
A k’óol’náx̱ akawliwaal.
Wudixwétl!
Wé lingit’aaní daa yéijiné ash wulixwétl.
Aag̲áa áwé tsáa
yéi adaayak̲á wé ts’ítsgux’ sáani,
«Tláakw! Tláakw! Sh x̱’adaa yoo jikaÿil.á. Tláakw! Tláakw!»

he was stringing up cod by the gills,
cod.
Having strung them up cheek to cheek on such a lo-o-o-ong line,
he started to drag up the string of cod.
The place—
the place where the spring tide was going to go out
is where he kept cutting the corners of the cods' mouths.
Here he would start to drag the string of cod up again.
As the tide was about to start coming up, at the place where
it was going to flow up to,
he cut into the corner of a cod's mouth
indicating how large
the spring tide was to be.
The last time—
the third time, it was at the base of a tree
where he cut into a cod's mouth.
This is how
he was working on
regulating how far the floodtide would rise.
Once that great quantity of seafood had been brought up, he said, "Now!
You will now start coming up, O tide, I have finished it.
The tide will always flow up to
eight places,
at neap tide—
at neap tide and spring tide."
At this point
he went inside, and that was that.
He lay there exhausted.
He had saved a bunch of little cod stomachs.
He kept grease in them. Raven made himself comfortable underneath
a cod stomach and the grease dripped down into his mouth.
He had put a hole in the bottom.
He was exhausted!
Working on the world had tired him out.
Only then
did he tell the little birds,
"Hurry! Hurry! Help yourselves to the food. Hurry! Hurry!"

Shkalneek vi. Yéil Du Waag̱í Ḵut Akakawulsóosi

Aadáx̱ g̱unayéi góot áwé haanaa niyaadé tsu
haandé g̱unayéi uwagút.
Aag̱áa—aag̱áa kwshéwéigé awsiteen gíwé
wéi—
wé shaanák'w.
Du shátx̱ awliyéx̱. Aan g̱unéi uwaḵúx̱ tle.
Yaakw—gootx̱ sáwé yaakw du jeet wujix̱ín?
Aag̱áa áwé ldakát ÿéix̱ ÿaawaḵúx̱ haandé.
Ldakát ÿéix̱ ÿaa naḵúx̱, ldakát ÿé, ldakát ÿé,
ldakát ÿé, goot'á sá.
Wáanéeskwshéwé
de a náḵ daaḵ has uwa.át.
«Ḵuk'éet' nax̱too.aadí.»
Ÿan has uwaḵúx̱. «Ḵuk'éet' nax̱too.aat.»
Tle aan woo.aat
wé du x̱úx̱ wé shaawát.
«Ax̱ waaḵ, áwé ch'a yáa ÿánde kakḵwatée ax̱ waag̱í.
Kéi kg̱wa.íx'ch yaakw ÿaa naḵúx̱u.
‹Haakw déi-éi, yaakw ÿaa naḵúx̱!› yóo—
yóo x̱'ayakg̱waḵáa.»
Áwé tle aax̱ daaḵ has uwa.át.
Kanat'á áwé s a.een.
Kanat'á agakg̱wastáa.
Agakg̱wastáa.
Áwé yáade kdunéek du ḵ'wádli yéi éexnax̱.á.
{…} Ch'a a káwu á,
a kát tléiḵw akawsitayi át áwé.
Áwé tle aadé kéi oo.éex'ch wé du waaḵ, «Haakw déi-éi!
Haakw déi-éi! Yaakw wéix̱ ÿaa naḵúx̱.»
L ḵ'adaat tooshtí.
«Haakw déi-éi!»
Tle a x̱ánde daaḵ an̲agút.
«De aax̱ x̱at kawduwatee,» du waag̱í áwé.
«Haaá?»
Aag̱áa áwé tsá aadé wjixeex
Gwáa!
Yaakw gwáawé áwu.

Episode vi. Raven Loses His Eyeballs

When Raven set out from there in this direction,
he again began coming this way.
That was when—I suppose that was when he saw
that—
that little old woman.
He made her his wife. He then set out with her by boat.
A boat—where did this boat come from that he got his hands on?
And then he went all over the place, coming this way.
He was going everywhere, all over the place, everywhere,
everywhere, wherever.
I guess eventually
they left the boat behind and went inland.
"Let's go berry picking."
They came ashore. "Let's go berry picking."
That woman just went
with her husband.
"My eyes, I'll just set my eyes down right here.
My eyes are going to yell out every time a boat comes by.
'Come here no-ow, a boat is coming by!'
they're going to say."
So they left and went upland.
They were picking blueberries.
She was going to boil the berries for their meal.
She was going to boil them for their meal.
They say that his cooking pot was here like this on the downstream side.
{...} It's right on top of it.
That's the thing in which he boiled the berries.
And then his eyes would yell out to him, "Come he-ere!
Come he-ere! A canoe is coming by over there."
Raven didn't pay attention to what they were saying.
"Come he-ere!"
Just then someone was walking up from the beach toward his eyes.
"I've just been taken away," his eyes said.
"Huh?"
And only then did he run there.
Behold!
Lo and behold, there was a boat there.

«Néi! Cha aank̲wáani, haahée! Haahée!
Ax̲ waak̲ áwé, ax̲ waak̲, ax̲ waak̲ áw[é].»
Tléik'. Tle du x̲'anák̲ áwé tle yóot k̲aa loowagúk̲ aan.
Á áwé kanat'á áwé du waak̲x̲ awliyéx̲.
«Daa sáyá i waak̲x̲ yiliyéx̲?»
du shátch yéi daaÿak̲á.
«Ch'a wéidáx̲ át áwé.»
Ch'u kanat'á wé du waak̲x̲ {dax̲ kasitee}.
(**AT.SHOOK̲**)
É-éh! Háháh! Haaá.é!
Tléil at ÿáx̲ k̲oonook.
K̲unaa,
K̲unaa yéi duwasáakw, wéix' k̲waawé
wudix'án.
Tsu s woo.aat atgutóode,
héen—héen yík.
Áwé yú naakéex' áwé
du kadaadzaaÿeidí kaadé áwé kaltátskw du shát,
kadaadzaaÿeit tlèin.
A jeedé áwé asyáa áwé wé kan̲at'á, a jeedé.
Wáananée sáwé yéi ash ÿawsik̲aa, «Déi áwé déi!
De tléil aadé déi áa gax̲tuwasháadi yé, ch'a k̲útx̲
áwé yakoogéi.
Ha ch'a a g̲óot wé táal, haakw déi!
Haakw déi!
Ch'a wéix'
ch'a a daadé yéi gax̲tusanéi.»
Áwé ch'a át tán du táali K̲unaa yík.
Du táali ch'a áwu á wé shaawát.
(**AT.SHOOK̲**)

Shkalneek vii. Yéil K̲uwu.éex'i

Yáax' áwé át uwak̲ux̲u ÿé áwé
áx' k̲oowa.éex'.
Ldakát át aawa.éex'.
Ldakát yéide át aawa.éex' áx',
woosh g̲unayáade át.
Ch'a yá héen tak.áditín aawa.éex'.

"Hey! Good townsfolk, give them here! Give them here!
Those are my eyes, my eyes; those are my eyes."
No. They ran off somewhere with the eyes to escape his tirade.
So he used blueberries for his eyes.
"What did you use for your eyes?"
his wife said to him.
"It's just something from over there."
Blueberries were his eyes.
(LAUGHTER)
Eh! Haha! Oh gosh!
Raven behaves unconventionally.
Redoubt Bay,
it's called Redoubt Bay; that's where
he was in a bad mood.
They went again into the forest
along the river—the river valley.
So, way upstream there,
his wife was shaking berries off the bush onto her berry pan,
a *huge* berry pan.
She was packing the blueberries toward Raven to give them to him.
At some point he told her, "That's enough now!
There's no way we can snatch up any more berries there now;
there are just too many.
Well, just leave that berry pan alone, come here now!
Come here already!
We're going to work on them
right there."
Her berry basket is just sitting there in Redoubt Bay.
That woman's basket is still sitting there.
(LAUGHTER)

Episode vii. Raven Hosts a Potlatch

So, at this point he held a potlatch
at the place where he had paddled to.
He invited every creature.
He invited all sorts of creatures there,
different kinds of creatures.
He invited them along with undersea creatures.

Kéet aawa.éex'
ḵa Tl'étl'—
Tl'étl', héen táak aa,
Tsaa.
Ldakát át áwé
aawa.éex' aadé.
Áwé wáanée sáwé
yéi ash yawsiḵaa wé—
wé du shát ḵu.aa,
«Cha wáa sá, wáa sá ḵeeyanóok?
Wáa sá, wáa sá kaawahayi át áwé haat keeyajél?»
L ash ḵ'adaat tooshtí
wé du x̱úx̱.
(VISITOR ENTERS AND MOMENTARILY INTERRUPTS)
L ash ḵ'adaat tooshtí wé du x̱úx̱.
Át yagóo áwé wé—
wé aantḵeení tlèin shaawahík wé neil.
Tatóok áyú yéi kdunéek, tatóok.
Ch'u áwu á yú íxde, yóo.
Áwé neildé áwé ÿanduwaxoon.
ḴAATÉIX̱': *Goo sáwé aadé ḵoowa.éex'?*
Goo sáwé aadé ḵoowa.éex'? Yú tliyaanax̱.á, Lawáak
tliyaanax̱.á gíwé, deikée.
Áwé tatóok áwu á, ldakát át a yeewú yóo kdunéek.
Ldakát át a yeewú á:
Náaḵw,
Kéet.
Ch'a yá gil'tú áwé yéi kaaxát.
Ldakát át áwu, Tsàa,
ldakát yéide át áwé áwu á.
Du ḵu.éex'i áwé.
Wáanée sáwé
neildé áwé shikawduwashee.
«Haa, shux'áanáx̱ has kax̱wlawóowag̱u aa hás
áwé neildé s ÿagux̱daxóon.
Áwé gax̱ÿilatéen.»
Tle héide kei shuwdux̱eijí áwé kéi kawduwashée wé shí.

He invited Killerwhales,
and Moonfish—
Moonfish from underwater,
and Seals.
He invited every creature
to the potlatch.
Eventually
his wife
said to him,
"Say, what—what are you doing?
What are all these creatures you've assembled here for, huh?"
Her husband
didn't pay any attention to what she said.
(VISITOR ENTERS AND MOMENTARILY INTERRUPTS)
Her husband didn't pay attention to what she said.
When the canoes arrived
the house was filled with a *huge* crowd of townspeople.
They say it was a cave, a cave.
It's still there way down south, they say.
The guests proceeded inside.
PELAYO: *Where did he invite them to?*
Where did he invite them to? Way farther over there, down past Klawock, I guess, down south.
There's a cave there; all the creatures were inside it, they say.
Every creature was in there:
Octopus,
Killerwhale.
The inside of the cliff is shaped like this.
Every creature was there, Seals,
all kinds of creatures were there.
They were his potlatch guests.
At some point,
they entered the house singing a song.
"Well, the first to proceed inside will be those from whom I have removed the sterna.
You will watch them."
As soon as they threw open the door, they began singing that song.

(AT.SHÍ)

Ahaa ahaa
X'áat'idaaÿéejayi
Ahaa ahaa
X'áat'idaaÿéejayi
Yéil du k̲'ush.eetí káa yawlishóo
Yéil keilk'i hás
Aha aha aha

Yóo áwé neil kawdliyích wé X'áat'idaaÿéejayi.

Ahaa, ahaa,
X'áat'idaaÿéejayi,
Ahaa, ahaa,
X'áat'idaaÿéejayi,
Yéil du k̲'ush.eetí káa yawlishóo
Yéil keilk'i hás
Aha aha aha aha
Ahaa ahaa
X'áat'idaaÿéejayi
Ahaa ahaa
X'áat'idaaÿéejayi
Yéil du k̲'ush.eetí káa yawlishóo
Yéil keilk'i hás
Aha aha aha aha

«Yeeytéen ágé yóo—
yú Tl'étl' neil uwagút. Yóo áwé át wootlóox' yú x̲'aháat k'í.
Yeeytéen ágé yú át wootlóox'u aa?
Kax̲wlawóowák̲w áyú akawliseek.
Ách áyú yéi yatee.
Wéit'aa hás k̲wás kax̲wliÿóowagu aa hás
áwé wéix' has al'eix̲.
Tlél uwadaléyáx̲ has al'eix̲.»
Yú Kéet áwé aan yéi sh kalneek.
(CH'ÉEN YAN WUDIYÍK̲)
Aagáa áwé tle—
tle «Yak'éi,» yóo k̲uyaawak̲aa.
K̲aa tóonáx̲ yaawaxíx,
«Yak'éi—haa kawulwóowagu yak'éi.»

(SINGING)

Ahaa ahaa
The Plovers
Ahaa ahaa
The Plovers
Their trail follows Raven's tracks around
Raven's sister's children
Aha aha aha

This is how the Plovers flew in.

Ahaa ahaa
The Plovers
Ahaa ahaa
The Plovers
Their trail follows Raven's tracks around
Raven's sister's children
Aha aha aha aha
Ahaa ahaa
The Plovers
Ahaa ahaa
The Plovers
Their trail follows Raven's tracks around
Raven's sister's children
Aha aha aha aha

"Can you all see that—
that Moonfish that came inside. It's rolling around at the foot of the door.
Can you all see the one that's rolling around?
He shied away from having his sternum removed by me.
That's why he's like that.
But those over there, the ones whose sterna I removed
  are dancing over there.
They're dancing as if weightless."
He told this story to the Killerwhales.
  (END OF TAPE)
So then
someone said, "It's good."
This thought passed through the people's minds,
"That would be good—if he removed our sterna, that would be good."

Áwé tle yóo áwé yax̱ shaÿawdudzix̱éx'w yú.á wé áwé Kéet.
Tle yá Kéet shóot áwé s shawdzix̱éx'w wé—
wé Tsaax'w sáani—
yées ḵáax'w sáani.
Tle yóode, tle wé—
tle wé Yáay tsú ḵaa x̱oo.
Á áwé hú ḵu.aa,
hú ḵu.aa áwé tle—
tle k'óox̱' du jee.
Gootx̱ sákwshíwé du jeet kawdiyáa wé k'óox̱' wé Yéil ḵu.aa?
Áwé tle ḵaa jeet awsi.ín.
«Yee waaḵ x̱á gax̱yeek'óox̱' yéi yee waaḵ,
yee waaḵ,» wé Tsaax'w sáani,
«Yee waaḵ gax̱yeek'óox̱'.»
Tle ldakát yóo yax̱ ashaÿawsix̱ex'u ḵu.éex'i tlein áwé ḵaa waaḵ wuduwak'óox̱'.
Áwé yóo Tsaax'w sáani ḵu.aa yéi s x̱'ayaḵá, «Hadáa!
Ha dei shígí ts'as ḵaa waaḵ gé, ḵudzitee gé?»
Tle ldakát yé sdu daat áwé has aléet wé k'óox̱'.
Ách áwé yú.á kadlich'éch'x̱ tsaa.
Hasdu daadé s aawalít, tlél ch'a sdu waaḵ has awuk'óox̱'.
Áwé yú kasayedéin yaa s at ga.áax̱ áwé át has aawat'úk.
Gwáa!
Ch'u tle gwáawé shé ḵaa x̱'atáanáx̱ ṉaadaa wé Kéet.
Tle yá ḵaa éeneenáx̱ síwégé tlákw ḵaa téix̱' tóox̱ atsaaḵ wé g̱ákw.
Tle yéi ásíwégé ḵutx̱ ÿaa ḵaa shunalxíx gé?
Áwé de x'oonk'í hasdu niÿaadé uyéx̱i sáwé s awsiteen.
Ḵaa téix̱' tóode, hé'! Á tsú hé—
hé g̱ákw.
«Góok!
Héent yee lugúḵ!
Óu, {gushtéx̱'}!»
Héent has loowagúḵ.
A {ítdáx̱} altín wé Tsaax'w sáaṉi, hóoch', át has kawduwax'aak tle.
Du ḵu.éex'i áwé yéi yoo akwsineek.

So in this way all the Killerwhales were hypnotized, they say.
So those little Seals—
those young men—
were hypnotized at the foot of the Killerwhales.
Then way over there,
Humpback Whales were among them as well.
So he,
he just—
he just had some pitch.
From where did Raven get his hands on that pitch?
So he gave them a container of pitch.
"You all are going to put pitch on your eyes like this—your eyes,
your eyes," Raven said to those little Seals,
"You all are going to put pitch on your eyes."
All of the great crowd of guests whom he hypnotized had pitch put on their eyes.
Those little Seals said, "Oh my!
Is that all there is to it, nothing but eyes?"
Then they were flinging the pitch all over their bodies.
They say that's why seals are spotted.
They flung it over their bodies, it wasn't only their eyes that they pitched up.
When they started to hear something strange, they took a quick glance at it.
Behold!
Lo and behold, blood was gushing through the corners of the Killerwhales' mouths.
It turns out that he had been stabbing a tree spine into their hearts through their armpits.
So that's how he was killing the people off, wasn't it?
Then the Killerwhales saw that a few of their number were missing from their side.
Into another person's heart, heh! And another with that—
that tree spine.
"Go on!
You folks run into the water!
Oh, {…}!"
They ran into the water.
{After that} he was watching those little Seals, and that was that; they were just swimming around there.
That's what he does to his potlatch guests.

K̲utx̲ ashuwlixeex wé Kéet ÿakugé.
Aag̲áa áwé tsá at uwax̲áa k̲únáx̲.
K̲únáx̲ at uwax̲áa.

Shkalneek viii. Yéil Kéetx' Sh Wulshaayí

Ÿax̲ aÿasax̲áa áwé
wé Kéet, aax̲ áwé ch'a g̲unéi uwagút.
Yú sdu niÿaade áwé ÿaa nagút.
Áwé léint uwagút.
Éh!
Léin áwé
ÿan uwaláa.
Léin áwé kaháa,
aag̲áa áwé yéi ash ÿawdudzik̲aa, «Héi!
Tle de Yéil k̲u.aa {tsé}.»
Kei tux̲'akasteech.
«{K'idaxwáach} yáx̲ tle yatee hé Yéil,» yú.á.
«Hadáa!
Hadáa!
Chookanshá k̲a {Skunsháa} káalk'w x̲áayá x̲át,
ách áyá.»
«‹{Dzéex} k'óol',› yéi gé yaawak̲aa?»
Haaá!
Haaá! Tle ch'a yáax' áwé yan aawashát du yak̲aayí,
«Yaax̲ x̲at g̲aysagú!»
Hé'! Yax̲ shayawlihík taay wé—
wé Kéet.
Taaych yax̲ shaÿawlihík wé yaakwx'.
«Dák̲de s'é kk̲washéex.»
Du shóode yan dul.áat áwé tle yóo,
áwé aawasháadi Leineitk'óoxk'u áwé tle du jee.
Aan áwé tsá wé yeek̲ká du tóoch wulichéesh
áa wunoogú
wé yaakw s'aatí x̲án.
Tle áwé g̲unéi kawduwanáa wé yaakw, hé'!
Kadunáa áwé wé ax̲áa.
Wé Lukshiyáank'i gúkx'u áwé aax̲ yax̲ ayatáx'.
«Tsx̲x̲x̲! Tsx̲x̲x̲!»

He killed off that large quantity of Killerwhales.
And finally, he ate really well.
He really ate.

Episode viii. Raven Gets Herself Married to a Killerwhale

When he had eaten up all of
the Killerwhale meat, he just started walking off.
He was walking in the direction of the surviving Killerwhales.
He walked to some tideflats.
Eh!
The tide had completely receded from
the tideflats.
When the tideflats were exposed,
that was when someone said to Raven, "Hey!
But {…} Raven."
Raven kept raising her asshole.
"That Raven seems to {have a supple rear end}," they said.
"Oh my!
Oh my goodness!
I am the fraternal niece of the women of the Chookaneidí and
of the {Skunsháa} clans, that's why."
"Did she say, '{…}'s rear end'?"
Aha!
Aha! Just then Raven latched on to this Killerwhale's words, saying,
"Take me aboard with you!"
My! The Killerwhales' boats
were crammed full of fat.
The boats were plugged with fat.
"I've got to run up into the woods first."
When they steered ashore for her,
she had that Little Mink whom she had caught.
Now that she had the Mink, she thought it would be possible
to sit on the rear seat
by the skipper of the boat.
The person in charge started giving orders to the boat, hey!
They were giving orders to the paddles.
She was trying to bite off the ears of that Little Mink.
"Waaa! Waaa!"

Ash jeedé kdag̱áax̱.
«Wáa sá, wáa sá daa.eeṉé? Wáa sáwé x̱'ayaḵá?
Wáa sáwé i yátk'u?»
«Ha de ch'a wé taay x̱áawé akawdzig̱áax̱,
wé taay.»
Hé'! Wé tsaa taayí.
«Du jeet aa xásh! Du jeet aa xásh!»
Daa sákwshéiwé lítaax̱ has awliyéx̱? Tle du jeet wuduwat[ée].
Ch'a yóo {ḵaa wax̱'akaÿáx̱} gíwé tle a x̱'aṉáḵ aṉaṉút'ch. Tlél tsú ch'a du x̱'éix̱
aa koodaa áwé ch'a wé—
wé Lukshiyáank' ḵu.aa.
Ch'a hóoch áwé aṉaṉút'ch a x̱'aṉáḵ.
Ch'a l yeewuwáat'i áwé tle tsu ash jeedé kei kwdag̱aax̱ch.
X'ooṉ.aa du jeet duxáash sáwé déi
yéi yawdudziḵaa
wé yaakw s'aatích,
wé t'ika.aach,
«Wáa sáwé iyasáakw wé i yátk'u, wáa sá?
Wáa sáwé iyasáakw?»
«G̱ayes'katleiḵwtík'i áhéi.»
Aadóoch sákwshé gí du een kaṉéek g̱ayéis' yei ḵukg̱wasteeyí,
k'e aadé kdag̱axádi yé.
«G̱ayes'katleiḵwtík'i áhé,
G̱ayes'katleiḵwtík'i,» yú.á,
«G̱ayes'katleiḵwtík'i.»
Cha ch'a yú—
yú a t'iká Kéetch—
Kéet, hóoch asháa
ag̱áa gúshíwé tsá G̱ayes'katleiḵwtík'i Éeshx̱ wusitee
wé Kéet ḵu.aa.
Wé yaakw ayasatáṉi áwé át sh jiwdliháa de
du x̱úx̱ sákw.
Ÿan yakwḵóox̱, ÿan ḵuyagóo áwéi yeisú déi—hé'!—
wé aantḵeení tlèin,
a x̱'éit at ÿawdudziḵúx̱ wé taay.
Ÿax̱.atg̱waḵú áwé tláakw at kaaxát.
Á áwé tle hú ḵu.aa
yéi a daa kéi tuwdishát du x̱úx̱ k'e ag̱ajaag̱í,
k'e ag̱ajaaḵ.

Little Mink was crying in Raven's arms.
"What—what are you doing? What is he crying about? What's wrong with your baby?"
"Well, he's been crying for some of that fat,
that fat."
My! That seal fat.
"Cut some off for her! Cut some off for her!"
I wonder what they used for a knife. They just gave it to her.
I suppose she would just swallow it {out of their view} before Little Mink had a chance to. Not even a drop of it ever ran down into
Little Mink's mouth.
It was she who kept swallowing it before Little Mink had a chance to.
Before long he would be crying in her arms again.
After they had cut off a number of pieces and given them to her, she was asked
by the skipper of the boat,
by the one on the seaward side,
"What do you call that child of yours, huh?
What do you call it?"
"This is Iron-Berry-Rope."
I wonder who told her that iron was going to come into existence,
things being as they were back then.
"This is Iron-Berry-Rope,
Iron-Berry-Rope," she said,
"Iron-Berry-Rope."
Finally,
that Killerwhale on the seaward side,
that Killerwhale, when he married Raven,
I suppose that was when that Killerwhale at last became Father of Iron-Berry-Rope.
As her husband-to-be was steering the boat
Raven wormed her way into his affections.
When the boat came ashore, when the fleet came ashore, now at last—heh!—
they transported food
for that *huge* crowd of villagers to eat, the fat.
As the proverb says, the situation was rapidly unfolding.
But Raven, though,
was suddenly struck with the idea that she should kill her husband;
she should just kill him.

Áwé tle g̲ákwg̲aa áwé woogoot.
Ch'u taat áwé
a téix̲' tóode aawatsaak̲ wé—
wé a luwalak'áats'ani g̲ákw.
Tle ách áwé awlijták̲ du x̲úx̲.
Ch'a yák'udé áwé kéi kawdig̲áx̲ Yéil,
«Hhhh!
Hhhh!
Hhhh!
Hhhh!»
«Wáa sá ikawdiyaa?» yóo ÿawdudzik̲aa.
«Ax̲ x̲úx̲ tax̲'.wook'oots!
Ax̲ x̲úx̲ tax̲'.wook'oots!
Hhhh!»
Hú kadag̲áax̲.
Tle ash jin̲ák̲ woosheex gíwé wé Lukshiyáan ÿádi.
«Yéi x̲'ayak̲áayin̲ ax̲ x̲úx̲,
‹X̲at n̲an̲áan̲i x'wán, ch'a hé x'aa lukan̲ax̲ x̲at kag̲aax̲dus.haa.
Ch'a hé x'aa lukáa kéi x̲at g̲adusháat,›
yóo x̲'ayak̲áayin ax̲ x̲úx̲.
Ayáx̲ x'wán du een yéi jinayné.
Ch'a wé x'aa lukáx' kéi ag̲asháadi, wé tliyaa,
aadé an̲g̲asháat.»
Du x̲'éig̲aa tsú dulnoogóon.
Áwé wé Kéet tlein áwé wé x'aa lukáa kéi wduwashát.
Aadé áwé nagútch g̲ax̲shóode.
De ax̲á síwéigé, de yaa anask'ít' ásíwéigé wé
Kéet tlein.
Aag̲áa áwé tle kéi akoog̲aax̲ch aadé,

(AT.SHÍ)

G̲ayes'katleik̲wtík'i Éesh éi-éi-éi
Haanaa gu-gu, gu-goo-oo-oo, gu-gu-gu-goo-oo-oo

Yóo áwé g̲ax̲ nooch aadé,

G̲ayes'katleik̲wtík'i Éesh éi-éi-éi
Haanaa gu-gu, gu-goo-oo-oo

Shí kát áwé g̲ax̲ nooch,

Haanaa gu-goo-oo-oo

And then she went walking after a tree spine.
While it was still night
she stabbed him through the heart with
a sharp-pointed tree spine.
She used it to kill her husband.
All of a sudden Raven started wailing,
"Waaah!
Waaah!
Waaah!
Waaah!"
"What happened to you?" people said.
"My husband had a heart attack!
My husband had a heart attack!
Waaaa!"
It was she who was crying out.
Maybe that is when that baby Mink just ran away from her.
"My husband always used to say,
'When I die, please just let me be buried on that peninsula.
Just let me be taken up to that peninsula,'
my husband would say.
Please do right by him.
Just let them take him up to that point, the one over there;
let them take him there."
They were satisfied with what she said.
This huge Killerwhale was taken up to that peninsula.
She would go there so she could mourn.
But actually she was eating him; she was in fact devouring
  that huge Killerwhale.
That was when she would cry out wailing over him,

(SINGING)

O-o-o Father of Iron-Berry-Rope
Come this way, co-o-ome, co-o-ome, co-o-me

This is how she would cry over him,

O-o-o Father of Iron-Berry-Rope
Come this way-ay-ay, co-o-ome, co-o-me

She would cry to the song,

Come this way-ay-ay

Anax̱ haat g̱agút áwé yaa ax̱'akaklatáx'ch
wé k'óox̱'.
Áwé tle yá aan x̱'ayeet na.aadích áwé tle yéi yanasḵéich, «Shéi!
Haa x̱'éit aa x̱'eelts'ík' i k'óox̱'oo!
«Jáa!
L góot ḵáa x̱'éig̱aa uwatiyi N̲aachook'óox̱'u
áyá x̱atáax'.»
Tle yóo áwé yanaḵéich hú ḵu.aa,
«L góot ḵáa x̱'éig̱aa uwatiyi Naachook'óox̱'u
áyá x̱atáax'.»
Hóh!
Aadé kaaxát de.
Wáananée sáwé
a daa ḵuyaawa.aa aadé yoo kwdzigitgi yé.
Aadáx̱ sh jiwdlihaa.
Tsu aax̱ g̱unéi sh kawdziyáa áwé
wé Kéet áx'—
áx' ḵutx̱ ashuwlixeexi yé.

Shkalneek ix. Yéil ḵa Yáay

Wé—
át sh jiwdliháa wé—
wé yáay
anax̱ kei x'akji yé.
Hí'!
Yáaÿ tlèin.
Éh!
Awsikóo ḵu.aa yóo yaaw áwé tle—
tle ÿaa ashanalhík
yú [yáay].
«K'e yan ÿaḵayeik, a yíkde nḵadaḵeení,» tle yóo tuwatee.
Tle kéi wux'aagí áwé ÿan aÿaawayék, áwé tle a yíkde wdiḵeen,
tle hóoch'.
De du jeewú áwé x̱'aan ḵu.aa,
K'áxwch du jeenáx̱ ÿan ÿawsiÿig̱i x̱'aan—
du ux̱ganḵáas'i.
A yíx' áwé tle shóot awdi.ák,
gwál gán tsú yéi awsinei.

When she would come back around she was always chewing away on some gum.
So the people walking around the village would say to her, "Say!
Pinch us off some of your gum to chew!"
"Hush!
I'm chewing this *N̲aachook'óox̱'u,* which is not suitable for anybody else to chew."
That's what she would say,
"I'm chewing this *Naachook'óox̱'u,* which is not suitable for anybody else to chew."
Ho!
She was latched onto it.
At some point
people started figuring out what she was up to.
Raven extricated himself from there.
He began again to venture off from
the place
where he wiped out those Killerwhales.

Episode ix. Raven and the Whale

So,
Raven spirited himself away to the—
the place where
that humpback whale kept surfacing.
Heh!
A *huge* whale.
Eh!
He knew that those herring
were filling up
the whale.
"I should get myself in position so that I can fly into it," he thought.
When the whale swam up, he was ready for it and then just flew into it;
just like that, he was in.
He already had the fire,
the fire that Pygmy Owl had brought for him to have control over—
his matches.
He just made a fire inside it;
he probably also brought firewood.

A yíx' áwé tle shóot awdi.ák.
Hé'! Tle wé du x̱'aaních áwé hú ḵu.aa wé yaaw,
tláakw woonei atgaltóos', tláakw.
Tláakw!
Tláakw!
Gwál ch'a wáa sákwshíwé èex̱ tle yóo asinút'kw,
wé yaaw.
Wáananée sáwé shoowaxeex wé yaaw, hóoch'.
Hé'! Ch'a ÿaa nax'ák,
ch'a ÿaa nax'ák.
Yeisú déi a yik.ádi ḵu.aa
atx̱ axáash áwé yaandéin nanéi, t'óos',
t'óos'.
Wáananée kwshéiwé tlax̱ ḵúnáx̱ a téix̱'t ayaawashát.
Hóoch'.
(DU JÍN AAWAT'ÁCH)
Haahá,
du een g̱unayéi wlitít, tóo aawanúk.
Du een kéi uwatán.
Hé'! Gasgítch.
De wé a téix̱'t lítaa aÿasháat ásíwéigé—
daa sákwshíwé lítaax̱ awliyéx̱?—
yáax' áwé g̱unéi wulitít du een.
«Lik̲'ayiyéide shéi-éi-éi-éi
x̱aan g̱alahaashée-ée-ée!» yú.á.
«Lik̲'ayiyéit kwshé x̱aan g̱alahaashée-ée-ée!»
yóo alx̱éis'.
«Lik̲'ayiyéit kwshé x̱aan g̱alahaashée-ée-ée!
Lik̲'ayiyéit kwshé x̱aan g̱alahaashée-ée-ée!»
Yú át áwé ash een át wulihásh,
Ltu.áa tliyaanax̱.á áwé shéiyú, ch'a á gíwé yéi duwasáakw Lik̲'ayiyé, yóo.
L'éi-éiw kuwát' áwé tle a ÿát wulihásh, áx' áwé tle
tóo aawanúk ash een aax̱ daaḵ naltít.
Ch'a yéi sh kawjix'aaḵw.
Wáananée sáwé adátx'i du daadé aseiwa.áx̱, «Héhéhéi!
Yáay yáat satáan!
Yáay yáat satáan!»
Hé'! Áwé ashkadulgút, *ball* gíwé woosh jeet kawdusg̱éex'.
Áwé tle neildé s at'aawoogoot.

He just made a fire inside it.
Heh! Due to his fire
he just went to town barbecuing the herring, quickly.
Quickly!
Quickly!
He must have been guzzling the oil in prodigious quantities—I mean the herring.
At some point the herring were all gone—that was the end of that.
Heh! The whale just kept on swimming,
just kept on swimming.
Now at last he was slicing off pieces
of the innards since he was ravenous for barbecue,
barbecue.
Eventually, I suppose, he managed to penetrate to its very heart.
That was the end of the whale.
(SLAPS HANDS)
Aha,
it began to drift with him; he could feel it.
It breached with him.
Hey! It kept dropping.
I guess when he took a knife to its heart—
I wonder what it was that he used as a knife—
this was when it began to roll in the swell with him.
"May it float to *Lik̲'ayiyé-é-é-é*
with me-e-e!" he said.
"May it float to *Lik̲'ayiyé* with me-e-e!"
he wished.
"May it float to a *Lik̲'ayiyé* with me-e-e!
May it float to *Lik̲'ayiyé* with me-e-e!"
That creature floated there with him;
the far side of Lituya Bay, I guess, might be the place they call *Lik̲'ayiyé*.
The whale just drifted up against a lo-ong sandy beach; and there
he felt it getting rocked up onto the beach by the waves with him inside.
He just settled himself down comfortably.
Eventually he heard the voices of children around him, "Hey-hey-hey!
There's a dead whale lying here!
There's a dead whale lying here!"
Heh! They were playing; maybe they were playing catch with a ball.
So they ran home with the news.

«Aa sgí ḵaa kaṉax̱ angaxaasháḱóo-óo-óo yáaÿ yíkdáx̱—
yáaÿ yíkdáx̱ kei x̱duḵee-ee-een?» yóo áwé
x̱'ayaḵá a yíkde.
«Aadóo sgí ḵaa kaaṉáx̱ angaxaasháḱóo-óo-óo
yáaÿ yíkdáx̱ kei x̱duḵeenée-ée-ée?» yóo áwé x̱'ayaḵá.
«Iya.áx̱ch ágé?» adátx'i,
«t'aax̱toogoot neildé!»
Tle neil has luwugoog̱óo tle yéi s x̱'ayaḵá,
«Yáaÿ áyú yóot satáan, yáaÿ.
Áyú a yíkde áyóo
yéi x̱'ayaduḵá,
‹Aa sgí ḵaa kaanáx̱ angaxaasháḱ'u,
yáaÿ yíkdáx̱ kei x̱duḵeení?› yóo áyá
x̱'ayaduḵá a yíkde.»
«Háa!»
Tle sdu x̱'éix̱ akdudliyáakw. «Tléiḱ, haadé
haat yi.á,
ḱe aadé gax̱yisa.áax̱.»
Tle guṉéi s uwa.át aadé wé aaṉtḵeeṉí.
Gwáa!
Ch'a ayáx̱ áwé.
«Aa sgí ḵaa kanax̱ angaxaasháḱóo-óo-óo
yáaÿ yíkdáx̱ kei x̱duḵeenée-ée-ée?» yóo áwé x̱'ayaḵá.
Tle wé shaaṉák'w tsú jiwduwataaṉ aadé. Gwál ax̱ yáx̱ áwé
wdishán wé shaaṉák'w.
Ag̱áa áwé tle kawduwa.aaḵw kéi wduxaashí yóo.
Ḵóok yáx̱ áwé kéi wduwaxásh.
Aadóo sá jiwdixwétl tle tsu góot ḵáa áx̱ goot wé
kei nduxáshi.
Daa sákwshéiwé lítaax̱ wududliyéx̱?
Ch'a yák'udéi, á áwé du tóogaa áx̱ ḵukaṉalgéi áwé ḵaa
yát wudiḵín.
Áh-hó-hó-hó-hó-hó, hú'!
Wé shaaṉák'w ḵwáwé tle kéi shikaawashée,

(AT SHÍ ḴA NADÁAKW AKAGWÁLS')

X̱'unéi, X̱'unéi,
Ch'a kéi gidaḵeen!
Ch'a kéi gidaḵeen!

"Who could cut open a li-i-ittle hole over a fellow
so a fellow could fly-y-y up out of a whale?" That is what he was saying inside it.
"Who could cut open a li-i-ittle hole over a fellow
so a fellow could fly-y-y out of a whale?" he was saying.
"Do you hear that," said the children,
"Let's go home and tell the news!"
Then as they came running home, they said,
"There's a dead whale lying over yonder.
And inside it
someone is saying,
'Who could cut open a li-i-ittle hole over a fellow
so a fellow could fly-y-y out of a whale?' this is what someone's saying inside it."
"Hah!"
The people had no faith in what the children were saying.
"No, come here with us,
you all will hear it," the kids said.
So the townspeople started walking toward it.
Behold!
It was really true.
"Who could cut open a li-i-ittle hole over a fellow
so a fellow could fly-y-y out of a whale?" he was saying.
Then a little elder was led over there as well. Maybe that little elder was as old as I am.
So then the people tried cutting a hole, like this.
They cut a box-shaped hole.
Whoever got tired of working, another one would come to take their place as they were cutting it up.
I wonder what the people used for a knife.
All of a sudden, when he was satisfied with the size of the hole, he flew out right in the people's faces.
Ah-ho-ho-ho-ho-ho, hoo!
The little elder began singing,

(SHE BEGINS SINGING AND TAPPING THE TABLE)

X̱'unéi, X̱'unéi,
Just fly on up!
Just fly on up!

X̱'uṉéi, X̱'uṉéi,
Ch'a kéi gidaḵeen!
Ch'a kéi gidaḵeen!
X̱'uṉéi, X̱'uṉéi,
Ch'a kéi gidaḵeen!
Ch'a kéi gidaḵeen!
Ḵuwáx̱ ṉidaḵeen!
X̱'uṉéi, X̱'uṉéi,
Ch'a kéi gidaḵeen!
Ḵuwáx̱ ṉidaḵeen!
Ḵuwáx̱ ṉidaḵ[een]!

Tle yá x'aa t'éide áwé wudzigeet, tle hóoch'.
Haahá!
Yeisú déi tláakw ḵoowaṉei wé yáaÿ taayí xaash.
Daatx̱ yaa ndutéen wé yáaÿ.
A yeex̱ ḵuwawsinák̲ ḵaa hítx'i x̱ánde.
Tláakw at ÿatee
wé yéijiné.
Tlax̱ naak'w yáx̱ ÿatee hú ḵu.aa,
wé yáaÿ yíkdáx̱ kei daḵéen.
Yax̱.atg̱wakú,
«Du x̱aawú tóotx̱ kawlix'áas
wé eex̱.»
Áwéi-éi k'e sh daa.ilg̱éi-éikw
wé x'áat'ák'w wat'éik.
Sh daa.ilg̱éikw.
Adudáakw.
Taat kanax̱ tlél oox̱éx'wx̱ wé adaakw.
Áwé dus.ée wé dleey.
Dus.ée wé yáaÿ dleeyí, kawdudlixaash.
Du tóog̱aa ṉatée áwé tsáa aaṉ
ÿáa uwagút.
«Daa sá, daa sá yéi daayné?» tle yóo ḵuyawsiḵaa.
«Ha yáaÿ áwé wduwat'ei, yáaÿ.
Yáaÿ áwé wduwat'ei.
Aatlein! Aatlein! Aatlein!
A daa yéi jiduṉé,» yú.á.
«Haaw! Haaw!

X̱'unéi, X̱'unéi,
Just fly on up!
Just fly on up!
X̱'unéi, X̱'unéi,
Just fly on up!
Just fly on up!
Fly however you want!
X̱'unéi, X̱'unéi,
Just fly on up!
Fly however you want!
Fly however you want!

Then he dropped behind this peninsula and was gone.
Aha!
Now at last everyone was bustling about cutting up the whale blubber.
They were carrying it away from the carcass of the whale.
They had people lined up inside it ready to take it to the houses.
Things were proceeding at a furious pace
with the work.
But poor Raven was nearly dead from exhaustion, though,
when he flew up out of the whale.
There's a proverb,
"Oil
was gushing out of his fur."
So-o-o, he felt he should wipe himself off
behind that little island.
He was wiping himself off.
They were rendering fat.
They went without sleep all night long rendering fat.
And they were cooking the meat.
They were cooking the whale meat that had been cut up.
Only when he was satisfied with the way things were progressing
did he appear before the village.
"What's that, what are you doing?" he said to them.
"A whale was found, a whale.
A whale was found.
A huge one! A huge one! A huge one!
People are working on it," they said.
"Well! Well!

Ha tlél shéigé l daa sá a yíkde wdu.aax̱ gí wé yáaÿ gé?»
    tle yóo ḵuyawsiḵaa.
    (AT.SHOOḴ)
«Héigíl ch’a ḵukawdu.áax̱ákw a yíkde?»
«Ha a yíkde at wuduwa.áx̱, a yíkde,
a yíkde at wuduwa.áx̱.
‹Aa sgí ḵaa kaṉax̱ angaxaashák’u yáaÿ yíkdáx̱ kei x̱duḵeeṉ?›
    yóo x̱’ayaduḵá a yíkde.
Á áwé du kaṉax̱ anduxáash áwé ch’a wé x’aa ÿat’éide woogwáatl a yíkdáx̱.»
«Tlaagóo!
Ha yú haa aaníx’ x̱áa tsú yéi at kawdiÿaa,
yú haa aaníx’.
Áwé tle ḵutx̱ ḵaa shoowaxeex.
Wé yáaÿ,
a yíkdáx̱ kéi wduwaḵiṉi yáaÿ
has awux̱aayí wé aantḵeeṉí ḵwá
yax̱ has ÿawsix’áḵw tle.
Ḵutx̱ has shoowaxeex.
Ch’as a náḵ—
a ṉáḵ ṉaawulgáas’i sgíwé, yak’éi wé át
a náḵ ṉaawulgáas’i.»
«Hú-hu-hoo!
Góok!
Naagax̱la[gáas’]» Ch’a wáa sá du x̱’éik’ aduhíngeen.
«Góok! Naagax̱lagáas’.»
Tle ṉaawligáas’. Goo sákwshíwé át ṉaawligás’
    du x̱’ayáx̱?
Aag̱áa áwé yeisú déi,
tláakw woonei hú ḵwá wé yáaÿ taayí x̱á.
Tláakw yatee ḵúnáx̱.

Shkalneek x. Yéil Du Loowú Kéi Wdusyeig̱í

Aag̱áa áwé
tléil yéi áyá a kát ḵee.á ḵoostí yú.á yá lingit’aaní.
Kawjigidéyáx̱ áwé yatee, ch’a kawjigidéyáx̱. Tlél
    a kát ḵee.á ḵoostí.
Tle yóode áwé a tóode yaa nagút, wéi—
wé kag̱ít yáx̱ ḵuteeyí.

So, by the way, no one happened to hear anything inside the whale, did they?" he said to them.
(LAUGHTER)
"Mightn't any mysterious sounds have been heard coming from inside it?"
"Well, something was heard inside it, inside it;
something was heard inside it.
'Who could cut open a little hole over a fellow so a fellow could fly out of a whale?' is what somebody said inside it.
When he was cut out he just rolled out of sight behind that peninsula."
"Amazing!
You know, this happened in our village too,
in our village.
Then everyone died off.
That whale,
when the townspeople ate
the whale that a fellow had flown out of,
they just died off en masse.
They all perished.
Just—
for the villagers to move away from it, I suppose—it would be good
for the villagers to move away from that thing."
"Hoo-hoo-hoo!
Get going!
Let the villagers relocate!" They were gullible enough to believe him.
"Get going! Let the villagers relocate."
The villagers relocated. Where was it, I wonder, that they relocated to per his directions?
And so now at last,
he got busy eating the whale fat.
He was in a veritable feeding frenzy.

Episode x. Raven Gets His Nose Yanked Off

At that time
daylight did not exist in the world as it does now, they say.
It was as if the world were in darkness—just completely dark. There was no daylight in the world.
Then, way over that way, he was going into the world
as it lay in darkness.

Át uwagút wé
taaych áa woosh yaduldzeit yé.
Taaÿ áyú *ball*-x̱ sitee,
wé *football.*
Kadux̱ísht.
Kei kdulk̲'íshch.
Hé! Tle ashkoolyát tsaa taayí.
Áwé tle k̲aa x̱oot wujixíx hú tsú.
Tle [du] jeet kawuxeexí áwé taay tle an̲an̲út'ch.
Hóoch'! K̲ut kagaxíxch wé *ball.* Aag̱áa k̲udushee nooch.
Aag̱áa áwé tsu ch'a g̱óot.aa daak koodutéeych.
Football áyá aan ash kadulyát.
Aadóoch sá kei kawlik̲'ísh, tle tláakw áyóo
woosh káa yei k̲udak̲óoshch
a n̲iyaadé át k̲aa luwugoog̱ú.
Ch'a aan̲ áwé tlél áx̱ jiwdusdaa yóo an̲út'gu hóoch k̲u.aa.
Áwé tsu ashkadulyádi áwé awsiteeni át áwé anax̱ yéik̲ wududzi.ín wé—
wé k̲ílaa,
l'oowú k̲ílaa.
A káx' áwé yéi duwa.óo wé—
wé taay.
Wé aan k̲ugax̱dust'ex̱ át tsú ÿaa yéi ndusnein,
gwál x̱aat tíx' gíyú.
Tle a kát ÿaa wunadéin, tle wé yaakw ÿíx̱ ÿaa aawa.aat, tle daak uwak̲úx̱ wé yaakw.
Wé deikéex' áwé
ÿadunák̲ws'.
Wé taay áwé ách ÿadulnák̲ws'.
Haahá!
Du tóoch wulichéesh, «K'e aadé nk̲agoot.
K'e aadé nk̲agoot.»
Tle ÿatx̱ ashoowa.áx̱ wé héen.
Tle aadé woogoot
yú yaakw tayee.
Awsiteen wé taay át kawlidzéidzi yé.
Tle át uwagút tle.
A yaax̱ akakéil' tle.
Ha ch'al yéi koogeix̱ kát yú taaÿ,

He came to the
place where people were throwing fat at each other.
Fat was used for a ball—
a football.
They were hitting it with a stick.
They were batting it up in the air.
Heh! They were playing with seal fat.
Then he, too, ran to join them.
When the ball of fat came to him he'd just swallow it.
It was gone! The ball kept disappearing. They would be searching for it.
Then they would bring out another one.
They were playing with a football.
When anybody would bat it up,
they would quickly pile onto one another
as people milled around toward the ball.
Despite this, they weren't watching his actions when he would swallow it.
While they were still playing, something that had caught his eye
    was brought down to the beach, a—
a platter,
a wooden platter.
They had the—
the fat on it.
They were readying those things people were going to use to hook fish,
perhaps line made from spruce roots.
As he was observing them, the people just got aboard a boat
    and the boat went out to sea.
Way out on the sea,
they were baiting their lines.
They were baiting hooks with the fat.
Aha!
He thought it would be readily accessible, "I ought to go out there.
I should go out there."
Then he lifted the water by one end like a blanket.
He just walked down
below the boat.
He saw the place where the fat was wafting about in the water.
Then he just walked up to it.
He was untying it from the hook.
Hah, as if those pieces of fat were all that big,

at yanáag̱u.
Tle aax̱ awuteeyí áwé tle ananúťch.
Anax̱ kéi x̱dusÿéḵ áwé tlél daa sá a ÿáa yei uteex̱.
Cháatl x̱'ayeex' áwé s daṉáḵws'
hás ḵu.aa.
Tle tsu aṉax̱ ÿaa kax̱dulyéich.
«Tléik', tlél daa sá.
Wé a yaṉáag̱u tle tlél ayáx̱ yéi ḵoosteech. »
Ÿan has uwats'úk. Tlél daa sá.
Wé taay ḵwá tle ldakát has akaawajeil.
«Haa.
Ch'a de wéidu wé aadé yee yateeyi yé.
Dáa,
dáa,
ts'óots' jee wuskóowu daak ÿaÿx̱á!
Ts'óots' jee wdzikuwu aa daak ÿaÿx̱á!»
Ách áwé tle—
tle yéi ḵuyaawaḵaa,
«Aanÿádi áyú
ts'óots' jee wdzikóo.»
Hú áwé tle daak ÿawduwax̱áa,
wé daṉáḵws'i kaadé.
Tle ayáx̱ awuteeyí áwé tle—
gwál x̱aatch gíwé yax̱ koodus.aax̱w—
tle yínde akawliyaa.
Tle ch'a shux'áa aayí yéi akanalyéini áwé tle jee awdinúk
wé át ÿawusheeyí wé tíx'.
Haahá!
Át yaawashée.
Ha ch'a tle tlax̱ yáat, du luwax'aan kwshéiwégé,
akakéil' gé?
Ch'a yák'udé áwé g̱unayéi wdudzix̱úť.
Há'! Du lutóox̱ áwé kei yawdlig̱ích, áwé {…} áwé ťeix̱áax̱ sitee.
Haahá!
Hóoch'!
Kínde áwé g̱unayéi wduwax̱úť.
Ḵoosh kadáan á!
Tle yú yaakw tayee áwé, {… a} tayeedé áwé
yax̱ sh kadlix̱ít.

the bait.
Then when he removed it, he would swallow it.
Whenever the line was pulled up there was never anything on it.
Those people, for their part, were setting their hooks where they could expect the halibut to bite.
They would lower one after another.
"Nope, nothing.
The bait on the hooks is never all there as it should be."
They pulled the lines in. Nothing.
As for the fat, they put it all away.
"Hah.
Right there, that's the problem with you people.
Please,
please,
take out somebody who has a feel for fish nibbles!
Take out somebody who has a feel for fish nibbles!"
So
someone just said,
"A certain nobleman
has a feel for fish nibbles."
So he was the one they took out
to where they were setting their hooks.
Then when he had placed a hook in the proper way—
perhaps roots were used to tie on bait—
he just lowered it on down.
As he was lowering the first one, he felt Raven touch the line.
Aha!
He touched it.
So it was right here, right at the very tip of his nose, I guess, that he was untying the fat, wasn't it?
All of a sudden someone began to jerk on the line.
Hah! He was hooked right through the beak; {…} it was a hook.
Aha!
He was a goner!
They were starting to pull him upward.
What a fine mess!
Then, under the boat, {…} he was trying to wriggle himself down
under the boat.

Hél x̱á ooshgóok wé át wux'aak, ch'a daa sá tsú tlél ooshgóok.
Tle héen táat wugoot tsú tlél ooshgóok, ch'a aan áwé yóo áwé óot yaanwuhá ḵwá yéi kaaxát.
Tle yá yaakw tayee áwé àawatséx̱, yóo.
Haahá!
Wáananée sáwé tle aax̱ wool'éex' du loowú, tle kínde wdudzix̱óot'.
Hóoch'.
Yínde áwé, ch'a yéi yei ndag̱át' diyínde.
Éh! Ÿan ÿadux̱áa áwé a daa yoo ÿakdudzi.éik,
«Daa sáyá?
Daa sáyá? Daat loowú sáyá?»
Tsu héit ḵáach áwé a keekánde
anaa.aat.
«Daat loowú sáwé?»
Wáananée sáwé,
hú ḵu.aa,
taÿas'áaxu—
taÿas'áaxu áwé s'áaxwk'ux̱ awliyéx̱. Du ḵ'alukáx̱ akaawat[ee].
A eetéet áwé aawatsáḵ aas k'óox̱'u.
Yú du lú yáx̱ akaawachúx.
A eetéex̱ kéi aawatsáḵ, yóo.
Aan áwé tsá g̱unayéi uwagút,
tle a shóonáx̱ áwé át uwagút wé hítx'.
«Goo sáyá? Goo sá?
G̱uneit loowú aadé kéi wdudziyéḵ, goot'á sá?»
«Ha!
Cha tléil wutusakú daa sáwé yéi iyasáakw.
Hél wutusakú.
Kei at wudusyeig̱í tlél wutusakú. Gwál k'idaaká gíwé.»
Tle k'idaakáx' áwé neil uwagút.
«Goo sáyá? Goo sá? G̱uneit loowú aadé kei wdudziyéḵ, yéi sh kadulneek.»
«Ha! Gwál yú k'idaaká gíwé, tléil wutusakú.»
Haahá! A shunaaÿát ÿaa nagút wé hítx'.
Wáananée sáwé a shóot tle ḵúnáx̱ át uwagút.
«Goot'á sáyá? Goot'á sá G̱uneit loowú aadé kéi wdudziyéḵ sh kadulneek?»
G̱uneit loowú yóo áwé ayasáakw.

He didn't know how to swim, you see; he didn't even know how to do anything.
He didn't even know how to walk into the water, but he was driven by hunger.
He just kicked the underside of the boat, like this.
Aha!
Eventually his nose broke off and they pulled it up.
No more nose.
Downward, he was just slinking downward.
Eh! When the people brought it ashore, they kept examining it, "What is this?
What is this? What kind of nose is this?"
The other people
were walking by to get a good look at it.
"What kind of nose is that?"
Eventually
Raven used
a limpet shell—
he used a limpet shell for a little hat. He pulled it over the end of his beak.
He stuck tree pitch in place of his beak.
He kneaded it to look like his own nose.
He stuck it in place of his nose, like so.
He finally started off with his new nose
and came to the houses at the end of town.
"Where is it? Where?
The Alien's nose was pulled up; where exactly is it?"
"Hah!
We don't know what you're referring to.
We don't know what it is.
We don't know whether something was pulled up. Maybe next door."
So he went into the next house.
"Where is it? Where? The Alien's nose has been pulled up, that's the story people are telling."
"Hah! Maybe it's over there next door, we don't know."
Aha! He was walking about the houses at the very far end.
Eventually he came to the very end.
"Where exactly is it? Where is it that people are saying that the Alien's nose was pulled up and taken to?"
He was calling it the Alien's nose.

«Ha yáat áwé yáat,» tle yóo yawdudzik̲aa, «yáat áwé.»
«Hadá, k'e, k'e, k'e, k'e k̲aak̲asateen k'e!
K'e k̲aak̲asateen!
Haa.
Tlax̲ yoo kwx̲aajeek x̲á.
Yú haa aaníx' yéi at n̲an̲ée x̲áayóo,
yú ách kéi at wusiyeg̲i k̲áa á ch'u tle tlél k̲uwustee.
Á áwé ÿax̲atínni áwé, yéi áwé yánde kagux̲dayáa, yéi.»
«Haa,
ha likoodzée shéigé!
Tlaagóo!
Shéigé taay k'át ax̲á G̲un̲eit áwéigé?»
G̲un̲eit loowú—
G̲uneit loowú yóo asáakw nuch.
(AT.SHOOK̲)
Xwéi!
Tle du jeet kawduwakél',
yax̲ áwé wdudzi.áx̲w yú t'áa yáx̲.
Du jeet wuduwatée. «Tlaagóo!
Éh! Tlél yéi x̲wateen.
Yú gan̲yigeidí s'é héide kan̲ax̲latsaak̲
k̲a héide.»
«Aax̲ yakaylatsák̲ aax̲ wé gan̲yigeidí!»
Du eetíg̲aa áx̲ k̲ukan̲ax̲lageit
ásíwéigé.
Aag̲áa áwé
du eetíg̲aa aax̲ gadutáan
áwé,
«G̲áa!»
Aan gáant wudik̲ín.
«Dlóow!
Yéil Tl'éetl'i Kuháatl'i ldakát yéide ÿaa gasgítch,»
yóo g̲íwé yawdusk̲aa.
Tle aan gáant wudik̲ín. Hóoch'.

"Hah, this is the place here," someone said to him, "This is the place."
"Holy cow! I must, must, must, must see it, I must!
I must see it!
Well.
I'm really curious about it, you see.
At our village when this happened, you see,
the man who pulled it up did not live.
If I recognize it as that thing, that's what is going to happen."
"Well,
that's amazing, isn't it!
Incredible!
Could it be that the Alien eats a lot of fat?"
The Alien's nose—
the Alien's nose, that's what he was calling it.
(**LAUGHTER**)
Whew!
They untied it and gave it to him;
they had tied it up on the wall.
They gave it to him. "Incredible!
Eh! I can't get a good look at it like that.
First let the smoke-spreading boards be pushed apart to this side and to that side."
"Push the smoke-spreading boards out of the way!"
He said that so that the space would be big enough for him to fit through, apparently.
So then,
when they had moved the boards far enough out of the way for him to fit through,
"Caw!"
He flew outside with it.
"Damn!
Shitty Crap-Tailed Raven is always up to something," I guess that's what they said to him.
He flew outside with it. That was that.

Shkalneek xi. Yéil k̲a K̲ei.á

Aadáx̲—
aadáx̲ áwé tle gun̲ayéi uwagút tle tliyaadé.
Tliyaat góot áwé
g̲ákw áa dust'ex̲ yéit uwagút.
Kawjig̲ít.
«Héi-éi-éi! Há há há há há há hé'!»
Héen x̲ukaadé áwé k̲aa ÿayík duwa.áx̲ch.
«Héi-éi-éi! Hó hó hó hó hó hó!
Héi-éi-éi! Hó hó hó hó hó!
Ax̲ x̲'éit aÿwóo!»
aadé éex' wé k̲aa t'aak̲.
«Ax̲ x̲'éit aÿwóo!
Daa sá yéi daaÿné,
ax̲ x̲'éit aÿwóo!»
L k̲'adaat k̲aa tooshtí. Hé'!
K̲aa ÿayík duwa.áx̲ch
wé héen x̲ukaadé.
«Yee káa k̲ei.á nk̲waak'oots!
Ax̲ x̲'éit aÿwóo!
Hé hé héi-éi-éi!»
«Naasshagiÿát
K̲ei.á Daakeit ang̲a.oo!»
tle yóo yawdudzik̲aa.
Haahá!
Tlél awuskú K̲ei.á Daakeit goox' sá yéi teeyí.
Tle yú G̲ákw Sax̲a K̲u.oo x̲'éitx̲ áwé
tsá awsikóo.
«Haahá, likoodzí!
Naas Sháagu shígé K̲ei.á Daakeit gé?» tle yóo
áwé tuwatee.
«{K'e héi-éi tle} áa x̲'akaawaháa,» du x̲'éidáx̲ {duwa…}—yoo akuwajeek
yú deikée k̲aa ÿayík aadé duwa.ax̲ji yé.
«Dáa ax̲ x̲'éit aÿwóo! Dáa ax̲ x̲'éit aÿwóo!»
«Du x̲'éide aa ÿan̲aÿx̲á, du x̲'éide aa ÿan̲aÿx̲á!»
tle yóo k̲uyaawak̲aa.
Tle wé a x̲ánde yaa nak̲úx̲ wé yaakw.
Tle daat kát sákwshígé du jeet wududzi.ín. «Náa!

Episode xi. Raven and the Daylight

From there—
from there he started walking to the next place over.
When he got over there,
he came to a place where people were fishing for gnarly driftwood.
It was dark.
"He-e-ey! Ha ha ha ha ha ha, hey!"
People's voices could be heard over the water.
"He-e-ey! Ho ho ho ho ho ho!
He-e-ey! Ho ho ho ho ho!
Send me something to eat!"
he was yelling to the people on the other side.
"Send me something to eat!
Whatever you're working on,
send me some to eat!"
They didn't pay attention to anything he said. Heh!
You could hear their commotion
from across the water.
"Watch out or I might break daylight on you folks!
Send me something to eat!
Hey hey he-e-ey!"
"This Child-of-the-Head-of-the-Nass
is evidently supposed to own the Container of Daylight!"
they said to him.
Aha!
He didn't know where the Container of Daylight was.
He only came to know this from what the
People-Who-Eat-Gnarly-Driftwood said.
"Aha, amazing!
Oh, so I suppose the Container of Daylight is at the Head of the Nass,
right?" he thought.
{...}—he was curious about the noises people were making
way out on the water.
"Please send me something to eat! Please send me something to eat!"
"Transport some over for him to eat; transport some over for him to eat!"
someone said.
So the boat was coming his way.
I wonder what sort of container they brought it to him in. "Here!

Yáadu á.
Héidoo á.»
Yéi kwdigeyi shaaḵ ÿátx'i áyú.
Aganastée tlél aadé akoox̱lix̱'aali yé, tle yú du lakáa yaa analtúl.
Yéi ash yayeet wududzi.ín.
«Kaylix̱'ál ágé?» yóo ash yawsiḵaa.
«Tléik'.»
«K'aahée.»
Ash jeetx̱ anastée áwé tle agawdzitee.
K'e yú kadux̱'al.aa dux̱aayí tle yóo x̱'ayikduwa.áx̱ch hú ḵu.aa.
«Ha yéi x̱áawé dux̱a át áwé. Wáa sáwé tsú tlél kaÿlax̱'aal?»
«Tlél x̱á ÿax̱wadlaaḵ.»
Yáax' áwé tle a jee ḵux̱ awsi.ín.
Yáax' áwé tle g̱unayéi uwagút tsu.
Akakgwa.aaḵw yú Náas Sháakt wugoodí, yóo tuwatee.
Ch'a yaa nagút, ch'a yaa nagút.
Tle ldakát át aÿatéen, ldakát át.
Ldakát át x̱oot woogoot.
Wáanée sáwé
át uwagút wé héen,
Naas.
Tle a sháakde áwé
g̱unéi uwagút.
Ax̱'eiwawóos' wé ḵáa,
ash géit uwagudi ḵáa,
«Goot'á sáwé,
Naas Sháak du hídi áwu á?» yóo aÿawsiḵaa.
«Áyá héen kaanáx̱ ÿánde kg̱eegóot, aatx̱ áwé tsás nánde áyú kg̱eegóot.
Naakée—tlax̱ naakée áwé át la.áa du hídi.
Naas Sháak Aanḵáawu áwé wé ḵáa,»
yóo ash ÿawsiḵaa.
Aag̱áa áwé, ayáx̱ áwé tle a kanax̱ ÿan uwagút wé héen.
G̱aadlàan
wé héen,
Náas.
A kanax̱ ÿan góot áwé
a x̱'awoolt uwagút tle, a x̱'awoolt áwé áa.

Here it is.
There it is right there."
They were big bits of driftwood.
When he took it and put it in his mouth there was no way he could munch it; he was just rolling it around in his mouth.
They set a container of it before him like that.
"Did you munch it?" one of them said to Raven.
"No."
"Give it here."
When he took it from Raven he put it in his own mouth.
His chewing sounded just like he was eating turnips, for example.
"Well, it's something that is eaten like this, you see. Why didn't you crack it with your teeth?"
"I couldn't do it, see."
At this point Raven gave the container back to him.
Now he began walking again.
He thought he would try to get to the Head of the Nass.
He was walking along, just walking along.
He could see everything, everything.
He walked about amidst everything.
Eventually
he arrived at the river
Nass.
Then he started up
toward the headwaters.
He asked a certain man,
a man he encountered,
"Where exactly is
Head-of-the-Nass' house?" Raven asked him.
"You'll cross over this river, and from there you'll go upstream.
It's upstream—his house is located way upstream.
That man is the Headman of the Head of the Nass,"
he told him.
So then he crossed over the river as he had been told.
That river
was *deep*,
the Nass.
When he crossed over
he came to his door; he sat at the door.

Tle ash x̱ánt uwagút wé—
ash x̱áni yux̱ woogoot wé ḵáa.
«Wáa sá ḵeeyanóok?» tle yóo ash ÿawsiḵaa.
«Ha yá Náas Sháak Aanḵáawu x̱ánt áyá x̱waagút.»
«Áa-áa!
Ch'a yáax' g̱anú, yánde ikakḵwanéek neilx'.»
Neildé nagóot áwé tle akan[éek],
«Ḵáa áwé i x̱ánt uwagút, ḵáa.
Hé gáant áa.
Hé gáant áa
wé ḵáa.»
«Haa, haa.
Neildé g̱aÿx̱oox̱, neildé.
Neildé g̱aÿx̱oox̱.»
Tle áa neil wugoodí áwé tle
du weex̱ shakawduwaÿaa.
«Du ÿeex̱ shakax̱yiyá!»
Hé'! S'eek doogú áwé áx̱ kawduwayaa áa yei kg̱wanuk wé.
Tle a káx' áwé wdudzinook, «Yáax' g̱anú!
At yisa.í!»
Hé'.
Yú kax̱yee ḵu.aa áwé kawditéx̱' wé
dleey,
dleey.
Ḵ'wátl daak wuduwatán,
a káx' áwé kduxásht.
Yá yeedádi té ḵ'wádli yáx̱ gíyú utí yú—.
Gankáa kéi wdudzi.ín.
Ÿan ée áwé tle du x̱'aÿee.
De at x̱aayí áwé, wé shaatk'i x̱'eis héeng̱aa ḵukawduwaḵaa,
wé Náas Sháak du sée,
«Héeng̱aa nakw s'é, héen!»
Hasdu kooḵénayi áwé.
«Haagú!
Héeng̱aa nagú!
Ax̱ séek' at gug̱ax̱áa.»
Láḵdi ÿádi áwé du jeet wuduwatán wé x'eesháa,
tle gánde.
Haaw.

He came to him—
a man came out to greet him.
"What are you doing here?" he said to Raven.
"Well, I came to see the Headman of the Head of the Nass."
"Oh, yes!
Sit right here, I'll announce you inside."
When he went inside he reported,
"A man has come to see you, a man.
He's sitting right outside.
He's sitting right outside,
that man."
"Well, well.
Ask him in, into the house.
Ask him in, you folks."
When he came inside
a pelt was spread out for him.
"Spread out a pelt for him!"
Heh! A black-bear pelt was spread out where he was to sit.
Then he was seated on it, "Sit here!
Cook something, you folks!"
Heh.
Twisted above in the rafters was
meat,
meat.
A pot was brought out,
and the meat was sliced into it.
Maybe it was like today's cast-iron pot.
It was put on the fire.
When it was done, he was served.
While he was eating, someone was sent to get water for that girl,
the daughter of Head-of-the-Nass,
"Go for water first, water!"
He was their messenger.
"Come!
Go get water!
My daughter is going to eat."
He was handed a small bentwood box as a dipper
and went outside.
Well.

Yú eetkát dus.áa, yées kaÿát áwé at gugax̱áa.
«K'e gítg̱aa tóox̱ sh ḵuḵaaḵal.oo.»
Ch'a—yóo—
du x̱'éix̱ at duteex̱. Ch'a aan áwé yú héengaa nagoodí ítde wjixeex,
wé gítg̱aa tóox̱ sh ḵug̱aag̱al.oowóot.
Tle wé héen kaadé áwé sh wudig̱éex'.
Neil dus.éen áwé tle wé eetkaadé tle téil a kináa.
«Ée-á!
G̱ítg̱aa a kát wulihaash!»
tle yóo kéi yaawaḵáa woosh ít
wé shaatk', eetkaadé.
«G̱ítg̱aa a kát wulihaash!
Ée! Ée!
Tléik', tlél ushk'é!
A kaax̱ yóot kax̱[ích]!
Wáa sá? Wáa sá?
Téil ÿaksatí, téil!"
K'idéin tsú
a daa yoo akdudlig̱ínk [wé] át,
«Tle gítg̱aa een áwé tle héen haat isa.eench.
Kaax̱ yóot kasaxá.»
Tle kaax̱ yóot akaawax̱ích, tle woogoot, téil ayawsitee.
Át góot áwé héen tle—
tle awsi.een.
Káa yoo kawdligán.
Yáax' áwé tle neildé.
Yá anax̱ wóosht ÿawduwatsuwu ÿ[é] áx̱ dux̱ás'ch, láḵt áyú.
Tle a t'éix̱ áwé kei sh wuditsáḵ.
«Ax̱ niÿaanáx̱ shé x̱'éit ashakg̱al.aayée-ée-ée!» tle yóo áwé tuwatee hú ḵu.aa.
Ch'a yóo atx̱á yaax̱t áa yú neilx' hú ḵu.aa.
«Ax̱ niÿaanáx̱ shé x̱'éit ashakg̱al.aayée-ée-ée!»
Tle ḵúnáx̱ yáa áx̱ kei sh wuditsag̱i yé, *corner*,
áx' áwé,
a x̱'éit ÿawdzi.áa wé át.
Tle aawanóot' wé g̱ítg̱aa,

They had her sit in the side-room; the young girl was going to eat.
"How about I fit myself inside an evergreen needle."
Just so,
they were feeding the young girl. Nevertheless, he ran out after the water carrier
so he could fit himself inside an evergreen needle.
He just threw himself onto the water.
When the water container was brought into the room, they shone torchlight above it.
"That's just disgusting!
A tree needle is floating in it!"
the young woman spoke up time after time
in the room.
"A tree needle is floating in it!
Ew! Ew!
No, it's no good!
Dump it out!
What's the matter? What's the matter?
Get a torch, a torch!»
The dipper was again
carefully inspected,
"You just keep bringing water with tree needles in it.
Pour it out."
He just threw it out and left; he took a lit torch.
When he arrived there, he—
he got some water.
He shone his torch back and forth over it.
At this point he took it home.
A bentwood box is lashed up where the sides are butted up against each other.
Raven just shoved himself back up behind the lashing.
"Let her tip it from my side into her mouth!" that's what he wanted to happen.
The girl, though, was just sitting before the meal in the house.
"Let her tip it from my side into her mouth!"
There,
at the very place he had shoved himself up into, the corner,
she put her lips to it.
She just swallowed the needle

tle tsu aadé kei kawdigáx̲, «Hhhh!
G̲ítg̲aa x̲waanóot'!
G̲ítg̲aa x̲waanóot'!»
Du tláach yéi yawsik̲aa,
«Hadáa! Ch'al igux̲sanei kát.
Ch'a daat ÿan x̲'eedats'én déi-ei!
Ch'al ikg̲wajak̲ kát wé g̲ítg̲aa.»
Ách áwé k̲ushtúyáx̲ wáa sá aan at dux̲aayí tlél wáa sá yoo k̲oosneik g̲ítg̲aa.
Náakwx̲ sitee k̲wá i jiyís, g̲ítg̲aa.
Áwé ch'a tlákw áwé Bob x̲'éide sax̲ahéi nuch
wé g̲ítg̲aa téix̲i héen ax̲danaa. Wé du x̲'óol' tlákw jikawdigug̲wéyáx̲ tóo ayanook.
Wáananée sáwé tle yéi yawdudzik̲aa,
«Háa!
Ch'u tle—
ch'u tle ásíwéigé
ÿát du káa yéi wootee gé?
K̲a a káa uwawát tle.»
Wáannée sáwé kei kg̲wanéekw.
Hé'! Ch'as k'óox áwé du daadé kdusyáa,
x̲'alitseeni at doogú.
Tléi-éi-éi-éil aadé kg̲waanéegu yé ch'a yú eetká.
Tlél aadé k̲ug̲waax̲dziteeyi yé yú atk'átsk'u.
«Lyóo.at.uwajeegi Shaanák'wg̲aa ang̲agoodée,
Lyóo.at.uwajeegi Shaanák'w.»
Tle át du een aawa.át tle.
«Wáanáx̲ sáwé l yei k̲oosteech wé atk'átsk'u?»
Aaa,
yéi áyá du tundatáani yatee yá atk'átsk'u,
k̲'anashgidéi k̲áa kagéyís áyá ax̲layeix̲ít tuwatee,
aadé ÿánde sh kakg̲wasyaa yé.
Yá k'óox tlél du tuwáa ushgú a káa k̲uwusteeyí, yá x̲'alitseeni at doogú.
«Du daadáx̲ yéi anax̲sanei,» yóo áyá tuwatee yá atk'átsk'u.
«Aasyiks'íx'g̲ayi k̲u.aa
du daax' yéi ng̲atee,
k̲a gáan
chashtuhít g̲alayeix̲ée,

and started to wail, "Hhhh!
I swallowed a tree needle!
I swallowed a tree needle!"
Her mother told her,
"Goodness gracious! That's not going to do anything to you.
Just quiet down about it now!
As if that tree needle could kill you."
That's why, no matter what quantity of evergreen needles people consume
in the process of eating, they don't do anything harmful to humans.
To the contrary, evergreen needles are medicine for you.
That's why I'm always wanting Bob
to drink evergreen-needle tea. He feels like his stomach
is always clenched up.
Eventually someone said,
"Hah!
It would—
it would appear that
she has gotten pregnant, right?
And the child is growing inside her."
Eventually she was about to have labor pains.
Heh! Only marten skins were spread on the floor around her,
expensive pelts.
There was no-o-o-o way she could progress into labor right in that room.
No way could that baby be born.
"Let someone go fetch Unfazable-Little-Elder,
Unfazable-Little-Elder."
Then she was escorted there.
"Why won't the baby come out?"
Yes,
this is what the baby boy's thoughts were:
he wanted to make the way he was going to lower himself
to the ground to be born
to be of benefit to poor people.
He didn't want to be born on these marten skins, these expensive pelts.
"Let them take it away from around her," is what the child was thinking.
"Instead, let tree moss
be put around her;
and outdoors,
let a brush hut be built;

chashtuhít g̱alayeix̱.»
A yeex' tsá yei ḵukg̱wastée, yóo áyá du toowú yatee yá atk'átsk'u,
ách áyá l yei ḵoosteech.
Ḵ'anashgidéi ḵáa
kagéyís.
Ḵaa-aa
ḵustí yéi kuwát' du jee yéi kg̱watée yéi ḵuwdziteeyi ḵáa.
Yú gáan chashtuhídix' ḵuwdziteeyi ḵáa,
ḵa yú s'íx'g̱aa káx' ḵug̱astéeni,
ḵustí yéi kuwát' du jee yéi kg̱watée.
Yóo áhé yoo tuwatánk yá ḵaa kayádi.
Yóo áwé sh kalneek wé Lyóo.at.uwajeegi Shaanák'w ḵu.aa,
«Ách gáanx' g̱alayeix̱í du ya.áak, chashtuhít.
A yeedé du een ang̱a.aadí yá neildáx̱.»
Yéi áwé
yoox̱'atánk yéi awsinei.
Ayáx̱ áwé tle gáanx' wududliyéx̱ wé hit,
cháash hít,
ḵa wé s'íx'g̱aa—aasyiks'íx'g̱ayi áa ÿax̱ kawdudlijél.
Tle a káx' áwé—
a káx' áwé tsá ḵuwdzitee wé atk'átsk'u.
Áwé yá kóoḵdáx̱—
a táadáx̱ kei dusnóok áwé tle
tle altín wé shawat.shaanák'wch ḵwá.
«Tlaagóo-óo-óo!» yóo x̱'ayaḵá.
«Tlaagóo-óo-óo! Ax̱ dachx̱ánk'!
Ch'a Yéil waaḵ x̱áashé, ax̱ dachx̱ánk'.»
Du toowúch áwé shé kax̱'aal, wé shawat.shaaṉák'w.
(AT.SHOOḴ)
Tle ÿan ash kaawaṉík.
«Ch'a Yéil waaḵ x̱áashé, ax̱ dachx̱ánk'.»
Tle áwé a yís x'áant uwaṉúk.
Ách áwé haa datsáagun yéi ḵutoosteet'í.
Yá yeedát ḵwá neil,
tlél haa jiyís atk'éix̱ ustí.
Ách áyá Lingít ḵutx̱ ÿaa shunaxíx yeedát.
Yú a shukát yú Yéilch aadé haa wliyex̱i yé haa shagóon, á ḵwá k'éiÿeen.
Shawat.shaanx' ḵuwdzitee ḵa ḵáa shaanx'.
Has wudishánx̱.

let a brush hut be built."
Only in a brush hut would he be born; that's how the boy felt,
  and that's why he refused to be born.
It was for
the poor people.
A-a-and
a person born this way will have a long life.
A person who is born outside in a brush hut
and born on moss
will have a long life.
This is what the fetus was thinking.
This is how Unfazable-Little-Elder was laying out the story,
"So let a place be made for her outside, a brush hut.
Let someone escort her into the brush hut from the house."
Those were
the words she used.
Accordingly, a hut was built outside,
a brush hut,
and moss—they lined the pit with tree moss.
Right on top of this—
it was, at last, right on top of this that the boy was born.
And when he was brought out
from the bottom of the pit,
the old woman was gazing at him.
"Incredible!" she said.
"Incredible! My dear grandchild!
Now those must be Raven's very eyes, my dear grandchild."
He was probably chewing out this little old woman in his mind.
  (LAUGHTER)
She exposed his secret.
"Now those must be Raven's very eyes, my dear grandchild."
He was angry with her.
That is why we lived so long when we were born this way.
But now, giving birth inside
is not a good thing for us.
This is why so many Tlingits are perishing now.
The way Raven first made our ancestors, *that* was good.
There were old women around, and old men.
They always grew old.

Yá yeedát k̲u.aa yá neilx’ k̲aa k̲usteet’ích
tlél aadé aa x̲wdishaani yé.
Yéi áyá yatee yá shkalneek,
yá Yéil du daat,
ÿan awsineyi át haa jiyís.
Aadáx̲ yaa gawáat áwé
du hídi yeex̲ áwé dák̲de yéi awsinei.
G̲agaan áx̲ daak̲ aawatée,
dís,
k̲utx̲.aÿanahá.
Yéi koogeÿi át áwé du hídi yeex̲ daak̲ yéi awsinéi
Náas Sháak k̲u.aa,
Naas Sháak Aank̲áawu.
Naas Sháak yóo áwé duwasáakw wé k̲áa,
Naas Sháak á.
Á áwé deisgwach g̲unayéi wdig̲wát’ wé *baby*.
Aag̲áa áwé tle at kadag̲áax̲.
yóox̲ dák̲de awli.aadi át daadé áwé kdag̲áax̲,
akawlix̲óox̲.
Tléi-éil du k̲’adaat k̲aa tooshtí.
Tle taat kanax̲ dagax̲ nuch.
Ch’u tle déi dax̲ek̲ji nuch.
Wáananée sáwé déi tle déi du tláa tsú tle du x̲’éi kdag̲áax̲.
Aag̲áa áwé déi yéi yaawak̲aa,
«Du jeet kaÿlakél’ déi!»
(CH’ÉEN YAN WUDIYÍK̲)
Tle yú k̲utx̲.ayanahá
shux’áanáx̲ aawax̲oox̲.
Wáananée sáwé
aan át wudig̲wáat’.
Át akawlijoox.
Yú—yú k’wát’ yáx̲ áwé kawdax̲dixwás’ a daaká.
Ch’u yéi k̲unoogú áwé gáant kaawajúx, gáant akawlijúx.
Tle ch’as yax̲ ÿakawusxáat’i áwé k̲utx̲.aÿanahá wdudziteen.
Háa!
K̲utx̲.aÿanaháax’w áwé dikée yax̲ yakawdzixát’.
(AT.SHOOK̲)
De wé gáant akawlijúx.
(AT.SHOOK̲)

But these days, since people are born inside,
none of them can grow old.
This is how this story is,
about Raven,
and the things that he prepared for us.
After that, as Raven was growing up,
Head-of-the-Nass put them away inside his house.
He had hung up the sun,
the moon,
and the stars.
Head-of-the-Nass had hung up all these great things
inside his house,
the Headman of the Head of the Nass.
That man's name is Head-of-the-Nass;
it's Head-of-the-Nass.
The baby eventually began crawling.
Then he was just wailing away.
He was wailing for the things that Head-of-the-Nass had put away;
    he kept on asking for them.
They didn't pay any attention to him.
He would just cry all through the night.
It got to the point where he couldn't ever get any sleep.
Eventually it got to the point where his mother was crying with him.
Then finally Head-of-the-Nass said,
"Untie it for him now!"
    (END OF TAPE)
He asked first
for the stars.
Eventually
he was crawling around with the container.
He would roll it around.
The—the outer surfaces of the containers were spherical.
While he was doing that, it rolled outside; he rolled it outside.
Once they were stretched out across the sky, the people beheld the stars.
Hah!
The innumerable stars were stretched across the sky.
    (LAUGHTER)
He had rolled it outside.
    (LAUGHTER)

A niyaadé áwé aawax̱oox̱ dís.
A daadé kdagax̱ nooch.
Ch’u tle déi-éi-éi ÿaa ash gajáḵch yá gaax̱.
Tle x’oon gwax̱éen sáwé ch’a góot yéide
gax̱ nooch.
Déi-éi aan gax̱satée nuch du wátk’u wé shaawát.
«Du jeet kaÿkél’ déi ax̱ dachx̱ánk’!
Du jeet kaÿkél’!
Du jeet kaÿkél’!»
Ách áwé du jeet koodukéil’ch tle.
Aahá!
Sagú áwé!
Ÿanáatx̱ yaa ax̱út’jin, ách áwé neil tle áa ḵee.éix̱.
Ḵei.á neilx’ áyú {…}.
Wáageen sáwé gunayéi akooljooxch.
Aahá.
Yeedát áwé «Yan jiy.ín dé, de
át akawlijoox.»
(AT.SHOOḴ)
Át akawuljooxú áwé
gáant akawlijúx tle tsu.
Ch’as dei áx̱ galxáat’ áwé wé dís wududziteen.
Yóot áx̱ wulixáat’.
«Hóoch’!
Ax̱ adée!
Ax̱ duwuweidí wuyíde yaa akanajél wé ax̱ dachx̱án!»
X’oon ux̱ée sáwé yeisú déi tsu wé—
tsu wé gagaan
akawlix̱óox̱.
«Haahée!
Haahée!
Haahée!
Haahée!»
Tléi-éi-éil du tuwáa ushgú ḵaa jeet awuteeyí.
Tle tlél wé ḵei.á áwé du jeedé akagux̱lakéil’.
Áwé tle eetkaadé áwé aan wudzigaax̱.
Eetkáx’ áwé aan gax̱satí du wátk’u wé shaawát.
Eetkáx’ áwé aan gax̱satí.
Ách áwé déi

Next, he asked for the moon.
He kept crying for it.
This relentless crying kept ju-u-st about killing him.
Whenever some number of nights passed, he would cry
with renewed intensity.
By now that poor woman was weeping with her little child.
"Untie it for my dear grandchild now!
Untie it for him!
Untie it for him!"
So they would just untie it and give it to him.
Aha!
What joy!
He kept prying the lid off, so daylight kept breaking inside of the house.
In the house, daylight {…}.
Sometimes he would start rolling it around.
Aha.
Now Head-of-the-Nass said, "You folks keep an eye on him to see
what he does next; he's already rolling it around."
(LAUGHTER)
While rolling it here and there,
he rolled it right outside again.
Once it became suspended in the sky, the people beheld the moon.
It was suspended far off yonder.
"No more!
My goodness!
My grandchild is strewing my wealth into thin air!"
After however many nights passed, at last he again—
he again set to ceaselessly begging
for the sun.
"Gimme!
Gimme!
Gimme!
Gimme!"
Head-of-the-Nass didn't want to give it to anybody.
He wasn't going to untie the daylight for him.
At that point she went with him into the room weeping.
The woman was in the room weeping with her little child.
She was in the room weeping with him.
So now, finally,

tle wé du tláa tsóos du x̱'éitx̱ gáax̱.
Ách áwé déi yéi ayawsiḵaa, «Du jeet kaÿlakél' déi!
Du jeet kaÿlakél' déi ax̱ dachx̱ánk'!
Du jeet kaÿlakél'!»
Yeisú déi, yeisú déi,
yeisú déi, yeisú déi du tóotx̱ ÿaa ḵuṉahéiṉ áwé.
Yéi áwé wé g̲agaan áwé de du jeewú, a daakaḵóogu.
Ch'u tle—
yax̱.atg̲wakú {x̱á...} yaa yanasxíx.
Déix̱ yagiyee x̱'áanáx̱ gíwé aan ashkawdliyát wé neilx̱'.
Yáax' áwé tsú tle aan gaan—
gaankát wudiḵín,
gáant wudiḵín aan tle wé ḵóok.
«G̲áa-áa-áa!»
Hóoch'.
«Déi!
Wuyít akaajéil ax̱ duwuweidí
Yéil Tl'éetl'i!» yóo.
(ATLEIN AT.SHOOḴ)
Yeisú—
yeisú déi wé g̲ákw áa dusx̱a yé du tóo kei uwaxíx,
tle aadé áwé
G̲ákw Sax̱a Ḵu.oo t'áade
«Ax̱ x̱'éit aÿwóo!» aadé éex'.
«Ax̱ x̱'éit aÿwóo!
Yee káx' ḵei.á nḵwaak'oots!
Ax̱ x̱'éit aÿwú!»
«Dláa!
Naasshagiyátk'w Ḵei.á Daakeit ang̲a.oo!»
tle ásí yéi yawdudziḵaa aadé,
wéide.
Hé'! Áyá tle ḵaa yayík du.áx̱ji yanáatx̱ ayaawax̱út'.
«Aháháháa!»
Áwé ch'u tle áwé wduwatl'ékw a náḵ wé kagán.
Tsu yaṉáatx̱ ayaawax̱út'.
Tlax̱ nas'gidahéen yanáatx̱ awoox̱óot',
daax'oon.aa ḵu.a gíwé tsá déi tle—
tle de gáant—gáant aawax̱út'.
{...} wé g̲agaan.

his mother, too, was crying for his pain.
So, finally, he said to them, "Untie it for him now!
Untie it for my dear grandchild now!
Untie it for him!"
Now at last, at last,
at last, at last, his sadness was disappearing.
He now held the sun in his grasp, its box.
Well, there—
there is a proverb, {...}.
For perhaps two days he played with it inside the house.
Now at this point he flew with it—
he flew up with it to the smokehole and
and just flew outside with the box.
"Ca-a-aw!"
That was that.
"Ugh!
Shitty Raven managed to strew my wealth into thin air!"
  that's what he called him.
  (MUCH LAUGHTER)
Now—
now at last, the place where people eat gnarly driftwood popped into
  Raven's mind, so he went that way,
to the shore above the People-Who-Eat-Gnarly-Driftwood.
"Send me something to eat!" he howled to them.
"Send me something to eat!
Watch out or I might break daylight on you folks!
  Send me something to eat!"
"Give me a break!
This Precious-Little-Child-of-the-Head-of-the-Nass is evidently
  supposed to own the Container of Daylight!" is what they
  actually said to him from over there.
Heh! When he heard those people gabbing away, he pulled the lid off.
"Oh no-o-o-o!"
As this happened they recoiled from the light.
He pulled the lid off again.
After he had pulled the lid off precisely three times,
finally, on the fourth time, I guess, he just—
he just pulled it into the outside world.
{...} the sun.

Íh!
Aax̱ ásíwé k̲eiwa.aa yá lingit'aaní.
Haahá.
Wuyít akaawajél du ádi.

Eh!
Then, in fact, dawn poured over the world.
Hah.
He strew his possessions into thin air.

Naakil.aan X̱'éidáx̱ Tlaagú

Stories by Frank Dick

FIGURE 13. Frank Dick, Juneau, September 1986. Photo by M. Bryan Thompson. Courtesy of Sealaska Heritage Institute, PO004, box 9, item 68.

OUR NEXT STORYTELLER is Naakil.aan, Frank Dick Sr., of Yakutat, Alaska. Dick was a member of the L'uknax̱.ádi clan and a child of the Kaagwaantaan. He was born in Sitka on August 10, 1899, and passed away on June 17, 1992, in Juneau. His first wife was Maggie Dick, the younger sister of Frank Italio. A short biography of Dick's life can be found in the Dauenhauers' *Haa Ḵusteeyí*.*

This extended tale containing twelve episodes was told in a single sitting and consists of two recordings (originally taken on two sides of a cassette tape), each of which is slightly over thirty minutes in length. The performance was recorded in the fall of 1983 in Juneau by Dick's grandson G̱unaak'w, Fred White, who also drafted the first transcription and translation of the texts.†

Taken as a whole, this extended tale was originally given the title «Yéil Sákw» by the Dauenhauers (which translates as 'Raven-to-Be' or 'Future Raven') due to the fact that Dick uses the phrase *Yéil sákw* early on in the first episode to speak of the 'future Raven' or the 'makings of Raven' prior to his birth. We have since revised the title to «Haa Aanéex' Yóo Kawdzigidi Yéil» with the English title "Raven Who Acted Upon Our Land". This title, based on the concluding statements with which Dick punctuates the performance,‡ reflects a theme present throughout each episode—that of Raven performing his antics in the setting of the Dry Bay region, the ancestral homeland of Dick's house group, and thereupon affecting this landscape and the distribution of its resources.

Dick recounts these stories in a straightforward manner, sticking closely to the narrative timeline with little commentary and few excursions. In many places Dick does not flesh out every detail of the story, but merely outlines the plot. When recounting an abstract of a large collection of stories in this manner, the listener is expected to

---

* Dauenhauer and Dauenhauer, *Haa Ḵusteeyí*, 185–88.

† Digitized copies of these recordings were made available for this publication by Fred White.

‡ FD xii, 38–40, 49.

supply the missing details from previous experience and exposure to the story. Dick sometimes omits details that he apparently felt his audience could fill in with their background knowledge of the story. For example, in "Raven Deceives His Younger Brother" (FD viii) during a sequence in which Raven explains to a crew of little birds that he will pretend to have a prophetic dream about a coming battle and specifies the words he will use as a signal for the birds to descend on the house in order to make it seem as though the battle has really begun, Dick does not go on to narrate what happens next; he simply jumps straight into the mock-battle scene. The listener is required to fill in all of these crucial details: Raven pretends to toss in his sleep in the grip of a nightmarish dream; his younger brother, X̱ashak'ákwk', wakes him up; and Raven narrates the dream, cueing the birds to initiate the mock-battle (these details are elaborated in Italio's version of the same story, FI I, iii).

In Dick's texts we find a few notable lexical items that do not occur elsewhere in this volume. One is a verb theme attested in two forms: «yóo dudlisaayée» (or «yóo dudlisaayí»)[*] 'it is known by this name'; also «yóo dudlisaayi át»[†] 'these things known as [sea urchins]' and «yóo tudlisaayí»[‡] 'we know it (a place) by this name'. Our consultants were unable to verify these verb forms and were unsure of their intended meaning; however, based on the context, we have settled on the translations given above. In Naish and Story's *Tlingit Verb Dictionary*, we find «ee sàayee toolisàayee» (i.e., *i saayí tulisaayí*) "we glorify your name (we honor it and make it well-known and holy)".[§] The verb theme in this case is *O-S-l-saayí*, meaning more or less 'for S to make O('s name) renowned'. But the verb forms from Dick have an additional *d-* element in the classifier and seem to require an adverb of manner complement, namely *yóo=* 'like this/that'. So although these verb themes seem to be related to each other, we cannot specify the exact nature of this relationship.

Another feature of Dick's speech is the way he pronounces the first-person plural independent pronoun. For most speakers, this is *uháan* 'we, us'; and indeed, he uses the form «uháan»[¶] and the corresponding ergative form «uháanch».[**] But in one instance we seem to hear him say, «Yuháanch yéi wtuwasáa»[††] 'We were the ones who named it that' and in another we hear «Yooháanch ḵu.áyáas yéi wtuwasáa yáa x̱'aan»[‡‡] 'But we were the ones who named the fire', both of which surprisingly have /y/ at the onset of the word. *Wuháan* is a known variant, with initial /w/ (presumably underlyingly /ÿ/), but it is never known to occur with /y/. Fred White indicated

* FD viii, 46; xi, 63.

† FD vii, 16.

‡ FD viii, 116.

§ Naish and Story, *Tlingit Verb Dictionary*, 101.

¶ FD xii, 47.

** FD i, 4, 28.

†† FD vi, 26.

‡‡ FD iv, 34.

that Dick had suffered a stroke prior to the recording of this performance, which left part of his jaw paralyzed and hindered his speaking ability, which is the probable cause of this unexpected pronunciation.* We have nonetheless transcribed the instances with initial /y/ as we heard them.

In Dick's texts we also find several instances of a special construction that we refer to, for lack of a better term, as 'the *ch'u yé k̲áa áx'* ... *yé* construction' (which requires an attributive verb form before *yé* 'place'), translating, 'everybody is/was out VERB-ing; every last one of them is/was out there VERB-ing'. Examples include:

FD vi, 44:	ch'u yé k̲áa áx' daxash yé	every last person was out flensing [the whale]
FD vi, 73:	ch'u yé k̲áa áx' adakw yé	every last person was out rendering fat
FD vi, 108:	ch'u yé k̲áa áx' at wooxooni yé a nák̲	every last one of them was getting ready to leave it behind
FD ix, 91:	ch'u yé k̲áa áx' k̲ukdahaa yé	every last one of them was out digging

This construction is found in the speech of Elizabeth Nyman as well, though she pronounces *ch'u yeik̲áa*... where Dick pronounces *ch'u yé k̲áa*..., and she does not include the word *áx'* 'there' as Dick does. Examples from Nyman include:

ch'u yeik̲áa núkt ax̲a yé†	[e]verybody was eating grouse
ch'u yeik̲áa yakashxit yé‡	every one of them painted up her face

Finally, the oldest example we can point to is that rendered by Swanton from a story told by Deikenaak'w in 1905, «tc!ū´ye qā´awe dudugu´ tū´de wudjix̣ī´x̣iyA», i.e., *ch'oo yé k̲áa* (or possibly *ch'oo yeik̲áa* or *ch'oo yéi k̲áa) áwé du doogú tóode wjixeexi yé* 'every person ran into his skin' (that is, every animal-spirit quickly ran to reinhabit its body).§

We find a few examples of the obsolete phoneme /ÿ/ in Dick's speech, but not nearly as many as we find with Italio and Susie James. As found in the speech of Italio, James, and Katherine Mills, and occasionally in the speech of Austin Hammond, the tones of certain preverbs are raised from low to high (*kéi*=, *yéi*=, *yóo*=, and *yéik̲*=). Like Italio, Dick alternates between *P yáx̲* and *P yéx̲* 'like P', which for most speakers is only found as *P yáx̲*. Also like Italio, he alternates between the forms *deisgwach* and *deisguch* 'gradually', though he uses *deisgwach* more frequently. We have done our best to transcribe these as we heard them in each specific case rather than applying a standardized form.

* In a recording from February 11, 1978, before his stroke, we again hear «uháan» multiple times. MC005, tape 4, side a; cf. 01:13 on the recording.

† Nyman and Leer, *Gágiwduł.àt*, 70–71; original spelling, «ch'u yèkhâ núkt axha yé».

‡ Ibid, 244–45; original spelling, «ch'u yèkhâ yakashxit yé».

§ Swanton, *Tlingit Myths and Texts*, 272; from text 91, "The Shaman who Went into the Fire, and the Heron's Son".

Haa Aanéex’ Yóo Kawdzigidi Yéil

Shkalneek i. Yéil ḵa Du Káak

…Hél ḵu.as x̱wasakú du saayée yáa shaawát.
De ch’a hóoch’ áyáa aadé x̱wsikuwu yé áyáa.
Ch’a ldakát yéide át wududzikóo a x̱oo.aa.
Uháanch aadé wtusikuwu yé,
á áyáa
yeedát yáat’át
yáa ax̱ dachx̱án jiyís ax̱ tuwáa sigóo kawx̱aneegí.
Aadé x̱wsikuwu yé ayéx̱ áyá yaa kakḵwanéek.
Tléil ch’a ḵushtuyéx̱ áyá kakḵwaneek.
Shúx’waanáx̱
Yéil—
Yéil sákw,
yáa du káak áyáa
ḵuwdzitee, du tláa éek’,
du tláa sákw éek’.
Á áyáa
yéi x̱’ayaḵáa nukch
gugaḵoox̱ú—.
Naḵúx̱ch
lkeeyiyáag̱aa.
Wáag̱een sáwé haat uḵoox̱ch.
Wáananée sáyáa
du sákw
yáa shaawát—.

Raven Who Acted Upon Our Land

Episode i. Raven and His Uncle

…I don't, however, know the name of this woman.
This is all I know of them.
Some people know all kinds of things.
The way that we know it ourselves,
this is
what I now want
to tell for my grandchild's sake.
I am going to proceed to tell it the way that I know it.
I am not just going to tell it for the sake of telling it.
In the beginning,
Raven—
Raven-to-be
had a maternal uncle,
his mother's brother,
the brother of the one who would become his mother.
Now,
this is what he would say
when he was going to travel in his boat—.
He would leave
for an unusually long time.
Sometimes he would come here.
Eventually
the woman
through whom he would be born—.

Ch'u yáa yagiyeedéi yéi at kaaxát, ch'áakw ku̱.aa
ḵoogáa áyáa at naseich,
yóo áyá a shukát tuwasáakw.
Yáa yeedát uháanch ḵwaawés yéi tuwasáakw,
«Dikyáanḵáawuch áyáa haa jeet wusiháa.
Dikyáanḵáawuch áyá aan haa kawlixétl,»
yóo tuwasáakw yáa yeedát.
Há', yéi áyá wootee yáa shaawát.
Du eegáa áyá woosoo wéi—
wé ch'a ksiyéiyi át áyá du eegáa woosoo.
Ash shukaawajáa
yáa shaawát,
«Éeḵdáx̱
shanyaateiÿí daaḵ tí!
Shanyaateiÿí daaḵ tí!
Yakgisat'áa áwés.
Tléil tlax̱ yakgwat'aa.
Kakgwat'áa áwé.
Aagáa áwé tsáas kakgeenóot'.»

A x̱'ayáx̱ áyáas
ayaksat'áa áyá tsáa
akaawanóot'.
Tle du x̱ánx̱ ḵukooḵaa wé du éek'
ash wuḵeedée.
Ash x̱'einawóos'ch,
«Daaḵwéit sáwé ḵuwdzitee?»
«Ḵáa áhé.»
«Yiják!
Yiják,
ax̱ shát éex̱ oongaanóok.»
Ách áwé ch'a du x̱'ayáx̱ dujaaḵch.
Haa, yáat'aa ḵu.aayáa ch'u tle, tle a yáa awlisín.
Tléil tsu gági awusnook.
Ch'u tle—ch'u tle yaa nalgéini, yaa nalgéini déi,
ha wáananée sáyá ayáx̱—
ayáx̱ du daa kéi yaa ḵushunasgéin.
Ax̱'eiwawóos' du tláa,
«Wáa sáyáa, ch'a tléináx̱ ákyáa ḵeedzitee, atléi?»

To this very day this is how the situation is; but long ago
people would be given supernatural assistance,
this is what we first called it.
But nowadays we refer to this by saying,
"It was God who gave this to us.
It was God who blessed us with it,"
this is what we call it now.
Well, this is how it was for that woman.
A being came to give her supernatural assistance;
it was a strange being that came to give her supernatural assistance.
It instructed
the woman,
"Bring up a low-tide stone
from the beach!
Bring up a low-tide stone!
You are to heat it.
It won't be very hot.
It will be warm.
Then you must swallow it."

As she was told,
she didn't swallow it
until she had heated it.
Her brother would send people to check on her
when he was suspicious of her.
He would ask her,
"What was it that was born?"
"It's a male."
"Kill it!
Kill it,
or it might bother my wife."
So they would kill it just as he had ordered.
But this particular child she just hid from him.
She never even brought him out into the open.
As he was growing up, as he was already growing up,
eventually
he began to understand the situation for what it was.
He asked his mother,
"What's the matter, do you live alone, mom?"

«Tléik'.
Yá i káak,
i káak x̱'ayáx̱ áyáa
yát wux̱a.oowú
ch'u tle du x̱'ayáx̱ dujáḵx̱ ḵáa aa,
du shát—
du shátx̱ oonanóokg̱aa.»
Haa, á áyáa du tóon wooteeyéyáx̱ wootee hú ḵwa Yéil.

Ách áyáa akaawa.aaḵw,
a daa yéi jeewanei,
a daa yóo toowatán wáa sá agux̱saneeyí, wáa sá yéi jikg̱waneiyí.
Yóo dikée
s'eiyatóox̱ oos.áx̱wch du shát
gugaḵoox̱ú.
Dís,
Yóoḵis'kooḵéik á.
Yéi duwasáakw.
Át akaawa.aaḵw yáa dís.
Yá ḵées'
du x̱'ayáx̱
daaḵ déich.
Á áyá yéi áyóo—wáag̱eens a eeti.aa
ḵées'—tle ch'u yaa yanawádi
yéi áyá át akaawa.aaḵw,
ayáx̱ áyáa.
Ách áwéis,
yá hóoch tsú yá a daa yóo toowatán,
«Haahá!
akakg̱wa.aaḵw áwé.»
Ách áwé du tláa daa yéi jeewanei tle.
A tóox̱ gugagut át,
a tóox̱ gugagut át sákw
yéi awsinei.
Ḵaa hú tsú,
hú tsú,
Gus'x̱lugooḵ,
a lú yéi koowáat' yóo kdunéek wéit'át.
Aag̱áa áwé tsáa yan asnée áwé tsáa aax̱ akawlikéil'

"No.
This uncle of yours,
at your uncle's command,
when I bear a child
the males are killed at his command,
so the child won't bother his wife—
his wife."
So now Raven seemed to have been offended.

So he made a plan
and worked on it;
he thought about what he was going to do and how he would go about it.
Raven's uncle always tied his wife
way up there up in the eaves
when he was going to travel.
The moon,
in fact that's Tide-Commander.
That's his name.
The moon has command over the tide.
At his word
the floodtide
rises.
So in that way—sometimes the next floodtide—
while the moon is still waxing
he commands the tide in this way,
accordingly.
So,
Raven began thinking about it as well,
"Aha!
he's going to try it."
So he set right to work on his mother.
Something for her to don,
he prepared
what would become something for her to don.
And for himself too,
he prepared one for himself too:
Pokes-Nose-Into-Clouds,
they say that creature has a very long beak.
And only after he was done did he untie

du káak shát.
Aax̱ akaklakéil' áwé a éenyee kóoni
aawax'úl'.
Á áyáa tle
sh t'aawdigoot.

Du x̱einéenáx̱ kawdliyeech.
«Ax̱ adée!»—
ch'a yaadachóon áwéi yéi—
«Ax̱ adée!»
L awuskú daatch sáwéi yéi wusneiÿí.
Ách áwé haat ḵóox̱,
haat ḵóox̱,
akawsidaa ḵées'.
Aag̱áa yáa ḵées' kaawadaa.
X'oon yagiyee x̱'áak sá, x'oon dís sáyá
    yan shaawahík?
Yankát uwadáa yá lingit'aaní, ḵées'.
Akawsidaa yáa ḵées',
Yóoḵis'kooḵéik á.

Hé'!
Wáannée sáwéi
ḵúx̱de yóo wdinei, haahá!
Woolaa.

Shkalneek ii. Yéil ḵa Ḵei.á

Woolaa.
Héi-éi-éih!
Áwé ch'a áyáa át woogoot, ch'a át woogoot,
ch'a wáa sá.
Wáananée sáwé áa tlein áwé áa daak uwagút wéi—
wéi Shaḵyátx'i Isdik Ḵu.oo.
Adusdèek.
Hó-hóu.
Ch'áakw dateeyí,
«Ax̱ shóodéi-èiy!»

his uncle's wife from the eaves of the house.
After he untied her, he plucked out
the flickers in her armpits.
Then
he went to report on what he had done.

The flock of flickers caught up with his uncle.
"My precious stuff!"—
they were just going straight ahead like that—
"My precious stuff!"
He didn't know what had caused this.
So when he came back in his boat
when he came back,
he made the tide rise.
Then the tide rose.
Over the course of many days, of many months,
  the whole world was covered with water.
It was flooded by the tide.
Tide-Commander himself
made the tide rise.

My!
Eventually
it subsided, aha!
The tide went down.

Episode ii. Raven and the Daylight

The tide went down.
He-e-ey!
So he was just walking around, just walking around,
for no particular reason.
At some point he came out to a large lake
across from the People-Who-Dipnet-Bits-of-Driftwood.
They were dipnetting.
Ho-ho!
After a long time he said,
"Come and get me-e!"

Hé'!
X'óol' yáx̱ yatee asdeek.
Hél du x̱'adaat ḵaa too[shtí].
Tsóok',
tsu akaawa.aaḵw.
Yáax' áwé tsáa tsu,
haahá,
[du] x̱'éináx̱ yóot akaawag̱íx',
«Ax̱ shóodéi-èiy!
Yee káx' ḵei.á nḵwaak'oots.»
«Héhéhé!
Goodáx̱ Naasshagiyát
Ḵei.á Daakeit du jee yéi ng̱atee?»
Now,
he got it.
Aawat'ei k'idéin tle.
Ách áyáa woogoot
ch'a koogéiyi, goodéi sákwshé woogoot.

Gwáa!
Wáannée sáwé át uwagút Náas Sháak.
Haahá!
X̱'awoolt uwagút, ch'a altín, ch'a áwu hú,
ch'a át áa.
Deisguch,
wáananée sáwé wéi du ḵáa goox̱ú,
wé du sée daa yóo jikwli.atgi,
yáanáx̱ yux̱ woogoot.
Ax̱'eiwóos', ax̱'eiwóos', ldakát yéide ax̱'eiwóos'.
Haa, yéi áwés ash een akanéek, «X̱áach áwé du daat x̱at yawsitáḵ.
Gánde kg̱wagoodí du shukáx̱ yóo x̱aagútkw,
ḵaa at gug̱ax̱aayée tsóo,
x̱áach áwé a daa yóo jikux̱li.átk.
Héen agux̱danaayée tsóo, tléil aadé yóo a kát sa.in
héen oox̱dinaa[yi] yé,
ch'u tle éeḵdáx̱ aa—ch'u tle tléix'
kanaadaayi aa.»

Haa, ách áwé yan ayaawayék.
Haahá.

My!
They were dipnetting like crazy.
Nobody was paying attention to him.
Once again
he tried calling out.
At this point, finally,
aha,
he flung the words out of his mouth,
"Come and get me-e!
Watch out or I might break daylight on you folks."
"Heh-heh-heh!
From where does the Child-of-the-Head-of-the-Nass hail
that he should possess the Container of Daylight?"
Now,
he got it.
He surely found it.
So now he was walking around,
just aimlessly walking around; I wonder where he went.

Just imagine!
Eventually he came to the Head of the Nass.
Aha!
He came to the doorway; he was just watching it; he was
just there, just sitting there.
After a while,
the headman's male slave,
the one who attended to his daughter,
eventually came out through the door here.
Raven was asking him, asking him, asking him all kinds of questions.
Well, this is what he told him, "I'm the one who takes care of her.
When she's about to go out, I go ahead of her,
and when she's going to eat too,
I'm the one who attends to her.
And when she is going to drink water, she can't drink water that's
sitting in a container;
just water from the riverbank—only that which comes from a single
flowing source."

So Raven lay in wait for the slave.
Aha.

Ch'a l ák' ooheení áwéi anax̱ yux̱ woogoot.
Yaa anatán wé láḵdi x'eesháa.

Gwáa!
Tle ayawdagoodée, ayawdagoodí áwé
a kát sh wudix̱ích.
  G̱UNAAK'W: *Oh.*
Ch'a yéi áyáa akaawax̱áax', a wax̱'at'eex'.wánt
  áwé wulihaash.

Tle yawduwatín.
«Ée! Ée! A kát at wulihaash.»
Yóot kawduwax̱ích
du x̱'ayáx̱.
Haahá.
«G̱una.aa a shayadáax̱!»
Yá a wax̱'at'eex'.wán,
anax̱ x̱'éide ashakakg̱wal.aa yé du toowóoch,
áx' áwéi a yáx̱ kéi sh wuditsáḵ.
Adana nóok áwé
a lakaadé sh wudlihaash.
«Héi-ei!
At x̱waanóot'!
At x̱waanóot'!»
«Ax̱ séek'!
Ax̱ séek'!»

Haaw.
X'óol' yáx̱ woonei.
Du ée dulḵú.
Héi-éil tsu—
héil aadé kéi g̱waaxeexi yé.
Tlei ch'a yéi déi tle yan kawdu{wa.éts'}, tlél tsu wáa sá utí.
Hóhó.
Deisgwach, deisgwach,
deisgwach dís yaa anas.át, deisgwach dís yaa anas.át.
Héil kéi unóokch.
Deisgwach du x̱'óol'—
du x̱'óol' yéi ḵunastéen.

Before he could believe his eyes, the slave came walking out.
He was carrying the bentwood bucket.

Gosh!
Then when he turned back, when he turned back,
Raven flung himself into the bucket.
FRED WHITE: *Oh.*
Just like that, he pried apart a flap of wood from the bentwood bucket
and drifted about where the corner was lashed together.

Then they noticed it.
"Yuck! Yuck! Something's floating on it."
They tossed out the contents
at her command.
Aha.
"Get another one, better than the last!"
This inner corner of the bentwood bucket,
he thought this was where she would tip it into her mouth;
it was there that he stuck himself up against the side of it.
As she was drinking it,
he made himself float into her mouth.
"He-ey!
I swallowed something!
I swallowed something!"
"My daughter!
My daughter!"

Well.
Everything was in turmoil.
They were making her vomit.
There was no way
to get it out.
Finally, they just gently laid her down to rest; she was okay again.
Hoho.
Gradually, gradually,
the months were gradually passing; the months were gradually passing.
She wasn't getting her period.
She was gradually—
she was getting a baby bump.

Du éet yaan.wuhaayée la.oos nukch,
i yit.shát aayí yáx̲.

Haa,
haahá.
Wáananée sáwé,
haahá,
yoo sh tudinúkk wé shaatk’.
Yoo sh tudinúkk.
Éh!
Kei kawduwaháa
wé kóok̲.
A táade áwé kawdudziyaa áwé k’óox.

Du yaak̲oosgeiyée áyáa hú k̲u.aa,
yáa k̲’anashgidéix̲ siteeyi k̲u.oo,
tléil yá k’óox átx̲ agux̲layeix̲.
Ách áyáa hú k̲u.aa,
«K̲’anashgidéi k̲áa jeeg̲áa yá s’íx’g̲aa.»
Ldakát át tle ch’as s’íx’g̲aax̲ wududliyéx̲. Du daax’ aan yéi jiduné.
Héil shaÿawdahaa.
Tle k̲uwdzitee wé atk’átsk’u.
Éh!
Dleit k̲áa atk’átsk’u áwé yóo oowayáa
i sáni
k̲ug̲astée.
Éh!

Aaa,
wáanée sáwé
wuduwax̲oox̲
Lyóo.atkoowajeegi Shaanák’w.
I don’t know.
Héil x̲wasakú daak̲wéit sá yéi s asáagu.
Tléil yóo at koojeek.
Tle yax̲ at kaneek.
Wududliyéx̲ ch’a hásch.
Du jeet wududzinúk.
Wooch kát awdzinúk.

When she got hungry her belly would get restless,
like your daughter-in-law's.

Well,
aha.
Eventually,
aha,
the young woman went into labor.
She went into labor.
Eh!
They dug out
a pit.
They lined the bottom with marten skins.

But herein lies Raven's wisdom:
people who are poor
won't be able to use marten skins.
This is why he thought,
"Moss is suitable for poor people."
Moss was used for everything. They were treating her body with it.
It wasn't a large amount.
Then the child was born.
Eh!
Your paternal uncle
looked like a white boy
when he was born.
Eh!

Yes,
eventually
Unfazable-Little-Elder
was summoned.
I don't know.
I don't know what sort of being it is they refer to by that name.
She doesn't get perplexed.
She just tells things the way they are.
They made it themselves.
They handed the baby to her.
She held it in her arms.

Ch'áakw wooch kát awusnoogú áwéi
ash yalatín.
«Hehéi-ei! Héi-ei, ax̱ dachx̱ánk'.»
Goox' sáyú awsiteen Yéil?
«Dei ch'u Yéil waaḵ x̱áashé ax̱ dachx̱ánk'.»
Aaa.

Atx̱ áyáa
ḵuwdzitèe-ee, ḵuwdzitee, ḵuwdzitee, deisguch—
deisguch g̱unéi yaa nashḵáḵ, deisguch g̱unéi yaa nashḵáḵ.
Wáanée sáwé g̱unéi wjiḵáḵ.
Haahá.
Éh!
Ooltínch yóo kax̱yee yóot'át.

Aaa.
«Du jeet kiylakél' ax̱ dachx̱ánk'!
Du jeet kiylakél'!»
Du jeet kawdudlikél'.

Gwáa!
Du jeet kadulkéil' áwéi-éi-éi, át akanalgíx'ch.
Át akanalgwátlch, gwál wéi *balloon* yáx̱
gíyú kakoodagei.

Át akanalgwátlch.
Hou-ou, tle ch'a a x̱ánx' natèi-eich.
A x̱ánee g̱anúkch.
Haaw, kéi gasgídín
yáax' áwé yéi asaawahaa kéi akg̱ag̱éex'i.
Gaankaanáx̱ tle kéi kaawaxíx.
Éh!
Yax̱ yakawdziḵinyéyéx̱ áwéi woonee
ḵutx̱.ayanahá.
A daadé kdag̱áax̱.
Du jíni
a ítx̱ yéi aya.óo.
Du jináḵ áwé kéi kawlis'ís.
A daadé kdag̱áax̱.

After she had held it in her arms for a long time,
the little old woman gazed at its face.
"Hey-he-ey, he-ey, my dear grandchild."
Where had she seen Raven?
"Now those must be Raven's very eyes, my dear grandchild."
Yes.

After that,
he was bo-orn, he was born, he was born; gradually—
he gradually started toddling along; he gradually started toddling along.
Eventually he started toddling.
Aha.
Eh!
He kept watching that thing way up there in the rafters.

Yes.
"Untie it for my dear grandchild!
Untie it for him!"
It was untied for him.

Wow!
When it was untied for him, he would thro-o-ow it around like a ball.
He would roll it around—maybe the containers were spheres
the size of balloons, I suppose.

He kept rolling it around.
Ho-o, he always slept ri-i-ight by it.
He always sat right by it.
Well, whenever he would wake up,
he would immediately want to toss it up.
It went right up through the smokehole.
Eh!
The stars
began to twinkle.
He was crying after them.
He had his hands
upstretched after them.
They had sailed up out of his hands.
He was crying over them.

Ei-eih!
Hóoch', tle táach ujaak̲ch.

Yáax' áwé tsáa
k̲ei.á
awdzig̲áax̲ á.

Tlex̲ wáa-áa-áa yóo kooneigée sáyáa yéi yaawak̲aa,
«Du jeet kiylakél' déi ax̲ dachx̲ánk'!
De g̲aax̲ch uwaják̲, du jeet kiylakél' déi!»
Á áwé du jeet kawdudlikél', hou-ou-ou!
Daa sáwé yéi wdudzinei?
Tle ch'a yá a x̲ánx' áwé sh k̲'analtèich, áa nateich.

Haahá.
Yáax' áwé tsáa deisgwach chush daatx̲ yaa
  k̲aa tanas.héin.
Tléil du káx̲ *watch* k̲oostí.
Yáax' áwé yéi tuwdisháat,
«Góok áyá.»
Ch'u tle tléix' áwé kéi sh wudlitséx̲ kínde.
«G̲áa-aa!»
Haaw.

Aan gáant sh wudlitséx̲.
«Ax̲ adée!
Ax̲ adée!
Kaawayíkt akaajéil ax̲ ádi yóo Yéil Tl'éetl'i!»
Ash wulitl'ítl'.
Haaw,
atx̲ áwéi woogoot,
haaw,
aax̲ haat uwagudi yéidachóon.
Tlax̲ wáa-áa-áa yóo koogútgoo sáyáa
át uwagút Aakwéi.
Aakwéi á—
du ta.eetí,
át tux̲'ada.àayi yé.

Oh-h-h!
Eventually he would tire and fall fast asleep.

Finally at this point,
he begged for
the daylight.

After he had carried on for so-o-o long, his grandfather said,
"Untie it for my dear grandchild now!
He's crying himself to death; untie it for him now!"
So they untied it and gave it to him, ho-o-o!
What had they done?
He would pretend to sleep right by it; he would sleep there.

Aha.
At this point he was gradually lulling them into lowering their guard around him.
No one kept watch over him.
This is when the thought popped into his mind,
"It's go time!"
All at once he kicked himself upward.
"Ca-aw!"
Well.

He propelled himself outside with it by kicking his feet.
"My precious stuff!
My precious stuff!
That Shitty Raven managed to strew my possessions into thin air!"
He dubbed Raven "shitty".
Well,
then he set out walking,
well,
straight towards the place he had come from.
After walking here and there for a lo-o-ong time,
he came to the Akwe River.
Indeed, the Akwe—
this is where you find the imprint of where he lay,
the place where he had been sitting on his butthole.

Gwáa.
Áwéi-éi-éi ch'áakwx̱ sateeyée áwéi
tsoo yéi,
«Ax̱ shóodéi-èiy!
Ax̱ shóot yiḵúx̱!»
Héi-éi! Náanáx̱ áwé x'óol' yáx̱ yatee asdeek.

Nás'gi.aayí yéi aan yánde ag̲ax̱oox̱ áwéi, tléik'.
Aag̲áa áwé tsáa,
«Ax̱ shóodéi-èiy!
Yee káa ḵei.á nḵwaak'oots.»
«Hé'-ei.
Gootx̱
Naasshagiyát
Ḵei.á Daakeit du jee yéi ng̲atee?»

Ách áwéi
a yanáa awlis'úx̱.

A yanáa awlis'úx̱.
«Du shóode! Du shóode! Du shóode! Du shóode!»
Gwáa!
Tsaatsguyéig̲aa áwé
du shóode.

Wáannée sáwé ḵúnáx̱,
ḵúnáx̱ x'éig̲aa a yanáax̱ ayaawax̱út'.
Éh!
Ḵeiwa.àa.
Yáa tsaa naa.át,
x'óow s'aatx'í, at doogú
naa.át s'aatx'í, héendei.
Yá dzix̱áawu át yáx̱ yateeyi aa ḵwás dáḵde atkaawa.át.
Yáa té tsú,
ldakát yéide wdudlikéil',
tle yáa aasx', ldakát,
ḵei.á jináḵ.
Lituya Bay-t áyáa shukatán ldakát át.
X̱áay át shukatán, ldakát, laax̱ tsú.

Wow.
So after a long time
he hollered again like that,
"Come get me-e!
Boat over to me, you folks!"
He-ey! Everyone upstream was dipnetting like crazy.

The third time he called for them to come ashore, nothing.
Finally he hollered,
"Come get me-e
or I might break daylight on you folks!"
"Heh-hey.
From where does
the Child-of-the-Head-of-the-Nass hail
that he should possess the Container of Daylight?"

So
he nudged it open a little.

He nudged it open a little.
"Go pick him up! Go pick him up! Go pick him up! Go pick him up!"
Wow!
Belatedly
they went to pick him up.

Eventually he really,
he really pulled the lid all the way off.
Eh!
It *dawned*.
Those wearing seal clothing,
the owners of blankets and the owners of
skin clothing made of sea mammal hides went into the water.
But the ones that were like fur-bearing mammals rushed inland.
The rocks, too,
fled in all directions,
as well as the trees, everything,
to escape the daylight.
The range of all kinds of trees extends as far as Lituya Bay.
Yellow cedar are in that range, and red cedar too.

Ldakát yéide át áwu á.
Haa, yáade k̲wás, tléik',
tlél daa sá k̲oostí.
Ch'as yáa aas áyá yáadu.
Háa!
Haaá!

Shkalneek iii. Yéil k̲a Kudatankahídi

Hei-ei-ei.
Aag̲áa áyáa ch'a át wugoodée,
ch'a át wugoodée-ée-ée
ldakát yéide,
haahá,
yáax' áyáa,
yáax' áyáa awsiteen
yóo-óo-óo deikéenáx̲ át lahashji hít.
Haahá.
A daa yéi jikg̲wanéi áyú dei.
Wáa sá agux̲saneiyée daa yoo tuwatánk.
Wáananée sáyáa a káx̲ tuwditaan.

He ch'a yéi kdunéek,
ts'ítskw,
ts'ítskw x̲'eitákw aa tás,
á áyáa wóoshde awlitsóow
yáa náak̲w tl'eig̲ée, déex̲ a x'aan yatee,
aadé kdlixwás'.
Ách áyáa yan awsiyík̲.
{K̲oo[wa]shee}.
Dushí a daasheeyí, tlél k̲wá x̲wa.aax̲ín.
Dushí a kát yánde yaa anasyik̲ shí.
Haa-aa-aaw, deisgwach yán,
deisgwach yán,
deisgwach yán.
Yan asyéek̲—yáa G̲aaw Aanée yóo duwasáakw,
G̲aaw Aanée—
á áyáa,
anax̲ áyáa yan awsiyík̲.

All kinds of things are there.
But over this way, there are no cedar trees;
there isn't anything.
Just these spruce trees are here.
Ha!
Aha!

Episode iii. Raven and the Salmon Box

He-e-ey.
Then as he was just walking around,
just wa-a-alking around
all over the place,
aha,
it was at this point,
it was at this point that he saw
a house floating around wa-a-ay out on the ocean.
Aha.
He was going to do something about this now.
He was thinking about how to go about it.
Eventually he came up with an idea.

Okay, they tell it just like this,
a songbird—
the tendon from a songbird's heel
was what he used to connect
the octopus tentacles; it has two tips
that hang from it.
This is what he used to pull it ashore.
{He was looking for help}.
People sing the song that goes with this, but I've never heard it.
They sing the song to which he pulled it ashore.
We-e-ell, it was gradually approaching the shore,
gradually approaching the shore,
gradually approaching the shore.
When he pulled it ashore—the place is called *G̱aaw Aanée*,
G̱aaw Aanée—
this is the place
where he pulled it ashore.

Áx' áyáa yéi téeyeen yáa Yakwdèiyée,
áyá yá hít a kaanáx̱ yan awsiyig̱i Yakwdèiyée,
áwé ldakát yéide
tle yáa haa aanée,
haa aanée sákw.
Ách áyáa ch'u tle ch'oo aadáx̱ áyáa
Lingítx̱ haa wsitee.
Gus'éix̱ á,
a káx' áyáa wdudliyéx̱ tle
yáa Diginaa Hít.
Yáat'aa tsús,
yóo a shaká yáx̱ kaaxadi yé,
át áyáa la.áa yáa tléix'.aa.
Ách áyáa yéi aawasáa
A Shaká Hít.
Shakahít
yóo aawasáa.
Yéi déix̱ áyáa wootee Diginaa Hít.
Ldinax̱k'iyéide yan asnée wéi hít,
yan adax̱sanée áyáa,
tsu a daa yóo toowatán
wáa sá ḵukg̱wanoogóo.

Shkalneek iv. Yéil ḵa X̱'aan

G̱UNAAK'W: {...} *wé x̱'aan.*
Wáa sá?
G̱UNAAK'W: *Haa, ák.wé x̱'aan?*
Hmmm.
Yáa—yáa x̱'aan
áa ḵaa jikawliník,
á tsú.
Yú deikéenáx̱ kéi kagánch wéi x̱'aan.
Áyá yáa k'ákw—
ách áyáa X̱ashak'ákwk'
du xwáayi
-x̱ wusitee,
yáa k'ákw.
Du lú yéi kuwáat'een.

It is here that this Canoe Trail used to be,
the Canoe Trail over which he pulled the house,
every which way
onto our land,
onto what would become our land.
So it was from this very event that
we became Tlingit.
It was at *Gus'ëix̱*;
there they built
Far-Out House.
And this one,
the place which is shaped like a canoe prow,
this is where it stands, the house that replaced the original one.
This is why he named it
"Its Prow" House.
Prow House
is what he named it.
In this way there came to be two Far-Out Houses.
Sooner or later, once he finished the houses,
when he finished each of them,
he thought again about
what he would do next.

Episode iv. Raven and Fire

WHITE: {…} *fire.*
What?
WHITE: *So, is it fire you were going to talk about?*
Hmmm.
He talked someone into getting
the—the fire
as well.
The fire kept flaring up way out at sea.
This pygmy owl—
so this pygmy owl named
X̱ashak'ákwk'
became
his sidekick.
His beak used to be long.

Á áyáa,
«Héi!
Ax̲ shax̲aawúch kéi kg̲wagáan.»
«Tléik̓.
Ei-ei.
Yées aa áa yéi kk̲wa.oo.
Yées aa áa yéi kk̲wa.oo.»
Héi-éi. Wáanée sáwé aadé akaawak̲aa, héi!
Daak wudik̲ín.
Hei-ei-ei.
Wáanée sáwé atx̲ ayawsiyeik̲.
Yánde ÿaa ndak̲ín.
Aag̲áa áwé yéi ayanask̲éich,
«X̲ashak̓áa-áa-áakwk̓,
ch'a tlágu at yanéekw.
Áa yáx̲ x'wán, líl x̲'eenák̲x̲ik̲!
Ch'a tlágu at yanéekw.
Aandachóon.»
Ch'u yéi adaayak̲aayí du x̲ánnáx̲ yan
    aÿawsiyék̲ yáa x̲'aan.
Yoohá anch k̲u.áyáas yéi wtuwasáa yáa x̲'aan,
    «yanax̲ kéi kaganji x̲'aan».
Yóo wtuwasáa yáa x̲'aan.
Yóo deikéex' yanax̲ kéi kagánch.
«Yanax̲ kéi kaganji x̲'aan»
yéi wtuwasáa yáa x̲'aan.

Shkalneek v. Yéil k̲a Héen

Atx̲ á yan asnée, yáat'aa yan asnée—
haahá—
aag̲áa áyá tsáa tsoo—
tsu akaawa.aak̲w.
Tsu a daa yóo toowatán daa sá.
Wáannée sáyá a káx̲ tuwditaan yáa héen.
Haahá, héen á.
Héen ashukg̲watée
hítx'i x̲oodé.
Aawa.áx̲

So he said,
"Hey!
Because of my hair, my beak will get burned up."
"No.
Ei-ei.
I'll put a new beak on there for you.
I'll put a new beak on there."
He-ey. Eventually Raven sent him there, hey!
He flew out.
Hei-ei-ei.
Eventually he picked it up in his beak.
He was flying toward shore.
Then Raven would say to him,
"X̱ashak'áa-áa-áakwk',
things worth doing are always painful.
Take courage, don't release it from your mouth!
Things worth doing are always painful.
Straight for the land now!"
As he was telling him these things X̱ashak'ákwk' set the fire down by him using his beak.
We ourselves have named this fire "the fire that flares up from underground".
This is what we named the fire.
It would flare up from underground way out on the ocean.
"The fire that flares up from underground"
is what we named this fire.

Episode v. Raven and Fresh Water

After that, when he finished it, when he finished this—
aha—
now it was at this point that he again—
he again devised a scheme.
Again he thought about what he would do.
Eventually he settled on the idea of fresh water.
Aha, water.
He was going to divert the water
so that it would flow among the houses.
He had heard

yú G̱anook Héeni.
Goon áyóo
du x̱'ax̱ánoo.
Ách áyáa
sh tóon wuditee, aadé wooḵoox̱
a x̱ánde du káani.
Ho-ho-ho.
A x̱áni daak góot áwé, «Ax̱ káani!»
«A-á.»
«Ch'a ltooshgú áyáa ax̱ káani, ch'a ltooshgú.
I kayaag̱áa yéi ḵux̱aanóok, ltooshgú.
Ch'a ltooshgú tléináx̱ satéen.»
A x̱áni daak uwagút.
Haaw.
Du daa yóo jikwli.átk du káani wáa
sá du daa.
Haaw.
Du x̱'éix̱ yan at dutée áyá,
«Éi, yan sh g̱atool.aadée ax̱ káani,
sh kanax̱toolneegée wóoshtin,
ch'a daatx'i sáani sá.»
Haahá.
Yéi asakg̱wahéa táach ax̱lajaaḵ.
Ei-ei-ei-ei, ldakát yéide.
Haaw.
Deisgwach yóo yóo waneek
táach las'úx̱x̱.
«He, líl s'é eeteix̱éeḵ, ax̱ káani. I yáx̱ x̱at taa.uwa.ás, ách
áyá i x̱ánde yéi ḵux̱aanóok,
ch'as ḵaa sé—ch'as sh katoolneegí.
De x̱át tsú de héide tsu
kḵwaḵóox̱ dei.»
Gwáa.
Wáannée sáwé ch'a tleix̱,
ch'a tleix̱,
ch'a tleix̱ táach uwajáḵ.
Haahá.
Át jiwdigút wé héen.
Héide a yanáa aawax̱óot'.

of Petrel's Water.
There was a spring
nearby for him to drink from.
This had
offended Raven so much that he boated there
to his brother-in-law's place.
Ho-ho-ho.
When he came up to him Raven said, "My brother-in-law!"
"Yes."
"I'm just feeling so bad, my brother-in-law, just feeling so bad.
I've come to visit you, feeling so bummed out.
Sitting alone by oneself is such a drag."
Raven walked out to him.
Well.
He was doing chores for his brother-in-law, doing anything he could do for him.
Well.
When he was finished being fed,
"Hey, let's lie down and rest, my brother-in-law. Let's tell each other some stories,
just any little things."
Aha.
He was going to will Petrel to fall asleep.
He-e-e-ey, Raven tried every which way.
Well.
Eventually, that's what kept happening to him;
he kept nodding off.
"Hey, don't go to sleep just yet, my brother-in-law. I'm lonesome for you, so I've come to visit you,
just to hear another human voice—just for us to tell some stories.
Me too, now, since I'm sleepy I'm going to be taking my boat back over there again soon."
Wow.
Eventually Petrel fell asleep for good,
for good;
he fell asleep for good.
Aha.
Raven charged over to the water.
He dragged the lid off.

Tláakw, tláakw, tláakw.
Ch'u tle ḵúnáx̱, ch'u tle aax̱ kéi ndaḵíni tin áwéi
ash káa kéi wdzigít.
«Shée!
Gasháat, ax̱ gaankayéigi!»
Ách áwé áx' ash woosháat.
Áx̱ wulixáat' yú kaawayík.
Ha yéi asaawahaa du káani
du tayeet ag̱a.aagí.
Shóot awdi.ák.
Ash éex̱ aklakwáatx̱.
Ldinax̱k'iyéide ash eedéi sh ilháa áwé
tsáa ajeewanáḵ.
Yóo naakéenax̱.aanáx̱, íxdei gíyá,
át wudiḵeen
héinax̱.aanáx̱,
Iḵhéeni,
ḵa tliyáanax̱.á aa.
Iḵhéeni ḵu.áyáas yáat,
Aalséix̱,
T'aaḵú,
wáa sá yakoogéi yáa héen tlénx',
a saayéetin.
A saayée sákw ch'a a yáx̱ yaa anal.át.
Du x̱'atáadáx̱ kadutl'oog̱ú áyáa héen
ÿátx'ix̱ dax̱sitee, yóo kdunéek,
tle ch'u yéi.
Kadutl'őoḵ du x̱'atáanáx̱.
Áyáa dei tlax̱ a yáanáx̱ wooneeyi aa áyáa a
shunaayát wudiḵeen.
Áyáa ax̱'eiwanáḵ
yá éil' tlein sákw.
Áyá éil' tleinx̱ wusitee.

Shkalneek vi. Yéil ḵa Yáay

Haa, yáa aadáx̱,
áyáa yáa—yáat'aa yan awusneeyée áyáa
akaawa.aaḵw tsoo

Quick, quick, quick.
Just as he was flying up,
Petrel woke up on him.
"Watch out!
Grab him, my smokehole spirit!"
So it caught hold of him there.
He was suspended in mid-air.
Well, what his brother-in-law wanted
was for his servant to build a fire under Raven.
He built the fire.
He was blackening Raven with soot.
Sooner or later, once Petrel finally yielded to Raven, the smokehole spirit released him.
Way over from the northern side toward the south, perhaps,
he flew around
along this side,
by the Copper River,
and the one on the other side of it.
Now here is the Copper River,
the Alsek River,
the Taku River,
however many of those big rivers there are,
with their names.
He was assigning them the names that they were to have.
When the water dripped from the corner of his mouth, each of the drops would become a little stream—that's how they tell it—then on to the next one.
Drops kept falling from his mouth.
He flew around where the sea floor drops off with an amount of water that was way too much for him to carry.
Then he released from his mouth
the water that was to become the ocean.
It became the ocean.

Episode vi. Raven and the Whale

Well, after this,
when he finished this task,
he again made

tsoo g̲óot yéidei.
Á áyáa yaa nagúdi áyáa awsiteen
wéi yáay tlein wé diginaanáx̲ kéi x'ákch.
Haahá!
Du tóoch lichéesh.
Tle yéi áyá áx̲ k̲uklageix̲ wé anax̲ kéi daséich yé.
Kéi wdasaayée yáa aadé wdiyeig̲i yé
  {kawditóow}. Áx' áwé ayaawayék,
  a yíkde wdik̲een.
Haaw.
Áwé hóoch'.
A yée yéi wootee.
Yéi kdunéek at gas.ée.
Gwáa!
Wáananée sáyóo
ldakát á kéi nas.át'.
Wus.áat'ee—wudzi.át'—
haahá, woonaa áyá.
Haa, áyáa awdlix̲éis',
«Yak'éiyi l'éiwdéi-éi-éi!
Aalséix̲ wát!»
Ách áwé Aalséix̲ wátnáx̲ ÿan wulihásh.
Áwoo á yáa yeedát,
wéi yáay.
Yuháanch yéi wtuwasáa
G̲altseenawáa.
Daa sá yéi wdusaayí tléil x̲wasakú.
Yéi wduwasáa
G̲altseenawáa.
Yáa a daadéi yaa ana.át
wéitadee, déex̲.
Wooweidi k̲u.oo áyóo yú.á.
Keitl hasdu een yaa na.át.
Áyá tle ch'a áx' téix̲ has wusitee.
Tle ch'a yéi anax̲ kawda.áayin.
Yáa yeedát k̲u.aa,
yáa—
yáa naa.aayeit yóo duwasáagu át k̲ut woog̲éex'.
Yá x'áat' tlein

a different plan.
Now, while he was walking along, he caught sight of
a huge humpback whale surfacing offshore.
Aha!
He thought he could pull it off.
The hole it breathes through is always so big across.
When it took a breath, {he calculated} how long it took the whale's spray to abate. He positioned himself there, waiting for his chance, then flew inside it.
Well.
So that was that.
He was inside of it.
They say he was cooking for himself.
Gosh!
At some point
the whole thing began getting cold.
When it became cold—it was cold—
aha, it had died.
Well now, he made a wish,
"To a fine sand bea-ea-each!
The mouth of the Alsek!"
So he drifted ashore along the mouth of the Alsek.
It is there now,
that whale.
We are the ones who named it
Ga̱ltseenawáa.
I don't know what it was that they gave the name to.
It was named
Ga̱ltseenawáa.
People were gathering around
women in menarche, two of them.
It's said that they were people undergoing their first menstrual cycle.
A dog was walking along with them.
On that very spot they just turned to stone.
They used to jut out just so.
Now, though,
this—
this thing called a *naa.aayeit* has been lost.
A big island

ch'u tle tsá át satánin,
G̲íl' X'áat'i.
Á áwé wéi yáay yéeyi.
Áwé ch'u yé k̲áa áx' daxash yé,
duxáash.
Aag̲áa áwé wduwa.áx̲, haahá!
Ei-ei.
«Aadóo sá k̲aa kaanáx̲ ang̲axaashée-ée-ée
yáay yíkdáx̲ kéi x̲duk̲een?»
Haahá!
Tle wduwa.áx̲
a yíkdei áwé.
Ách áwéi
k̲únáx̲ yáa—áyú, áyú, áyú, áyú, áyú—
k̲aa kagéix' áwé káx̲ daak̲'awdudlixásh.
Tle kei wdudlitl'ét'.
Ch'oo l g̲adustínji áwéi
a tóonáx̲ kéi wdik̲ín.
Daat yáx̲ sá wdlit'íx', daakootláa eex̲.
A yíknáx̲ kéi dak̲éen áyáa wduwa.áx̲,
«X̲'ún! X̲'ún! X̲'ún! X̲'ún! X̲'ún! X̲'ún! X̲'ún! X̲'ún!» ch'u tle yóo kínde.
Tléil k̲uwustee.
Ách áyáa
yéi wduwasáa—yéi k̲uwduwasáa—yéi wduwasáa
X̲'unyéi.
Yáay yíkdáx̲ X̲'unéi.
Lingít saayíx̲ wusitee yáa X̲'unéi.
Ldinax̲k'iyéide yan awusnée á,
haaw, tle hóoch', tle k̲ut woogoot.
Hél tsú wduskú goodéi sá wugoodí, ch'u tle yú kínde tléil k̲uwustee.
Hou-ou, tláakw at kaaxát.
Tláakw at kaaxát adaakw,
ch'u yé k̲áa áx' adakw yé.
Ha ch'a aag̲áa áwé tsá
k̲aa x̲oot uwagút. Haaw.
Hou-ou-ou.
Hé'!
{...} aadé yóo oolg̲énk wé—
wé eex̲

used to be there originally,
Cliff Island.
That is what used to be the whale.
Every last person was out flensing the whale,
flensing it.
Then they heard it, aha!
Eh-h.
"Who could cut a hole over a fello-o-ow
so a fellow could fly up out of a whale?"
Aha!
That's what they heard
from inside it.
Because of that—
really, this—so, so, so, so, so—
they cut the whale open wide enough for the person to get out.
Then someone climbed up on top of the whale.
Before anyone saw him
he flew up out of it.
He had become extremely stiff; the oil was thick all over him.
When he flew up out of it, people heard him call out,
"*X̱'ún! X̱'ún! X̱'ún! X̱'ún! X̱'ún! X̱'ún! X̱'ún! X̱'ún!*" then he just went up.
He was gone.
Because of this
he was named—a person was given the name—he was named
X̱'unyéi.
X̱'unéi from inside the whale.
X̱'unéi became a Tlingit name.
Sooner or later, once he finished with this,
well, that was that; he just disappeared.
No one knew where he had gone; he just up and disappeared.
Ho-oh. There was a frenzy.
There was a frenzy to render fat.
Every last person was out rendering fat.
Well, only then
did he go among the people. Well.
Ho-o-oh.
Heh!
He was examining the {…}—
they were rendering

dudáakw.
«Héhe!
Tléil shéyákwshé a yíkde k̲ukawdu.áax̱ákw?
. . . .áax̱ákw?»
«Hé'!
A yíkde at wuduwa.áx̱,
‹Aadóo sá k̲aa kaanáx̱ angaxaashée-ée
yáay yíkdáx̱ kéi x̱duk̲een?›
yóo x̱áa wduwa.áx̱.»
«Haa,
aadé sh kayeelnik yé,
cha aank̲wáani,
ihí, ihí!
Á áyá yáa—
yá aax̱ haadé yaa nx̱agut yé—
ch'u tle áyá tléináx̱ ch'a koogéiyi áyá yaa nx̱agút,
  tléil tsu x̱wsakú goosóo lingít.
Ch'a koogéiyi áyáa yaa nx̱agút.
Áyáa yee kagéit x̱waagút yáax̱'.
Ihí!
Á áwé,
yéi áwé, a yíkde at wuduwa.ax̱i át áwé.
Áwé ch'a aan wuduwax̱áa.
Á áyáa yéi k̲uwsinee, k̲utx̱ k̲aa shuwlixeex, hóoch'!
Héil tsu tléináx̱ k̲áa k̲oostí.
A nák̲ yee klagáas'!
Ihí! Ihí!»

Haaw.
Ayáx̱ áwé,
ch'u yé k̲áa áx' at wooxooni yé a nák̲.
Tle a nák̲ naawligáas'.
A shóo yéi wootèe hóoch k̲u.aa.

Shkalneek vii. Yéil Geesh Daax̱ Wugoodí

Ldinax̱k'iyéide {yan at dax̱} sanée—
haahá—
aagáa áyáa tsáa tsoo

the oil.
"Hey-hey!
Mightn't any mysterious sounds have been heard coming from inside it?
... any mysterious sounds?"
"Heh!
People did hear something from inside it saying,
'Who could cut a hole over a fello-ow
so a fellow could fly up out of a whale?'
Indeed, that's what they heard."
"Well,
the way you are telling it,
good townspeople,
don't eat it; don't do it!
Now this—
this place from which I am coming—
this whole time I've been walking along aimlessly all by myself,
  not knowing where any people are.
I was walking along aimlessly,
and now I have come upon you folks here.
Don't eat it!
That is the very thing
from which these other people had heard something calling.
Despite this bad omen, the people ate it.
That's what did the people in; it killed off all the people, they were all gone!
Not a single person was left.
Move away from it, you folks!
Don't eat it! Don't!"

Well then.
Accordingly,
every last one of them was getting ready to leave it behind.
The whole clan just moved away.
Raven, on the other hand, sat down to eat it.

Episode vii. Raven Goes Down Along the Bull Kelp

Sooner or later, once he was finished with everything—
aha—
it was only then that,

tsu g̱óot yéide,
aa, de yéi át tsu du jeet uwaxíx.
Áwé át wulihaash geesh.
Ch'a át wugoodí áwé awsiteen wé geesh,
ách a káa wjiḵaaḵ.
Á áwé akaawa.aaḵw.
Tle aawa.áx̱ ḵu.aa wéi—
wéi shaanák'w,
wé Ḵées' Yax̱ Shakawdzinugu Shaanák'w.
A daax̱ áwé woogoot,
yáa geesh daax̱.
Aag̱áa áyáa yáa nées',
yóo dudlisaayi át,
du jeet kaawasóos, gwál déex̱.
Ách áyá g̱altóo yéi awdi.oo tle.
Haahá!
Aan a x̱ánde woogoot,
wé shawat.shaanák'w x̱ánde.
Ḵées' Yax̱ Shakawdzinugu Shaanák'w á.
Yóo áwé sh disáakw.
Haaw, a x̱áni neil uwagút.
Hé'! Yéi áwé yakwligéi wé du x̱'aaní.
Hé'! Yáanax̱.á áwé yáa a keekánx̱ áwé áx'
  yan sh wudzitáa.
Hé'!
«Ḵúnáx̱—
ḵúnáx̱ x̱at seiwa.át'.
Nées' g̱ehéenak'u áyá x̱at sawli.át'.
Ho-ho.
Nées' á!
Á áyá,
nées' x̱á áyáa a héenak'u áyá x̱at sawli.át'.»
X'oon.aa yéi yanaḵáa sáyá yéi ash yawsiḵaa, «Héhéi!
Daag̱u x̱'áanáx̱ sá woolaayi
  léin áwé keenéek?»
Haaw.
Ash een ḵunáax̱ daaḵ akaawaník.
Ách áwé át jiwdigút.
Kindaatóog̱un aawasháat.

in a different way,
ah, he got his hands on something else like that.
Now, there were bull kelp drifting about.
While he was walking around, he caught sight of the bull kelp,
so he flew there and landed upon it.
Then he devised a scheme.
He had heard about
that little elder,
that Little-Elder-who-Enlarged-the-Tide.
He went down along
the bull kelp.
And then he got ahold of
these things known as sea urchins,
maybe two of them.
So he just put them in his pocket.
Aha!
He took them and went to her,
to that little old woman.
She is Little-Elder-Who-Enlarged-the-Tide.
That's what she named herself.
Well, he entered her house.
Heh! That fire of hers was pretty big.
Heh! Right along here, he lay down right where he could
    keep an eye on her.
Heh!
"I'm really—
I'm really cold.
Sea-urchin juice has made me chilly.
Ho-ho.
It's sea urchins!
You know,
it's these sea urchins, their juice has made me so chilly."
After he had said this so many times, she said to him, "Heh-hey!
What stretch of time are you talking about during which a tideflat
    would have been exposed by low tide?"
Well.
She explained it to him.
That is why he attacked her there.
He seized her and held her upside down.

Tláakw áwé a x'aash áyú adax̱nax̱ícht wé,
wé nées',
«Tóo nú nées' nóox'u!
Tóo nú nées' nóox'u! Yáadu yáa nées' nóox'u.»
Ho-ho-ho-ho tláakw kaaxát aan.
Tláakw kaaxát.
Haa, aax̱ áwé yéi kéi ayawu.aayí tle
yéi ash yawsiḵaa,
«Déi g̱aag̱waalaa, Yéi-éi-éil!
Déi g̱aag̱waalaa.»
Haaw, gootx̱ sáwé du x̱ánt wujixíx
du xwáak'u,
X̱ashak'ákwk'.
«X̱ashak'ákwk',
aag̱áa yux̱ neesheex!
Wáa sá woolaa?»
Daaḵw.aa sá yéi aawasáa ḵaa shoowú yáx̱,
«Ḵaa shoowú yáx̱ woolaa.»
Yeisú déi tsu a káa ajiyawdigút.
Tláakw
ash jiyeet kadag̱áax̱.
Haahá, yáax' áwé,
«Naaléi át uwalayi yé.»
Haa, aag̱áa áwé tsá ajeewanáḵ.
A náḵ woogoot, hé'!

Shkalneek viii. Yéil Du Kéek' Ḵut Awulyeilí

Ldakát át áwé a x̱oot uwaláa.
Haaw.
Ldakát át áwé ashasaḵéet'.
A daa yóo kagax̱du.áat.
Wuduwadákw.
Daaḵwéit sá, ldakát yéide át a x̱oodáx̱ woolaa,
dag̱aataayi át.
Áwé, haaw, goodáx̱ sáwé du jeet uwaxíx
wé s'áax̱' yook'óo?
Á áwéi
yax̱ awsi.áx̱w.

After he had spanked each of her buttocks vigorously with
those sea urchins, he said to her,
"Feel the burn of the sea-urchin shell!
Feel the burn of the sea-urchin shell! Here is the sea-urchin shell."
Ho-ho-ho-ho, she was suffering from it.
She was under duress.
Well, after he had detained her like that for quite a while,
she cried out to him,
"Enough! The tide could go out any minute, Ra-a-aven!
Enough! The tide could go out any minute!"
Well, Raven's little buddy,
X̱ashak'ákwk',
ran up to him from somewhere.
"X̱ashak'ákwk',
run outside and check it out!
How far has the tide gone down?"
X̱ashak'ákwk' referred to a certain tide level as 'like half a person',
"The tide has gone out as far as half a person."
Now at last Raven turned back and attacked her.
She was wailing in pain
under his torture.
Aha, and now X̱ashak'ákwk' said,
"The tide has gone down a long way."
Well, then he finally released her.
He left her and walked off, hey!

Episode viii. Raven Deceives His Younger Brother

The tide went out, revealing many things.
Well.
He was rousing up all the creatures.
They were to gather around it.
They rendered the fat from it.
The tide had receded to reveal a great variety of creatures,
each of them full of fat.
Then, well, he got ahold of a
little cod stomach from somewhere or other.
Then
he tied it in a bundle.

Daa sákwshíwé aawadákw?
Aawatawu át gíwé wé eex̱.
Áwé tsá
yéi shanáax̱ awdzi.áx̱w, a tayeet ishḵúx̱.
Du lakaadéi kdutl'óoḵ.
A daa yóo tuwatánk wáa sá kg̱wasgeedée tsu.
Gwáa!
Haahá!
A káx̱ tuwditaan.
Hou, shawdinúk.
Shawdinúk, gánde woogoot.
Gáanx' áwé tle ldakát yéide át áwé, wé—
wé s'óos'ani, ldakát yéide át áwé hít daa
    yaa adax̱natsúw.
Aan áwé yóo dax̱ x̱'adax̱li.átk.
«Ax̱ jóoni kakḵwalaneek.
Ax̱ jóoni kakḵwalaneek.
Yéi akḵwajóon,
‹Hei-ei-ei-ei!
X̱áa aan káa wdinaaḵ!
X̱áa aan káa wdinaaḵ!
Hou!
X̱ashak'áa-áa-áakwk'!
Yux̱ neeshee-ee-eex!›
Tle yáat'aa yéi yaa yanx̱aḵéini teen áwé
tláakw yee kg̱wanéi.»
Haahá,
wuduwa.áx̱,
«Xw-xw-xw-xw!»
wé aantḵeení.
Hm!
Hou-ou-ou-ou!
Neilnax̱.á áwé át yóo dzigítk,
neilnax̱.á.
Wé éenaa—
yóo duwasáakw.
Yóo dudlisaayée,
éenaa.
Wé té aan dull'at' át,

I wonder what he rendered the oil from.
That oil might have been something that he stole.
So then,
he tied it up over his head like this and made himself comfortable below it.
The oil was slowly dripping into his mouth.
Raven was thinking about what he was going to get up to next.
Wow!
Aha!
He came up with an idea.
Ho, he got up.
He got up and went outside.
Then outside, all kinds of things, those—
those pinecones, he began placing all kinds of things upright
around the house.
He was conversing with each of them about it.
"I'm going to narrate my dream.
I'm going to narrate my dream.
This is how I'm going to dream,
'He-e-e-ey!
A war party has made a stand upon the land!
A war party has made a stand upon the land!
Ho!
X̱ashak'áa-áa-áakwk'!
Run outside!'
Just as soon as I start saying this
you guys better get busy."
Aha,
a noise was heard,
"Wh-wh-wh-wh!"
a noise made by the pinecone townspeople.
Hm!
Ho-o-o-o!
Raven kept flailing around in the house,
in the house.
Those wooden tongs—
that's what they are called.
That's the name they are known by,
tongs.
That thing people use to handle hot rocks,

aan dull'at' át áwé,
á áwé yéi wduwasáa,
éenaa.
X̲'wéinaa áwé yóo.
Shál yáx̲ kadudzixát, yóo áwé de a káa kdultáx'ch wé té.
A kaadé duxwéinch.
Á áwé yá neilx' ÿan yóo ax̲'ayax̲íchk.
(DU JÍN AAWAT'ÁCH)
«O-ho-ho-ho-ho.
K̲aa s'aagí {… een} x̲aat'óok!»
Aan dak̲áan áwé,
yan ax̲'eix̲eechch.
«X̲ashak'áa-áa-áa-áakwk'w!
I gu.aa yáx̲ x'wán! Hmm!
Hou-ou-ou!
Ho-ho-ho-ho-ho-ho-ho!»
Tle yáat'aa táax̲ ÿawdageejée áwé,
«K̲aa s'aagí {… een} x̲aat'óok!»
Áwé tle hóoch'i aayí yaa akanall'úx'u áwé du káa
neil wujixíx du xwáak'u.
«De yéi ágí yéi at k̲ushinóokk'?»
Aaa.
A táade kát ashakaawax̲ích
du káak.
Haahá.
Áwé wéi lák̲t aan daadus.ax̲w át,
wé x̲aat,
á áwé.
Hé-he!
Kaldaagéináx̲ áwé aawa.éex',
«X̲ashak'ákwk'!
Lí s'é!
Daa sáwé ách x̲at keesa.aax̲w kík'?»
«X̲aat áyáa.»
«Lée!
Lée, kík'! Ilí!
Lí!
Áwoo.

an implement used to handle them,
these were named
tongs.
It's a forked roasting stick, like this.
They shape them like spoons; this is how they use them to grip rocks.
They ladle water over the hot rocks to create steam.
So there in the house he was smacking the tongs up and down.
(SLAPS HANDS)
"Ah-ho-ho-ho-ho.
Wow, I shot a person's bone {with a …}!"
When X̱ashak'ákwk' was out there fighting, Raven kept smacking the tongs on the ground.
"X̱ashak'áa-áa-áa-áakwk'w!
Be of good courage! Hmm!
Ho-o-o!
Ho-ho-ho-ho-ho-ho-ho!"
When he dunked his face into the box of oil, he said, "Wow, I shot a person's bone {with a …}!"
And now when he was drinking up the very last one, his little buddy ran inside and came upon him.
"Is this really what this darned little creature is doing now?"
Yes.
X̱ashak'ákwk' flipped his uncle
headlong into the box of oil.
Aha.
Then X̱ashak'ákwk'w used those spruce roots
that they tie up bentwood boxes with;
that's what he used.
Heh-heh!
Raven called out to him cautiously,
"X̱ashak'ákwk'!
Wait!
What are you using to tie me up, little brother?"
"These are spruce roots."
"Don't
Don't, little brother! Don't!
Don't!
They're there.

Áwu i tlaakáak hás ách wooch
kas.aax̱u át.»
Haaw, goox' sáyú du tlaakáak hás ách kas.aax̱u át?
«Áwoo.
Yanshukáx̱ kalxwás'[ch].
Wéi yanshukáx̱ koolxwás'ch wé
chookán kax̱aadí kulyát'.
Á áwéi.»
Ách áwé adaawsi.áx̱w.
Aadáx̱ áwé tsáa
yan aksa.áax̱w áwéi
aawayaa.
Haahá.
Goodéi sákwshí yaa anayáan, goodéi sákwshé?
Áwu áwé Aalséix̱.
Yáa yeedát
G̱éelk'uwá yóo tuwasáakw,
Nánde Aa G̱éelk'uwá.
Ḵúnáx̱ áwé yayát', aawayàa
wéi a séetnáx̱,
héinax̱.aadáx̱.
Tle yéi yatee,
héen táade tle.
Áx' áwé ch'a aan aawayàa.
Áx' áwé yéi asaawahaa
daak ax̱sag̱éex'i.
Daak awsig̱íx'.
Yeisú tléix' yan wusxeexí áwé kawliwál', akawlik'úts.
«G̱áa!»
Yóode áwé yaa ndaḵín,
aa, a yíknáx̱.
Yéi wtuwasáa wéi tl'átk,
yéi wtuwasáa
Ch'eek'áa,
yóo tudlisaayí.
Tlákw daak wusitanéyáx̱ yatee wéi téix' a yaadáx̱.
Ch'a aan áwé hé yaakw áx̱ kéi akg̱aḵúx̱ún, tléil aadé yaakw
yée aa g̱aagwaaxeexi yé.
Du shátch yéi yawsiḵaa,

They're there, the stuff that your mother's uncles would use
to tie each other up."
Well, where was this stuff his mother's uncles used to tie things up with?
"They're there.
They hang down along the edges of the beach.
They hang down along the edges of the beach, those
long grass roots.
That's the stuff."
That's what X̱ashak'ákwk' used to tie him up.
Then finally,
when he got him securely tied up,
he started packing him.
Aha.
I wonder where he was packing him to; I wonder where to.
The Alsek River is there.
Nowadays
we call it Face-of-Little-Mountain-Pass,
the Northern Face-of-Little-Mountain-Pass.
It's a really long pass; he packed him
through the channel,
from this side over here.
It's just like this,
leading down into the water.
Nonetheless, he packed him through there.
That's where Raven wanted X̱ashak'ákwk'
to toss him off.
He tossed him off.
The moment it hit the ground, it broke to pieces; he snapped the ties.
"Caw!"
He was flying off into the distance,
yes, along the river valley.
We named that land—
we named it
Ch'eek'áa;
that is the name by which we know it.
It's like those rocks are always raining down from the side of it.
Nonetheless, whenever someone takes a boat up along it, there is no way
that any of those rocks can fall down into the boat.
Raven's wife said to him,

«Hé'!
Haa yée yéi aa kg̱waxéex wéi té!»
«Dé, ilítl'!»
Wé yaakw aax̱ ḵux̱ dax̱ alshéet' áwé.
Déi áwé, tléil yaakw yée yéi aa uxíxch áx'.

Shkalneek ix. Yéil ḵa T'á

Aaa.
Atx̱ áwé tsu a daa yoo toowatán wáa sá ḵukg̱wanóok.
Tle yéi a daa yóo tutángi áwé,
«Éeḵ!»
Wéi—
wé Aalséix̱ tliyaanax̱.á,
á áwé yeedát
wé G̱éelák'w yóo tuyasáagu yé.
Tléil ḵu.aa áwé aag̱áa—tlél G̱éelák'w yóo dusáagun.
Tle yáa yeedát áwé g̱eelák'w ḵudzitee.
Áx' áwé a kát uwagút wé aan eetí.
Haahá.
Tle ákwshé x̱á akaxeet, akaxeet, akaxeet.
Áwé yéi koogéi áwé, yéi kawligéik' wé s'òowk', yóo aawasáa.
Áwé kéi akawlixít.
Áwé tle adáx̱ a daa jiwli.aat.
Yáa at goowú yáx̱ yateeyi yé tle a kináax' áwé yan aawatée.
Ayatéen de wé t'á diginaanáx̱ kéi x'ákch.
Á áwé,
de du tóoch lichéesh.
Akaawa.aaḵw, haahá.
«Héi, chaa t'á tlein!
K'e hé s'oowk' aadé idaayaḵa yé!
‹Du táax̱'u yiktl'eexí gí!
Du x'éix'u x̱ootl'eexí gí!
Du yat'ootl' tl'eex tlein ltín!›
Ldakát yéide.
Haanaanáx̱ yan sh idagúḵ!»
Héi-éi, x'oon.aa yéi adaayaḵaayí sáwéi

"My!
One of those rocks is going to drop down into our boat!"
"Can it already!"
He kept cramming the rocks back into place, away from the boat.
That put an end to it; no rocks ever fall down into a boat at that place.

Episode ix. Raven and the King Salmon

Yes.
After that he considered what to do next.
As he was contemplating it,
"The beach!"
There,
over beyond the Alsek,
this is
the place we now call Little-Mountain-Pass.
Though at that time it wasn't—it wasn't formerly named
Little-Mountain-Pass.
Nowadays there is a little mountain pass.
It was there that he walked onto the site where the village used to be.
Aha.
Then I suppose he was just poking around, poking around,
poking with a stick.
It was this big; the little greenstone, as he called it, was a bit large.
He poked it up with the end of a stick.
Then after that he tended to it.
He set it down atop a stump-like natural feature.
Then he could see a king salmon surfacing offshore.
So now,
he thought he could get it.
He made a plan, aha.
"Hey, big king salmon!
You should check out what this little greenstone is saying to you!
'Isn't there filth in his warts!
Isn't there filth within his gills!
Look at his big filthy black face!'
He's calling you all kinds of names.
Push ashore over this way!"
So-o, after saying that to him so many times,

du eeg̱ayáanáx̱ guxkáa [woox'aak].
«Lí s'é! Lí s'é x̱á x̱áawé! Lí s'é! Lí s'é!
Gánde s'é kḵwagóot,
gánde.
Al'éel' kuḵagóot,»
yóo áyáa aawasáa. Áa
yeiḵ gug̱agóot.
Áwé x'ús' áwéi aag̱áa áwé át sh kawdiḵáa.
Haahá.
Du jeet wujix̱én wé x'ús' sákw.
Chaa ch'a aag̱áa áwé tsá tsu wé át aayi yé,
áa woonook.
Haahá, atx̱ áwé tsu
yéi áyá asaawahaa
aan g̱adaḵaant.
Wáananée sáwé tsu yanax̱ guxkáa wdlitsees, haahá!
(NAS'GIDAHÉEN DU JÍN AT'ÁCHT)
Ashakaawat'íx̱',
daaḵ awsixát'.
Hí'! T'á tlèin
Áwé tlei,
tle adax̱,
adax̱ a daa jiwli.aat.
Yá a koowóo,
yá a leet,
yáanax̱.áx' áyá ḵóode áwéi.
Yéi kwligéi, áwé áa yan awsitée.
Tle x̱'áal' a daa yéi aawa.oo, tle ldakát,
unanéeg̱aa.
Yá a shoowú ḵu.aawé
agux̱ladáak.
Á áwé du xwáax'u sákw ashawsiḵée,
«X̱'áal'g̱aa nay.á, ax̱ xwáax'u sáani!
X̱'áal'g̱aa nay.á!»
Ayáx̱ áwé aawa.aat x̱'áal'g̱aa.
Aaa, ch'a yáag̱aa, gootlk'i yá, dax̱
nadag̱átch x̱'áal'.
«Hé.e!
Goodáx̱ sá yéi yeeysinei?»

the king salmon beached himself below Raven.
"Wait! Wait, just hang on a second! Wait! Wait!
First I'm going to go to the bathroom,
to the bathroom.
I'm going to go poop,"
that's what he called it. He was going to come back down
there to the beach.
So, Raven sent himself on a mission to find a club.
Aha.
He got his hands on something he could use as a club.
Finally the king salmon sat down
where Raven had been sitting.
Aha, after that, too,
Raven wanted the king salmon
to quarrel with the greenstone.
Eventually he swam aground, aha!
(**SLAPS HANDS THREE TIMES**)
He conked it on the head
and dragged it up from shore.
My! It was a *huge* king salmon.
So then,
then after that,
after that he set to work on it.
Its tail and
the ridge of its back
he took into a den nearby.
That salmon was big; he set the tail and the ridge of its back down there.
Then he put skunk cabbage around the whole thing,
so that nothing would happen to it.
The rest of it, though,
he was going to cook in a pit.
So then he roused himself up a posse,
"Go get some skunk cabbage, my little buddies!
Go get some skunk cabbage!"
Accordingly they went after skunk cabbage.
Well, around here, on the side of a little mound were strewn
a bunch of skunk cabbage.
"Goodness!
Where did you get it from?"

«Héi gutlshutuwanyee.»
«Ée! Ée! Ée!
Áx̱ shát anax̱ kéi wdusgaani yé áwé.
Ée!
Du xóosht'i aadé yax̱ shakawuyaayéen.
Déex̱ shaa kaanáx̱ kei y.á!»
Ách áwé du x̱'ayáx̱ déex̱ shaa kaanáx̱ aawa.aat.
A t'éináx̱ áwé hú ḵu.aa
awlidaak.
Gòon yít ishḵúx̱.
Yan sa.éex' áwé—
l'éiw tóonáx̱ duldákx̱in áwé, x̱'áal' a daa yéi du.úx̱x' áwé—
sdoox tóonáx̱ a yáanáx̱ u.éeych tle k'óox̱' yáx̱ nateech a s'aag̱ée—
áwé wduldaagée
wé x̱áat.

Héh.
Ask'éet' áwé tsáa,
a s'aag̱ée, a s'aag̱ée yáa a díx̱'i yéi
x̱'áal' tóo ayawsitee.
Héil tlax̱ naaliyéide kawus.há.
Yéi kwsigéink' áwé wé x̱'aan, a wanáadei satéen.
«Hé.e, hé.e!
Ha, gwál ch'a yéi yikuwáat' déi wu.aadéen!
Kéi yladaak déi!
De—dei shákdéi dei hóoch'!»
Hou-ou-ou, ch'u yé ḵáa áx' ḵukdahaa yé.
Anax̱ kéi kawdudzihá a.
Ch'as a s'aaḵx'ée sáani, a díx̱'ee áwé a tóot satéen. Tlél daa sá á, {...} ch'a ldakát á
awsik'ít'.
Áwéi-éi-éi ldakát át yéi kdunéek
g̱aax̱.
Gax̱dustí,
ldakát át.

"Tucked under the end of this mound over here."
"Ew! Ew! Ew!
That's the place where my wife was cremated.
Ew!
Her ashes were spread over there.
Climb over two mountains!"
So they climbed over two mountains as he had instructed them.
But Raven, though,
cooked it in a pit behind there.
He was relaxing in a spring.
When it was done cooking—
people used to cook it under the sand, putting skunk cabbage
    all around it—
it gets overcooked in the stove and the bones become
    gooey like tree pitch—
when they would cook
the salmon in a pit.

Heh.
Only when he had gobbled it all up,
the bones, the bones, its backbone,
did he wrap them inside the skunk cabbage.
He didn't dig the pit very far down.
The fire was quite small; the bundle of bones lay there away from the fire.
"Heh-eh! Heh-eh!
Well, some other people probably left some time ago!
Dig it up out of the pit!
Already—it's probably already finished by now!"
O-o-o-oh, every last one of them was out digging.
They dug it up from the pit.
There were only tiny bones, the backbone, lying in the skunk cabbage.
    There was nothing there;
he had gobbled the whole thing up.
Well, every creature, they say,
was crying.
All the creatures
were crying.

Shkalneek x. Yéil ḵa Xóots Wooshdasháay

Háh.
Aadáx̱ áyáa—
aadáx̱ áyáa tsoo a daa yóo toowatán wáa sá ḵukg̱wanoogú.
Haahá, a káx̱ tuwditaan.
Woogoot.
Wooḵoox̱.
Ho-ho-ho.
Du aatx̱úx̱ x̱ánt uwaḵúx̱.
Cháatl yéi adaané áwé, ch'a yéi
 tléil daa sá.
Wáannée sáwé,
«Daak g̱atooḵoox̱ú, ax̱ aatx̱úx̱.
I een daak kuḵaḵóox̱.»
Á áwé wé t'á koowóo,
á áwé.
Wé t'á koowú
tle áwé yú a waḵ{x̱oo} yáx̱—yéi áwé a yáx̱ anateech.
Aag̱áa áwé ash x̱'eiwóos' nukch,
«Daaḵwéit sáwé ách yeelnáḵws'
kélk'?»
«Hehéi!
Tléik', tléik'!
Kéi kg̱isanóok
i tl'íl,
daax̱ yakanadúch't.
K'e x̱át tsú.»
Gwáa.
Wáananée sáwé hú tsú a yáx̱ awsinei
wé aadé sh kalnik yé.
Ajáaḵ áwé, áyú tle wé x'aa yat'éináx̱
 yan ayaawax̱áa.
Á áwé wé du xwáak'oo
wé Yooḵ—
Yooḵk' áwé du xwáak'u.
Tle yaa naḵúx̱u áwé, «Héi!
Yooḵk', k'aandé, haandé i shá!
Wáa sáyá tlél yóo sheeda.ús'kw?

Episode x. Raven and the Brown Bear Couple

Hah.
After this—
after this, he considered what he would get up to next.
Aha, he came up with an idea.
He set out walking.
He set out by boat.
Ho-ho-ho.
He went to his auntie's husband.
The latter was working on getting halibut, but kept coming up with nothing.
Eventually Raven said,
"Let us go out in the boat, my auntie's husband.
I'll take the boat out with you."
So, it was that king salmon tail;
that's what it was.
He kept flashing glimpses of that king salmon tail
to the Male Brown Bear.
Then he kept asking Raven,
"What kind of thing are you using to bait your halibut hooks,
nephew?"
"Hey-hey!
No, no!
You need to pick up
your penis and
cut off the folds of flesh around it.
See, I'm doing it too."
Wow.
Eventually he, too, did likewise,
according to the way Raven was spinning the story.
Once Raven had killed him, he took him ashore in the boat to a secluded place behind a point.
So then his little sidekick,
Cormorant—
Little Cormorant was his little sidekick.
As he was just boating along, Raven called out, "Hey!
Little Cormorant, let's see it; bring your head over here!
How is it that you never wash your hair?

Wéis'x' ágí i daax̲ naa.aat?
I l'óot' daak tsaak̲!»
A l'óot'—a l'óot'—yáax' áwé de agux̲sanóok yá a
l'ut'yax'aanéede, aax̲ aawats'éek',
ash koonanéekg̲aa á
yóo du aat teen.
Aaa.
«K'e x̲'eendataan!»
«Mmmmmmmmm,» yóo áwé du.ax̲ji nukch
yóo shaltláax̲ kaadé.
«Mmmmmmmmm.
Mmm!»
«Haaw.
Yéi áwé yóo x̲'ayatangi át áwé xwáa.
I yeeg̲áa át uwanúk.
Hou-ou.»
Aan a x̲ánt ask̲óox̲ áwé
tláakw x̲'ayak̲áa nukch,
tláakw akanéek.
Áwé tléik'. Tlél yax̲
x̲'akoodul.aax̲.
«Ho-ho-ho.
‹Héende aa kanataan!› akanéek Yook̲k'.
‹Héende aa kanataan!› akanéek.»
«Ho-ho-ho, sagú!
Sagú! Haa goosú i aatx̲úx̲ k̲u.aa?»
«Ho-ho-ho-ho.
Wéi x'aak'w yat'éix' shakals'óow,»
yóo áwé aawasáa.
«Wé x'aak'w ÿat'éix' x̲'akal.eesh,»
yóo áwé aawasáa.
«Áx' shakals'óow,»
yóo aawasáa hóoch k̲u.aa.
«Áx' shakals'óow,
wé x'aak'w yat'éix'.»
Aaa.
«A yoowú {…} wé cháatl,
a yoowú.»
Ayáx̲ áwé.

Is that a horde of lice crawling all over you?
Stick your tongue out!
Its tongue—its tongue—at this point he acted like he was about to put
a louse onto the tip of its tongue, but instead he pinched it off
so Cormorant couldn't go to his auntie
and snitch on him, that's why.
Yes.
"Speak up, why don't you!"
"Mmmmmmmmm," is the noise cormorants always make
out there on the lichen-covered shoals.
"Mmmmmmmmm.
Mmm!"
"Well.
That's the way a sidekick is supposed to talk.
She has been sitting there waiting for you.
Ho-o."
After guiding his canoe to her with Cormorant,
Cormorant kept jabbering on, blabbering on about what had
really happened.
But it was to no avail. No one could make sense of what
Cormorant was saying.
Raven then lied to her, saying, "Ho-ho-ho.
Little Cormorant is saying, 'Put a hook in the water!'
He is saying, 'Put a hook in the water!'"
"Ho-ho-ho, what fun!
What fun! So where is your auntie's husband, anyhow?"
"Ho-ho-ho-ho.
He is behind that little point chopping limbs off trees,"
that's how Raven described it.
"He's stringing fish heads behind that little point,"
that's what he called it.
"He's there cutting tree limbs,"
that's what he called it.
"He's there cutting tree limbs,
behind that little point."
Yes.
Raven said, "Their stomachs {…} the halibut,
their stomachs."
That's how it went.

Hm.
Haahá.
Wé té,
té áwé dax̲ awsit'áa.
«Tlél dutáax' aat.
Tlél dutáax'
ax̲ jig̲eit.
A káx̲ jiyadultáx'ch,
tle dunút'x'w.»
Ash x̲'ayáx̲ áwé tle anút'x'w, tléil ootáax'.
Haaw.
«Yook̲k',
yá ax̲ aat x̲'éit héen lashát!»
Tláakw áwé héen a x̲'éit awlishát.
Mmm.
Du yíx' áwé wdli.úk.
Ch'a koogéiyi jiwdigoot.
Tle hóoch'.
Aag̲aa áwé wéi du xwáak'oo,
«Héi!
Yóo deikée shaltláax̲ kaadé nag̲idak̲een.»
Shaltláax̲ káa yéi nukji át áwé
yook̲.
Du x̲'ayáx̲ áwé shaltláax̲ káa yéi
    yatee yú yook̲.
Aadé akaawanáayi yé áwé.

Shkalneek xi. Yéil k̲a K̲aa Yahaayí Hídi

Haaw.
Ch'a koogéiyi ldakát yéi-éit woogoot.
Áwé ch'a yéi át wugoodí áwé ásíyá
hít át la.áa.
A x̲ánt uwak̲úx̲.
Aag̲áa áwé áa daak̲ uwagút.
Hél lingít á.
Hél dak̲áatk'.
Hé'!
Wé dlèey k̲u.aas, daak̲wéit dleeyí sáwé?

Hm.
Aha.
Stones—
he heated up some stones.
"People don't chew this, auntie.
They don't chew
my catches.
They close their mouths over them and bite down
and just swallow them whole."
Just like he said, she just swallowed them whole; she didn't chew them.
Well.
"Little Cormorant,
grab some water for my auntie!"
He dashed off and got some water for her.
Mmm.
The water was boiling inside her.
She was flailing around erratically.
She was done for.
Then Raven called to his little sidekick,
"Hey!
You should fly over onto those lichen-covered shoals out there."
The cormorant
is a creature that sits on the lichen-covered shoals.
Just as Raven directed him, the cormorant stays out on the
 lichen-covered shoals.
That's where he sent him.

Episode xi. Raven and the House of Souls

Well.
He walked aimlessly all o-over the place.
So, while he was walking about like that, lo and behold,
a house was standing there.
He boated over to it.
Then he walked up there from shore.
There were no people there.
It was a little ghost town.
Heh!
That meat though, what kind of meat was that?

Tle tléil duteen
    yú ganyayíx'.
Á ch'a a daa yóo tuwatánk.
Áwé át ḵutées' ldakát yé.
Há!
Yá át tan át áwé ch'u tle
yóot wujix̱ín.
A káx' áwé woonook.
Áwé ch'a yéi—
ch'a yéi át aayí, ch'a yéi, ch'a yéi,
ch'a yéi át aayée áwé—
á tsú,
ha, áwé yóo—
yóo a kát yéi at daadune át,
át yoo dax̱ kaawasóos.
Ho-ho-ho!
Wéi
dleey—
yataayi át áwé du x̱'eis wududzi.ée.
Du x̱'aseiyée yawdudzi.ín.
Hél lingít yéi oostínch, ch'a aan áwé
akg̱wax̱aa átx' hé du x̱'aseiyée tle yéi daaduné.
Yan shukawditáx'.
Yáax' áwéi
gáani yux̱ woogoot.
Ch'u gáani yux̱ nagóot áwé tle at géide kéi tuwdishát.

Tlél lingít á.

Ch'a yéi a daa kéi tuwdishát.
Jé!
Ch'a át uwagút.
Tlax̱ wáa
dag̱aatáay áwé jánwu.
Jánwu daa.ádi áwé.
Jig̱eit áyá yéi daaduné.
Tle anlinaa íḵde.
Dei áwé yak'éi áwé yóo tsú.

It was hard to see it through the column of smoke
  going up to the smokehole.
So he just thought about it.
He took a look around the whole place.
My!
Something wooden lying there
had just flown off and landed.
He sat on it.
So as he was just—
just like that as he was sitting on it, just so, just so,
as he's sitting there just so—
and furthermore,
now, those—
those worktables on which they prepared things
were teetering and falling.
Ho-ho-ho!
The
meat—
someone had cooked fatty meat for him to eat.
Someone placed it right in front of him.
He couldn't see any people, but nonetheless
someone was preparing dishes for him to eat right in front of him.
He bit down on the end.
At this point
he walked out of the house.
As he was walking outside, it struck him that something was wrong.

There were no people there.

He suddenly realized something about it.
Gee!
He just walked up to it.
Mountain goats
are so very fat.
There were various parts of a mountain goat.
Someone was working on their kill.
Raven then began packing them in bundles down toward the beach.
There's a nice trail like this too.

De áa k̲ux̲ awdigút.

Tsu jig̲eit áyá yéi aa daaduné.

Gwá'!
Du yaagú yíkde yéi awsineiyi aa tléil á.
Yú neilóo á.
Wáa sáyú?
Áwéi ch'a aan tsoo.
Aag̲áa áwé hóoch'i aa[yí]—yáa dax̲.aa,
dax̲.aa daakeit áyá—ách kandu{ll'úx'}ch—{yéi tle} gánde yaa nagút. Tle aan gánde yaa nagúdi áwé
éech' du shanáa wooxeex.

Haa.
A tayeex̲ wudzigeet wé té.
Du shanáa wooxeex.
Tle atx̲ wook̲oox̲.
Goodé sá wook̲oox̲? Tlél wuduskú
goodé sá wukoox̲ú.
K̲aa Yahaayée Hídee á,
yóo áyóo dudlisaayée,
K̲aa Yahaayée.
Tléil lingít á.
K̲aa yahaayée k̲u.aa áyú.

Shkalneek xii. Yéil Sh K̲'awuldaax̲í

Á áwé ch'a yéi át wugoodée,
ch'a yéi át wugoodée áwé tsoo,
tsu a káx̲ woogoot.
Daak̲wéit sáyú tlél x̲wasakú yú a káx̲ woogoodi át.
Du sée k̲udzitee.
Haaw.
He'!
Áwé tle,
tle aawasháa wé a sée.
Áa sh wudlisháa tle.
Hou-ou.

Someone turned around and went back to the house with Raven's bundles.

They were still working on some of their kill.

Gosh!
The ones Raven had put in his boat weren't there.
They were in the house.
How was that possible?
Nonetheless, he made another trip.
Then the final one—the second one,
the second container—the people would use it to {guzzle out of}—he was heading outside with it. As he was just walking outside with it
a boulder went over his head.

Well.
He fell to the ground as the rock passed over.
It went over his head.
Then he boated off.
Where did he go? Nobody knows
where he went.
That's the House of Souls;
that is the name it is known by,
Souls.
There are no people there.
What they are are souls.

Episode xii. Raven Pretends to Build a Canoe

Then as he was just walking around,
as he was just walking around again,
he came across something else.
I don't know what kind of being it was that he came across.
She had a daughter.
Well.
Heh!
So then,
he just married the daughter.
He got her to marry him.
Ho-o-o.

Áwé yéi áyá tle kéi tuwdishát
kei ag̱adaax̱ée,
yaakw ag̱ax̱óot'.
Héh.
{…}
De yánde {yaa a[n]dag̱as.ín, daawdudlitsín}. Awux̱aayée áwé nagútch.
(DAAX'OONDAHÉEN DU JÍN AT'ÁCHT)
Yagiyee yáag̱aa áwé adaax̱ishdi nukch wé aas.
Yaakw áyú ax̱óot'.
Yaakw adáax̱ du chaan yeeyís.
Yóo áwé.
Hó!
{De yax̱ g̱agúdín} áwé aan akanik nukch,
«Hé!
K̲únáx̱—
k̲únáx̱ x̱at jiwdixwétl.
Ax̱ shaawádi, k̲únáx̱ x̱at jiwdixwétl.
De yánde s'é sh kuk̲astáa.»
Éh!
Gánt utáaych.
Ldinax̱k'iyéide a jeet at shulaxéex áwé a nák̲ k̲ut wujixeex.
Goosóo wéi yaakw?
Ash een at koonáa nukch wé du [shát].
Tle, «Ilí! Ilí!»
{Tlákw du ítx̱ yaa [sh] nalx̱án}.
Héil du tuwáa ushgú du een wu.aadée
wéi shaatk'.
Áwé tle ch'a hú
ldakát yéide—
ldakát yéide yóo kawdzigít.
Aan áyá tlax̱ tléil k̲wá dax̱ x̱wasakú
a x̱oo—
a x̱oo.aa á tsú.
Á áyá aadé dax̱ x̱wasikuwu yé áyá, tlax̱ wooyíkg̱aa wuteeyí áyá
yáat kax̱wliník de ch'a hóoch'.
Ách áyáa

So then he came up with the idea
to hew out a canoe,
to adze out a canoe.
Heh.
{...}
She was already {setting out the dishes of food; they nourished their bodies}; after eating the meal, he would leave.
(SLAPS HANDS FOUR TIMES)
He would be out beating on the tree all day long.
He was adzing out a canoe.
He was hewing a canoe for his mother-in-law to sit in.
Or so he said.
Ho!
{Whenever he came back down} he would always say to her,
"Heh!
I'm really—
I'm really tired from working.
Milady, I'm really tired from working.
I'm going to lie down for a while now."
Eh!
He would sleep by the fire.
Sooner or later, once he had used up all of her provisions, he ran off and left her.
Where was that boat?
She always wanted to tag along with him.
He just said, "Don't! Don't!"
{She was always tagging along behind him.}
He did not want the young woman
to come with him.
Just he alone
performed all kinds—
he performed all kinds of acts.
However, I really don't know
some—
some of these stories.
So this is how I know them; since they have been scattered to the four winds
I've told this much and that's all for now.
This is why

uháan yáa G̱unaax̱oo Ḵwáanx̱ haa sateeyí,
haa daa yaa ḵushusigéi ldakát yéide át.
Haa aanéex' áyáa yóo kawdzigít Yéil.
Áa haa wliyéx̱.
Tle ldakát yéide áa haa wliyéx̱.

we who are Dry Bay People
understand all kinds of things.
It was upon our land that Raven performed all these antics.
He shaped us there.
In so many ways, he shaped us there.

Daanawáak X̱’éidáx̱ Tlaagú

Stories by Austin Hammond

FIGURE 14. Austin Hammond in 1984, participating as master storyteller in the eighteenth annual Festival of American Folklife at the Smithsonian Institution in Washington, DC. He wears a ceremonial headdress called a *shakee.át* featuring the image of a kingfisher, alluding to *Tlax̱aneis' Noow* 'Kingfisher Fort', an important site along the Chilkat River in history of the Lukaax̱.ádi clan. Photo by Dane Penland. Courtesy of Sealaska Heritage Institute, PO004, box 12, item 94, and the Ralph Rinzler Folklife Archives and Collections, Center for Folklife and Cultural Heritage, Smithsonian Institution.

AUSTIN HAMMOND, whose principal name was Daanawáak̲, was a leader of the Chilkat Lukaax̲.ádi clan and a child of the Kaagwaantaan. He was born on October 18, 1910, and passed away on July 3, 1993. A biography of Hammond can be found in *Haa K̲usteeyí*.* The texts presented here were recorded on two separate occasions.

The bulk of Hammond's material here comes from a recording made at the KHNS radio station in Haines, Alaska, sometime during the winter of 1985, during which he told an extended tale consisting of four episodes. The premiere of the program in 1986 was broadcast live in the old Klukwan tribal house, with a substantial sound system, so the overflow audience could hear it outside. The audio source was originally labeled "Yeil Kooklak, Raven Legends",† which uses an approximate spelling of *Yéil K̲utlaakw*—translatable as 'Raven Myth(s), Ledgend(s), Tale(s)'—and is a fitting title. We have applied the alternative title «Yéil Yóo Tuwasáagu» "He Whom We Call Raven",‡ which is a line we take to be emblematic of the tone of Hammond's tale taken as a whole, in which Raven is depicted with a sense of grandeur and quasi-theological majesty; the headless relative clause used in this title, *yóo tuwasáagu* 'whom/which we call', is a rarely attested syntactic formulation that Hammond uses numerous times throughout the tale.

This first tale is told in stylized oratorical fashion, with lines of narration frequently punctuated with affirmations *aaa* 'yes' and *aa*, a shortened form of *aaa* that we translate as 'ah'. He makes it clear that in order to tell a story properly, the storyteller's duty is not simply to recount the story, but also to explain what the story means for the listener. Indeed, Hammond was a devout Christian who believed that these Raven stories contained moral teachings that hold true in a Christian context

---

* Dauenhauer and Dauenhauer, *Haa K̲usteeyí*, 207–50.

† MC005, tapes 502, side a, and 502, side b; the audio is also found in MS052, series 077, item 045.

‡ The lines the title is taken from are AH I, i, 6-7.

as surely as they held true in the pre-Christian Tlingit worldview. In particular, Hammond made a point of drawing a comparison between three manifestations of Raven—*Yéil Tlein* 'Great Raven', *Yéil Yádi* 'Raven's Child', and *Yéil Dleit* 'White Raven'—and the Christian Holy Trinity: Father, Son, and Holy Spirit. In recounting the story of Raven's birth to the young woman at the head of the Nass, he goes on to provide a comparison between the birth of Raven to the young virgin woman and the birth of Christ to the Virgin Mary. In the former case, Raven set free the stars, and in the latter case, the Wise Men followed the star to Bethlehem; in the former case, Raven was born not on precious pelts but on lowly moss, and in the latter case, Christ was born not in the comfort of home but in a manger. He also compares the world that lay in darkness before Raven broke the daylight to present-day people who walk metaphorically in darkness, and implicitly likens Raven's breaking of the daylight to the dawn of the light of Christ in the seeker's heart. In telling the story of how Pygmy Owl was persuaded to fly out to sea, set on fire a stick held in his beak, and fly back to the mainland with the fire while enduring the pain of his beak burning away, Hammond repeatedly pointed out that Pygmy Owl performed this sacrificial deed for the good of all the people of the world, and went on to compare it with sacrifices to be made by his grandson he refers to by name as Daax̱ḵuwadéink'.*

Despite the fact that Hammond sometimes drew parallels between these stories and Christian teachings, he tells the legends themselves in classical Tlingit fashion and often goes into great detail. The suite of stories selected by Hammond does not appear to be random; as he tells these four myths, they are largely serious in nature—he avoids the more scurrilous of Raven's adventures—and Hammond finds morals and lessons in each of them. In sum, readers will find of interest both the classical Tlingit legends themselves and the Christian Tlingit worldview in which Hammond has embedded them.

Hammond told the second tale included here, «Yéil Du Loowú Kei Wdusyeigí» "Raven Gets His Nose Yanked Off", during a conference on Alaska Native art, held at the Portland Art Museum, May 15–17, 1989.† At the end of the first day of the conference, Hammond told this discrete tale to explain the form and meaning of an art object that depicts Raven's detached nose.‡ On the recording, K̲'óots'i, Anna Katzeek, gives a live line-by-line English translation, often with additional

* It is not clear what specific task Daax̱ḵuwadéink' was to set out on and endure for the betterment of the Tlingit people; a likely possibility is participation in a legal battle over rights to land, hunting, and fishing.

† MC005, tape 81, side a.

‡ We were unable to identify the specific art object in question. Video recordings were taken of a significant portion of the conference (held in SHI's archive, MC029), but the object and storytelling relevant to this text do not appear to have been captured on video.

explanatory commentary. She usually speaks during a pause following Hammond's phrases, but at times the two speak simultaneously. The result is a dynamic performance that showcases Katzeek's fluency in both languages and with her sometimes adding details drawn from her own distillation of the story that differ somewhat from what Hammond had just said. This amounts to a bilingual oral-literary performance involving Hammond and Katzeek as side-by-side co-performers, rather than simply a performance by Hammond that Katzeek interpreted. Also present were Katherine Mills (Yakwx̱aan Tláa), Amy Marvin (K̲ooteen), Jimmie George (Wóochx̱kaduhaa), Lydia George (Kudeisgé), Judson Brown (Shaakakóoni), and David Katzeek (Kingeistí),* all of whom were invited, in addition to Hammond, by the Portland Art Museum to provide information on objects held in the Axel Rasmussen Collection. Everyone present can be heard laughing as this story unfolds. Much of the conference was recorded by Sealaska Heritage Foundation and Museum staff (probably by Tim Wilson).

For the sake of comparison, the tale is presented below in two forms: first (AH 11a), it is transcribed as heard on the recording with Hammond's Tlingit and Katzeek's English in the spoken order and form without any translation supplied by the editors; second (AH 11b), the Tlingit lines of Hammond's tale are presented without Katzeek's interpretation and with the usual more-or-less literal translation provided by the editors. The Tlingit transcriptions of Hammond's Tlingit are identical in both of these presentations, though the line numbers and translations differ.

On the recording, a little while after Hammond and Katzeek complete the story, Katherine Mills can be heard saying that there is a song that goes with the Raven-nose object, and the song is then sung by her and K̲ooteen, Amy Marvin. Mills states that the song was composed by her great-uncle K̲aalg̲aa, Charlie Charles.

* David Katzeek was Anna Katzeek's son and a leader of the Shangukeidí. Before his passing on October 28, 2020, he served as a key fluent consultant for this volume, assisting Geiger and Leer with translating many stories in this volume.

I. Yéil Yóo Tuwasáagu

Shkalneek i. Yéil ḵa G̱anook

Aa, yáa yeedát
ax̱ tuwáa sigóo tsoo
a daa x̱'ax̱wdataanée,
aaa, yá lingit.aanée
shux'áa a daa yéi jinanéi
yáa Yéil
yóo tuwasáagu,
du káanitín.
Aa, yéi áyá kdunéek
ax̱ léelk'úch.
Wooshkáakeiydagwéich yéi duwasáakw.
Hóoch áyá x̱aan aklaneegéen.
Aaa, yáa deikéex'
át has yaawagoowu yé,
aa, aag̱áa áwé woosh kát has yawdigóo.
Aaa, yéi kunaaliyéide áwé awsiteen du x̱ánde yaa naḵúx̱u yáa Yéilch,
áwé tle ḵaa x̱ánde wooḵoox̱.
Aag̱áa áyáa
a x̱ánt ḵóox̱ áyá aawa.éex', «Ax̱ káani!
Wa.á ákyáa?»
«Aaa, x̱át áyáa.»
«Ax̱ káani,
yak'éi x̱á ix̱wsateení.»
Aaa, woosh een yóo s x̱'adli.átk.

I. He Whom We Call Raven

Episode i. Raven and Petrel

Ah, now
I would again like
to speak about
when he whom we call
Raven
first set to work
on this world
with his brother-in-law.
Ah, this is how it was told
by my grandfather.
Jim David is his name.
It was he who used to tell it to me.
Yes, far out to sea,
where they were traveling around in canoes,
yes, they pulled up alongside one another then.
Raven could see someone in the distance paddling toward him,
so he paddled toward the guy.
Then,
when he paddled up to him he called out to him, "My brother-in-law!
Is that you?"
"Yes, it's me."
"My brother-in-law,
it's sure nice to see you."
Yes, they conversed with each other.

Ách haa een kadulneek át yá shkalneek.
Aaa, tlél yáa
aadéi woosh yát has x̱'awdliyuwu yéyáx̱
g̱unéi yawuxeex.
Woosh kaanáx̱ toowú datí yáx̱ áyá g̱unéi
s akawliník x̱aan.
Ách áwé a yáx̱ kakḵwalaneek tsoo.
Aaa, yéi áwé yoo x̱'ayatánk yáa Yéil,
«Ax̱ káani,
[goot'a]gáan sáyá ḵiydzitee?»
Aaa, aag̱áa áwé yéi yaawaḵaa hú ḵu.aa,
«Ch'u kaat'tín x̱á ḵux̱wdzitee.»
Aaa, yáa kaat'
yéi s ayasáagu át
ldakát átx̱ áyá átx̱ dulyéix̱.
Áwé aan ḵuwdzitee yóo sh kalneek.
Aag̱áa hú ḵwá yéi yaawaḵaa wé Yéil, «Há.
Atk'átsk'oo síyá wa.á yeisú!
X̱át ḵu.aa ch'ul Haayeetl'óoḵk'u daak sh ulhaashjí áyá ḵux̱wdzitee—
aaa, ldakát át ch'ul daa sá
gági uxeexjée.»
Áwé yéi aawasáa,
«Ch'a Haayeetl'óoḵk'utín ḵux̱wdzitee.»
Aaa, woosh kaanáx̱ yoox̱'al.átgi yáx̱ áyá s x̱'awli.aat.
Aag̱áa áwé wé—
wé du káani ḵwá ch'u tle
yóode kei ayaawax̱ích du yaagú.
«Wa.é shgé ax̱ shukát ḵiydzitee.»
Ách áwé du déx̱'de wooshee
du s'áaxug̱áa.
Ḵugwáas' S'áaxw yóo áwé wduwasáa.
Tle sháax̱ awditee.
Sháax̱ ax̱datée áyá tlax̱ tlél tsu goo sá duteen.
Tsu du yaagú taká tlél ooteen yáa Yéil.
Aaa, aag̱áa áwé tsá sh daa yoo tuditánk,
aaa, aadé ḵwáaḵt yaawaḵayi yá.
Aaa, akoolx̱éitl' du tóo yéi yaa naneen.
Aa, aag̱áa áwé
yéi áyá haa nateech, yóo áwé x̱at daayaduḵáa nuch.

This story is a means by which principles are conveyed to us.
Yes, the event didn't
begin with them
addressing each other as kin.
They began telling me the story with Raven and his brother-in-law each feeling that they were better than the other.
So I will tell it like that again.
Yes, that's how Raven spoke,
"My brother-in-law,
about when were you born?"
Yes, then his brother-in-law said,
"I was born a contemporary of primitive digging sticks."
They used what they call a
digging stick
for every purpose.
So his story was that he was born a contemporary of these digging sticks.
Then Raven said, "Hah.
Well now, you're just a boy yet!
I, however, was born before the Little-Liver-Beneath-Us floated itself out—
yes, before anything at all
emerged."
That's what he called it,
"I was born a contemporary of the Little-Liver-Beneath-Us."
Yes, they were conversing in such a way as to verbally dominate each other.
So then,
his brother-in-law
whipped his boat around in a different direction.
"You must have been born before me."
So he reached behind his back
for his hat.
It was named the Fog Hat.
He put it on his head.
When he put it on his head nobody could see anything anywhere.
Raven couldn't even see the bottom of his boat.
Yes, then at last he admitted to himself,
yes, that he had misspoken.
Yes, fear was creeping into him.
Ah, since that time,
that's how we've been; that's what they always tell me.

K̲wáak̲t yax̲took̲éiní[n] áwé tsá
sh daa yoo tutudatangi nuch.
Aaa, yéi áwé woonee wé Yéil.
Akoolx̲éitl' du káa yaa gatée
aawa.éex' du káani,
«Ax̲ káani.
Ax̲ káani.
Wa.é shgé ch'a ax̲ shukát k̲iydzitee.»
Aag̲áa áyá
tlél tsu óo ushxweix̲k hú k̲u.aa.
Aaa, du yaagú yíkt áa.
Aa, aag̲áa áyá
ch'u yáa sh wulk'áatl'i áyá akoolx̲éitl' k̲únáx̲ du káa yéi yaa naneen.
Tsu aawa.éex' du káani, «Ax̲ káani,
ax̲ káani,
aa, wa.é shgé ch'áakw k̲iydzitee ax̲ shukát.»
Aag̲áa áyá yáa—
yá k̲áa k̲wa ch'u tle
sh kawjix'aak̲w.
Tlél tsu g̲unéi unúkx̲.
Aaa, áyá g̲aax̲déin du toowú woonee
yáa Yéil.
Du satóox' yéi woonee,
«Ax̲ káanée-ée,
ax̲ káanée-ée,
wa.á sgí ch'áakw k̲iydzitee.
L daa sá ux̲ané,» gíwé g̲aax̲ yáx̲ woonee
 du satú.
«Ax̲ káanée-ée.
Ax̲ káanée-ée.
Wa.á sgí ch'áakw k̲iydzitee.»
Aag̲áa áyá du yaagú x̲'atóot uwashée,
yá du t'ak̲kát wulihaashi,
«Wáa sáyá x̲'ayeek̲á, wáa sá?»
Sháatx̲ kei awditée.
Goosú wé k̲uwdagwáas'i?
Du kaax̲ kei aawadák̲.
«Ax̲ káani, wa.é sgí ch'áakw k̲iydzitee ax̲ shukát.»
Yéi áyá haa nateech, yóo áyá x̲aan kadulneek.

Only when we speak out of line
do we really consider our behavior.
Yes, this is what happened to Raven.
As fear was coming over him
he called out to his brother-in-law,
"My brother-in-law,
my brother-in-law,
you must have been born before me."
All the while
Petrel didn't even utter a peep in reply to him.
Yes, he was sitting in his boat.
Ah, then,
as Petrel stayed silent here, great fear was coming over Raven.
Again he called to his brother-in-law, "My brother-in-law,
my brother-in-law,
ah, you must have been born long before me."
So then this—
this man just
went limp.
He didn't even budge.
Yes, Raven
felt like crying.
It crept into his voice,
"My brother-in-la-aw,
my brother-in-la-aw,
you must have been born long ago.
I'm not doing anything," his voice must have been quavering
as if he were crying.
"My brother-in-la-aw,
my brother-in-la-aw,
I suppose you were born long ago."
Then Petrel put his hand on the inside of the gunwale of Raven's boat,
which was floating alongside him,
"What are you carrying on about, huh?"
He took his hat off.
Where did the fog go?
The fog lifted off him.
"My brother-in-law, you must have been born long before me."
This is how we are, so I'm told the story.

Woosh kaanáx̱ yoox̱'adatánk,
ách áwé a x̱ánt x̱at yadujeeyín,
«Hél lingít kaanáx̱ yoo x̱'eetángiḵ.
Ch'a wáa sá Lingít
át kawdiyaa, a káax' át ikandayá.»
Aaa, áyáa ax̱ sháan tóo woogei.
Ách áwéi ch'a oowayáa daak sh x̱wadlixixi yáx̱ x̱at nateech.
Aaa, yáa yeedát yáa Yéil,
a ítnáx̱ áwé tle wóoshtin yéi s jiwdinei.
Wóoshtin át has kawdiyaa.
Aaa, yáa át has kawdiyaayi yéix' tle yá lingit.aaní daax'
    yéi s jeewanei.
G̱unéi s awliyéx̱.
Aa, yáa
gíl'x̱ siteeyi yá
l'éiw áyá kunag̱eey táa yéi s ana.eich.
X'aa, gíl'x̱ nasteech wáayteeyi yá,
wáaytiyéix' sá téix̱ nasteech.
Yéi áyá yaa s analyéx̱.
Aaa, yéi kunaaliyéitx̱ áwé s ooltínch, yak'éi.
Aa, aag̱áa áyá g̱unéi s awliyéx̱ yáa aas tsóo,
ldakát yáa aas woosh g̱uwanáadei,
á tsóo.
Aaa, yéi x̱aan has akanéek ax̱ léelk'w,
«Uháan haa shuká áyá yáa aas.
X̱'aséikw a tóo yéi yatee.»
Aag̱áa yá gaaw shux'áa yaa s aklayéix̱ ḵwá
    tlél x̱'aséikw a tú.
Aa, áwé
yáa a k'iyee kakg̱wa.aa chookán
ḵa yáa ḵ'eikaxwéin,
keishísh, ch'áal', ldakát át
áyá át has ooltínch.
Aaa, ḵukawjig̱ít ḵu.aa áyá, tlél ch'u yéi kunaaliyéitx̱ duteen nuch.
Áwé a daa yoo s tuli.átk wáa sá s agux̱saneeyí.
Áwé wéi Yéil áwé
yéi kunaaliyéitx̱ altíni
ldakát,
aag̱áa áwé a daa yoo tuwatánk.

That's why people used to admonish me about
dominating one another verbally,
"Don't try to dominate another person verbally.
However the Tlingit people
go about their lives, use this as a guide to conduct yourself."
Yes, this has really been on my mind.
That's why it always seems that I have let myself down.
Yes, now Raven and Petrel
worked together after that.
They journeyed about together.
Yes, at the places where they journeyed about,
  they worked on this world.
They began to shape it.
Yes,
in cliffy areas
they would put sand at the head of the cove.
Points are cliffy in some places;
in other places they are rocky.
This is how they were shaping it.
Yes, they kept gazing at it from afar; it was wonderful.
Ah, then they started making the trees as well,
all different kinds of trees
as well.
Yes, this is what my grandfather tells me,
"The trees came before us.
There is life within them."
At this time, as they were first beginning to create them,
  there was no life in them.
Ah, so,
they kept gazing at
the grass that was to grow at the base of the trees
and the flowers,
alders, willows, everything.
Yes, but it was dark, so these things could not be seen from afar.
So they considered what they were going to do about it.
Now, as Raven
was looking at it all
from afar,
he was contemplating it at this time.

Aaa, yá aanáx̱ has ayawliyex̱i yá,
kunag̱eey,
áa yéi s aya.óo.
Yakwdeiyí haa Lingídich yéi yasáakw.
A x̱oo.aa áwé x'áat' a yakáa yax̱ satee
óoxjaa yanaa.
Ldakát woosh g̱uwanáade
x̱'al.át,
aaa, yá kunag̱eey.
Á ḵu.aa yéi x̱aan kawduwaneek
ax̱ léelk'úch,
«A yáanáx̱ yayeeḵoox̱ú yakwdeiyí, i káa ayawdateeyí,
tlél naliyéi kg̱eeḵoox̱, i een áa yax̱ gugashx̱éen i yaagú.»
Aag̱áa áwé yéi x̱at daayaḵá, «A táanáx̱ yan yiḵoox̱ú ḵwás
yei ikg̱wanéex̱.
Yéi áyá yatee yá átk'.aheen woosh g̱uwanáadei,»
yóo áwé x̱at daayaḵá.
Kunag̱eeyx̱ sitee, woosh g̱uwanáade x̱'al.át
daaḵw.aa óoxjaa yís sá.
Aaa, yéi áyá ḵunáax̱ daaḵ has akaníkch x̱aan.
Aaa, ách áwé yeedát ax̱ dachx̱anx'isáanich has akg̱wa.áax̱ yá
shkalneek, ách áwé ax̱ tuwáa sigóo ḵunáax̱ daaḵ kax̱aníkji.
Hasdu kagéyís áyá a daa yéi jix̱ané ax̱ dachx̱anx'isáani,
aaa, ch'u tle l ax̱ gaawút koodaxéetji.
«Aaa, yá kunageey tséi x'wán a yáanáx̱ yeeḵóox̱,
yáa óoxjaa aadé wduwanugu yé káax'
a t'éinax̱.áx' yei ikg̱waneex̱í.»
Aa, ách áwé ax̱ léelk'úch x̱aan has aklaneek.

Shkalneek ii. Yéil ḵa Kei.á

Aag̱áa áyá has ayatéen
yáa hít át la.aa yá.
Aaa, áwé a daa yóo tuwatánk,
ḵa awsikóo a yeex' yéi yateeyi át,
aaa, yá át la.aa hít.
Du sháttin ḵa du sée
ḵa yáa du kéilk' du daa yoo jikwli.atgi—.
Du een át kawdiyaa.

Yes, they had placed
coves
along the course they took in shaping the landscape.
Canoe trails are what our Tlingit people call them.
Some of them have an island located out in front of them,
providing shelter from the wind.
Yes, these coves
have entrances facing
all different directions.
But this is what I was told
by my grandfather,
"When you're passing by a canoe trail and a storm overtakes you,
you won't get far; your boat will capsize."
Then he told me, "But if you come ashore at the head of the cove,
you will be safe.
This is how all different aspects of faith are,"
he told me.
They are coves, with entrances facing in different directions
suitable for whichever direction the wind blows from.
Yes, that is how they always explained it to me.
Yes, that is why my grandchildren will hear this story now;
that is why I like to explain it.
It is for the benefit of my dear grandchildren that I perform this labor,
yes, before my time is up.
"Be sure not to bypass the cove;
proceed according to the way the wind is blowing;
you will come to safety behind it."
Yes, this is why my grandparents told the story to me.

Episode ii. Raven and the Daylight

At that time they could see
where this house was standing.
Yes, he was contemplating,
and he knew what was inside of,
this house that was standing there.
With his wife and his daughter
and his nephew who attended to her—.
The nephew moved about with her.

Aag̲áa áyá ts’ootaat has shax̲dak̲éenín áyá,
aaa, shóot uda.aakch
wé sdu kéilk’.
Aag̲áa tsá daak ugootch wé du káak.
Atx̲ áwé du shát daak g̲agúdín áwé yéi ayanask̲éich du shát,
«Haa sée haat g̲agoot déi,
aaa, yáa héen ax̲danaayí.»
Ách áwé wdudzikóo haa Lingídich
tlél ch’a koogéiyi héen áyá tudanáayin ch’áakw,
hél yá naadaayi aa héen.
Goon yóo áwé duwasáakw.
Kei kduháaych, a táatx̲ áwé héen duyáa.
Aaa, áwé a yís ag̲ax̲oox̲ch du sée,
aaa, «Wé héen ax̲danaa déi haa sée!»
A tóonáx̲ áyá x̲’aséikw haa jee yéi yatee,
aa, yá yak’éiyi aa héen.
Aaá, aag̲áa áyá
áwé wé sdu sée jeet ax̲sa.ín—
t’aaw áwé du jeewú—
t’aaw
a táax̲ yei altsák̲ch.
A daatx̲ yóot kawujeexóo wé héen, aag̲áa áwé yak’éi.
Yáa a daax̲ wugoowú k̲u.aa áwé,
l ushik’éiyi aa héen áwé.
Aag̲áa yóode koodusxáaych, tsu yak’éiyi aa héeng̲aa nagútch.
Aaa, yéi áyá yatee haa k̲usteeyí.
Shayadihéini aa
yá haa k̲usteeyí tóox’ hél ayáx̲x̲ haa ustí.
Aaa, a daax̲ kei g̲wéich yá t’aaw yóo tuwasáagu,
wáaytiyi aa sá a daax̲ yóox̲ kagwáatl.
Áyá lingít éex̲ dashee.
Yáa yeedát a daa yoo x̲’ax̲aatangi aa gwál ax̲ dachx̲anx’isáani eedé gux̲dashée.
Ách áwé kx̲anéek,
aaa, k̲aa een kax̲anéek, k̲unáax̲ daak̲ kax̲aníkch.
Gu.aal kwshé a daatx̲ yóot kawugwáadlik̲.
Aaa, aag̲áa áwé kei gux̲lagéi i k̲usteeyí.
Yak’éiyi yéi ikakg̲waháa.

At that time, when they would get up in the morning
their nephew
would always make a fire.
Only then would his uncle come out.
Then, when his wife came out, he would say to his wife,
"Let our daughter come here now;
yes, let her drink water."
That is why our Tlingit people knew that
it wasn't just any old water that we would drink long ago,
not the water that flows in streams.
It's called springwater.
They would dig out the spring and pack water from it.
Yes, this was what she called her daughter over for,
yes, "Let our daughter drink water now!"
Through this we have life,
ah, this good water.
Yes, then,
whenever he would give water to their daughter—
he had a feather—
he would stick
the feather down inside the water.
If the water rolled off it, then the water was okay.
If it soaked in, though,
it was bad water.
Then they would dump it out and he would go back
    to fetch good water.
Yes, that is how our way of life is.
Many of us
are unrighteous in the way we live.
Yes, sometimes what we call a feather soaks up the water; but
at other times the water rolls off.
This is what helps people.
What I am talking about now might help my
    dear grandchildren.
That is why I am telling it,
yes, I tell people; I keep explaining it.
I hope the water rolls off and away from the feather.
Yes, then your life will shine brightly.
You will find yourself in a good place.

Aaa, yóo áyá x̱aan kadunik nooch.
Aaa, áwéi
wé Yéil
áa neil góot áwé altín.
Hú ḵu.aa áyá yáa Yéil, Yéil Dleit áyáa.
Tle du tóonáx̱ akdziganéyáx̱ yatee, tlél duteen.
Lingítch yéi yasáakw ḵaa yakg̱wahéiyagu.
Tlél duteen nuch.
Yéi áwé wootee hú, wéi Yéil.
Aag̱áa áwé ooltínch,
aa, wé du sée aadé a daa yéi jine yá.
Hóoch ḵu.aasgíwé a daa yoo tuwatánk wé Yéil,
aaa, yá yées shaawát,
yá daak gutji aa.
Eetkaadé s na.áat áwé át uwagút.
Ḵákw áwé yú.á, gúx'aax̱ sitee ḵákw.
Áx' áx̱ ÿas.aa yá—
anax̱ áx̱ ÿas.aa yá áa yéi yatee.
Áyá yáa
haa Lingídich wusikóo yá yán.
Aaa, yá gítg̱aa yóo tuwasáakw.
Áwé áx̱ ayakaawatée.
A tóode áwé ajeewanáḵ du latseenée
yá daak gug̱agut aa yá yées shaawát jiyís.
Yá héen a kaax̱ agux̱danáa.
Áwé yan aawatán tsoo.
Aag̱áa áwé áa daaḵ góot áwé altín.
Aaa, has shawdiḵée wé ts'ootaat.
Daak has áat áwé yú ḵáa tsu yéi yaawaḵaa,
«Góok déi haa sée daak g̱agoot,
yá héen ax̱danaa.»
A táax̱ áwé yei altsáḵch wé t'aaw.
Aa, «Tlél wáa sá utí,» yú.á,
«Yak'éi yá héen.»
Ách áwé a jeet aa wdudzi.ín du sée jee.
Sdu sée adana nóok áwé
shux'áa aayí tlél wáa sá utí.
Déix̱ aa áwé tsá aawanóot'
wé gítg̱aa.

Yes, that is what I'm told.
Yes,
when Raven
went inside, he was studying the situation.
But this Raven here, this was White Raven.
It was like he was transparent; he was invisible.
The Tlingit call it a human spirit.
He was invisible.
That's how he turned out, Raven.
At that time he would watch,
ah, the way that the father cared for his daughter.
I suppose Raven had designs on her,
yes, this young woman,
the one who kept coming out from her room.
When they went to the room, Raven approached.
It was a basket, they say; a basket was used as a dipper.
The place where he kept peeking into the dipper—
he was there at the place where he kept peeking into it.
Now,
our Tlingit people knew about hemlock.
Yes, a hemlock needle is what we call it.
He maneuvered the needle into place along the side of the dipper.
He released his power into it
for this young woman that was to come out.
She was going to drink water from the dipper.
So Raven set the dipper down again.
Then, when he retreated, he watched.
Yes, they got up that morning.
Once they came out, the man again said,
"Go ahead now, let our daughter come out
and drink water."
He would stick the feather into the water.
Ah, "It's alright," he said,
"The water is fine."
So they handed some to his daughter.
As their daughter was drinking it,
the first one was alright.
She didn't swallow
the needle until she sampled the second dipperful.

Aagáa áyá yéi yaawak̲aa wéi shaawát,
wé yées shaatk',
«At x̲waanóot' a kaadáx̲.»
Áwé yan awsi.ín.
Aagáa áwé wé k̲áa,
wé du sháttin a daa yoo s x̲'ali.átk, «Wáa sá yá t'aawch tlél kooneek?»
Wé sdu sée k̲wá dák̲de woogoot tle wé sdu eetí kaadéi.
«Wáa sá yáa t'aawch tlél kooneek,
aaa, yá héen l ayáx̲x̲ usteeyí?»
Á áwé
yá a tóox̲ ayakawuteeyí a tóode ajeewanag̲i
yáa l.ultook,
yóo tuwasáakw Lingítch,
Dleit K̲áach k̲wáwé *spirit*
yóo yasáakw.
Áwé a tóode ajeewanák̲.
Ách áwé tlél wé t'aawch kooneek.
Aaa,
aagáa áwé
eetkaadéi unayéix̲ áwé
ch'a altín
aadé át has kawdiyaayi yá.
Yáax' áwé tsá
yéi yaawak̲aa,
«Haa sée x̲áayá kát yat.áa.
Goonáx̲ sáyá?
Tlél tsu k̲áa á.
Hél tsu goonáx̲ sá du x̲ánx̲ oogoot.»
K̲a yá shkalneek
aaa, Dikyáank̲áawu shkalneegí áyá.
A daa aniyilgeen, ax̲ x̲oonx'ée,
yáa shkalneek
Dikyáank̲áawu aadé k̲uwdziteeyi yá.
Á áyá yáa Lingítch kalaneek,
aaa, yáa yées shaatk'
du káx' yat.áa.
Aagáa áyá a daat has tukawdixíl' hasdu sée.
Aagáa áwé du éesh k̲u.aa tlax̲ yáa x̲'alitseeni aa at doogú áwé
daak yéi awsinée,

Then the woman said,
the young virgin,
"I swallowed something from the dipper."
So she set it down.
Then the man
and his wife talked it over, "Why didn't the feather predict it?"
Their daughter went back into their room, though.
"Why didn't the feather predict
that the water was unsuitable?"
That's what it was
that he released into it as he maneuvered it along the inside of the dipper:
purity;
this is what we Tlingit call it.
White people, though,
call it spirit.
That's what he released into it.
That is why the feather didn't predict it.
Yes,
and then,
when she had retreated to her room,
he just watched
what they were going about doing.
Finally
he said,
"Our daughter is pregnant.
Where from?
There's not a man around.
Nobody ever comes to her from anywhere."
And this story,
yes, is the story of God.
Consider the story,
my friends,
of how God was born.
This is the story that the Tlingit tell;
yes, this virgin
was pregnant.
At this time they were worried about their daughter.
Then her father brought out
the most precious furs

wé du sée a káa yatnag̱a.oot.
Áx̱ akawsiyàa.
Aaa, tléik'—
tléil yei ḵoosteech wé atk'átsk'u.
Deisgwach a kát a yáanáx̱ ḵuyaawaháa.
Tsu ch'a g̱óot.aa.
Tsu tléik'.
X'oon.aa yéi s anasnée sáyáa—
yáa shawat.shaan át áa—
hú áyá
yéi yaawaḵaa,
«Aax̱ yéi niysaní.
Aax̱ yéi niysaní.
Yú dáaḵde aa ng̱agoodée yihwáan.
Yáa yán yíx' yéi yatee s'íx'g̱aa, haat yéi ysaní.
Kúlt'u yáx̱ dag̱aatee,
kúlt'u yáx̱.
Haat yéi ysaní.»
Ách áwé aag̱áa aawagoot.
Aaa, haat yéi wduwdzinée.
Áwé tsá áa yéi wduwa.oo.
A káx' áyá tsá yatwoo.oo.
Aa, yáa atk'átsk'u a káa ḵuwdzitee.
Ách áwé Lingítch átx̱ layéix̱ s'íx'g̱aa,
ch'áakw,
aaa, yáa atk'átsk'u a káa ḵuwusteeyéech.
Aaa, áwé k'e yáa—ḵúx̱de át ayilg̱ín
yá a kaax̱ haa een sh kadulnik aa.
Dikyáanḵáawu du Yéet
yei ḵukg̱wastee nóok,
ldakát áyá a x̱oox̱ yaa ana.át
yá hítx',
yá klig̱éiyi aa hítx',
áa yatnag̱a.oo.
Áyá yax̱ shayawlihík.
Tlél goo sá
ḵoostí.
X'oon.aa x̱oox̱ ayoo.áat sáwé yéi yaawaḵaa wé ḵáa,
«Yóot áwé

so his daughter could birth the child upon them.
He spread them out.
Yes, but no—
the child kept refusing to be born.
Eventually it was overdue in her womb.
They laid another skin down.
Still, no luck.
After they had put so many skins down—
there was an old woman sitting there—
it was she
who said,
"Remove them.
Remove them.
One of you go up into the woods.
There is moss in the hemlock tree; bring some here.
They are like *kúlt'*,
like *kúlt'*.
Bring some here."
So someone went to get it.
Yes, they brought it back.
Then finally the moss was put there.
It was finally upon this that she had the baby.
Ah, the child was born on it.
That is why the Tlingit use moss,
because long ago,
yes, this child was born on it.
Yes, for example—look back on
the Book from which we are told the stories.
When the Son of God
was about to be born
they were walking in the midst of
these houses,
these beautiful houses,
to give birth there.
But they were all full.
There was
nowhere.
After they had walked among so many houses, the man said,
"Over there

gawdáan daakahídi k̲a wasóos,
a sá áwé áwoo á.»
Ách áwé aadé s woo.aat.
A ya.áak yéi awsinee,
aa, wé du éeshch.
Wé Joseph yóo tuwasáakw.
Aag̲áa áyá yan asnée áwé tsáa
a káa yatwoo.oo.
A káa k̲uwdzitee wé atk'átsk'u.
Yéi áyá yatee haa shkalneegí, tlél yá klig̲éiyi yéix' k̲uwustee,
aaa, yáa—
yá Yéil.
Aaa, yá s'íx'g̲aa káx' áyá tsá yatwoo.oo.
Ách áwé yéi yee daayax̲ak̲á, a daa aniyilg̲een haa k̲usteeyí.
Shiyadihéini aa a géide yoo x̲'ali.átk
haa shkalneegée.
De ch'a á áwé wé X'úx' kaax̲ haa een kadulneek—
yáa X'úx' kaax̲.
Ách haa een kalanik átch haa een k̲unáax̲ daak̲ kaníkch.
Aaa, yáa yeedát yá shkalneek,
aaa, yáa neilx' yéi dag̲aateeyi át shagóon áyáa.
Yá Yéilch—
aa, yá du yádi k̲uwdzitee.
Yéil Tlein
yóo wtuwasáa. Nás'k áyá yatee yáa saa:
Yéil Dleit,
Yéil Tlein,
Yéil Yádi áyá k̲uwdzitee.
Hóoch áyá tsáa a daa yéi jeewanei
yá neilx' yéi dag̲aateeyi yá k̲óok:
K̲utx̲.ayanahá Daakeit,
k̲a yáa Dís Daakeit—yóo tuwasáakw yá dís—
k̲a yáa gag̲aan
a daakeidí yík,
k̲ei.á
a daakeidí yík.
Yóo áyá x̲aan has aklaneek.
Aadéi yá lingit.aanituk̲wáani eedé gux̲dashee yé áyá a daa yéi jiné yáa Yéil.
Ách áwé yee een k̲unáax̲ daak̲ kax̲aníkch

is a horse and cow stable;
their voices are coming from there."
So they went there.
His father,
ah, prepared a place for it.
We call him Joseph.
Only after he had prepared the manger
did she have her child on it.
The boy was born on it.
That's how our story is; he wasn't born in a nice fancy place,
yes, this—
this Raven.
Yes, she ended up giving birth on moss.
That's why I am telling you folks, consider our culture.
Many people are speaking out against
our stories.
This is precisely what we are told from the Book—
from this Book.
The Book that tells us the story explains it to us.
Yes, now this story,
yes, it is the history of the boxes in the house.
Raven—
ah, he had a child.
Great Raven
is what we named him. There are three names:
White Raven,
Great Raven,
Raven Child, who was born.
It was this last one who got to work on procuring
the boxes inside the house:
the Container of Stars,
and the Container of the Moon—this is what we call the moon—
and the sun
in its container,
the daylight
in its container.
This is how they tell the story to me.
Raven was working on a way to assist the people of the world.
That is why I keep explaining this to you,

sh daa anax̲toolg̲einéet.
Aaa, yá atk’átsk’u k̲ug̲astéedáx̲,
aaa, yáa
k̲óok—.
Tle du yoox̲’atángitín áwé tléwnlé k̲uwusteeyí.
Yá k̲uwusteeyí áyá yáa—
yá shawat.shaan jeet wududzinúk.
Yá shawat.shaanch áwé siháan.
Aag̲áa áwé ayalatíni áyá du waak̲x’isáani át kawduwagwáatl.
«Ée!
Cha Yéil waak̲ x̲áashé!»
yóo áwé x̲’ayak̲á hú k̲u.aa.
Aag̲áa áyá yá atk’átsk’u k̲u.aa—
éh!—du toowúch aklax̲’aal.
«Wáa sáwé ch’a l sh yilk’áatl’!»
Aaa, ách áwé
yáa k̲utx̲.ayanahá áyáa shux’aanáx̲,
aaa, yá g̲unéi dag̲áat’ awdzig̲áax̲.
Yú du jínx’i sáani a yinaadé kéi awlitsúw yá k̲óok.
Áyá du léelk’w,
yáa ank̲áawux̲ siteeyi yá aanyádi,
áyá yéi ayawsik̲aa,
«Ax̲ dachx̲ánk’i jeet yisa.ín, aan ashkang̲alyádi wé k̲óok.»
Aaa, ách áwé du jeet wududzi.ín yá k̲óok.
Aaa, áyáa
aan ashkoolédi áyá
yanáatx̲ ayaawax̲út’.
Yáa gaanéili áyá k̲udzitee.
Anax̲ áwé tle gáant kaawaxíx yú k̲utx̲.ayanahá.
Tle yú xáats’x̲ wulixáat’.
Aa, áyá Dikyáank̲áawu Shkalneegí áyá.
Aaa, yá nás’ginác̲ yateeyi yóo yaak̲usgéix’i,
has ax̲satéen,
aaá, aag̲áa áwé yéi s yaawak̲aa,
«Haa G̲aneex̲í k̲uwdzitee.
Haa G̲aneex̲í k̲uwdzitee.
Téengé yú k̲utx̲.ayanahá yóox̲ yawlixáat’?
Aaa, yá Éesh yóo s ayasáagu yáx̲ áwé yawlixáat’ yú.á,
k̲utx̲.ayanahá tlein.»

so that we can examine ourselves.
Yes, after the boy was born,
yes, this
box—.
He was soon to be born with his words.
When he was born,
they handed him to this old woman.
The old woman was holding him.
And then as she was looking at his face, his little eyes were rolling around.
"Ew!
Now those must be Raven's very eyes!"
she said.
But the child, though—
eh! he was chewing her out in his mind.
"Why don't you just shut up!"
Yes, so
he first began crying for these stars,
yes, once he started crawling.
He lifted his little hands up toward the box.
So his grandfather,
a nobleman who was the headman,
said,
"Hand my dear grandchild the box so he can play with it."
Yes, so they gave him the box.
Yes, so,
as he played with it,
he pulled off the lid.
There was a smokehole.
The stars poured outside through it.
They were just suspended in the sky.
Yes, so this is the Gospel.
These three wise men,
when they saw the star,
yes, that was when they said,
"Our Savior is born.
Our Savior is born.
Do you see that star suspended way up there?
Yes, a great star is suspended, they say,
over the face of the one they call the Father."

A yinaadé á tsú g̱unéi s uwa.át.
Yéi áyáa haa shagóon yatee,
átk'.aheenéex̱ haa sateeyí.
Aadóoch sá wsiteen yóo ḵutx̱.ayanahá,
hú áyá a yinaadé g̱unéi gútx̱.
Aa, aadóoch sá tlél át awulg̱ein,
hú áyá tlél g̱aneex̱ du jee.
Aaa, yá lingit.aanitóox' ḵut kei nasgít.
Aaa, ách áwé yá ḵutx̱.ayanahá shux'aanáx̱ yatx̱ yawsixíx.
Uháanch a daa yoo tux̱tula.aadée.
Aa, yáa yeedát áwé
yee een kax̱anéek,
gu.aal shé, ax̱ dachx̱anx'isáani, yeeysateenéeḵ
yú ḵutx̱.ayanahá.
A yinaadé g̱unéi x̱yee.aadée
yihwáan tsú.
Yéi yís áyá yeedát yee een kax̱laneek.
Aa, yáax' áwé át ḵoowaháa.
Aaa, yá ḵutx̱.ayanahá dikéex̱ yax̱laxáat'dáx̱,
a daadé kdag̱aax̱ ítnáx̱ áwé,
aa, yáa tleiknax̱.át áwé sa.ín,
aaa, yáa dís yóo tuwasáagu
áwé asg̱áax̱ tsu.
«Du jeet yisa.ín ax̱ dachx̱ánk'
aan ash kang̱alyádee!»
Ách áwé du jeet wududzi.ín yá déix̱ aa.
Ayáx̱ áwé aan át sh wudligwáatl,
ashkoolét aan.
Du tóotx̱ ḵoowahaa, du toowú sigóo wé atk'átsk'u.
Ch'as yéi áyá asayahéi du dachx̱ánk'
yá ḵáa ḵu.aa,
aaa, sagú a tóo yéi ng̱ateet. Ách áwé a jeedé
akananáach yá ḵóok,
aaa, du at.ooweidée—
Lingítch yéi yasáakw—
aaa, yá du jeex' yéi yateeyi át.
A jeet oos.eench,
aaa, du dachx̱ánk'.
Ayáx̱ áwé aan ashkoolet nooch.

They began walking in that direction.
That is how our history is,
for those of us who are believers.
Whoever has seen that star
starts walking toward it.
Whoever hasn't looked at it
doesn't have salvation.
Yes, he is stumbling about lost in this world.
Yes, that is why the stars were the first to appear.
Let us consider them.
Ah, at this time
I am telling you folks,
I hope, my dear grandchildren, that you see
that star.
May you folks begin to go in that direction,
you as well.
I am telling you this now for this reason.
Yes, the moment has now arrived.
Yes, after the stars had stretched across the heavens,
after Raven was crying for it,
yes, sitting off to one side in its container
was what we call the moon;
he was begging for it as well.
"Hand it to my dear grandchild
and let him play with it!"
So they gave him the second one.
Accordingly, he rolled around with it;
he played with it.
His agony had vanished; the boy was happy.
That is all this man wanted
for his dear grandchild,
yes, that joy would be in his heart. That's why he would tell them
    to give him the box every time,
yes, his precious things—
which is what the Tlingits call them—
yes, these things he had.
He gave,
yes, his dear grandchild the box every time.
Just so, he would play with it.

Aaa, ch'a yéi aan ashkoolyédi áyá tle tsu yanáatx̱ ayaawax̱út'.
Aaa, yanáatx̱ ayax̱óot' áyá tle yóo dikéet uwaxíx tsu.
Ag̱áa áyá, «Ax̱ adée!»
yóo áwé yanaḵéich,
«Ax̱ adée!»
Aaa, yóo du dachx̱ánk' ḵu.aasgíwé ḵúnáx̱ a daa tuwatee
yóo góos' tóode yaa akanajel át
du jináḵ.
Áwé
yú dikéex̱ yax̱laxáat' áwé a daadé kdag̱áax̱ wé atk'átsk'u.
Nas'gi.aa áwé,
yáa ḵóok át sa.in yé áyá du jín áa yéi aya.óo.
Ag̱áa áyá yéi x̱'ayaḵá—.
Aaa, tlax̱ ásgíyú asix̱án du dachx̱án,
aaa, yá ḵáa ḵu.aa.
Aaa, yéi áyá ḵunáax̱ daaḵ akaník[ch] ax̱ léelk'w,
haa dachx̱anx'iyán áyá tusix̱án,
haa dachx̱anx'iyán
haa aayée yáanáx̱ a daa haa tutée nuch—
haa dachx̱ánk'.
Ách áwé a shagóon yéi yatee,
aaa, yá du dachx̱ánch yáa kéede yaa kanajel át.
Aaa, tlax̱ áyáa tlél tsu
aadé oonax̱sineeyi yé ḵoostée nich a daadé kdag̱aax̱í.
Aaa, yá g̱agaan
daadé kdagax̱ nóok áyá,
«Du jeet yisa.ín ax̱ dachx̱ánk' yá ḵóok.
Aaa, du jeet yisa.ín.»
Ách áwé du jeet wududzi.ín.
Aaa, tle tsu a tóotx̱ at wooxeex wé atk'átsk'u,
aan ashkoolét.
Ch'a ooltínch du dachx̱ánk'.
Aaa, awsikóo wáa sáyá kagux̱dayaayí.
Ch'a aan áwé a jeet oos.eench
aadé asix̱ani yéich.
Aaa, ch'a yáa aan át sh wulgwáadli áyá
tle tsu yanáatx̱ ayaawax̱út'.
Tle tsu yú dikéex̱ wulixáat'.
Ag̱áa áyá yéi x̱'[ayaḵá], «Ax̱ adée!

Yes, just as he was playing with it he pulled the lid off again.
Yes, when he pulled off the lid it went straight up to the sky again.
So then, "My precious stuff!"
he kept saying,
"My precious stuff!"
Yes, but I suppose his grandchild's mind was focused on
the things he was taking from his grandfather
and strewing into the clouds.
Now,
when it became suspended up above, the boy was wailing about it.
He held his hands outstretched toward
where the third box sat.
Then he said—.
Yes, this man,
yes, must have really loved his grandchild.
Yes, this is how my grandfather would explain it to me:
we love our grandchildren;
we are more concerned with our grandchildren's welfare
than anything we own—
each of our dear grandchildren.
That's why the history of these things is as it is,
yes, these things his grandson was strewing up into the sky.
Yes, there was never anything else
he could do with them when Raven was wailing for them.
Yes, after he had been wailing for
the sun, his grandfather said,
"Hand my dear grandchild the box.
Yes, hand it to him."
So they gave it to him.
Yes, the boy's agony just faded away again,
and he played with it.
He would just watch his dear grandchild.
Yes, he knew what his grandchild was going to get up to.
Even so, he always gave it to him,
because of the way he loved him.
Yes, as he was rolling himself around with the box
he just pulled the lid off again.
Then it was suspended up above as well.
Then his grandfather said, "My precious stuff!

Ax̱ adée!
Aaa, yú dikéede yaa kandak’íť ax̱ ádee,
aaa, yá ax̱ dachx̱ánk’.»
Aaa, tlax̱ a yáx̱ x̱’alyoo du dachx̱ánk’.
Aaa, yú dikéet wuxeexí áwé ḵwá kdagax̱ nuch áwé Yéil.
Aaá, áwéi
yá ḵei.á ḵu.aasgíwé
ch’a a daa yoo tuwatánk, tlél a jeex̱ oos.een.
Aaa, ch’a hú sgé tsú a daa yoo tuwatánk
yá sdu léelk’w,
aaa, wáanáx̱ sáyóo keenaadé yaa akanajéli.
Yá ch’a g̱óot yéide yoo ḵuyaneek, tle yáa—
yáa dís
ḵeiwu.aa yáx̱ ḵuwatee, ḵa yá g̱agaan
k’idéin áa ḵeiwu.aa yáx̱ wootee.
Á áyá a daa yoo tuwatánk.
Wáannée sáwé
wé atk’átsk’u x’oon.aa yagiyee kdagaax̱í sáwé tle táach ujaaḵch wé ťáa káx’.
A kaadé s akoos.háaych.
Hóoch’i aayí áwé g̱agaan
a ítnáx̱ áwé kaawaháa,
aaa, yá ḵei.á yóo tuwasáagu.
Aaa, á tsú kawdudlineek
yá ḵei.á
ax̱ léelk’úch x̱aan.
Aaa, x̱aan akagux̱lanik nóok áwé yéi x̱’ayaḵá, «K’e yá ḵei.á,
haa, Dikyáanḵáawuch áyá haa jeet uwatée yá Yéil.»
Tlél Dikyáanḵáawu yóo ooséix̱, Yéil yóo áwé ayasáakw
haa Lingídich.
«Aaa, aadé a daa yéi jine yé,
aaa, yá keenaadé yaa akanajélee,
yá ḵei.á áyá a tóox̱ haa woodaa,»
yóo áyá x̱’ayaḵá ax̱ léelk’w,
«Yá ḵei.á áyá a tóox̱ haa woodaa.»
Yá taat—
ha yéi x̱aasáakw—
taat tú, sheyadihéini aa
jiyísx̱ áyá sitee, yá uháan.
X̱át áwé yéi x̱at téeyeen.

My precious stuff!
Yes, all my possessions are flocking to the sky,
yes, my dear grandchild."
Yes, he consistently acknowledged him as his dear grandchild.
Yes, but when the sun flew up into the sky, Raven kept on wailing.
Yes, but it was the daylight,
I suppose,
that he set his mind on; his grandfather wouldn't give it to him.
Yes, and I suppose his grandfather as well
was asking himself,
yes, why Raven was strewing these things up in the sky.
The sky would change;
when the moon came out
it was like the dawning of the day; and the rising of the sun
was like the full dawn.
This is what he was contemplating.
Eventually,
after wailing for so many days, the boy would just fall asleep on the floor.
They would arrange him on the floor.
The last one,
that which we call the daybreak,
yes, came after the sun.
Yes, I was also told the story of
the daybreak
by my grandfather.
Yes, when he was going to tell it to me he said, "Consider the daybreak,
well, God gave it to us—Raven, that is."
My grandfather never called him God; our Tlingit people
call him Raven.
"Yes, this is the way he was arranging it;
yes, as he was strewing these things up in the sky,
we became accustomed to living in the daylight,"
my grandfather says,
"We became accustomed to living in the daylight."
The night—
this is how I refer to it—
the middle of the night is the preferred time
for many people, for many of us.
Me, too, I used to be that way.

Ts'as áa kawjigidi yéide yax̱ x̱agúdin.
Aa, wáannée sáwé
yéi a daadé kdagax̱ nóok áwé yéi ayawsiḵaa,
  «Ax̱ dachx̱ánk' du jeet yisa.ín!
Tlax̱ ax̱ dachx̱ánk'i yáx̱ ák.wé?
Aaa, wé ḵei.á du jeet yisa.ín!
Ash g̱waajaaḵ wé g̱aax̱.»
Aadé asix̱ani yé du dachx̱ánk'.
Ách áwé a jeet awsi.ín tsú,
aaa, hóoch'i aayí.
Wé shawat.shaan tsú ch'a át áa, altín.
Tlax̱ wáa yeekunayáat' sáwé, x'oon.aa yagiyee sáwé tsáa,
yá gaanéilináx̱ aan gáant wudiḵín.
«G̱áa!» yóo wduwa.áx̱
wé Yéil.
Aag̱áa áwé tsá wé shawat.shaan yéi yaawaḵaa,
«Yeisú g̱aax̱ x̱áa l yéi eex̱ají
  Yéilx̱ isateeyí.»
Ách áwé Yéilch átx̱ layéix̱
Naasshagiyéil.
Aaa, áx̱ kawdudlisáy Naasshagiyéil.
Náasdáx̱ shkalneek áyáa,
Náasdáx̱.
Ách áwé áx̱ kawdudlisáy
Naasshagiyéil.
Aaa, ách áwé aan gáant daḵéen,
aaá, aan yaa nagút
yá Ḵei.á Daakeit.
Tlél ch'a yóo neilnáx̱ ayawuyeesh,
tle yá gáanx' áwé tsáa
yá lingit.aaní káa ḵeinga.aat. Ách áwé tlél
  yanáatx̱ ayawuyeesh wé neilx',
aaa, yá lingit.aanikáa yoo ḵeinga.éigit.
Ách áwé aan yaa nagút.
Yeeytéen yá ḵugóos'—
a káx̱ yaa ax̱út'ch
yáa ḵei.á.
Tlax̱ ḵukooshgítch haa káx',
ách áwé aadé kakḵwalanéek á,

I used to try to go exclusively to dark places.
Yes, eventually,
as Raven was wailing over it, his grandfather said to them,
  "Hand it to my dear grandson!
Isn't that just like my dear grandchild?
Yes, hand him the container of the daylight!
He might cry himself to death."
That is how he loved his grandchild.
So he gave that one to him as well,
yes, the last one.
That old woman, too, was just sitting there watching him.
After a very long time, only after so many days
did he fly outside through the smokehole with it.
"Caw!" is what they heard
Raven cry.
Only then did that old woman say,
"I don't buy all this constant crying coming from you,
  you being Raven and all."
That is why Raven uses the name
Raven-of-the-Head-of-the-Nass.
Yes, from this he became known as Raven-of-the-Head-of-the-Nass.
This is a story from the Nass,
from the Nass.
That is why he became known as
Raven-of-the-Head-of-the-Nass.
Yes, so when he flew outside with it,
yes, he walked along carrying
the Container of Daylight.
He didn't pull the lid off while inside the house,
but only once outside,
so that it would dawn on the world. That is why
  he didn't pull the lid off inside the house,
yes, so that it could always dawn over the world.
That is why he was walking along carrying it.
You see these clouds—
the wind keeps pulling them
over the daylight.
It always gets very dark on us;
that's why I am going to tell the history of it

a shagóon.
Aaá, aag̱áa áyá aan yaa nagúdi áyáa, yá saak isdeegí áyáa
át uwagút.
Yá deegáa
hasdu jeex' yéi yatee.
Há'! Tlax̱ áyóo yagéi yú.á yú saak.
Aaa, aadé kdulneek yá a shagóon yá saak.
Hasdu toowú sagóo nuch yáa saak,
aaa, yá deegáa tóox' yéi ng̱atéen, shag̱ahígín.
Aaa, aag̱áa áyá yax̱ kax̱dusxéinín, át kanduk'énch.
Toowú sagú áwé sdu jee yéi nateech, yóo áwé kdunéek.
Ách áwé yá asdeegée yéi x̱'ayaḵáa nuch,
«Óo-oo-oo-oo.»
Hintáax' yei x̱'andustáni wéi deegáa,
«Óo-oo-oo-oo.»
Ch'a yáa át át kaduwak'éini yáx̱ áwé s du.ax̱ji nuch hás tsú,
yá saak isdeegée.
A yáx̱ áwé shahíkx̱.
Shahíkx̱ yá deegáa tú.
Yéi áwé wdudzikóo Lingítch,
a shagóon
aa, yáa saak isdeek.
Aag̱áa wé Yéil át góot áyá yéi x̱'ayaḵá, «Dá x̱áat aywú!
X̱áat aywú!»
Tléil a x̱'adaat ḵaa tooshtí.
Wáanée sáwé
yéi ḵuyawsiḵaa—x'oon.aa yéi yanaḵáa sáyá, «X̱áat aywú!»—
aag̱áa yéi yaawaḵaa yú.á wé Yéil,
«Ḵei.á yee káa nḵwaak'oots!»
Aag̱áa áwé yá asdeegí áwé yéi yaawaḵaa,
«Goodáx̱ Naasshagiyéil?»
Ách áwé
tle áx̱ wusitee
Naasshagiyéil,
yáa Yéil Yádi.
Náas du saayíx̱ wusitee: Naasshagiyéil.
Aaa, yéi áyá wtusikóo haa Lingídich.
Yáa shkalneek
woosh g̱uwanáade kdulneek.

into the microphone.
Yes, then as he was walking along carrying it,
he went up to some eulachon dipnetters.
They had
dipnets.
Hah! There were so many eulachon, they say.
Yes, this is the way the history of the eulachon is recounted.
They were always happy,
yes, when the eulachon were in the dipnets, when the nets were full.
Yes, then when they dumped them out, the eulachon would jump about.
They would always experience happiness; this is how they tell it.
That's why the dipnetter would say,
"Oo-oo-oo-oo."
While they were lowering the dipnets into the water, they would say,
"Oo-oo-oo-oo."
They, too, would make sounds like eulachon jumping about,
these eulachon dipnetters.
In that way it gets full.
The inside of the dipnet gets full.
This is how the Tlingit know
the history,
ah, of dipnetting eulachon.
When Raven got there, he said, "Do send me some eulachon!
Send me some!"
They didn't pay attention to what he said.
Eventually
he said to them—after saying, "Send me some!" so many times—
Raven then reportedly said,
"Watch out or I might break daylight on you folks!"
Then these dipnetters said,
"Where does this Raven-of-the-Head-of-the-Nass hail from?"
From that,
this Child of Raven
became
Raven-of-the-Head-of-the-Nass.
Nass became his name: Raven-of-the-Head-of-the-Nass.
Yes, this is how our Tlingit people know it.
This story
is told in various ways.

Aaa, yá ixkéex' tsú át x̱wasi.áx̱
yá shkalneek.
Aadé x̱aan kadulnik yá ḵu.aa áyá ax̱ léelk'úch,
ách áwé yeedát yee een kax̱laneek.
Ḵa a shagóon
aadé
áx̱ yaa kanax̱lanik yá,
ách
haa een kadulneek át, a káax' ḵugaax̱dudziteeyi aa.
Ách áwé—
aag̱áa áyá yáa ḵei.á
át awsi.een, yá l du jeex̱ at du.oo nóok áwé
ch'a yéi gugéink' yanáatx̱ ayaawax̱út'.
Kawdzig̱aax̱,
«Ágánáa!» yóo s yaawaḵaa.
Has tuwlidlékw
yá ḵei.á.
Tle yanáatx̱ ayaawax̱út'.
Ách áwé ḵugóos'
tóonáx̱ haa káa yoo ḵeiya.éik.
Ḵugóos' a káx̱ yaa ayíshch
ḵei.á.
Ách áwé a kaax̱ yax̱las'ísín áwé tsáa
haa káa ḵeina.éich.
Yéi áyá wootee yá ḵei.á.
Aaa, l du jeex̱ at du.oo nóok áyá tsá yanáatx̱ ayaawax̱út'.
Aaa, aag̱áa yóot ḵaa luwagúḵ.
Héende aa atkaawa.át
ḵa dáḵde aa atkaawa.át.
Aaa, tsaax̱ aa wsitee.
Taanx̱ aa wsitee,
cheech,
ḵa yá yáay, woosh g̱uwanáade át,
yá héen táade atkaawa.adi aa.
Dáḵde aa,
tsu a x̱oo.aa s'eek,
xóots—
daa sáyá dáḵde át luwagoog̱u át,
áx̱ aa wsitee.

Yes, I have listened to this story
down south.
This is the way my grandfather told it to me;
that's why I am now telling the story to you folks.
And the way
I am explicating its history
as I continue my story,
this is what they use
to convey to us principles that people can live by.
So,
then he carried the daylight around,
and when people wouldn't leave anything for him
he pulled the lid open a little bit.
They wailed;
"Oh no!" they said.
The daybreak
startled the wits out of them.
He just yanked the lid off.
That's why the day breaks on us
through the clouds.
The wind pulls clouds over
the daybreak.
So the day breaks on us
only when the clouds are blown off.
That is how the dawn came to be.
Only when people weren't leaving anything for him did he pull the lid off.
Yes, then the people ran away.
Some rushed into the water
and some rushed up into the forest.
Yes, some of them became seals.
Some of them became sea lions,
porpoises,
and whales, various creatures,
the ones who rushed into the water.
The ones going into the forest,
some of them black bears,
brown bears—
whatever creatures mill about in the forest,
that's what some of them became.

Aaa, áyá kóoshdaa
ch'a yá dáak̲de yaa lugagúk̲ch.
Áx̲ aa wsitee k̲uwakaan—
daa sáyá dáak̲ ádi.
Yá haa Lingídi k̲u.aa áyá yóo aas t'éinác̲ áwé s at latín.
Yéi áyá haa nateech haa Lingídi.
Aaa, aas t'éix' atoolsínch, ch'as áa k̲ukawjig̲idi yéide yax̲ haa kwdaya nuch.
Ách áwé
haa kookáx̲ sitee
haa shkalneegée.
Ách áyá ax̲ léelk'w yéi x̲at daayak̲áa nuch,
«A daa yoo tután
yáa shkalneek,
yagéiyi át a tóotx̲ gax̲yeet'eeyéet.
Aadóo sá [du] een keelaneek aa x'wán
hasdu een k̲unáax̲ daak̲ kaneek.»
Ách áyá yeedát yáat.át tóode yee een k̲unáax̲ daak̲ kanx̲aník.
Aaa, a x̲oo.aa uháan áwé
kag̲ít tóox' tsá
gági too.átx̲.
A x̲oo.aa wé k̲ei.á tóot natoo.átch.
Áyá átk' aheeníx̲ sitee.
Aaa, yá átk' aheeníx̲ dax̲ has sitee, hás.
Aaa, yá kag̲ít tóo yéi yateeyi aa k̲u.aa áyá, l ayáx̲x̲ usiteeyi aa a tóox' áwé yéi s yatee,
ách áwé taat tóox' tsá gági s átx̲.
Aaa, yéi áyá yee een kax̲laneek yeedát.
Aaa, yáa aadé g̲ayeeysikóowéyáx̲ yee een k̲unáax̲ daak̲ kanx̲aník,
aa, yáa a shagóon,
aaa, yá Náasdáx̲ shkalneek áyá.
Aaa, ách áyáa
haa een kadulneegí haa Lingídich,
aaa, kunáax̲ daak̲ has akaníkch haa een.
Aaa, sheyadihéini yéix' yéi haa daayaduk̲á,
aaa, «Ch'áagu k̲usteeyí áwé tlél daatx̲ sá ustí.»
Tléik'!
Haa dachx̲anx'isáani x̲á
kei s nawát.

Yes, and land otters,
they would just keep running up into the forest.
Some became deer—
whatever is a creature of the forest.
Our Tlingit people would watch from behind the trees.
That is how our Tlingit people are.
Yes, we always hide behind the trees; we would always try to make our way into dark places.
So,
our stories
are a reflection of our lives.
This is why my grandfather always told me,
"Consider
these stories well
so that you may find from within them things of great significance.
Be sure to explain the story to
whomever you tell it to."
This is why I am explaining it to you all now into this microphone.
Yes, some of us
emerge
only in the darkness.
Some of us always walk in the daylight.
These are believers.
Yes, they are believers.
Yes, the ones who are in the darkness; those who are unrighteous are in darkness,
so they only emerge in the night.
Yes, this is how I am telling it to you folks now.
Yes, I am explaining this to you in such a way that you might know,
yes, its history,
yes, this story from the Nass.
Yes, that is why,
when our Tlingit people tell it to us,
yes, they explain it to us.
Yes, on many occasions we have been told,
yes, "The old way of life isn't worth anything."
No!
Our dear grandchildren, you see,
are growing up.

Hás tsú s ax̲sakóowu.
Hasdu ée niylatóow.
Ag̲áa s agux̲sakóo
tsu yá l ayáx̲x̲ usiteeyi át.

Shkalneek iii. Yéil k̲a X̲'aan

K̲a yá héen—
át kax̲wliník—
aaa, yá héen
yá a ítx' kakg̲waháa, a tóox' yéi kg̲watée.
Ldakát át a x̲oox̲ yaa x̲'agax̲tudatáan.
Aaa, yáa
a daa yoo x̲'ax̲aatangi aa,
yáa aas,
tlél áyáa ch'a daa sá latseen a tú,
yáa kaawahaayi aa.
A eeti.aa tóox' áwé yéi kg̲watée,
yá latseen a tóode ajikg̲wanak̲ núknee,
a tóox'.
K̲a yáa té
tlél tsu daa sá a tóo yéi utí.
Á yeisú áyáa
k'e yáa kanax̲toohéinín—
tlél ch'u wé yagiyee.
…
K̲a yá té yóo tuwasáagu át
tlél tsu daa sá a tóo yéi utí,
aaa, yáa
yan awsiniyi át.
Ách áwé a daa yoo tuwatánk.
«Aaa, daa sá uyéx̲ a tóode,
aa, yáax' yan x̲wasiniyi át?»
Ách áwe át woogoot hú k̲u.aa,
a daa yoo tuwatánk.
Wáannée sáyá awsiteen yóo deikéenáx̲ kei ganch x̲'aan.
Yóo deikée, yá éil' ká,
a kaanáx̲ áyá kei kagánch
yá x̲'aan.

Let them know it too.
Teach it to them, you folks.
Then they will again recognize
the things that are unrighteous for what they are.

Episode iii. Raven and Fire

And the water—
I've told it up to this point—
yes, the water
will come after this; it will be included in the narration.
We will proceed to talk about all the various events.
Yes, these
things I am talking about,
the trees,
none of the things that were located here
had any power within them.
It was to be within the ones to be created next,
when he was going to release power into them,
within them.
And these rocks,
there was no life force within them.
These days, for example,
when we plant them here, they have life force within them,
but not in those days.
. . .
And what we call rocks
had no life force in them,
yes, these
things that Raven had prepared.
So he was contemplating the matter.
"Yes, what is missing within,
ah, the things I have prepared here?"
So he walked around
contemplating it.
Eventually he saw the fire that kept flaring up way out at sea.
Way out in the ocean
fire
was flaring up through the water.

Áyá a daa yoo tuwatánk ch'a át woogoodi yéix'
wáa sá ayakg̲wadlaag̲ée.
Aag̲áa áyáa
yá át woo.aadi át x̲oot woogoot hú tsú.
K̲utées'.
Ax̲satínch anax̲ kei koogaanch.
Aaa.
Aag̲áa áyá
a daa yoo tuwatánk,
aa, yá uyex̲ át,
yá kaawahaayi át:
yá aas
k̲a yá téix'.
Tlél tsu daa sá
a tú.
Tlél aadé kg̲waagaani yé yáa aas,
k̲a tlél tsu daa sá k̲oostí.
Dleit K̲áach k̲u.aa áwés
spirit yóo yasáakw.
Tlél tsu yéi yateeyi át a tóo yéi utí ldakát át.
Ách áwéi
yú deikéenáx̲ kei kaganch x̲'aan a daa yoo tuwatánk hóoch k̲u.aa.
«Aaa, wáa sá yakk̲wadláak̲?»
Ách áwéi
yá át woogoodi yéix' áyá awsiteen yáa
yées k̲áa.
Tlax̲ yayát' áyú du lú yú.á.
Tlax̲ áyú a kaax̲ du toowú klig̲éi.
Tlél tsu daa sá du toowútin utí.
Lingítch yéi yasáakw ch'a hú sh daa tukawdijél.
Aaa, áyá áa yaa gútch,
áa awsiteen.
Áyá yaa nagúdi áyá
ch'a a daa yoo tuwatánk,
«Gwál hú shákdé x̲aadé gux̲dashée,
héit woogoodi aa.»
Tle ash yáanáx̲ woogútch.
Wáannée sáwé yéi ayawsik̲aa,

So, right where he was walking around
he was contemplating how he could get his hands on that fire.
Then
he, too, went among those creatures that were walking about.
He searched.
He kept seeing the fire flaring up there.
Yes.
At this time
he was contemplating,
ah, what was missing
from the situation as it was:
the trees
and the rocks.
There was nothing
within them.
It was impossible for trees to burn,
and there was nothing else.
The white man
calls it spirit.
There was no such thing within anything.
This led
Raven to contemplate the fire that kept flaring up
way out at sea.
"Yes, how will I get my hands on it?"
So
right where he was walking around, he caught sight of a
young man.
He had a very long nose, they say.
He was really proud of it.
He wasn't concerned about anything else.
The Tlingit would call him self-absorbed.
Yes, he kept walking by
and he saw him there.
As Raven was walking along
he was still contemplating the issue,
"Perhaps he will be the one to help me,
this guy walking over here."
The guy kept walking past him.
Eventually he said to him,

«X̱áat idashí!
X̱áat idashí!»
Du waḵshóonáx̱ áwé du yát awdlig̱én, ch'a yaadachóon at shooḵ,
du yáanáx̱ yaa nagúdi.
Tle yóode woogoot du náḵ tsu.
Ách áwé wáannée sáwé tsu anax̱ haat uwagút tsu, aag̱áa áyá
déix̱ aa áyá ax̱'eiwawóos',
«X̱áat idashí!
Aaa, i yáx̱ yateeyi ḵáa áyá ax̱ tuwáa sigóo x̱áat wudasheeyí.»
Ch'a yaadachóon ash yashooḵ,
tle yóode woogoot tsu.
Lingítch áyá yéi wsikóo
nás'gi aa
áyá tsáa
aadé yoo ḵutudzi.áx̱k
daa sá haa tuwáa sagoowú.
Yéi áwé yatee yá K'ákw, yóo áyá tuwasáakw
yá ash yáanáx̱ át woogoodi át áyá yées ḵáax̱ siteeyi.
Á lú yéi koowáat'.
Wáannée sáwé nes'gi.aa yaa nagúdi áyá yéi ayawsiḵaa tsu,
«Dá x̱áat idashí!»
Aag̱áa áwé ash x̱áni ḵux̱ wudihán,
«Daa sáyú i tuwáa sigóo
i jiyís yéi x̱wsaneeyí.»
Aag̱áa áyá
yéi ayawsiḵaa, «Iyatéen gé yóo deikéenáx̱ kei kagánch yú x̱'aan?
Áyá ax̱ tuwáa sigóo aan x̱áat yidasheeyí, yá ax̱ jiyís yang̱eedlaag̱ée.
Yáax' ax̱ jiyís, yáanáx̱ aan
yan g̱idaḵeen.»
«Ha wáa sáyú kḵwasanée?»
«Ha x̱áach i jiyís yéi kḵwasanée.»
Ách áwé aag̱áa woogoot tle yáa Yéil,
Lingítch áyá yéi yasáakw téil.
Áwé tlax̱ liyát',
gwál tlax̱ tléix' waat yáx̱ kuliyáat'.
Áwé yéi awsinei a jiyís, yá a shú
kíts yáx̱ aawa.oo.
Aag̱áa áyá yéi adaayaḵá, «Yú deikéenáx̱ kei kawugaaní,
a tóox̱ áyá yá a lú

"Help me.
Help me."
He was watching him out of the corner of his eye; he laughed out loud
as he walked past him.
Then he walked away from him again.
So eventually he just came up to him again, and then
Raven asked him a second time,
"Help me.
Yes, I want a fellow like yourself to help me."
He just laughed out loud at him
and walked away again.
This is the Tlingit perspective:
it is only on
the third time
that we listen closely
to what we want.
That is how Pygmy Owl was; this is what we call
the creature who walked past him, who was a young man.
His nose was this long.
Eventually he asked him a third time,
"Please help me!"
Then he stopped by him,
"What is it that you want
me to do for you?"
This was when
Raven said to him, "Do you see that fire flaring up way out at sea?
Well, I want you to help me with it—to get it for me.
Here, along here,
I want you to fly ashore with it for me."
"Well how am I supposed to do that?"
"Well, I'll fix it up for you."
So Raven went to get
what the Tlingit call pitchwood.
It was very long,
maybe as long as an armspan.
This is what he made for him; he left
the end of it rough like tinder.
Then he said to him, "While the fire is flaring up way out at sea,
you must fly through it

aan yakg̱idaḵéen
yá x̱ʼaan akg̱asháat.»
Á áyá kx̱anéek.
Tlél daa sá *spirit* a tóo yéi utí,
latseen tlél a tóo yéi utí.
Hóoch ḵu.aa áyá a tóode ajeewanáḵ yáa a lóode aksa.ax̱w át.
Du latseení a jeet aawatée,
aa, yá x̱ʼaan
aan yan g̱adaḵeenít.
Ách áyá yéi adaayaḵá—a lóode aksa.aax̱óo
yéi ayawsiḵaa,
«Ldakát yá lingit.aanituḵwáani
káx̱ áyá,
yá x̱ʼaan haadé—yá ax̱ jeedé yakg̱eedláaḵ
yá lingit.aanituḵwáani káx̱.»
Chʼa yá a lóode yéi adaaneiyí, «I gu.aa yáx̱ xʼwán!
I gu.aa yáx̱ xʼwán!
Aaa, ax̱ jeet yadláḵ wé x̱ʼaan.»
Aag̱áa áyá chʼa ash yashooḵ
a lóode aksa.aax̱ú.
Aag̱áa áa ashukoojeisʼ
aadé yínde yakg̱was.aa yá
yá x̱ʼaan agashátni.
Aaa, ách áwé
daak gadaḵéen
yéi adaayaḵá, «I gu.aa yáx̱ xʼwán!
Ax̱ jeet yadláḵ wé x̱ʼaan.
Yá lingit.aanituḵwáani káx̱ áyáa
yéi yoo ikayasheik.»
Ách áwé daak wudiḵín
yá Kʼákw yóo tuwasáagu aa.
Aaa, wáanée sáwé a kanax̱ kei akaawagán yá x̱ʼaan yú deikée.
Tle a tóox̱ aan yawdiḵín, yáa
kíts yáx̱ yateeyi yá
aawasháat.
Át akaawagán.
Aag̱áa áwé yánde aan yaa ndaḵín.
Chʼul a katʼóot káa daak udaḵeenjí áyá du yax̱áng̱aa yaa akanagán.
«I gu.aa yáx̱ xʼwán!

with the tip of the torch in your beak
so it can catch the fire."
This is what I am telling.
Nothing had spirit within,
nor power within.
But Raven released it into the torch he was tying onto Pygmy Owl's beak.
He gave his power to him,
ah, so he could fly to shore
with the fire.
So Raven said to him—as he was fastening it onto his beak,
 he said to him,
"On behalf of
all of the people of this world,
you will obtain the fire and bring it here—to me,
on behalf of the people of the world."
As Raven was putting it onto his beak, he said, "Be of good courage!
Be of good courage!
Yes, secure the fire for me."
Then he was just smiling at Raven
as he was fastening it onto his beak.
Then he instructed him as to
how to lower his head
when he grabs the fire.
Yes, that is why
as he was flying out to sea
Raven told him, "Be of good courage!
Secure that fire for me.
It is on behalf of the people of the world
that you are suffering so."
So the one we call Pygmy Owl
flew out to sea.
Yes, eventually the fire flared up over the open ocean.
He just flew through the flames with it
and the fire took hold of
the rough end.
The torch caught fire.
Then he started flying toward shore with it.
Before he had flown halfway out it was burning close to his face.
"Be of good courage!

I gu.aa yáx x'wán!
Lingit.aanitukwáani káx áyá eeshandéin yoo ikayasheik,»
yóo áwé adaayaká.
Kdagáax
yá K'ákw,
yá du lú yéi koowat'i,
tle áwé daak nagán yá du lú.
Áwé kdagáax hú ku.aa.
Aa, «I gu.aa yáx x'wán!
Aaa, yá lingit.aanitukwáani káx,
aaa, hás áyá
hasdu káx eeshandéin yoo ikayasheik
ka i kaax hasdu toowú kei kgwak'éi.
Ách áwé i gu.aa yáx x'wán!»
Ách áwé aan yan wudikín K'ákwch.
A lóotx yéi anasnée yú x'aan
aagáa áyá yá aas tóode aléet.
Ldakát át tóode aléet.
Yá gíl' tóode aléet.
Ldakát a tóode aléet áyá
aan yoo x'ali.átk, «Hé lingit.aanitukwáani káx áyá
eeshandéin yoo ikaawashòo.
Aaa.
Lingit.aanitukwáanich i eedé
toowú kei kgwak'éi.»
Aaa, yá du lú daak uwagani,
tlax wáa sá adaatuwusinóok yá K'ákw.
Ách áwé K'ákw a lú,
aa, naaléi áa daak uwagani yá, hóoch áwé yéi awsinee Yéilch.
Aa, ách áwé yéi adaayaká,
«Yá lingit.aanikwáanich i yaadé kgwatéen,
aaa, yá x'aan yayidlaagí.
Tlél daa sá itukawuxéel'ik hé i lú daak wugaanée.
Ch'as yá lingít aanitukwáani
i kaax toowú k'eiyí
a kát isanatí.
Aagáa áyá kéex' yéi kgwatée i saa.»
Aa, yéi áyá adaayaká yáa K'ákw,
aa, yá Yéilch.

Be of good courage!
You are suffering on behalf of the people of the world,"
he was telling him.
Pygmy Owl
was wailing;
his long beak
was burning away.
He was wailing.
Yes, "Be of good courage!
Yes, on behalf of the people of the world,
yes, they are the ones
you are suffering for,
and because of you they will be happy.
So be of good courage!"
That's why Pygmy Owl flew ashore with it.
When Raven took the fire from his beak,
he then flung the flames into the trees.
He flung them into everything.
He flung them into cliffs.
After he had flung all of the flames into them
he spoke to Pygmy Owl, "It is on behalf of the people of the world
 that you have suffered.
Yes.
The people of the world
will be grateful to you."
Yes, Pygmy Owl really mourned the loss of
his beak that had burned away.
So Pygmy Owl's beak
was burnt way back; Raven had caused this.
Ah, so he said to him,
"The people of the world will see by your face,
yes, that you obtained the fire.
Don't fret about anything now that your beak has burnt away.
Just remember the joy
that will come to the people of the world
because of you.
Then your name will be held up high."
Ah, this is what,
ah, Raven told Pygmy Owl.

Aagáa áwé
tlax̱ du toowóox̱ wusitee,
aa, yá K'ákw ku.aa,
yáa Yéilch aadé daayaka yá.
Du toowú nóogu tle a kát seiwax'ákw.
Ách áwé K'ákw—
aaa, kuwdzitee,
X̱ashak'ákwk' yóo wduwasáa—
du eenx̱ wusitee.
Goodé sá ash een át kawdiyaa tle?
Hú áyá X̱ashak'ákwx̱ sitee.
Aa, ách áwé Lingít
woosh yáx̱ awoolx̱'éix'w, «I gu.aa yáx̱ x'wán!
I gu.aa yáx̱ x'wán!»
Aa, yáa yeedát
yá a daa yoo x̱'ax̱aatangi aa—
ldakát át áyá a tóonáx̱ kudzitee haa Lingít yoox̱'atángi—
aaa, a tóonáx̱ shdaayootudatánk haa jee yéi yatee
eeshandéin yoo haa kawushoowú.
A ídu á lax̱éitl.
Yóo áyá sh kadulnik nuch x̱aan
ax̱ léelk'úch Wooshkáakeiydagwéich.
Aaa, a ídu lax̱éitl.
Yéi áyá yee kgwatée, ax̱ dachx̱anx'iyán.
Aaa, eeshandéin yoo yee kakgwashóo.
Yáa yeedát a káx̱ yéi jitoone át—
aa, yáa yeedát
a káx̱ yux̱ wutuwa.aat yá lingit.aanitu.ádi,
haa kagéi kakgwahaa át.
Ách áwé
tlél aadé kei x̱tudileedi yá.
Ch'u yáa Yéilch áyá yéi haa shukaawajáa.
«I gu.aa yáx̱ x'wán!» yóo haa daayakáa nuch tlákw.
Ách áwé shdaayootudatánk a tóonáx̱ kudzitee haa shkalneegée.
Yáa yeedát yá kax̱lanik aa haa shkalneegí áyáa.
Aaa, gwál de wéidoo
a tóonáx̱
sh daa yakushusigéiyi aa.
Sh daa yoo tuditangi aa a tóotx̱ kei akgwat'ee.

So then,
Pygmy Owl,
yes, really took to heart
what Raven had told him.
He just forgot about his sorrow.
So Pygmy Owl,
who was named X̲ashak'ákwk'—
yes, he was really something—
he joined Raven.
Where did he venture to with Raven then?
He is X̲ashak'ákw.
That is why the Tlingit
shore each other up, saying, "Be of good courage!
Be of good courage!"
Ah, at present,
these stories I am talking about—
everything exists within the scope of our Tlingit language—
we have introspection through this
as we undergo suffering.
Good fortune follows suffering.
That is what my grandfather Jim David
used to tell me.
Yes, good fortune follows suffering.
This is how you will be, my grandchildren.
Yes, you folks will suffer.
The things we are working toward these days—
ah, these days
we have gone forth on behalf of the creatures of the world,
such things as we may encounter.
That is why
we can't give up.
Raven himself has shown us the way.
"Be of good courage!" he keeps telling us all the time.
That is why self-examination lies within the scope of our stories.
The stories I am narrating now are our stories.
Yes, maybe there are already people out there
who understand themselves
by way of this story.
Those who are introspective will find understanding through it.

Ách áyáa haa een kadulneek yá shkalneek.
Aaa, yáa ax̱ dachx̱án,
aaa,
gwál hóoch kei akg̱wat'ei a tóodáx̱.
Aaa, yáa yeedát haa káx̱ yux̱ gug̱agóot.
Ch'a yá X̱ashak'ákw yáx̱ áyá kg̱watée,
aaa, yux̱ nagútni haa káx̱,
aaa, daaḵ nagáni
áx' yanóogu yéide kg̱wagáan,
aaa, yáa haa káx̱ yéi jine núkni.
Daax̱ḵuwadéink'
yóo tuwasáakw ax̱ dachx̱ánk'.
Hú áyá haa káx̱
eeshandéin yoo kakg̱washóo.
Aaa.
Ách áwé,
áx̱ daaḵ nadaḵin yá,
aaa, kadag̱ax̱ núkni,
á yéi áyá yéi x̱'ayakḵwaḵáa x̱át ḵu.aa,
«I gu.aa yáx̱ x'wán chx̱ánk'!
Yá lingit.aanituḵwáani káx̱ áwé eeshandéin yoo ikayasheik.»
Yóo áyá ax̱ toowú kg̱watée x̱át ḵu.aa.
Aa, ách áwé yeedát
tlél sh x̱'awux̱dawóoḵ
yá át tóode a daa yoo x̱'ax̱atángi.
Aaa, yéi áyá ax̱ tuwáa sigóo yee jeet x̱wateeyí, ldakát ax̱ dachx̱anx'isáani.
Aaa, yáa yee húnx̱w
yee káx̱ eeshandéin yoo kakg̱washóo.
Aa, áyá yeedát,
a shagóon áyá yeedát
yáax' a daa yoo x̱'ax̱aatánk.
Yá lingit.aanituḵwáani káx̱ eeshandéin yoo kakg̱washóo yá yee húnx̱w,
yee éek'.
Ách x'wán sh daa yee tiyil.á!
A tóot aniyilgein yihwáanch tsú,
aadé yux̱ gug̱agut yá.
Aaa, yéi áyá ax̱ tuwáa sigóo yee een kax̱waneegí ax̱ dachx̱anx'isáani.
Aadóoch sá át wus.aax̱ée
yá shkalneek,

This is why these stories are told to us.
Yes, my grandchild here,
yes,
maybe he will find understanding through it.
Yes, now he is going to go forth on our behalf.
He will be just like X̱ashak'ákw,
yes, when he goes forth on our behalf;
yes, when his beak is burning away,
it will burn back to where it is painful,
yes, while he is working on our behalf.
Daax̱ḵuwadéink'
is what we call my dear grandchild.
He is the one that
will suffer on our behalf.
Yes.
That is why,
at the place he is flying out over,
yes, just as he is wailing,
this is when I will say,
"Be of good courage, grandson!
You are suffering on behalf of the people of the world."
That is how I myself am going to feel.
Ah, that is why now
I have full confidence in my words
as I speak about it into this microphone.
Yes, this is what I would like to give to you, all of my dear grandchildren.
Yes, your older brother
will suffer on your behalf.
Ah, now
I am talking about
the history of it here.
Your older brother will suffer on behalf of the people of the world,
your brother.
So be sure to reflect on yourselves!
Meditate upon how he will go forth,
you folks, too.
Yes, this is what I want to tell you, my dear grandchildren.
Whoever listens to
this story,

aa, yihwáan yee kagéi kakgwaháa,
aaa, a ítx' kakgwahaa aa
haa shkalneegée.
Aaa, yáa—
yáat'aa ítx' kakgwaháa
yáa héen daat,
aadéi a tóonáx latseen haa jee yéi teex yá.

Shkalneek iv. Yéil ka Héen

Ách áwé
haa tuwáa sigóo
ldakát át
yee een yan kawtulaneegí.
Ax kéek',
aa, Lingít x'éináx yéi tuwasáakw Jakwteidu.oo,
hóoch áyá kunáax daak akaníkch.
Aaa, yá ax yoox'atángi, Lingít x'éináx yoo x'axatángi
    dleit káa x'éináx akanéek.
Hóoch áyá tsu kunáax daak akakgwanéek yee een.
Aa, ax kéek' áyá.
Dáxnáx áyá ktoo.aakw
yan wutusaneeyí
yá haa yéijineiyí.
Yáa yeedát yá haa een yéi jiné yá dleit káa.
Tlax wáa sá haa een tuli.aan.
Ách áyá yeedát
yáat'át tóode yoo x'axatángi
gunalchéesh yéi ax toowú yatee du eedéi,
aadé haa éet wudishiyi yá—
dikée haa lashádi.
Yihwáan tsú yéi yee toowú natí,
gunalchéesh.
Aaa, yáa yeedát yá haa eenx sitee.
Aa, yáa—
yáat'át
ax jiyís átx awliyéx,
aa, yá Gordon.
Du yéijineiyí

yes, our stories,
yes, and the stories to come after this one,
will be available for you folks.
Yes,
after this story is to come the one
about the water,
about how we gain power through it.

Episode iv. Raven and Fresh Water

That is why
we would like
to tell you folks
the whole story.
My younger brother,
ah, in Tlingit we call him Jak̲wteidu.oo,
he's the one that always explains it.
Yes, my speech, when I speak in Tlingit
    he recounts it in English.
It is he that will explain it to you folks again.
Yes, he is my younger brother.
The two of us are trying
to complete
our work.
At this time a white man is working with us.
How very kind he is to us.
That is why now,
as I am speaking into this microphone,
I feel grateful to him
for the way he has helped us—
elevating us.
You folks, too, should feel that way,
thankful.
Yes, now he is with us.
Yes, this—
he is operating
this microphone for me,
ah, Gordon.
It is as if he has donated

ch'a oowayáa akaawagéex'éyáx yatee.
Ka du yéijineiyí—
yáa a tóode yoo x'axatángi yáa yées át
woosh kaanáx kei anatéen.
Ách áyá
«Gunalchéesh,» yéi yaxwaakaa.
Yéi áyá ax tuwáa sigóo yee een kaxwaneegí.
...
Aaa, yáa—
yáa yeedadi aayí,
yá kaawahaayi át,
tlél áyáa héen koostí.
Ách áyá a daadé sh kakkwalneek yeedát.
Aaa, yáa
lingit.aanitú áyá uwaxúk.
Ách áwéi
a daa yóo tuwatánk
wáa sá ayakgwadlaagí.
Aa, át woogoodi yá áwé,
aa, ayatéen,
aya.áxch
goot'á sá áa yéi teeyí wé héen.
Ách áwé a daa yoo tuwatánk hóoch ku.aa,
wáa sá ayakgwadlaagí.
Yá aan x'ayee ch'a át woogoodi yé,
wáanée sáwé
yéi a daa tuwditaan,
«Shk'e aadé nkagoodée.»
Aagáa áyá yá aan x'ayeegáa wooteeyi ketlháatl'i áyá
aax aa wootee.
Á yá át tóo ayatée áwé aadé woogoot.
Aaa, ldakát káa áwé du káani yóo a yáx x'alyoo.
Ách áwé a xáni neil góot,
aa, yáa Ganook
du héeni ká
áwé át tá.
Aa, tlél aadóoch sá áx ushee
yáa héen.
Aaa, ách áwé

his labor.
And his work—
as I am speaking into this new invention
he is compiling these stories.
That is why
I say, “Thank you.”
That is what I would like to tell you folks.
. . .
Yes, this—
the current story about
this situation:
there was no water.
So I am going to tell the story about it now.
Yes, the
world was dried up.
So
he was contemplating
how he could get his hands on it.
Ah, at that place where he walked around,
ah, he could see and
he could hear
just where the water was.
So he was contemplating
how he could get his hands on it.
In the village where he was walking about,
eventually
he came up with an idea,
“How about I go on over there.”
Then he picked up some of the dog poop that was lying here and there
in the village.
So once he had taken up this stuff, he went there.
Yes, he would address everyone as his brother-in-law.
So when he entered Petrel’s house,
ah, Petrel
was sleeping
on top of his fresh water.
Ah, nobody ever touched
the water.
Yes, that is why

hú k̲u.aa a kanáak áwé át tá.
Aaa, ách áwé hóoch k̲u.aa tle
wé G̲anook x̲ánde yaa gagóot
yá ketlháatl'i yaa anatèen
a daax' yoo akg̲ahaat.
Yéi áwé awsinee, a tuk̲daa yoo akaawaháa.
Aag̲áa áyá,
áyá kei awsigít.
«Ax̲ káani,
sh daa x̲'ayditee.
Nagú!
Sh daanida.óos', yú ík̲de nagú!
A g̲óotx̲ sitee i naa.ádi.»
Ách áwé hú k̲u.aa kei isgéet sh daat wudlinúk ayáx̲ gwáayá.
Ách áwé éek̲de woogoot,
aa, sh daang̲ada.óos'it.
Aag̲áa áyá hú k̲u.aa
ch'u yéi sh daa yéi jidaneiyí áyá yá Yéil k̲wá tle yá héen táax̲ yawdzi.aa, yanáatx̲ ayaawatán.
Tle wáa sá litseen, a yáx̲ áwé
adaná.
Aaa, yáa—
yá yax̲ adana nóok áwé neil uwagút hú k̲u.aa,
G̲anook.
Aag̲áa áyá tlél a yanáax̲ ayawux̲óot' wé goon kanaak.áat'ani.
Tle hú áwé
gáant wudik̲ín yáa gaanéilinteam.
Aag̲áa hú k̲u.aa yéi yaawak̲aa G̲anook,
«Ax̲ kanaakyéigi,
gasháat!»
Tle tliyeitiyéix̲ áwé wdik̲ín wé Yéil.
Tlél tsu g̲unéi udak̲ínx̲.
A tayeex' áwé hú k̲u.aa yá G̲anook,
téil wóoshde yaa akanajél,
aa, yáa Yéil tayeex'.
Dleit yáx̲ áwé téeyin yú.á yáa Yéil—
dleit yáx̲.
Áyá yá—
yáa a tayeex' wóosht akaawajeli yáa

he was sleeping above it.
Yes, so as Raven
was walking up to Petrel,
he was carrying the dog poop
so that he could smear it on Petrel's body.
That's what he did; he smeared it around Petrel's butt.
So then,
Raven woke him up.
"My brother-in-law,
you got poop all over yourself.
Go!
Go on down to the beach and wash yourself clean!
Your clothes are trashed."
So when he woke up Petrel felt around himself; lo and behold, it was true.
So he went down to the beach,
ah, to wash himself clean.
And then Raven—
while Petrel was occupied with cleaning himself, Raven just stuck his head in the water and removed the cover.
He was drinking it
with all his might.
Yes,
as he was trying to drink it up
Petrel came in.
Raven hadn't yet pulled off the cover over the spring.
He just
flew out through the smokehole.
Then Petrel said,
"Spirit above me,
grab him!"
Raven was just flapping his wings in place.
He couldn't even manage to fly.
Below him, Petrel
was assembling pitchwood,
ah, below Raven.
Raven used to be white, they say—
white.
So,
he lit

téil,
aaa, át akawligán.
Tle t'ooch' yáx̱ yaa naneen
yá Yéil ḵu.aa.
Ách áwé Yéil—wé Yéil ḵwá tle t'ooch' yáx̱ wootee.
Aaa, du éex̱ akawdudlikwáat.
De ch'a hóoch' áyá déi yax̱ wudiḵín hú ḵu.aa,
hél tsu g̱unéi udaḵínx̱.
Dei ch'a hóoch'i daséiguch áyá ayaawadlaaḵ
gáande.
Aaa, t'ooch' yáx̱ wootee Yéil.
Hú áyá aan yaa ndaḵín
yáa héen, yá goon,
aaa, yáa ixkéenáx̱.
Náas—
aaa, a saa a yáx̱ ayawli.át
yá Náas,
tle yá nánde
áx̱ kei ndaḵin yá.
Du x̱'atáatx̱ kadutl'uḵgu aa áyá shaanax̱héenix̱ sitee.
Áyá áx̱ yaa ndaḵin yá,
goo sáwé áa yan aawakóo
áyá tle saax̱ sitee.
Aa, yá áax̱ dax̱sitee tle áa yan aawakuwu yá.
Áyá yáa—
tle nánde áx̱ kei ndaḵíni,
aaa, yáa
Shtax'héen yóo wduwasayi yá
héen tleinx̱ wusitee.
Aa, goot'á sá
yá gidéin áa yan aawakuwu yá,
a saayée dax̱ ḵudzitee.
Aaa, yá T'aaḵú,
tle yá Lḵoot, Jilḵáat,
tle yú nánde, *Yakutat*,
áx' áyáa
yan aawakóo.
Ách áwé

the pitchwood he had assembled below him,
yes, and set it ablaze.
And Raven
just started turning black.
So Raven—Raven turned black.
Yes, he was blackened from the soot.
All he could do now was flap his wings in place;
he couldn't even manage to fly.
With his last breath he succeeded
in flying outside.
Yes, Raven had turned black.
He was flying along
with this water, this springwater,
yes, from the south on up.
The Nass River—
yes, he assigned the names to the rivers,
the Nass,
and the places along which he was flying
northward.
The drops that fell out of his mouth were now rivers
within mountain valleys.
So, at the places along which he was flying,
wherever he spit that water out
is a name.
Yes, each place where he dropped water from his beak is now a lake.
So,
just as he was flying north through there,
yes,
the place that was given the name Stikine
became a great river.
Yes, whichever locations
where he released a large quantity of water,
they each have names.
Yes, the Taku River
and the Chilkoot, the Chilkat,
and Yakutat to the north,
this is where
he released the water from his beak.
That is why

haa Lingídee
yá shaanax̱héeni tlél duná.
Du jeetx̱ áyá wtusikóo Yéil
yá shaanax̱héeni tlél haa ée ushk'eiyí.
Aa, yá shaanax̱héeni—yáa
kawusg̱áadi kayaanée yaa kandutl'úg̱u,
ldakát át yá kada.eix̱ át áyá yaa kakdutl'úk̲ch.
Ách áwé
séew daak g̱asatánín
yá shaanax̱héeni kaadé aa nadéich.
Ách áwé tlél yáa naadaayi héen dunáayeen,
yú shaanax̱héeni yóo tuwasáagu.
Aaa, yáa a kaadé kaawadaayi aa yá shaa yaadáx̱.
áyá nóokx̱ haa jee sateex̱.
Ách áwé tlél tudaná.
Gòon áwé dunáayin,
goon.
Tlél a tóonáx̱ nóok k̲oostí.
Aaa, yóo diyée tl'atgitóox' áwé yéi nateech yá goon.
Ách áwé haa Lingídich kei kooháaych goon,
nax̱tudanáat.
Yéi áyá téeyin haa jeex', haa Lingídi.
Aa, yá goon
a tuwáatx̱ daséikw haa jee yéi yatee.
Ldakát yá lingit.aanituk̲wáani
ch'a s adaná yáa héen.
Aa, yáa yeedát áyá dleit k̲áa jeedáx̱,
aaa, yá shaanax̱héeni haa x̱'éit shuwduwatée.
Aaa, yáa haa x̱'éit shuwduteeyí shaanax̱héeni
áyá aa naadaa yóo shaa yaadáx̱ yú áa kaadé,
áyá tudaná.
Áyá nóok haa jee yagéi yeedát.
Aa, a x̱oodé yéi s at nasneech,
aa, yá nóok ag̱ajaag̱ít, yá l ayáx̱x̱ usiteeyi át ag̱ajaag̱éet.
Uháan haa éex' k̲u.aas tlél ushk'é.
Aaa, yáa Yéilch aadé yan haa wsiniyi yá
yá goon tudanaayée k̲wáayá haa ée yak'éi.
Aa, ách áwéi,
aa, yá shaanax̱héeninàx̱

our Tlingit people
don't drink water from mountain valley rivers.
It is from Raven's actions that we know
that water from mountain valley rivers is bad for us.
Yes, this water from mountain valley rivers—
when the fallen leaves are dripping with rainwater,
all these plants keep dripping.
So
when it rains,
some of that water flows into the mountain valley river.
That is why people never used to drink flowing river water,
that which we call mountain valley river water.
Yes, the water that flows into the valley from the mountainsides
becomes a sickness for us.
That is why we don't drink it.
People used to drink springwater—
springwater.
No sickness arises from it.
Yes, springs are down below inside the earth.
That is why our Tlingit people always dig up the springs,
so we can drink from it on a regular basis.
This is how it was for us, for our Tlingit people.
Ah, because of springwater
we have life.
All of the people of the world
just drink this water.
Yes, nowadays, under the management of white people,
yes, this river water from the valley has been piped to us.
Yes, when this water from mountain valley rivers is piped to us
some of it flows from the mountainsides down onto the lake
and we drink it.
So we have a lot of disease now.
Yes, they are always mixing something in it,
ah, so it can kill the disease, so it can kill the pathogens.
But it is bad for us.
Yes, due to how Raven programmed us,
when we drink springwater it is good for us.
Yes, that is why,
ah, there is sickness in the world

yá lingit.aanitóox' yéi yatee yá nóok.
Ách áwé yeedát
haa Lingídich yéi wsikóo,
aa, a tóonáx̱ haa daséigu haa jee yéi teex̱éech
ách áyá goon átx̱ tulayéix̱.
A tóonáx̱ haa x̱'aséigu yax̱ yoo yaateek.
Aaa, ách áyá
aa, ldakát át,
yá ḵuwakaan
yóo tuwasáagu át, haa aayí, haa at.sheeyí tóo yéi yatee.
Aa, yá g̱agaan—.
Goon yóo tuwasáakw.
Áyáa
átx̱ tulayéix̱,
aa, yá ḵuwakaan jeex'.
Aaa.
Ách áyá a táax̱ g̱aax̱tootán yá héen
    a yahaayí tudanaayí,
yéi yantooḵéich,
aaa,
«Xwéi!»
Aaa, yá goon wutudanaayí haa x̱'aséigu haa jee yéi naneech.
Aaa, yéi áyá haa Lingídich wusikóo,
ax̱ dachx̱anx'isáani.
Yihwáan áyá yee een sh kax̱alneek yeedát,
yihwáan
g̱iysakóot haa Lingít ḵusteeyée.
Dleit ḵáa ḵusteeyí tóonáx̱ áyá
    haa jee yaa nagéin nóok.
Áyá kx̱anéek yá héen.
A tóonáx̱—
yá
a tóonáx̱ naadaa yáa—
yá g̱iyéis'x̱ siteeyi át.
Tle tsu á áyá,
tlél ayáx̱ haa ée utí.
Aa, ách áyá nóok haa jeex' yéi yatee.
Aaa,
yáa yeedát,

due to the water from mountain valley rivers.
So now,
this is how our Tlingit people know it to be:
ah, we use springwater
because through it our life force is always present for us.
Our breath of life is restored through it.
Yes, this is why,
ah, everything,
what we call a deer, for example,
is reflected in our possessions, our songs.
Yes, the sun—.
We call it springwater.
So,
we use it,
ah, sharing it with the deer.
Yes.
So whenever we lower a dipper into the water,
  when we drink the sun's reflection,
yes,
we always say,
"Whew!"
Yes, when we drink springwater, our life force always comes back to us.
Yes, this is the way our Tlingit people know it,
my dear grandchildren.
I am telling this story to you folks now,
so that you
may know our Tlingit way of life.
Through the white man's way of life
  there is getting to be more and more disease.
So I am telling about this water.
Through these—
the water
flows through
these iron pipes.
That, too,
is not right for us.
Ah, that is why we have disease.
Yes,
nowadays,

aa, ch'a ldakát át áyá—
tlél ayáx̱ utí yáa héen
yóo tuwasáagu át—
tle tsu yá duna átt kawdiyáa.
Aa, a tóonáx̱ áyá kaxéel' haa jee yéi teex̱
yá tudana át.
Tlél héen áyá.
Ch'áakw áyá wduskóowun.
Ch'áakw,
aaa, yá ḵuklasheix̱ át átx̱ tulayeix̱í yá héen
tlél nóok a tóonáx̱ ḵoostéeyin.
Yeedadi aayí wdudliyex̱i aa dleit ḵáach
a x̱oodé áyá yéi at daaduné,
aag̱áa áyá haa ée s ahóon.
Ách áwé tlél haa ée ushk'é
yá dleit ḵáach haa jeex̱ tee át,
tlél yá uháan haa éex' uk'é.
Aaa, tlax̱ wáa sá
shdaayootudatánk óosh haa jee yéi yatee.
A daa aniyilg̱een!
Aa, yáa yeedát yáa tudana át,
a tóonáx̱ kaxéel' haa jee yéi teex̱,
aa, yá héen.
Aadéi l ayáx̱x̱ usiteeyi aax̱ wusiteeyi átx̱
siteeyi yá náaw yóo tuwasáagu át.
Ách áwé
haa Lingídich
a daadéi ḵutées' daa sá átx̱ gax̱tulayeix̱í,
hél ch'a koogéiyi.
Ách áwé sh daa anax̱yilg̱eenéet áyá ax̱ dachx̱anx'isáani yee een kax̱anéek yeedát.
Aa, yá héenx̱ siteeyi át,
aa, yá ḵuklasheix̱ átx̱ wududliyéx̱ haa jiyís.
Aa, áyá tlax̱
átx̱ tulayeix̱í a tóonáx̱
kaxéel' haa jee yéi teex̱.
Sheyadihéini aa ḵuwujaaḵ a tóonáx̱ ḵudzitee.
A tóonáx̱ shḵ'awulyeil haa jeex' yéi yatee
yá tudana át.

ah, all kinds of stuff—
this so-called water
is toxic—
has even ended up in the drinking water.
Ah, due to what we drink
we always have problems.
It's not water.
Long ago they knew it.
Long ago,
yes, when we used this springwater for homebrew,
sickness would not come about through it.
The water systems of today, those made by white people,
they put additives in them;
then they peddle the water to us.
That is why
the things white people give us are detrimental to us;
they are no good for us.
Yes, if only
we had enough self-awareness.
Examine it, you folks!
Yes, we always have problems with
what we drink nowadays,
ah, due to this water.
What we call liquor
is a substance that has become something that is so very destructive.
That is why
our Tlingit people
keep an eye on whatever we are going to use;
it's not just haphazard.
That is why I am telling it to you now, my dear grandchildren,
so that you will examine yourselves.
Yes, this supposed water,
yes, has been made into alcoholic beverages for us.
Yes, so
when we use it a lot
we have trouble with it.
Many murders arise through it.
We have deceit due to
what we drink.

Lingít tlél a yáa ayatooné a tóonáx̱
yáa yeedát átx̱ tulayex̱ át.
Aaa, yá náaw tóonáx̱
lingít tlél a yáa ayatooné.
Sh daa aniyilg̱een, ax̱ dachx̱anx'isáani.
Yeehwáan áyá yee een sh kax̱alneek yeedát.
Aaa, tlax̱ wáa sá kei kg̱wak'éi
yá ch'áakw kaduneegi aa gòon
átx̱ tulayeix̱í.
Aaa.
Aadé haa ée kg̱waak'éiyéyáx̱ átx̱ tulayéix̱,
tlél yá naadaayi aa,
yá dleit ḵáach yéi daane aa,
átx̱ tulayeix̱í.
Ách áwé yeedát
ax̱ tuwáa sigóo yeey.aax̱ée,
aa, yáa héen daat át.
Yá lingit.aanitóox̱ áyá ayaawakóo yá Yéilch
haa jiyís,
lingit.aanituḵwáanich nax̱danáat.
Aa, ch'a uháanch átx̱ wutuliyéx̱, a daat wutuwa.aat.
Ách áwé
a x̱oo.aa nanáax̱ sitee haa jeex'.
Aaa, ách x'wán
shdaayootudatánk
yee jee yéi natí!
Aaa, ách áyá yeedát yá kax̱lanik át,
a tóode aniyilg̱een.
Aaa, yá lingit.aanituḵwáanich dana héen
haa Yéilich haa jeet uwatiyi,
yá goon átx̱ tulayeix̱í áyá
tlax̱ haa x̱'aséigu haa jeex' yeekg̱wayáat'—
tlél yá dleit ḵáach haa jeet uwatiyi aa—
a tóonáx̱ latseen haa jee yéi kg̱watée.
Aaa, tsu yá Dikyáanḵáawu yóo tuwasáagu,
hóoch,
aaa, yáa—
yaa gagóot,
yá shaawát át aa yéix',

We don't respect people due to
what we are using now.
Yes, due to liquor,
we don't respect people.
Examine yourselves, my dear grandchildren!
It is you people that I am telling stories to now.
Yes, how much better it would be
for us to use
the springwater that they used to tell us about long ago.
Yes.
We use it in a way that could be good for us,
not using tap water,
the kind that white people
supply.
So now
I would like you folks to hear,
ah, this story about the water.
Raven carried the water in his beak around the world
for us,
so the people of the world could drink it as needed.
Yes, we've come to use it ourselves; we've adopted it.
That is why
it's the death of some of us.
Yes, so
be sure to have
self-awareness, you folks!
Yes, so take a good look into
this story I am telling you.
Yes, the water that the people of the world drink,
which our Raven gave to us,
when we use this springwater,
our lifespans will become long—
not that which the white people give to us—
we will obtain power through it.
Yes, and the one we call God,
he,
yes,
as he was walking along,
at the place where the woman was sitting,

aaa, yéi x̲'a[yak̲á], «Ax̲ jeet aa sa.ín yee héeni.»
Aaa, aag̲áa áyá
ch'a ash yalatín,
aa, tlél ash jeex̲ aa us.eenée, aag̲áa áyá yéi yaawak̲aa Dikyáank̲áawu,
«X̲áach i jeedé kk̲wasa.in aa héen,
aaa, tleix̲ x̲'aséikwx̲ siteeyi héen,
á áyáa,
x̲áach i jeedé kk̲wasa.éen.
Aaa, yáa yeedát yá ax̲ jeedé kg̲isa.in aa k̲wá tlél áyáa
yeekg̲wayáat'.»
Yéi áyá haa een kadulneek.
Haa Lingídich tsú ch'u yéi wsikóo.
Ách áyá yeedát,
yá át tóode a daa yoo x̲'ax̲aatánk.
Gu.aal kwshé
a daax'
ayiyiyilg̲eeník̲
yáa shkalneek—
yáa yeedát yánde kk̲watee aa yee jiyís.
Yèehwáan yá ax̲ dachx̲anx'isáani yee een yoo x̲'ax̲li.átk
yee x̲sax̲ánich.
Yeedát óosh l yee x̲wsax̲ánich
tlél tle yee een koonk̲alaneegín yá shkalneek.
Yee daatoowú x̲a.oowúch yee een kax̲laneek,
ux̲ kei aa utéeg̲aa yihwáan.
Sh daa aniyilg̲een.
Ách áyáa
yáa yeedát gunalchéesh,
yáa yeedát yá xáanaa ax̲ jeex' yéi wootee,
yáat'át tóode yoo x̲'ax̲atángi yee een.
Yéi áyá ax̲ tuwáa sigóo yee een yan kax̲wlaneegí x̲áach tsú yá shkalneek.

yes, he said, "Give me some of your water!"
Yes, then
she was just looking at him;
ah, when she wouldn't give him any, then God said,
"The water that I shall give you,
yes, water that is everlasting life,
this is what
I shall give to you.
Yes, the water that you will give me now
will not last long."
This is how the story is told to us.
Our Tlingit people, too, know it the same way.
That is why now,
I am speaking about it into this microphone.
My hope is
that you
will examine
this story—
this story that I will now set to completion for you folks.
I am conversing with *you* who are my dear grandchildren
because I love you.
If I didn't love you now,
I would not have told you this story.
I'm telling you this because you folks are on my mind,
lest some of you spin out of control.
Consider yourselves.
This is why
at this time,
now, this evening, I am grateful
to have had the opportunity to speak to you folks through this microphone.
This is how I, too, wish to finish telling this story to you folks.

IIa. Yéil Du Loowú Kei Wdusyeigí K̲'óots'ich X̲'akaawaneegi

Raven Gets His Nose Yanked Off Translated Live by Anna Katzeek

Okay?[*]

Yes.

Yéil tlél héen táak át yoo udat'áchk.

Ravens does not swim in the water.

Ch'a aan áyá yáat'aa,
a daat shkalneek k̲udzitee.

But still we have the Raven nose, we have a story behind it.

Aawa.áx̲ áwé yú.á,

He heard about it,

wé taaych áa yadusnak̲wx'u yá.

he heard about a place where they threw fat to each other—
at each other.

Ch'as taay áyá k̲únáx̲ k'át ax̲á Yéil.

Raven really liked fat.

Ch'a aan áwé ch'u shóogu aadé wlixooni yá.

But still he never gained weight; he's always slim.
He was always hungry.

---

* Hammond's lines of speech are given flush left in Roman.
Katzeek's are italicized and indented.

Áwé awsiteen áwé áa dunaḵws'i yá cháatl x̱'ayeex'.

He saw the people jigging for halibut.

Aag̱áa áwé
aadéi—
yá héen, k'e yáat'aa yatx̱ shux̱waa.áx̱,

And then he looked at the water, and it was just as if he lifts it up like a blanket to look under,

a tayeedé—a tayeedé woogoot.

so he walked underneath the water.

Aadáx̱
a náatx̱ akakel' nooch anax̱ yínde s aksixadi yá.
Ch'as a náadei kdus.aax̱wx'ún ch'áakw
wé t'eix̱áa náadei wé náaḵw.

He's talking about the old-timer halibut hook, they used to tie it on, and he was looking—examining the halibut hooks while he was down there.

Áwé
tlél tsu jee dunúkx̱
a náatx̱ akawukéil'i.

And the person who was holding it above, that was fishing, didn't even feel the jigging on the line when he untied it.

Áwé kei x̱dusyég̱ín áwé wé t'eix̱áa

When they pull up the line,

tlél daa sá a náak.

there wouldn't be anything on there.

Tsu yawdunaag̱ú áwé tsu héende.

Then they would put another bait on—that's what he said, they used to tie it on—tie the bait on and then they would throw the halibut hook over.

Áwé
ch'áakw
tsu tsu ch'u yé.

And he would do the same to it, the halibut hook.

A náatx̱ akakéil' tsu.

He would untie the bait.

X'oon.aa yéi ndusnée sáyá,

He did that so many times.

aa, yá Yéil
l jee dunúkx̱u áwé wéit,
aag̱áa áyá a daa yóo tuwatánk wé k̲áa, wé ast'eix̱í.

And the man that was fishing was wondering, "What's going on?
Who takes the bait off our hook?"

Ách áwé
yáa ts'óots' jee ayawdzikuwu k̲áa áwé

So they went for an expert who could feel a very slight tug on the line.

du eeg̱áa yan yakw.uwak̲úx̱ yú.á.

They went ashore to find the person who was an expert at feeling
things when there's a little jerk on the line.

Áwé tsu
aadé daak k̲óox̱ áwé, tsu {...} aadéi woogoot.

And the Raven went underneath again. He went under the water.

Ha dei ch'u tle—
tle kagéinámx̱ a daatx̱ yéi adaané.

He thought he was just so clever, see, he was taking it off
as smoothly as he can do it—untie the bait.

Tlax̱ a yáanáx̱ k̲u.aa át yawdzi.áa a náatx̱ yéi adaaneiyí.

He said when he was taking the bait off, he had his nose
too close to it, too close to the hook.

Á wé k̲áach
jee ayawdinúk.

That expert felt there's something going on on this line, you know,
he felt a little
wriggling.

Jee ayadanóok áwé yák'wde áa ajikaawax̱óot'.

And then he pulled—you have to pull the line.

Aag̱áa áwé du lóonáx̱ woojeil yú.á wé t'eix̱áa.

They said that the halibut hook
got right on his nose, on Raven's nose.

Kei ndusyéḵ.

Then they were bringing him up.

Altín wé yaakw tayee, k'e hé dikée.

He could see under the bottom of the boat, just like you see the ceiling.

Tle yáa diyée yaa kagooséi áwé a tayee aawatséx̱ wé yaakw.
Kawdudzixát.

As soon as he came closer, he kicked up underneath the boat.
That man was pulling it.

Aadóo sánix̱ sá sateeyí ch'a aadé yéi x̱át nay.oo!
(LAUGHTER)

Whosever uncle Raven is, he says, "Forgive me!" for telling this story.

(LAUGHTER)
A tayee áwé aawatséx̱. Kawdudzixát.

He was kicking underneath, bracing himself under there
so they won't pull him in.

A yíkde áwé ḵaa jeet uwaxíx.
A náax̱ wulixáat' áwé du loowú.

Here was the Raven nose, on a hook; they pulled his nose off.

Tlél wuduskú daatx̱ sá sateeyí.

They didn't know what it was; the fishermen did not know exactly
what it was.

Áwé yan has ḵóox̱ áwé ldakát—

When the fishermen went ashore,

ldakát wé lingítch áwé a daa woos.éix̱.

all the people came down and they were examining this thing they
brought up.

Eesháan, wé Yéil ḵu.aa áwé du loowú g̱óot áwé yan uwax'ák.

Poor Raven came ashore, came out from in the water without a nose.

Áwé loon áwé akaawayéx̱.

And he found a bark, and he shapened it.

Át aawatsáḵ du lú.

He stuck it to where his bill usually goes, his nose.

Gootx̱ sákwshíwé du jeet uwaxixi át? Ḵ'alux̱út'aa s'áaxw yóo duwasáakw.

He said that he had on a hat with a bill on it.

G̱unéi uwagút tsu.

They didn't know he got this hat that had a bill.
And he started to walk.

Tle a shóonáx̱ áwé át uwagút wé hít.

And he went from one house that began—coming to the village,

Áwé awóos',

one house at a time. And then he asked.

«Goodéi sá kei wdudziyéḵ?»
G̱uneit loowú yóo áwé aséix̱.

"I wonder who got the G̱uneit's nose?"
He gave it a name. He wasn't saying, "It's my nose," you know.
"I wonder who pulled it up?" he said.

Áwé a x̱oox̱ yaa nagút.
«K'idaakaadé áwé kei wududziyéḵ,» yóo yanduskéich.

"We heard it was next door." So he went to the next-door house.

Ách áwé tsu aax̱ g̱unéi ugootch. Át ugootch.

And then he would go to the next door and say,

«Yáat ák.wé kei wdudziyéḵ
G̱uneit loowú?»

"Is this where they caught—where someone
brought up the G̱uneit's nose?"

«Tleik'. K'idaakaadé áwé.»

And they said, "No, not here. Try next door."

A x̱oox̱ yaa nagút wé hítx'.

He's walking through the houses.

Yáax’ áwé át uwagút k̲únáx̲ áwé át tin yá. Aaa.

Finally he came to the house where his nose was,

Awóos’,

and he was asking,

«G̲uneit—yáat ák.wé kei wdudziyék̲ G̲uneit loowú?»

"Are you the people who brought up the G̲uneit's nose?"

«Aaa. Yáadu á. Wéidu.»

He said, "Yes. This is—we did. It's right there."

Yáa x̲’wáal’ áwé a daa yéi duwa.óo.

They put down—the downy part of a bird feathers around it.

Aag̲áa áwé a daa yoo yakwdzi.éik.

And he was looking at it. He was looking at it.

«Háh!» Ash yáa k̲ut woonei tsu, «Hóh!

He said, "My! This looks ..."
It looks strange to him.

Gwál tlél kawdakei kwshé yéi—aadéi yateeyi yá.»

He said, "Isn't this something!
It's amazing!"

Tle a daa yoo yakoos.éigi áwé aax̲ yóot aawax̲út’ wé loon.

While he was looking at it, while people looked at him—
blinked their eye,
he pulled the other one off,

A eetéet aawagúk̲.

and then he put his nose back.

Aag̲áa áwé gáant wujixíx hú k̲u.aa.

He ran out the door.

Ách áwé yá yéil a lú,
tlél aax̲—yeeytéen aadéi yateeyi yá,
tlél *fit*-x̲ ustí áx’.

That's why when you see a raven,
it doesn't look like it really fits onto his nose.

(LAUGHTER)

Ha yéi áwé kawdudlineek x̱aan.

That's the way the story went, as it was told to him.

Aa, ch'a aadé x'wán yéi x̱at nay.oo, ax̱ aat hás.[*]

Yéi kg̱watée, gunalchéesh.[†]
That's just one of the cute little things he did.

AMY MARVIN: Wéidu, i sáni loowú áwé.
(MUCH LAUGHTER)

That's your uncle's nose—
your uncle Raven's nose.

---

* Translation: 'Ah, please do forgive me, my aunties.'

† Translation: 'It will be so, thank you.'

IIb. Yéil Du Loowú Kei Wdusyeigí
Yoox̱'atánk Yéidaanéiyich X̱'aawaneegi

Okay?
Yéil tlél héen táak át yoo udat'áchk.
Ch'a aan áyá yáat'aa,
a daat shkalneek ḵudzitee.
Aawa.áx̱ áwé yú.á,
wé taaych áa yadusnaḵwx'u yá.
Ch'as taay áyá ḵúnáx̱ k'át ax̱á Yéil.
Ch'a aan áwé ch'u shóogu aadé wlixooni yá.
Áwé awsiteen áwé áa dunaḵws'i yá cháatl x̱'ayeex'.
Aagáa áwé
aadéi—
yá héen—k'e yáat'aa yatx̱ shux̱waa.áx̱—
a tayeedé—a tayeedé woogoot.
Aadáx̱
a náatx̱ akakel' nooch anax̱ yínde
    s aksixadi yá.
Ch'as a náadei kdus.aax̱x'ún ch'áakw,
wé t'eix̱áa náadei wé náaḵw.
Áwé
tlél tsu jee dunúkx̱
a náatx̱ akawukéil'i.
Áwé kei x̱dusyégín áwé wé t'eix̱áa
tlél daa sá a náak.
Tsu yawdunaagú áwé tsu héende.

IIb. Raven Gets His Nose Yanked Off

Translated by the Editors

Okay?
Raven doesn't swim in the water.
But still there is a story about it,
this very story.
They say he heard about
a place where people were using fat to bait halibut hooks.
Raven really loved to eat only fat, a lot of it.
But even so, he was still as thin as ever.
He saw where people were setting their hooks for halibut.
So then,
toward the—
the water—see, for instance, how I've lifted the edge of this cloth—
Raven did just so and walked underneath the water, underneath it.
After this
he would untie the bait from the body of the hooks where they had the line dangling down.
Long ago, they just tied octopus used as bait
over the hooks when fishing for halibut.
Now,
the people couldn't even feel it
when he untied the fat from the hooks.
So whenever they pulled up the hooks
there was never anything on them.
So once they rebaited the hooks, they would cast them back into the water.

Áwé
ch’áakw
tsu tsu ch’u yé.
A náatx̲ akakéil’ tsu.
X’oon.aa yéi ndusnée sáyá,
aa, yá Yéil
l jee dunúkx̲u wéit,
aag̲áa áyá a daa yoo tuwatánk wé k̲áa, wé ast’eix̲í.
Ách áwé
yáa ts’óots’ jee ayawdzikuwu k̲áa áwé
du eeg̲áa yan yakw.uwak̲úx̲, yú.á.
Áwé tsu
aadé daak k̲óox̲ áwé, tsu {…} aadéi woogoot.
Ha dei ch’u tle—
tle kagéináx̲ a daatx̲ yéi adaané.
Tlax̲ a yáanáx̲ k̲u.aa át yawdzi.áa
    a náatx̲ yéi adaaneiyí.
Á wé k̲áach
jee ayawdinúk.
Jee ayadanóok áwé yák’wde áa ajikaawax̲óot’.
Aag̲áa áwé du lóonáx̲ woojeil yú.á wé t’eix̲áa.
Kei ndusyék̲.
Altín wé yaakw tayee, k’e hé dikée.
Tle yáa diyée yaa kagooséi áwé a tayee aawatséx̲ wé yaakw.
Kawdudzixát.
Aadóo sánix̲ sá sateeyí ch’a aadéi yéi x̲at nay.oo!
    (AT.SHOOK̲)
A tayee áwé aawatséx̲. Kawdudzixát.
A yíkde áwé k̲aa jeet uwaxíx.
A náax̲ wulixáat’ áwé du loowú.
Tlél wuduskú daatx̲ sá sateeyí.
Áwé yan has k̲óox̲ áwé ldakát—
ldakát wé lingítch áwé a daa woos.éix̲.
Eesháan, wé Yéil k̲u.aa áwé du loowú g̲óot áwé yan uwax’ák.
Áwé loon áwé akaawayéx̲.
Át aawatsák̲ du lú.
Gootx̲ sákwshíwé du jeet uwaxixi át? K̲’alux̲út’aa s’áaxw
    yóo duwasáakw.
G̲unéi uwagút tsu.

So,
it went on just the same
for a long time.
He was still untying the fat from the hooks.
After the people had gone through this process a number of times,
ah, since
nobody ever felt Raven there
that man, that fisherman, was thinking the situation over.
So
a boat went ashore to pick up
a top-notch nibble-feeler, they say.
So once again,
after the boat went out there, Raven went back to the hooks.
This time he was just
ever so stealthily removing the fat from the hooks.
But he put his face too close to the hook
    as he was removing the bait from it.
That man, the nibble-feeler,
felt him.
When the nibble-feeler felt him, he up and jerked on the line.
That was when the hook worked its way through his nose, they say.
The people were hauling him up.
He was watching the bottom of the boat just like this ceiling above us.
Down below, as the boat drew closer, he kicked the bottom of it.
They pulled the line taut.
Whoever's uncle Raven is, please forgive me.
    (**LAUGHTER**)
He kicked the bottom of it. They pulled the line taut.
It fell aboard and into their hands.
His nose was dangling from the hook.
They didn't know what it was.
So when they came ashore, all—
all the people were examining it.
But poor Raven wriggled ashore without his nose.
He whittled a piece of bark.
He stuck it on, his wooden nose.
I wonder where it came from, this thing he got ahold of. It is called
    a "visor hat".
He started walking again.

Tle a shóonáx̲ áwé át uwagút wé hít.
Áwé awóos',
«Goodé sá kei wdudziyék̲?»
G̲uneit loowú yóo áwé aséix̲.
Áwé a x̲oox̲ yaa nagút.
«K'idaakaadé áwé kei wududziyék̲,» yóo yandusk̲éich.
Ách áwé tsu aax̲ g̲unéi ugootch. Át ugootch,
«Yáat ák.wé kei wdudziyék̲
G̲uneit loowú?»
«Tleik'. K'idaakaadé áwé.»
A x̲oox̲ yaa nagút wé hítx'.
Yáax' áwé át uwagút k̲únáx̲ áwé át tin yá. Aaa.
Awóos',
«G̲uneit—yáat ák.wé kei wdudziyék̲
    G̲uneit loowú?»
«Aaá. Yáadu á. Wéidu.»
Yá x̲'wáal' áwé a daa yéi duwa.óo.
Aag̲áa áwé a daa yoo yakwdzi.éik.
«Háh!» Ash yáa k̲ut woonei tsu, «Hóh!
Gwál hél kawdakei kwshé yéi—aadéi yateeyi yá.»
Tle a daa yoo yakoos.éigi áwé aax̲ yóot aawax̲út' wé loon.
A eetéet aawagúk̲.
Aag̲áa áwé gáant wujixíx hú k̲u.aa.
Ách áwé yá yéil a lú,
tlél aax̲—yeeytéen aadéi yateeyi yá,
tlél *fit*-x̲ ustí áx'.
Ha yéi áwé kawdudlineek x̲aan.
  (AT.SHOOK̲)
Aa, ch'a aadé x'wán yéi x̲at nay.oo, ax̲ aat hás.
  K̲'ÓOTS'I: *Yéi kg̲watée, gunalchéesh.*
    That's just one of the cute little things he did.
  K̲OOTEEN: *Wéidu, i sáni loowú áwé.*
  (AATLEIN AT.SHOOK̲)
  K̲'ÓOTS'I: *That's your uncle's nose—*
    your uncle Raven's nose.

He came to a house at the end of town.
He was inquiring about it,
"Where did they take it when they pulled it up?"
He kept calling it "the Alien's nose".
So he went from door to door.
"They took it next door when they pulled it up," people kept telling him.
So he'd start out again. He'd come to another house and ask,
"Was it here that they brought it to when they pulled up
the Alien's nose?"
"No. That was next door."
He was walking through the houses.
He finally came to the very place where his nose was lying. Yes.
He asked for it,
"The Alien's—is it here that they brought the Alien's nose when they
pulled it up?"
"Yes. It's here. Over there."
Down feathers had been put all around it.
So then Raven was giving it a look-over.
"Hah!" He was amazed by it too. "Hoh!
I guess it's not too shabby, is it, the way it is?"
As he was looking it over, he yanked the bark off.
He stuck his nose back on where it used to be.
Then he ran outside.
That's why a raven's beak—
you can see the way it is—
it doesn't fit very well there.
Well, this is how the story was told to me.
(LAUGHTER)
Ah, please do forgive me, my aunties.
ANNA KATZEEK: *It will be so, thank you.*
That's just one of the cute little things he did.
AMY MARVIN: *There it is; that's your uncle's nose.*
(MUCH LAUGHTER)
ANNA KATZEEK: *That's your uncle's nose—*
your uncle Raven's nose.

Yakwx̱aan Tláa X̱'éidáx̱ Tlaagú
Stories by Katherine Mills

FIGURE 15. Mills wearing a headband and vest displaying her clan's crest, the kittiwake. Hoonah, c. 1980s. Courtesy of Huna Heritage Foundation, Paul Rudolph Collection.

OUR FINAL STORYTELLER is Yakwx̲aan Tláa, Katherine Mills, of Hoonah, Alaska. She was a woman of the T'ak̲deintaan clan from Tax̲'hít' 'Snail House' and a child of the K̲ookhittaan clan. She was born on June 14, 1915, and passed away on August 16, 1993. Mills was a gifted storyteller who loved to make her audience laugh. Her versions of these stories are sometimes serious in tone, but at other times she delights in the scurrilous details of Raven's romps and the reactions of his victims. Her delivery of these stories is rapid and straightforward, with few pauses and little pomp, yet her speech is full of marvelous examples of the creativity possible in Tlingit storytelling. Her style for Raven stories was characterized by a classic 'deadpan' tone of voice contrasting with the outrageous antics of Raven underway in the stories. It is evident in these texts that she enjoyed punctuating her stories with classical formulas such as «Yéi áwé kaawagei»* 'That's the whole story' (literally, 'That is how big it came to be') and «Yéi áwé yan shuwjix̲ín yáat'aa»† 'That is how this one ends.'

Mills was literate in Tlingit and well-practiced with the writing system. She was a major player in early efforts to teach the language and develop popular Tlingit literacy. Along with Andrew Hope III, Nora and Richard Dauenhauer, and Henry Davis, she was a founder of Tlingit Readers Inc. and served until her death as a charter member of its board of directors. She taught Tlingit language and culture in the Hoonah public schools for many years. During the course of her teaching, she composed many materials for classroom use. Of these, the best known is her *Wooch Yáx̲ Yaa Datúwch: Tlingit Math Book*, published in 1973 by Tlingit Readers Inc., which features basic arithmetical problems formulated in Tlingit and which has remained popular in classrooms for decades. She participated in the first Tlingit Language Workshop at Sheldon Jackson College in 1971 as well as subsequent iterations; her

* KM III, 167; IV, 62; VI, 84.

† KM II, 114; V, 113.

math book was published during the third such workshop. In the 1980s she collaborated with Wally and Marie Olson on a bilingual pamphlet called "Tlingit Thinking / Lingit Tundataanee,"[*] published by Southeast Alaska Regional Health Corporation (now Southeast Alaska Regional Health Consortium). She made many contributions to Sealaska Heritage Foundation (now Sealaska Heritage Institute). She was active in one of the foundation's very first Tlingit transcription and translation projects and she served as a charter member of the Elders Advisory Council (since renamed the Council of Traditional Scholars). Among her unpublished works are a short play in Tlingit and English titled "Eagle Boy";[†] a draft manuscript titled «Keinei at K'atsk'oo», which is a Tlingit translation of *Cannery Kid*, a short book written in English by her grandson Gussie Mills;[‡] and numerous miscellaneous transcriptions, including, importantly, of Tlingit songs.[§]

In contrast to her record of achievement, Mills was a very quiet person, so low-key and low-profile as to be easily overlooked by outsiders. Mills was a lifetime member of Hoonah Alaska Native Sisterhood Camp No. 12, serving as president for many years and as a convention delegate. She was also a convention delegate for Central Council of the Tlingit and Haida Indian Tribes of Alaska and served on the Hoonah City Council. She was a lifelong member of the Russian Orthodox Church.

Mills told the six tales presented here on February 4, 1989, in Anchorage and was recorded by Ḵaalyát', Edna Belarde Lamebull. While Mills was recorded telling all six tales on the same day and in the same location, she appears to have told them as discrete performances with the recorder having been switched off at the end of each story and an unknown amount of time elapsing between each recording. Most of these narratives are internally complete and lack a discernible connection between the surrounding stories from the recording. The exceptions are "Raven and the King Salmon" (KM II) and "Raven and the Brown Bear Couple" (KM III), which can be logically connected in this order by the fact that the king salmon tail that Raven salvages in the former story becomes his halibut bait in the latter. We have presented Mills' material as six discrete tales in the order we believe they were told, reflecting the order of the individual tracks on the archival holding.[¶]

---

* MS052, box 65, file unit 004.

† MS052, box 46, file unit 028.

‡ MS052, box 65, file unit 005. «Keinei at K'áts'oo» (standardized as *Keinei Atk'átsk'u*) is literally 'Cannery Kid' (*keinei* being a Tlingit borrowing of English 'cannery').

§ MS052, box 15.

¶ MC005, tape 253, tracks a, b, d, e, f, g (track c is an English telling of "Raven and the Brown Bear Couple").

FIGURE 16. A ceremony in Hoonah, c. 1980s. Mills stands dancing among a group of T'ak̲deintaan women while Amy Marvin (furthest left, holding drum) of the Chookaneidí leads the drumming and singing. Front row dancing women, left to right: UNK, Mary Wilson, Irene Lampe, Sue Belarde, Hilda See, Katherine Mills (wearing black vest), and Marlene Johnson. The gifts lying before Mills and the other T'ak̲deintaan women indicate that they are honored guests at a potlatch hosted by a clan of the opposite Eagle moiety, perhaps the Chookaneidí. Courtesy of Huna Heritage Foundation, Paul Rudolph Collection.

FIGURE 17. Mills (second from left) teaching a Tlingit language course in a classroom in Hoonah, c. 1970s. Courtesy of Huna Heritage Foundation, Marlene Johnson Collection.

I. Yéil ḵa Kudataankahídi

Yakwx̱waan Tláa yóo x̱at duwasáakw.
T'aḵdeintaan Sháawu áyá x̱át,
Xunaadáx̱.
Tax̱'hít
a sháawu áyá x̱át, Tax̱'hittaan Sháawu.
Áwé yee een áwé sh kakḵwalneek ch'a yéi yguwáatl'.
Tleidahéen áwé yú.á yóo Yéil—
x̱áat áwé tlél ḵaa x̱'ax̱áni yéi uteex̱éen ch'áakw,
áwé
yú Yéilch a daa yóo tutangi nuch. Ch'as yóo deikéex' áwé isx̱ítt'
yá x̱áat.
Áwé a daa yóo tuwatánk yú Yéil. Ḵ'anashgidéi ḵu.oo yá haa yáx̱,
áwé tlél aadé hasdu kagéi aa kg̱waaháayi yé.
Ách áwé
a daa yóo toowatán yú Yéil.
G̱útl,
gútl áwé du jeewú á, sáḵs.
Áwé tléináx̱ yateeyi aa ḵáa ḵu.aa áwé,
Náaḵw Tl'eig̱í Wootsaag̱áa áwé du jeewú.
Aag̱áa áwé
yú Yéil ḵwás wáa sá óosh du jeet wudzinée yá Náaḵw Tl'eig̱í Wootsaag̱áa yóo áwé tuwditaan tlákw.
Tlákw át nagútch. Wáanée sáwé dé a x̱ángaa woogoot wé
wootsaag̱áa s'aatí.

I. Raven and the Salmon Box

My name is Yakwx̱waan Tláa.
I'm a woman of the T'ak̲deintaan clan
from Hoonah.
I'm a woman
of the Snail House, a Snail-House Woman.
Now I'll tell you some stories for a little while.
Once upon a time, it is said, Raven—
there were no salmon accessible for people to eat long ago,
so,
Raven kept contemplating this. The salmon
would spawn only out in the ocean.
Now Raven was contemplating this. There was no way poor people like us
could ever access any.
That's why
Raven was contemplating it.
Blunt-tipped arrows,
he had some blunt-tipped arrows and a bow.
But there was one man
who had the Octopus Tentacle Cane.
And so,
Raven was fixated on figuring out how to get his hands on this
    Octopus Tentacle Cane.
He was always walking around. Eventually he wandered up to the
owner of the cane.

Aag̲áa áwé yéi yaawak̲aa,
«Hél gé aadé yáa—?
Shk'e latín yáa
ax̲ sák̲si.
Yá g̲útl áyá k̲únáx̲ átx̲ sitee.
Yú shaa shakéet woogoodi
jánwu aadé kk̲wat'óok.
K'e latín!»
Áwé tle aadé kéi awli.ún wé du g̲údli yú shaa shakée.
Áwé tle aawat'úk yú—
yú jánwu,
tle daak wudzigít,
tle sdu x̲ángaa áwé wdzigeet.
Aag̲áa áwé tsá yóo wootsaag̲áa s'aatéech x̲'eiwawóos',
«Yá i g̲údli daséix'án ágí seeyahéi
ax̲ Náak̲w Tl'eig̲í Wootsaag̲áyi?»
«Aaá! Aaá!
Yéi áwé ax̲ tuwáa sigóo!
K̲únáx̲ áyá yak'éi yá ax̲ sák̲si
k̲a yá g̲útl,» yóo x̲'ayak̲á Yéil.
«K̲únáx̲ i jeex' kéi kg̲wak'éi.
X̲át k̲wás i wootsaag̲áyi ax̲ jeex' kéi kg̲wak'éi.»
Ách áwé tle—
tle woosh daséix' yéi s ayawdzinée.
Aag̲áa áwé tsá yéi ayawsik̲aa
Yéil aan g̲unayéi kg̲wagoodí,
«Tlél áwé du latseení k̲oostí wé wootsaag̲áa,
tle ch'a x̲át ax̲ saayí
a x̲'áax̲ kéi nilasáyi áwé tsáa a latseení áa yéi kg̲watée.»
Naaliyéix̲ yóo ksa.aa yú.á du wootsaag̲áyi k̲u.aa
ch'a g̲unáa yateeyi át aan akg̲waasháat.
Ách áwé
tle yéi yaawak̲aa Yéil,
«Yéi x̲á kg̲watée, yéi kg̲watée.»
Aag̲áa áwé tsá aan gáande woogoot.
Du een yéi jine aa,
du kéilk' k̲u.aawé—Gidzanóox yóo áwé duwasáakw wé yéil.
Aag̲áa áwé
át has uwa.át wé héen wát,

So then he said,
"Isn't there some way—?
Well, why don't you take a gander at this
bow of mine?
This blunt-tipped arrow is really something.
I'll launch my arrow at that mountain goat
walking about the mountain top.
Just watch!"
Then he shot his blunt-tipped arrow up there toward the mountain top.
It struck the—
the mountain goat;
it just fell down
and landed by them.
So then at last the owner of the cane asked him,
"Do you want to trade your blunt-tipped arrow
for my Octopus Tentacle Cane?"
"Yes! Yes!
That's what I want!
This bow of mine is really good,
and this blunt-tipped arrow," Raven said.
"It will be good for you to have.
And your cane will be good for me to have."
So they just—
they just made the trade.
Then just when Raven was getting ready to leave with it,
he told Raven,
"The cane itself is powerless;
only when you go along intermittently saying my name as you use it
will its power be present."
It is said that the cane would extend over a great distance,
and no matter what it was, he could grab it with the cane.
So
Raven said,
"Indeed, it will be so; it will be so."
Then finally he went outside with it.
The guy who was working with Raven,
his nephew, in fact—Gidzanóox' was the name of that raven.
Then
they came to the mouth of the river,

Aalséix̱ wát áwé yú.á.
Áwé tle—
tle héenx̱ ak'eewataan wé wootsaag̱áa.
Áwé tle—
tle daak kanas.éin tle yóo deikéede yú x̱áat—
x̱áat daakahídi, yéi duwasáakw
Kudataankahídi,
yú x̱áat a yee yéi yateeyi
hít,
yú yax̱'áak, tlax̱ yú deikée.
Á áwé
yánde asayahéi.
Tle aanáx̱ ax̱'awshik'éix̱'.
Deisgwach át ash jinaasháat
yóo taashuká.
Du x̱'us.eetí tlénx' tle áa yéi yatee.
Ch'u yeedát de tlél aax̱ unahéich. K̲ushtuyáx̱ wáa koogeyi héen a káa yóo jisatángi sá, yóo teet tlénx', ch'a aan hél aadé kéi shaag̱aaheegi yé du x̱'us.eetí.
Aadóo sá áx̱ k̲uyawuteení yú héen wát yan wulaayí yéi gax̱dustéen
yú átch aadé át woox̱óot'i yé.
Áwé
wáanée sáwé Gidzanóox'ch yéi yawsik̲aa, «Cha dáa déi kéi kashí!
Cha dáa déi du saayí
sá déi.»
Áwé hél ch'a yéi awusá, kéi áwé shikaawashée,
«X̱'anax̱g̱aatwaayáa,»
yóo ashukawlix̱oox̱ yóo shí.
Tléix' ashukawulx̱oox̱ú áwé tle naaliyéix' yánde yaa asyík̲ch yú Kudataankahídi.
Tle yaa sh nalk'átl'i áwé tle tsu kéi akooshéeych. Tle tlákw áwé yánde yaa anasyík̲.
Tlax̱ wáa yeekunayáat' sá yán ayaawadlaak̲
wé hít.
Aag̱áa áwé tle yéi k̲uyawsik̲aa,
«Ldakát yá lingít,
daak̲w héen yaax̱x' sá yéi iteex̱ée,
ldakát yeehwáan áwé haadé gax̱yeek̲óox̱ yeedát yee yaakwx'u sáani yíkt,

the mouth of the Alsek River, they say.
Then he—
he just dipped the butt of the cane into the water.
Then it—
it began extending out, all the way out to the salmon—
the salmon house; it's called the
Salmon Box,
the house
that the salmon live in,
way out in the deep ocean, far out at sea.
That was what
he wanted to get to shore.
Then he hooked the crook of the cane through it.
By degrees it jerked him here and there
on the beachfront.
His huge footprints are still right there.
They haven't been erased even to this day. No matter how much water rolls over them, even with those huge breakers, there's no way his footprints can get filled in.
Whoever travels through the mouth of the river when the tide is low can see
the place where that thing dragged him around.
So,
at some point Gidzanóox' said to him, "Please, sing it right now!
Please say his name
right now."
He didn't just utter the name; he began to sing,
"X̱'anax̱gaatwaayáa,"
is how he chanted that song.
With one chant, he was making progress hauling that Salmon Box a great distance toward shore.
And just as he was falling silent, he would start singing it again. He was steadily pulling it ashore.
After a very long time
the house reached the shore.
Then he told the people,
"All the people,
whatever stream you live along,
all of you are to come here now in your little boats,

k̲ushtuyáx̲ wáa koogeyi héen yaax̲x' sá yéi iteeyí, tsu aa yátsx'i,
 k̲a tsu aatlénx'
naadaayi héen,
aag̲áa áwé i jeedé yéi kk̲wasanée yá x̲áat.»
Ách áwé tle ldakát yú aandáx̲ k̲u.oo áwé
tle át k̲uyaawagóo.
Aag̲áa áwé
daak̲w.aa héen sá—
wáanganeens ch'as g̲aat a yíx̲ hèen—
g̲aat áwé k̲aa jeet yéi awsinée,
k̲aa l'ook,
k̲aa téel',
cháas',
saak.
Ách áwé,
ách áwé tle ldakát yáa héen—
k'e aadé k̲ux̲ has ayaawax̲ayi yé—
tlákw k̲utaan
áa k̲ux̲ kadahéich yá héen yík
yá x̲áat.
Yú Yéilch aadé yan wusiniyi yé áwé.
Yá héen k̲u.aa áwé wóoshi ax̲'akaawadúx'.
Ách áwé tlél aadé shoong̲aaxeexi yé, k̲ushtuyáx̲ wáa sá
k̲uk'é
yaa shayandahéini yá sínde x̲'áaknáx̲, k̲ukawuxoogú, tlél aadé yínde
 yóo ng̲waaneeyi yé k'idéin
yá héenx'.
Ách áwé yá x̲áat ch'u shóogu yáa áa s ajeewanag̲i yé ch'u shóogu áx̲
 has ya.aa,
x'oon jinkaat táakw x̲'áaknáx̲ sá.
Áwé
yáa—yá Yéil aadé haa éet wudishiyi yé áyá.
Ách áyá k̲'anashgidéi k̲u.oo kagéi kaawaháa
yá shkalneek.

no matter what size of stream you live along,
    whether tiny creeks or huge
rivers;
then I'll give salmon to you."
So the people from all those villages
came in their boats.
So then,
whichever stream—
in some cases only sockeye swim up the stream—
he gave sockeye to the people,
and coho,
and chum,
humpies,
eulachon.
This is why,
this is the reason fish migrate back to all these rivers—
just look how many fish they hauled back home—
the salmon
show back up in the rivers
every summer.
That's the way Raven arranged it.
He tied each river up in a loop.
That's why they can never become depleted; no matter how many
nice days
accumulate through the week when it's dry weather, there's no way
    that the water level can recede much
in these rivers.
So these salmon still migrate to the very same place
    where they had left them,
many decades after the fact.
Well,
this—this is how Raven helped us.
This is how poor people came to have access to salmon,
this very story.

II. Yéil k̲a T’á

Yá Yéil áwé neecht woogoot.
Ch’a át wugoodí awsiteen yáa t’á
át wootáan yá g̲eey ká.
A daat áwé tle
át tuwditaan, «Wáa sá óosh x̲wasinei yú t’á,
yáanáx̲ yan kak̲aladootl.»
Tlax̲ wáa yóo koogóot sáwé
aawat’ei wé s’oow.
Tle at gook’ú shakéex’,
té shakéex’ gíwé kéi awutí.
Aag̲áa áwé tsáa
tle x̲’wáal’ a daa yéi aya.óo.
Aag̲áa áwé tsá yéi ayawsik̲aa wé t’á,
«Cha t’á
haadé k̲inees.aax̲!
Yá s’oowk’úch áwé yéi idaayak̲á,
‹x’éix’u x̲ootl’eex›.»
Áwé yá t’á k̲u.aa áwé tlél du x̲’éit wus.aax̲.
Tle tsu ch’a át wootáan.
Aag̲áa áwé tle tsu yéi ayanask̲éich,
«Cha t’á,
yá s’oowk’ áwé tláakw idaayak̲á.
Du x̲’éit sa.áx̲. Yáanáx̲ yan x’ák.»
Ch’a át woox’aak wé deikée wé t’á k̲u.aa.

II. Raven and the King Salmon

Raven was walking around on the beach.
While he was walking around, he saw a king salmon
jumping out there in the bay.
He just pondered
the situation, "What could I do to that king salmon
to lure it into coming ashore here?"
After walking quite a ways
he found a greenstone.
He just put it on top of a little stump
or maybe on top of a rock.
Next
he placed down feathers around it.
Then he said to the king salmon,
"O king salmon,
listen here!
This little greenstone is calling you
'trash-in-the-gills.'"
But the king salmon didn't listen to him.
It just started jumping around again.
Then he'd say to it again,
"O king salmon,
this little greenstone is insulting you.
Listen to what he's saying! Swim on in here!"
But the king salmon just kept swimming around out there.

Hél du x̱'éit wus.aax̱.
Wáannée sáwé tlax̱ aan kéi u.éex'[ch],
«Cha t'áa-áa-áa-áa!
Yáanáx̱ yan x'áa-áa-áa-áak,
yá s'oowk' aadé idaayaḵa yé k'idéin g̱ee.aax̱éet!»
Aag̱áa áwé tsá du x̱ánde yóot uwax'ák.
Ch'u l ák' ooheení áwé, tle guxkáa woox'aak wé t'á.
Aag̱áa áwé yéi ayawsiḵaa,
«Ḵoosh kadáan á!
Ḵoosh kadáan á!
Gánde x̱áat tuwdishát.
Dag̱inaadé s'é kḵwashéex.»
Áwé tle dáḵde wujixeex.
Yú dáaḵdáx̱ ḵach x'ús'gaa ásíwéigé wjixeex. Yéiḵ aawashát tle wé x'ús', tle aan áwé ashaawax̱ích wé t'á.
Áwé du jikayáanáx̱ kawlidaal wé x'ús'.
Áwé wé át kawdliyeeji átx'i sáani ḵu.aa wé du dachx̱anx'iyánx̱ sitee.
Aag̱áa áwé yéi ayawsiḵaa wé du dachx̱anx'iyán,
«X̱áat yidashí,
héi daaḵ g̱atoox̱óot'i.
Yéi g̱ax̱tuladáak áyá yá x̱áat.»
Há', tle kéi kawduwaháa du dachx̱anx'iyánch du ji.een,
a ya.áak.
«Dag̱inaadé yee lunagooḵ!
X̱'áal' yéiḵ yéi ysané.
A taká, yá kóoḵ takáa yéi g̱ax̱too.óo.
A daadé kag̱ax̱tooyéiḵ, aag̱áa áwé tsá
ch'a x̱'aank'átsk'u a kináakde ag̱ax̱too.áak.»
Áwé tle ḵukawdliyeech wé ts'ítsgux' sáani.
Tle yéiḵ yéi wdudzinée
wé x̱'áal'.
Áwé tle ḵux̱'eiwawóos',
«Goodáx̱ x̱'áal' sá yéiḵ yéi yeeysinée?»—«Ch'a hé dag̱inaa áwé, wé gooch seiyí.»
Aag̱áa yéi yaawaḵaa Yéil ḵu.aa,
«Ch'a hé dag̱inaa yóo gé?»—«Aaá.
Áx' shayadihéin. Ḵúnáx̱ yak'éi.

It didn't listen to him.
Eventually he really started hollering out,
"Hey king sa-a-a-a-almon!
Swim in over he-e-e-ere
so you can clearly hear what the little greenstone is saying about you!"
Only then did it swim off toward him.
Before Raven could believe his eyes, the king salmon swam up onto the sand.
Then Raven said to him,
"What a fine mess!
What a fine mess!
I need to go to the bathroom right away!
I'll run up into the woods first."
So he just ran on up.
Actually, he ran up to get a club from the woods. He grabbed one and went down to the beach and just clubbed the king salmon over the head with it.
Well, the king salmon was too heavy for him.
The birds of the air are his grandchildren.
So then he said to his grandchildren,
"Help me.
Let's pull it up over here.
We'll bake this salmon in a pit under a fire."
Well, with his grandchildren helping him, they dug up
a pit for it.
"Run up in the woods, guys!
Bring down some skunk cabbage leaves.
We'll put them in the bottom of the pit.
We'll wrap them around the fish and then
we'll build a little fire up on top of it."
Then the little birds flew off.
They brought down
the skunk cabbage.
Then he asked them,
"Where did you get the skunk cabbage that you brought down?"—
"Back over here, at the base of the hill."
Then Raven said,
"Just back over there?"—"Yes.
There's a lot there. It's really good.

Ách áwé tle haa waaḵg̱áa wootee.
Ha wáa sáwé?»
tle yóo yawdudziḵaa wé Yéil.
Yá Yéil ḵwá tle yéi yaawaḵaa,
«Cha ée!
Ax̱ shát aadé gánde yóo gútgu yé áwé!
Ch'a g̱óot.aag̱áa nay.á!
Déix̱ shaa kaanáx̱ áwé yéi gax̱yee.áat,
aag̱áa áwé tsá kéi kg̱wak'éi.»
Áwé tle ḵukawdliyeech du jiyís, tle áa jiwduwanáḵ wé x̱'áal'.
Aag̱áa áwé hú ḵu.aa tle yú kóoḵ takaadé akawsiyáa,
tle wé x̱áat tsú aax̱ awsitaa.
Aag̱áa áwé tsá a daat aawa.ák.
Ch'ul yeenayát'ji áwé, tle yan uwa.ée wé x̱áat tlein.
Áwé tle aawax̱áa,
a koowú ḵu.áwé tle awsineex̱.
Daat yís sákwshíwé awsineex̱ a koowú?
Tle ch'as a tuxaagí áwé át astéen.
Áwé
tle a kát ḵushakaawaháa.
Wé at goowú tsú tle a kát awligwátl.
Ch'ul yeenayát'ji áwé—há'!—haat has kawdliyích tle yées aa x̱'áal'tin.
Áwé tle yéi ḵuyawsiḵaa, «Aatlein át áyá haa woonee,
  ax̱ dachx̱anx'isáani.
Yá at goowú a káa daak sh wudligwátl yá haa x̱áadi. Tle hóoch'k',
  hóoch'kíx̱ wusitee.»
Áwé yáa—
yá ts'ítskw ḵu.aawé tle has gax̱satí
a x̱oo.aa.
Yá hasdu waḵgandaa dleit yáx̱ dag̱aatee has waḵ.ilg̱éigu.
Yá shoox̱' ḵu.aa gánt uwanúk,
tle du x̱'ul'yáx̱ akawdlikwáat,
tle x̱'aan yáx̱ yatee.
Yá ts'eig̱eenéi ḵu.áwé hasdu jeedáx̱ kéi daḵínch,
  áwé ḵúx̱de s alshát.
Agashátch.
Áwé yéi ayawsiḵaa wé ts'eig̱eenéi,
«X̱áat ḵusteeyí yá héenx'i x̱oo
tlél yéiḵ idaḵínjiḵ!

That's why it looked suitable to us.
What's wrong?"
they said to Raven.
But Raven just said,
"Ugh! Yuck!
That's where my wife used to go to the bathroom!
Go get a different batch!
You must go over two mountains;
only then will it be satisfactory."
So then they flew off to do his bidding and left the skunk cabbage there.
But then he himself spread the skunk cabbage out in the bottom of the pit
and picked up the fish too.
Next he made a fire around it.
Before long the huge salmon was cooked.
Then he just ate it,
but he saved the tail.
I wonder what he saved the tail for.
He left only the skeleton there.
So,
he just covered it with a mound of earth.
He also rolled a tree stump on top of it.
Before long—hah!—they flew back with some fresh skunk cabbage.
So he said to them, "Something dreadful has happened to us,
  my dear grandchildren.
This tree stump rolled itself over onto our salmon. It's just
  gone, all gone."
So these—
these birds were just weeping,
some of them were.
The rims of their eyes were white as they wiped their eyes.
But the robin sat close to the fire;
the face of her belly was singed by the fire;
it was red.
The magpie, on the other hand, kept trying to fly away from them,
  but they were holding her back.
He would grab her.
Then he said to the magpie,
"Don't fly down to the beach
while there are salmon in the creeks!

Cha ch'a héen yíx̱ shuwulxeexí yá x̱áat, aag̱áa tsá
yéi kg̱idaḵéen.»
Yáax' áwé tsu
yéi ayawsiḵaa woolnáx̱.wooshḵáḵ,
«Tlákw áyá woolnáx̱ át gag̱eeshḵáaḵ.
Goot sá ydiḵín, áx' woolnáx̱ yaa kg̱eeshḵáḵch.»
Yá ḵaatoox'u sáani yéi ayasáagu aa tsú
yan ayawdax̱siḵáa.
Ḵa yá x̱'éishx'w ḵu.aa áwé
ḵúnáx̱ ashaksayéikw,
woosh g̱unayáade ashaksayéikw
du shadaa.
Du x̱'wáal'i ḵúnáx̱ ḵ'asigóo aadé yan awsineyi yé yá Yéilch.
Aag̱áa áwé tsá
ch'a áa yéi wootee ch'a yéi yguwáatl', du náḵ ḵut ḵaa loowagooḵ tle.
Yéi áwé yan kawdiyáa.
Du dachx̱anx'isáani áwé du daa yóo kaawa.át. Áwé tle
tlél tlax̱ aan wuk'éi á ḵu.aa.
Ashukawdag̱aajáa ḵu.aa ldakát yéide.
Yéi áwé yan shuwjix̱ín yáat'aa,
yá shkalneek.

Only when there are no more salmon in the creek are you
to fly down there."
Here again
he said to the wren,
"You will always hop through holes.
Wherever you fly to, you'll be hopping through holes."
And he gave instructions to
the ones he named chickadees as well.
And as for the blue jay,
Raven was thoroughly combing the feathers on his head,
combing each side up differently
around his head.
It's really fun the way that Raven fixed up his feathers.
Then,
Raven stayed there for a little while, and they just ran away from him.
That's how it turned out.
His little grandchildren flocked to him. But
he didn't treat them right at all.
Still, he instructed each of them in various ways.
That's how this one ends,
this story.

III. Yéil k̲a Xóots Wooshdasháay

Yá at koowú, wé Yéilch wusineex̲i at koowú,
ch’a g̲óot yéide áwé a daa yóo tuwatánk.
Áwé yaa nagút. Awsikóo k̲u.aa yá wooshdasháay—
yá Xóots wooshdasháay áa yéi yateeyi yé.
Áwé
a x̲áng̲aa nagóot áwé tle
du tuwáa sigóo aan wooch isx̲áni.
Yá Xóots k̲a yáa
du shátch k̲wás has akawshik’án yá Yéil.
Du kaneek áyá has aawa.áx̲. Ách áwé hél hasdu tuwáa ushgú, k̲únáx̲ has akawshik’án.
Ch’a aan áwé Yéil k̲u.aa tle sdu ée sh wudlix̲án.
Áwé tle s ash yaawadlaak̲.
Áwé ch’a
k’idéin a daa s tutee nóok áwé
yéi yaawak̲aa Yéil k̲u.aa,
«I een daak shukk̲alx̲aajée, ax̲ aatx̲úx̲.
Aag̲áa áwé
aatlein atx̲á i x̲’ax̲áni yéi kg̲watée.
I een daak
k̲ukk̲wast’eix̲.»
Áwé tle
yá Xóots k̲wáawé tle yéi yaawak̲aa, «Ha góok!
Ha góok!»

III. Raven and the Brown Bear Couple

This salmon tail, that salmon tail that Raven salvaged,
he had a novel idea about what to do with it.
So he was walking along. But he knew where this married couple—
where this Brown Bear couple lived.
So,
when he drew nigh to them
he wanted to ingratiate himself with them.
But this Bear
and his wife didn't want Raven around.
They had heard of his reputation. That was why they didn't like him; they really didn't want him around.
Even so, Raven made friends with them.
They just took him into their good graces.
So,
when they were feeling better about him,
Raven said,
"Let me go out trolling with you, my auntie's husband.
Then
there'll be a lot of food on hand for you to eat.
I'll go out
fishing with you."
So then,
this Bear just said, "Let's go!
Let's go!"

Ách áwé tle daak has uwak̲úx̲ ch'u ts'ootaat.
Yáa
Yook̲ yóo áwé duwasáakw
yá Yéil een
át kawdiyaayi aa yá gaaw.
Áwé tle hú tsú tle tsu sdu een tle
áwé tle daak has uwak̲úx̲.
Ch'a góot.át daax' yéi jineiyée áwé yá Xóots,
yá Xóots k̲u.aa yá du t'eix̲í x̲'adaa yéi jineiyée áwé,
yá Yéilch k̲u.a yá t'á koowú áwé tle
aax̲ yóo aa yaxáshk tle,
tle du t'eix̲í a náa yéi ana.eich, tle yínde akanalgútch.
Áwé tle ch'a tlákw áwé kéi anast'éx̲ yú cháatl.
Deisgwach shaawahík hasdu een
wé yaakw.
Wáanée sáwé yá Xóotsch x̲'eiwawóos',
«Daa sáwé? Daa sáwé náak̲wx̲ yiliyéx̲? Tlax̲ yéi eest'eix̲! X̲át k̲wá tlél tsu kéi x̲at jeeduyík̲ch.»
«Ch'a k̲udzitèe,
ch'a k̲udzitee, ax̲ aatx̲úx̲,
aadé yax̲danak̲ws'i yé.
Ch'a k̲udzitee.
Hél aadé i een koonk̲aaneegi yé.»
«Dá x̲aan kananeek,
dá x̲aan kananeek, ax̲ yak̲áawu.» Deisgwach a yát x̲'awdliyóo.
Wáanée sáwé déi wé Yéilch yéi yawsik̲aa, «Yanéekw.
Yanéekw, ax̲ aatx̲úx̲.
Yá aan yax̲danak̲ws'i át yanéekw.
Hél ák' oox̲aheen a yát eeháni.»
«Kakk̲wa.aak̲w x̲á,
kakk̲wa.aak̲w.
Áa x̲at shukoojáa dé.»
«Yanéekw, a jiyeet át gageeshk'éin,
ldakát yéide ikagux̲daxéel'.»
«Ha ch'a aan
wa.é x̲á tlél wáa sá eetí,
wé át aan yeedanák̲ws'i.»
Ách áwé tle—
tle—

So they went out fishing early in the morning.
This guy's
name is Cormorant,
the guy traveling about
with Raven at the time.
And he, too, was with them
when they canoed out.
While this Bear was working on other things,
while this Bear was adjusting the spacing of his fishhooks,
Raven just kept cutting pieces off
the king salmon tail
and putting them on his hook and just sending them on down.
He just kept bringing up halibut every time.
Their boat
eventually filled up on them.
At some point Bear asked him,
"What is that? What is it that you're using for bait? You're hooking so many! But me, I'm not even getting a tug."
"It's really something,
it's really something, my auntie's husband,
my style of baiting.
It's *really* something,
but I can't tell you."
"Please tell me,
please tell me, partner." By now he's addressing him as kin.
Finally Raven told him, "It's painful.
It's painful, my auntie's husband.
This stuff I'm baiting the hooks with is painful.
I don't believe that you can stand it."
"I'll sure try,
I'll try.
Show me already."
"It's painful; you'll hop around from the pain;
you'll have all kinds of problems."
"Well, even so,
you're doing just fine
when you bait with that stuff."
So Raven just—
just—

tle yéi ayawsiḵaa,
«Ḵúnáx̱ yanéekw yá át,
tlél ḵwá yee.uwát'x̱ ḵúnáx̱ néegu.»
«Ha yan x̱á x̱at uwanée de a yís,» tle yéi yaawaḵaa wé Xóots.
Ách áwé tle yéi ayawsiḵaa,
«Ch'a yá i lawyadaadookx'u sáani áwé aax̱ gag̱eexáash.
Aag̱áa áwé tle aan yakgidanáaḵw.
Aag̱áa áwé ax̱ yáx̱ akg̱eest'eix̱ ḵúnáx̱.
I tóoch lachéeshi áwé yéi kg̱isanée.»
Áwé tle wé Xóotsch ḵu.aawé tle aax̱ wooxaash,
tle aan yawdináḵw.
Tlél a yát uhán yú a néegu, tle éex',
tle kéi dagútch.
«Ch'a g̱aa iyatee ax̱ aatx̱úx̱,» yóo áwé ayanasḵéich,
«Ch'a g̱aa iyatee.
Yanéegu át áwé yéi daa.eené, yéi áwé x̱at wootee x̱át tsú.»
Wáanée sáwé tle woonaa wé Xóots ḵu.aa.
Tle wé x'aak'w yat'éináx̱ áwé yan aawax̱ách.
Aag̱áa áwé tsá wé Yooḵch yéi daayaḵá,
«Ikakḵwanéek, du shát een ikakḵwanéek.
Wáa sáwé tsú ḵeeyanéekw?» yóo,
«Ikakḵwanéek.»
Áwé tle a x̱ánt uwagút.
«I l'óot' daak tsaaḵ,
ch'u tle ḵúnáx̱ daak tsaaḵ.»
Áwé tle yú Yooḵ ḵu.áwé tle du l'óot' daak aawatsáḵ tle ḵúnáx̱.
Ch'u tle a k'óol' áwé át uwajél wé Yéil,
tle aax̱ aawats'éek'w.
«Haaw, shk'e x̱'eendataan.»
«R-r-r-r-r-r-r-r,» yóo duwa.áx̱ch, hél aadóoch sá x̱'awu.aax̱.
Hél aadóoch sá x̱'akg̱wa.aax̱. Áwé tle a tóoḵt jiwsigóo. «Hé deikée shaltláax̱ áwé i aaníx̱ gux̱satée.» Tle aadé akaawanáa.
Ách áwé
yooḵ ḵeení a yáa yeeyḵoox̱ú
has x̱'akgee.áax̱ yóo s x̱'ala.átgi,
«R-r-r-r-r-r-r-r.»
Wé Xóots ḵu.áwés tle anax̱ yan aawax̱ách wé x'aa t'éik.
Aag̱áa áwé tsá
aadé aksixát.

just said to him,
"This stuff is very painful,
but the intense pain doesn't last very long."
"Well, I'm quite ready for it now," the Bear said.
So Raven said to him,
"You have to cut off these little folds of foreskin around your penis.
Then you'll use that for bait.
Then you'll be catching lots of fish like me.
If you think you can handle the pain, you can do it."
So the Bear cut it off
and baited his hook with it.
He couldn't stand the pain; he was just hollering,
and lurching up and down.
"You're alright, my auntie's husband," Raven kept telling him,
"You're alright.
You're doing a painful thing; that's how it was for me, too."
Eventually the Bear just died.
So, Raven towed him ashore to the far side of the little point.
Then finally Cormorant said to him,
"I'm going to tell on you, I'm going to tell on you to his wife.
What on earth are you doing?" he said,
"I'm going to tell on you."
Then Raven went up to him.
"Stick out your tongue,
stick it way out."
Then Cormorant stuck his tongue all the way out.
Raven just reached in and grabbed the root of Cormorant's tongue
and pinched it off.
"Now, let's hear you speak."
"R-r-r-r-r-r-r," is how he sounded; nobody could understand his speech.
Nobody could understand him. Raven jabbed him in the butt. "That reef out there will be your territory." Then he sent him out there.
That's why
when you go by a rookery of cormorants
you'll hear them talking,
"R-r-r-r-r-r-r."
As for that Bear, he towed him behind the point.
At last
he tethered him there.

Áwé tle—
tle ayaawax̱aa wé x̱áat ḵu.aa wé—
wé shaawát aa Xóots x̱ánde.
Áwé tle a eeg̱ayáakt ḵóox̱ áwé, «Haat at yax̱wsiḵúx̱, ax̱ aat.
Yáadu á yá át.»
«Ha goosóo
wé i aatx̱úx̱ ḵu.aa?»
«Héinax̱.á x'aak'w yat'éix' áwé
t'eix̱áa sákw aklax̱óot'.» yú.á.
«Yéi agux̱sanée áx'.
Tlax̱ yawdi.aa, haa jeex̱ áyá at yawlik'wách
yá x̱áat.»
Áwé tle a jeex' yéi akanajél.
«Tle ch'as wé digéix'i aa wé cháatl yoowú ax̱ jeedéi g̱ích.
X̱át áwé at gakḵwas.ée,
wa.é ḵwá
tle kéi kg̱idaxáash.»
Áwé tle kéi anaxásh wé cháatl
ldakát.
Wé Yéilch ḵu.aa tle wé at yoox'ú dáḵde akaawajeil.
Tle téix' sáani áwé tle ayawsiháa, ch'a aan daakdigéix'i aa.
Áwé tle wé at yoowú a daakáa—
a daakáa akaawadúx' wé
cháatl yoowú.
Aag̱áa áwé tsá ḵ'wátl kát akaawajél,
tle awli.úk.
Wáannée sáwé ḵúnáx̱ yadag̱at'áa áwé wé téix' sáani, wé át tóox',
tle wé
cháatl yoowú tsú tle a daa uwa.ée.
Aag̱áa áwé tsá yéi ayawsiḵaa wé du aat,
«Daaḵ gú déi! De yan at x̱wasi.ée.»
Áwé tle sh yáa wdiwútl wé du aat,
tle daaḵ uwagút.
Aag̱áa áwé yéi ayawsiḵaa,
«Tlél áwé kdutáax' daa sá x̱wsa.eeyí, tle ch'a hú kwdagé áwé dunút'x'w.
Tlél koodutáax', lig̱aas.
Shux'áanáx̱ at x̱wasa.eeyích áwé i x̱'eis,
hél kakg̱eetáax'.»
A yáx̱ áwé tle—

Then he—
he loaded up the fish and took them
to the Female Bear.
When he came up to the beach, "I brought over a boatload, my auntie.
Here are all the things."
"So where is
your auntie's husband, anyhow?"
"He's on the other side of that little point,
chopping wood to be made into fishhooks," he said.
"He's going to do it over there.
It's taking a very long time; our gear was broken to bits
by the fish."
Meanwhile he was offloading the halibut and giving them to her.
"Toss me over just the large halibut stomachs.
I'll do the cooking myself.
and you
will cut them up."
So then she was cutting up the halibut,
all of it.
Meanwhile Raven brought the stomachs up from the beach.
He gathered pebbles that were relatively small, yet large in circumference.
Then he knotted the stomachs—
he knotted the halibut stomachs
around the stones.
Then finally he put them into a pot
and boiled them.
Eventually, when the pebbles got piping hot inside those halibut stomachs, the
halibut stomachs enclosing the rocks were cooked as well.
Then he said to his auntie,
"Come up now! I'm done cooking."
So his auntie
hurried up to him.
Then he said to her,
"People don't chew my cooking; they just swallow it whole.
They don't chew it; it's forbidden.
Since this is the first time I've cooked for you,
you mustn't chew it."
Accordingly—

ḵúnáx̱ du éet yaan.uwaháa wé shaawát—
tle ch'a hú kwdagé áwé anút'x'w wé cháatl yoowú.
Tle ch'a ldakát áyá
du yíx' yaa gagéi áwé tle,
tle si.áat'i héen a x̱'éit awsi.ín. «Yáat'át! Yáat'át!
Si.áat'i héen yáadu. A ítde áyú
duneix̱.»
Áwé tle—
tle awdináa wé—
wé du aatch,
áwé tle du yée yaa nal.úk
wé yaawat'ayi téix'.
«Yáadu aa tsu héen, tsu idaná,» yóo.
Ch'as eetiyáanáx̱ yaa nal.úk, tle g̱unayéi yawji.ák wé neil yee.
Ch'áakw át yawush.áagi áwé tle wdzigeet, tle hóoch'.
Ldakát du yik.ádi gíwé tle yax̱ yawsi.ée.
Aag̱áa áwé tsá
wé Yéilch
tle yóo—
yú ḵáa aa yú Xóots át ayaawax̱áa yú du aatx̱úx̱.
Át aawax̱ách.
K'e a shóo yéi wootee wé—
wé Xóots dleeyí ḵa wé—
wé du aat dleeyí ḵaa
ldakát wé cháatl.
Tle ch'a tléináx̱ hóoch áwé a shóo yéi wootee.
Yú Yooḵk' tsú tlél du x̱áng̱aa wdaḵeen.
Tle yú deikéex' shaltláax̱ káa yéi yatee.
Yéi áwé kaawagei.

the woman was very hungry—
she swallowed those halibut stomachs whole.
Then as everything
was expanding in her stomach,
he just brought her some cold water to drink. "Here! Here!
Here's some cold water. People drink it
afterward."
So then—
then his auntie
drank it,
and those hot rocks just
started boiling inside her,
"Here's some more water; drink some more," he said.
It just started boiling harder than ever, and she began to
stagger around inside the house.
After staggering around for quite some time, she fell;
she was a goner.
All her innards must have gotten cooked.
Then finally
Raven
brought that
Male Bear there, his auntie's husband.
He towed him there.
He stayed there, you see, to feast on the—
the Bear's flesh and his—
his auntie's flesh and
all that halibut.
He was the only one there feasting on it.
Little Cormorant didn't fly anywhere near him either.
He stayed on the reef out there.
That's the whole story.

IV. Yéil k̲a G̲uwakaan

There's just a little short one.
The Raven and Deer,
they were pretty chummy people.
They walked around together.
But the Raven was already planning ahead because
he wanted to get that Deer so he can have him for dinner.
And so—
I'm supposed to be talking in Tlingit!
Yáa—
yá Yéil áyá G̲uwakaan
du yak̲áawoox̲ awliyéx̲.
Aag̲áa áwé tsá
a daax' k̲wá yóo tuwatánk
wáa sáyá akgwajáak̲ du atx̲aayí sákw.
K̲únáx̲ du éet yaan.uwaháa.
Áyá yá du yak̲áawux̲ k̲wáyá sitee yá G̲uwakaan.
Ách áwé tle—
tle aan g̲unayéi uwa.át. Át has woo.aat
ldakát yé.
K̲ach áa oog̲aajaag̲i yéig̲aa
    ásíwéigé k̲ushée.
Wáanée sá awsiteen wé x̲'aak.
A táade naaléi, tlél k̲wá káx̲ k̲oolgé.

IV. Raven and the Deer

There's just a little short one.
The Raven and Deer,
they were pretty chummy people.
They walked around together.
But the Raven was already planning ahead because
he wanted to get that Deer so he can have him for dinner.
And so—
I'm supposed to be talking in Tlingit!
The—
the Raven made Deer
his partner.
And only then
did he start scheming about
how he could kill him for his dinner.
Raven was very hungry.
But this Deer was his partner.
So,
Raven just started strolling with him. They strolled about
everywhere.
Raven was actually searching for a place where he could kill him,
as it turns out.
At some point Raven saw a ravine.
It was a long way to the bottom, but not very far from side to side.

Áwé
wudinag̱u aas áwé a kaanáx̱ yan uwashóo.
A kaanáx̱ yan uwashóo. Ch'áakw ḵu.aa gíwé deix̱ satéeyin a ká.
Áwé tlax̱ ḵúnáx̱ áyú wdináḵw yú aas.
Ayatéen yú Yéilch aadé yateeyi yé.
Áwé tle a kaanáx̱ áwé yan ushḵaaḵch,
«X̱at latín!
Ax̱ yaḵáawu, x̱at latín!»
Tle daak gashḵáḵch—há'!
Át wujiḵaaḵ.
Ḵúnáx̱ yaa ashukdaḵéen du yáx̱ áwé adaané du yaanashḵág̱i.
Tle a kaanáx̱ áwé diyáanax̱.aadé yan ushḵaaḵch.
«Haaw! Wa.é áwé déis, ax̱ yaḵáawu.
Wa.é áwé déis.
A kaanáx̱ yan gú!»
Yú G̱uwakaan ḵwá át tukawjiyáa a kaanáx̱ yan wugoodée yú aas.
Ayatéen aadé yateeyi yé. «Tlél wáa sá ikg̱wanei, ax̱ yaḵáawu.
X̱at latín, ax̱ yaḵáawu.» Tle tsu a kaanáx̱ yan ushḵaaḵch.
Ch'áakwx̱ nastée áwé a dayéen át wushḵaag̱í akaawa.aaḵw wé G̱uwakaanch.
Tle daak nagút.
Ch'a yák'wdéi wool'éex'
wé aasák'w.
Tle diyéede wdzigeet wé—
wé G̱uwakaan ḵwá,
tle woonaa.
Aag̱áa áa yaa wdiḵeen.
Hél tsu aadé oonax̱sineiyi yé. Tlél lítaa oowayawu át du jee.
«Goonáx̱ sá óo-óo-óosh x̱wasix̱áa ax̱ yaḵáawu,»
yóo yanaḵéich.
Wáanée sáwé a daa awdlig̱een.
Tle ḵúnáx̱ yá G̱uwakaan tóoḵ áyá x̱á du tóogaa yatee. (AT.SHOOḴ)
Aag̱áa áwé tsá
aanáx̱ áwé gunayéi awsix̱áa hé G̱uwakaan du tóoḵnáx̱.
Yéi áwé ayaawadlaaḵ.

Now,
there was a rotten tree extending across it.
It led across the ravine. I suppose it used to serve as a trail leading over it long ago.
That tree was very rotten.
Raven could see what shape it was in.
So he just kept hopping across it.
"Watch me!
My partner, watch me!"
He just kept on hopping out—hah!
He was hopping around.
As he was flying along leading Deer, he made his hopping conform to the way Deer walked.
He just kept hopping over to the other side.
"Well! It's your turn now, partner.
It's your turn now.
Walk across it!"
But Deer was reluctant to cross the tree.
He could see the shape it was in. "Nothing will happen to you, partner.
Watch me, partner." Then Raven would hop across it again.
After Raven had been hopping about while facing him for a long time, Deer gave it a try.
He just started walking out.
All of a sudden
the little tree broke.
The Deer just—
he just fell down below
and died.
Then Raven flew down there.
There was still no way he could get at it. He didn't have anything resembling a knife.
"I wo-o-onder what I could use as an entry point to eat my partner,"
he kept saying.
Eventually he took a close look at it.
Deer's anus suited his fancy to a T.
(LAUGHTER)
At last
he began to eat his way into Deer through his anus.
That's how he accomplished it.

Tle awsik'ít'.
Tle tlél tsu áa yan aa wusháat.
Áwé kallítaaḵ
ch'a hú du satoowúch áwé g̱unayéi ayawsixíx yú atx̱á,
tle ḵúnáx̱ a tóoḵnáx̱.
Yéi áyá kaawagei.

He devoured him completely.
Raven didn't even leave a single scrap behind.
Knifeless,
relying on his wits alone, he started conducting his private feast,
right through the anus.
That's the whole story.

V. Yéil k̲a Yáay

Tléix' yateeyi aa áwé.
Yáa—
yá Yéil áwé át woogoot,
áwé awsiteen yá yáay.
Héennáx̲ kéi aklakél'ch yú yaaw.
Áwé ch'a wáa-áa sáyú tsú du x̲'éit aa g̲asnee wé yaaw?
Wáanée sáwé yéi tuwdisháat,
«Shk'e áa daak kuk̲adak̲éen.
Tle yá yaaw x̲'ayeex' x̲'awut'aax̲í áwé, x̲át tsú du yíkde kk̲wadak̲éen. Yéi áwé tsá aa yakk̲wadláak̲ yá yaaw wusx̲á.»
Áwé tle áa daak wudik̲ín. Tle k̲únáx̲
yá yaaw du yíkt kawu.aayí áwé wé yáay,
tle a yíkde hú tsú wdzigeet yá yaaw x̲oo.
Tle yá yáay
du yoowú k'óol' áwé áwu á yá Yéil.
Tle áx' shóot awdi.ák.
Tle áx' áwé agalt'óos'
wé Yáaych
sax̲a yaaw.
Tle k'idéin
ch'u tle oosk'éet'ch.
Tle ldakát á yax̲ awoosx̲áaych, yáax' áwé tsú neil aa koo.áaych.
Yú yáay k̲u.aa

V. Raven and the Whale

There's this one story.
This—
this Raven was walking around
and saw this whale.
It was chasing herring up through the water.
Just ho-ow could Raven get a taste of the herring?
Eventually he came up with an idea,
"How about I fly out there.
Then when the whale's jaws open to receive the herring, I'll fly inside him too. It's the only way I'll get to eat the herring."
So he flew out there. When
the herring were really just streaming into the whale,
Raven, too, tumbled into it among the herring.
Raven was
right in the pit of the stomach of the whale.
He made a fire there.
Right there he was roasting
the herring
that the whale was eating.
He would just gobble them up
with no problem.
He would eat the whole lot, and here another load would come streaming in.
Herring would come streaming

yú yaaw tle neil koo.áaych
yá Yéil át aa yé,
tle yax̱ ayagoos.éeych.
Áyá yeedát *barbecue* yóo duwasáakw,
yasátk aadé at gas.ee yé.
Wáananée sáwé
x̱'awdzinák̲ wé yáay
wé yaaw neilx̱ kalasóosi.
Aatlein yaaw áyú aawax̱áa yú Yéil.
Ch'a aan áyú
yóo yáay yíx̱ dixwás'
yú taay
ḵa ldakát du yik.ádi,
tle ch'u tle yú—
yú yáay yoowú tsú tle—
tle yax̱ ayawsix̱áa,
ḵa yá taay,
ldakát át.
Ldakát yú yáay yik.ádi áyú ax̱á.
Ts'as du x̱'éi kéi nak'éin yú atx̱á.
Wáanée sáwé a téix̱' aax̱ aawaxaash, tle woonaa yú yáay.
Du een áwé át wulihaash.
Áwé tle a yíkde áwé éex',
«Yak'éiyi l'éi-éi-éiwt kwshé x̱at g̱alahaash.
Yak'éiyi l'éiwt g̱alahaash yá yáay,» yóo áwé a yíkde éex'.
Ch'áakw éex'i áwé
tóo aawanúk yan wulihásh yú yáay.
Yá teet du een át x̱'awdiyeeḵ.
Awsikóo yan áyú wlihásh.
Ách áwé tle tsu a tóode éex',
«Aadóo sgí ḵaa kaanáx̱ kéi ag̱axaash?
Aadóo sgí ḵaa kaanáx̱ kéi ag̱axaash?»
Ch'a yéi x̱'ayaḵaayée áwé
adátx'ich áwé seiwa.áx̱.
Át ḵaa loowagooḵ wé áa yéi yateeyi ḵu.oo.
Áwé tle s at'aawjixeex neildé.
Áyú wé atyátx'i tle yéi has sh kalneek hasdu tláa ḵa hasdu éesh hás een,
«Yáay tlein á yóonáx̱ yan wulihásh. A yíkde kasayedéin
at duwa.áx̱ch.»

into that whale
where Raven was sitting;
and he just kept cooking it all up.
Nowadays it's called a barbecue;
it was fast the way he cooked.
Eventually
the whale quit eating
as the herring kept falling in.
Raven had eaten a huge amount of herring.
Nevertheless,
the fat
and all of its internal organs
hung inside the whale;
he just—
the whale's stomach, too—
he just ate it all up,
fat and all,
everything.
He was eating up everything inside the whale.
The food was tasting better and better to him.
At some point he cut out its heart and the whale died.
The whale floated around with him.
Then he was hollering inside it,
"Oh, let me float to a fine sand bea-ea-each.
May this whale float to a fine sand beach," he was hollering inside it.
After hollering for a long time
he felt the whale float ashore.
The undertow was pulling it about in the breakers with Raven inside.
He knew he had floated to the beach.
That's why he was hollering inside it again,
"Who could cut a fellow out of here?
Who could cut a fellow out of here?"
Just as he was saying this
some children heard his voice.
The people who lived there were running around.
They just ran home to tell the news.
So those children were telling the story to their mothers and fathers,
"There's a huge whale that floated ashore way over there. Strange sounds are coming from inside."

Ách áwé tle aadé aawa.aat,
ldakát k̲aa jishagóoni een.
Át a.áat áwé sawduwa.áx̲ wé Yéil,
«Aadoo sgí k̲aa kaanáx̲ kéi k̲ug̲axaash?»
Áwé tle a daa wduwanaak̲, tle kawdudlis'úw tle wé yáay tlein.
Tle—
tle du eetée yáx̲ áx̲ k̲ukunalgéi, áwé anax̲
kéi wdik̲ín, «G̲áa!»
Tle ch'a kei ndak̲ín áwé,
ch'a kei ndak̲ín kindachóon. Áwé tle ldakát á yú
a k̲wáan áwé tle yéi s x̲'ayak̲á,
«Ch'a kéi gidak̲een!
Ch'a kéi gidak̲een!»
Ch'a kínde kéi ndak̲ín.
Wáanée sáwé, «K̲uyáx̲ nidak̲een!
K̲uyáx̲ nidak̲een!»
Tle yant'éide wdik̲een.
Yant'éit dak̲éen áwé tle—
tle
daada.ús'kw.
Tláakw yatee, daada.ús'kw. Ldakát yú eex̲, ldakát át áwé
du daatx̲ a.ús'kw.
Wáanée sáwé ayaawadlaak̲, tle k'idéin sh wudzinee.
Yáax' áwé tle aan yáa uwagút.
Há! Ldakát áwé neildé yaa kandujél wé yáay daa.ityeidí,
dleey, k̲a yú taay, ldakát át.
Áwé tle yéi k̲uyawsik̲aa,
«Hóu! Yáay tlein áyá yeeyják̲.»
«Tléik', tléik'.
Hél wutoojaak̲.
Haa eeg̲áa at woosoo.
Yáanáx̲ yan wulitidi yáay áyá.»
«A tóode gé at duwa.áx̲ch?»
«Aaá.
A tóode x̲á at duwa.áx̲ch.
A tóodáx̲ kéi at wudik̲ín.»
«Haaw.
Haaw.
Yóo áwé duwa.áx̲ch.

So the people went over there
with all their implements.
When they got there they heard Raven's voice,
"Who could cut an opening over a fellow?"
Then the people stood around it and chopped up the huge whale.
Then—
then, when the opening was just wide enough for Raven to fit through,
    he flew out through it, "Caw!"
He was just flying up,
flying straight up. Then the whole
tribe said,
"Just fly on up!
Just fly on up!"
Then he was flying upwards.
At some point they said, "Fly however you want!
Fly however you want!"
Then he flew out of sight.
When he flew out of sight
he was
just washing his body.
He quickly washed his body. He was washing all the grease
    and everything off his body.
Eventually he got it done and primped himself right up.
At this point he appeared before the village.
My! The people were taking home all the parts of the whale,
the meat and the blubber, everything.
Then he said to them,
"Ho! You folks have killed a huge whale."
"No, no.
We didn't kill it.
We had supernatural assistance.
This is a whale that was carried to shore here by the waves."
"Was anything heard inside it?"
"Yes.
Something certainly was heard inside.
Something flew up out of it."
"Well.
Well.
That's what it sounds like.

Ch'áakw tsú yéi at woonee,
áwé yú aantḵeenéech has aawax̱áa,
tle ḵutx̱ has shoowaxeex.
Ách áwé yéi ḵuyawaḵaa,
ách uwa.ax̱i ḵu.ooch,
‹Yáay yan wulhaashí,
wunaawú,
a tóodáx̱ kéi at wudaḵeení, hél aadé x̱duwax̱aayi yé.
Tle a náḵ yóo naaligás'k.›»
Ách áwé tle—
tle a náḵ at wuduwaxoon.
Tle ldakát yóo neildé kawduwajeili yáay
daa.ityeidí tle a náḵ ḵuwligáas'.
Áwé Yéil ḵu.aa tle áa yéi wootee.
Yú yáay tlein a shóox' yéi wootee. Tle ldakát á shunaxéex áwé tsá
aax̱ wudiḵeen.
Yéi áyá yan shuwjix̱ín yáat'aa.

Something like this happened a long time ago too,
and the townspeople ate it,
and they all just died off.
And so the people said,
the people who heard this,
'Should a whale float ashore,
dead,
and should something fly up out of it, the people shan't eat any of it.
The whole clan just up and migrates away from it.'"
Owing to this,
the people just made preparations to leave it behind.
The people just packed up and moved away from all
the parts of the whale that they had brought into their homes.
But Raven stayed there.
He settled down to eat that huge whale. Only when the whole thing was gone did he fly away.
That's how this one ends.

VI. Wáanáx̱ Sá Yéil Éet Yaan.uháaych

Yáat'aa,
yáat'aa shkalneek ḵu.aa, wáanáx̱ sáyá
yá Yéil ch'a tlákw du éet yaan.uháaych.
Tléináx̱ yateeyi aanḵáawu tlein áwé
x'ús' áwé aya.óo.
Ḵúnáx̱ k'idéin
daakawduwach'ák'w.
Yá aanḵáawu tlein
tle ch'as héenx̱ áyá yéi ax̱'atánch yá x'ús'. Daa sá aag̱áa tuwditaan áyá tle du eeg̱aayáaknáx̱ tle yax̱ x'aak.
Áwé
ch'a g̱óot.át een ḵu.áwés ashax̱íchx̱. Tle neildé yóo asitaak,
tle agoos.éeych.
Yá du x'ús'i ḵwáwé tle dikéex̱ áwé daaḵ awootaanch.
Tlél aadé daa sá a déint g̱waaxeexi yé du x'ús'i yá ḵáa.
Áwé yá aawajag̱i yá yées x̱áat áwé tle hú ḵu.aa
tle awux̱aayí áwé tle yú gánt utáaych. Du díx̱' áa oos.háaych yá gant'áx̱'i,
tle k'idéin nateich.
K'idéin tsú shaahíkch, aag̱áa áwé tle k'idéin nateich.
Áwé yú Yéilch
a daadé ḵukawdlits'éek'w.

VI. Why Raven Is Always Hungry

This one,
this story is about why
Raven perpetually gets hungry.
A certain great nobleman
owned a club.
Its exterior was very nicely
carved.
This great nobleman
would just dip the business end of his club into the water. Whatever he had his mind set on would just swim up to the beach below him.
So,
he would club it over the head with something else. Then he would take it home
and cook it up.
But he would hang his club up high.
Nothing could get near this man's club.
When he ate freshly killed salmon
he would sleep close to the fire. He would position his back toward the heat of the fire
and have a nice sleep.
He would get comfortably full, too; then he would sleep well.
So Raven
was chipping away at the idea.

Du tuwáa sigóo—
wáa sá du jeet ux̲dzinee yú x̲áat aan shadux̲isht x'ús'.
K̲únáx̲ áwé yak'éi aadé wdudliyex̲i yé.
Wáanée sáwé át k̲oowaháa.
Tle k̲únáx̲
tlákw ooltínch yú Yéilch.
De tsu shawdinúk.
K̲únáx̲ du éet yaan.wuhaayí áwé shaadanookch, tle yú ík̲de anatánch yú du x'ús'i.
Daa sá aag̲áa tuwditaan—
wáag̲eens cháatl,
wáag̲eens t'á,
wáag̲eens g̲aat—
tle yéi tle du x̲ánnáx̲ yan ux'aakch.
Tle ashanax̲íshdích yú k̲áach. Tle neildé yéi anasneech, tle agoos.éeych.
Wáang̲een sáwé tsaa.
Yéi áwé tle tlákw du x̲'ax̲áni yéi at yateeyéyáx̲ áwé yatee.
Áwé tle dikéex̲ daak̲ awootaanch.
Áwé at g̲ax̲éinín tle nateich k'idéin.
Áwé tle k'idéin yan sh wustaayée Yéil k̲wá tle át uwagút.
Tle aax̲ yux̲ awliseen wé x'ús'.
Áwé tle ík̲de aan woogoot.
Áwé tle x'oon x̲áat sáwé aag̲áa tuwditaan.
Há'!
T'á,
tle x'oon t'á sáwé tle du x̲ánnáx̲ yan uwahín.
Áwé tlél ch'a góot.aa k̲áas' een áwé ashawux̲ísht Yéilch k̲u.aa.
Tle k̲únáx̲ yú x̲áat yánde aan yadudlak̲wx'u át een áwé ashaawax̲ísht.
Tle yú a daanéegwál'i k̲a yú a daadé wdudli.adi át ldakát á aax̲ kaawasóos.
Aag̲áa áwé tsáa yú Yéilch k̲u.aa áa k̲ux̲ aawatán, áx̲ daak̲ ayawutéeyi yé,
yú a s'aatí x̲ánx'.
Hú k̲u.aas tle neildé woogoot, tle yax̲ ayagawdzi.ée, tle yax̲ ayawsix̲áa yú x̲áat.
Áwé gánt áwé uwatáa, hú tsú tle wé Yéil,
ch'a yú k̲áa yáx̲.
Áwé yú k̲áa kéi isgéet áwé tle át awdlig̲ín yú du x̲áat—
du x̲áat x'ús'i.

He wanted
to figure out how he could get his hands on the club used for hitting salmon over the head.
It was very beautifully wrought.
Eventually the time came.
Raven just
watched him closely all the time.
The man got up again.
When he was really hungry he would get up and take his club down yonder to the beach.
Whatever he had his mind set on—
sometimes halibut,
sometimes king salmon,
sometimes sockeye—
just like that it would swim ashore by him.
Then the man would club it. He would just take it home and cook it up.
Sometimes it was seal.
So he lived high on the hog.
Then he would hang his club up high.
After he ate, he would sleep well.
Now, once the man was lying down comfortably, Raven went there.
He took the club and sneaked it outside.
Then he went down the beach with it.
He had his mind set on catching who knows how many salmon.
Wow!
King salmon,
so many king salmon swam ashore by him.
But Raven didn't hit them with a different stick.
He clubbed those salmon with the very same one that he had used to get them to come ashore.
Then the paint and the things that were inlaid around it all fell off.
After that, Raven finally put it back where it had been hung,
in its owner's house.
The Raven just went home, cooked it up, and devoured all the salmon.
Raven, too, slept with his back to the fire,
just like that man.
When the man woke up he looked at his salmon—
his salmon club.

Ldakát a daatx̱ kaawasóos yú aadé duwa.uwu yé.
Áwé tle—tle awsikóo yú Yéilch. Ch'u tle ḵúnáx̱ a yís a yaadé yaḵatí k'idéin.
Áwé tle aadéi woogoot.
Hél awutaan yú x'ús'.
Yéil gwáawégé tá.
Áwé ch'a yeisú taayí áwé yú Yéil ḵu.aa
tle yú Yéil tóoḵnáx̱ áwé tle daak akaawajél
ldakát yú Yéil naasí,
ldakát át.
Tle héinax̱.aadé aawalít ldakát yéide.
Áwé
tle aag̱áa áwé tsá neildéi woogoot.
Ch'áakwx̱ nastée áwé Yéil kéi wdzigít.
«Óu!
X̱at seiwa.át'! Ch'u tle yéi áwé sh tux̱dinook, ax̱ yíknáx̱ át agoowasháat.»
Aag̱áa áwé tsá
x'oon aa yéi yanaḵáa sáwé sh daax̱ ayawdlig̱ín.
Tle ayaawatín du yik.ádi ldakát yéig̱aa koowáat'.
Áwé tle sawu.áat'i sóox̱ áwé tle—
tle aax̱ tóot akaawajél.
Áwé du naasí ḵwá ch'u tle yéi kawliyáatl'k'.
Ách áwé tlél aadé shaag̱aaheegi yé.
Du tóo ḵux̱ akaawajél.
Ách áwé yeedát
yá lingítx̱ haa sateeyí aa wunéegu,
ḵaa yík wunéegu, wáangeens ḵaa naasí a shóotx̱ yóo aa dudlixáshk,
ch'a aan ḵwá ḵushahíkx̱ yeedát.
Yú Yéil ḵwá tlél shawuheek. Ch'u yáa yeedát de tlákw át ḵunasgúkch.
Yéi áwé kaawagei.

All the inlay had fallen off from where it had been set.
So then he knew it was Raven who had done this. He cursed him up and down about it.
Then he went over there.
He didn't take the club.
Behold, Raven was asleep.
While that Raven was still sleeping
he pulled out all of Raven's intestines
through Raven's anus,
everything.
Then he tossed them aside all over the place.
So,
now finally he went home.
After a long while Raven woke up.
"Oh!
I'm cold! I feel just like gusts of wind are blowing right through me."
Only after
he'd said this a number of times did he inspect his body.
He recognized his innards stretched all over the place.
Before he got too cold he hurried
to gather them unto himself.
But his poor little intestines had just shriveled up.
That's why he can never get full.
He stuffed them back up inside himself.
This is why now
when one of us humans gets sick,
when a person has an internal ailment, sometimes part of their intestines are cut out,
but even so, people get full now.
That Raven, though, he never did get full. To this very day he's always pecking around.
That's the whole story.

Notes to the Stories

Notes to Frank Italio's Stories

EDITORIAL BACKGROUND. The original audio recording of August 29, 1952, is Frederica de Laguna's reel 4, side 2; that of September 13, 1952, is her reel 7, side 2; and that of May 7, 1954, is her reel 2-2E. These recordings were deposited in the American Philosophical Society Archives and digitized copies were given to Sealaska Heritage Institute. These copies were used in preparing the text of this volume and can be found in the institute's William L. Paul Sr. Archives in the Frederica de Laguna Fieldwork Recordings Collection, MC047, identified as "04-03 Raven Cycle", "07-05 Continuation of Raven Stories, Raven's Theft of Daylight", and "02-16 Raven Story and Songs"; these correspond to FI I, i–iii, 133 (August 29, 1952); FI I, iii, 134–v (September 13, 1952); and FI II (May 7, 1954), respectively.

The texts of these stories of Frank Italio were first transcribed and translated by Nora Dauenhauer, who was herself his direct descendant.[*] The oldest renditions that could be located in the Dauenhauers' collected papers are handwritten drafts by Nora with labels indicating the years 1995 and 1998.[†] The transcription was reviewed in the early 2000s by Jeff Leer while on a trip to Juneau and visiting with the Dauenhauers, but because time was short, this review was conducted without listening to the audio recordings, so many issues were not resolved at the time. The transcription and translation were later proofread by Keri Eggleston, James Crippen, and Lance Twitchell. In 2018–2019, Twitchell reviewed much of the material with

---

* Italio was both Nora's mother's father's brother and her mother's mother's father. Italio and his wife, a Lukaax̱.ádi woman named Seigeigéi, had six children. Their daughter Leetkwéi, Kathy Dalton, was married to Italio's own younger brother Naag̱éi, George Frances, and one of the five children resulting from this marriage was Emma Marks, also named Seigeig̱éi, Nora's mother. See the biography of Emma Marks in Dauenhauer and Dauenhauer, *Haa K̲usteeyí*, 378–406, for further details on this genealogy and some biographical remarks about Italio.

† MS052, box 25, file unit 004.

George Davis and Marge Dutson and corresponded separately on the material with Will Geiger, who reviewed it independently. In February of 2019, Geiger noticed that the majority of the portion of the third episode from the August 29, 1952, recording "Raven Deceives His Younger Brother" (FI I, iii, 8–133) had not been transcribed in the existing manuscript and so prepared the draft transcription and translation, which was subsequently edited by Twitchell and then by Leer. In 2020–2021, Geiger and Leer jointly reviewed all of Italio's material, comparing the original audio, making further revisions to the texts and translations, and expanding the notes; they consulted David Katzeek, Kenneth Grant, Bessie Cooley, Sam Johnston, Florence Sheakley, and Ruth Demmert on particularly difficult issues of grammar and translation.

Notes to Frank Italio's tale I, episode i, "Raven and His Uncle"

The English interpretations of Italio's performances that Minnie Johnson provided to de Laguna yielded essential insights for the transcription and translation of Italio's texts.* We cite many instances where we were able to correlate her English interpretations with specific lines or groups of lines of Italio's text, in part to show how a native speaker and contemporary of Italio would interpret the Tlingit material, but also to trace the intellectual history that these specific performances have given rise to and show our indebtedness to it.

LINE 1. *Yéil, {...}x̱ siteeyi át:* The opening line of the story is difficult to hear clearly. Johnson does not give a literal interpretation, but comments, "He start with what Yeł [Yéil] is made out of",† so the phrase Italio uses here could mean something along the lines of 'Raven is a being that is made out of stone', but we cannot verify it from the recording and it does not sound like *téix̱ siteeyi át* 'a being that is stone' (compare FI II, 31, «Shanyaateiyí áwé Yéilx̱ sitee», 'A low-tide stone, that is Raven'). Because the crucial word of this phrase is unclear, all we can discern from it is 'Raven, a being who is a [?]' or, 'Raven, a being who is made out of [?]'. An older draft of the manuscript had the line transcribed as «Yéil adátx'ix̱ siteeyi át», translated as 'Raven, a being who is a child'—the word in question does sound quite close to *adátx'i* or *adátx'ee* on the recording, but *adátx'i* (a contracted form of *atÿátx'i*) means 'children', not 'child', so if that were the case the phrase would seem to mean 'Raven, a being who is [of] children'. We ultimately felt that all of our renderings were too tenuous, so we leave the resolution of this line to future listeners.

LINE 3. *Dei ÿaa kanilaník áwé*: Johnson is apparently addressing Italio in this line.

* The text of Johnson's interpretations are published in de Laguna, *Under Mount Saint Elias*, 848–55.

† Ibid, 848, bracketed spelling ours.

LINE 8. *{...}*: This line is difficult to hear to the point that we did not even venture a guess. Leer heard it as *x̱waawóos'* 'I asked for it, enquired about it', but could not determine what comes before it. We also considered the possibility that he may be saying *ách áyá i yayee wux̱aawóoḵ* 'this is why I doubt you', as a sort of friendly challenge of Johnson's interpretation skills. At any rate, Italio is pausing to ask how the interpretation will be handled; Johnson then instructs him to continue the narration into the recording device.

LINE 10. Note Johnson's reference to the microphone with the phrase «yá a tóode yoo x̱'eeyatangi át», 'this thing you are speaking into', as well as her use of a progressive imperative «ÿaa kaklaneek», 'continue telling the story of it' or 'continue narrating it'.

LINE 15. *lingit'aantuḵwáanich:* Typically, we find this noun as *lingit'aanituḵwáani* 'inhabitants within the world', where *lingit'aaní* 'world' is compounded with the following *tu-* 'inside, within' and *ḵwáani* 'inhabitants, people of'. Italio's pronunciation is unusual in that he suppresses the *-i* of *lingit'aani-*, yielding *lingit'aantuḵwáani.*

LINES 16–17. *Yáa ḵées' / du jeenáx̱ kawuhaaÿích:* It is not entirely clear whether this subordinate clause, meaning 'because the tide was under his control, authority', forms a sentence with lines 12–15 before, or with line 18 after it. We have transcribed it as connected with the line after it, as an explanation for why the moon is named *Yooḵis'kooḵéik* 'Tide-Commander'. If it relates to lines 12–15, it would be an explanation for why all the beings of the world were so fearful of him.

LINE 18. *Yooḵis'kooḵéik:* This refers to the man who is to become Raven's maternal uncle. See §2.3 of the editors' introduction for discussion of this character.

LINE 19. *Lingítch yéi yasáakw:* Because the word *lingít* can mean either 'people' or 'human being(s)' generically, or 'Tlingit people' specifically, this statement is ambiguous. We have translated the phrase as 'Tlingit people call him Tide-Commander', but other equally valid translations are 'Tlingits call him Tide-Commander' or 'people call him Tide-Commander'. Johnson interprets this line as "They call that brother yu qíṡ kuqék [Yooḵis'kooḵéik] [...]—'in charge of the tides.' And people are afraid of him, that he might get the tides stay up and destroy the whole thing."*

LINE 24. *du dlaak' jeex' tlél yát awuswáat:* The crucial question that kept arising in this and other very similar constructions that we find in Italio's performances is: who is the subject of the verb and what is their semantic role? If Tide-Commander is the subject, the implication is that he 'is causing the child not to grow up', meaning that he is intentionally preventing the child from growing up (by having it killed). If

* Ibid, bracketed spelling ours.

the woman is the subject, the implication is that she 'is not causing the child to grow up', meaning that, try as she may, she does not succeed in raising the child (because her brother has them sought out and murdered). In some contexts, we prefer the latter interpretation, but in other contexts the former seems preferable. Compare the following:

FI I, i, 24:	du dlaak' jeex' tlél yát awuswáat	He prevented a child from growing up in his sister's care
FI II, 36–37:	Du éek' jiyeex' tle tlél ch'oo ÿát ooswátx̱ du jeex'	Under her brother's control she still never raised a child in her [own] care
FI II, 40:	Áwé tlél ÿát awuswáat	He caused a child never to grow up *or* She never managed to raise a child
FI II, 118:	Du dlaak' jeex' ÿét l awuswáadeech	because he never let a child grow up in his sister's care

FI I, i, 24, seems best interpreted with the subject of the verb being Tide-Commander, i.e., the subject 'has prevented a child from growing up', as opposed to 'has not raised a child'. However, FI II, 36–37, seems best interpreted with the woman as the subject of the verb, i.e., the subject 'has not raised a child', as opposed to 'has prevented a child from growing up'. In FI II, 40, both 'She never managed to raise a child' (the woman as subject) and 'He caused a child never to grow up' (Tide-Commander as subject) seem equally plausible (we have adopted the latter interpretation). Finally, in FI II, 118, Tide-Commander as the subject seems best to fit the context.

LINE 26. Johnson's interpretation of this line: "Every time that woman, his sister, give birth to a child, he send one of his slaves out to find out whether it's a boy or a girl."*

LINE 27. *du goox̱x'ú yéi ayanask̲éich—:* This line literally means 'thus he would say to his slaves', but Italio seems to want to fill in several details about his slaves and his sister before stating what Tide-Commander would say to them. Tide-Commander's statement eventually comes in line 39, with him saying to his slaves, «Aadé naÿ.á!» 'Go there!' (i.e., go check on my sister).

LINE 29. *k̲ées'i akoolx̱éitl':* If our hearing of this noun phrase is correct, the word *k̲ées'i* is the truncated form of *k̲ées'-x'* 'floodtide-at', so that the whole phrase translates 'the fear of the floodtide'. The verb *akwdlix̱éitl'* 's/he/it is afraid' is commonly preceded by a noun phrase with the locative postposition *-x'*, e.g., *áa akwdlix̱éitl'* 's/he/it is afraid of it', where *áa* is the truncated form of *áx'*.

* De Laguna, *Under Mount Saint Elias*, 848.

LINE 31. *tle ch'a hú:* The independent human third-person pronoun *hú* could refer either to Tide-Commander or to the subject of the verb in the preceding line, «du jeex̱ goot» '[whomever Tide-Commander told to do so] would submit to his power' (lit. 's/he/it walks into his hands'). So, it could alternatively mean '[whomever Tide-Commander would tell to do so] would submit to his (Tide-Commander's) power of their own volition' or some such.

LINE 34. *yéi yaawak̲aa—:* Italio again prepares to impersonate Tide-Commander (see note to line 27) but interrupts himself to discuss the situation of the woman and resumes by explaining that Tide-Commander was speaking to his slaves as we see in line 38.

LINES 42–43. *Ag̲ajaak̲:* This is a hortative form with third-person object and third-person subject, meaning 'let him/her/it/them kill him/her/it/them'. The implied object is the woman's child, and the implied subject is evidently the moon's slaves. Because slaves are treated grammatically as non-human entities, and therefore do not take the human pluralizer *has=* when more than one is involved, the same verb form would be used if the subject were one slave or multiple slaves. Compare line 27, «du goox̱x'ú yéi ayanask̲éich» 'he would tell his slaves [to kill it]', where it is explicit that the order is given to multiple of Tide-Commander's slaves and, again, there is no pluralizer *has=* or *s=* in the verb.

LINES 48–51. *du shát eedé ÿax̱ ÿagax̱dusk̲áa:* Johnson's interpretation of this phrase is apparently "[the girl] will be some messenger to his wife". However, we note that the verb appears to contain the exhaustive derivational string *ÿax̱=ÿa-u-s-* (*Ø*) 'all, a bunch', so it is possible that the translation is '[the child] will divulge everything to his wife'. Johnson: "If it's a boy, he give orders to kill it. And when it's a girl, he orders them to kill it anyhow. He's afraid the girl will be some messenger to his wife, he's so jealous."* Note the consistency in the interpretation provided two years later by John Ellis for a similar statement in Italio's 1954 performance (FI II, 48, «du shátdei woondusk̲aag̲áa» 'so no one could smuggle a message to his wife'.), "Even when she have little baby girls, he always kills them because they might carry a message to his wife."† In the *Tlingit Verb Dictionary* we find a phrase with a remarkably similar form, «doo èe-dei kei yagax̱doosk̲áa» (i.e., *du eedé kei yagax̱dusk̲áa*), which Constance Naish and Gillian Story translate there as "they'll charge him"‡ (i.e., monetarily), but it is difficult to reconcile that translation with the interpretations of Johnson and Ellis here.

* Ibid.

† Ibid, 856.

‡ Naish and Story, *Tlingit Verb Dictionary*, 45.

LINE 54. *Tlél k̲waayú ín áyú du x̲'awoolnáx̲ unashú:* This line is difficult to hear, and we've written it as best as we were able to hear it. We have translated it literally, but it likely has an idiomatic meaning. This may be a sort of proverbial expression denoting that she lived in something like a cave and was defenseless. We find such a notion stated plainly by Shotridge, who writes, "Jealousy [Shotridge's title for Tide-Commander] also had a sister, a being who represented Hope, from whom came forth disappointment and regret; anxiety and confidence. *Hope was unguarded*, and always subject to temptations of joys of other beings."*

LINE 55. *áa yóo k̲aa jikung̲ak̲éigín:* This appears to be a repetitive contingent form but seems to have unexpected low tone on the final -(*n*)*ín* suffix used with the contingent, so we actually hear *áa yóo k̲aa jikung̲akéigin* on the recording. This is likely simply an effect of pitch downdrift at the end of the sentence. For further discussion of this phenomenon see §3.10.6 of the editors' introduction.

LINE 61. *wáananée sáwé:* This formulaic phrase, often translated as 'eventually', is used ubiquitously in Tlingit oral narrative in transitioning between scenes. Italio's pronunciation here and in many (but not all) other instances is striking in that the last two syllables, *sáwé*, are significantly lower in tone than the preceding syllable, *née*, which is given the greatest emphasis of the whole phrase.

LINE 62. *ÿát du jeet shoowaxíx:* More literally, 'she ran out of children'. The implication here may not only be that her brother has murdered all her children, but that she is or believes herself to be no longer capable of conceiving or bearing any more children.

LINE 63. *Ei-ei áyáa-áa-áa:* This is chanted, with the first word at a lower pitch than the second word, and the second word rising on the second syllable. This represents the woman's lamentation.

LINE 67. *Kéet du eeg̲iyáa yaawagóo:* The verb *ÿaawagoo* 'the fleet/pod traveled'—here with the derivational string *N eeg̲aÿáa* (Ø) 'out from the beach below N'—can refer to the motion of multiple boats or of a group of sea mammals, especially a pod of killerwhales. The image is thus initially ambiguous (is it a pod of killerwhales or is it a fleet of canoes paddled by Killerwhale People?) until line 72, which follows shortly after, where we find the verb *ÿan uwak̲úx̲* 'he arrived to shore by (a single) boat'. The initially hazy image is thus resolved into that of the Killerwhale People traveling in a fleet of boats, rather than a pod of killerwhales swimming along, and the focus then turns to a single boat landing on shore below the woman, then to a single individual from among the Killerwhale People: their leader *Gushtuwool* 'Hole-in-the-Dorsal-Fin'.

* Shotridge, "Raven In Eyre", emphasis ours.

LINE 69. *Gushtuwool:* See §2.4 of the editors' introduction for discussion of this character. This is the name of the leader of the Killerwhale People who comes to the aid of the ailing woman.

LINE 74. *Wáa sáyá x̲'ayeek̲á yáat?:* The question here, *wáa sá x̲'ayeek̲á?*, literally means 'what are you saying here?', though the implication is closer to 'what are you crying about?' or 'why are you crying?' In some Athabaskan languages the verb for 'to say' is used more generally for 'producing oral noise'. So for example in Koyukon Athabaskan the question *Dodenee?*, literally, 'What is s/he saying?', can be answered by *Etsaah* 'S/he is crying'. So, we can infer that *Dodenee?* in this case actually means 'What oral noise is s/he making?' and would correspond to English 'What is s/he carrying on about?' in this usage. Likewise, the question *wáa sá x̲'ayeek̲á?* here is to be thought of as meaning 'What are you making oral noise about?' or 'What are you carrying on about?'

LINE 77. *Hasdu ítde áyá yéi x̲'ayax̲ak̲á:* This is more literally, 'toward their absence I am saying this'. Here again the verb *yéi x̲'ayax̲ak̲á* 'I am saying (so)' can in some instances be interpreted as referring to making oral noise of any sort, in this case weeping.

LINES 84–85. *Du kinaak.ádi tle kaax̲ kéi awditée, / yú du doogú áyá:* Here, as throughout much of Tlingit mythology, animal or animal-like entities are viewed as having overlying skins that they can remove like coats so as to reveal their underlying human-like form. Note, however, that the situation in the narrative is slightly more complicated than this. If we adhere directly to the language and order of events in Italio's performance, we are never actually presented with the image of an animal removing its skin and thereupon revealing its underlying human self; rather, what we find is a man canoeing ashore, walking up the beach, speaking to the woman, and then removing his coat. The image is thus that of a man removing his jacket and thereupon still appearing as a man. No apparent changes in his corporeal form take place when he removes 'his skin'. In the imagery of the narrative (which we might take to represent the perceptual experience of the woman) Hole-in-the-Dorsal-Fin never appears directly in the form of a killerwhale. It is only with Italio's statement, «du doogú áyá» 'this (the jacket) is his skin', that a relationship is established between Hole-in-the-Dorsal-Fin's jacket and his skin. We also find the converse process throughout Tlingit mythology, in which a person dons an animal's skin and thus takes on the animal's bodily form; a recurring example in this volume is when Raven has his mother don the skin of a duck, which enables her to assume its form and float over the flooded earth without issue. Compare the statement from a version Johnson told in English on February 16, 1954, in which Hole-in-the-Dorsal-Fin explicitly changes from a killerwhale to a human before approaching the woman;

Johnson states, "The killerwhale heard a girl weeping and crying because she lost all her children. [...] He came ashore and turned into a human being."*

LINE 88. *at géide s wudzigeet:* This is literally approximately, 'they performed an unnatural act'. The implication seems to be that Hole-in-the-Dorsal-Fin and the woman have intercourse.

LINE 92. *k̲ées' áx̲ laa ÿé:* This line contains a false start, «k̲ées' át—áx̲ laa ÿé», in which Italio first uses *át* 'to there', with the punctual *-t* postposition, but revises this to *áx̲* '(repeatedly) contacting there', with the pertingent *-x̲* postposition. The postposition *-x̲* takes the place of *-t* in repetitive imperfectives of Ø-conjugation motion verbs.

LINE 100. *tl'éx̲ yáx̲ ÿawut'aaÿí:* The precise meaning of the phrase *tl'éx̲ yáx̲* 'resembling tl'éx̲, tl'éx̲-like' used in lines 100 and 113 is unclear to us and was unrecognizable to every elder we consulted. The noun *tl'éx̲* refers to usnea, a type of lichen that grows on trees, colloquially called 'old man's beard'. Johnson told de Laguna in a context unrelated to Italio's recording, "Lichens from the ground in the woods are good for sores. Smash it up and heat it on rocks with seal oil and mountain goat tallow."† The apparent idiom used by Italio in the text could refer to usnea that is heated to a comfortable temperature in the manner Johnson describes, but we have no way of verifying this hypothesis. If you listen closely, you will hear Italio pronounce the word *tl'éx̲* as *tl'.éx̲*, with an appreciable gap between the glottalization of the /tl'/ and the release of the glottalization. This appears to be a means of emphasizing the word *tl'éx̲*. One can compare a similar phenomenon in the Navajo language, where the stem of a word beginning in a glottalized stop may be emphasized in the same way, so, for example, the emphatic form of the word *tł'oh* 'grass' sounds like *tl''oh*.‡

LINE 101. *kikgeenóot':* We would expect *kakgeenóot'* here, with *ka-* specifying that the thing swallowed is round and/or small. We hear the first syllable as /kik/ rather than /kak/; perhaps the vowel of *ka-* is raised from /a/ to /i/ according to some vowel-harmony rule we are not aware of, or perhaps this is not a rule but simply an anticipatory vowel-raising phenomenon that might happen from time to time in Italio's speech.

LINE 103. *yóo áwé ash daaÿak̲á:* The third-person salient pronoun *ash* marks the main character of a story or sequence, and in this part of the story Raven's mother is treated as the main character.

LINE 104. *Ayéx̲ áwé yéi jeewanei:* Johnson: "So she did. [...] She follow the instructions the Killerwhale gave her."§ This is a critical turning point in the narrative, on

* De Laguna, *Under Mount Saint Elias*, 858.

† Ibid, 656.

‡ Personal communication, Martha Austin to Leer.

§ De Laguna, *Under Mount Saint Elias*, 848.

either side of which there is a very close reflection between, first, what the woman is instructed to do and, second, what she does.

LINE 109. *yéi kugoogek'i té:* Italio pronounces this phrase as «yéi kugoogek'i té» 'a stone that is this small'. This would typically be said with an initial /ka/ rather than /ku/, but we write it in the text as he pronounced it here.

LINE 110. *daakdidúk:* The core meaning of this verb is 'it is solid', but the verb carries the implication that the object in question is solid, has no holes or cracks, and in general is impenetrable.

LINE 111. *Tle dáakx' daak uwagút:* This line contains a false start: «Tle a x̱áni daak̲— dáak̲x' daak̲ uwagút.» Italio seemed to begin saying *tle a x̱áni daak̲ uwagút* 'she just walked up from the beach [and went] next to s/he/it' (possibly referring to Hole-in-the-Dorsal-Fin) but decided to revise *a x̱áni* to *dáak̲x'* 'further up (inland from beach)'.

LINE 114. *a yeenáx̱ ayaawatsák̲ tsu daa sá:* Johnson: "She got something to scoop it up from the fire—'ínA [*éenaa*]."* Johnson suggests that the woman is using *éenaa* 'tongs' to remove the stone from the fire. Note Italio's use of the verb *kéi kg̱ilaxwéin* 'you will ladle it up, dish it out' based on the root *xwéin~* 'ladle, spoon, shovel, dish out' during Hole-in-the-Dorsal-Fin's instructions, but *a yeenáx̱ ayaawatsák̲* 'she poked it (some stick-like implement) down under it (the hot stone)' based on the root *tsaak̲~* 'push, prod, poke (with stick-like object, end first)' in describing the woman's actions.

LINE 115. *Du lakát akaawag̱íx'i:* We could not determine the syllable following *du lakát* 'into her mouth'. We have interpreted it as a false start at the beginning of the verb, *ak— akaawag̱íx'i*. The final portion of the verb, heard as *g̱íx'i*, is also hard to account for because an attributive verb form would be expected to have low tone on the stem, i.e., *g̱ix'i*, but on the recording it sounds like *g̱íx'i*. Further, if this were an attributive verb form, there is no head noun with which it could be associated. It cannot be a subordinative form, as this would be *akawug̱éex'i*, which lacks the *i-* element of the classifier and has a long high-toned stem. Alternatively, it could simply be that Italio says the verb *akaawag̱íx'* 'she tossed it' followed by an incidental and non-phonemic release.

LINES 116–17. Johnson: "And she swallow it right down. It didn't hurt. She didn't even feel the effect of it."†

LINE 119. *tlél daa sá du yíkde tóo oonook:* It would appear that, just as one says *aadé awsiteen* 's/he saw her/him/it there' and *aadé aawa.áx̱* 's/he heard her/him/it there', likewise one can say *aadé tóo aawanook* 's/he felt it there' where *NP-de* 'toward NP'

* Ibid, bracketed spelling ours.

† Ibid.

specifies the location where the sensation is felt. Also compare the phrase in line 120, «aadé tóo akg̱wanóok» 'she will feel it there', as well as FI I, v, 64, «Tlél du yíkde tóo oonookch» 'She (the daughter of Raven-of-the-Head-of-the-Nass) didn't feel it (Raven in the form of an evergreen needle) inside her'.

LINE 120. *aadé tóo akg̱wanóok:* Note that the verb stem in the phrase *tóo akg̱wanóok* is expected to be high for the future form, but sounds low on the recording; that is, we hear *tóo akg̱wanook*. This is a striking example of tone downdrift.

LINE 125. *du dísi yaa shunaxíx:* This is more literally, 'her months were disappearing', but here *du dísi* 'her months' refers to her menstrual cycles. Johnson: "Shortly after—she's pregnant."*

LINES 128–29. Since there is no verb used in this quotation, we are doing our best to translate the overall implied meaning of what Hole-in-the-Dorsal-Fin is instructing the woman to do. There is a false start after the quotation in line 129, namely «ÿan yóo—ÿan yóo ash yasiḵéik». Ruth Demmert translates *yan yóo ash yasiḵéik* as "he keeps telling or warning her beforehand".

LINE 130. *du wadák'u:* Italio here refers to Hole-in-the-Dorsal-Fin as 'her (the woman's) young man', which implies something more like 'her boyfriend'.

LINE 133. *ÿatwoo.oo:* Note that in this verb the noun *ÿát* 'child' has been incorporated into the verb as prefixed *ÿat-*. If *ÿát* 'child' were unincorporated, the phrase would be *ÿát aawa.oo*.

LINE 140. *a waaḵ náḵ oolsínch:* Note that the third-person intransitive form of this verb is identical with the transitive form with third-person subject and third-person object in this habitual verb form, so this could translate as either 'she would hide (herself) from them' or 'she would hide him/it from them'; *a waaḵ náḵ* is literally 'away from their (the slaves') eyes'.

LINE 142. *káx̱ akanasteech:* If this is correctly transcribed, the possessor of *káx̱* is the null reflexive possessor meaning 'self('s)', so the verb refers to Raven wearing toy arrows on himself as if in a quiver, with the verb denoting multiple small objects strung together; this typically refers, for example, to a string of beads, but it may apparently refer to a string of any small objects. Johnson: "Pretty soon the boy start to creep and walk. And pretty soon he start to make a bow and arrow out of the bushes. His mother taught him how to do it and he practice."†

* De Laguna, *Under Mount Saint Elias*, 848.

† Ibid.

LINE 144. *Yax̱.atgwakú keitl yaanawádi yéx̱ áwé ÿatee:* The opening of this line with *yax̱.atgwakú* 'proverb, saying' indicates that this is a proverbial expression. The implication seems to be that Raven was 'like a dog('s) growing up', in the sense that he grew into maturity very rapidly in comparison to a normal human. We have written the phrase *keitl yaanawádi* with *yaanawádi* as one word assuming that *yaanawádi* in this phrase is a possessed progressive verbal noun, *keitl yaanawádi* meaning 'a dog's growing up', but it is possible to interpret this as a subordinative progressive imperfective, i.e., *keitl yaa nawádi* 'when/as a dog is growing up'. Raven's rapid growth into maturity seems to form a broader theme beyond this moment in this story. Compare FI I, V, 141, «daaḵwéit yaanawádi yáx̱ sáwé yatee?» 'what sort of thing grows [so fast] as this?', which Johnson interpreted as "Raven grows like a weed."* Johnson told de Laguna about another instance in which Italio remarked on Raven's rapid growth, "Frank Italio this afternoon said, 'I wish everybody grow up fast as Raven, just like the minutes go round the clock, the way he wants to give people daylight.'"†

LINE 146. *Shde ḵáax̱ sateeyí:* We have not been able to verify the word *shde*, but we take it to be a variant or elaboration of *de* 'now, already'.

LINE 155. *ash een ÿan akaawaník:* The use of the salient pronoun *ash* for Raven instead of his mother shows him now emerging as the protagonist of the narrative. Johnson: "His uncle don't know yet that he's a big boy. His mother explain everything what he done to her children, so he (the boy) is going to fix him (his uncle) good and plenty."‡

LINE 160. *alx'éesh:* The third-person verbal object prefix *a-* is barely audible, if at all. It would seem that Italio pronounced this vowel so softly that de Laguna's recorder failed to capture it. Since Tlingit does not allow a verb to begin with a bare consonantal classifier (*l-*, *s-*, *sh-*), we conclude that Italio did pronounce the verb as *alx'éesh* and not **lx'éesh*. This raises the possibility that instances of the third-person possessive pronoun *a*, which the transcribers did not hear and therefore did not write, were likewise softly pronounced by Italio and unrecorded.

LINE 168. *K'e tóox̱ nagú:* Here again we might expect *a tóox̱* 'through/into it', but we do not hear the possessive pronoun *a*. We find the theme of Raven putting his mother into the skin of a duck so that she can assume the form and function of the bird and float unharmed over the flooding tide in every version of this story told in this volume. Compare:

* Ibid, 854.

† Ibid, 842.

‡ Ibid, 848.

FI I, i, 168:	«K'e tóox̲ nagú, atléi, k'e tóox̲ nagú.»	"You should get inside [this duck skin], mother, you should get inside it."
AW i, 46:	«Yá s'ús' tóode áwé kg̲eeshéex,»	"You must quickly get inside this harlequin duck,"
SJ i, 155–56:	[«]Yá gáaxw tóox̲ daak̲ gú! Yá gáaxw doogú tóox̲ daak̲ gú!»	["]Get inside this duck! Get inside this duck skin!"
RZ II, v, 35–37:	yá a doogóo— yá a doogú tóox̲ áwé awsinook du tláa	its skin— he put his mother inside [this bufflehead] skin
FD i, 94–95:	a tóox̲ gugagut át sákw yéi awsinei	he prepared what would become something for her to don

LINES 173–74. Johnson: "And then when the water breaks over her, it don't seem to hurt her. She comes out on top and she keeps going on top of the water. She floats—just like she's on top of the ground to her. It don't seem to feel any different to her."*

LINE 175. *Du kaanáx̲ kéi u—:* The complete verb in this phrase was either not pronounced or was pronounced so quietly that it was not captured on the tape. One suggestion for completing the verb would be *du kaanáx̲ kéi ultéetch* 'the waves would wash over her'.

LINE 176. *át wulitéet:* Note the long high verb stem. For most speakers the basic stem-form of the verb is *teet*, but for Italio it is *téet*, which is consistent with Tongass Tlingit *ti't*.

LINE 182. *Tle ch'u shóogu yáax' {k̲ux̲wasteeyéyéx̲} x̲á x̲áa ÿatee:* The crucial verb form of this line is exceedingly difficult to hear, and our transcription of this line changed repeatedly. We have written it as *k̲ux̲wasteeyéyéx̲*, which, if transcribed correctly, would be based on the perfective decessive verb form *k̲ux̲wasteeyín* 'I had been born, had come into existence', but we are at a loss as to why Raven's mother would compare her experience in the duck skin to being 'born' (rather than 'existing' or 'living') at a time before donning the duck skin. We have settled for the rather free translation, 'To me, you see, it's just like it was when I lived my life here before'. Johnson interprets this as, "And when his mother get off the water and come home, he asks his mother, 'How does it feel to be on top of the water?' She went and answer, 'It don't make any difference. It's just the same as walking on the ground. It's all right,' she told her son."†

* De Laguna, *Under Mount Saint Elias*, 848–49.

† Ibid, 849.

LINE 189. *Gus'x̱lugook̲:* Johnson: "And he took his bow and arrow and he went around on the beach. He run onto the snipes and killed the biggest snipe amongst them. And he done the same thing as he done to the duck. He cut it on the back, and after he got through skinning he got into it."* Johnson distinguishes the species here as a "snipe" for Raven and a "duck" for his mother. Compare this line from a separate version Johnson told in English to de Laguna: "So Raven go to work when he know his uncle is out. He's got the skin of some kind of sharp-nosed bird, and he hangs it up for hours and hours, and he practice, and then twists and get free."† This creature is discussed further in §2.7 of the editors' introduction.

LINE 191. *yóo lukoowáat':* This statement, which means 'its beak was this long', was likely accompanied by a hand gesture.

LINES 193–204. Johnson's interpretation aligns nicely with this sequence of lines, "And he fly and fly up high, and finally he get to the sky and he just stick his bill into the solid part of the sky. And he hang there and swing back and forth, and he swing back and forth. And he thinks that will work. And finally he give a sudden jerk and his bill come loose, and he fell down on the ground. So he thinks that it will work. He got he and his mother prepared for the flood that the Moon is going to make."‡

LINE 194. *Tle yú xáats't áwé wdik̲ín:* We have translated *xáats'* here unconventionally as 'firmament'. The word *xáats'* is usually translated as 'blue sky' or 'open sky'. It is evident from the description of Raven sticking his beak into the *xáats'* that the Tlingit perception of the *xáats'* was as a solid but permeable substance above the earth and the clouds. George Thornton Emmons, writing in the late 1800s, stated that "the sky is believed to be an inverted dome over a flat earth."§ De Laguna states the same, "The lower surface [of the sky] is presumably like an inverted hard bowl."¶ Note Johnson's interpretation "he just stick his bill into *the solid part of the sky.*"** In Gerhard von Rad's study of the Old Testament, *Genesis: A Commentary*, he writes that "the ancients imagined [the firmament] as a gigantic hemispherical and ponderous bell."†† The English word 'firmament' is based on the Latin *firmamentum*, which is the word used in the Vulgate version of the Bible to translate the Hebrew *rāqīa'*. Von Rad explains, "*Rāqīa'* means that which is firmly hammered, stamped (a word of the same root in Phoenician means 'tin dish'!). The meaning of

* Ibid.

† Ibid, 845.

‡ Ibid, 849.

§ Emmons, *The Tlingit Indians*, 289.

¶ De Laguna, *Under Mount Saint Elias*, 795.

** Ibid, 849, emphasis ours.

†† Von Rad, *Genesis*, 53.

the verb *rq*ʿ concerns the hammering of the vault of heaven into firmness."[*] The word 'firmament' thus carries a latent image of the heavens as a sort of hammered bell or dome-like object, which makes for a fitting parallel with Emmons' and de Laguna's descriptions of the *xáats'* as something akin to an "inverted dome" or "inverted hard bowl".

LINE 196. *du lú:* This line appears to contain a false start, «yú du lú k—», likely for *yú du lú kuwát'* 'that long beak of his'.

LINE 201. *áa g̱unéi akawlitéx̱':* In discussing the recurring theme of Raven 'twisting' or 'unscrewing' his beak from the sky, we considered the quite speculative idea that this detail could relate to the way the night sky appears to spin around us due to Earth's rotation on its axis.

LINE 205. *De a kát woosh kát ÿawdidaa yú du káak ḵu.aa:* Johnson interprets this line as "He's laying around and watch his uncle."[†] We can compare a documented form such as «a kát (át) y̱aawadaa», translated as "kept an eye on him/her/it",[‡] which is the basis of Italio's form, but this does not account for the elements *woosh kát ... d-* (and the long high-toned open stem in the perfective, indicative of zero-conjugation) that we hear in his. We can point to two examples of this combination from the stories Deikeenaak'w told to Swanton in Tlingit: «adê´ wuckᴀt wudigu´t diyē´dî»[§] (i.e., *aadé woosh kát wudigút diyéede*) 'she paced back and forth (toward) there below' and «wūckᴀ´t wudîqê´n yuî´xt!»[¶] (i.e., *woosh kát wudiḵín yú íx̱t'*) 'the shaman flies (or flew) back and forth'. These forms from Italio and Deikeenaak'w are notable in that they are all intransitive with a singular subject and there is no way to construe the reciprocal possessive pronoun *woosh* 'each other' with any argument of the verb, as would usually be the case. These seem to be special idiomatic cases in which *woosh kát...d-* (lit. 'on top of one another') means something along the lines of 'repeatedly retracing one's steps or path'. In Italio's line it would seem to imply that Raven would periodically return to the same vantage point to watch his uncle and keep an eye on his movements. Once Raven sees his uncle make preparations and depart in his boat, Raven takes the opportunity to go to his uncle's house and seize his wife.

---

* Von Rad, *Genesis*, 53.

† De Laguna, *Under Mount Saint Elias*, 849.

‡ Leer, "Verb Books."

§ Swanton, *Tlingit Myths and Texts*, 262. This line comes from text 90, "The Man Who Was Abandoned". Swanton translated it as "she was walking around back of the fire". Ruth Demmert and Sam Johnston independently confirmed the meaning of *woosh kát wudigút* as 's/he was pacing back and forth'.

¶ Ibid, 340. This line occurs in text 104, "Story of the Kā´gwᴀntān". Swanton translated it as "a shaman can fly about".

LINE 207. *dulnáax'w íḵdé:* We seem to hear an unaccountable high tone on the *-de* suffix, pronounced as *íḵdé*. Johnson: "He watched him. Finally, he sees his uncle get his big canoe down on the water, and everything they're going to use on the way on the trip to the other town."* The verb *dulnáax'w* 'people are carrying/taking/bringing bundles' is a multiple imperfective form; the corresponding perfective form is *wududlinaa* 'people carried, took, brought bundles'. The fourth-person subject pronoun *du-d-* 'people' here almost certainly refers to the slaves of Tide-Commander.

LINE 209. *G̱una.aant wuḵoox̱ akwshitán:* Note that here *wuḵoox̱* 'travel by (single) boat' is a perfective verbal noun serving as a complement to the main verb *akwshitán*, which usually translates as 's/he/it frequents it (a place)'. The combination *wuḵoox̱ akwshitán* loosely translates here 'he is fond of, or in the habit of, going by boat', or 'he is wont to go by boat'.

LINE 213. *Tsu yeekawliyáat'éyáx̱ áwé:* This line could also possibly be *Tsu yeekawliyáat', ayáx̱ áwé*. We have opted for the transcription with *-éyáx̱*, which is the reduced form of *-ÿéyáx̱* (see appendix 1, §13.1.2, for discussion on these kinds of constructions). The implication seems to be Tide-Commander was out travelling for a significant amount of time. Literally, the line reads, 'It seems to have taken a long time again' (with *tsu* 'again'), but since no other situation has been described as having taken a long time, we have omitted the word 'again' from the translation. In terms of the theme of Tide-Commander travelling away from his home for long periods of time, compare FD i, 19–20, «Naḵúx̱ch / lkeeyiyáag̱aa» 'He (Tide-Commander) would leave / for an unusually long time'. In terms of the formulaic phrasing Italio uses here, compare FI I, iv, 74, «Tle yeekawliyáat'éyáx̱ áwé tlei tsu» 'It went on for a long time, so once again...', referring to the passage of time while Raven was stuck inside the dead beached whale.

LINE 216. *aax̱ at wujix̱einéyáx̱ áwé ÿatee wé neil:* This could also be translated as 'The house was like a place where things (trees, containers, various wooden objects) had fallen off' or much more freely 'It looked like a tornado had swept through the house' or 'things in the house were in total shambles'. The image seems to be that of the interior of a house in which everything had fallen out of place.

LINE 222. *ḵóokt yíkt—:* Italio ends this line with a false start heard as «ḵóok yíkt dus—», certainly anticipating *ḵóok yíkt dus.áa* 'she (the wife of Tide-Commander) was made to sit in a box' (with fourth-person subject). He revises this to «ḵóok yíkt as.áa» 'he (Tide-Commander) had her sit in a box' in the following line (with third-person subject).

* De Laguna, *Under Mount Saint Elias*, 849.

LINE 223. *k̲óok yíkt as.áa:* Tide-Commander would apparently keep his wife tied up in a box and hoisted into the rafters of the house when he would leave. Johnson's interpretation of this scene: "And that man's slaves—there's a whole pile of them—the house is full of them—they got so fear of this man come to visit there—they point to the box up in the ceiling."[*] Compare with a line from a different version told in English to de Laguna by Johnson herself, "Then when his uncle is gone he goes in there and asks the other people, 'Where does my uncle keep his wife?' 'Right up there in a box all tied up tight with ropes and roots.' Then he ordered the people to get the box down. He got the woman out and he pulled out all the hair from under her arms. And then he threw it up the smokestack (i.e., smokehole). The hair was flicker feathers (kun tȧ we) [*kóon t'aawú*])."[†] Compare also this line from a separate version told to de Laguna by Maggie Harry: "He had a cage and kept his wife in it, hanging from the roof."[‡]

LINES 231–32. *ÿanáax̲ aÿawlik'úts. / Daax̲ aÿawlik'úts:* The verb phrases in these two lines contain the derivational string *P-x̲ ÿa-u-s/l-* (Ø) 'all/a bunch in relation to P'; occurring first as *ÿanáax̲ aÿawlik'úts* 'he snapped (the lines) over it' (where P is *N ÿanáa* 'over, covering N'), second as *daax̲ aÿawlik'úts* 'he snapped (the lines) around it' (where P is *N daa* 'around N'). Note that in both cases the relational noun that serves as the postpositional object lacks a possessive pronoun. This derivational string is most commonly attested in the form *ÿax̲=ÿa-u-s/l-* (Ø) 'all/a bunch', where the postpositional object is *ÿan* and *ÿan-x̲* contracts to *ÿax̲*; Italio's forms here provide rare examples of relational nouns that can occur as the postpositional object of *-x̲*. Johnson: "And he got a ladder and take the box down and take it outside and tear up all the lines that man tie up the box with. And he tear it up and get ahold of his uncle's wife."[§]

LINE 235. *A jín yéi awsinei:* Literally, 'He did so to her hand/lower arm'. The implication seems to be that Raven lifted his uncle's wife's arms to expose the flickers in her armpits.

LINE 236. *Éeneekóon:* This is the name of Raven's uncle's wife. The name literally means 'Armpit-Flicker(s)', i.e., someone who has northern flickers in her armpits. We have translated her name as 'Flicker-Pits', since 'Armpit-Flicker' sounds like 'a person who flicks armpits', and 'Flicker-Pits' simply sounds better in English than 'Flicker-Armpits'. We hear the name pronounced as «Éenyeekóon» in FI II, 120. See §2.6 of the editors' introduction for discussion of this character.

* De Laguna, *Under Mount Saint Elias*, 849.

† Ibid, 845, bracketed spelling ours.

‡ Ibid, 857.

§ Ibid, 849.

LINES 237–41. *tle atx̱ áwé ax'óol':* Johnson: "He went to work and pull all her feathers off, and he just throw [them] up in the air, and it fly around the air."* In Johnson's interpretation, it seems that she perceives the uncle's wife to have flicker feathers in place of her armpit hair, and Raven plucks these feathers out and casts them into the air. However, we are interpreting this scene as involving flickers residing in the armpits of the uncle's wife and Raven yanking the birds out whole from there (rather than plucking the birds' feathers or the feather-like armpit hair of the woman). We can point to three instances in which this scene takes place in the texts of this volume: FI I, i, 237, «tle atx̱ áwé ax'óol'» 'he (Raven) plucked them (flickers) from there (from under his uncle's wife's arms)'; FI II, 117, «a éenyee kóoni wuyíkt aawax'úl' wé du káak shát» 'he (Raven) plucked the flickers of his uncle's wife's armpits [and cast them] into the air'; and FD i, 102–03, «Aax̱ akaklakéil' áwé a éenyee kóoni / aawax'úl'» 'After he untied her, he plucked out / the flickers in her armpits'. All examples having to do with 'plucking feathers' that we could find in our reference materials occur with the fricative classifier element *l-* (which makes sense on classificatory grounds when the object is a mass of hair or feathers). In each of the three examples from Italio and Dick, we find the verbs occurring with no fricative element in the classifier; we might speculate that this is because what is being plucked are whole birds, not feathers. Note also that the phrase in line 238, «gáant kanalÿichji át» 'things that fly about outside' is actually pronounced by Italio as «gáant kanalÿitji át», in which the coda consonant /ch/ of the verb stem *ÿich* is altered to /t/ before /ji/; in addition to this, in Italio's pronunciation the stop /t/ (which has taken the place of /ch/) is unreleased before /ji/, making it difficult to discern. See §3.10.8 of the editors' introduction for further discussion of the rule responsible for changing /ch/ to /t/ here.

LINE 239. *«Gáant,» yóo áwé x̱'aÿak̲á:* We are not sure if the subject of the verb here is Raven or the flickers. If it is Raven, he would seem to be telling the flickers to fly around outside. If it is the flickers, it would seem to be an imitation of the birds' call.

LINE 243. *du x̱einínáx̱ kawdliyeech:* The relational noun *N x̱einí* means 'even with, alongside N'. When combined with *ji-* 'hand', the compound *N jix̱einí* means 'working alongside N' or 'assisting N in work'; and when combined with *x̱'a-* 'mouth', the compound *N x̱'ax̱einí* means 'verbally supporting N' or 'reinforcing N by speech'. The combination *N x̱einí-náx̱* translates as 'catching up to, overtaking N'. Note the use of the same phrase in FD i, 106.

LINE 244. *«Ax̱ adée!»:* This is an affective variant of *ax̱ ádi* 'my thing(s)'. We have followed Johnson's interpretation of *ax̱ adée!* as 'my precious stuff!', but other valid interpretations could be 'my precious!' or 'my goodness!' (although the latter translation does not convey the sense of loss and grief implicit in this interjection).

* Ibid.

Johnson: "'Somebody's got my precious stuff!' His wife's hair was flying in his face. He just got so mad he give an order to have the flood—just over that hair from under her arms! (Hearty laughter by MJ and ourselves)."* What Johnson describes as "His wife's hair" is, in her interpretation, the flicker feathers that Raven plucked from his uncle's wife's armpits and cast into the air; while the imagery is not perfectly clear to us, we are taking Italio to be referring to actual flickers residing in the woman's armpits.

LINES 247–48. Line 247 ends with the false start «Daa sákwshé a tóonáx̱ yéi adaa—». Italio revises the portion after *daa sákwshé* as «a tóonáx̱ ayadlak̲x'u át» in the following line. A substantial question remains as to the referent of the head noun *át* 'thing(s)' in *a tóonáx̱ ayadlak̲x'u át*. Here *át* could be coreferential with the postpositional object *a* in *a tóonáx̱* (which would mean 'the thing from which it is getting bunches of it'), the verbal object *a-* in *ayadlak̲x'u* (which would mean 'the thing of which it is getting bunches from there'), or the unexpressed third-person subject in *ayadlak̲x'u*. We have here opted for the latter analysis and translated the sentence accordingly as 'the creature that is getting bunches of [flickers] from in there'.

LINE 258. Johnson: "So that's why the Moon went up to the sky. And he stayed there, and the tide start to come up and destroy all the people but that boy and his mother."†

Notes to Frank Italio's tale I, episode ii, "Raven Goes Down Along the Bull Kelp"

LINE 4. *Tlél du tóon at utí:* The pronominal reference in this line does not make it clear whether it was Raven's mother or Raven's uncle who was unconcerned. We have interpreted it as referring to Raven's mother, floating worrilessly over the flood in the duck skin. This line begins with a false start; the unaltered line is «Tóon at— Tlél du tóon at utí».

LINE 16. *A kináak k̲wá k̲ukaawak̲ín:* The verb *k̲ukaawak̲ín* appears to be based on an unattested theme. We could not determine the exact form or meaning to our satisfaction and our consultants did not recognize this form. It may indicate Raven 'hovering' above the bull kelp once he had flown into a position above it.

LINE 23. *geesh daax̱ áwé yéi woogútch aadé:* This appears to be the perfective counterpart to the repetitive imperfective in *geesh daax̱ áwé yéi gútch* 'he keeps going (or trying to go) down the bull kelp'. Such repetitive perfectives are exceedingly rare in today's language, although we find occasional examples in these texts, e.g., FI II, 165,

* De Laguna, *Under Mount Saint Elias*, 845.

† Ibid, 849.

«k'idéin xeewa.átx̲» 'dusk would now keep recurring in proper fashion', and SJ xi, 215, «Has wudishánx̲» 'They always grew old'.

LINE 33. *Anallúk'ch:* The theme used here is *O-S-l-lóok'~* (*na*) 'for S to suck O (meat, out of shell creature)'.

LINES 34, 40, 41. *x̲'akandukeich / aadé x̲'akdukaa ÿé / k̲aa x̲'akwdakaa:* The theme used in these lines is *O-x̲'e-ka-u-S-d-kaa* (*na*) 'for S to copy, reproduce O's speech, words, oral sounds', an elaboration of *O-ka-u-S-d-kaa* (*na*) 'for S to motion, gesture to O'. Line 34 is a habitual form, line 40 an imperfective attributive, and line 41 a basic imperfective. Here the sound of Raven slurping up the sea-urchin meat is echoing off the surrounding mountains and cliffs, leading Raven to assume that someone is copying his sounds to mock him. De Laguna notes that Italio explained after the narration:

> It's his own echoes. This sound goes around in every place and he thinks somebody is watching him. That's why when you go to a large place and make a loud noise, you think somebody is copying you. You say, "Xó," and it's like somebody answering you, imitating you. That's what they believe a long time ago. [...] Echo is x̣ᴀduqa [*x̲'akdukaa* or perhaps *x̲'akwdakaa*].
>
> Finally he give up. He didn't see a soul. He didn't even find out who's imitating his swallowing niṡ [*nées'*].*

LINE 44. *nís'aa:* Raven evidently was using a *nís'aa* 'sea-urchin knife' to open the urchins he was eating and then proceeded to use this instrument to jab into the face of the cliff. Johnson: "And he make some kind of a can opener—we call it niṡᴀ [*nís'aa*]—just like the table knife. I don't know what it's made of. They used to use it. It's got a round point that goes in the back of a sea egg and it twist open. I saw them made of a stick."† Note the consistency with the Raven story Deikeenaak'w told in English to Swanton, "Finally Raven became angry, seized the knife he was cutting up the sea urchins with and slit up the front of the cliff."‡

LINES 46–51. Johnson's interpretation: "He gets so mad! [... H]e goes to part of the mountain and he makes cuts here and there on the mountain. [...] It shows on the mountain on the other side of Lituya Bay today. They call in Yeł a'awᴇ niṡiyᴀ [*Yéil Áa Aawanis'i Yé*]—'where Raven eat niṡ [*nées'*] and cut the mountain up in strips.'"§ The form used by Italio in the narration, *áx' aawanis'i yé* 'place where he ate sea urchins', does not appear to be an actual placename as such; the form provided by Johnson in the interpretation, however, has the appearance of a formal placename,

* Ibid, 850, bracketed material ours.

† Ibid, 849, bracketed spelling ours.

‡ Swanton, *Tlingit Myths and Texts*, 10.

§ De Laguna, *Under Mount Saint Elias*, 850, bracketed material ours.

Yéil Áa Aawanis'i Yé 'The Place Where Raven Ate Sea Urchins'. Note that when Italio says «Ltu.áa tliyaanax̱.áwu» 'it is on the far side of Lituya Bay' in line 46, this is the 'far side' relative to Yakutat, which is consistent with de Laguna's description of it being a peak "southeast of Lituya Bay".* De Laguna suggests further that this "may be Mount Crillon or Mount La Pérouse",† but this has not been confirmed. We seem to hear Italio pronouncing the name of the specific cliff that Raven cut into as «Naalx̱'»; this name has not been attested elsewhere and its form and meaning are unclear to us and our consultants.

LINE 51. This line contains a false start. The unaltered line is «ayakaawahani—Yéilch ÿakaawahani g̱íl'».

LINE 52. *Tlél yéi dusáakw Yéil, yóo:* Johnson: "He was never called Yeł that time"‡ (i.e., …at that time).

LINE 54. *Yax̱ K̲ées' Shakawdzinugu Shaanák'w:* This character is discussed in §2.9 of the editors' introduction.

LINE 55. *Ash yáa aawasáa:* Johnson: "It was that old man called him Yeł."§ Note that in Johnson's own version of this story which she told in English to de Laguna, she refers to an "old woman" and generally uses the pronouns "she" and "her".¶ However, in Johnson's interpretation of this narrative by Italio, she uses "he", "him", and "old man".** Because Italio uses *k̲áa shaanák'w* 'old man' in line 64, and because Johnson interprets Italio's telling as involving a man, we interpret it as an elderly man rather than woman, even though a woman may be a more common reference in other versions of this story. Nora Dauenhauer's mother Seig̱eig̱éi, Emma Marks, also uses the term *k̲áa shaanák'w* in her telling of this story, but the Dauenhauers nonetheless interpreted this as a woman in a published text of Marks' performance of this story.†† The interested reader should compare Marks' telling with FI I, ii, and FD xii, the three of which have a strong thematic correspondence.

LINE 57. *Lyóo.atkoowajeegi Shaanák'w:* See §2.8 of the editors' introduction for discussion of this character's name and significance.

* De Laguna, *Under Mount Saint Elias*, 93.

† Ibid.

‡ Ibid, 850.

§ Ibid.

¶ Ibid, 845.

** Ibid, 850.

†† Dauenhauer and Dauenhauer, "Raven and the Tide". A revised text of Emma Marks' story will be included in an eventual second volume of Raven stories, with some adjustments from the Dauenhauers' 2000 publication. The audio of her telling is found in the Alaska Native Language Archive identified as "Emma and Jenny Marks; Telling stories", ANLC1919, recording b.

LINE 61. *Daa sákwshíyáagé yéi sitee:* Our consultants were unfamiliar with the fairly obscure phrase *yéi sitee*, which is not equivalent with the more usual *áx̲ sitee* 'that's what s/he/it is'. Compare FI I, v, 100, which is a quotation of Unfazable-Little-Elder, «K'e s'íx'g̲aa wéit'át shákdéwé yéi sitee» 'Maybe moss would be the right thing'. There are two examples in the speeches in *Haa Tuwnáagu Yís* that use the same verb theme but with the addition of the prefix *tu-* 'inner being, mind, thoughts, soul', and (in the metaphysical sense) 'heart'. The first is from Jessie Dalton, «yee tula.eesháani káx̲ áwé gági uwagudi yáx̲ ax̲ tusitee / yá yee éesh du s'áaxu»,[*] translated by the Dauenhauers as, "I feel as if your father's hat / has come out for your grief".[†] The second is from George Jim, «Yéi áwé ax̲ tusitee yeedát», translated as "That's how it seems to me now".[‡] We can infer from these examples that the verb *yéi sitee* denotes a sense of 'seeming to be'. Johnson: "When he enter there he see a real old, old lady. She's all by herself. And the old lady ask him what he wants; what is he looking for, she asks him. 'I wonder—I just want to find out who's in charge of the tide. Are you the one who's in charge of the tide?' he ask the old lady."[§]

LINE 64. *K̲áa shaanák'w ... yóot'aa aÿa.óo:* This phrase might alternatively be *K̲áa shaanák'w ... yóot aÿa.óo* 'An old man ... owns that place over yonder.' Johnson: "And she [Unfazable-Little-Elder] said, 'No, there's an old man not so very far from here. He's the one in charge of the tide.'"[¶]

LINE 66. *yánde kux̲lakóox:* The only sense we could make of this is that it is a future form meaning 'the tide will completely recede'. Note that here Italio actually says «yánde kux̲lakóox» where we would expect the future form to be *yánde kagux̲lakóox*. Interestingly enough, in Tongass Tlingit we find a number of future forms where the thematic prefix *ka-* is omitted before the string of prefixes denoting the future, just as Italio has apparently done here. Tongass examples we can point to are *a kaa`x̲ k̲ukux̲sahaa˙* (rather than *a kaa`x̲ k̲ukakux̲sahaa˙*) 's/he will polish it', corresponding to perfective form *a kaa`x̲ k̲ukaws.haa`* 's/he polished it'; *sh g̲walnee`k* (rather than *sh kakg̲walnee`k*) 's/he will tell a story, stories', corresponding to perfective *sh kawtlnee`k* 's/he told a story, stories'; and *akux̲shaxee˙t* (rather than *akakux̲shaxee˙t*) 's/he will write it', corresponding to perfective *akawshixit* 's/he will write it'.[**]

---

* Dauenhauer and Dauenhauer, *Haa Tuwunáagu Yís*, 252. On comparing with the original audio of Dalton's speech, we actually hear her pronounce this line as «gági uwagudéyáx̲ ax̲ tusitee», in which *gági uwagudéyáx̲* is another fine example of what we are calling the quasi-attributive *-ÿéyáx̲* construction (see appendix 1, §13.1.2). Our source of the audio is MC005, tape 255, side a; cf. 44:03 on the recording.

† Dauenhauer and Dauenhauer, *Haa Tuwunáagu Yís*, 253.

‡ Ibid, 300–01.

§ De Laguna, *Under Mount Saint Elias*, 850.

¶ Ibid.

** All Tongass forms in this note come from Leer's "Lexical Binders".

LINE 68. *{keitl k̲unáax̲i}x̲ awliyéx̲:* We are unable to hear or decipher this utterance to any satisfaction. It sounds to us rather like the form written above, which could mean that the old man who watches over the tide (or Unfazable-Little-Elder or Raven) made it (whatever 'it' is) into a *keitl k̲unáax̲i* (whatever that is), but this is a very tenuous rendering of something poorly heard. It may be that this sentence is the concluding part of Unfazable-Little-Elder's answer to Raven's inquiry about why the tide won't go down.

LINE 69. This line begins with the false start «Tle aadé wjixee[x]—» 'then he (Raven) ran there', which Italio revises to «aadé woogoot a x̲ánde» 'he (Raven) walked there to him (the little old man)'.

LINES 71–72. *Gwáawé gánt uwatáa du díx̲'—:* Italio cuts off after pronouncing *du díx̲'* 'his back', but we can infer that this is an incomplete pronunciation of *du díx̲'náx̲* 'along his back'. Compare the line Swanton rendered from a Kiks.ádi man named K̲'alyáan as «G̣Aʹndawe utāʹîtc dudAʹq!anAx»* (i.e., *Gánt áwé utáaych du déx̲'náx̲*).

LINE 75. *a dzúkde yanax̲ ayaawataan:* The implication here seems to be that Raven positioned a piece of firewood so that it would block the heat of the fire from radiating onto the old man in order to make the old man uncomfortable and aggravated. We have interpreted the possessive pronoun *a* of *a dzúkde* 'toward behind him' as referring to the old man. Compare FI II, 92, «a dzúkde yanax̲ aÿag̲atánch wé gán» '[Raven] kept sticking the firewood in the ground behind [the old man's] back', which is an identical phrase other than that the verb is in the habitual and specifies the object of the verb as *wé gán* 'the firewood'. We rely again on Johnson's interpretation: "So he come to this old man and he find it out that he's got a fire going. He's laying down and he turn his back. He turn his back to the heat. And this here snipe (Raven is still wearing the snipe skin) went there, and he's a man to that old man. So he went there. *He turn the wood. He turn it around so the old man wouldn't get heat.* He want some heat and he start to warm up his hands."† Note that for Johnson, in this scene Raven is still wearing the skin of the Gus'x̲lugook̲ 'Pokes-Nose-Into-Clouds', yet he nonetheless appears in the eyes of the old man to be a human being. Compare also SJ V, 46, «yá a gáni áwé tle a díx̲'náx̲ ayag̲atánch tle» 'he (Raven) would shove a piece of her firewood down along her back'.

LINE 80. *ash x̲'akaadáx̲ áa yéi nasgéet áwé tsá:* The meaning of this clause was not clear to our consultants. We have provisionally translated it so that it fits with the narrative context.

---

* Swanton, *Tlingit Myths and Texts*, 297; from text 97, "The Four Brothers". See Jones, "Haa Daat Akawshixít", especially note 6, for some background on the Kiks.ádi man K̲'alyáan from whom Swanton recorded "The Four Brothers" and "How the KîksAʹdî Came to Sitka".

† De Laguna, *Under Mount Saint Elias*, 850, emphasis ours.

LINE 81. *Cha goot'ayéigaa sá wulaay̆i léin áwé a kát eeyanís'*: Compare FI II, 96–97, and see §2.9 of the editors' introduction for comparison of this formulaic expression with those used in the same narrative context by James and Dick.

LINE 82. *Yéil Tl'éetl'i:* The postnominal modifier *tl'éetl'i* 'shitty' is based on the verb root *l'éel'*~ 'defecate', with sound-symbolic substitution of the glottalized stop /tl'/ in place of the glottalized fricative /l'/. We translate it here quite literally. Johnson interprets it along the lines of 'a piece of raven shit' rather than a 'raven who is shitty', stating, "That old man says, 'Since when the tide goes out? You're nothing but Raven's poop!—Yeł x̌itłi (or tł'itł'i) [*Yéil Tl'éetl'i*].'—Excuse me for mentioning this!"* We have retained Nora Dauenhauer's preferred translation, 'Shitty-Ass Raven'. According to Italio, this is how the name *Yéil* 'Raven' was first bestowed on the illustrious character who is the subject of this volume. Johnson continues, "That's how that old man named that Yeł. That's the first time he heard his own name."†

LINE 85. *«Tsu g̱unayéidi igax̱dusáakw ltín.»:* The particle *ltín* is a shortened form of *latín* 'look!' Leer notes that it has been attested in Interior Tlingit in fossilized form in the expression *juwáak'w ltín!* 'look at its cute little face! (speaking of a baby)'. Italio uses it multiple times throughout his narratives in quotations of various characters.

LINES 91–92. *Tóo nú! Nées' nóox'u tóo nú!* 'Feel it (inside yourself)!' is an imperative form which has the corresponding imperfective *tóo ayanook* 's/he feels it (inside self)'. Raven is telling the little old man to feel the sting of the sea-urchin spines that he has stabbed into his rear end. 'Feel the burn!' could be a rough idiomatic equivalent in English. This is clearly formulaic, as we find the phrase in the same moment of this scene in FD vii, 43–44, simply with the verb phrase and the object reversed, «Tóo nú nées' nóox'u! / Tóo nú nées' nóox'u!» 'Feel the burn of the sea-urchin shell! / Feel the burn of the sea-urchin shell!' This phrase demonstrates two notable grammatical phenomena. First, *tóo* here is not the locative form of *NP tú* 'inside NP', but rather the locative form of a comparatively rare pronominal stem *tu-* 'self' (cognate with Tongass *du-*), which does not require the *d-* element of the classifier; so *tóo ayanook* (cognate with Tongass *doo' ayanee`kw*) literally means 's/he feels it in her/himself'. The same pronominal stem is found in *tóot awsinúk* (cognate with Tongass *doo`t aw`snuk*) 's/he took it (e.g., a child) to her/himself, adopted it'. The progressive counterpart is *toodé yaa anasnúk* 's/he is taking it to her/himself, adopting it'; note that the stem *too-* here has low tone, in contrast with *NP tóode* 'into NP'. Second, there are four verb roots which lose the final consonant in the imperative form, namely *goot~*, *.aat~*, *nook~* (also *nook~* in Southern Tlingit), and *nook~* (*neekw~* in Southern Tlingit); compare *aadé woogoot* 's/he went there' with

* Ibid, 850, original brackets altered to parentheses, bracketed spelling ours.

† Ibid, 850.

aadé nagú! 'go there!', *aadé s woo.aat* 'they went there' with *aadé nay.á!* 'you folks go there!', *woonook* 's/he sat down' with *ganú!* 'sit down!', and *tóo aawanúk* 's/he felt it (inside self)' with *tóo nú!* 'feel it (inside yourself)!' (and note that even though the Southern Tlingit form of the latter perfective form is *tóo àawanikw*, the imperative form is *tóo nu*, with the same stem as in Northern Tlingit).

LINE 96. *G̱aag̱waalaa:* This potential form more typically occurs as *gwaag̱aalaa*, with the irrealis *u-* combining with the conjugation prefix *g̱a-* rather than the following mode prefix *g̱a-* that characterizes the future, hortative, potential, and contingent modes; that is how we find it in SJ v, 55 and 56, «gwaag̱aalaa dei, Yéil!» Italio, however, pronounces it here as «G̱aag̱waalaa», and we find him pronouncing it the same way in FI II, 102, «Déi, Yéil, gwaag̱aalaa!» Notably, Dick pronounces it this way as well; in FD vii, 48–49, we hear «Déi g̱aag̱waalaa, Yéi-éi-éil!» This phrase is included as part of the discussion of Little-Elder-Who-Enlarged-the-Tide in §2.9 of the editors' introduction.

LINE 98. *yóo ÿawuḵaayí:* The pronunciation of this sounds nearly like *yóo guwuḵaaÿí* on the recording, with the initial syllable resembling /gu/ where we expect /ÿa/ or /wa/. We have written it in the text according to its expected morphophonemic form, *yóo ÿawuḵaaÿí* '(lit. 'when [Raven] spoke thusly'), but we are not entirely sure what transpired from an articulatory point of view.

Notes to Frank Italio's tale I, episode iii, "Raven Deceives His Younger Brother"

LINE 5. *X̱ashak'ákwk':* See §2.10 of the editors' introduction for discussion of this character.

LINE 8. *{...} he does remember all that:* We were unable to hear the beginning of Johnson's English statement here, but we assume she is saying something along the lines of 'I just don't see how he does remember all that', referring to Italio's ability to ornament his stories with such wonderful detail.

LINE 9. *So that's the end of that story:* De Laguna may have correctly meant here that the previous episode, "Raven Goes Down Along the Bull Kelp", recently ended; or, she may have mistakenly taken Italio's pause to laugh and Johnson's interjection in line 8 to mean this was the end of Italio's narration.

LINE 11. Johnson: "So that driftwood stand up and start to walk lame."*

LINE 12. *yanax̱ yéi oogooḵch:* We would have expected this phrase to appear as *yanax̱ yéi agúḵch*, which would be the normal *g̱a*-conjugation repetitive imperfective. The preverb *ÿanax̱=* 'moving into the ground' (from *ÿán-náx̱* 'shore/ground-through')

* De Laguna, *Under Mount Saint Elias*, 850.

typically imposes g̲a-conjugation on the verb and denotes downward motion, but here the verb is clearly Ø-conjugation. It would thus appear that Italio can treat *yéi=* 'down' as a Ø-conjugation derivational string like *kéi=* 'up'. We can see this also in line 47, «a ÿaanáx̲ yéi akootsaak̲ch» 'he kept poking it (a bone fragment) down through the side of it (a cod stomach)', where *yéi akootsaak̲ch* is a Ø-conjugation habitual verb form with *yéi=*. We find this as well in RZ II, ii, 30, «Yanax̲ yei aawagúk̲» 'He (Raven) pushed him (his brother) down into the ground'.

LINE 13. *yóot ixkéex':* We hear Italio saying «yóot ixkéex' ka.éix̲» 'it (yew) grows way down south' here, but Johnson seems to have heard him as saying *deikéex'* 'far out at sea' rather than *ixkéex'* 'in the south', leading her to interpret this moment as, "And he come to a place where he pick up some kind of hard wood that drift from a long ways—must be from the Hawaiian Island or some place—That hardwood, you can't hardly cut it with a knife. It's just so hard!"* The wood in question is *sák̲s* 'yew'.

LINES 20–21. *Ts'as yáaÿ x'wán x̲'akla.ísh, kík'!:* Raven is telling X̲ashak'ákwk' to 'string up whales' in the manner that would run a line through the gills of a number of fish. We find the same theme employed by both Deikeenaak'w and John Kadashan. In the Deikeenaak'w text we find, "After that the sea went down so far that it was dry everywhere. Then Raven went about picking up the smallest fish, as bull heads and tom cod, which he strung on a stick, while a friend who was with him at this time, named CAk!Ak^{u}, took large creatures like whales. With the grease boiled out, CAk!Ak^{u} filled an entire house, while Raven filled only a small bladder."† And from Kadashan:

> After the flood Raven stayed in a town of considerable size. A man there, named CAq!^{u}k!^{u}, collected all kinds of big sea animals, as whales and seals, at the time of this great ebb and made a great quantity of grease out of them, while Raven collected only small fishes like cod and red cod and obtained but a few stomachs full of oil. He would eat this up as fast as he made it, but his companion worked hard so as to have a large quantity on hand.‡

LINE 24. *l at yéx̲ yóo unasgít yís:* The verbal noun *l at yéx̲ yóo unasgít* 'misbehavior' is formed in a way that we do not fully understand, containing as it does the prefix *na-* and a short high stem. The corresponding negative perfective form would be *tlél at yéx̲ yóo wusgeet* 's/he/it acted improperly, misbehaved' and the corresponding negative imperfective attributive form would be *l at yéx̲ yóo udzigitgi NP* 'NP which misbehaves, goes against the grain, breaks all the rules'. This is the basis of the title

* Ibid.

† Swanton, *Tlingit Myths and Texts*, 17.

‡ Ibid, 121.

we have applied to Italio's tale taken as a whole, «L At Yéx̱ Yóo Udzigitgi Yéil» "Raven Who Breaks All the Rules". The prefix *na-* in this instance is not the *na-*conjugation prefix, but rather an element used in the formation of verbal nouns derived from motion verbs—including zero-conjugation motion verbs.

LINE 26. *Awliyéx̱:* Literally, 'he made it'. It is unclear who is acting on what here. The frame of reference could be associated with lines 23–24 just prior, «Yéi du ÿáa wuduwasáa— / e-eh—l at yéx̱ yóo unasgít yís» 'He had been given the name Raven— / e-eh—for his inappropriate behavior', which refers to the original instance of the name *Yéil* 'Raven' being bestowed on Raven by Little-Elder-Who-Enlarged-the-Tide (see FI I, ii, 79–83); if this were the case, *awliyéx̱* here could be taken to mean 'he (Little-Elder-Who-Enlarged-the-Tide) made/concocted it (the name Yéil)'. On the other hand, if the frame of reference is to the present narrative, with Raven and X̱ashak'ákwk' working on gathering up sea creatures for food, it would seem to either mean that Raven has made something such as food for himself, or that X̱ashak'ákwk' has finished making something such as a box of oil, though it is totally unclear what has been made.

LINE 42. *Ash x̱'éix̱ at gugateex̱ yóo áyú oowajée:* Typically, the verb *oowajée* 'he thinks, considers it' would occur with either an adverb of manner like *yóo=* 'thus, so' or the essive *-x̱*, but here we find both. The essive postposition *-x̱* here specifies what Raven was thinking or considering, namely that 'he (X̱ashak'ákwk') was going to feed him (Raven)'; the future form *ash x̱'éix̱ at gugatee* has a non-assertive irrealis form (with the long low stem *tee*) due to it being a subordinative clause.

LINE 43. *Atk'é yáx̱ ágé x̱'éix̱ at gugatée?:* Ruth Demmert translated this line as "Was he going to feed him something good?" *Atk'é yáx̱* literally means 'like a good thing', 'like something good', or 'like good stuff', but it is difficult to work this wording into the translation.

LINE 55. *adaangwaanéiyi:* This verb is notable in that it has invariable stem *néi* except in the imperfective where it has the usual stem variants (e.g., *yéi adaané, yéi adaanéiyin, yéi adaaneiyí*). It occurs here in the potential attributive.

LINE 56. *Wáa óosh daax̱ané:* Note the use of *wáa óosh* here (without *sá*) instead of *wáa sá óosh* 'how might…?'

LINE 58. *Héik'!:* Our first thought was to consider this a variant of *tléik'* 'no' in the same way that *hél* 'not' is a variant of *tlél* and *ihí* 'don't' is a variant of *ilí*; however, we have never encountered *héik'* as a variant of *tléik'* and our consultants do not recognize it as such. Alternatively, perhaps *héik'* is a diminutive form of the interjection *héi!* 'hey!', which is normally used to call or answer a call; in this case Raven may be excitedly calling his own attention to the scheme he just concocted. We find the same interjection in FI I, v, 171, where it seems to be emphasizing baby Raven's excitement and wonder after having released the stars into the sky from their container.

LINE 60. *woogoot x̱aaÿasahéix̱:* The word *x̱aaÿasahéix̱* is a combination of *x̱áa* 'war party', incorporated into the verb as the prefix *x̱aa-*, plus the imperfective verbal noun *ÿasahéix̱* 'gathering', which is formed from the verb theme *O-ÿa-S-s-haa~* 'for S to gather O'. The verbal noun here serves as a compliment to the verb. *X̱aaÿasahéix̱ woogoot* 'he went war-party gathering' can be compared with more common expressions like *al'óon woogoot* 'he went hunting' and *ast'eix̱ wooḵoox̱* 'he went fishing'.

LINES 66–68. The quote within the quote represents Raven quoting his future self in a ploy to relate a fake nightmare to X̱ashak'ákwk' in order to fool him into running out of the house, leaving Raven alone and free to guzzle all the stored oil his brother has prepared in boxes. The description of his dream is thus meant to serve as the cue for his crew of birds and other animals to descend on the house and create the illusion of a war party coming to attack. Johnson interprets this scene as, "And he consider to himself he must tell some kind of story to [X̱ashak'ákwk']."*

LINE 69. *hít k'iyee:* The exact pronunciation of the term following *hít* 'house' was difficult to discern on the tape, so this is one possible rendering. The phrase *hít k'iyee* 'back of the house' can refer to a place inside the house at the rear, or a place outside the house at the rear. We use the latter reading here, since it is clear that X̱ashak'ákwk' runs outside the house to attack the supposed invaders.

LINES 73, 76. *«Mmm, mmm, mm, mm, mm.»:* It would appear that Raven is pretending to have a nightmare causing him to moan and thrash about in his sleep. This is, of course, a ploy to get X̱ashak'ákwk' to wake him and ask him what he was dreaming about. When Raven recounts his 'dream' to X̱ashak'ákwk', the words will serve as the cue for the mock attack to begin.

LINE 74. *át nax̱dux̱íjín:* On the tape this sounds very much like *át dax̱dux̱íjín*. This is a contingent form of a *na*-conjugation verb, so the morphophonemic form is *át nax̱dux̱íjín*. Italio has an occasional tendency to slightly denasalize his pronunciation of /n/, which results in a sound that comes close to an unaspirated plosive /d/. Another example is his pronunciation of *nées'* 'sea urchin' in FI I, ii, 15, which was transcribed in a previous draft of the manuscript as *dís* 'moon' due to this same phenomenon.

* De Laguna, *Under Mount Saint Elias*, 851, bracketed spelling ours.

LINE 81. *Ash t'éini woojeil:* Ruth Demmert interpreted this phrase as "he (X̲ashak'ákwk') reached behind him (Raven)". Johnson: "[X̲ashak'ákwk'] went over there and shook him. 'What's wrong with you?'"*

LINES 84–85. *G̲unéide awx̲aajoon:* Johnson interprets this as, "I got a funny dream, the funniest dream I ever dreamt."† This is a contraction of *g̲unaÿéide*, meaning 'a strange way' or 'in a strange manner'.

LINE 86. *{...}:* We could not hear the beginning portion of this line clearly and cannot offer a transcription. What we seem to hear is something like *sh daaka(l)tseen*, which might have to do with strengthening the body. However, if that were the case, we would rather expect something like *sh daageeltseen* 'strengthen your body', but this is clearly not what Italio says here.

LINE 92. *yóo x̲at dzigítk:* Italio utters this sentence in a monotone fashion, so we cannot clearly hear the tones. This is another line that is challenging to interpret. The phrase *yóo x̲at dzigítk* seems to literally mean 'I keep falling back and forth' or 'I keep getting buffeted back and forth'. The implication seems to be that Raven is pretending to be in something resembling a shamanic trance and combatting the supposed invaders telepathically from within the house. Johnson interpreted this as Raven saying, "I going to do my (spirit?) work inside. I going to kill them inside."‡ Compare FD viii, 42, «Neilnax̲.á áwé át yóo dzigítk», which we have translated as '[Raven] kept flailing around in the house'.

LINE 93. *ax̲ lakaadé kanax̲lal'úx':* We can only interpret this as a progressive imperfective form, so we would expect *ax̲ lakaadé ÿaa kanax̲lal'úx'* 'I am going along gulping it; I am in the process of gulping it down'. For reasons that we cannot explain, we do not hear the progressive proclitic *ÿaa=* here. Note that we also seem to hear «shk'e aadé ndagat yé» 'consider how they are piling up' in FI I, v, 103, where *ÿaa=* is likewise absent. This is a topic of ongoing research. Another less likely possibility is that the verb written as *kanax̲lal'úx'* might actually be the habitual form *kanax̲lal'úx'ch* 'I gulp it down (every time)', with the final habitual suffix *-ch* being inaudible.

LINE 97. *kéex':* We heard this on the tape as sounding closer to *téex'*, but we could not make any sense of this, so we rendered it as *kéex'* 'up above, out loud'.

LINE 101. Johnson: "Just then those birds come on top of the house and make a noise."§

---

* De Laguna, *Under Mount Saint Elias*, 851, bracketed spelling ours.

† Ibid.

‡ Ibid.

§ Ibid, 852.

LINE 102. *sh x̱'adajunéyáx̱:* The construction here is similar to the dissimulative derivation *sh=ḵ'e-S-d-l-* 'for S to pretend to …' and the way this verb is used hints at a sense of 'pretending'; however, we note that Italio clearly pronounces *x̱'a-* rather than *ḵ'a-* here and that there is no *l-* element in the classifier.

LINES 108–17. This seems to be the scene that prompted Johnson to remark on Raven's ability to consume seemingly infinite quantities of food, "No sooner does [X̱ashak'ákwk'] go out than [Raven] open one of the łAkt [*láḵt*] and drink it all up. And the next one! Where in the world did he put all that? It's wonderful! (Johnson had also referred to Raven's extraordinary capacity when we were making the recording)."*

LINE 113. Italio is laughing as he delivers this line, so it is hard to determine exactly what he said here.

LINE 118. *Éenaa áwé wooch ítx̱ akoox̱áat'ch:* We have not been able to identify the verb theme with certainty. In Leer's "Verb Books" we find «kawdix̱áat'», translated as "(board, pole, twig, etc.) bent down under pressure", but we were unable to find a transitive counterpart. Also, we do not understand the function of the postposition *-x̱* in *wooch ítx̱*. Johnson: "He got one of them 'inA [*éenaa*] (tongs). There is no (….?) on it, but he just snap it. It sounds like a gun went off."† Compare FD viii, 55, 58.

LINE 119. *Ḵaa s'aagí {… een} x̱aat'óok:* We do not know exactly what Italio is saying here. Johnson seems to think that this is in "[Raven's] own language."‡ De Laguna gives her rendition of Johnson's interpretation as, "'Ha, ha, ha, qatṡ 'aq̇eduɬihadut(?),' he said in his own language. 'I got him in the legs and broke the legs.' He makes believe that he is killing with the bow and arrow."§ If our transcription is correct, this would literally mean 'Wow, I shot a human bone with a [?].' However, the Dauenhauers published a version of this story by Emma Marks, in which they transcribed her version of this formulaic expression as, «Ḵaa s'aagí tóoli nx̱aat'óok», which they translated as "I'm hitting someone through the bone with my arrow", though they noted that the words and imagery were puzzling to them and to the audience members present at the performance.¶ The hardest part of this expression to resolve is what have transcribed as {… *een*}; we were tempted to render it as *dóol een* 'with a sandhill crane', but we ultimately felt this was too tenuous. First, note that there is no /n/ in de Laguna's rendition of Johnson's restatement of the phrase, «qatṡ 'aq̇eduɬihadut» (unless, by chance, de Laguna's ⟨h⟩ was a typographical error

* Ibid, 851, bracketed material ours.

† Ibid, original brackets altered to parentheses.

‡ Ibid.

§ Ibid.

¶ Dauenhauer and Dauenhauer, "Raven and the Tide", 140, 148.

for original ⟨n⟩); Johnson makes no reference to a crane. Furthermore, in Italio's version, these two syllables sound more like *dóodleen*, so our rendering as *dóol een* is exceptionally speculative. Note that *x̱aat'óok* 'wow, I shot it' or 'sure enough, I shot it' (i.e., I hit it with an arrow) is an instance of the realizational mode. We also find this same formulaic phrase in FD viii, 57, 63; the exact wording in both of those cases is also very difficult to discern from the recording.

LINE 121. Just prior to this line, Johnson can be heard letting out a little laugh.

LINE 130. *Tle du waak̲ tsú {...}:* The portion in braces is problematic and hard to hear. We seem to hear *klax'ís* or the like, but we cannot make any sense out of this.

LINE 133. *{...}:* This is the end of the first recording that makes up this story. Italio can be heard continuing into the next line of the story here as the tape runs to its end, but the disturbance in the tape rendered the line unintelligible.

LINE 134. *Áwé {...}:* This is the first line of the second recording that makes up this story. The reader should note that fifteen days pass between lines 133 and 134. As Italio begins the narration de Laguna blows her pitchpipe and there is a disturbance in the microphone, rendering a short portion after *áwé* unintelligible.

LINES 135–36. There is a false start at the end of line 135, in which Italio first refers to X̱ashak'ákwk' as «du kéilk'» 'his (Raven's) maternal nephew' but then corrects this to *du kéek'* 'his younger brother' in line 136.

LINE 138. *Ch'eek'áa:* This placename may refer to the southeastern face of the Brabazon Range—the mountainside across what would have in the relatively recent past, before Alsek Lake became so large, been a chokepoint of the Alsek River to the northwest of Gateway Knob. The name is pronounced by Italio as «Ch'eek'áa» and it is pronounced exactly the same by Dick in FD viii, 115. This name was recorded differently by de Laguna, who wrote, "This portage is apparently over the point of land on the west bank of the Alsek, opposite Alsek Glacier. The mountain on the west was called G̨eł'uwa [*G̨éelk'uwá*], while the hill on the east side of the Alsek, Gateway Knob, was called K̓itča [evidently *K'eech'áa*] in Athabaskan, or YAdagwAł in Tlingit, referring to the stones that continually 'rolled down' from it (or from the glacier)."* Note that the form *K'eech'áa* that de Laguna cites as the Athabaskan name for Gateway Knob indicates that either the Athabaskan name she provides or the Tlingit name provided by Italio and Dick exhibits metathesis of /k'/ and /ch'/.

LINES 139–144. It would appear that lines 139–44 are an aside about *Ch'eek'áa*—which Italio refers to in descriptive terms as «Yéil a ÿaatx̱ daak wudusg̱éex'i yé» 'the

* De Laguna, *Under Mount Saint Elias*, 87, bracketed material ours.

place from the face of which Raven had been thrown off'—rather than an advancement of the plot. Raven is thrown off the cliff only once. When Italio resumes the narrative in line 145, Raven is still in the box and has not yet been thrown off the mountainside. *Yéil a ÿaatx̱ daak wudusg̱éex'i yé* may be one variant of an actual placename. The verb *wudusg̱éex'i* is in the decessive attributive form (corresponding to *wudusg̱éex'in*).

LINE 145. *tlél du túg̱aa ushteex̱:* Normally this is pronounced *tóog̱aa*, but here it is pronounced with the first syllable short as *túg̱aa*. Note also that a third form, *tug̱áa*, is standard in the phrase *sh tug̱áa ditee* 's/he is satisfied', although *sh tóog̱aa ditee* also occurs frequently.

LINE 147. *yóo wanak̲éich:* Underlyingly this is *yóo ÿanak̲éich*, but as Italio pronounces it here the /ÿ/ is rounded to /w/ after *yóo*.

LINES 152–53. *yéi x̱á taashukáx̱ kalxwás'ch gé?:* Two utterances from Johnson have been removed from the transcription for the sake of clarity. In line 152, Italio is impersonating Raven asking X̱ashak'ákwk' if the material they formerly used to tie one another with hangs down along the beach fringe; Johnson seems to think that Italio is asking her this question, so she replies «Aaa» 'Yes.' In the middle of the following line, Johnson says "Oh, I see," seemingly realizing that Italio was not addressing her in the first place.

LINE 153. *Lax̱'éis'i:* This is a genus of grasses colloquially called 'beach rye' or 'beach wildrye', which is variously identified as *Leymus mollis* and *Leymus arenarius*; the former seems to be the most current scientific name. The variant *lax̱'ées'i* is attested from Nellie Willard and other speakers. We were unable to resolve the middle portion of this line; what Italio says between *Lax̱'éis'i kax̱aadí* and *á áwé* is almost completely obscured by Johnson exclaiming "Oh, I see!" Johnson to de Laguna: "When anything caves in you can see the roots hanging down",* i.e., when the sand on the edge of the beach erodes the roots get exposed.

LINE 155. *ách kadus.áax̱w:* We seem to hear a short vowel in the stem of *kadus.áax̱w*, but are writing it this way because it is in a context where only the consecutive mode would be appropriate, i.e., preceded by *chaa ch'a* and followed by *tsá*, which combination is interpretable as 'not until NP had V-ed'.

LINE 156. *Taashukáx̱ kalxwás'[ch] x̱áayá:* Comparing with line 152, «taashukáx̱ kalxwás'ch gé?», we suspect that the verb here might have been *kalxwás'ch* 'they (beachgrass roots) hang down', but that the final *-ch* was below the threshold of audibility. In this instance, the referent of the term *taashuká* seems to be what is called in English

* Ibid, 852.

terms of beach topology the 'backshore' or 'backshore berm', which is the section of a beach just above the highest reach of the waves and tide; when beach grasses grow above the upper edge of the beach, the gradual erosion of sand at the backshore exposes their roots. Compare FD viii, 86–88, «Yanshukáx̱ kalxwás'[ch]. / Wéi yanshukáx̱ koolxwás'ch wé / chookán kax̱aadí kulyát'.» 'They hang down along the edges of the beach. / They hang down along the edges of the beach, those / long grass roots.'

LINE 157. *haa tlaakáak hás ách woosh kas.aax̱u át:* This is a decessive attributive form meaning 'thing our mother's uncles formerly used to bind each other with', the implication being that in the olden days their mother's mother's brothers supposedly used to make use of beach-grass root for tying each other up. Raven is exploiting the traditional respect reserved for the special kinship relation to one's mother's mother's brother(s): If that's how their uncles of old did things, X̱ashak'ákwk' should feel inclined to follow suit. Unless there is a traditional practice of 'binding one another' that we are overlooking, it seems that all aspects of the notion that their mother's uncles would tie each other up using the roots of beach grass are entirely fabricated by Raven. Compare the two references to this theme in Deikeenaak'w's Raven story told in English to Swanton, "Then Raven called out, 'My brother, do not tie the box up very strongly. Tie it with a piece of straw such as our forefathers used to use'";* and, "But the man came back, saw what Raven was doing, and threw him into a grease box, which he started to tie up with strong rope. Raven, however, called out, 'My brother, do not tie me up with a strong rope, but take a straw such as our forefathers used to employ.' He did so."†

LINE 159. *Aadé at ḵukg̱wanuk yé áyá ch'u tle tsu súg̱aa aawatee:* More literally, 'The way things (i.e., events) were going to behave (or act, i.e., how things would unfold), he just picked it up in advance again.' The implication seems to be that Raven 'picked up on' events that were going to happen and dealt with them proactively, i.e., he knew X̱ashak'ákwk' was going to throw him off a cliff in a box, so Raven cajoled him into using inferior lashings. Johnson: "So Hacaguk [X̱ashak'ákwk'] went way back on top of the mountain, want to get rid of his uncle, Raven, because he tells lies, makes trouble."‡

Notes to Frank Italio's tale I, episode iv, "Raven and the Whale"

LINE 3. *eex̱ x̱oot aay̆í y̆éey̆ich:* The verb here occurs in the decessive subordinative, which is formed by adding *y̆éey̆i* 'former(ly)' to the ordinary subordinative form.

* Swanton, *Tlingit Myths and Texts*, 12.

† Ibid, 17.

‡ De Laguna, *Under Mount Saint Elias*, 852, bracketed spelling ours.

LINE 7. This line begins with the false start «Teet x̲'—», evidently for *teet x̲'atóode* 'into the curl of the waves', which Italio pronounces in full immediately after. An alternative possible rendering of what we heard as *teet x̲'atóode* would be *teetx'i tóode* 'into the waves', with the plural suffix *-x'* followed by the epenthetic vowel *-i*, which is inserted to break up clusters of three consonants.

LINES 8–9. Johnson: "Then he run into the big whale just taking a swim, diving up and down, just schooling."*

LINES 13–14. Johnson: "Finally he come to conclusion, fly around and watch. Fly around and round. Every time that whale come up to breath, that big hole get wide open. He scoop all the fresh air down in that hole."†

LINE 19. *Tle neil[x̲] áwé du waak̲x' wusitee wé yáaÿ yík:* We do not clearly hear the essive suffix *-x̲* in this line, but we have inserted it in brackets because it is required with the verb *wusitee* here. The only logical place for it is joined to the noun *neil* 'home'. As we have written it, the line literally means, 'The inside of the whale just became a home in his (Raven's) eyes'. Raven's perception of the inner space of the whale as that of the inner space of a home comes through in Italio's 1954 tale as well. Compare FI II, 62–63, in which the inner space of the whale is compared to the home they were sitting in during the storytelling session, «Yáaÿ yíkde wdak̲eení, / áyá aadé tuligéiyi yé yáat» 'When he flew into the whale, [the interior of the whale was] as spacious as this [house]'; the second clause, *áyá aadé tuligéiyi yé yáat* is elliptic, literally meaning 'the way it is large inside here'.

LINE 25. Italio and Johnson are both laughing here. Johnson interjects something while Italio delivers this line, making it difficult to hear the full phrase. Johnson begins with *goodáx̲* 'from where', so she might be starting to say something like 'where did Raven get the supplies to build a fire in there?' while they are both laughing. Note this detail in a version of the same story told by Johnson to de Laguna in English, "There's lots of fat. He could live in there for days and days. He build a fire. How come he could build a fire? Why didn't he suffocate?"‡

LINE 28. *du een át wootáan:* Johnson: "Finally he begin to bounce up and down—the whale goes up and down. It is getting sick and wounded. Whale is restless."§

LINE 35. Johnson: "Raven is wondering which way he's going to get out."¶

---

* Ibid.

† Ibid.

‡ Ibid, 845.

§ Ibid, 852.

¶ Ibid.

LINE 39. *Yóo wunaawóoch áwé yéi wsinei:* Here we have a very interesting example where a subordinative verb form (*wunaawóo* '[the fact] that it (the whale) died') appears in the ergative form (with *-ch*) as the subject of *yéi wsinei* 'it (the whale dying) caused it (the hole Raven entered through closing shut) to happen'. It seems likely that *yóo wunaawóo* here means '[the fact] that it died like this' (with *yóo* 'like this'), a less probable alternative interpretation being '[that fact] that it died over yonder' (with *yóo* being the truncated form of *yóox'* 'over yonder'). This sentence seems to mean that the death of the whale caused the blowhole to seal shut, apparently on account of rigor mortis.

LINES 42, 44. *«Yak'éiyi l'éiwdéi-éi-éi!»:* These lines impersonating Raven are chanted. The verb *oolx̱éis'* used in lines 41 and 43 means 's/he is wishing, praying for it'—this refers to the traditional manner of Tlingit prayer (as opposed to the Christian versions, e.g., (*a yís*) *sh káa x̱'adagáax'* 's/he is praying (for it)' and *du káa x̱'adagáax'* 's/he is praying for him/her'); it is often found pairing with speech acts by Raven that are chanted and drawn out (and the wishes Raven makes in this manner seem to always materialize). Johnson describes Raven as 'singing', reflecting the chanted quality of Raven's wishmaking, "Raven is starting to sing: 'Łen kʷedi [*l'éiw k'éide*]—nice sandy beach!' He notice that thing is going to touch. He just keep still and sing that song."* There is a comical anecdote from Johnson about her interactions with Italio regarding this point, which she apparently related to de Laguna later in the evening after doing the translation from the tape, "After Yeł gets through with that whale business, I almost get into argue with Frank (Italio). 'Łeyun q̓ʷe·de [*l'éiw k'éide*]—wish for good sandy beach' is correct. But Frank Italio say it that way: 'yk̓eyi łeyude [*yak'éiyi l'éiwde*].'"† In Johnson's form, we find the archaic postnominal modifier *k'é* 'good' instead of the attributive verb form *yak'éiyi* 'which is good', used by Italio. Also note that both of de Laguna's transcriptions of Johnson's pronunciation of *l'éiw k'éide*, indicate nasalization of the final /w/ of *l'éiw*, which nasalization is still found in the Teslin dialect, where the word is written *l'éiw̃*. Additionally, de Laguna apparently recorded a snatch of a L'uknax̱.ádi song from Italio that uses *Yak'éiyi l'éiwdéi* as the lyrics.‡ All the performances of "Raven and the Whale" in this volume use a version of this formulaic phrase, though not all instances are perfectly identical; compare SJ ix, 40–45; FD vi, 21; and KM v, 46–47.

LINE 45. *l'éiw kaléit wulihásh:* Note here the lengthening of the final short high vowel of *l'éiw kalé* 'a beautiful sand beach' in combination with the punctual postposition *-t*, yeilding *l'éiw kaléit*.

* De Laguna, *Under Mount Saint Elias*, 852, bracketed spelling ours.
† Ibid, 853, bracketed spelling ours.
‡ Ibid, 1152.

LINE 49. *K̲ul.áx̲s'*: The verb used in this line, *k̲ul.áx̲s'* 'he is listening', is the imperfective form corresponding to the perfective *k̲uwdzi.aax̲* 'he listened'. Note that the fricative element of the classifier is *s-* in the perfective, but *l-* in the imperfective due to cooccurrence restrictions: the imperfective stem *.áx̲s'* contains an affricate-series consonant, /s'/, thus requiring the use of the classifier element *l-* rather than *s-*.

LINE 57. This line is very challenging to hear and interpret, to the point that we did not venture a transcription. We seem to hear the word following *Aalséix̲* 'Alsek River' resembling *wát* 'river mouth', but with low tone; for *Aalséix̲ wát* 'mouth of the Alsek', we would expect high tone. A previous draft of the manuscript had estimated Italio's pronunciation «Alséix̲ wat Gasg̲éex' Altín». We cannot locate any documented or recorded forms of this placename that resemble Italio's pronunciation. It seems to refer to the same location that Dick refers to as *G̲altseenawáa* in FD vi, 27, 30; see the note to those lines for discussion.

LINE 58. *Yéilch yíkde wdak̲eeni yáaÿ:* The fact that *Yéil* occurs with the ergative suffix *-ch* would normally indicate that Yéil is the subject of a transitive verb, but here the verb is intransitive, and we note that there is no resumptive pronoun *a* 'it' before *yíkde* 'into', which leads us to believe that Italio here has deleted the possessor *a* of *yíkde* in the same way as one would automatically delete the object *a-* of a transitive verb. This is a striking and exceedingly rare syntactic phenomenon; see appendix 1, §6, for further discussion.

LINES 59–60. *Duléich wé l'éiw—. / L'éiwx̲ sateeyí:* Taken at face value, these two lines seem to say, 'people were yelling that it was sand[y]', but we do not understand how this would figure into the story. It is possible that the first word of line 59, which we have written *duléich* 'people are yelling' is in fact a different verb, but we cannot find a suitable alternative. Lacking any alternative, we take *wé l'éiw* to be a false start in line 59.

LINES 67–68. *Aadóo sá k̲aa kaanáx̲ ang̲axaashée / yáaÿ yíkdáx̲ kéi x̲duk̲een?:* This is one of the classical formulas of the Raven genre. See §1.4.2 of the editors' introduction for discussion and comparison.

LINES 69–70. Johnson: "He could hear them saying they're puzzled, never heard whale making that noise before."*

LINE 69. *Géh!:* We cannot hear exactly what this interjection is and we do not know what it means.

* Ibid, 852.

LINE 71. *tle yóo k̲uwaawak̲aa:* This intransitive verb is highly irregular in that the prefix *k̲u-*, which is ordinarily an object prefix, here replaces the fourth-person subject prefix combination *du-d-* 'someone', 'one', or 'people'. The form *yéi k̲uyaawak̲aa* or *yéi k̲uwaawak̲aa* 'a person, people, someone said' was standard, but nowadays we find examples of even elderly speakers using the form *yéi yawduwak̲aa*. Outside this peculiar fourth-person form, this verb takes only a subject prefix. Most Athabaskan languages also share this striking peculiarity, showing the reflex of Proto-Athabaskan [*qʊ-niː] 'one says; it is said', with [*qʊ]-, which is normally a fourth-person object pronoun (like Tlingit *k̲u-*); elsewhere, the usual fourth-person subject prefix is [*t͡ʂ'ə]-.

LINE 74. *yeekawliyáat'éyáx̲:* We could not determine to our satisfaction whether Italio says «yeekawliyáat'éyáx̲ áwé» or «yeekawliyáat', ayáx̲ áwé». We have written it with *-éyáx̲*; see appendix 1, §13.1.2, for discussion of this construction. We find the same formulaic phrase in FI I, i, 213, where we were likewise unsure whether we were hearing *...yáat'éyáx̲ áwé* or *...yáat', ayáx̲ áwé*. Whichever it is, the difference in meaning and function within the narrative is inconsequential. In her own telling of the same story to de Laguna in English, Johnson similarly refers to Raven being inside the beached whale for a notable length of time, "Raven is in there 2 or 3 days."*

LINES 76, 79. *K̲aa yéx̲ aanÿédi súk:* Johnson pronounces «súk» 'future (N), (N)-to-be' instead of the more common *sákw*. We find this sort of vowel variation also in *k'wát'* 'egg' varying with *k'út'*, *yáxwch'* varying with *yúxch'* 'sea otter', and *shákw* varying with *shúk* 'strawberry' in Yakutat. Italio himself varies between sometimes saying *sákw* and sometimes *súk*; compare FI II, 173, «lyax̲dats'éini súk» 'a troublemaker in the making'. There is no clear grammatical or phonological motivation for Italio's variation.

LINE 79. *Aadóo sgé k̲aa yéx̲ aanÿédi súk k̲aa kaanáx̲ angaxaa[sh]?:* Here Johnson interjects in the middle of Italio's narration in order to suggest her slightly different version of what Raven calls out from inside the whale. Her formulation can be confirmed by comparison with the version of this story Johnson told to de Laguna in English on April 6, 1954:

> He sing a song in there and he says he wish that whale . . .
>
> "'Adúskᴇ ('adúsgɪ, who perhaps) gayeẋ (qayᴀẋ, a man like) 'anyᴀdi (high-class person) sύk (sᴀkʷ, destined to be) qaqanᴀẋ 'anquxáx (?-to cut open), yaẏ-yɪk-dᴀẋ (out of the whale) keẋduqin (I will fly out)."

* De Laguna, *Under Mount Saint Elias*, 846.

That's the song he's singing inside there. He's wishing: "I wish somebody as high-class as I am, I wish somebody come around as high-class as I am, so to cut that whale open so I can fly out."*

Compared with the audio of the Italio recording, de Laguna's transcription of Johnson's phrasing can be reconstructed as *Aadóo sgé ḵaa yéx̱ aanÿédi súk ḵaa kaanáx̱ angaxaash yáaÿ yíkdáx̱ kéi x̱duḵeen?* 'Who, being nobility material like a certain fellow, could cut a hole over a fellow so a fellow could fly out from inside a whale?' Note the close affinity between Johnson's «ḵaa yéx̱ aanÿédi súk» 'nobility-to-be like a person' (in which Raven refers to himself in the fourth person), which she renders in English as "somebody as high-class as I am", and the phrasing used by Kadashan in the Raven story he told to Swanton in English, "The he sang: 'Let *the one who wants to be high-born like me* cut the whale open and let me out, and he will be as high as I am.'"†

LINE 82. Italio is laughing through the delivery of this line, making it difficult to hear. He seems to find the idea, implicit in Johnson's version of Raven's exhortation from inside the whale, that the *aanÿádi* 'nobility, aristocracy' existed during the time of the events in the narrative humorous.

LINE 92. *aadé kunaskakch yé:* We could not hear the final clause of this line to our satisfaction. We seem to hear an unexplained consonant sounding like /x̱/ between *aadé* and *kunaskakch.* It is likely an artifact of the recording process or of rapid speech.

LINE 95. *Kée—:* We are interpreting the first syllable of this line as a false start, possibly for *kéenax̱.á* 'the area up above' and revised to *ḵaa yax̱oot* 'among (the) people's faces', but we are not completely convinced of our interpretation here.

LINES 96, 100. *X̱'óo!:* Italio repeatedly pronounced this utterance with extra-high pitch and a fair degree of nasalization. We find it pronounced as «X̱'ún! X̱'ún! X̱'ún!...» in FD vi, 61. Johnson elaborates on the meaning of this sound, which would have otherwise been impossible for us to determine:

"Yay̧yɪk-dᴀx̱ x'one" [*yáaÿ yíkdáx̱ x̱'unéi*] (whale-inside-from top, or "spinning wheel"). He just give himself that name so they won't know he's Yeł.

(Q[uestion]:) That thing sounds like xun [*xóon*], North wind. Do they say it brings it if kids play with it?

(A[nswer]:) Yes, but I don't believe it. (MJ then mentioned some Eskimo or "Aleut" gadget, but refused to repeat the native word or explain.)‡

---

* Ibid, 860.

† Swanton, *Tlingit Myths and Texts*, 91, emphasis ours.

‡ De Laguna, *Under Mount Saint Elias*, 852, bracketed material ours.

Note the references in the quote from de Laguna to a "top", a "spinning wheel", and a "gadget". These words strongly imply that Johnson was describing a bullroarer, which is called *xóon kayénaa*. As de Laguna suggests, some (though not Johnson herself) believed that this *xóon kayénaa* would bring the north wind (*xóon*). Given this understanding, it is easy to see that Raven's repeated exclamation, «x̱ʼóo! x̱ʼóo! x̱ʼóo! x̱ʼóo!», imitates the sound of a bullroarer being spun in successive rotations. We might have expected Italio to mention the personal name X̱'unéi, but he does not. Compare FD vi, 60–67, and the notes to FD vi, 61 and 65. Johnson related to de Laguna later in the evening after her interpretation of this performance, "When he drift ashore from the whale, he flew out, but Frank Italio didn't tell that part of it. He sing a song, flew way up so nobody notice him, and sing: 'Yaỵyıkdᴀx̣ x̣ʼoné' [*Yáaÿ yíkdáx̱ X̱'unéi*] he call himself. Tłʼᴜknax̣ᴀdi [*Lʼuknax̱.ádi*] have that name, 'Xoné' [*X̱'unéi*]."[*] Dick uses the same full form of this name as Johnson, «Yáay yíkdáx̱ X̱'unéi» 'X̱'unéi from inside the whale' (FD vi, 66). It is interesting that Johnson states that the name belongs to the Lʼuknax̱.ádi, whereas we understand the name to be claimed by the Lukaax̱.ádi. The name is still in use today; it is currently the name of Lance Twitchell, a member of the Lukaax̱.ádi clan and a contributor to this volume.

LINE 102. *xáats' tóode:* This line seems to contain a false start, possibly *xáats' tʼak̲[kaadé]* 'up to right next to the sky', but Italio quickly revises the portion after *xáats'* to *tóode* 'toward inside'. An alternative interpretation of the false start would be that Italio was actually preparing to say *xáats't dak̲[éen]* 'when/after he [flew] to the sky'.

LINES 115, 120, 123. *Tlél shéyágúshé a yíkde k̲ukawdu.áax̱ákw:* This formula is discussed and compared in §1.4.2 of the editors' introduction.

LINES 115–30. We quote Johnson at length here because there is such a nice correspondence between these lines and her interpretation:

> After they get everything put up, he get to one end of the town and go to each house.
>
> "I wonder if anybody hear anything in that whale that drift ashore?"
>
> "No, no, not in this house. Maybe in next one."
>
> He went to the next house and asked the same question.
>
> "No, nobody from this house. Go to next one."
>
> Next one, same thing.
>
> Next one to the last, he requiring [i.e., inquring] if they ever hear noise inside of that whale—[...]
>
> This time he question (the one who heard him inside the whale).
>
> They answer him right away. "That's right." The person what heard him is the one he question. "I notify the others I hear it." Raven come to the right place then.[†]

* De Laguna, *Under Mount Saint Elias*, 853, bracketed spellings ours.

† Ibid, 852, original brackets altered to parentheses, brackets ours.

LINE 119: *tliÿa.aa ÿé:* This is very hard to hear, and Italio's pronunciation falls away after *tliÿa.aa ÿ—*.

LINE 127. *Wáa sá ák.wéigé?:* It is hard to translate sentences like this, where the wh-question interrogative phrase *wáa sá* 'how' is followed by the enclitic string *ák.wéigé*, which contains two instances of the yes/no-question enclitic *gí/gé*, which are also interrogatives—the string *ák.wéigé* is underlyingly *á-gí-wéi-gé*; the /í/ of *gí* is regularly deleted between *á* and a demonstrative element like *wé*(*i*), yielding *ák.wé*(*i*). The effect of all these interrogatives piled on top of one another seems to convey great astonishment.

LINES 131–32. *«Gwáa! Gwáa!» Du x̲'éit uwashée:* Johnson: "'Oh, my!' He put his hand to the side of his face (MJ covered her mouth, and said it meant surprise)."*

LINES 136–37. *Ch'a.aan:* This is an obscure made-up name that Raven uses to refer to the whale. Raven seems to simply make up this strange word and claim that what the villagers are working on is not really a whale so as to fool them into believing that it is no good to eat and will bring harm to the entire village if they don't leave all the meat in place and move away. The name is either a nonce word (a made-up word created for one-time use) or a pun on the phrase *ch'a aan* 'nonetheless'. See §2.22 of the editors' introduction for further discussion.

LINES 139–40. *t'áatx̲ kei naalagás'ch:* The phrase *N t'áak* 'uphill from, behind (inland from) and above N' should be distinguished from *N t'éik* 'behind (the back of) N' and *N kináak* 'above (overhead of) N'. Note also that the expectable possessive pronoun *a* 'it' either does not occur before *t'áatx̲* 'from behind (inland of)' or was pronounced but inaudible on the recording in both lines here. If the village was situated above the beach, which is the normal configuration, then it would have been located uphill and behind (*a t'áak*) the beached whale, so here Raven is angling for the villagers to move away from their current residence and leave the whale and all the processed meat and fat in place. He is simply exploiting the fact that the whale just so happened to land below the village and is trying to make this sound like an especially ominous configuration.

LINES 141, 143. *K̲utx̲naax'ák̲wx̲ sitee:* The verbal noun *k̲utx̲naax'ák̲w* 'the dying-off of the clan/tribe' corresponds to the unattested verb phrase **k̲utx̲ naawoox'aak̲w* 'the clan/tribe died off'. Note that the noun *naa* 'clan, tribe' has been incorporated into the verb.

LINE 142. *K̲ashde sh x̲'alk'átl'x̲ áwé:* This seems to be a joking ironic aside, followed by laughter.

* Ibid.

LINE 148. *Tliyéix' aan wudiláx̱:* Literally approximately, 'The town withered up at a standstill.' *Tliyéix'*, literally 'in one place', more idiomatically translates as 'at a standstill, (standing) still', as in *tliyéi(x')* *yéi inatí!* 'stop!' (lit. 'you be in a single place!'). The image is of the town suddenly and immediately going quiet and motionless, being entirely abandoned after the major hustle-and-bustle that was taking place while the people processed the whale.

LINE 153. *a shóo ÿan x̱'eiwatée:* We are not exactly sure what this phrase means, but *a shóo(x')* usually means 'poised to eat/drink/work on it' and *ÿan x̱'eiwatée* appears to mean 'he (Raven) positioned his mouth' or 'he got into position with his mouth wide open.' Raven is thus poised to devour the whale meat, fat, and oil that the villagers left behind. This formulaic expression, along with the theme of Raven settling down for a feast after tricking his interlocutors, is discussed and compared in §1.4.2 of the editors' introduction.

Notes to Frank Italio's tale I, episode V, "Raven and the Daylight"

LINE 1. *Haaw:* This episode continues directly after the preceding one. Italio pronounces «Haaw» 'Well' here with a heavy sigh, which seems to punctuate the end of the preceding narrative and the beginning of this one.

LINE 3. *Ÿax̱taattuḵwáani:* See §2.16 of the editors' introduction for discussion of the beings known as the *Ÿax̱taattuḵwáani* 'Night-Dwellers.'

LINES 6–12. Johnson: "And he's howling and he call someone to come across and get him, otherwise he's going to break daylight on them."*

LINE 9. *{...}:* We hear a single syllable here, but we were unable to resolve it.

LINE 12. *Yee káa ḵei.á nḵwaak'oots!:* This may be the most distinctive formulaic expression in the whole Raven genre. Italio uses it also in line 233 and FI II, 75, 77, 132. See §2.16 of the editors' introduction for some discussion and comparison.

LINE 18. *Chaa goodáx̱ Naasshagiyét sáyú:* Calling Raven a *Naasshagiyét* 'Child-of-the-Head-of-the-Nass' here is ironic and meant to poke fun at him. It is somewhat akin to calling a rude and demanding person 'Your Highness.' However, Raven takes this insult as a useful piece of information; his next move is to become exactly what they call him: a child born at the headwaters of the Nass River. This is a formulaic expression used by numerous storytellers; see §2.16 of the editors' introduction for discussion and comparison.

* De Laguna, *Under Mount Saint Elias*, 853.

LINE 19. *áa shukawdujaaÿéyáx̱ áwé woonei:* Note that here Italio uses a rarely encountered decessive attributive form. The non-attributive decessive form of the first verb would be *áa shukawdujaaÿín* 'he had been instructed how to do, get it'. The attributive form of this decessive verb is *áa shukawdujaaÿi* (*aa*) '(the one) who had been instructed how to do, get it' (in which *aa* 'the one' is simply a placeholder in the position of the head noun). Finally, by adding *-ÿéyáx̱* to the decessive attributive form we arrive at the form used here by Italio, «áa shukawdujaaÿéyáx̱» 'as if he had been instructed [as to where the daylight resided]'. We have described this as a quasi-attributive *-ÿéyáx̱* construction; see appendix 1, §13.1.2, for discussion.

LINE 20. *Náas Sháakde:* This Tlingit name of the Nass River is most commonly attested with low tone, as *Naas*, yet here Italio clearly pronounces the placename with high tone. He pronounces it high again in FI II, 80, 227, and 228. It is pronounced high also by James, Dick, and Hammond.

LINE 23. *Nasshagiyéil:* The character Naasshagiyéil 'Raven-of-the-Head-of-the-Nass' (whose name Italio pronounces unconventionally here with short initial *Nas-*) is discussed in §2.14 of the editors' introduction.

LINE 30. *wé du sée:* This refers to the daughter of Naasshagiyéil. She is briefly discussed in §2.15 of the editors' introduction.

LINE 31. *x̱'wáal' tóox̱ s'é sh ḵuwdli.oo:* We considered a number of alternative translations for the verb phrase (*a*) *tóox̱ sh ḵuwdli.oo*, including 'he fit himself into (it)', 'he spirited himself into (it)', 'he hid (or concealed) himself inside (it)', and 'he ensconced himself inside (it)'. In the "Verb Books" we find the forms «a tóox̱ sh ḵuwdli.oo», glossed as "fit self into it, changed into it", and «a tóox̱ aḵuwli.oo», glossed as "fit into it", with a note added in the handwriting of John Marks that reads, "didn't normally fit, but was made to fit, such as a witch taking over a dog's body. Could also be a shaman spirit taking over some object."

LINE 45. *Atx̱ áwé tsu ḵeina.áa:* The consecutive verb form *ḵeina.áa*, literally 'when it dawned', is a standard formula meaning 'the next day', 'the next morning', or 'at dawn'. The use of this formula may seem ironic or contradictory at this point in the narrative because Raven has yet to release the daylight from its container. The major thematic 'lack' that Raven is working to liquidate is, after all, the dawn-dusk cycle. Formula (if taken to mean 'at break of daylight') and theme ('lack of daylight') would seem to have a kind of topsy-turvy relationship in this instance. Because the story explains the origin of daylight and the formula relies on the image of the same, this narrative context creates a unique situation in which the figure of the metaphor is the very thing that is absent from the world of the story. This formula is such a conventionalized way of narrating the passage of time that here it does not literally mean daylight (as if somehow simultaneously in the container and in the sky) is spreading over the horizon; it has become a metaphor indicating that time has elapsed, the actors have recuperated, a scene transition has taken place, and the plot is advancing. A comparison can be made between this Tlingit formula and Homeric formulas such as *ἦμος δ' ἠριγένεια φάνη ῥοδοδάκτυλος Ἠώς* 'when appeared the early-born rosy-fingered dawn'.* Milman Parry comments on Homer's formula, "the formulaic line which expresses the idea 'at dawn' always brings in the epithet *ῥοδοδάκτυλος* ['rosy-fingered']. [...] Now the bearing of the practice on the meaning of the metaphor is clear: a phrase which is used because it is helpful is not being used because of its meaning."† Homer's use of the epithet *ῥοδοδάκτυλος* 'rosy-fingered' is "helpful" in practice because it serves the Greek oral composer in meeting the metrical requirements of their verse-form; it does not strictly mean that beams of the rising sun are creating reddish-pink tones on the horizon. Italio's *k̲eina.áa* and Homer's *ῥοδοδάκτυλος* are parallel traditional oral-formulaic means of advancing time in the narrative using the image of the rising sun as a metaphor.

LINES 50, 54. *k̲'watlgeigi̲anx̲áas'i:* This is a vocabulary item that we do not have an exact translation for. We are also uncertain of its exact phonetic form. What we have given here is our best estimate based on Italio's two pronunciations. We settled on the interpretation *k̲'watlgeigi̲anx̲áas'i* 'the place where the box is mended together', but should note that Johnson refers in her interpretation to a 'crack', which led us to consider that instead of *x̲áas'* 'mend crack (esp. in canoe)', the stem could be *k̲áas'* 'crack'. Nevertheless, we seem to hear a fricative /x̲/ in both of Italio's pronunciations, but we are keeping open the possibility that it is /k̲/. Leer suggests that this term could refer to the segment of spruce root that lashes together the corner of the box; on the other hand, it could refer to the crack that is joined together with spruce roots or other means. Some boxes join the non-bent corner with wooden pegs, rather than spruce roots, which is how Johnson perceived it, "He turn himself into a sticker of that spruce limb. This time he study up and down and he knows the easiest way to get inside the girl. That place where the bucket gets together—the three corners are just bent; the fourth corner is wooden pegs—he watches for that. And he turns to spruce sticker in the crack in the little square bucket."‡ Note that by "spruce sticker", Johnson means a *gítgaa* 'evergreen needle'. It is a consistent theme in the versions of "Raven and the Daylight" in this volume for Raven to position himself, in the form of an evergreen needle, in the corner of the bentwood drinking vessel from which the young woman would sip the water and thereupon swallow

* *Iliad* 1.477, *Odyssey* 2.1. We give Parry's translation from *The Making of Homeric Verse*, 383.

† Parry, *The Making of Homeric Verse*, 373.

‡ De Laguna, *Under Mount Saint Elias*, 853.

him. The choice of words to describe this location in the box varies between each storyteller. Compare the following:

FI I, V, 49–54:	Awsikóo yáa k̲'watlgeig̲anx̲áas'ináx̲ adaná yú aanÿédi. Anax̲ áwé oodanáaÿch. Anax̲ adana yé k̲udzitee. Tle yá k̲'watlgeig̲anx̲áas'i tayeex̲ áwé kei sh wuditsák̲, g̲ítg̲aa tóox̲ sh k̲uwdli.oo.	He knew that the noble child drank from the place where the bentwood pail was lashed together. She always drank from there. There was a place from which she drank. Then, concealed inside an evergreen needle, he just shoved himself up under the place where the box was lashed together.
AW ii, 25–28:	A gukshitú áa yéi sh wudi.oo. Awdlix̲éis' wé yées yát anax̲ ax̲danaa. Ách áwé a niyaanáx̲ awdináa wé héen. Du ulx̲éis'i áa uwaháa.	He positioned himself in the corner. He prayed that the young woman would drink from that side. So she drank the water from that side. His prayer came true.
SJ xi, 134–35:	Yá anax̲ wóosht ÿawduwatsuwu ÿ[é] áx̲ dux̲ás'ch, lák̲t áyú. Tle a t'éix̲ áwé kei sh wuditsák̲.	A bentwood box is lashed up where the sides are butted up against each other. Raven just shoved himself back up behind the lashing.
SJ xi, 139–41:	Tle k̲únáx̲ yáa áx̲ kei sh wuditsag̲i yé, *corner*, áx' áwé, a x̲'éit ÿawdzi.áa wé át.	There, at the very place he had shoved himself up into, the corner, she put her lips to it.
FD ii, 53:	a wax̲'at'eex'.wánt áwé wulihaash	he drifted about where the corner was lashed together
FD ii, 60–62:	Yá a wax̲'at'eex'.wán, anax̲ x̲'éide ashakakg̲wal.aa yé du toowóoch, áx' áwéi a yáx̲ kéi sh wuditsák̲.	This inner corner of the bentwood bucket, he thought this was where she would tip it into her mouth; it was there that he stuck himself up against the side of it.

LINE 55. *koodlidéin:* This appears to be a variant of *koodzidéin* 'a tremendous amount', but it sounds close to *kootldéin* on the recording.

LINE 56. *Tlél áx̲ jiyawuxaash:* When asked about this phrase, Ruth Demmert provided the form «tlél du éex̲ k̲aa jiyawuxaash», which she translated as "nobody could anticipate him doing that", as well as «ch'ul du éex̲ jiyawuxaashí», which she translated as “before s/he knew what was happening.” The recessive pronoun *á* that Italio uses here could refer either to Raven or to the situation in general. Compare also line 193, «Ch’ool du éex̱ ḵaa jiyawuxaashí» ‘Before anyone could anticipate him doing so’, it which *du* clearly refers to Raven.

LINE 57. {*X’éigaa*}: Geiger hears the first few syllables of this line as *ch’a yég̱aa* and not *x’éigaa* ‘truly’, even though none of us are familiar with *ch’a yég̱aa* and we have not been able to elicit it from our consultants. For this reason, Leer suggested transcribing this as *x’éigaa*, citing the poor quality of the recording at this point. We also considered the possibility that what he actually said was *ch’a g̱ég̱aa* ‘in vain’, but we do not hear the initial /g̱/ of *g̱ég̱aa*.

LINE 61. *yan ilḵóo:* We could not discern whether the verb was *yan ilḵóo* or *yan wulḵóo*. We settled on *yan ilḵóo* ‘when she finished vomiting’ because this is the ordinary consecutive form. If this were *yan wulḵóo*, it would be a very rare example of a *wu-* consecutive.* There is a minor false start in this line, «áwé át—át akandulgánch».

LINE 68. *yaa anastúw, ÿaa anatúw, ÿaa anatúw:* Note that Italio uses «yaa anastúw» (with the *s-* element of the classifier) the first time, but «ÿaa anatúw» (with no classifier) the second and third times. Our consultants are unclear as to the difference in meaning. Because he repeats it twice as *ÿaa anatúw*, it is possible that Italio meant for this to serve as a correction of the first form. In both pronunciations of *ÿaa anatúw* ‘she is counting (months passing)’, the preverb *ÿaa* sounds like *waa* because it follows a /w/.

LINE 76. *cháash hít:* This is a reference to the practice of women giving birth in a brush hut or bough hut that was secluded from others. Elizabeth Nyman describes this practice in her narrative «T’aaḵú Yanyeidí Daat Shkalneek» published in *Gágiwduł.àt*:

Ch’âkw tlêł nèłx’ yát du.èxhín.	Long ago, they did not bear children at home.
Chashhít	They would [stay] in a brush hut
ḵà ít yû nàłiyê	some distance away from the people
áwé áx’ t’akwanêyi du.èxh.	[and] have their babies.†

LINE 77. *a yee kéi kawduwaháa kóoḵ:* There is a brief false start in this line, «a yee kei—kei kawduwaháa».

LINE 87. *du éet toodataanch:* This conveys the image of a fetus communicating with its mother by mental telepathy. Literally approximately, ‘it (Raven in the form of a

* For a description of the *wu-* consecutive see Story, *Morphological Study of Tlingit*, 216.

† Nyman and Leer, *Gágiwduł.àt*, 20, 21. Converted to the standard orthography: *Ch’áakw tléil neilx’ yát du.eix̱ín. / Chashhít / ḵaa ít yóo naaliyéi / áwé áx’ t’akwanéiyi du.eix̱.*

fetus) sent a thought to her'. This is the traditional Tlingit way of referring to labor pains: the fetus is said to be sending thoughts to the mother. Johnson: "The minute she moves out she gets the pain again. It keep on like that."* The same concept applies in line 112, «tuwditaan» 'it communicated its desire to come out', literally 'he had a thought'.

LINE 100. *yéi sitee:* See the note to line FI I, ii, 61, for a discussion of the verb phrase *yéi sitee*. This is a fairly obscure verb, the meaning of which seems to be 'seems to be'.

LINE 102. *tlél yéi k̲oosteech:* This verb phrase, which is a negative repetitive form, literally means 'it never gets born', but this sounds awkward in English. The translation we have used, 'it hasn't been born yet', would correspond best to a negative habitual form, e.g., *tlél k̲oog̲asteech*.

LINE 103. *shk'e aadé ndag̲at yé k'óox doogú káa {...}:* We cannot resolve the last portion of this line to our satisfaction. Leer suggests *...k'óox doogú káa ch'u k̲usteet' lingít* 'people were still being born on marten hides', but notes that what comes after the stem syllable *teet'* is completely unclear. Geiger hears something like *...k'óox doogú káa dax̲ k̲udusteet'í...*, but could not even wager a guess at the final syllable. Specifics aside, the overall implication seems to be that Raven is setting the standard for actual childbirth, and had Raven been born on the marten hides or other expensive pelts it would have set a precedent in which only the very wealthy could have a successful birth (this causes Italio and Johnson to laugh heartily). By holding out to be born on a plentiful and freely accessible material like moss, Raven made the conditions for childbirth readily available to everyone. Johnson: "Frank laugh! Suppose we all have to be born like that! We wouldn't grow up! Poor people—Raven looks after the poor ones. That's why the babies not born on precious skins like that girl's father had."† Note further that the expected progressive proclitic *ÿaa=* does not occur after *aadé* and before *ndag̲at* here; why this is the case is unclear to us and the topic of ongoing research. We seem to find another such instance of the progressive *ÿaa=* being absent in FI I, iii, 93.

LINE 108. *S'íx'g̲aa atx̲ kawdudli*[*jeil*], *kéi shawdudli*[*.át*]: Italio does not pronounce the stem on either of the verbs in this line. We are assuming the first verb theme to be *O-ka-S-jeil~* 'for S to carry plural O in loose bunches', referring to the bunches of *s'íx'g̲aa* 'sphagnum moss' being brought over to line the birthing pit, and the second theme to be *O-S-l-.aat~* 'for S to carry plural O (especially in an orderly or controlled manner)'.

* De Laguna, *Under Mount Saint Elias*, 854.

† Ibid.

LINES 108–10. During her interpretation, Johnson described the practice of preparing a pit for a child to be born into, "Funny! I saw my grandmother fix it up for my mother lots of times! They dig a square hole about a foot deep (extend hands about 12 inches apart), and they fill it with moss all around, spongy soft moss. There are two boards on each side of the moss, on the sides. They put a cloth of any soft kind over the moss."*

LINE 110. *a x̱'adaaÿax̱t'áayi:* This word can be analyzed as follows: 'the edge-boards (*ÿax̱-t'áaÿi*) around (*daa-*) the opening (*x̱'a-*) of it (*a*)', i.e., around the opening occupied by the birthing pit. Note that the *ÿax̱-* of *N ÿax̱-t'áaÿi* 'edgeboards of N' is a reduced form of *N ÿaax̱* 'the side, border, edge of N (especially of a stream, of a trail, of a table, or the like)'.

LINE 115. *Ch'ul áx' áwé udaxeechjí:* On the recording the way Italio pronounces this verb it really sounds like *udaxeetjí* rather than *udaxeechjí*. This appears to be an instance in which /ch/ is modified to /t/ when followed by a sibilant or a shibilant (here the habitual suffix *-ch*, which forms the syllable /jí/ in combination with the subordinative suffix *-í*). In Leer's "Verb Books" we find the form «aawaxích» glossed as "put all one's strength/power/concentration into it, try w. all one's might to do it, hold it down"; to this we might add that the translations 'bear down' or 'strain' would be appropriate in referring to giving birth. In Italio's form here, the verb occurs with the *d-* element of the classifier in place of an object, which evidently forms the antipassive of the transitive verb attested by Leer.

LINE 116. *kawdigáx̱ a táade:* Here *a táade*, literally 'toward the bottom of it (the pit)', specifies where the baby is heard crying, not toward where the baby is crying.

LINE 125. *Ch'a yéi jidu.aax̱w:* Traditionally babies would be tied into a *t'ook* 'cradleboard' with their arms strapped down.

LINE 133. *Wak̲ltáax̱ at kasg̱ix'x̱éyéx̱ áyá k̲uwanóok:* We find a seemingly related motif of Raven 'shooting' thoughts from his eyes at Unfazable-Little-Elder in Shotridge's notes on the Raven adventures; there we find "The Ancient Wisdom" (Shotridge's moniker for Unfazable-Little-Elder) admonishing "Master Maul" (the name Shotridge attributes to Raven before he was named Yéil). The account in Shotridge does not take place in the same scene, in which the old woman holds Raven in the form of a human baby, but at some prior time when Raven appeared before her, "Master Maul came upon the Ancient Wisdom, and when he appeared in her presence he was abashed, because he did not have the power to conceal from her, his intentions. Thus, came forth perplexity. The Ancient Wisdom received Master Maul in an indifferent attitude; she appeared suspicious: '*Steady thy eyeshots Raven,* they

* De Laguna, *Under Mount Saint Elias*, 854.

betray thy mission.' Warned the ancient One."[*] In terms of the grammar in this line, *at kasgix'x̲éyéx̲* is another example of what we are calling the quasi-attributive *-ÿéyáx̲* construction (discussed in appendix 1, §13.1.2).

LINE 134. *Daag̲áa de ch'a ayak'w.uwagwál:* This is the only instance of *daag̲áa* in these texts. We have been unable to verify its meaning with our consultants, but interestingly enough, in Leer's "Stem List" we find *gwaag̲áa* given as a synonym for *gu.aal* (*kwshé*)... 'I wish...', so we suspect this *daag̲áa* is synonymous with what Leer recorded as *gwaag̲áa*, the implication being that Raven wishes that he could smack Unfazable-Little-Elder in her little face in order to get her to stop saying that he has 'Raven's eyes'. Note the incorporated diminutive inalienable noun *yak'w-* 'little face'. Johnson: "Raven's heart is just beating! He just feel like slapping that little old lady."[†]

LINES 138–39. *ch'a tléix' ÿan uwatée / k̲wáak̲x̲ daak̲ ÿawdusk̲aaÿí:* The phrase *ch'a tléix' ÿan uwatée* seems to mean something like 'it (the whole matter) was laid to rest' or 'it was laid to rest all at once'. The dependent clause *k̲wáak̲x̲ daak̲ ÿawdusk̲aaÿí* literally means '[the fact] that a person misspoke to him (Raven)', but here the implication seems to be that Unfazable-Little-Elder 'spilled the beans' or 'let the cat out of the bag' in the sense that she divulged Raven's true identity, which could have foiled his whole plan. Therefore, we take the whole sentence to indicate that her disclosure failed to register among the other people and was never brought up again. Johnson: "So it's all over—they all forget it. The old lady goes home. Nobody mention it."[‡]

LINE 141. *daak̲wéit yaanawádi yáx̲ sáwé yatee:* Johnson: "Raven grows like a weed."[§] There appears to be a theme in Italio's texts of Raven growing with remarkable rapidity. Compare FI I, i, 144, «Yax̲.atg̲wakú keitl yaanawádi yéx̲ áwé ÿatee» 'As the proverb goes, he (Raven) was growing up as [fast as] a dog'.

LINE 151. *Dei shé kei kdig̲áax̲ á:* The verb *kei kdig̲áax̲* appears to be a realizational forms, which would correspond to the perfective *kei kawdigáx̲* 'he started crying'. This realizational form could be translated 'at last he started crying', the implication perhaps being that Raven had to go through all the prior stages (finding where the Container of Daylight was, being swallowed by the young woman, gestating inside-her, being born, and growing to a suitable size) and can now finally set to the task of crying inconsolably in order to get the Container of Daylight into his hands. It is possible that the opening particles *dei shé* require (or prefer) that the following verb occur in the realizational mode, but we do not have other examples of a construction like this to support such a claim.

---

* Shotridge, "Raven In Eyre".

† De Laguna, *Under Mount Saint Elias*, 854.

‡ Ibid.

§ Ibid.

LINE 152. *ḵaa jee shukdax̱'ax̱'w nuch:* This is using an apparently rather obscure verb, the root of which Leer wrote in the "Stem List" as «x̱'ax̱'» and glossed as "have convulsions, fits". However, after checking Italio's phrase and this verb with a number of elders, we believe the root is actually *x̱'áax̱'w~*.

LINE 163. *K'út' yéx̱ kaaxát:* Italio's pronunciation of the word for 'egg' sounds very close to *k'út'* here rather than the more usual *k'wát'*. Note that here Italio pronounces «k'út' yéx̱ kaaxát», but in line FI I, i, 110, he pronounces «k'wát' yáx̱ kaaxát». We also find Italio varying between *N sákw* and *N súk* 'future N, N to-be'. There is no clear grammatical or phonological motivation for the variations. A Yakutat informant reports that Lena Farkas of Yakutat always pronounced this word as *k'út'*. The phrase *k'út' yéx̱ kaaxát* literally means 'it is shaped like an egg' or 'it resembles an egg', but idiomatically translates as 'it is round'. While the containers of the heavenly bodies are often referred to as 'boxes' in English, we find a number of instances such as this in which the containers appear to be spherical rather than cubic. Various references and descriptions about the physical configuration of the containers are discussed in §2.13 of the editors' introduction.

LINE 171. *Héik'!:* We have taken this to be a diminutive variant of the exclamation *héi!* 'hey!', in which case it would seem to be emphasizing baby Raven's excitement and wonder. The same interjection occurs in FI I, iii, 58; we discuss the term further in the note to that line.

LINE 172. *du yoowú du x̱'éi ÿan uwatée:* This appears to be an idiomatic expression similar in construction, but not in meaning, to the English 'his heart was in his throat'. Johnson's interpretation, "Raven is more than tickled",* likely corresponds to this line, but we are not certain.

LINE 174. *Ḵuwlix̱'aanéyáx̱ áwé ḵuwatee:* This is another good example of what we are calling a quasi-attributive *-ÿéyáx̱* construction, which we discuss in appendix 1, §13.1.2. This line is a clear example of why such constructions are syntactically so striking and unusual: normally, the head noun of an attributive clause must be coreferential with a resumptive pronoun within the attributive clause; here there is no such resumptive pronoun.

LINE 178. *a kayaax̱ yaawaḵeich:* The only thing that we can identify from this verb phrase is *a kayaa* 'something like it'. We cannot identify the verb stem and it was unknown to all our consultants. Italio clearly pronounces a low-toned *ḵeich*; it cannot be *ḵaa* 'say' because with the suffix *-ch* this would yield high-toned *ḵéich*. This verb might contain the obliquative derivational string *NP-x̱ ÿa-u-* (Ø) 'moving along NP',

* De Laguna, *Under Mount Saint Elias*, 854.

though we would expect the stem to be *k̲éch* in such a form (assuming the final /ch/ is the coda consonant of the root itself). Johnson seems to interpret this line as, "He make a motion that he wants to get hold of it",* and since we cannot identify the verb phrase we have approximated her interpretation in the text.

LINE 183. *ash ujaak̲ch sh.iltí:* Literally 'joy (or gladness) would kill him'. The verbal noun *sh.iltí* 'joy, gladness' here corresponds to the verb *sh dlitée* 's/he/it is joyful, glad', attested from Elizabeth Nyman.

LINES 185–86. *«Goodé sáwé wuduwadzòo / wéit'aa k̲wá?» hú gí yéi x̲'[ayak̲á]?:* We could not hear this line very well due to Italio's laughter, and we are not certain of the translation. What we have written as *yéi x̲'ayak̲á* 'he says so' is only audible on the recording as *yéi x̲'*—. We have taken this to be an impersonation of Raven-at-the-Head-of-the-Nass grumbling about baby Raven's manner of playing with the Container of Daylight. We are not clear on what may have been thrown or launched. We are told that Raven is playing with the container by cracking the lid open a bit; perhaps a few beams of light escape in these moments. Also note the emphatic tone modification on the verb stem of *wuduwadzòo* 'someone threw, launched it (as a projectile)'.

LINE 193. *jig̲eit awdish*[*át*]: Italio either did not finish pronouncing the stem (*shát*) of the verb here, or he uttered it below the threshold of the microphone. Note that in *awdishát* (which is not a self-standing word), the *d-* element of the classifier denotes the null reflexive possessor (i.e., Raven) of *jig̲ei-t* 'in the crook of (self's) arm'.

LINE 204. *kéi shikaawashée:* Note the noun *shí* 'song' incorporated into the verb here as prefixed *shi-*.

LINE 208. *Seiwusx̲'een:* We could not hear this name well at all, so this is an approximate rendering. Italio was born on July 7, 1870, making him eighty-two years old at the time of this recording. One begins to gain an appreciation of the antiquity of the song and the process of its oral transmission through specific individuals by imagining a young Frank Italio in Dry Bay learning this song from his grandfather who must have been born near the turn of the nineteenth century, and who in turn likely learned the song from his grandparents before him, and so on.

LINE 210 ONWARD. The two songs: De Laguna's notes, including a free interpretation by Johnson, to the two songs Italio sings here can be found in Volume III of *Under Mount Saint Elias.*† Comparing the recording against the transcriptions in

* Ibid.

† Ibid, 1152–53.

de Laguna,* there are some inconsistencies in her rendering. This seems largely due, as de Laguna notes, to the fact that "Frank Italio sang in such a quavering style it is hard to tell whether some of the syllables of the song are intended to be separate vocables or simply quavers",† and also that "he was in the habit of interrupting his singing, sometimes even in the middle of a word, in order to tell the story or make a comment on it, and then would resume singing."‡ This is indeed what we find on the recording. For instance, across lines 221–23, Italio breaks up the word *k̲ee.á* 'daylight' in the lyrics in order to state «De du jeehú á yú k̲ei.á» 'He already has possession of the daylight' between the syllables *k̲ei-* and *-.á*. Further, in, for example, the opening line of the first song, which we have rendered as *K̲ee.á haa aa haa aa haa*, it is not clear whether *haa aa haa aa haa* represents a chain of discrete vocables or if this amounts to a stylized, melodic elongation of the final vowel of *k̲ee.á* 'daylight' (i.e., *k̲ee.á-há-.á-há-.á-há*). The issue could be posed in English as whether the line more closely resembles *Daylight la da la da la* or *Dayli-hi-li-hi-li-hight* (we suspect the latter). We have generally transcribed vocables where we perceived a significant 'pulse' in Italio's delivery and we have not attempted to 'translate' the vocables in the English, whether as elongated words or as more familiar English vocables such as *lala*, *nana*, *dada*, etc. We have offered translations to the lyrics where they seemed relatively transparent and have drawn inspiration from Johnson's free interpretation. Italio sings the same pair of songs at the conclusion of FI II.

LINE 219. *sh toodé shukalx̲úx̲s'*: The first two words here, pronounced *sh toodé*, are difficult to make sense of. If this were to mean 'into self', we would expect the tonal pattern to be the opposite: *sh tóode*. This is clearly not an error on Italio's part, though, because we find the same phrase with identical tonal pattern in FI II, 247, told two years later. One possibility is that *sh toodé* is an irregular contraction of *sh toowúde*, which would mean something like 'into his own mind/soul' or even 'to his own satisfaction', but this interpretation is quite speculative, and we have not been able to resolve the question. We can compare lines 233–34, «á áyá shukawdlix̲úx̲ ch'a hú / chush tóot» 'these were the very lyrics he himself composed / in his own mind' (which has nothing unusual about it). The *-dé* in *sh toodé shukalx̲úx̲s'* and the *-t* in *shukawdlix̲úx̲ … chush tóot* may denote the location of the eventuality expressed by the verb; i.e., the composition of the song may have taken place 'in his own mind; internally'. The 1952 interpretations by Johnson and the 1954 interpretation by Ellis do not provide any clear insights about this wrinkle. The verb *shukalx̲úx̲s'* denotes the composition of the lyrical content of a song; it can have a fairly generic meaning, i.e., 'he's composing (a song)', but it can have more culturally specific meaning

* De Laguna, *Under Mount Saint Elias*, 1152–53.

† Ibid, 1153.

‡ Ibid.

pertaining to the 'love songs' that are composed about people of the opposite moiety (typically the clan's 'children', i.e., those who are related to the clan of the composer through their father); Naish and Story, for example, gloss *shukalx̱úx̱s'* as "he composes tribal love-songs which call forth a response".[*] Raven's actions, and the lyrics themselves, here better align with the more generic meaning; as Italio states earlier in lines 204–05, «kéi shikaawashée / ch'a hú chush daat x̱á» 'he started singing a song / about himself, you see'.

LINE 222. *De du jeehú á yú k̲ei.á:* Here Italio pronounces the locative-predicative suffix following the vowel of *du jee-* 'his (Raven's) possession' as *-hú*; this suffix is now almost exclusively heard pronounced *-wú* (i.e., *du jeewú á* 'he has it'). He uses this archaic variant *-hu* ~ *-hú* following a vowel in three other instances in these texts: «du jeehú á wé k̲ei.á» 'he had possession of the daylight' (FI II, 127); «dei du jeehú á yóo k̲ei.á» 'he already had possession of the daylight' (II, 226); «Héinax̱.áhu hú» 'He's over this way' (II, 53); and «Áhu hú» 'He's there' (II, 202). We find the variant also in material taken down in 1862–83 by Leopold F. Radloff, a German academic working in Saint Petersburg, who worked with a Tlingit elder identified as Tikhontin,[†] who travelled from Alaska to Saint Petersburg to work with Radloff. Examples (with Radloff's glosses in German) include, «ttís wăk-jík tlinkít áhu. im [Mondes]Auge ist ein Mensch» (i.e., *Dís wak̲yík lingít áhu.* 'In the eye of the moon is a person.');[‡] «tlinkít kíki tsūk áhu. ½ Mensch ist auch da.» (i.e., *Lingít kígi tsóo(k') áhu.* 'A half person is there too.');[§] «iknāḱ sáku xāt túhu. Kupfererz ist in d[en] Inseln.» (i.e., *Ik̲náach' sákw x'áat' tóohu.* 'Copper ore is in the islands.');[¶] «tís ká tlinkít áhu, tu x̆īšá-gi tu k̆ĭhú. auf d[em] Mond ist e[in] Mensch, seine Flasche ist in s[einer] Hand.» (i.e., *Dís ká lingít áhu, du x'eesháÿi du jeehú.* 'On the moon is a person; he has his bucket.').[**] Examples of this archaic variant are also found in Swanton's texts, such as the line he rendered from Don Cameron as «Wuts!ā´g̣a acdjī´ hu yu-cāwa´t»[††] (i.e., *Wootsaag̱áa ash jeehú yú shaawát* 'that woman had a cane') and the line he rendered from Deikeenaak'w as «Aēq!g̣ayā hoē´k!ᵘ» (i.e., *a eeg̱ayáahu eix̱'* 'below the beach of it was a slough').[‡‡] Leer notes that this pronunciation with *-hu* ~ *-hú* rather than *-wu* ~ *-wú* after a vowel was, until recently, standard in Carcross as well.

---

* Naish and Story, *Tlingit Verb Dictionary*, 40.

† The name Tikhontin may be interpreted as *Deix̱eintéen* based on the spelling «Dèx̣ìntí·´n», which name appears in the genealogical material Teresa Mayer Durlach obtained from Louis Shotridge (Durlach, *The Relationship Systems of the Tlingit, Haida, and Tsimshian*, 173).

‡ Radloff, "Tlingit linguistic materials", 114l.

§ Ibid.

¶ Ibid, 240l.

** Ibid, 247l.

†† Swanton, *Tlingit Myths and Texts*, 292; from text 94, "The L!ênAxx̣ī´dAq" (i.e. *Tl'anaxéedák̲w*). Swanton identifies this man as "Don Cameron of the Chilkat Kā´gwAntān" (ibid., 1, 414).

‡‡ Ibid, 308; from text 99, "Moldy-End".

LINE 224. Johnson: "And now he get it. He's sitting on the bank on the box of daylight."*

LINE 236. Johnson: "The old people amongst them [who] scoop up driftwood caught on all right."†

LINE 244. *k̲únáx̲ a kát k̲ei.á aawak'oodzi aa:* This phrase literally means 'the very one (i.e., the song) to which he broke daylight'. The use of *a kát* 'to it' in this clause implies that this is the song 'to which' (i.e., not 'onto which') Raven broke daylight, as in the phrase *at.shí kát aawal'eix̲* 'he danced to the song'.

LINES 248–50 AND THROUGHOUT SONG. *Yee hee hee / A káa haa k̲ee.á haa haa yaa / Unax̲duwak'oots shéi:* An issue arises here with the interpretation of the first syllable in each of the first two of these lines, namely: which is to be taken as a vocable and which as the nominal object of *N ká* 'on N'? First, recalling Raven's formulaic threat to the Night-Dwellers (*yee káa k̲ei.á nk̲waak'oots!* 'watch out or I might break daylight on you folks!'),‡ it is tempting to take *Yee hee hee* as an elongated form of *yee* 'you folks' and the opening syllable of the following line as a vocable. We could then perceive the words *yee káa* 'upon you folks' in the song, just as in Raven's threat. This would align to an extent with the narrated line 233 in which Italio states, «‹Yee káa k̲ei.á nk̲waak'oots!› á áyá shukawdlix̲úx̲ ch'a hú» '"Watch out or I might break daylight on you folks!"—these were the very lyrics he himself composed'. However, the verb in Raven's threat uses a first-person singular subject (*nk̲waak'oots* 'I might break it') while the verb in Raven's song uses a fourth-person subject (*unax̲duwak'oots* 'someone could break it' or 'it could be broken'); if the subject of the verb has changed, it is reasonable to expect other changes of person elsewhere in the phrase. As a second interpretation, if we take *Yee hee hee* as vocables, *A káa* can be interpreted as 'on them (the Night-Dwellers)'. This interpretation seems favorable in light of Italio's narrated line 277, «A ká wé k̲ee.á», which we have interpreted as 'the daylight was upon them'; in this line Italio seems to be simultaneously narrating the story and stating the lyrics of the song before he resumes singing. We have taken the latter interpretation, assuming the underlying phrase in these lines of the song to be *a káa k̲ee.á unax̲duwak'oots kwshéi*, which could be translated as 'someone could presumably break daylight on them' or 'daylight could presumably be broken on them'. As a final thought, a notable feature of the potential-mode verb form *unax̲duwak'oots* 'it could be broken; someone could break it' is that the irrealis prefix *u-* occurs overtly before the fourth-person subject prefix *du-*. This *u-* is normally precluded by subject prefixes other than the first-person singular.

* De Laguna, *Under Mount Saint Elias*, 855.

† Ibid.

‡ See FI I, V, 12; II, 75, 77, 132; and §2.16 of the editors' introduction.

LINE 259. *Aadé a kaax̱ ÿawjik̲ák̲:* We do not know exactly toward 'where', 'what', or 'whom' Raven was scooting, i.e., we are not certain of the referent of *á* in *aadé*. We have interpreted it as referring to the Night-Dwellers.

LINE 260. *Héende yóo atkaawa.át:* The verb used here, *atkaawa.át* 'they rushed (en masse)', is a formulaic element that we find used by Italio, Wanamaker, Dick, and Hammond exclusively in this scene in each of their performances of "Raven and the Daylight". See §2.16 of the editors' introduction for discussion and comparison of each of their formulations. See also §3.11 on the reasoning for combining the pronominal *at-* with the verb word in the case of this specific verb theme.

LINE 276. *Aaa:* Just as at the opening of this episode, there is a clear note of exhaustion in Italio's breath here. This may in fact simply be a sigh rather than *aaa* 'yes'.

LINE 290. *Wóosht k̲eeya.ayi saa.* This attributive verb phase is apparently based on the form *wóosht k̲eeya.áa*. If this were a perfective form, we would expect *wóosht k̲eewa.áa* 'the dawn has gathered together', the corresponding attributive form being *wóosht k̲eewa.ayi* (or *k̲eiwa.ayi*), but instead of /wa/, we hear /ya/ as the classifier syllable in this case. It might be possible to interpret *wóosht k̲eeya.ayi* as a attributive realizational verb modifying *saa* 'name' and taking Ø-conjugation with the punctual postposition *-t*, but this would be the only example of an attributive realizational verb that we are aware of. In any case, since *k̲eewa.áa* is an impersonal verb, with neither a subject nor an object, we find no third-person pronoun eligible to serve as the antecedent referent for *saa* 'name', which further complicates this interpretation. It is as if one were to say, 'the name such that the dawn gathered together' or the like. We find it exceedingly difficult to translate this phrase.

LINE 294. Pitchpipe: De Laguna notes regarding her practice of recording Tlingit songs, "A standard pitchpipe was blown before and after songs so that it might be possible to allow for variations in the speed of the tape."* She notes elsewhere that her pitchpipe produced an A and that when the tapes were played back for analysis the pitchpipe was heard to be a half-tone high.† We did not adjust the speed or tone of the audio in order to achieve an A on playback, but future listeners and researchers may find it enriching for the study and appreciation of the songs and in order to hear a more precise rendering of Italio's pacing and tone of voice.

* De Laguna, *Under Mount Saint Elias*, 565.

† Ibid, 1169.

Notes to Frank Italio's tale II, "Raven the Troublemaker"

LINES 1–7. Just prior to telling this extended Raven tale, Italio had sung two spirit songs composed by G̱oochdáa, a famous *íx̱t'* 'shaman' of the Lukaax̱.ádi clan.* De Laguna asks if Italio wants to sing another of G̱oochdáa's songs. He replies that though there are many, he only knows two and then proceeds to change the subject in the direction of Raven. We could not resolve the phrase that comes after what sounded like *X̱áat Ḵwáan[i]* 'Salmon People'. *X̱áat Ḵwáani, Sheen X̱'ayeeyéigi*, and *Yakwshakaháadi* would appear to be names or features of G̱oochdáa's songs. De Laguna glosses the name G̱oochdáa as 'Wolf-Weasel' numerous times throughout *Under Mount Saint Elias*, thus treating it as a compound of the nouns *g̱ooch* 'wolf' and *dáa* 'ermine, weasel'. Another consideration is that Interior Tlingit has a dual marker *dáa* 'pair of' that is used after animal names to denote specifically a pair of animals, so this name could also be analyzed as 'Pair of Wolves'.

LINES 8–17. Ellis describes this opening discussion, "He was asking if you know about (how) that Yeł (was) born in this world. She (HB [Helen Bremner], who was acting as interpreter during the recording) just said yes, they know."†

LINE 22. *Kéet Ḵwáani:* Ellis interpreting this moment: "Guc-tu-wuł [Gushtuwool] (Killerwhale with a 'Hole in the Fin')—that's Raven's father—kit quwani [*kéet ḵwáani*] (Killerwhale spirit)."‡ The inalienable noun *ḵwáani*, or *ḵuháani*, used especially after animal names, refers to the animals viewed as a collective entity or tribe, so that *Kéet Ḵwáani* could translate as 'the Killerwhale People' or 'the Killerwhale Tribe'.

LINE 29. *ḵuwdzitee:* This sounded close to *ḵuwudzitee* with an uncontracted *wu-* perfective prefix, which is quite possible. The Orthodox Christmas greeting is *Xrisdós ḵuwudzitee!* 'Christ is born!'

LINE 31. *Shanyaateiyí:* Ellis' interpretation: "CAnya tEyi [*Shanyaateiyí*]—that's the rock at the lowest tide."§ De Laguna also cites John Peabody Harrington's records from George Johnson, "The old people, 200 years ago, mebbe, used to call the beach cAnyàa [*shanyaa*], but now we call the beach łèen-'iitthíi [*lein.eetí*] ('low tide place of')."¶ *Lein.eetí* is literally, '[place] where the tideflats had been'.

LINE 37. *tlél ch'oo ÿát ooswátx̱:* There is a false start here that has been edited out of the text, «tlél ÿát—ch'oo ÿát ooswátx̱ du jeex̱».

* MC047, "02-14", "02-15".

† De Laguna, *Under Mount Saint Elias*, 856, bracketed material ours.

‡ Ibid, bracketed spellings ours.

§ Ibid, bracketed spelling ours.

¶ Ibid, 857, bracketed spellings ours.

LINE 41. *Du shátt x̱'eitáangaa:* The verb in the clause *du shátt x̱'eitáangaa* is a dependent admonitive form with the postposition *-g̱aa* meaning 'lest s/he (the child) address his wife', or 'so that s/he would not address his wife'. Ellis' interpretation: "Even when she have little baby girls, he always kills them because they might carry a message to his wife."*

LINE 42. *x̱áa ḵoodé tle ajáḵx̱:* The exact meaning of this sentence is elusive. Taken literally, it seems to be 'A war party (*x̱áa*) [goes] to someone or to some people (*ḵoodé*) [and] just (*tle*) kills them customarily (*ajáḵx̱*)'.

LINE 43. The opening of this line is very unclear and barely audible at all. We've supplied *du* 'his', which is the usual pronoun Italio uses to refer to Tide-Commander elsewhere. There are many instances in the de Laguna recordings where the initial syllable of a line of speech is faint to the point of being inaudible or nearly so.

LINE 45. Ellis: "But that tide, he controls the tide [flood]; that's why she's scared of him."†

LINE 48. *du shátdei woonduskaagáa:* The verb here, *woonduskaagáa*, is a dependent admonitive form with postposition *-g̱aa*, translatable as a 'lest' clause in English. Note that irrealis prefix *u-* occurs here along with the fourth-person subject *du-*; it is striking to see the retention of irrealis *u-* before *du-* in a *na-*conjugation admonitive form. Finally, the admonitive normally requires a long high-toned verb stem (compare line 41, «Du shátt x̱'eitáangaa» 'Lest s/he speak to his wife'), so we would expect *…ḵáagaa* rather than *…ḵaagáa* here; this is the only instance we have found so far of a long low-toned admonitive verb stem. We also do not understand the function of the postposition *-de* 'toward' in du *shátdei* 'toward his (Tide-Commander's) wife'; we had earlier transcribed this as *du shát yéi…*, but the syllable after *shát* is clearly low and we do not hear a /y/.

LINES 53–54. *Héinax̱.áhu hú:* This is very likely a reference to the placename *Yéil Hídi* 'Raven's House'. It is listed in the Tlingit placename atlas *Haa Léelk'w Hás Aaní Saax'ú*, edited by Thomas Thornton, as «Yéil Hít» (lacking the possessive suffix) with the location given as "Cave at Cape Suckling".‡ De Laguna, however, spelled it as «Yeł hıdi»§ (i.e., *Yéil Hídi*), with the possessive *-i*, and identified it with the same location. Italio refers to this again later in the narrative in lines 206–07 where he says that Raven uses a rock for a house. We believe that the correct form of this placename is the possessive construction *Yéil Hídi* 'Raven's House', since *Yéil Hít*

* Ibid, 856.

† Ibid.

‡ Thornton, *Haa Léelk'w Hás Aaní Saax'ú*, 17 m#24.1.

§ De Laguna, *Under Mount Saint Elias*, 101.

'Raven House' is the name of several clan houses. Note also the use of the archaic form of the locative-predicative suffix, *-hu* rather than the now-standard *-wu*, following a vowel in *héinax̱.áhu* 'his is there over this way' (see the note to FI I, V, 222, for further discussion).

LINE 57. *lingit'aanig̱ei yóo kaawagút:* There are several ways to refer to being 'on' or 'in' the world: *lingit'aaniká* 'on the world', *lingit'aanig̱ei* 'enclosed within the world' and *lingit'aanitú* 'in the world'. The phrase *yóo kaawagút* implies that Raven was walking back and forth 'proudly' or 'fancily', or even 'strutting' or 'parading', as opposed to the ordinary *yóo uwagút* 'he walked back and forth'.

LINE 70. This line contains a false start. Italio begins to say «ḵei.á áa yéi teeyí» '[the fact] that the daylight was there', but then revises this to «goox' sá yéi teeyí» 'where [the daylight] was' in the following line. Raven seems to know that the daylight is out there somewhere, but he needs to figure out exactly where.

LINE 72. *yóox̱'atángích áwé ax̱'awliwóos':* Italio pronounces «yóox̱'atángích» with high tone on the preverb *yóo=* as well as high tone on the epenthetic vowel *-í-*; such a high-toned epenthetic vowel is inserted when a word ending in two consonants is followed by a postposition or a relational noun. Note also that the verb phrase here is an instrumental applicative derivative of *ax̱'eiwawóos'* 'he asked him/her', with the instrumental *-ch* suffix added to the noun *yóox̱'atánk* 'speech, language' and the insertion of the *l-* classifier element into the verb. This sentence therefore more literally translates, 'he (Raven) asked them (the Night-Dwellers) using speech'.

LINE 79. *Tle aawa.áx̱:* This line simply means 'He just heard it.' We have translated it more freely so as to convey the implication that Raven picked up something useful in what the Night-Dwellers said to him, namely, the whereabouts of the daylight, rather than that he simply heard their statement.

LINES 83–85. *ḵáa shaanák'w:* Line 83 contains a false start. Italio says, «Wé Yax̱ Ḵées'—» and then simply goes on to lines 84 and 85 with «ḵées' káx̱ duldél / ḵáa shaanák'w». Italio was apparently about to refer to the 'little old man' by the name *Yax̱ Ḵées' Shakawdzinugu Shaanák'w* 'Little-Elder-Who-Enlarged-the-Tide', which is how he pronounces the name in FI I, ii, 54. This character is discussed in §2.9 of the editors' introduction.

LINE 92. *a dzúkde yanax̱ aÿag̱atánch wé gán:* On the recording this verb sounded to us like *ayakgatánch*, but we do not expect the *ka-* prefix and the stop-like sound may simply be Italio momentarily hesitating before the pronunciation of *g̱a-*. This verb is a habitual form with aspectual derivational string *ÿanax̱=* (*g̱a*) 'down into the earth'. The initial word, written as *a* here, is practically inaudible, but we can hear something before *dzúkde*. Compare FI I, ii, 75, «De a dzúkde yanax̱ ayaawataan» '[Raven] stuck a piece of firewood behind [the old man's] back', which is otherwise identical except that the line begins with *de* 'now' and the verb is in the perfective. Ellis' interpretation: "And he lay right close to the fire. And he [the old man] took that fire off; he push him away from it. He lay too close to it."*

LINES 104–05. *Yáat'aach kei lagwaal:* Note the instrumental derivation, with the instrumental suffix *-ch* added to the noun and the *l-* classifier element in the verb. Italio seems here to be speaking to someone present in the room as he narrates. De Laguna explains, "On May 8, 1954, Frank Italio again told the whole story of Raven in Tlingit, though evidently a shorter and confused version. Then he was asked to sing the songs that referred to the Theft of Daylight, which he did, using a cigar box as a drum. The tape ran out while he was singing the second song."†

LINE 113. *héen tak.ádi:* This noun phrase refers to 'creatures of the water'. Here *héen táak* 'in the water' is reduced to *héen tak-*, so that *tak.ádi* forms a compound. Another variant is *hintaak.ádi*, where *héen* is reduced to *hin-* and *táak* is lowered in tone but not reduced. Yet another variant is *hintak.ádi*, where both *héen* and *táak* are reduced.

LINES 114–15. Ellis: "His uncle tried to kill him by making a flood. The tide was just about halfway up the mountain. Flooded all over (yu qiṡ kanada) [*yú ḵées' kanadá* 'the flowing of the floodtide']. That's when he was trying to kill that Yeł."‡

LINE 120. We understand *Éenyeekóon*, literally meaning 'Armpit Flicker', to be the name of the wife of Tide-Commander. This character is discussed in §2.6 of the editors' introduction. It is possible that here Italio actually said, *Éenyeekóon yóo áwé aawasáa* 'He called her Flicker-Pits' rather than *Éenyeekóon áyú aawasháa* 'he had married Flicker-Pits', as we have transcribed it in the text. Note that Ellis' interpretation aligns with the transcription and translation we have adopted: "His uncle, the Moon, was married to some kind of bird. And Raven did something in revenge, too, because some of his brothers and sisters were always killed off. That's why he did that."§

LINE 128. *ch'a g̱una.aa shaÿadáax̱:* The phrase a *shaÿadáax̱* can usually be translated as 'better than before' or 'more (intensely) than before'. The whole phrase *ch'a g̱una.aa shaÿadáax̱* could be translated 'better (or more intensely) than the other time', (i.e., better, more intensely, more boldly than the first time Raven

* De Laguna, *Under Mount Saint Elias*, 856.

† Ibid, 1152.

‡ Ibid, 856, bracketed material ours.

§ Ibid.

emerged across from the Night-Dwellers). Raven is emboldened in this instance because he is now in possession of the daylight, whereas he was previously just fishing for information.

LINE 140. *k̲ei.á yéx̲:* Italio is implying here that Raven is nudging the cover off the container slightly, releasing just a hint of dawn from the container, in the same way that dawn begins to break over the horizon. This comparison is striking because the daylight is compared to the daylight, once referring to the (mythical) daylight in the container and once referring to the (empirical) daylight in the sky.

LINE 144. *Hhhh!:* Ellis: "He slipped the cover off and just like lightning. … (The narrator's explosive 'pow!' can be heard on the recording)."*

LINE 151. *S'eták̲:* This is the placename for the Sitak River. It sounds like Italio pronounces the name with an /e/ as the first vowel, although it is commonly documented as *S'iták̲*. We received reports that Lena Farkas of Yakutat consistently pronounced this name, like Italio, as *S'eták̲*.

LINE 154. *Laak̲'ásgi X'aaÿí*: This placename literally means 'Black-Seaweed Point'; the corresponding English placename is Cape Spencer.† We cannot tell with certainty whether Italio pronounces the other placename in this line as *Diyáayi* or *Diyáay*, but it sounded more to us like the latter. This placename is listed in the Thornton atlas as «Diyáayi», translated there as "Looks Like a Whale";‡ however, Leer notes that the expected meaning of *diyáaÿ* would be 'it has humpback whales', not 'looks like a whale', and the expected nominalized form of that verb would be *dayáaÿ* 'having whales', which would be suitable for a placename. We do seem to hear *di-* rather than *da-* in Italio's pronunciation, so we are unable to analyze this name with much certainty. In the "Xunaa K̲áawu" chapter of the Thornton atlas the location is given as "Bear Island";§ in the "Yaakwdáat, G̲alyáx̲, and G̲unaax̲oo" chapter the location is given as "East River/Deception Hills".¶

LINE 155. *át áwé shukatán wé téix'*: According to Sam Johnston, *át shukatán* means "that is where the range or extent of it ends", so here this means that there are no more rocks past this point; the rocky area ends here. Compare FD ii, 218, «*Lituya Bay*-t áyáa shukatán ldakát át» 'The range of all kinds of things (trees) ends at Lituya Bay'.

* De Laguna, *Under Mount Saint Elias*, 856.

† Thornton, *Haa Léelk'w Hás Aaní Saax'ú*, 40, m#39.

‡ Ibid, 24, m#277; 39, m#12.

§ Ibid, 39, m#12.

¶ Ibid, 24, m#277.

LINES 165. *xeewa.átx̱:* The verb *xeewa.átx̱* appears to be a repetitive perfective, apparently meaning something like 'it came to regularly fade to dusk' or 'it regularly faded to dusk'. The corresponding repetitive imperfective is *xee.átx̱* 'it regularly fades to dusk'. The implication is that the recurring pattern of dawn and dusk, day and night, has now been established in the world. Ellis: "After he break daylight, [...] then it gets dark and daylight."*

LINE 168. *yú ḵáa shaanák'wch aadé uwasayi yé yáx̱:* Here again (as in FI I, ii), Italio states that the being known as Yéil, i.e, Raven, only came to have this name once Little-Elder-Who-Enlarged-the-Tide bestowed it on him. Ellis: "[T]hey call him 'Yeł,' just the way the old man call him 'Yeł.'"† We had two theories about the construction *aadé uwasayi yé yáx̱*. First, it could conceivably be an uncontracted *-ÿéyáx̱* construction equivalent with *aadé uwasayéyáx̱* (see appendix 1, §13.1.1, for discussion of the *-ÿéyáx̱* construction); however, if this were the case, we might expect *aadé uwasayéyáx̱* to mean 'as if (or, as though) he had named him'. Alternatively, it could be simply what it looks like: in the phrase *aadé uwasayi yé* 'the way he named him', the head noun *yé* 'place, manner' is coreferential with the *a-* of *aadé* and taken together such constructions mean 'the way in which...' (since *a-* and *yé* are coreferential, this is therefore what we are calling a 'truly attributive' construction), and the following *yáx̱* means 'like', so all taken together the phrase means 'in the way that the old man had named him'. We have opted for the second analysis.

LINE 172. *akawusgóowuch:* The only analysis we can come up with for this verb is that it appears to be an irregular decessive perfective subordinative form with *-ch* 'because', but the exact construction here is open to question, since the expected decessive subordinative perfective form would be *akawusgoowú ÿéeÿich*, using the modifier *ÿéeÿi* 'former(ly)'. In fact, we find an example using such an expected form with the *-ch* suffix in FI I, iv, 3, «eex̱ x̱oot aaÿí ÿéeÿich» 'because he (Raven) had been sitting in oil'. The non-decessive subordinative perfective form of this verb would be *akawusgoowúch* 'because he jabbed it', which differs from the form Italio gives only in the tone marking. It seems possible that Italio formed this verb from the decessive perfective *akawusgóowun* 'he had jabbed it'. However, if this is indeed a decessive subordinative, we have no way of explaining why he would omit *ÿéeÿi* in this instance but not in the example from FI I, iv.

LINE 173. *lyax̱dats'éini:* The negative repetitive verbal actor noun used here, *lyax̱dats'éini* 'troublemaker', denotes someone who just won't 'quit it' or 'knock it off'—someone who generally never settles down or ceases with foolishness. This is the basis upon which we derive the title of this tale, «Lyax̱dats'éinix̱ Siteeyi Yéil»

* De Laguna, *Under Mount Saint Elias*, 856.

† Ibid.

"Raven the Troublemaker". Compare the affirmative perfective form *yan wudits'ën*, which Leer in the "Verb Books" glossed as "stopped (doing it), left off, 'cut it out'; (machine) stopped". The corresponding repetitive form would be *yax̱ dats'ëin* 's/he/it keeps stopping, leaving off, "cutting it out"'. The negative repetitive form would be *tlél yax̱ udats'ëin* 's/he/it never stops, etc.' It is this latter form from which Italio derives the actor noun used here (with the actor-noun suffix *-ÿi* as found in, e.g., *shkalneegí* 'preacher' and *at.shéeyi* 'singer'); being a negative form, it is surprising that Italio's form lacks the negative/irrealis prefix *u-*. We can point to a few other sporadic cases where where *u-* is suppressed, such as *tlél nalé* alongside *tlél unalé* 'it won't be long (until…)' and *tlél da.át* alongside *tlél uda.át* 'it is empty'.

LINES 175–76. *Káayaakw … du [di]yeegooleidée:* The word *Káayaakw* is apparently Italio's rendering of the English word 'kayak', with the last syllable apparently reinterpreted as *yaakw* 'boat' (i.e., Raven's boat). This seems to be a reference to Wingham Island, which is noted in the Thornton atlas to be Raven's kayak (rather than canoe).* Ellis: "That Kayak [Wingham Island]—that's Yeł's boat—deyagułet—that's the kayaks they use. I guess it's made out of skins."† De Laguna's approximate spelling probably actually represents *diyaagooleit* or *diyeegooleit*. She writes it elsewhere as «deyaguwułet»‡ (evidently *diyaaguwuleit*). Harrington recorded the word in Yakutat as «tíikuułèet» (i.e., *deegooleit*) as well as the possessed form «'αx̣-tiikuułeetí» (i.e., *ax̱ deegooleidí*), which is translated there as "my kayak".§ In line 176, Italio's pronunciation sounds like «du yeegooleidée» (we do not hear the initial *di-*, but supply it in brackets, assuming that it was pronounced below the recorder's threshold), and in line 180 it sounds like «diyeegooleit». The word *Káayaakw* is not listed in the Thornton atlas as a placename, but there are comments on the region, "The area between Cape Suckling and Katalla is another place where Raven was active. Raven stories explain the formation of the Controller Bay area. For example, Kayak Island (Yáay Ká, 'On the Humpback Whale,' #17) is a whale Raven was hunting, Wingham Island (#13) is Raven's kayak, Okalee Spit (#18) is Raven's harpoon line, and so on."¶ Leer notes that the Tlingit word for the Sugpiaq people was *Giyak̲wk̲wáan*, where *Giyak̲w-* comes from the Sugpiaq name for Kayak Island, *Kayaaq* 'Whetstone' (referring to the overall shape of the island), which is entirely unrelated to the Sugpiaq word *qayaq* 'kayak'. (The rounding of /k̲/ in *Giyak̲w-* is evidently due to the following

* Thornton, *Haa Léelk'w Hás Aaní Saax'ú*, 5.

† De Laguna, *Under Mount Saint Elias*, 856–57, brackets original.

‡ "Another word, deyaguwułet (dex̣ yagu wułet ?), may possibly refer to the two-man baidarka, (cf. dex̣ 'two'), but my informants were very uncertain of the words." De Laguna, *Under Mount Saint Elias*, 331, parentheses original. Her etymology of *di-* as being from *déix̱* 'two' is entirely unlikely.

§ Harrington, "Tlingit and Eyak materials from George Johnson", 860–61, page reference is to the digitized manuscript.

¶ Thornton, *Haa Léelk'w Hás Aaní Saax'ú*, 5.

/k̲w/ of *k̲wáan*, i.e., the original form must have been *Giyak̲-*, which more directly reflects Sugpiaq *Kayaaq*.)

LINES 178–79. *a shaká:* Wingham Island is here metaphorically Raven's boat, and the end of the island is thus the prow of the boat. Since Raven was said to be shooting a harpoon at the whale (Kayak Island), we can safely assume that the 'prow of the boat' is the south end of Wingham Island.

LINE 181. *Yá «Atx̲án» yóo duwasáagu át:* We are interpreting *Atx̲án* as meaning 'Near the Creature'. *Yáaÿ* 'Whale' here is the name of Kayak Island. There are two projections on the northwest side of Kayak Island that could correspond to this description. De Laguna wrote, "Kayak Island [...], or 'Big Kayak,' is referred to as 'On the Whale,' Yay̱kA [*Yáaÿ Ká*], and it is said that one can smell the fat on it. The meat is black and the fat is white. Raven's harpoon is stuck into it somewhere."* This name appears in the Thornton atlas as «Yáay Ká», translated as "On the Humpback Whale".† Although de Laguna's and Thornton's renditions of the name include the noun *ká* 'horizontal surface' after *Yáaÿ*, we find *Yáaÿ* without following *ká* in Italio's sentence «wé Yáaÿ t'ak̲kaadé duwatéen» 'it (the thing called *Atx̲án*) is visible along the side of the Whale (Kayak Island)'. Therefore, we can conclude that the island can be named either *Yáaÿ* or *Yáaÿ Ká*. Italio describes the thing alongside the island as «du áadayi», meaning 'his (Raven's) spear/harpoon'. Ellis: "Kayak Island is supposed to be a whale. Something sticks out of a nearby one—it's a spear."‡

LINE 192. *K̲aataanaa wát:* The noun *wát* refers to the mouth of a body of water, so other translations could be 'the shores of the Katalla estuary' or 'the mouth of the Katalla River', which would be the place near Katalla where the fresh water enters the ocean. De Laguna notes, "The settlement is called Qatánà. (Note that n and l are frequently interchanged by Tlingit speakers)."§ The English 'Katalla' is borrowed from the the Tlingit placename *K̲aataanaa* (phonetically [qʰaːtʰaːnaː]), which is itself Eyak in origin. Krauss documents the Eyak placename as «qa˙ta˙lah» (phonetically [qʰaːtʰaːlah]) and suggests the final *lah* in this instance may denote 'place, town, village'.¶ As de Laguna remarked, the Eyak sonorant [l] is replaced by [n] in Tlingit.

LINE 196. Ellis: "His house (Yeł hıdi) {*Yéil Hídi*} is on that side—Cape Suckling, I think. {...} The buoy (kAsi̇s) {*katsees*} was sticking out; they were sailing right by it. Raven is up westward, right at the end ('acu) {*a shú*}. His house is a rock, where

---

* De Laguna, *Under Mount Saint Elias*, 102, bracketed spelling ours.

† Thornton, *Haa Léelk'w Hás Aaní Saax'ú*, 5, m#17.

‡ De Laguna, *Under Mount Saint Elias*, 857.

§ Ibid, 104.

¶ Krauss, "Eyak Dictionary", 2219.

he's staying—Aleutian Islands, I guess [added the translator]. Yeł is still alive. It's up westward some place."*

LINE 199. *a daax̱ aa ÿawlis'ís:* The translation here is our interpretation based on the context in which Raven was slicing pieces of fat from the Whale (Kayak Island); compare de Laguna's description of Kayak Island as having black meat and white fat, which one can smell.† On the other hand, it is quite possible that Italio is referring to something else being blown around the buoy.

LINE 208. Italio pauses briefly after this line and then he, Helen Bremner, and de Laguna can be heard laughing. This is likely the point described in de Laguna's notes to her song recordings as follows, "During the recording of the story, Frank Italio kept his face turned away from the mike and towards Helen, and she listened intently and nodded several times. At one point, Frank turned around and pretended to bite F[rederica de Laguna]'s hand holding the mike, then laughed delightedly."‡

LINE 220. *gaaw:* The laughter following the discussion of the drum may be due to the fact that Italio used a cigar box as a make-shift drum for the performance of the two songs. De Laguna writes, "[H]e was asked to sing the songs that referred to the Theft of Daylight, which he did, using a cigar box as a drum. The tape ran out while he was singing the second song."§

LINE 239. *Áwé a ítdei tlél óosh sh dajáḵx̱ ugaax̱:* The phrase *tlél óosh sh dajáḵx̱ ugaax̱* literally translates, 'if only he weren't crying [to the point of] killing himself', but the implied meaning is 'he is nearly crying himself to death'.

LINE 247. *sh toodé shukalx̱úx̱s':* We have not been able to confirm the meaning or confidently classify the form of *sh toodé*, which Italio pronounces identically both here and in FI I, V, 219. See the note to that line for discussion of this phrase.

LINES 248–END. The two songs: From this point forward Italio concludes the performance by singing the same two songs, in the same order, that he had sung at the conclusion of his 1952 performance (FI I, V, 210–92)—the first song evidently composed by Raven as he sat on the Container of Daylight on the bank of the Akwe River just prior to releasing its contents, the second song sung by Raven while in the act of breaking daylight over the Night-Dwellers and the rest of the world. Helen Bremner has prompted Italio by asking if he would like to sing the song known as «A Kát Ḵei.á Aawak'oodzi Shí», "The Song to Which He Broke Daylight". This

* De Laguna, *Under Mount Saint Elias*, 857, parentheses and brackets original, material in braces ours.

† Ibid, 102.

‡ MC047, "APS MSS.REC.30, Yakutat audio transcript (ACLS N2.3b)".

§ De Laguna, *Under Mount Saint Elias*, 1152.

appears to be the title given to the second of the two songs sung here and in FI I, V; the first song is never referred to with a formal title. The tape goes silent for a portion of the first song and then cuts out while Italio is in the middle of the second. The noise-reduced audio file of this performance does not contain the recorded portions of the second song. To hear the whole performance containing both song fragments, we consulted a digital copy of Laguna's larger reel, which does not have any extraneous noise removed.*

Notes to Andrew Wanamaker's Stories

EDITORIAL BACKGROUND. Jeff Leer originally transcribed these stories in addition to three others in handwritten manuscript form. Unfortunately, the audio recordings were lost, and Leer sent the original manuscript to Nora Dauenhauer so she could use it to learn how to read Tlingit. Most of these manuscript pages were later found in an attic, but along the way the final pages of most of the stories had been lost or discarded. The extant material includes three Raven stories as well as a handful of other transcribed texts unrelated to Raven and is accessible in the Alaska Native Language Archive.† At the time Leer transcribed the tapes, he did not have a comprehensive grasp of Tlingit grammar, and as a result he made many of the types of errors that beginning students of Tlingit make. At the time, for example, he apparently did not understand that verb roots ending in a glottalized consonant always have high tone in their long-vowel forms, and erroneously marked a number of these long-vowel stems with low tone—in other words, he wrote his preconceived notion of what he thought the tone should be when he should have been listening to what the tone actually was. These instances, together with other problems with Leer's original transcriptions, are pointed out in the notes. Leer originally transcribed the stories using the older Naish–Story orthography, which has been converted into the current practical (a.k.a. 'Revised Popular') orthography for this volume. Leer's revised transcriptions and translations were subsequently reviewed by Will Geiger. Kenneth Grant, Bessie Cooley, Ruth Demmert, and Sam Johnston were consulted on issues of grammar and translation.

Notes to Andrew Wanamaker's episode i, "Raven and His Uncle"

LINES 7, 8. *Yéi ash yawsiḵaa:* Note that in line 7 Heron is referred to with the salient pronoun *ash=*, indicating that at this early point in the narrative he is viewed as the

* MC047, B1, item 5.

† Leer, "Miscellaneous transcriptions, 1969–1974". In addition to those about Raven included here, Leer's material from Wanamaker includes the three stories «Ḵaaḵ'ex'wtí», «Ḵaakáa», and «Nus'gudooshonux̱ Has Wootee» (i.e., *Nas'gadooshóonáx̱ Has Wootee* 'They Became Three People').

protagonist, being addressed by the woman. In the following line their status with respect to saliency is reversed: the woman is referred to with the salient pronoun *ash=* in line 8. In line 11, Heron is referred to with the recessive pronoun *a*.

LINE 21. *du káa kawdix̲'áx̲'w:* This is corrected from Leer's original «doo káh kuwdix̲'úx'w» (i.e., *du káa* **kawdix̲'áx'w*).*

LINE 36. *Aak'wáchk'u:* Leer transcribed this word as «àh k'wúchk'oo» (i.e., *aak'wáchk'u*). If correct, it would appear to be an affective variant of *aak'wátsk'u* 'a little tiny one' (a compounded form of *aak'w* 'little one' plus *ÿátsk'u* 'tiny').

LINE 46. *Yá s'ús' tóode áwé kgeeshéex:* This literally translates as 'You will run into (i.e., to the inside of) this harlequin duck'.

LINE 50. *Gus'tú awlisháat:* This is corrected from «gos'tóo uwlishát» (i.e., **gus'tóo awlisháat*).

LINE 52. *Yéil tsu yá diyée yawdik̲een:* We are not sure how to interpret the verb form here. If Leer originally wrote this incorrectly and Wanamaker actually said *diyée yawdik̲ín*, the verb would be in the obliquative form with a locative PP preceding it: *P-x' ÿa-u-* (∅) 'appearing at P', so the sentence would translate approximately, 'Raven again appeared flying low' or the like. Leer originally wrote «diyée yuwdik̲èen» (i.e., *diyée yawdik̲een*), which clearly indicates a long low stem. If Wanamaker actually pronounced it this way, the long low stem would suggest that this is a *na*-conjugation obliquative, of which we can find no further examples.

LINE 55. *yá lingit'aanée wooneix̲i aa:* Here *lingit'aanée* appears to be the truncated form of *lingit'aaníx'* 'in/on the world', so the phrase here is equivalent to *yá lingit'aaníx' wooneix̲i aa* 'those who were spared in the world'.

Notes to Andrew Wanamaker's episode ii, "Raven and the Daylight"

LINE 2. *a shóo yéi wootee:* This sentence is virtually impossible to translate intelligibly into English. It literally means, 'he came to be at the end of it', but in contexts like this *a shóo*(*x'*) 'at the end of it' actually means 'in a position ready to act on it (i.e., poised to work on it, poised to eat or drink it, ready and waiting to transport or to be transported)'. We find similar formulations used by Italio, Dick, and Mills at the conclusion of each of their tellings of "Raven and the Whale". As discussed in §1.4.2 of the editors' introduction, although Wanamaker is telling a different story, "Raven and the Daylight", there is continuity here in that these all share the theme

* Leer, "Miscellaneous transcriptions, 1969–1974". This is the source for all references to Leer's original spellings.

of Raven convincing villagers to leave behind their stocks of food, enabling him to gorge on them.

LINE 6. *Du ádix̱ sitee:* This literally translates, 'They are his things (i.e., possessions)'.

LINE 9. *yá hintaak.ádi yéi adaane aantḵeení:* Leer originally wrote «yéi uh dàh neiyi antḵeenée» (i.e., *yéi adaaneiyi aantḵeení*), evidently due to confusion from two factors: first, because he did not understand the formation of attributive verb forms; and second, because he had just encountered the subordinative verb form *yéi s adaaneiyí* 'as they were gathering/processing it' in the preceding line.

LINE 13. *Kawduwashooḵ:* In Leer's original transcription he erroneously marked the verb stem *shooḵ* with high tone.

LINE 17. *yées yát:* This is literally 'a young child', which is Kenneth Grant's preferred translation. However, the young woman was of childbearing age. She is discussed in §2.15 of the editors' introduction.

LINE 23. *Wé shaatk'ích wusteení:* Leer's original transcription of the verb was «uh woosteenée» (i.e., *awusteení*), which was evidently a naïve hypercorrection of what Wanamaker originally pronounced as *wusteení* (without *a-*), since Leer did not understand the ergative construction at that time.

LINE 25. *A gukshitú:* See the note to FI I, v, 50, 54, for comparison of the descriptions of Raven in the corner of the young woman's drinking vessel.

LINE 29. *awunóot'i:* Leer's original transcription erroneously had the verb stem *nóot'* marked with low tone.

LINE 31. *Du káa yan wuwáadi:* Here again, Leer's original transcription erroneously had the verb stem *wáad* marked with low tone.

LINES 35, 40. *shawat.shaanák'w:* Leer's original transcription was «shawút shanúk'w» (i.e., *shaawát shaanák'w*), but it is safe to assume that Wanamaker actually pronounced it in the more usual compounded form *shawat.shaanák'w* as did his contemporaries. While Wanamaker does not use the more elaborate title for this character used by some storytellers, i.e., Lyóo.at.uwajeegi Shaanák'w or Lyóo.atkoowajeegi Shaanák'w, we can readily identify her as Unfazable-Little-Elder; see §2.8 of the editors' introduction for discussion of this character.

LINE 41. *De ch'a Yéil waaḵ x̱áashgé:* When asked about the enclitic combination *=x̱áa=shgé*, Kenneth Grant noted, "It's like a suspicion."

LINE 44. *aawagáx̲t:* Kenneth Grant noted that this verb can be translated, "he was begging for it".

LINE 46. *Du jeet yití!:* Wanamaker mentions *k̲utx̲.ayanaháa* 'stars' and *dís* 'moon' but never specifies that they are in containers. However, the use of the verb theme *O-S-tee~* 'for S to carry, take, bring, put a single O' implies that the stars are regarded as a single compact entity. The containers of the celestial bodies are discussed in §2.13 of the editors' introduction. Here the grandfather is speaking to more than one of his servants or slaves.

LINE 48. *Aan k̲us.ook':* The verb *k̲us.ook'* specifically refers to situational play, which is comparatively sedentary, similar to English 'playing house'. Later in the episode, Wanamaker switches to *ashkoolyát*, the term for physically active playing.

LINE 58. *yoo akligwátlk:* Here and in the following line, Leer's original translation erroneously records the verb as «ukwl… » (i.e., **akwl…*) where it should have been «ukl… » (i.e., *akl…*).

LINE 59. *neilx̲ aklagwáatl du léelk'uch unak̲éetg̲aa:* The verb phrase *neilx̲ aklagwáatl* is a repetitive imperfective verb form meaning roughly, 'he kept rolling it inside'. Furthermore, the dependent admonitive form with *-g̲aa*, namely *unak̲éetg̲aa* 'lest he be suspicious of him/it', was originally written *unak̲eetg̲áa* in Leer's original transcription, apparently erroneously.

LINE 60. *akawligwáatl:* Leer's original transcription erroneously had the verb stem *gwáatl* marked with low tone; this verb root is invariably high.

LINE 65. *Tlél sh wulk'áatl':* Here again, Leer's original transcription erroneously had the verb stem *k'áatl'* marked with low tone; it is necessarily high due to the fact that the root contains a final glottalized consonant.

LINE 72. *aadé aan ashkoolyat yé:* Leer's original transcription had «adéi àn ush koolyudee yéh» (i.e., *aadé aan ashkoolyadi yé*) rather than *…yat yé*, evidently because he did not clearly understand how attributive clauses are formed. It is just possible that Wanamaker used the decessive attributive form of the verb, i.e., *aadé aan ashkoolyádi yé* 'the way he used to play with it, had played with it', but this seems unlikely on two grounds: Leer did not write «yadee» with high tone, and the following high unrounded sonorant /y/ of *yé* could have tricked Leer's ear into believing the verb ended in the relative suffix—which he, like Naish and Story, was writing with long *-ee* rather than as its actually occurring form *-i*. For further discussion of attributive verb forms see appendix 1, §13.

LINE 78. *kag̲ít tú áwé:* Leer originally transcribed this erroneously as «kug̲ít tóo» (i.e., *kag̲ít tóo*), but here it should be *kag̲ít tú*.

LINE 82. *Goodáx̱ Naasshagiyéil sá?:* Toward the beginning of this episode (line 14), the townspeople fishing in darkness address Raven mockingly as «Naasshagiyéil yádi» 'the child of Raven-of-the-Head-of-the-Nass'. Here they refer to him directly (though ironically) as «Naasshagiyéil» 'Raven-of-the-Head-of-the-Nass'. Wanamaker also refers to Raven as «Yéil—Naasshagiyéil» 'Raven—[that is,] Raven-of-the-Head-of-the-Nass' in the first line of the following episode (AW iii, 1), so it would appear that at that point Raven has appropriated the name Naasshagiyéil as his own. See §2.14 of the editors' introduction for discussion of the name and character Naasshagiyéil 'Raven-of-the-Head-of-the-Nass'; see also §2.16 for a discussion of this and related formulaic expressions used in this context.

LINES 86–87. *Héende aa atkaawa.át…atgutóode atkaawa.át:* Leer's original transcription erroneously has a high tone on the «út» of «…út kawu.út» (i.e., **át kaawa.át*), no doubt due to his misanalysis of the construction of (*héende*) *aa atkaawa.át*, which on the surface of things would seem to contain two proclitic pronouns, *aa=* 'one(s)' and *at=* 'thing(s)'. For further discussion of this curious verb theme see §3.11 of the editors' introduction; see also §2.16 for discussion and comparison of its use as a formulaic expression in this narrative context.

Notes to Andrew Wanamaker's episode iii, "Raven and the Brown Bear Couple"

LINE 6. *ásíwéigé:* This was originally written as «uséiweh géh» (i.e., **aséiwé gé*); this has been corrected to *ásíwéigé*. The noun *xóots* refers specifically to 'brown bear(s)' or 'grizzly bear(s)' rather than black bears, polar bears, or any other kind of bears. Throughout the rest of the episode we simply use 'bears', since the type of bear is established here.

LINE 10. *Tlél aag̲áa yoo toodatángin wáa sáyá yakg̲wak̲aayí:* The first phrase here, «Tlél aag̲áa yoo toodatángin», could be interpreted in two ways depending on how *aag̲áa* is construed. Originally it was assumed that *aag̲áa* here means 'at that time'; however, if this were the case, we might expect it to be the first word in the sentence. An alternative interpretation, which we have adopted in the text, would take *aag̲áa* to mean '(searching) for it (i.e., what he was going to say)'; in this case, a more literal interpretation of the whole line would be 'He never used to ponder in search for what he was going to say'. The second phrase in this line was originally written as «wah súh yéi yukg̲wuk̲ayée» (i.e., **wáa sá yéi yakg̲wak̲aayí*); however, either *wáa sá* 'how' or *yéi* 'so, thus, like this/that' can serve as the adverb of manner here, but not both. Therefore *yéi* has been removed.

LINE 18. *Du x̱'aseiyée yawdudzi.ín:* The form *du x̱'aseiyée* here is the truncated form of *du x̱'aseiyí-x'* 'before him/her (i.e., positioned where s/he is poised to eat)', with the locative postposition, whereby the high-toned suffix *-ÿí* (or *-ÿée*) is obligatorily lengthened to *-ÿée* in the truncated form; for further discussion see appendix 1, §3. Kenneth Grant translated *du x̱'aseiyí* as "right by or under his mouth".

LINE 20. *chush yáax' x̱'éix̱ at wuditee:* This was originally written «choosh yáx' x̱'éix̱ wododitèe» (i.e., *chush yáax' *wududitee*). When Leer was preparing this text for the present volume, he could not parse this as written. It is particularly confusing because **wududi...* looks like a perfective form with the fourth-person human pronoun *du-* followed by the classifier *di-*; however, this combination is scrupulously avoided in Tlingit—underlying *du-di-* must surface as *duwa-*. Only when said out loud did it become apparent that Wanamaker actually says «...x̱'éix̱ at wuditee», and in the process he elides the /ÿ/ of the perfective prefix *ÿu-* (which is usually written *wu-* since /ÿ/ becomes /w/ next to a rounded vowel, i.e., /u/ or /oo/); see §3.10.2 of the editors' introduction for further discussion of /ÿ/ in this regard. It is important to keep in mind that what are written as aspirated stops (e.g., /t/, the IPA form being $[t^h]$) at the end of a syllable are phonemically plain stops (e.g., /d/, the IPA form being [t]), so what we write as *at* 'thing(s)' is phonemically /ad/ (see appendix 1, §14 for further discussion). In the phrase *x̱'éix̱ at ÿuditee*, when the /ÿ/ is suppressed following what is underlyingly /d/, the last two words are syllabified as *a-du-di-tee*. What Leer wrote as *wo-* (i.e., *wu-*) was a mishearing of the /a/ of *at=*.

LINE 27. *Yook̲:* The character *Yook̲* 'Cormorant' is discussed in §2.21 of the editors' introduction.

LINES 31–33. *héeni aawataan ... héeni anatáan ... héeni awutaaní:* Leer's original «héen awutàn» (i.e., **héen aawataan*) and the corresponding subordinative form «héen uh wootànée» (i.e., **héen awutaaní*) are corrected to *héeni aawataan* and *héeni awutaaní*. Leer was apparently unfamiliar with the truncated form *héeni* 'into the water', which is equivalent with *héenx'* (see appendix 1, §3, for discussion of truncated locative forms). He did, however, perceive the suffix *-i* in one instance, rendering it impressionistically as «yei» when he wrote *héeni anatáan* as «héenˀ yei uh nután» (i.e., **héenˀ yei anatáan*).

LINE 37. *ax̱ leiwadaaleilx'isáani:* Leer wrote this phrase as «ux̱ leiwudàh leilx'ee sánee». We have for the most part directly transliterated his original rendering but have conjoined the words into a single compounded form. He may have heard and transcribed this term incorrectly, or it may correctly reflect an authentic variant of the form we have obtained from our consultants: *ax̱ lawyadaaleilx'isáani* 'the little (*-x'=sáani*) folds/wrinkles [of skin] (*leil*) around (*daa-*) the side/face (*ÿa-*) of my (*ax̱*) penis (*law-*)'. This seems to be the Tlingit word for 'foreskin'; but for all we know, it may more generally refer to any or all of the folds of skin around the penis. Compare:

FD x, 22–24:	[«]Kéi kgisanóok i tl'íl, daax̱ yakanadúch't.[»]	["]You need to pick up your penis and cut off the folds of flesh around it.["]
KM iii, 67:	«Ch'a yá i lawyadaadookx'u sáani áwé aax̱ gageexáash.[»]	"You have to cut off these little folds of foreskin around your penis.["]

LINE 38. *wé Xóotsch ḵu.aa aax̱ wulixaash wé du láaw:* Leer's original transcription of this line has two errors. He did not hear the ergative postbase *-ch* on *Xóotsch*, but we know it must have been there because of the non-occurrence of the third-person object pronominal *a-* in the verb *wulixaash*. Being unfamiliar with the term at the time, he also wrote *láaw* 'penis' as «láh» (i.e., ˣ*láa*).

LINE 39. *gunayéi jiwdigút:* Note that *jiwdigoot* more generally means 'went to fight' or 'went to war', but here the Bear begins 'fighting' with the air, i.e., flailing about.

LINES 41–42. *katsees yát idaḵín...katsees yát wudiḵín:* Leer originally wrote «yát» (i.e., *yáat*) where he should have written «yút» (i.e., *yát*) in both instances. In the orthography used at the time, ⟨a⟩ corresponded to the long vowel now written as ⟨aa⟩ (phonetically [aː]) and ⟨u⟩ corresponded to the short vowel now written as ⟨a⟩ (phonetically [a]).

LINE 43. *du jig̱eit ash uwajáḵ wé Xóots:* Kenneth Grant translates *du jig̱eit* as "his handiwork". Bessie Cooley similarly translates this as "what he has acquired by killing or buying". She recalls a hunter once saying to her, «ax̱ jig̱eit áyá», which she translated as "this is my kill". The relational noun *jig̱eit* seems to be a lexicalized combination of *ji-gei-.át* 'arm-crook-thing'. Since this word highlights Raven's trickery all three times it occurs in this story, we translate one instance as 'my special recipe' and the other two as 'his artifice', meaning something Raven has secretly acquired and is using in an underhanded way. The translations given by Grant and Cooley would indicate that *(du) jig̱eit* is an inalienable noun, evidently a contraction of *(du) ji-g̱ei-.át* '(his/her/its) arm-crook-thing' and in line 64 we find «ax̱ jig̱eit áyá tlél dutáax', tle dunút'x'w» 'one does not chew my catch; one simply swallows it in mouthfuls', where *ax̱ jig̱eit* is clearly the object of both verbs. Note also that in lines 43 and 74 the syntax is quite unusual. In both cases we find «du jig̱eit ... ash uwajáḵ» rather than *du jig̱eitch ... uwajáḵ* 'his artifice killed him/her'. See the following note for discussion of this syntactic wrinkle.

LINES 43, 73, 74, 76. *ash uwajáḵ:* There is something peculiar at work in Wanamaker's use of (what looks like) the salient pronominal *ash=* in the verb theme *O-S-jaaḵ~* (Ø) 'for S to kill O' throughout this narrative. Typically, the only way to interpret the verb phrase *ash uwajáḵ* would be 's/he/it (recessive) killed him/her (salient)', where *ash=* is a syntactic object and denotes the semantic patient (i.e., the one who has been killed). Compare:

line 58:	du aat ash x̱'eiwawóos'	his auntie asked him (Raven)
line 69:	tlél ash wuḵeet	she wasn't suspicious of him (Raven)
line 70:	du aat ash x̱'awuwóos'i	when his auntie asked him (Raven)

In each of these cases, the salient object *ash=* functions as usual and clearly refers to Raven as the object of the verb. It would be odd (to the point of being illogical) for the salience to suddenly shift from Raven to the Bears at the moment Raven kills each of them. In addition, we have not found any other clear cases where the object pronominal *ash=* may occur with a coreferential noun phrase in the same clause; such a construction may in fact be ungrammatical. Compare Wanamaker's surprising uses of *ash=*:

line 43:	Áwé tle du jig̱eit ash uwajáḵ wé Xóots.	So Raven's artifice killed the Bear.
line 73:	Áwé tle ash uwajáḵ wé Shéech Xóots.	So that's what killed the Female Bear.
line 74:	Yéil áwé ch'a du jig̱eit hú tsú ash uwajáḵ	She, too, was killed by Raven's artifice
line 76:	Ash jáaḵ áwé tsáa	After this had killed her

If it is in fact ungrammatical for *ash=* to be coreferential with an overt NP, in line 43 *ash=* and *Xóots* 'Bear' cannot be coreferential; likewise, in line 73 *ash=* and *Shéech Xóots* 'Female Bear' cannot be coreferential; again, in line 74 the independent pronoun *hú* 'she' (referring here to the Female Bear) necessarily refers to the object of the transitive verb (it would have to be ergatively marked *hóoch* to refer to the subject) and cannot be correferential with *ash=*. We would thus be forced to conclude that in these cases *ash=* is in fact not a verbal object pronoun. We cannot say with certainty how it could be accounted for in these cases. Speculatively, we can imagine *du jig̱eit ash uwajáḵ* to be a deformation of *du jig̱eit, ách uwajáḵ* 'his artifice, it [was what] killed him/her/it', where *á* 'it' is the subject marked for ergativity and is coreferential with the NP *du jig̱eit* 'his artifice';* if that were correct we would end up with the very counterintuitive situation in which *ash=* denotes the ergatively-marked subject of the verb (the semantic agent, i.e., the secret recipe), rather than the object of the verb (the semantic patient, i.e., the Female Bear). This peculiarity is specific

* See Leer, "Tlingit Anaphoric System", 36–38, where he argues that *ash=* historically derives from procliticized *á-ch*.

to the instances in which Raven kills each of the Bears in this narrative. The object pronominal *ash=* occurs numerous other times in Wanamaker's two preceding narratives; all such cases are syntactically and semantically perfectly normal with one possible exception: AW i, 42, «du kéilk' tlél ash g̱waajaag̱i át» '[there was] nothing [that] could kill his nephew'. This is either another case in which *ash=* strangely enough seems to denote the ergatively-marked subject (i.e., is equivalent to *du kéilk', tlél ách g̱waajaag̱i át* 'his nephew, [there was] nothing that could kill him', which interpretation fits the context) or a case which invalidates the premise that an overt NP referring to the object (in this case *du kéilk'*) and an overt object pronominal (in this case *ash=*) cannot co-occur in the same clause.

LINE 52. *Úsh:* Leer originally transcribed this as, «Húsh! k'ei x̱'uneedutàn» (i.e., *Húsh! k'e x̱'anidataan!*). Ruth Demmert interprets this as «Úsh k'e x̱'anidataan!», which she translated as "Now let's hear you talk!" (alternatively, 'Now just you try to say something!'). The interjection or particle *úsh* occurs in Nora Dauenhauer's performance of "Raven and the Deer" (to be included in an eventual second volume of Raven stories): «Úsh x̱at latín!» 'Just you watch me!' Note that Dauenhauer's form similarly uses an imperative following *úsh*.

LINE 56. *Yéi áwé altin k̲áa yoo x̱'ayatánk:* Literally, 'Thus it is [that the] person watching him speaks.'

LINE 59. *goo sákwshé gwé:* We suspect that what Leer wrote as «gwéh» (i.e., *gwé*) may not be exactly what Wanamaker said, since our consultants find it puzzling in this context.

LINE 59. *i aatx̱úx̱:* Here the Female Bear refers to 'your auntie's husband' when she could have simply said 'my husband'; both formulations would refer to the same person. This illustrates a Tlingit tradition whereby the speaker often references the addressee's relationship to the person in question rather than their own relationship to this person.

LINE 64. *ax̱ jigeit áyá tlél dutáax':* Here again we find *ax̱ jigeit* meaning perhaps 'my catch' or perhaps 'my handiwork, my artifice'. This time we translate it as 'my special recipe'.

LINE 65. *sayahéi:* We might expect the verb to be in the form *asayahéi* here. The ergative postposition *-ch* regularly requires the omission of the third-person pronominal object *a-* from its verb as long as the verb is syntactically more or less adjacent to the ergatively marked agent. But in this case the ergatively marked agent *du kook̲énayi-ch* 'his messenger' is separated from the main verb *sayahéi* (in place of *asayahéi*) by the intervening purposive clause *akang̱aneegít*, which is not part of the main clause. As spoken by Wanamaker, this sentence provides an impressive instance of long-distance application of the rule dealing with the omission of *a-* after *-ch*.

LINE 67. ‹*Héende aa kanataan,*› *akanéek:* Here Raven is acting as though he is interpreting Cormorant's garbled speech for the Female Bear, maintaining that Cormorant is simply indicating that now is the right time to set the halibut hooks, when in fact Cormorant is trying to tell her that Raven has murdered her husband and stashed the body.

LINE 70. *ash x̱'awuwóos'i:* In Leer's original version he wrote «ush x̱'eiwuwóos'ee» (i.e., *ash x̱'eiwawóos'i*), which would be an attributive verb form *ash x̱'eiwawóos'i* 'who had asked him (Raven)'. It seems more likely that Wanamaker would have used the corresponding subordinative form *ash x̱'awuwóos'i* 'when she asked him' instead. Nevertheless, the possibility remains that Leer's original version is correct, in which case the sentence would read, 'His aunt, who asked him, thought it was the truth.'

LINE 72. *Yax̱ yakawdlichák:* Leer originally wrote «Yux̱ hus yukuwdzichúk» (i.e., *Yax̱ has *yakawdzichák*). The classifier was undoubtedly misheard, since *dzi-* cannot occur before a stem containing an affricate-series consonant such as /ch/. Then comes the thornier problem: the human plural proclitic *has=* is totally incongruous here, since stones could not be viewed as human or even animate in this context, and Raven acted alone in placing the rocks in the stomachs, so *has=* couldn't refer to Raven in addition to Cormorant and/or the Female Bear. Perhaps «Yax̱ has—» was a false start; Wanamaker could have started to say *yax̱ has ayakawlichák* 'they packed a bunch of them (stones, inside the stomach)', but then changed his mind (since the only one packing the stones in the stomach was Raven) and decided to say *yax̱ yakawdlichák* 'they (the stones) were all packed (inside it)'. Without the original audio we can only make an educated guess.

LINE 76. *yóot ayawsinák̲:* Leer's original manuscript had «yóodei uwsinúk̲.?» (i.e., **yóode awsinák̲.?*), which is clearly incorrect since *yóode* would require a *na-*conjugation form of the verb (i.e., *yóode ayawsinaak̲* 'he chased him way over there'), but *yóot=* 'away' takes Ø-conjugation, which accounts for the short high-toned stem *nák̲* in *yóot ayawsinák̲* 'he chased him away'. Leer must have simply misheard *yóot ay…* as *yóodei….*

Notes to Robert Zuboff's Stories

EDITORIAL BACKGROUND. The text of Robert Zuboff's first tale was originally transcribed by Gabriel George and Crystal McCay under Henry Davis' direction as a class project for second semester Tlingit at Sheldon Jackson College in Sitka, Alaska, in the spring of 1973. The result was printed in June 1973 by Tlingit Readers Inc. at the college print shop during the third annual Tlingit Language Workshop. The booklet, which did not feature an English translation, included a musical transcription by McKay of the song Zuboff sings to impersonate Raven singing the song of X̱'enax̱gaatwaayáa* in order to activate the power of the Náak̲w Tl'eegí Wootsaag̲áa 'Octopus Tentacle Cane' and drag the Kutatankahídi 'Salmon Box' ashore.

Although the original audio recording is no longer extant, the transcription given in this volume differs in a few ways from the original paperback. It has been adjusted for orthographic standardization and modified in a number of instances based on characteristics of Zuboff's speech attested in other recordings; the reasonings for specific modifications are described in the notes to RZ I. A clear example of this is the title of the story. Whereas the original title was «K̲udatan Kahídee», the title applied here is «Yéil k̲a Kutatankahídi», in which we add *Yéil k̲a* 'Raven and', which is commonly used in titles of Raven stories; the initial consonant is altered from ⟨k̲⟩ to ⟨k⟩ per Zuboff's and others' pronunciation; *Kutatankahídi* is compounded; the suffix *-ee* is standardized to short *-i*; and Zuboff's unique pronunciation of the Tlingit name for the Salmon Box (plainly audible throughout RZ II, iii), with *kutatan-* rather than usual *kudatan-*, is used. The paperback publication did not include an English translation; the translation provided here was initially done by Nora Dauenhauer. In the final stages of editing, Geiger and Leer made few revisions to her translation.

Nora Dauenhauer did the initial transcription of most of RZ II and her transcriptions were subsequently edited by herself, Richard Dauenhauer, and Keri Eggleston. The text of episode iii ("Raven and the Salmon Box (telling 2)"), however, was initially drafted by Richard, who transcribed lines 1–43 and then passed the project on to Ishmael Hope, who worked through the remaining material of the story. This draft was proofread and edited by participants in the University of Alaska Southeast course Heritage Language Teaching Methods and Materials Development in the fall of 2009.† The manuscript was subsequently edited in Intermediate Tlingit Transcription in the spring of 2010.‡ In 2020–2021, Geiger and Leer worked through

* Zuboff is the only storyteller known to us to pronounce this name with initial *x̱'e-* rather than the more usual *x̱'a-*. The substitution of *x̱'e-* in place of *x̱'a-* appears to be a stylization Zuboff employs often but not uniformly. For example in RZ II, iii, 131, he says «anax̱ ax̱'ewutaaní» with *x̱'e-*, but later in the same story, in RZ II iii, 215, he says «a daa yoo x̱'ax̱atangi nooch» with *x̱'a-*.

† Participants in this course included Linda Belarde, Kassandra and Roby Littlefield, Virginia Oliver, Emma and Norma Shorty, Daphne Wright, Ralph Wolfe, Gloria Anderstrom, Amanda Bremner, Ishmael Hope, and Joe Thomas.

‡ Participants in this course included Gloria Anderstrom, Linda Belarde, Keri Edwards, Vaughn Eide, Cory Grant, Ishmael Hope, Jessica Isturis, David Katzeek, Elizabeth Kunibe, Kassandra and Roby Littlefield, Paul Marks, Dan Monteith, Virginia Oliver, Eva Rowan, Alice Taff, and Fred White.

all of Zuboff's material, comparing the transcription against the original audio, revising the translation wherever necessary, and expanding and revising the commentary. On the whole not a lot of revision was necessary. The recording is of excellent quality. There are only a few places where we were unable to determine exactly what he said. This team consulted David Katzeek, Kenneth Grant, Bessie Cooley, Sam Johnston, and Ruth Demmert on particularly difficult issues of grammar and translation.

Notes to Robert Zuboff's tale 1, "Raven and the Salmon Box (telling 1)"

TITLE, LINE 110, AND THROUGHOUT. *Kutatankahídi:* The recording on which this text is based is no longer extant, so we were unable to compare the transcription against the original audio. In the recording of Zuboff's other telling of this story included in this volume (RZ II, iii), he consistently pronounced this word as «Kutatankahídi», with initial *kutatan-* [$k^{wh}ut^{h}at^{h}an$] rather than the more common *kudatan-* [$k^{wh}utat^{h}an$]. Further confirmation is provided in a recording of Zuboff telling this story in English where he pronounces the name there again as «Kutatankahídi».[*] We have revised all instances to *Kutatankahídi.* The original paperback publication spelled the name throughout as «Ḵudatan Kahídee».[†] See §2.18 of the editors' introduction for discussion of the Salmon Box.

LINE 29. *Pafísifik:* In the original publication this was spelled "Pafacific".[‡] We adjusted to "Paficific" based on Zuboff's pronunciation in the audio recording of his other version of this story in this volume.

LINE 44 AND THROUGHOUT. *X̱'enax̱gaatwaayáa:* In the original publication this name was written as «X̱'anax̱gaatwaayáa»[§] and the sung form was transcribed as «X̱'aa naax̱ gaat waa yaa».[¶] In RZ II, iii, we hear him pronounce «X̱'enax̱gaatwaayáa», with initial *x̱'e-*, in all cases other than the sung forms, which he pronounces there as «X̱'ei-naax̱-gaa-twaa-yáa», lengthening *x̱'e- to x̱'ei-*. We have adjusted all instances of the name in this version according to Zuboff's pronunciations in the other.

LINE 88. *yóo yax̱'áagi yéi yatee:* Literally, 'it was way out on the open ocean'. Note that in the phrase «yax̱'áagi yéi yatee» 'it is on the open ocean', *yax̱'áagi* is the truncated form of *yax̱'áak-x'* 'on the open ocean'; see appendix 1, §3, for discussion of truncated locative forms.

---

* MC005, tape 121, side b, occurs at 29:40 on the recording.

† Tlingit Readers Inc., *Ḵudatan Kahídee.*

‡ Ibid, 6.

§ Ibid, 7, 8, 10, 14.

¶ Ibid, 13–14.

LINES 96–99. These lines form a chiasmus. Lines 96–97 are repeated with slight variation and with the order of dependent and subordinate clauses reversed in lines 98–99.

LINE 102. *átx̱ guḵalayéix̱:* Note the use of *guḵa-* rather than the more usual *kuḵa-* in this future form with first-person singular subject and no consonant preceding the prefix string (which is underlyingly *ga+u-g̱a-x̱a-*). It was correctly written «átx̱ guḵalayéix̱»[*] in the original publication, but, being unable to compare the transcription against the audio, we had to look to other recordings to find an example that corroborates how Zuboff pronounces such constructions. In his performance of the story about *K̲aakáa* (an ancestor of the Kiks.ádi clan who lived among the *Kóoshdaa K̲wáani* ‘Land Otter People’ and became a powerful *íx̱t’* ‘shaman’), Zuboff can be heard pronouncing «ách guḵalatáaḵ» ‘I will use it to pierce it’, with *guḵa-*.[†]

LINE 118. *Gidzanóox’:* See §2.12 of the editors’ introduction for discussion of the character Gidzanóox’.

LINES 124, 126. *Shukanalx̱oox̱ déi:* This is literally approximately, ‘sing it (the words of the song) out now’. In this case Gidzanóox’ is telling Raven to sing the song that invokes the name of X̱’enax̱gaatwaayáa in order to activate the power of the Octopus Tentacle Cane.

LINES 127–36. The song: The song lyrics here are essentially the same as found in the original paperback rendition. The only revision we made is altering their «O» to the corresponding long form «Ou», because we clearly hear it as being long in Zuboff’s recorded performance of the same song. Compare the song in the second telling (RZ II, iii, 135–60), which is slightly more elaborate.

LINES 139, 141. *naaléi áa yaa asyiḵji yé:* Literally, ‘it is far, the place at which he is dragging it around (circuitously)’. The implication is that Raven was able to maneuver the box a great distance, or at least shift its position, by invoking the name of X̱’enax̱gaatwaayáa. Here is another instance of an obliquative motion verb form preceded by *P-x’*; the obliquative prefix string *ÿa+u-* has been modified to the preverb *ÿaa=* in the repetitive imperfective.

LINE 145. *l’éiw kalag̱é:* The original publication had this transcribed as «l’éiw kasag̱é»[‡] with the *s-* rather than *l-* classifier element. We have revised to *kalag̱é* because that

---

* Ibid, 11.

† MC005, tape 115, side b, occurs at 27:15 on the recording. Thanks to Matthew Spellberg for directing us to this example.

‡ Tlingit Readers Inc., *K̲udatan Kahídee*, 15.

is how we heard Zuboff pronounce it in RZ II, iii, 166, and because this is the expected form.

LINE 152. *du x̱'us.eetí áa yéi teex̱:* Literally, 'his footprints are always there'. *Áa yéi teex̱* is a repetitive imperfective verb form meaning roughly 's/he/it is always (i.e., customarily) there'.

LINE 154. *Yáa gus'yaadáx̱ jinli.aadi yé:* Note that there is no resumptive pronoun in this attributive clause. We might expect *Yá áa gus'yaadáx̱ jinli.aadi yé*, which Zuboff may in fact have said; the first two words could easily have been run together and heard as *yáa* by the transcribers Gabriel George and Crystal McCay. Without the original audio, we cannot resolve this question. The phrase *gus'yaadáx̱* literally means 'from the face of the clouds'. Since the geographic setting of this story is at or near the Alsek River delta, the reference here involves looking out to the horizon across the open ocean, specifically the Gulf of Alaska. Such a view is not available from a great portion of Tlingit Country, which lies within the sheltered inside waters of the Alexander Archipelago.

Lines 175–76. *You tig it wherever you wand it:* This was written in the original publication as "You tik it wherever you wand it, / wherever you wand it."* Tlingit does not allow for a distinction between an unaspirated and unaspirated stop at the end of a syllable; all such stops are inherently unaspirated. In earlier generations, this carried over also into English speech, so, for example, when a speaker said something that can be rendered in the Tlingit orthography as *áay hídít*, this could represent either 'I hid it' or 'I hit it'. Likewise above, what Zuboff pronounces as «tígít» stands for 'take it' and what he pronounces as *wáandít* stands for 'want it'.

Notes to Robert Zuboff's tale II, episode i, "Raven and Fire"

LINE 3. *A eetée:* This is the truncated form of *a eetíx'* (or *a eetéex'*) 'in its aftermath; where it had been, happened'; see appendix 1, §3, for further discussion. The implication of this line seems to be that everything had been disturbed during the flood but had not entirely disappeared from the face of the earth.

LINE 22. *áa tlein:* It is not clear if Zuboff is simply referring to a big lake or to the village of *Áa Tlein*, which literally means 'Big Lake' but refers to Atlin Lake and the village of Atlin in British Columbia. We have interpreted it as the former because Atlin Lake is south of Teslin; therefore, when Zuboff says «A t'áak áyá yáa áa tleinx̱ sitee» in line 25, meaning 'it is a big lake inland from it (Teslin)', we assume he is not talking about Atlin Lake.

* Tlingit Readers Inc., *K̲udatan Kahídee*, 16.

LINE 24. *Tás̲lan:* The Teslin people actually pronounce the name of their village as *Deis̲leen*, which is borrowed from Tagish or another of the local Athabaskan languages, meaning "the outlet of the lake"; compare Southern Tutchone *Délin*, from earlier **dédhlin* 'it flows out'; we would expect (unattested) Tagish **Dèezlį̨į̨* as the immediate source. Some Coastal Tlingit speakers refer to the village as *Tás Tlein*, literally meaning 'Large Thread', resulting from a folk etymology of the English name.

LINE 26. *teyak̲áash áyá kamdziyík̲:* The exact meaning of *teyak̲áash* is unclear. It might be a variant of *tayax̲áax'w* 'slate' (Teslin dialect). *Kamdziyík̲* appears to mean '(the stone) is striped/striated', apparently in a pattern that resembles Raven's tracks.

LINE 33. *gaaw kei has akg̲watan g̲anúgún:* The verb group *kei has akg̲watan g̲anúgún* is an example of a future verb form (with the usual stem *táan* reduced to *tan*) followed by the contingent auxiliary *g̲anúgún*; this combination means 'whenever … is/was going to …'. The reference here is to a ceremony involved in the process of mourning a deceased relative. A passage from Louis Shotridge's piece "My Northland Revisited" provides a reference, "In the latter part of the autumn I made my second visit to Klaku-aun [*Tlákw.aan*], my birthplace, an ancient town situated about twenty-three miles up the Chilkat River. I came this time to pay my respects for a 'Call together' ceremony, which had been proposed by my family. The call together is a revival of what has been known as a 'Drum-bearing' ceremony (interpretation of the Tlingit name for a mourning ceremony). In former times it was performed immediately after a death."* We can readily understand Shotridge's references here to be first to the *k̲u.éex'*, which he refers to as a "call together", and second to be the *gaaw wutaan*, which he translates literally as "drum-bearing". See also the section titled "Taking Up the Drum" in *Haa Tuwunáagu Yís* for discussion of these ceremonies.†

LINE 37. *k̲áa x̲'us.eetí:* Contrast *k̲áa x̲'us.eetí* 'a man's footprints' with *k̲aa x̲'us.eetí* 'human footprints'.

LINES 43–44. *Kéetx' áyá tsú / sh wulsháayin:* The theme used here, *P-x' O-S-l-shaa~ (Ø)* 'for S to get P (man) to marry O (woman); for S to cause P to marry O', is the applicative causative form of the transitive theme *O-S-shaa~ (Ø)* 'for S (man) to marry O (woman)' (see further appendix 1, §11). *Kéetx'* is homophonous with the explicit plural of *Kéet* 'Killerwhale', but here *-x'* is the locative postposition and *Kéet* is the embedded agent, namely the person whom Raven got to marry himself (or, in this case, 'herself'). Note that the verb for 'to marry' is traditionally understood to have a man as the subject and a woman as the object (but in modern Tlingit speech this

* Louis Shotridge, "My Northland Revisited", 106, parentheses original, bracketed spelling ours.

† Dauenhauer and Dauenhauer, *Haa Tuwunáagu Yís*, 44–73.

conventional understanding is only a tendency, not a rule). Zuboff clarifies that Raven is the woman in this situation by stating, «Shaawátx̱ wusitee» 'he (Raven) became a woman'. See SJ viii for a more fleshed-out account of this story.

LINE 47. *Aadé át ḵuwdi.oowu yé:* This means something along the lines of, '[This is] the way he went about in [various] forms' or '[This is] the way he went around changing physical forms'.

LINE 60. *Tléik':* As is customary for many Tlingit speakers, Zuboff pronounces *tléik'* as [tɬǽːk'] or [tɬǽːjk']; the vowel written as [ǽː(j)] is similar to the vowel of English 'rag'.

LINE 66. *yan áwé ayakaawaḵáa:* We do not know why this verb contains the prefix *ya-*.

LINE 92. *yíḵdlaa áa yéi yoo yaneek:* Literally, 'sparks happen there (customarily)'.

Notes to Robert Zuboff's tale II, episode ii, "Raven Makes Humans"

LINE 6. *té áyá ashawsigút:* The normal way to speak of rousing or getting someone out of bed is *ashawsinúk* 's/he caused him/her to get up'. In contrast, the form used here by Zuboff, «ashawsigút», seems to imply that the person is being roused up ready for action.

LINES 10–11. *yiwooyáat' / aag̱áa yei ḵutoosteech yé:* Literally, 'it came to be a long time that we customarily live for'.

LINES 13, 15. *dax̱atwooshú ... nas'gatwooshú:* These are more original variants of the numbers now usually pronounced as *dax̱adooshú* 'seven' and *nas'gadooshú* 'eight'; Zuboff can be heard using the pronunciation «dax̱adooshú» in line 40, as well as «tleidooshú» 'six' in line 39. In more modern speech, the /w/ (underlyingly /ÿ/) of *-wooshú* is suppressed after a stop consonant (the suppression of the morphophone /ÿ/ following an obstruent consonant is discussed in §3.10.2 of the editors' introduction).

LINE 30. *Yanax̱ yei aawagúḵ:* Note the unusual use of *yéi=* here as a Ø-conjugation derivational string meaning 'down', akin to *kei=* 'up'. The more usual form would be *yanax̱ aawagooḵ* (*g̱a*) 'he stuck it in the ground'. Compare FI I, iii, 12, «yanax̱ yéi oogooḵch» 'he (Raven) kept poking them (pieces of driftwood) down into the ground', where we likewise find *yéi=* 'down' with Ø-conjugation in place of the usual *g̱a*-conjugation form, which in this case would be *yanax̱ ag̱agúḵch*.

LINE 41. *yéi áyá haa kanax̲ yoo at yateek:* Literally, 'this is how things overcome, overtake us; this is how we are overcome'. We have supplied 'old age' in the translation for clarity, but the Tlingit line simply uses the verbal pronoun *at=* 'thing(s), something'.

LINES 42–43. *Yáa kayaank'ée áyá / haa éex̲ awliyéx̲ yáa Yéil:* Here *kayaank'ée* 'little leaf' is the object of the verb *awliyéx̲* 'he (Raven) made it' and *haa éex̲* 'into us' has the essive postposition *-x̲*, which denotes what the object of the postposition is identical to, is used as, becomes, or is turned into. So the whole phrase means that Raven turned a little leaf into us, i.e., into humans.

Notes to Robert Zuboff's tale II, episode iii, "Raven and the Salmon Box (telling 2)"

LINE 8. *Atkookeidí:* This term is generally translated as 'allegory', 'parable', or 'metaphor'. This opening frame connects to the allusion to the Alaska Native Claims Settlement Act at the story's conclusion, suggesting that Zuboff intended this performance of a traditional story as a political commentary on contemporary events. For more on this aspect of storytelling see Cruikshank's *The Social Life of Stories*; Hensel's *Telling Our Selves*; Morrow and Schneider's *When Our Words Return*; Greg Sarris' *Keeping Slug Woman Alive*; and Schneider's *... So They Understand* and *Living with Stories.*

LINES 20, 24, 44, 180, 186. 'Have access to': There was considerable discussion among Tlingit speakers over how to translate Tlingit sentences like *Du x̲'éix̲ aa kdahaa* and *haa kagéix' kaawaháa*. The meaning of the verb in these lines was variously translated as 'to have access to', 'to get a share of', and 'to get some to eat'.

LINES 30, 32. *Déivín:* This is Zuboff's Tlingitized pronunciation of the English 'Devil'.

LINE 37 AND THROUGHOUT. *Kutatankahídi:* Zuboff uses a unique form of the name of the Salmon Box, pronouncing it as «Kutatankahídi» rather than the more conventional *Kudatankahídi*. See §2.18 of the editors' introduction for discussion of this entity and its name.

LINE 40. *yáa Yéil:* Zuboff may have said *Yéilch* here, with ergative *-ch*, but we weren't certain that we really heard the *-ch* or if it may be a sound introduced by the poor recording quality.

LINE 47. *Náak̲w Tl'eegée Wootsaag̲áa:* Alternative translations of *wootsaag̲áa* could be 'staff' or 'cane'. Because this implement is an octopus tentacle, it can hook onto objects with suction cups without necessarily requiring the hook associated with a cane. See §2.17 of the editors' introduction for discussion of this entity.

LINE 49. *X̱'enax̱g̱aatwaayáa:* We seem to hear Zuboff pronouncing this name as «X̱'enax̱g̱aatwaayáa» in all cases other than the sung forms, which he pronounces there as «X̱'ei-naax̱-g̱aa-twaa-yáa». We would typically expect *x̱'a-* rather than *x̱'e-* here, but we have written it as we heard it. We are unable to analyze or translate this name. See §2.17 of the editors' introduction for discussion of this character.

LINES 51, 52. *Sáḵs:* This literally means 'bow' (additionally, 'yew'), but could be more loosely translated 'bow and arrow(s)'. As far as we are able to determine, both *chooneit* 'arrow(s)' and *sáḵs* 'bow' can be used to generally to refer to 'bow and arrow(s)' together.

LINE 54. *át kawdiy[aa]*: The stem of this verb is inaudible, either because the recorder failed to capture it or it was scrubbed out in the remastering process, or perhaps because Zuboff simply did not fully pronounce the whole word.

LINE 82. *a t'éinax̱.áx̱ áyá yamdiḵín:* Here Zuboff uses the perfective *m-* (rather than *w-*) after a vowel and before a CV- classifier (here *di-*).The verb theme is a motion derivative formed with *P-x̱ ÿa+u-* 'moving (sideways, in an arc, circuitously) around P', where *ÿa+u-* is the obliquative derivational string.

LINES 89–91. *Tléil gé aadé yáa ax̱ chooneidée / i Náaḵw Tl'eeg̱ée Wootsaag̱áa / daséix' wooḵasitaani yé:* This is more literally, 'Couldn't I trade my arrow for your Octopus Tentacle Cane?' Note that Zuboff uses the second-person singular possessive pronoun *i* 'your', but uses the unpossessed form *wootsaag̱áa* 'cane'. This is not simply a slip-up on Zuboff's part; we find the identical construction in RZ I, 82, «i Naaḵw Tl'eeg̱í Wootsaag̱áa», and we also find «du Naaḵw Tl'eeg̱í Wootsaag̱áa» in RZ I, 108. We would expect the possessed form *wootsaag̱áyi* in each of these instances and we do not have a principled explanation for Zuboff's use of the non-possessed form.

LINES 99–102. *ax̱ éex̱ shikeelx̱oox̱ú:* In *shikeelx̱oox̱ú* and *yaa shikanilax̱úx̱u*, the prefix *shu-* becomes *shi-* due to the following second-person subject prefix *ee-*.

LINE 107. *I éex̱ shukakḵwalx̱oox̱:* The root *x̱oox̱~* is documented as fully variable, so we are surprised to hear the long low stem in the future here, especially because we hear Zuboff also pronouncing «Akawulx̱óox̱udáx̱» 'After asking him over and over' (RZ II, iv, 178). The form «shukakḵwalax̱oox̱» hints at an invariable long low stem, while the form «Akawulx̱óox̱udáx̱» hints at an invariable long high stem. Leer documented similar future forms with a long high vowel from Tongass consultants, who treated this as a fully variable stem. A real possibility is that the low tone on *x̱oox̱* is simply due to a greater degree of downdrift than usual.

LINES 114–15. *gus'yaadáx̱ jinli.aadi / teet tlénx':* The verb *jinli.aadi* is an attributive processional imperfective meaning roughly '(swells) that roll one after the other'; see further appendix 1, §12.

LINE 131. *anax̱ ax̱'ewutaaní:* We heard *x̱'e-* here instead of usual *x̱'a-*. The more usual pronunciation would be *anax̱ ax̱'awutaaní.*

LINE 134. *kei shukaawashée:* Zuboff vacillates here, saying first «kei akaaw—» (likely for *kei akaawashée* 'he started singing it') and then what sounds like *kei shukaawashée* 'he began singing a song' (a variant of *kei shikaawashée*), although this last form was extremely garbled on the tape. There appears to have been an airplane flying overhead during this moment of the performance.

LINE 148. *yóo áwé ash daaÿaḵá:* This verb contains the prefix string *daa ÿa-*. For many speakers, the underlying /ÿ/ of *ÿa-* is simply suppressed in ordinary speech after *daa-* in this particular verb, the result being that this verb form is pronounced *yóo ash daaaḵá*, as we can hear in Zuboff's pronunciation here. To avoid visual confusion, we write this verb form as *yóo ash daaÿaḵá.*

LINE 161. *Gwál jinkaat kaay yéi gíyá yaa oosyíḵch:* The irrealis verb form used here is conditioned by both *gwál* 'maybe' and *gíyá* 'I guess'. The verb here, *yaa oosyíḵch* 'he would pull it', is a repetitive imperfective of an obliquative verb form containing the prefix string *ÿa+u-*, which in the repetitive imperfective irregularly contracts to the preverb *ÿaa=*. Such obliquative verb forms are normally preceded by postpositional phrases (*P-x̱*, *P-náx̱*, or even *P-x'*). We cannot account for the fact that there is no postpositional phrase before *yaa oosyíḵch* here.

LINE 165. *du x̱'us.eetí (Raven's footprints):* There is an area of sand dunes devoid of trees just north of Dry Bay. In the spiritual and cultural geography of the Yakutat and Dry Bay people, this is where Raven dug in his heels pulling in the Salmon Box. Where the box was pulled ashore is said to be the peninsula between the ocean and Cannery Creek, which is called 'Canoe Prow'. The Lukaax̱.ádi clan house called Shakahít '[Canoe] Prow House' commemorates this, as does the L'uknax̱.ádi clan house Diginaa Hít 'Far-Out House'.

LINE 171. *Ch'a goo sá i tuwáa sigóo x'wán aadé:* Literally approximately, 'Wherever you want, do [go] thither!'

LINE 173. *Yadusḵúx̱x':* This is a multiple imperfective form meaning 'they (bunches of harvested salmon) are being transported in loads by boat'.

LINE 175. *ldakát yéi kaawaháa:* Here *ldakát yéi* is the truncated locative form corresponding to *ldakat yéix'* 'at every place'; see further appendix 1, §3.

LINES 191–92. *Tléil áyá ayáx̱x̱ usiteeyi ḵáa / dénageit:* This has a number of possible interpretations. It could be 'an unrighteous person', 'an unworthy person', 'an immoral person' or the like. *Dénageit* is Tlingitized pronunciation of the English 'delegate'.

LINE 194. *aag̱áa yáa* Alaska *dulgeiyág̱u yé:* Literally, 'when people were making a claim to Alaska, suing for Alaska'.* The reference here is to the legal battle carried out by Tlingit and other Native peoples of Alaska to receive just compensation for the illegitimate appropriation of their land by the United States through the Treaty of Cession. This legal process culminated in the Alaska Native Claims Settlement Act, which passed Congress in 1971, the year prior to this recording.† Zuboff's reasoning is that this story is a kind of covenant, and that the fish belong to the Tlingit people who have been disenfranchised by newcomers through permit systems. He asserts that if he had been a delegate in the legal battle, he would have been more assertive in defending Native fishing rights. He uses the remaining lines of the performance to explain that he knows where the evidence is that qualifies him to speak with authority on the Tlingit claim to the land and resources. This claim is supported by evidence of a cairn on a certain mountain behind Angoon, the remains of a fortress where people took refuge during the flood. See the note to RZ II, V, 72–73, for further discussion of the cairns and mountains.

LINE 202. *yáa haa jineiyí:* Zuboff clearly says «haa jineiyí» here instead of the usual *haa yéijineiyí* 'our work'. We have no explanation for the lack of *yéi=* here, which is an integral part of the verb theme *yéi=ji-S-nei*` 'for S to work, labor', from which the noun *yéijiné* 'work, labor' is derived.

Notes to Robert Zuboff's tale II, episode iv, "Raven and His Uncle"

LINES 7–8. *Du dlaak' / yádi áyá ch'u tle ajáḵx̱:* The object of the verb here is *du dlaak' yádi*, which literally translates as 'his sister's child' in the singular, and the verb *ajáḵx̱* 'he kills it (customarily)' indicates that the killing of an individual child was repeated, so the sentence indicates that Tide-Commander would kill each successive child as soon as it was born.

LINES 43. *gunayéi dís wusi.át:* Note that here *dís* 'moon' occurs in what would normally be the position for an incorporated noun, in this case following the preverb *g̱unayéi* 'beginning'; we have not found the verb theme *O-s-.aat~* outside this idiom.

* Compare the example from Leer's "Verb Books", «(ash éex̱) algeiyáḵw», translated there as "is claiming it (from him) as just payment; is suing (him) for it".

† Much has been written on the history and implications of ANCSA. See, for instance, the introduction to Dauenhauer and Dauenhauer, *Haa Ḵusteeyí*; Paul, *Then Fight For It!*; Metcalfe and Ruddy, *A Dangerous Idea*; and Case and Voluck, *Alaska Natives and American Laws*.

This case appears to parallel other forms like *du kát yát áa* 'she is pregnant', literally 'on her a child is sitting' (this is the form that some people provide; other people use the form *du kát yat.áa*, where the *yat-* is completely incorporated into the verb).

LINE 49. *Yéil tle yóo aawasáa tsu:* We had trouble translating *tsu* here. Most commonly *tsu* translates as 'again', but it may sometimes translate as 'even'. Since we have no evidence that the woman gave the name *Yéil* 'Raven' to any other children, we have translated *tsu* here as 'even'.

LINES 63–64. *Gwál wudashee / ash tuwáa usgú, i káak:* Contrast this phrase *gwál ash tuwáa usgú* 'maybe he wants it', in which the dubitative *gwál* 'maybe' triggers the irrealis form of the verb, with the more commonly encountered *tléil ash tuwáa ushgú* 'he doesn't want/like it; he despises it', which uses the negative pejorative form of the verb with the *sh-* classifier element in place of *s-*. Note also that the third-person salient possessive pronoun *ash=* here is used to refer to Raven's uncle. From line 88 onward *ash=* is used to refer to Raven as the salient actor.

LINE 67. *át ishéex áwé:* Note that in the consecutive form Zuboff uses here, «át ishéex» 'when he ran to there', if *shéex* were the actual verb stem we would not expect the peg prefix *i-* [ʔi]. The fact that *i-* is present indicates that the initial consonant /sh/ is still regarded as the underlying classifier, and *xéex* as the underlying verb stem. As a general rule in Northern Tlingit, a classifier consisting of only a fricative must form the coda of a syllable. In the uncontracted form *át ishxéex*, the peg prefix *i-* is inserted in order to avoid the occurrence of a word-initial consonant cluster (i.e., /shx/). In the contracted form *át ishéex*, the onset consonant /x/ of the verb root *xeex~* is deleted, whereby the classifier *sh-* has become the onset of the verb stem; so even though the peg prefix no longer functions to break up a consonant cluster at the beginning of the verb word, its retention preserves lexical information about the underlying form of the verb. Note that the deletion of stem-initial /x/ occurs with this verb when the classifier is *sh-* (e.g., *tlél aadé wusheex* 's/he/it didn't run there', though some speakers prefer the form *tlél aadé wushxeex* 'id.'), but never when it is *ji-* (e.g., *aadé wjixeex* 's/he/it ran there').

LINES 88, 89. *yaa ash kanatáx':* This phrase literally means, 'it (the canoe) was in the process of gripping him' (as if clenching him in its jaws).

LINE 113. *yéi kwdiyáat':* Nora Dauenhauer noted that at this point Zuboff indicated the length of his hand, from fingertips to wrist, in order to demonstrate the length of the shards of *ín* 'obsidian' or *ít'ch* 'glass'.

LINE 144. There is a short interruption in the narrative here in which someone enters the house looking for an absent resident. Zuboff falls silent while Nora Dauenhauer dismisses the interrupter. Zuboff immediately resumes with the next line, entirely undisturbed, as though someone had pressed his pause button.

LINE 148. *du táanayi:* A *táanaa* is a type of gaff hook used specifically for hunting octopus. De Laguna described this implement as "a variety of gaff hook".* Emmons writes, "[Octopus] were taken with a dull hook, formerly of deer horn and later of iron, lashed to the end of a pole. (At Yakutat this was described as being of wood, like a huge v-shaped trout hook.) This hook, *tar-nar* (tá·na·) [*táanaa*], was thrust under submerged rocks and into underwater holes, and twisted around, entangling the tentacles of the devilfish, so that it could be drawn to the surface."†

LINES 150–51. *Ashalach'ú<u>k</u>s':* We heard this verb pronounced in two different ways. The first instance, in line 150, sounded like *ashalach'ú<u>k</u>s'* (or perhaps *ashalats'ú<u>k</u>s'*), but the second time, in line 151, it sounded like *ashalach'ú<u>x</u>'s'* (or perhaps *ashalats'ú<u>x</u>'s'*); we were uncertain as to whether the stem began with /ts'/ or /ch'/. The Dauenhauers noted that they did not know how to translate this verb, but guessed that it had something to do with adjusting the 'head' (*sha-*) of the octopus hook. Leer subsequently found what, in his opinion, must be an instance of this verb theme in Story's *Morphological Study of Tlingit*, with the example «ʌ šʌ́włıč'ʊ́G» (i.e., *ashawlich'ú<u>k</u>*), which she glossed as "he let down halibut hooks".‡ Based on Story's example, we settled on the transcription *ashalach'ú<u>k</u>s'*. The verb root *ch'oo<u>k</u>~* is otherwise undocumented and was unrecognizable to our consultants. Although we have translated this as 'he was raising and lowering it (the octopus hook)', based on Story's gloss of «ʌ šʌ́włıč'ʊ́G», the context calls this translation into question. Why would Raven be lowering and raising his octopus hook if he is not even at the octopus hole? And Raven is using a *táanaa* 'octopus gaff', which consists of a long pole with a hook affixed to the end, rather than a halibut hook. Perhaps at this point Raven was testing the octopus hook for structural integrity and/or balance, found that the barb was not securely lashed on, and then retied the barb (line 153 being «A<u>x</u>'akas'eet áyá» 'He was lashing/hafting the hook [to the shaft]'), but this is all fairly tenuous speculation.

LINE 168. *yáa du káak hídi:* This simply means 'this house of his uncle's', but is an elliptic way of saying something like *yáa du káak hídi yeex'* 'in his uncle's house'.

LINE 172. *du koolgeiyí:* We expect the form *du kulgeiyí* 'his large size', but Zuboff clearly pronounces *kool-* long, and in fact we seem to hear the rest as something roughly like *géiyu*, which is extremely puzzling.

---

* De Laguna, *Under Mount Saint Elias*, 389.

† Emmons, *The Tlingit Indians*, 121, bracketed material ours; an illustration of a *táanaa* can be seen in ibid, 120.

‡ Story, *Morphological Study*, 77.

LINE 178. *Akawulx̱óox̱udáx̱:* In Leer's "Verb Books" as well as his "Lexical Binders", the stem for this theme is documented as variable, so we would expect *akawulx̱oox̱údáx̱* here, with a long low stem in the subordinative, but Zuboff clearly pronounces the stem with high tone. See the note to RZ II, iii, 107, for further discussion.

LINE 179. *kei x̱'ayadlúxch á ḵúnáx̱:* The verb root here appears to be *dloox~* (varying with *dleexw~* in Southern Tlingit), which has to do with skin peeling off (of, e.g., a dead or cooked fish) and perhaps delamination in general. In Leer's "Verb Books" we find such forms as «kei shoowadlúx», glossed as "(skin of dead creature) peeled off, tore off", and «kei ÿaawadlúx», translated as "[s/he] messed up". The translation 'messed up' is rather puzzling in view of the fact that we find the same verb theme in the *Tlingit Verb Dictionary* in the example sentence «kei has yadlúxch» with the translation "they tore away (at the Boston Tea Party)",* presumably referring to the American colonies 'tearing away' or 'peeling away' from England. This verb form is the same as what Zuboff says except that he adds the prefix *x̱'e-* referring to oral activity. Although we do not know exactly how to translate this verb form, there is a strong implication that Tide-Commander's speech betrayed his extreme irritation.

Notes to Robert Zuboff's tale II, episode V, "Raven and the Flood"

LINE 31. *hintaakx'wás'g̱i:* The bufflehead (*Bucephala albeola*) is a small sea duck related to the goldeneye.

LINE 36. *A doogú tóox̱ áwé awsinook:* This is literally 'he caused her to sit (or, to move in a sitting position) down along the inside of its skin'. By donning the skin of the bufflehead, Raven's mother takes on its physical form and is able to float safely and unhindered over the flooding waters.

LINES 44, 45. *xáats':* See the note to FI I, i, 195, for discussion of the translation 'firmament' as applied to *xáats'*.

LINE 55. *Aag̱áa áyá uháan tsóo:* This is the beginning of a long parenthetical discursus on how Tlingit people survived during the flood caused by Raven's uncle. The chronology presented here by Zuboff is not universal among tradition-bearers. For him the episodes of Raven's uncle and the flood happen after the ancestral people migrate from the interior of the continent to the coast, settling in Angoon. In this section of the narrative he connects the mythic events to the ancestral population and local landscape features, describing rock cairns on a mountain top where people took refuge. This section was omitted in earlier drafts but has been reinstated for this edition of the text.

* Naish and Story, *Tlingit Verb Dictionary*, 244.

LINE 69. *S'ex'aayihéen Shaa:* This placename as Zuboff pronounces it literally means 'Silt-Point-River Mountain'. In Thornton's placename atlas, *Haa Léelk'w Hás Aaní Saax'ú*, we find the form «Sax'aayi Héen», translated as "Stream with a Point" and located at "Hood Bay entrance"* or alternatively located at "Creek, North Arm Hood Bay",† but no names for a mountain containing the name for this creek or stream. We cannot account for the initial *sa-* of that form, but the *s'e-* in Zuboff's is clearly the combining form of *s'é* 'alluvial silt, clay'. Zuboff's form implies the likely existence of the placenames *S'ex'aayí* 'Silt Point' and *S'ex'aayihéen* 'Silt-Point River'. Zuboff was recorded telling this story in English, and there he refers to this mountain as "Hood Bay Mountain",‡ which is what we have used in the text of the present story's translation. See the next note as well for de Laguna's remarks on the mountains in the Angoon area which have ancient rockpiles and rope up their peaks.

LINES 72–73. *A shakéewu aa yáa xóow / ka̲ yáa tíx':* Zuboff mentions the mountain, the rockpile, and the rope in another version of this story that he told in English:

> When we got the top of this Hood Bay Mountain from behind Angoon,
> it was blowing.
> It was raining.
> It was blowing heavy, heavy southeast.
> We making a shelter.
> We putting up rockpile.
> The rockpile up in Hood Bay Mountain is four feet high.
> On the south end of this rockpile is a coil of rope in there today.§

The *xóow* 'rockpile(s), cairn(s)' and *tíx'* 'rope' that Zuboff refers to here are also mentioned in de Laguna's *Story of a Tlingit Community*, which is based on archeological and ethnographic work she performed in Angoon in 1949 and 1950. There are evidently a number of peaks in the Angoon area that are reported to have cairn-like structures along with ancient strands of rope or its remnants. De Laguna writes, "From Hood Bay Cannery a high mountain, evidently a volcanic neck, is visible above the end of South Arm. It is called 'Box Mountain' from its shape. Like many peaks in the Angoon area, this is supposed to be one of the mountains where people took refuge during the Flood. The natives told us that there is a rope coiled up around the top of the peak, by means of which the people moored their raft or canoe, and that it is now so old that if touched it turns to ashes."¶ She writes of another peak, "A mountain south of Chaik Bay (elevation 3,400 feet as marked on the U. S.

* Thornton, *Haa Léelk'w Hás Aaní Saax'ú*, 118, m#155.

† Ibid, m#166.

‡ MC005, tape 6, side a, occurs at 05:00 on the recording.

§ Ibid, occurs at 05:00 on the recording.

¶ De Laguna, *Story of a Tlingit Community*, 52.

Coast and Geodetic Survey Chart No. 8252) is called canaq̇Áts̓. This was also a Flood refuge mountain, and there is a rope at the summit, now reduced to ashes, according to the informant who claims to have seen it."* The placename de Laguna renders as «canaq̇Áts̓» is found in Thornton's atlas as «Shalak'áts'» and translated there as "Sharp Head".† De Laguna also reports that a Deisheetaan man "said that Table Mountain, a 2,400-foot peak south of [Whitewater Bay], was another refuge place during the Flood. There are ropes and ashes on top, which he has touched, and piles of stone, which are the remains of walls to keep out the bears that attacked those who took refuge on the summit."‡

LINE 75. *aa kamdi.áa:* Here Zuboff again uses the perfective *m-* (rather than *w-*) after a vowel and before a CV- classifier (here *di-*).

LINES 78–79. *xóots / nakwaanée:* This could be translated as 'swimming bears', 'swimmer bears', or more literally 'bear swimmers'. *Nakwaaní* exemplifies a type of verbal noun known as an 'agent noun' formed from motion verbs, which is characterized by the conjugation prefix *na-* and the suffix *-ÿi*, referring to the agent or actor, in this case, the swimmer. Another example of this type of verbal noun is *du ítx̱ na.aadí* 'his disciples' (lit. 'the walkers following him'). For non-motion verbs, agent nouns are formed with the imperfective stem plus the suffix *-ÿi* and do not take the *na-* prefix, e.g., *at.shéeyi* 'singer', *shkalneegí* 'preacher', *at'eegí* 'steersman'. Note also Zuboff's repetition with the terms reversed in line 82, «nakwaaní, yáa xóots» 'the swimmers, these bears'.

LINE 95. *áa yoo akamlitíx̱':* Here Zuboff again uses the perfective *m-* (rather than *w-*) after a vowel and before a CV- classifier (here *li-*).

LINE 98. *Ch'a wé diyée áwé áx̱ wulixáat'i dís áwé:* Literally, 'It's down below; it's the moon which was suspended there'. The implication here seems to be that from Raven's perspective the moon was 'suspended below' him such that the moon was between him and Earth.

LINES 100–03. *yáa yaa ndak̲in át / nás'k ux̱éeych / ... yá dís daadé:* Zuboff literally states here that 'this thing that flies along / it thrice overnights / towards the moon's periphery'. The phrase «yáa yaa ndak̲in át» literally means, 'this thing that flies

* Ibid, 55.

† Thornton, *Haa Léelk'w Hás Aaní Saax'ú*, 120, m#237. Also note the companion name «Shalak'áts' Yádi», translated as "Sharp Head Baby" and given the same location (ibid, 120, m#234); this could also be translated 'Little Sharp Head' or 'Smaller Sharp Head'. It is possible that de Laguna originally rendered the name as «całaq̇Áts̓», with ⟨ł⟩ being mistakenly altered to ⟨n⟩ during retranscription or typesetting. On the other hand, if de Laguna rendered this consonant faithfully, and she in fact heard *shanak'áts'*, we would be unable to analyze this form.

‡ De Laguna, *Story of a Tlingit Community*, 57.

along', but evidently refers to a spacecraft; it almost certainly refers more specifically to one or more of the Apollo missions 11, 12, 14, 15, and 16, which had successfully gone from Earth to the moon and back prior to Zuboff's performance of this story. The verb *ux̱éeych* 'it overnights' refers the passage of nights rather than days, but we have used the translation 'it takes three days' because in English it is more natural to refer to the passage of days than nights. We take *dís daadé,* which literally means 'towards around the moon' or 'towards the moon's periphery', to denote '[achieving] lunar orbit'. The successful Apollo missions did in fact take roughly three days between launch and lunar orbit.

LINE 104. *Hú ḵu.aa áyá naaléi áyá aadáx̱ yei nasgit yé:* The implication here seems to be that the place that Raven fell from was even further away from Earth than the place to which spacecrafts go when in lunar orbit, but Zuboff does not say this in so many words here.

LINES 110, 111. *geesh, sú:* Zuboff begins to say «geesh kadootl» 'a bed of bull kelp', but seems to change his mind and then says «sú kadootl» 'a bed of giant kelp' here as well as in lines 120–21. These terms refer to two different species of sea plants. *Geesh* is 'bull kelp' although it is sometimes misidentified as giant kelp particularly when referring to detached leaves that can be difficult to distinguish. According to George Davis and Marge Dutson (who were consulted by Lance Twitchell for the translation of Susie James' texts), *sú* refers to 'giant kelp'. Naish and Story glossed «s'óh» (i.e., *sú*) as "long seaweed".*

LINE 114. *Gwál yeewuyáat':* Note the use of the irrealis form of the verb following *gwál* 'maybe'. The corresponding realis form would be *yeewooyáat'* 'it was a long time'.

LINE 124. *Éil' tlèin:* Note the emphatic pronunciation of *tlèin* 'great, big' with precipitously falling tone.

LINE 128. *Naasa.áa yáx̱ ash een kayaxát:* Literally, 'It (the kelp bed) was shaped like a *naasa.áa* with him'. The obsolete word *naasa.áa* refers to a kind of container; it is glossed separately as "woman's tool box (sewing box)" and "tool case" (the latter attributed to Yakutat) in Leer's "Lexical Binders". The word is borrowed most likely from some Athabaskan language (compare Proto-Athabaskan **na:səʔa:* 'container; pot, kettle', literally, 'it extends around; it encircles, surrounds'; compare also Navajo *názʼá* 'it extends in a circle; it loops around'), which was also borrowed into Eyak as *la:səʔah* '(large) pot'. It seems likely that the Athabaskan word originally had the broader sense of 'container', and the Tlingit adopted the word in the narrower sense of a specialized tool kit or a sewing kit. The original meaning of the Athabaskan word also changed into the more specific sense of 'pot, kettle', which we find in

* Naish and Story, *English-Tlingit Dictionary: Nouns*, 17.

Eyak as well. It thus appears most likely that the Athabaskan word in the original broad sense of 'container' was borrowed at an early date by the Tlingit—which would provide for enough time to narrow down the original meaning of the word—and was subsequently borrowed at a later date by the Eyak, among whom the word has essentially the same meaning as it does among the present-day Athabaskan peoples in Alaska and the Yukon Territory. De Laguna refers to Raven's wife's "sewing basket" as «Yeł nasA 'ayi»* and «Yeł naṡi' ayi».† The standardized spelling of de Laguna's forms would be *Yéil naasa.áayi*. De Laguna also appears to offer a picture of a woman's *naasa.áa*, consisting of a bag made from fish skin,‡ so we have translated Zuboff's usage as 'sewing kit'.

Notes to Robert Zuboff's tale II, episode VI, "Raven Makes the Aleutian Islands"

LINE 19. *l'éiw:* The translation of this word is usually 'sand' or even 'sand/y beach', but it can also mean 'gravel', as in this context where Raven later tosses *téix' sáani* 'small stones, pebbles'.

LINE 45. *yóo naakée:* The word *naakée* is usually translated 'north' in modern times but originally referred to 'upcurrent' in general. The Aleutian Islands are actually located to the west and southwest of Tlingit Country and the major current that flows through the Gulf of Alaska circulates northwest along Tlingit Country and southwest toward the Aleutian Islands, so Zuboff's use of *naakée* in this instance cannot be based either on magnetic North or on a sense of heading 'upcurrent' through the Gulf of Alaska. Rather, we take it to refer to the direction opposite of *ixkée*, which is often translated as 'down south' and tends to refer to the continental US. Hence, we have translated *naakée* unconventionally as 'west' in the text.

LINE 50. *lingit'aani teen:* We might expect *lingit'aaní teen* here and do not have a principled explanation for the loss of the tone on *-aaní*. The loss of tone in forms like *lingit'aanitukwáani* 'inhabitants of the earth' is explainable by the fact that this is a noun compound, but we do not regularly find instances of such tone loss before a postposition like *teen* 'with'.

Notes to Susie James' Stories

EDITORIAL BACKGROUND. Nora Dauenhauer copied the original recording of Susie James' performance onto cassettes in 1972 and transcribed the stories in

* De Laguna, *Under Mount Saint Elias*, 100.

† Ibid, 847.

‡ Ibid, 1045, plate 128, upper right.

1995. The manuscript was word processed with a printout date of February 21, 1995. It was proofread March 9, 1995 and reprinted March 22, 1995. The work lay dormant until a file update of May 14, 2006, and renewed activity began on September 13, 2011, with revisions by Lance Twitchell working with George Davis and Marge Dutson in 2012 and proofreading by James Crippen in 2017–18. The first two and a half minutes of the eighth episode, "Raven Gets Herself Married to a Killerwhale", were not originally transcribed by Dauenhauer, who presumably overlooked this portion in the process of transcribing it from cassette tape. This segment of the narrative was initially transcribed and translated by Crippen and Bessie Cooley in July of 2015. The final revisions to the whole of James' material—the transcriptions, translations, and notes—were done by Will Geiger and Jeff Leer in 2021–2023. In October 2023, Geiger located the segment used to complete the final episode and drafted the transcription and translation, which was subsequently reviewed and edited by Leer. Geiger and Leer consulted Kenneth Grant, Bessie Cooley, Sam Johnston, Florence Sheakley, and Ruth Demmert on particularly difficult issues of grammar and translation.

Notes to Susie James' episode i, "Raven and His Uncle"

LINES 2, 147. *K̲inyukookook̲éik:* James is the only storyteller in this volume to attest a name for Raven's mother. This character is discussed in §2.2 of the editors' introduction.

LINE 5. *tle a.een wé du káakch:* Here James says «du káak» 'his/her maternal uncle', in which we would have to interpret *du* 'him/her' as referring to Raven, so the line would mean 'his (Raven's) uncle slaughters her children'. However, James could have possibly misspoken here and intended to say *du éek'*, in which case *du* would refer to Raven's mother, and the line would mean 'her (Raven's mother's) brother slaughters her children'; this seems plausible based on the fact that in line 20 James impersonates the woman as saying, «ax̲ káak áwé» 'it's my uncle', but then abruptly revises this to «ax̲ éek' áwé» 'it's my brother'. We have transcribed the line as James pronounced it, rather than editorialize the line as *Du ÿátx'i áwé tle a.een wé du éek'ch* 'Her brother slaughters her children'. In the latter, the referent of *du* in *du ÿátx'i* 'her children' and in *du éek'ch* 'her brother' would be the same person.

LINE 8. *tle ash ják̲x̲:* Although the child was referred to in the preceding line with the pronoun *du*, here the child is referred to with the salient object pronoun *ash=*. The identity of the salient character regularly shifts throughout the beginning of James' narrative. Compare:

line 14:	yéi ash yawsik̲aa	he (Heron) said to her (the woman)
line 25:	ash ják̲x̲	it (the canoe) kills him (the woman's child)
line 37:	yóo ash yawsik̲aa	he (Heron) said to her (the woman)
line 61:	ash jeet awsitán	he (Tide-Commander) handed it to him (Raven)

The salient character referred to by *ash=* is initially the woman; it then shifts momentarily to the woman's successively murdered children, then back again to the woman, and finally to Raven. Upon line 61, Raven has become the salient character and remains so through the rest of the story. Curiously enough, it is particularly in conjunction with the verb *O-S-jaak̲~* 'for S to kill O' that we seem to find a predilection for the use of *ash=* referring to a character that we would not expect to be identified as the salient actor; see the note to AW iii, 43, 73, 74, 76, for discussion of that peculiarity.

LINE 13. *aatlèin:* James pronounces the final syllable of this word at an emphatic elevated pitch level. In other similar cases, the pitch starts at a fairly high level and then sharply fades, but here it sounds closer to a sustained high pitch.

LINE 15. *Wáa sáwé tsú x̲'ayeek̲á:* James pronounces the verb here with non-phonemic rounding of /x̲'/, sounding something like *x̲'wayeek̲á.*

LINE 20. *Ha yú ax̲ éek' áwé:* This line contains a false start that has been edited for clarity. The unaltered utterance is «Ha yú ax̲ káak áwé Yook̲is'kook̲éik—ax̲ éek' áwé Yook̲is'kook̲éik yóo duwasáakw» 'Well it's my uncle; Tide-Commander—my brother; Tide-Commander is his name', with James revising *ax̲ káak* 'my uncle' to *ax̲ éek'* 'my brother'. The character Yook̲is'kook̲éik is discussed in §2.3 of the editors' introduction.

LINE 26. *du eedé yóo x̲'ayax̲ak̲á:* Here *yóo x̲'ayax̲ak̲á* means roughly 'I am making oral noise like this', or 'I am carrying on like this (with oral noise)', referring to the fact that she is crying. *Du eedé* 'toward him/her' seems to refer to each of her children who have been sequentially murdered, and it is they that the woman is crying for, or literally 'toward'.

LINES 30–31. *Ch'a yaa k̲igeelt'éet ... yaa k̲ugatées':* Note the use of the progressive imperative forms «yaa k̲igeelt'éet» 'keep going along beachcombing' and, in the following line, «yaa k̲ugatées'» 'keep searching', both of which contain the non-imperfective progressive string *ÿaa=ga-.*

LINES 43–44. *yátx̲ du jee wsitee wé té, yátx̲:* Note the unusual afterphrase with essive suffix *-x̲* in line 44, which normally occurs only before the verb requiring an essive-case argument. We would expect an afterphrase such as this to lack the *-x̲* suffix, as simply *yát* 'child'.

LINE 83. *Ch'a yák'w {…} tle kéi awli̱gích:* This line was transcribed as «Ch'a yák'w áwé hú tle kéi awli̱gích» in an early draft of the manuscript and was accordingly translated 'He felled it in short order.' Upon relistening we did not hear *áwé hú* following *ch'a yák'w* 'right away', but we were unable to definitively resolve it. Leer thought he might have heard *Ch'a yák'w áyá a góo tle kéi awli̱gích*, which would translate something like, 'Right away he felled it at the base (of the tree)'. Geiger heard the line as *Ch'a yák'w {…} áwé tle kéi awli̱gích*, being unable to resolve one syllable after *ch'a yák'w*.

LINE 87. This line contains a false start. The unaltered utterance is «Át góot áwé, ‹Náa! Yáadu i x̱út'a—i shunax̱wáayi…›», where James clearly is about to say *i x̱út'ayi* 'your adze' but revises this to *i shunax̱wáayi* 'your axe'.

LINES 108–10, 112. These lines are whispered, impersonating Tide-Commander being squeezed against the wall as the octopus expands and fills the entire space of his house.

LINE 111. *ch'al cháa eex̱oox̱ kát!:* In the texts of James, alone among speakers in this volume, we find four instances of a special construction, which for convenience's sake we call the *ch'al … kát* construction. This construction begins with *ch'al* (underlyingly *ch'a=l*, literally 'just=not') followed by a negative attributive verb form plus *kát*. None of our consultants recognized this construction, so we are unable to translate it definitively, but it seems to have the flavor of '[You're acting] as if V (but this is a ridiculous notion)'. In James' "Raven Gets His Nose Yanked Off", we find «Ha ch'al yéi koogeix̱ kát yú taaÿ» (SJ X, 42) which we translate as 'Hah, as if those pieces of fat were all that big'; James seems to be humorously remarking on the fact that Raven went to great lengths in order to steal what were ultimately rather meager pieces of fat from fishermen's hooks. Two other instances are found in James' "Raven and the Daylight" in the voice of the mother of the young woman who has to console her daughter after she swallows (Raven in the form of) an evergreen needle and causes a commotion; James impersonates the woman as saying, «Ch'al igux̱sanei kát. … Ch'al ikgwajaḵ kát wé g̱ítgaa» (SJ XI, 147, 149), which we translate as 'That's not going to do anything to you. … As if that evergreen needle could kill you'. James' first example from this story, «ch'al cháa eex̱oox̱ kát», is especially challenging, since it includes the word *cháa*, which is unknown to us in this form; none of our consultants could recognize it either. This line had previously been translated as 'Well, isn't this what you asked for?', which suits the context. However, when taken alongside James' other examples, and while considering that *cháa* occurs in the expression *tlél cháa x̱'eití* 's/he is crabby, cantankerous' (more literally, 'his/her speech is not [of the] *cháa* [variety]', which implies that speech of the *cháa* variety is pleasant and ingratiating), and that (low-toned) *chaa* is a polite vocative term used by men to address other men, we have opted to translate this as, 'Well, as if that were a polite way to ask for it!' Raven appears to be acting as though he simply did what his uncle asked of him and that his uncle is now overreacting by aggressively insisting that Raven get rid of the octopus; of course, his uncle expected the giant creature to kill Raven and never wanted it inside his house.

LINE 123. *wé k̲[ées']*: James only pronounces the initial consonant of the word *k̲ées'* 'floodtide' here.

LINE 158. This line contains a false start. The unaltered utterance after the quotation is «yóo ash ÿawsik̲aa—aÿawsik̲aa» in which James initially says «yóo ash ÿawsik̲aa» 'she (Raven's mother) said to him (Raven)' but revises this to «yóo aÿawsik̲aa» 'he (Raven) said to her (his mother)'.

LINE 170. *Xáats't k̲adak̲eení:* See the note to FI I, i, 195, for discussion of the term *xáats'* being translated as 'firmament'.

LINE 172. *ei-ei-ei-ei:* This is said with a quavery voice, and you can almost imagine James moving a hand through the air like 'jazz hands' accompanying an image of Raven flying along high in the sky. It seems nearly translatable as 'look at him go-o-o-o!' Note that Italio makes the very same vocalization when Raven is flying up to the sky; compare FI I, ii, 1–2.

LINE 178. *yoo akayikkasinúkk:* We could not determine exactly what this verb phrase means with incorporated *kayik-* 'noise'. Compare the documented forms «tóo akayikkaawanúk» and «[tóo] akayikyanook», glossed as "had a premonition of it".* Perhaps Raven had to judge what was going on on the surface of the world by sound because his eyes were pointed up while he dangled by his beak from the sky.

LINE 179. *Gwál yéi unaléin gíyáa {...} de:* Before *de* 'now, already' we hear two syllables that sound approximately like *gu.á(h)* or *gu.áx̲*; the consonant we seem to hear following /á/ could be a distortion in the tape or some extraneous sound, so this might be a variant of the enclitic *gú.á* attested in Leer's "Verb Books" as «á gú.á», translated there as "or (what about) that one? (as an afterthought, something not previously considered)". Note also the irrealis form *yéi unaléin* following *gwál* 'maybe' and before *gíyáa* 'I suppose', both of which tend to select the irrealis form of the verb.

Notes to Susie James' episode ii, "Raven Makes the Aleutian Islands"

LINE 3. *Sú:* This seems to refer to giant kelp (*Macrocystis pyrifera*), according to photo identification with Marge Dutson and George Davis. A 'kelp bed' or 'kelp forest'

* Leer, "Verb Books".

is an underwater region with high densities of kelp. The tangled, matted surfaces of these beds and forest are referred to as 'kelp paddies'. Massive kelp paddies that are thoroughly enough matted and tangled can become island-like formations protruding from the surface of the ocean. It is this sort of formation that Raven is wishing to land on. The Tlingit names *sú kadootl*, literally 'tangle of giant kelp', *geesh kadootl* 'tangle of bull kelp', and *ḵájaa* 'kelp island' seem to refer to the paddy-like surface structures of kelp forests. Dutson also called these «kóoshdaa yaagú» 'land otter boat(s)' because the Land Otters would use these kelp islands as boats to lure people into coming with them.

LINES 5–6. *yóo áwé / tután:* Line 5 ends with a false start that cuts off just before the verb stem, with James uttering «yóo áwé ool—», almost certainly for *yóo áwé oolx̱éis'* 'that's what he's wishing' but revising this to *yóo áwé tután* 'that's what he's hoping for'.

LINE 12. *geesh:* Bull kelp or *geesh* is a large, monotypic species of kelp found along the Pacific coast of North America from about Monterey, California, to the Aleutian Islands. It is also known in English as ribbon kelp or bullwhip kelp, and is a long, tubular seaweed with a pod or air bladder at the end. From one end of the pod hang broad, ribbonlike blades, and from the other end extends a tube or stipe (stalk) up to thirty or forty feet long that resembles a bullwhip from which the popular name derives. Bull kelp is one of the most common seaweeds in its range.

LINE 20. *a káx' áwé wdzigeet:* James slaps her hand here as a sound effect for Raven landing on the kelp.

LINE 21. *Kudaseig̱ákw áwé tlax̱ niyís:* This phrase literally means 'He is catching his breath for good.'

LINE 22. *a kát satáan:* This phrase refers to a person or animal lying dead, unconscious, or unable to move, as opposed to *a kát sh istáan*, which refers to a person or animal that is conscious and capable of acting. This presents the image of Raven lying limp and motionless like a corpse on the surface of the kelp island after his freefall from the sky and hard landing.

LINE 23. *du daadé áwé aya.ax̱ji át:* The verb in this line is difficult to hear. We could clearly hear the stem *.ax̱ji*, so we construed it to be *aya.ax̱ji át* 'something (a creature) that he could hear'.

LINES 24, 39. *H-h-h-h!:* James produces what we have written as *H-h-h-h!* by drawing in breath with the vocal cords not completely apart, but this effect cannot be duplicated in writing.

LINE 28. *Yáxwch':* This is the name of the sea otter—also pronounced *yúxch'*. The sea otter was once prolific on the coast but was hunted nearly to extinction during the Russian colonial era. They are relatively common in certain areas of Tlingit Country and Alaska maintains the largest population of sea otters in the Pacific.

LINES 37–38. *k'aagú:* James impersonates Raven saying «k'aagú», which is a contraction of *k'e* 'why not...?', 'how about...?', '...should...', or 'it would be a good idea to...', which is a sentence-initial particle used for suggesting, combined with the imperative verb phrase *haagú!* 'come here!' A similar contraction *shk'áay* 'give (it) here!' occurs in Tongass Tlingit, from *shk'e haahée* 'give it here, why don't you'; *haahée* is the Hinyaa equivalent of Northern Tlingit *haadé ~ haandé* 'give (it) here'. Marge Dutson translated *k'aagú* with a diminutive meaning as, "come here, cutey!" Ruth Demmert understood *k'aagú* to be equivalent with *shk'e haagú*.

LINE 45. *Wáa sás i ÿát x̱'ex̱wdliyóo:* Note that James pronounces the verbal prefix here as *x̱'e-* rather than the more usual *x̱'a-*.

LINE 51. *Ch'áakw dateeyí:* We were unable to satisfactorily resolve this verb. On the recording it sounds like something close to *datseeyí* or *dadzeeyí*, which has an unrecognizable meaning. We were unable to verify the phrase *ch'áakw dateeyí*, as none of our Coastal or Interior consultants were able to confirm this phrase. Compare FD I, ii, 9, where we also appear to have heard *ch'áakw dateeyí*; however, in that case as well, it is a tenuous rendering of something poorly heard.

LINE 53. *ach x̱án:* Here James seems to pronounce the *ach* variant of the proximate pronoun, rather than the more commonly heard *ash*. It is possible that she does pronounce *ash*, but the sound might have gotten distorted on the recording, making it sound like *ach*. In all other cases, she pronounces *ash*; for example, *ash jeet* in line 56 shortly after.

LINE 54. *anax̱ kei sh wudix̱ích:* It is hard to hear the beginning of this line clearly because another present individual, presumably James' daughter Mary Pelayo, clears their throat loudly, obscuring the audio. James usually raises the tone of *kéi=* 'up', but it is pronounced low in this line and the next; this may possibly be conditioned by the preceding *anax̱* 'along it/there' in both lines.

LINES 59–60, 83. *Anóoshan Áanan tliyaanax̱.á:* We do not understand the exact reference here. The phrase *Anóoshan Áanan tliyaanax̱.á* literally means 'the far/other side of the Aleutian Islands', so it would seem that James is stating that the long rocky peninsula/island chain (*tax'aayí*) that Raven created is somewhere on the far side of the Aleutian Islands, rather than itself being the Aleutian Islands. Alternatively, it is possible that when James says *Anóoshan Áanan*, she is referring to the Alaska Peninsula and/or the nearest Aleutian Islands and is therefore claiming that the island chain is located on the far side of the Alaska Peninsula, which is geographically accurate. Raven appears to have formed the chain of islands starting from the furthest reaches of the chain and working toward the mainland, so we can picture him beginning perhaps somewhere between Attu Island and the Russian Commander Islands.

LINE 63. *daak áwé akanalít:* Note that the proclitic *daak=* 'inland' is followed here by the enclitic *áwé* before the verb word, which has the effect of emphasizing *daak=* 'inland'. Compare the more typical ordering in line 73, «Wé té áwé daak akanalít» '[Raven] was casting the rocks toward the mainland'.

LINE 82. *tax'aayí kwlaÿát':* James' choice of verb in «tax'aayí kwlaÿát'» 'a long rocky peninsula', which contains the *l-* classifier element, indicates that a rocky point or island chain is classified as a composite object, namely a strung-out object, such as a long beach or a village that looks like a string of houses to an observer on the ocean.

Notes to Susie James' episode iii, "Raven and Fire"

LINE 2. *ayagaaxdatéen:* This is a truncated contingent form equivalent to *ayagaaxdatéenín* 'whenever it is stormy' (the contingent is briefly discussed in appendix 1, §9.12).

LINE 8. *héit'át:* The demonstrative *héit'át* is literally 'that thing (nearby) over there' or 'this thing over here', referring to something (or more than one thing) not at hand but further away, somewhere in the general vicinity. The reference in this context is to the living things that are near Raven out on the peninsula.

LINE 14. *K'áxwk':* This character is discussed in §2.10 of the editors' introduction.

Notes to Susie James' episode iv, "Raven and the Salmon Box"

LINE 6. *tle a kaadé sixát wé kéidladi:* The word *kéidladi* refers to any kind of bird in the genus *Larus*, which are the gulls proper. Southeast Alaska is home to several species of gull, particularly the mew gull, herring gull, Thayer's gull, and glaucous-winged gull. Tlingit people do not generally differentiate between these different gull species. The verb phrase *aadé sixát* means something like 'it sticks out toward there'. The gulls are being described as an extended composite object that points toward the 'house' (i.e., the Kudatankahídi, or 'Salmon Box'), acting as a path to the site of interest. This is significant because gulls are often seen out on the water flying in circles around schools of fish. They try to catch fish as they near the surface and prey on injured fish when marine animals hunt from below. Raven has taken note of this because a large flock of gulls flying around over water means they have likely found food, and since Raven is always hungry this is a great opportunity for him.

LINE 8. *tlax̱ áwé l yóo akoojeek:* The verb phrase James uses here, *l yóo akoojeek*, could be literally translated as 'he exhibited no curiosity toward it' or 'he wasn't wondering about it', the implication being that Raven didn't need to ponder the situation and already understood the significance of what he was looking at. But how to translate this sentence in the context where Raven is asking «Daa sákwshíyúgé?» 'Whatever can that be?' remains a challenge for us. Note that if this is a declarative statement it is interesting that James uses the negative particle *l* rather than the more usual *tlél*. We can compare an instance in the story «Aak'wtaatseen» told by Cyril George on April 18, 2013, where he states, «Hasdu íx̱t'ích tléil yoo kawujeeyí áyá»,* which literally seems to mean 'when their shaman came to be incurious about it'; in practical terms, however, this means something closer to 'when their shaman came to the point of no longer wondering about it', i.e., 'when their shaman knew what it was and what to do about it'. In that context, the shaman has determined that a salmon wearing a necklace was in fact the boy named Aak'wtaatseen who had disappeared from their village.

LINES 13–14. *aadóo sgé ḵaa x̱ooníx̱ nax̱sateeyí:* As usual, Raven wants to find 'relatives' who can assist him, willingly or not, in his schemes. The term *ax̱ x̱ooní* 'my relative' traditionally refers to any person of the same moiety as the speaker. In modern Tlingit it has become extended to refer to any person with whom the speaker has a friendly relationship, i.e., 'my friend'.

LINE 15. *yaa ḵunalwás' áwé, «Aadóo sgé ḵóot g̱adashee?»:* The postpositional phrase *ḵóo-t* 'to someone, people' is the classical Tlingit form that now coexists alongside the more modern form *ḵaa ée-t*.

LINES 20–22. These lines are whispered, apparently for dramatic effect.

LINE 37 AND THROUGHOUT. *X̱'anax̱.waatg̱waayáa:* The usual name given to this character is *X̱'anax̱gaatwaayáa*. In James' version of the name, the consonants /g̱/ and /w/ are metathesized and the /g̱/ is rounded to /g̱w/. This character is discussed in §2.17 of the editors' introduction.

LINE 43. *a kat'óotx̱ áwé daaḵ ÿaawatán:* The relational noun (*a*) *kat'óot* 'partway, halfway up (it)' here refers to partway up the side of the house and thus up along the wall. It is especially to be noted that the final /t/ of *kat'óot* is not the punctual postposition *-t*; rather, it is part of the noun stem. Here *a kat'óot* is followed by the pertingent

* MC032, series 4, box 4, item 1.

postposition -*x̱*, forming part of the derivational string *NP-x̱ daak̲=ÿa-u-* (∅) 'hanging up along NP'. Compare the sentence with a transitive form of the same verb, *áx̱ daak̲ ayaawatán* 'he (X̱'anax̱.waatg̱waayáa) hung it (the Octopus Tentacle Cane) there', which occurs two lines below.

LINE 48. *k̲aax̱'awóos' ash jeet aawatée:* Literally this means 'he (X̱'anax̱.waatg̱waayáa) handed a question to him (Raven)'. In Leer's "Verb Books" we find the possessed forms «du atx̱'awóos'i» and «du k̲aax̱'awóos'i», which look like 'his thing's question' and 'his person's question', respectively, but both, according to Leer's gloss, apparently simply mean "his question".

LINE 51. *Tlél aadé i jeetx̱ nak̲waataani yé ch'a tleix̱:* Literally this means, 'I couldn't take it from you forever.' Raven is of course lying here. The first thing he does upon entering the Salmon Box is hide the Octopus Tentacle Cane inside of it.

LINE 57. *ash ée akawdli.aax̱ wé shí:* James begins rapidly knocking on the table at this point. She may either be mourning her loss of memory for the song or perhaps trying to 'drum up' the song in her mind.

LINE 59. *yú hít g̱unayéi saxíxni yánde:* At the end of this line James trails off her drumming, raps sharply, and then says the next line. This seems to be a kind of punctuation indicating that she is unable to recall the song she has mentioned and at this point gives up.

LINE 66. *ch'a yá haanaa:* The word *haanaa* is a contraction of *haa-niÿaa*, which means 'this direction'. The element *haa*(*n*)- here is not the first-person plural possessive pronoun but rather the cislocative pronoun that indicates a location nearby the speaker, i.e., 'over here, over this way'. This is the same cislocative pronoun seen in, e.g., *haan-dé* '(give it) here' and *haa-t uwagút* 'he came here'. In this sentence we translate *haanaa* as '[toward himself,] this way'. Compare also line 68, «haanaa kaawaháa» 'it shifted this way'.

LINE 66. *ch'a a yahaayí kát áwé ax'aatán:* We can reconstruct the verb phrase used here as follows: beginning with *a kát atán* 's/he has it (wooden object) lying/resting on it' and adding the incorporated noun *x'aa-* 'point, tip' we arrive at *a kát ax'aatán* 's/he has the tip of it (wooden object) lying/resting on it'. In this case, Raven has the tip of the Octopus Tentacle Cane resting on the silhouette (*a yahaayí*) of the Salmon Box.

LINE 67. *daak̲ k'ul'gasteech:* The classificatory verb pair of the positional theme *O-s-tee*` 'for (composite) O to lie' and the motion theme *O-S-s-tee*` 'for S to move (composite) O' refers to objects such as woven bags, among other things. So we find, e.g., *daak̲ awsitée* 's/he put it (composite object) away'. This can be modified by adding one of two incorporated nouns, *x̱'e-*, referring to a top-heavy bag, for instance; and *k'ul'-*, referring to a bottom-heavy bag. So in this instance *daaḵ k'ul'gasteech* refers to the Salmon Box as if it were a bottom-heavy bag. Similarly, the original *Ishkahít*, said to have been built with a platform extending over a deep hole in the Chilkat River, was described by David Johnston to Leer as «át k'ul'satéen» 'it sits there (like a bottom-heavy bag)'.* Note also that *daaḵ k'ul'gasteech* is a progressive habitual verb form; the prefix *ga-* here is the mark of the non-imperfective progressive modes.

LINE 76. *X̱'aṉax̱.waatg̱waayáa-áa-áa-áa, x̱áat idashée-ée-ée-ée!:* This line is chanted, impersonating Raven singing.

LINES 79–81. *Ch'u yéi adaaÿaḵaayí áwé deisgwách {...} / ÿán ÿaa aÿanadláḵ. / Deisgwach ÿán ÿaa aÿanadláḵ, ch'u yéi adaaÿaḵaaÿí:* These lines together provide an excellent example of a chiasmus, with the same complex sentence repeated but with the order of clauses reversed.

LINE 88. *Héi'!:* James claps once right after this exclamation, presumably a gestural punctuation of the astonishment that Raven experiences when walking inside the Salmon Box, perhaps along the lines of exclaiming 'I'll be darned!'

LINE 92. *s'áax̱':* This refers to gray cod or Pacific cod. It is related to the famous Atlantic cod and may be the same species as Greenland cod.

LINE 96. *át kawdziheeni át áyú shaawahík:* The verbs *O-sha-heek~* (∅) 'for O to be full' and *O-sha-tl'éet'~* (∅) 'for O to be full (of liquid)', together with their causative counterparts, regularly take an unmarked complement without postposition, denoting what the container is full of. In this case the Salmon Box is full of «át kawdziheeni át» 'creatures that swim around'.

LINE 100. *shaakaḵáaw̱oo:* This sounded to us like *shaakḵáanu*, but we believe that the beginning of the word was actually *shaa-ka-* 'mountain-on', rather than *shaak-* 'head (of river)', and what we write as ⟨w̱⟩ actually sounds more or less like an /n/; as far as the latter point is concerned, we don't really understand what transpired from an articulatory point of view.

LINE 104. *shikax̱úx̱s'i tóox':* James clearly says «shikax̱úx̱s'» rather than the more common form *shukax̱úx̱s'* 'lyrics'.

LINE 107. *i shatx̱ix̱úx̱:* We do not know the identity of the person James is referring to. It is apparently the husband of an older sister of James' daughter Mary Pelayo, who recorded this performance.

* Personal communication, David Johnston to Leer.

LINE 112. *yéi ash yawsik̲aa:* This line comes after a long discursus about the song Raven uses to activate the power of the Octopus Tentacle Cane by invoking the name of X̲'anax̲.waatg̲waayáa, so the identity of the participants in the activity has not been established. We can justifiably only take the salient object pronoun *ash=* to refer to Raven here; the identity of the subject remains unclear, but we take it to refer to a member of Raven's crew, which James goes on to discuss in the lines immediately following.

LINES 123–24. *ldakát yéide / aléet yá aanx'i tóode:* The point of this section, translating 's/he was (or, they were) flinging them into all the villages every which way', remains a mystery to us. We are unable to determine who is throwing what, and what significance this has in the sequence of events. From the surrounding lines, it seems most likely that Raven is scattering barbecue sticks, but the songbirds seem to already be using the barbecue sticks to cook the food that Raven will go on to steal from them.

LINE 128. *S'íx'g̲aa sháax̲ awdzitee:* In Charlie Joseph's telling of "Raven and Eulachon",* Raven similarly places moss on his head to scare people away from a fish barbecue. This thus appears to be one of Raven's recurring tricks, perhaps hearkening back to a now forgotten dance or performance where a man would put moss on his head and scare people. Other Northwest Coast groups have dances involving a wild man covered with moss and lichen, so this may be distantly related to Raven's behavior. In the phrase *S'íx'g̲aa sháax̲ awdzitee*, the *d-* element of the classifier stands in for the null reflexive possessor of *shá* 'head'. To this is added *P-x̲* (*g̲a*) 'down onto P'. The underlying verb theme is *O-S-tee*ˋ 'for S to handle O (generic object)', to which is added the configurational fricative classifer element *s-*, which refers to a composite object, in this case moss. Putting them all together, we end up with *sháa-x̲ a-ÿu-d-s-i-tee* 'head-down·on·to it-PERF-self's-COMPOSITE-REALIS-put', i.e., 'he (Raven) put it (moss) down onto his own head'.

LINE 132. *At gaÿis.í! Kk̲watáa:* It would be quite usual for *kuk̲atáa* 'I will sleep' to contract to *kk̲watáa* after a word ending in a vowel in the same clause, but here the contraction occurs even though there is an intervening clause boundary.

LINE 137. *yú l'éiw:* James uses the word *l'éiw* 'sand' here to refer to a beach. Although Tlingit has two words *éek̲* and *neech* that can be translated as 'beach', as well as *yán* 'shore, mainland', none of these terms immediately conjures up the conventional English image of a sandy beach from a Tlingit perspective. Most beaches in Tlingit Country are either rocky or gravelly as the result of the relatively gentle sheltered waters, along with many tidal mudflats where shallow bays and river mouths have

* MC005, tape 16.

silted up. Sandy beaches are rare and even more rare are those with white sand. The greatest sandy beaches in Tlingit Country are found along the Gulf Coast near Yakutat where rivers dump their great burdens of glacial silt and the winter storms of the Gulf of Alaska and the northern Pacific relentlessly hammer the shore.

LINE 140. *móon:* The recording is distorted at the beginning of this line, so it is not entirely clear what James is saying. It seems like she uses the English word 'moon', as we have transcribed it, but we do not understand how she is connecting the position of the 'moon' with the location of the sand beach or why she would choose to code-switch rather than use the Tlingit word *dís* 'moon'.

LINE 142. *yóo k̲uwanéekw du x̲'oos:* Literally, 'his feet were behaving like that.' Phonetically, the stem here sounds something like *nyóokw*.

LINE 147. *yú Atkudatankahídi:* This is apparently a variation on the name *Kudatankahídi*. See §2.18 of the editors' introduction for further discussion of this entity and its name(s).

LINES 150–51. *yú yaakw—yú hít:* These lines contain a false start that we did not edit out of the text because it seems to demonstrate that, even for James herself, the physical form of the Salmon Box is not entirely clear. Referring to the Salmon Box, James first calls it «yú yaakw» 'that ship (or canoe, boat)', pauses, and then seems to correct this to «yú hít» 'that house'.

Notes to Susie James' episode v, "Raven Goes Down Along the Bull Kelp"

TITLE. This story was originally given the Tlingit title «Yéil K̲ées' Akanasdáa» (literally, 'When Raven Set the Floodtide Flowing') and the English title "Raven and the Tide Lady" by Nora Dauenhauer. It has been changed here to «Yéil Geesh Daax̲ Wugoodí» (literally, 'When Raven Went Down Along the Bull Kelp') with the English title "Raven Goes Down Along the Bull Kelp"; the Tlingit title is an allusion to the formal title used for the crest image of Raven descending down along the bull kelp in this story, *Geesh Daax̲ Woogoodi Yéil* 'Raven Who Went Down Along the Bull Kelp'. For an example of a reference to an item of *at.óow* which depicts this crest and bears this title in its name, see Jessie Dalton's speech in *Haa Tuwunáagu Yís*, in which she mentions the *Geesh Daax̲ Woogoodi Yéil K'oodás'* 'Raven-Who-Went-Down-Along-the-Bull-Kelp Tunic',* a woven tunic depicting Raven in the process of descending.

* Photographs of the tunic can be found in Dauenhauer and Dauenhauer, *Haa Tuwunáagu Yís*, 91–92, and it is mentioned in Jessie Dalton's speech (ibid, 244–45, 248–51, 385).

LINE 3. *K̲ées' Yax̲ Ashakawdzinugu Shaanák'w:* See §2.9 of the editors' introduction for discussion of this character.

LINE 7. *Leineitk'óoxk'u:* See §2.11 of the editors' introduction for discussion of the character Little Mink, whom James refers to variously as «Leineitk'óoxk'u» and «Lukshiyáank'», both of which mean 'Little Mink'.

LINE 15. *Kakax̲duk̲éin k'oodás' káx':* On the one hand, Geiger points out that *kakax̲duk̲éin* has the appearance of a contingent verb form (equivalent with *kakax̲duk̲éinín*; the variation between the contingent suffix forms -(*n*) and -(*n*)*ín* is briefly described in appendix 1, §9.12). In this case, we would translate *kakax̲duk̲éin* as 'whenever [beads] are sewn' and lines 15–16 could be interpreted as «Áwé kakax̲duk̲éin k'oodás' káx' yéi / Geesh Daax̲ Woogoodi Yéil yóo duwasáakw» 'When beads are sewn on a tunic like this / it is referred to as Raven Down Along the Bull Kelp'. On the other hand, Leer suggests that *kakax̲duk̲éin* may be a variant of what appears in the *Interior Tlingit Noun Dictionary* as «kaxhdukhés'ákw» (i.e., *kax̲duk̲és'ákw*), glossed as "patchwork blanket, crazy quilt",* and in Naish and Story's *English-Tlingit Dictionary* as «kux̲dook̲és'uk̲w» (i.e., *kax̲duk̲és'ák̲w*), glossed as "crazy quilt"† where perhaps the suffix *-ákw* was misheard as *-ák̲w*. If Leer's supposition is correct, *kakax̲duk̲éin k'oodás'* would be a noun compound referring to a jacket with quilting. Regardless, we are taking James' reference to be to a ceremonial tunic displaying the image of Raven going down the bull kelp. A photograph of such a tunic can be seen in Dauenhauer and Dauenhauer, *Haa Tuwunáagu Yís*, 91–92.

LINE 17. *Héen takaadé ÿax̲ ÿagút:* The verb form *ÿax̲ ÿagút* 'he tried going' is an example of the now rarely encountered conative derivation, which is formed with *ÿax̲=i-* plus an invariably short high-toned stem. In all examples we have found, it translates 'trying to V' (see appendix 1, §12).

LINE 22. *G̲altóode awditee:* The inalienable noun *g̲altú* 'pocket' is the most common variant of a word that also appears as *g̲atltú* or *k̲atltú*. This is composed of the reduced form of the inalienable noun (*du*) *k̲aatl* '(his/her flank' plus (*a*) *tú* 'inside (it)'. The *d-* element of the classifier in *awditee* refers to the covert reflexive possessor (i.e., Raven) of *g̲altú*; compare *du g̲altóode aawatee* 's/he put it in his/her pocket', (i.e., into a different person's pocket).

LINE 23. *Gwál x̲'waash gíyú:* The word *x̲'waash* is glossed in the second edition of *English-Tlingit Dictionary: Nouns* as "large sea urchins".‡ In his *Tlingit Dictionary*, Lance Twitchell glosses *x̲'waash* as "red sea urchin | largest urchin found in the Pacific

* Leer, Hitch, and Ritter, *Interior Tlingit Noun Dictionary*, T·34.

† Naish and Story, *English-Tlingit Dictionary: Nouns*, 42.

‡ Davis, *English-Tlingit Dictionary: Nouns*, 36.

Northwest • color of spines varies: may be red, brick red, pink, purple, or even maroon. [...] (*Strongylocentrotus franciscanus*)".* As Twitchell suggests, the red sea urchin is the larger of the two commercially harvested species of urchins in Southeast Alaska and so can be identified as *x̱'waash*, and the green sea urchin as *nées'*.

LINE 28. *neil wujiḵáḵ:* This verb is a subtle pun. When used in reference to birds (and airplanes) the verb phrase *áa wjiḵaaḵ* means 'it landed there'. When a human or other flightless animal is the subject the same verb phrase instead means 'he squatted (i.e., assumed a squatting position) there'.

LINE 31. *X̱at sawli.áat':* This verb form appears to be an unexpected variant of *x̱at sawli.át'* 'it made me cold', which occurs in line 44. The slime or juice of some crustaceans is called *áat'lani* which appears to contain the verb root *.áat'*~ 'cold'; compare *áat'ch x̱at uwajáḵ* 'I'm hypothermic' (lit. 'cold has killed me'). Perhaps this linguistic consideration ties in with the theme of Raven claiming to have been chilled by consuming the sea urchins. Further, the Dauenhauers had noted in their draft manuscript of this story that a side effect of consuming sea urchins as well as some other shellfish is that one becomes or feels cold.

LINE 35. *Gwátk sá woolaay̱i léin áwé a kát eeyaṉís'?:* The intransitive verb *aawanís'* means 'he ate sea urchins', and *eeyanís'* is the same verb with a second-person singular subject. To gather sea urchins the normal way there must be a very low tide. The little old lady addressing Raven here is keeping the tidewaters elevated, so she does not believe that Raven could have obtained sea urchins. But Raven has obtained them by having Little Mink go down along the kelp stalk to the bottom of the ocean. Compare line 41, which is in essence the same formula with a few minor differences. This formula as used by Italio, James, and Dick is compared in §2.9 of the editors' introduction.

LINE 37. *{...} nagú gánde!:* We were unable to make out the first word in this line on the recording.

LINE 46. *a díx̱'náx̱ ayag̱atánch:* James plunks her finger on the table a few times during this line. See note to FI I, ii, 75, for further discussion of this moment in the plot.

LINE 49. *{...}:* This verb phrase is nearly unintelligible on the recording. To us it sounds approximately like *wux̱ gút*, but we can find no clear resolution. What sounds like *wux̱* could be *yux̱=* 'outside', but this proclitic requires *na-* conjugation, so we would expect *yux̱ nagóot* 'when he went outside' in a consecutive form.

* Twitchell, *Tlingit Dictionary*, 169, accessed online with date of last modification given as November 28, 2023.

LINE 51. James begins clapping her hands here as a sound effect for Raven repeatedly stabbing the urchin spines into the little elder's butt. She continues the slapping until the beginning of line 53.

LINE 52. *A dex̱'k'idaat:* The relational noun *dex̱'k'idaa* is composed of *dex̱'-* 'back', *k'i-* 'base', and *daa* 'around'. Here the combination is translated as 'over her butt', but perhaps the phrase 'over her sacral curve' would be more technically accurate. Nora Dauenhauer revised 'back' to 'butt' in an earlier draft, which translation we have retained here.

LINE 58. *Yéex̱:* This appears to be a rare interjection that we have not been able to verify with our consultants.

LINE 59. *Ch'a goox' sáwé, «Gidzanóok'!:* The phrase preceding the quote is elliptic and we are unsure of its exact meaning. On the name and character Gidzanóok', see §2.12 of the editors' introduction.

LINE 66. *Aag̱áa áwé yeisú dé:* James again slaps her hands a few times during this line as a sound effect for Raven stabbing the spines into the little elder's butt. Each of the four fluent elders we consulted about the phrase *yeisú déi*—Ruth Demmert, Kenneth Grant, Florence Sheakley, and Sam Johnston—independently confirmed the translation of *yeisú déi* as 'finally' or 'at last'; the contrast presented to them was between *yeisú neil uwagút*, which was uniformly interpreted as "he just came inside" (i.e., only a moment ago), and *yeisú déi neil uwagút*, which was translated as "at last he came inside" or "he finally came inside" (i.e., after being delayed or out longer than expected). Demmert suggested that the manner in which James uses *yeisú déi* in the narrative imparts a sense of incredulity or amazement, in Demmert's words, "almost like she [Susie James, the narrator] couldn't believe it". This phrase appears to be quite formulaic for James, occurring eleven times throughout this extended tale.* We have tried to reflect this formulaic quality of the phrase by translating it consistently as 'now at last'.

LINE 71. *Á áwé tsu:* James again slaps her hands for sound effect in this elliptical sentence.

LINES 89, 94, 97. *a x̱'atóox̱ axáash … a x̱'atóode axáash:* The implication here seems to be that the locations along the beach at which Raven sliced into the cods' mouths marked off certain extremes to which the tide was to rise once it resumed its proper cycle. See note to lines 103–06 for further discussion.

* SJ v, 66; viii, 60; ix, 28, 100, 147; xi, 274, 91–92, 305.

LINE 91. *Daak̲ kagadéini:* Note the progressive conditional form *daak̲ kagadéini* 'when the tide starts coming up'; the corresponding non-progressive conditional form would be *daak̲ kadéini* 'when the tide comes up'. Conditional forms are typically interpreted as 'if V' or 'when V (in the future)'; when used in a narrative that is set in a past, the reference is to the future relative to the 'now-window' of the events in the narrative, rather than the now-window of the narrator's performance. That is, *daak̲ kagadéini* here means 'when the tide starts coming up (in the future relative to Raven's actions in the narrative sequence)' rather than 'when the tide starts coming up (in the future relative to James' utterance)'.

LINES 95–96. *hóoch'i aayí—nas'gi.aa:* We don't know what the relationship is between the *hóoch'i aayí* 'last one' and the *nas'gi.aa* 'third one', which refer to iterations of Raven cutting the cods' mouths to mark points to which the tides will rise and recede. She seems to either be saying, 'the last one—[or rather,] the third one...' or, 'the last one—[by which I mean] the third one...'. She has already described Raven marking the extreme high and low points of the spring tide, the extreme high of which would reach the *aas shuwee* 'base of the tree(s)'.

LINE 101. *Daak̲ at kadujéil tlein:* This is an interesting and unusual instance of *tlein* following a verb, which in this case is a consecutive verb form.

LINES 103–06. *Nas'gidooshú yeekáx' áwé / daak̲ kakg̲wadéich, ... / léin wúx̲ k̲a léin ÿát':* It is difficult to determine with much certainty the significance of this statement, which is attributed to Raven as a command to the tide about how its cyclic movements would be structured after the period of tidal stagnation caused by Little-Elder-Who-Enlarged-the-Tide. In the world today, tides vary over the course of the day, the month, and the year. Tlingit Country experiences 'mixed semidiurnal' tides, so there are generally two high tides and two low tides each day, and the amplitude of these two tidal swings are typically not equal—one of the high tides will usually be higher than the other. The variation in tidal amplitude that occurs over the month is influenced by many factors, and it matters which kind of 'month' one considers. The calendar month does not track well with the tidal cycles; however, the lunar 'synodic' month (the passage of time between two identical successive phases of the moon, e.g., from one full moon to the next full moon) follows, or rather, generates, a meaningful tidal cycle. Each synodic month there are two spring tides (*léin ÿát'* lit. 'long tideflat') and two neap tides (*léin wúx̲* lit. 'neap tide tideflat'). Spring tides are those with the greatest amplitude (highest high tides and lowest low tides) of the synodic month and neap tides are those with the least amplitude (lowest high tides and highest low tides) of the synodic month. Because there are numerous other astronomical forces that affect tidal amplitude and the tidal cycles in general, such as the varying angle of declination of the moon's ecliptic path around the Earth relative to the Earth's ecliptic plane around the sun, the cycle of the tides is not a perfectly repetitious pattern, so finding a clear pattern of eight involves a fair amount of abstraction from the observable behavior of the tide. Bear in mind that four and eight are considered 'whole', 'ideal', or 'complete' numbers in Tlingit. If one were to consider the two tidal cycles that occur each day as individual units, at a fairly abstract and impressionistic level one could discern a repeating cycle of: spring tide, six intervening tides, and then neap tide—eight in total. This is a fairly speculative hypothesis, but we suggest here that James' account of Raven cutting the cods' mouths in certain locations and commanding the tide that it is to always rise to eight places refers to the general pattern of eight diurnal tidal cycles between each quarter of the synodic month, e.g., from the new moon (spring tide) to the first quarter moon (neap tide).

LINE 111. *át ishk̲úx̲:* This is an instance of the relatively obscure positional verb theme *S-d-sh-k̲oox̲~* 'for S to be in a comfortable position'. Compare the entry in Leer's "Lexical Binders", *a shóox' isk̲úx̲x̲* 'is making himself comfortable for it (e.g., food)' (perhaps mistranscribed for *a shóox' ishk̲úx̲x̲*).

Notes to Susie James' episode vi, "Raven Loses His Eyeballs"

LINES 15–16. *Tle aan woo.aat / wé du x̲úx̲ wé shaawát:* The pronominal reference here is not clear, but we feel that the subject is likely the woman and *aan* means 'with him', i.e., 'with her husband', i.e., 'with Raven'. Note that the plural verb stem *.aat~* indicates that more than one person was walking, even though the subject *wé shaawát* 'the woman' is singular; this use of a plural verb stem is usual when *P een* 'with P' (in this case, *aan* 'with him/her/it') precedes the verb.

LINE 17. *Ax̲ waak̲ … ax̲ waagí:* Note that at the beginning of this line Raven uses the unalienated form *ax̲ waak̲* 'my eyes', but at the end of the line he uses the alienated form *ax̲ waagí* 'my eyes (detached from self)', indicating that he has now removed his eyes from the sockets.

LINE 20. *yóo x̲'ayakg̲wak̲áa:* Typically, this verb theme takes the prefix *x̲'e-* 'mouth' (which usually surfaces as /x̲'a-/) only in the basic imperfective, e.g., *yéi x̲'ayak̲á* 'he says so'. Here James surprisingly includes this prefix in a future form. The expected future form would be *yóo yakg̲wak̲áa* 'so they (my eyes) will say'. Note that we find the same phenomenon in AH I, iii, 241, «yéi x̲'ayakk̲wak̲áa» 'I will say so'.

LINE 26. *{...:}:* The first part of this line was too difficult for us to decipher from the recording, so we didn't venture a transcription. We can gather from the context that it is likely a statement having to do with the location of the cooking pot.

LINE 45. *Ch'u kanat'á wé du waaḵx̱ {dax̱ kasitee}:* James is laughing during this line, making it difficult to hear the final verb to our satisfaction. If our rendering is correct, *du waaḵx̱ dax̱ kasitee* would translate 'they each (two blueberries) were his eyes', but we have set the verb phrase in braces to indicate our uncertainty.

LINE 47. *Tléil at ÿáx̱ ḵoonook:* This line is the basis for the overall title of the tale, «L At Yáx̱ Ḵoowanoogu Yéil» "Raven Who Flouts Convention" (the title being the attributive form corresponding to James' declarative negative imperfective form used in this line). On the recording it sounds like James pronounces *at yáx̱* 'like things' as *adáx̱*, which is why we have written this as *at ÿáx̱*. In nearly all cases, the postposition (*a*) *yáx̱* 'like (it)' is attested with initial /y/ (phonetically [j]), but instances such as this, in which the initial approximant is suppressed following an obstruent consonant, suggest that in James' speech the underlying form is (*a*) *ÿáx̱*, with initial/ÿ/ (phonetically [ɰ]). There are occasional references that suggest some other speakers also used this form. For instance, Leer's "Lexical Binders" contain the Tongass form «ay̱ax̱ awe» alongside the Hinyaa «áy̱éx̱ áwé», both of which are glossed as "that's right" (Leer's ⟨y̱⟩ is an older notation that was later replaced by ⟨ÿ⟩); all other entries there are written with initial ⟨y⟩.

LINES 48, 49, 63. *Ḵunaa:* This is the Tlingit placename for Redoubt Bay.*

Notes to Susie James' episode vii, "Raven Hosts a Potlatch"

LINE 1. James pronounces «át uwaḵux̱u wé» here, with *ÿé* 'place' rounded to *wé*.

LINE 17. *wáa sá kaawahayi át áwé haat keeyajél:* The phrase *wáa sá kaawahayi át* is difficult to translate. Possible translations of *wáa sá kaawaháa* include 'how is it?' and 'what condition is it in?' The translation in the text is based on Ruth Demmert's translation of the whole line, "what are they for, these things you've brought?"

LINE 19. *wé du x̱úx̱:* James seems to pronounce a syllable between *du* and *x̱úx̱* in this line, but we could neither decipher it nor think of what element could be inserted between the possessor *du* 'his/her' and the inalienable noun *x̱úx̱* 'husband'. During this line, someone apparently enters the room where the recording was taking place and asks James' daughter if she is ready to go home, momentarily interrupting the narration. After this brief pause James resumes by repeating the sentence «L ash ḵ'adaat tooshtí wé du x̱úx̱», where she clearly pronounces «wé du x̱úx̱» with no intervening syllable.

LINE 25. *neildé áwé ÿanduwaxoon:* Leer points out that Swanton's *Tlingit Myths and Texts* contains examples of verb forms where we seem to find /n/ instead

* Thornton, *Haa Léelk'w Hás Aaní Saax'ú*, 102, m#457.

of a syllable-final /w/ in perfective forms; two such examples found in the story "Moldy-End" told in Tlingit by Kadashan are «tc! A wā´SA cū´KAn duwAdjā´ tc!A ayA´x qōwanū´k^{u}»[*] (i.e., *ch'a wáa sá shukanduwajáa ch'a ayáx̱ ḵoowanook*, 'just as he was instructed, that's how he acted') and «Dugā´wu dūłi yêx kandudjîxî´t»[†] (i.e., *Du gaawú dóol yéx̱ kandujixít* 'He painted his drum like a loon'). Note that these verb themes for 'instructing' and 'painting, writing' are both inherently Ø-conjugation, so the *na-* prefix cannot be taken to be a conjugation marker in these forms. In the case of James' *ÿanduwaxoon*, however, this verb has the appearance of a 'processional' imperfective, like, e.g., *has naa.aat* 'they are going in procession' or *góos' naagáas'* 'clouds are passing by'. We agree that the latter interpretation is preferable; from the context it is clear that people are entering in procession.

LINE 32. *yá g̱il'tú áwé yéi kaaxát:* James likely gestured with her hands while saying *yéi kaaxát* 'it is shaped like this'.

LINE 33. *Tsàa:* James pronounces the noun *Tsaa* 'Seal(s)' here with dramatically falling tone, going rapidly from quite high to quite low. This is another example of emphatic tone modification, discussed further in §3.10.4 of the editors' introduction.

LINE 38. *has kax̱wlawóowag̱u aa hás:* This phrase contains the decessive attributive perfective form *has kax̱wlawóowag̱u* 'from whom I have removed the sterna'. The verb theme here is formed with the derivational string *O-ka-u-S-l-*NOUN*-áḵw* 'for S to remove NOUN from O; for S to de-NOUN O'; here the noun is the inalienable noun *wóow* 'chest, sternum'. This same verb theme occurs in lines 66, 68, and 76. When checking this form with Ruth Demmert, she provided the form *kax̱wlis'aag̱áḵw* 'I de-boned it', in which the noun is *s'aaḵ* 'bone'.

LINE 42. *X'áat'idaaÿéejayi:* In his manuscript "Tlingit and Eyak Flora and Fauna Terms", Harrington identified this bird as a black turnstone and rendered the name as «ç'wat' […] taa íitja ii» (i.e., *x'wat'daaÿéejaÿi*) with unexplained rounding of the initial consonant.[‡] Naish and Story translate this as "plover; sandpiper".[§] In Leer's "Lexical Binders" we find a number of variants from various sources: Nikolai Petrovich Rezanov and Saint Veniaminov provided forms that can be interpreted either as *x'áat'daaÿéejaÿi* or more likely *x'at'daaÿéejaÿi*; Kelly and Willard attested

---

* Swanton, *Tlingit Myths and Texts*, 313.

† Ibid, 318.

‡ Harrington, "Flora and Fauna Terms", 146.

§ Naish and Story, *English-Tlingit Dictionary: Nouns*, 22. Their original spellings are «x'ut'dah yéejeiyee» and «x'ut'dah yeejuyee», which would be standardized as *x'at'daayéejeiyi* and *x'at'daayéejayi,* respectively (tone supplied in the latter). We strongly suspect that the first of these forms was misheard and that in both instances the speakers with whom Naish and Story worked actually said *x'at'daayéejayi.*

«x̱'al'daayéiyi»; and Leer attested the Tongass form «x̱'aldaa`ye̱e˙ji».* Elizabeth Nyman attested the form «x'at'daayéejayi», with short *x'at'*-, and identified it as a "black turnstone".† It is noteworthy that here James pronounces this word in the same way that it occurs in the song, *X'áat'idaaÿéejayi*, with no reduction of the vowel length or tone of *x'áat'*- and with the vowel /i/ following it; the vowel /i/ seems likely to have been introduced for the purpose of fitting the words to the melody of the song.

LINE 45. *Yéil du ḵ'ush.eetí káa yawlishóo:* Note that instead of the usual *du x̱'us.eetí* 'his footprints', the song lyrics contain the pejorative variant *du ḵ'ush.eetí*. The fricative element *l*- of the classifier in the verb *yawlishóo* is configurational and thus seems to convey an image of the Plovers' multiple individual trails converging and diverging so as to form a network of tracks superimposed over Raven's footprints. Note that *káa* is a truncated form of *ká-x'* and that it is followed by an obliquative verb form containing the string *ÿa+u*- (*Ø*); we are not entirely sure of the semantic implications of such a combination. Minnie Johnson interprets this song in an English version of this story told on August 13, 1952:

> Yeł compose this song:
> The snipes are his servants—all the birds.
> When they find the footprints of Raven,
> They always follow him.‡

LINE 66. *Kax̱wlawóowáḵw áyú akawliseek:* It would appear that the *Tl'étl'* 'Moonfish' in this sentence is embarrassed about what is described in the first verb of the sentence, but we cannot determine what the syntactic relationship between the two verbs is. *Kax̱wlawóowáḵw* appears to be an irrealis perfective form with first-person subject based on the realis perfective form *kax̱wliwóowáḵw* 'I removed its sternum'. We do not understand the function of this irrealis perfective form *kax̱wlawóowáḵw*; it cannot be interpreted as a verbal noun since it is inflected for subject. Judging by the narrative context, it would seem that Raven has *not* removed the sternum of this particular Moonfish and is claiming that this is the reason it is rolling about awkwardly at the foot of the door in contrast to the rest of the Moonfish from which he has removed the sterna and which are seen to be dancing beautifully into the house as if weightless. This seems to be a ploy by Raven to convince the rest of the potlatch guests that it is in their best interest to let Raven do the same, or whatever other bodily modifications, to them.

---

* Cited in Leer, "Lexical Binders".

† Leer, Hitch, and Ritter, *Interior Tlingit Noun Dictionary*, M·139. Elizabeth Nyman is the only Atlin speaker mentioned in the front matter (vii), and Leer confirms that all Atlin forms that were published in this source were confirmed with her.

‡ De Laguna, *Under Mount Saint Elias*, 870.

LINE 68. *kax̱wliÿóowag̱u aa:* The word for 'chest' occurs as *wóow* on the coast and in Atlin, in Teslin as *yóow*, and in Carcross as *ÿóow*. The form James uses in this line with *kax̱li-ÿóow-áḵw* thus seems to be identical with the Carcross form. In all other instances of this verb theme in this narrative, James pronounces the stem with an initial /w/.

LINE 74. *Yak'ëi—haa kawulwóowag̱u yak'ëi:* This line contains a false start. The unaltered utterance is, «Yak'ëi haa wóow aadé—haa kawulwóowag̱u yak'ëi», literally 'It's good, our sterna the way—that he remove our sterna is good.' The use of the phrase *haa wóow* 'our chests, sterna' in the false start here confirms that *wóow* 'chest, sternum' is the noun used in the verb stem position in the various forms of this verb. Here the Killerwhales are thinking that it would be a good idea to have Raven remove their sterna, as he claims to have done to the Moonfish. We can compare two relevant sources in regards to the theme at work here in James' performance. The first is from a Raven story told in English by Minnie Johnson on August 13, 1952:

> People at the feast wonder how he get the flying birds to obey his orders. They wonder why they mind that Yeł. And he get up to get that snipes. All the birds come in when he is going to sing and dance for all that eats. What's the little birds to get out of it? What benefit they going to get?
>
> He got a chopping block. He kick at that chopping block and then that block can't dance. Every once in a while he kick it, and then it roll right over.
>
> They believe him. Oh that confounded Raven!
>
> That is the town of Kit [Killerwhales]. They are all nice and fat, having a feast. The reason he got that chopping block he give a kick to is to fool that Kit. He didn't fix them, but Raven claims that's why all those little birds can fly. But of course they fly by themselves. He says [however] that he plugs up their behinds. He takes a sharp stick and he pokes their ass hole up till it touches their heart. Raven explained that the chopping block wouldn't get cleaned up, so he don't dance. So then the Kits want to be fixed up like the birds.*

We might infer from this that in James' text the means by which Raven claims to have removed the birds' sterna, which Raven claims is the reason they are able to dance so elegantly before the guests, is with the use of a sharp stick; in line 98 we find Raven skewering the Killerwhales with such an implement, «Tle yá ḵaa éeneenáx̱ síwégé tlákw ḵaa téix̱' tóox̱ atsaaḵ wé g̱ákw.» 'It turns out that he had been stabbing a tree spine into their hearts through their armpits.' The Killerwhales may have believed that this was the way Raven rendered the birds light and graceful, and therefore willingly submitted to the strange procedure. Since Raven claims to be removing a bone of the chest, he uses the armpit as the entry point in James' narrative, rather than the anus as in Johnson's. It would be interesting to know how Johnson would have referred to a 'chopping block' in Tlingit; perhaps in James' narrative,

* De Laguna, *Under Mount Saint Elias*, 870, brackets original.

what Raven refers to as the Moonfish that did not have its sternum removed is in fact not a Moonfish at all, but some inert object or other creature. The next variation on this theme to consider comes from Kadashan in 1904:

> While sitting outside one day a kē´kᵘ [*k̲'eik̲'w* 'kittiwake'] (a small sea gull with black head and white body) flew past, and Raven said, "Here comes the man I made white." By and by she saw another, called kuL!ê´ta [*k̲utl'éit'aa* 'small white seagull'], also white, and repeated the same words." Then some swans came along far up in the sky, and she said the same thing about them. The killerwhales heard all this and said, "Since you have made them white, can't you make us white also?" "It will hurt you to be made white," said Raven. "Those people that came along were made white because they were brave." Then she sharpened the same hardwood stick with which she had killed her husband and told all of the killers to lie in a row. She began pounding into their ears, and so killed all of them but the last one. This looked up in time to see what she was doing and rushed into the sea saying, "Raven has finished us sure enough" (QothagAsînī´yēł [*K̲ut haa gasinée Yéil*]). Raven remained there for some time eating the whales she had killed.*

Between the tellings of James and Kadashan a sequence of episodes is reversed: in James' narrative, Raven first hosts a potlatch (at which his wife is in attendance) where he performs the deadly procedure on the Killerwhales and then turns into a woman in order to marry into the Killerwhales and murder her Killerwhale husband; in Kadashan's, Raven turns into a woman, kills and eats her Killerwhale husband, and then convinces the Killerwhales to let her perform a procedure on them. There is a notable difference in the procedures that Raven performs: in James' narrative Raven claims to have removed birds' sterna; in Kadashan's Raven claims to have turned birds white. James uses form such as *kax̲liwóowag̲u aa* 'those of which I removed the sternum' (with *wóow* 'chest, sternum' as the root). We do not have a Tlingit form from Kadashan, but we can relate the notion of 'making white' to the verb *dliwóo* 's/he/it is whitish, fair, pale' (with *wóo* 'have fair complexion' as the verb stem), which would presumably have the causative form *aliwóo*, meaning approximately 's/he keeps him/her/it whitish' (i.e., '...is the cause of its being whitish'). A plausible historical explanation is that these expressions, which are so different semantically ('cause to be whitish' and 'remove sternum'), stem from a common oral formula containing the fricative element *l-* of the classifier and a verb stem with the phonological shape *wóo*, though we cannot say which (if either of these) would have constituted the older formula. And yet, even with these wildly different semantic outcomes at the level of the sentence, the general thematic structure (trickery–complicity) and the functional relationships between the characters at the level of the

* Swanton, *Tlingit Myths and Texts*, 116, parentheses original, bracketed spellings ours. Naish and Story attest «kootl'éit'ah» (i.e., *kootl'éit'aa*), glossed as "small white seagull" (*English-Tlingit Dictionary: Nouns*, 22).

narrative remain largely intact: Raven falsely attributes innate features of birds to his own quasi-surgical actions (trickery); Killerwhales believe him and request the same be done to them (complicity); Raven kills them off by impaling them with a sharp stick.

LINE 75. *yax̱ shaÿawdudzix̱éx'w:* This is a puzzling verb form, which none of our consultants recognized. If we combine the verb theme *O-S-s-x̱éix'w~* 'for S to cause (plural) O to sleep' with the exhaustive derivational string *ÿax̱=ÿa-s-* 'all, a bunch' we get forms like *ÿax̱ ÿawdudzix̱éx'w* 'they were all put to sleep'. However, this verb also contains the prefix *sha-* 'head', which as a thematic prefix could refer to a 'pile' or 'heap' of objects, so it would follow that this refers to a heap of sea creatures being put to sleep (i.e., the big group of Seals present at the potlatch). Since these Seals were able to act on Raven's command by putting pitch on their eyes, and then their bodies, they do not appear to be asleep per se, and so we take this to mean that the Seals were 'hypnotized' by Raven. This translation is a bit tenuous, though, because none of our consultants could confirm the existence of the verb *has ashawsix̱éx̱'w*, let alone provide a gloss for it. Compare also line 76, «kéet shóot áwé s shawdzix̱éx'w», and line 89, «ldakát yóo yax̱ ashaÿawsix̱ex'u ḵu.éex'i tlein.»

LINE 83. *tle k'óox̱' du jee:* Here we would expect *tle k'óox̱' du jeewú*. Normally the locative predicative suffix -*(w)ú* would not occur only if the clause were negative, but in this case the clause is affirmative. We do not know why the -*(w)ú* was not included here, but we cannot explain it away as an isolated aberrance because there is another example of this unexpected lack of -*(w)ú* in SJ viii, «aawasháadi Leineitk'óoxk'u áwé tle du jee» 'she (Raven [in the form of a woman]) had the Little Mink she had caught'.

LINE 91. *Ha dei shígí ts'as ḵaa waaḵ gé, ḵudzitee gé?:* The implication of this line seems to be that the little Seals are asking if the only appropriate place for the pitch is the eyes. They go on to fling the pitch all over their bodies, which is the mythic explanation for the spotted coats of empirical harbor seals. Note that there are three instances of the yes/no interrogative enclitic *gí* or *gé* here; this seems to underline the birds' confusion.

LINE 95. This line contains a false start. The unaltered utterance is «Áwé yú kasayedéin yaa at gas—yaa s at ga.áax̱ áwé át has aawat'úk», in which *yaa at gas—* is a false start that James revises to *yaa s at ga.áax̱* 'when they started hearing something', which is a progressive consecutive form.

LINE 95. *át has aawat'úk:* The meaning of this phrase was independently confirmed by Ruth Demmert and Sam Johnston, both of whom translated it as "They glanced at it." It appears that *át aawat'úk*, literally meaning 'he shot it (an arrow) at it', can be used as a lexicalized idiom meaning 'he shot a glance at it'; this fact is, to our knowledge, undocumented in any Tlingit lexical materials.

LINE 97. *shé k̲aa x̲'atáanáx̲ n̲aadaa wé Kéet:* The end of this line contains a series of false starts. After the phrase *shé k̲aa x̲'atáanáx̲* 'blood through the corners of people's mouths' James struggles to complete the line and ultimately resolves the false start as «n̲aadaa wé Kéet» 'it flowed, those Killerwhales', so the complete clause can be reconstructed as *shé k̲aa x̲'atáanáx̲ n̲aadaa wé Kéet* 'blood was flowing through the mouths of those Killerwhales'. Note that the fourth-person human possessive pronoun *k̲aa* 'people('s)' and the noun *Kéet* 'Killerwhales' are coreferential here.

LINE 105. *Óu, {gushtéx̲'}!:* We could not hear the end of this line to our satisfaction. What is written is an impressionistic rendering of what we seemed to hear and we are very skeptical of its accuracy. This appears to be the final utterance of a dying Killerwhale whom Raven has stabbed through the heart—the final syllable *téx̲'* is reminiscent of *téix̲'* 'heart'.

Notes to Susie James' episode viii, "Raven Gets Herself Married to a Killerwhale"

LINE 10. *Tle de Yéil k̲u.aa {tsé}:* This entire line is unclear. Although we agree on the beginning part of the line, *Tle de Yéil k̲u.aa*, we are less certain of the final syllable. We have written it as *tsé*, which normally occurs with an admonitive verb form meaning 'be careful not (to do something)', but in this case might be construable as elliptic, with the admonitive verb being understood; perhaps it was a warning to watch out for Raven, who had just massacred a number of Killerwhales in the preceding story. Alternatively, James might have said *Tle de Yéil k̲u.aa sá* 'just say Raven's name now', but this phrase would not make much sense to us here.

LINE 11. *Kei tux̲'akasteech:* This line would appear to describe Raven flaunting 'herself' (specifically her ass) to the Killerwhales in the form of a woman in order to get invited aboard and marry their leader. Although James never says outright that Raven transformed himself into a woman, by the narrative context and James' use of a high-pitched voice to impersonate Raven in quotations, the listener is meant to understand that this change has taken place. From this point through line 112, we use the feminine pronouns 'she' and 'her' to refer to Raven in the guise of a woman. Compare Kadashan, "Raven went to another place and turned himself into a woman,"* and Zuboff:

Kéetx' áyá tsú	He even got a Killerwhale
sh wulsháayin.	to marry him.
Shaawátx̲ wusitee.†	He became a woman.

* Swanton, *Tlingit Myths and Texts*, 114.

† RZ II, i, 44-46.

Note also James' use of the incorporated inalienable noun *tux̱'e-* 'anus' (from *tuḵ-x̱'é* 'butt-mouth, butt-opening', usually contracted to *tux̱'e-*) with the verb theme *O-ka-S-s-tee*` 'for S to carry O (small stick-like object; string of small objects like beads)', indicating that Raven's anus is described as a string of small objects, perhaps hinting at the presence of dingleberries.

LINE 12. *{K'idaxwáach} yáx̱ tle yatee hé Yéil:* We were unable to resolve the first three syllables of this line to our satisfaction. The unattested verbal noun **k'idaxwáach* we have provided here is simply an educated guess based on the verb *wudixwách* 'it (hide, leather) is soft, flexible, supple' and the incorporated noun *k'i-* 'rear end'. Since the previous line mentions Raven flaunting her ass, this interpretation would fit contextually, with the Killerwhales admiring how fine a rear end she has.

LINE 15. *{Skunsháa}:* We were unable to clearly make out this word on the recording. It sounded to us like *Skunsháa* or *Shkunsháa*, which would evidently be a feminine counterpart of a clan name such as **Skuneidí* or **Shkuneidí*, though we have never encountered such a clan name. Raven seems to be trying to convince the Killerwhales that she comes from a prestigious lineage, and is therefore worthy of marriage, being a fraternal niece of the Chookansháa (the women of the Chookaneidí) and of the so-called Skunsháa or Shkunsháa (that is, Raven is claiming that the Chookansháa and the Skunsháa are her father's sisters); it is likey that the latter is a fake clan name that Raven simply made up to create a false impression of prestige.

LINE 16. *«‹{Dzéex} k'óol',› yéi gé yaawaḵaa?»:* The first two syllables of this line are very difficult to decipher. We examined many possibilities based on what we seemed to hear and the context, and none were all that satisfactory. Based on the context, the mention of *k'óol'* 'rear end' would seem to fit with the fact that Raven was raising her ass repeatedly to attract the Killerwhales' attention, but the syllable before *k'óol'* remains a mystery. We considered the possibility of this being *dzée k'óol'* 'a cur's rear end', but we can't account for why a cur (a type of dog) would be invoked here. Another possibility would be *dzéexw k'óol'* 'butter clam butt(s)', which likewise seems incongruous. Whatever this first word may be, it appears that the Killerwhales were mocking or charmed by Raven's freshly minted clan affiliations.

LINES 28–29. *gunéi kawduwanáa … Kadunáa:* Note that in line 28 it would appear that orders are given to the boat itself, «gunéi kawduwanáa wé yaakw» 'they (or someone) began giving orders to the boat', and that in line 29 the orders are given to the paddles, rather than to 'paddlers' per se, «kadunáa wé ax̱áa» 'they were giving orders to the paddles'.

LINE 30. *aax̱ yax̱ ayatáx':* This is another instance of the rare conative imperfective, meaning 'trying to V'; see appendix 1, §12.

LINES 48, 51. *G̱ayes'katleiḵwtík'i:* This name is included in the discussion of Little Mink in §2.11 of the editors' introduction The first two times James mentions this name (lines 48 and 51) she actually says «G̱ayes'katleiḵwtík'i Éesh». It becomes clear as the narrative progresses that the name meant for Raven's 'baby' (Little Mink) is *G̱ayes'katleiḵwtík'i*, apparently meaning 'Iron-Berry-Rope', and that through marriage to the supposed mother of *G̱ayes'katleiḵwtík'i*, the Killerwhale skipper becomes *G̱ayes'katleiḵwtík'i Éesh* 'Father of Iron-Berry-Rope' by marrying Raven and thus taking Raven's 'baby' as his own child. In lines 52 and 53 James repeats the name *G̱ayes'katleiḵwtík'i* as a correction for the listener to clarify that her baby's name does not contain *Éesh* 'Father of'. We have therefore removed *Éesh* in lines 48 and 51 in the text.

LINE 61. *wé aantḵeení tlèin:* There is a sharply fading tone on *tlèin* 'big, large' here, apparently denoting a very large number or quantity, which is another example of emphatic tone modification (mentioned in §3.10.4 of the editors' introduction).

LINE 62. *a x̱'éit at ÿawdudziḵúx̱ wé taay:* This appears to be an instance of the verb theme *O-ÿa-S-s-ḵoox̱~* 'for S to transport O by boat'. We considered the possibility that this is a form based on the verb theme *O-S-d-sh-ḵoox̱~* 'for S to bring O (food) to a potlatch or other gathering', but the classifier sounds like *s-* on the recording, and there is no motivation for the prefix *ÿa-* to be added to the latter theme; the former theme, however, is completely unproblematic since it includes both *ÿa-* and *s-*.

LINE 68. This line contains a false start. The unadjusted utterance is «A luwalak'áa— ch'u taat áwé.» This is an incomplete pronunciation of the phrase *a luwalak'áats'ani gákw* 'a sharp pointed tree spine', which James uses two lines later.

LINES 106, 108. *Ṉaachook'óox̱'u:* This sounded to us like *Ṉaachook'óox̱'u* on the recording; *k'óox̱'u* in this phrase is clearly the possessed form of *k'óox̱'* 'pitch, sap', but *Ṉaachoo* is not identifiable as a word, although the first syllable *naa-* might refer to a 'clan'. Note the parallel theme in Kadashan's English version, "Raven stayed there mourning for a long time, but she was really eating the killer-whale's body. After she had remained by it for a very long time, she would come home chewing gum, but, when the husband's relations asked for a piece, she would say, 'No, no one can chew this gum but Maca'', which was the name she gave to herself."[*] Although «Maca'» (which would directly transliterate from Swanton's system as *Maasháa* [tones uncertain]; compare Eyak *Maashah* 'Little Mother') and *Ṉaachoo* are phonetically quite different, if we take the theme in Kadashan's version as the basis for the interpretation of this moment in James' narration, we could imagine *Ṉaachoo* to be an invented name that Raven applies to herself; so when Raven says, «Ṉaachook'óox̱'u

* Swanton, *Tlingit Myths and Texts*, 115.

áyá x̱atáax'», this could mean, 'I am chewing the gum of *Ṉaachoo*', i.e., 'I am chewing gum that belongs only to someone with the name *Ṉaachoo*'.

LINE 112. *a daa ḵuyaawa.aa:* In this phrase, *ḵu-* (normally the fourth-person human object prefix) appears to denote the semantic agent of the verb. When we brought this phrase to Ruth Demmert she provided the contrasting examples «a daa ḵuyaawa.aa» (using *ḵu-* rather than *du-* as the fourth-person human pronominal), which she translated as "they were gathered around it, examining it", and «a daa yawtuwa.aa» (using the subject prefix *tu-* 'we'), which she translated as "we were gathered around it, examining it". This verb theme thus apparently shows the same irregularity as the intransitive verb theme *(yéi)=ÿa-S-ḵaa~* 'for S to say (so)', where likewise the *ḵu-* pronominal refers to a fourth-person human agent, i.e., *yéi ḵux̱'ayaḵá* 'someone says so'.

LINE 113. From this point onward, now that Raven has extricated himself from among the Killerwhales and presumably no longer inhabits the form of a woman, we again refer to him with male pronouns 'he', 'him', and 'his'.

Notes to Susie James' episode ix, "Raven and the Whale"

LINES 8–10. These lines form a single sentence, but we have found it difficult to match the noun phrases to the verbs that reference them. There appear to be two false starts in line 9. The unaltered utterance of lines 9–10 is «tle—tle—tle du káa neil—ÿaa ashanalhík wé Yéil, / yú kéet.» The first portion, *tle du káa neil* is clearly a false start, which James revises to *yaa ashanalhík* 'it was causing it to become full'. Furthermore, we suspect that *wé Yéil* is also a false start; *(yaaw) ÿaa ashanalhík wé Yéil* would normally translate 'it is causing Raven to become full of (herring)'; by contrast, *(yaaw) ÿaa ashanalhík wé Yéilch* would translate 'Raven is causing it to become full of (herring)'. Neither of these interpretations make sense in the narrative context, therefore we suspect that *wé Yéil* is simply a false start here, subsequently revised to *yú kéet* 'that killerwhale', which appears to be a performance error for *yú yáay* 'that humpback whale'. We have supplied [*yáay*] in place of *kéet* in the text for this reason. It seems possible that *wé Yéil* in line 9 is meant to be the subject of the verb *awsikóo* 'he knows it' in line 8, but it would be very unusual for these two phrases to be separated by so much intervening material.

LINE 16. *du ux̱ganḵáas'i:* The word *ux̱ganḵáas'* is usually translated as 'matches'. It is composed of an element *ux̱gan-* and the noun *ḵáas'* 'stick'. The element *ux̱gan-* is said by speakers to be a contraction of *úx̱ akagan*, which is the attributive form of *úx̱ akagaan* 'it is flammable'. This same element *ux̱gan-* is also seen in a couple of other terms for flammable items such as *ux̱ganhéen* 'kerosene' (with *héen* 'water'), *ux̱ganté* 'coal' (with *té* 'rock'), and *ux̲ganl'oowú* 'matches' (with *l'oowú* 'wood'). Raven is often described as having matches derived from his obtaining fire, even though matches are a nineteenth-century European invention. Although Raven stories occur in the mythic past, they are also in another way timeless so that they can incorporate phenomena from the present day of the storyteller.

LINE 21. *tláakw woonei atgalt'óos'*: James seems to be using a rare and poorly understood syntactic construction here and a handful of other times in this narrative. Compare:

line 21:	tláakw woonei atgalt'óos'	he just went to town barbecuing the herring
line 100:	tláakw k̲oowan̲ei wé yáaÿ taayí xaash	everyone was bustling about cutting up the whale blubber
lines 103–04:	tláakw at ÿatee wé yéijiné	things were proceeding at a furious pace with the work
line 148:	tláakw woonei hú k̲wá wé yáaÿ taayí x̲á	he got busy eating the whale fat

What is remarkable in these sentences is that the verbal nouns *atgalt'óos'* 'barbecuing', *yáaÿ taayí xaash* 'cutting whale fat', *yéijiné* 'work', and *yáaÿ taayí x̲á* 'eating whale fat' are not coreferential with the object of the verb that they follow and appear to have no ordinary syntactic relationship with the verb. We find a similar issue in line 114, «Taat kanax̲ tlél oox̲éx'wx̲ wé adaakw» 'They went without sleep all night long rendering fat', where the verbal noun *adaakw* 'rendering (fat)' has no ordinary syntactic relationship with the verb *tlél oox̲éx'wx̲* 'they never slept'.

LINE 24. *èex̲*: Note the emphatic falling tone on *èex̲* 'oil'. It is possible that *èex̲* is a false start here, which James revises to *wé yaaw* 'the herring' at the end of the line. This particularly makes sense since in the following line she states that the herring were all gone.

LINES 40, 42, 44, 45. *Lik̲'ayiyéit/yéide (kwshé) x̲aan galahaashée:* These lines impersonate Raven 'wishing' (or 'praying') for the whale to drift ashore at a place apparenty called *Lik̲'ayiyé*. The exact form of this word was difficult to resolve based on the recording. The first three syllables sound something like *lik̲'ayi* or *lak̲'ayi*, but both forms are unrecognizable and unanalyzable. The phrase Raven uses here is formulaic, and where James seems to use a placename *Lik̲'ayiyé*, most others (including Italio, Dick, and Mills) use *yak'éiyi l'éiw* 'a fine sand beach'. Minnie Johnson, in her interpretation of Italio's 1952 recording (FI I), seems to have provided the form *l'éiw k'éide* 'toward a fine beach' to de Laguna: "Raven is starting to sing: 'Łen kʷedi [*l'éiw k'éide*]—nice sandy beach!' He notice that thing is going to touch. He just keep still and sing that song."[*] In Johnson's form, we find the archaic postnominal modifier *k'é* 'good' instead of the usual attributive verb form *yak'éiyi* 'which is good'. It is possible that James' form *lik̲'ayiyé* is somehow a variant based on *l'éiw k'é* or the compounded form *l'awk'é*, but it is hard to see how either of these forms could evolve into *lik̲'ayiyé*. Note also that we seem to hear *Lik̲'ayiyé* with no postposition in line 47.

LINE 52. *Yáay yáat satáan!:* James (presumably) drums on the table while impersonating the children here. One possibility is that this is a sound effect representing the sound of a ball being caught, as the children are said to be playing catch with a ball in line 54.

LINE 54. *ashkadulgút:* Here James is clearly talking about some form of 'play', but we cannot identify the specific verb stem that she used. We might expect *ashkadulÿát* 'they, people are playing', but we clearly hear the stem as *gút*.

LINES 56, 58, 66, 74, 128. *Aa sgí k̲aa kan̲ax̲ angaxaasháák'óo-óo-óo:* This is a widely shared formula, which is compared in §1.4.2 of the editors' introduction. Note the use in James' form of the diminutive verb suffix *-ák'w*, which is an unusual variant of the diminutive *-k'(w)*; here it is affixed to a hortative verb form. Normally *-ák'w* is added to certain nouns only, e.g., *héenák'w* 'creeklet', *x'áat'ák'w* 'islet'.

LINE 61. *t'aax̲toogoot neildé:* We do not understand why this verb is Ø-conjugation here. We might expect instead *t'aanax̲too.aat neildé* 'let's go home and report', with the verb root *.aat~* 'go, walk (of several individuals)'. The use of the verb root *goot~* 'go (of one individual)' here might imply that the children said they should each go home separately rather than going as a group; however, in the next line we find the verb theme *O-lu-gook̲~* 'for (plural) O to run', where the children appear to be running in a group.

LINE 65. *yéi x̲'ayaduk̲á:* The usual form of this verb phrase would be *yéi k̲ux̲'aÿak̲á*, using the prefix *k̲u-* rather than the usual fourth-person subject pronoun *du-*. While *yéi k̲ux̲'aÿak̲á* is lexicalized in this way, it is a highly irregular form; we have so far found only one other verb that seems to use *k̲u-* in this way (see the note to SJ viii, 112).

LINE 81. This line contains a false start. The unaltered utterance is «Ch'a yák'udéi, á áwé k̲aa yát wudik̲—du tóogaa áx̲ k̲ukan̲algéi áwé k̲aa yát wudik̲ín.»

LINE 85 AND THROUGHOUT SONG. *ch'a kéi gidak̲een!:* This is a Ø-conjugation progressive imperative form addressed to Raven and meaning 'keep flying up!' The corresponding perfective form would be *kéi ydik̲ín* 'you flew up'.

---

* De Laguna, *Under Mount Saint Elias*, 852, bracketed spelling ours.

LINE 93 AND THROUGHOUT SONG. *Ḵuwáx̱ nidaḵeen!:* The initial word here, heard as *ḵuwáx̱*, is undocumented and was unrecognized by our consultants. Note also the use of this phrase in KM V, 74–75, «Wáanée sáwé, ‹Ḵuyáx̱ nidaḵeen! Ḵuyáx̱ nidaḵeen!›» We have translated it as 'fly however you would like'. Though we have no way of confirming or denying it, we considered the possibility that this passage from the Raven story told in English by Deikeenaak'w to Swanton contains an English approximation of this phrase, "They began to cut a hole just over the place these came from and presently they heard some one inside say, 'Xōnē´-ē [*X̱'unéi-éi*].' When the hole was large enough, Raven flew straight up out of it until he was lost to sight. And they said to him, '*Fly to any place where you would like to go*.'"*

LINE 105. *Tlax̱ naak'w yáx̱ ÿatee hú ḵu.aa:* The literal meaning of this sentence is, 'He, though, is very much like a little corpse.'

LINE 118. *«Daa sá, daa sá yéi daayné?»:* The more common form of this verb would be *yéi daayeené* instead of *yéi daayné*. Outside of the imperative mode, the second-person plural subject pronoun is usually *yee-* if it occurs in the syllable just before the stem, but James reduces it here to *y-*. In the imperative mode, this prefix occurs as *y-* after a vowel and either directly before the stem or before a CV- classifier; elsewhere in the imperative it occurs as *yi-*. Note that James uses the same form in SJ xi, 13.

LINE 125. *Héigíl ch'a ḵukawdu.áax̱ákw a yíkde?:* This is another important formula. See §1.4.2 of the editors' introduction for some discussion and comparison.

Notes to Susie James' episode x, "Raven Gets His Nose Yanked Off"

LINE 4. This line begins with a false start. James begins the line saying, «Tlél tlax̱—Tlél tlax̱—Tle yóode áwé…».

LINE 12. *ashkoolyát tsaa taayí:* This sentence is unusual in two ways. First, we might expect *ashkadulyát* 'they, (the) people are playing' or *has ashkoolyát* 'they are playing', but there is no indication of plurality in the verb as it is. Second, there is no clear syntactic relationship between the noun phrase *tsaa taayí* 'seal fat' and the verb; we might have expected something like *ashkadulyát tsaa taayítin* 'they were playing with seal fat'. For further examples of noun phrases that are 'stranded' in this way see the note to SJ ix, 21.

LINE 14. *Tle* [*du*] *jeet kawuxeexí áwé:* We were unable to hear the words after *Tle*, but it appears to be a false start, so we supply *du* 'his' (i.e., 'Raven's) here.

* Swanton, *Tlingit Myths and Texts*, 13, emphasis and bracketed spelling ours.

LINE 22. *anax̱ yéik̲ wududzi.ín:* We were unable to hear most of the pronunciation of the verb *wududzi.ín* 'it (a container bearing contents) was carried' because the microphone was moved or bumped.

LINE 27. *aan k̲ugax̱dust'ex̱ át:* Typically, this verb, meaning 'for S to fish with a hook', occurs with the thematic prefix *a-* (e.g., *ast'eix̱* 'he's fishing with a hook') rather than the prefix *k̲u-* that James uses here. We cannot determine the difference in meaning implied by the use of *k̲u-*. Note, though, that we find the same *k̲u-* prefix in KM III, 19-20, «I een daak / k̲ukk̲wast'eix̱» 'I'll go out / fishing with you'.

LINE 32. *ách ÿadulnáák̲ws':* The classifier of this verb is underlyingly *s-*, but this is altered to *l-* because the stem in this case, *nák̲ws'*, contains an affricate-series consonant (i.e., a lateral, sibilant, or shibilant consonant), namely the suffix *-s'*. Compare AH IIa/b, 10/6, «wé taaych áa yadusnak̲wx'u yé» 'the place where people were using bits of fat to bait halibut hooks', where the stem is *nák̲wx'*, containing the suffix *-x'(w)*, and the classifier is *s-*.

LINE 39. *Awsiteen wé taay át kawlidzéidzi yé:* Here we find a verb theme that has not been attested elsewhere. The theme appears to be *O-ka-l-dzéits~* 'for O to waft (or to move somehow) in the water' or the like. Since the fat and the wooden hooks themselves are buoyant, we would expect the baited hooks to float a few feet above the sinker on the ocean floor. Based on this consideration we have used the word 'wafting' in the English translation; however, the reader should not take this translation as definitive.

LINE 40. James begins whispering here and through the next few lines, apparently for dramatic effect.

LINE 42. *ch'al yéi koogeix̱ kát:* The elements *ch'al ... kát* employed in this phrase are discussed in the note to SJ I, 111. James seems to be remarking on the fact that the bits of fat Raven peruses here were quite meager when compared to the effort he had to expend in going after them. Raven simply cannot resist the opportunity to eat some fat.

LINE 45. *Anax̱ kéi x̱dusÿék̲:* This is a shortened variant of the contingent verb form *anax̱ kéi x̱dusyég̲ín* 'whenever it (the line) was pulled up'.

LINE 50. *Ÿan has uwats'úk:* This stem is not attested elsewhere in our lexical corpus, and our consultants did not recognize it. An earlier team of editors translated this as 'they were pulling the lines in', and we have retained this translation.

LINE 56. *ts'óots' jee wuskóowu:* We seem to hear «ts'óots' jée wuskóowu» 'somebody who has a feel for fish nibbles' with high tone on *jée*, and likewise «ts'óots' jée wdzikuwu aa» 'one who knows the feel of fish nibbles' in line 57. Four lines later in line 61 we do not clearly hear high tone in «ts'óots' jee wdzikóo» 'he (a nobleman) knows the feel of fish nibbles'. Note also that we seem to hear a similar high tone in line 67, which sounds like «jée awdinúk» 'he (the nobleman) felt it (Raven touching the line)'. These apparent high tones are puzzling because *jee(x')* is never expected to take high tone; they could be emphatic modifications, in which case they would be pronounced with dramatically falling tone and written *jèe* rather than *jée*. Compare Hammond's form «ts'óots' jee ayawdzikuwu ḵáa» 'a man who knew how to feel for a bite', or, 'a top-notch nibble-feeler', in AH IIa/b, 52/33. The noun *ts'óots'* 'fish nibble' is based on the root *ts'óots'~*, which refers to a fish nibbling on or jerking the end of a fishing line.

LINES 67, 69. *át ÿawusheeyí ... Át ÿaawashée:* Ruth Demmert interpreted *át yaawashée* as "he was feeling around for something".

LINE 72. *áwé {...} áwé t'eix̱áax̱ sitee:* We were unable to resolve three syllables in this line, which we have simply left untranscribed as '{...}'. The final portion is either /sáa/, /...s.áa/, or /...s.háa/.

LINE 76. *Ḵoosh kadáan á!:* The word *ḵoosh* refers to a festering sore or something unclean. *Ḵoosh kadáan!* is a fixed idiom, like 'What a fine mess!' in English.

LINES 77–78. *{... a} tayeedé áwé / yax̱ sh kadlix̱ít:* We could not clearly hear the two syllables in braces. The first syllable sounded something like *dzée*, which we could only interpret as *dzée* 'cur (type of dog)', but this does not fit the context in any clear way. The second syllable sounded something like *ax̱* or *yakw* or the like, but *a* 'it (i.e., the boat)' fits the context better. The form *yax̱ sh kadlix̱ít* is another example of the rare conative form (discussed in appendix 1, §12) meaning 'he is/was trying to wriggle'. Ruth Demmert interpreted *a tayeedé áwé yax̱ sh kadlix̱ít* as "he's trying to wriggle himself under the boat", the implication being that Raven is trying to stay under the boat instead of getting yanked to the surface.

LINE 80. *óot yaanwuhá:* This is a spectacular instance of a perfective verbal noun meaning 'him having become hungry' or 'him getting hungry' with *óot* (consisting of the archaic third-person postpositional object *oo-* plus postposition *-t*) in place of modern *du éet* (composed of *du=ee-* plus *-t*). The statement James uses in this line, «óot yaanwuhá ḵwá yéi kaaxát» 'but him having become hungry shaped this situation' (i.e., Raven's hunger was the driving force in this situation), could readily explain many of Raven's other antics. Raven's hunger is often the essential 'lack' which propels many plots forward in the 'lack–lack liquidated' theme discussed in §1.4.1 of the editors' introduction.

LINE 81. *àawatséx̱:* This phrase is difficult to hear. We have interpreted it as a drawn out, emphatic pronunciation of *aawatséx̱* 'he (Raven) kicked it (the bottom of the boat)', with an unusual modification of the prefix string. Another possibility would be that James actually said *aÿaawatséx̱*, but our consultants were unable to confirm such a verb form.

LINES 87, 90. *Daat loowú sáyá?:* Literally, 'what's nose is this?', but this form of question is ungrammatical in English so we have used 'what kind of nose' instead.

LINE 101. *G̱uneit loowú:* The first word here, *G̱uneit*, is a contraction of *g̱una.át* 'alien being'. In line 124 we also find *G̱uneit* as a self-standing noun phrase. Anna Katzeek consistently translated *G̱uneit loowú* as 'the G̱uneit's nose' in her live interpretation of AH 11a. *G̱uneit* 'Alien' is thus the name Raven used for what the people believed to be a mysterious creature from which the fishermen pulled the nose. In this interpretation, this noun phrase would be written *G̱uneit loowú* or *g̱uneit loowú*, depending on whether we take *G̱uneit* to be a proper noun or a common noun. Note that in the Raven stories Deikeenaak'w told to Swanton in English, we find reference to the nose of the sea monster *G̱unakadeit*, "All at once his nose came off, and they pulled it up. When they landed, they took it to the chief's house and said, 'We have caught a wonderful thing. It must be the nose of the Ḳonaqadē´t.' [...Raven] went through the houses saying, 'I wonder in what house are the people who caught that Ḳonaqadē´t's nose.'"* Although Deikeenaak'w told this story in English, we can readily restore his original Tlingit phrase as *G̱unakadeit loowú* 'the nose of G̱unakadeit'. There is clearly a resemblance between *g̱uneit loowú* and *G̱unakadeit loowú*, but we have no way to definitively trace the pedigree of the use of these names in the story. We can note, though, that the former has been instantiated as a personal name belonging to a Raven clan; Clara Peratrovich (Gux̱tlèn) states in an interview that Wilbur Ketah of the G̱àanax̱.adi had the name G̱unèit Lòowu—a "big name", Clarence Jackson (Tag̱ooch) responds.†

LINE 110. *A shóot tle ḵúnáx̱ át uwagút:* This is a semi-false start for *a shú tle ḵúnáx̱ át uwagút* 'then he (Raven) came to the very end (of town)'.

LINES 132, 133. *gaṉyigeidí:* Raven is asking for the house dwellers to move the *gaṉyigeidí* 'smoke-spreading boards' aside, which are devices used to cause the smoke from the fire to spread out throughout a smokehouse. Speaking of smokehouses as opposed to larger community houses, de Laguna writes, "Above the fire (or fires) was a false ceiling or 'table' (ganigédì [*ganyigeidí*]), made of boards, to catch the soot and the direct heat and to spread the smoke throughout the upper part of the

* Swanton, *Tlingit Myths and Texts*, 8, bracketed material ours.

† MS055, box 9, file 4, item 2. These spellings reflect her use of the Southern dialect of Hèinyàḵwàan.

house. Above this were the racks for drying fish."* The *ganyigeidí* are distinct from the moveable board screen that was used to block the smokehole of a traditional house from wind and weather, which is called *gaanyéili* or *gaanéili*; de Laguna provides the following description, "Above the fireplace was the smokehole (ganka [*gaanká*]). This was provided with a moveable board screen (ganyétłi [*gaanyéili*], ganka t'ayi [*gaankat'áayi*], ganka yix̣i [possibly *gaankaÿéegi*]). This could be tilted on one side or the other, depending on the wind."† The first element in *gaanká* 'smokehole' and *gaanyéili* 'smokehole screen' is *gaan* 'smokehole', which is evidently related to (*du*) *gaan* '(his/her) fontanel'. On the other hand, *ganyigeidí* appears to be a compounded form of *ganyik-(ÿee-).ádi* 'over the fire-(under-)thing' (note that *ganyík* means 'over/in the fire', not 'in the firewood'). Because James uses the term *ganyigeidí* here, rather than *gaanyéili* or one of its variants, it appears to us that Raven is asking the people to push aside the smoke-spreading boards, which would presumably have formed a low false ceiling in the house, rather than asking them to push aside a smokehole screen.‡

Notes to Susie James' episode xi, "Raven and the Daylight"

LINE 11. *aadé éex' wé ḵaa t'aaḵ:* James whispers this line. We do not understand how *wé ḵaa t'aaḵ* 'beside those people' fits into this sentence.

LINE 15. *L ḵ'adaat ḵaa tooshtí:* The word *ḵ'adaa* here is a pejorative variant of (*du*) *x̱'adaa* 'about/concerning (his/her) speech'. Note first that she uses *l* in place of usual *tlél* 'not' in this declarative statement, and second that the expected possessive pronoun *du* is missing before *ḵ'adaat* (discussed in appendix 1, §6.1). This sentence therefore appears to be a formulaic expression passed down from antiquity.

LINES 19–20. *Naasshagiÿát / Ḵei.á Daakeit anga.oo:* See §2.16 of the editors' introduction for comparison and discussion of this formulaic expression.

LINE 24. *G̱ákw Sax̱a Ḵu.oo:* We would have expected James to use an attributive verb form here (i.e., *g̱ákw asx̱a* 'who eat gnarly driftwood'), but she forms the name using the combining form of the verbal noun *g̱ákw sax̱á* 'eating gnarly driftwood', which modifies the following noun *ḵu.oo* 'people'. The *s-* element of the classifier here is configurational, indicating that the driftwood is has a gangly and gnarled shape. Compare Dick's name for the same figures, «Shaḵyátx'i Isdik Ḵu.oo» 'People-Who-Dipnet-Bits-of-Driftwood' (FD ii, 6), which uses different words but an identical structure (*ḵu.oo* modified by a verbal noun). The reference here is to the people

* De Laguna, *Under Mount Saint Elias*, 303, parentheses original, bracketed spelling ours.

† Ibid, 297, parentheses original, bracketed material ours.

‡ For more details on the traditional structure of Tlingit houses see especially Shotridge, "Indians of the Northwest", 81–99, as well as Emmons, *The Tlingit Indians*, 103–12, and de Laguna, *Under Mount Saint Elias*, 295–302.

often known as the *Yax̱taattuḵwáani* 'Night-Dwellers'; see §2.16 of the editors' introduction for discussion of these figures. This line contains a false start. The unaltered line is «tle yú hás t—G̱ákw Sax̱a Ḵu.oo…» with an interruption after *hás.*

LINE 26. *Naas Sháagu:* Here James pronounces the Tlingit name of the Nass River with low tone. We find her varying evenly between high-tone and low-tone pronunciations of the placename throughout this tale and we are unable to discern anything conditioning these tonal alterations.

LINE 27. *«{K'e héi-éi tle} áa x̱'akaawaháa,» du x̱'éidáx̱ {duwa…}—:* None of our consultants were able to find a meaning for *áa x̱'akaawaháa*, which sounds to us like it might mean something like 'he was in a situation where he was prepared to speak (or to eat)', but we are unable to confirm this impression. Also, there was discussion about what we have written as *K'e héi-éi tle*, which might actually have been *K'e héi-éitl'* 'Check it out, it's huge'. Finally, the syllables after *du x̱'éidáx̱* sounded possibly like *duwa-*, which would likely have been a false start for *du x̱'éidáx̱ duwa.áx̱ch* 'the sound came from his mouth'.

LINE 34. *Yéi kwdigeyi shaaḵ ÿátx'i:* Presumably this line was accompanied by a hand gesture showing how large the pieces of driftwood were, but of course we cannot discern this from the recording. Otherwise, this would seem to be 'large small bits of driftwood'. This phrase helps explain the reference of the term *g̱ákw* used earlier in the narrative, which we translated as 'gnarly driftwood'. James' pronunciation of *shaaḵ ÿátx'i*, lit. 'driftwood children', but functionally meaning 'small pieces of driftwood' sounds like *shaag̱átx'i* here, with the semivowel /ÿ/ essentially disappearing.

LINE 41. *kadux̱'al.aa:* The word *kadux̱'al.aa* is an uncommon term for a dense root vegetable like a turnip or rutabaga. It is based on the verb root *x̱'aal~* 'crunch with mouth' and is a relative clause meaning literally 'one that people crunch'. James' use of this word here is a kind of subtle pun because in this scene of the narrative she also uses forms of the verb *akawlix̱'ál* 'he crunched it' that are based on the same verb root.

LINE 64. *G̱aadlàan:* James pronounces the stem of this verb with sharply fading tone to emphasize that the water was very deep.

LINE 86. *áa yei kg̱wanuk wé:* James rounds the head noun *ÿé* 'place' to *wé* here, retaining the labial shape of the verb stem.

LINE 100. *Héeng̱aa nakw s'é:* This is a reduced equivalent of *héeng̱aa nagú s'é* 'go for (i.e., fetch) water first'.

LINE 115 AND THROUGHOUT. James impersonates the young woman who is to become pregnant with Raven in a higher pitched, girlish voice.

LINE 139. *áx̱ kei sh wuditsag̱i yé, corner:* See the note to FI I, V, 50, 54, for comparison of the descriptions of Raven in the corner of the young woman's drinking vessel.

LINES 147–49. *Ch'al igux̱sanei kát … Ch'al ikg̱wajak̲ kát:* For discussion of the *ch'al … kát* construction, see the note to SJ i, 111. Note, in this instance, the lack of an adverb of manner such as *yéi=* before *igux̱sanei*. We know that alongside *yéi woonei* (or … *nee*) 'it happened to him/her/it', one can say *woonei* (or …*nee*) 's/he died', so it would seem that alongside *yéi awsinei* (or …*nee*) 's/he/it did so to him/her/it' one can say *awsinei* (or …*nee*) to mean 's/he/it caused him/her to die'.

LINE 150. *wáa sá aan at dux̱aayí:* The implication here is that it is okay when people eat foods in which some evergreen needles are consequently ingested. A prime example of a traditional Tlingit food in which this would happen is herring roe on hemlock boughs.

LINES 152–53. *Bob x̱'éide sax̱ahéi nuch:* We do not know who Bob is in this short aside. One possibility is Robert Zuboff, who often went by Bob.

LINE 165. *Lyóo.at.uwajeegi Shaanák'w:* This character is discussed in §2.8 of the editors' introduction. James is the only storyteller in this volume to use the form *Lyóo.at.uwajeegi Shaanák'w* to refer to Unfazable-Little-Elder (though we find this form used by others such as Charlie Joseph, Shotridge, Deikeenaak'w, and Kadashan). Italio and Dick, on the other hand, use *Lyóo.atkoowajeegi Shaanák'w*.

LINE 167. *át du een aawa.át:* Note *du een* 'with her' intervening between *át* 'to there' and *aawa.át* 'people came'. A similar construction occurs in line 191, «A yeedé du een ang̱a.aadí» 'Let someone escort her inside'.

LINES 178, 179. *chashtuhít galayeix̱ée:* James clearly says this verb in both lines without the third-person object prefix *a-*; i.e., we would expect *ax̱layeix̱ée* 'let him/her build it' or *gadulyeix̱í* 'let it be built' rather than *galayeix̱ée*. This is the only instance we have encountered of a transitive verb becoming object-intransitive with a passive meaning. When we asked Ruth Demmert about this line she confirmed the verb form *wuliyéx̱*, which she translated as "it is made". A similar construction is also found in a 1974 recording of George Dalton; when speaking about the place *L'awshaashakee.aan* 'Village-Upon-the-Sand-Mount' (in the Bartlett Cove area) he states, «Yeedát tle yéi *cover*-x̱ wuliyéx̱»* 'Now it's just been covered up'. The term used in this line by James, *chashtuhít* 'brush hut', is a kind of temporary shelter built from

* MC041, tape 7.

freshly cut boughs. Traditionally these would be constructed on the back side of a house as a kind of lean-to in which birthing would occur. Also note the similar construction in line 190, «Ách gáanx' galayeix̱í du ya.áak, chashtuhít» 'So let a place be made for her outside, a brush hut', where the object *du ya.áak* 'a place for her' occurs as an afterphrase.

LINE 215. *Has wudishánx̱:* The verb form here is a rare instance of the durative perfective. The corresponding imperfective is *has dashánx̱* 'they (customarily) grow old'. For further discussion see appendix 1, §10.

LINE 216. *neilx' ḵaa ḵusteet'ích:* Note that here James uses the object pronoun *ḵaa=* 'people' with this verb. Typically, this verb takes only subjects, so we might have expected *neilx' ḵudusteet'ích* 'because people are born inside'. However, we have instances from a variety of speakers who treat this as an object-intransitive verb rather than a subject-intransitive verb when meaning 'to be born'. Some people say, for instance, *Sheet'káx' x̱at ḵuwdzitee* 'I was born in Sitka' rather than *Sheet'káx' ḵux̱wdzitee*. When used to mean 'to exist', on the other hand, all speakers use exclusively subject pronominals.

LINE 239. As discussed in the introduction to James' tale, line 239 is the last line from the recording taken September 1972; at the end of this line the tape ran out, cutting James' performance short in the midst of the action. Lines 240 to the end of the text are taken from a separate recording made by Nora Dauenhauer roughly four months prior on May 14, 1972.

LINE 263. *Ḵei.á neilx' áyú {...}:* After the first few words of this line, James' words become too quiet for us to comprehend.

LINES 277–80. *Haahée!:* These lines are pronounced in a high-pitched near-whisper to impersonate baby Raven begging for the Container of Daylight.

LINE 295. *yax̱.atg̱wakú {x̱á...} yaa yanasxíx:* We were unable to resolve the portion in between *yax̱.atg̱wakú* 'proverb' and *yaa yanasxíx*; as for this latter verb, we could not tell if James pronounced *yaa yanasxíx* or *yaa ayanasxíx*. There are a range of possible interpretations of these forms; *yaa yanasxíx* translated as 'the light was moving' seems pertinent to the context of Raven being on the cusp of stealing the daylight, but we were too uncertain to venture a translation in the text.

LINE 303. *Wuyít akaajéil ax̱ duwuweidí Yéil Tl'éetl'i!:* Upon comparison with Dick, this line—an impersonation of Naas Sháak 'Head-of-the-Nass' (a.k.a. Naasshagiyéil 'Raven-of-the-Head-of-the-Nass)—appears to be another formulaic expression occurring in the speech of a character. Compare FD ii, 174, «Kaawayíkt akaajéil ax̱ ádi yóo Yéil Tl'éetl'i!» 'That Shitty Raven managed to strew my possessions into thin air!' In addition to the moniker *Yéil Tl'éel'i*, literally 'Shitty Raven' (used also by Italio in FI I, ii, 82; II, 97), these lines use the rare realizational verb mode (see appendix 1, §9.3, for discussion of this verb mode), which here we translate as 'he (Raven) managed to strew them'.

LINE 319. {...} *wé gagaan:* The poor recording quality coupled with James speaking very softly at the beginning of this line made it impossible for us to resolve this line. We believe she said *wé gagaan* 'the sun', but entertained the idea that she may have actually said *wé kagán* 'the light'.

Notes to Frank Dick's Stories

EDITORIAL BACKGROUND. Fred White, Frank Dick's grandson, drafted the first transcription and translation in 1983–1984.* The manuscript in its early state was divided into 'part 1' and 'part 2' (now FD i–v and FD vi–xii, respectively), with these two parts corresponding to the two sides of the original cassette recording. White confirmed in 2023 that the tale was told in a single sitting, with the tape cassette simply being flipped in the recorder when time required. We thus consider this to be a single extended tale consisting of twelve episodes. The original 'part 1' was included in an early field test edition of Raven stories in June 1984 and was proofread by Jeff Leer on May 16, 1985. The manuscript then lay dormant until 1994 when Richard Dauenhauer returned to work on it, doing further work on the text in 1995, 1998, and 1999, and again in 2002. Nora and Richard Dauenhauer worked on it again in 2011. Keri Eggleston reviewed the manuscript with George Davis on May 7, 2015, and James Crippen did a review May 21–24 of the same year. Lance Twitchell and Will Geiger independently reviewed the text and corresponded on revisions in 2019. Finally, in 2020–2021, Geiger and Leer reviewed all of the material, listening to the original audio and making final revisions to the transcription, translation, and notes. They consulted Kenneth Grant, Bessie Cooley, Sam Johnston, and Ruth Demmert on particularly difficult linguistic issues.

Notes to Frank Dick's episode i, "Raven and His Uncle"

LINE 1. *yáa shaawát:* The recording appears to have started after Dick was already in the process of speaking. The woman referred to here is to become the mother of Raven. This character is discussed in §2.2 of the editors' introduction.

LINE 6. «Áwé» can vaguely be heard pronounced at the end of this line, but it is clearly not Dick speaking. It is likely Fred White. We left it untranscribed.

* Printouts of these early renditions can be found in MS052, box 25, file unit 004.

LINE 9. *kushtuyéx̱:* This word could also be translated as 'for no reason' or 'for nothing'. Compare also *kushtuyáx̱ déi!* 'so what?' or 'who cares?'

LINES 1–9. These initial remarks do not advance the plot of the "Raven and His Uncle" story, but rather serve to form an opening narrative frame that sets the tone for the performance of the tale. This opening frame can be indexed with the final lines of the tale, FD xii, 38–51; the concluding remarks are likewise not inherent to the plot of "Raven Pretends to Build a Canoe", but form a closing narrative frame that brings resolution to the entire multi-episodic tale. For a detailed analysis of this sort of 'narrative frame' as a Tlingit oral-literary compositional device see Richard Dauenhauer's doctoral dissertation, "Text and Context of Tlingit Oral Tradition", 78–122.

LINE 10. *Shúx'waanáx̱:* Of particular note in Dick's pronunciation is the high tone on the first vowel; this word is normally pronounced with low tone on the first vowel. Dick's variant, *shúx'waanáx̱*, seems to be restricted to the Yakutat dialect; a Yakutat informant reports hearing this similarly as *shúx'aa(náx̱)* in Yakutat. Note also that Dick pronounces this with a rounded /x'w/, as do some other Coastal and Interior Tlingit speakers, resulting from progressive rounding following the vowel /u/ of *shú-*. Italio, however, who is also of Yakutat, can be heard pronouncing this as «shux'áanáx̱» (FI II, 237) (with low-toned *shu-*, high-toned *-x'áa*, and unrounded /x'/) alongside «shux'aa» (FI I, V, 232; II, 224) (with both *shu-* and *x'aa* low). Ruth Demmert pronounces this as «shux'áanáx̱» and Sam Johnston as «shux'wáanáx̱». When working with living speakers it is possible to ask them to say the word syllable-by-syllable so as to ascertain whether the consonant following the /u/ is fully (i.e., phonemically) rounded or incidentally rounded; the speaker may perceive it as *shu-x'áa-náx̱* or *shu-x'wáa-náx̱*.

LINES 16–17. *Á áyáa / yéi x̱'ayak̲áa nukch:* Line 16 contains a false start. The unaltered line is «Á áyáa yéi ash daaya—», the false start apparently being for *yéi ash daayak̲áa nukch* 'he would say to him/her', but revised in line 17 to «yéi x̱'ayak̲áa nukch» '(this is what) he would say'. The particular habitual auxiliary used here, =*nukch*, appears to be confined to Yakutat;* most Coastal Tlingit speakers use the variants =*nooch* ~ *nuch*, whereas the Interior Tlingit use =*neech*.

LINE 20. *lkeeyiyáagaa:* This is an obscure word that Leer in his "Stem List" transcribed from Tongass Tlingit as «łki`ÿi-ÿa˙-ga̱'», and glossed as "for longer (than necessary, seemly)".

LINE 23. *du sákw:* This is a difficult phrase to translate, especially because the sentence includes two phrases (*du sákw* and *yáa shaawát*) which may or may not be

* Leer, "Schetic Categories", 154, note 64.

connected and Dick cut off mid-sentence in order to clarify another aspect of the woman’s situation. The word *sákw* can occur as both a noun modifier (*N sákw* ‘future N; N-to-be’) and as a postposition (*P sákw* ‘for future P; to be used for P’). Therefore, it would be possible to interpret *du sákw* either as ‘the future him, him-to-be’ or ‘for the future him, in order for him to come about in the future’; the lack of context leaves it unclear which interpretation is to be preferred. A comparable example can be found in *Haa Tuwunáagu Yís* from a speech by Charlie Joseph, «Has du sákw», translated there as “Their ancestor”.[*] The Dauenhauers explained in a note to this translation, “We have paraphrased here. The Tlingit word ‘sákw’ is more literally ‘ingredients,’ ‘raw materials,’ or ‘makings for.’”[†] Our consultants have rejected forms with *sákw* preceded by a human possessor, e.g., *ax̱ sákw*, presumably meaning ‘what-is-to-be(come)-me’; nevertheless, the instances noted here from Joseph and Dick leave little doubt that such phrases were acceptable in classical Tlingit.

LINES 25–31. This is an explanatory discursus. Dick resumes talking about the woman in line 32.

LINE 26. *ḵoog̱áa áyáa at naseich:* This is the affirmative habitual mode of the verb *P-g̱aa O-soo`* (*na*) ‘for O to provide supernatural aid to P’, with the fourth-person human postpositional pronoun *ḵu-* ‘people, someone’ as the object of the postposition *-g̱aa* (denoting the semantic patient), and the fourth-person non-human pronoun *at=* ‘(some)thing(s)’, here the verbal object (denoting the semantic agent).

LINE 27. *yóo áyá shukát tuwasáakw:* This sounds on the recording possibly like *yóo áyá shukatuwasáakw*. We can neither verify a form with incorporated *shuka-*, nor can we make sense out of how *shukát* would fit syntactically into this phrase as currently transcribed.

LINES 29–30. *Dikyáanḵáawuch:* Setting aside the ergative postposition *-ch*, Dick pronounces this as «Dikyáanḵáawu», syllabified as *Di-kyáan-ḵáa-wu*, whose second syllable has the non-canonical onset /ky/ and where the end of *-kyáan-* sounds like English /ng/ in ‘long’; his pronunciation can be rendered phonetically as [tiˈkʲʰáːŋˈqʰáːwu]. It is more usually pronounced as *Dikáanḵáawu* (phonetically [tiˈkʰáːŋˈqʰáːwu]), where what is written as ⟨n⟩ likewise sounds like English /ng/. Both forms are contractions of the phrase *Dikée Aanḵáawu* which is normally translated as ‘God’ but more literally means ‘Chief (or Headman) of the Heavens’. This may be a calque of the Chinook Jargon name *Sáχali Táyi* ‘Above Chief’ which was used to refer to the Christian God as opposed to other spirits and deities in various Indigenous religions of the Pacific Northwest. Aurel Krause in his diary of 1881

* Dauenhauer and Dauenhauer, *Haa Tuwunáagu Yís*, 176–77.

† Ibid, 337.

refers to early Protestant Christian missionaries using Chinook Jargon to preach to Tlingit people because the missionaries were incapable of or unwilling to learn Tlingit.* However, this name for the Christian God is found in the earliest Russian translations into Tlingit, well before Chinook Jargon gained traction in Southeast Alaska. The noun *aank̲áawu* 'headman, chief' refers to a leader of the Tlingit aristocracy who could traditionally speak on behalf of the whole town. This word is a compound of *aan* 'town, land' and *k̲áa* 'man' with the possessive suffix *-wu*, and so literally means 'man of the town'.

LINES 38–39. *Shanyaateiÿí:* The word *shanyaateiÿí* 'low-tide stone' is now relatively rare, but generically refers to a rock visible only at extreme low tide. Whereas all versions of this story included in this volume attribute the name *Yook̲is'kook̲éik* to Raven's uncle, Harrington recorded «CAny̯aa-ttheeyyíi» (i.e., *Shanÿaateiyí*) as the name of Raven's maternal uncle from George Johnson; Johnson also says that the word «cAnyaa or cAny̯aa» (i.e., *shanyaa* or *shanÿaa*) means "down at the beach".† The technical English term corresponding to *shanÿaa* would be 'lower littoral zone', especially the very lowest region of the lower littoral zone. One can say, for instance, *shanyaax̲ woolaa* 'the tide has gone completely out' (lit. 'the tide flowed out over the shanyaa').

LINE 47. *du x̲ánx̲ k̲ukook̲aa:* This is the repetitive form corresponding to perfective *du x̲ánt k̲ukaawak̲áa* 'he sent people to her'. We can infer that the people (*k̲u-*) whom Tide-Commander sends to check on his sister are his slaves, but Dick never specifies who or what these people are.

LINE 49. *Ash x̲'einawóos'ch:* It is not clear whether the subject of the verb here, 'he', refers to Tide-Commander or to the person or people he sent to check on the woman.

LINE 50. *Daak̲wéit sáwé:* The phrase *daak̲wéit sá?* 'what kind of thing?' is functionally equivalent with *daa sá?* 'what?' In Yakutat, *daak̲wéi sá?* (from **daak̲w yéi sá?*) 'how?' or 'in what way?' appears to be roughly equivalent with *wáa sá?* 'how?', and *daak̲wéit sá?* appears to be a contraction of **daak̲wéi át sá?*

LINES 52–53. *Yiják̲!:* Here, again, we can infer that the referent of *yi-* 'you all' is Tide-Commander's slaves.

---

* "[M]any persons were attracted to the missionary work who were not suited to their posts and had no understanding of the Indian character and customs and so satisfied themselves with superficial results. Only a few made a serious effort to learn the language of the natives; most of them contented themselves with the meager Chinook jargon, the common trade language of the Northwest Coast from the Columbia River northwards to the Alexander Archipelago, which is sufficient for trading purposes but totally unsuitable for the expression of religious and moral ideas." Krause, *The Tlingit Indians*, 231.

† Cited in de Laguna, *Under Mount Saint Elias*, 857.

LINE 69. *du shátx̱ oonanóokg̱aa:* This is a dependent admonitive form with the postposition -*g̱aa*. Note that here *du shátx̱* should not be confused with the homophonous *du shátx̱* 'her older sister'; rather, *du shát-x̱* 'affecting his wife', with the postposition -*x̱*, is equivalent to *du shát éex̱* in line 54 («ax̱ shát éex̱ oongaanóok» 'it might bother my wife', in which case the verb is in the potential mode, so we would expect the stem to have low tone, i.e., *oong̱aanook*, and we cannot account for the audible high tone in Dick's pronunciation).

LINE 75. *s'eiyatóox̱ oos.áx̱wch:* The word *N s'eiÿatú ~ s'eeÿatú* refers to the inside corner or angle formed by the gable of the house. This word is composed of *N s'eiÿ ~ s'eeÿ* 'gable of N (roof)' (ultimately identical with *N s'eiÿ ~ s'eeÿ ~ s'ee* 'eyebrow of N') plus *N ÿa-tú* 'inside the corner, angle, or curve of N's peak'. Traditionally there was a platform formed of boards laid across the two main rafter logs. This platform was used for storage and for temporary sleeping space.*

LINES 93–94. *A tóox̱ gug̱agut át:* This passage alludes to a bird Raven kills so that his mother can crawl into the bird's skin, assume the form and function of the bird, and thus float safely upon the flooding waters.

LINE 106. *Du x̱einéenáx̱ kawdliyeech:* The relational noun *N x̱einí* generally refers to motion or position 'even with N, alongside and keeping pace with N'. Note the use of the same phrase in the same moment of the plot in FI I, ii, 44.

Notes to Frank Dick's episode ii, "Raven and the Daylight"

Between the end of the previous episode and this one, Dick pauses and lets out a deep sigh.

LINE 6. *Shak̲yátx'i Isdik K̲u.oo:* A more commonplace way of forming this name would have been *Shak̲yátx'i Asdik K̲u.oo* 'People Who Dipnet Bits of Driftwood', where *shak̲yátx'i asdik* is the attributive form of *shak̲yátx'i asdeek* '[they] dipnet little pieces of driftwood'. In this case, however, the third-person object pronominal *a*- is missing; therefore we must take *shak̲yátx'i isdik* to be a compounding form of the verbal noun *shak̲yátx'i isdeek* 'dipnetting bits of driftwood' (verbal nouns are incompatible with any pronominals except the fourth-person objects *at=* 'thing(s)' and *k̲aa=* '(some)one, people') where the stem -*deek* is reduced to -*dik* due to its being compounded with the following noun *k̲u.oo* 'people'. Notably, James' name for these people, «G̱ákw Sax̱a K̲u.oo» 'People-Who-Eat-Gnarly-Driftwood' (SJ xi, 24, 306) uses different words but an identical structure; hers likewise modifies *k̲u.oo* with

* For more details on the traditional structure of Tlingit houses see especially Shotridge and Shotridge, "Indians of the Northwest", 81–99, as well as Emmons, *The Tlingit Indians*, 103–12, and de Laguna, *Under Mount Saint Elias*, 295–302.

the combining form of a verbal noun (in her case *g̱ákw sax̱a* 'eating gnarly driftwood') rather than an attributive verb form. These figures, known also as the *Yax̱taattuḵwáani* 'Night-Dwellers', are discussed in §2.16 of the editors' introduction.

LINE 8. *Hó-hóu:* This line is intoned as a soft chant, almost like a song.

LINE 9. *Ch'áakw dateeyí:* It is hard to hear exactly what Dick says here, and no speaker we have checked with recognizes *ch'áakw dateeyí.* However, from the context it would appear that this phrase would be virtually synonymous with *ch'áakwx̱ sateeyí* 'it being a long time' (i.e., 'after a long time'). Compare SJ ii, 51, where we also appear to hear *ch'áakw dateeyí*; this, however, is also a tenuous rendering of something poorly heard.

LINE 12. *X'óol' yáx̱ yatee asdeek:* Literally approximately, 'the dipnetting is frenzied, chaotic'. The same phrase occurs again in line 190. Compare also line 71, «X'óol' yáx̱ woonei» 'It (the situation) was frenzied, chaotic, in turmoil'.

LINE 13. *ḵaa too[shtí]:* Dick never actually finishes pronouncing this verb, only saying «...ḵaa too—too—too—».

LINE 26. *Aawat'ei k'idéin tle:* The implied object of the verb *aawat'ei* 'he (Raven) found it' is the whereabouts of the daylight and how to go about getting it; *k'idéin* 'well' seems to imply that what Raven heard was entirely sufficient for him to go about his task.

LINE 30. *Náas Sháak:* The name of the Nass River is pronounced with high tone here. This placename is most commonly attested with low tone, *Naas*, but we find this high-tone variant used also by Italio, James, and Hammond.

LINES 34–35. The pronoun *du* 'his' in both *du ḵáa gooxú* 'his male slave' and *du sée* 'his daughter' refers to Naasshagiyéil, the man who possesses the Container of Daylight at the head of the Nass River (discussed in §2.14 of the editors' introduction).

LINE 35. *wé du sée daa yóo jikwli.atgi:* This is a great example of a postposed relative clause. In most cases the head noun of a relative clause comes immediately after the verb, but postposed relative clauses are not uncommon in Tlingit. Here *wé du sée daa yóo jikwli.atgi* 'who waits on his daughter' modifies the preceding *wéi du ḵáa gooxú* 'his male slave'.

LINE 41. *x̱áach áwé a daa yóo jikux̱li.átk:* What is interesting is that the ergative independent pronoun *x̱áach* refers to the subject of an intransitive verb here, whereas normally it refers to the subject of a transitive verb. What appears to be happening is that the possessive pronoun *a* 'her (the young woman)' of *a daa* is interpreted as a quasi-object of the verb. This is discussed in appendix 2, §6.

LINES 50–51. *ayawdagoodí áwé / a kát sh wudix̲ích:* Dick concludes line 50 saying, «ayawdagoodí áwé tl'eex a ká—a kát sh wudix̲ích.» We are taking *tl'eex a ká* 'debris/rubbish on it' to be a false start here.

LINES 53, 60. *a wax̲'at'eex'.wán:* This term appears to refer to the inside corner of a bentwood box. Leer's "Stem List" contains the penciled entry, «+wak̲.at'i`x'.wán», translated there as "(inside) corner (of bentwood box)", which was in fact most likely copied from a draft manuscript of Dick's text. However, upon relistening to Dick's two pronunciations, we hear *wax̲'a-* (from *wax̲'é* or *wak̲x̲'é* '(inside) corner of eye') rather than *wak̲.a-*. Moreover, the prefix sequence *wak̲.a-* does not make sense, since there is no known prefix *a-* that would occur in this position. Interestingly enough, this very word appears in a romanized transcription of an anonymous Russian word list that Leer found in one of his notebooks: «auakat'ixún», evidently a romanization of ауакатихýн (i.e., *a wax̲'at'eex'.wán*) glossed "outer angle", even though in the context of this story, Raven has to have been positioned *inside* the bentwood dipper. Raven is thus hiding himself in the *ták̲di x'eesháa wax̲'at'eex'.wán* 'inside corner of the bentwood dipper'—a wonderfully specific and now rare vocabulary item. This might refer to any inner corner of a bentwood box, or it could refer specifically to the single lashed or pegged corner. The latter seems more likely because in lines 61–62 Dick says that Raven thought that *a wax̲'at'eex'.wán* would be the specific section of the box from which the girl would take a sip and so Raven strategically positioned himself there. If it were the case that this term referred to any of the four inner corners, it would be unclear why Raven selected the particular corner that he did. See the note to FI I, V, 50, 54, for comparison of the descriptions of Raven in the corner of the young woman's drinking vessel.

LINE 54. *yawduwatín:* While the verb would usually mean 'he was recognized' or 'someone/people recognized him', here this seems to refer to the fact that the people notice the little speck of debris (which Raven is hiding in) floating on the surface of the drinking water, the implication being that the people noticed the debris that Raven hoped would go undetected, not that they recognized Raven himself.

LINE 59. *a shayadáax̲:* This means 'better than before', here in the sense that after pouring out the bentwood pail that contained the rubbish, the young woman wanted the slave to get another one so as to get a rubbish-free, and therefore improved, batch of water.

LINE 63. *Adana nóok áwé:* This is an imperfective verb form *adaná* 'she drinks it; she is drinking it' followed by the consecutive auxiliary *=nóok*. Note that the verb stem *ná* simply loses its tone before *=nóok*, whereas before the habitual auxiliary *=nukch~nuch~nooch~neech* the stem is lengthened: *adanáa nu(k)ch* 's/he drinks it (habitually)'.

LINE 74. *héil aadé kéi g̲waaxeexi yé:* Literally, 'it can't come [back] up'.

LINE 75. *yan kawdu{wa.éts'}:* We can't hear anything beyond «yan kawdu…». We have retained Fred White's initial transcription, *yan kawduwa.éts'*, meaning 'they gently, delicately, carefully laid her down'.

LINE 78. *deisgwach dís yaa anas.át:* The literal meaning of this would seem to be 'she was letting the months go by gradually'.

LINE 81. *du x̲'óol' yéi k̲unastéen:* This is literally 'her belly was coming into existence', the implication being she was 'starting to show', i.e., was becoming visibly pregnant.

LINE 82. *la.oos nukch:* The verb root *.oos* is invariable, and it is notable that it is not shortened here before the auxiliary habitual =*nukch*. We can't tell if the object of *la.oos nukch* 's/he/it would be restless' is the woman or her belly (i.e., the growing fetus), but the phrase *i yit.shát aayí yáx̲* 'like your daughter-in-law's one' in the following line hints that he is talking about the baby bump.

LINE 83. *i yit.shát:* This line is an aside to Fred White. The compound *yit.shát* means literally 'son's wife', but the functional equivalent in English is 'daughter-in-law'.

LINE 100. *Héil shay̆awdahaa:* Literally, 'they were not many'.

LINE 104. *i sáni:* Dick is referring to Raven as Fred White's 'paternal uncle', since White belongs to the Shangukeidí clan, which is of the Eagle moiety.

LINE 105. Right after this line Fred White says something ending in …*yáx̲*, but we could not confirm anything beyond that.

LINE 110. *Lyóo.atkoowajeegi Shaanák'w:* This character, whose name we translate as 'Unfazable-Little-Elder', is discussed in §2.8 of the editors' introduction.

LINE 113. *Tléil yóo at koojeek:* This is more literally, 'She doesn't puzzle over things', 'She isn't curious', or 'She doesn't get mystified, perplexed, baffled'. The implication is that she has a certain attitude of disinterestedness and is never unsure of the truth or identity of what confronts her.

LINE 114. *Tle yax̲ at kaneek:* This is a repetitive verb phrase that would seem here to mean something like 'she (customarily) announces, reports (the identity of) things'; the corresponding perfective form is *yan at kaawaník*.

LINE 115. *Wududliyéx̲ ch'a hásch:* This literally means 'it was made just by them', but it is not clear what was made by whom. We suspect that Dick is stating that some unspecified group of people in the past was responsible for creating the name

Lyóo.atkoowajeegi Shaanák'w for this being. Note that here the fourth-person human subject prefix *du-* 'they, (the) people' is correfferential with the ergatively-marked third-person human plural independent pronoun *hás* 'them'.

LINE 117. *Wooch kát awdzinúk:* This is somewhat of a grammatical puzzle. Our consultants were stumped by this construction. The only way we can make sense out of this is by comparing it with other instances where *woosh kát* with the *d-* element of the classifier indicates 'retracing one's path', such as *woosh kát wudigút* 'he paced back and forth' and *woosh kát wudik̲ín* 'it flew back and forth' (see the note to FI I, i, 205, for discussion of these forms). Accordingly, we might translate this as 'she shifted the baby from side to side (in her arms)' or even 'she rocked the baby from side to side'. However, this is quite speculative, especially because the only examples with *woosh kát* and *d-* meaning 'retracing one's path' use intransitive verbs, whereas the verb in this case is transitive.

LINE 125. *k̲uwdzitèe-ee:* Dick pronounces the first verb in this line with emphatic falling tone and an overlong vowel.

LINE 126–27. *gunéi yaa nashk̲ák̲ … gunéi wjik̲ák̲:* This is a sort of pun. Even though this verb most naturally translates 'he started scooting' in this context, the theme *S-d-sh-k̲aak̲~* usually translates 'for S (a bird) to land', 'for S to perch', or 'for S to waddle, move in a squatting position' and so superimposes the image of a raven waddling upon the image of a human child toddling. The preverb *gunéi* 'beginning, starting to V' is rarely attested before the progressive, but here Dick repeats this phrase twice.

LINES 132, 133, 158, 159. *Du jeet kiylakél':* Note the contraction here of *ka-ÿi-* to *kiy-*, as in the Teslin dialect, rather than *kay-*, as in most of Coastal Tlingit.

LINE 139. *Natèi-eich:* This is an exceptionally emphatic and drawn-out pronunciation of *nateich* 'he would sleep'.

LINE 145. *Yax̲ yakawdzik̲inyéyéx̲ áwéi woonee:* The phrase on which this line is based is found in Leer's "Lexical Binders" as «yax̲ yakawdzik̲ín», glossed there as "stars are twinkling". This verb is embedded in what we refer to as a quasi-attributive *-ÿéyáx̲* construction (described in appendix 1, §13.1.2). Fred White translated the whole sentence in the manuscript of this text as "They're out shining like a moonless night", which captures the image implied by this phrase—an event resulting in the stars shining brilliantly and vividly against the dark sky with no other competing light. This line ends with the false start «k̲ei[.á]—» 'dawn, daylight', which Dick corrects to «k̲utx̲.ayanahá» 'stars' in the following line.

LINE 148. *Du jíni:* We might expect Dick to say *du jín* 'his hand(s)/arm(s)' here, but instead he says «du jíni», which would usually translate 'his foreleg(s)/paw(s) (speaking of an animal)'.

LINE 157. *Tlex̲ wáa yóo kooneigée sáyáa:* Note that the repetitive string *yóo=...(-k)* together with the thematic prefix combination *ka+u-* found in this verb occurs in similar phrases such as *wáa yóo koogóot sáwé* 'after s/he/it had walked for so long' and *a daa yóo akwdligínk* 'he looked it over'. Note that *yóo=* (or *yoo=*) requires the verb stem to take the suffix *-k* only in the imperfective forms such as the subordinative imperfective form *yóo kooneigée* (underlyingly *yóo=ka+u-nei-k-ee*); *-k* is not found in the other modes, such as the consecutive form *yóo koogóot.*

LINE 159. *De gaax̲ch uwaják̲:* Literally, 'crying has already killed him'.

LINE 162. *Sh k̲'analtèich:* This is a rare example of a verb of pretending with the dissimulative derivational string *sh=k̲'e-d-l-* (*na*) 'pretending to V'. Additionally, this is a habitual form with emphatic falling tone on the stem.

LINE 174. *Kaawayíkt akaajéil ax̲ ádi yóo Yéil Tl'éetl'i!:* The verb *akaajéil* is an instance of the realizational mode, which takes the conjugation prefix (here Ø-), the *i-* element of the classifier, and a long high stem. See appendix 1, §9.3, for brief discussion of this verb mode. The moniker *Yéil Tl'éetl'i* literally means 'Shitty Raven'. Note the consistency with this passage from the Raven story told in English by Deikeenaak'w, "When the child had this in his hands, he uttered the raven cry, 'Ḳā [*G̲áa*],' and flew out with it through the smoke hole. Then the person from whom he had stolen it said, 'That old manuring raven has gotten all of my things.'"*

LINE 175. *Ash wulitl'ítl':* The verb form *ash wulil'íl'* would literally mean 'he caused him to shit'. But the verb here is clearly pronounced «ash wulitl'ítl'» and in the preceding line the man curses Raven by calling him «Yéil Tl'éetl'i» 'Shitty Raven'. These are both formed from the root *tl'éetl'~*, which would appear to be a pejorative variant of ordinary *l'éel'~* '(to) shit'. Therefore we have translated *ash wulitl'ítl'* as 'he dubbed [Raven] shitty', namely by calling him *Yéil Tl'éetl'i* 'Shitty Raven'.

LINE 179. *aax̲ haat uwagudi yéidachóon:* The phrase *aax̲ haat uwagudi yé* means 'the place from which he came to here'; this refers to the place from which Raven set out before his arrival at the house of Naasshagiyéil; Dick specifies two lines later that it was in fact the Akwe River, which lies between Yakutat and Dry Bay, where Raven initially learned of the whereabouts of the Container of Daylight from the Night-Dwellers and back towards which he is now journeying with the container in his possession. We might rather expect *aax̲ haat uwagudi yé dachóon*, with

* Swanton, *Tlingit Myths and Texts*, 4, bracketed spelling ours.

P dachóon 'straight towards P' treated as a separate word like the relational postpositions, e.g., *P nák̲* '(getting) away from P' and *P g̲óot* 'without P'. However, it appears that *-dachóon* is treated as a suffixal postposition by Dick here, since he uses the lengthened form *yéi-* before *-dachóon*, as is normal before true postpositions, e.g., in the locative form *yéi-x'* 'at the place' and the allative form *yéi-de* 'toward the place'.

LINE 191. *yéi aan yánde ag̲ax̲oox̲:* This is a consecutive form. Usually consecutives end with a long high stem, but *x̲oox̲* is an invariable root, so it remains long and low. Also note that in this line Raven has tried calling to the Night-Dwellers three times without success; four being the 'magic number' or 'complete number' in Tlingit culture, it is only on Raven's fourth attempt that he gets the response he is after.

LINES 196–97. *Naasshagiyát:* There is a false start in line 196 with Dick pronouncing «Naasshagiyéil» 'Raven-of-the-Head-of-the-Nass', but immediately correcting this to «Naasshagiyát» 'Child-of-the-Head-of-the-Nass' in the next line. On the name and character *Naasshagiyéil* see §2.14 of the editors' introduction, and on the use of the term *Naasshagiyát* by the Night-Dwellers see §2.16.

LINE 209. *K̲eiwa.àa:* The fading pronunciation of the stem is so prominent here that it actually sounds like *k̲eiwa.àh*.

LINE 213. *dák̲de atkaawa.át:* See §§1.7 and 2.16 of the editors' introduction for discussion of the unique verb *atkaawa.át* 'they rushed'. Note that *at* (normally a proclitic meaning 'something, things' which is written as a separate word) is here a thematic element of the verb; that is, it has no morphological function and no discernable meaning. Accordingly, it is written as part of the verb word.

LINE 215. *Ldakát yéide wdudlikéil':* More literally, 'they (the rocks) were chased in all directions'.

LINES 218–19. *át shukatán:* According to Sam Johnston, *át shukatán* means "this is the limit of their range", speaking, for example, of trees. Compare FI II, 155, «Tle át áwé shukatán wé téix', át wudikel'i yé áwé» 'The rocks extend to there, which is the place [the rocks] fled to'.

Notes to Frank Dick's episode iii, "Raven and the Salmon Box"

LINE 1. *Hei-ei-ei:* Dick starts this episode immediately after the last one and begins with a deep, trailing sigh.

LINES 13–18. *yáa náak̲w tl'eigée ... Ách áyá yan awsiyík̲:* The reference here is to an implement known as the *Náak̲w Tl'eeg̲í Wootsaag̲áa* 'Octopus Tentacle Cane' with which Raven pulls ashore the *Kudatankahídi* 'Salmon Box' at the mouth of the Alsek River (discussed in §§2.17 and 2.18 of the editors' introduction).

LINE 20. *{K̲oo[wa]shee}:* We cannot hear this verb clearly, nor can we assign an unambiguous meaning to it. Fred White wrote this phrase as «K̲oowshee» and translated it as "He's getting help." We are unable to hear /wa/ here, but have supplied it because this is clearly not an imperfective form and there is a verb *k̲oowashee* 's/he searched' attested. However, this verb form is normally preceded by a postpositional phrase such as *P-g̲aa* 'for P'. Perhaps *k̲oowashee* is more or less equivalent to *k̲oog̲áa k̲oowashee* 'he searched for someone/people', i.e., searching for someone to help him, with the *k̲oog̲áa* 'for someone/people' understood. We have also explored the possibility that this verb could have the root *shee`* 'to sing', but have rejected this hypothesis because there is no lexical item containing the root *shee`* 'to sing' and preceded by *k̲u-*, and because of White's translation.

LINE 21. *tlél k̲wá x̲wa.aax̲ín:* Sam Johnston translated this phrase as, "But I never heard it." Because this is a negative decessive verb form, we might expect the phrase to mean, 'But I hadn't heard it before' (with the implication: 'nevertheless, I have since heard it'). However, Johnston was very clear about the interpretation, and his has a much better fit with the narrative context, so we use his translation here.

LINES 26, 27. *G̲aaw Aanée:* In line 26, we clearly hear «G̲aaw Aanée» with initial /g̲/ rather than /g/. In line 27, the initial consonant is not as clearly audible. In Thomas Thornton's placename atlas the name is given as «Gaaw Aaní» (with initial /g/) with the translation "Time (Drum) Land" and the location "Akwe River area, Raven's land of creation".* The word *gaaw* means both 'drum' and 'time'; assuming our transcription *G̲aaw Aanée* is correct, we are unable to assign a meaning to *G̲aaw*. Fred White similarly transcribed the name in the initial drafts with initial /g̲/ in both instances.

LINES 30–31. *Yakwdèiyée:* There are numerous places throughout Tlingit Country with the name *Yakwdeiyí* 'Canoe Trail'.† It is a common name used to mark places to go ashore when needing to escape bad weather or to land a canoe near a village.

---

* Thornton, *Haa Léelk'w Hás Aaní Saax'ú*, 39.

† From ibid: "Yakwdeiyí, Canoe Road, Inside Cape Yakataga" (17, m#35); "Yakwdeiyí, Canoe Road, Inside the berm on Ocean Cape" (18, m#64); "Yéil Yakwdeiyí, Raven's Canoe Trail, Alsek River" (25, m#283); "Yeil Yakwdeiyí, Raven's Canoe Trail, Cape Fairweather Area" (25, m#298); "Yakwdeiyí, [Raven's] Canoe Trail, Above Lituya Bay" (25, m#304); "Yakwdeiyí, Canoe Trail, Portage Creek above La Chaussee Spit" (40, m#56); "Yéil Yakwdeiyí, Raven's Canoe Trail, Safe anchorage above Icy Point" (42, m#121); "Yakwdeiyí, Canoe Path, Across from Taku Glacier" (75, m#78); "Yeilkíji Yakwdeiyí, Raven's Wings Boat Road, Passage through rollers, Chichagof Island" (92, m#123); "Yeil Yakwdeiyí, Raven's Canoe Trail, Beach at cove in Larch Bay" (141, m#279); "Aanyádi Yakwdeiyí, Nobles' Canoe Landing, Old Wrangell" (153, m#88).

LINE 37. *Gus'éix̱:* Thornton has a short section titled "The Lost Village of Gus'eix̱".[*] The location of the village is described as being somewhere up the Akwe River.[†] The syllable *s'éix̱* was heard with high tone here; Fred White wrote it high as well.

LINE 39. *Diginaa Hít:* This is the name of a L'uknax̱.ádi clan house. We have translated it with a commonly used English form 'Far-Out House', though 'Seaward House' or 'Offshore House' could be suitable literal alternatives. The word *diginaa* or *daginaa* (depending on dialect) comes from earlier *dag-i-nÿaa* 'out-EPENTHETIC·VOWEL-vicinity', where *-i-* is the epenthetic vowel inserted by rule to break up a cluster of three consonants, here /g/-/n/-/ÿ/.

LINE 45. *Shakahít:* This is the name of a Lukaax̱.ádi clan house. As Dick says in line 44, this name is a compounded form of *A Shaká Hít* 'Its Prow House'. We find Dick etymologizing a compound noun in a directly parallel manner in the story of "The Woman Who Married the Bear", «Taakw.eetí / yóo áyá wduwasáa; táakw a eetí áyá», translated by the Dauenhauers as "Spring / is what they call it; the remains of winter".[‡]

LINE 47. *Yéi déix̱ áyáa wootee Diginaa Hít:* Here Dick seems to pronounce «déix̱» 'two' with the vowel /éi/, whereas in line 17 we hear «déex̱», with /ée/. This sentence translates most naturally, 'In this way there came to be two Far-Out Houses', but it is not entirely clear why Dick would say this, since he just distinguished *Diginaa Hít* from *Shakahít*, unless he is referring to both the *Diginaa Hít* in Dry Bay and the *Diginaa Hít* in Sitka, both of which are houses of the L'uknax̱.ádi.

LINE 48. *Ldinax̱k'iyéide yan asnée wéi hít:* The word *ldinax̱k'iyéide* is an obscure term with a poorly understood meaning. The use of *ldinax̱k'iyéide* in combination with a consecutive verb form is a recurring formula we find throughout Dick's storytelling. In his "Stem List", Leer documented this term from Charlie Joseph, who used it in the phrase «ldinax̱k'iyéide woogoot» and translated it as "he went somewhere (but we don't know where)." In that instance it seems to refer to an indeterminate place; we surmise that this can refer also to an indeterminate time, so that it might also mean 'at some time (we don't know when)'. We have opted for the translation 'sooner or later' and applied it to each of the five cases in Dick's tale (FD iii, 48; v, 57; vi, 68; vii, 1; xii, 31). Its use as a formula is discussed in §1.4.2 of the editors' introduction.

* Ibid, 10–12.

† Ibid, 24, m#250.

‡ Dauenhauer and Dauenhauer, *Haa Shuká*, 194–95.

Notes to Frank Dick’s episode iv, “Raven and Fire”

LINE 1. *{…} wé x̱’aan:* There is a pause after the last story and someone, presumably Fred White, appears to prompt Dick to tell the story of “Raven and Fire” after the completion of the previous episode. The only part of this line that was intelligible on the tape was the end of the sentence, «wé x̱’aan» ‘the fire’.

LINE 10. *X̱ashak’ákwk’:* This character is discussed in §2.10 of the editors’ introduction.

LINES 11–12. *du xwáayi / -x̱ wusitee:* The noun *NP xwáayi* is a somewhat old-fashioned term meaning ‘NP’s sidekick, lackey, henchman’, or colloquially, ‘homie’. As an example, Nora Dauenhauer used it to describe Tonto’s relationship to the Lone Ranger. This noun also appears in the phrase *Dikée Aanḵáawu Xwáax’u* ‘Prophets of God’. Note also that Dick pauses between *du xwáayi* and *-x̱ wusitee*; Leer notes that he has heard this same phenomenon from other speakers on various occasions.

LINE 17. *Ax̱ shax̱aawúch kéi kg̱wagáan:* The verb *kéi kg̱wagáan* ‘it will burn up’ is intransitive, therefore *ax̱ shax̱aawúch* cannot be interpreted as an ergative argument; instead, it is to be translated as ‘because of my hair’.

LINE 29. *ch’a tlágu at yanéekw:* Here *ch’a tlágu* appears to be an archaic form of *ch’a tlákw* ‘always, anciently’. Ruth Demmert used this older variant when asked how to say ‘as usual’, replying «ch’a tlagu yáx̱», literally ‘as always’. Leer also found this phrase *ch’a tlágu* in a manuscript of Tlingit prayers from St. Nicholas Russian Orthodox Church in Juneau, where it is used to translate ‘now and ever and unto ages of ages’. Compare *tlagoo* (*aayí*) ‘ancient (one)’, where *tlagoo* is a contracted form of *tlaguwu*, which is composed of *tlagu* ‘anciently’ plus the time-noun suffix *-ÿi*; compare *ts’ootaadi atx̱aayí* ‘breakfast’, literally ‘morning food’, where the noun *ts’ootaat* ‘morning’ takes the suffix *-i* in combination with the following possessed noun.

LINE 30. *Áa yáx̱ x’wán:* This is chanted, so the underlying tones are obscured. *Áa yáx̱ x’wán* is presumably a shortened form of *i gu.aa yáx̱ x’wán* ‘be of good courage’, ‘stay strong’, or the like.

Notes to Frank Dick’s episode v, “Raven and Fresh Water”

LINE 1. *Atx̱ á:* This would more usually occur as *atx̱ áyá*, but here Dick omits the demonstrative element (*yá*, *wé*, etc.)

LINE 15. *sh tóon wuditee:* Dick begins this line with the word *aadé*, which appears to be a false start, as we see by the following *aadé wooḵoox̱*. However, Ruth Demmert confirmed the phrase «du éede sh tóon wuditee»,* which she translated as "s/he was offended by him/her", so it is marginally possible that Dick intentionally said «aadé sh tóon wuditee» 'he (Raven) was offended by it (Petrel hoarding the fresh water)'.

LINES 20–22. *Ch'a ltooshgú:* The word *ltooshgú* 'feeling wretched' is a verbal noun corresponding to the negative-pejorative verb phrase *tlél tooshgú* 's/he feels unhappy, wretched'.

LINE 21. *I kayaagáa yéi ḵux̱aanóok:* The translation 'I've come to visit you' is Fred White's. Swanton rendered a sentence containing a similar use of *N kayaa* from Deikeenaak'w as «Atcaya′ îkā′yade wutū′waāt» (i.e., *ách áwé i kayaadé wtuwa.aat*), which Swanton translated as "This is why we came to find you";† Ruth Demmert, however, translated this phrase as "[we have come] to spend some time with you, to pass the time with you". The database upon which the *Interior Tlingit Noun Dictionary* was based includes a note indicating that Lucy Wren provided the sentence «du keyaadé x̱waagoot» and translated this as "I went to where I thought he would be". Compare also line 36, «ách áyá i x̱ánde yéi ḵux̱aanóok» 'so I've come to visit you like this'.

LINE 22. *tléináx̱ satéen:* The verb *satéen* normally applies to a composite object, often composed of strands, such as a bag or basket. The word *satéen* 'lying (as a bag)' is a verbal noun homophonous with the positional imperfective (*át*) *satéen* 'it (e.g., a bag) is lying (there)'. In this case *tléináx̱ satéen* appears to refer to a person sitting alone, wretched and pitiful, like a floppy and useless sack.

LINE 25. *Du daa yóo jikwli.átk du káani wáa sá du daa:* The pronominal references here do not make it clear who is tending to whom and who is feeding whom. It could be that Raven is coddling his brother-in-law by tending to him in the hopes that he will gain Petrel's trust. Alternatively, it could be that Petrel is tending to Raven, who has made himself appear pitiful before his brother-in-law; therefore Petrel feels a duty to take care of Raven who has come to visit him. Here *wáa sá* appears to have the force of *tlax̱ wáa sá* 'how very [diligently]'.

LINE 36. *I yáx̱ x̱at taa.uwa.ás:* For most speakers, the verb form would be *x̱at taawa.ás*, with short-vowel thematic prefix *ta-*, which combines with *uwa-* to form *taawa-*. However, we clearly hear «x̱at taa.uwa.ás» on the recording, with long-vowel thematic prefix *taa-*. We received a report that Lena Farkas of Yakutat pronounced this verb in the same way as Dick.

* Note that Ruth Demmert consistently pronounces *du éede* rather than more usual *du eedé*. The same was true of George Davis, also of Kake.

† Swanton, *Tlingit Myths and Texts*, 286; from text 92, "Mountain Dweller".

LINE 36. *i x̲ánde yéi k̲ux̲aanóok:* The translation of this phrase was not clear to us or our consultants. It literally seems to mean 'I am acting like this toward you (or, toward where you are)', but the import of this phrase seems to be 'I am coming to you in this manner (i.e., pitiful and lonesome)'.

LINE 49. *Shée!:* This word is not clearly audible. Fred White transcribed it as *Lée!* 'No!', which, if correct, would be a rhetorically lengthened variant of *lí!* 'don't!' (but such a variant is elsewhere unattested). The exclamation *shée!* 'watch out!; be careful!' was attested from Elizabeth Nyman.

LINES 53–54. *Yéi asaawahaa du káani / du tayeet ag̲a.aagí:* We have supplied 'his (i.e., Petrel's) servant' in the translation even though it is not mentioned in Dick's utterance. Syntactically this phrase involves three persons, '[His (Raven's) brother-in-law]$_1$ wanted [him/her/it (unspecified)]$_2$ to build fire beneath [him (Raven)]$_3$'; we assume that the unspecified subject of *ag̲a.aagí* 'for him/her/it to build a fire' is a servant of Petrel, though it could also be his smokehole spirit.

LINE 57. *Ldinax̲k'iyéide ash eedéi sh ilháa:* The crucial verb in this line, which we have written as *sh ilháa*, is quite unclear on the recording. We went through various possible interpretations of what we might have heard and in researching the possibilities we found the phrase «aadé sh eelháa» in Leer's "Verb Books", which was translated as "Resign yourself to it!" Our transcription and translation of the verb are based on this entry. Note the use again of *ldinax̲k'iyéide* followed by a consecutive verb form. There is a false start in this line; the unaltered utterance is «Ldinax̲k'iyéide yáa du—ash eedé…».

Notes to Frank Dick's episode vi, "Raven and the Whale"

LINE 10. *aadé wdiyeig̲i yé {kawditóow}:* The verb we have transcribed as *kawditóow* is very unclear on the recording. Further, we have no known examples of the verb stem *tóow* 'to count' with the prefix *ka-*, so the translation 'he calculated' is speculative. Based on Leer's entry «wudiyeek̲», glossed as "(water, smoke) backed up, (storm) slacked off, abated, (there was an) undertow",* we have interpreted *aadé wdiyeig̲i yé* 'the way it abated' as referring to the spray from the whale's blowhole.

LINE 13. *A yée yéi wootee:* Note that *a yée* is the truncated form of *a yíx'* (or *a yíkx'*) 'inside it' (i.e., inside the whale).

LINE 14. This line begins with the false start, «Du kát—», which has been omitted from the text.

* Leer, "Verb Books".

LINES 24–43. These lines form an excursus from the narrative proper. Here it would seem that Raven's dramatic arrival at the mouth of the Alsek River prompts Dick to name the village and recount important events and landmarks of the region.

LINES 27, 30. *G̱altseenawáa:* The placename *G̱altseenawáa* does not appear in Thornton's atlas. The English reference would apparently be Bear Island in Dry Bay. According to one of Swanton's informants (we are unsure who exactly this was, Swanton only ever seems to say "the writer's informant"), "the Q!At!kaā´y̨î [X'at'ka.aayí] (island people) received their name from an island at the mouth of Alsek river said to be called ǪAłtsē´nîwâ [G̱altseenawáa], and were part of the L!ūk!naxA´dî [L'uknax̱.ádi] of the same region."* De Laguna writes:

> The rocky island in the middle of the bay is called "Bear Island," because it is frequented by so many bears that it is dangerous to go there without a gun. The native name is ǪÁłtcinuwu [untranslated; perhaps a typographical error for ǪÁłtcinuwa]. Swanton's Sitkan informant (1908, p. 413) gave it the name ǪAłtsē´nîwâ [...]. The island looks like a stranded whale, and is in fact *the* whale down whose blowhole Raven flew, and which he caused to wash ashore at Dry Bay. The Alsek delta is sandy because Raven wished the Whale to strand on a fine sandy beach. The people that flensed the Whale and whom Raven cheated of the blubber lived on the east side of the bay, at Yay̨ tay̨i [*Yáay̱ Taay̱í*], 'Whale Fat.'†

Minnie Johnson also mentions the same name in her telling of an extended Raven tale recorded in English by de Laguna, "I forgot the name of the village. GAłtsenewa [...] is where the whale drift ashore. It's a sand island."‡

LINE 31. *A daadéi yaa ana.át:* Dick does not make it clear what the people are gathering around. It could be that *a* in *a daadéi* 'toward its periphery' refers to the place named *G̱altseenawáa*, or it could be that it refers to the two women who were turned to stone.

LINE 33. *Wooweidi ḵu.oo:* Most speakers would pronounce this as *wooweidi ḵu.oo*, but Dick clearly pronounces the stem *weid* with low tone here.

LINE 35. *téix̱ has wusitee:* Thornton comments, "A moral lesson is also inscribed here in the form of five rocks off Bear Island [which we take to be *G̱altseenawáa*], representing an adolescent girl, her two brothers, and their two dogs. All were turned to stone because the girl violated her puberty rites by looking at the boys. This event is also commemorated in a carved ceremonial hat possessed by the

* Swanton, "Social Condition", 413, bracketed spellings ours.

† De Laguna, *Under Mount Saint Elias*, 84, parentheses original, bracketed material ours.

‡ Ibid, 846.

L'uknax̱.ádi (de Laguna 1972: 84)."[*] We might add that the girls violated the menarchic restrictions by walking around rather than staying in seclusion, as suggested in line 34 when Dick says, «Keitl hasdu een yaa na.át» 'A dog was walking along with them'. Swanton's plate XLIX in "Social Condition" illustrates the hat, which was drawn in crayon "by an old woman of the T!A'q!dentān [T'ak̲deintaan] at Sitka";[†] Swanton describes it as, "A hat illustrating the story of a man (the figure in the center), and two girls (on the sides) who turned into stone while trying to cross Alsek river. Used by the LuqāxAdî [Lukaax̱.ádi]."[‡] Both de Laguna and Swanton say that this hat belongs to the Lukaax̱.ádi, rather than the L'uknax̱.ádi. De Laguna notes,

> On or very close to the island are rocks that were once an adolescent girl in her puberty hood, her two brothers, and their two dogs, all turned to stone because she looked at them. To approach these rocks will cause stormy weather. Swanton (1908, pl. XLIX, c) figures a Tłukwax̣Adi [Lukaax̱.ádi] hat which illustrates "the story of a man (the figure in the center), and two girls (on the sides) who turned to stone while trying to cross Alsek river".[§]

Thornton and de Laguna suggest there was one girl; Swanton and the drawing of the hat are more in agreement with Dick, who says that there were two. It is interesting that Dick uses the non-human form of the numeral *déex̱* for the two *wéitadi* rather than *dáx̱náx̱*, the specifically human form with suffix *-náx̱*. This may have to do with the fact that these are stone figures, but is also reminiscent of the traditional practice of using non-human forms of numerals when referring to humans of particular social status such as slaves, e.g., *déix̱ goox̱* 'two slaves' (rather than [×]*dáx̱náx̱ goox̱*).

LINE 39. *naa.aayeit yóo duwasáagu át k̲ut woog̲éex'*: None of our consultants were able to identify the meaning of *naa.aayeit* and we searched numerous older texts for it in vain. One possibility is that it could be an archaic word referring to a hat or hood of some sort worn during a young woman's first menstruation, akin to the Koyukon *ts'ehtlekk* 'puberty hood with fringes'. We find such a reference in de Laguna, but it does not corroborate the form or meaning of the word in question, "On or very close to the island are rocks that were once an adolescent girl *in her puberty hood*, her two brothers, and their two dogs."[¶] Emmons relates that in 1855 the Finnish ethnographer Heinrich Johan Holmberg wrote, "at the first signs of puberty a girl was confined in a dark, cramped place; because she was considered unclean, she must not look at the sky, to prevent which *she had to wear a hat with a wide brim*."[**] As for the final verb of this line, heard as «k̲ut woog̲éex'», we have no oth-

* Thornton, *Haa Léelk'w Hás Aaní Saax'ú*, 9, parentheses original, bracketed material ours.

† Swanton, "Social Condition", 419, bracketed spelling ours.

‡ Ibid, plate XLIX, bracketed spelling ours.

§ De Laguna, *Under Mount Saint Elias*, 84, parentheses original, bracketed spelling ours.

¶ Ibid, emphasis ours.

** Emmons, *The Tlingit Indians*, 266, emphasis ours.

er examples of an intransitive verb form with the root *géex'*~; normally, the verb is transitive in its basic form, as in *kut aawagéex'* 's/he lost it'.

LINE 44. *ch'u yé káa áx' daxash yé:* This construction with *ch'u yé káa* + attributive clause + *ÿé* is syntactically a relative clause, but it seems to nonetheless have a simple declarative force, in this case the translation being 'every last person was out flensing [the whale]'. See the introduction to Dick's texts for further discussion and examples.

LINES 48–49, 86–87. *Aadóo sá kaa kaanáx angaxaashée / yáay yíkdáx kéi xdukeen?:* We find remarkable consistency from one storyteller to another with this formulaic expression that Raven calls out from inside the beached whale. See §1.4.2 of the editors' introduction for some discussion and comparison.

LINE 56. *Tle kei wdudlitl'ét':* This line is very difficult to hear. We considered two possibilities. The first was *tle wdudlik'átl'*, which would mean 'they (the villagers) just quieted him/her down'; however, it would be unclear how or why the villagers quieted Raven down, and if it were someone else they quieted down, it wouldn't be clear who it might have been. If it were referring to the villagers quieting themselves down we would expect *tle sh wududlik'átl'*, but we do not hear *sh* or the vowel of *wu-*. The other possibility, which we have used in the text, is *tle kei wdudlitl'ét'* 'they just climbed up (i.e., they climbed up on top of the whale)'.

LINE 59. *Daat yáx sá:* Here *daat yáx sá* 'like what?' or 'how very much' is the adverb of manner to be construed with *daakootláa* 'it is thick around him' or 'he has a thick coating of it', in which case *w[u]dlit'íx'* 'it solidified' would be a kind of false start or parenthetical remark. Leer reports that rhetorical questions like this would often occur in Elizabeth Nyman's speech; in all cases they were to be interpreted as 'how very much' or the like (rather than as questions meaning 'how much?' or 'like what?').

LINE 61. *X'ún! X'ún!…:* On the recording, these vocalizations sound closer to *x'úw̃*, with nasalized /w/, or *x'úŋ*, with [ŋ] like the /ng/ in English 'sing'. Based on the interpretation Minnie Johnson provided to de Laguna regarding Italio's narratives, this sound appears to be an onomatopoetic imitation of the sound made by a bullroarer; see the note to FI I, iv, 96, for further discussion.

LINE 65. *X'unyéi:* In line 65, the first time Dick pronounces this name, he says «X'unyéi». This may be an explanatory pronunciation of the name, i.e., *X'un yéi [wduwa.áx]* '*X'un* is how [they heard it]'. But the second and third time he pronounces this name, in lines 66 and 67, he pronounces the name in its usual spoken form, X'unéi. This is a personal name among the Lukaax.ádi clan, the name today of Lance Twitchell.

LINE 68. *Ldinax̱k'iyéide yan awusnée á:* The word written here as *awusnée* actually sounds to us like *awsnée*, and we are not sure whether this should be interpreted as *awusnée* or simply as *asnée*. If the former interpretation is correct, then this verb would be an instance of the poorly attested *wu-* consecutive. Dick does not state what it is that Raven finished doing in this line, but a good guess would be that he was removing the stiffened whale grease that had caked up all over his body.

LINE 78. *{...} aadé yóo oolg̱énk:* We are unable to make out the first three syllables of this line. The verb form *yóo oolg̱énk* here is puzzling in several respects. First, it looks like a negative verb form, since there is no *i-* element in the classifier and there is a *u-* prefix (which has combined with *a-* to produce *oo-*). Second, the more common verb form that would be used here is *a daa yóo akwdlig̱énk* 's/he is examining it', with the prefix string *ka+u-* following thematic *a-*.

LINE 82. *Tléil shéyákwshé a yíkde ḵukawdu.áax̱ákw?:* See the note to FI I, iv, 115, 120, 123, for discussion of this formulaic expression.

LINE 93. *Á áyá yáa—:* Dick has changed the quality of his voice in this impersonation of Raven and his voice rapidly trails off here. The quality of Dick's voice seems to present Raven as attempting to sound like an aged and rugged traveler. We cannot clearly make out this line. Alternatively, it could be something like *ahé ahé ahé* or *he-he-he* or the like.

LINE 101. *ch'a aan wuduwax̱áa:* This phrase, and especially the element *ch'a aan*, are discussed in §2.22 of the editors' introduction.

LINE 110. *A shóo yéi wootèe hóoch ḵu.aa:* Note the emphatic fading tone on *wootèe*. Furthermore, the use of the ergative suffix *-ch* in *hóoch* 'he, him' following an intransitive verb preceded by a relational noun plus postposition combination is striking here; Raven is marked as ergative while being the object of the verb. See §1.4.2 of the editors' introduction for discussion of the formulaic use of *a shóo(x')* *yéi wootee* 'he was poised before it (i.e., to feast on it)' by Italio, Wanamaker, Mills, and Dick at the conclusion of the theme of Raven tricking people into leaving behind a mass of food for him to gorge on.

Notes to Frank Dick's episode vii, "Raven Goes Down Along the Bull Kelp"

LINE 1. *Ldinax̱k'iyéide {yan at dax̱} sanée:* The material in braces is very difficult to resolve. What we have written may not be what he originally said but it makes grammatical sense.

LINES 12, 22. *Ḵées' Yax̱ Shakawdzinugu Shaanák'w:* See §2.9 of the editors' introduction for discussion of this character.

LINE 26. *a keekánx̱ áwé áx' yan sh wudzitáa:* We do not understand why the pertingent postposition *-x̱* is added to *a keekán* 'going to see, check up on it'; note that because the following word *áx'* 'there' has the locative postposition *-x'*, which is normal before the preverb *yan* 'to rest', we do not know how to construe *a keekánx̱* with the rest of the sentence. We might surmise, however, that the postposition is something of a false start; Dick might have had another ending to the sentence in mind, but diverted the sentence midstream.

LINE 31. *Ho-ho:* We believe Dick is impersonating Raven pretending to shiver here.

LINE 36. *Daag̱u x̱'áanáx̱ sá woolaayi léin áwé keenéek?:* Literally, approximately, 'The tideflat exposed by the receded tide during which time interval are you telling of?' Note that the attributive clause *daag̱u x̱'áanáx̱ sá woolaayi* 'that the tide receded during which time interval' (which modifies the head noun *léin* 'tideflat') contains an interrogative word. Due to the rules for wh-question formation in English, such a translation would be virtually unintelligible. Other instances of this formulaic expression, used also by Italio and James, are compared in §2.9 of the editors' introduction.

LINE 41. *a x'aash áyú adax̱nax̱ícht:* If this were a declarative sentence, we would expect *adag̱ax̱ícht* or *adag̱ax̱ísht* 'he is spanking each of them'. If we are correct that there is a *na-* prefix here, then the verb must be in the durative consecutive mode (i.e., it is inflected for both consecutive aspect and durative epiaspect), meaning 'once he had (thoroughly) spanked each of them (i.e., each butt cheek)'.

LINES 43–44. *Tóo nú!:* This is the imperative of the verb whose imperfective form is *tóo ayanook* 's/he feels it'; the same phrase occurs in the same scene in Italio's telling, so this is clearly a formulaic element of the story (the only difference is that *tóo nú!* 'feel it!' and *nées' nóox'u* '[the] sea-urchin shell' are reversed); see the note to FI I, ii, 91–92, for grammatical discussion.

LINE 47. *aax̱ áwé yéi kéi ayawu.aayí tle yéi ash yawsik̲aa:* The first verb of this line is puzzling because we find the form *ayaawa.aa* 's/he detained him/her', but we have been unable to attest a form with the preverb *kéi*. As for the second clause, we seem to hear *kéi ash yawsik̲aa*, but here again the preverb *kéi* is puzzling, and since this preverb imposes Ø-conjugation on the verb we would expect the long high stem *k̲áa*, but we hear a long low *k̲aa*. We have therefore retained Fred White's transcription, *tle yéi ash yawsik̲aa* 'she said to him'.

LINE 56. *Daak̲w.aa sá yéi aawasáa k̲aa shoowú yáx̱:* Literally, 'He named whichever one (i.e., whichever level the tide was at a certain time) "like half a person".' The implication is that X̱ashak'ákwk' went down to check the tide level a number of times, and one of those times he said the tide level had receded an amount corresponding to half the height of a person. Compare SJ V, 63, «K̲aa shoowú yéx̲ ÿaa woolaa!» 'It has gone down as far as half a man!', which, in James' story, is the voice of the character Gidzanóok'.

Notes to Frank Dick's episode viii, "Raven Deceives His Younger Brother"

LINE 42. *Neilnax̲.á áwé át yóo dzigítk:* This phrase differs only in slight details from FI I, iii, 92, «neilnax̲.á áyú ch'a yóo x̲at dzigítk» 'I keep getting buffeted back and forth'; see the note to that line for more details.

LINE 55. *neilx' ÿan yóo ax̲'ayax̲íchk:* The prefix *x̲'a-* 'mouth, opening' here appears to refer to the opening or 'jaws' of the *éenaa* 'tongs', which Raven is smacking to make noise.

LINES 57, 63. *K̲aa s'aagí {... een} x̲aat'óok:* These lines are very difficult to hear, so both the transcription and translation are tenuous. Compare the identical phrase in FI I, iii, 119; see the note to that line for further discussion.

LINE 65. *De yéi ágí yéi at k̲ushinóokk'?:* This verb form has three notable features: the fourth-person non-human object proclitic *at=* 'something' denotes the agent of the verb here; the *sh-* element of the classifier is used for pejorative affect; and the verb includes the diminutive suffix *-k'*. From the context, it is clear that X̲ashak'ákwk' is referring to Raven here.

LINES 83–84. *i tlaakáak hás ách wooch kas.aax̲u át ... du tlaakáak hás ách kas.aax̲u át:* The ergative postposition *-ch* in *ách* here is part of the instrumental applicative derivational string *P-ch s/l-* 'by means of P'. The verb *kas.aax̲u* is in the attributive decessive imperfective form (corresponding to *kas.aax̲ún*). Note also that the subject of the verb is not marked as plural with the proclitic *has=*. This is clearly not an accident, since we find the sentence replicated almost exactly in FI I, iii, 158, «haa tlaakáak hásch ách woosh kas.aax̲u át». It may simply be because the subject ... *tlaakáak hás* '...mothers' uncles' is already specified as plural. Finally, in line 83, the reciprocal object *wooch=* 'each other' is lacking, yet the verb still contains the *d-* element of the classifier. Therefore, we have interpreted this form as an antipassive with the *d-* element of the classifier, referring to documented form «yax̲ daawdzi.aax̲w», which is translated as "he made bundles";* compare the transitive form, «du káak eex̲ yee.átx'i yax̲ adaawsi.aax̲w», translated as "he tied up his uncle's oil containers".†

* Leer, "Verb Books".

† Ibid.

LINE 84. *Haaw, goox' sáyú...:* This seems to be an aside showing X̲ashak'ákwk''s internal confusion about the location of the material his mother's uncles purportedly used to use to tie stuff up with, which Raven answers by saying, «Áwoo» 'They are there', referring to the edge of the beach.

LINE 86. *Yanshukáx̲ kalxwás'[ch]:* We did not hear the repetitive suffix *-ch* in line 86, but have supplied it since it appears in the following line. Compare FI I, iii, 152 and 158, «taashukáx̲ kalxwás'ch» 'they hang down along the beach', where Italio uses *taashuká* 'end of flat area (sandflat, tideflat, etc.)' rather than *yanshuká*; the latter often translates as 'campsite' or '[out in] the bush', but here it seems more felicitous to translate *yanshuká* as 'shorefront'. Even though the words *taashuká* and *yanshuká* have different meanings, in these stories they seem to refer to the same location, namely, the 'backshore' or 'backshore berm'. We also find the term *taashuká* in KM I, 77, referring also to the 'backshore' region of the beach, in that case being the location where Raven was jerked around by the Salmon Box once he had hooked it with the Octopus Tentacle Cane.

LINE 95. *sákwshí:* Note that *sákwshí* in the first instance is probably *sákwshé* influenced by the following *yaa*. The second instance is clearly *sákwshé*.

LINE 99. *Nánde Aa G̱éelk'uwá:* The prenominal modifier *nánde aa* 'the northern one' is commonly used in placenames, contrasting against *íxde aa* 'the southern one'. Compare the placename pair, «Nánde Aa Kéet Áak'u», translated as "Northern Killer Whale Lagoon", and «Íxde Aa Kéet Áak'u», "[Southern] Killer Whale Lagoon."* The name used here by Dick, *G̱éelk'uwá* 'Face-of-Little-Mountain-Pass', is composed of the noun *g̱éel* 'mountain pass', the diminutive suffix *-k'w* 'small, little, dear', and the inalienable noun *ÿá* 'face, side', with the epenthetic vowel *-u-* intervening in order to break up the three-consonant cluster (/l/-/k'w/-/ÿ/) that would otherwise result. De Laguna writes,

> This portage is apparently over the point of land on the west bank of the Alsek, opposite Alsek Glacier. The mountain on the west was called Ģeł'uwa [*G̱éelk'uwá*], while the hill on the east side of the Alsek, Gateway Knob, was called K̇itċa [which corresponds to Italio's and Dick's *Ch'eek'áa*] in Athabaskan, or YAdagwAł [*Yadaagwál* or *Yadagwál*[*t*]] in Tlingit, referring to the stones that continually 'rolled down' from it (or from the glacier).†

One inconsistency here is that de Laguna's form would be transliterated as *K'eech'áa*; compared to Italio's and Dick's pronunciations, «Ch'eek'áa», the consonants are metathesized (see FD viii, 115, and FI I, iii, 134). De Laguna notes that this is the

* Thornton, *Haa Léelk'w Hás Aaní Saax'ú*, 60 m#102 and m#105 respectively. Location of both places described as "East side Lutak Inlet".

† De Laguna, *Under Mount Saint Elias*, 87, parentheses original, bracketed material ours.

"Athabaskan" name (if that is correct, presumably from Ahtna or Southern Tutchone) and lists an alternative name «YAdagwAł», which would be directly transliterated as *Yadaagwál*. This name appears in two places in the Thornton atlas, with different spellings and meanings; first, in the "Yaakwdáat, G̱alyáx̱, and G̱unaax̱oo K̲wáan" chapter, as «Yadagwált», translated as "Raven's Rocks Falling Down" with the location "Gateway Knob area";* second, in the "Xunaa K̲áawu" chapter, as «Yadak'wát'», translated as "Bird Eggs on the Face" with the location "Gateway Knob".† Following de Laguna, one might be inclined to identify «YAdagwAł» with *Ch'eek'áa* as a pair of Tlingit/Athabaskan names that both refer to Gateway Knob and take *G̱éelk'uwá* to refer to a different location on the opposite side of the Alsek River. However, Dick seems to suggest that *G̱éelk'uwá* and *Ch'eek'áa* refer to the same general area, namely, the location where Raven was packed to and thrown off the mountainside by X̱ashak'ákwk', and further, that this is the same place from which rocks are known to fall. In the "Yaakwdáat, G̱alyáx̱, and G̱unaax̱oo K̲wáan" chapter of the atlas, the forms «G̱ílguwaa» and «G̱ílkw.uwaa» are given with the translation "Pass That Resembles G̱ílkw" and the location "Mountain west of Gateway Knob;"‡ in the "Xunaa K̲áawu" chapter, the forms «G̱elk.uwaa» and «G̱elguwaa» are given with the translation "Looks like a Small Pass" and the location "Mountain pass east of Gateway Knob."§ In both cases, the Tlingit spellings and English translations assume that de Laguna's «uwa» in «G̣eł'uwa» is to be interpreted as the suffix -*.uwaa* 'resembling'; Dick, however, clearly pronounces it twice with a short high final vowel *wá* (this being the labialized pronunciation of *ÿá* 'face'). De Laguna quotes an unnamed informant who had lived in Dry Bay, "When they were going up the river, they used to cross the glacier the whole way across. They took their cottonwood dugouts with them. They took their canoes up a gully between two mountains, like a v, with a ravine, gẹł' [*g̱éel*] or gẹł'k̓ʷ [*g̱éelk'w*], like a steep place between the two mountains. They carry the canoes over. It takes them two or three days."¶ This would seemingly be the *g̱éel*(*k'w*) '(little) mountain pass' that forms the basis of the name *G̱éelk'uwá*; however, the exact location of the mountain pass in question is not certain. Further complicating the matter, Minnie Johnson appears to have told de Laguna that it was from Mount Reaburn "that Raven's partner threw him down a cliff in a box, after Raven had cheated him","** but that mountain stands far to the west of Gateway Knob. In sum, this placename has been attributed to a variety of locations by different sources (Gateway Knob and passes both considerably to its east and to the west) and has been spelled and interpreted in a variety of irreconcilable ways.

* Thornton, *Haa Léelk'w Hás Aaní Saax'ú*, 25, m#285.
† Ibid, 39, m#9.
‡ Ibid, 25, m#284.
§ Ibid, 39, m#11.
¶ De Laguna, *Under Mount Saint Elias*, 87, bracketed spellings ours.
** Ibid, 81.

LINE 115. *Ch'eek'áa:* Italio pronounces this placename the same way in FI I, iii, 134; see the note to that line for further discussion.

LINES 117–124. Here Dick segues for this brief period into a different story involving Raven and his wife traveling by boat underneath the place from which he was thrown off in the box. De Laguna quotes an unnamed informant:

> Of Gateway Knob: "That's where the rocks fall all around and they call it Yeł tsunayɪ ('Raven's work?') [*Yéil Dzoonáyi* 'Raven's Sling (or missile, projectile)']. There are rocks that big (the size of golf balls) coming down. It's funny they don't go in the boat. They just fall around the boat. When you are going to die—that's the time they go in the boat. Old Crow (Raven) made it like that. His wife is just scared. 'Oh, it's going to drop on our boat and go through!' (she said). 'Don't worry about it,' said Raven. 'Oh no, they won't go through.' I believe it (my informant added.) When my father was going up to Tɪnx kayani [*Tínx Kaÿaaní* 'Bearberry Leaves'], it touched his boat. That same summer they drowned."*

LINE 121. *Haa yée yéi aa kg̲waxéex:* Note that here *haa yée* 'inside our [boat]' is the truncated form of *haa yíx'* (or *haa yíkx'*), which literally means 'inside us', but the context means 'inside our boat'. The student of Tlingit grammar should pay special attention to the fact that *a yée* 'inside it', which is the truncated form of *a yíx'* or *a yíkx'*, is to be distinguished from *a yee*, the truncated form of *a yeex'* 'inside it (e.g., a building)'.

LINE 122. *ilítl'!:* Note that *ilítl'!* 'knock it off!' is a pejorative variant of *ilí!* 'don't!' Compare *héitl'!* 'how big!' and *gushéil'!* 'I don't know, darn it!', which is a pejorative form of *gushé* 'I don't know'.

Notes to Frank Dick's episode ix, "Raven and the King Salmon"

LINE 4. «*Éek̲!*»: We are not sure if this is a quotation or, if the transcription is correct, why Raven or anyone else would yell out 'The beach!' Nonetheless, we have interpreted it as a quotation attributed to Raven. It is likely that Dick is leaving a certain number of details unstated, expecting the listeners to fill in the surrounding narrative gaps, but here we are unable to do so ourselves.

LINES 8–9. *G̲éelák'w:* This is possibly a variant of *G̲éelk'w* 'Little-Mountain-Pass'. The latter is attested in combination with *ÿá* 'face' in the placename *G̲éelk'uwá* (see FD viii, 99) and by de Laguna, who quotes an unnamed informant's son, "The Tłukʷax̣ʌdi [Lukaax̲.ádi] lived in Dry Bay, and used to go up the Alsek, and take their canoes over a point called Ġeł'k̓ʷ [*G̲éelk'w*], through a v-shaped notch."†

* Ibid, 87, parentheses original, bracketed material ours.

† Ibid, bracketed spellings ours.

LINE 14. *yéi kawligéik'*: We might expect *yéi kawsigéi(n)k'* 'it was/became small', but we hear *yéi kawligéik'*, with the classifier element *l-*. Noting first that *yéi kwligéi* means 's/he/it is big; s/he is an adult', we would expect the perfective counterpart *yéi kawligei* 's/he/it was/became big, an adult'. It is possible that Dick added the diminutive suffix to this word, yielding *yéi kawligeik'* 'the little [thing] was large', but the actual stem pronounced by Dick seems to be *géik'*. However, we still cannot account for the fact that the fricative element of the classifier is present even though it is referring to a stone, which is not normally considered a composite or animate entity; however, in this case Dick might have been ironically referring to the little greenstone as an animate entity, since Raven will go on to pretend that the stone is capable of insulting the king salmon. Note also the emphatic fading tone on *s'òowk'* 'little greenstone'.

LINES 24–26. These three 'curses' are hard to hear in places; we have restored them as best we could. In line 29, note first we find the stem *t'ootl'*, an affective variant of ordinary *t'ooch'* 'black', as in the personal name *Dukt'ootl'* 'Black Skin'. Secondly, we find unpossessed *tl'eex* 'filth' instead of possessed *tl'eexí*. Finally, note *ltín!* 'see! behold!', of which we find more examples in Italio's texts.

LINE 30. *du eeg̱ayáanáx̱ guxkáa [woox'aak]:* We cannot hear the final verb and the word we transcribe as *guxkáa* 'running aground (on the beach)' is not clearly audible. Compare KM II, 31, «guxkáa woox'aak» '[the king salmon] swam up onto the sand'.

LINE 39. *wé át aayi yé:* This is an attributive decessive positional imperfective; the corresponding phrase with an attributive positional imperfective verb form is *wé át aa yé* 'the place where he is sitting'. The ordinary decessive form of this verb is *aayín* 's/he was, had been sitting'.

LINE 44. *yanax̱ guxkáa wdlitsees:* This phrase is hard to capture in English. It portrays the fish as swimming powerfully (*wudlitsees*) ashore (*yanax̱*, from *yán náx̱*) so that it charges up onto dry ground (*guxkáa*).

LINE 53. *ḵóode:* Compare *ḵóot áa* 'it (e.g., a bear) is sitting in a den'. In this instance, we suspect that *ḵóode* 'into a den' describes Raven stashing the king salmon's tail and dorsal fin in a nearby cave or den for later use. The noun *a leet* refers to the 'dorsal ridge' or more specifically to the 'dorsal fin'. Raven will make use of these components of the salmon as halibut bait in the next narrative ("Raven and the Brown Bear Couple").

LINE 54. *áa yan awsitée:* The classifier element *s-* in this verb refers to a composite object, so we suspect that the tail and the ridge meat were attached to each other.

LINE 55. *x̱'áal':* This refers to skunk cabbage. The plant grows to three or four feet tall on wet, marshy sites and has broad, waxy leaves that are the largest of any plant in the region. It has flowers in a spadix surrounded by a single bright yellow spathe and emits a fetid, skunky odor when blooming. The leaves are used to wrap food for steaming and baking in much the same way as banana leaves and taro leaves are used in the tropics.

LINE 63. This line contains two false starts. The unaltered utterance is «Aaa, yáa—ch'a yáag̱aa, ga—gootlk'i yá, dax̱ nadag̱átch x̱'áal'.»

LINE 76. *Yan sa.éex':* This is an extremely rare example of a consecutive with locative postposition *-x'*;* it is essentially equivalent to *yan sa.ée* 'when it (the king salmon) was completely cooked'. Note also that here the *s-* element of the classifier does not form a causative, but indicates that what is being cooked (the king salmon) is classified as a composite object.

LINE 88. *wu.aadéen:* Raven is addressing his crew that has returned from gathering skunk cabbage, but here he uses a decessive perfective verb form with a third-person subject, possibly to emphasize the length of time that Raven claims has elapsed since these unnamed people left. We gather that he is suggesting that some other people had previously come by and gobbled up all the flesh, which is a lie meant to cover up the fact that he has eaten it all himself.

LINE 91. *ch'u yé ḵáa áx' ḵukdahaa yé:* We are familiar with the verb *ḵukaháa* 's/he is digging', where the areal object *ḵu-* effectively detransitivizes the verb theme *O-ka-S-haa~* 'for S to dig O'. We do not understand why Dick uses the *d-* element of the classifier here.

Notes to Frank Dick's episode x, "Raven and the Brown Bear Couple"

LINE 8. *Du aatx̱úx̱:* The term *du aat* refers to 'his paternal aunt'; here we use the informal translation 'his auntie'. This term is used in English by Tlingit people to speak of a paternal aunt who belongs to the opposite moiety. *Du aatx̱úx̱* 'his auntie's husband' would in theory be of the same moiety as Raven and could be considered his clan brother, uncle, or the like; however, the fact that he is a bear (an Eagle-moiety crest) makes it difficult to associate him with the Raven moiety.

LINE 16. *a waḵ{x̱oo} yáx̱, ... a yáx̱ anateech:* We were unable to resolve the syllable in brackets to our satisfaction. The phrase *a yáx̱ anateech*, which would seem to mean 's/he keeps passing it by its face', apparently refers to the fact that Raven was flashing the Brown Bear glimpses of what he will eventually claim to be a chunk of his penis without letting him see what it really was: the tail of the king salmon from the previous episode.

* For another example see Leer, "Schetic Categories", 445–46, note 60.

LINES 22–23. *Kéi kg̲isanóok i tl'íl:* Raven instructs the Male Bear to pick up his penis with the verb theme *O-S-s-nook~* 'for S to pick up (animate) O', as if his penis were a living being.

LINE 24. *Daax̲ yakanadúch't:* In researching this verb, we examined two possibilities. First, in the *Tlingit Verb Dictionary* and in Leer's "Verb Binders" we find the theme *O-ka-S-l-dóoch'~* (Ø) 'for S to cut O (esp. fish for boiling) into chunks'; we only seem to find examples of this verb theme that include the *l-* classifier element. On the other hand, we find another theme in Leer's "Verb Books" and "Lexical Binders", *O-ka-S-(l-)dóoch'~ (na)* 'for S to roll and pinch, tweak O (esp. flesh)'; the *l-* element of the classifier alternates with no fricative element in Leer's examples from Tongass Tlingit. The meaning 'cutting up fresh fish' seems better suited to the narrative than 'tweaking flesh' here—though the Bear is cutting up the skin or flesh of his own penis rather than fresh fish—but we would be more confident in our interpretation of this verb if we could find a form with no fricative element in the classifier, since the form used by Dick has no fricative element. Dick's form, *daax̲ yakanadúch't,* contains the obliquative derivational string *P-x̲ ÿa+u-* (Ø) '(moving sideways, in an arc, circuitously) around P'. Further, in Dick's form, where the repetitive suffix *-t* is added to the verb stem, forming a repetitive imperfective, the repetitive epimode requires that the prefix *na-* (which in this case does not function as a conjugation maker but rather as an epimode marker) override the underlying conjugation marker of the verb, which in this case is Ø- due to the obliquative derivational string. This analysis remains speculative, however, since we have found no other cases of any repetitive form other than the ordinary one ending in *-ch* created from an obliquative verb form; certainly we have no other examples with *-t.*

LINE 31. *Yook̲ … Yook̲k':* The Character *Yook̲(k')* '(Little) Cormorant' is discussed in §2.21 of the editors' introduction.

LINE 36. *i daax̲ naa.aat:* The verb *naa.aat* is a *na*-conjugation processional form. The phrase here *i daax̲ naa.aat* 'they (lice) are crawling all over you' provides a mental picture of lice moving in procession over the body.

LINE 42. *K'e x̲'eendataan!:* More literally, 'How about you speak?' The introductory particle *k'e* indicates that the speaker is making a suggestion or proposal to the addressee. Note the verb form *x̲'eendataan* in place of *x̲'anidataan,* where the second-person singular subject is surprisingly displaced to the left of the *na-* conjugation prefix. This phenomenon seems to be restricted to certain common imperative forms, e.g., *jeenda.óos'* alongside *jinida.óos'* 'wash your hands'.

LINE 50. *Aan a x̲ánt ask̲óox̲:* As written, the text reads: *aan* 'with him (Cormorant)', *a x̲ánt* 'to her (the Female Bear)', *ask̲óox̲* 'after he (Raven) had guided it (the boat)'. However, given the poor quality of the recording, we also considered the possibility of interpreting this line as *aan a x̲ánt has k̲óox̲* 'after they (Raven and Cormorant) had come to her (the Female Bear) with it (halibut)'.

LINE 57. *Haa, goosú i aatx̲úx̲ k̲u.aa:* We find the same formulaic expression in KM III, 105–06. This expression is discussed in §2.20 of the editors' introduction.

LINE 68. *A yoowú {…} wé cháatl:* This line is spoken rapidly and is very difficult to decipher on the recording. We are unable to venture a transcription of the middle portion. We gather that this is Raven speaking to the Female Bear based on Dick's intonation, which is typical for quotations from Raven.

LINE 77. *ax̲ jig̲eit:* In AW iii, we find Raven repeatedly talking about «ax̲ jig̲eit». From the context there, it seems to mean 'my special way of preparing (a catch)'. In Wanamaker's section of the story involving the Male Bear, *ax̲ jig̲eit* refers to Raven's special bait that he uses to catch a lot of halibut; he falsely claims that he is cutting folds off the skin of his penis. In the section involving the Female Bear, *ax̲ jig̲eit* refers to Raven's special way of cooking halibut, which he tells her is not to be chewed but rather swallowed whole. In both sequences, Raven's *jig̲eit* results in the death of the Bear. However, when we consulted Sam Johnston and Bessie Cooley of Teslin, they indicated that *ax̲ jig̲eit* means "my kill" or more generally "my acquisition", i.e., what I have obtained or made with my own hands or acquired by trade or by buying. Compare FD xi, 43 and 47, where the term appears simply as *jig̲eit*, with no possessor.

LINE 78. *A káx̲ jiyadultáx'ch:* This is a remarkably complex verb form. The configurational string *ji-s/l-* refers to a long rope-like or withe-like object, in this case, this is referring to the halibut stomach. Superimposed on this is the Ø-conjugation obliquative derivational string *P-x̲ ÿa+u-* '(going sideways, in an arc, circuitously) around NP', where P is *a ká* 'its surface'. Raven is instructing the Female Bear as to how she should consume the stomach by saying that 'one' or 'a person' (Raven uses the fourth-person human subject pronoun *du-*) reaches their jaws over the entirety of the strung-out stomach before closing their teeth together. Raven wants her to avoid sinking her teeth into it so that she will swallow the stomach whole without noticing that it contains hot rocks.

LINE 91. *nag̲idak̲een:* Hortatives with second-person subjects are hardly found outside of purposive constructions. We thought about interpreting this as a potential form, *nag̲idik̲een* 'you could fly', but we clearly hear *da-* on the tape rather than *di-*.

Notes to Frank Dick's episode xi, "Raven and the House of Souls"

For those interested in the comparative analysis of oral literature, there are a number of consistencies between the story told here by Dick and a moment in the extended Raven tale told in English by John Kadashan to Swanton.*

LINE 8. *Hél dak̲áatk':* In Leer's "Verb Books", we find «tl[él] k̲oodak̲âat», translated there as "there's nobody there". Assuming that this verb can occur also without the areal prefix *k̲u-*, we could expect *tlél udak̲áat* 'it is uninhabited', but Dick seems to omit the negative prefix *u-*. It is marginally possible that Dick does say «Hél udak̲áatk'», but with the /u/ so quiet as to be inaudible on the recording. The omission of negative *u-* is found in the common expression *tlél nalé* (with *u-* as *tlél unalé*) 'soon' (lit. 'it is not far'), usually pairing with a subordinative form such as *tlél (u)nalé haat wugoodí* 'soon s/he will come'. Note also the diminutive suffix *-k'*. We find another case in which *u-* is omitted in a lexicalized negative verb form, namely the phrase «lyax̲dats'éini súk»† 'a troublemaker in the making', used by Italio in this volume.

LINE 32. *Yan shukawditáx':* This particular verb theme is not documented in our lexical resources, and our consultants did not recognize it. The closest form we can find is «du l x̲'eishk'eiyée a káa x̲'akawditáx'», which is translated as "he has chewed down on his foul mouth".‡ In both verb forms, it would appear that in the core portion of the verb, *kawditáx'*, the *d-* element of the classifier creates an antipassive verb, which would correspond to the transitive verb *akaawatáx'* 'he bit it' or 'he got a grip on it (with teeth or pliers)'. To this *kawditáx'* is added *shu-* 'end', apparently referring to the fatty portions of meat on the platter before him; the initial *yan=* implies completion of action.

LINES 40–41. *Tlax̲ wáa dagaatáay áwé jánwu:* We would expect the wh-question enclitic *sá* to occur after *wáa* 'how', i.e., *tlax̲ wáa sá dagaatáay wé jánwu* 'how very fat the mountain goats are', but we do not hear it on the tape. The enclitic *sá* is sometimes omitted though; compare, for example, FI I, iii, 56, (Raven wondering to himself) «Wáa óosh daax̲ané?» 'What could I do about this?'

LINES 43, 47. *Jig̲eit:* See the note to FD X, 77, for a more detailed discussion of the term *jig̲eit*. Note that here the word *jig̲eit* occurs unpossessed; we have translated it as '[their] kill'. We might also glean a clue to the interpretation of this word from Kadashan's English version of the same story, when he says "*the goods* were all carried up to the house by invisible hands."§

* Swanton, *Tlingit Myths and Texts*, 92.

† FI II, 173.

‡ Leer, "Lexical Binders".

§ Swanton, *Tlingit Myths and Texts*, 92, emphasis ours.

LINE 44. *Tle anlinaa ík̲de:* The verb *anlinaa* is a processive imperfective form. We take this line to mean that Raven is carrying the bundles of mountain goat meat one after another down to the beach and storing them in his boat. Another possibility would be to interpret this as referring to the ghosts carrying the bundles down, but these ghosts are elsewhere referred to with the fourth-person pronoun *du-* 'people, someone' throughout the narrative, so if Dick were referring to the ghosts we would have expected him to say *tle ndudlinaa.*

LINE 46. *áa k̲ux̲ awdigút:* The prefix *a-* denotes a fourth-person human agent, meaning 'someone' or '(some) people' and referring to one of the ghosts. The most common fourth-person subject pronoun is *du-*, but *a-* is used instead with simple intransitive motion and positional verbs, e.g., *aadé aawak̲oox̲* 'someone (or some people) went there by boat', *át ahán* 'someone is standing there', and *át anák̲* 'people are standing there'. We interpret this line as meaning that one of the ghosts returned to the house, the implication being that the ghost was taking the bundles out of Raven's boat and back up to the house.

LINE 54. *ách kandu{ll'úx'}ch—{yéi tle} gánde yaa nagút:* The stem and classifier of the verb written as *ách kandu{ll'úx'}ch* were very difficult to discern on the recording; if transcribed correctly, it would seem to mean 'people use it (the container) to drink it up' or 'people use it to guzzle'. The theme *O-ka-S-l-l'óox'~* 'for S to guzzle O' is normally ∅-conjugation; however, we have seen that certain verbs (such as verbs of eating, drinking, and swallowing) which usually take ∅-conjugation have a special subtheme with *na*-conjugation referring to consumption on a regular basis. If this verb is transcribed correctly, it includes the instrumental derivational string *P-ch s/l-* 'using P', where the P *á-* would refer to the container mentioned at the beginning of the line, but we do not know what the unexpressed object of the verb would be. Furthermore, the two syllables before *gánde yaa nagút* 'he (Raven) was walking outside' are difficult to hear.

LINE 62. *K̲aa Yahaayée Hídee:* The reference here is to a specific location. In de Laguna, we find this description:

> Kayak Island (Kaye's Island), or "Big Kayak," is referred to as 'On the Whale,' Yaỵka [*Yáaÿ Ká*], and it is said that one can smell the fat on it. The meat is black and the fat is white. Raven's harpoon is stuck into it somewhere. Lemesurier Point, at the northeast end, is 'Whale Head,' Yaỵ ca [*Yáaÿ Shá*]. A crack where "steam" comes out is the whale's blowhole. Also on the island, is a "Spirit House," S'eg̣e qawu hıdi [*S'igeek̲áawu Hídi*], literally 'dead person's house.' This is probably a cave. It is slippery in front of the "house," and if you fall when walking past, you must scream like a fox, or you will die. A human "spirit" (ghost) lives there, and the rock looks like a curtain tied up for a door.*

* De Laguna, *Under Mount Saint Elias*, 102, parentheses original, bracketed material ours.

The form de Laguna provides is *S'igeek̲áawu Hídi*, rather than Dick's *K̲aa Yahaayhí Hídi*. The phrase *k̲aa yahaayí* normally refers to 'a person's shadow', 'a person's image', or 'a person's soul'—the person may be alive or dead—whereas *s'igeek̲áawu* (from *s'eek̲-ÿee-k̲áawu* 'smoke-under-person') refers exclusively to the shades of the dead and is generally translated as 'ghost(s)'. In the story Kadashan told to Swanton, we find, "It was a ghost house, and the town was called the Town of Ghosts (Qay̨ahāy̨î' ānî') [*K̲aa Ÿahaayí Aaní*]",* using *aaní* 'town of' rather than *hídi* 'house of'. The Thornton atlas lists both «K̲aa Yahaayí», translated as "Ghosts" and located "Near Copper River",† and «S'igeek̲áawu Hídi», translated as "Dead Person House" and located at a "Cave on Kayak Island."‡

Notes to Frank Dick's episode xii, "Raven Pretends to Build a Canoe"

Notes on other 'versions': Deikeenaak'w§ and Kadashan¶ both tell short English versions of a story in which Raven encounters a woman named *X̲áatkak̲ugáas'i* 'Fog-Over-Salmon',** he marries her, she brings salmon about, and they proceed to put up lots of salmon-derived provisions. Kadashan's version continues: Raven quarrels with his new wife, provisions are lost, she abandons him and turns into fog. There are some common themes between those and Dick's story here: marriage, (loss of) provisions, quarrelling, wife running away. In his tome "Tsimshian Mythology", Franz Boas documented a similar Tsimshian story, "Txä'msEm and the Salmon Woman",†† which likewise involves Txaamsm‡‡ (who is the Tsimshian mythological equivalent to Tlingit Yéil) encountering a woman, marriage, bringing salmon about, quarrelling, loss of provisions, and the wife running away. The stories in "Tsimshian Mythology" were told to Boas in Sm'algyax̲ by Henry W. Tate at Port Simpson around 1910 and translated by Boas. Similar to Kadashan's story, in Tate's telling, Txaamsm's bride's name, "Bright-Cloud Woman", is related to fog/clouds and she also turns into fog when she runs away from him. Boas also documented a story titled "Txä'msEm Pretends to Build a Canoe".§§ In Tate's telling, Txaamsm marries a

---

* Swanton, *Tlingit Myths and Texts*, 92, bracketed spelling ours.

† Thornton, *Haa Léelk'w Hás Aaní Saax'ú*, 16, m#3.

‡ Ibid, m#20.

§ Swanton, *Tlingit Myths and Texts*, 14–15.

¶ Ibid, 108.

** Spelled by Swanton as «XātkA-kogā's!î», with the translation "Fog (or Cloud)-on-the-Salmon" in the Deikeenaak'w text, and as «Xāt-kA-kogā's!î», translated as "Fog-over-the-salmon" in the Kadashan text. Ibid, 14, 108.

†† Boas, "Tsimshian Mythology", 76, 668.

‡‡ *Txaamsm* is the spelling of the name in the orthography adopted by the Sm'algyax̲ Language Authority.

§§ Boas, "Tsimshian Mythology", 84, 720.

widow's daughter, and, claiming to love her so much, proposes that he build a canoe for the mother of his new bride; he's really only doing this so that they'll prepare dryfish soup for him while he's away 'working' on the canoe. This is the critical detail for the Ravenesque comedy of the story: Raven is only *pretending* to build a canoe by just smacking a rotten tree all day to make noises, "Then her daughter went to the place where her husband was working. Unseen she arrived at the place where he was, and saw him standing at the end of an old rotten cedar tree beating it with a stone ax to make a noise like a man who is working with an ax. His wife saw that there was a large hole in the rotten cedar tree, and therefore it made so much noise when TxämsEm was striking it."* Dick never says outright that Raven is only pretending to make the canoe, but (and this may only be because Tate's version resolves the obscurities in Dick's in such a satisfying way) we nonetheless get the impression that the same deception is at work in Dick's story, even if it is only barely visible. The background understanding of Raven being a total fraud in the process of supposedly constructing the canoe is necessary for this story to be funny at all. A comprehensive comparative analysis of the stories and themes found in Tlingit Raven stories and the Tsimshian Txaamsm stories would be a worthy endeavor.

LINES 3–5. Dick specifies that Raven came across something («a káx̱ woogoot») and says that it is some kind of being; in line 9 he says that this being had a daughter («du sée k̲udzitee»). Tate clarifies, "TxämsEm did still another thing. After he had visited every country, he found a little hut in which were two women—a widow and her daughter."†

LINE 10. *Áa sh wudlisháa:* This verb form contains the causative string *P-x' s/l-* 'causing P (to do something)', and thus could translate either as 'she (the daughter) caused him (Raven) to marry herself' or 'he (Raven) caused her (the daughter) to marry himself'. We have chosen the latter interpretation simply on the grounds that it seems to make more sense with Raven controlling the situation. Compare RZ II, i 43–44, «Kéetx' áyá tsú / sh wulsháayin» 'She even got a Killerwhale / to marry her', in which Raven is a woman enticing a male Killerwhale to marry her, so the sexes are reversed but the syntactic structure is the same.

LINES 12–14. Again we can compare with Tate, "After a while TxämsEm said to his young wife, 'Now, my dear, you know that I love you so very much, and therefore I shall build a nice little canoe for your mother. I shall go away tomorrow to look for red cedar. Then I will build a canoe for her. I want you to get ready, for I want to start early in the morning.' Then the young woman repeated this to her mother."‡

* Ibid, 58.

† Ibid, 84.

‡ Ibid.

LINE 16. *{…}:* On listening to this line we kept hearing something like «G̲ak̲ee, g̲ak̲ee, g̲ak̲ee [y]áax'». This sounds temptingly close to *g̲aÿk̲í, g̲aÿk̲í, g̲aÿk̲í yáax'* 'sit, sit, sit here', but there was the persistent problem that we heard the first syllable simply as /g̲a/, without /ÿ/, and the second syllable as /k̲ee/, and both syllables were difficult for us to resolve. Accordingly we decided against wagering a definitive transcription and translation, and leave it to future scholars to decipher.

LINE 17. *De yánde {yaa a[n]dag̲as.ín, daawdudlitsín}:* Both these clauses were difficult for us to resolve, so the portion in braces is tentative, but the final clause of the line, «Awux̲aayée áwé nagútch» 'After eating it (the meal), he would leave', makes it clear that a meal is involved. Dick begins slapping his hands together here after line 17 and continues doing so while delivering line 18. In Tate's tale, we find Raven beating an old rotten cedar tree with an axe, pretending to be building a canoe. Dick doesn't say outright that Raven is only pretending, but his slapping noises hint that this is exactly what is happening at this point in the narrative (i.e., simply slapping the log instead of actually adzing it into a boat).

LINE 18. *Yagiyee yáag̲aa áwé adaax̲ishdi nukch:* There are two moments in Tate's tale that could correspond to this moment in Dick's. The first is Raven going into the woods under the pretense that he's going to cut down a red cedar that will then be hewn out to form the canoe. Note the consistency between Dick's «yagiyee yáag̲aa» 'all day long' with Boas' translation of Tate, "all day long": "After he had taken his meal, he took his mother-in-law's stone tools and went; and *his mother-in-law and his wife heard him cut the tree with stone ax.* He came home before it was evening, weary and sore on account of the hard work that he had been doing *all day long*."* Further along in Tate's tale, Raven's wife trails him and sees that he is only smacking a dead and rotting hollow tree to make noises like someone adzing a canoe:

> A few days later TxämsEm started again, and on the following morning he went to take along some food for his dinner. Now, the widow said to her daughter, "Go, my dear daughter, and see how long it may take until your husband has finished the canoe that he is building, but go secretly." Then her daughter went to the place where her husband was working. Unseen she arrived at the place where he was, and saw him *standing at the end of an old rotten cedar tree beating it with a stone ax to make a noise like a man who is working with an ax.* His wife saw that there was a large hole in the rotten cedar tree, and therefore it made so much noise when TxämsEm was striking it.†

If Dick's line «yagiyee yáag̲aa adaax̲ishdi nukch wé aas» 'he (Raven) would be out beating on the tree all day long' is to correspond to a moment in Tate's tale, we think

* Boas, "Tsimshian Mythology", 84, emphasis ours.

† Ibid, 85, emphasis ours.

it is the former quote above, in which Raven creates the auditory illusion that he is chopping down a tree—hence *adaax̱ísht* 'he's beating on it (all around)'. The next two sentences (lines 19–20) would then allude to Raven's pretending to adze and hew out the tree.

LINE 21. *Yóo áwé:* This simple verbless phrase could be interpreted as equivalent to *yéi áwé*, meaning 'that is how it was', which would seem to indicate that Raven really was laboriously hewing out a canoe for his mother-in-law. Alternatively, it could be interpreted as equivalent to *yú.á*, meaning 'so he said', suggesting that Raven had really only claimed to be building the canoe. We have taken this latter interpretation, since it much better aligns with Tate's version of the story and Raven's disposition as a habitual liar.

LINE 23. *{De yax̱ g̱agúdín}:* We were not at all sure of the first syllable here. If the verb *yax̱ g̱agúdín* is correctly transcribed, it has the appearance of a conative verb form in the contingent mode, meaning 'whenever he would try to go'; however, this translation hardly fits the context. The hypothesis that the contingent verb form *yax̱ g̱agúdin* could correspond to the perfective form *yax̱ uwagút* 'he walked in place' fares no better.

LINES 31–32. *Ldinax̱k'iyéide a jeet at shulaxéex áwé a nák̲ k̲ut wujixeex:* In the versions of the story from Tate and Kadashan, Raven's wife runs away, abandoning him; however, from the pronominal reference here, where *a* appears to refer to Raven's wife in both instances, we gather that Raven depleted his wife's supply of food and then abandoned her. Tate's version similarly has Raven depleting the provisions, abandonment, and a canoe being taken in the process (presumably a different canoe than the one Raven is pretending to make):

> Therefore they took the canoe and moved to their tribe. They took away all the provisions that were left. Txämsem went back before it was evening. Before he reached his mother-in-law's hut he was glad and whistled, because he thought his mother-in-law had prepared him supper. But when he went in, he saw that everything was gone. Nothing remained except empty boxes and a little fire. Then he was hungry again.*

LINE 33. *wé du [shát]:* Dick does not say anything after *du* in this line. We have supplied *shát* 'wife' in order to complete the sentence and because in the following line Raven is clearly speaking to his wife.

LINE 35. *{Tlákw du ítx̱ yaa [sh] nalx̱án}:* This line is very difficult to hear. We have considered a range of possibilities in trying to restore this line. The phrase *du ítx̱* 'following him (Raven)' is possible, but not certain. Also, we do not hear the reflexive

* Ibid.

pronoun *sh=* before *nalx̱án*, but all examples of this verb theme we have been able to locate include the reflexive pronoun. Further, we seem to hear a consonant, sounding like /x̱/, after *nalx̱án*, but this could simply be an artifact of the recording.

LINES 38–51. These final lines are not inherent to the plot of "Raven Pretends to Build a Canoe", but form a closing narrative frame in which Dick brings the entirety of the tale to a resolution. Compare the opening narrative frame established in FD i, 1–9.

Notes to Austin Hammond's Stories

EDITORIAL BACKGROUND. The executive producer of the radio program that produced Austin Hammond's stories for KHNS was Gordon Sandy. Transcriptions of these recordings were initially drafted by Richard Dauenhauer. A more detailed transcription and a translation were later drafted by Ishmael Hope, Keri Eggleston, and George Davis. The texts were then reviewed by Lance Twitchell and James Crippen. Finally, the transcription, translation, and notes were reviewed by Will Geiger and Jeff Leer, who consulted Kenneth Grant, Bessie Cooley, Sam Johnston, Florence Sheakley, and Ruth Demmert on particularly difficult issues of grammar and translation.

Nora Dauenhauer transcribed and translated the text of AH II in December of 1999; she revised the manuscript in March of 2001 and further in 2009. Richard Dauenhauer and Lance Twitchell later independently reviewed and edited the manuscript. It was given final review and revision in 2022 by Geiger and Leer, who consulted Ruth Demmert and Sam Johnston on issues of grammar and translation.

Notes to Austin Hammond's tale I, episode i, "Raven and Petrel"

LINES 6–7. *yáa Yéil / yóo tuwasáagu:* This is an example of an attributive clause without a head noun, which is usually referred to as a 'headless relative clause', literally meaning 'who we call Raven'. For details, see appendix 1, §13.

LINE 11. *Wooshkáakeiydagwéich yéi duwasáakw:* Hammond is referring to his maternal grandfather (Hammond's mother's mother's husband) whose English name was Jim David. The Dauenhauers write, "After his father's death, Austin was raised by his maternal grandparents, Jim and Martha David. Jim David was totally blind. According to family estimates, he lived to be over one hundred years old. His Tlingit name was Woosh Káa Kei Yadagwéich."* We have written the name the way we heard Hammond pronounce it both times on the recording (here and AH I, iii, 205), «Wooshkáakeiydagwéich» where *ya-* has been reduced to *y-*.

* Dauenhauer and Dauenhauer, *Haa Ḵusteeyí*, 209.

LINE 20. *Wa.á ákyáa?: Wa.á* is a slight variant of *wa.é* 'you (singular)'. In most cases we also heard *yá* 'place, time, manner' as a variant of usual *ÿé*. This was a feature of Chilkat Tlingit found also, according to a Yakutat informant, in some Yakutat idiolects. Leer reports that stem-final /é/ was usually—but not always—replaced by /á/ in the speech of Nellie Willard (e.g., *du x̱'á* 'his/her mouth' and *du sá* 'his/her voice'), who was also from the Chilkat area. However, in William Kelly and Frances Willard's "Grammar and Vocabulary of the Hlingit Language of Southeastern Alaska" from 1905, the Chilkat speaker and co-author Frances Willard appears to consistently keep stem-final /é/ as such; for example, they write the words meaning 'blood', 'mouth', 'voice', and 'you' as «Shĕ», «G̈ĕ´», «Sĕ´», and «Wă-ĕ´»* (i.e., *shé, x̱'é, sé, wa.é*), respectively, all with final /é/.

LINE 25. *Ách haa een kadulneek át yá shkalneek:* There are two ways to interpret *ách haa een kadulneek át*, depending on what we take to be the underlying verb theme. The instrumental derivational string *N-ch...s/l-* 'by means of N' is applied either to the attributive clause based on the verb phrase *haa een kaduneek* 'they tell it to us' or on the verb phrase *haa een kadulneek* 'they tell the story of it to us'. So the whole phrase *ách haa een kadulneek át* would translate as 'the thing by means of which they tell it (or, the story of it) to us'. This phrase thus constitutes the predicate complement of a verbless copular sentence and *yá shkalneek* 'this story' is the subject of this sentence, so the whole line would translate 'this story is the means by which they tell it (or, the story of it) to us'. The third-person object of the verb *kadulneek* (which simply means 'it') could be taken to refer to generalities such as culturally appropriate conduct, or it could refer to the theme of the narrative that immediately follows, specifically, the characters' use of language as a means of establishing dominance; or both could be true.

LINE 31. This line contains a false start. Hammond begins by saying «yéi áwé yoo s x̱'a[li.átk]» and then revises to the singular verb «yoo x̱'ayatánk» 'he (Raven) was speaking'.

LINE 33. *[Goot'a]g̱áan sáyá ḵiydzitee?:* This line contains a false start. Hammond begins by saying «gwátk sáyá» 'when (in the past)?', but then starts over and only pronounces «-g̱áan», so we can assume that he intended *goot'ag̱áan sáyá* 'about when, during what time span?'

LINES 35, 36. *kaat':* The rare word *káat'* 'clam-digging stick' is attested by Naish and Story as «kát'» (i.e., *káat'*) with high tone, glossed as "digging stick for clams (also a pick)",† but in both cases we hear Hammond pronounce *kaat'* with low tone. Based

* Kelly and Willard, "Grammar and Vocabulary of the Hlingĭt Language of Southeastern Alaska", 753, 756, 758.

† Naish and Story, *English-Tlingit Dictionary: Nouns*, 42.

on Hammond's usage of the term we suspect that, for him, *kaat'* refers to a pointed stick used as an all-purpose tool.

LINE 42. *ch'ul Haayeetl'óok̲k'u daak sh ulhaashjí:* What we appear to hear is either … *daak sh ulhaashjí* or …*daak sh wulhaashjí.* The first possibility is the more preferred grammatically, with *ch'ul* followed by a verb in the negative perfective subordinative, which is the form used to mean 'before V'. *Haayeetl'óok̲k'u* literally translates 'Little-Liver-Beneath-Us'. This entity is breifly discussed in §1.2.1 of the editors' introduction.

LINE 64. *sh daa yoo tutudatangi nuch:* The fact that the singular verb for 'think' is used here indicates that each person is thinking over their own actions as a solitary individual. The plural counterpart would be *sh daa yoo tutool.atgi nuch* 'we consider ourselves (every time)'.

LINE 72. *tlél tsu óo ushxweix̲k:* The word *óo* here (truncated from *óox'*) is an archaic form corresponding to modern *du ée*(*x'*), here translatable as 'to him'. The verb *tlél ushxweix̲k* means 's/he doesn't say a word, doesn't make a peep', so the whole phrase here translates 'he (Petrel) didn't even utter a peep to him (Raven)'.

LINE 80. *yá k̲áa:* It is not clear whether *yá k̲áa* 'this man' here refers to Raven or to Petrel. If it refers to Raven, the following two lines, «sh kawjix'aak̲w. / Tlél tsu g̲unéi unúkx̲», could be translated 'he went limp. / He didn't even budge.'* In this reading, being fearful and unable to navigate in the thick fog, Raven has bedded down in his canoe to wait for Petrel to come to his aid; one nearly pictures him in the fetal position. On the other hand, if *yá k̲áa* refers to Petrel, the same two lines could be translated 'he made himself comfortable. / He didn't even budge.' In this reading, Petrel, who is perfectly at ease in the fog he has conjured with his hat, would be sitting comfortably and motionless in his canoe while watching Raven cower in terror. We have taken it to refer to Raven in the text.

LINE 89. *L daa sá ux̲ané:* This appears to be an extremely archaic phrase, as we can see first by the negative *l* instead of the usual *tlél* in a declarative statement, as well as the verb itself, which lacks the usual preverb *yéi* as well as the prefix *daa-*. In modern speech the phrase *tlél daa sá yéi daax̲wané* (or *tlél daa sá yéi daa.ux̲ané*) means 'I'm not working on, harvesting, preparing anything', but based on the narrative context, the phrase *l daa sá ux̲ané* appears to mean something more like 'I'm not doing anything'. So far this is the only instance of the putative theme **O-S-nei`* 'for S to do something to O' that we have encountered.

LINE 95. *Wáa sáyá x̲'ayeek̲á, wáa sá?:* Here again, *wáa sá x̲'ayeek̲á* means 'what are

* The interpretation of *sh kawjix'aak̲w* as 'he went limp' is based on Sam Johnston's interpretation of the verb, "He relaxed, *really* relaxed."

you doing (orally)?', or more colloquially, 'what are you carrying on about?' or 'what are you crying about?'

LINE 97. *Goosú wé kuwdagwáas'i:* Literally approximately, 'where is it that it was foggy?', but more colloquially translatable as 'how is it that it was foggy before but now it's not?' or even 'where did the fog go?' Other rhetorical questions like this are discussed in §3.10.7 of the editors' introduction.

LINE 102. *ách áwé a x̲ánt x̲at yadujeeyín:* The meaning of this phrase was clarified by Sam Johnston, who translated it as "they used to warn me against it; there was a time when they told me, 'don't do it'". We do not understand the meaning or function of the phrase *a x̲ánt*, including the referent of *a*.

LINE 106. *ax̲ sháan tóo woogei:* Literally approximately, 'Yes, so inside my head it has become great'. Note that Hammond does not say *ax̲ shantóo* here, but rather breaks it into *ax̲ sháan tóo*.

LINE 107. *ch'a oowayáa daak sh x̲wadlixixi yáx̲ x̲at nateech:* None of our consultants understood the meaning of *daak sh x̲wadlixíx*; moreover, in our lexical materials we find forms with the *s-* element of the classifier with this stem *xeex~*, but none with the *l-* element of the classifier. In short, we don't understand exactly what this expression means, but from the context it appears that he is saying that it was as if he had fallen down, and this impression is reinforced by the fact that the preverb *daak=*, when combined with verbs of moving through space such as *xeex~*, refers specifically to falling down.

LINE 117. *wáaytiyéix' sá:* This is a truncated pronunciation of *wáayteeyi yéix' sá*, which is itself a conventionalized truncated pronunciation of *wáa yateeyi yéix' sá* 'at some places/times; sometimes'.

LINE 123. *yéi x̲aan has akanéek ax̲ léelk'w:* Literally approximately, 'thus they tell me, my grandfather'. Hammond uses the human plural marker *has=* in the verb phrase, but then specifies the agent of the verb as *ax̲ léelk'w*, which is singular.

LINE 126. *Yaa s aklayéix̲:* This line contains a false start. Hammond seems to begin saying «shux'áa yaa aklayéix̲» 'when he was first making it' but revises this to «shux'áa yaa s aklayéix̲» 'when they were first making it' so as to refer to both Raven and Petrel. *Yaa s aklayéix̲* is a progressive consecutive verb form containing the string *ÿaa=ga-*, which is required for non-imperfective forms in the progressive epiaspect.

LINE 131. *át has ooltínch:* The implication seems to be that Raven and Petrel were watching to see if the plants would grow. Hammond specifically references grass, flowers, alders, and willows—all things that would have green leaves.

LINE 142. *a yakáa yax̱ satee:* The verb in this phrase is in the repetitive imperfective form corresponding to the perfective (*a yakáa*) *yan wusitée* 'it became situated (out in front of it)'. The *s-* element of the classifier here refers to the extended, string-like shape of an island as viewed from sea.

LINE 160. *yá kunag̱eey tséi x'wán a yáanáx̱ yeek̲óox̱:* This is an admonitive verb form preceded by the enclitic *tséi* 'be careful (not to)', meaning 'do not bypass the cove (or else…)'. This motion verb contains the obliquative derivational string *ÿa+u-* (∅); the corresponding perfective form of the verb phrase is *a yáanáx̱ yeeyak̲úx̱* 'you bypassed it (by boat)'.

LINE 162. *a t'éinax̱.áx' yei ikg̱waneex̱í:* We do not know exactly how to interpret the subordinative future verb form *yei ikg̱waneex̱í* '(the fact) that you will be saved/safe' here, but the phrase seems to have a force similar to that of a *t'éinax̱.áx' ig̱aag̱aneex̱í*(*t*) 'so that you will be safe behind it'.

Notes to Austin Hammond's tale 1, episode ii, "Raven and the Daylight"

LINE 7. *yáa du kéilk' du daa yoo jikwli.atgi:* Here the attributive clause *du daa yoo jikwli.atgi* 'who attends to, waits on her' comes after the head noun *du kéilk'* 'his nephew'; for further discussion of attributives see appendix 1, §13.

LINE 26. *wé sdu sée jeet:* This sounds like *wé sdu séech jeet*, but we think what sounds like the ergative suffix *-ch* is simply a false start for the following /j/ of *jeet*.

LINE 53. *Tlél duteen nuch:* Literally, 'People could never see him' or 'he was never visible'.

LINES 62–63. *Áx' áx̱ ÿas.aa yá— / anax̱ áx̱ ÿas.aa yá:* This sequence is difficult to interpret. It would be tempting to take the verb forming the basis of the attributive clause in both lines to be (*át*) *as.áa* 'he has her sit (there)', i.e., the young girl's father has her sit in a specific location. However, this positional verb only occurs with the postposition *-t*, never with *-x̱*. To account for the occurrence of *-x̱* here, we considered the possibility that Hammond actually said *áx̱ ÿas.aa* 'he keeps peering/peeking in there' (literally, 'moving his face to it repeatedly') with /ÿ/ suppressed after the /x̱/ of *áx̱* (as discussed in §3.10.2 of the editors' introduction); if this interpretation is correct, Raven would seem to be peering into the empty drinking vessel. Since Hammond has established just prior to this scene that this is *Yéil Dleit* 'White Raven', who is an invisible and translucent spirit, it could be that Raven is right out in the open examining the drinking vessel to find a good place at which to position the needle for the young woman to unwittingly swallow.

LINE 67. *áx̱ ayakaawatée:* This verb phrase contains the obliquative derivational string *P-x̱ ÿa+u-* (∅) 'moving sideways, in an arc, circuitously along P' as well as the configurational prefix *ka-* 'round or tiny object', which we take to refer to the evergreen needle. We therefore interpret *áx̱ ayakaawatée* as 'he (Raven) moved (or maneuvered or transferred) it (the needle) [into position] along it (the inside corner of the dipper)'. Compare the subordinative form of the same verb in line 95, «a tóox̱ ayakawuteeyí» 'when he maneuvered it (the needle) along the inside of it (the dipper)'.

LINE 71. *Áwé yan aawatán tsoo:* The subject of the verb here is (the invisible) Raven, *yan aawatán tsoo* 'he (Raven) set it (the empty dipper) down again'. However, the drinking vessel that Raven sets down here contains the evergreen needle that the girl will swallow, and which will become her baby—the baby whose identity we know to be Raven. Most other storytellers typically describe Raven assuming the form of a *gítgaa* 'evergreen needle', finding his way into the young girl's drinking vessel in that form, being swallowed by her, and finally becoming a baby in her womb; in such cases, Raven is a single, discrete entity throughout the process. Hammond's narrative stands apart in that Raven himself seems to have a different ontological status—multiple entities *are* Raven. Hammond presents the image of Raven secretly placing the needle inside the drinking vessel, releasing some of 'his power' (*du latseení*) into the needle, setting the cup (which now contains the power-laden needle) back in its place, and then stepping back to become an observer. While Raven watches the woman swallow the needle, it is in fact also Raven who inhabits the needle that she swallows. The power that Raven released into the needle therefore *is* Raven in a separate personage—Raven the son born of a virgin. We are thus confronted with the image of Raven existing 'in multiple persons'; the Christian theological counterpart to such an image is, of course, the Holy Trinity, in which God is one substance but three persons (The Father, The Son, and The Holy Ghost). Numerous Biblical motifs and comparisons occur throughout the four episodes of Hammond's performance, but this apparent 'Raven Trinity' is one of the most striking. See the note to lines 185–89 for further discussion.

LINE 72. *áa daaḵ góot áwé altín:* The pronominal reference here is unclear. The phrase *áa daaḵ góot* could translate 'when she went back there', or alternatively, 'when he (Raven) went back there' (i.e., up against the back wall or into the back room or the like).

LINE 81. *adana nóok áwé:* This verb form illustrates an interesting fact about stem variation before auxiliary verbs. If *adaná* 'she is drinking it, drinks it' is followed by the habitual auxiliary verb form =*nuch* (or the variants =*nooch*~*nukch*~*neech*), the result is *adanáa nuch* 's/he drinks it (habitually)', with a long high stem before this auxiliary verb form; however, it appears as *adana* with a short low stem before the other forms of the auxiliary verb: consecutive =*nóok*, conditional =*núkni*, and contingent =*g̱anúgún*.

LINE 114. *Dikyáank̲áawu:* This is a contraction of *Dikée Aank̲áawu* 'Headman of on High'. See the note to FD i, 29–30, for discussion of this word.

LINE 115. *A daa aniyilg̱een:* Hammond appears to pronounce this verb as «aniyilg̱een» rather than the usual Coastal way, *anayilg̱een*. Here the vowel of *na-* is retrogressively assimilated to the vowel of *yi-*.

LINE 119. *yées shaatk':* This refers to a young woman of marriageable age who is not yet married. We have translated it as 'virgin' to complement the explicit biblical comparisons Hammond makes throughout this performance. Since Tlingit has no direct equivalent for the English 'virgin', *yées shaatk'* would be the closest approximate equivalent.

LINE 120. *du káx' yat.áa:* The usual way of saying this is *du kát yat.áa* or *du kát yát áa* 'she is pregnant', literally, 'a child sits on her', where the postposition *-t* occurs before the positional verb *áa* 's/he/it is sitting'. Perhaps *du káx'* was a false start that Hammond didn't bother to correct to *du kát*. Compare «a káa yatwoo.oo» 'she gave birth to her child on it' in line 169, where *a káa* (equivalent to *a káx'* 'on it') is expected; there, however, *a káa* means 'on it (the moss)', whereas *du ká* in *du kát yat.áa* refers to 'on her (i.e., in her womb)'.

LINE 131. *yáa shawat.shaan:* Hammond simply refers to this individual as an 'old woman', but we can readily understand this character to be Unfazable-Little-Elder. See §2.8 of the editors' introduction for discussion of this character.

LINES 134, 135. *Aax̲ yéi niysaní:* This is normally said *aax̲ yéi naysané* or *aax̲ yéi naysaní* on the coast, but in Teslin we find exactly the same form that Hammond uses here, where *niy-* replaces the usual Coastal Tlingit prefix combination *nay-* (underlyingly *na-ÿi-*), and in general *Ciy-* replaces *Cay-* (underlyingly *Ca-ÿi-*). According to a Yakutat informant, some Yakutat speakers also use *Ciy-* in place of *Cay-*. Compare the similar case of *aniyilg̱een* in place of usual *anayilg̱een* in lines 115 and 175.

LINES 138, 139. *Kúlt'u yáx̲:* Here Hammond is impersonating the 'old woman' (Unfazable-Little-Elder), who is instructing the people as to what type of moss she wants them to gather. She clearly wants them to gather moss of a specific type or quality, namely, that which is *kúlt'*-like, so we might speculate that here *kúlt'u yáx̲* means something like 'curly' or 'soft'. Hammond pronounces «kúlt'u yáx̲» both times where we would expect *kúlt'i yáx̱* with epenthetic /i/ rather than /u/ breaking up the three consonant cluster. We are not sure of the meaning of *kúlt'*; it appears to occur also in a noun found in Leer's "Stem List", namely, *N ḵ'alukakúlt'i*, glossed there as "hole in rawhide for pulling end of same through", i.e., a hole cut in N (a strip of rawhide) through which the end of N is pulled, thereby forming a slip-loop.

LINE 150. *yá a kaax̱ haa een sh kadulnik aa:* Literally, 'this one from which stories are told to us'. This is a reference to the Bible.

LINE 160. *X'oon.aa x̱oox̱ ayoo.áat sáwé:* This is a variant of *x'oon.aa x̱oox̱ awoo.áat sáwé* 'after they/people had gone through the midst of so many [houses]', with the obliquative derivational string *P-x̱ ÿa+u-* (Ø) 'moving sideways, in an arc, circuitously along P'. We find *yoo-* in place of, or varying with, *woo-* in this prefix combination among other Coastal and Interior Tlingit speakers.

LINES 185–89. *Yéil Tlein ... Yéil Dleit ... Yéil Yádi:* Here Hammond touches on his concept of what we might call the 'Raven Trinity': *Yéil Tlein* 'Great Raven', *Yéil Dleit* 'White Raven', and *Yéil Yádi* 'Raven's Child'. From the general context, it would appear that in Hammond's quasi-theological framework, *Yéil Tlein* corresponds with God the Father, *Yéil Dleit* with the Holy Spirit (keeping in mind the fact that Hammond described *Yéil Dleit* as a transparent and invisible spirit in lines 44–46), and *Yéil Yádi* with God the Son.

LINE 205. *Tle du yoox̱'atángitín áwé tléwnlé ḵuwusteeyí:* First note that what we write as *tléwnlé* here is one of various possible contractions of *tlél unalé* 'it is not far off (in distance or time)', which with a following subordinative verb form translates 'soon'; other attested contractions are *tlél nalé, tléinlé, tléilí*. Hammond's variant as we have transcribed it contains the consonant cluster /wnl/, which is impermissible in ordinary words; *tléwnlé* seems to be syllabified *tléwn-lé*. Furthermore, we are not entirely sure what Hammond meant to imply by saying Raven would soon be born «du yoox̱'atángitín» 'with his word(s), speech, language'. He may have meant that Raven was able to speak at birth. Compare AH I, i, 35, «Ch'u kaat'tín x̱á ḵux̱wdzitee» 'I (Petrel) was born a contemporary of primitive digging sticks', or more literally, 'Even with digging sticks I was born', implying that these digging sticks were used at the time of Petrel's birth.

LINE 209. *át kawduwagwáatl:* The verb *át kawduwagwáatl* 'they are rolling around' is the explicitly plural counterpart to *át kaawagwáatl* 'it is rolling around', according to Ruth Demmert.

LINE 214. *du toowúch aklax̱'aal:* This literally appears to mean something like 'he was crunching/munching on her in his mind'.

LINE 226. *aan ashkoolédi áyá:* Note the contraction of classifier *l-* plus stem *ÿát ~ ÿét* to *lét* here. We similarly find «ashkoolét» in lines 267 and 308 as well as «ashkoolet nooch» in line 277; however, we find forms of this verb pronounced with the stem-initial /y/ as «ashkangalyádi» in line 223 and «ashkoolyédi» in line 278. The contraction of *l-ÿát* or *l-ÿét* to *lét* is normal in Interior Tlingit and fairly common in Coastal Tlingit; compare also *adétx'i* 'children', a contraction of *atÿátx'i* or *atÿétx'i*, in which /ÿ/ is likewise suppressed after the consonant /d/ of *at* (what is written as ⟨t⟩ is phonemically /d/, i.e., the unaspirated stop [t], not [tʰ]).

LINE 228. *Yáa gaanéili áyá k̲udzitee:* The noun *gaanyéili* or *gaanéili* refers to the smokehole screen, which was typically propped up over the smokehole to block weather and wind.

LINE 229. *Gáant kaawaxíx yú k̲utx̲.ayanahá:* Given that this deals with the stars, it is interesting in terms of the narrative imagery that Hammond uses *gáant kaawaxíx* instead of *gáant kaawasóos*; the former refers to a single round object moving through space, while the latter is the plural counterpart. Perhaps in Hammond's mind, this scene involves the image of a single object flying out of the box and passing through the smokehole, then proliferating into numerous stars only after having exited.

LINE 237. *Téengé:* This is a stylized contraction of *iyatéen gé*? 'you see?' Leer recalls Nora Dauenhauer saying this as *héengé*?

LINES 237, 38. *yóox̲ yawlixáat' / ... yáx̲ áwé yawlixáat':* On first glance, these verb phrases looks like obliquative forms with *P-x̲ ÿa+u-* (*Ø*) 'moving sideways, in an arc, circuitously along P', but if that were the case the expected stem would be *xát'*, not *xáat'*. On researching the verb theme, we find *P-x̲ O-l-xáat'~*(*g̲a*) 'for O to be suspended from P'. To this is added *ÿa-*, a configurational prefix referring to objects considered to contain fire in themselves: the moon, the stars, comets, or sparks—but curiously, not the sun—as well as firewood.

LINE 238. *yá Éesh yóo s ayasáagu yáx̲ áwé yawlixáat' yú.á:* First, note that *Éesh* 'Father' occurs here without a possessor, which is extremely unusual. We take it to mean that Hammond is speaking of God the Father. This is the object of the 'headless' attributive clause *yá Éesh yóo s ayasáagu* 'whom they call the Father'. After this comes *N yáx̲*, which appears to be *N ÿa-x̲* 'along/over the face of' and not *P yáx̲* 'like P'. But since there is no head noun after *yóo s ayasáagu* 'whom they call', *N ÿá-x̲* has no overt possessor; i.e., the *N* is not fully specified, as it would have been if he had said *yá Éesh yóo s ayasáagu **aa** yáx̲ ...* '... across the face of **the one** they call the Father'. Finally, we don't know what the astronomical or theological implications of this sentence are.

LINE 272. *du at.ooweidée:* This is a variant of *du duwuweidí* 'his wealth', seemingly influenced by *at.óow* 'clan possession(s)'.

LINE 288. *Nas'gi.aa áwé:* This line begins with a couple false starts, «Hóoch'i aa[yí]—yáa dax̱[.aa]—nas'gi.aa áwé» 'The last one—the second [one]—the third one'.

LINE 289. *yáa ḵóok át sa.in yé áyá:* There are multiple false starts in this sequence; it was difficult for us to determine exactly what Hammond intended to say.

LINES 300–01. *tlél tsu / aadé oonax̱sineeyi yé ḵoostée nich:* There is an apparent false start in these lines. Hammond pronounces, «Aaa, tlax̱ áyáa tlél tsu a—a jeex' aa—aadé oonax̱sineeyi yé ḵoostée nich a daadé kdagaax̱í». We have interpreted *a jeex' aa* as a false start based on Hammond's hesitation both before and after this phrase. We plainly heard Hammond pronounce the habitual auxiliary here as *=nich*, even though elsewhere he consistently pronounces it as *=nuch* or *=nooch* and in general *=nooch* is the variant most commonly found in Coastal Tlingit; for Interior Tlingit speakers in general the habitual auxiliary is *=neech*.

LINE 307. *tle tsu a tóotx̱ at wooxeex wé atk'átsk'u:* Literally this means 'then something fell from the boy's mind (or spirit) again'. The implication is that little Raven's misery immediately disappeared as soon as he was handed the sun's container. With *tsu* 'again' here, Hammond is referring back to line 268 when Raven received the previous box containing the moon, «Du tóotx̱ ḵoowahaa, du toowú sigóo wé atk'átsk'u» 'His anguish had vanished; the boy was happy'. *A tóotx̱ at wooxeex* 'concern passed from his mind' and *du tóotx̱ ḵoowahaa* 'his spirit cleared up' are different in form but basically identical in meaning. The recurring image is that of a frantic, wailing, unconsolable toddler becoming contented, calm, and unencumbered.

LINE 316. *yéi x̱'[ayaḵá]:* Here Hammond does not finish pronouncing the verb, so we supply the remaining portion of the complete form in brackets.

LINE 321. *yú dikéet wuxeexí áwé:* As Hammond tells the story, there appears to in fact be a container of the sun in addition to a container of the daylight. Here Raven seems to have already released the sun, but he clearly has yet to release the daylight.

LINES 325–26. *yá sdu léelk'w:* This literally means 'their grandfather', with the plural possessive *sdu* 'their'. We translated it in the text as 'his (i.e., Raven's) grandfather' assuming that it was simply a discourse error. Raven appears to be the only grandchild of the man who possesses the boxes.

LINE 335. *A kaadé s akoos.háaych:* To us this sounded like «a kaadé s akoosáaych», but our consultants were unable to interpret such a sentence, although they have no difficulty interpreting *a káa s akoos.háaych* 'they would position/situate him/her/it on it', with the locative postposition *-x'* 'at, on, in' rather than the allative postposition *-de* 'to(ward)' used by Hammond. Therefore, we think Hammond actually says «a kaadé s akoos.háaych», which would seem to mean either 'they would situate him (Raven) on it (the floor)' or 'they would situate it (the container) on it (the floor)'. We have taken it as referring to the people 'arranging' Raven on the floor, in the sense that they would adjust his position after he had cried himself to sleep.

LINES 336–38. *Hóoch'i aayí áwé g̱agaan / a ítnáx̱ áwé kaawaháa, / aaa, yá ḵei.á yóo tuwasáagu:* We are unable to make sense of the sequence of events here without interpreting Hammond's story as involving both the sun and the daylight, understood as separate entities that are released from their respective containers at different times. Abstracted from the narrative context, it would be equally plausible to interpret these lines as, 'The last one was the sun; it came after what we call the daylight'. The ambiguity lies in whether the *a* of *a ítnáx̱* 'following it' refers to the daylight or rather to the sun, and likewise which of these entities correspond to *hóoch'i aayí* 'the last one'. In lines 194–97 Hammond lists what the various containers held, relating them in order as the stars, the moon, the sun, and, lastly, the daylight; we also find the Container of Daylight is referred to again as «hóoch'i aayí» in line 364. We have thus interpreted *a ítnáx̱ áwé kaawaháa* as meaning 'it (the daylight, i.e, the last one) came after it (the sun)'. Note also Hammond's use again of a headless relative clause in «yá ḵei.á yóo tuwasáagu» 'that which we call the daylight'; such a phrase would more ordinarily end with *aa* 'one' or *át* 'thing'. For a comparison of how different storytellers refer to the containers and what lies within them see §2.13 of the editors' introduction.

LINE 356. *Ts'as áa kawjig̱idi yéide yax̱ x̱agúdin:* This appears to be a decessive of the rare conative imperfective, meaning 'I used to try to go…'. See appendix 1, §12, for further discussion.

LINE 358. *yéi ayawsiḵaa, «Ax̱ dachx̱ánk' du jeet yisa.ín!:* The pronominal reference in *yéi ayawsiḵaa* is not clear; the usual translation of this passage would be 'he said to him/her, "Give it to my grandson, you folks!"', where we might expect *yéi s ayawsiḵaa* 'he said to them' (rather than 'he said to him/her'). But since slaves were traditionally classified grammatically as non-human entities, and thus were not pluralized with the human pluralizer *has=*, we could take *yéi ayawsiḵaa* to mean 'he said to them (his slaves)', which would harmonize with the plural subject of *du jeet yisa.ín!* 'give it to him, you folks!'

LINE 360. *wé ḵei.á du jeet yisa.ín!:* Because this phrase uses the noun *ḵei.á* 'daylight' (rather than the proper noun *Ḵei.á Daakeit* 'Container of Daylight') as the object in the verb form based on the theme *O-S-s-.een~* 'for S to handle O (container bearing contents)', we translate it as 'hand him the container of the daylight'.

LINE 363. *a jeet awsi.ín tsú:* It is unusual to have high-toned *tsú* after a verb. In this sentence we might alternatively expect *a jeet awsi.ín tsu* 'he gave it to him again' or *a jeet awsi.ín á tsú* 'he gave it to him as well'.

LINE 371. *«Yeisú g̱aax̱ x̱áa l yéi eex̱ají Yéilx̱ isateeyí»:* This crucial line was extremely hard to parse and even harder to translate. The phrase *yeisú g̱aax̱ x̱áa* would seem to translate literally, 'constant (or recent) crying, you see'. This is followed by *l yéi eex̱ají* 'I don't have that opinion of you', and finally *Yéilx̱ isateeyí* 'you being Raven'. Although the exact meaning of this combination of elements eludes us, we have provided a translation that reflects the narrative reality: the old woman, whom we know as Unfazable-Little-Elder, has already recognized Raven by his eyes (see line 211) and knows what he is up to. With this in mind, we have rejected alternative translations that would construe *l yéi eex̱ají* together with *Yéilx̱ isateeyí*, which would convey the meaning, 'I don't believe that you are Raven'.

LINES 374, 377. *áx̱ kawdudlisáy Naasshagiyéil:* This verb theme does not appear in our corpus and our consultants are unfamiliar with it. We suspect that the essive applicative derivational string *P-x̱ s/l-* 'being P; (claiming something) to be P' is a part of this verb theme, but we cannot account for the prefix *ka-* here. The stem here, *sáy*, is (or looks like) that which would take the place of *sáa* (meaning 'to name') in motion derivations, but this fact does not help resolve our uncertainty. We have retained the translation from the manuscript as we inherited it, 'he became known as'.

LINE 375. *Náasdáx̱ shkalneek áyáa:* Note here (as well as AH ii, 376, 427, 498; iv, 119, 121) the high-tone pronunciation *Náas*, this being the Tlingit placename for the Nass River. This placename is largely attested with low tone, but Hammond along with Italio, James, and Dick all use the high-tone variant.

LINE 385. *yoo ḵeinga.éigit:* This is a purposive verb form corresponding with the repetitive imperfective form *yoo ḵeiya.éik* 'it (customarily) dawns; it keeps dawning', which is a repetitive of the *yoo=i-...-k(w)* variety.

LINE 388. *a káx̱ yaa ax̱út'ch:* The verb phrase *a káx̱ yaa ax̱út'ch* is a repetitive obliquative form; the corresponding perfective is *a káx̱ ayaawax̱út'* 'he dragged it over onto it'. Note also «ḵugóos' a káx̱ yaa ayíshch / wé ḵei.á» 'It (the wind) pulls clouds over / the daylight' in lines 451–52; there likewise the perfective form corresponding to *a káx̱ yaa ayíshch* is *a káx̱ ayaawayísh* 'it pulled it over onto it'.

LINE 393. *saak isdeegí:* Strictly speaking, there is a contrast between *saak isdeegí* 'eulachon dipnetter' and *saak isdeekx'í* 'eulachon dipnetters'. Hammond uses the form that is technically a singular here as well as in lines 408 and 413; perhaps it is to be interpreted as a collective noun in these cases. These 'eulachon dipnetters' are known also as the *Yax̱taattuḵwáani* 'Night-Dwellers', though Hammond never refers to them as such. See §2.16 of the editors' introduction for discussion of these figures.

LINES 404, 406. *«Óo-oo-oo-oo.»*: These lines are chanted as an impersonation of the dipnetters.

LINE 439. *a káax' ḵugaax̱dudziteeyi aa:* Hammond pronounces what sounds like «a káa g̱aax̱—ḵux̱dudziteeyi aa» here. This is evidently a performance error; we have revised the phrase to *a káax' ḵugaax̱dudziteeyi aa* 'one that people can live by'.

LINE 442. *yá l du jeex̱ at du.oo nóok áwé:* There appears to be at least one false start in this line; however, this passage as we have resolved it seems to fairly represent what Hammond is saying.

LINE 445. *Ágánáa!:* The interjection *aganáa* typically has low tone on the first two syllables, but here the people are screaming.

LINES 451–52. *Ḵugóos' a káx̱ yaa ayíshch / ḵei.á:* If all we had to rely on were this one sentence, the identities of the three third-person pronominals in this sentence would be quite obscure; the verb phrase *a káx̱ yaa ayíshch* literally means 'it pulls it over it', with no direct clues as to what pulls what over what. However, immediately after this in lines 453–54, we are told «a kaax̱ yax̱las'ísín áwé tsáa / haa káa ḵeina.éich» 'only when it blows off of it / does it dawn on us'. This implies that the clouds are pulled over (*a káx̱*) the daylight and that the wind is what pulls them (even though the wind is never directly named); our translation of 451–52, 'the wind pulls clouds over the daybreak', is therefore dependent on the interpretation of lines 453–54.

LINE 458. *Héende aa atkaawa.át:* See §3.11 of the editors' introduction for discussion of this grammatical construction and §2.16 for comparison of its use as a formulaic expression.

LINE 476. *yax̱ haa kwdaya nuch:* This appears to be an imperfective conative form followed by the habitual auxiliary *=nuch*, which has the effect of deleting the *i-* element of the classifier in the expected plain imperfective conative form *yax̱ haa kwdiyá* 'we are trying to travel'. If this analysis is correct, note especially that the stem *yá* is not lengthened to *yáa* before *=nuch*, which would be the normal process (compare, e.g., *ax̱á* 's/he/it is eating it' vs. *ax̱áa nuch* 's/he/it habitually eats it'); instead, *yá* loses its tone and is reduced to *ya*.

LINE 496. *aadé gayeeysikóowéyáx̱:* We actually hear something more like «aadé g̱ayeeysikóoyáx̱» here, but we expect *...kóowéyáx̱* (itself a truncated form of *...kóowu yé yáx̱*).

LINE 502. This line contains a false start. The unaltered utterance is «Aaa, sheyadihéini yéix' yéi kduln—yéi haa daayaduḵá», where *yéi kduln—* was surely an interrupted and revised pronunciation of *yéi kdulneek* 'so the story of it is told, so they tell the story of it'.

LINE 508. *Hasdu ée niylatóow:* The ordinary imperative form for this verb phrase is *hasdu ée ylatúw* (with ∅-conjugation). We have found a few instances where verb themes that ordinarily take ∅-conjugation also take a special *na*-conjugation imperative, hortative, and potential forms: *x̱á!* 'eat it!' vs. *nax̱áa!* 'eat it! (on a daily basis, so many times a day, etc.)', *idaná* 'drink it!' vs. *nidanáa* 'drink it! (on a daily basis, etc.)'. It is therefore possible that *hasdu ée niylatóow!* refers to teaching on a daily or regular basis.

Notes to Austin Hammond's tale I, episode iii, "Raven and Fire"

LINE 10. *yáa kaawahaayi aa:* This could be equivalent to *yáax' kaawahaayi aa* 'one that is situated, located, found here' or 'ones that are situated/located here', or it could be equivalent to *yá kaawahaayi aa* 'this one (or these ones) situated, located, found'. We would expect the attributive verb form to have a short vowel in the stem, that is, we would expect *kaawahayi* rather than *kaawahaayi*, but in line 43 Hammond again says «kaawahaayi».

LINE 19. There is a long pause in the audio here. In line 18 the audio seems to be sharply cut off at the end of the line. There is a discernably different quality to the audio beginning in line 20, so this may have been a different recording situation.

LINE 49. *ḵa tlél tsu daa sá ḵoostí:* We are not sure whether this means 'there was nothing else [that had life force inside of it]' (i.e., no other entities other than the trees and rocks) or 'there was nothing else [that could provide life force]' (i.e., no spirit, power, inner potency).

LINE 69. *ash yáanáx̱ woogútch:* This habitual verb form contains the obliquative aspectual derivational string *P-náx̱ ÿa+u-* (∅) 'moving sideways, in an arc, circuitously by way of P'. The corresponding perfective verb phrase is *ash yáanáx̱ yaawagút* 'he walked past him'.

LINES 81–85. *Lingítch áyá yéi wsikóo / nás'gi aa / áyá tsáa / aadé yoo ḵutudzi.áx̱k / daa sá haa tuwáa sagoowú:* It would appear that Hammond has changed the referent of the first-person plural here from 'the ones who listen' to 'the ones who want'. The rather free interpretation of what Hammond seems to be saying is, 'This is the Tlingit perspective on the matter: when some stimulus is perceived by us, we only pay attention to it the third time it is apprehended.'

LINES 95, 97. *ax̲ jiyís yang̲eedlaag̲ée, yan g̲idak̲een:* These verbs are in the hortative mood. Hortative verb forms with second-person subject are quite rare; we suspect that in these cases *yang̲eedlaag̲ée* and *yan g̲idak̲een* are equivalent to the purposive forms *yang̲eedlaag̲éet* 'so that you will attain it' and *yan g̲idak̲eent* 'so that you may fly ashore', where the *-t* characteristic of purposive forms has been omitted. For further discussion see appendix 1, §9.8.

LINE 101. *téil:* The word *téil* refers to pitchwood as well as torches made of pitchwood.

LINE 105. *kíts yáx̲ aawa.oo:* We think that *kíts* is probably a variant of the word Leer recorded in the "Lexical Binders" from a Kake speaker as «kích», which was translated as "tinder, bark of fir, red cedar, for starting fire, also, dried grass roots"; *kích* appears to be a dialect variant of *kíts*. We find the similar phrase «kích yáxh yatì» (i.e., *kích yáx̲ yatee*) translated as "[It] 'is dry and crumbly', literally, 'is like tinder'" in the *Interior Tlingit Noun Dictionary*.*

LINE 109. *yá x̲'aan akg̲asháat:* Here again, as in lines 95 and 97, *akg̲asháat* appears to function as a purposive but lacks the postposition *-t*. But in this case, it may be that Hammond actually said *akg̲asháatt*, with the first /t/ unreleased and the second /t/ released, which would be hard to distinguish from *akg̲asháat*.

LINE 113. *a lóode aksa.ax̲w át:* There are two possible ways to interpret *a lóode ksa.ax̲w át*, depending on the referent of *a* in *a lóode*. If we take this *a* to refer to the torch, then we get the interpretation we have provided. If we take this *a* to refer to Pygmy Owl, the translation of the whole line would be 'But [Raven] released it (power) into the creature onto whose beak Raven was tying the torch'.

LINE 129. *yá x̲'aan agashátni:* This sounds close to *agashád^{i}ni*, with Hammond releasing the plain stop /d/ before *-ni* (Leer recalls a similar instance where Wanamaker pronounced *a yíknáx̲* 'along the (concave) inside of it' approximately as a *yíg^{a}náx̲*). This line could be interpreted in two ways; it could mean 'when he (Pygmy Owl) grabbed the fire' or 'when it (the torch) grabbed the fire'. The interpretation 'when the fire grabbed it (the torch)' seems less likely; in that case we would expect rather *yá x̲'aanch gashátni*.

LINE 135. *yéi yoo ikayasheik:* We can't clearly hear the *i-* object pronominal prefix pronounced, but we are confident that it is present, especially since we hear *i-* very clearly in line 166, «eeshandéin ikaawashòo» 'you have suffered'.

LINE 165. *Ldakát a tóode aléet áyá:* The verb *aléet* could be a consecutive form ('when he threw them') or an imperfective form ('he is/was throwing them'). Since

* Leer, Hitch, and Ritter, *Interior Tlingit Noun Dictionary*, M·21.

aléet is followed by the enclitic *áyá* here, and since the consecutive, conditional, and contingent verb moods are most frequently followed by enclitics such as *áyá* and *áwé*, we interpret *aléet* here as a consecutive form.

LINE 166. *eeshandéin yoo ikaawashòo:* Hammond pronounces the stem *shòo* here with emphatic falling tone.

LINES 168–69. *Lingit.aanituḵwáanich i eedé / toowú kei kg̱wak'éi:* Here we find an interesting example of an ergative NP marked with the postposition *-ch* and followed by an intransitive verb. If the ergative NP *lingit.aanituḵwáanich* 'inhabitants within the world' were omitted—or if simply the ergative suffix *-ch* were omitted—we would expect that the relational noun *toowú* would take a possessive pronoun, e.g., *i eedé hasdu toowú kei kg̱wak'éi* 'they will be grateful to you', more literally, 'their minds/hearts/souls (*hasdu toowú*) will be good (*kei kg̱wak'éi*) toward you (*i eedé*)'; it would not be grammatically possible to omit the possessive pronoun *hasdu* 'their' in that case. We therefore take this as a rare case where an ergative subject preceding an intransitive verb has 'zeroed out' the possessive pronoun before a relational noun; otherwise, the possessive pronoun would be obligatory. The semantic implications of this, if any, are not clear to us. See appendix 1, §6, for further discussion and examples.

LINE 175. *Yá lingit.aaniḵwáanich i yaadé kg̱watéen:* Since the verb *O-S-téen* 'for S to (be able to) see O, to have O in sight' is a *ga*-conjugation verb, we would expect the future form here to be *kéi kg̱watéen*; we do not understand why *kéi=* is missing here. We also considered the possibility that the verb might be in the potential mode: ... *i yaadé kg̱waatéen* '(the people of the world) might see it on/by your face', but we hear short /g̱wa/ rather than long /g̱waa/ here.

LINE 181. *i saa:* Here Hammond uses what appears to be the absolute form of the noun *saa* 'name' rather than the expected possessed form *saayí* after the second-person singular possessive pronoun *i*. We find the same usage as well as in AH I, iv, 120, «a saa a yáx̱ ayawli.át» 'he assigned the names to them (the rivers)'. In all other instances Hammond uses *N saayí.*

LINE 196. *woosh yáx̱ awoolx̱'éix'w:* In Leer's "Lexical Binders" we find the Tongass form «du wax̱ awoo`lx̱'ey̱s'», which is translated as "he's encouraging him". In the *Tlingit Verb Dictionary* we also find «doo yáx̱ ayax̱wlix̱'éyx'», translated there as "I encouraged him/told him not to be a coward".* We would be tempted to write Hammond's form here as *woosh yáx̱ awoolx̱'éyx'w* based on the stems in the cited materials, but we clearly hear Hammond pronounce the suffix with labialization, as /x'w/ rather than /x'/, and we would not expect the suffix *-x'* to be labialized following a /y/; that is, we would expect the stem *x̱'éyx'*, but not **x̱'éyx'w*. We find another

* Naish and Story, *Tlingit Verb Dictionary*, 79.

form in the "Lexical Binders" which is very similar to Hammond's; the phrase «a yáx̱ awoolx̱éix'» is translated as "he's talking to his hook (encouraging it to catch fish)" and attributed to the Stikine area, though it lacks the final labialization which we hear from Hammond. It would appear that Hammond's form and the Stikine form are based on a historical reanalysis of the root as *x̱'éi~* rather than *x̱'éiy~*.

LINES 209–12. *yá lingit.aanitu.ádi, / haa kagéi kakg̱wahaa át:* This is likely a reference to defending Tlingit people's fishing and hunting rights. The biography of Hammond in *Haa K̲usteeyí* discusses the various ways he was involved in defending Tlingit lands and rights.* The compound noun *lingit.aanitu.ádi* literally means 'things in the world', but in cases like this *át* often specifically denotes 'creatures, animals'. The attributive clause *haa kagéi kakg̱wahaa át* literally means something along the lines of 'things which will appear before us', but could better be translated 'animals that we will gain access to' or even more freely, 'animals that we will be able to harvest'. Compare the example sentence from Naish and Story, «tléil gé daa sá ee kagéi kawoohá?» (i.e., *tléil gé daa sá i kagéi kawuhá?*), which is translated there as "didn't anything come before your eyes/didn't you see anything (when hunting)?"†

LINE 221. *sh daa yak̲ushusigéiyi aa:* We would expect *sh daa yak̲ushudzigéiyi aa*, with the *d-* element added to the classifier because of the reflexive possessive pronoun in *sh daa*, but we hear *si-*. For discussion of the reduction of the prefix string *ÿaa=k̲u-* to *ÿa-k̲u-* see §3.11 of the editors' introduction.

LINE 240. *kadag̱ax̱ núkni:* We seem to hear «chush kadag̱ax̱ núkni» here, but we have no way of accounting for *chush* as the direct object of the verb, which is intransitive. Therefore, we take *chush* to be a false start.

LINE 241. *yéi x̱'ayakk̲wak̲áa:* Usually this verb takes the prefix *x̱'e-* exclusively in the basic imperfective but in no other moods (e.g., the future form is usually said *yéi yakk̲wak̲áa* 'I will say so'), but we have here an example where *x̱'e-* is used in a future form. We find this same phenomenon in SJ vi, 20, «yóo x̱'ayakg̱wak̲áa» 'he will say that'.

LINES 254–55. *yee húnx̱w ... yee éek':* Hammond is using both male and female kinship terms here, which means this could be translated as 'the older brother of all you males and the brother for all you females'. In Tlingit, the kinship terms for siblings are gender specific. A female speaks of *ax̱ shátx̱* 'my older sister', *ax̱ kéek'* 'my younger sister', and *ax̱ éek'* 'my brother (either older or younger)', and a male speaks of *ax̱ húnx̱w* 'my older brother', *ax̱ kéek'* 'my younger brother', and *ax̱ dlaak'* 'my sister (either older or younger)'.

* Dauenhauer and Dauenhauer, *Haa K̲usteeyí*, 207–50.

† Naish and Story, *Tlingit Verb Dictionary*, 133.

LINE 256. *sh daa yee tiyil.á:* There is a false start in the verb word; the unaltered utterance is «sh daa yee tiyil—il.á». It seems that the vowel of the preverb *yoo=* has been altered from /oo/ to /ee/ in order to harmonize with the vowel of *ti-*, which has itself been altered from *tu-* before the second-person plural subject prefix *yi-*. We can point to another example of *yoo=* being altered to *yee=* by vowel harmony, in this case with the second-person singular subject; George Davis can be heard saying «Wáa sá sh daa yee teeditánk?» 'What do you (singular) think of yourself?' twice as well as «aadé sh daa yee teeditangi yé» 'the way you think of yourself' in a speech recorded at Celebration 1982.*

LINE 257. *yihwáanch tsú:* Here, with *yihwáanch tsú* 'you folks, too', Hammond is addressing the radio audience at large, not just the people physically present with him in the studio.

LINE 260. *Aadóoch sá:* This is pronounced here as «aadóot sá», with /ch/ altered to an unreleased /t/ before the /s/ of *sá*. See §3.10.8 of the editors' introduction for further discussion of this phonological phenomenon.

Notes to Austin Hammond's tale I, episode iv, "Raven and Fresh Water"

LINE 6. *Jak̲wteidu.oo:* This is the name of Hammond's younger brother, Horace Marks. He also had the Tlingit names Sk̲uwadál and X̲'adánjaa.†

LINE 36. There is another long pause in the recording here. An early draft of the manuscript indicated that it was Horace Marks speaking from here on, but the voice is clearly that of Hammond.

LINE 76. *sh daa x̲'ayditee:* The reflexive pronominal *sh* before *daa* requires the *d-* element of the classifier here. Note also that *x̲'e-* here does not refer to 'mouth' but is rather a configurational prefix referring to viscous substances such as oil, grease, honey, muck, or, as in this case, dog poop.

LINE 82. *sh daangada.óos'it:* Hammond appears to be struggling as he puts this phrase together. There are two false starts in this line. We would expect *sh daanax̲da.óos'it*, but Hammond breaks the word into syllables as he attempts to put the words together.

LINE 88. *yax̲ adana nóok:* This is an instance of an imperfective conative form followed by the consecutive auxiliary verb *nóok*. For further discussion of conatives see appendix 1, §12.

* MC002, box 1, item 10, "Angoon Dancers, First Performance"; these phrases occur at 48:35 and 49:35 on the recording.

† Dauenhauer and Dauenhauer, *Haa K̲usteeyí*, 208.

LINE 90. This line contains a false start, «Aag̱áa áyá tlél a yanáax̱ ayawuyeesh—ayawux̱óot' wé goon kanaak.áat'ani» 'At that time he hadn't pulled off—he hadn't dragged off the cover over the well'.

LINE 96. *tliyeitiyéix̱:* This appears to be a contraction of *tleiyéi yateeyi yé* 'one place' plus the postposition -*x̱*, which here denotes motion in place (i.e., flapping wings in place without being able to fly). A more common variant is *tleiyateeyiyé* (from *tléix' yateeyi yé* 'a place which is one').

LINE 98. *A tayeex' áwé hú ḵu.aa yá G̱anook:* This section is hard to hear, especially what we have transcribed as *A tayeex' áwé*, so we have simply made our best estimate of what Hammond is saying here.

LINE 110. *du éex̱ akawdudlikwáat:* We weren't sure if Hammond said *du éex̱* or *du yáx̱* here. If he actually said *du yáx̱ akawdudlikwáat*, this would mean 'his face was blackened from the soot'; however, Raven's whole body turned black, not just his face.

LINE 113. *ch'a hóoch'i daséiguch áyá ayaawadlaaḵ:* The postpositional phrase *hóoch'i daséiguch*, with postposition -*ch*, is not an ergative subject here; otherwise, the verb would appear as *yaawadlaaḵ*, without *a*-. Therefore we take *hóoch'i daséiguch* to be a fixed idiom meaning 'with one's last breath' (i.e., with the last bit of energy available before one would have perished).

LINE 124. *Du x̱'atáatx̱ kadutl'uḵgu aa:* We do not understand why the attributive verb form *kadutl'uḵgu* (underlyingly *ka-du-tl'uḵ-k-u*) has the repetitive suffix -*k*. In Leer's "Verb Books", we find the imperfective form «kadutl'óoḵ», translated as "is dripping (one drop at a time)", without -*k*.

LINE 148. *kawusg̱áadi kayaanée:* The verb *kawusg̱áadi* could be interpreted in two ways. We are taking it to be a perfective decessive attributive meaning 'which had fallen', referring to the leaves and plant matter; *kawusg̱áadi* could also be interpreted as a subordinative form meaning 'when they fell', but given the cadence of Hammond's speech we favor the former analysis.

LINE 149. *kada.eix̱ át:* This sounds like «kat.eix̱ át» in Hammond's pronunciation. Note also that we might expect the more common term *ka.éix̱ át* 'growing thing(s)'; the presence of the *d*- element of the classifier and the low tone on the suffixed stem *.eix̱* of Hammond's form *kad*[*a*]*.eix̱* here are presently unclear to us. Perhaps there is a split-second false start here, where Hammond started to say *kad*[*us.éix̱ át*] 'planted thing(s)'and switched gears, trying to land on *ka.éix̱ át* 'growing thing(s)'.

LINE 163. *nax̲tudanáat:* The imperative verb form *idaná!* means 'drink it!' (normally referring to just one time), whereas *nidanáa!* means 'drink it!' (on a regular basis, for example three times a day). Likewise, *g̲atudanaat* 'in order that we drink it' contrasts with Hammond's form *nax̲tudanáat* 'in order that we drink it (on a regular basis)'; these are purposive verb forms with the postposition *-t.*

LINE 187. *yax̲ yoo yaateek:* We are interpreting this as equivalent to *yax̲ yoo yaateeyánk* 'it (customarily) gets restored', which contains the restorative aspectual derivational string *ÿax̲=ÿa-. . . -ÿán (na)* 'restoring to proper condition'.

LINE 192. *yá g̲agaan:* This could be a false start. We do not understand how this line and the next could possibly fit together. We are interpreting the following five lines as a parenthetical excursus.

LINE 196. *yá k̲uwakaan jeex':* The phrase *k̲uwakaan jeex'* 'in the possession of the deer' here makes it sound like the deer are in control of the springs and that people use them under their authority. The Tlingit relational noun *N jee* '(in) the possession of N, (in) the hands/custody of N, (under) N's control' is often fiendishly difficult to translate idiomatically into English but there is a close equivalent in the Latin preposition *penes* 'under the government or command of; at the disposal of; in the custody of'.

LINE 198. *a yahaayí tudanaayí:* We don't know for sure what the referent of *a* is in *a yahaayí* 'its shadow'. We assume it refers to the shadow cast by the sun, but this whole section is difficult to interpret.

LINE 228. *k̲uklasheix̲ át:* The attributive clause *k̲uklasheix̲ át* literally means 'that which intoxicates people'; however, our consultants indicate that *k̲uklasheix̲ át* is regularly translated as 'homebrew'.

LINES 242–43. *Aadéi l ayáx̲x̲ usiteeyi aax̲ wusiteeyi átx̲ siteeyi yá náaw yóo tuwasáagu át:* Note the unusual degree of embedding of attributive clauses here. The innermost attributive clause together with the generic head noun *aa* 'one' is *l a yáx̲x̲ usiteeyi aa* 'one that is improper/immoral'; this is embedded in *P-x̲ wusiteeyi át* 'the thing that has become P', which is in turn embedded in *aadéi P-x̲ siteeyi yá* 'the way it is P; how it is P'. The final noun phrase is *yá náaw yóo tuwasáagu át* 'this thing we call booze', which also contains an attributive clause. So, the whole sentence translates literally, 'How [very much] it is a thing that has become one that is improper/immoral, this thing which we call booze'.

LINE 264. *ch'áakw kaduneegi aa:* The verb form *kaduneegi* 'who used to tell it' here is an attributive decessive imperfective form, corresponding to *kaduneegín* 'it used to be told, people used to tell it'.

LINE 270. *átx̱ tulayeix̱í:* Hammond pronounces what sounds like *átx̱ tulayeix̱íx̱* here, but what we hear as the final /x̱/ is probably just an extraneous sound.

LINE 279. *a x̱oo.aa nanáax̱ sitee haa jeex':* This passage is hard to translate. It literally translates 'some of them (*a x̱oo.aa*) are death(s) (*nanáax̱ sitee*) in our possession (*haa jeex'*)'. He seems to be implying that some of the people die from alcoholism, leaving it to the survivors to pick up the pieces.

LINES 291–305. This is a reference to Jesus' interaction with the Samaritan woman at Jacob's Well, as related in John 4:4–42.

LINE 296. *yéi x̱'a[yaḵá]:* Hammond left out the final two syllables of this verb, which we have supplied in brackets.

LINE 312. *ayiyiyilgeeníḵ:* The underlying morphological breakdown of this verb is *a-ÿa-ÿu-ÿi-d-l-g̱een-íḵ*. The /i/ of the second-person plural subject prefix *ÿi-* causes the preceding /u/ of the perfective prefix *ÿu-* to assimilate to /i/, giving *a-ÿa-ÿi-ÿi-d-l-g̱een-íḵ*. In addition, the /a/ of the thematic prefix *ÿa-* 'face' is likewise found to assimilate to /i/ in this instance, giving *a-ÿi-ÿi-ÿi-d-l-g̱een-íḵ*; this is not a standard practice among Tlingit speakers, although we do find such sporadic assimilations in the speech of other Northern Tlingit speakers, such as George Davis (see the note to AH I, iii, 256). The standard convention (inherited from the early writing system of Naish and Story) has been to write the second-person plural subject prefix plus the perfective prefix and/or the *i-* element of the classifier with a long vowel, i.e., as *ÿeeÿ-*, in all situations, but because all four syllables before the verb stem in this case (*a-yi-yi-yil-*) are clearly pronounced by Hammond with identical short length, we write it as we hear it.

LINE 315. *Yèehwáan:* There is an emphatic falling tone on the first syllable of *yèehwáan*.

LINE 318. *tlél tle yee een koonḵalaneegín:* The verb *koonḵalaneegín* is a negative decessive potential form. Decessive potential verb forms have a result-contrary-to-fact implication; Hammond is saying that if he didn't love them, he wouldn't have told them the story (but he does love them and he did tell it to them).

LINE 320. *ux̱ kei aa utéegaa:* The verb in this phrase is in the dependent admonitive form with the postposition *-g̱aa*; such constructions translate 'lest …' or 'so that … won't/wouldn't …'.

LINE 326. *x̱áach tsú:* The implication of *x̱áach tsú* 'I too' here seems to be that Hammond recognizes that he is following in the footsteps and acting in a similar capacity as his grandparents and other storytellers before him from whom he learned the stories that he has just told and explained.

Notes to Austin Hammond's tale II, "Raven Gets His Nose Yanked Off"

The line numbers below that are given before or without the slash symbol refer to the verbatim transcription of the joint performance by Hammond and Katzeek (AH IIa). The numbers given after the slash symbol refer to the editorialized version of Hammond's Tlingit with the editors' translation (AH IIb).

LINES 10/6. *taaych áa yadusnak̲wx'u yá:* The verb root *naak̲w~*, referring to fishing with or baiting halibut hooks, is related to the noun *náak̲w* 'octopus'.

LINES 20/12. *yatx̲ shux̲waa.áx̲:* The verb root here is *.aax̲~*, which refers to a sheet-like object lying or being handled. The verb theme here is specifically *O-shu-S-.aax̲~* 'for S to move O (sheet-like obj.) by the end'. By 'sheet-like objects' we refer to blankets, sheets, hides, coats, mats, etc. Without video evidence, it is unclear exactly what Hammond is doing with his hands here, but it would appear that he is lifting the end of some kind of cloth or blanket as he speaks.

LINE 28. After Katzeek speaks here, Jimmie George asks a question in Tlingit in a side conversation. We hear *shóogu* at the beginning and *kwshé* at the end, but we can't make out the middle portion. A woman, likely Lydia George, quietly replies «aaá» 'yes'.

LINES 52/33. *ts'ôots' jee ayawdzikuwu k̲áa:* This is a technical idiom based on the verb theme *O-S-s-koo`* (Ø) 'for S to know O'. There is an unexpressed reflexive possessor before *jee*, which in this case means 'in his/her own hands'; this accounts for the *d-* element of the classifier in the verb. The direct object of the verb appears to be *ts'ôots'* 'fish nibble/tug'. We are not sure how to account for the element *ÿa-* here, but we find it also in lines 66/41, «jee ayawdinúk» 'he felt it on the line'. The entire expression seems to translate 'person who knows/recognizes a tug/nibble in his/her hands'.

LINES 54/34. *du eeg̲áa yan yakw.uwak̲úx̲:* In the verb *yan yakw.uwak̲úx̲* there is an incorporated noun *yakw-* 'boat, canoe' embedded in the verb; in the verb theme *yakw k̲oox̲~*, *yakw-* functions as the subject of the verb, referring not only to the boat but also to the people inside it.

LINES 57/36. *{...}:* This appears to be a false start, but Katzeek is talking at the same time, making it hard to discern.

LINES 71/43. *du lóonáx̲ woojeil:* Literally, 'it (the hook) felt its way through his nose'. The verb *woojeil* typically refers to humans (or animals) groping or feeling their way along with the hand. So, it would appear that the hook is viewed as an animate being here.

LINES 76/45. *k'e hé dikée:* This roughly means 'take for example this place right above here'. Katzeek translates this as referring to the ceiling. Hammond seems to be inviting the audience to use the ceiling above their heads as a way of imagining Raven looking up at the bottom of the boat's hull.

LINES 78/46. *yaa kagooséi:* This verb is in the progressive consecutive form, so means 'as it (the boat) was getting nearer'. The corresponding perfective would be *kaawasei* 'it became near, drew close', and the verb theme is *O-ka-u-sei*` 'for O to become near'. The progressive epiaspect requires *ÿaa=ga-* here, so the morphological analysis of this word is *ÿaa=ka-ga+u-séi.*

LINES 82/48. *Aadóo sánix̱ sá sateeyí:* This is a jokingly apologetic aside from Hammond, who is a member of the Raven moiety, to the members of the Eagle moiety in the audience, greeted with much laughter.

LINES 95/55. *yan uwax'ák:* Here the verb *yan uwax'ák* implies that Raven swam ashore in the manner of a fish as opposed to the manner of a bird or a mammal; we have translated it as 'he wriggled ashore'. For a single human swimming we might rather expect *yan uwahóo* or *yan wudit'ách.*

LINES 101/58. *K̲'alux̱út'aa s'áaxw:* The noun *k̲'alux̱út'aa* has not been attested elsewhere. This is a combination of the relational noun (*a*) *k̲'alú* 'the pointed end of (its) opening' (e.g., the tip of the nose, the spout of a pitcher, or the visor of a cap) and *x̱út'aa* 'adze', so the combination *k̲'alux̱út'aa* literally translates as 'visor-adze'; so *k̲'alux̱út'aa s'áaxw* refers to a hat with a visor that looks roughly like an adze. Katzeek translates this as "hat with a bill on it". Nowadays it is often used to refer to a baseball cap.

LINES 110/63. *G̲uneit loowú:* For discussion of the term *g̲uneit* see the note to SJ X, 101.

LINES 150/82. *yá yéil a lú:* The use of the possessive pronoun *a* 'its' rather than *du* 'his' here implies that Hammond is referring to generic ravens' beaks rather than the character Raven's nose. Note also that Katzeek translates this as "when you see a raven" (not 'when you see Raven').

LINES 156/86. *ax̱ aat hás:* Having jokingly apologized to the Eagle moiety in lines 82/48, Hammond now makes a similar apology specifically to the women of the opposite moiety. There is more laughter and a pause with some background talking, after which a woman's voice is heard ironically exclaiming «Wéidu, i sáni loowú áwé!» 'There it is, your paternal uncle's nose!', leading to much more laughter. We believe this to be the voice of Amy Marvin, but it could possibly be Katherine Mills or Lydia George. She is referring to an object presented to the group of elders from the Portland Art Museum's collection, the form and meaning of which Hammond's story was meant to explain.

Notes to Katherine Mills' Stories

EDITORIAL BACKGROUND. Nora Dauenhauer transcribed and translated these stories in the early 1990s.* They were eventually transposed into a digital manuscript and edited by Keri Eggleston in the summer of 2015. Lance Twitchell subsequently reviewed and edited the manuscript. Lastly, in 2021–2022, Will Geiger and Jeff Leer made final revisions to the transcription, translation, and notes while referencing the original audio and consulting Kenneth Grant, Bessie Cooley, Sam Johnston, and Ruth Demmert on particularly difficult linguistic issues.

Notes to Katherine Mills' tale I, "Raven and the Salmon Box"

LINE 4. *Tax̱'hít:* The name of this clan house is usually translated in English as 'Snail House'; under this interpretation, the first component of the name, *tax̱'-*, would be the compounding form of *táax̱'* 'slug, snail'. This word, however, is homophonous with *táax̱'* 'tier, level of housepit', which describes a level of the stepped platforms leading down to the fireplace in the center of a traditional Tlingit house. The word *táax̱'* 'tier' would presumably have an identical compounding form *tax̱'-*.

LINE 13. *tlél aadé hasdu kagéi aa kg̱waaháayi yé:* Note that open verb stems belonging to the subtype of zero-conjugation verb themes illustrated here with the theme *P-x' O-ka-haa~* 'for O to become situated, located at P' form their imperative, hortative, and potential modes with a long high stem, here illustrated by the stem *háa* in the attributive potential form *aa kg̱waaháayi.*

LINES 16–17. *gútl:* This word refers to an arrow hafted with a blunt head. These were used especially for hunting birds and other small animals and functioned by inducing a lethal blunt-force trauma, rather than the broadhead-tipped arrows that work by cutting through the vital organs so as to cause the animal to bleed to death.† A blunt-tipped arrow is not at all suitable for hunting big game like a mountain goat. Nonetheless, Raven fares just fine with his unorthodox equipment.

LINE 21. *wáa sá óosh du jeet wudzinée:* There are a couple of puzzling aspects to this verb. First, although the motion theme *yéi=O-S-s-nee`* 'for S to carry, take, bring multiple O' is well known, Mills' verb phrase lacks *yéi=* and furthermore contains the *d-* element in the classifier, which we take to have the function of converting a transitive verb into a 'passive' intransitive verb, which means that the logical subject of the verb is rendered indeterminate, i.e., *du jeet wudzinée* here translates as 'it (the Octopus

* MS052, box 25, contains a range of drafts, both printed and handwritten, from as early as 1992.

† See, e.g., Emmons, *The Tlingit Indians*, 138, and de Laguna, *Under Mount Saint Elias*, 368–69, for some discussion of these kinds of arrows.

Tentacle Cane) wound up in his (Raven's) possession' or 'it was brought into his possession'. The other puzzling aspect of this verb is that the motion theme cited above refers to multiple objects, whereas the Octopus Tentacle Cane is only one object. The use of *wáa sá óosh* with a perfective verb form regularly translates as 'how could (such and such happen)?' Compare Mills' other uses of this verb theme in KM V, 6, «wáa-áa sáyú tsú du x̱'éit aa g̱asnee wé yaaw?» 'ho-ow could Raven get a taste of the herring?' (using a hortative form), and KM VI, 22, «wáa sá du jeet ux̱dzinee» 'how might he get ahold of it' (using a potential form, here again referring to a single object).

LINE 60. *Gidzanóox' … wé yéil:* The word *yéil* 'raven' is not capitalized here because it refers to a certain particular *yéil* 'raven', not the character named *Yéil* 'Raven'. In Mills' telling, Gidzanóox' appears to be a raven rather than some other bird or entity. Like Zuboff, Mills describes Gidzanóox' as the sororal nephew (*kéilk'*) of Raven. See §2.12 of the editors' introduction for further discussion of this character.

LINE 63. *Aalséix̱:* This is the name of the river that empties into *G̱unaax̱oo* (Dry Bay) near Yakutat.* The river is identical with the Alsek River in English up to its confluence with the Tatshenshini River. Above this confluence, the Tlingit name *Aalséix̱* corresponds to the English name 'Tatshenshini' and the Tlingit name *Tachaans.héeni* corresponds to the English name 'Alsek', according to Nora Dauenhauer. The placename *Tachaans.héeni* was obtained by Leer from Jim Kane; no one else that Leer asked was able to identify this placename taken down by Lt. Frederick Schwatke circa 1883 from an 1869 map created by Chilkat Tlingit leader Koklux. The first part of that name, *Tachaans-*, looks like it comes from a local Athabaskan language (with the prefix *ta-* 'water'); *héeni* is Tlingit, being the possessed form of *héen* 'river, creek, water'.

LINE 68. *x̱áat:* Although translated here as 'salmon', the word *x̱áat* can also refer to fish of any kind. In this version of the story, Mills states in line 109 that the Salmon Box contained *saak* 'eulachon' in addition to salmon. This inclusion of eulachon is significant because besides salmon it is the only anadromous fish in the Tlingit diet.

LINES 69, 89. *Kudataankahídi:* Mills' pronunciation of this name, with the long stem *-taan-*, is unique among the storytellers in this volume. See §2.18 of the editors' introduction for discussion of this entity.

LINE 76. *Deisgwach át ash jinaasháat:* The verb in *át ash jinaasháat* appears to be a rare instance of the realizational mode with *deisgwach* 'eventually, finally'. Alternatively, it could be interpreted as a processional form—in either case, the surface form of the verb would be identical; see appendix 1, §12, for further discussion of processional imperfectives. The verb theme here is *O-ji-S-sháat~* 'for S to lead O

* See Thornton, *Haa Léelk'w Hás Aaní Saax'ú*, 7–9, for a discussion of this geographic area.

by the hand quickly or abruptly; for S to jerk O (in a certain direction) by the hand', which forms a contrastive pair with the more common *O-ji-S-taan~* 'for S to lead O by the hand (calmly and deliberately)'.

LINE 77. *taashuká:* The technical English term corresponding to *taashuká* would be the 'backshore' or 'backshore berm'. In FI I, iii, 152, 156, Raven manipulates X̱ashak'ákwk' into going to the *taashuká* to fetch the roots of beach ryegrass that hang down from the backshore berm; Dick uses the slightly different term *yanshuká* in FD viii, 86–87, which appears to have the same general reference as *taashuká* here.

LINE 78. *Du x̱'us.eetí tlénx':* Many of Raven's adventures are associated with the Dry Bay area at the mouth of the Alsek River. The sand dunes along the Akwe River are said to be where Raven dug in his heels pulling the Salmon Box ashore; a placename in Thornton's atlas «Yéil Áx̱ Daaḵ Uwanugu Yé», translated as "Where Raven Scooted Back",* refers to this event. The peninsula between the coast and *Sduhéenák'w* (Cannery Creek) is called *Yaakw Shaká* 'Canoe Prow' (does not appear in Thornton), which is a reference to the *Kudataankahídi*, the prow of which points to Dry Bay. At the Cannery Creek village site there were two clan houses named after this story: the *Shakahít* 'Prow House' of the Lukaax̱.ádi and the *Diginaa Hít* 'Far-Out House' of the L'uknax̱.ádi.

LINE 87. *X̱'anax̱gaatwaayáa:* See §2.17 of the editors' introduction for discussion of this character.

Notes to Katherine Mills' tale II, "Raven and the King Salmon"

LINE 10. *té shakéex' gíwé kéi awutí:* Note the irrealis form of the verb following *gíwé* 'I suppose' here. The corresponding realis form would be *kéi aawatée* 'he put it up'.

LINE 12. *x̱'wáal' a daa yéi aya.óo:* Raven is treating the greenstone like a precious artifact, displaying it in a place of honor and putting down feathers around it.

LINE 17. *x'éix'u x̱ootl'eex:* This phrase literally means 'filth among gills' with *x'éix'u* 'gills', *x̱oo* 'among', and *tl'eex* 'trash, dirt, filth'. This situation illustrates one of Raven's favorite tricks that Richard Dauenhauer would refer to as 'Let's You and Him Fight'. By feeding lies and disinformation to people, Raven manipulates them into fighting with each other. The fight then either frees something for Raven to steal or otherwise allows Raven to take advantage of the combatants. We can identify such a sequence as another instance of the 'tickery–complicity' theme discussed in §§1.4.1–2 of the editors' introduction. Compare the insults in FD ix, 24–26.

* Ibid, 24, m#260. The location is described there as "Dunes on Akwe River".

LINE 35. *Gánde x̱áat tuwdishát:* The Tlingit euphemism for defecation and urination is 'going outside'. Raven is already outdoors and therefore has no need to go outside, so this can only be the euphemism. In modern-day Tlingit, these two concepts are expressed differently: *gánde woogoot* 's/he went to the bathroom' is distinguished from *gáande woogoot* 's/he went outside', but in older recordings we find *gánde woogoot* used for both meanings. The verb used here has not been found elsewhere; *x̱áat tuwdishát* 'the urge has suddenly come over me'; note that *x̱áat* 'to me' is an older form of modern *ax̱ éet*.

LINE 39. *du jikayáanáx̱ kawlidaal wé x'ús':* Mills says «x'ús'» 'club' here, but we believe this to be a performance error, i.e., that she meant to say *t'á* 'king salmon' instead. She had evidently intended to refer to the fact that the king salmon was too heavy for Raven alone to carry, which is why he recruits the birds to help him pull up the fish. This may be an ironic statement, in which case Raven would be capable but simply too lazy to do it on his own. On the other hand, the image in the story could be that of a truly massive fish. The largest king salmon on record was caught in a fish trap in Petersburg, Alaska, in 1949, weighing 126 pounds.* It is safe to assume that equivalent and even larger king salmon must have been periodically encountered and harvested by Tlingit people over the course of their long occupation of the coast. One could thus remain within the domain of realism while imagining the king salmon in this story to be roughly the size of an adult person.

LINE 40. *wé át kawdliyeeji átx'i sáani:* This phrase is a relative clause that literally means 'little things (or creatures) that fly around (in flocks)'. Raven has various passerine birds as his companions or 'gang', often referred to as *du xwáax'u* 'his sidekicks, posse, gang, crew'.

LINE 43. *héi daak̲ gatoox̱óot'i:* The word *héi* here is the truncated form of the locative *héix'* '(located) just over here/there'; for further discussion of truncated locative forms see appendix 1, §3.

LINE 46. *a ya.áak:* While we have translated this phrase as 'a pit for it' in the text, the phrase *a ya.áak* literally means 'a place/space for it'.

LINE 56. *gooch seiyí:* Here *gooch seiyí* is actually pronounced as *goot seiyí*. For discussion of the reason for the change of /ch/ to /t/ here see §3.10.8 of the editors' introduction.

LINE 70. *kóok̲ takaadé akawsiyáa:* We cannot account for the high tone on the verb stem. It could be an emphatic tone modification.

* Marsh, "The Chinook Tradition", 6.

LINE 79. *tle a kát k̲ushakaawaháa:* Compare «du kaanáx̲ k̲ushayakawduwaháa», translated as "they buried/covered him up completely".* The incorporated noun *sha-* (literally, 'head') in this verb refers to a heap (here, the heap or mound of dirt that Raven piled over the remnants of the salmon); the theme *k̲u-ka-S-haa* 'for S to dig' appears to be an antipassive of *O-ka-S-haa* 'for S to dig O'.

LINE 87. *Yá hasdu wak̲gandaa dleit yáx̲ dag̲aatee has wak̲.ilg̲éigu:* The phrase *du wak̲gandaa,* attributed to an Atlin speaker, occurs in the *Interior Tlingit Noun Dictionary* with the translation "wrinkles in skin of his/her eyelids above the eyelashes".† It was also elicited from a Teslin speaker who gave the form *du wak̲dandaa* with the gloss "the area around his/her eyes".‡ Among Louis Shotridge's notes we find this word written as «wɑggan dà» (i.e., *wak̲gandaa*) and translated as "'eye-light-circle', ground [sic for 'round'] orifice of eye, Palperbral";§ the anatomical term 'palpebral' means 'pertaining to the eyelids'. We have translated *hasdu wak̲gandaa* in the text simply as 'the rims of their eyes'. The verb form *has wak̲.ilg̲éigu* is in the subordinative imperfective; the corresponding plain imperfective is *has wak̲.ilg̲éikw* 'they are wiping their eyes', and the corresponding perfective is *has wak̲.wudlig̲oo* 'they wiped their eyes'. The rest of this story is a good example of the explanatory nature of some Raven stories, describing how the small birds acquired their present forms because of Raven; in the study of folklore and mythology, a narrative that explains the origin of the world or its features is known as an etiological myth or 'aition'.

LINE 89. *tle du x̲'ul'yáx̲ akawdlikwáat:* In the *Tlingit Verb Dictionary* we find «s'eenáa x̲'atsáagee áx̲ akawlikwáat» glossed as "the lamp chimney got black with smoke",¶ i.e., with soot, so we might expect *du x̲'ul'yáx̲ akawlikwáat* 'the surface of her belly got blackened with soot'; however, we clearly hear the classifier *dli-* on the recording.

LINE 91. *ts'eig̲eenéi:* This refers to the American magpie. The Tlingit name varies widely among dialects, having forms like *ts'eig̲einéi, ts'eig̲eenée, ts'eeg̲eení, ts'ig̲eení,* and *ts'eig̲éeni,* among others. Magpies are common in coastal and inland Tlingit Country especially near human settlements.

LINE 98. *woolnáx̲.wooshk̲ák̲:* The Pacific wren (*Troglodytes pacificus*) has the scientific name of its genus taken from the Greek τρωγλοδύτης (*trōglodýtēs*) 'troglodyte, cave-dweller'. This refers to the wren's tendency to feed and hide in cavities and

* Leer, "Verb Books".

† Leer, Hitch, and Ritter, *Interior Tlingit Noun Dictionary*, M·108. This phrase must have been reelicited from Elizabeth Nyman; she is also the only Atlin speaker mentioned in the front matter (vii), and Leer confirms that all Atlin forms that were published in this source were confirmed with her.

‡ Ibid, M·108.

§ Shotridge, "Tlingit Language Notes from the University of Pennsylvania".

¶ Naish and Story, *Tlingit Verb Dictionary*, 30.

crevices. The Tlingit name *woolnáx̱.wooshk̲ák̲* 'squatting, landing, hopping through a hole' refers to the same behavior. In a passage from the Raven story Swanton recorded from Deikeenaak'w in English, we find reference to a very specific 'hole' that the wren came to hop through:

> One time Raven assembled all the birds in preparation for a feast and had the bears in the rear of his house as guests. All the birds had canes and helped him sing. As he sang along Raven would say quietly, "Do you think one of you could fly into the anus of a bear?" Then he would start another song and end it by saying much in the same language, "One of you ought to fly up into that hole" (i.e., anus). He kept taunting the birds with their inability to do this, so, when the bears started out, the wren (wu´łnaxwūckaq [*woolnáx̱.wooshk̲ák̲*], 'bird-that-can-go-through-a-hole') flew up into the anus of one of them and came out with the intestines. Before it had pulled them far out the bear fell dead. Then Raven chased all of the small birds away, sat down, and began eating.*

LINE 100. *woolnáx̱ yaa kg̲eeshk̲ák̲ch:* The verb *yaa kg̲eeshk̲ák̲ch* 'you will keep hopping through holes' is a future repetitive form of a verb with the obliquative derivational string.

LINE 101. *k̲aatoox'u sáani:* The name *k̲aatoowú* refers to the chickadee, either the chestnut-backed chickadee or the black-capped chickadee, or in some locations the boreal chickadee. The form *k̲aatoox'u sáani* used in this narrative is the plural diminutive of *k̲aatoowú*. The word *k̲aatoowú* comes from *k̲aa toowú* 'a person's inner being, mind, feelings, soul'. The name refers to the traditional belief that when a chickadee suddenly starts singing in the forest it means that someone elsewhere is thinking of the hearer. This belief is also found in Ahtna Athabaskan, where the chickadee has the name *ne'iine'*, literally 'a person's thoughts, mind' or 'our thoughts'.†

LINE 103. *x̱'éishx'w:* This name refers to the Steller's jay, which is locally referred to as 'blue jay', though the blue jay is technically a distinct species. The phrase *x̱'éishx'u yáx̱ yatee* 'it is dark blue' literally means 'it is like a Steller's jay', referring specifically to the striking blue feathers of its body and tail. Mills' narrative focuses on the origin of the Steller's jay's other prominent physical feature, the crest feathers that stand vertically on top of its blackish-brown head.

Notes to Katherine Mills' tale III, *"Raven and the Brown Bear Couple"*

LINE 2. *ch'a g̲óot yéide áwé a daa yóo tuwatánk:* Literally, 'he was thinking about it in a different way'. The implication is that Raven was working out a novel scheme for

* Swanton, *Tlingit Myths and Texts*, 17, bracketed spelling ours.

† Kari, *Ahtna Athabaskan Dictionary*, 93.

how to use the tail of the king salmon in a way that would be useful for the purpose of killing the Bears.

LINE 9. *has akawshik'án:* This verb also means 'they shooed, drove him away; they rejected him'.

LINE 12. *tle s ash yaawadlaak̲:* This verb phrase contains one of only a couple of recorded examples of the combination *has=ash=* preceding the verb word. The proclitic *has=* is the human pluralizer, and *ash=* is the salient object pronoun. Here *has=* could be taken to pluralize either the third-person subject or the salient object *ash=*, so *has ash yaawadlaak̲* could be translated either 'he (Raven) won them (Bears [salient]) over' or 'they (Bears) won him (Raven [salient]) over'. The former translation makes sense contextually, since Raven is trying to ingratiate himself to the Bears; however, it would be unclear why the Bears would be treated as salient characters here. The latter translation also makes sense in that we expect Raven to be the salient character; however, it would be unclear why Mills would say that the Bears succeeded in winning Raven over while Raven was the one making the overtures. A separate recording of Mills telling this story in English may lend some credence to the interpretation in which Raven is the referent of *ash=*. She states, "and then the Bear kept trying to be friendly";* this is not enough to confirm the semantic structure of the Tlingit line, but if we take it as Mills' way of expressing the same idea in English, (*ha*)*s ash yaawadlaak̲* could be interpreted as something like 'they (Bears) established contact with him (Raven [salient])', 'they took to him', 'they took him [into their good graces]', or the like. If, on the other hand, (*ha*)*s=ash=* were taken to refer to the Bears as plural salient characters, with the translation 'he (Raven) won them (the Bears [salient]) over', the unexpected use of *ash=* referring to the Bears rather than Raven here would be reminiscent of the unexpected use of *ash=* in Wanamaker's version of "Raven and the Brown Bear Couple" (see the note to AW iii, 43, 73, 74, 76). While we do not wish to imply that the same syntactic process is involved in this line of Mills' text as the one we see in Wanamaker's sentences like «du jig̲eit ash uwaják̲», it would seem remarkable that both these unexpected uses of *ash=* occur in the story of "Raven and the Brown Bear Couple". These questions aside, Elizabeth Nyman provides another textual example of the combination *has=ash=* (which combination is actually *has=ach=* in Nyman's speech) referring to a non-salient plural agent acting upon a salient character, namely, «Has ach xh'awûs' áwé yût'à Tom Williams» (i.e., *Has ach x̲'awóos' áwé yóot'aa*, Tom Williams), translated as "They had asked about him, Tom Williams".†

* MC005, tape 253, track c.

† Nyman and Leer, *Gágiwdul.àt*, 60. See also Leer's "Tlingit Anaphoric System"; this example from Nyman is discussed in ibid, 14.

LINE 13. This line contains a false start. The unaltered utterance is «Áwé ch'a yáa du—».

LINE 14. *k'idéin a daa s tutee nóok:* Note the low tone on the stem of *tutee* before the consecutive auxiliary *=nóok* here. But in combination with the habitual auxiliary *=nooch ~ nuch ~ nukch ~ neech*, the stem is high-toned: *a daa s tutée nuch*. Compare also Hammond's phrase «ya<u>x</u> adana nóok áwé» 'as he was trying to drink it up' (AH I, iv, 88), where the low-toned stem *na* appears before the consecutive auxiliary *=nóok* (but this time the stem is short, not long as in *tutee nóok*).

LINE 15. *yéi yaawa<u>k</u>aa:* Mills starts by saying *yéi ayawsi<u>k</u>aa* 'he said to him/her' but then revises this to *yéi yaawa<u>k</u>aa* 'he said'.

LINES 19–20. *I een daak / <u>k</u>uk<u>k</u>wast'ei<u>x</u>:* Although the verb theme *a-S-d-s-t'ei<u>x</u> (na)* 'S hook-fishes' by default has an invariable long low-tone stem *t'ei<u>x</u>*, the preverb *daak=* 'out' requires that the following verb become Ø-conjugation with fully variable root. Therefore, we would expect the long high-tone stem *t'éi<u>x</u>* here as would be appropriate for the affirmative future stem of a variable root, but Mills pronounces the stem low as *t'ei<u>x</u>*. We note that Mills paused after uttering *daak* here, which may indicate that *daak* is a false start. Finally, we cannot account for the use of the prefix *<u>k</u>u-* in place of usual *a-* here, but we note that in SJ X, 27, we find «aan <u>k</u>uga<u>x</u>dust'e<u>x</u> át» 'things people were going to use to hook fish', also with *<u>k</u>u-*.

LINE 32. *yá du t'ei<u>x</u>í <u>x</u>'adaa yéi jineiyée áwé:* Literally, 'while he was working on the mouths of his fishhooks', evidently implying that he was adjusting the barb and/or getting the bait worked into place. We have translated *du t'ei<u>x</u>í <u>x</u>'adaa* as 'the spacing of his hooks', due to the fact that we construe the element *<u>x</u>'a-* 'mouth' to refer to the gap between the tip of the barb of the hook and the wooden body of the hook. On a traditional Tlingit halibut hook, called *náxw*, the spacing between the tip of the hook's barb and the wooden arm opposite that to which the barb is affixed influences the size of the halibut that the hook can catch. Halibut above a certain size cannot pass their lips though the set spacing, and so cannot get hooked, while smaller halibut are unable to reach their mouths over the body of the hook. Halibut range in size from a few pounds to over 400. Hooking massive halibut risks loss of gear and trying to bring a lively one of this size into a canoe could lead to capsizing or injury.

LINE 35. *yínde akanalgútch:* Note that the usual classifier with this verb is *s-*, as in *yínde akawsigoot* 'he sent it (the hook) down'. However, when a verb stem (here *gútch*) contains an affricate-series consonant (here the habitual suffix *-ch*), the *s-* element of the classifier is replaced by *l-*.

LINES 37–38. *Deisgwach shaawahík hasdu een / wé yaakw:* Here *hasdu een* means 'with them (Raven, Bear, and Cormorant)', not 'with them (the halibut)'. The line is literally, 'Eventually the boat got full with them', meaning that the boat—with Raven, Bear, and Cormorant aboard—became full of halibut. The verb *O-sha-heek~* (Ø) 'for O to become full' most frequently takes a bare NP complement denoting what O is full of, e.g., *yaaw shaawahík* 'it's full of herring', but it is also quite possible to add one of the synonymous postpositions *P-tin*, *P-teen*, or *P-een* 'with P' to the NP complement, e.g., *yaawtín shaawahík* 'it's full of herring'; likewise the causative counterpart *yaaw(tín) ashawlihík* 's/he filled it with herring'.

LINE 40. *tlél tsu kéi x̲at jeeduyík̲ch:* Note that here the *jee-* of *jeeduyík̲ch* is a contraction of *ji-u-*. In most cases the irrealis/negative prefix u- does not occur before the second-person subject prefixes, the first-person plural subject prefix, nor the fourth-person human subject prefix *du-*. Here we have the negative/irrealis prefix occurring with the fourth-person human subject prefix *du-*. We again find Mills using this combination in line 135, «tlél koodutáax'» 'they don't chew it; one does not chew it' (with the underlying prefix string *ka-u-du-*). We also find *u-* and *du-* occurring together in the lyrics to the song sung by Italio of when Raven broke daylight; in FI I, V, 250, we find, «unax̲duwak'oots» 'it (the daylight) might break' (underlyingly *u-na-g̲a-du-i-k'oots*).

LINES 41–42, 44. *Ch'a k̲udzitèe:* While *k̲udzitee* literally means 'it exists', here it seems to have the force of 'it's really something', i.e., it's rather spectacular, in which 'it' refers to Raven's purported manner of baiting his halibut hooks (namely, by the skin of one's own penis). In the same scene in Mills' English telling of this story she impersonates Raven saying, "It's [a] very crucial thing", which may correspond to her use of *ch'a k̲udzitee* here. Note also the emphatic pronunciation in line 41, in which the tone of the stem *tèe* begins high and is sharply lowered.

LINE 47. *ax̲ yak̲áawu:* There is a certain humorous irony here with the Bear being the one calling Raven 'my partner' rather than the other way around. Raven often addresses those he encounters as *ax̲ yak̲áawu* 'my partner' when he's looking to scam someone, but the Bear really means to imply friendship and cooperation in an honest, earnest way. At the end of this line Mills highlights this situation by pointing out how the Bear is now using kinship terminology.

LINE 61. This line contains a false start. The unaltered line is «tle aan—».

LINE 67. *i lawyadaadookx'u sáani:* We have not been able to definitively determine the anatomical reference of *N lawyadaadookx'u sáani*, literally meaning 'little skins around the face of N's penis', but 'foreskin' seems like the most likely candidate. In her English telling of the same story Mills impersonates Raven as saying, "You have to cut part of your penis out." See the note to AW iii, 37, for comparison with Wanamaker and Dick.

LINE 96. *R-r-r-r-r-r-r:* The people listening to Mills' performance can be heard laughing at the end of this line.

LINES 105–06: *Ha goosóo / wé i aatx̱úx̱ ḵu.aa?:* We find the same formulaic expression in FD x, 57. This expression is discussed in §2.20 of the editors' introduction.

LINE 135. *Tlél koodutáax', ligaas:* Here again, as in line 40, we find Mills using the negative/irrealis prefix *u-* in combination with the fourth-person human subject prefix *du-*, this time in a negative imperfective form. It is interesting that in line 134 just prior, Mills says «Tlél áwé kdutáax'» 'One does not chew it', which is the very same negative imperfective with *du-*, but that time lacking the negative/irrealis *u-*. In her English telling of this story, Mills states this as "It's no good to chew my cookin'."

LINE 164. *Tle ch'a tléináx̱ hóoch áwé a shóo yéi wootee:* This is a notable instance of an ergatively marked pronoun (*hóoch*) before an intransitive verb preceded by a relational noun plus postposition (*a shóo yéi wootee*). See appendix 1, §6, for further discussion.

Notes to Katherine Mills' tale IV, "Raven and the Deer"

LINE 33. *yaa ashukdaḵéen:* The verb theme *O-shu-S-d-ḵeen~* 'S leads O by flying' has not been attested so far aside from this example. It is formed in the same way as, e.g., *O-shu-S-goot~* 'S leads O (by walking)'. Mills uses the verb here in its progressive habitual form, with the string *ÿaa=ga-*.

LINE 43. *Ch'a yák'wdéi:* Mills' pronunciation of this sounds to us like *Ch'ák'wdéi.* Other speakers use the forms *ch'a yák'wde*, *ch'a yák'udé*, and *ch'a yáak'udé*. Mills' variant is apparently based on *ch'a yák'udé*, with the loss of the vowel /u/ and consequent rounding of the preceding /k'/.

LINE 45. *diyéede:* This is an unusual variant of *(di)yínde* 'downward'.

LINE 49. *lítaa oowayawu át:* The relative verb form *oowayawu* (*át*) '(thing) that resembles it' (compare *oowayáa* 'it resembles it') is notable in that the relative suffix is *-wu* rather than *-ÿi*, as might be expected. The few other verbs that show this irregularity are *woonaawu* (*ḵaa*) '(person) who has died', *yatleiwu* (*át*) '(thing) that is stout' (compare *yatlei* 'it is stout'), *yéi kootlawu* (*át*) '(thing) that is so stout' (compare *yéi kootláa* 'it is so stout'), and *koosawu* (*áa*) '(lake) that is narrow' (compare *koosáa* 'it is narrow').

LINE 50. *Goonáx̱ sá óo-óo-óosh x̱wasix̱áa ax̱ yaḵáawu:* Literally, 'Through where could I po-o-ossibly eat (the flesh of) my partner.' The *s-* classifier element functions as a configurational prefix, specifically denoting that the object of the verb is red meat or flesh.

LINE 59. *kallítaak̲:* This is an example of the productive string *ka-l-*NOUN*-k̲* 'lacking, without NOUN; NOUN-less'. Other examples of this construction are provided in §3.11 of the editors' introduction.

LINE 60. *du satoowúch:* Here the ergative postposition *-ch* has no direct syntactic relationship with the verb; it simply means 'because of', or in this case 'relying on'. The phrase *du satoowú* 'his wits, cleverness' is the possessed form of the hypothetical noun *satú* 'wits, cleverness', which would be the verbal noun corresponding to the stative imperfective verb form *sitóo* 's/he is clever' (literally, 's/he is mind-ed; s/he has a mind, spirit, inner life').

Notes to Katherine Mills' tale V, "Raven and the Whale"

LINE 6. *wáa-áa sáyú tsú du x̲'éit aa g̲asnee:* See the note to KM I, 21, for discussion of this interesting verb.

LINE 25. *yax̲ ayagoos.éeych:* This spectacular verb form combines the exhaustive aspectual derivational string *yax̲=ya-s/l-* (∅) 'all, a bunch, a lot' with the self-benefactive non-aspectual derivational string *ga-d-* 'for self' along with the elements *u-…-ÿ-ch* which are required for the ∅-conjugation habitual mode. These are all superimposed on the verb theme *O-S-s-.ee~* 'for S to cook O', resulting in the underlying string, in the order required by the verb template, *ÿax̲=a-ÿa-ga-u-d-s-.ée-ÿ-ch* (*a-* is the third-person object prefix).

LINE 29. *x̲'awdzinák̲:* This is an uncommon and interesting verb form. In Leer's "Verb Books" we find the transitive verbs «ax̲'eiwanák̲» ("he quit drinking [it]") and «ajeewanák̲» ("[s/he] left it/him, let it go, gave (it) up, quit (it)") as well as the latter's antipassive partner «jiwdinák̲» ("[s/he] gave up, quit"), so we can expect also the antipassive form *x̲'awdinák̲* 's/he quit eating, drinking, speaking'. This leaves us with the question of where the *s-* element of the classifier figures in. In this case, *s-* appears to function as a configurational prefix, referring to the mass of herring. Compare line 9, «yaaw wusx̲á» 'the eating of herring', and line 30, «yaaw neilx̲ kalasóosi» 'as the herring kept falling in', in which the fricative element of the classifier (*s/l-*) has the same configurational connotation.

LINES 53–54. *Aadóo sgí k̲aa kaanáx̲ kéi ag̲axaash?:* Literally approximately, 'Who should it be that cuts it up over a person?' The verb is in the hortative mode. *Aadóo sgí* conveys the meaning 'Who could it be?' Compare also line 64. See §1.4.2 of the editors' introduction for discussion of this formulaic expression.

LINE 58. *tle s at'aawjixeex neildé:* The non-aspectual derivational string *O-t'aa-* 'bearing O (news, word), announcing O (words)' is added to a variety of motion verb themes; examples from the *Tlingit Verb Dictionary* include, «hàa t at'aa oowagút» (i.e., *haat at'aa.uwagút*), translated there as "he came here bearing news", «doo géi t at'aa oowa.át» (i.e., *du géit at'aa.uwa.át*), translated there as "they met him with the news",* and «ax̱ yoox̱'atángee yeey.áx̱ch: yaa t'aanx̱a.íx'», translated there as "you hear my sayings: I announce them loudly/I call them out".† Note particularly that, although the subject of *(ha)s at'aawjixeex* is plural, the verb theme *S-d-sh-xeex~* 'for (one) S to run' itself refers to a single entity running. We suspect that the reason the corresponding plural theme *O-lu-goo*k̲*~* 'for (several) O to run' is not used here is that the latter theme is object-intransitive, and that the derivational string *O-t'aa-* can be added only to subject-intransitive motion verbs.

LINE 64. *Aadoo sgí* k̲*aa kaanáx̱ kéi* k̲*ugaxaash?:* This differs from Raven's statements in lines 53 and 54 only in that the prefix k̲*u-* is used instead of the third-person object prefix *a-*.

LINES 71–72. *Ch'a kéi gida*k̲*een:* These two lines are sung, apparently impersonating the villagers. The verb is in the progressive imperative form. Compare SJ ix, 84–97, where James sings the same song.

LINES 74–75. K̲*uyáx̱ nida*k̲*een!:* These two lines are sung as well. Our consultants were unable to provide a meaning for the adverb k̲*uyáx̱*. We find the same phrase in SJ ix, 93 and 96–97 (though it is pronounced there as «k̲uwáx̱ n̲idak̲een»); see the note to SJ ix, 93, for discussion.

LINE 78. This line contains a false start. The unaltered utterance is «tle daa—». Mills restarts in the next line to complete the pronunciation of the verb *daada.ús'kw* 'he was washing his (own) body'.

LINE 83. *yáay daa.ityeidí:* The noun *(a) daa.ityeidí* '(its) body parts (viewed as a connected whole)' is usually contracted to *(a) daa.ideidí*; Mills uses the more original form here.

LINE 103. *Yáay yan wulhaashí:* It is possible that Mills alternatively says *yáa yan wulhaashí* 'when it floated ashore here' (where *yáa* is the truncated form of *yáax'*), but we believe we hear *yáay* 'whale' rather than *yáa*.

* Naish and Story, *Tlingit Verb Dictionary*, 222.

† Ibid, 19. A more literal translation of *yaa t'aanx̱agút* would be 'I'm going along announcing them'.

Notes to Katherine Mills' tale VI, *"Why Raven Is Always Hungry"*

LINE 11. *neildé yóo asitaak:* The expected form of this verb is *yóo asiteik*. We cannot explain why the verb root does not undergo ablaut before the repetitive suffix *-k*.

LINE 22. *wáa sá du jeet ux̱dzinee:* See the note to KM I, 21, for discussion of this and similar phrases.

LINES 30–32. *wáag̱eens:* This is a variant of *wáang̱aneens* 'sometimes'. Line 35 contains yet another variant.

LINE 34. *ashanax̱íshdích:* This is a habitual form based on the theme *O-sha-S-x̱ísht(na)* 'for S to hit/beat O repeatedly on the head', as opposed to *O-sha-S-x̱eech~* (Ø) 'for S to hit O on head (once)'. Notice also that because the root *x̱ísht* ends in two consonants, the epenthetic vowel *-í-* has been inserted before the habitual suffix *-ch*, yielding the stem *x̱íshdích*.

LINE 35. *Wáang̱een sáwé:* In this instance we can barely hear the consonant /g̱/, if at all. To Geiger, what we write as ⟨ng̱⟩ here sounded like a voiced uvular nasal, i.e., [ɴ].

LINE 36. *tlákw du x̱'ax̱áni yéi at yateeyéyáx̱ áwé yatee:* This is more literally, 'it was like he always had food on hand'. This is an example of what we are referring to as a quasi-attributive *-ÿéyáx̱* construction. See appendix 1, §13.1.2, for further discussion.

LINE 37. *dikéex̱ daak̲ awootaanch:* This is the habitual form corresponding to the perfective form *dikéex̱ daak̲ ayaawatán* 'he hung it (e.g., a container) up high'.

LINE 49. *áx̱ daak̲ ayawutéeyi yé:* This is a perfective decessive attributive form corresponding to perfective *áx̱ daak̲ ayaawatée* 'he hung it up there'. The whole phrase means 'the place where [the owner] had (previously) hung it up'.

LINE 57. *tle awsikóo yú Yéilch:* The first sentence in this line, «Áwé tle—tle awsikóo yú Yéilch», is elliptic, apparently a short-hand way of saying something like *...awsikóo yú Yéilch yéi wusneeyí* 'he (the owner of the club) knew that it was Raven who did this'.

LINE 73. *ldakát yéig̱aa koowáat':* The phrase *aag̱áa koowáat'* means 'it is long enough, of sufficient length for it'; therefore, *ldakát yéig̱aa koowáat'* literally means 'it is long enough for the whole place', implying that Raven's innards stretched out over the whole area.

LINE 76. *yéi kawliyáatl'k':* Literally, 'they (Raven's innards) became short', with the diminutive suffix *-k'* emphasizing how especially pitiful and tiny Raven's innards had become.

LINE 81. *k̲aa naasí a shóotx̲ yóo aa dudlixáshk:* Mills seems to be comparing Raven's condition to the medical procedure known as a colectomy, in which all or a part of a person's colon is surgically removed. But whereas a person who undergoes a colectomy can still be satiated and become full by eating, Raven's hunger can never be satisfied; he is a bottomless pit.

LINE 84. After the final line of Mills' story, a woman, presumably Edna Belarde Lamebull, can be heard saying «Wáa sá duwasáakw wé k̲áa?» 'What is that man's name?' right before the tape cuts off.

Appendixes

Appendix 1. Linguistic Exposition

1 *'Classical' Tlingit*

In the notes to the stories the reader will find reference to 'classical Tlingit'. This term is used to refer to patterns of speech used by Tlingit speakers born, roughly speaking, prior to 1950 and found in the written archival record as far back as the earliest non-Native explorers who visited the Northwest Coast.* The most substantive of the earliest transcriptions of Tlingit come from Nikolai Petrovich Rezanov (1764–1807), who in 1805 gathered an extensive vocabulary list consisting of translations of 1,200 Russian words into the languages of the most important trading partners with the Russians, including Tlingit and Eyak. An even more important source of Tlingit lexicon was left to us by Leopold Karl Friedrich Radloff (1819–1865), who in and around 1862 collected roughly 350 pages of vocabulary and sentences from a Chilkat elder whose name he wrote as Tikhontin (evidently to be interpreted as *Deix̲eintéen*, based on the spelling «Dèx̣ìntí·ńn»,† which name appears in the genealogical material Teresa Mayer Durlach obtained from Louis Shotridge), along with a 147-page manuscript of German-Tlingit vocabulary. Another early source of Tlingit vocabulary is Aurel Krause (1848–1908), who wrote his memoirs entitled *Die*

* Writing in 1980, about a century after US English-only assimilation programs were initiated in Tlingit Country, Michael Krauss stated, "The number of Tlingit speakers is at most 2,000, the youngest in their thirties." Krauss, "Alaska Native Language: Past Present, and Future", 34. That youngest thirty-year-old cohort would have been born in approximately 1950. Roughly a decade later, the Dauenhauers wrote, "There are no speakers that we know of under the age of forty." Dauenhauer and Dauenhauer, *Beginning Tlingit*, xix. The latter was written as a third-edition preface in 1991, again roughly pointing to 1950 as a major turning point for the Tlingit language. On a broad population scale, the transmission of the language was effectively halted for the generations born after 1950.

† Durlach, *The Relationship Systems of the Tlingit, Haida, and Tsimshian*, 173.

Tlinkit-Indianer, published in German in 1885, which were translated into English and published in 1956 with the title *The Tlingit Indians: Results of a Trip to the Northwest Coast of America and the Bering Straits.*

One characteristic these earliest documenters of Tlingit all share is the consistent distinction between the phonemes /y/ and /ÿ/—the latter is the unrounded back high semivowel [ɰ].* But in John Swanton's *Tlingit Texts and Myths* of 1909, the distinction between /y/ and /ÿ/ is not strictly maintained; in many cases original /ÿ/ appears as /y/ in his texts.† The merger of /ÿ/ with /y/ had begun. (Leer had found that the distinction between /ÿ/ and /y/ was consistently maintained in the Taant'ak̲wáan (Tongass) dialect of Tlingit but nowhere else in Southern Tlingit; original /ÿ/ was only sporadically attested from certain speakers of Northern and Interior Tlingit.) Other than this gradual merger of /ÿ/ with /y/, speakers of classical Tlingit are notable for their full use and control of all the modes, epimodes, and epiaspects of the Tlingit verb. This may not be true of modern speakers, who rarely use the circumstantial modes (consecutive, conditional, and contingent) and may have trouble with rarely used verb forms such as negative and/or decessive attributive forms. Speakers of classical Tlingit are also notable for their ability to freely create predictable verbal derivatives such as the exhaustive, the self-benefactive, the conative, and other derivatives that may be difficult for modern speakers to produce. Finally, speakers of classical Tlingit preserve certain rare constructions that cannot be replicated by modern speakers. Some specific examples of such constructions from this volume are Frank Dick's elaborations using *ch'u yé k̲áa áx' … yé* 'everyone is/was …' (e.g., «ch'u yé k̲áa áx' daxash yé»‡ 'every last person was out flenzing [the whale]') and Susie James' various phrases based on *ch'al … kát* 'as if …' (e.g., «Ch'al ikg̲wajak̲ kát wé gítg̲aa»§ 'As if that evergreen needle could kill you').

Some specific individuals we can point to as representatives of the latter generation of classical speakers are K̲aalk̲áawu, Cyril George (1922–2014); K̲eixwnéi, Nora Marks Dauenhauer (1927–2017); Kaxwaan Éesh, George Davis (1927–2017);

* In Radloff's and Krause's transcriptions using the Roman alphabet, /y/ is consistently transcribed as ⟨j⟩, whereas /ÿ/ is transcribed as ⟨g⟩; the phoneme /g/, on the other hand, is transcribed as ⟨k⟩. Similarly, in the Cyrillic transcriptions of Rezanov, Radloff, and other early Russian explorers and traders, /ya/ and /yaa/ are transcribed as ⟨я⟩, /ye/ and /yei/ as ⟨е⟩, /yi/ and /yee/ as ⟨и⟩, and /yu/ or /yoo/ as ⟨ю⟩ (these Cyrillic characters are romanized as *ya*, *ye*, *yi*, and *yu*, respectively); on the other hand, /ÿ/ is consistently transcribed as ⟨г⟩ (this character is romanized as *g*; the Tlingit phoneme /g/ is transcribed as ⟨к⟩, which is romanized as *k*).

† It should be noted, though, that in cases where /y/ is expected, Swanton's text has /ÿ/ (Swanton represented the phonemes /y/ and /ÿ/ with the characters ⟨y⟩ and ⟨y̨⟩ respectively). Because Swanton's original notes and transcripts are no longer extant, it is impossible to know if Swanton originally indicated /ÿ/ in these cases. It is possible that typographical errors were introduced in the process of transcribing Swanton's handwritten notes or in the final typesetting of the book.

‡ FD vi, 44. For further examples and discussion see the introduction to Dick's stories.

§ SJ xi, 149. For further examples and discussion see the note to SJ i, 111.

Seidayáa, Elizabeth Nyman (1915–1999); Lugóon, Sophie Smarch (1930–2020); Wooshjix̲oo Éesh, George Ramos (1930–2019); Achkwéi, Lena Farkas (1933–2017); and Kootax̲'teek, or K'óox, Johnny Marks (1943–2008). Some eloquent speakers of the classical language alive today are La.oos Tláa, Ida Calmegane (1928–); L'eiwtuyéil, Herman Davis (1933–); Anáalahaash, Sam Johnston (1935–); K̲aanák̲, Ruth Demmert (1937–), K̲aakal.aat, Florence Marks Sheakley (1940–); and Keiyeeshí, Bessie Cooley (1944–). This is a representative but far from exhaustive list.

2 *Prefixes, Suffixes, Proclitics, and Enclitics*

In morphological breakdowns, prefixes and suffixes are indicated with hyphens, e.g., the prefix *ka-* and the suffix *-x̲* (similarly for ordinary postpositions like *-t*, *-de*, and *-náx̲*). Proclitics and enclitics, which are written as separate 'words', are indicated with the equals sign, e.g., the proclitics *kei=* 'up' and *x̲at=* 'me', and the enclitics *=sáani* 'little (plural)' and *=tsú* 'also'; to this category belong also relational postpositions such as *=yáx̲* 'like' and *=g̲óot* 'without'. Proclitics and other phrases that are grammatically associated with the verb and that must occur before the verb word are said to be 'bound' to the verb.

We furthermore introduce a new convention here: namely, the use of a plus sign to denote three special prefix combinations containing the thematic prefix *u-*; these combinations act as a unit and not as we would expect if each of their component parts were combined according to the ordinary prefix combination rules. These are *ÿa+u-*, *ka+u-*, and *ga+u-*, which occur as (1) *ÿa-*, *ka-*, and *ga-* if there is a subject pronominal other than the first-person singular *x̲a-* as well as in all perfective forms; otherwise, (2) *woo-*, *koo-*, and *goo-*, respectively, in the syllable just before the stem (with or without a following *s-*, *l-*, or *sh-* classifier), but (3) *wu-*, *ku-*, and *gu-* in any preceding syllable—and *ku-* contracts to *kw-* after a vowel and before a CV- prefix (where C is a stop consonant).* The rules are different for *ÿa-u-*, *ka-u-*, and *ga-u-* (where *u-* is the negative/irrealis prefix); these combinations regularly contract as *woo-*, *koo-*, and *goo-*, no matter how far they are from the stem syllable.

3 *Truncated Locative Forms*

The locative postposition *-x'* has variants that lack the *-x'* suffix per se, which we call **truncated locative forms**. These forms are used when the locative postpositional

* This generalization unfortunately does not apply to the combinations *ka+u-* and *ga+u-* in comparative stative verb forms and in verbal nouns. 'Comparative' *ka+u-* and *ga+u-* always yield *ku-* and *gu-*, respectively, never **koo-* and **goo-*. (However, *koo-* and *goo-* do appear in comparative verb forms, but only as contractions of *ka+u-ÿa-* and *ga+u-ÿa-*, respectively.) Compare *yéi googéink'* (*ga+u-ÿa-géink'*) 'it is small', *yéi kwsigéink'* (*ga+u-si-géink'*) 's/he/it (e.g., a child) is small' and *ch'a yéi gugéink'* (*ga+u-géink'*) 'a little bit'.

phrase immediately precedes the verb together with its bound elements. Perhaps the most familiar truncated locative form is *tuwáa* in *ax̱ tuwáa sigóo* 'I want, like, enjoy it', which is directly equivalent to *ax̱ tuwáx' sigóo*. The truncated locative forms are constructed as follows: *CV́(V)-x'* > *CV́V* (e.g., *ká-x'* > *káa*), *CVV-x'* > *CVV* (e.g., *daa-x'* > *daa*), *CVVC-x'* > *CVVC-i* (e.g., *ÿaax̱-x'* > *ÿaax̱i*), *CV́VC-x'* > *CV́VC-i* (e.g., *dáaḵ-x'* > *dáag̱i*). Certain relational nouns like *P yí(k)* 'inside cavity of P' and *P táa(k)* 'bottom surface of P' always take this *-k* where either (1) there is no postposition added, or (2) followed by the predicative-locative suffix *-(w)u* (e.g., *a yígu* 'it is inside it'). When followed by a postposition, however, the final, *-k* is optional; for example, *yaakw yíkx'* and *yaakw yíx'* are synonymous, both meaning '(located) in the boat/canoe'. However, this *-k* never occurs in the corresponding truncated locative forms, for example in *yaakw yée woonook* 's/he sat down in the boat' (not **yaakw yígi woonook*).

4 *Verb Theme and Root Notation*

We use the term **verb theme** to refer collectively to the prefixes required by the verb and the verb root, followed by a description of the essential attributes of the verb: its conjugation prefix and whether it is an event, an act, a position, or a state. Within the verb word, we use the cover symbols **S-** for the subject pronominal prefix or proclitic and **O-** for the direct object pronominal prefix or proclitic. The lexical classifier elements are represented as *d-* and (for the fricative element of the classifier) *l-*, *s-*, or *sh-*. The verb root is given in its basic stem form—this is the stem form we find, for example, in the negative future. For **variable verb roots**, we use the representations *CVV~* for open roots and *CVVC~* or *CV́VC~* for closed roots. Open variable roots have several subtypes; we will not discuss all of them in detail here. These normally undergo ablaut when a consonantal suffix is added to the root: /aa/ becomes /ei/ and /oo/ becomes /(w)ei/. Just plain *CVV~* indicates that obstruent-suffixed forms of the root have long high tone, whereas *CVV`* indicates that the obstruent-suffixed forms of the root have long low tone. **Invariable verb roots** are written out, with vowel length and tone indicated, and without the symbol '~'. The term 'invariable' is somewhat misleading, since there are degrees of invariability. First, all *ga*-conjugation stative verb roots are invariable, but if they have the form *CV́V*, the stative imperfective is almost always of the variable type that has affirmative and decessive stem *CV́V* but negative stem *CV́* and subordinate stem *CVV* before the suffix *-ÿi*. Second, open 'invariable roots' almost always take ablaut before a consonantal suffix. Finally, attributive forms of 'invariable roots' may undergo reduction (whereby a long vowel changes to a short vowel—this happens only with closed roots), and/or loss of tone, so that whereas *O-S-s-x̱án* (*ga* state) 'for S to love O' shows only high-tone *x̱án* in non-attributive forms such as *x̱asix̱án* 'I love him/her/it'; the attributive form *x̱asix̱ani* (*aa*) '(one) that I love' has lost its tone.

5 *Citation of Verb Themes*

Descriptions of rarely occurring verb forms are provided in the notes where we feel the reader may have trouble parsing the form without additional information and grammatical explanation. The vocabulary used to describe such grammatical issues is generally consistent with that found in Leer's 1991 dissertation, "The Schetic Categories of the Tlingit Verb". Note also that we use the abbreviations **S** (subject of verb), **O** (object of verb), **P** (postpositional object), **N** (nominal object, also known as the possessor of a possessed noun; if a nominal object is specifically a pronoun, we will refer to this as a 'possessive pronoun' rather than using the confusing label 'pronominal nominal object'), as well as **NP** (noun phrase, regardless of its external grammatical relationships). When we speak of the **absolutive argument** of the verb, we refer to the subject of a subject-intransitive verb but the object of a transitive or object-intransitive verb. Nouns themselves are divided into two categories: **alienable** (meaning that the basic form of the noun is intransitive, i.e., non-possessed; most alienable nouns also have transitive, i.e., possessed, forms), and **inalienable** (meaning that the noun occurs only in its transitive, i.e., possessed, form). **Relational nouns** comprise a subcategory of inalienable nouns that denote a spatial or temporal relationship, such as *N ká* 'N's (horizontal) surface, on N', *N taÿee* 'underneath N', and *N ít* 'after/following N (in space or time)'.

6 *Ergativity and Omission of Third-Person Possessive Pronouns After Ergative NPs*

We use the phrase **ergative argument** to refer to a noun phrase that functions as the subject of a verb when it is marked as ergative (which means that it refers to the agent doing something to someone or something else) by means of the postposition *-ch*. If the ergative argument more or less immediately precedes a transitive verb, the third-person object pronoun *a-* will normally be omitted from the verb; compare, for example, ***a**daná* 'she's drinking it' vs. *wé shaawát**ch** daná* 'the woman is drinking it'.

But, as we have begun learning while working through these texts, we find the situation more complex and nuanced than this. In some cases we find an ergative noun phrase before an intransitive verb preceded by an oblique argument consisting of a relational noun followed by a postposition; in such cases the third-person possessive pronoun that serves as the object of the relational noun (i.e., *a* 'it, its' and apparently even *hasdu* 'them, their', and presumably also *du* 'his, her') may be omitted. The first such construction to catch our attention was Frank Italio's formulation «Yéilch yíkde wdaḵeeni yáaÿ»* 'the whale inside which Raven had flown', in which the possessive pronoun *a* 'it' of *a yíkde* 'towards inside of it (the whale)' has been

* FI I, iv, 58.

deleted following *Yéilch*;[*] the more ordinary form of this phrase would be *Yéil a yíkde wdak̲eeni yáaÿ*, which is identical in meaning. We find another example from Austin Hammond,

Lingit.aanituk̲wáanich i eedé toowú kei kg̲wak'éi.[†]	The people of the world will be grateful to you.

in which the possessive pronoun *hasdu* 'their' of *hasdu toowú* 'their spirit, mind, inner being' has been deleted after *Lingit.aanituk̲wáanich*;[‡] the ordinary construction here would be *Lingit.aanituk̲wáani i eedé hasdu toowú kei kg̲wak'éi*.

We can point to two other examples from outside the texts of this volume. In a speech at Celebration 1982, Charlie Jim states, «a x̲oo.aa k̲u.ooch k̲wá tlél daa yak̲ushoosgé»[§] 'some people, however, don't understand it', in which the possessive pronoun *hasdu* of *hasdu daa* has been deleted after *k̲u.ooch*; the ordinary construction would be *a x̲oo.aa k̲u.oo k̲wá tléil hasdu daa yak̲ushoosgé*. The second example comes from the text Swanton took down from a man named K̲'adasteen, «Ye do-wasā´kᵘ Tā´y̥ākᵘtc-y̥îx-wugū´dî-hīn», i.e., *Yéi duwasáakw Tayaakwch Yíx̲ Woogoodi Héen*; Swanton translated this accurately as "They call it River-the-stone-canoe-came-down-through."[¶] In this placename, the possessive pronoun *a* 'it' of *a yíx̲* (from *a yík-x̲*) 'down along inside it (the river)' has been deleted after *Tayaakwch* 'Stone-canoe' (from *té-yaakw-ch*).

Ergatively marked independent pronouns never result in the deletion of third-person object pronominals, but we find interesting cases where such ergatively marked pronouns occur before—or in conjunction with—intransitive verbs preceded by a relational noun plus postposition combination similar to the examples cited above.

---

* Italio's phrase uses the attributive form of the decessive verb phrase *a yíkde wdak̲eenín* 'he had flown toward the inside of it'.

† AH I, iii, 168–69.

‡ We can be confident that *hasdu* 'their' is the relevant pronoun of choice here (rather than *a*) because just prior to uttering this line Hammond uses *hás* 'them' and *hasdu* 'their' in reference to the *lingit.aanituk̲wáani* 'people of the world': «Aaa, yá lingit.aanituk̲wáani káx̲, / aaa, hás áyá / hasdu káx̲ eeshandéin yoo ikayasheik / k̲a i kaax̲ hasdu toowú kei kg̲wak'éi.» 'Yes, on behalf of the people of the world, / yes, they are the ones / you are suffering for / and because of you they will be happy' (AH I, iii, 155–58).

§ MC002, box 1, item 10, "Angoon Dancers, First Performance." This phrase occurs at 2:00:15 on the recording. As discussed briefly in §3.11 of the editors' introduction, in Charlie Jim's pronunciation the 'mental activity' proclitic *ÿaa=* is reduced to *ya-* in this instance, which is normal, though not obligatory, when this morpheme occurs after *daa* and before *k̲u-*.

¶ Swanton, *Tlingit Myths and Texts*, 360; from text 105, "Story of Kâ´ck!e qoan" (i.e., Story of Kwáashk'i K̲wáan). Note that both instances of ⟨y̥⟩ (corresponding to /ÿ/ [ɰ]) in Swanton's transcription are erroneous. The words *yaakw* [jaːkʷ] 'canoe, boat' and *N yík* [jík] 'inside N (a shallow concave landform, boat, structure)' begin with /y/ [j], not /ÿ/ [ɰ].

Dick provides two such examples: in «x̱áach áwé a daa yóo jikux̱li.átk»[*] 'I'm the one that attends to her', *x̱áach* is the ergative counterpart to *x̱át* 'I, me', and the *a* of *a daa* 'around her' is retained; in «A shóo yéi wootèe hóoch ḵu.aa»[†] '[Raven], on the other hand, sat down to eat [the whale meat]', the ergatively marked pronoun occurs in the afterphrase position, where *hóoch* is the ergative counterpart to *hú* 's/he, him/her'. Katherine Mills provides an example which is closely parallel to the latter of Dick's, but with the ergatively marked pronoun in the forephrase position, «Tle ch'a tléináx̱ hóoch áwé a shóo yéi wootee»[‡] 'He (Raven) was the only one there feasting on it (the meat of the Brown Bear couple and their halibut catch)'. We are still investigating these rare twists on the ergative construction and provide notes pointing out examples illustrating it in the texts.

6.1 *Other Cases of Omission of Possessive Pronoun* a

We also find cases where we would expect the non-human third-person possessive pronoun *a* before a relational noun plus postposition, but we do not hear it. In some cases, this may be due to the poor quality of the recording—unstressed syllables without any consonants may be below the threshold of reproducibility on the recording. This may be the case in «Ch'a daat ÿan x̱'eedats'én déi-ei!»[§] 'Just quiet down about it now!' Here we might expect *Ch'a a daat* … 'just/simply about it …', and perhaps this is what James said but we couldn't hear the unstressed *a*; it could have been swallowed up by the preceding word *ch'a*. In other cases, we are more sure that *a* is omitted, e.g., «K'e tóox̱ nagú»[¶] 'You should get inside it', where we might expect *a* before *tóox̱* '(moving) along into'; another example is «Tle t'áatx̱ kei naalagás'ch»[**] '[In this situation] the clan just picks up and moves away from behind [the *ch'a.aan*]', where again we might expect *a* before *t'áatx̱* 'from [a place] behind/upland from [where the *ch'a.aan* lies]' (*ch'a.aan* being the made-up word Raven uses for a dead humpback whale in order to trick the villagers into abandoning it).

7 *Third- and Fourth-Person Pronominals*

Tlingit has several types of third-person postpositional object pronouns and possessive pronouns. The most common type, referring to humans (including anthropomorphized animals), is the **neutral** human possessive pronoun *du* 'his/her' and postpositional object *du=ée/ee-* 'him/her'. These are pluralized with preceding *has-*,

* FD ii, 41.
† FD vi, 110.
‡ KM III, 164.
§ SJ xi, 148.
¶ FI I, i, 168.
** FI I, iv, 139.

i.e., *hasdu* 'their' and *hasdu=ée/ee-* 'them'. Especially in narratives, however, speakers may distinguish between a **salient** actor (referring to the protagonist—the person around whom the narrative revolves at the moment) and a **recessive** actor (referring to a person who is placed in opposition to the salient actor). The salient nominal and postpositional object pronouns are *ash* and *ash=ée/ee-*, respectively; whereas the recessive pronouns are the same as the pronouns referring to non-humans: *a* and *á/aa-*, respectively. The reader should take special notice of the fact that pronouns referring to non-humans (as well as recessive actors) may refer indifferently to one or more than one non-human (or recessive actor); for example, *wé tléiḵw aawax̱áa* can mean either 's/he/it ate the berry' or 's/he/it ate the berries', and *aawax̱áa* can mean either 's/he/it ate it (one thing)' or 's/he/it ate them (more than one thing)'. Likewise, *awsiteen* can translate 's/he/it saw him/her/it' or, if the object is non-human or recessive, 's/he/it saw them'; but if the subject or object is human plural we would say *has awsiteen* 'they saw him/her/it/them' or 's/he/it saw them'.

The Tlingit language also distinguishes a set of 'fourth-person' pronominal prefixes and proclitics. The **human fourth person** (subject prefix usually *du-(d-)* but sometimes *a-* instead, verbal object *ḵu-* or *ḵaa=*, possessive pronoun *ḵaa*, and postpositional object *ḵóo/ḵoo-*) refers to an unspecified person or group of people; compare *ax̱á* 's/he/it is eating it' and *dux̱á* 'someone is eating it; (the) people are eating it; they (an indeterminate group) are eating it; it is being eaten', and compare *du éet wudishée* 's/he helped him/her' and *ḵóot wudishée* 's/he helped someone; s/he helped (the) people'. The **non-human fourth person** with proclitic *at=* refers to an unspecified thing or things. Although Tlingit lacks a sex distinction in third-person pronouns (like English 'he' vs. 'she'), we can see that the language has its own ways of distinguishing which actor or group of people is being referred to.

8 *Transitivity Types*

The verb system in particular is extremely complex and multidimensional. There are four transitivity types: **impersonal** (with neither S- nor O-), **subject-intransitive** (with S- but without O-), **object-intransitive** (with O- but without S-), and **transitive** (with both S- and O-). Tlingit object-intransitive verbs normally correspond to English intransitive verbs. Most commonly, subject-intransitive verbs refer to situations under the control of the actor, whereas object-intransitive verbs usually refer to situations where the actor lacks control over what is going on; compare the subject-intransitive verb *x̱waditúw* 'I read (in the past)' and *x̱at wudixwétl* 'I'm tired'. In some cases, however, object-intransitive verbs are used even when the actor (typically a plural actor) has control of the situation, compare subject-intransitive *S-d-sh-xeex* 'for (a single) S to run' vs. object-intransitive *O-lu-gooḵ* 'for (more than one) O to run'—English 'to run' is intransitive in either case.

9 *Verb Modes*

There are twelve verb modes (listed below), many of which can combine with other dimensional categories, namely: **negative or irrealis status** (required in negative sentences, optional with *gwál* or *=gíwé* 'maybe, perhaps'); the **decessive epimode** (which basically indicates that the situation described by the verb is no longer in force); and the attributive, subordinative, and prohibitive epimodes. An **attributive** verb form is used to modify a head noun, although 'headless relative clauses' do occur (see §13 below). A **subordinative** verb form functions as the head of a subordinate clause. The imperfective and perfective modes also feature the **prohibitive/optative** epimode with the distinctive suffix *-ÿiḵ* (with the variant form *-ḵ* also possible after a stem ending in a vowel), which serves, with sentence-initial *líl* or *tlél*, to form negative commands, and with sentence-initial *gu.aal* (*kwshé*), to express a hope or wish. The attributive, subordinate, and prohibitive/optative epimodes are mutually exclusive and therefore take up a single dimension in the verbal manifold. However, negative/irrealis status and the decessive epimode occupy separate dimensions, meaning that they can combine with each other as well as with the attributive or subordinative categories; for example, *l x̱wax̱aayích* 'because I didn't eat it' is a negative subordinative verb form followed by the postposition *-ch*, and *l x̱wax̱aayí yéeyich* 'because I hadn't eaten it' is a negative decessive subordinate verb form followed by the postposition *-ch* 'because', and *l x̱wax̱áayi* (*aa*) '(the one) which I hadn't eaten' is a negative decessive attributive verb form followed by *-ch*. In contrast, the prohibitive/optative epimode is inherently negative and does not combine with the decessive epimode, e.g., *gu.aal x̱wax̱aayíḵ* (or *gu.aal x̱wax̱aaḵ*) 'I hope I eat it'—there is no corresponding decessive form meaning 'I hope I had eaten it'. Following is a list of the Tlingit verb modes together with rough descriptions.

9.1 *Imperfective*

For **active verbs**, the basic imperfective denotes ongoing or customary activity, e.g., *ax̱á* 's/he is eating it; s/he eats it (customarily)'; for **stative verbs,** it denotes an ongoing state, e.g., *ÿak'éi* 'it is good/nice'; and for **positional** verbs, it denotes a resting position or posture, e.g., (*át*) *hán* 's/he/it is standing (there)'. **Eventive verbs** lack a basic imperfective. We distinguish three types of imperfectives based on their semantic properties: **basic imperfectives**, like *ax̱á*, *ÿak'éi*, and (*át*) *hán* mentioned above, which denote ongoing (and sometimes also customary) activity; **repetitive imperfectives**, like *yei ḵusteech* 's/he/it always comes into being, is always born', which denote repeated or customary actions or repeated attempts to act; and **multiple imperfectives**, like *has ḵusteet'* 'they (successively) come into existence, are born', which denote that the absolutive argument of the verb consists of multiple entities. (This combines with all epimodes.)

9.2 *Perfective*

For active and eventive verbs, the perfective denotes a situation that came to fruition in the past, and (if not decessive) implies that the state resulting from the past event still applies in the present, e.g., *aawax̱áa* 's/he ate it', *wudixwétl* 's/he got tired (and still is); s/he is tired'. For stative verbs, this denotes a situation whereby the state has come into existence, e.g., *wook'éi* 'it was/became good/nice; it improved'. (This combines with all epimodes.)

9.3 *Realizational*

The realizational is similar in meaning to the perfective, although it seems to convey a sense of achievement, of finally realizing a goal after protracted effort. Leer wrote in his 1991 dissertation that this mode "is generally translated like the perfective, but seems to convey a sense of vividness or immediacy."* Compare, for instance, the realizational *ÿanax̱tuwadláak̲* '(sure enough) we (finally) reached it!' with the perfective *ÿawtuwadlaak̲* 'we reached it'. The realizational mode is extremely rare; most examples we have collected are from old songs. An example of a realizational form from this volume occurs twice in a formulaic expression attributed to Raven's grandfather, who curses Raven while lamenting the loss of his most valuable possessions; from Dick we hear «Kaawayíkt akaajéil ax̱ ádi yóo Yéil Tl'éetl'i!»† 'That Shitty Raven managed to strew my possessions into thin air!'; and from James, «Wuyít akaajéil ax̱ duwuweidí Yéil Tl'éetl'i!»‡ 'Shitty Raven managed to strew my wealth into thin air!' (Negative and epimodal forms have not been found.)

9.4 *Future*

The future mode denotes a situation that will apply or is expected to apply in the future, e.g., *akg̱wax̱áa* 's/he will eat it, is going to eat it, is (supposed) to eat it, can/could/should eat it'. (This combines with all epimodes.)

9.5 *Potential*

The potential mode denotes a situation that could potentially apply if circumstances allow, e.g., *aadé nax̱tuwa.aat* 'we can/could go there', *tlél aadé g̱atuwax̱aaÿi yé* (*k̲oostí*) 'we can't eat it' (lit., '(there is) no way we can/could eat it'), *tlél g̱atuwax̱aaÿi át* (*k̲oostíl*) 'there is nothing for us to eat' (lit., '(there is) nothing we can/could eat'). The decessive potential is used for the apodosis in a condition-contrary-to-fact

---

* Leer, "The Schetic Categories of the Tlingit Verb", 379.

† FD ii, 174.

‡ SJ xi, 303.

construction, e.g., (*Yáax' óosh yéi x̱at teeyí*) *i eedé ḵwadasheeÿín* '(if I had only been here) I would/could have helped you'. The plain potential is most often used after an imperative or hortative verb form to denote negative consequences if the command or exhortation is not heeded. Dick's impersonation of Tide-Commander provides such an example:

«Yijáḵ!	"Kill it!
Yijáḵ,	Kill it,
ax̱ shát éex̱ oongaanóok.»*	or it might bother my wife."

(This mode combines with all epimodes except the subordinative.)

9.6 *Habitual*

The habitual mode denotes a situation that habitually applies, particularly a situation that is conditional on something else happening, e.g., (*haat gagúdín*) *haa een at ux̱áaÿch* '(when s/he comes) s/he eats with us (every time)', *ch'a tlákw ts'ootaat x̱áat has oox̱áaÿch* 'they eat fish every morning'. (This mode combines with all epimodes.)

9.7 *Imperative*

The imperative voices a direct command to one or more addressees, e.g., *at x̱á!* 'eat!', *at ÿix̱á!* 'eat, you folks!', *igak'éi!* 'be good!' (Only second-person subjects occur with this mode. No negative or epimodal forms are possible.)

9.8 *Hortative*

The hortative mode expresses an indirect command or suggestion, e.g., *aadé nax̱too.aat* 'let's go there', *at ḵax̱aa* 'let me eat', *gagak'éi* 'let it be good/nice'. No decessives nor epimodal forms are possible, but the suffix *-ÿi* may be added to a hortative verb form without change in meaning. The postposition *-t* added to a hortative verb form creates a purposive clause, e.g., *at ḵax̱aat áyá haat uwagút* (or *at ḵax̱aaÿít ...*) 'I came to eat', more literally, 'I came in order that I eat'. Occasionally, however, as found in the texts of this volume, it seems that hortatives without this postposition *-t* can function as purposive clauses. (Negative purposive clauses are possible but rare; the admonitive with *-g̱aa* is normally used instead.)

9.9 *Admonitive*

In conjunction with the enclitic *=tsé*, the admonitive mode serves to warn someone to be careful not to do something, e.g., *eex̱áa tsé* 'be careful not to eat it',

* FD i, 52–54.

k̲ut tsé geejóon 'beware lest you have bad dreams'. It also combines with the postposition *-g̲aa* to form a dependent clause meaning 'lest V', e.g., (*du éet wudishée*) *daak usgéetg̲aa* '(s/he helped him/her) lest s/he fall down' or '(s/he helped him/her) so that she won't/wouldn't fall down'. (No epimodal forms are possible; this mode is inherently negative, and seems to occur only with second-person subjects.)

9.10 *Consecutive*

The consecutive mode refers to a condition that was met in the past. It translates 'when, after V (in the past)', e.g., *át góot* (*at uwax̲áa*) 'when/after s/he came there (s/he ate)'. A verb in this mode forms a dependent clause. The meaning 'after V (in the past)' can be unambiguously expressed by adding the postposition *-dáx̲* to the consecutive verb form. (Negative forms occur, but no epimodal forms are possible.)

9.11 *Conditional*

The conditional mode refers to a condition that is expected to occur in the future. It translates 'when, if V (in the future)', e.g., *át gútni* (*at gug̲ax̲áa*) 'when/if s/he comes there (s/he will eat)'. A verb in this mode forms a dependent clause. (Negative forms occur, but no epimodal forms are possible.)

9.12 *Contingent*

The contingent mode refers to a condition that habitually recurs. It translates 'when(ever) V', e.g., *át gag̲údín* (*at ux̲áaÿch*) 'whenever s/he comes there (s/he [habitually] eats)'. A verb in this mode forms a dependent clause. (Negative forms occur, but no epimodal forms are possible.)

10 *Epiaspect*

Another dimension that overlies the categories of mode and epimode is called **epiaspect**, which is comprised of two mutually exclusive categories: progressive and durative. The **progressive epiaspect** denotes that the situation is in the process of unfolding. It can denote motion in progress, e.g., *ÿaa nagút* 's/he/it is walking/going along'; events in progress, e.g., *ÿaa ndaxwétl* 's/he/it is getting tired' (cf. *wudixwétl* 's/he/it is tired'); a state coming into effect, e.g., *kei nakʼéin* 'it is getting good/better/nice(r)' (cf. *ÿakʼéi* 'it is good/nice' and *wookʼéi* 'it was good/nice; it became good/better/nice(r)'); and it can have an inchoative meaning, e.g., *daak nastán* 'it is starting to rain' (cf. *daak wusitán* 'it is raining'). The progressive epiaspect requires that the verb word be preceded by a preverb such as *ÿaa=*, *kei=*, or *ÿei=*; the progressive imperfective takes the prefix *na-*, whereas the other modes take the prefix *ga-* (and note that the perfective progressive does not occur), as we see in the progressive habitual forms *ÿaa gagútch* 's/he/it keeps walking and walking (along)' and *daak gastánch* 'it keeps starting to rain'. The **durative epiaspect** refers to situations where the event is ongoing for some time, especially relevant to an event involving repeated episodes. Durative verb forms most frequently have a suffix such as *-ch*, *-x̲*, or *-k(w)* added to the root. Outside the imperfective and perfective modes, durative verb forms are marked with the prefix *na-*, e.g., *nat'úkt* 'shoot at it (repeatedly)!' (repetitive imperfective *at'úkt* 's/he is shooting at it with arrows (repeatedly)'; cf. *t'úk!* 'shoot it (with an arrow)!'); *naják̲x̲* 'keep killing it!, keep trying to kill it!' (repetitive imperfective *aják̲x̲* 's/he keeps killing it, is trying to kill it'; cf. *ják̲!* 'kill it!'); *has woonáat'* 'they died off one after another' (multiple imperfective *has náat'* 'they are dying off one after another'; cf. *has woonaa* 'they died'). A third epiaspect, rarely encountered, is the **conative**, which we will discuss below in §12.

11 *Derivational Strings*

Atop this richly-endowed apparatus that serves to generate thousands of potential verb forms, Tlingit makes ample use of **derivational strings**, i.e., strings of elements that combine to impart a difference in meaning to the verb. Some of these are called **non-aspectual derivational strings**, meaning that they do not affect the conjugation class of the verb nor alter the verb stem variation. Of these, some, like *ka-* 'round/tiny object', *ÿa-* 'firewood', *x̲'e-* 'viscous substance', and the classifier element *s/l-* 'composite object', are **configurational** in nature, meaning that they are used to designate the spatial configuration of the absolutive argument. A few such strings serve to form important **causative and 'applicative' derivatives**. For example, many object-intransitive verbs form causatives with the string *S-s/l-* 'for S to cause O to VERB', e.g., *awsixúk* 's/he dried it', cf. *uwaxúk* 'it is dry'; furthermore, many transitive verbs form an 'causative applicative' with the string *P-x'=S-s/l-* 'for S to cause P to VERB O', e.g., *ax̲ ée(x')* *awsitáw* 's/he made me steal it'; cf. *x̲waatáw* 'I stole it' and *aawatáw* 's/he stole it'. Another common non-aspectual derivational string is the **self-benefactive** derivational string *ga-d-* 'for self', e.g., *awsi.ée* 's/he cooked it' vs. *agawdzi.ée* 's/he cooked it for her-/himself, for immediate consumption'.

Much more numerous are the **aspectual derivational strings**, which overwrite the underlying conjugation class and repetitive imperfective type of the verb, supplanting it with the conjugation class and repetitive imperfective type innate to the aspectual derivational string. Most strings of this type are properly added to motion verb themes, which have no innate conjugation class nor default repetitive imperfective type; these typically specify the direction of motion, e.g., *át wudik̲ín* 'it flew (up to) there; it arrived there by flying' (Ø-conj., repetitive imperfective *áx̲ dak̲een* 'it keeps flying (up to) there'); *kei wdik̲ín* 'it flew up' (Ø-conj., repetitive imperfective *kei da<u>k</u>ínch* 'it keeps flying up'), *át wudi<u>k</u>een* 'it is/was flying around/about' (*na*-conj.; there appears to be no corresponding repetitive imperfective), *ÿaa wdi<u>k</u>een* 'it flew down' (*<u>g</u>a*-conj., repetitive imperfective *yei da<u>k</u>ínch* 'it keeps flying down'), *<u>k</u>ut wudi<u>k</u>een* 'it flew astray; it got lost (or went out of sight) by flying' (*<u>g</u>a*-conj., repetitive imperfective *<u>k</u>ut kei da<u>k</u>ínch* 'it keeps flying astray'), and what we call **obliquative** derivatives such as *ana<u>x</u> ÿawdi<u>k</u>ín* 'it flew through there' (Ø-conj. with prefixes *ÿa+u-*, repetitive imperfective *ana<u>x</u> ÿaa da<u>k</u>ínch* 'it keeps flying through there').* Some Ø-conjugation aspectual derivational strings can be added to non-motion verbs as well; compare the motion verb form *ÿan aawatée* 's/he set it down (i.e., to an end-point, to a position of rest)' (Ø-conj.) vs. the active verb form *ÿan aawatúw* 's/he finished reading it' (Ø-conj.), more literally, 's/he read it to the end-point' (compare *aawatóow* 's/he read it', *na*-conj.). Similarly, referring to the starting-point of an activity is indicated by the preverb *<u>g</u>unaÿéi=* or *<u>g</u>unéi=* (Ø-conj.), e.g., *<u>g</u>un(aÿ)éi aawatúw* 's/he started to read it'. Another important aspectual derivational string is the **exhaustive** *ÿa<u>x</u>=ÿa-s/l-* (Ø-conj.), which denotes that all or most of the absolutive argument is affected by the action or event, e.g., *uwa.ée* 'it is cooked' vs. *ÿa<u>x</u> ÿawsi.ée* 'all/lots of it is cooked' and *awsi.ée* 's/he cooked it' vs. *ÿa<u>x</u> aÿawsi.ée* 's/he cooked up all/lots of it'.

12 *The Conative and the Processional Imperfective*

Of great interest because of their rarity are instances of the conative epiaspect attested with certainty only in imperfective forms, where the verb has the proclitic *ÿa<u>x</u>=*, the *i-* element of the classifier, and the conative stem, which is short and high-toned for both open and closed roots, e.g., *ya<u>x</u> ayatí* 's/he is trying to set it (ordinary object) in place', *ya<u>x</u> a<u>x</u>'ayatí* 's/he is trying to link/hook it on (e.g., onto a chain)', *ya<u>x</u> alitl'ít* 's/he is trying to get rid of it, divorce, fire him/her', *ya<u>x</u> ayatán* 's/he is trying to set it (e.g., an empty container) in place', and *aadé ya<u>x</u> ayashí* 's/he is trying to reach/touch it'. Examples from this volume include two lines from James, «wé nées'<u>g</u>aa wé héen takaadé ÿa<u>x</u> ÿagút»† 'he (Raven) was trying to go to the sea floor for urchins' and «Wé Lukshiyáank'i gúkx'u áwé aa<u>x</u> ayatáx'»‡ 'She (Raven) was trying to bite the ears off that Little Mink'. Hammond uses a decessive conative form in the statement «Ts'as áa kawjigidi yéide ya<u>x</u> <u>x</u>agúdin»§ 'I used to try to go only to dark places'; he also

* These obliquative verb forms generally refer to motion with a sideways, arc-like, or circuitous trajectory; compare also *daa<u>x</u> ÿaawatúl* 'it is spinning in a circle', *haandé ÿaawanúk* 's/he scooted over this way (while sitting)', *héide ÿaawanúk* 's/he scooted over that way', *a tóo aÿaawatée* 's/he transfered it into it'.

† SJ v, 17.

‡ SJ viii, 30.

§ AH I, ii, 356.

uses a form with the habitual auxiliary in «ch'as áa ḵukawjigidi yéide yax̱ haa kwdaya nuch»[*] 'we always try to make our way into dark places'.

In these texts we also find a fair number of what we call 'processional' imperfectives. These are formed like the extension verbs *anax̱ naashóo* 'it extends, sticks up through there' and *(ka)naadaa* 'it flows', with the conjugation prefix (here *na-*) and the *i-* element of the classifier in affirmative forms, except that they can be formed from any verb of motion with a plural absolutive argument. Only forms with *na-* conjugation prefix have been found, e.g., *aadé s naa.aat* 'they are/were going there in procession' and *aadé s anli.aat* 'they are bringing them there in procession'. Some examples from the texts:

i daax̱ naa.aat[†]	They (lice) are crawling all over you
Tle anlinaa íḵde[‡]	he then began packing them in bundles down towards the beach
gus'yaadáx̱ jinli.aadi teet tlénx'[§]	these huge breakers that are constantly rolling in from the cloud banks
neildé áwé ÿanduwaxoon[¶]	[the guests] proceeded inside

13 *Attributive Verb Forms*

Attributive verb forms are an indispensable feature of Tlingit speech. In the notes to the texts we often comment on attributive clauses (more often called 'relative clauses' by linguists) and how they are used in a given passage. They are most usually followed by a head noun. If the head noun is coreferential with the subject of a subject-intransitive verb or the object of the verb in the attributive clause, this subject or object will take the third-person form, e.g., *x̱at wusiteeni ḵáa* '(the) person who saw me' (in which *ḵáa* is coreferential with the covert third-person subject), *x̱wasiteeni ḵáa* '(the) person whom I saw' (in which *ḵáa* is coreferential with the covert third-person object), and *awsiteeni ḵáa* '(the) person whom s/he/it saw' (in which the *ḵáa* 'person' is coreferential with the third-person object *a-*). Likewise, if the head noun is coreferential with a postpositional object or possessive pronoun, this object will usually be expressed with 'resumptive' third-person pronominals: *á-* or *du=ée/ee-* as postpositional object and *a* or *du* as possessive pronoun. In particular, if the head noun is coreferential with a third-person subject of a transitive

* AH I, ii, 476.
† FD X, 36.
‡ FD xi, 44.
§ RZ II, iii, 114–15.
¶ SJ vii, 25.

verb, the resumptive pronoun will take the ergative suffix *-ch*, e.g., *ách wusiteeni ḵáa* 'the person who saw him/her/it'. Other examples with resumptive pronominals are *x'óow du jee yéi yateeyi ḵáa* 'a person who has a blanket' (more literally, 'a person such that a blanket is in his possession (*du jee*)') and *aadé x̱wsiteeni ÿé* 'the place where I saw it' (more literally, 'the place (*ÿé*) such that I saw it there (*aadé*)'). The combination *aadé ... ÿé* can also translate 'in the way/manner that ...', so *aadé x̱wsiteeni yé* also means 'the way I saw it' or 'how I saw it'. Furthermore, the combination *aag̱áa ... ÿé* almost always translates '(at the time) when ...', so *aag̱áa x̱wsiteeni yé* means '(at the time) when I saw it'.

It can often prove difficult for students of the Tlingit language to distinguish between the attributive form and the subordinative form of a given verb. Here is a useful tip for the learner: if the verb has the suffix *-ÿi* (or the long-vowelled counterpart) and if there is a high tone on this suffix, then the verb is most likely in the subordinative epimode, whereas the attributive suffix *-ÿi* will never have high tone. Another clue is that the classifier of subordinative verb forms always lacks the *i-* element. Not all attributive forms take the *i-* element of the classifier, but those that do will end in the suffix *-ÿi* (which, however, will never be long); in non-decessive attributive verb forms, moreover, neither the stem nor the suffix takes high tone, except in rare cases where the stem is completely invariable. (Note that the suffix *-ÿi* is not added to non-decessive attributive forms of verb modes or epimodes that do not take the *i-* element of the classifier, e.g., *ax̱a át* 'what s/he/it is eating', more literally 'the thing (*át*) such that s/he/it is eating it'; the corresponding subordinative form is *ax̱aayí* 'the fact that s/he/it is/was eating it; while s/he/it is/was eating it'.) Compare, for example, the perfective attributive form ***x̱wasiteeni*** *keitl* '(the) dog **that I saw**' (with the *i-* element of the classifier and without high tone on the stem or suffix) and the perfective subordinative form *x̱wasateení wé keitl* '(the fact) that I saw the dog' or 'when I saw the dog' (without the *i-* element of the classifier and with high tone on the suffix). Postpositions may be attached to the subordinate verb form, e.g., *x̱wasateení**ch*** '**because** [of the fact that] I saw him/her/it' and *x̱wasateení**dáx̱*** '**after I** saw him/her/it', but postpositions are never added to attributive verb forms.

Attributive clauses most commonly precede the head noun which they modify. However, if the attributive form of the verb has the *i-* element of the classifier and the suffix *-ÿi*, it can be postposed, that is, it may come after the head noun, sometimes at the end of the entire sentence. Dick provides an example:

wáananée sáwé wéi du ḵáa goox̱ú,	eventually his male slave,
wé du sée daa yóo jikwli.atgi,	**who waited on his daughter,**
yáanáx̱ yux̱ woogoot.*	came out through here.

* FD ii, 34–36.

Hammond's narratives in particular provide a number of examples of postposed attributive clauses, for example:

Yéi áwé yatee yá K'ákw,
  yóo áyá tuwasáakw
yá ash yáanáx̱ át woogoodi át áyá
  yées ḵáax̱ siteeyi.[*]
	This is how Pygmy Owl was;
	  this is what we call
	the creature who walked past him,
	  who was a young man.

This is not the case if the attributive form of the verb lacks the *i-* classifier element as well as the suffix *-ÿi*, in which case the attributive clause usually precedes the head noun; however, such an attributive clause may be postposed if it is followed by the generic head noun *aa* '(the) one (such that ...)', e.g., *ax̱ jeet tán wé ḵóok,* ***wé naa.át a tóode kagax̱duchak aa*** 'give me the box, **the one into which clothes will be packed**'. Hammond's narratives also contain a few instances of what are called 'headless' attributive clauses, where there is no head noun either before or after the attributive clause. Compare:

yá t'aaw yóo tuwasáagu[†]	what we call a feather
yáa dís yóo tuwasáagu[‡]	what we call the moon
yá ḵei.á yóo tuwasáagu[§]	what we call the daybreak

The more usual way of formulating these would involve a noun after the attributive verb, e.g., *yá t'aaw yóo tuwasáagu* ***át*** 'the **thing** we call a feather' or *yáa ḵei.á yóo tuwasáagu* ***aa*** 'the **one** we call the daylight'. Robert Zuboff, as well, omits a head noun in the lines

yáa Yooḵis'kooḵéik yóo sh disáagu[¶]	this [man] who calls himself Tide-Commander

rather than *yáa Yooḵis'kooḵéik yóo sh disáagu* ***ḵáa*** 'the **man** who calls himself Tide-Commander' or ... *yóo sh disáagu aa* 'the **one** who calls himself...'. Interestingly, the only headless attributive clauses we have identified in this volume use the verb theme *(yéi=)O-S-sáakw (na)* 'for S to call O (by name a certain name)'.

13.1 *The Two Types of* -ÿéyáx̱ *Construction: Truly Attributive and Quasi-Attributive*

What we are calling the *-ÿéyáx̱* construction is formed by adding *-ÿéyáx̱* (composed of the noun *ÿé* 'place, manner' and the postposition *yáx̱* 'like') to the attributive form of a verb minus the attributive suffix *-ÿi* if it would otherwise occur. There are

---

* AH I, iii, 86–87.

† AH I, ii, 37.

‡ AH I, ii, 261.

§ AH I, ii, 338.

¶ RZ II, iv, 5–6.

two types of *-ÿéyáx̱* constructions: truly attributive and quasi-attributive. The only difference between the attributive *-ÿéyáx̱* construction and an ordinary attributive construction is the fact that (1) the combination *ÿé* place, manner' plus *yáx̱* 'like, as, similar to' forms a lexicalized unit; (2) the attributive suffix *-ÿi* is omitted if it would occur in the normal attributive form; and (3) the /ÿ/ of *ÿé* is omitted when following a consonant, whether this consonant is the final consonant of the attributive verb form or whether it becomes the final consonant due to the omission of the attributive suffix. The combination *-ÿéyáx̱* always forms two syllables and can surface in four possible ways, the only difference being the onset of the first syllable: (1) *-ÿéyáx̱* [ɰé.jáχ], with unaltered /ÿ/; (2) *-yéyáx̱* [jé.jáχ], with underlying /ÿ/ pronounced as /y/; (3) *-wéyáx̱* [wé.jáχ], with underlying /ÿ/ pronounced as /w/, which only occurs when directly preceded by a labial vowel; and (4) ...*Céyáx̱* [Cé.jáχ], in which /ÿ/ is suppressed when following a consonant.

13.1.1 *The Truly Attributive* -ÿéyáx̱ *Construction*

The 'truly attributive' *-ÿéyáx̱* construction is syntactically much like an ordinary attributive construction as described above in §13: the head noun, underlyingly *ÿé* 'place, manner', is referred to by a resumptive third-person pronoun in the attributive clause, most often specifically the *a-* of *aadé*. The only difference here is that the attributive suffix *-ÿi* may be omitted in cases where it would be obligatory in an ordinary attributive construction. Examples of truly attributive *-ÿéyáx̱* constructions in this volume include «Aadé haa ée kg̱waak'éiyéyáx̱ átx̱ tulayéix̱»* 'We use it (spring water) in a way that could be good for us' and «Ch'a yá ax̱ káak aadé at koo.ag̱wéyáx̱ g̱unéi ikadá»† 'Start flowing as my uncles commands' (i.e., '... in the manner that my uncle commands'). If *yáx̱* were absent in these examples we would get uncontracted verbs followed by *ÿé* (or one of its variants), i.e., *aadé haa ée kg̱waak'éiyi yá* 'the way it could be good for us' (Hammond consistently uses the variant *yá* in place of *ÿé* 'place') and *aadé at koo.aḵw ÿé* 'the way that he commands'.

13.1.2 *The Quasi-Attributive* -ÿéyáx̱ *Construction*

What we are calling the 'quasi-attributive' *-ÿéyáx̱* construction, on the other hand, is like the truly attributive *-ÿéyáx̱* construction discussed above in that it is built on the attributive form of the verb, but differs in that the attributive verb phrase altogether lacks a resumptive third-person pronominal coreferential with the head noun *ÿé*; specifically, the phrase *aadé* 'the way, manner (in which)' is missing. This construction is syntactically unique within Tlingit grammar; this is the only situation in which the

* AH I, iv, 267.

† SJ i, 164.

head noun of an attributive clause lacks a coreferential resumptive pronoun within the attributive clause.* The quasi-attributive *-ÿéyáx̱* construction is usually followed by a generic verb, e.g., *…-ÿéyáx̱ ÿatee* 'it is as if …' or *…-ÿéyáx̱ woonee* 'it happened as if …'. This construction occurs numerous times throughout this volume. Examples include «Tle ch'u tle áa shukawdujaaÿéyáx̱ áwé woonei ḵei.á áa yéi yateeyi yé»† 'It was as if they had given him directions to where the daylight resided'; «Ḵuwlix̱'aanéyáx̱ áwé ḵuwatee»‡ 'It was like the whole atmosphere was aflame'; «Haa, á áyáa du tóon wooteeyéyáx̱ wootee hú ḵwa Yéil»§ 'So now Raven seems to have been offended'; «tlákw du x̱'ax̱áni yéi at yateeyéyáx̱ áwé yatee»¶ 'he lived high on the hog' (more literally, 'it is as if things are always available for him to eat'). Further examples from outside this volume are found, for instance, in the famous speech given by Naatláa, Jessie Dalton, at the 1968 potlatch for Jim Marks in Hoonah, Alaska; she can be heard using at least six of these constructions in the course of her speech, one being

[G]ági uwagudéyáx̱ ax̱ tusitee	I feel it's as if your father's hat
yá yee éesh du s'áaxu.**	has come out.

* Naish and Story attest a number of examples of these constructions, but they mistakenly perceived a long vowel /éi/ where it is really the short vowel /é/ followed by the approximant consonant /y/ in the sequence /é/-/y/ of *-ÿéyáx̱*, i.e., /éy/ [ej] was mistakenly perceived as /éiy/ [é:j]. This presumably is what led them to represent these forms with a hyphen as «-éi yáx̱» in their *Tlingit Verb Dictionary*. They write, for example, «àa-dei yawdoodziḵàay-éi yáx̱ woodzigèet» (i.e., *aadé yawdudziḵaayéyáx̱ wudzigeet*), translated as "he did as he was told" (72), which is a 'truly attributive', and «a yík-t at kawdiyáay-éi yáx̱ ax̱ toowáa yatèe» (i.e., *a yíkt at kawdiyaayéyáx̱ ax̱ tuwáa yatee*), translated as "I've come to the conclusion there's something moving round on it (boat, way out at sea)" (136), which is a 'quasi-attributive'. Naish made note of this construction in what was originally her master's thesis, there likewise considering the vowel of the modified *ÿé* to be /éi/ rather than /é/, and never remarking on the strikingly unusual syntax in the quasi-attributive instantiations (i.e., the lack of any resumptive pronoun internal to the attributive clause which would be coreferential with the clause-external head noun *ÿé*). She writes, "When the following syntactic marker is the adjectival *yʌ́X* [i.e., *yáx̱*] 'similitudinal', the nominal phrase is very frequently a type B noun phrase with nucleus the noun *yɛ́* [i.e., *yé*] 'place'; the noun has the variant form *é* [i.e., *éi*] and the attributive suffix immediately preceding it (if present) is elided with the noun" (Naish, *A Syntactic Study of Tlingit*, 126). She provides the example sentence, «ʌX gé-de wʊdɪhané yʌ́X wutì», which she translates as "It was as though everything was against me"; this would directly transliterate as *ax̱ géidei wudihaanéi yáx̱ wootee*, but is probably best represented by *ax̱ géide wudihaanéyáx̱ wootee*, and would appear to be best translated as 'it was as if s/he had stood up against me'.

† FI I, V, 19.

‡ FI I, V, 174.

§ FD i, 70.

¶ KM VI, 36.

** The given transcription is ours; the translation is the Dauenhauers' from *Haa Tuwunáagu Yís*, 253. The phrase is transcribed there as «gági uwagudi yáx̱», but Dalton can clearly be heard pronouncing «gági uwagudéyáx̱» at 44:03 on the recording (MC005, tape 255, side a; Dalton's speech occurs at 37:17–46:13 on the recording). Other examples (all quasi-attributive) transcribed as we heard them from her speech include «ch'a ldakát áwé gági yawdixunéyáx̱ ax̱ tuwáa yatee» (39:21); «gági yawdixunéyáx̱ hasdu daa yoo tux̱aatánk» (40:56); «ch'a oowayáa yee waḵshiyeex' gági gutx̱éyáx̱ áwé yatee yeedát» (41:28); «has ayakawdliyijéyáx̱ áwé hasdu daa ax̱ tuwatee yee aat hás» (43:14).

14 *A Note on Spelling and Pronunciation of Tlingit Stop Consonants*

In the standard (a.k.a. Revised Popular) Tlingit orthography, the stop consonants written as ⟨t⟩, ⟨ts⟩, ⟨tl⟩, ⟨ch⟩, ⟨k⟩, ⟨kw⟩, ⟨k̲⟩, and ⟨k̲w⟩ are somewhat ambiguous in that they can denote either aspirated or unaspirated stops depending on whether they occur at the beginning or the end of a syllable. These symbols denote aspirated stops (phonetically [tʰ], [tsʰ], [tɬʰ], [tʃʰ], [kʰ], [kʷʰ], [qʰ], and [qʷʰ] respectively) when they occur at the onset of a syllable, as in, e.g., ***té*** [**t**ʰé] 'rock', ***tsaa*** [**ts**ʰa:] 'seal', and ***kwéiy*** [**k**ʷʰé:j] 'marker'. The same symbols, however, denote unaspirated stops (phonetically [t], [ts], [tɬ], [tʃ], [k], [kʷ], [q], and [qʷ]) when occurring at the end of a syllable, as in, e.g., ***át*** [ʔát] 'thing(s)', *xóo**ts*** [xʷú:**ts**] 'brown bear', and *née**kw*** [ní:**k**ʷ] 'sickness'; additionally these same consonants are represented by different symbols (⟨d⟩, ⟨dz⟩, ⟨tl⟩, ⟨j⟩, ⟨g⟩, ⟨gw⟩, ⟨g̲⟩, and ⟨g̲w⟩) when they occur syllable-initially, as in the corresponding possessed forms *du á**di*** [tu ʔáti] 'his/her stuff', *du xóo**dz**i* [tu xʷú:**ts**i] 'his/her brown bear', and *du née**gu*** [tu ní:**k**ʷu] 'his/her sickness'. Still further, related issues can arise when words containing a final unaspirated stop are followed by *á*, *áyá*, *áwé*, *ásgíwé*, etc. As a general rule, words written beginning with a vowel are expected to begin with a glottal stop [ʔ], but these usually do not. Readers could reasonably construe the spelling and word boundary, e.g., *x̲át áyá* 'it's me' to necessarily imply the pronunciation *x̲át.áyá* [χátʔájá], but it is usually pronounced as *x̲ádáyá* [χátájá]; the same holds for, e.g., *gooch áwé* 'that's a wolf', which is usually pronounced as *goojáwé* [qu:tʃáwé] rather than *gooch.áwé* [qu:tʃʔáwé]. In summary, a single Tlingit orthographic symbol such as ⟨t⟩ can denote two different phonemes, aspirated [tʰ] or unaspirated [t], depending on syllable position; additionally, two different Tlingit orthographic symbols, ⟨t⟩ and ⟨d⟩, can denote the same phoneme, unaspirated [t]. These conventions often cause confusion for students of the language as they try to understand the relationship between the phonemic composition of Tlingit words and the symbols used to represent them. In cases such as unpossessed *hí**t*** [hít] 'house' vs. possessed *hasdu hí**di*** [hastu híti] 'their house', because the written symbol has changed from ⟨t⟩ to ⟨d⟩, it may appear as if the sound has 'changed' from an aspirated stop to an unaspirated stop upon adding the possessive suffix; it is really the same (unaspirated) phoneme in both cases.

Appendix 2. Style & Symbol Conventions

Table i: Conventions Used in the Stories

STYLE/SYMBOL	ROLE
« » ‹ ›	Double guillemets are used in the Tlingit texts in place of ordinary double quotation marks for quotations of characters' speech. Single guillemets are used in place of ordinary single quotation marks (i.e., quotes within quotes). Guillemets allow for a visually obvious contrast between quotation marks and the Tlingit orthographic symbol ⟨'⟩, which is used to denote glottalization and can easily be confused with quotation marks.
" " ' '	Double quotation marks are used in the English translations for quotations from the characters' speech, with single quotation marks for quotes within quotes.
—	The em dash is used both in the Tlingit transcriptions and in the English translations to set off a parenthetical excursus or side-comment on the part of the speaker, particularly when it interrupts the narrative sequence. The em dash is also placed immediately after false starts that have not been edited out of the texts. The em dash is also placed between repetitions and other transitions that interrupt the syntax in some way; in many such cases, these are not strictly speaking false starts, but a stylization found regularly throughout Tlingit storytelling.*

* The most common example of this is the repetition of a determiner (usually long yáa, wéi, or yóo—more rarely héi), often with a slight pause between each instance, e.g., SJ vii, 63–64, «Yeeytéen ágé yóo— / yóo tl'étl' neil uwagút?» 'Can you all see that— / that moonfish that came inside?'; RZ I, 55–56, «Iyatéen ágé yóo— / yóo jánwu?» 'Can you see that— / that mountain goat over yonder?'; RZ II, i, 1–2, «Shayadihéin yáa— / yáa shkalneekx'i sáani» 'There are a lot of these— / these little stories'; and FD iv, 5–6, «Yáa—yáa x̲'aan, / áa k̲aa jikawliník» 'He (Raven) talked someone into getting / the—the fire.'

STYLE/SYMBOL	ROLE
(·)	Some performance notes are signaled to the reader in parentheses, by far the most common being laughter. Others include singing, the storyteller slapping their hands as a sound effect, an interviewer blowing a pitchpipe, and the abrupt ending of a tape.
{ · }	Braces are placed around sections of the Tlingit transcription that we were unable to resolve to our satisfaction. The same applies to the English translations. If words or phrases are set within braces, this represents our best guess as to what the speaker said or how to translate it. If we cannot even venture a guess as to what was said, we indicate the missing section with an ellipsis within braces, '{…}'. In such cases we provide a note discussing the problems we encountered in trying to resolve the bracketed section.
italics	Italics are used in the narratives for English words that were spoken in the original Tlingit performance as well as for Tlingit terms that found their way into the English translations. Switching languages in midstream like this is called 'code-switching'. Exceptions are made for frequently occurring Tlingit names of characters, people, and clans, which are for the most part left in roman throughout the book. Song lyrics are set in italics, as are interjections by interviewers and interlocutors. On a few occasions, italics are used in the translations in order to indicate special intonational emphasis on a particular word; the corresponding Tlingit emphasis is handled by tone marking indicated by a grave accent (discussed in §1.6.4 of the introduction).
bold	Bold, small-cap type is used in the stories for performance notes, such as laughter, sound effects, a tape recording's lapse, etc.

Table ii: Conventions Used in the Editors' Introduction, Notes, and Linguistic Exposition

STYLE/SYMBOL	ROLE
italics	Non-quoted Tlingit material under discussion is set in italics with the gloss following in 'single quotes'. In the case of direct Tlingit quotations, the Tlingit material is left in roman and set within «guillemets», also with the gloss following in single quotes.
«·» ‹·›	Double guillemets are used for direct quotations of Tlingit speech or writing, including in-line quotations of speech from within this volume, quotations of fluent consultants who clarified matters of grammar and translation, quotations of Tlingit from archival audio sources, and quotations of written Tlingit from published and archival sources. Titles of Tlingit stories are also set within guillemets.

STYLE/SYMBOL	ROLE
“·” ‘·’	Double quotation marks are used for direct quotations from written source material as well as direct English quotes from fluent elders who advised us on matters of grammar and translation. They are also used for titles of works in English, including the translated titles of the stories in this volume. Single quotes are used in all other cases, most often indicating English glosses following Tlingit words and phrases.
(·)	Parentheses are used to insert a word or phrase that clarifies or disambiguates what is being referred to, e.g., ‘He (Raven) said. . . .’ Without these clarifications, many descriptions in the notes would result in unhelpfully vague and abstract glosses—especially with third-person references—such as, ‘he gave it to him’, or worse yet, ‘s/he/it told him/her/it/them to go to him/her/it’.
[·]	Square brackets serve a few roles. They are used in order to supply words or phrases that do not directly correspond to the Tlingit words or phrases in question, but which are useful or even essential for providing an illuminating English translation. For example, a phrase such as «Ax̱’akas’eet»,[*] literally means simply ‘he was lashing the mouth/opening of it’; since this is quite abstract when taken out of its narrative context, we gloss it in the notes as ‘[Raven] was lashing the hook [to the shaft]’ while noting that in this situation Raven is preparing an implement for gaffing octopus. Square brackets are also similarly used when we insert a clarifying word or statement into a quotation; for example, in de Laguna’s quotation of Minnie Johnson, “They call that brother yu qíṡ kuqék [Yooḵis’kooḵéik]”,[†] we supply the standard spelling of Raven’s uncle’s name in square brackets immediately after the cited rendering. Finally, sounds or words rendered phonetically using the International Phonetic Alphabet (IPA) are always set within square brackets.
⟨ · ⟩	Angle brackets denote a graphemic rendering of a written unit of a specific orthography, i.e., the way a symbol or groups of symbols are employed according to a specific orthographic tradition.
/ · /	Forward slashes are used in a phonemic or morphophonemic rendering using a standard non-technical orthography.
*	An asterisk placed at the beginning of an italicized particle, word, or phrase indicates a reconstructed or unattested form.
×	A raised × placed at the beginning of an italicized particle, word, or phrase indicates an ungrammatical or otherwise problematic form.

* RZ II, iv, 153.

† De Laguna, *Under Mount Saint Elias*, 848.

Notes

Notes to the Guest Introduction

1 De Laguna, *Under Mount Saint Elias*, 101.
2 Kawaky, *Haa Shagóon.*
3 Interestingly, a taboo in Tlingit, *ligaas*, is also interpreted as 'against nature', with prohibitions (taboos) and prescriptions on behavior serving to define the laws of nature and how to live with it without causing too much trouble. See de Laguna, *Under Mount Saint Elias*, 811–14.
4 Bateson, *Steps to an Ecology of Mind.*
5 Thornton and Malhi, "The Trickster in the Anthropocene".
6 Pelton, *The Trickster in West Africa*, 1.
7 Boas, *Tsimshian Mythology.*
8 Swanton, "Social Condition, Beliefs, and Linguistic Relationships of the Tlingit Indians" and *Tlingit Myths and Texts.*
9 Radin, "Religion of the North American Indians" and *The Trickster: A Study in American Indian Mythology.*
10 Radin, *The Trickster*, 168.
11 Ibid, x.
12 Ibid, 209.
13 See Carroll, "The Trickster as Selfish-Buffoon and Culture Hero", 105.
14 Radin, The Trickster, 168–69, emphasis mine.
15 Cf. Witzel, *The Origins of the World's Mythologies.*
16 Hymes, "Mythology", 594.
17 Radin, *The Trickster*, x.
18 E.g., Cruikshank, *Life Lived Like a Story* and *The Social Life of Stories*; Dauenhauer and Dauenhauer, *Haa Ḵusteeyí*; de Laguna, *Story of a Tlingit Community* and *Under Mount Saint Elias*; McClellan, *My Old People Say*; Nyman and Leer, *Gágiwduł.àt*; Thornton, "Person and Place: Lessons from Tlingit Teachers" and *Being and Place Among the Tlingit.*
19 De Laguna, *Story of a Tlingit Community*, 161.
20 De Laguna, *Under Mount Saint Elias*, 210.
21 Nelson, *Make Prayers to the Raven*, 16–19.
22 Thornton, Deur, and Bert, "Raven's Work in Tlingit Ethno-geography".
23 Cf. Krause, *The Tlingit Indians.*
24 Cf. Thomson, *Motif-Index of Folk-literature*, 146–47.
25 Cf. Swanton, *Tlingit Myths and Texts.*
26 See ibid. and Thornton, *Being and Place Among the Tlingit* and *Haa Léelk'w Hás Aaní Saax'ú.*
27 Thornton, *Being and Place Among the Tlingit.*
28 See Thornton, *Haa Léelk'w Hás Aaní Saax'ú*, 125–26.
29 Cf. de Laguna, *Under Mount Saint Elias* and Thornton, Deur, and Adams, "Raven's Work in Tlingit Ethno-geography".
30 Thornton, *Haa Léelk'w Hás Aaní Saax'ú*, 24, m#271.
31 Cf. de Laguna, *Under Mount Saint Elias*, 84.
32 Thornton, *Haa Léelk'w Hás Aaní Saax'ú*, 24, m#'s 260 and 270.
33 De Laguna, *Under Mount Saint Elias*, 84. The name rendered by de Laguna as «'Atuqka» is probably *Áa Tuḵká* 'On the Outlet of the Lake', referring to an island point between Cannery and Muddy Creeks.
34 KM I, 124–27.
35 Compare Frank Italio's and Frank Dick's stories in this volume with de Laguna, *Under Mount Saint Elias*, 84, and Bert Adams Sr., Fred White, et al, Project Jukebox, 1998, https://jukebox.uaf.edu/drybay, quoted in Thornton, Deur, Adams, "Raven's Work in Tlingit Ethno-geography", 46–47.
36 Thornton, Deur, and Adams, "Raven's Work in Tlingit Ethno-geography", 47.

37 FI II, 173.
38 Thornton and Malhi, "The Trickster in the Anthropocene", 3.
39 Swanton, *Tlingit Myths and Texts*, 81.
40 Ibid, 81.
41 RZ II, ii, 36–45.
42 SJ i, 52–53.
43 RZ II, v, 64.
44 RZ II, v, 69. Cf. de Laguna, *Story of a Tlingit Community*.
45 Thornton and Malhi, "The Trickster in the Anthropocene".
46 Thornton and Thornton, "The Mutable, the Mythical, and the Managerial: Raven Narratives and the Anthropocene".
47 Scott, *Seeing Like a State: How Certain Schemes to Improve the Human Condition have Failed*, 6.
48 Thornton and Malhi, "The Trickster in the Anthropocene".
49 Cf. Babcock-Abrahams, "A Tolerated Margin of Mess".
50 Star and Griesemer, "'Translations' and Boundary Objects".
51 Schwartz and Sharpe, *Practical Wisdom: The Right Way to do the Right Thing*, 43.
52 Ibid, 280.
53 Basso, *Wisdom Sits in Places: Landscape and Language Among the Western Apache*.
54 Other stories suggest Raven returned to live at the head of the Nass River but is now "inaccessible to humans as well as ghosts" (see Krause, *The Tlingit Indians*, 183; Veniaminov, *Notes on the Islands of the Unalashka District*; and Jensen, "A Structural Approach to the Tsimshian Raven Myths: Lévi-Strauss on the Beach").

Notes to the Editors' Introduction

1 Especially relevant are the introductions to Dauenhauer and Dauenhauer, *Haa Shuká* and *Haa Tuwunáagu Yís*. For further analytical discussion, see Richard Dauenhauer's doctoral dissertation, "Text and Context of Tlingit Oral Tradition".
2 FI II, 181.
3 FI II, 175.
4 FD ii, 180–84. The grave accent in *tux̱'ada.àayi* denotes emphatic tone modification of the long low-toned syllable, discussed in §3.10.4.
5 FI I, v, 296–302; II, 150–55; FD ii, 214–23.
6 FI I, iv, 41–45, 57–58. Ideas about the location are discussed in the note to FI I, iv, 57.
7 FD vi, 20–25, 40, 43.
8 KM V, 45–51.
9 KM V, 1, 113.
10 RZ I, 180–84.
11 KM I, 124–27.
12 RZ I, 156–61.
13 KM I, 78–81.
14 FD iii, 26, 27. The form and interpretation of this placename is discussed briefly in the note to these lines.
15 FD iii, 30–31.
16 Thornton, *Haa Léelk'w Hás Aaní Saax'ú*, 25.
17 FD iii, 37–39. See Thornton, *Haa Léelk'w Hás Aaní Saax'ú*, 10–12, for discussion of this village.
18 FD iii, 41.
19 FD iii, 35–36.
20 RZ II, i, 18–24, 27–30.
21 Dauenhauer, "Text and Context of Tlingit Oral Tradition", 79.
22 Ibid.

23 See, for instance, Zuboff's «Táax'aa», "Mosquito", in Dauenhauer and Dauenhauer, *Haa Shuká*, 72–81. There are numerous additional examples in the recordings of Zuboff in the Dauenhauer Tlingit Oral Literature Collection, some of which will be published in a forthcoming volume on Zuboff edited by Ishmael Hope and Matthew Spellberg.

24 Swanton, *Tlingit Myths and Texts*, 83, parentheses original, bracketed spelling ours.

25 The orthography here reflects Peratrovich's use of the Southern dialect of Hèinyàḵwáan. This is from an interview discussion of placenames in the Craig–Klawock area on December 6, 1997 (MC062, file unit 1, item 33). Her description of *héen ànax̱ kèi déich yé* 'a place through which water flows up' (clearly referring to a spring) is consistent with the reference in Dick's telling of this story, in which he states, «Goon áyóo / du x̱'ax̱ánoo» 'There was a spring / nearby for him (Petrel) to drink from' (FD V, 12–13).

26 We find this high-tone variant in the speech of Italio, James, Dick, and Hammond. James is notable in that she varies regularly between low-tone and high-tone pronunciations with a perfectly even split. The single instance from Wanamaker is low.

27 Leer documented the Tongass form with a fading vowel in the "Stem List" as «na`s» (Tongass fading vowels correspond to long low-toned vowels in Northern Tlingit).

28 SJ ix, 47.

29 FI I, ii, 46.

30 AH IIa/b, 76/45.

31 AH IIa, 77.

32 Small-scale gatherings of this sort are common in many oral literary traditions. Albert Lord comments, "The circumstances will be different to some extent in each traditional culture, but speaking for the one that I know best, that of the Slavic Balkans, I would find one of the most normal places for singing to be the house in a small village where neighbors gather for an evening and sit and talk and listen to a singer." Lord extends this to the performance setting of the ancient Greek epic traditions of which Homer was a part, "I see no reason why what I have said about traditional performer and traditional audience cannot apply just as well to the singer in a small king's court as to the singer in a neighborhood gathering. The kingdoms in ancient Greece were small, the number of listeners surely not very great" (*The Singer Resumes the Tale*, 2).

33 De Laguna writes:

> On my return [to Yakutat] in 1952, with Catharine McClellan, we were fortunate in being able to live in a nice little house on the main street, right in the center of town, between the church and the ANB (Alaska Native Brotherhood) Hall on the one hand, and the post office and jail on the other. Across the street was the new house in which Minnie Johnson was living with her little granddaughter, Catharine ('Tiny') Cranston, so we naturally saw a great deal of her and her friends. Her house was, in fact, a center for the social life of the older people in the community. Catharine and I also tried to make our house a place where all the people could feel welcome, and there we enjoyed many visits from native friends and neighbors. (*Under Mount Saint Elias*, 8)

In 1954 de Laguna's mother and her assistant Mary Jane Downs may also have been present, "In February, 1954, I returned to Yakutat, accompanied by my mother and Mary Jane Downs. The latter served as ethnographic assistant. This time we rented a house, belonging to John Ellis, which was situated on top of a steep bank well above the main road" (ibid, 9).

34 AH I, i, 32–35, 40–44.

35 Вениаминов, *Записки объ атхинскихъ алеутахъ и колошахъ*, 53.

36 Veniaminov, *Notes on the Islands of the Unalashka District*, 395, bracketed spelling ours. Veniaminov's footnote to this passage reads, "What is this liver which emerged from below? I was not able to learn anything about it."

37 Swanton, *Tlingit Myths and Texts*, 10. Swanton writes elsewhere, "The earth was in a measure conceived of as a live thing, and a 'great liver of the world' is spoken of" (*Social Condition*, 452).

38 Leer "Lexical Binders". Leer rendered the phrase as «ch'oo l haa yee tl'ooḵk'[óo] daak sh ulhaashjí» and provided the literal translation, "before the (?) under us floated out".

39 In their draft materials for this volume, the Dauenhauers referred to "Early myth time", which was distinct and prior to "Raven myth time". They described early myth time as "a convenient way to group what are essentially the 'odds and ends' of Tlingit creation accounts dealing with cosmic phenomena (sun, moon, thunder, earthquakes, winds, etc.) that existed before the birth of Raven" (MS052, box 48, file unit 27). "Early myth time" would be an appropriate category for the Haayeetl'óok̲k̲'u.

40 De Laguna, *Under Mount Saint Elias*, 798.

41 MC047, "01-03 How the Russians gave whiskey to Raven".

42 FI II, 201–07.

43 Many aspects of the Raven stories can be productively related to Sergei Kan's ethnopsychological description of the Tlingit model of the person, which is extended by homology to the structure of the house, elaborated in *Symbolic Immortality* and his article "Why the Aristocrats Were 'Heavy'". A basis of this model is the oppositions between a noncorporeal inside and a corporeal outside, a contrast implying a permanent spirit and an impermanent body. Further oppositions develop on this basis, such as dry vs. wet, hard vs. soft, heavy vs. light; homologous to these are, for example, good luck vs. bad luck, pure vs. impure, life vs. death. He writes:

> The stone was a perfect symbol of dryness, hardness, and weightiness, as well as longevity. It was the hardest, and most stationary and long-lasting object in the Tlingit universe. [...] The [...] opposition [between life and death] was dramatically expressed in one of the myths describing the birth of Raven, the Tlingit Creator-Transformer, as well as the one describing his creation of man. In this myth, Raven's wicked maternal uncle kept destroying his sister's children, until she was advised to swallow a smooth stone from the bottom of the sea exposed at low tide. [...] Being made of stone, Raven was very strong and would not age or die, so that his uncle failed to destroy him. The original human population of the world, destroyed by the Flood, was transformed by Raven into rocks that cover the present surface of the earth. After the Flood, he created a new race out of leaves, which made them mortal. ("Why the Aristocrats Were 'Heavy'", 85)

Entities such as stones and leaves in the stories may take on symbolic meaning through their relationship and opposition to one another; thus, stone as opposed to leaf, or Raven as opposed to humans, may be the symbolic material used to express more abstract concepts such as immortality and mortality, invincibility and vulnerability, permanence and finitude, etc.

44 Italio was eighty-two and eighty-four. Wanamaker was eighty. Zuboff was eighty. James was eighty-two. Dick was eighty-four. Hammond was seventy-five and seventy-nine. Mills was seventy-three.

45 The source of life-span data on these men is Jones, "Haa Daat Akawshixít, He Wrote About Us: Contextualizing John R. Swanton's 1904 Fieldwork on the Tlingit Indians", 130, 133.

46 See appendix 1, §1, for discussion of some grammatical elements of 'classical' Tlingit grammar.

47 After a long legal battle led by Tlingit and other Alaska Native people, this Treaty of Cession was proven illegal in the court of law of the United States, resulting in the Alaska Native Claims Settlement Act of 1971, a topic which is foregrounded in Zuboff's Raven stories.

48 See especially the introduction to Dauenhauer and Dauenhauer, *Haa K̲usteeyí*, 3–121, as well as Dauenhauer and Dauenhauer, "Technical, Emotional, and Ideological Issues in Reversing Language Shift: Examples from Southeast Alaska", and R. Dauenhauer, *Conflicting Visions in Alaskan Education*.

49 Dauenhauer and Dauenhauer, *Haa Tuwunáagu Yís*, 148.

50 We note that the Dauenhauers used the same characterization, "The language of the speeches is often popularly described as 'old time Tlingit,' which might be called 'classical' Tlingit" (ibid, 74).

51 Ibid, xxi.

52 The exception that proves the rule is the Neix̲.ádi clan, which does not fall under either moiety and was the sole clan traditionally permitted to marry into clans of the Raven and Eagle moieties.

53 For more detailed discussion of such changes, see Dauenhauer and Dauenhauer, "Evolving Concepts of Tlingit Identity and Clan" and "Tlingit Clans and Shifting Patterns of Socio-political Discourse", as well as Richard Daunhauer, "Syncretism, Revival, and Reinvention: Tlingit Religion, Pre- and Postcontact".
54 Emmons, *The Tlingit Indians*, 34.
55 De Laguna, *Under Mount Saint Elias*, 809.
56 Dauenhauer and Dauenhauer, "Evolving Concepts of Tlingit Identity and Clan", 255.
57 In this vein, see especially the section "At.óow in Action: Levels of Mediation in Tlingit Oratory", in Dauenhauer and Dauenhauer, *Haa Tuwunáagu Yís*, 80–108.
58 Dauenhauer and Dauenhauer, *Haa Shuká*, 28.
59 Dauenhauer, "Text and Context of Tlingit Oral Tradition", 209, note 1, emphasis original.
60 MS052, box 48, file unit 27, brackets ours.
61 SJ viii, 15.
62 KM I, 1–5.
63 Shotridge, "War Helmets and Clan Hats of the Tlingit Indians", 45–46, plate 1. The hat can be seen in de Laguna, *Under Mount Saint Elias*, 1134 and 1138, worn by a L'uknax̱.ádi man whom de Laguna described as the leader of the Whale House of Sitka, and whose name she rendered as «Q̇ex̣ix̣».
64 This piece is pictured and briefly discussed in Brown, *Native Visions: Evolution in Northwest Coast Art from the Eighteenth through the Twentieth Century*, figure 4.44, 90–92. It is held in the Seattle Art Museum with the label "Lkaayaak yeil s'aaxw (Box of Daylight Raven Hat)" and item number 91.1.124.
65 Shotridge, "The Journey of the Raven", bracketed material ours.
66 Ibid, bracketed material ours.
67 In "The Journey of the Raven" Shotridge continues, "It is generally known that the average pupil in whose mind, from childhood, had been fixed that the native people of our continent, all alike, were none but harshness in their moral character. Hence, to them was bestowed only a credit which is within the limits of any primitive man. Thus, it might appear, at first, strange that there really existed, among the aborigines, philosophy, the underlying subject of which was treated, as is known, only in primitive forms." Shotridge interprets the characters of the stories as a kind of pantheon of virtues, dispositions, and forces: Raven's uncle represents Jealousy, begetting hate and homicide; the uncle's wife is Vanity, combining outward beauty with inner conceit and evil design; Raven's mother represents Hope, from whom comes disappointment, regret, and anxiety, but also endurance and confidence; Mercy comes to the aid of Hope, their combination begetting the representative of Justice (Raven); Justice must consult with Destiny; etc.
68 The relevance of oral-formulaic theory to Tlingit oral literature was first proposed by Richard Dauenhauer in his doctoral dissertation, but with limited application. It was further discussed in the Dauenhauers' *Haa Tuwunáagu Yís* in connection to the structure of Tlingit oratory. Ishmael Hope, a contributor to this volume, maintains that oral formulas are much more extensive in Tlingit oral literature than has been generally recognized; referring to perhaps the most ubiquitous formula in Tlingit oral narrative, he notes, "*Wáananée sáwé* is a pivotal Tlingit oral formula in the way 'wine-dark sea', 'rose-fingered dawn', and 'grey-eyed goddess Athena' are for Homeric oral formula" (personal communication, Hope to Geiger). Our awareness of the existence of a body of relatively fixed phrases in the Raven stories arose organically through editing this volume (one's ears can't help but perk up after hearing Raven utter the same words in the same situation on three or more occasions), but it was through discussions with Hope that we came to describe and understand them using the terms and concepts of oral-formulaic composition. Robert Bringhurst also has discussed formulas in the context of Haida mythology,

> Formulaic phrases are used in oral literature worldwide, especially for starting and ending stories. Perhaps they are used in every realm of human and nonhuman communication. *Once upon a time* and *happily ever after* are two examples born in the oral world. *To whom it may concern* and *Yours sincerely* are examples from the world of writing. Handshakes and waves are gestural examples. Some traditions are

richer than others in such formulae, and some oral poets take obvious delight in them while others shy away. (*A Story as Sharp as a Knife*, 117)

69 Dauenhauer and Dauenhauer, *Haa Tuwunáagu Yís*, xxv–xxvi.

70 Lord, *The Singer of Tales*, 30.

71 Ibid, 54.

72 Ibid, 68–69. Lord further defines his use of the term theme as "a structural unit that has a semantic essence but can never be divorced from its form, even if its form be constantly variable and multiform" (ibid, 198). One such theme Lord discusses in Homeric and Slavic songs (and which is prolific in the Raven genre) is 'disguise'. This theme necessarily involves the identity of character or entity being concealed so as to appear as something other than itself. The character who dons the disguise as well as the purpose and substance of the disguise are constantly variable, but the structure remains stable.

73 This idea originated with the Russian folklorist Vladimir Propp. In *Morphology of the Folktale*, Propp enumerates what he describes as the morphological 'functions' within Russian fairy tales; among a series of thirty-one such functions, 'lack' and 'lack liquidated' are functions 8a and 19 (35–36, 53–55). The folklorist Alan Dundes adapted Propp's work in application to Native American folklore. Dundes redefined Propp's 'functions' as 'motifemes' (by analogy to grammatical morphemes), and pays special attention to the prominence of the 'lack–lack liquidated' structure in the Native North American material (cf. Dundes, *The Morphology of North American Indian Folktales* and "Structural Typology in North American Indian Folktales"). Richard Dauenhauer wrote in the early draft material for this volume, "The pattern of 'lack–lack liquidated' identified by Dundes is the fundamental episodic or 'motifemic' structure of Raven and other Trickster stories" (MS052, box 48, file unit 22). The profusion of terminology is admittedly problematic: Propp refers to 'functions'; Dundes and Dauenhauer refer to 'motifemes'; Parry and Lord refer to 'themes'; also relevant are Lévi-Strauss' 'mythemes'. We have used 'theme' simply for the sake of continuity with Parry and Lord's discussion of the relationship between formula and theme. Lord writes, "The most interesting work on themes […] with which I am acquainted has been done not in the field of epic but in the related fields of folktale and myth. In folktale see V. Propp, 'Morphology of the Folktale[.' …] In myth the work of Claude Lévi-Strauss, 'The Structural Study of Myth,' […] is very significant" (*The Singer of Tales*, 284, note 1). Our discussion of theme through examples such as 'lack–lack liquidated' and 'trickery–complicity' is in the style of Propp and Dundes and still extremely cursory.

74 Dundes, *The Morphology of North American Indian Folktales*, 62.

75 Propp identified "trickery" and "complicity" as his functions 6 and 7 (*Morphology of the Folktale*, 29–30). Dundes redefined these as the motifemes "deceit" and "deception" (*The Morphology of North American Indian Folktales*, 63).

76 These two themes may be reiterated and combined multiple times within a single narrative. For instance, in "Raven Gets His Nose Yanked Off", Raven is hungry (lack$_1$), so he slips beneath the ocean and eats bait from fishermen's halibut hooks (lack liquidated$_1$). Raven has used the ocean to avoid detection and so makes it appear as though a halibut has managed to take the bait but shake the hook (trickery$_1$). The fishermen continue to rebait the hooks for a time (complicity$_1$), allowing Raven to have a nice meal. The fishermen become confounded by the hooks being stripped of bait but lacking any catch (lack$_2$), and so change tactics. While Raven is eating another piece of bait, an expert fish-nibble feeler yanks the line and hooks Raven through the nose. His nose is dislodged from his face and pulled aboard the villagers' boat. Here the initiation of a new lack, that of Raven's nose going missing from his face (lack$_3$), is simultaneously the liquidation of a different lack felt by the fishermen, the answer to the riddle of the missing bait (lack liquidated$_2$). The villagers take the nose home and conclude that it must be a *G̱uneit Loowú* 'Alien Nose'. Raven goes to the village in a disguise to trick the villagers into placing the nose back in his hands (trickery$_2$); the villagers succumb to his guise (complicity$_2$) and Raven seizes the opportunity to return the nose to his face and escape (lack liquidated$_3$).

77 Lord, *Epic Singers and Oral Tradition*, 76, emphasis ours.

78 Lord, *The Singer of Tales*, 99.
79 Ibid, 63.
80 Parry, "Studies in the Epic Technique of Oral Verse-Making: I", 80. Lord, *The Singer of Tales*, 30.
81 Parry demonstrated this especially in the case of the Homeric epithets, in which the formulas tend to consist of a noun and one or more fixed adjectives. For example, depending on how many metrical feet remain to be filled at the end of a given line involving Athena, the poet may conclude the line with *Ἀθήνη* 'Athena', *γλαυκῶπις Ἀθήνη* 'grey-eyed Athena', or *θεὰ γλαυκῶπις Ἀθήνη* 'the goddess grey-eyed Athena'. He observed, "of eleven different adjectives used in the Iliad to describe Athene, only two [...], each of them used only once, have the same metrical value. Homer had to hand a particular word for each of the ten metrical exigencies that might arise" (*The Making of Homeric Verse*, 427).
82 Dennis Tedlock writes, "there is no meter—in the strict sense of recurrent quantification of stresses, vowel lengths, or syllables, all at the segmental level—in the indigenous verbal arts of the New World" (*The Spoken Word and the Work of Interpretation*, 218). Munro Edmonson notes, "Outside of Oceania (and possibly West Africa), the use of rhyme and versification is confined to the areas of the Old World that are now literate. This is not to say, of course, that some of the more elaborate poetic techniques may not have preceded literacy in at least some parts of this area" (*Lore*, 114).
83 Tedlock, *The Spoken Word and the Work of Interpretation*, 143.
84 Ibid, 145.
85 The linguist and literary theorist Roman Jakobson comments, "Rhyme is only a particular, condensed case of a much more general, we may even say the fundamental, problem of poetry, namely *parallelism*" ("Linguistics and Poetics", 82, emphasis original).
86 Parry, "Studies in the Epic Technique of Oral Verse-Making: I", 81.
87 Foster, "From the Earth to Beyond the Sky", 203. The Dauenhauers discuss Foster's work and formulaic composition in the context of Tlingit ceremonial oratory in *Haa Tuwunáagu Yís*, 137–46. On Foster's definition of the formula, they write, "this modification seems important not only for Iroquois studies, but for the study of Tlingit and other Native American traditions as well" (ibid, 143).
88 The braces in this example indicate uncertainty on our part due to noise in the recording.
89 Dauenhauer and Dauenhauer, *Haa Shuká*, 201–05. Dick's Raven stories were recorded sometime in the fall of 1983. His "Woman Who Married the Bear" was recorded April 3, 1984.
90 FI I, ii, 99.
91 FD V, 57.
92 FD vi, 110.
93 KM V, 112.
94 FI I, iv, 153.
95 AW ii, 2.
96 KM III, 160–64.
97 Discussing comparable whole fixed verses in Homer, Parry writes, "[T]he art of the oral poet is largely that of grouping together whole fixed verses. These fixed verses themselves are, of course, no work of the single singer, but the gradual work of time and of countless singers" (*The Making of Homeric Verse*, 389).
98 FI I, iv, 67–68; repeated in 75–77 and 128–129.
99 Johnson's complete formula as given here is reconstructed based on FI I, iv, 76 and 79, along with de Laguna, *Under Mount Saint Elias*, 860. See the note to FI I, iv, 79, for discussion of her formula.
100 SJ ix, 56–57; repeated with slight variation in SJ ix, 58–59, 66–67, 74–75, 128.
101 FD vi, 48–49; repeated in FD vi, 86–87.
102 KM V, 53; repeated in KM V, 54.
103 KM V, 64. The formula occurs in other versions of the story outside this volume, for instance, once in a 1972 recording of Willie Marks, «Aadóo sgí ḵaa kaanáx̱ angaxaa-aa-aash?» (MC005, tape 74, side b). We can also recognize the spirit of this Tlingit formula in the English Raven stories

recorded by Swanton from dictation in 1904. Deikeenaak'w states, "I wonder who will make a hole on the top so that he can be my friend" (*Tlingit Myths and Texts*, 13); and, reminiscent of Minnie Johnson's rendering, Kadashan states, "Let the one who wants to be high-born like me cut the whale open and let me out, and he will be as high as I am" (ibid, 91).

104 FI I, iv, 115, 120, 123.

105 SJ ix, 125.

106 FD vi, 81–83.

107 In many grammatical environments *a shóox'*, literally 'at its end', regularly takes the truncated form *a shóo* (eliding the locative *-x'*); see appendix 1, §3, for discussion.

108 Swanton, *Social Condition*, 452.

109 Personal communication, Selina Everson to Geiger. More literally, 'Every thing's indwelling spirits exist; because of that, people steady their own mouths.'

110 Eliot, "Tradition and the Individual Talent", 44. This essay was the source of the epigraph with which the Dauenhauers set the tone for volume one in this series, "Tradition … cannot be inherited and if you want it you must obtain it by great labour" (Dauenhauer and Dauenhauer, *Haa Shuká*, vi; from Eliot, "Tradition and the Individual Talent", 43).

111 Eliot, "Tradition and the Individual Talent", 43.

112 The Dauenhauers discuss the spiritual theme of 'imitating one's ancestors' throughout *Haa Tuwunáagu Yís*, describing those who do so as "following the actions of their departed ancestors" (377). They refer often to the words of David Kadashan and Jessie Dalton from a ceremony in 1968. Kadashan stated, «[C]h'a a kayaa áyá yéi gax̱tusanéi», translated by the Dauenhauers as "We will only imitate (our ancestors)" (238–39). The Dauenhauers comment, "The living people present are imitating their ancestors, from whom many of them inherited the at.óow in which they are standing. In this way the departed are made spiritually present. We have supplied 'our ancestors' for clarity in translation; the Tlingit has 'them'" (383). Naa Tláa, Jessie Dalton, stated later in the same ceremony:

Ha yáa yeedát	And now
aaa,	yes,
ch'a yax̱ at g̱wakú "a kayaa áyá s ootee	it is like the saying "they are only imitating
tlax̱ kaawaȳíkt jeenaxéexg̱aa"	lest they grope aimlessly"
yá yee léelk'w hás aadé x̱'āyaḵáayi yé.	the way your grandparents said. (252–53)

The Dauenhauers summarize their understanding of such 'imitation' as, "they are following cultural tradition, and also […] are spiritually engaged in ritual activity, because it is through ritual action that more abstract mythic patterns are expressed. Myth and ritual provide models for human behavior. Without them, we grope aimlessly in a spiritual void" (xxi).

113 FI I, v, 204–07, 219.

114 FI II, 246–47.

115 FI I, v, 208–09.

116 FI II, 218.

117 The relationship of the song to place is also notable here. From the mythic era of Raven on the banks of the Akwe River, to the historical time of Italio's grandparents in Dry Bay, to the live performance by Italio in Yakutat, the song has remained within a roughly sixty-mile radius.

118 Some people do directly perceive Raven as having the identity of a bird. Maggie Adams Harry, for instance, speaking in English in 1952, states plainly, in reference to Raven, "The Creator was a bird" (De Laguna, *Under Mount Saint Elias*, 858).

119 FI I, i, 146.

120 AW i, 16.

121 RZ II, iv, 55.

122 For instance, SJ xi, 76 (in which James impersonates a messenger announcing Raven to Head-of-the-Nass), «Ḵáa áwé i x̱ánt uwagút, ḵáa» 'A man has come to see you, a man', and RZ II, i, 41, «Yei sh kalhéich yáa ḵáa. / He's invisible man.» 'This man makes himself disappear. / He's the invisible

man.' Other relevant examples include when Zuboff identifies imprints in the rocks near Teslin, British Columbia, as Raven's own footprints, breaking into English to state, "It is a human being['s] tracks" (RZ II, i, 36), and when Mills begins her performance of "Raven and the Deer", also speaking in English, stating that Raven and Deer would walk about together and that "they were pretty chummy people" (KM IV, 3). Veniaminov as well writes, "But under the term Yéil [sic], or the raven, is understood not the bird raven but a person who bore such name" (*Notes on the Islands of the Unalashka District*, 383).

123 MC002, series 17, item 47. The recording is available on SHI's YouTube channel.

124 Italio uses «shanyaateiyí» 'low-tide stone' in three instances in the 1954 performance (FI II, 31, 50, 55), but not once in those of 1952; in the latter, when the woman finds the stone, Italio states «Tle k'wát' yáx̱ kaaxát, daakdidúk tle» 'It was just round and entirely solid' (FI I, i, 110). Wanamaker uses the term «Té k'wát'» 'a round stone' (AW i, 10) in one instance, but more frequently «shanyaateiyí» 'a low-tide stone' (AW i, 12, 15, 29). Dick impersonates the instructions issued by the being who came to the aid of Raven's mother-to-be, «shanyaateiÿí daak̲ tí!» 'Bring up a low-tide stone from the beach!' (FD i, 38, 39). James does not use the term *shanyaateiyí*, but refers to «daakdidugwéyáx̱ yateeyi aa té» 'a stone that is completely solid' (SJ i, 32) and «daakdidugu téik'» 'a small, solid little pebble' (SJ i, 39). Zuboff also does not use *shanyaateiyí*, describing it similarly as «K̲únáx̱ daakdidugu aa té» 'A stone that is really solid' (RZ II, iv, 32, 34, 35, 39).

125 FI II, 31.

126 AW i, 15.

127 FI II, 55-56.

128 RZ II, iv, 48–49.

129 The first example from Zuboff, in which Raven's mother gives her son the name, advances the plot of the story; it is internal to the narrative proper. The second example, in which Raven is compared with Lucifer, does not serve to advance the plot and is a more of a commentary on the character Raven in the storyteller's own voice; it is external to the narrative proper, though still an integral part of the composition. These together provide an excellent example of a distinction Richard Dauenhauer would make, following the work of Alan Dundes (see, for instance, Dundes, "Metafolklore and Oral Literary Criticism"), between 'oral literature' and 'oral literary criticism.' The texts in this volume contain many valuable examples of such 'oral literary criticism,' in which the storytellers offer their thoughts, commentaries, comparisons, and contextualizations, analogous to the function of literary criticism in relation to written works.

130 RZ II, i, 13–17. As a supreme example of Raven's flexibility as a literary figure, note that while Zuboff likens Raven to Lucifer and the Devil, Hammond likens him to Jesus and God himself (see, for instance, the notes to AH I, ii, 71 and 185–89).

131 FI II, 82.

132 FI I, ii, 82; II, 97.

133 De Laguna, *Under Mount Saint Elias*, 850, bracketed spelling ours.

134 FI I, iii, 23–24.

135 Swanton, *Tlingit Myths and Texts*, 82. An important article providing biographical information on K̲aadashaan and Swanton's other Tlingit informants is Jones, "'Haa Daat Akawishixít, He Wrote About Us': Contextualizing Anthropologist John R. Swanton's 1904 Fieldwork on the Tlingit Indians".

136 Shotridge, "Raven in Eyre". The title of Shotridge's piece "Raven in Eyre" is apparently a play on the concept of 'Justices in eyre,' which referred to magistrates in medieval England that travelled through a circuit of courts. Shotridge likely selected 'eyre' as an ornate parallel to the idea of Raven's 'journey' or 'adventure'; the English term 'eyre' is derived from Latin *iter* 'route, journey, course.' Shotridge's "Raven in Eyre" presents a fitting image of Raven journeying, wandering, meandering, etc., in a sort of circuitous path from one adventure to the next.

137 Ibid, emphasis ours.

138 Along these lines, in relating Raven to the Biblical figure of the Devil, Zuboff concedes in RZ II, iii, 32–33, «Ch'a Déivínx̱ sateeyí teen ('Even being that he's the Devil'), / *he done a lot of good for us.*»

139 Harrington, "Tlingit and Eyak materials from George Johnson", 1083, page reference is to the digitized manuscript. The manuscript of this story is handwritten by Harrington and often difficult to make out. Johnson's story is rich in detail and consists of numerous episodes of Raven's adventures all woven together; the manuscript merits a careful retranscription.

140 SJ i, 2, 147.

141 In both of these cases, however, we would have no way of explaining the reduction of *yoo=* to *yu-* and, furthermore, we could explain neither the redoubling of *koo-* as *kookoo-* in James' form nor the change from *k̲ukoo-* to *kookoo-* in the other.

142 FD i, 1.

143 Veniaminov, *Notes on the Islands of the Unalashka District*, 388.

144 Вениаминов, *Записки объ атхинскихъ алеутахъ и колошахъ*, 39–40. The cited spellings would be romanized as *Kitxugínsi*, *kitxuginsi*, and *kitxugínsa*, respectively.

145 Veniaminov, *Notes on the Islands of the Unalashka District*, 388.

146 Veniaminov's initial Кит is clearly *Kéet* 'Killerwhale' and the final си is *sée* 'daughter of', but the middle two syllables, х8ги́н, are more difficult to account for. Our hypothesis is that ⟨и́⟩ was a typesetter's mistranscription of Veniaminov's handwriting, which should have been rendered as ⟨á⟩. This would yield the Cyrillic form Китх8гáнси; note that the final ⟨и⟩ (corresponding to the Tlingit vowels /i/ and /ee/) is rendered once erroneously as ⟨a⟩ (corresponding to the Tlingit vowels /a/ and /aa/), providing a clear example of ⟨a⟩ and ⟨и⟩ having been confused. Next, Veniaminov's ⟨г⟩ typically corresponds to the Tlingit phoneme /ÿ/, but sometimes corresponds to /h/. If we take ⟨г⟩ to denote a Tlingit /h/ in this name, the hypothetically correct Cyrillic form Китх8гáнси would yield *Kéet K̲uháan Sée*, literally meaning 'Daughter of Killerwhale People', in which *k̲uháan* is the archaic uncontracted form of *k̲wáan* 'tribe, people, collectivity'. We are unable to explain why this would occur as *Kéet K̲uháan* rather than *Kéet K̲uháani*. It would be reasonable to speculatively reconstruct the name as *Kéet K̲uháani Sée*, but with the limited and already tenuous nature of the source material we cannot do so with much confidence.

147 Kamenskii, *Tlingit Indians of Alaska*, 59. Kamenskii's form as romanized by Kan, "kukhin", presents many of the same issues as Veniaminov's, and was quite possibly influenced by Veniaminov's published spelling; the fact that Kamenskii's contains the romanized ⟨kh⟩, which corresponds to Cyrillic ⟨x⟩, lends some credence to the hypothesis that Veniaminov's ⟨г⟩ actually represents Tlingit /h/ rather than /ÿ/.

148 Ibid, 60, brackets original.

149 FI I, i, 130.

150 FI I, i, 18, 20, 246, 258; SJ i, 10, 20, 90; RZ II, iv, 3, 5, 13, 79, 101, 132.

151 FD i, 78, 118.

152 AW i, 1.

153 AW i, 43.

154 FD i, 77–83.

155 FI I, i, 4–6.

156 FI I, i, 28.

157 FI I, i, 255–58.

158 FI II, 24.

159 FI I, i, 71.

160 FI II, 23.

161 FI I, i, 130.

162 De Laguna, *Under Mount Saint Elias*, 858.

163 FD i, 34.

164 Kamenskii, *Tlingit Indians of Alaska*, 60, brackets original.

165 SJ i, 47–50.

166 FD i, 52–54.

167 We find this theme playing out in a remarkably different manner in the Raven story that Kadashan told to Swanton in English, "Then he [Raven] went to Nās-ca′kî-yēł's [Naasshagiyéil's] house,

took down the box which contained his mother, and liberated the flickers (kūn [*kóon*]) which she always kept under her arms" (*Tlingit Myths and Texts*, 119). In this case we find the name Naasshagiyéil where we would usually expect Yoo<u>k</u>is'koo<u>k</u>éik; we find Raven's mother in the box with flickers under her arms where we would usually expect the uncle's wife; and we find Raven coming to the aid of the woman in the box rather than gaining access to her as a form of revenge against her husband.

168 FI I, i, 236; FI II, 120.
169 FD i, 102.
170 See the note to FI I, i, 237–41, for discussion of the verb forms used by Italio and Dick.
171 De Laguna, *Under Mount Saint Elias*, 845, parentheses original, original brackets altered to braces, material in brackets ours.
172 Shotridge, "Raven in Eyre", parentheses original, bracketed material ours.
173 Veniaminov, *Notes on the Islands of the Unalashka District*, 387, original brackets altered to parentheses, bracketed material ours.
174 Kamenskii, *Tlingit Indians of Alaska*, 59.
175 FI I, i, 189; FD i, 98.
176 MC005, tape 64, side b.
177 FI I, i, 191.
178 FD i, 99.
179 De Laguna, *Under Mount Saint Elias*, 849.
180 Ibid, 845.
181 Swanton, *Tlingit Myths and Texts*, 119.
182 Ibid, 120.
183 Veniaminov, *Notes on the Islands of the Unalashka District*, 389.
184 Вениаминов, *Записки объ атхинскихъ алеутахъ и колошахъ*, 41.
185 FI I, V, 129–32.
186 AW ii, 41.
187 FD ii, 120, 122.
188 SJ xi, 203–04, 207.
189 AH I, ii, 210–11.
190 Note, though, that the grandparent-grandchild relationship in Tlingit culture does not necessarily entail heredity (though it can). The relationship may exist by affinity through marriage or clan genealogy (including that of one's namesake); it may also exist through other social bonds or on generational grounds.
191 AH I, ii, 131, 207, 208, 365, 370.
192 AW ii, 35, 40.
193 SJ xi, 165, 166, 189.
194 MC005, tape 16, occurs at 28:55 on recording.
195 FI I, ii, 57; I, V, 92, 95, 127; FD ii, 110.
196 FD ii, 112–14.
197 Veniaminov, *Notes on the Islands of the Unalashka District*, 391.
198 Kamenskii, *Tlingit Indians of Alaska*, 58.
199 Swanton, *Tlingit Myths and Texts*, 80, 82; from myth 31, "Raven".
200 Swanton, *Tlingit Myths and Texts*, 102.
201 Ibid, 80, 102.
202 Ibid, 102.
203 Ibid, 34; from myth 8, "The Wolf-chief's Son".
204 Shotridge, "Raven in Eyre", parentheses original, bracketed material ours.
205 Shotridge, "The Journey of the Raven".
206 Harrington, "Tlingit and Eyak materials from George Johnson", 1049–1101.
207 Ibid, 1072.
208 Ibid, 1085.

209 De Laguna, *Under Mount Saint Elias*, 860. This comes from a story John Ellis told to de Laguna on March 3, 1954.

210 Shotridge's form as well as Swanton's renderings of the name as spoken by Deikeenaak'w and Kadashan appear to use the low-toned variant of the preverb *yoo=*, while James and Charlie Joseph both use the high-toned variant *yóo=*. This is a purely dialectal variation with no difference in meaning.

211 MC047, "06-13 Raven Cries for Daylight".

212 A final consideration, the details of which are beyond the scope of this this volume, is that Unfazable-Little-Elder can be meaningfully connected (in some cases entirely identified) with the figure known to not only the Tlingit, but also to the Haida and Tsimshian, as Mouse Woman.

213 SJ V, 74; FD vii, 21.

214 FI II, 85, 168.

215 FI I, ii, 64–66.

216 FI I, ii, 54. We find a very similar pronunciation from Emma Marks (Nora Dauenhauer's mother and a descendant of Italio), «yax̱ ḵís'shakawdzinugu shaanák'w» (in "Emma and Jenny Marks; Telling stories"; cf. 08:04 on recording). The only difference from Italio's form is that Marks has shortened the vowel of the noun *ḵées'* 'floodtide', but (surprisingly) has retained the high tone.

217 SJ V, 3.

218 FD vii, 12, 22.

219 These are based on entries in Naish and Story, *Tlingit Verb Dictionary*, 220. The first example is spelled there as «xákwl'ee shakawdinòok» and glossed as "soapberries swell up (when beaten)"; the second example is unaltered from the original, their gloss being "the rice is still swelling". The long low-toned stem in the perfective form *shakawdinook* alongside the use of the preverb *yaa=* in the progressive imperfective form *yaa shakandanúk* indicate that this is a *na*-conjugation verb.

220 The addition of the *s*- element of the classifier could be explained as forming a causative (i.e., transitive) structure with the addition of a subject; *ḵées'* 'floodtide' would then be the object and *shaanák'w* 'little elder' the subject; this would yield *Ḵées' Ashakawsinoogu Shaanák'w* 'Little-Elder-Who-Enlarged-the-Tide'. From this point, though, we are unable to determine the roles played by *yax̱=* and *d-* in the name or why the verb takes ∅-conjugation (the latter is indicated by the short low-toned stem *nug* in the perfective attributive). It is tempting to view *yax̱=* and ∅-conjugation as stemming from the exhaustive derivational string *ÿax̱=ÿa-s-* (∅) 'all, a lot, a bunch', but this would yield *Ḵées' Ÿax̱ Ashaÿakawsinugu Shaanák'w* 'Little-Elder-Who-Enlarged-the-Entirety-of-the-Tide'; this analysis is either incorrect or incomplete due to the fact that the element *ÿa-* is not used by any of the storytellers in this volume and it leaves the *d-* element of the classifier unexplained. We do, however, seem to find a form containing *yax̱=ÿa-s-* in the speech of Minnie Johnson, who told a series of Raven stories to de Laguna on June 23, 1952. De Laguna writes, "She's the Head of the Tide [qiṡ 'ax̣cuwu katsinuq gu canukʷ—old lady who watches the tide]" (*Under Mount Saint Elias*, 845, brackets original). De Laguna's rendering «qiṡ 'ax̣cuwu katsinuq gu canukʷ» would seem to represent *ḵées' ÿax̱ shuwakadzinugu shaanák'w*; this form appears to contain the prefix *shu-* 'end' where Italio, James, and Dick use *sha-* 'head', and contains the prefix *ÿa-* (rounded to *wu-* following the vowel of *shu-*), which is not present in the others' forms. Johnson's form shares features of Dick's, namely *ḵées'* occurring before *ÿax̱=* and there being no object prefix *a-* on the verb. An alternative explanation is that the *ÿax̱-* of *ÿax̱ḵées'* may actually be the same element that we find in *Yax̱taattuḵwáani* 'Night-Dwellers' (discussed in §2.16) and in the *Yanyeidí* personal name *Yax̱góos'*, which belonged to Billie Williams among other people. The hypothesis in this case would be that *ÿax̱-* is the combining form of the relational noun *ÿaax̱* 'side, edge (of body of water, trail, table, etc.)', but we do not clearly understand what compounds like *yax̱taat* or *yax̱ḵées'* would mean, and none of our fluent consultants have been able to provide an answer. A problem for this analysis is the fact that James and Dick order the elements as *ḵées' yax̱* rather than *yax̱ḵées'*.

221 SJ V, 19.

222 FD vii, 17.

223 A photograph of a ceremonial tunic—belonging originally an Ishkeetaan man named Weihá (Jim Fox)—is pictured in Dauenhauer and Dauenhauer, *Haa Tuwunáagu Yís*, 91, 92. The tunic is known by the name *Geesh Daax̱ Woogoodi Yéil K'oodás'* 'Raven-Who-Went-Down-Along-the-Bull-Kelp Shirt' and is mentioned in Jessie Dalton's famous oration during the memorial for Jim Marks (ibid, 244–45; 248–251; 388, note 27).

224 FI I, ii, 76.

225 FI II, 90.

226 SJ V, 31.

227 FD vii, 30.

228 FI I, ii, 81–82.

229 FI II, 96–97.

230 SJ V, 35, 41.

231 FD vii, 36.

232 FI I, ii, 95–96. Italio's and Dick's pronunciation of this potential verb form as *gaagwaalaa* is irregular. The combination of the underlying prefix string *u-ga-ga-i-* is more typically pronounced as *gwaagaa-* (as in James' form *gwaagaalaa*), with the irrealis *u-* combining with the conjugation prefix *ga-* rather than the following mode prefix *ga-* that characterizes the future, hortative, potential, and contingent modes.

233 FI II, 102.

234 SJ V, 54–55.

235 FD vii, 48.

236 Shotridge, "The Journey of the Raven".

237 "[T]here existed a being who represented Jealousy, this being possessed great power, and from him came forth hate and homicide." After this introductory statement Shotridge refers to Raven's uncle simply as "Jealousy" (Shotridge, "Raven in Eyre"). If Shotridge does mean that Little-Elder-Who-Enlarged-the-Tide is the mother of Tide-Commander, this would therefore make her Raven's mother's mother.

238 De Laguna, *Under Mount Saint Elias*, 850.

239 Though the term is attested in numerous sources the specific identity of *k'ákw* remains unclear. Writing of when Raven obtained fire, Shotridge refers to "a bird, perched on a limb of a tree, it was one with a long bill, and its gray coat was spotted with specks of black and white" ("The Journey of the Raven"). He states that this bird is "now known as 'Chicken Hawk'", and writes the name "Kaku" (ibid.), which is clearly based on K'ákw. The term 'chicken hawk' is an unofficial designation that can refer to the Cooper's hawk, the sharp-shinned hawk, or the red-tailed hawk. Only the sharp-shinned and the red-tailed hawks occur within Tlingit Country; the range of the Cooper's hawk is further south. The sharp-shinned hawk has a grey back with a brown speckled chest, which is the closest match to Shotridge's description. We also find references to the character K'ákw when Raven obtained fire in Swanton; Deikeenaak'w refers to, "a chicken hawk (KA!kᵘ) which had a very long bill" (*Tlingit Myths and Texts*, 11). Note that Swanton's spelling «KA!kᵘ» contains a typographical error in which the symbol ⟨!⟩ (used to mark glottalization of a consonant) and the vowel ⟨a⟩ mistakenly traded places; Kadashan says that Raven tied "a piece of pitch-wood to a chicken hawk's bill" (ibid, 83). De Laguna recorded John Ellis staying "Yeł sent this hawk out to bring in the fire" (*Under Mount Saint Elias*, 865). Harrington lists *k'ákw* alongside the Eyak word he spelled as «taxọyuuka' 'ịixiila'», which he glosses as "lit. face shaped like a person"; to this entry he writes, "Described as a hawk, brown and gray color, can grab a duck. It's Atch. [i.e., Eyak] name is said to be applied because it has a face pretty near that of a person. It can also turn this face around so it looks backward from the way its body is pointed" ("Tlingit and Eyak Flora and Fauna Terms", 147). Krauss documents this word in his "Eyak Dictionary" manuscript with the variants «dəx̣ųhgaˀ ˀį·łilah», «dəx̣ųhyu·gaˀ ˀį·łilah», and «dəx̣ųhyu·gaˀ ˀį·łila·ˀ», which he glosses literally as "it has a face like a person, like people" and describes it as "a small owl species or some kind of hawk" ("Eyak Dictionary", 2202). Harrington also listed *k'ákw* under the heading "Hoot Owl" with the description "Speotyto cunicularia Hypugaea Bonaparte (Burrowing Owl)

does not extend [sic] as far north as Alaska, but from a picture was included under the name Lh. [i.e., Tlingit] k'ákw, and of the picture was also stated: it has a face like a person" ("Tlingit and Eyak Flora and Fauna Terms", 150). Naish and Story list «k̲'ákw» (sic for *k'ákw*) with the gloss, "owl without ear tufts" (*English-Tlingit Dictionary: Nouns*, 21); a later version of their dictionary altered the spelling to «k'ákw» with the same gloss (Davis, *English-Tlingit Dictionary: Nouns*, 29). The same gloss is found in Edwards, *Dictionary of Tlingit*, 155. Leer glosses it as "small owl" in the "Stem List" and as "owl (earless)" in the "Lexical Binders". In the *Interior Tlingit Noun Dictionary*, there is no specific entry for *k'ákw*, but we find a set of opposed terms, one containing *k'ákw* and the contrasting term containing *dzísk'w*, the latter being the most common and generic word for 'owl': *du ludíx̲' (shu)k'águ*, glossed as "bone at the base of his/her skull that looks like a small owl (k'ákw)", is contrasted against *du ludíx̲' (shu)dzísk'u*, glossed as "bone at the base of his/her skull that looks like a larger owl (dzísk'w)" (M·107). The original spellings are «du łudíxh' shuk'águ» (attributed to Atlin), «du łudíxh' k'águ» (Teslin), «du łudíx̲' shudzísk'u» (Atlin), and «du łudíxh' dzísk'u» (Teslin). These would seemingly represent the C1 and C2 vertebrae respectively. J.B. Fawcett can be heard mentioning K'ákw in his telling of "Raven and Fire", and switching to English to refer to the bird as a "fish hawk" (MC005, tape 175, side a), which is often a colloquial name for the osprey. A final source we can point to is Zuboff himself. In his Tlingit performance of "Raven and Fire" in this volume he uses the name K'ákw; in an English performance of the same story (not included in this volume) he refers to the character as an "owl" (ibid, tape 121, side b).

240 In attempting to determine what species *k'ákw* might refer to, Geiger consulted Mark Schwan, former president of the Juneau Audubon Society. "The great horned owl is a resident species in the Pacific Northwest, but it has ears. The barred owl is earless and established here now, but only recently extended its range to the Pacific Northwest. Great gray owls are large and earless, but would likely have been extremely rare along the coast in the past. Smaller resident owls include the western screech owl, which has ear tufts; the pygmy owl, which is earless; and the saw-whet owl, which is also earless. The short-eared owl is larger, though it is mainly a spring and fall migrant; as the name suggests, this owl does have ear tufts, but they are small enough that they are often overlooked. The Northern Harrier is a fairly common raptor that is also a spring and fall migrant; it has a rather flat face and an appearance rather like an owl" (Personal communication, Schwan to Geiger, May 9, 2023).

241 In this interpretation of *X̲ashak'ákwk'*, the noun *x̲aaw* 'fur' is incorporated as prefixed *x̲a-*; the following *sh(a)-* is the fricative element of the classifier, possibly with a pejorative connotation; *k'ákw* 'pygmy owl' occurs in the position of the verb stem; and the final *-k'* is the diminutive suffix.

242 RZ II, i, 53–54, 56, 66.

243 SJ iii, 14, 20.

244 SJ iii, 27; ix, 15. Because James never pronounces the name without a consonantal suffix, we cannot be sure if for her the underlying noun form really is *k'áxw*, or if it is actually *k'ákw* but with the final consonant having undergone lenition, altering the final stop /kw/ to the fricative /xw/.

245 FI I, iii, 3–5.

246 FI I, iii, 13.

247 FI I, iii, 42; iv, 5.

248 FI I, iii, 20, 66, 146.

249 FD iv, 9–13.

250 FD viii, 77, 80.

251 Swanton, *Tlingit Myths and Texts*, 121.

252 Ibid, 17. Swanton placed a footnote on the first instance of «shAk!A´kᵘ» in this passage, "Said to be a kind of bird. K!Akᵘ [i.e., *k'ákw*] alone would mean 'chicken hawk.'"

253 RZ II, ii, 42–43.

254 AH I, iii, 87.

255 AH I, iii, 189, 191, 194.

256 SJ v, 19; viii, 30.

257 SJ viii, 82.

258 SJ v, 7; viii, 25.
259 Leer, Hitch, and Ritter, *Interior Tlingit Noun Dictionary*, M·134. The prenominal modifier *leineit* ~ *leeneit* is also found in the noun phrases *leineit shál* 'sheep- or goat-horn spoon' and *leineit s'íx'* 'sheep- or goat-horn bowl'.
260 SJ viii, 25.
261 SJ viii, 48, 51–53.
262 SJ viii, 57, 95, 98.
263 Compare "TxämsEm and the Hunter" in Boas, "Tsimshian Mythology", 75, 692.
264 Swanton, *Tlingit Myths and Texts*, 84.
265 Because the forms pronounced by James, Zuboff, and Mills always end in a glottalized consonant (/k'w/ or /x'w/), we infer here that Swanton's «…q!u» is a typographical error for «…q!ᵘ». There are numerous instances in Swanton's *Tlingit Myths and Texts* in which it is clear that the «u» should have been superscript but was written on the line.
266 SJ v, 59.
267 RZ II, iii, 144–45.
268 RZ I, 116–18.
269 KM I, 59–60.
270 FI I, v, 24, 197; SJ xi, 20, 23; FD ii, 23, 198; AH I, ii, 381.
271 AW ii, 6, 63, 72.
272 AW ii, 65, 84.
273 AW ii, 75.
274 FI I, v, 26, 162; II, 237.
275 AH I, ii, 192.
276 SJ xi, 225, 247, 249.
277 FD ii, 146.
278 AW ii, 6, 43, 50. Wanamaker is the only speaker in this volume to use a long high stem *háa* with this noun.
279 AH I, ii, 193.
280 FI I, v, 27.
281 AW ii, 6, «Du ádix̱ sitee ḵutx̱.ayanaháa ḵa dís ḵa Ḵee.á Daakeit» 'He owned the stars and the moon and the Container of Daylight'.
282 SJ xi, 20, 23, 26, 311.
283 SJ xi, 223, 275, 293.
284 AH I, ii, 194–95.
285 AH I, ii, 196–97.
286 Hammond refers numerous times to the containers using the noun «ḵóok» 'box(es)' (AH I, ii, 191, 219, 223–24, 271, 289, 304); in Wanamaker we only find it used more sparingly and only as the head noun in the compounds «Ḵee.á Daakaḵóok» 'Box of Daylight' (AW ii, 65, 84) and «Ḵee.á Daakaḵóogu» 'Box of Daylight' (AW ii, 75).
287 SJ xi, 293.
288 FI I, v, 163.
289 SJ xi, 245.
290 FD ii, 137.
291 Examples of Raven 'rolling' the containers around include: FI I, v, 168, «Tle gáant akawlijúx» 'He just rolled it outside'; SJ xi, 244, «Át akawlijoox» 'he rolled it around'; SJ xi, 250, «De wé gáant akawlijúx» 'He had rolled it outside'; AW ii, 58, «Át akanalgwátlch, aan shóode yoo akligwátlk» 'He would roll it around; he kept rolling it (moon) to the end of the town and back'; FD ii, 138, «Át akanalgwátlch» 'He kept rolling it (container of stars) around'; AH I, ii, 266, «aan át sh wudligwáatl» 'he rolled around with it (the moon)'.
292 SJ xi, 262.
293 FI I, v, 176.
294 Shotridge, "The Journey of the Raven", bracketed material ours.

295 Ibid.
296 Ibid.
297 Ibid.
298 Ibid.
299 Swanton, *Tlingit Myths and Texts*, 3.
300 Ibid., 4.
301 FI I, V, 160–61.
302 AW ii, 46.
303 FD ii, 132–33. Dick's form is interesting in that the prefix sequence *ka-ÿi-* is pronounced as *kiÿ-* (which is regular in the Teslin dialect but not typically elsewhere).
304 SJ xi, 239.
305 SJ xi, 256–58.
306 SJ xi, 288–90.
307 Compare the phrase from Leer's "Lexical Binders", «daa kx̱akéil'» translated as "I'm untying it (box)", which lacks the fricative element.
308 AH I, ii, 304.
309 SJ xi, 223–25.
310 FI I, V, 167.
311 FI II, 141
312 FD ii, 207. Compare also AW ii, 85, «Aagáa áwé déi ldakát yanáatx̱ ayaawax̱út'» 'Then finally he yanked the lid off altogether', and AH I, ii, 448, «Tle yanáatx̱ ayaawax̱út'» 'He just yanked the lid off'.
313 One may liken this to Lord's statement, "It is certainly possible that a formula that entered the poetry because its acoustic patterns emphasized by repetition a potent word or idea was kept after the peculiar potency which it symbolized and which one might say it was even intended to make effective was lost—kept because the fragrance of its past importance still clung vaguely to it and kept also because it was now useful in composition." It is also certainly possible that all this concern with *l-* in the verb *kaylakél'* amounts to the kind of criticism Lord castigated, "in that it attributes to an innocent epithet a pathos felt only by the critic, but not acknowledged or perhaps even dreamed of by either the poet or his audience. Being part of the tradition, they understand its characteristics and necessities" (*The Singer of Tales*, 65–66).
314 AW ii, 14, 82. From Italio we hear this man's name pronounced with all the possible variations of the initial vowel: «Náasshagiyéil» (FI II, 235) with long high-toned *Náas-*, «Naasshagiyéil» (FI II, 241) with long low-toned *Naas-*, and, most surprisingly, «Nasshagiyéil» (FI I, V, 23) with short low-toned *Nas-*, all of which translate as 'Raven-of-the-Head[waters]-of-the-Nass[-River]'.
315 FI II, 235–36.
316 AW ii, 14.
317 AW ii, 82.
318 SJ xi, 229. *Naas Sháak* could also be translated 'Headwaters of the Nass'. Note that Zuboff agrees here with James; he refers to this man by the name Naas Sháak in an English performance of this story not included in this volume (MC005, tape 121, side b).
319 SJ xi, 61.
320 AW ii, 5.
321 AH I, ii, 372–73. The verb phrase Hammond uses here, *áx̱ kawdudlisáy*, has left us and our fluent consultants puzzled, so the translation 'he became known as…' is a tentative approximation.
322 AW iii, 1.
323 Shotridge, "Raven in Eyre". What Shotridge refers to as "less fortunate beings" we can infer to be the Night-Dwellers.
324 Harrington, "Tlingit and Eyak materials from George Johnson", 1085.
325 Swanton, *Tlingit Myths and Texts*, 80.
326 Ibid, 374–75.
327 FI I, V, 51, 58. In FI II, 230, we hear «aanÿádi».

328 FI I, V, 82, 114.
329 SJ xi, 98, 118.
330 SJ xi, 108.
331 SJ xi, 237.
332 AW ii, 17.
333 AW ii, 17, 18, 26.
334 AW ii, 19, 23, 29.
335 FD ii, 35.
336 FD ii, 88.
337 AH I, ii, 6, 56, 80, 123.
338 AH I, ii, 81, 91, 121.
339 AH I, ii, 58, 69.
340 AH I, ii, 86, 119.
341 AH I, ii, 85
342 According to Italio and Dick it was specifically the Akwe River. FI I, V, 296; II, 67–69; FD ii, 181–82.
343 The name is pronounced variously by Italio as «Ÿax̱taattuḵwáani» and «Yax̱taattuḵwáani». John Ellis clearly recognized the term in his translation of Italio, "He break daylight over that Akwe [River], near Dry Bay. He came to those yɪx̣tat-tu-qwani—that's 'People in the Dark'" (de Laguna, *Under Mount Saint Elias*, 856). Minnie Johnson likewise interpreted Italio's use of the name as "the people in the dark" (ibid, 53). In Leer's "Lexical Binders" we find the form «taat tuḵuháani» (lacking *yax̱-* and, as in Charlie Joseph's form, with the uncontracted form *ḵuháani* in place of modern *ḵwáani*); interestingly, it is translated there as "person of the night (raven before he brought light into the world)", suggesting that—at least according to the source of the entry, which was unfortunately not recorded—Raven himself could be considered a member of the Night-Dwellers due to the fact that he, too, was a person living in the world of darkness.
344 MC005, tape 16, occurs at 17:15 on recording.
345 Shotridge, "The Journey of the Raven".
346 FI I, V, 5.
347 FD ii, 6.
348 SJ xi, 24, 306.
349 SJ xi, 34.
350 AH I, ii, 393. The phonological similarity of the two words that are variously used to refer to what the Night-Dwellers were dipnetting is notable: *shaaḵ* [ʃa:q] 'driftwood' and *saak* [sa:k] 'eulachon'.
351 AW ii, 9.
352 FI I, V, 12, 233; II, 75, 77, 131; SJ xi, 17, 309; AW ii, 12, 81; FD ii, 20, 194; and AH I, ii, 420. These are all identical with three exceptions: in FD ii, 20, and SJ xi, 309, the non-truncated locative form *káx'* is used in place of the truncated form *káa*, which is directly equivalent in meaning (note that these two storytellers use the truncated form *káa* in FD ii, 194, and SJ xi, 17); and in AH I, ii, 420, the object *ḵei.á* is placed at the beginning of the sentence, «Ḵei.á yee káa nḵwaak'oots!», which has no effect on the meaning. Maggie Dick (Italio's sister and Frank Dick's wife) says the line once with *káx'* and once with *káa* and in her introduction to a song about Raven breaking daylight (MC047, "06-13 Raven Cries for Daylight").
353 FI I, V, 17–18; repeated in FI II, 78. John Ellis interpreted the recording of Italio's formulation as "Who's that Nas-cAki-yɪt [*Naasshagiyát*] to have the daylight" (de Laguna, *Under Mount Saint Elias*, 856)? De Laguna's «yɪt» would directly transliterate as *yit*, but this probably represents *yét* or *yát* 'child', especially considering that on the same page she wrote «yɪx̣» (i.e, *yix̱*) where we would have expected her to write *yAx̣* (i.e., *yax̱*) in the name *Yax̱taattuḵwáani*.
354 FD ii, 21–23; repeated in FD ii, 196–98. An example from outside this volume (identical with Dick's formulation) comes from Emma Ellis, recorded by de Laguna April 1, 1954, «Gudáx̱ Nas-caki-yat qe'a daket du tciyen gati» (de Laguna, *Under Mount Saint Elias*, 861), the standardization being *Goodáx̱ Naasshagiyát Ḵei.á Daakeit du jee yéi ngatee?* Compare also the parallel scene in Boas, "Tsimshian Mythology", 62.

355 SJ xi, 310–11; repeated in SJ xi, 19–20.

356 AW ii, 14.

357 MC047, "06-13 Raven Cries for Daylight". The original audio recording of May 17, 1955, is de Laguna's 6-2-B; see de Laguna, *Under Mount Saint Elias*, 1155, for discussion of the song. Maggie Dick pronounces the name as «Naasshakeeyéil», which would seemingly be based on *Naas Shakée* 'Above the top/peak of the Nass', rather than *Naas Sháak* 'Head(waters) of the Nass'; this does, however, appear to be a genuine variant of the name, as we find «Goodáx̱ Naas shayee yát?» in Leer's "Lexical Binders", translated there as "Are you the child of the chief from the head of the Nass (that you should have the daylight)?" We are unable to explain Maggie Dick's use of a *-ch* suffix in the form *ḵei.ách*.

358 In "The Journey of the Raven", Shotridge writes of when Raven initially cracked off the lid in this scene, "Raven moved, only a bit, the cover of the magic case that he carried, and there flashed forth a glare of light. There was a great outcry of fright from the ensuing darkness, and then a dead silence. – From fright the beings-of-darkness became dumfounded, thus remained dumb on to eternity." In Shotridge's account, the breaking of daylight not only brought about animal speciation, but a extinguished a prior condition in which animals and humans spoke a common language.

359 The thought process behind combining *at-* with the verb word in these cases is discussed in §3.11.

360 FI I, V, 260–62.

361 FI II, 149.

362 AW ii, 86–87.

363 FD ii, 213.

364 AH I, ii, 457–64.

365 FD iii, 15–18.

366 De Laguna, *Under Mount Saint Elias*, 866.

367 RZ I, 30–35.

368 SJ iv, 89.

369 SJ iv, 147.

370 RZ II, iii, 37, 94, 104, 124. Further confirmation is provided in a recording of Zuboff telling this story in English where he can be heard to again pronounce the name as «Kutatankahídi» (MC005, tape 121, side b).

371 KM I, 69, 89.

372 FD iii, 8.

373 De Laguna, *Under Mount Saint Elias*, 866. Minnie Johnson's form is curious for two reasons: first, unless de Laguna transcribed the vowel incorrectly (which is certainly possible), she seems to use *ka-* in place of usual *ku-*; second, this is the only form we have encountered that contains the element *yax̱-*, which we cannot definitively analyze, though it calls to mind the homophonous element found in *Yax̱taatuḵwáani* and *Yax̱ Ḵées' Shakawdzinugu Shaanák'w*.

374 This was de Laguna's impression; see *Under Mount Saint Elias*, 43.

375 Shotridge, "The Emblems of the Tlingit Culture", 352.

376 We find this notion in Veniaminov's notes from 1840, "The Koloshi (i.e., the Tlingits) of the wolf moiety acknowledge as their first ancestor not the beast wolf, but also a person, someone [named] Kanuk [G̣anook]" (*Notes on the Islands of the Unalashka District*, 383, brackets original, parentheses ours). However, this is contradicted by, Swanton, among others, "The Petrel (G̣Anū´k [*G̣anook*]) from whom the culture hero Raven obtained fresh water appears on both sides [i.e., is claimed by clans of both moieties]. According to Kadashan it was owned by the Wolves; but an old Sitka woman said the petrel hat (tc!īt s!āx̣^{u}) belonged to the Ravens of Chilkat" (Swanton, "Social Condition", 416, bracketed spelling ours). While Swanton glosses «tc!īt s!āx̣^{u}» as "petrel hat", this is clearly *ch'eet s'áaxw* 'murrelet hat'.

377 FD V, 16, 25, 53; AH I, i, 8, 49, 67, 76; iv, 59.

378 AH I, i, 102.

379 AH I, iv, 137–39.

380 FD V, 61–66.
381 FD V, 74.
382 AW iii, 59.
383 FD X, 57.
384 KM III, 105–06.
385 KM III, 26–28.
386 FD X, 37, and KM III, 85, are uniformly «I l'óo't daak̲ tsaak̲!» 'Stick out your tongue!' AW iii, 50, is identical other than the addition of the sentence-initial particle *k'e* 'how about…', « K'e i l'óot' daak tsaak̲!» 'Go ahead and stick your tongue out!' Compare the scene with Raven and Cormorant in Swanton, "Haida Texts—Masset Dialect", 300–01, which contains many overlapping elements with AW iii, FD X, and KM III, including Raven ripping out Cormorant's tongue in this manner after halibut fishing.
387 FI I, iv, 133–38.
388 FD vi, 101.
389 Swanton, *Tlingit Myths and Texts*, 13.
390 Compare "TxämsEm Frightens Away the Owners of a Whale" in Boas, "Tsimshian Mythology", 71, 687–89.
391 The one exception in this chronology is Hammond's "Raven Gets His Nose Yanked Off", which is the most recent recording in the book, being from May 1989. It is grouped together with the rest of Hammond's material, the bulk of which is a lengthy multi-episodic performance from 1985, and so comes before that of Mills.
392 In the terminology used by professional folklorists, the narratives of this volume would most typically be classified as 'prose narratives' or 'tales'. As spoken in performance, Tlingit oral narrative is characterized by regular pauses; these pauses are reflected with the use of line breaks in the standard method of transcription. This produces a written form which visually more closely resembles poetry than prose. Some scholars contend that Indigenous oral narrative may be better characterized as 'poetry' than 'prose'. Dennis Tedlock and Dell Hymes, for example, have made compelling cases—on different grounds—for treating Indigenous oral narrative as poetry rather than prose. Tedlock, in, e.g., *The Spoken Word and the Work of Interpretation*, tends to focus on the narratives' dramatic qualities and their structuring through repetition, parallelism, pause, and intonation. Hymes, on the other hand, in, e.g., *"In vain I tried to tell you"*, perceives numerically 'measured' (rather than 'metered') structuring of 'verse' at the level of grammar and syntax. The folklorist William Bascom writes, "When the term prose narrative proves clumsy or inept, I suggest that *tale* be used as a synonym" (*The Forms of Folklore: Prose Narratives*, 4). We prefer the term 'tale' to 'prose narrative' for its simplicity and because it avoids the poetry-prose debate. We use the term 'tale' with the restricted definition of the category of verbal art which takes the form of spoken narrative.
393 Alan Dundes writes, "Extended tales consist of essentially complete tale units told in succession. Usually, one lack is liquidated before another lack is introduced. Similarly, the consequences from violating an interdiction usually occurs before a new interdiction is introduced" (*The Morphology of North American Indian Folktales*, 94–95).
394 AW i, 59, 66.
395 AW iii, 44.
396 This description of the line is adapted from Tedlock's discussion in the context of Zuni song and speech-making. His comments to distinguish the line from the breath-group and the utterance apply equally in the Tlingit case:

> Each line is an uninterrupted sequence of sounds, falling between two silences. The line is not to be confused with the "breath group": Many silences in extended discourse, Zuni or otherwise, are not accompanied by the taking of breath—indeed, they may be accompanied by a closing of the glottis. Nor is the line to be confused with the "utterance," unless we can free ourselves from the linguistic notion that

the utterance must necessarily mesh directly with syntactical units. The line I am speaking of is the line as actually delivered. (*The Spoken Word and the Work of Interpretation*, 180)

397 The Dauenhauers noted in the first volume in this series, "The lines are split according to the pauses and punctuated according to the intonation. [...] Where there is a pause, there is a line turning. Heavier and longer pauses are marked with a period, comma, or semicolon" (*Haa Shuká*, 8).

398 Ibid, 32.

399 FI I, V, 210–41, 245–92; II, 248–79.

400 RZ I, 127–36; II, iii, 135–60.

401 SJ vii, 14–62.

402 SJ viii, 95–101.

403 SJ ix, 84–97.

404 Note that throughout this volume we provide only the unrounded version of suffixes beginning with *-ÿi*, which is a shorthand way of saying that the suffix is *-ÿi* (modern *-yi*) after an unrounded vowel and *-i* after an unrounded consonant, and that the suffix is *-wu* after a rounded vowel and *-u* after a rounded consonant. We have adopted this practice so as to avoid the proliferation of complex formulae such as *-(ÿ)i* ~ *-(w)u*. Furthermore, although the possessive, subordinative, agent-noun, prohibitive/optative, and decessive suffixes, as well as the optional hortative suffix, may occur long or short and accented or unaccented, the attributive and time-noun suffixes are always short and unaccented.

405 It seems probable that this phenomenon of pronouncing /n/ without clear and unambiguous nasalization may have arisen in individuals with chronic sinus inflammation, whereby nasals are hard to produce because of nasal congestion. In English, a similarly occluded /n/ (e.g., due to a cold) conventionally results in a sound similar to /d/, i.e., 'no' sounds like 'dough', whereas in Tlingit, the occluded /n/ sounds more like /l̠/ (phonetically [l]).

406 The fading vowel of Tongass Tlingit is produced by rapidly lowering the volume of air from the lungs passing through the vocal cords. These fading vowels are acoustically similar to the aspirated vowels of Eyak, but there is a significant difference in how they are produced. An aspirated vowel is produced not by rapidly lowering the volume of air coming from the lungs, but rather by opening the vocal cords while air is still coming from the lungs.

407 SJ iv, 3.

408 Story, *A Morphological Study of Tlingit*, 23.

409 FI I, i, 117.

410 FI I, V, 165.

411 AH I, i, 97.

412 FD vi, 59.

413 SJ iv, 42.

414 SJ vi, 7.

415 FD viii, 7–8.

416 FI I, V, 141.

417 FD ii, 121.

418 KM V, 6.

419 FI I, i, 238.

420 FI I, V, 115.

421 If these nouns are consistently written as several words, we would end up with undesirable written forms like *kalyéi jinéik̲*, *kalyoo x̱'atángik̲*, and *kalsh yáa awudanéik̲*.

422 Truncated locative forms are discussed in appendix 1, §3.

423 Crippen, "The Syntax in Tlingit Verbs", 779.

424 The notation *ka+u-* is discussed in appendix 1, §2.

425 We find similar Tongass forms in the text of "The Lazy Woman" told by Emma Williams:

Wei' aa`de at kaw`dwa.at,	They rushed to it in a body,
we shaa˙ ḵa at y̲atx'i[...].	the woman and children[...].
Ch'u tle at kaw`dwa.at wei shaa˙ nei`lde.	Then the women rushed home,
Daa` sa has aa`washaa't s'íx',	They grabbed whatever (they could), dishes,
ee`x̲ y̲inaa`de at kaw`dwa.at.	(and) rushed (down) toward the oil.
	(Williams and Williams, *Tongass Texts*, 102–03)

Leer's translation "they rushed to it in a body" makes for a fitting image when carried over to the Night-Dwellers fleeing in groups according to the skins they wore; those wearing blankets 'rushed as a body' to the mountainside, those wearing seal skins 'rushed as a body' to the water, etc.

Bibliography

Alaska State Archives. US Commissioner Vital Stats Records, Birth Certificates (Sitka) 1884–1960. AS29459.

Alaska State Library, Historical Collections. "Act to define the political status of certain Native Indians within the Territory of Alaska." ASL-KFA1225.A31915-P52. Accessed online April 20, 2024. https://vilda.alaska.edu/digital/collection/cdmg22/id/86/rec/2.

———. MS SJC, Sheldon Jackson College Collection.

Bryn Mawr College Special Collections. BMC-1975-06, Frederica de Laguna Papers.

Babcock-Abrahams, Barbara. "'A Tolerated Margin of Mess': The Trickster and His Tales Reconsidered." *Journal of the Folklore Institute*, vol. 11, no. 3 (March 1975): 147-186.

Bascon, William. "The Forms of Folklore: Prose Narratives. *The Journal of Folklore*, vol. 78, no. 307 (January–March 1965): 3–20.

Basso, Keith H. *Wisdom Sits in Places: Landscape and Language among the Western Apache.* Albuquerque: University of New Mexico Press, 1996.

Bateson, Gregory. *Steps to an Ecology of Mind.* New York: Ballantine, 1972.

Boas, Franz. "Tsimshian Mythology." In *Thirty-first annual report of the Bureau of American Ethnology, 1909–1910*, 29–1037. Washington, DC: United States Government Printing Office, 1916.

Bringhurst, Robert. *A Story as Sharp as a Knife: The Classical Haida Mythtellers and Their World.* Vancouver: Douglas and McIntyre, 1999.

Brown, Steve C. *Native Visions: Evolution in Northwest Coast Art from the Eighteenth through the Twentieth Century.* Seattle: The Seattle Art Museum and University of Washington Press, 1998.

Carroll, Michael P. "The Trickster as Selfish-Buffoon and Culture Hero." *Ethos*, vol. 12, no. 2 (Summer 1984): 105–31.

Case, David S., and David A. Voluck. *Alaska Natives and American Laws.* 3rd edition. Fairbanks: University of Alaska Press, 2012.

Crippen, James A. "The Syntax in Tlingit Verbs." PhD diss., University of British Columbia, 2019.

Cruikshank, Julie. *Life Lived Like a Story: Life Stories of Three Yukon Native Elders.* Lincoln: University of Nebraska Press, 1990.

———. *The Social Life of Stories: Narrative and Knowledge in the Yukon Territory.* Lincoln: University of Nebraska Press, 1998.

Dauenhauer, Nora Marks, and Richard Dauenhauer, eds. *Beginning Tlingit*. 4th edition. Juneau: Sealaska Heritage Institute, 2000.

———. "Evolving Concepts of Tlingit Identity and Clan." In *Coming Ashore: Northwest Coast Ethnology, Traditions, and Visions*, 253–78, edited by Marie Mauzé, Michael E. Harkin, and Sergei Kan. Lincoln: University of Nebraska Press, 2004.

———, eds. *Haa Shuká, Our Ancestors: Tlingit Oral Narratives*. Vol. 1 of *Classics of Tlingit Oral Literature*. Seattle: University of Washington Press; Juneau: Sealaska Heritage Foundation, 1987.

———, eds. *Haa Tuwunáagu Yís, for Healing Our Spirit: Tlingit Oratory*. Vol. 2 of *Classics of Tlingit Oral Literature*. Seattle: University of Washington Press; Juneau: Sealaska Heritage Foundation, 1990.

———, eds. *Haa Ḵusteeyí, Our Culture: Tlingit Life Stories*. Vol. 3 of *Classics of Tlingit Oral Literature*. Seattle: University of Washington Press; Juneau: Sealaska Heritage Foundation, 1994.

———. "Raven and the Tide: A Tlingit Narrative" in *Worldviews and the American West: Life of the Place Itself*, 135–50, edited by Polly Stewart, Steve Siporin, C. W. Sullivan III, and Suzi Jones. Logan: Utah State University Press, 2000.

———. "Technical, Emotional, and Ideological Issues in Reversing Language Shift: Examples from Southeast Alaska." In *Endangered Languages: Language Loss and Community Response*, edited by Lenore Grenoble and Lindsay Whaley, 57–98. Cambridge: Cambridge University Press, 1998.

———. "Tlingit Clans and Shifting Patterns of Socio-political Discourse." In *Discourses in Search of Members: Festschrift in Honor of Ron Scollon*, 335–60, edited by David S.C. Li. Landham MD: University Press of America, 2002.

Dauenhauer, Richard. *Conflicting Visions in Alaskan Education*. Juneau: Tlingit Readers, Inc., 1997.

———. "Syncretism, Revival, and Reinvention: Tlingit Religion, Pre- and Postcontact." In *Native Religions and Cultures of North America: Anthropology of the Sacred*, 160–80, edited by Lawrence E. Sullivan. New York: Continuum, 2000.

———. "Text and Context of Tlingit Oral Tradition." PhD diss., University of Wisconsin-Madison, 1975.

Davis, Henry, ed. *English-Tlingit Dictionary: Nouns*. Sitka: Sheldon Jackson College, 1976.

De Laguna, Frederica. *Story of a Tlingit Community: The Problem in the Relationship Between Archeological, Ethnological, and Historical Methods*. Smithsonian Institution Bureau of American Ethnology Bulletin 172. Washington, DC: United States Government Printing Office, 1960.

———. *Under Mount Saint Elias: The History and Culture of the Yakutat Tlingit*. Vol. 7 of *Smithsonian Contributions to Anthropology*. Washington, DC: Smithsonian Institution Press, 1972.

Dundes, Alan. "Metafolklore and Oral Literary Criticism." *The Monist*, vol. 50, no. 4 (October 1966): 505–16.

———. *The Morphology of North American Indian Folktales*. Folklore Fellows Communications no. 195. Helsinki: Suomalainen Tiedaekatemia, 1980.

———. "Structural Typology in North American Indian Folktales." *Southwest Journal of Anthropology*, vol. 19, no. 1 (Spring 1963): 121–30.

Durlach, Theresa Mayer. *The Relationship Systems of the Tlingit, Haida and Tsimshian*. Vol. 11 of *Publications of the American Ethnological Society*, edited by Franz Boas. New York: American Ethnological Society, 1928.

Edmonson, Munro S. *Lore: An Introduction to the Science of Folklore and Literature*. New York: Holt, Rinehart, and Winston, Inc., 1971

Edwards, Keri. *Dictionary of Tlingit*. Juneau: Sealaska Heritage Institute, 2009.

Eliot, T.S. "Tradition and the Individual Talent." In *The Sacred Wood: Essays on Poetry and Criticism*, 42–53. New York: Alfred A. Knoff, 1921.

Emmons, George Thornton. *The Tlingit Indians*. Seattle: University of Washington Press, 1991.

Foster, Michael K. "From the Earth to Beyond the Sky: An Ethnographic Approach to Four Longhouse Iroquois Speech Events." Canadian Ethnology Service Paper no. 20 in National Museum of Man Mercury Series. Ottawa: National Museums of Canada.

Harrington, John Peabody. "Tlingit and Eyak materials from George Johnson." Unpublished manuscript, 1940. EY940H1940d. Alaska Native Language Archive.

———. "Tlingit and Eyak Flora and Fauna Terms." Unpublished manuscript, 1940. EY940H1940a. Alaska Native Language Archive.

Hensel, Chase. *Telling Our Selves: Ethnicity and Discourse in Southwestern Alaska*. New York: Oxford University Press, 1996.

Hymes, Dell. *"In vain I tried to tell you": Essays in Native American Ethnopoetics*. Philadelphia: University of Pennsylvania Press, 1981.

———. "Mythology." In *Handbook of North American Indians, Volume 7: Northwest Coast*, 593–601, edited by Wayne Suttles. Washington DC: Smithsonian Institution, 1990.

———. "Tlingit Poetics." *Journal of Folklore Research*, vol. 26, no. 3 (September–December 1989): 236–48.

Jakobson, Roman. "Linguistics and Poetics." In Jakobson, *Language in Literature*, ch. 7, 62–94, edited by Krystyna Pomorska and Stephen Rudy. Cambridge: The Belknap Press of Harvard University Press, 1987.

Jensen, Allan. "A Structural Approach to the Tsimshian Raven Myths: Lévi-Strauss on the Beach." *Anthropologica*, vol. 22, no. 2 (1980): 159–86.

Jones, Zachary R. "'Haa Daat Akawishixít, He Wrote About Us': Contextualizing Anthropologist John R. Swanton's 1904 Fieldwork on the Tlingit Indians." *Alaska Journal of Anthropology*, vol. 15, nos. 1–2 (2017): 126–40.

Kamenskii, Anatolii. *Tlingit Indians of Alaska*, translated by Sergei Kan. Fairbanks: University of Alaska Press, 1985.

Kan, Sergei. *Symbolic Immortality, The Tlingit Potlatch of the Nineteenth Century*. Washington, DC: Smithsonian Institution Press, 1989.

———. "Why the Aristocrats Were 'Heavy' or How Ethnopsychology Legitimized Inequality Among the Tlingit." *Dialectical Anthropology*, vol. 14, no. 2 (1989): 81–94.

Kari, James, ed. *Ahtna Athabaskan Dictionary*. Fairbanks: Alaska Native Language Center, 1990.

Kawaky, Joseph, producer. *Haa Shagóon*. Film presented by Chilkoot Indian Association. Juneau: Sealaska Heritage Foundation, 1981.

Kelly, William A., and Frances H. Willard. "Grammar and vocabulary of the Hlingît language of Southeastern Alaska." In *Report of the Commissioner of Education*, ch. 10, 715–66. (Annual reports of the Department of the Interior for the fiscal year ended June 30, 1904, vol. 1). Washington, DC: US Government Printing Office, 1905.

Krause, Aurel. *The Tlingit Indians: Results of a Trip to the Northwest Coast of America and the Bering Straits*, translated by Erna Gunther. Seattle: University of Washington Press, 1956.

Krauss, Michael E. "Alaska Native Languages: Past, Present, and Future." Alaska Native Language Center Research Papers, no. 4, 1980. G961K1980. Alaska Native Language Archive.

———. "Eyak Dictionary." Unpublished manuscript, 1970. EY961K1970b. Alaska Native Language Archive.

———. "Eyak Dictionary (revised)." Unpublished manuscript, 2011. EY961K2011. Alaska Native Language Archive.

Leer, Jeff. "Miscellaneous transcriptions, 1969–1974." Unpublished manuscript, 1969. TL962L1969. Alaska Native Language Archive.

———. "The Schetic Categories of the Tlingit Verb." PhD diss., University of Chicago, 1991.

———. "The Tlingit Anaphoric System and its roots in Na-Dene." Unpublished manuscript, 1993. CA965L1993b. Alaska Native Language Archive.

Leer, Jeff. "Tlingit Lexical Binders." Unpublished manuscript, 1976. TL962L1976e. Alaska Native Language Archive.

———. "Tlingit Stem List." Unpublished manuscript, 1975. TL962L1975m. Alaska Native Language Archive.

———. "Tlingit Verb Books 1 and 2." Unpublished manuscript, 1974. TL962L1974h. Alaska Native Language Archive.

Leer, Jeff, Doug Hitch, and John Ritter. *Interior Tlingit Noun Dictionary: The Dialects Spoken by Tlingit Elders of Carcross and Teslin Yukon, and Atlin, British Columbia.* Whitehorse: Yukon Native Language Center, 2001.

Lord, Albert Bates. *Epic Singers and Oral Tradition.* Ithaca: Cornell University Press, 1991.

———. *The Singer of Tales.* 2nd edition. Cambridge: Harvard University Press, 2000.

———. *The Singer Resumes the Tale*, edited by Mary Louise Lord. Ithaca: Cornell University Press, 1995.

Marks, Emma. "Emma and Jenny Marks; Telling stories." Audio recording, 1972. ANLC1919. Alaska Native Language Archive.

Marsh, Ken. "The Chinook Tradition: Feeding Alaskans, the Economy, and a Hungry World." *Chinook News*, 1 (Summer 2014): 6–8.

McClellan, Catharine. *My Old People Say: An Ethnographic Survey of Southern Yukon Territory.* Ottawa: National Museum of Man, 1975.

Metcalfe, Peter, and Kathy Kolkhorst Ruddy. *A Dangerous Idea: The Alaska Native Brotherhood and the Struggle for Indigenous Rights.* Fairbanks: University of Alaska Press, 2014.

Morrow, Phyllis, and William Schneider, eds. *When Our Words Return: Writing, Hearing, and Remembering Oral Traditions of Alaska and the Yukon.* Logan: Utah State University Press, 1995.

Naish, Constance M. *A Syntactic Study of Tlingit.* No. 6 in *Language Data, Amerindian Series.* Texas: Summer Institute of Linguistics, 1976.

Naish, Constance M., and Gillian L. Story. *English-Tlingit Dictionary: Nouns.* Fairbanks: Summer Institute of Linguistics, 1963.

———. *Tlingit Verb Dictionary.* College: Alaska Native Language Center, 1973.

Nelson, Richard K. *Make Prayers to the Raven: A Koyukon View of the Northern Forest.* Chicago: University of Chicago Press, 1983.

Nyman, Elizabeth, and Jeff Leer. *Gágiwduł.àt: Brought Forth to Reconfirm: The Legacy of a Taku River Tlingit Clan.* Whitehorse: Yukon Native Language Center; Fairbanks: Alaska Native Language Center. 1993.

Parry, Milman. "Studies in the Epic Technique of Oral Verse-Making: I. Homer and Homeric Style." *Harvard Studies in Classical Philology*, vol. 41 (1930): 73–148.

———. *The Making of Homeric Verse*, edited by Adam Parry. Oxford: The Clarendon Press, 1971.

Paul, Fred. *Then Fight For It!: The Largest Peaceful Redistribution of Wealth in the History of Mankind and the Creation of the North Slope Borough.* Bloomington: Trafford Publishing, 2004.

Pelton, Robert. D. *The Trickster in West Africa: A Study of Mythic Irony and Sacred Delight.* Berkeley: University of California Press, 1989.

Propp, Vladimir. *Morphology of the Folktale.* 2nd edition. Translated by Laurence Scott, revised and edited by Louis A. Wagner. Austin: University of Texas Press. 1968.

Radin, Paul. "Religion of the North American Indians." *The Journal of American Folklore*, vol. 27, no. 106 (October–December 1914): 335–73.

———. *The Trickster: A Study in American Indian Mythology.* New York: Philosophical Library, Inc., 1956.

Radloff, Leopold F. "Tlingit linguistic materials." 1861 Unpublished manuscript. TL860R1861. Alaska Native Language Archive.

Sarris, Greg. *Keeping Slug Woman Alive: A Holistic Approach to American Indian Texts.* Berkeley and Los Angeles: University of California Press, 1993.

Schneider, William. *...So They Understand: Cultural Issues in Oral History.* Logan: Utah State University Press, 2002.

Schwartz, Barry and Sharpe, Kenneth. *Practical Wisdom: The Right Way to do the Right Thing.* New York: Riverhead Books, 2010.

Scott, James C. *Seeing Like a State: How Certain Schemes to Improve the Human Condition have Failed.* New Haven: Yale University Press, 1998.

———, ed. *Living with Stories: Telling, Re-telling, and Remembering.* Logan: Utah State University Press, 2008.

Shotridge, Louis. "My Northland Revisited." *The Museum Journal*, vol. 8, no. 2 (June 1917): 104–15.

———. "The Emblems of the Tlingit Culture." *The Museum Journal*, vol. 19, no. 4 (December 1928): 350–76.

———. "War Helmets and Clan Hats of the Tlingit Indians." *Museum Journal*, vol. 10, nos. 1–2 (March–June 1919): 43–48.

———. "Raven in Eyre." Unpublished manuscript. Louis Shotridge Digital Archive, University of Pennsylvania Museum of Archeology and Anthropology, Philadelphia (website), 2011. Accessed May 6, 2024. Shot0616.

———. "The Journey of the Raven." Unpublished manuscript. Louis Shotridge Digital Archive, University of Pennsylvania Museum of Archeology and Anthropology, Philadelphia (website), 2011. Accessed May 6, 2024. Shot0615.

———. "Tlingit Language Notes from the University of Pennsylvania." TL914Sh1912. Unpublished notes, c . 1912–15. Alaska Native Language Archive.

Shotridge, Louis, and Florence Shotridge. "Indians of the Northwest." *The Museum Journal*, vol. 4, no. 3 (September 1913): 71–99.

Sitka Public Library. Romain Hardcastle Collection.

Star, Susan Leigh, and James R. Griesemer. "Institutional Ecology, 'Translations' and Boundary Objects: Amateurs and Professionals in Berkeley's Museum of Vertebrate Zoology, 1907-39." *Social Studies of Science*, 19, no.3 (August 1989): 387–420.

Story, Gillian L. *A Morphological Study of Tlingit.* No. 7 in *Language Data, Amerindian Series.* Texas: Summer Institute of Linguistics, 1979.

Swanton, John R. "Haida Texts—Masset Dialect." In Volume 10 of *The Jesup North Pacific Expedition: Memoir of the American Museum of Natural History*, edited by Franz Boas. Leiden: E. J. Brill Ltd., 1908.

———. "Social Condition, Beliefs, and Linguistic Relationship of the Tlingit Indians." In *Twenty-sixth annual report of the Bureau of American Ethnology, 1904–1905*, 391–485. Washington, DC: Government Printing Office. 1908.

———. *Tlingit Myths and Texts*, Smithsonian Institution Bureau of American Ethnology Bulletin 39. Washington, DC: Government Printing Office, 1909.

Tedlock, Dennis. *The Spoken Word and the Work of Interpretation*. Philadelphia: University of Pennsylvania Press, 1983.

Thompson, Stith. *Motif-Index of Folk-literature: A Classification of Narrative Elements in Folktales, Ballads, Myths, Fables, Mediaeval Romances, Exempla, Fabliaux, Jest-books and Local Legends.* Bloomington: Indiana University Press, 1966.

Thornton, Thomas F. *Being and Place Among the Tlingit.* Seattle: University of Washington Press, 2008.

———. *Haa Léelk'w Hás Aaní Saax'ú: Our Grandparents' Names on the Land.* Seattle: University of Washington Press; Juneau: Sealaska Heritage Institute, 2012.

Thornton, Thomas F. "Person and Place: Lessons from Tlingit Teachers." In *Celebration 2000: Restoring Balance Through Culture*, 79–86. Juneau: Sealaska Heritage Foundation, 2000.

Thornton, Thomas F., Doug Deur, and Bert Adams. "Raven's Work in Tlingit Ethno-geography." In *Language and Toponymy in Alaska and Beyond: Papers in Honor of James Kari*, 39–55, edited by Gary Holton and Thomas F. Thornton. Language Documentation and Conservation Special Publication no. 17. Honolulu: University of Hawaiʻi Press, 2019.

Thornton, Thomas F. and Patricia M. Thornton. "The Mutable, the Mythical, and the Managerial: Raven Narratives and the Anthropocene." *Environment and Society: Advances in Research*, vol. 6, no. 1 (September 2015): 66–86.

Thornton, Thomas F. and Yadvinder Malhi. "The Trickster in the Anthropocene." *The Anthropocene Review*, vol. 3, no. 3 (December 2016): 201-204.

Tlingit Readers Inc. *Ḵudatan Kahídee, Shaadaax' X̱'éidáx̱ Shkalneek: The Salmon Box, told by Robert Zuboff.* Sitka: Sheldon Jackson College, 1973.

———. *Woosh Yáx̱ Yaa Datúwch: Tlingit Math Book.* Sitka: Sheldon Jackson College, 1973.

Twitchell, X̱'unei Lance, ed. *Tlingit Dictionary.* Last modified November 28, 2023. Juneau: Goldbelt Heritage Foundation and X̱'unei Lance Twitchell (website). Accessed May 6, 2024. https://tlingit-language.com/resources/dictionary-2/.

Veniaminov, Ivan. *Notes on the Islands of the Unalashka District*, edited by Richard A. Pierce, translated by Lydia T. Black and R.H. Geoghengan. Kingston: The Limestone Press, 1984.

Вениаминовъ И. Записки объ атхинскихъ алеутахъ и колошахъ. Санктпетербургъ: Россійско-Американская Компанія, 1840.

Von Rad, Gerhard. *Genesis: A Commentary.* Revised edition, translated by John H. Marks. Philadelphia: The Westminster Press, 1972.

White, Fred. "Interview on Dry Bay, Alaska." Audio recording, 2001. Archive number 2001-10-03. Project Jukebox, Elmer E. Rasmuson Library. University of Alaska, Fairbanks. Accessed online May 6, 2024. https://jukebox.uaf.edu/interviews/3520.

William L. Paul Sr. Archives, Sealaska Heritage Institute. MC002, Celebration Recordings Collection.

———. MC005, Dauenhauer Tlingit Oral Literature Collection.

———. MC029, Tlingit Art at the Portland Art Museum Recordings Collection.

———. MC032, Sealaska Heritage Institute Operational Recordings.

———. MC041, Wilsey & Ham, Inc. 14(h)1 Historic Sites Recordings Collection.

———. MC047, Frederica de Laguna Fieldwork Recordings Collection.

———. MC062, SENSC Native Place Name Project Recordings Collection.

———. MS052, Dauenhauer Literary Estate Collection.

———. MS055, Rick Harris Papers.

———. PO004, Dauenhauer Photograph Collection.

———. PO077, Cyril George Photograph Collection.

Williams, Frank, and Emma Williams. *Tongass Texts*, edited by Jeff Leer. Fairbanks: Alaska Native Language Center, 1978.

Witzel, E.J. Michael. *The Origins of the World's Mythologies.* Oxford: Oxford University Press, 2012.